New Perspectives on

MICROSOFT®
OFFICE XP

What does this logo mean?

It means this courseware has been approved by the Microsoft® Office User Specialist Program to be among the finest available for learning Microsoft Word 2002, Microsoft Excel 2002, Microsoft Access 2002, and Microsoft PowerPoint® 2002. It also means that upon completion of this courseware, you may be prepared to become a Microsoft Office User Specialist.

What is a Microsoft Office User Specialist?

A Microsoft Office User Specialist is an individual who has certified his or her skills in one or more of the Microsoft Office desktop applications of Microsoft Word, Microsoft Excel, Microsoft PowerPoint, Microsoft Outlook®, or Microsoft Access, or in Microsoft Project. The Microsoft Office User Specialist Program typically offers certification exams at the "Core" and "Expert" skill levels. * The Microsoft Office User Specialist Program is the only Microsoft approved program in the world for certifying proficiency in Microsoft Office desktop applications and Microsoft Project. This certification can be a valuable asset in any job search or career advancement.

More Information:

To learn more about becoming a Microsoft Office User Specialist, visit **www.mous.net**

To purchase a Microsoft Office User Specialist certification exam, visit **www.DesktopIQ.com**

To learn about other Microsoft Office User Specialist approved courseware from Course Technology, visit www.course.com/NewPerspectives/TeachersLounge/mous.cfm

* The availability of Microsoft Office User Specialist certification exams varies by application, application version and language. Visit **www.mous.net** for exam availability.

Microsoft, the Microsoft Office User Specialist Logo, PowerPoint and Outlook are either registered trademarks or trademarks of Microsoft Corporation in the United States and/or other countries.

New Perspectives on

MICROSOFT® OFFICE XP

First Course

JUNE JAMRICH PARSONS
DAN OJA

PATRICK CAREY
Carey Associates, Inc.

ROY AGELOFF
University of Rhode Island

JOSEPH J. ADAMSKI
Grand Valley State University

ROBIN M. ROMER
ANN SHAFFER
LISA RUFFOLO
KATHLEEN T. FINNEGAN

S. SCOTT ZIMMERMAN
Brigham Young University

BEVERLY B. ZIMMERMAN
Brigham Young University

COURSE
TECHNOLOGY
™
THOMSON LEARNING

Australia • Canada • Mexico • Singapore • Spain • United Kingdom • United States

COURSE TECHNOLOGY

™

THOMSON LEARNING

New Perspectives on Microsoft® Office XP—First Course
is published by Course Technology.

Managing Editor:
Greg Donald

Senior Editor:
Donna Gridley

Senior Product Manager:
Kathy Finnegan

Product Manager:
Melissa Hathaway

Technology Product Manager:
Amanda Young

Editorial Assistant:
Jessica Engstrom

Marketing Manager:
Sean Teare

Developmental Editors:
Kim Crowley, Jessica Evans, Mary Kemper, Rose Marie Kuebbing, Jane Pedicini, Lisa Ruffolo

Production Editors:
Daphne Barbas, Jennifer Goguen, Kristen Guevara, Elena Montillo, Aimee Poirier

Composition:
GEX Publishing Services

Text Designer:
Meral Dabcovich

Cover Designer:
Efrat Reis

Preface

New Perspectives

Course Technology is the world leader in information technology education. The New Perspectives Series is an integral part of Course Technology's success. Visit our Web site to see a whole new perspective on teaching and learning solutions.

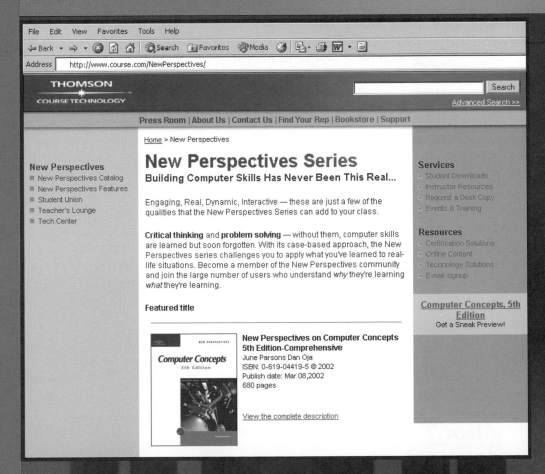

New Perspectives—Building Computer Skills Has Never Been This Real

Why New Perspectives will work for you.

Critical thinking and **problem solving**—without them, computer skills are learned but soon forgotten. With its **case-based** approach, the New Perspectives Series challenges students to apply what they've learned to real-life situations. Become a member of the New Perspectives community and watch your students not only **master** computer skills, but also **retain** and carry this **knowledge** into the world.

New Perspectives catalog
Our online catalog is never out of date! Go to the Catalog link on our Web site to check out our available titles, request a desk copy, download a book preview, or locate online files.

Complete system of offerings
Whether you're looking for a Brief book, an Advanced book, or something in between, we've got you covered. Go to the Catalog link on our Web site to find the level of coverage that's right for you.

Instructor materials
We have all the tools you need—data files, solution files, figure files, a sample syllabus, and ExamView, our powerful testing software package.

How well do your students know Microsoft Office?
Experience the power, ease, and flexibility of SAM XP and TOM. These innovative software tools provide the first truly integrated technology-based training and assessment solution for your applications course. Click the Tech Center link to learn more.

Get certified
If you want to get certified, we have the titles for you. Find out more by clicking the Teacher's Lounge link.

Interested in online learning?
Enhance your course with rich online content for use through MyCourse 2.0, WebCT, and Blackboard. Go to the Teacher's Lounge to find the platform that's right for you.

Your link to the future is at
www.course.com/NewPerspectives

What you need to know about this book.

- Student Online Companion takes students to the Web for additional work.

- ExamView testing software gives you the option of generating a printed test, LAN-based test, or test over the Internet.

- New Perspectives Labs provide students with self-paced practice on computer-related topics.

- This edition includes NEW tutorial cases and case problem scenarios throughout!

- Each Word tutorial emphasizes the importance of planning the work to be done in the document.

- Our coverage of Excel functions is more extensive and complete than that of other texts. Students work with financial functions to calculate the cost of mortgages and loans; calculate a payments schedule using financial and logical functions; and work with text and date functions.

- Students will appreciate our clear and concise coverage of database concepts, which gives them the solid foundation they need as they progress to creating and working with Access database objects.

- Our coverage takes full advantage of the new PowerPoint Task Pane, Slides Tab, and Outline Tab.

- This edition includes three Integration tutorials, giving students even more opportunity to learn how the Office programs work together.

- This text, when used in conjunction with the *New Perspectives on Microsoft Office XP Second Course* and the *New Perspectives on Microsoft Office XP Third Course*, will prepare students for Expert-level certification for Microsoft Word 2002, Microsoft Excel 2002, Microsoft Access 2002, and Microsoft PowerPoint 2002.

CASE	TROUBLE?	SESSION 1.1	QUICK CHECK	RW
Tutorial Case Each tutorial begins with a problem presented in a case that is meaningful to students. The case sets the scene to help students understand what they will do in the tutorial.	**TROUBLE? Paragraphs** These paragraphs anticipate the mistakes or problems that students may have and help them continue with the tutorial.	**Sessions** Each tutorial is divided into sessions designed to be completed in about 45 minutes each. Students should take as much time as they need and take a break between sessions.	**Quick Check Questions** Each session concludes with conceptual Quick Check questions that test students' understanding of what they learned in the session.	**Reference Windows** Reference Windows are succinct summaries of the most important tasks covered in a tutorial. They preview actions students will perform in the steps to follow.

BRIEF CONTENTS

TABLE OF CONTENTS

Exploring the Basics

Investigating the Windows 2000 Operating System

Tutorial 2   **WIN 2000 2.01**

Working with Files

Creating, Saving, and Managing Files

Tutorial 3   **WD 3.01**

Creating A Multiple-Page Report

Writing a Recommendation for Tyger Networks

Tutorial 4   **WD 4.01**

Desktop Publishing a Newsletter

Creating a Newsletter for Wide World Travel

Creating Web Pages with Word — WEB 1

Creating a Web Page for Bayside Health Inc.

Microsoft Excel 2002—
Level I Tutorials — EX 1.01
Read This Before You Begin — EX 1.02

Tutorial 1 — EX 1.03

Using Excel to Manage Financial Data

Creating an Income Statement

Tutorial 2   EX 2.01

Working with Formulas and Functions

Analyzing a Mortgage

Tutorial 3   EX 3.01

Developing a Professional-Looking Worksheet

Formatting a Sales Report

Tutorial 4   EX 4.01

Working with Charts and Graphics

Charting Sales Data for Vega Telescopes

Creating Web Pages with Excel   WEB 1

Publishing Workbooks to the Web

Integrating Microsoft Office XP   INT 1.01

Tutorial 1   INT 1.03

Integrating Word and Excel

Creating a Customer Letter that Includes a Chart and Table for Country Gardens

Microsoft Access 2002—

Level I Tutorials   AC 1.01

Tutorial 1   AC 1.03

Introduction to Microsoft Access 2002

Viewing and Working with a Table Containing Employer Data

SESSION 1.1   AC 1.04

SESSION 1.2   AC 1.13

Tutorial 2   AC 2.01

Creating and Maintaining a Database

**Creating the Northeast Database, and Creating,
Modifying, and Updating the Position Table**

Tutorial 3   AC 3.01

Querying a Database

Retrieving Information About Employers and Their Positions

New Perspectives on

ESSENTIAL COMPUTER CONCEPTS

CREDITS

OBJECTIVES

In this chapter, you will:

- Describe the components of a computer system

- Compare the types of computers

- Define microcomputer hardware in terms of its functions: input, output, processing, and storage

- Examine data representation and the ASCII code

- Describe how peripheral devices are connected to a microcomputer

- Identify the hardware and software that are used to establish a network connection

- Explain how Internet access, e-mail, and the World Wide Web affect the use of computers

- Discuss the types of system software and their functions

- Identify popular application software

- Describe how data is shared among different types of application software

ESSENTIAL COMPUTER CONCEPTS

CASE

Paik's Oriental Rug Gallery

Paik's Oriental Rug Gallery, located in the university town of Lake Thompson, specializes in the sale of new and used Oriental carpets. Paik's also does beautiful renovations of damaged or old Oriental rugs. Thanks to his excellent customer service and professional reputation, Owner Sang Kee Paik has broadened his customer base over the course of the last two years and is finding it hard to keep up with the paperwork. He recently hired you, a college graduate of the school of business, to assist him.

After several days on the job, you suggest to Mr. Paik that he would find it much easier to manage his inventory and payroll if he purchased several computers. He tells you he's considered that before, but hasn't had time to shop around. He asks you to research the features and prices of today's personal computers and recommend what he should consider purchasing for himself and his employees.

You go to the library and start paging through computer trade magazines so that you can examine the features of current models. Computers and their prices are constantly changing, but most of today's computers are well-suited to running a small business. You are sure you will be able to find computers that will meet Mr. Paik's needs.

LABS

Using a Mouse | Using a Keyboard | Peripheral Devices | Using Files | The Internet: World Wide Web | User Interfaces | Multimedia

What Is a Computer?

Computers have become essential tools in almost every type of activity in virtually every type of business. A **computer** is defined as an electronic device that accepts input, processes data, stores data, and produces output. It is a versatile tool with the potential to perform many different tasks.

A **computer system** includes a computer, **peripheral devices**, and **software**. The physical components of a computer are referred to as **hardware**. The design and construction of a particular computer is referred to as its **architecture**, or **configuration**. The technical details about each component are called **specifications**. For example, a computer system might be *configured* to include a printer; a *specification* for that printer might be a print speed of eight pages per minute or the capacity to print in color. The computer itself takes care of the processing function, but it needs additional components, called **peripherals**, to accomplish its input, output, and storage functions. In this chapter, you will learn more about the hardware that performs these basic computer functions.

Software refers to the intangible components of a computer system, particularly the **programs**, or lists of instructions, that the computer needs to perform a specific task. Software is the key to a computer's versatility. When your computer is using word processing software—for example, the Microsoft Word program—you can type memos, letters, and reports. When your computer is using accounting software, you can maintain information about what your customers owe you and display a graph showing the timing of customer payments.

The hardware and the software of a computer system work together to process data—the words, figures, sounds, and graphics that describe people, events, things, and ideas. Figure 2 shows how you, the computer, the data, and the software interact to get work done. Suppose that you want to write a report. First, you instruct the computer to use the word processing program. After activating the word processing program, you begin to type the text of your report. What you type into the computer is called **input**. You might also need to issue commands that tell the computer exactly how to process your input. Perhaps you want to center the title and double-space the text. You use an input device, such as a keyboard or a mouse, to input data and issue commands.

Figure 2	DATA IS INPUT, PROCESSED, STORED, AND OUTPUT

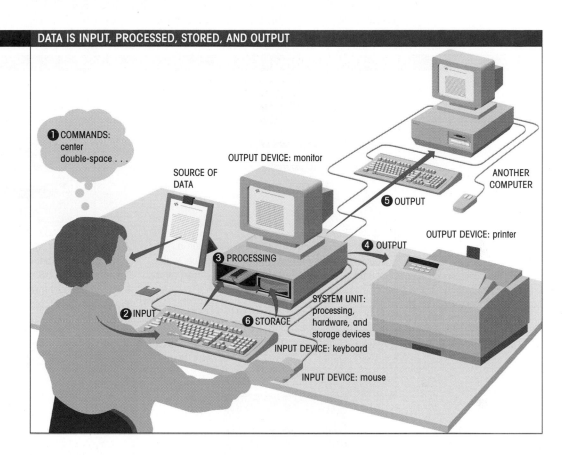

The computer processes the report according to your commands and the instructions contained in the software—the title becomes centered and all the text double-spaced. **Processing** changes the data you have input, for example, by moving text, sorting lists, or performing calculations. Or, you might choose to import from another computer an illustration, text, or numeric data such as stock prices. This processing takes place on the **main circuit board** of the computer, also referred to as the **motherboard**, which contains the computer's major electronic components. The electronic components of the main circuit board are referred to as **processing hardware**.

Using a computer to type your report has several advantages. The first is the speed at which you can perform the task. Second, the capability of storing the answer and using it over and over again, in so many different ways, makes using a computer the most effective way to perform many personal and clerical tasks. Finally, an important advantage is sharing data and output with others. You make a note to find out whether Paik employees will need to share their data.

Types of Computers

Personal computers are not the only way to compute; there are other types of computers, which are classified by their size, speed, and cost. **Microcomputers**, also called **personal computers** (PCs), are the computers typically used by a single user, usually at home or at the office. They come in many shapes and sizes, as you can see in Figure 3.

Figure 3	MICROCOMPUTERS

A standard desktop microcomputer fits on a desk and runs on power from an electrical wall outlet. The display screen is usually placed on top of the horizontal desktop case.

A microcomputer with a tower case contains the same basic components as a standard desktop microcomputer, but the vertically oriented case is large and allows more room for expansion. The tower unit can be placed on the floor to save desk space.

A notebook computer is small and light, giving it the advantage of portability that standard desktop computers do not have. A notebook computer can run on power from an electrical outlet or batteries.

A personal digital assistant (PDA), or palm-top computer achieves even more portability than a notebook computer by shrinking or eliminating some standard components, such as the keyboard. On a keyboardless PDA, a touch-sensitive screen accepts characters drawn with your finger. PDAs easily connect to desktop computers to exchange and update information.

A **desktop** or **tower** microcomputer can cost between $1,000 and $3,000. A **notebook** computer with similar capability is usually much more expensive. The **personal digital assistant** (PDA) has limited capability, and not always a lower price.

You assume that your recommendation to Mr. Paik will include microcomputers because most daily tasks can be performed very efficiently using them. However, you wonder whether some employees might need the portability of notebook computers, and whether others might need a PDA. You add these notes to your list of questions to ask Mr. Paik.

Small and large businesses use microcomputers extensively. But some businesses, government agencies, and other institutions also use larger and faster types of computers: **minicomputers**, **mainframes**, and **supercomputers**. Unlike most microcomputers, these can have multiple input and output devices so that more than one user can work simultaneously.

Minicomputers, like the one in Figure 4, are somewhat larger than microcomputers. Physical size, however, is not the deciding factor when buying a minicomputer. The computing capability of a microcomputer may be more than a minicomputer, and a fairly typical minicomputer may cost between $20,000 and $250,000. Usually, a company decides to purchase a minicomputer when it must carry out the processing tasks for many users, especially when the users share large amounts of data. Each user inputs processing requests and views output through a terminal. A **terminal** is a device with a keyboard and screen used for input and output, but is not capable of processing on its own.

Figure 4	A TYPICAL MINICOMPUTER HANDLES PROCESSING TASKS FOR MULTIPLE USERS

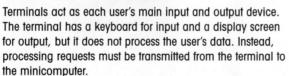

Terminals act as each user's main input and output device. The terminal has a keyboard for input and a display screen for output, but it does not process the user's data. Instead, processing requests must be transmitted from the terminal to the minicomputer.

The minicomputer stores data for all the users in one centralized location.

Mainframe computers, like the one shown in Figure 5, are larger and more powerful than minicomputers. As with a minicomputer, one mainframe computer performs processing tasks for multiple users on terminals. However, the mainframe can handle many more users than a minicomputer. Mainframes are typically used to provide centralized storage, processing, and management for large amounts of data. The price of a typical mainframe computer can be several hundred thousand dollars.

Figure 5   **THE SYSTEM UNIT FOR THE IBM S/390 G4 MAINFRAME COMPUTER**

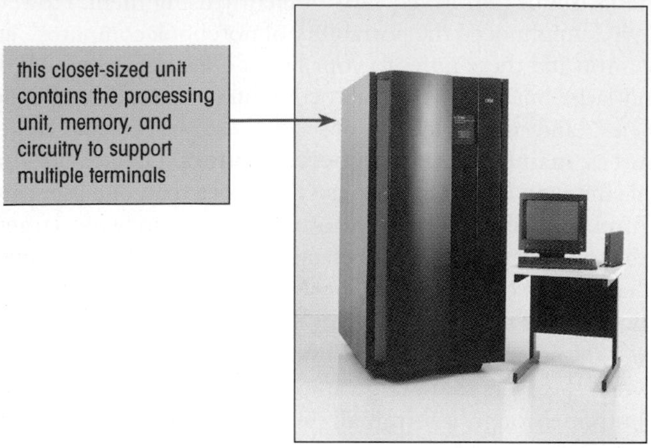

this closet-sized unit contains the processing unit, memory, and circuitry to support multiple terminals

The largest and fastest computers, called **supercomputers**, were first developed for high-volume computing tasks such as weather prediction. Supercomputers like the one shown in Figure 6 are also being used by large corporations when the tremendous volume of data would seriously delay processing on a mainframe computer. Although its cost can be several million dollars, a supercomputer's processing speed is so much faster than that of microcomputers, minicomputers, and mainframes that the investment can be worthwhile.

Figure 6   **A CRAY SUPERCOMPUTER**

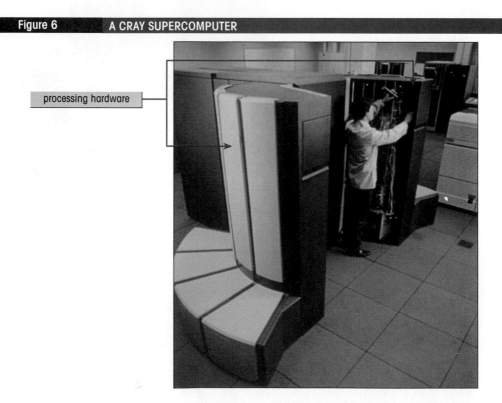

processing hardware

How would you classify the computer in the advertisement shown in Figure 1 at the beginning of the chapter? If your answer is a desktop microcomputer, you are correct. The computer in that ad fits on a desk and is not portable.

Based on what you have learned about the computing process and types of computers, you decide to recommend that Mr. Paik purchase some microcomputers. When you look at the ad, however, you realize that there are several specifications that Mr. Paik may not understand. Your recommendation will have to explain what each listed component does, and why it is important. The remainder of this chapter will focus on microcomputer hardware and software in more detail, so you can learn what you need to know to make a better recommendation.

Computer **Hardware**

Using a Mouse

Peripheral Devices **Using a Keyboard**

As you've already learned, computer hardware can be defined as the physical components of a computer. Now look at the hardware you might use in a typical microcomputer system.

Input Devices

You input data and commands by using an input device such as a keyboard or a mouse. The computer can also receive input from a storage device. This section takes a closer look at the input devices you might use. Output and storage devices are covered in later sections.

The most frequently used input device is a keyboard. The top keyboard in Figure 7 is a standard 101-key keyboard. Newer keyboards such as the bottom keyboard in Figure 7, are **ergonomic**, which means that they have been designed to fit the natural placement of your hands and should reduce your risk of repetitive-motion injuries. All keyboards consist of three major parts: the main keyboard, the keypads, and the function keys.

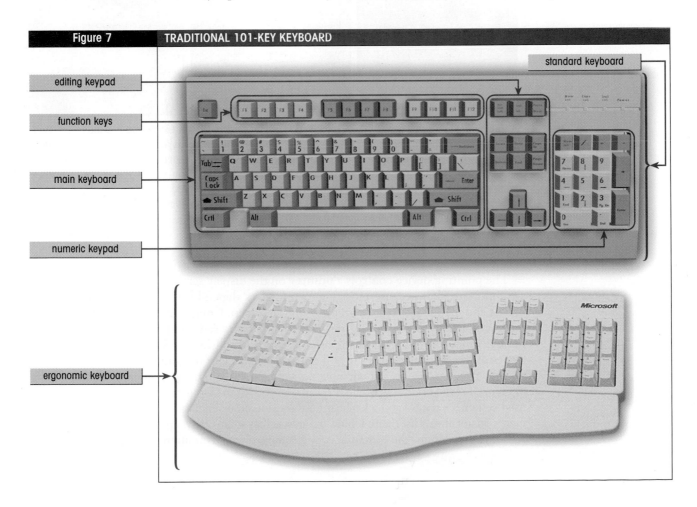

| Figure 7 | TRADITIONAL 101-KEY KEYBOARD |

editing keypad

function keys

main keyboard

numeric keypad

ergonomic keyboard

standard keyboard

All microcomputers also should be equipped with a pointing device. The most popular is a mouse such as the one in Figure 8, but your computer might be equipped with one of the other options pictured in Figure 9.

Figure 8   **A MOUSE**

Figure 9   **NOTEBOOK POINTING DEVICES**

Track point

Track ball

Touch pad

A **track point** is a small eraser-like device embedded among the typing keys. To control the on-screen pointer, you push the track point up, left, right, or down. Buttons for clicking and double-clicking are located in front of the spacebar.

A **track ball** is like an upside-down mouse. By rolling the ball with your fingers, you control the on-screen pointer. Buttons for clicking are often located above or to the side of the track ball.

A **touch pad** is a touch-sensitive device. By dragging your finger over the surface, you control the on-screen pointer. Two buttons equivalent to mouse buttons are located in front of the touch pad.

The pointing device controls a **pointer** on the display screen. Using a pointing device is an important skill because most microcomputers depend on such devices to select commands and manipulate text or graphics on the screen. Computers that input from terminals do not normally use pointing devices. Computers used for presentations often feature remote input devices, such as the remote control used for a TV/VCR. The remote input device allows you to control the pointer from the back of the auditorium.

Now that you have read about input devices, refer back to the computer advertisement shown in Figure 1 at the beginning of the chapter. Can you list the input devices included with the advertised system? A mouse and a keyboard are considered essential peripheral devices, so advertisements do not always list them. Unless the ad specifies some other input device, such as a track ball, you can safely assume the computer comes equipped with a traditional keyboard and mouse.

Output Devices

Output is the result of processing data; output devices show you those results. The most commonly used output devices are monitors and printers. A **monitor** is the TV-like device that displays the output from a computer, as shown in Figure 10.

Figure 10	A COLOR MONITOR

Factors that influence the quality of a monitor are screen size, resolution, and dot pitch. **Screen size** is the diagonal measurement in inches from one corner of the screen to the other. Common measurements for today's monitors are 15", 17", and 21". The first microcomputer monitors and many terminals still in use today are character-based. A **character-based display** divides the screen into a grid of rectangles, one for each typed character. A monitor that is capable of displaying graphics, called a **graphics display**, divides the screen into a matrix of small dots called **pixels**. **Resolution** is the maximum number of pixels the monitor can display. Standard resolutions are 640 × 480, 800 × 600, 1,024 × 768, 1,280 × 1,024, and 1,600 × 1,200. The resolution you use depends on your monitor size. If your screen is small, 1,600 × 1,200 resolution will make the objects on the screen too small to see clearly. Resolution is easy to adjust on most monitors. **Dot pitch** measures the distance between pixels, so a smaller dot pitch means a sharper image. A .28 or .26 dot pitch (dp) is typical for today's monitors.

A computer display system consists of a monitor and a **graphics card**, also called a **video display adapter** or **video card**. This card is installed inside the computer, and controls the signals the computer sends to the monitor. If you plan to display a lot of images on the monitor, you may also need a **graphics accelerator card** to speed up the computer's ability to display them. When purchasing a monitor, you must be sure that it comes with a video card that is compatible with your computer.

Notebook computers use a different display technology because monitors are too bulky and heavy. Instead, they use a **liquid crystal display** (LCD) similar to a digital watch or the time display on a microwave oven. The size of these screens is also measured diagonally, typically 11.3" to 12.1" across. An **active matrix screen** updates rapidly and provides resolution similar to that of a monitor. If you want to display a lot of images, especially video, on a notebook computer, it should have an active matrix screen.

Refer back to the computer ad in Figure 1. Does this microcomputer include a monitor and video card? The correct answer is yes, both are included. What are the size and resolution of the monitor? The monitor is a 19" 1,600 × 1,200 .26 dp color monitor.

A **printer** produces a paper copy of the text or graphics processed by the computer. A paper or acetate transparency copy of computer output is called **hard copy**, because it is more tangible than the electronic or magnetic copies found on a disk, in the computer memory, or on the monitor. There are three popular categories of printers, and each has special capabilities.

The most popular printers for business use are **laser** printers, like the one shown in Figure 11, because they use the same technology as duplicating machines. A temporary laser image is transferred onto paper with a powdery substance called **toner**. This produces high-quality output quickly and efficiently. The speed of laser printers is measured in **pages per minute** (ppm). Color laser printers use several toner cartridges to apply color to the page. Non-color laser printers are less expensive than color laser printers.

Figure 11   A LASER PRINTER

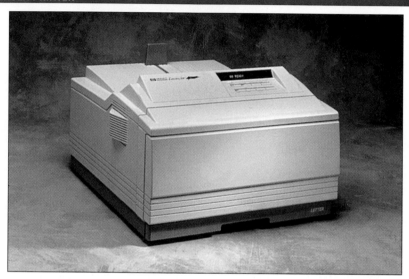

A less expensive alternative is to use a color **ink-jet** printer such as the one shown in Figure 12. These printers carefully spray ink onto paper. The quality of the ink-jet output is almost comparable to a laser printer's output, but it is produced much more slowly. Ink-jet printers, with and without color capabilities, are very popular printers for home use.

Figure 12   AN INK-JET PRINTER

Figure 13 shows a **dot matrix** printer, an example of the oldest technology currently found on the computer market. These printers transfer ink to the paper by striking a ribbon with pins. Using more pins controls the quality of the print, so a 24-pin dot matrix printer produces better quality print than a 9-pin. Dot matrix printers are most often used when a large number of pages need to be printed fairly quickly. The speed of dot matrix printers is measured in **characters per second** (cps). Some examples of their usefulness are the printing of grade reports, bank statements, or payroll checks. Also, they are the only type of printer that can print on multipart forms, so they continue to be useful to all kinds of businesses.

Figure 13	A DOT MATRIX PRINTER

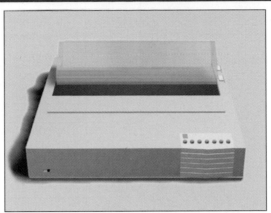

You are not sure if Mr. Paik needs you to consider the purchase of printers to go with the recommended microcomputers. You notice that the computer ad in Figure 1 does not include a printer, so you make a note to ask if your recommendation should include one. If so, you decide to recommend both a color laser printer to print correspondence, advertisements, and brochures, and a high-speed dot matrix printer for clerical tasks.

Multimedia devices are another category of peripheral devices. **Multimedia** is an integrated collection of computer-based media including text, graphics, sound, animation, and video. Most microcomputers come equipped with a sound card and speakers that can play digital sounds. The sound card converts sounds so that they can be broadcast through speakers.

The computer advertised in Figure 1 includes a sound card and speakers. These are also output devices that you need to mention in your recommendation. You wonder what purpose these devices might serve at Paik's Oriental Rug Gallery. Mr. Paik might participate in teleconferences on product availability attended by suppliers in widespread locations, or record announcements that employees can play back at their convenience. Later in this chapter, you will learn how business users are sharing a variety of data resources, including digital sound.

Using Files

Processing Hardware

The most important computer function is processing data. Before you can understand this function and the hardware that executes it, you first need to learn how the computer represents and stores data.

Data representation

The characters used in human language are meaningless to a computer because it is an electronic device. Like a light bulb, the computer must interpret every signal as either "on" or "off." To do so, a microcomputer represents data as distinct or separate numbers. Specifically, it represents "on" with a 1 and "off" with a 0. These numbers are referred to as **binary digits**, or **bits**.

Microcomputers commonly use the **ASCII** code to represent character data. ASCII (pronounced "ASK-ee") stands for **American Standard Code for Information Interchange**.

A series of eight bits is called a **byte**. As Figure 14 shows, the byte that represents the integer value 0 is 00000000, with all eight bits "off" or set to 0. The byte that represents the integer value 1 is 00000001, and the byte that represents 255 is 11111111.

| Figure 14 | BINARY REPRESENTATION OF THE NUMBERS 0 THROUGH 255 |

Number	Binary Representation
0	00000000
1	00000001
2	00000010
3	00000011
4	00000100
5	00000101
6	00000110
7	00000111
8	00001000
⋮	⋮
253	11111101
254	11111110
255	11111111

Each byte represents a unique character such as the number 8, the letter *A*, or the symbol $. For example, Figure 15 shows that ASCII code represents the letter *A* by the byte 1000001, and the lowercase *a* by 1100001. The symbol $ is represented by 0100100. Even a space has its own unique value: 0100000. The phrase "Thank you!" is represented by 10 bytes. Each of the eight letters requires one byte, and the space and the exclamation point also require one byte each.

| Figure 15 | SAMPLE ASCII CODE REPRESENTING LETTERS AND SYMBOLS |

Character	ASCII
(space)	0100000
$	0100100
A	1000001
B	1000010
a	1100001
b	1100010

As a computer user, you don't have to know the binary representations of numbers, characters, and instructions, because the computer handles all the necessary conversions internally. However, because the amount of memory in a computer and its storage capacity are expressed in bytes, you should be aware of how data is represented. **Storage** and **memory capacity** is the amount of data, or number of characters, that the device can handle at any given time. A **kilobyte** (KB) is 1,024 bytes, or approximately one thousand bytes. A **megabyte** (MB) is 1,048,576 bytes, or about one million bytes. A **gigabyte** (GB) is 1,073,741,824 bytes, or about one billion bytes. You will see the symbols KB, MB, and GB refer to both processing and storage hardware.

The Microprocessor

The two most important components of microcomputer hardware are the **microprocessor**, a silicon chip designed to manipulate data, and the **memory**, which stores instructions and data. The type of microprocessor and the memory capacity are two factors that directly affect the price and performance of a computer.

The **microprocessor**, such as the one shown in Figure 16, is an integrated circuit (an electronic component called a **chip**) which is located on the main circuit board inside the computer.

Figure 16	AN INTEL PENTIUM III MICROPROCESSOR, FOUND IN MANY IBM-COMPATIBLE COMPUTERS

The terms **processor** and **central processing unit** (CPU) also refer to this device that is responsible for executing instructions to process data.

The speed of a microprocessor is determined by its clock speed, word size, and cache size. Think of the **clock speed** as the pulse of the processor. It is measured in millions of cycles per second, or **megahertz** (MHz), a measurement of electrical impulses. The microprocessor in the first IBM PC models operated at 4.77 MHz. Today's microprocessors are capable of speeds over 500 MHz.

Word size refers to the number of bits that are processed at one time. A computer with a large word size can process faster than a computer with a small word size. The earliest microcomputers had an 8-bit word size, but now a 64-bit word size is common.

Cache, sometimes called **RAM cache** or **cache memory**, is special high-speed memory reserved for the microprocessor's use. It speeds up the processing function by accessing data the computer anticipates you will request soon, while you are still working on something else.

Take another look at the computer advertised in Figure 1. What is the type and speed of its microprocessor? Your answer should be that it has a Pentium III microprocessor that can operate at 500 MHz and has 512 KB cache.

Memory

Computer **memory** is a set of storage locations on the main circuit board. Your computer has four types of memory: random access memory, virtual memory, read-only memory, and complementary metal oxide semiconductor (CMOS) memory.

Random access memory (RAM) is active during the processing function. It consists of electronic circuits on the motherboard that temporarily hold programs and data while the computer is on. Each circuit has an address that is used by the microprocessor to transmit and store data. Figure 17 illustrates how each byte of data is stored in a separate RAM address.

Figure 17 THE MICROPROCESSOR AND RAM ARE ACTIVE DURING THE PROCESSING FUNCTION

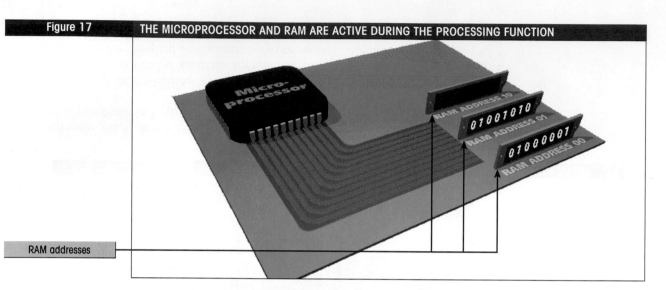

RAM addresses

RAM is constantly changing as long as the computer is on. The microprocessor is constantly using RAM to store and retrieve instructions and data as they are needed. The term **volatile** is used to describe this constantly changing state of RAM.

For example, if you are writing a paper, the word processing program that you are using is temporarily copied into RAM so the microprocessor can quickly access the instructions that you will need as you type and format your paper. As you type, the characters are also stored in RAM, along with the many fonts, special characters, graphics, and other objects that you might use to enhance the paper. How much you can include in your paper depends on the RAM capacity of the computer you are using.

Look at the computer ad in Figure 1. Notice that this computer has 128 MB of RAM. In other words, it has the capacity to temporarily store over 128 million characters at any one time. Although your paper might not be that long, the computer uses a lot of that available memory for programs and other data it needs to process your paper. The notation "expandable to 768 MB" tells you that you can add more RAM to this computer. Expandability is an important feature of any computer; you need to be able to change your computer's capability as your needs change. You don't have to worry about running out of RAM, however. Today's microcomputer software uses space on your computer's storage devices to simulate RAM if more is needed. This extra memory is called **virtual memory**. Figure 18 explains how it works.

Figure 18 HOW VIRTUAL MEMORY WORKS

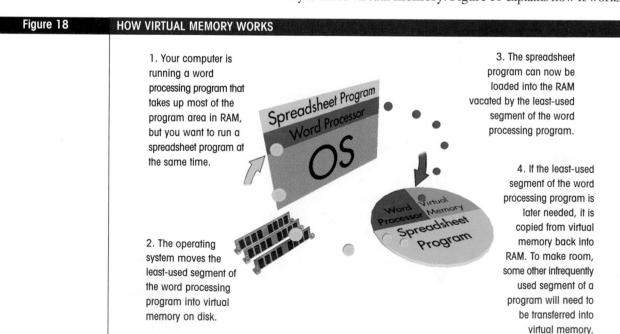

1. Your computer is running a word processing program that takes up most of the program area in RAM, but you want to run a spreadsheet program at the same time.

2. The operating system moves the least-used segment of the word processing program into virtual memory on disk.

3. The spreadsheet program can now be loaded into the RAM vacated by the least-used segment of the word processing program.

4. If the least-used segment of the word processing program is later needed, it is copied from virtual memory back into RAM. To make room, some other infrequently used segment of a program will need to be transferred into virtual memory.

The disadvantage of using virtual memory is that it is much slower than RAM, so expanding the RAM capacity of a microcomputer will improve its performance. **Read-only memory (ROM)** is another set of electronic circuits on the motherboard inside the computer. Although you can expand your RAM capacity, you cannot add to ROM capacity. In fact, the manufacturer of the computer permanently installs ROM. It is the permanent storage location for a set of instructions that the computer uses when you turn it on.

The events that occur between the moment you turn on the computer and the moment you can actually begin to use the computer are called the **boot process**, as shown in Figure 19. When the computer is off, RAM is empty. When the computer is turned on, the set of instructions in ROM checks all the computer system's components to make sure they are working, and activates the essential software that controls the processing function.

Figure 19	ROM BOOT PROGRAM ACTIVATED

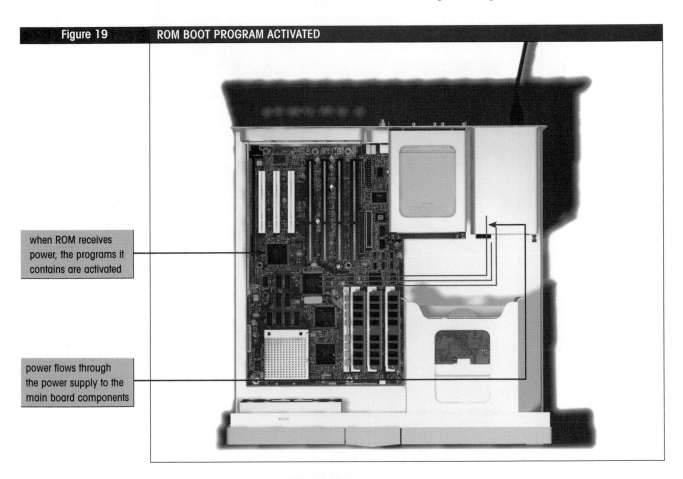

when ROM receives power, the programs it contains are activated

power flows through the power supply to the main board components

Complementary metal oxide semiconductor (CMOS) memory (pronounced "SEE-Moss") is another chip that is installed on the motherboard. It is also activated during the boot process and contains information about where the essential software is stored. A small rechargeable battery powers CMOS so its contents will be saved between computer uses.

Unlike ROM, which cannot be changed, CMOS must be changed every time you add or remove hardware to your computer system. Thus, CMOS is often referred to as semipermanent memory, ROM as permanent memory, and RAM as temporary memory.

Storage Devices and Media

Because RAM retains data only while the power is on, your computer must have a more permanent storage option. As Figure 20 shows, a storage device receives data from RAM and writes it on a storage medium, such as a disk. Later the data can be read and sent back to RAM to use again.

Figure 20	STORAGE DEVICES AND RAM

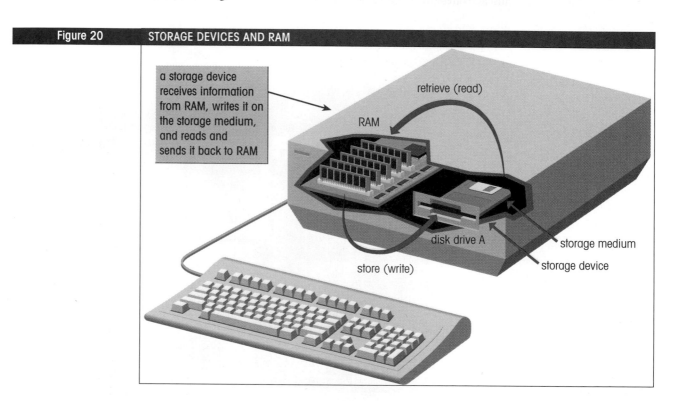

a storage device receives information from RAM, writes it on the storage medium, and reads and sends it back to RAM

retrieve (read)

RAM

disk drive A

storage medium

storage device

store (write)

Before you can understand the hardware that stores data, you need to know how data is stored. All data and programs are stored as files. A computer **file** is a named collection of related bits that exists on a storage medium. There are two categories of files: executable files and data files. An **executable file** contains the instructions that tell a computer how to perform a specific task. The files that are used during the boot process, for instance, are executable. Users create **data files**, usually with software. For instance, your paper that you write with a word processing program is data, and must be saved as a data file if you want to use it again.

The storage devices where computer files are kept can be categorized by the method they use to store files. **Magnetic storage devices** use oxide-coated plastic storage media called mylar. Figure 21 illustrates the process of storing data on magnetic media.

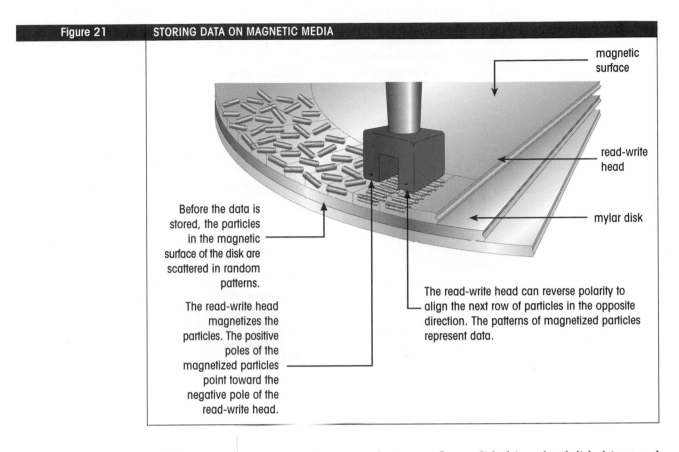

Figure 21 | **STORING DATA ON MAGNETIC MEDIA**

magnetic surface

read-write head

mylar disk

Before the data is stored, the particles in the magnetic surface of the disk are scattered in random patterns.

The read-write head magnetizes the particles. The positive poles of the magnetized particles point toward the negative pole of the read-write head.

The read-write head can reverse polarity to align the next row of particles in the opposite direction. The patterns of magnetized particles represent data.

The most common magnetic storage devices are floppy disk drives, hard disk drives, and tape drives. **Floppy disks**, sometimes called **diskettes**, are flat circles of iron oxide-coated plastic enclosed in a hard plastic case. The most common size of floppy disks for microcomputers is 3.5". You may also see floppy disks in other sizes. For instance, 5.25" and 8" are used in older microcomputers. However, physical size is not the best way to describe floppy disks. Instead, the capacity of the disk is more important. The floppy disk in Figure 22 is a **high-density** disk, which means it has the capacity to store 1.44 MB. In contrast, older **low-density** disks of the same physical size can store only 720 KB. As a user, you need to know what capacity of floppy disk your microcomputer can accept.

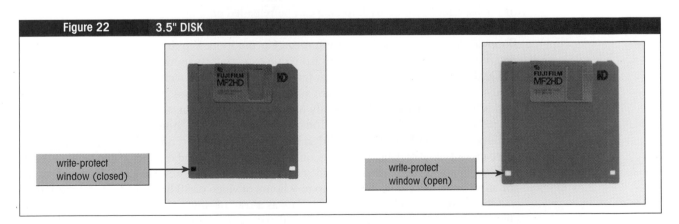

Figure 22 | **3.5" DISK**

write-protect window (closed)

write-protect window (open)

Write protection prevents additional files from being stored on the disk, and any file from being erased from the disk. To write protect a 3.5" floppy disk, you open the write-protect window, as shown in Figure 22.

The other most common magnetic storage device is a **hard disk drive**, such as the one shown in Figure 23. This drive contains several iron oxide-covered metal platters that are usually sealed inside the computer. Hard disk storage has two advantages over floppy disk storage: speed and capacity.

Figure 23	HARD DISK DRIVE OPENED TO ILLUSTRATE INTERNAL COMPONENTS

The speed of a disk drive is measured by its **access time**, the time required to read or write one record of data. Access time is measured in **milliseconds** (ms), one-thousandths of a second. The hard disk drive included in Figure 1, for instance, has 10 ms access time. Its capacity is 21 GB. Although this seems like a very high number, a Windows-based micro-computer fully loaded with typical software can use up to 1 GB, and the addition of data files can quickly add up.

Another magnetic storage device is a **tape drive** that provides inexpensive archival storage for large quantities of data. Tape storage is much too slow to be used for day-to-day computer tasks; therefore, tapes are used to make backup copies of data stored on hard disks. If a hard disk fails, data from the backup tape can be reloaded on a new hard disk with minimal inter-ruption of operations. Some microcomputers include a **Zip drive**, a special high capacity floppy disk drive manufactured by Iomega Corporation. Zip drives can make copies of data, and transport large amounts of data from one computer to another.

Optical storage devices use laser technology to read and write data on silver platters. The first standard optical storage device on microcomputers was the **CD-ROM** drive, which stands for **Compact Disk Read Only Memory**. One CD can store up to 680 MB, equivalent to more than 450 floppy disks. Today's microcomputers, however, are more commonly equipped with **DVD**, or **Digital Video Disk**, drives. DVDs, though the same size as CDs, can store up to 17 GB of data, depending on whether data is stored on one or two sides of the disk, and how many layers of data each side contains. DVD has more than enough storage capacity for an entire feature-length film—up to 9 hours of video or 30 hours of CD-quality audio.

Optical storage technology records data as a trail of tiny pits in the disk surface. The data that these pits represent can then be "read" with a beam of laser light. Figure 24 shows how data is stored on optical media.

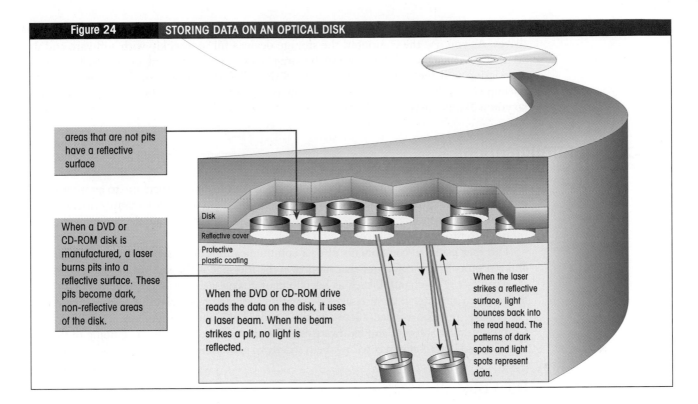

Figure 24   STORING DATA ON AN OPTICAL DISK

areas that are not pits have a reflective surface

When a DVD or CD-ROM disk is manufactured, a laser burns pits into a reflective surface. These pits become dark, non-reflective areas of the disk.

Disk

Reflective cover

Protective plastic coating

When the DVD or CD-ROM drive reads the data on the disk, it uses a laser beam. When the beam strikes a pit, no light is reflected.

When the laser strikes a reflective surface, light bounces back into the read head. The patterns of dark spots and light spots represent data.

The disadvantage of optical storage technology is that the surface of the CD is not usually rewriteable like magnetic media. Once the laser cuts a pit in the CD surface, the pit cannot be recut, so the data stored there cannot be changed. The most common uses of CDs or DVDs are for software distribution and storing large files that typically include graphics, animation, and video. Optical storage media are very durable. Unlike magnetic media, such as floppy and hard disks, CD and DVD platters are not susceptible to humidity, dust, fingerprints, or magnets. They are not indestructable, however. Take care not to scratch the disk surface or expose the disk to high temperatures.

The original CD-ROM drive had a relatively slow access time: 600 ms. As the technology has improved, that access time has decreased to less than 200 ms. A lower number means faster access. Also consider the drive's data transfer rate, measured in kilobits per second (Kbps), to classify it as 1X (the original), 2X (twice the original), 3X, and so on. The computer in Figure 1 comes with a 6X DVD-ROM drive. DVD-ROM drives can read DVDs and CDs.

Figure 25 shows the typical storage configuration of a microcomputer. It includes a DVD-ROM drive, a floppy disk drive, and a hard drive.

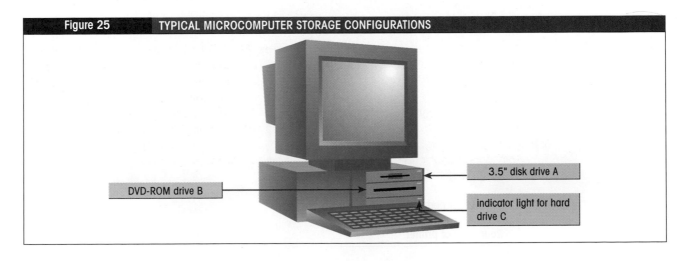

Figure 25   TYPICAL MICROCOMPUTER STORAGE CONFIGURATIONS

DVD-ROM drive B

3.5" disk drive A

indicator light for hard drive C

You decide that your recommendation should include microcomputers with DVD-ROM drives. As you use the computer, the storage devices fill up quickly with software and data, so it's a good idea to purchase as much storage capacity as your budget allows. Your recommendation will include high-capacity hard disk drives, and tape or Zip drives to use for backup copies. Most microcomputers come equipped with 3.5" 1.44 MB floppy disk drives, so you will include them, too.

Data Communications

The transmission of text, numeric, voice, or video data from one machine to another is called **data communications**. This broad-based definition encompasses many critical business activities, from sending a letter to the printer upstairs to sending an electronic mail (e-mail) message to the company offices around the globe.

The four essential components of data communications are a sender, a receiver, a channel, and a protocol. The computer that originates the message is the **sender**. The message is sent over some type of **channel**, such as telephone or coaxial cable, a microwave signal, or optical fibers. The computer at the message's destination is called the **receiver**. The rules that establish an orderly transfer of data between the sender and the receiver are called **protocols**. Communication software and hardware establish these protocols at the beginning of the transmission, and both computers follow them strictly to guarantee an accurate transfer of data.

Data Bus

Peripherals are devices that can be added to a computer system to enhance its usefulness. Starting at the microprocessor, and passing through a continuous channel, the data travels out to the appropriate device. From an input device back to the microprocessor, the path is reversed. This communication between the microprocessor, RAM, and the peripherals is called the **data bus**.

An external peripheral device must have a corresponding **port** and **cable** that connect it to the back of the computer. Inside the computer, each port connects to a **controller card**, sometimes called an **expansion** or **interface card**. These cards, which provide an electrical connection to a variety of peripheral devices, plug into electrical connectors on the main board called slots or **expansion slots**. Figure 26 shows the data path that connects a printer to a computer. An internal peripheral device such as a hard disk drive may plug directly into the motherboard, or it may have an attached controller card. The transmission protocol is handled by a **device driver**, a computer program that can establish communication because it contains information about the characteristics of your computer and of the device.

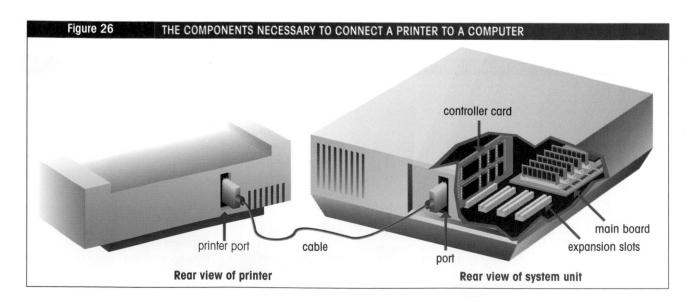

Figure 26 | THE COMPONENTS NECESSARY TO CONNECT A PRINTER TO A COMPUTER

controller card

main board

expansion slots

printer port   cable   port

Rear view of printer   **Rear view of system unit**

Microcomputers can have several types of ports, including USB, parallel, serial, SCSI, and MIDI. Figure 27 diagrams how the ports on a desktop microcomputer might appear.

A **parallel port** transmits data eight bits at a time. Parallel transmissions are relatively fast, but increase the risk for interference, so they are typically used to connect a printer that is near the computer. A **serial port** transmits data one bit at a time. Typically, a mouse, keyboard, and modem are connected with serial interfaces.

SCSI (pronounced "scuzzy") stands for **small computer system interface**. One SCSI port provides an interface for one or more peripheral devices. The first is connected directly to the computer through the port, and the second device is plugged into a similar port on the first device. SCSI connections can allow many devices to use the same port. They are particularly popular on Macintosh computers and notebook computers.

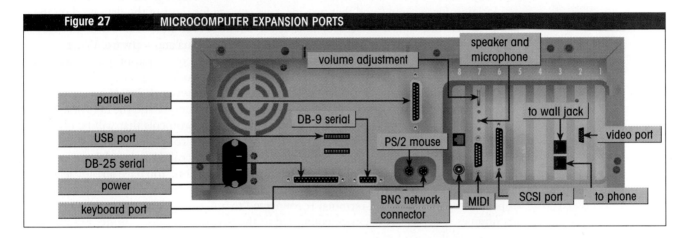

Figure 27   MICROCOMPUTER EXPANSION PORTS

Figure 27 shows some other ports for telephone cables to connect a modem, a video port to connect a monitor, and a network connection. The interface to a sound card usually includes jacks for speakers, a microphone, and a **musical instrument digital interface** (MIDI), which is pronounced "middy." MIDI ports are used to connect computers to electronic instruments and recording devices.

Notebook computers may also include a **Personal Computer Memory Card International Association** (PCMCIA) slot. PCMCIA devices are credit-card-sized circuit boards that plug directly into the PCMCIA slot, and can contain additional memory, a modem, or a hard disk drive.

Today's computers also usually include **USB**, short for **Universal Serial Bus**, ports. USB is a high-speed technology that facilitates the connection of external devices, such as joysticks, scanners, keyboards, video conferencing cameras, speakers, modems, and printers, to a computer. The device you install must have a **USB connector**, a small rectangular plug. You simply plug the USB connector into the USB port, and the computer recognizes the device and allows you to use it immediately. USB-compatible computers thus work more like stereo systems, in that you don't have to completely disassemble the unit to add a component. Any USB device can use any USB port, interchangeably and in any order. You can "daisy chain" up to 127 devices, plugging one device into another, or you can connect multiple devices to a single inexpensive hub. Data is transferred through a USB 10 times faster than, for example, through a serial port. For many USB devices, power is supplied via the port, so there is no need for extra power cables. Older computers can have a plethora of connectors— a keyboard connector, a mouse port, a parallel port, a joystick port, two audio ports, and two serial ports. USB computers replace this proliferation of ports with one standardized plug and port combination.

Look at Figure 1 at the beginning of the chapter. Does this computer include any of the ports illustrated in Figure 27? It mentions RS-232, USB, and parallel ports. Ports for speakers, a monitor, the mouse, and a modem are probably included, because the advertisement lists those devices.

Networks

One of the most important types of data communications in the business world is a network connection. A **network** connects one computer to other computers and peripheral devices, enabling you to share data and resources with your coworkers. There are a variety of network configurations, too many to discuss thoroughly here. However, any type of network has some basic characteristics and requirements that you should know.

In a **local area network** (LAN), computers and peripheral devices are located relatively close to each other, generally in the same building. If you are using such a network, it is useful to know three things: the location of the data, the type of network card in your computer, and the communication software that manages protocols and network functions.

Some networks have one or more computers, called **file servers**, that act as the central storage location for programs and that provide mass storage for most of the data used on the network. A network with a file server is called a **client/server** network. These networks are dependent on the file server because it contains most of the data and software. When a network does not have a file server, all the computers essentially are equal, and programs and data are distributed among them. This is called a **peer-to-peer network**.

Each computer that is part of the network must have a **network interface card** installed. This device creates a communication channel between the computer and the network. **Network software** is also essential, establishing the communications protocols that will be observed on the network and controlling the "traffic flow" as data travels throughout the network.

A microcomputer that is not connected to a network is called a **standalone computer**. When it is connected to the network, it becomes a **workstation**. You have already learned that a **terminal** is a device with a keyboard and screen used for input and output, but is not capable of processing on its own. A terminal is connected to a network that uses minicomputers and mainframes as servers. Any device connected to the network is called a **node**. Figure 28 illustrates a typical network configuration.

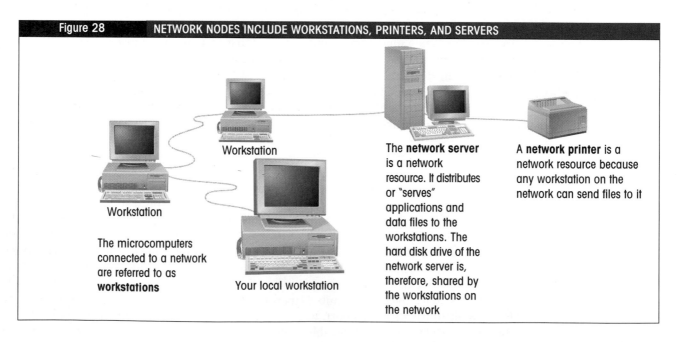

Figure 28   NETWORK NODES INCLUDE WORKSTATIONS, PRINTERS, AND SERVERS

Workstation

Workstation

The microcomputers connected to a network are referred to as **workstations**

Your local workstation

The **network server** is a network resource. It distributes or "serves" applications and data files to the workstations. The hard disk drive of the network server is, therefore, shared by the workstations on the network

A **network printer** is a network resource because any workstation on the network can send files to it

Look at the computer ad in Figure 1. Is this computer networked? Can it be networked? Why or why not? Your answer should be that the computer is not currently part of a network and is not shipped with a network card. However, it should be possible to connect this computer to a network with the appropriate network card and software, which would have to be purchased separately.

Telecommunications

Telecommunications means communicating over a comparatively long distance using a phone line. When it is not possible to connect users on one network, then telecommunications allows you to send and receive data over the telephone lines. To make this connection, you must use a communications device called a **modem**. A modem, which stands for *mo*dulator-*dem*odulator, is a device that connects your computer to a standard telephone jack. The modem converts the **digital**, or stop-start, signals your computer outputs into **analog**, or continuous wave, signals (sound waves) that can traverse ordinary phone lines. Figure 29 shows the telecommunications process, in which a modem converts digital signals to analog signals at the sending site (modulates) and a second modem converts the analog signals back into digital signals at the receiving site (demodulates).

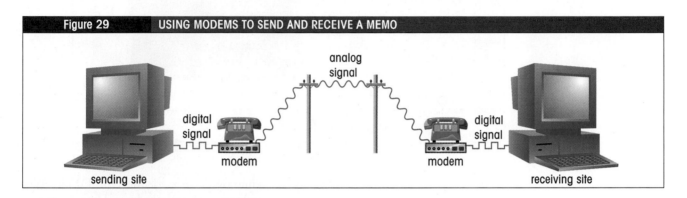

Figure 29   USING MODEMS TO SEND AND RECEIVE A MEMO

Look again at Figure 1. Although this computer ad doesn't list a network interface card, it does include a 56K bps fax/modem. The number 56 represents the modem's capability to send and receive 57,600 **bits per second** (bps). This speed is adequate for Paik employees to connect to suppliers at other locations around the world.

The Internet: World Wide Web

The Internet

In the mid-1990s, the expansion of the Internet greatly enhanced the possibility of connecting to your global offices. The Internet was originally developed for the government to connect researchers around the world who needed to share data. Today, the Internet is the largest network in the world, connecting millions of people. It has become an invaluable communications channel for individuals, businesses, and governments around the world.

The first Internet experience most people have is to use **electronic mail**, more commonly called **e-mail**. This is the capability to send a message from one user's computer to another user's computer where it is stored until the receiver opens it. The vast network of networks that make up the Internet pass the message along through electronic links called **gateways**. E-mail has become such an integral part of business that you know that you must recommend it to Mr. Paik. Your recommendation will list its advantages: lower postage costs, lower long-distance charges, and increased worker productivity.

The newest commercial benefit of using the Internet is the emergence of the **World Wide Web**, sometimes referred to simply as the **Web**. The Web is a huge database of information that is stored on network servers in places that allow public access. The information is stored as text files called **Web pages** that can include text, graphics, sound, animation, and video. Figure 30 shows a sample Web page.

Figure 30   A HOME PAGE ON THE WORLD WIDE WEB

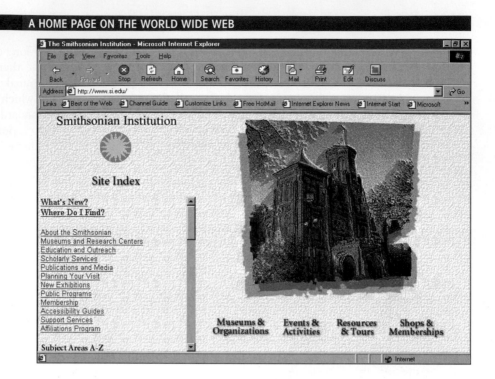

The evolution of multimedia and Internet technologies has made the World Wide Web the perfect communication tool for marketing business services and products. Hyperlinks are the primary resource for making the Web possible. A **hyperlink** is a place on a computer screen that is programmed to connect to a particular file on the same network server, or even on a network server on the other side of the globe. The communications software that helps you navigate the World Wide Web is called **Web browsing** software, or a **Web browser**. You decide to include the benefits of Internet and World Wide Web access in your recommendation to Mr. Paik. Specifically, you plan to convince him that he could sell carpets and advertise his carpet renovation services through the Web.

Computer Software

Just as a tape player or DVD player is worthless without tapes or DVDs, computer hardware is useless without software. Many people think the word *software* applies to any part of the computer system that is not hardware, but that is not an accurate definition. **Software** is defined as the instructions and associated data that direct the computer to accomplish a task. Sometimes the term *software* refers to a single program, but often the term refers to a collection of programs and data that are packaged together, as shown in Figure 31. The software you use determines what type of computer you can use and what you can do with the computer.

Software can be divided into two major categories: system software and application software. **System software** helps the computer carry out its basic operating tasks. **Application software** helps the user carry out a variety of tasks.

Figure 31	A SOFTWARE PRODUCT

A **software package** contains disks or a CD-ROM and a reference manual.

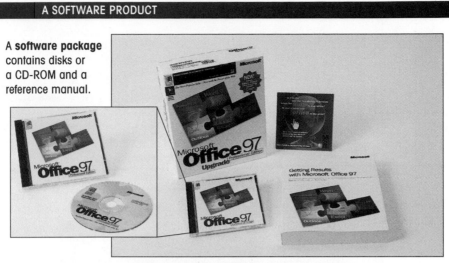

The CD-ROM contains one or more **programs**, and possibly some data. For example, the Microsoft Office 97 software includes programs that help you draw graphics, write documents, and make calculations. The software also includes some data, such as a thesaurus of words and their synonyms.

System Software

User Interfaces

System software manages the fundamental operations of your computer, such as loading programs and data into memory, executing programs, saving data to disks, displaying information on the monitor, and transmitting data through a port to a peripheral device. There are four types of system software: operating systems, utilities, device drivers, and programming languages.

An **operating system** controls basic input and output, allocates system resources, manages storage space, maintains security, and detects equipment failure. You have already learned the importance of data communications, both inside a standalone computer and from a workstation to other users on a network. The flow of data from the microprocessor to memory to peripherals and back again is called basic **I/O**, or **i**nput/**o**utput. The operating system controls this flow of data like an air-traffic controller manages airport traffic.

A system resource is any part of the computer system, including memory, storage devices, and the microprocessor, that can be used by a computer program. The operating system allocates system resources so programs run properly. Most of today's computers are capable of **multitasking**—opening and running more than one program at a time—because the operating system is allocating memory and processing time to make multitasking possible. An example of multitasking is producing a document in your word processing program while you check a resource on the Internet. Both the word processing program and the Web browsing program are allowed to use parts of the computer's resources, so you can look at the resource periodically while you are writing about it in your paper. The operating system is also responsible for managing the files on your storage devices. Not only does it open and save files, but it also keeps track of every part of every file for you and lets you know if any part is missing. This activity is like a filing clerk who puts files away when they are not being used, and gets them for you when you need them again. Figure 32 illustrates how the operating system assists word processing software to print a document.

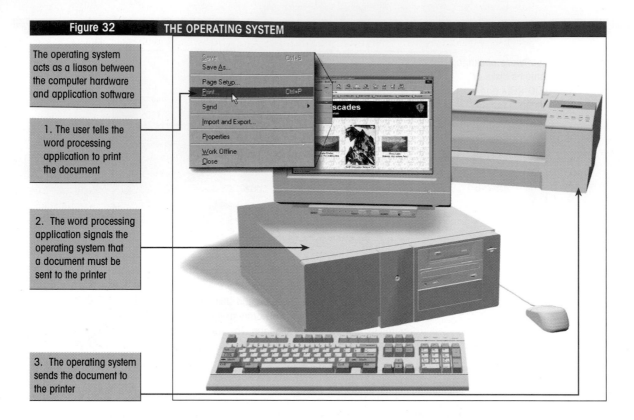

Figure 32 THE OPERATING SYSTEM

The operating system acts as a liason between the computer hardware and application software

1. The user tells the word processing application to print the document

2. The word processing application signals the operating system that a document must be sent to the printer

3. The operating system sends the document to the printer

While you are working on the computer, the operating system is constantly guarding against equipment failure. Each electronic circuit is checked periodically, and the moment a problem is detected, the user is notified with a warning message on the screen.

The operating system's responsibility to maintain security may include requiring a username and password or checking the computer for virus infection. Unscrupulous programmers deliberately construct harmful programs, called **viruses**, which instruct your computer to perform destructive activities, such as erasing a disk drive. Most viruses are more annoying than destructive, but computer users should protect themselves by using virus protection software. **Virus protection software** searches executable files for the sequences of characters that may cause harm and disinfects the files by erasing or disabling those commands.

Microsoft Windows is referred to as an **operating environment** because it provides a **graphical user interface** (GUI, pronounced "goo-ey") that acts as a liaison between the user and all of the computer's hardware and software. In addition to the operating system, Windows also includes utilities, device drivers, and some application programs that perform common tasks. Since the mid-1980s, Windows has become one of the most popular operating environments because its graphics and menus make it easy to learn and quick to use.

Utilities are another category of system software that augment the operating system by taking over some of its responsibility for allocating hardware resources. There are many utilities that come with the operating system, but some independent software developers offer utilities for sale separately. For example, Norton Utilities is a very popular collection of utility software.

Each peripheral device requires a **device driver**, system software that helps the computer communicate with that particular device. When you add a device to an existing computer, part of its installation includes adding its device driver to the computer's configuration.

The last type of system software is **computer programming languages**, which a programmer uses to write computer instructions. The instructions are translated into electrical signals that the computer can manipulate and process. Some examples of popular programming languages are BASIC, Visual Basic, C, C++, COBOL, Ada, FORTRAN, Java, JavaScript, CGI, and Perl.

As you get ready to make your recommendations to Mr. Paik, you realize that the primary factor in deciding the computer specifications you choose to purchase is the software his employees will be using.

Application Software

Application software enables you to perform specific computer tasks. In the business world, some examples of tasks that are accomplished with application software are document production, spreadsheet, and database management. In addition, businesses may sometimes use graphics and presentation software, including multimedia applications.

Document production software includes word processing software, desktop publishing software, e-mail editors, and Web authoring software. All of these production tools have a variety of features that assist you in writing and formatting documents. Most offer **spell checking** to help you avoid typographical and spelling errors, as shown in Figure 33.

Figure 33	IN-LINE SPELL CHECK

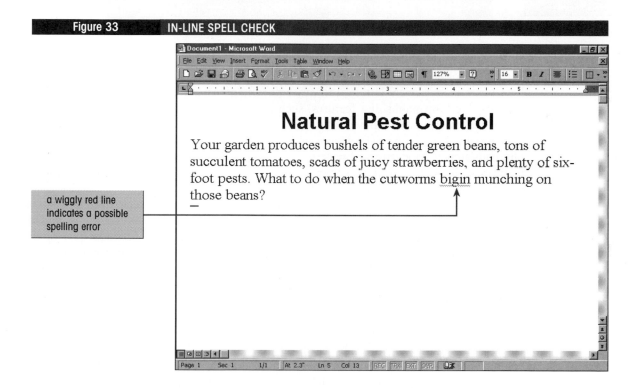

a wiggly red line indicates a possible spelling error

Many also assist you with **grammar-checking** and **thesaurus** tools to improve your writing by offering suggestions and alternatives. Most document production software allows you to perform **block operations**, an editing tool that quickly reorganizes your words after they have been typed. Block operations may also be called **copy-and-paste** or **cut-and-paste**, which is exactly what they allow you to do: copy or move words around. Document production software may also include **search** or **replace** features that allow you to look for a sequence of characters and substitute new text.

A **document template** is a preformatted document into which you type your text. A template might include format settings such as margins, line spacing, **font** (the style of type), and font size. Templates makes it easier to produce consistent documents, such as letterhead or business cards that make a business familiar. Figure 34 shows some of the document templates available with Microsoft Word, a popular word processing software package.

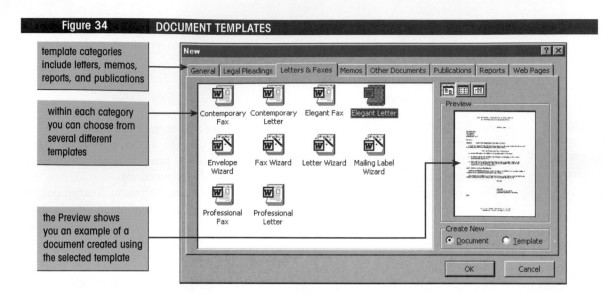

Figure 34 DOCUMENT TEMPLATES

template categories include letters, memos, reports, and publications

within each category you can choose from several different templates

the Preview shows you an example of a document created using the selected template

Desktop publishing software is a variation of word processing software that focuses on the format or printed appearance of documents. It is particularly useful for the design of brochures, posters, newsletters, and other documents that are printed in special sizes and formats. Desktop publishing features, such as automatic page numbering and the use of styles, facilitate the development of multiple-page documents. A **style** is a collection of formatting options that are given a name and used repeatedly throughout a document to maintain consistency. Modern word processing software now includes many desktop publishing features such as the automatic generation of a table of contents or index and the ability to insert graphics.

Data communications makes possible the production of documents referred to as **electronic publishing**. Instead of printing and distributing documents on paper, many businesses and individuals are transmitting them electronically by including them in e-mail messages, posting them to the World Wide Web, or participating in electronic conferences where participants can view documents simultaneously. **Web authoring software** transforms word processing documents into a format that can be viewed electronically on remote computers.

Spreadsheet software is a numerical analysis tool that both businesses and individuals use extensively. You can use spreadsheet software, for example, to maintain your checkbook register. Most people use a calculator to keep track of their bank accounts, but using a spreadsheet has several advantages. Spreadsheet software creates a **worksheet**, composed of a grid of columns and rows. Each column is lettered, and each row is numbered. The intersection of a column and row is a **cell**, and each cell has a unique address, called its **cell reference**. Figure 35 shows a typical worksheet that includes a simple calculation.

You type numbers into the grid, then create formulas that perform calculations using these numbers. In many ways, a spreadsheet is the ultimate calculator. Once your numbers are on the screen, you don't have to reenter them when you want to redo a calculation with revised or corrected numbers. As an additional benefit, spreadsheet software provides you with excellent printouts of the raw data or of graphs created from the data.

With the appropriate data and formulas, you can use an electronic spreadsheet to prepare financial reports, analyze investment portfolios, calculate amortization tables, examine alternative bid proposals, and project income, as well as perform many other tasks involved in making informed business decisions.

Figure 35   **A TYPICAL WORKSHEET**

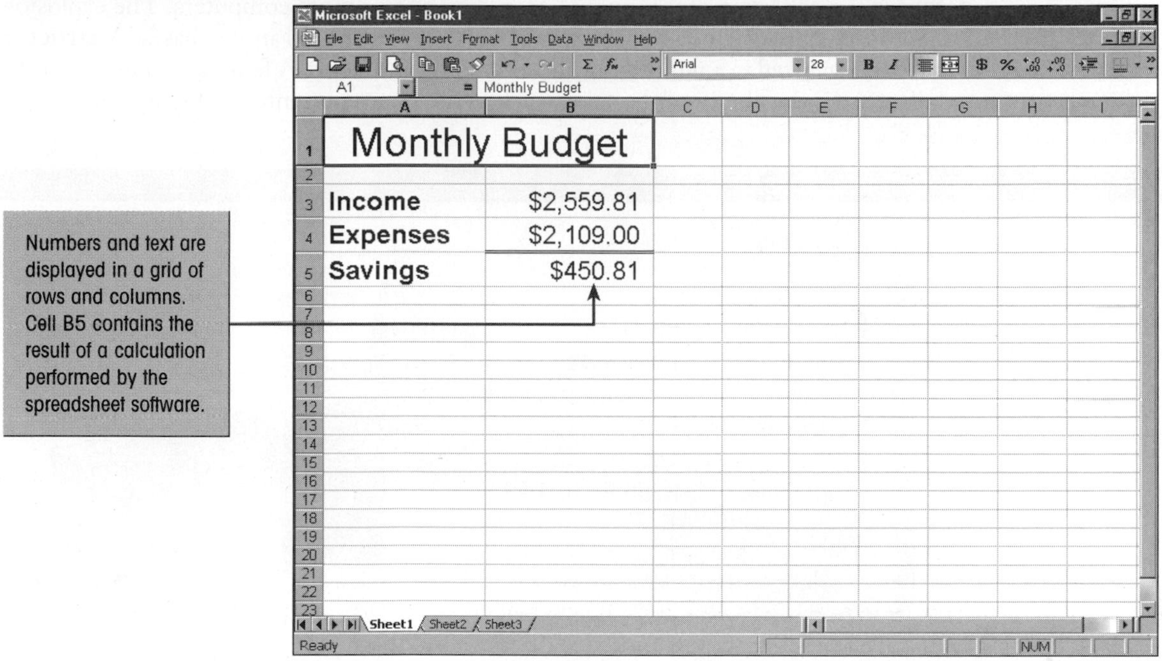

Numbers and text are displayed in a grid of rows and columns. Cell B5 contains the result of a calculation performed by the spreadsheet software.

	A	B
1	Monthly Budget	
2		
3	Income	$2,559.81
4	Expenses	$2,109.00
5	Savings	$450.81

Graphs provide a quick, visual summary of data. With spreadsheet software it is simple to create attractive graphs. Because they are so easy to produce, you have to be careful that the way you are presenting your data is a visual representation of the truth. Figure 36 shows how changing the shape of a graph can dramatically change the visual summary it provides. Although the data in these two graphs is the same, the graph on the right makes it look as if sales are climbing at a faster rate than the sales in the other graph.

Figure 36   **GRAPHS CAN "STRETCH THE TRUTH"**

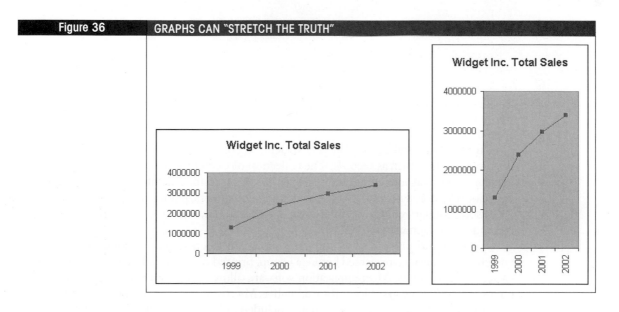

One of the most common types of application software is **database management** software. A **database** is a collection of information stored on one or more computers. The explosion of information in our society is primarily organized and managed in databases. A **structured database** is organized in a uniform format of records and fields. A familiar example of a structured database is the library card catalog, such as the one represented in Figure 37.

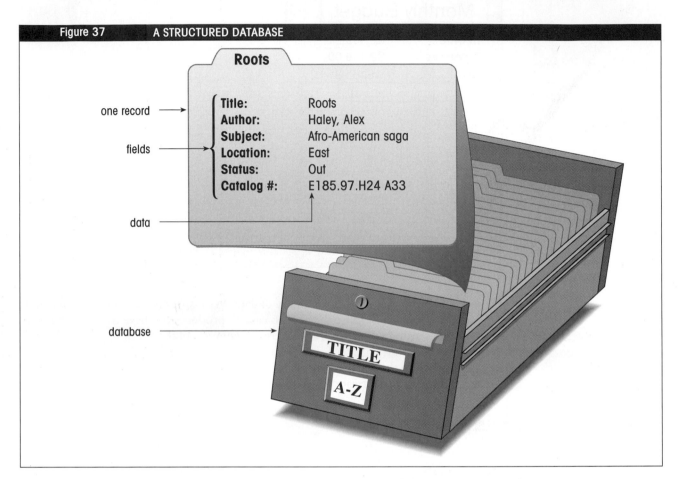

Figure 37   A STRUCTURED DATABASE

Structured databases typically store data that describes a collection of similar entities. Some other examples are student academic records, medical records, a warehouse inventory, or an address book.

A **free-form database** is a loosely structured collection of information, usually stored as documents rather than as records. The collection of word processing documents you have created and stored on your computer is an example of a free-form database. Another example is an encyclopedia stored on a CD-ROM containing documents, photographs, and even video clips. The most familiar example of a free-form database in our society is the World Wide Web with its millions of documents stored worldwide.

Graphics and presentation software allow you to create illustrations, diagrams, graphs, and charts that can be projected before a group, printed out for quick reference, or transmitted to remote computers. Most application software allows you to include graphics that you can create yourself using graphics software, such as Microsoft Paint or Adobe PhotoShop. You can also use **clip art**, simple drawings that are included as collections with many software packages. Microsoft PowerPoint is popular presentation software that allows you to create colorful presentations and transparencies. A Microsoft PowerPoint screen is shown in Figure 38.

Figure 38   **PRESENTATION SOFTWARE**

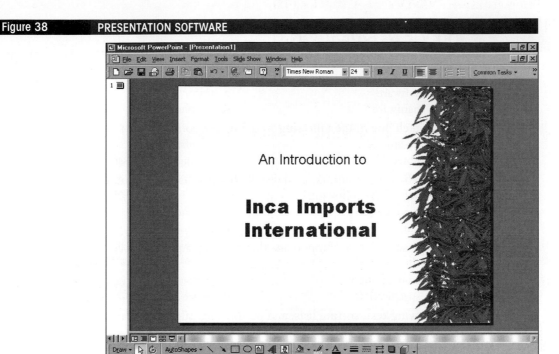

Multimedia authoring software allows you to record digital sound files, video files, and animations that can be included in presentations and other documents. Macromedia Director and MicroMedium Digital Trainer Professional are two examples of software that you can use to create files that include multimedia. You can sequence and format the screens into tutorials or presentations. Like Web authoring software, multimedia authoring software also uses hypertext to link documents so that the reader can jump from one document to another. Most modern application software allows users to integrate these multimedia elements into other types of files.

In the 1990s, one of the most powerful developments in computer use was the ability of users to use data created in one application in a document created by another application. For instance, it has become so easy to add a graphic to your word processing document that you forget the graphic was created and saved by someone using graphics software.

Applications that were designed for the Windows environment have added a new dimension to this merging capability. **Object linking and embedding** (OLE) refers to the ability to use data from another file, called the *source*. Embedding occurs when you copy and paste the source data in the new file. Think of embedding as taking a snapshot of the original. No matter what happens to the original, you still have the copy, as it appeared when you first copied it. Linking allows you to create a connection between the source data and the copy in the new file. The link updates the copy every time a change is made to the source data. The seamless nature of OLE among some applications is referred to as **integration**, and the ability to integrate data from all of your applications has become an important skill in business.

You are now ready to approach Mr. Paik with your recommendations for microcomputer hardware, network access, and software. Look back at Figure 1 to be sure that you understand each specification listed. Also consider the software options you should recommend. What will you include? The computer ad already lists Microsoft Windows, so your recommendation should include document production, spreadsheet, and database management software that is compatible with Microsoft Windows. Current versions of Windows include e-mail and network communication software, including Web browsing and Web authoring software. Here's hoping that Mr. Paik approves your recommendations. Good luck!

REVIEW QUESTIONS

1. What is the key to a computer's versatility?
   a. software
   b. hardware
   c. price
   d. peripherals

2. Which one of the following would not be considered a microcomputer?
   a. desktop
   b. notebook
   c. mainframe
   d. personal digital assistant

3. Keyboards, monitors, hard disk drives, printers, and motherboards are all examples of which of the following?
   a. input devices
   b. output devices
   c. peripherals
   d. hardware

4. The selection of components that make up a particular computer system is referred to as the _____.
   a. configuration
   b. specification
   c. protocol
   d. device driver

5. Moving text, sorting lists, and performing calculations are examples of which of the following?
   a. input
   b. output
   c. processing
   d. storage

6. What do you call each 1 or 0 used in the representation of computer data?
   a. a bit
   b. a byte
   c. an ASCII
   d. a pixel

7. What usually represents one character of data?
   a. a bit
   b. a byte
   c. an integer
   d. a pixel

8. What is a megabyte?
   a. 10 kilobytes
   b. about a million bytes
   c. one-half a gigabyte
   d. about a million bits

9. Which one of the following microprocessors is fastest?
   a. 200 MHz Pentium
   b. 166 MHz Pentium Pro
   c. 200 MHz Pentium with MMX
   d. 233 MHz Pentium II

10. Which of the following temporarily stores data and programs while you are using them?
    a. ROM
    b. a floppy disk
    c. RAM
    d. a hard disk

11. What do you call a collection of data stored on a disk under a name that you assign it?
    a. a file
    b. the operating system
    c. a protocol
    d. a pixel

12. Which of the following storage media does not allow you to recycle by writing over old data?
    a. hard disk
    b. floppy disk
    c. CD
    d. tape

13. What connects a monitor to a computer?
    a. a parallel port
    b. a network card
    c. a graphics adapter
    d. new letter-quality mode

14. A microcomputer that is attached to a network is called a _____.
    a. desktop
    b. workstation
    c. terminal
    d. PDA

15. What telecommunications hardware is needed to convert digital signals to analog signals?
    a. mouse
    b. device driver
    c. modem
    d. slot

16. Which one of the following is system software?
    a. Microsoft Excel   c. Microsoft Paint
    b. Microsoft Windows   d. Microsoft Word

17. Which of the following is not a function of an operating system?
    a. controls basic input and output   c. manages storage space
    b. allocates system resources   d. carries out a specific task for the user

18. Random access memory (RAM) is measured in _____.

19. Disk access time is measured in _____.

20. The clock speed of a microprocessor is measured in _____.

21. _____ is the maximum number of pixels a monitor can display.

22. The transmission of text, numeric, voice, or video data from one computer to another is called _____.

23. Connecting a microcomputer to peripheral devices is called

    _____.

24. The capability to send a text message from one user to another user's account where it is stored until the receiver opens it, is called _____.

25. The _____ is a huge database of information that is stored on network servers around the world, and which users access by using browser software.

26. For each of the following data items, indicate how many bytes of storage would be required:

Data Item	Number of Bytes
North	
U.S.A.	
General Ledger	

27. Read the following requirements for using Microsoft Office 2000 Premium (taken from the documentation that accompanies the software). Then turn back to the computer advertisement shown in Figure 1 at the beginning of the chapter and determine if the computer specifications listed in the ad are sufficient to run Office 97.

    To use Microsoft Office 2000 Premium, you need:
    - PC with a Pentium 75 MHz or higher processor
    - Pentium 166 MHz or higher is required for PhotoDraw
    - User of Windows 95 or Windows 98 will require 16 MB of RAM for the operating system, plus an additional 4 MB of RAM for each application running simultaneously (8 MB for Outlook)
    - Users of Windows NT Workstation version 4.0 or later will require 32 MB of RAM for the operating system, plus an additional 4 MB of RAM for each application running simultaneously (8 MB for Outlook)

    Hard Disk Space Requirements for Office 2000 Premium:
    - 252 MB for Disc 1 (Word, Excel, Outlook, PowerPoint, Access, FrontPage)
    - 174 MB for Disc 2 (Publisher, Small Business Tools)
    - 100 MB for Disc 3 (PhotoDraw)

28. Using the system requirements listed in Question 27, look through a recent computer magazine and find the least expensive computer that will run the Microsoft Office 2000 Premium software. Make a photocopy of the ad showing the specifications, price, and vendor. Write the name of the magazine and the issue date at the top of the photocopied ad. Write a two-page paper that supports your selection.

29. In this chapter, you learned that the use of multimedia requires special hardware and software. Look for current prices and specifications of multimedia hardware in advertisements in magazines or in your local newspaper. What are the highest priced devices, and why are they so expensive? In the following chart, add the specifications and price for the most expensive examples of these devices that you can find. Look at the computer advertisement shown in Figure 1 at the beginning of the chapter and determine if the computer specifications listed in the ad are sufficient to run multimedia. If not, write a statement that justifies adding the cost of the higher-quality device you listed here.

Multimedia Device	Specifications	Price
DVD-ROM drive		
Speakers		
Headphones		
Large, high-resolution monitor		

LAB ASSIGNMENTS

The New Perspectives Labs are designed to help you master some of the key computer concepts and skills presented in each chapter of the text. If you are using your school's lab computers, your instructor or technical support person should have installed the Labs software for you. If you want to use the Labs on your home computer, ask your instructor for the appropriate software.

Each Lab has two parts: Steps and Explore. Use Steps first to learn and review concepts. Read the information on each page and do the numbered steps. As you work through the Lab, you will be asked to answer Quick Check questions about what you have learned. At the end of the Lab, you will see a Summary Report of your answers to the Quick Checks. If your instructor wants you to turn in this Summary Report, click the Print button on the Summary Report screen.

When you have completed Steps, you can click the Explore button to complete the Lab Assignments. You can also use Explore to practice the skills you learned and to explore concepts on your own.

Using a Mouse

A mouse is a standard input device on most of today's computers. You need to know how to use a mouse to manipulate graphical user interfaces and to use the rest of the Labs.

1. The Steps for the Using a Mouse Lab show you how to click, double-click, and drag objects using the mouse. Click the Steps button and begin the Steps. As you work through the Steps, answer all of the Quick Check questions that appear. When you complete the Steps, you will see a Summary Report that summarizes your performance on the Quick Checks. Follow the directions on the screen to print the Summary Report.

2. In Explore, demonstrate your ability to use a mouse and to control a Windows program by creating a poster. To create a poster for an upcoming sports event, select a graphic, type the caption for the poster, then select a font, font styles, and a border. Print your completed poster.

Using a Keyboard

To become an effective computer user, you must be familiar with your primary input device—the keyboard.

1. The Steps for the Using a Keyboard Lab provide you with a structured introduction to the keyboard layout and the function of special computer keys. Click the Steps button and begin the Steps. As you work through the Steps, answer all of the Quick Check questions that appear. When you complete the Steps, you will see a Summary Report that summarizes your performance on the Quick Checks. Follow the directions on the screen to print the Summary Report.

2. In Explore, start the typing tutor. You can develop your typing skills using the typing tutor in Explore. Take the typing test and print out your results.

3. In Explore, try to improve your typing speed by 10 words per minute. For example, if you currently type 20 words per minute, your goal would be 30 words per minute. Practice each typing lesson until you see a message that indicates you can proceed to the next lesson. Create a Practice Record as shown here to keep track of how much you practice. When you have reached your goal, print out the results of a typing test to verify your results.

Practice Record

Name: _____

Section: _____

Start Date: _____ Start Typing Speed: _____ wpm

End Date: _____ End Typing Speed: _____ wpm

Lesson #: _____ Date Practiced/Time Practiced _____

Peripheral Devices

A wide variety of peripheral devices provide expandability for computer systems and provide users with the equipment necessary to accomplish tasks efficiently. In the Peripheral Devices Lab you will use an online product catalog of peripheral devices.

1. Click the Steps button and begin the Steps. Complete the Steps to find out how to use the online product catalog. As you work through the Steps, answer all of the Quick Check questions. When you complete the Steps, you will see a Summary Report of your performance on the Quick Checks. Follow the directions on the screen to print the Summary Report.

2. After you know how to use the product catalog to look up products, features, and prices, use the catalog to do the following:
   a. List the characteristics that differentiate printers.
   b. List the factors that differentiate monitors.
   c. Describe the factors that determine the appropriate type of scanner for a task.
   d. List the peripheral devices in the catalog that are specially designed for notebook computers.

3. Suppose that the company that produces the peripheral devices catalog selected your name from its list of customers for a free scanner. You can select any one of the scanners in the catalog. Assume that you own a notebook computer to which you could attach any one of the scanners. Click the Explore button and use the catalog to help you write a one-page paper explaining which scanner you would select, why you would select it, and how you would use it.

4. Suppose you are in charge of a new college computing lab. The lab will include 25 computers that are used by students from all departments at the college. You have a $3,000 budget for printers. Use the product catalog to decide which printers you would purchase for the lab. Write a one-page memo to your boss that justifies your choice.

5. Suppose you own a basic computer system. You have an idea that you can earn the money for your college tuition by using your computer to help other students produce spiffy reports with color graphs and scanned images. Your parents have agreed to "loan" you $1,000 to get started. Click the Explore button and look through the online peripheral devices catalog. List any of the devices that might help you with this business venture. Write a one-page paper explaining how you would spend your $1,000 to get the equipment you need to start the business.

In this Lab you manipulate a simulated computer to view what happens in memory and on disk when you create, save, open, revise, and delete files. Understanding what goes on "inside the box" will help you quickly grasp how to perform basic file operations with most application software.

1. Click the Steps button to learn how to use the simulated computer to view the contents of memory and disk when you perform basic file operations. As you proceed through the Steps, answer all of the Quick Check questions that appear. After you complete the Steps, you will see a Quick Check Summary Report. Follow the instructions on the screen to print this report.

2. Click the Explore button and use the simulated computer to perform the following tasks.
   a. Create a document containing your name and the city in which you were born. Save this document as NAME.
   b. Create another document containing two of your favorite foods. Save this document as FOODS.
   c. Create another file containing your two favorite classes. Call this file CLASSES.
   d. Open the FOOD file and add another one of your favorite foods. Save this file without changing its name.
   e. Open the NAME file. Change this document so it contains your name and the name of your school. Save this as a new document called SCHOOL.
   f. Write down how many files are on the simulated disk and the exact contents of each file.
   g. Delete all the files.

3. In Explore, use the simulated computer to perform the following tasks.
   a. Create a file called MUSIC that contains the name of your favorite CD.
   b. Create another document that contains eight numbers and call this file LOTTERY.
   c. You didn't win the lottery this week. Revise the contents of the LOTTERY file, but save the revision as LOTTERY2.
   d. Revise the MUSIC file so it also contains the name of your favorite musician or composer, and save this file as MUSIC2.
   e. Delete the MUSIC file.
   f. Write down how many files are on the simulated disk and the exact contents of each file.

One of the most popular services on the Internet is the World Wide Web. This Lab is a Web simulator that teaches you how to use Web browser software to find information. You can use this Lab whether or not your school provides you with Internet access.

1. Click the Steps button to learn how to use Web browser software. As you proceed through the Steps, answer all of the Quick Check questions that appear. After you complete the Steps, you will see a Quick Check Summary Report. Follow the instructions on the screen to print this report.

2. Click the Explore button on the Welcome screen. Use the Web browser to locate a weather map of the Caribbean Virgin Islands. What is its URL?

3. A SCUBA diver named Wadson Lachouffe has been searching for the fabled treasure of Greybeard the pirate. A link from the Adventure Travel Web site www.atour.com leads to Wadson's Web page called "Hidden Treasure." In Explore, locate the Hidden Treasure page and answer the following questions:
   a. What was the name of Greybeard's ship?
   b. What was Greybeard's favorite food?
   c. What does Wadson think happened to Greybeard's ship?

4. In the Steps, you found a graphic of Jupiter from the photo archives of the Jet Propulsion Laboratory. In the Explore section of the Lab, you can also find a graphic of Saturn. Suppose one of your friends wanted a picture of Saturn for an astronomy report. Make a list of the blue, underlined links your friend must click in the correct order to find the Saturn graphic. Assume that your friend will begin at the Web Trainer home page.

5. Enter the URL http://www.atour.com to jump to the Adventure Travel Web site. Write a one-page description of this site. In your paper include a description of the information at the site, the number of pages the site contains, and a diagram of the links it contains.

6. Chris Thomson is a student at UVI and has his own Web pages. In Explore, look at the information Chris has included on his pages. Suppose you could create your own Web page. What would you include? Use word-processing software to design your own Web pages. Make sure you indicate the graphics and links you would use.

User Interfaces

You have learned that the hardware and software for a user interface determine how you interact and communicate with the computer. In the User Interfaces Lab, you will try five different user interfaces to accomplish the same task—creating a graph.

1. Click the Steps button to find out how each interface works. As you work through the Steps, answer all of the Quick Check questions. When you complete the Steps, you will see a Summary Report of your performance on the Quick Checks. Follow the directions on the screen to print the Summary Report.

2. In Explore, use each interface to make a 3-D pie graph using data set 1. Title your graphs "Cycle City Sales." Use the percent style to show the percent of each slice of the pie. Print each of the five graphs (one for each interface).

3. In Explore, select one of the user interfaces. Write a step-by-step set of instructions for how to produce a line graph using data set 2. This line graph should show lines and symbols, and have the title "Widget Production."

4. Using the user interface terminology you learned in this Lab, write a description of each of the interfaces you used in the Lab. Then, suppose you worked for a software publisher and you were going to create a software package for producing line, bar, column, and pie graphs. Which user interface would you use for the software? Why?

Multimedia

Multimedia brings together text, graphics, sound, animation, video, and photo images. In this Lab you will learn how to apply multimedia and then have the chance to see what it might be like to design some aspects of multimedia projects.

1. Click the Steps button to learn about multimedia development. As you proceed through the Steps, answer the Quick Check questions. After you complete the Steps, you will see a Quick Check Report. Follow the instructions on the screen to print this report.

2. In Explore, browse through the STS-79 Multimedia Mission Log. How many videos are included in the Multimedia Mission Log? The image on the Mission Profile page is a vector drawing; what happens when you enlarge it?

3. Listen to the sound track on Day 3. Is this a WAV file or a MIDI file? Why do you think so? Is this a synthesized sound or a digitized sound? Listen to the sound track on page 8. Can you tell if this is a WAV file or a MIDI file?

4. Suppose you were hired as a multimedia designer for a multimedia series on targeting fourth- and fifth-grade students. Describe the changes you would make to the Multimedia Mission Log so it would be suitable for these students. Also, include a sketch showing a screen from your revised design.

5. When you view the Mission Log on your computer, do you see palette flash? Why or why not? If you see palette flash, list the images that flash.

6. Multimedia can be effectively applied to projects such as Encyclopedias, atlases, and animated storybooks; to computer-based training for foreign languages, first aid, or software applications; for games and sports simulations; for business presentations; for personal albums, scrapbooks, and baby books; for product catalogs and Web pages.

Suppose you were hired to create one of these projects. Write a one-paragraph description of the project you would be creating. Describe some of the multimedia elements you would include. For each of the elements indicate its source and whether you would need to obtain permission for its use. Finally, sketch a screen or two showing your completed project.

New Perspectives on

MICROSOFT®
WINDOWS® 2000
PROFESSIONAL

Read This Before You Begin

To the Student

Make Data Disk Program

To complete the Level I tutorials, Review Assignments, and Projects, you need three Data Disks. Your instructor will either provide you with Data Disks or ask you to make your own.

If you are making your own Data Disks you will need three blank, formatted high-density disks and access to the Make Data Disk program. If you want to install the Make Data Disk program to your home computer, you can obtain it from your instructor or from the Web. To download the Make Data Disk program from the Web, go to **www.course.com**, click Data Disks, and follow the instructions on the screen.

To install the Make Data Disk program, select and click the file you just downloaded from **www.course.com**, 6548-9.exe. Follow the onscreen instructions to complete the installation. If you have any trouble obtaining or installing the Make Data Disk program, ask your instructor or technical support person for assistance.

Once you have obtained and installed the Make Data Disk program, you can use it to create your Data Disks according to the steps in the tutorials.

Course Labs

The Level I tutorials in this book feature three interactive Course Labs to help you understand Using a Keyboard, Using a Mouse, and Using Files concepts. There are Lab Assignments at the end of Tutorials 1 and 2 that relate to these Labs. To start a Lab, click the **Start** button on the Windows 2000 taskbar, point to **Programs**, point to

Course Labs, point to **New Perspectives Course Labs**, and click the name of the Lab you want to use.

Using Your Own Computer

If you are going to work through this book using your own computer, you need:

■ **Computer System** Microsoft Windows 2000 Professional must be installed on a local hard drive or on a network drive. This book is about Windows 2000 Professional—for those who have Windows 2000 Millennium, you might notice some differences.

■ **Data Disks** You will not be able to complete the tutorials or exercises in this book using your own computer until you have your Data Disks. See "Make Data Disk Program" above for details on obtaining your Data Disks.

■ **Course Labs** See your instructor or technical support person to obtain the Course Lab software for use on your own computer.

Visit Our World Wide Web Site

Additional materials designed especially for you are available on the World Wide Web. Go to **http://www.course.com**.

To the Instructor

The Make Data Disk Program and Course Labs for this title are available in the Instructor's Resource Kit for this title. Follow the instructions in the Help file on the CD-ROM to install the programs to your network or standalone computer. For information on using the Make Data Disk Program or the Course Labs, see the "To the Student" section above. Students will be switching the default installation settings to Web style in Tutorial 2. You are granted a license to copy the Data Files and Course Labs to any computer or computer network used by students who have purchased this book.

OBJECTIVES

In this tutorial you will:

- Start and shut down Windows 2000

- Identify the objects on the Windows 2000 desktop

- Practice mouse functions

- Run software programs, switch between them, and close them

- Identify and use the controls in a window

- Use Windows 2000 controls such as menus, toolbars, list boxes, scroll bars, option buttons, tabs, and check boxes

- Explore the Windows 2000 Help system

LABS

EXPLORING THE BASICS

Investigating the Windows 2000 Operating System

CASE

Your First Day on the Computer

You walk into the computer lab and sit down at a desk. There's a computer in front of you, and you find yourself staring dubiously at the screen. Where to start? As if in answer to your question, your friend Steve Laslow appears.

"You start with the operating system," says Steve. Noticing your puzzled look, Steve explains that the **operating system** is software that helps the computer carry out operating tasks such as displaying information on the computer screen and saving data on your disks. (Software refers to the **programs**, or **applications**, that a computer uses to perform tasks.) Your computer uses the **Microsoft Windows 2000 Professional** operating system—Windows 2000, for short.

Steve explains that much of the software available for Windows 2000 has a standard graphical user interface. This means that once you have learned how to use one Windows program, such as Microsoft Word word-processing software, you are well on your way to understanding how to use other Windows software. Windows 2000 lets you use more than one program at a time, so you can easily switch between them—between your word-processing software and your appointment book software, for example. Finally, Windows 2000 makes it very easy to access the **Internet**, the worldwide collection of computers connected to one another to enable communication. All in all, Windows 2000 makes your computer effective and easy to use.

Steve recommends that you get started right away by starting Microsoft Windows 2000 and practicing some basic skills.

Starting Windows 2000

Using a Keyboard

Windows 2000 automatically starts when you turn on the computer. Depending on the way your computer is set up, you might be asked to enter your username and password.

To start Windows 2000:

1. Turn on your computer.

TROUBLE? If you are asked to select an operating system, do not take action. Windows 2000 will start automatically after a designated number of seconds. If it does not, ask your technical support person for help.

TROUBLE? If prompted to do so, type your assigned username and press the Tab key. Then type your password and press the Enter key to continue.

TROUBLE? If this is the first time you have started your computer with Windows 2000, messages might appear on your screen informing you that Windows is setting up components of your computer. If the Getting Started with Windows 2000 box appears, press and hold down the Alt key on your keyboard and then, while you hold down the Alt key, press the F4 key. The box closes.

After a moment, Windows 2000 starts. Windows 2000 has a **graphical user interface** (**GUI,** pronounced "gooey"), which uses **icons,** or pictures of familiar objects, such as file folders and documents, to represent items in your computer such as programs or files. Microsoft Windows 2000 gets its name from the rectangular work areas, called "windows," that appear on your screen as you work (although no windows should be open right now).

The Windows 2000 Desktop

In Windows terminology, the area displayed on your screen when Windows 2000 starts represents a **desktop**—a workspace for projects and the tools needed to manipulate those projects. When you first start a computer, it uses **default** settings, those preset by the operating system. The default desktop, for example, has a plain blue background. However, Microsoft designed Windows 2000 so that you can easily change the appearance of the desktop. You can, for example, add color, patterns, images, and text to the desktop background.

Many institutions design customized desktops for their computers. Figure 1-1 shows the default Windows 2000 desktop and two other examples of desktops, one designed for a business, North Pole Novelties, and one designed for a school, the University of Colorado. Although your desktop might not look exactly like any of the examples in Figure 1-1, you should be able to locate objects on your screen similar to those in Figure 1-1. Look at your screen and locate the objects labeled in Figure 1-1. The objects on your screen might appear larger or smaller than those in Figure 1-1, depending on your monitor's settings.

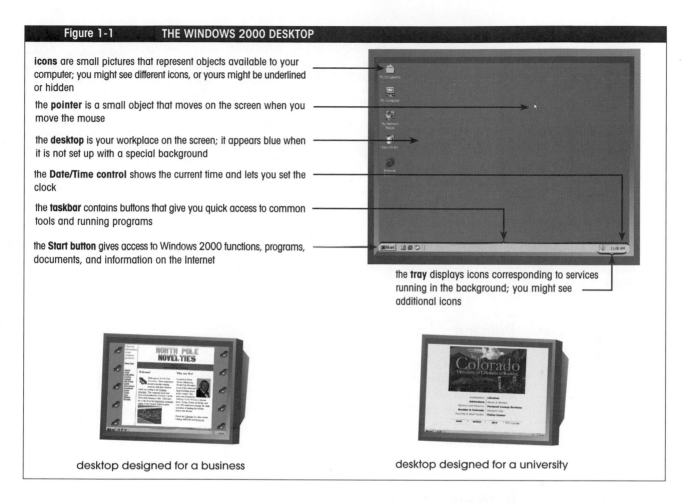

Figure 1-1 THE WINDOWS 2000 DESKTOP

icons are small pictures that represent objects available to your computer; you might see different icons, or yours might be underlined or hidden

the **pointer** is a small object that moves on the screen when you move the mouse

the **desktop** is your workplace on the screen; it appears blue when it is not set up with a special background

the **Date/Time control** shows the current time and lets you set the clock

the **taskbar** contains buttons that give you quick access to common tools and running programs

the **Start button** gives access to Windows 2000 functions, programs, documents, and information on the Internet

the **tray** displays icons corresponding to services running in the background; you might see additional icons

desktop designed for a business

desktop designed for a university

If the screen goes blank or starts to display a moving design, press any key to restore the Windows 2000 desktop.

Using a Pointing Device

Using a Mouse

A **pointing device** helps you interact with objects on the screen. Pointing devices come in many shapes and sizes; some are designed to ensure that your hand won't suffer fatigue while using them. Some are directly attached to your computer via a cable, whereas others function like a TV remote control and allow you to access your computer without being right next to it. Figure 1-2 shows examples of common pointing devices.

The most common pointing device is called a **mouse**, so this book uses that term. If you are using a different pointing device, such as a trackball, substitute that device whenever you see the term "mouse." Because Windows 2000 uses a graphical user interface, you need to know how to use the mouse to manipulate the objects on the screen. In this session you will learn about pointing and clicking. In Session 1.2 you will learn how to use the mouse to drag objects.

You can also interact with objects by using the keyboard; however, the mouse is more convenient for most tasks, so the tutorials in this book assume you are using one.

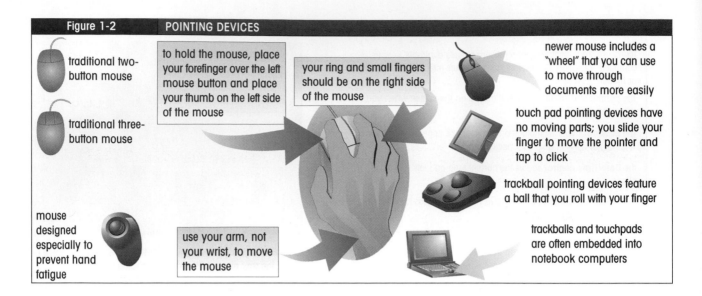

Figure 1-2   POINTING DEVICES

traditional two-button mouse

traditional three-button mouse

mouse designed especially to prevent hand fatigue

to hold the mouse, place your forefinger over the left mouse button and place your thumb on the left side of the mouse

your ring and small fingers should be on the right side of the mouse

use your arm, not your wrist, to move the mouse

newer mouse includes a "wheel" that you can use to move through documents more easily

touch pad pointing devices have no moving parts; you slide your finger to move the pointer and tap to click

trackball pointing devices feature a ball that you roll with your finger

trackballs and touchpads are often embedded into notebook computers

Pointing

You use a pointing device to move the pointer over objects on the desktop. The pointer is usually shaped like an arrow $\leftthreetimes$, although it can change shape depending on where it is on the screen and on what tasks you are performing. Most computer users place the mouse on a **mouse pad**, a flat piece of rubber that helps the mouse move smoothly. As you move the mouse on the mouse pad, the pointer on the screen moves in a corresponding direction.

You begin most Windows operations by positioning the pointer over a specific part of the screen. This is called **pointing**.

To move the pointer:

1. Position your right index finger over the left mouse button, as shown in Figure 1-2, but don't click yet. Lightly grasp the sides of the mouse with your thumb and little fingers.

TROUBLE? If you want to use the mouse with your left hand, ask your instructor or technical support person to help you use the Control Panel to swap the functions of the left and right mouse buttons. Be sure to find out how to change back to the right-handed mouse setting, so that you can reset the mouse each time you are finished in the lab.

2. Place the mouse on the mouse pad and then move the mouse. Watch the movement of the pointer.

TROUBLE? If you run out of room to move your mouse, lift the mouse and place it in the middle of the mouse pad. Notice that the pointer does not move when the mouse is not in contact with the mouse pad.

When you position the mouse pointer over certain objects, such as the objects on the taskbar, a "tip" appears. These "tips" are called **ScreenTips**, and they tell you the purpose or function of an object.

To view ScreenTips:

1. Use the mouse to point to the **Start** button 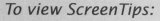, but don't click it. After a few seconds, you see the tip "Click here to begin," as shown in Figure 1-3.

   TROUBLE? If the Start button and taskbar don't appear, point to the bottom of the screen. They will then appear.

Figure 1-3	VIEWING SCREENTIPS

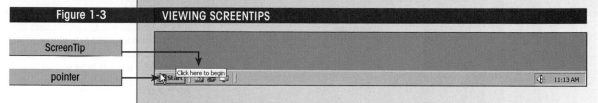

ScreenTip

pointer

2. Point to the time on the right end of the taskbar. Notice that today's date (or the date to which your computer's time clock is set) appears.

Clicking

Clicking is when you press a mouse button and immediately release it. Clicking sends a signal to your computer that you want to perform an action on the object you click. In Windows 2000 most actions are performed using the left mouse button. If you are told to click an object, click it with the left mouse button, unless instructed otherwise.

When you click the Start button, the Start menu appears. A **menu** is a list of options that you use to complete tasks. The **Start menu** provides you with access to programs, documents, and much more. Try clicking the Start button to open the Start menu.

To open the Start menu:

1. Point to the **Start** button 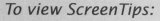.

2. Click the left mouse button. An arrow ▸ following an option on the Start menu indicates that you can view additional choices by navigating a **submenu**, a menu extending from the main menu. See Figure 1-4.

Figure 1-4	START MENU

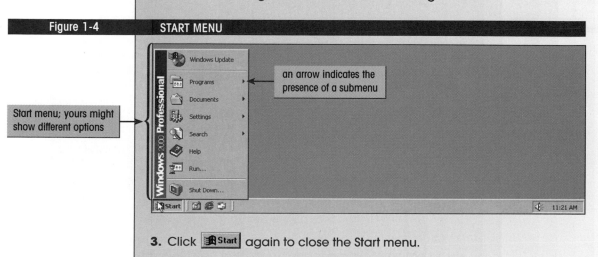

an arrow indicates the presence of a submenu

Start menu; yours might show different options

3. Click 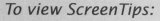 again to close the Start menu.

Next you'll learn how to select items on a submenu.

Selecting

In Windows 2000, pointing and clicking are often used to **select** an object, in other words, to choose it as the object you want to work with. Windows 2000 shows you which object is selected by highlighting it, usually by changing the object's color, putting a box around it, or making the object appear to be pushed in, as shown in Figure 1-5.

Figure 1-5	SELECTED OBJECTS

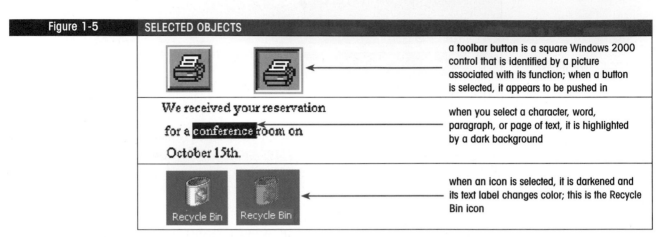

a **toolbar button** is a square Windows 2000 control that is identified by a picture associated with its function; when a button is selected, it appears to be pushed in

when you select a character, word, paragraph, or page of text, it is highlighted by a dark background

when an icon is selected, it is darkened and its text label changes color; this is the Recycle Bin icon

In Windows 2000, depending on your computer's settings, some objects are selected when you simply point to them, others when you click them. Practice selecting the Programs option on the Start menu to open the Programs submenu.

To select an option on a menu:

1. Click the **Start** button and notice how it appears to be pushed in, indicating it is selected.

2. Point to (but don't click) the **Programs** option. After a short pause, the Programs submenu opens, and the Programs option is highlighted to indicate it is selected. See Figure 1-6.

Figure 1-6	PROGRAMS SUBMENU

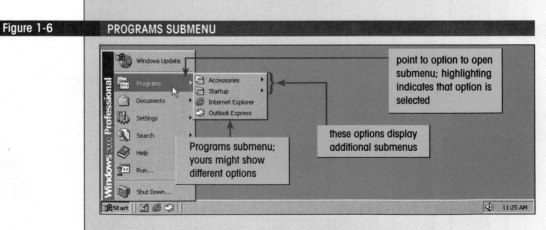

point to option to open submenu; highlighting indicates that option is selected

these options display additional submenus

Programs submenu; yours might show different options

TROUBLE? If a submenu other than the Programs menu opens, you selected the wrong option. Move the mouse so that the pointer points to Programs.

TROUBLE? If the Programs option doesn't appear, your Start menu might have too many options to fit on the screen. If that is the case, a double arrow ⌄ appears at the top or bottom of the Start menu. Click first the top and then the bottom arrow to view additional Start menu options until you locate the Programs menu option, and then point to it.

3. Now close the Start menu by clicking ▐▌Start again.

You return to the desktop.

Right-Clicking

Pointing devices were originally designed with a single button, so the term "clicking" had only one meaning: you pressed that button. Innovations in technology, however, led to the addition of a second and even a third button (and more recently, options such as a wheel) that expanded the pointing device's capability. More recent software—especially that designed for Windows 2000—takes advantage of the additional buttons, especially the right button. However, the term "clicking" continues to refer to the left button; clicking an object with the *right* button is called **right-clicking**.

In Windows 2000, right-clicking both selects an object and opens its **shortcut menu**, a list of options directly related to the object you right-clicked. You can right-click practically any object—the Start button, a desktop icon, the taskbar, and even the desktop itself—to view options associated with that object. For example, the first desktop shown in Figure 1-7 illustrates what happens when you click the Start button with the left mouse button to open the Start menu. Clicking the Start button with the right button, however, opens the Start button's shortcut menu, as shown in the second desktop.

| Figure 1-7 | CLICKING WITH THE LEFT AND RIGHT MOUSE BUTTONS |

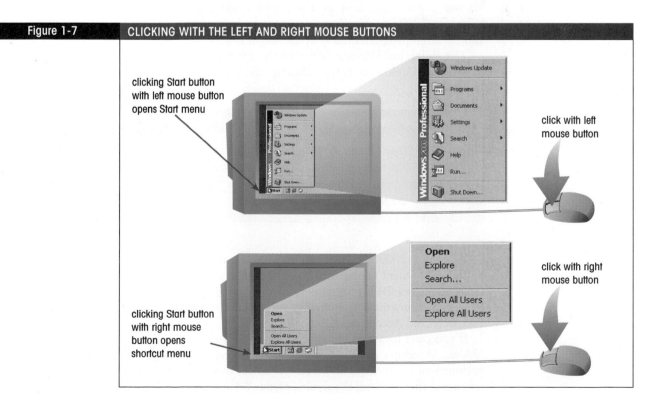

Try using right-clicking to open the shortcut menu for the Start button.

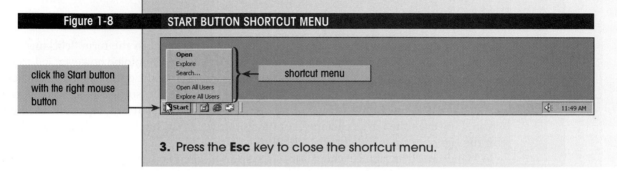

To right-click an object:

1. Position the pointer over the Start button.

2. Right-click the **Start** button [Start] . The shortcut menu that opens offers a list of options available to the Start button.

TROUBLE? If you are using a trackball or a mouse with three buttons or a wheel, make sure you click the button on the far right, not the one in the middle.

TROUBLE? If your menu looks slightly different from the one in Figure 1-8, don't worry. Different systems will have different options.

Figure 1-8	START BUTTON SHORTCUT MENU

click the Start button with the right mouse button

Open
Explore
Search...
Open All Users
Explore All Users

shortcut menu

Start   11:49 AM

3. Press the **Esc** key to close the shortcut menu.

You again return to the desktop.

Starting **and Closing a Program**

To use a program, such as a word-processing program, you must first start it. With Windows 2000 you usually start a program by clicking the Start button and then you locate and click the program's name in the submenus.

The Reference Window below explains how to start a program. Don't do the steps in the Reference Windows as you go through the tutorials; they are for your later reference.

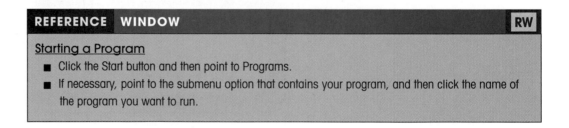

REFERENCE WINDOW   **RW**

<u>Starting a Program</u>

- Click the Start button and then point to Programs.
- If necessary, point to the submenu option that contains your program, and then click the name of the program you want to run.

Windows 2000 includes an easy-to-use word-processing program called WordPad. Suppose you want to start the WordPad program and use it to write a letter or report. You open Windows 2000 programs from the Start menu. Programs are usually located on the Programs submenu or on one of its submenus. To start WordPad, for example, you select the Programs and Accessories submenus.

If you can't locate an item that is supposed to be on a menu, it is most likely temporarily hidden. Windows 2000 menus use a feature called **Personalized Menus** that hides menu options you use infrequently. You can access hidden menu options by pointing to the menu name and then clicking the double arrow ⏷ (sometimes called a "chevron") at the bottom of the menu. You can also access the hidden options by holding the pointer over the menu name.

To start the WordPad program from the Start menu:

1. Click the **Start** button to open the Start menu.

2. Point to **Programs**. The Programs submenu appears.

3. Point to **Accessories**. The Accessories submenu appears. Figure 1-9 shows the open menus.

TROUBLE? If a different menu opens, you might have moved the mouse diagonally so that a different submenu opened. Move the pointer to the right across the Programs option, and then move it up or down to point to Accessories. Once you're more comfortable moving the mouse, you'll find that you can eliminate this problem by moving the mouse quickly.

TROUBLE? If WordPad doesn't appear on the Accessories submenu, continue to point to Accessories until WordPad appears.

Figure 1-9	START MENU

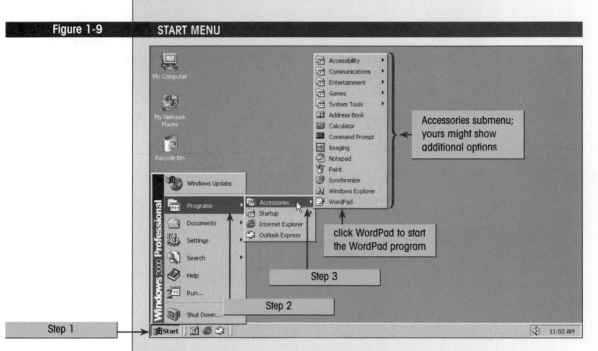

4. Click **WordPad**. The WordPad program opens, as shown in Figure 1-10. If the WordPad window fills the entire screen, don't worry. You will learn how to manipulate windows in Session 1.2.

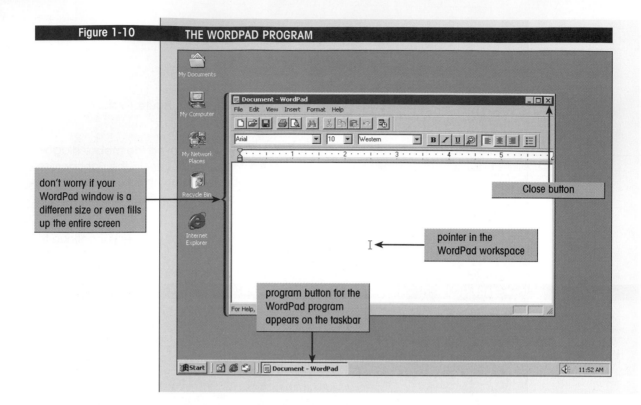

Figure 1-10   THE WORDPAD PROGRAM

don't worry if your WordPad window is a different size or even fills up the entire screen

Close button

pointer in the WordPad workspace

program button for the WordPad program appears on the taskbar

When a program is started, it is said to be **open** or **running**. A **program button** appears on the taskbar for each open program. You click program buttons to switch between open programs. When you are finished using a program, click the Close button ☒.

To exit the WordPad program:

1. Click the **Close** button ☒. See Figure 1-10. You return to the Windows 2000 desktop.

Running **Multiple Programs**

One of the most useful features of Windows 2000 is its ability to run multiple programs at the same time. This feature, known as **multitasking**, allows you to work on more than one project at a time and to switch quickly between projects. For example, you can start WordPad and leave it running while you then start the Paint program.

To run WordPad and Paint at the same time:

1. Start WordPad again and then click the **Start** button [Start] again.

2. Point to **Programs** and then point to **Accessories**.

3. Click **Paint**. The Paint program opens, as shown in Figure 1-11. Now two programs are running at the same time.

TROUBLE? If the Paint program fills the entire screen, don't worry. You will learn how to manipulate windows in Session 1.2.

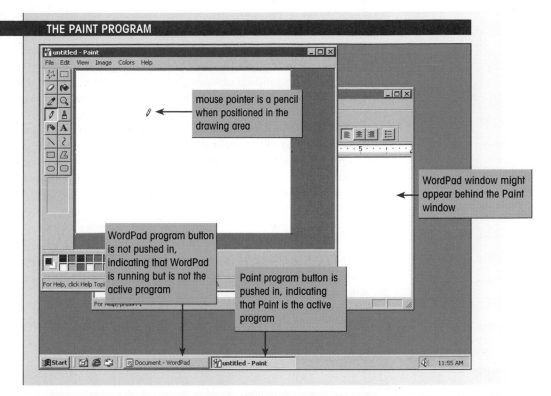

Figure 1-11   THE PAINT PROGRAM

mouse pointer is a pencil when positioned in the drawing area

WordPad window might appear behind the Paint window

WordPad program button is not pushed in, indicating that WordPad is running but is not the active program

Paint program button is pushed in, indicating that Paint is the active program

What happened to WordPad? The WordPad program button is still on the taskbar, so even if you can't see it, WordPad is still running. You can imagine that it is stacked behind the Paint program, as shown in Figure 1-12. Paint is the active program because it is the one with which you are currently working.

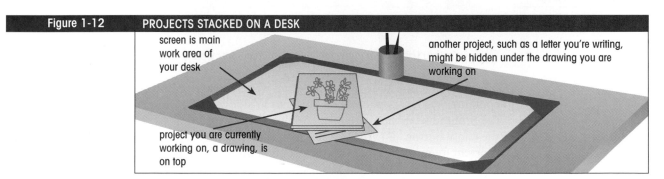

Figure 1-12   PROJECTS STACKED ON A DESK

screen is main work area of your desk

another project, such as a letter you're writing, might be hidden under the drawing you are working on

project you are currently working on, a drawing, is on top

Switching Between Programs

The easiest way to switch between programs is to use the buttons on the taskbar.

To switch between WordPad and Paint:

1. Click the button labeled **Document - WordPad** on the taskbar. The Document - WordPad button now looks as if it has been pushed in, to indicate that it is the active program, and WordPad moves to the front.
2. Next, click the button labeled **untitled - Paint** on the taskbar to switch to the Paint program.

The Paint program is again the active program.

Accessing the Desktop from the Quick Launch Toolbar

The Windows 2000 taskbar, as you've seen, displays buttons for programs currently running. It also can contain **toolbars**, sets of buttons that give single-click access to programs or documents that aren't running or open. In its default state, the Windows 2000 taskbar displays the **Quick Launch toolbar**, which gives quick access to Web programs and to the desktop. Your taskbar might contain additional toolbars, or none at all.

When you are running more than one program but you want to return to the desktop, perhaps to use one of the desktop icons such as My Computer, you can do so by using one of the Quick Launch toolbar buttons. Clicking the Show Desktop button returns you to the desktop. The open programs are not closed; they are simply made inactive and reduced to buttons on the taskbar.

To return to the desktop:

1. Click the **Show Desktop** button on the Quick Launch toolbar. The desktop appears, and both the Paint and WordPad programs are temporarily inactive. See Figure 1-13.

   TROUBLE? If the Quick Launch toolbar doesn't appear on your taskbar, right-click the taskbar, point to Toolbars, and then click Quick Launch and try Step 1 again.

Figure 1-13	ACCESSING THE DESKTOP

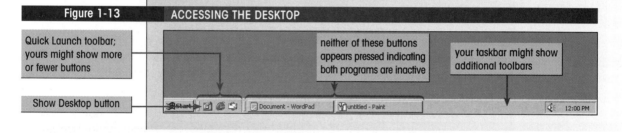

Quick Launch toolbar; yours might show more or fewer buttons

neither of these buttons appears pressed indicating both programs are inactive

your taskbar might show additional toolbars

Show Desktop button

Closing Inactive Programs from the Taskbar

It is good practice to close each program when you are finished using it. Each program uses computer resources, such as memory, so Windows 2000 works more efficiently when only the programs you need are open. You've already seen how to close an open program using the Close button ☒. You can also close a program, whether active or inactive, by using the shortcut menu associated with the program button on the taskbar.

To close WordPad and Paint using the program button shortcut menus:

1. Right-click the **untitled – Paint** button on the taskbar. To right-click something, remember that you click it with the right mouse button. The shortcut menu for that program button opens. See Figure 1-14.

2. Click **Close**. The button labeled "untitled – Paint" disappears from the taskbar, indicating that the Paint program is closed.

3. Right-click the **Document – WordPad** button on the taskbar, and then click **Close**. The WordPad button disappears from the taskbar.

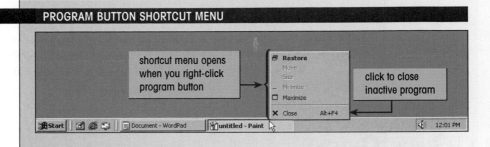

Figure 1-14 | PROGRAM BUTTON SHORTCUT MENU

shortcut menu opens when you right-click program button

click to close inactive program

Shutting **Down Windows 2000**

It is very important to shut down Windows 2000 before you turn off the computer. If you turn off your computer without correctly shutting down, you might lose data and damage your files.

You should typically use the "Shut Down" option when you want to turn off your computer. However, your school might prefer that you select the Log Off option in the Shut Down Windows dialog box. This option logs you out of Windows 2000, leaves the computer turned on, and allows another user to log on without restarting the computer. Check with your instructor or technical support person for the preferred method at your lab.

To shut down Windows 2000:

1. Click the **Start** button on the taskbar to display the Start menu.

2. Click the **Shut Down** menu option. A box titled "Shut Down Windows" opens.

TROUBLE? If you can't see the Shut Down menu option, your Start menu has more options than your screen can display. A double arrow ❣ appears at the bottom of the Start menu. Click this button until the Shut Down menu option appears, and then click Shut Down.

TROUBLE? If you are supposed to log off rather than shut down, click the Log Off option instead and follow your school's logoff procedure.

3. Make sure the **Shut Down** option appears in the box shown in Figure 1-15.

TROUBLE? If "Shut down" does not appear, click the arrow to the right of the box. A list of options appears. Click Shut Down.

Figure 1-15 | SHUTTING DOWN

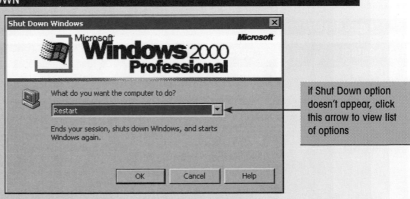

if Shut Down option doesn't appear, click this arrow to view list of options

4. Click the **OK** button.

5. Wait until you see a message indicating it is safe to turn off your computer. If your lab staff has requested you to switch off your computer after shutting down, do so now. Otherwise leave the computer running. Some computers turn themselves off automatically.

Session 1.1 QUICK CHECK

1. What is the purpose of the taskbar?

2. The _____ feature of Windows 2000 allows you to run more than one program at a time.

3. The _____ is a list of options that provides you with access to programs, documents, submenus, and more.

4. What should you do if you are trying to move the pointer to the left edge of your screen, but your mouse bumps into the keyboard?

5. Even if you can't see an open program on your desktop, the program might be running. How can you tell if a program is running?

6. Why is it good practice to close each program when you are finished using it?

7. Why should you shut down Windows 2000 before you turn off your computer?

SESSION 1.2

In this session you will learn how to use many of the Windows 2000 controls to manipulate windows and programs. You will also learn how to change the size and shape of a window; how to move a window; and how to use menus, dialog boxes, tabs, buttons, and lists to specify how you want a program to carry out a task.

Anatomy of a Window

When you run a program in Windows 2000, it appears in a window. A **window** is a rectangular area of the screen that contains a program or data. Windows, spelled with an uppercase "W," is the name of the Microsoft operating system. The word "window" with a lowercase "w" refers to one of the rectangular areas on the screen. A window also contains controls for manipulating the window and for using the program. Figure 1-16 describes the controls you are likely to see in most windows.

Figure 1-16	WINDOW CONTROLS
CONTROL	**DESCRIPTION**
Menu bar	Contains the titles of menus, such as File, Edit, and Help
Sizing buttons	Let you enlarge, shrink, or close a window
Status bar	Provides you with messages relevant to the task you are performing
Title bar	Contains the window title and basic window control buttons
Toolbar	Contains buttons that provide you with shortcuts to common menu commands
Window title	Identifies the program and document contained in the window
Workspace	Part of the window you use to enter your work—to enter text, draw pictures, set up calculations, and so on

WordPad is a good example of a typical window, so try starting WordPad and identifying these controls in the WordPad window.

To look at window controls:

1. Make sure Windows 2000 is running and you are at the Windows 2000 desktop.

2. Start WordPad.

TROUBLE? To start WordPad, click the Start button, point to Programs, point to Accessories, and then click WordPad.

3. On your screen, identify the controls labeled in Figure 1-17. Don't worry if your window fills the entire screen or is a different size. You'll learn to change window size shortly.

Figure 1-17	WORDPAD WINDOW CONTROLS

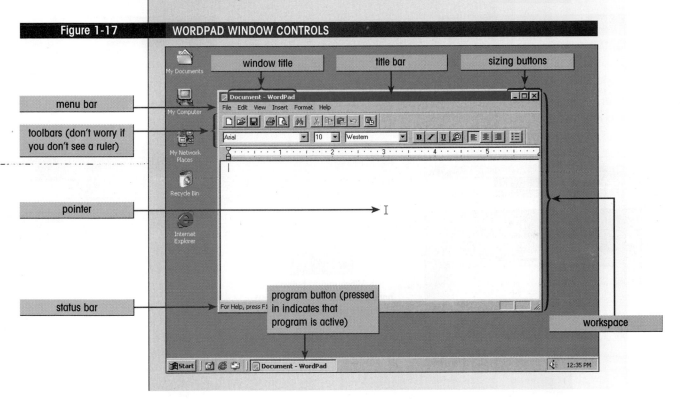

Manipulating a Window

There are three buttons located on the right side of the title bar. You are already familiar with the Close button. The Minimize button ▬ hides the window so that only its program button is visible on the taskbar. The other button changes name and function depending on the status of the window (it either maximizes the window or restores it to a predefined size). Figure 1-18 shows how these buttons work.

Minimizing a Window

The Minimize button hides a window so that only the button on the taskbar remains visible. You can use the Minimize button when you want to temporarily hide a window but keep the program running.

Figure 1-18   WINDOW BUTTONS

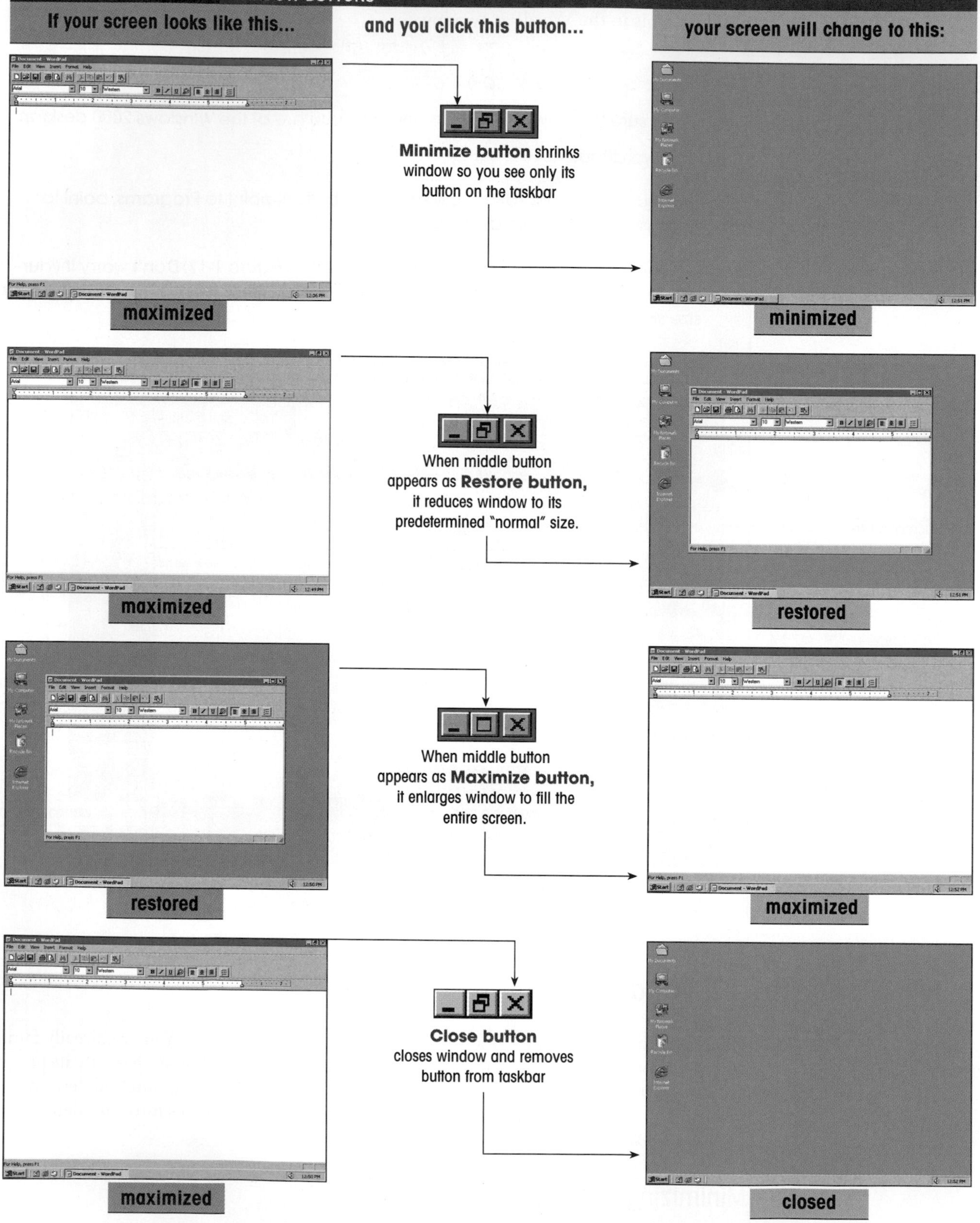

If your screen looks like this...   **and you click this button...**   **your screen will change to this:**

Minimize button shrinks window so you see only its button on the taskbar

maximized → minimized

When middle button appears as **Restore button,** it reduces window to its predetermined "normal" size.

maximized → restored

When middle button appears as **Maximize button,** it enlarges window to fill the entire screen.

restored → maximized

Close button closes window and removes button from taskbar

maximized → closed

To minimize the WordPad window:

1. Click the **Minimize** button [_]. The WordPad window shrinks so that only the Document - WordPad button on the taskbar is visible.

TROUBLE? If you accidentally clicked the Close button and closed the window, use the Start button to start WordPad again.

Redisplaying a Window

You can redisplay a minimized window by clicking the program's button on the taskbar. When you redisplay a window, it becomes the active window.

To redisplay the WordPad window:

1. Click the **Document - WordPad** button on the taskbar. The WordPad window is restored to its previous size. The Document - WordPad button looks pushed in as a visual clue that WordPad is now the active window.

2. The taskbar button provides another means of switching a window between its minimized and active state: Click the **Document - WordPad** button on the taskbar again to minimize the window.

3. Click the **Document - WordPad** button once more to redisplay the window.

Maximizing a Window

The Maximize button enlarges a window so that it fills the entire screen. You will probably do most of your work using maximized windows because they allow you to see more of your program and data.

To maximize the WordPad window:

1. Click the **Maximize** button [□] on the WordPad title bar.

TROUBLE? If the window is already maximized, it will fill the entire screen, and the Maximize button won't appear. Instead, you'll see the Restore button [⧉]. Skip Step 1.

Restoring a Window

The Restore button [⧉] reduces the window so it is smaller than the entire screen. This is useful if you want to see more than one window at a time. Also, because of its smaller size, you can drag the window to another location on the screen or change its dimensions.

To restore a window:

1. Click the **Restore** button [⧉] on the WordPad title bar. Notice that once a window is restored, [⧉] changes to the Maximize button [□].

Moving a Window

You can use the mouse to move a window to a new position on the screen. When you click an object and hold down the mouse button while moving the mouse, you are said to be **dragging** the object. You can move objects on the screen by dragging them to a new location. If you want to move a window, you drag its title bar. You cannot move a maximized window.

To drag the WordPad window to a new location:

1. Position the mouse pointer on the WordPad window title bar.

2. While you hold down the left mouse button, move the mouse to drag the window. A rectangle representing the window moves as you move the mouse.

3. Position the rectangle anywhere on the screen, then release the left mouse button. The WordPad window appears in the new location.

4. Now drag the WordPad window to the upper-left corner of the screen.

Changing the Size of a Window

You can also use the mouse to change the size of a window. Notice the sizing handle at the lower-right corner of the window. The **sizing handle** provides a visible control for changing the size of a window.

To change the size of the WordPad window:

1. Position the pointer over the sizing handle . The pointer changes to a diagonal arrow .

2. While holding down the mouse button, drag the sizing handle down and to the right.

3. Release the mouse button. Now the window is larger.

4. Practice using the sizing handle to make the WordPad window larger or smaller, and then maximize the WordPad window.

You can also drag the window borders left, right, up, or down to change a window's size.

Using **Program Menus**

Most Windows programs use menus to organize the program's menu options. The menu bar is typically located at the top of the program window and shows the titles of menus such as File, Edit, and Help.

Windows menus are relatively standardized—most Windows programs include similar menu options. It's easy to learn new programs, because you can make a pretty good guess about which menu contains the option you want.

Selecting Options from a Menu

When you click any menu title, choices for that menu appear below the menu bar. These choices are referred to as **menu options** or **commands**. To select a menu option, you click it. For example, the File menu is a standard feature in most Windows programs and contains the options typically related to working with a file: creating, opening, saving, and printing a file or document.

To select the Print Preview menu option on the File menu:

1. Click **File** on the WordPad menu bar to display the File menu. See Figure 1-19.

TROUBLE? If you open a menu but decide not to select any of the menu options, you can close the menu by clicking its title again.

Figure 1-19	FILE MENU

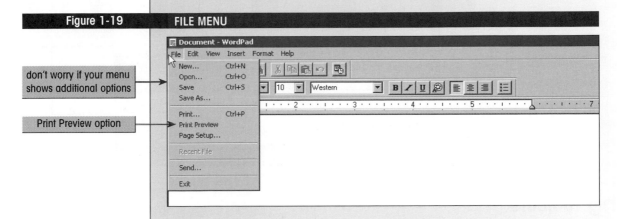

don't worry if your menu shows additional options

Print Preview option

2. Click **Print Preview** to open the preview screen and view your document as it will appear when printed. This document is blank because you didn't enter any text.

TROUBLE? If your computer is not set up with printer access, you will not be able to open Print Preview. Ask your instructor or technical support person for help.

3. After examining the screen, click the button with the text label "Close" to return to your document.

TROUBLE? If you close WordPad by mistake, restart it.

Not all menu options immediately carry out an action—some show submenus or ask you for more information about what you want to do. The menu gives you hints about what to expect when you select an option. These hints are sometimes referred to as **menu conventions**. Figure 1-20 describes the Windows 2000 menu conventions.

Figure 1-20	MENU CONVENTIONS

CONVENTION	DESCRIPTION
Check mark	Indicates a toggle, or "on-off" switch (like a light switch) that is either checked (turned on) or not checked (turned off)
Ellipsis	Three dots that indicate you must make additional selections after you select that option. Options without dots do not require additional choices—they take effect as soon as you click them. If an option is followed by an ellipsis, a dialog box opens that allows you to enter specifications for how you want a task carried out.
Triangular arrow	Indicates the presence of a submenu. When you point at a menu option that has a triangular arrow, a submenu automatically appears.
Grayed-out option	Option that is not available. For example, a graphics program might display the Text Toolbar option in gray if there is no text in the graphic to work with.
Keyboard shortcut	A key or combination of keys that you can press to activate the menu option without actually opening the menu
Double arrow	Indicates that additional menu options are available; click the double arrow to access them

Figure 1-21 shows examples of these menu conventions.

Figure 1-21   EXAMPLES OF MENU CONVENTIONS

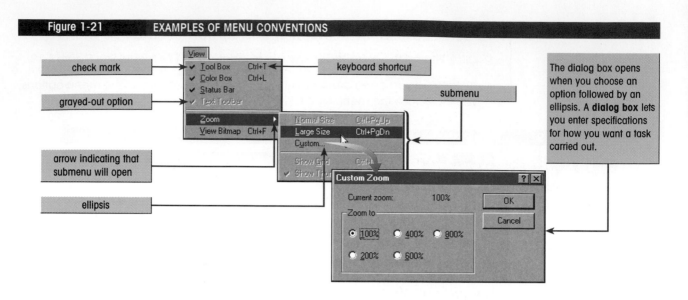

Using **Toolbars**

Although you can usually perform all program commands using menus, toolbar buttons provide convenient one-click access to frequently used commands. For most Windows 2000 functions, there is usually more than one way to accomplish a task. To simplify your introduction to Windows 2000 in this tutorial, we will usually show you only one method for performing a task. As you become more accomplished at using Windows 2000, you can explore alternate methods.

In Session 1.1 you learned that Windows 2000 programs include ScreenTips, which indicate the purpose and function of a tool. Now is a good time to explore the WordPad toolbar buttons by looking at their ScreenTips.

To find out a toolbar button's function:

1. Position the pointer over any button on the toolbar, such as the Print Preview button 🔍. After a short pause, the name of the button appears in a box near the button, and a description of the button appears in the status bar just above the Start button. See Figure 1-22.

Figure 1-22   TOOLBAR BUTTON AIDS

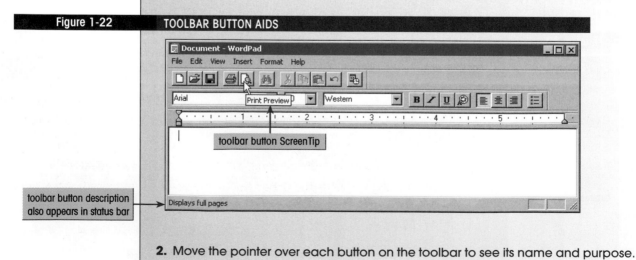

2. Move the pointer over each button on the toolbar to see its name and purpose.

You select a toolbar button by clicking it.

To select the Print Preview toolbar button:

1. Click the **Print Preview** button 🔍. The Print Preview screen appears. This is the same screen that appeared when you selected Print Preview from the File menu.

2. After examining the screen, click the button with the text label "Close" to return to your document.

Using **List Boxes and Scroll Bars**

As you might guess from the name, a **list box** displays a list of choices. In WordPad, date and time formats are shown in the Date/Time list box. List box controls usually include arrow buttons, a scroll bar, and a scroll box, as shown in Figure 1-23.

To use the Date/Time list box:

1. Click the **Date/Time** button 🔲 to display the Date and Time dialog box. See Figure 1-23.

Figure 1-23	LIST BOX

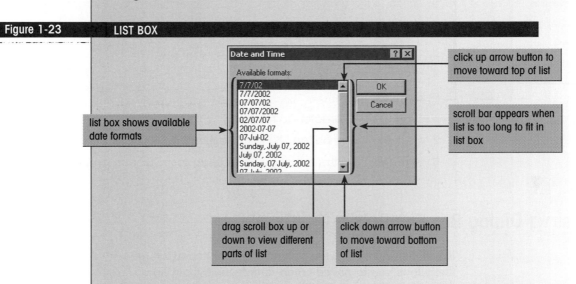

click up arrow button to move toward top of list

scroll bar appears when list is too long to fit in list box

list box shows available date formats

drag scroll box up or down to view different parts of list

click down arrow button to move toward bottom of list

2. To scroll down the list, click the **down arrow** button 🔽. See Figure 1-23.

3. Find the scroll box on your screen. See Figure 1-23.

4. Drag the **scroll box** to the top of the scroll bar. Notice how the list scrolls back to the beginning.

TROUBLE? You learned how to drag when you learned to move a window. To drag the scroll box up, point to the scroll box, press and hold down the mouse button, and then move the mouse up.

5. Find a date in the format "July 07, 2002." Click that date format to select it.

6. Click the **OK** button to close the Date and Time dialog box. This inserts the current date in your document.

You can access some list boxes directly from the toolbar. When a list box is on the toolbar, only the current option appears in the list box. A **list arrow** appears on the right of the box and you can click it to view additional options.

To use the Font Size list box:

1. Click the **Font Size** list arrow, as shown in Figure 1-24.

| Figure 1-24 | FONT SIZE LIST ARROW |

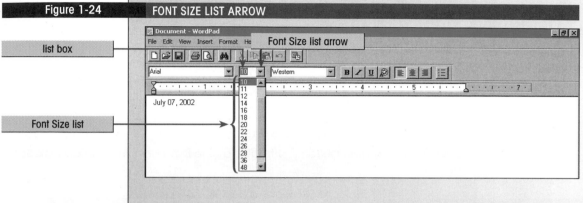

list box

Font Size list arrow

Font Size list

July 07, 2002

2. Click **18**. The list disappears, and the font size you selected appears in the list box.

3. Type a few characters to test the new font size.

4. Click the **Font Size** list arrow again.

5. Click **12**.

6. Type a few characters to test this type size.

7. Click the **Close** button ☒ to close WordPad.

8. When you see the message "Save changes to Document?" click the **No** button.

Using **Dialog Box Controls**

Recall that when you select a menu option or button followed by an ellipsis, a dialog box opens that allows you to provide more information about how a program should carry out a task. Some dialog boxes group different kinds of information into bordered rectangular areas called **panes**. Within these panes, you will usually find tabs, option buttons, check boxes, and other controls that the program uses to collect information about how you want it to perform a task. Figure 1-25 describes common dialog box controls.

| Figure 1-25 | DIALOG BOX CONTROLS |

CONTROL	DESCRIPTION
Tabs	Modeled after the tabs on file folders, tab controls are often used as containers for other Windows 2000 controls such as list boxes, radio buttons, and check boxes. Click the appropriate tabs to view different pages of information or choices.
Option buttons	Also called **radio buttons**, option buttons allow you to select a single option from among one or more options.
Check boxes	Click a check box to select or deselect it; when it is selected, a check mark appears, indicating that the option is turned on; when deselected, the check box is blank and the option is off. When check boxes appear in groups, you can select or deselect as many as you want; they are not mutually exclusive, as option buttons are.
Spin boxes	Allow you to scroll easily through a set of numbers to choose the setting you want
Text boxes	Boxes into which you type additional information

Figure 1-26 displays examples of these controls.

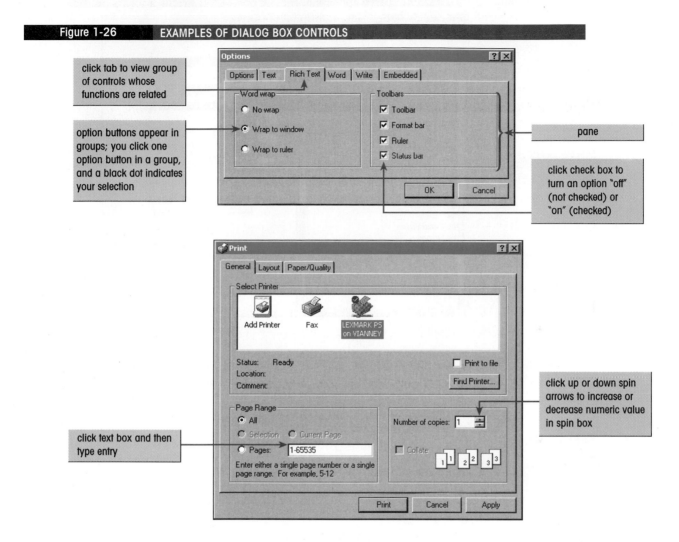

| Figure 1-26 | EXAMPLES OF DIALOG BOX CONTROLS |

Using **Help**

Windows 2000 **Help** provides on-screen information about the program you are using. Help for the Windows 2000 operating system is available by clicking the Start button on the taskbar, then selecting Help from the Start menu. If you want Help for a program, such as WordPad, you must first start the program, then click Help on the menu bar.

When you start Help, a Windows Help window opens, which gives you access to help files stored on your computer as well as help information stored on Microsoft's Web site. If you are not connected to the Web, you have access only to the help files stored on your computer.

To start Windows 2000 Help:

1. Click the **Start** button.

2. Click **Help**. The Windows 2000 window opens to the Contents tab. See Figure 1-27.

   TROUBLE? If the Contents tab is not in front, click the Contents tab to view the table of contents.

Figure 1-27   WINDOWS 2000 HELP

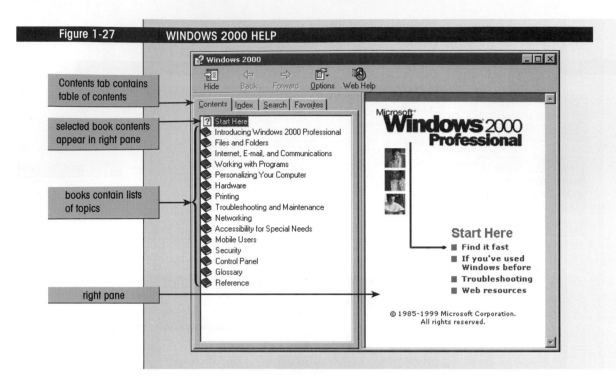

Contents tab contains table of contents

selected book contents appear in right pane

books contain lists of topics

right pane

Help uses tabs for the four sections of Help: Contents, Index, Search, and Favorites. The **Contents tab** groups Help topics into a series of books. You select a book 📖 by clicking it. The book opens, and a list of related topics appears from which you can choose. Individual topics are designated with the ❓ icon. Overview topics are designated with the 📖 icon.

The **Index tab** displays an alphabetical list of all the Help topics from which you can choose. The **Search tab** allows you to search the entire set of Help topics for all topics that contain a word or words you specify. The **Favorites tab** allows you to save your favorite Help topics for quick reference.

Viewing Topics from the Contents Tab

You know that Windows 2000 gives you easy access to the Internet. Suppose you're wondering how to connect to the Internet from your computer. You can use the Contents tab to find more information on a specific topic.

To use the Contents tab:

1. Click the **Internet, E-mail, and Communications** book icon 📖. A list of topics and an overview appear below the book title.

2. Click the **Connect to the Internet** topic icon ❓. Information about connecting to the Internet appears in the right pane. See Figure 1-28.

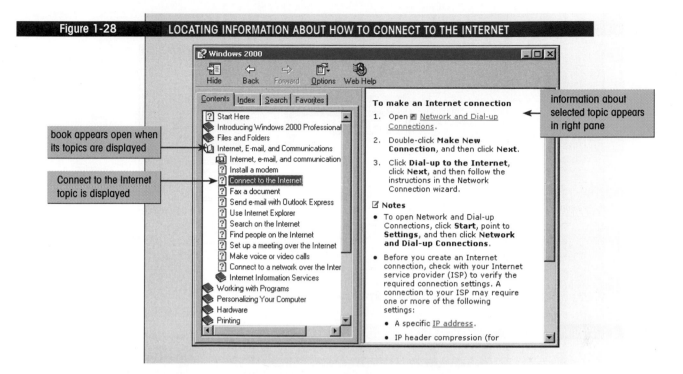

Figure 1-28 — LOCATING INFORMATION ABOUT HOW TO CONNECT TO THE INTERNET

Selecting a Topic from the Index

The Index tab allows you to jump to a Help topic by selecting a topic from an indexed list. For example, you can use the Index tab to learn more about the Internet.

To find a Help topic using the Index tab:

1. Click the **Index** tab. A long list of indexed Help topics appears.

   TROUBLE? If this is the first time you've used Help on your computer, Windows 2000 needs to set up the Index. This takes just a few moments. Wait until you see the list of index entries in the left pane, and then proceed to Step 2.

2. Drag the scroll box down to view additional topics.

3. You can quickly jump to any part of the list by typing the first few characters of a word or phrase in the box above the Index list. Click the box and then type **Internet**.

4. Click the topic **searching the Internet** (you might have to scroll to see it) and then click the **Display** button. When there is just one topic, it appears immediately in the right pane; otherwise, the Topics Found window opens, listing all topics indexed under the entry you're interested in. In this case, there are four choices.

5. Click **Using Internet Explorer** and then click the **Display** button. The information you requested appears in the right pane. See Figure 1-29. Notice in this topic that there are a few underlined words. You can click underlined words to view definitions or additional information.

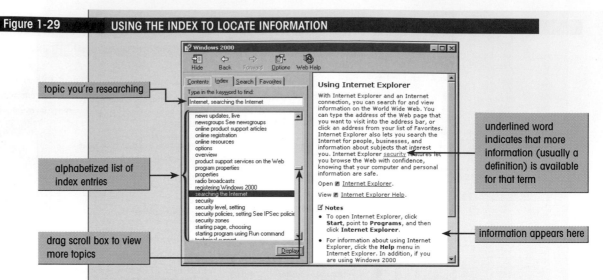

Figure 1-29 USING THE INDEX TO LOCATE INFORMATION

6. Click **security**. A small box appears that defines the term "security." See Figure 1-30.

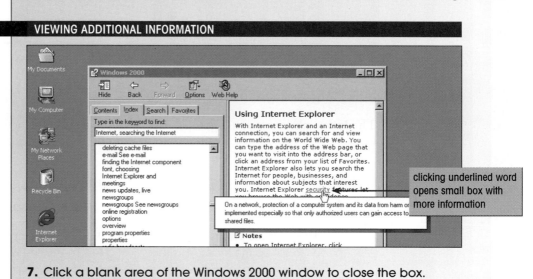

Figure 1-30 VIEWING ADDITIONAL INFORMATION

7. Click a blank area of the Windows 2000 window to close the box.

The third tab, the Search tab, works similarly to the Index tab, except that you type a word, and then the Help system searches for topics containing that word. You'll get a chance to experiment with the Search and Favorites tabs in the Review Assignments.

Returning to a Previous Help Topic

You've looked at a few topics now. Suppose you want to return to the one you just saw. The Help window includes a toolbar of buttons that help you navigate the Help system. One of these buttons is the **Back** button, which returns you to topics you've already viewed. Try returning to the help topic on connecting to the Internet.

To return to a Help topic:

1. Click the **Back** button. The Internet topic appears.

2. Click the **Close** button ⊠ to close the Windows 2000 window.

3. Log off or shut down Windows 2000, depending on your lab's requirements.

Now that you know how Windows 2000 Help works, don't forget to use it! Use Help when you need to perform a new task or when you forget how to complete a procedure.

You've finished the tutorial, and as you shut down Windows 2000, Steve Laslow returns from class. You take a moment to tell him all you've learned: you know how to start and close programs and how to use multiple programs at the same time. You have learned how to work with windows and the controls they employ. Finally, you've learned how to get help when you need it. Steve is pleased that you are well on your way to mastering the fundamentals of using the Windows 2000 operating system.

Session 1.2   QUICK CHECK

1. What is the difference between the title bar and a toolbar?

2. Provide the name and purpose of each button:
   a. [_]   b. [□]   c. [⊡]   d. [✕]

3. Describe what is indicated by each of the following menu conventions:
   a. Ellipsis...   b. Grayed-out   c. ▶   d. ✔

4. A(n) _____ consists of a group of buttons, each of which provides one-click access to important program functions.

5. What is the purpose of the scroll bar? What is the purpose of the scroll box?

6. Option buttons allow you to select _____ option(s) at a time.

7. It is a good idea to use _____ when you need to learn how to perform new tasks.

REVIEW ASSIGNMENTS

1. **Running Two Programs and Switching Between Them** In this tutorial you learned how to run more than one program at a time, using WordPad and Paint. You can run other programs at the same time, too. Complete the following steps and write out your answers to questions b through f:
   a. Start the computer. Enter your username and password if prompted to do so.
   b. Click the Start button. How many menu options are on the Start menu?
   c. Run the Calculator program located on the Accessories menu. How many program buttons are now on the taskbar (don't count toolbar buttons or items in the tray)?
   d. Run the Paint program and maximize the Paint window. How many programs are running now?
   e. Switch to Calculator. What are two visual clues that tell you that Calculator is the active program?
   f. Multiply 576 by 1457 using the Calculator accessory. What is the result?
   g. Close Calculator, then close Paint.

Explore ▶ 2. **WordPad Help** In Tutorial 1 you learned how to use Windows 2000 Help. Almost every Windows 2000 program has a Help feature. Many users can learn to use a program just by using Help. To use Help, start the program, then click the Help menu at the top of the screen. Try using WordPad Help:
   a. Start WordPad.
   b. Click Help on the WordPad menu bar, and then click Help Topics.
   c. Using WordPad Help, write out your answers to questions 1 through 4.
      1. How do you create a bulleted list?
      2. How do you set the margins in a document?
      3. How do you undo a mistake?
      4. How do you change the font style of a block of text?
   d. Close WordPad.

Explore 3. **The Search Tab** In addition to the Contents and Index tabs you worked with in this tutorial, Windows 2000 Help also includes a Search tab. Windows 2000 makes it possible to use a microphone to record sound on your computer. You could browse through the Contents tab, although you might not know where to find information about microphones. You could also use the Index tab to search through the indexed entry. Or you could use the Search tab to find all Help topics that mention microphones.

   a. Start Windows 2000 Help and use the Index tab to find information about microphones. How many topics are listed?
   b. Now use the Search tab to find information about microphones. Type "microphone" in the box on the Search tab, and then click the List Topics button.
   c. Write a paragraph comparing the two lists of topics. You don't have to view them all, but indicate which tab seems to yield more information, and why. Close Help.

4. **Getting Started** Windows 2000 includes Getting Started, an online "book" that helps you discover more about your computer and the Windows 2000 operating system. You can use this book to review what you learned in this tutorial and pick up some tips for using Windows 2000. Complete the following steps and write out your answers to questions d–j.

   a. Start Help, click the Contents tab, click Introducing Windows 2000 Professional, and then click Getting Started online book. Read the information and then click Windows 2000 Professional Getting Started.
   b. In the right pane, click New to Windows? Notice the book icons in the upper-right and upper-left corners of the right pane.
   c. Read each screen, and then click the right book icon to proceed through the Help topics. Alternately, you can view specific Getting Started Help topics by clicking them on the Contents tab. To answer the following questions, locate the information on the relevant Help topic. All the information for these questions is located in Chapter 4—"Windows Basics." When you are done, close Help.
   d. If your computer's desktop style uses the single-click option, how do you select a file? How do you open a file?
   e. What features are almost always available on your desktop, regardless of how many windows you have open?
   f. How can you get information about a dialog box or an area of the dialog box?
   g. How does the Getting Started online book define the word "disk"?
   h. If your computer is connected to a network, what Windows 2000 feature can you use to browse network resources?
   i. Why shouldn't you turn off your computer without shutting it down properly?

5. **Favorite Help Topics** You learned in this tutorial that you can save a list of your favorite Help topics on the Favorites tab. Try adding a topic to your list of favorites.

   a. Open a Help topic in the Help system. For this assignment, click the Contents tab, click Personalizing Your Computer, and then click Personalizing your workspace overview.
   b. Click the Favorites tab. The topic you selected appears on the right, and the topic name appears in the lower-left corner.
   c. Click the Add button. The topic appears in the box on the Favorites tab. This provides you an easy way to return to this topic.
   d. Click the Remove button to remove the topic from the Favorites list.

PROJECTS

1. There are many types of pointing devices on the market today. Go to the library and research the types of devices available. Consider what devices are appropriate for these situations: desktop or laptop computers, connected or remote devices, and ergonomic or standard designs (look up the word "ergonomic").

Use up-to-date computer books, trade computer magazines such as *PC Computing* and *PC Magazine*, or the Internet (if you know how) to locate information. Your instructor might suggest specific resources you can use. Write a one-page report describing the types of devices available, the differing needs of users, special features that make pointing devices more useful, price comparisons, and what you would choose if you needed to buy a pointing device.

2. Using the resources available to you, either through your library or the Internet (if you know how), locate information about the release of Windows 2000. Computing trade magazines are an excellent source of information about software. Read several articles about Windows 2000 and then write a one-page essay that discusses the features that are most important to the people who evaluated the software. If you find reviews of the software, mention the features that reviewers had the strongest reaction to, pro or con.

3. Upgrading is the process of placing a more recent version of a product onto your computer. When Windows 2000 first came out, people had to decide whether or not they wanted to upgrade to Windows 2000. Interview several people you know who are well-informed Windows computer users. Ask them whether they are using Windows 2000 or an older version of Windows. If they are using an older version, ask why they have chosen not to upgrade. If they are using Windows 2000, ask them why they chose to upgrade. Ask such questions as:

   a. What features convinced you to upgrade or made you decide to wait?
   b. What role did the price of the upgrade play?
   c. Would you have had (or did you have) to purchase new hardware to make the upgrade? How did this affect your decision?
   d. If you did upgrade, are you happy with that decision? If you didn't, do you intend to upgrade in the near future? Why, or why not?

   Write a single-page essay summarizing what you learned from these interviews.

4. Choose a topic to research using the Windows 2000 online Help system. Look for information on your topic using three tabs: the Contents tab, the Index tab, and the Search tab. Once you've found all the information you can, compare the three methods (Contents, Index, Search) of looking for information. Write a paragraph that discusses which tab proved the most useful. Did you reach the same information topics using all three methods? In a second paragraph, summarize what you learned about your topic. Finally, in a third paragraph, indicate under what circumstances you'd use which tab.

LAB ASSIGNMENTS

Using a
Keyboard

Using a Keyboard To become an effective computer user, you must be familiar with your primary input device—the keyboard. See the Read This Before You Begin page for information on installing and starting the lab.

1. The Steps for the Using a Keyboard Lab provide you with a structured introduction to the keyboard layout and the function of special computer keys. Click the Steps button and begin the Steps. As you work through the Steps, answer all of the Quick Check questions that appear. When you complete the Steps, you will see a Summary Report that summarizes your performance on the Quick Checks. Follow the directions on the screen to print the Summary Report.

2. In Explore, start the typing tutor. You can develop your typing skills using the typing tutor in Explore. Take the typing test and print out your results.

3. In Explore, try to improve your typing speed by 10 words per minute. For example, if you currently type 20 words per minute, your goal will be 30 words per minute. Practice each typing lesson until you see a message that indicates that you can proceed to the next lesson.

Create a Practice Record, as shown here, to keep track of how much you practice. When you have reached your goal, print out the results of a typing test to verify your results.

Practice Record
Name:
Section:
Start Date: Start Typing Speed: wpm
End Date: End Typing Speed: wpm
Lesson #:   Date Practiced/Time Practiced

Using a Mouse A mouse is a standard input device on most of today's computers. You need to know how to use a mouse to manipulate graphical user interfaces and to use the rest of the Labs. See the Read This Before You Begin page for information on installing and starting the lab.

1. The Steps for the Using a Mouse Lab show you how to click, double-click, and drag objects using the mouse. Click the Steps button and begin the Steps. As you work through the Steps, answer all of the Quick Check questions that appear. When you complete the Steps, you will see a Summary Report that summarizes your performance on the Quick Checks. Follow the directions on the screen to print the Summary Report.

2. In Explore, create a poster to demonstrate your ability to use a mouse and to control a Windows program. To create a poster for an upcoming sports event, select a graphic, type the caption for the poster, then select a font, font styles, and a border. Print your completed poster.

QUICK | CHECK ANSWERS

Session 1.1

1. The taskbar contains buttons that give you access to tools and programs.
2. multitasking
3. Start menu
4. Lift the mouse up and move it to the right.
5. Its button appears on the taskbar.
6. To conserve computer resources such as memory.
7. To ensure you don't lose data and damage your files.

Session 1.2

1. The title bar identifies the window and contains window controls; toolbars contain buttons that provide you with shortcuts to common menu commands.
2. a. Minimize button shrinks window so you see button on taskbar
   b. Maximize button enlarges window to fill entire screen
   c. Restore button reduces window to predetermined size
   d. Close button closes window and removes button from taskbar
3. a. ellipsis indicates a dialog box will open
   b. grayed-out indicates option is not currently available
   c. arrow indicates a submenu will open
   d. check mark indicates a toggle option
4. toolbar
5. Scroll bars appear when the contents of a box or window are too long to fit; you drag the scroll box to view different parts of the contents.
6. one
7. online Help

OBJECTIVES

In this tutorial you will:

- Format a disk

- Enter, select, insert, and delete text

- Create and save a file

- Open, edit, and print a file

- Create and make a copy of your Data Disk

- View the list of files on your disk and change view options

- Move, copy, delete, and rename a file

- Navigate a hierarchy of folders

LABS

Using Files

WORKING WITH FILES

Creating, Saving, and Managing Files

CASE

Distance Education

You recently purchased a computer in order to gain new skills so you can stay competitive in the job market. You hope to use the computer to enroll in a few distance education courses. **Distance education** is formalized learning that typically takes place using a computer and the Internet, replacing normal classroom interaction with modern communications technology. Distance education teachers often make their course material available on the **World Wide Web**, a popular service on the Internet that makes information readily accessible.

Your computer came loaded with Windows 2000. Your friend Shannon suggests that before you enroll in any online courses, you should get more comfortable with your computer and with Windows 2000. Knowing how to save, locate, and organize your files will make your time spent at the computer much more productive. A **file**, often referred to as a **document**, is a collection of data that has a name and is stored in a computer. Once you create a file, you can open it, edit its contents, print it, and save it again—usually using the same program you used to create it.

Shannon suggests that you become familiar with how to perform these tasks in Windows 2000 programs. Then she'll show you how to choose different ways of viewing information on your computer. Finally, you'll spend time learning how to organize your files.

SESSION 2.1

In Session 2.1, you will learn how to format a disk so it can store files. You will create, save, open, and print a file. You will find out how the insertion point differs from the mouse pointer, and you will learn the basic skills for Windows 2000 text entry, such as entering, selecting, inserting, and deleting. For the steps of this tutorial you will need two blank 3½-inch disks.

Formatting a Disk

Before you can save files on a floppy disk, the disk must be formatted. When the computer **formats** a disk, the magnetic particles on the disk surface are arranged so that data can be stored on the disk. Today, many disks are sold preformatted and can be used right out of the box. However, if you purchase an unformatted disk, or if you have an old disk you want to completely erase and reuse, you can format the disk using the Windows 2000 Format command. This command is available through the **My Computer window**, a feature of Windows 2000 that you use to view, organize, and access the programs, files, drives and folders on your computer. You open My Computer by using its icon on the desktop. You'll learn more about the My Computer window later in this tutorial.

The following steps tell you how to format a 3½-inch high-density disk, using drive A. Your instructor will tell you how to revise the instructions given in these steps if the procedure is different for your lab.

Make sure you are using a blank disk (or one that contains data you no longer need) before you perform these steps.

To format a disk:

1. Start Windows 2000, if necessary.

2. Write your name on the label of a 3½-inch disk and insert your disk in drive A. See Figure 2-1.

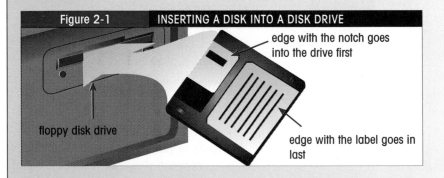

Figure 2-1   INSERTING A DISK INTO A DISK DRIVE

edge with the notch goes into the drive first

floppy disk drive

edge with the label goes in last

TROUBLE? If your disk does not fit in drive A, put it in drive B and substitute drive B for drive A in all of the steps for the rest of the tutorial.

3. Click the **My Computer** icon on the desktop. The icon is selected. Figure 2-2 shows this icon on your desktop.

TROUBLE? If the My Computer window opens, skip Step 4. Your computer is using different settings, which you'll learn to change in Session 2.2.

4. Press the **Enter** key to open the My Computer window. See Figure 2-2 (don't worry if your window opens maximized).

TROUBLE? If you see a list of items instead of icons like those in Figure 2-2, click View, and then click Large Icons. Don't worry if your toolbars don't exactly match those in Figure 2-2.

TROUBLE? If you see additional information or a graphic image on the left side of the My Computer window, Web view is enabled on your computer. Don't worry. You will learn how to return to the default Windows 2000 settings in Session 2.2.

Figure 2-2	MY COMPUTER WINDOW

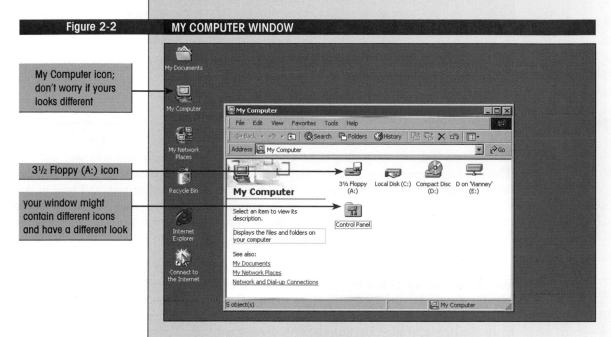

My Computer icon; don't worry if yours looks different

3½ Floppy (A:) icon

your window might contain different icons and have a different look

5. Right-click the **3½ Floppy (A:)** icon to open its shortcut menu, and then click **Format**. The Format dialog box opens.

6. Make sure the dialog box settings on your screen match those in Figure 2-3.

Figure 2-3	FORMATTING A FLOPPY DISK

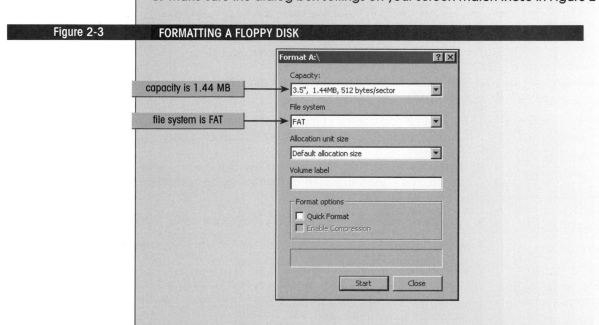

capacity is 1.44 MB

file system is FAT

By default, Windows 2000 uses the FAT (File Allocation Table) file system for floppy disks. A **file system** is the way files are organized on the disk. Windows 2000 supports other file systems such as FAT32 and NTFS, but this is a more advanced topic.

7. Click the **Start** button to start formatting the disk.

8. Click the **OK** button to confirm that you want to format the disk (the actual formatting will take a minute to perform). Click the **OK** button again when the formatting is complete.

9. Click the **Close** button.

10. Click the **Close** button ❌ to close the My Computer window.

Now that you have a formatted disk, you can create a document and save it on your disk. First you need to learn how to enter text into a document.

Working with Text

To accomplish many computing tasks, you need to enter text in documents and text boxes. This involves learning how to move the pointer so the text will appear where you want it, how to insert new text between existing words or sentences, how to select text, and how to delete text. When you type sentences of text, do not press the Enter key when you reach the right margin of the page. Most software contains a feature called **word wrap**, which automatically continues your text on the next line. Therefore, you should press Enter only when you have completed a paragraph.

If you type the wrong character, press the Backspace key to back up and delete the character. You can also use the Delete key. What's the difference between the Backspace and Delete keys? The **Backspace** key deletes the character to the left, while the **Delete** key deletes the character to the right. If you want to delete text that is not next to where you are currently typing, you need to use the mouse to select the text; then you can use either the Delete key or the Backspace key.

Now you will type some text, using WordPad, to practice text entry. When you first start WordPad, notice the flashing vertical bar, called the **insertion point**, in the upper-left corner of the document window. The insertion point indicates where the characters you type will appear.

To type text in WordPad:

1. Start WordPad and locate the insertion point.

TROUBLE? If the WordPad window does not fill the screen, click the Maximize button ▫ .

TROUBLE? If you can't find the insertion point, click in the WordPad **document window**, the white area below the toolbars and ruler.

2. Type your name, pressing the Shift key at the same time as the appropriate letter to type uppercase letters and using the Spacebar to type spaces, just as on a typewriter.

3. Press the **Enter** key to move the insertion point down to the next line.

4. As you type the following sentences, watch what happens when the insertion point reaches the right edge of the page:

This is a sample typed in WordPad. See what happens when the insertion point reaches the right edge of the page. Note how the text wraps automatically to the next line.

TROUBLE? If you make a mistake, delete the incorrect character(s) by pressing the Backspace key on your keyboard. Then type the correct character(s).

TROUBLE? If your text doesn't wrap, your screen might be set up to display more information than the screen used for the figures in this tutorial, or your WordPad program might not be set to use Word Wrap. Click View, click Options, make sure the Rich Text tab is selected, click the Wrap to window option button, and then click the OK button.

The Insertion Point Versus the Pointer

The insertion point is not the same as the mouse pointer. When the mouse pointer is in the text-entry area, it is called the **I-beam pointer** and looks like I. Figure 2-4 explains the difference between the insertion point and the I-beam pointer.

Figure 2-4	THE INSERTION POINT VS. THE POINTER

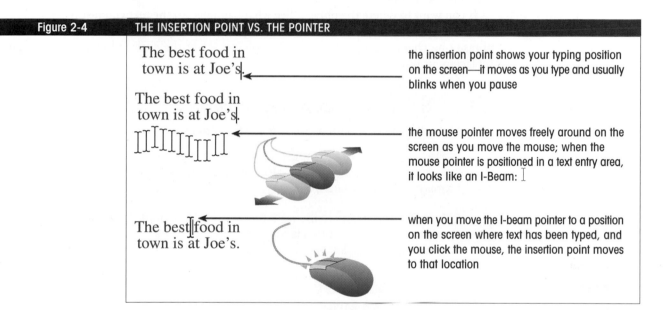

When you enter text, the insertion point moves as you type. If you want to enter text in a location other than where the mouse pointer is currently positioned, you move the I-beam pointer to the location where you want to type, and then click. The insertion point jumps to the location you clicked. In most programs, the insertion point blinks, making it easier for you to locate it on a screen filled with text.

To move the insertion point:

1. Check the locations of the insertion point and the I-beam pointer. The insertion point should be at the end of the sentence you typed in the last set of steps. The easiest way to locate the I-beam pointer is to move your mouse gently until you see the pointer. Remember that it will look like ⟨ until you move the pointer into the document window.

2. Use the mouse to move the I-beam pointer just to the left of the word "sample" and then click the mouse button. The insertion point should be just to the left of the "s."

   TROUBLE? If you have trouble clicking just to the left of the "s," try clicking in the word and then using the arrow keys to move the insertion point one character at a time.

3. Move the I-beam pointer to a blank area near the bottom of the workspace and then click. Notice the insertion point does not jump to the location of the I-beam pointer. Instead the insertion point jumps to the end of the last sentence or to the point in the bottom line directly above where you clicked. The insertion point can move only within existing text. It cannot be moved out of the existing text area.

Selecting Text

Many text operations are performed on a **block** of text, which is one or more consecutive characters, words, sentences, or paragraphs. Once you select a block of text, you can delete it, move it, replace it, underline it, and so on. To deselect a block of text, click anywhere outside the selected block.

If you want to delete the phrase "See what happens" in the text you just typed and replace it with the phrase "You can watch word wrap in action," you do not have to delete the first phrase one character at a time. Instead, you can select the entire phrase and then type the replacement phrase.

To select and replace a block of text:

1. Move the I-beam pointer just to the left of the word "See."

2. While holding down the mouse button, drag the I-beam pointer over the text to the end of the word "happens." The phrase "See what happens" should now be highlighted. See Figure 2-5.

   TROUBLE? If the space to the right of the word "happens" is also selected, don't worry. Your computer is set up to select spaces in addition to words. After completing Step 4, simply press the Spacebar to type an extra space if required.

Figure 2-5	SELECTING TEXT

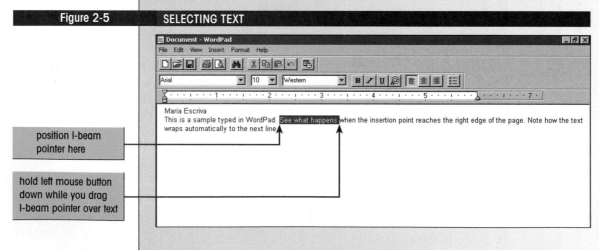

position I-beam pointer here

hold left mouse button down while you drag I-beam pointer over text

3. Release the mouse button.

   TROUBLE? If the phrase is not highlighted correctly, repeat Steps 1 through 3.

4. Type **You can watch word wrap in action**

The text you typed replaces the highlighted text. Notice that you did not need to delete the selected text before you typed the replacement text.

Inserting a Character

Windows 2000 programs usually operate in **insert mode**—when you type a new character, all characters to the right of the insertion point are pushed over to make room.

Suppose you want to insert the word "page" before the word "typed" in your practice sentences.

To insert text:

1. Move the I-beam pointer just before the word "typed" and then click to position the insertion point.

2. Type **page**

3. Press the **Spacebar**.

Notice how the letters in the first line are pushed to the right to make room for the new characters. When a word gets pushed past the right margin, the word-wrap feature moves it down to the beginning of the next line.

Saving a File

As you type text, it is held temporarily in the computer's memory, which is erased when you turn off the computer. For permanent storage, you need to save your work on a disk. In the computer lab, you will probably save your work on a floppy disk in drive A.

When you save a file, you must give it a name, called a **filename**. Windows 2000 allows you to use up to 255 characters in a filename—this gives you plenty of room to name your file accurately enough so that you'll know the contents of the file by just looking at the filename. You may use spaces and certain punctuation symbols in your filenames. You cannot use the symbols \ / ? : * " < > | in a filename, because Windows uses those for designating the location and type of the file, but other symbols such as & ; - and $ are allowed.

Another thing to consider is whether you might use your files on a computer running older programs. Programs designed for the Windows 3.1 and DOS operating systems (which were created before 1995) require that files be eight characters or less with no spaces. Thus when you save a file with a long filename in Windows 2000, Windows 2000 also creates an eight-character filename that can be used by older programs. The eight-character filename is created from the first six nonspace characters in the long filename, with the addition of a tilde (~) and a number. For example, the filename Car Sales for 1999 would be converted to Carsal~1.

Most filenames have an extension. An **extension** (a set of no more than three characters at the end of a filename, separated from the filename by a period) is used by the operating system to identify and categorize the file. In the filename Car Sales for 1999.doc, for example, the file extension "doc" identifies the file as one created with Microsoft Word. You might also have a file called Car Sales for 1999.xls—"xls" identifies the file as one created with Microsoft Excel, a spreadsheet program. When pronouncing filenames with extensions, say "dot" for the period, so that the file Resume.doc is pronounced "Resume dot doc."

You usually do not need to add extensions to your filenames because the program you use to create the file does this automatically. Also, Windows 2000 keeps track of file extensions, but not all computers are set to display them. The steps in these tutorials refer to files by using the filename without its extension. So if you see the filename Practice Text in the steps, but "Practice Text.doc" appears on your screen, don't worry—these refer to the same file. Also don't worry if you don't use consistent lowercase and uppercase letters when saving files. Usually the operating system doesn't distinguish between them. Be aware, however, that some programs are "case-sensitive"—they check for case in filenames.

Now you can save the WordPad document you typed.

To start saving a document:

1. Click the **Save** button 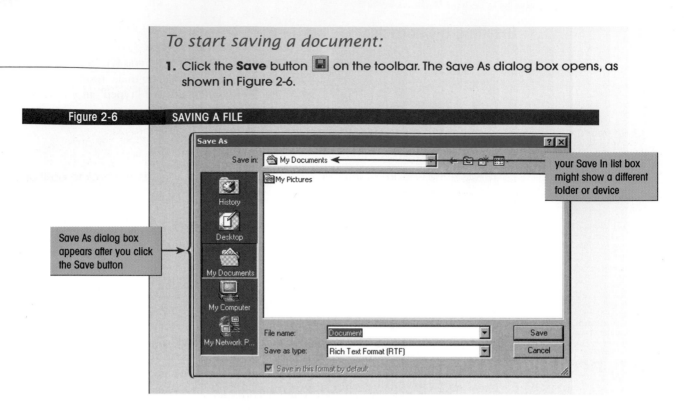 on the toolbar. The Save As dialog box opens, as shown in Figure 2-6.

Figure 2-6	SAVING A FILE

You use the Save As dialog box to specify where you want to save your file (on the hard drive or on a floppy disk, in a folder or not, and so on). Before going further with the process of saving a file, let's examine some of the features of the Save As dialog box so that you learn to save your files exactly where you want them.

Specifying the File Location

In the Save As dialog box, Windows 2000 provides the **Places Bar**, a list of important locations on your computer. When you click the different icons in the Places Bar, the contents of those locations will be displayed in the white area of the Save As dialog box. You can then save your document directly to those locations. Figure 2-7 displays the icons in the Places Bar and gives their function.

Figure 2-7	ICONS IN THE PLACES BAR

ICON	DESCRIPTION
History	Displays a list of recently opened files, folders, and objects
Desktop	Displays a list of files, folders, and objects on the Windows 2000 desktop
My Documents	Displays a list of files, folders, and objects in the My Documents folder
My Computer	Displays a list of files, folders, and objects in the My Computer window
My Network P...	Displays a list of computers and folders available on the network

To see this in action, try displaying different locations in the dialog box.

To use the Places Bar:

1. Click the **Desktop** icon in the Places Bar.

2. The Save As dialog box now displays the contents of the Windows 2000 desktop. See Figure 2-8.

Figure 2-8 | USING THE PLACES BAR

click to display the contents of the Windows 2000 desktop

contents of Windows 2000 desktop

3. Click the **My Documents** icon to display the contents of the My Documents folder.

Once you've clicked an icon in the Places Bar, you can open any file displayed in that location, and you can save a file into that location. The Places Bar doesn't have an icon for every location on your computer, however. The **Save in** list box (located at the top of the dialog box) does. Use the Save in list box now to save your document to your floppy disk.

To use the Save in list box:

1. Click the **Save in** list arrow to display a list of drives.

2. Click **3½ Floppy (A:)**.

Now that you've specified where you want to save your file, you can specify a name and type for the file.

Specifying the File Name and Type

After choosing the location for your document, you have to specify the name of the file. You should also specify (or at least check) the file's format. A file's **format** determines what type of information you can place in the document, the document's appearance, and what kind of programs can work with the document. There are five file formats available in WordPad: Word for Windows 6.0, Rich Text Format (RTF), Text, Text for MS-DOS, and Unicode Text. The Word and RTF formats allow you to create documents with text that can use bold-faced or italicized fonts as well as documents containing graphic images and scanned photos. However, only word-processing programs like WordPad or Microsoft Word can work with those files. The three text formats allow only simple text with no graphics or special formatting, but such documents are readable by a wider range of programs. The default format for WordPad documents is RTF, but you can change that, as you'll see shortly.

Continue saving the document, using the name "Practice Text" and the file type Word 6.0.

To finish saving your document:

1. Select the text **Document** in the File name text box and then type **Practice Text** in the File name text box. The new text replaces "Document."

2. Click the **Save as type** list arrow and then click **Word for Windows 6.0** in the list. See Figure 2-9.

Figure 2-9	COMPLETED SAVE AS DIALOG BOX

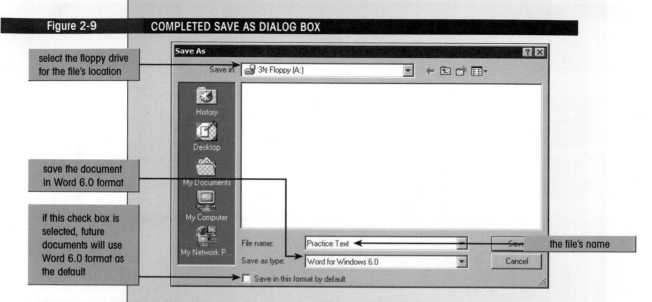

select the floppy drive for the file's location

save the document in Word 6.0 format

if this check box is selected, future documents will use Word 6.0 format as the default

the file's name

Note that if you want all future documents saved by WordPad to use the Word 6.0 format as the default format rather than RTF, you can select the Save in this format by default check box. If you select it, the next time you save a document in WordPad, this format will be the initial choice, so you won't have to specify it.

3. Click the **Save** button in the lower-right corner of the dialog box.

4. If you are asked whether you are sure that you want to save the document in this format, click the **Yes** button.

Your file is saved on your Data Disk, and the document title, "Practice Text," appears on the WordPad title bar.

Note that after you save the file the document appears a little different. What has changed? By saving the document in Word 6.0 format rather than RTF, you've changed the format of the document slightly. One change is that the text is wrapped differently in Word 6.0 format. A Word 6.0 file will use the right margin and, in this case, limit the length of a single line of text to 6 inches.

What if you try to close WordPad before you save your file? Windows 2000 will display a message—"Save changes to Document?" If you answer "Yes," Windows will display the Save As dialog box so you can give the document a name. If you answer "No," Windows 2000 will close WordPad without saving the document. Any changes you made to the document will be lost, so when you are asked if you want to save a file, answer "Yes," unless you are absolutely sure you don't need to keep the work you just did.

After you save a file, you can work on another document or close WordPad. Since you have already saved your Practice Text document, you'll continue this tutorial by closing WordPad.

To close WordPad:

1. Click the **Close** button ☒ to close the WordPad window.

Opening a File

Suppose you save and close the Practice Text file, then later you want to revise it. To revise a file you must first open it. When you open a file, its contents are copied into the computer's memory. If you revise the file, you need to save the changes before you close the program. If you close a revised file without saving your changes, you will lose them.

There are several methods to open a file. You can select the file from the Documents list (available through the Start menu) if you have opened the file recently, since the Documents list contains the 15 most recently opened documents. This list is very handy to use on your own computer, but in a lab, other student's files quickly replace your own. You can also locate the file in the My Computer window (or in **Windows Explorer,** another file management tool) and then open it. And finally, you can start a program and then use the Open button within that program to locate and open the file. Each method has advantages and disadvantages.

The first two methods for opening the Practice Text file simply require you to select the file from the Documents list or locate and select it from My Computer or Windows Explorer. With these methods the document, not the program, is central to the task; hence, this method is sometimes referred to as **document-centric**. You need only to remember the name of your file—you do not need to remember which program you used to create it.

Opening a File from the My Computer Window

If your file is not in the Documents list, you can open the file by selecting it from the My Computer window. Either way, Windows 2000 uses the file extension (whether it is displayed or not) to determine which program to start so you can manipulate the file. It starts the program, and then automatically opens the file. The advantage of both methods is simplicity. The disadvantage is that Windows 2000 might not start the program you expect. For example, when you select Practice Text, you might expect Windows 2000 to start WordPad because you used WordPad to create it. Depending on the programs installed on your computer system, however, Windows 2000 might start Microsoft Word instead. Usually this is not a problem. Although the program might not be the one you expect, you can still use it to revise your file.

To open the Practice Text file by selecting it from My Computer:

1. Open the **My Computer** window, located on the desktop.

2. Click the **3½ Floppy (A:)** icon in the My Computer window.

   TROUBLE? If the 3½ Floppy (A:) window opens, skip Step 3.

3. Press the **Enter** key. The 3½ Floppy (A:) window opens.

4. Click the **Practice Text** file icon.

   TROUBLE? If the Practice Text document opens, skip Step 5.

5. Press the **Enter** key. Windows 2000 starts a program, and then automatically opens the Practice Text file. You could make revisions to the document at this point, but instead, you'll close all the windows on your desktop so you can try the other method for opening files.

   TROUBLE? If Windows 2000 starts Microsoft Word or another word-processing program instead of WordPad, don't worry. You can use Microsoft Word to revise the Practice Text document.

6. Close all open windows on the desktop.

Opening a File from Within a Program

The third method for opening the Practice Text file requires you to open WordPad, and then use the Open button to select the Practice Text file. The advantage of this method is that you can specify the program you want to use—WordPad, in this case. This method, however, involves more steps than the method you tried previously.

You can take advantage of the Places Bar to reduce the number of steps it takes to open a file from within a program. Recall that one of the icons in the Places Bar is the History icon, which displays a list of recently opened files or objects. One of the most recently opened files was the Practice Text file, so it should appear in the list.

To start WordPad and open the Practice Text file:

1. Start **WordPad** and, if necessary, maximize the WordPad window.

2. Click the **Open** button 📂 on the toolbar.

3. Click **History** in the Places Bar.

The Practice Text file doesn't appear in the list. Why not? Look at the Files of Type list box. The selected entry is "Rich Text Format (*.rtf)". What this means is that the Open dialog box will display only RTF files (as well as drives). This frees you from having to deal with the clutter of unwanted or irrelevant files. The downside is that unless you're aware of how the Open dialog box will filter the list of files, you may mistakenly think that the file you're looking for doesn't exist. You can change how the Open dialog box filters this file list. Try this now by changing the filter to show only Word documents.

To change the types of files displayed:

1. Click the **Files of type** list arrow and then click **Word for Windows (*.doc)**

   The Practice Text file now appears in the list.

2. Click **Practice Text** in the list of files. See Figure 2-10.

| Figure 2-10 | THE OPEN DIALOG BOX |

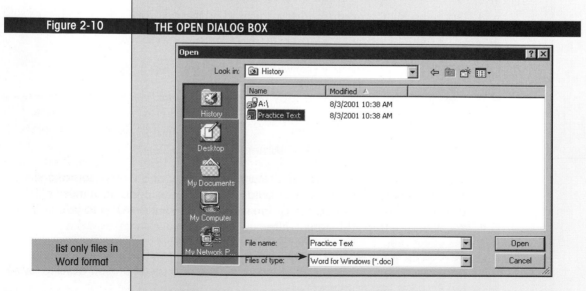

list only files in Word format

3. Click the **Open** button. The document should once again appear in the WordPad window.

Now that the Practice Text file is open, you can print it.

Printing a File

Windows 2000 provides easy access to your printer or printers. You can choose which printer to use, you can control how the document is printed, and you can control the order in which documents will be printed.

Previewing your Document Before Printing

It is a good idea to use Print Preview before you send your document to the printer. **Print Preview** shows on the screen exactly how your document will appear on paper. You can check your page layout so that you don't waste time and paper printing a document that is not quite the way you want it. Your instructor might supply you with additional instructions for printing in your school's computer lab.

To preview, then print, the Practice Text file:

1. Click the **Print Preview** button [icon] on the toolbar.

   TROUBLE? If an error message appears, printing capabilities might not be set up on your computer. Ask your instructor or technical support person for help, or skip this set of steps.

2. Look at your document in the Print Preview window. Before you print the document, you should make sure the font, margins, and other document features look the way you want them to.

   TROUBLE? If you can't read the document text on screen, click the Zoom In button as many times as needed to view the text.

3. Click the **Close** button to close Print Preview and return to the document.

Now that you've verified that the document looks the way you want, you can print it.

Sending the Document to the Printer

There are three ways to send your document to the printer. The first approach is to print the document directly from the Print Preview window by clicking the Print button. Thus once you are satisfied with the document's appearance, you can quickly move to printing it.

Another way is to click the Print button [icon] on your program's toolbar. This method will send the document directly to your printer without any further action on your part. It's the quickest and easiest way to print a document, but it does not allow you to change settings such as margins and layout. What if you have access to more than one printer? In that case, Windows 2000 sends the document to the default printer, the printer that has been set up to handle most print jobs.

If you want to select a different printer, or if you want to control how the printer prints your document, you can opt for a third method—selecting the Print command from the File menu. Using this approach, your program will open the Print dialog box, allowing you to choose which printer to use and how that printer will operate. Note that clicking the Print button from within the Print Preview window will also open the Print dialog box so you can verify or change settings.

To open the Print dialog box:

1. Click **File** on the WordPad menu bar and then click **Print**.

2. The Print dialog box opens, as displayed in Figure 2-11. Familiarize yourself with the controls in the Print dialog box.

Figure 2-11 THE PRINT DIALOG BOX

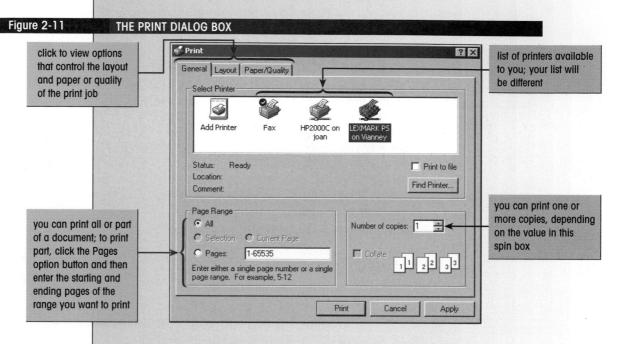

click to view options that control the layout and paper or quality of the print job

list of printers available to you; your list will be different

you can print all or part of a document; to print part, click the Pages option button and then enter the starting and ending pages of the range you want to print

you can print one or more copies, depending on the value in this spin box

3. Make sure your Print dialog box shows the Print range set to "All" and the Number of copies set to "1."

4. Select one of the printers in the list (your instructor may indicate which one you should select) and then click the **Print** button. The document is printed.

5. Close WordPad.

   TROUBLE? If you see the message "Save changes to Document?" click the No button.

You've now learned how to create, save, open, and print word-processed files—essential skills for students in distance education courses that rely on word-processed reports transmitted across the Internet. Shannon assures you that the techniques you've just learned apply to most Windows 2000 programs.

Session 2.1 QUICK CHECK

1. A(n) _____ is a collection of data that has a name and is stored on a disk or other storage medium.

2. _____ erases all the data on a disk and arranges the magnetic particles on the disk surface so that the disk can store data.

3. True or False: When you move the mouse pointer over a text entry area, the pointer shape changes to an I-beam.

4. What indicates where each character you type will appear?

5. What does the History icon in the Places Bar display?

6. A file that you saved does not appear in the Open dialog box. Assuming that the file is still in the same location, what could be the reason that the Open dialog box doesn't display it?

7. What are the three ways to print from within a Windows 2000 application? If you want to print multiple copies of your document, which method(s) should you use and why?

SESSION 2.2

In this session, you will learn how to change settings in the My Computer window to control its appearance and the appearance of desktop objects. You will then learn how to use My Computer to manage the files on your disk; view information about the files on your disk; organize the files into folders; and move, delete, copy, and rename files. For this session you will use a second blank 3½-inch disk.

Creating Your Data Disk

Starting with this session, you must create a Data Disk that contains some practice files. You can use the disk you formatted in the previous session.

If you are using your own computer, the NP on Microsoft Windows 2000 menu option will not be available. Before you proceed, you must go to your school's computer lab and find a computer that has the NP on Microsoft Windows 2000 program installed. If you cannot get the files from the lab, ask your instructor or technical support person for help. Once you have made your own Data Disk, you can use it to complete this tutorial on any computer running Windows 2000.

To add the practice files to your Data Disk:

1. Write "Disk 1 - Windows 2000 Tutorial 2 Data Disk" on the label of your formatted disk (the same disk you used to save your Practice Text file).

2. Place the disk in drive A.

3. Click the **Start** button 🏁Start.

4. Point to **Programs**.

5. Point to **NP on Microsoft Windows 2000 – Level I**.

   TROUBLE? If NP on Microsoft Windows 2000 - Level I is not listed, ask your instructor or technical support person for help.

6. Click **Disk 1 (Tutorial 2)**. A message box opens, asking you to place your disk in drive A (which you already did, in Step 2).

7. Click the **OK** button. Wait while the program copies the practice files to your formatted disk. When all the files have been copied, the program closes.

Your Data Disk now contains practice files you'll use throughout the rest of this tutorial.

My Computer

The My Computer icon, as you have seen, represents your computer, with its storage devices, printers, and other objects. The My Computer icon opens into the My Computer window, which contains an icon for each of the storage devices on your computer. My Computer also gives you access to the **Control Panel**, a feature of Windows 2000 that controls the behavior of other devices and programs installed on your computer. Figure 2-12 shows how the My Computer window relates to your computer's hardware.

Figure 2-12   RELATIONSHIP BETWEEN COMPUTER AND MY COMPUTER WINDOW

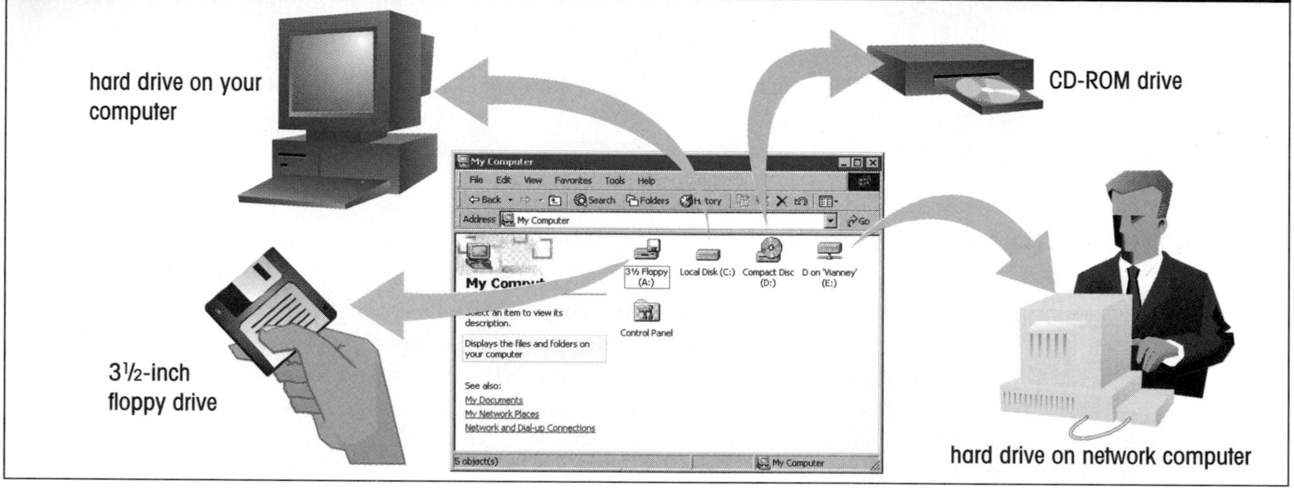

Each storage device that you have access to has a letter associated with it. The first floppy drive on a computer is usually designated as drive A (if you add a second floppy drive, it is usually designated as drive B), and the first hard drive is usually designated drive C. Additional hard drives will have letters D, E, F and so forth. If you have a CD-ROM drive, it will usually have the next letter in the alphabetic sequence. If you have access to hard drives located on other computers on a network, those drives will sometimes (though not always) have letters associated with them. In the example shown in Figure 2-12, the network drive has the drive letter E.

You can use the My Computer window to organize your files. In this section of the tutorial, you'll use the My Computer window to move and delete files on your Data Disk, which is assumed to be in drive A. If you use your own computer at home or work, you will probably store your files on drive C instead of drive A. In a school lab environment, you can't always save your files to drive C, so you need to carry your files with you on a floppy disk. Most of what you learn about working on the floppy drive will also work on your home or work computer when you use drive C (or other hard drives).

Now you'll open the My Computer window.

To open the My Computer window and explore the contents of your Data Disk:

1. Open the My Computer window.

2. Click the **3½ Floppy (A:)** icon and then press the **Enter** key. A window appears showing the contents of drive A; maximize this window if necessary. See Figure 2-13.

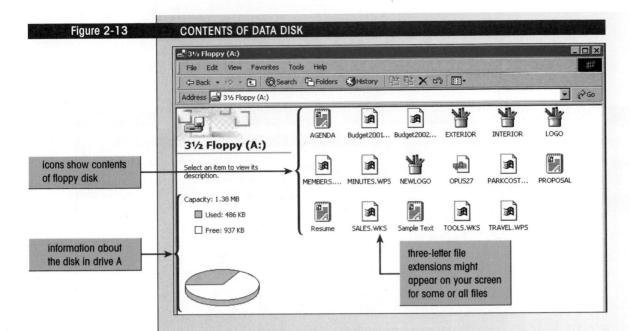

Figure 2-13   CONTENTS OF DATA DISK

icons show contents
of floppy disk

information about
the disk in drive A

three-letter file
extensions might
appear on your screen
for some or all files

TROUBLE? If the window appears before you press the Enter key, don't worry.
Windows 2000 can be configured to use different keyboard and mouse combinations to open windows. You'll learn about these configuration issues shortly.

TROUBLE? If you see a list of filenames instead of icons, click View on the menu
bar and then click Large Icons on the menu.

Changing the Appearance of the My Computer Window

Windows 2000 offers several different options that control how toolbars, icons, and buttons
appear in the My Computer window. To make the My Computer window look the same as
it does in the figures in this book, you need to ensure three things: that only the Address and
Standard toolbars are visible, that files and other objects are displayed using large icons, and
that the configuration of Windows 2000 uses the default setting. Setting your computer to
match the figures will make it easier for you to follow the steps.

Controlling the Toolbar Display

The My Computer window, in addition to displaying a Standard toolbar, allows you to display
the same toolbars that can appear on the Windows 2000 taskbar, such as the Address toolbar or
the Links toolbar. These toolbars make it easy to access the Web from the My Computer
window. In this tutorial, however, you need to see only the Address and Standard toolbars.

To display only the Address and Standard toolbars:

1. Click **View**, point to **Toolbars**, and then examine the Toolbars submenu. The
   Standard Buttons and Address Bar options should be preceded by a check mark.
   The Links and Radio options should not be checked. Follow the steps below to
   ensure that you have check marks next to the correct options.

2. If the Standard Buttons and Address Bar options *are not checked*, then click
   them to select them (you will have to repeat Step 1 to view the Toolbars
   submenu to do this for each option).

3. If the Links or Radio options *are checked*, then click them to deselect them (you will have to repeat Step 1 to view the Toolbars submenu to do this for each option).

4. Click **View** and then point to **Toolbars** one last time and verify that your Toolbars submenu and the toolbar display look like Figure 2-14.

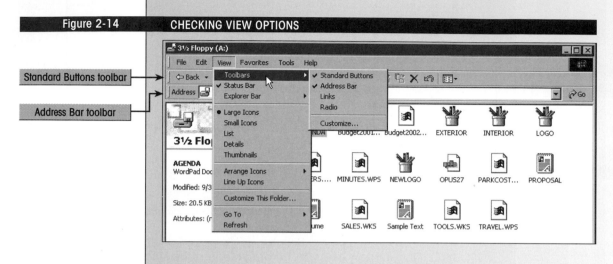

Figure 2-14 · CHECKING VIEW OPTIONS

Standard Buttons toolbar

Address Bar toolbar

TROUBLE? If the check marks are distributed differently than in Figure 2-14, repeat Steps 1–4 until the correct options are checked.

TROUBLE? If your toolbars are not displayed as shown in Figure 2-14 (for example, both the Standard and Address toolbars might be on the same line, or the Standard toolbar might be above the Address toolbar), you can easily rearrange them. To move a toolbar, drag the vertical bar at the far left of the toolbar. By dragging that vertical bar, you can drag the toolbar left, right, up, or down.

Changing the Icon Display

Windows 2000 provides five ways to view the contents of a disk—Large Icons, Small Icons, List, Details, and Thumbnails. Figure 2-15 shows examples of these five styles.

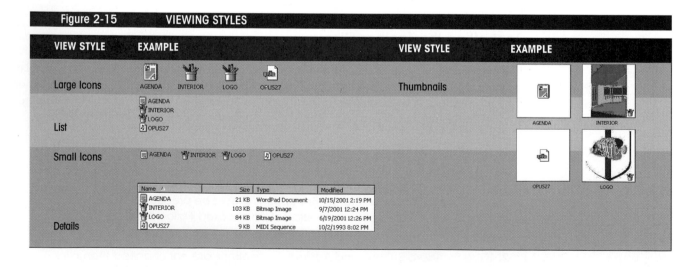

Figure 2-15 · VIEWING STYLES

The default view, **Large Icons view**, displays a large icon and title for each file. The icon provides a visual cue to the type of the file, as Figure 2-16 illustrates. You can also get this same information with the smaller icons displayed in the **Small Icons** and **List** views, but in less screen space. In Small Icons and List views, you can see more files and folders at one time, which is helpful when you have many files in one location.

Figure 2-16	TYPICAL ICONS IN WINDOWS 2000

FILE AND FOLDER ICONS

	Text documents that you can open using the Notepad accessory are represented by notepad icons.
	Graphic image documents that you can open using the Paint accessory are represented by drawing instruments.
	Word-processed documents that you can open using the WordPad accessory are represented by a formatted notepad icon, unless your computer designates a different word-processing program to open files created with WordPad.
	Word-processed documents that you can open using a program such as Microsoft Word are represented by formatted document icons.
	Files created by programs that Windows does not recognize are represented by the Windows logo.
	A folder icon represents folders.
	Certain folders created by Windows 2000 have a special icon design related to the folder's purpose.

PROGRAM ICONS

	Icons for programs usually depict an object related to the function of the program. For example, an icon that looks like a calculator represents the Calculator accessory.
	Non-Windows programs are represented by the icon of a blank window.

All of the three icon views (Large Icons, Small Icons, and List) help you quickly identify a file and its type, but what if you want more information about a set of files? **Details view** shows more information than the Large Icon, Small Icon, and List views. Details view shows the file icon, the filename, the file size, the program you used to create the file, and the date and time the file was created or last modified.

Finally, if you have graphic files, you may want to use **Thumbnails view**, which displays a small "preview" image of the graphic, so that you can quickly see not only the filename, but also which picture or drawing the file contains. Thumbnails view is great for browsing a large collection of graphic files, but switching to this view can be time-consuming, since Windows 2000 has to create all of the preview images.

To see how easy it is to switch from one view to another, try displaying the contents of drive A in Details view.

To view a detailed list of files:

1. Click **View** and then click **Details** to display details for the files on your disk, as shown in Figure 2-17. Your files might be listed in a different order.

Figure 2-17 | **DETAILS VIEW**

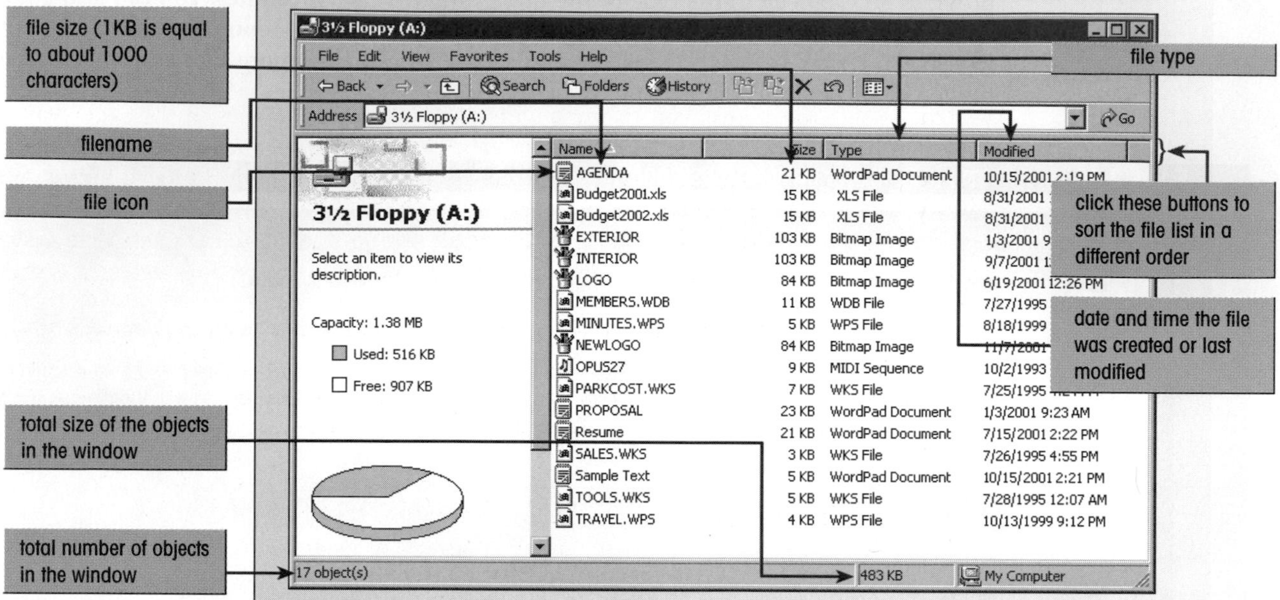

file size (1KB is equal to about 1000 characters)

filename

file icon

total size of the objects in the window

total number of objects in the window

file type

click these buttons to sort the file list in a different order

date and time the file was created or last modified

Name	Size	Type	Modified
AGENDA	21 KB	WordPad Document	10/15/2001 2:19 PM
Budget2001.xls	15 KB	XLS File	8/31/2001
Budget2002.xls	15 KB	XLS File	8/31/2001
EXTERIOR	103 KB	Bitmap Image	1/3/2001 9
INTERIOR	103 KB	Bitmap Image	9/7/2001 1
LOGO	84 KB	Bitmap Image	6/19/2001 12:26 PM
MEMBERS.WDB	11 KB	WDB File	7/27/1995
MINUTES.WPS	5 KB	WPS File	8/18/1999
NEWLOGO	84 KB	Bitmap Image	11/7/2001
OPUS27	9 KB	MIDI Sequence	10/2/1993
PARKCOST.WKS	7 KB	WKS File	7/25/1995
PROPOSAL	23 KB	WordPad Document	1/3/2001 9:23 AM
Resume	21 KB	WordPad Document	7/15/2001 2:22 PM
SALES.WKS	3 KB	WKS File	7/26/1995 4:55 PM
Sample Text	5 KB	WordPad Document	10/15/2001 2:21 PM
TOOLS.WKS	5 KB	WKS File	7/28/1995 12:07 AM
TRAVEL.WPS	4 KB	WPS File	10/13/1999 9:12 PM

3½ Floppy (A:)

Select an item to view its description.

Capacity: 1.38 MB

Used: 516 KB

Free: 907 KB

17 object(s)   483 KB   My Computer

2. Look at the file sizes. Do you see that Exterior and Interior are the largest files?

3. Look at the dates and times the files were modified. Which is the oldest file?

One of the advantages that Details view has over other views is that you can sort the file list by filename, size, type, or the date the file was last modified. This helps if you're working with a large file list and you're trying to locate a specific file.

To sort the file list by type:

1. Click the **Type** button at the top of the list of files.

The files are now sorted in alphabetical order by type, starting with the "Bitmap Image" files and ending with the "XLS File" files. This would be useful if, for example, you were looking for all the .doc files (those created with Microsoft Word), because they would all be grouped together under "M" for "Microsoft Word."

2. Click the **Type** button again.

The sort order is reversed with the "XLS File" files now at the top of the list.

3. Click the **Name** button at the top of the file list.

The files are now sorted in alphabetical order by filename.

Now that you have looked at the file details, switch back to Large Icon view.

To switch to Large Icon view:

1. Click **View** and then click **Large Icons** to return to the large icon display.

Restoring the My Computer Default Settings

Windows 2000 provides other options in working with your files and windows. These options fall into two general categories: Classic style and Web style. **Classic style** is a mode of working with windows and files that resembles earlier versions of the Windows operating system. **Web style** allows you to work with your windows and files in the same way you work with Web pages on the World Wide Web. For example, to open a file in Classic style, you can double-click the file icon (a **double-click** is clicking the left mouse button twice quickly) or click the file icon once and press the Enter key. To open a file in Web style, you would simply click the file icon once, and the file would open. You could also create your own style, choosing elements of both the Classic and Web styles, and add in a few customized features of your own.

In order to simplify matters, this book will assume that you're working in the Default style, that is the configuration that Windows 2000 uses when it is initially installed. No matter what changes you make to the configuration of Windows 2000, you can always revert back to the Default style. Try switching back to Default style now.

To switch to the Default style:

1. Click **Tools** and then click **Folder Options** on the menu.

2. If it is not already selected, click the **General** tab.

   The General sheet displays general options for working with files and windows. Take some time to look over the list of options available.

3. Click the **Restore Defaults** button.

4. Click the **View** tab.

   The View sheet displays options that control the appearance of files and other objects. You should set these options to their default values as well.

5. Click the **Restore Defaults** button.

6. Click the **OK** button to close the Folder Options dialog box.

Working with Folders and Directories

Up to now, you've done a little work with files and windows, but before going further you should look at some of the terminology used to describe these tasks. Any location where you can store files on a computer is referred to as a **directory**. The main directory of a disk is sometimes called the **root directory**, or the **top-level directory**. All of the files on your Data Disk are currently in the root directory of your floppy disk.

If too many files are stored in a directory, the list of files becomes very long and difficult to manage. You can divide a directory into **subdirectories**, also called **folders**. The number of files for each folder then becomes much fewer and easier to manage. A folder within a folder is called a **subfolder**. The folder that contains another folder is called the **parent folder**.

All of these objects exist in a **hierarchy**, which begins with your desktop and extends down to each subfolder. Figure 2-18 shows part of a typical hierarchy of Windows 2000 objects.

Figure 2-18 | PART OF A TYPICAL HIERARCHY OF WINDOWS 2000 OBJECTS

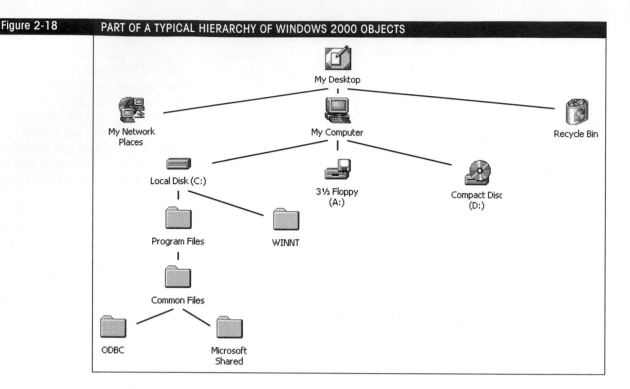

Creating a Folder

You've already seen folder icons in the various windows you've previously opened. Now, you'll create your own folder called Practice to hold your documents.

To create a Practice folder:

1. Click **File** and then point to **New** to display the submenu.

2. Click **Folder**. A folder icon with the label "New Folder" appears.

3. Type **Practice** as the name of the folder.

   TROUBLE? If nothing happens when you type the folder name, it's possible that the folder name is no longer selected. Right-click the Practice folder, click Rename, and then repeat Step 3.

4. Press the **Enter** key.

   The folder is now named "Practice" and is the selected item on your Data Disk.

5. Click a blank area next to the Practice folder to deselect it.

Navigating Through the Windows 2000 Hierarchy

Now that you've created a subfolder, how do you move into it? You've seen that to view the contents of a file, you open it. To move into a subfolder, you open it in the same way.

To view the contents of the Practice folder:

1. Click the **Practice** folder and press the **Enter** key.

2. The Practice folder opens. Because there are no files in the folder, there are no items to display. You'll change that shortly.

You've seen that to navigate through the devices and folders on your computer, you open My Computer and then click the icons representing the objects you want to explore. But what if you want to move back to the root directory? The Standard toolbar, which stays the same regardless of which folder or object is open, includes buttons that help you navigate through the hierarchy of drives, directories, folders, subfolders and other objects in your computer. Figure 2-19 summarizes the navigation buttons on the Standard toolbar.

Figure 2-19		NAVIGATION BUTTONS
BUTTON	**ICON**	**DESCRIPTION**
Back	⇐	Returns you to the folder, drive, directory, or object you were most recently viewing. The button is active only when you have viewed more than one window in the current session.
Forward	⇒	Reverses the effect of the Back button.
Up	⬆	Moves you up one level in the hierarchy of directories, drives, folders, and other objects on your computer.

You can return to your floppy's root directory by using the Back or the Up button. Try both of these techniques now.

To move up to the root directory:

1. Click the **Back** button ⇐.

   Windows 2000 moves you back to the previous window, in this case the root directory of your Data Disk.

2. Click the **Forward** button ⇒.

   The Forward button reverses the effect of the Back button and takes you to the Practice folder.

3. Click the **Up** button ⬆.

   You move up one level in hierarchy of Windows 2000 objects, going to the root directory of the Data Disk.

Another way of moving around in the Windows 2000 hierarchy is through the Address toolbar. By clicking the Address list arrow, you can view a list of the objects in the top part of the Windows 2000 hierarchy (see Figure 2-20). This gives you a quick way of moving to the top without having to navigate through the intermediate levels.

Figure 2-20 | **A HIERARCHY OF OBJECTS DISPLAYED IN THE ADDRESS LIST BOX**

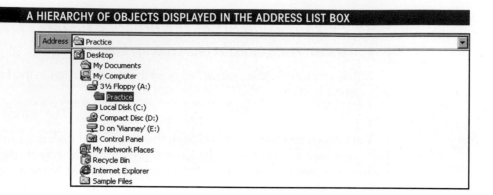

Now that you know how to move among the folders and devices on your computer, you can practice manipulating files. The better you are at working with the hierarchy of files and folders on your computer, the more organized the hierarchy will be, and the easier it will be to find the files you need.

Working with Files

As you've seen, the Practice folder doesn't contain any files. In the next set of steps, you will place a file from the root directory into it.

Moving and Copying a File

If you want to place a file into a folder from another location, you can either move the file or copy it. **Moving** a file takes it out of its current location and places it in the new location. **Copying** places the file in both locations. Windows 2000 provides several different techniques for moving and copying files. One way is to make sure that both the current and the new location are visible on your screen and then hold down the right mouse button and drag the file from the old location to the new location. A menu will then appear, and you can then select whether you want to move the file to the new location or make a copy in the new location. The advantage of this technique is that you are never confused as to whether you copied the file or merely moved it. Try this technique now by placing a copy of the Agenda file in the Practice folder.

To copy the Agenda file:

1. Point to the **Agenda** file in the root directory of your Data Disk and press the *right* mouse button.

2. With the right mouse button still pressed down, drag the **Agenda** file icon to the **Practice** folder icon; when the Practice folder icon turns blue, release the button.

3. A menu appears, as shown in Figure 2-21. Click **Copy Here**.

Figure 2-21   COPYING A FILE

TROUBLE? If you release the mouse button by mistake before dragging the Agenda icon to the Practice folder, the Agenda shortcut menu opens. Press the Esc key and then repeat Steps 1 and 2.

4. Double-click the **Practice** folder.

The Agenda file should now appear in the Practice folder.

Note that the "Move Here" command was also part of the menu. In fact, the command was in boldface, indicating that it is the default command whenever you drag a document from one location to another on the same drive. This means that if you were to drag a file from one location to another on the same drive using the left mouse button (instead of the right), the file would be moved and not copied.

Renaming a File

You will often find that you want to change the name of files as you change their content or as you create other files. You can easily rename a file by using the Rename option on the file's shortcut menu or by using the file's label.

Practice using this feature by renaming the Agenda file "Practice Agenda," since it is now in the Practice folder.

To rename the Agenda file:

1. Right-click the **Agenda** icon.

2. Click **Rename**. After a moment the filename is highlighted and a box appears around it.

3. Type **Practice Agenda** and press the **Enter** key.

> **TROUBLE?** If you make a mistake while typing and you haven't pressed the Enter key yet, you can press the Backspace key until you delete the mistake, then complete Step 3. If you've already pressed the Enter key, repeat Steps 1-3 to rename the file a second time.
>
> The file appears with a new name.

Deleting a File

You should periodically delete files you no longer need so that your folders and disks don't get cluttered. You delete a file or folder by deleting its icon. Be careful when you delete a folder, because you also delete all the files it contains! When you delete a file from a hard drive on your computer, the filename is deleted from the directory but the file contents are held in the Recycle Bin. The Recycle Bin is an area on your hard drive that holds deleted files until you remove them permanently; an icon on the desktop allows you easy access to the Recycle Bin. If you change your mind and want to retrieve a file deleted from your hard drive, you can recover it by using the Recycle Bin. However, once you've emptied the Recycle Bin, you can no longer recover the files that were in it.

When you delete a file from a floppy disk or a disk that exists on another computer on your network, it does not go into the Recycle Bin. Instead, it is deleted as soon as its icon disappears—and you can't recover it.

Try deleting the Practice Agenda file from your Data Disk. Because this file is on a floppy disk and not on the hard disk, it will not go into the Recycle Bin, and if you change your mind you won't be able to get it back.

To delete the Practice Agenda file:

1. Right-click the icon for the Practice Agenda file.

2. Click **Delete** on the menu that appears.

3. Windows 2000 asks if you're sure that you want to delete this file. Click the **Yes** button.

4. Click the **Close** button ⊠ to close the My Computer window.

If you like using your mouse, another way of deleting a file is to drag its icon to the Recycle Bin on the desktop. Be aware that if you're dragging a file from your floppy disk or a network disk, the file will *not* be placed in the Recycle Bin—it will still be permanently deleted.

Other Copying and Moving Techniques

As was noted earlier, there are several ways of moving and copying. As you become more familiar with Windows 2000, you will no doubt settle on the technique you like best. Figure 2-22 describes some of the other ways of moving and copying files.

Figure 2-22	METHODS FOR MOVING AND COPYING FILES	
METHOD	**TO MOVE**	**TO COPY**
Cut, copy, and paste	Select the file icon. Click **Edit** on the menu bar and **Cut** on the menu bar. Move to the new location. Click **Edit** and **Paste**.	Select the file icon. Click **Edit** on the menu bar and **Copy** on the menu bar. Move to the new location. Click **Edit** and **Paste**.
Drag and drop	Click the file icon. Drag and drop the icon in the new location.	Click the file icon. Hold down the Ctrl key and drag and drop the icon in the new location.
Right-click, drag and drop	With the right mouse button pressed down, drag the file icon to the new location. Release the mouse button and click **Move Here** on the menu.	With the right mouse button pressed down, drag the file icon to the new location. Release the mouse button and click **Copy Here** on the menu.
Move to folder and copy to folder	Click the file icon. Click **Edit** on the menu bar and **Move to Folder** on the menu bar. Select the new location in the Browse for Folder dialog box.	Click the file icon. Click **Edit** on the menu bar and **Copy to Folder** on the menu bar. Select the new location in the Browse for Folder dialog box.

The techniques shown in Figure 2-22 are primarily for document files. Because a program might not work correctly if moved into a new location, the techniques for moving program files are slightly different. See the Windows 2000 online Help for more information on moving or copying a program file.

Copying an Entire Floppy Disk

You can have trouble accessing the data on your floppy disk if the disk is damaged, is exposed to magnetic fields, or picks up a computer virus. To avoid losing all your data, it is a good idea to make a copy of your floppy disk.

If you wanted to make a copy of an audiocassette, your cassette player would need two cassette drives. You might wonder, therefore, how your computer can make a copy of your disk if you have only one floppy disk drive. Figure 2-23 illustrates how the computer uses only one disk drive to make a copy of a disk.

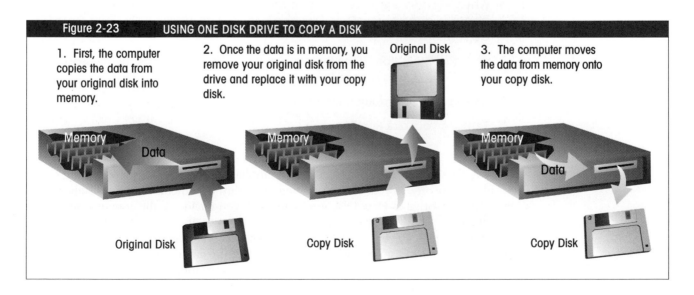

Figure 2-23	USING ONE DISK DRIVE TO COPY A DISK

1. First, the computer copies the data from your original disk into memory.

2. Once the data is in memory, you remove your original disk from the drive and replace it with your copy disk.

3. The computer moves the data from memory onto your copy disk.

Memory

Data

Original Disk

Original Disk

Memory

Copy Disk

Original Disk

Memory

Data

Copy Disk

Copying a Disk
- Insert the disk you want to copy in drive A.
- In My Computer, right-click the 3½ Floppy (A:) icon, and then click Copy Disk.
- Click Start to begin the copy process.
- When prompted, remove the disk you want to copy, place your second disk in drive A, and then click OK.

If you have an extra floppy disk, you can make a copy of your Data Disk now. Make sure you copy the disk regularly so that as you work through the tutorials in this book it will stay updated.

To copy your Data Disk:

1. Write your name and "Windows 2000 Disk 1 Data Disk Copy" on the label of your second disk. Make sure the disk is blank and formatted.

   TROUBLE? If you aren't sure if the disk is blank, place it in the disk drive and open the 3½ Floppy (A:) window to view its contents. If the disk contains files you need, get a different disk. If it contains files you don't need, you could format the disk now, using the steps you learned at the beginning of this tutorial.

2. Make sure your original Data Disk is in drive A and the My Computer window is open.

3. Right-click the **3½ Floppy (A:)** icon, and then click **Copy Disk**. The Copy Disk dialog box opens.

4. Click the **Start** button and then the **OK** button to begin the copy process.

5. When the message "Insert the disk you want to copy to (destination disk)..." appears, remove your Data Disk and insert your Windows 2000 Disk 1 Data Disk Copy in drive A.

6. Click the **OK** button. When the copy is complete, you will see the message "Copy completed successfully." Click the **Close** button.

7. Close the My Computer window.

8. Remove your disk from the drive.

As you finish copying your disk, Shannon emphasizes the importance of making copies of your files frequently, so you won't risk losing important documents for your distance learning course. If your original Data Disk were damaged, you could use the copy you just made to access the files.

Keeping copies of your files is so important that Windows 2000 includes a program called Backup that automates the process of duplicating and storing data. In the Projects at the end of the tutorial you'll have an opportunity to explore the difference between what you just did in copying a disk and the way in which a program such as the Windows 2000 Backup program helps you safeguard data.

Session 2.2 QUICK CHECK

1. If you want to find out about the storage devices and printers connected to your computer, what window could you open?

2. If you have only one floppy disk drive on your computer, it is usually identified by the letter _____.

3. The letter C is typically used for the _____ drive of a computer.

4. What information does Details view supply about a list of folders and files?

5. The main directory of a disk is referred to as the _____ directory.

6. What is the topmost object in the hierarchy of Windows 2000 objects?

7. If you have one floppy disk drive, but you have two disks, can you copy the files on one floppy disk to the other?

REVIEW ASSIGNMENTS

1. **Opening, Editing, and Printing a Document** In this tutorial you learned how to create a document using WordPad. You also learned how to save, open, and print a document. Practice these skills by copying the document called **Resume** into the Practice folder on your Data Disk. Rename the file **Woods Resume**. This document is a resume for Jamie Woods. Make the changes shown in Figure 2-24. Save your revisions in Word for Windows 6.0 format, preview, and then print the document. Close WordPad.

| Figure 2-24 | |

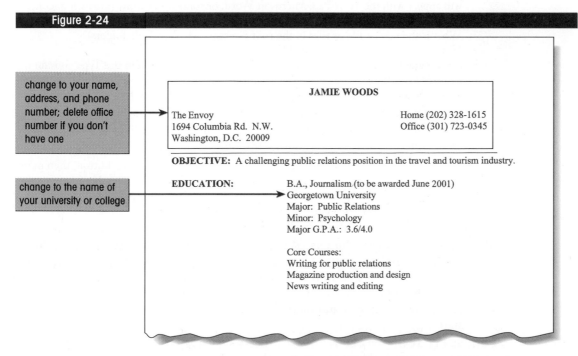

change to your name, address, and phone number; delete office number if you don't have one

change to the name of your university or college

JAMIE WOODS

The Envoy
1694 Columbia Rd. N.W.
Washington, D.C. 20009

Home (202) 328-1615
Office (301) 723-0345

OBJECTIVE: A challenging public relations position in the travel and tourism industry.

EDUCATION:

B.A., Journalism (to be awarded June 2001)
Georgetown University
Major: Public Relations
Minor: Psychology
Major G.P.A.: 3.6/4.0

Core Courses:
Writing for public relations
Magazine production and design
News writing and editing

2. **Creating, Saving, and Printing a Letter** Use WordPad to write a one-page letter to a relative or a friend. Save the document in the Practice folder on your Data Disk with the name **Letter**. Use the Print Preview feature to look at the format of your finished letter, then print it, and be sure to sign it. Close WordPad.

3. **Managing Files and Folders** Using the copy of the disk you made at the end of the tutorial, complete steps a through f below to practice your file-management skills, and then answer the questions below.
   a. Create a folder called Spreadsheets on your Data Disk.
   b. Move the files **Parkcost**, **Budget2001**, **Budget2002**, and **Sales** into the Spreadsheets folder.
   c. Create a folder called Park Project.
   d. Move the files **Proposal**, **Members**, **Tools**, **Logo**, and **Newlogo** into the Park Project folder.
   e. Delete the file called **Travel**.
   f. Switch to the Details view and write out your answers to Questions 1 through 5:
      1. What is the largest file or files in the Park Project folder?
      2. What is the newest file or files in the Spreadsheets folder?
      3. How many files (don't include folders) are in the root directory of your Data Disk?
      4. How are the Opus and Exterior icons different? Judging from the appearance of the icons, what would you guess these two files contain?
      5. Which file in the root directory has the most recent date?

4. **More Practice with Files and Folders** For this assignment, you need a third blank disk. Complete steps a through g below to practice your file-management skills.
   a. Write "Windows 2000 Tutorial 2 Assignment 4" on the label of the blank disk, and then format the disk if necessary.
   b. Create another copy of your original Data Disk, using the Assignment 4 disk. Refer to the section "Creating Your Data Disk" in Session 2.2.
   c. Create three folders on the Assignment 4 Data Disk you just created: Documents, Budgets, and Graphics.
   d. Move the files **Interior**, **Exterior**, **Logo**, and **Newlogo** to the Graphics folder.
   e. Move the files **Travel**, **Members**, and **Minutes** to the Documents folder.
   f. Move **Budget2001** and **Budget2002** to the Budgets folder.
   g. Switch to Details view and write out your answers to Questions 1 through 6:
      1. What is the largest file or files in the Graphics folder?
      2. How many word-processed documents are in the root directory? *Hint*: These documents will appear with the WordPad, Microsoft Word, or some other word-processing icon, depending on what software you have installed.
      3. What is the newest file or files in the root directory (don't include folders)?
      4. How many files in all folders are 5 KB in size?
      5. How many files in the root directory are WKS files? *Hint*: Look in the Type column to identify WKS files.
      6. Do all the files in the Graphics folder have the same icon? What type are they?

5. **Searching for a File** Windows 2000 Help includes a topic that discusses how to search for files on a disk without looking through all the folders. Start Windows Help, then locate this topic, and answer Questions a through c:
   a. To display the Search dialog box, you must click the _____ button, then point to _____ on the menu, and finally click _____ on the submenu.
   b. Do you need to type in the entire filename to find the file?
   c. How do you perform a case-sensitive search?

6. **Help with Files and Folders** In Tutorial 2 you learned how to work with Windows 2000 files and folders. What additional information on this topic does Windows 2000 Help provide? Use the Start button to access Help. Use the Index tab to locate topics related to files and folders. Find at least two tips or procedures for working with files and folders that were not covered in the tutorial. Write out the tip in your own words and include the title of the Help screen that contains the information.

7. **Formatting Text** You can use a word processor such as WordPad to format text, that is, to give it a specific look and feel by using bold, italics, and different fonts, and by applying other features. Using WordPad, type the title and words to one of your favorite songs and

then save the document on your Data Disk (make sure you use your original Data Disk) with the filename Song.

a. Select the title, and then click the Center ▤, Bold ▣, and Italic 𝑰 buttons on the toolbar.

b. Click the Font list arrow and select a different font. Repeat this step several times with different fonts until you locate a font that is appropriate for the song.

c. Experiment with other formatting options until you find a look you like for your document. Save and print the final version.

PROJECTS

1. Formatting a floppy disk removes all the data on a disk. Answer the following questions using full sentences:

   a. What other method did you learn in this tutorial for removing data from a disk?

   b. If you wanted to remove all data from a disk, which method would you use? Why?

   c. What method would you use if you wanted to remove only one file? Why?

2. A friend who is new to computers is trying to learn how to enter text into WordPad. She has just finished typing her first paragraph when she notices a mistake in the first sentence. She can't remember how to fix a mistake, so she asks you for help. Write the set of steps she should try.

3. Computer users usually develop habits about how they access their files and programs. Follow the steps below to practice methods of opening a file, and then evaluate which method you would be likely to use and why.

   a. Using WordPad, create a document containing the words to a favorite poem, and save it on your Data Disk with the name Poem.

   b. Close WordPad and return to the desktop.

   c. Open the document using a document-centric approach.

   d. After a successful completion of step c, close the program and reopen the same document using another approach.

   e. Write the steps you used to complete steps c and d of this assignment. Then write a paragraph discussing which approach is most convenient when you are starting from the desktop, and indicate what habits you would develop if you owned your own computer and used it regularly.

Explore ▶ 4. The My Computer window gives you access to the objects on your computer. In this tutorial you used My Computer to access your floppy drive so you could view the contents of your Data Disk. The My Computer window gives you access to other objects too. Open My Computer and write a list of the objects you see, including folders. Then open each icon and write a two-sentence description of the contents of each window that opens.

Explore ▶ 5. In this tutorial you learned how to copy a disk to protect yourself in the event of data loss. If you had your own computer with an 80 MB hard drive that was being used to capacity, it would take many 1.44 MB floppy disks to copy the contents of the entire hard drive. Is copying to floppy disks a reasonable method to use for protecting the data on your hard disk? Why, or why not?

   a. As mentioned at the end of the tutorial, Windows 2000 also includes an accessory called Backup that helps you safeguard your data. Backup doesn't just copy the data—it organizes it so that it takes up much less space than if you simply copied it. This program might not be installed on your computer, but if it is, try starting it (click the Start button, point to Programs, point to Accessories, point to System Tools, and then click Backup) and opening the Help files to learn what you can about how it functions. If it is not installed, skip Part a.

   b. Look up the topic of backups in a computer concepts textbook or in computer trade magazines. You could also interview experienced computer owners to find out which method they use to protect their data. When you have finished researching the concept of the backup, write a single-page essay that explains the difference between copying and backing up files, and evaluates which method is preferable for backing up large amounts of data, and why.

LAB ASSIGNMENTS

Using Files In this Lab you manipulate a simulated computer to view what happens in memory and on disk when you create, save, open, revise, and delete files. Understanding what goes on "inside the box" will help you quickly grasp how to perform basic file operations with most application software. See the Read This Before You Begin page for instructions on starting the Using Files Course Lab.

1. Click the Steps button to learn how to use the simulated computer to view the contents of memory and disk when you perform basic file operations. As you proceed through the Steps, answer all of the Quick Check questions that appear. After you complete the Steps, you will see a Quick Check Summary Report. Follow the instructions on the screen to print this report.

2. Click the Explore button and use the simulated computer to perform the following tasks:
   a. Create a document containing your name and the city in which you were born. Save this document as NAME.
   b. Create another document containing two of your favorite foods. Save this document as FOODS.
   c. Create another file containing your two favorite classes. Call this file CLASSES.
   d. Open the FOOD file and add another one of your favorite foods. Save this file without changing its name.
   e. Open the NAME file. Change this document so that it contains your name and the name of your school. Save this as a new document called SCHOOL.
   f. Write down how many files are on the simulated disk and the exact contents of each file.
   g. Delete all the files.

3. In Explore, use the simulated computer to perform the following tasks.
   a. Create a file called MUSIC that contains the name of your favorite CD.
   b. Create another document that contains eight numbers and call this file LOTTERY.
   c. You didn't win the lottery this week. Revise the contents of the LOTTERY file, but save the revision as LOTTERY2.
   d. Revise the MUSIC file so that it also contains the name of your favorite musician or composer, and save this file as MUSIC2.
   e. Delete the MUSIC file.
   f. Write down how many files are on the simulated disk and the exact contents of each file.

QUICK | CHECK ANSWERS

Session 2.1
   1. file
   2. Formatting
   3. True
   4. insertion point
   5. a list of recently opened files and objects
   6. The Files of Type list box could be set to display files of a different type than the one you're looking for.
   7. From the Print Preview window, using the Print button on the toolbar, and using the Print command from the File menu. If you want to print multiple copies of a file, use either the Print button from the Print Preview window or the Print command from the File menu—both of these techniques will display the Print dialog box containing the options you need to set.

Session 2.2
   1. My Computer
   2. A
   3. hard
   4. filename, size, type, and date modified
   5. root or top-level
   6. the Desktop
   7. yes

New Perspectives on

BROWSER AND E-MAIL BASICS

Read This Before You Begin

To the Student

Data Disks

To complete this tutorial, Review Assignments, and Case Problems, you need one Data Disk. Your instructor will either provide you with this Data Disk or ask you to make your own.

If you are making your own Data Disk, you will need **one** blank, formatted high-density disk. You will need to copy a set of files and/or folders from a file server, standalone computer, or the Web onto your disk. Your instructor will tell you which computer, drive letter, and folders contain the files you need. You could also download the files by going to www.course.com and following the instructions on the screen.

The information below shows you which folders go on your disk, so that you will have enough disk space to complete the tutorial, Review Assignments, and Case Problems:

Data Disk 1

Write this on the disk label:

Data Disk 1: Browser and E-mail Basics

Put this folder on the disk:

Tutorial.01

When you begin the tutorial, be sure you are using the correct Data Disk. Refer to the "File Finder" chart at the back of this text for more detailed information on which files are used in the tutorial. See the inside front or inside back cover of this book for more information on Data Disk files, or ask your instructor or technical support person for assistance.

Course Labs

This tutorial features an interactive Course Lab to help you understand World Wide Web concepts. There are Lab Assignments at the end of the tutorial that relate to this Lab.

To start a Lab, click the **Start** button on the Windows taskbar, point to **Programs**, point to **Course Labs**, point to **New Perspectives Course Labs**, and then click the name of the Lab you want to use.

Using Your Own Computer

If you are going to work through this book using your own computer, you need:

■ **Computer System** Microsoft Windows 98, NT, 2000 Professional, or higher must be installed on your computer. This book assumes a typical installation of Microsoft Internet Explorer 5.0 or higher and Outlook Express 5.0 or higher.

■ **Data Disk** You will not be able to complete this tutorial or exercises using your own computer until you have a Data Disk.

■ **Course Labs** See your instructor or technical support person to obtain the Course Lab software for use on your own computer.

Visit Our World Wide Web Site

Additional materials designed especially for you are available on the World Wide Web. Go to www.course.com/NewPerspectives.

To the Instructor

The Data Disk Files and Course Labs are available on the Instructor's Resource Kit for this title. Follow the instructions in the Help file on the CD-ROM to install the programs to your network or standalone computer. For information on creating Data Disks or the Course Labs, see the "To the Student" section above.

You are granted a license to copy the Data Files and Course Labs to any computer or computer network used by students who have purchased this book.

In this tutorial you will:

- Learn about Web browser software and Web pages

- Learn about Web addresses and URLs

- Save and organize Web addresses

- Navigate the Web

- Use the Web to find information

- Configure and use the Microsoft Internet Explorer Web browser

- Learn about e-mail and e-mail software

- Send and receive e-mail using Microsoft Outlook Express

LAB

The Internet: World Wide Web

BROWSER AND E-MAIL BASICS

Introduction to Microsoft Internet Explorer and Microsoft Outlook Express

CASE

Sunset Wind Quintet

The Sunset Wind Quintet is a group of five musicians who have played together for eight years. At first, the group began by playing free concerts for local charitable organizations. As more people heard the quintet and its reputation grew, the musicians were soon in demand at art gallery openings and other functions.

Each member of the quintet is an accomplished musician. The instruments in a wind quintet include flute, oboe, clarinet, bassoon, and French horn, which are all orchestral instruments. Each quintet member has experience as a player in a symphony orchestra as well. Three quintet members—the flutist, bassoonist, and the French horn player—currently hold positions with the local orchestra. The other two quintet members—the clarinetist and the oboist—teach classes in their respective instruments at the local university.

This past summer, a booking agent asked the quintet to do a short regional tour. Although the tour was successful, the quintet members realized that none of them had any business-management skills. Marianna Rabinovich, the clarinetist, handles most of the business details for the group. The quintet members realized that business matters related to the tour were overwhelming Marianna and that they wanted to do more touring, so they hired you as their business manager.

One of your tasks will be to help market the Sunset Wind Quintet. To do this, you must learn more about how other wind quintets operate and sell their services. At one of your early meetings with the group, you found that each member of the quintet had different priorities. In addition to marketing the quintet's performances, some members felt it would be a good idea to record and sell CDs, whereas others were concerned about finding instrument-repair facilities on the road when tours extended beyond the local area.

As you discussed these issues with the quintet members, you started thinking of ways to address their concerns. Your first idea was to find trade magazines and newspapers that might describe what other small classical musical ensembles were doing. As you considered the time and cost of this alternative, you realized that the Internet and World Wide Web might offer a better way to get started. You also recognized that e-mail provides an effective way for you to communicate with quintet members and others.

SESSION 1

In this session, you will learn how Web pages and Web sites make up the World Wide Web. You will learn about things to consider when you select and use a specific software tool to find information on the Web. Finally, you will learn about some basic browser concepts.

Web Browsers

The Internet: World Wide Web

As you start considering how you might use the Web to gather information for the Sunset Wind Quintet, you remember that one of your college friends, Maggie Beeler, earned her degree in library science. You meet with Maggie at the local public library, where she is working at the reference desk. She is glad to assist you.

Maggie begins by explaining that the Web is a collection of files that reside on computers, called **Web servers**, that are located all over the world and are connected to each other through the Internet. Most computer files connected to the Internet are private; that is, only the computer's users can access them. The owners of the files that make up the Web have made their files publicly available so you can obtain access to them if you have a computer connected to the Internet.

Client/Server Structure of the World Wide Web

When you use your Internet connection to become part of the Web, your computer becomes a **Web client** in a worldwide client/server network. A **Web browser** is the software that you run on your computer to make it work as a Web client. The Internet connects many different types of computers running different operating system software. Web browser software lets your computer communicate with all of these different types of computers easily and effectively.

Computers that are connected to the Internet and contain files that their owners have made available publicly through their Internet connections are called Web servers. Figure 1 shows how this client/server structure uses the Internet to provide multiple interconnections among the various kinds of client and server computers.

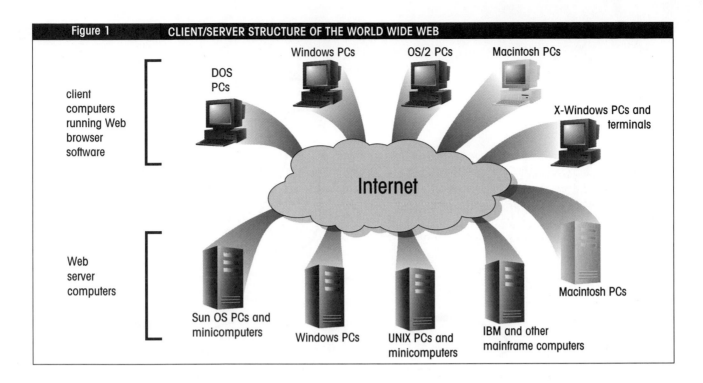

Figure 1 CLIENT/SERVER STRUCTURE OF THE WORLD WIDE WEB

Hypertext, Links, and Hypermedia

The public files on Web servers are ordinary text files, much like the files used by word-processing software. To allow Web browser software to read them, however, the text must be formatted according to a generally accepted standard. The standard used on the Web is **Hypertext Markup Language (HTML)**. HTML uses codes, or **tags**, to tell the Web browser software how to display the text contained in the document. For example, a Web browser reading the following line of text

<B>A Review of the Book <I>Wind Instruments of the 18th Century</I></B>

recognizes the <B> and </B> tags as instructions to display the entire line of text in bold and the <I> and </I> tags as instructions to display the text enclosed by those tags in italics. Different Web clients that connect to this Web server might display the tagged text differently. For example, one Web browser might display text enclosed by bold tags in a blue color instead of displaying the text as bold.

HTML provides a variety of text-formatting tags that you can use to indicate headings, paragraphs, bulleted lists, numbered lists, and other useful text formats in an HTML document. The real power of HTML, however, lies in its anchor tag. The **HTML anchor tag** enables you to link multiple HTML documents to each other. When you use the anchor tag to link HTML documents, you create a **hypertext link**. Hypertext links also are called **hyperlinks**, or **links**. Figure 2 shows how these hyperlinks can join multiple HTML documents to create a web of HTML text across computers on the Internet.

| Figure 2 | USING HYPERLINKS TO CREATE A WEB OF HTML TEXT ACROSS MULTIPLE FILE LOCATIONS |

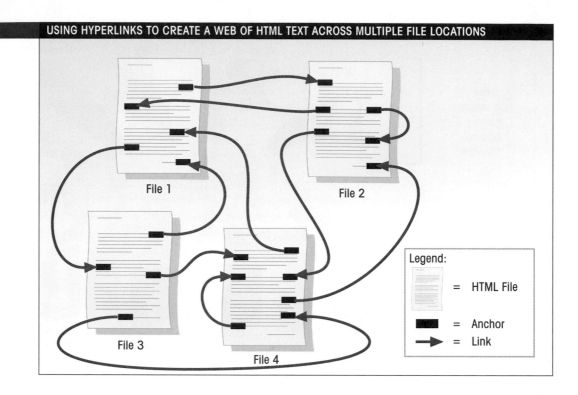

Most Web browsers display hyperlinks in a different color than other text on the page and underline them, so they are easily distinguished in the HTML document. When a Web browser displays an HTML document, people usually call the file a **Web page**. Maggie shows you the Web page shown in Figure 3 and suggests that it might be interesting to the Sunset Wind Quintet. The hyperlinks on this Web page are easy to identify because the Web browser software that displays this page shows the hyperlinks as red, underlined text.

| Figure 3 | WEB PAGE WITH HYPERLINKS |

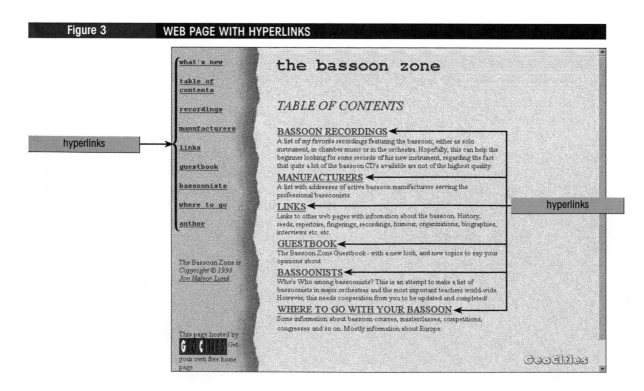

Each of the hyperlinks on the Web page shown in Figure 3 allows the user to connect to another Web page. In turn, each of those Web pages contains hyperlinks to other pages, including one hyperlink that leads back to the Web page shown in Figure 3. Hyperlinks usually connect to other Web pages; however, they can lead to other media, including graphic image files, sound clips, and video files. Hyperlinks that connect to these types of files often are called **hypermedia links**. You are especially interested in learning more about these hypermedia links, but Maggie suggests that you first need to understand a little more about how people organize the Web pages on their servers.

Maggie tells you that the easiest way to move from one Web page to another is to use the hyperlinks that the authors of Web pages embed in their HTML documents. Web page authors often use a graphic image as a hyperlink. Sometimes, it is difficult to identify which objects and text are hyperlinks just by looking at a Web page. Fortunately, when you move the mouse pointer over a hyperlink in a Web browser, the pointer changes to 🖑. For example, when you move the pointer over the Yellow Pages hyperlink shown in Figure 4, it changes shape to indicate that if you click the Yellow Pages text, the Web browser will open the Web page to which the hyperlink points.

Figure 4	MOUSE POINTER ON THE YELLOW PAGES HYPERLINK

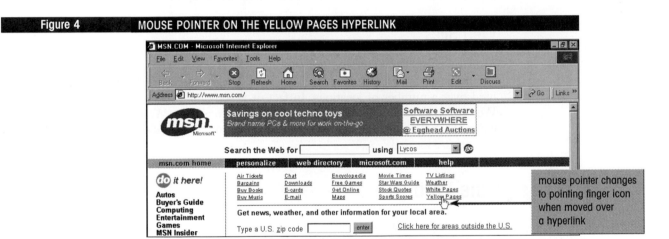

You might encounter an error message when you click a hyperlink. Two common messages that appear in dialog boxes are "server busy" and "DNS entry not found." Either of these messages means that your browser was unable to communicate successfully with the Web server that stores the page you requested. The cause of this inability might be temporary—in which case, you will be able to use the hyperlink later—or the cause might be permanent. The browser has no way of determining the cause of the connection failure, so it provides the same error messages in both cases. Another error message that you might receive is displayed as a Web page and includes the text "File not Found." This error message usually means that the Web page's location has changed permanently or that the Web page no longer exists.

Web Pages and Web Sites

Maggie explains that people who create Web pages usually have a collection of pages on one computer that they use as their Web server. A collection of linked Web pages that has a common theme or focus is called a **Web site**. The main page that all of the pages on a particular Web site are organized around and link back to is called the site's **home page**.

Home Pages

Maggie warns you that the term "home page" is used at least three different ways on the Web and that it is sometimes difficult to tell which meaning people intend when they use the term. The first definition of home page indicates the main page for a particular site; this use of "home page" refers to the first page that opens when you visit a particular Web site. The Bassoon Zone Table of Contents page shown in Figure 3 is a good example of this use. All of the hyperlinks on that page lead to pages in the Bassoon Zone site. Each page in the site links back to the Table of Contents page. The second definition of home page is the first page that opens when you start your Web browser. This type of home page might be an HTML document on your own computer. Some people create such home pages and include hyperlinks to Web sites that they frequently visit. If you are using a computer on your school's or employer's network, its Web browser might be configured to open the main page for the school or firm. The third definition of home page is the Web page that a particular Web browser loads the first time you use it. This page usually is stored at the Web site of the firm or other organization that created the Web browser software. Home pages that fall within the second or third definitions are sometimes called **start pages**.

Web Sites

Most people who create Web sites store all of the site's pages in one location, either on one computer or on one local area network (LAN). Some large Web sites, however, are distributed over a number of locations. In fact, it is sometimes difficult to determine where one Web site ends and another begins. Many people consider a Web site to be any group of Web pages that relates to one specific topic or organization, regardless of where the HTML documents are located.

Addresses on the Web

There is no centralized control over the Internet; therefore, no central starting point exists for the Web, which is a part of the Internet. However, each computer on the Internet does have a unique identification number, called an **Internet Protocol (IP) address**.

IP Addressing

The IP addressing system currently in use on the Internet uses a four-part number. Each part of the address is a number ranging from 0 to 255, and each part is separated from the previous part by a period, for example 106.29.242.17. You might hear a person pronounce this address as "one hundred six dot twenty-nine dot two four two dot seventeen." The combination of the four IP address parts provides 4.2 billion possible addresses ($256 \times 256 \times 256 \times 256$). This number seemed adequate until 1998, when the accelerating growth of the Internet pushed the number of host computers from 5 to 30 million. Members of various Internet task forces are working to develop an alternate addressing system that will accommodate the projected growth; however, all of their working solutions require extensive hardware and software changes throughout the Internet.

Domain Name Addressing

Although each computer connected to the Internet has a unique IP address, most Web browsers do not use the IP address to locate Web sites and individual pages. Instead, they use domain name addressing. A **domain name** is a unique name associated with a specific IP address by a program that runs on an Internet host computer. This program, which coordinates the IP addresses and domain names for all computers attached to it, is called **Domain Name System (DNS) software**, and the host computer that runs this software is called a **domain name server**. Domain names can include any number of parts separated by periods; however, most domain names currently in use have only three or four parts. Domain names follow a hierarchical model that you can follow from top to bottom if you read the name from left to right. For example, the domain name gsb.uchicago.edu is the computer connected to the Internet at the Graduate School of Business (gsb), which is an academic unit of the University of Chicago (uchicago), which is an educational institution (edu). No other computer on the Internet has the same domain name.

The last part of a domain name is called its **top-level domain**. For example, DNS software on the Internet host computer that is responsible for the "edu" domain keeps track of the IP addresses for all of the educational institutions in its domain, including "uchicago." Similar DNS software on the "uchicago" Internet host computer keeps track of the academic units' computers in its domain, including the "gsb" computer. Figure 5 shows the seven currently used top-level domain names.

Figure 5	TOP-LEVEL INTERNET DOMAIN NAMES
DOMAIN NAME	**DESCRIPTION**
com	Businesses and other commercial enterprises
edu	Postsecondary educational institutions
gov	U.S. government agency, bureau, or department
int	International organizations
mil	U.S. military unit or agency
net	Network service provider or resource
org	Other organizations, usually charitable or not-for-profit

In addition to these top-level domain names, Internet host computers outside the United States often use two-letter country domain names. For example, the domain name uq.edu.au is the domain name for the University of Queensland (uq), which is an educational institution (edu) in Australia (au). Recently, state and local government organizations in the United States have started using an additional domain name, "us." The "us" domain is also being used by U.S. primary and secondary schools as they begin to create Web presences, because the "edu" domain is reserved for postsecondary educational institutions. Figure 6 shows 10 of the most frequently accessed country domain names.

Figure 6	FREQUENTLY ACCESSED INTERNET COUNTRY DOMAIN NAMES
DOMAIN NAME	**COUNTRY**
au	Australia
ca	Canada
de	Germany
fi	Finland
fr	France
jp	Japan
nl	Netherlands
no	Norway
se	Sweden
uk	United Kingdom

The large increase in the number of host computers on the Internet has taxed the capacity of the existing top-level domain name structure, especially that of the "com" domain. A proposal to expand the available top-level domain names is currently under consideration by the Internet Policy Oversight Committee. The seven additional proposed top-level domain names are shown in Figure 7.

Figure 7	PROPOSED ADDITIONAL TOP-LEVEL INTERNET DOMAIN NAMES
DOMAIN NAME	**DESCRIPTION**
firm	Business firms
shop	Businesses that offer goods for sale
web	Entities that engage in World Wide Web-related activities
arts	Entities that engage in cultural and entertainment activities
rec	Entities that engage in recreational and entertainment activities
info	Entities that provide information services
nom	Individuals

Uniform Resource Locators

The IP address and the domain name each identify a particular computer on the Internet, but they do not indicate where a Web page's HTML document resides on that computer. To identify a Web page's exact location, Web browsers rely on Uniform Resource Locators (URLs). A **URL** is a four-part addressing scheme that tells the Web browser the following information:

- what transfer protocol to use when transporting the file
- the domain name of the computer on which the file resides
- the pathname of the folder or directory on the computer on which the file resides
- the name of the file

The **transfer protocol** is the set of rules that computers use to move files from one computer to another on an **internet**, which is a generic term used to describe *any* network of networks. The most common transfer protocol used on the Internet is the **Hypertext Transfer Protocol (HTTP)**. You can indicate the use of this protocol by typing http:// as the first part of the URL. People do use other protocols to transfer files on the Internet, but most of these protocols were used more frequently before the Web became part of the Internet. Two protocols that you still might see on the Internet are the File Transfer Protocol (FTP), which is indicated in a URL as ftp:// and the Telnet protocol, which is indicated in a URL as telnet://. FTP is just another way to transfer files, and Telnet is a set of rules for establishing a remote terminal connection to another computer.

The domain name is the Internet address of the computer, as described in the preceding section. The pathname describes the hierarchical directory or folder structure on the computer that stores the file. Most people are familiar with the structure used on Windows and DOS PCs, which use the backslash character (\) to separate the structure levels. URLs follow the conventions established in the UNIX operating system, which uses the forward slash character (/) to separate the structure levels. The forward slash character works properly in a URL, even when it is pointing to a file on a Windows or DOS computer.

The filename is the name that the computer uses to identify the Web page's HTML document. On most computers, the filename extension of an HTML document is either .html or .htm. Although many PC operating systems are not case sensitive, computers that use the UNIX operating system *are* case sensitive. Therefore, if you are entering a URL that includes mixed cases and you do not know the type of computer on which the file resides, it is safer to retain the mixed-case format of the URL.

Not all URLs include a filename. If a URL does not include a filename, most Web browsers will load the file named index.htm. The **index.htm** filename is the default name for a Web site's home page. Figure 8 shows an example of a URL annotated to show all four parts of the URL.

Figure 8   **STRUCTURE OF A UNIFORM RESOURCE LOCATOR (URL)**

The URL shown in Figure 8 uses the HTTP protocol and points to a computer at the Chicago Symphony. The Chicago Symphony's Web page contains many different kinds of information about the orchestra. The path shown in Figure 8 includes one level, which indicates that the information is about the orchestra's civic concerts. The filename (index.htm) indicates that this page is the home page in the civic concerts folder or directory.

You tell Maggie how much you appreciate all of the help she has given you by explaining how you can use Internet addresses to find information on the Web. Now you understand that the real secret to finding good information on the Web is to know the right URLs. Maggie tells you that you can find URLs in many places; for example, newspapers and magazines often publish URLs of Web sites that might interest their readers. Friends who know about the subject area in which you are interested also are good sources. The best source, however, is the Web itself.

You are eager to begin learning how to use a Web browser, so Maggie explains some elements common to all Web browsers. Most Web browsers have similar functions, which makes it easy to use any Web browser after you have learned how to use one.

Main Elements of Web Browsers

Now that you know a little more about Web sites, you start to wonder how you can make your computer communicate with the Internet. Maggie tells you that there are many Web browsers that turn your computer into a Web client that communicates through an **Internet service provider (ISP)**, which is a firm that sells access to the Internet, or a network connection with the Web servers. Two popular browsers are **Netscape Navigator**, or simply **Navigator**, and **Microsoft Internet Explorer**, or simply **Internet Explorer**.

Most Windows programs use a standard graphical user interface (GUI) design that includes a number of common screen elements. As you can see in Figures 9 and 10, the Navigator and Internet Explorer program windows share common Windows elements: a title bar at the top of the window, a scroll bar on the right side of the window, and a status bar at the bottom of the window. The menu bar appears below the title bar.

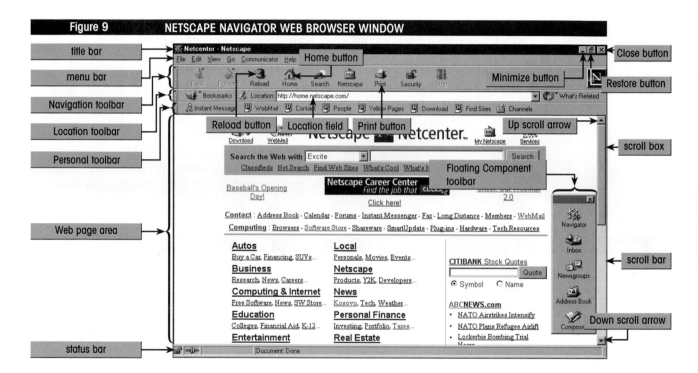

Figure 9   NETSCAPE NAVIGATOR WEB BROWSER WINDOW

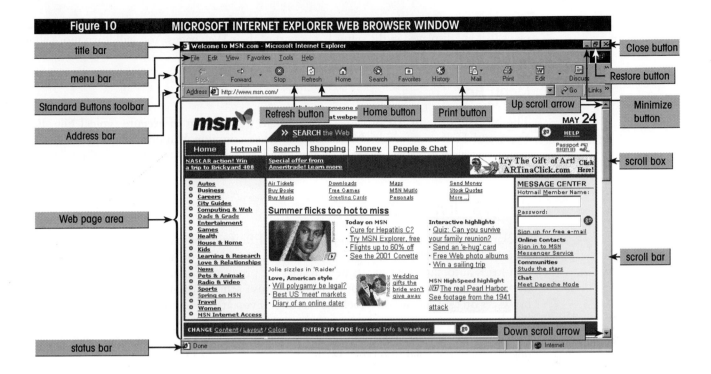

Figure 10   MICROSOFT INTERNET EXPLORER WEB BROWSER WINDOW

Next, Maggie describes each of these elements.

Title Bar

A Web browser's **title bar** shows the name of the open Web page and the Web browser's program name. As in all Windows programs, you can double-click the title bar to resize the window quickly. The title bar contains the Minimize ▬, Restore ▣, and Close ✖ buttons when the window is maximized to fill the screen. To restore a resized window to its original size, click the Maximize button ▢.

Scroll Bars

A Web page can be much longer or wider than a regular-sized document, so you usually need to use the **scroll bars** at the right side or bottom of the program window to move the page up, down, right, or left through the document window. You can use the mouse to click the **up scroll arrow** ▲ or the **down scroll arrow** ▼ to move the Web page up or down through the window's Web page area. Although most Web pages are designed to resize automatically when loaded into different browser windows with different display areas, some Web pages might be wider than your browser window. When this happens, the browser places another scroll bar at the bottom of the window and above the status bar, so you can move the page horizontally through the browser. You also can click and drag the scroll box in the scroll bar to move the Web page through the window.

Status Bar

The **status bar** at the bottom of the browser window includes information about the browser's operations. Each browser uses the status bar to deliver different information, but, generally, the status bar indicates the name of the Web page that is loading, the load status (partial or complete), and important messages, such as "Done." Some Web sites also send messages that are displayed in the status bar as part of their Web pages. You will learn more about the specific functions of the status bar in Session 2.

Menu Bar

The browser's **menu bar** provides a convenient way for you to execute typical File, Edit, View, and Help commands. In addition to these common Windows command sets, the menu bar also provides specialized command sets for the browser that allows you to navigate the Web.

Home Button

Clicking the **Home** button 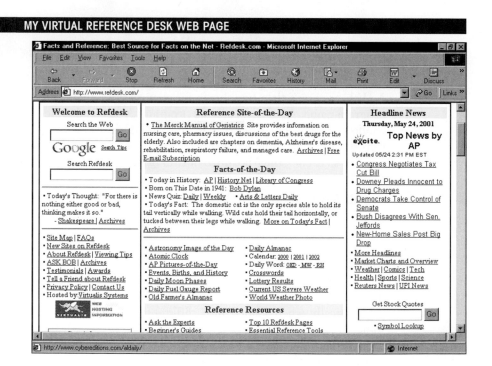 on the standard Buttons toolbar in Internet Explorer displays the home (or start) page for your browser. Most Web browsers let you specify a page that loads automatically every time you start the program. You might not be able to do this if you are in your school's computer lab, because schools often set the start page for all browsers on campus and then lock that setting. If you are using your own computer, you can use this program feature to choose your own start page. Some people like to use a Web page that someone else has created and made available for others to use. One example of a start page is the My Virtual Reference Desk Web page shown in Figure 11.

Figure 11   MY VIRTUAL REFERENCE DESK WEB PAGE

Web pages such as the one shown in Figure 11 offer links to pages that many Web users frequently use. The people and organizations that create these pages often sell advertising space on their pages to pay the cost of maintaining their sites.

Quick Access to Web Page Directories and Guides

You are starting to understand how to use the Internet to gather information about wind quintets. Maggie explains that a **Web directory** is a Web page that contains a list of Web page categories, such as education or recreation. The hyperlinks on a Web directory page lead to other pages that contain lists of subcategories that lead to other category lists and Web pages that relate to the category topics. **Web search engines** are Web pages that conduct searches of the Web to find the words or expressions that you enter. The result of such a search is a Web page that contains hyperlinks to Web pages that contain matching text or expressions. These pages can give new users an easy way to find information on the Web.

Web addresses can be very long and hard to remember—even if you are using domain names instead of IP addresses. In Internet Explorer, you save the URL as a **favorite** in the Favorites list. You realize that using the browser to remember important pages will be a terrific asset as you start collecting information for the quintet, so you ask Maggie to explain more about how to return to a Web page.

Using the History List

As you click the hyperlinks to go to new Web pages, the browser stores the location of each page you visit during a single session in a **history list**. You click the **Back** button ⬅ on the Standard Buttons toolbar in Internet Explorer, and the **Forward** button ➡ on the Standard Buttons toolbar in Internet Explorer to move through the history list.

When you start your browser, both buttons are inactive (dimmed) because no history list for your new session exists yet. After you follow one or more hyperlinks, the Back button lets you retrace your path back through the hyperlinks you have followed. Once you use the Back button, the Forward button becomes active and lets you move forward through the session's history list.

In most Web browsers, if you click and hold down the mouse button on either the Back or Forward button (or if you click the list arrow on either button), a portion of the history list appears. You can reload any page on the list by clicking its name in the list. The Back and Forward buttons duplicate the functions of commands on the browser's menu bar. You will learn more about the history list in Session 2.

Reloading a Web Page

Clicking the **Refresh** button 🗋 on the toolbar in Internet Explorer loads the same Web page that appears in the browser window. The browser stores a copy of every Web page it displays on your computer's hard drive in a **cache folder**, which increases the speed at which the browser can display pages as you navigate through the history list. The cache folder lets the browser load the pages from the client instead of from the remote Web server.

When you click the Refresh button, the browser contacts the Web server to see if the Web page has changed since it was stored in the cache folder. If it has changed, the browser gets the new page from the Web server; otherwise, it loads the cache folder copy.

Stopping a Web Page Transfer

Sometimes a Web page takes a long time to load. When this occurs, you can click the **Stop** button ⊗ on the Standard Buttons toolbar in Internet Explorer to halt the Web page transfer from the server; then you can click the hyperlink again. A second attempt may connect and transfer the page more quickly. You also might want to use the Stop button to abort a transfer when you accidentally click a hyperlink that you do not want to follow.

Returning to a Web Page

You use the Internet Explorer Favorites feature to store and organize a list of Web pages that you have visited, so you can return to them easily without having to remember the URL or search for the page again. Internet Explorer favorites work very much like a paper bookmark that you would use in a printed book: they mark the page at which you stopped reading.

You can save as many Internet Explorer favorites as you want to mark all of your favorite Web pages, so that you can return to pages that you frequently use or pages that are important to your research or tasks. You could even bookmark every Web page you visit!

Keeping track of many favorites requires an organizing system. You store favorites in a system folder. Internet Explorer stores *each* favorite as a separate file on your computer. Storing each favorite separately, instead of storing all bookmarks together, offers somewhat more flexibility but uses more disk space. You can organize your favorites in many different ways to meet your needs. For example, you might store all of the favorites for Web pages that include information about wind quintets in a folder named "Wind Quintet Information."

Printing and Saving Web Pages

You can use your browser to view Web pages, but sometimes you will want to store entire Web pages on disk; at other times, you will only want to store selected portions of Web page text or particular graphics from a Web page.

Printing a Web Page

The easiest way to print a Web page is to click the **Print** button 🖨 on the Standard Buttons toolbar in Internet Explorer. The current page (or frame) that appears in the Web page area is sent to the printer. If the page contains light colors or many graphics, you might want to consider changing the printing options so the page prints without the background or with all black text. You will learn how to change the print settings in Session 2.

Although printing an entire Web page is often useful, there are times when you need to save all or part of the page to disk.

Saving a Web Page

When you save a Web page to disk, you have an option to save only the text portion. If the Web page contains graphics, such as photos, drawings, or icons, you can select to save these graphics with the HTML document as well. To save only a graphic, right-click it in the browser window, click Save Image As or Save Picture As on the shortcut menu, and then save the graphic to the location that you specify. You will learn more about saving a Web page and its graphics in Session 2.

Reproducing Web Pages and Copyright Law

Maggie explains that there might be significant restrictions on the way that you can use information or images that you copy from another entity's Web site. The United States and other countries have copyright laws that govern the use of photocopies, audio or video recordings, and other reproductions of authors' original work. A **copyright** is the legal right of the author or other owner of an original work to control the reproduction, distribution, and sale of that work. A copyright comes into existence as soon as the work is placed into a tangible form, such as a printed copy, an electronic file, or a Web page. The copyright exists even if the work does not contain a copyright notice. If you do not know whether material that you find on the Web is copyrighted, the safest course of action is to assume that it is.

You can use limited amounts of copyrighted information in term papers and other reports that you prepare in an academic setting, but you must cite the source. Commercial use of copyrighted material is much more restricted. You should obtain permission from the copyright holder before using anything you copy from a Web page. It can be difficult to determine the owner of a source's copyright if no notice appears on the Web page; however, most Web pages provide a hyperlink to the e-mail address of the person responsible for maintaining the page. That person, often called a **webmaster**, usually can provide information about the copyright status of materials on the page.

Now that you understand the basic function of a browser and how to find information on the Web, you are ready to start using your browser to find information for the quintet.

Session 1   QUICK CHECK

1. True or False: Web browser software runs on a Web server computer.

2. Name two things you can accomplish using HTML tags.

3. Briefly define the term "home page."

4. Name two examples of hypermedia.

5. A local political candidate is creating a Web site to help in her campaign for office. Describe some of the things she might want to include in her Web site.

6. What is the difference between IP addressing and domain name addressing?

7. Identify and interpret the meaning of each part of the following URL: *http://www.savethetrees.org/main.html*

8. What is the difference between a Web directory and a Web search engine?

SESSION 2

In this session, you will learn how to configure the Microsoft Internet Explorer Web browser and use it to display Web pages. You will learn how to use Internet Explorer to follow hyperlinks from one Web page to another, how to record the URLs of sites to which you would like to return, and how to print and save Web pages. You will also learn about e-mail and use Microsoft Outlook Express to send and receive e-mail messages.

Starting Microsoft Internet Explorer

Microsoft Internet Explorer is the Web browser that installs with Windows 9X, Windows 2000, and Microsoft Office XP. This tutorial assumes that you have Internet Explorer 5 or later installed on your computer. You should have your computer turned on and open to the Windows desktop to begin.

To start Internet Explorer:

1. Click the **Start** button on the taskbar, point to **Programs**, and then click **Internet Explorer**. After a moment, Internet Explorer opens.

   TROUBLE? If you cannot find Internet Explorer on the Programs menu, check to see if an Internet Explorer shortcut icon appears on the desktop, and then double-click it. If you do not see the shortcut icon, ask your instructor or technical support person for help. The program might be installed in a different folder on your computer.

   TROUBLE? If a Dial-up Connection dialog box opens, enter your user name and password into the appropriate text boxes, and then click the Connect button. If you do not know your user name or password, ask your instructor or technical support person for assistance; you must have an Internet connection to complete the steps in this tutorial. After a connection is made, continue with Step 2.

2. If the program window does not fill the screen entirely, click the **Maximize** button on the Internet Explorer title bar. Your screen should look like Figure 12.

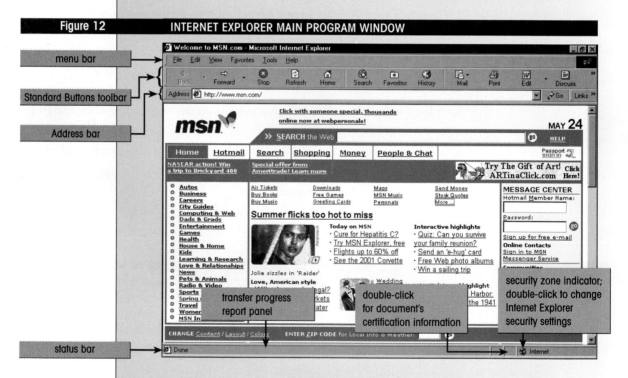

Figure 12 — INTERNET EXPLORER MAIN PROGRAM WINDOW

menu bar

Standard Buttons toolbar

Address bar

transfer progress report panel

double-click for document's certification information

security zone indicator; double-click to change Internet Explorer security settings

status bar

TROUBLE? Figure 12 shows the Microsoft home page, which is the page that Internet Explorer opens the first time it starts. Your computer might be configured to open to a different Web page or to no page at all.

TROUBLE? If you do not see the bars shown in Figure 12, click View on the menu bar, point to Toolbars, and then click the name of the bar that you want to turn on. When you turn on a toolbar, a check mark appears in front of its name.

Internet Explorer includes a Standard Buttons toolbar with 12 buttons. Many of these buttons execute frequently used commands for browsing the Web. Figure 13 shows these buttons and describes their functions.

Figure 13	STANDARD BUTTONS TOOLBAR BUTTON FUNCTIONS	
BUTTON	**BUTTON NAME**	**DESCRIPTION**
	Back	Moves to the last previously visited Web page
	Forward	Moves to the next previously visited Web page
	Stop	Stops the transfer of a new Web page
	Refresh	Reloads the current page
	Home	Loads the program's defined start page
	Search	Opens the Search Explorer bar in the Internet Explorer window, which displays a Web search engine chosen by Microsoft
	Favorites	Opens the Favorites Explorer bar in the Internet Explorer window, which allows you to return to Web pages that you have saved as favorites
	History	Opens the History Explorer bar in the Internet Explorer window, which allows you to choose from a list of Web pages that you have visited recently
	Mail	Opens the e-mail program specified in the Internet Options settings to read mail, to compose a new message, to send a link to the current page, or to send the current Web page to another recipient; also opens the specified newsreader program
	Print	Prints the current Web page
	Edit	Opens the current Web page for editing in Microsoft Word. Click the Edit button list arrow to choose to edit with Notepad or Microsoft Excel.
	Discuss	Opens the Discussion bar for using the specified discussion server

Now that you understand how to start Internet Explorer, you tell Maggie that you are ready to start using it to find information on the Internet. To find information, you need to know about the different Internet Explorer features and their functions.

Status Bar

The **status bar** at the bottom of the window includes four panels that give you information about Internet Explorer's operations. The first panel—the **transfer progress report**—presents status messages that show, for example, the URL of a page while it is loading. When a page is completely loaded, this panel displays the text "Done" until you move the mouse or execute a command. This panel also displays the URL of any hyperlink on the page when you move the mouse pointer over it.

When you are loading a Web page, the first panel contains a **graphical transfer progress indicator** that moves from left to right in the panel while a Web page loads, to indicate how much of a Web page has loaded from a Web server. This indicator is especially useful for monitoring progress when you are loading large Web pages.

The second panel is empty when you connect to the Internet. If you are working **offline**, which means that your browser is open but is not connected to the Internet, then an offline icon is displayed in the second panel to let you know the connection status.

If you double-click the third panel on the status bar, a Certificate Information dialog box opens and indicates whether the currently displayed Web page has a certificate and, if so, the certificate's type. A **certificate** is an indication of the security of a Web page. Certificate information is useful when you need to gauge the security level of a particular Web page, such as when you are conducting a financial transaction.

The fourth status bar panel reports to which **security zone** the page you are viewing has been assigned. As part of its security features, Internet Explorer lets you classify Web pages by the security risk they present. You can open the Internet Security Properties dialog box, shown in Figure 14, by double-clicking the fourth status bar panel. This dialog box lets you set four levels of security-enforcing procedures, including one that you can tailor to your specific needs. The default browser security level is Medium, which is adequate for most Web users.

Figure 14   CHECKING SECURITY SETTINGS

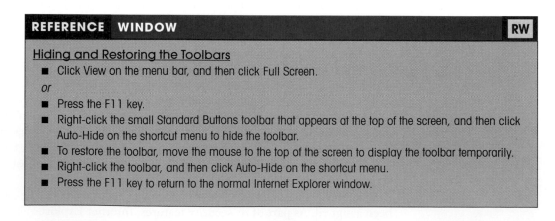

Menu Bar

In addition to the standard Windows commands, the menu bar also includes the **Favorites** menu command, which lets you store and organize URLs of sites that you have visited.

Hiding and Showing the Internet Explorer Toolbars

Internet Explorer lets you hide toolbars to show more of the Web page area. The easiest way to increase the display area for a Web page is to click View on the menu bar, and then click Full Screen (or press the F11 key).

REFERENCE WINDOW　　RW

Hiding and Restoring the Toolbars
- Click View on the menu bar, and then click Full Screen.

or
- Press the F11 key.
- Right-click the small Standard Buttons toolbar that appears at the top of the screen, and then click Auto-Hide on the shortcut menu to hide the toolbar.
- To restore the toolbar, move the mouse to the top of the screen to display the toolbar temporarily.
- Right-click the toolbar, and then click Auto-Hide on the shortcut menu.
- Press the F11 key to return to the normal Internet Explorer window.

To use the Full Screen and Auto-Hide features:

1. Press the **F11** key. The small Standard Buttons toolbar appears at the top of the screen, and the menu bar and title bar are hidden from view.

2. Right-click the small **Standard Buttons** toolbar that appears at the top of the screen to open the shortcut menu, and then click **Auto-Hide** on the shortcut menu.

3. Move the mouse pointer away from the top of the screen for a moment. Now, you can see more of the Web page area. When the toolbar disappears, return the mouse pointer to the top of the screen to display it again.

4. With the toolbar displayed, right-click the **toolbar** and then click **Auto-Hide** on the shortcut menu to turn on the toolbar again.

5. Press the **F11** key to return to the normal Internet Explorer window.

You can use the commands on the View menu to **toggle**, or turn on and off, the individual toolbars or the status bar. Also, you can use the Customize command on the View/Toolbars menu to show the Standard Buttons toolbar buttons with or without the text labels that describe each button's function.

Entering a URL in the Address Bar

Maggie tells you to use the Address bar to enter URLs directly into Internet Explorer. Marianna gave you the URL for the Pennsylvania Quintet, so you can see its Web page.

REFERENCE WINDOW   **RW**

Entering a URL in the Address Bar
- Click in the current URL that is displayed in the Address bar, and then press the Backspace key.
- Type the URL of the location that you want to load.
- Press the Enter key to load the URL's Web page in the browser window.

To load the Pennsylvania Quintet's Web page:

1. Click in the **Address bar** to select all of the text that is displayed, and then press the **Backspace** key to delete it.

   TROUBLE? If you double-click in the Address bar you will change to editing mode. If this occurs, press the Backspace key as many times as necessary to delete all of the text in the Address bar so the text you type in Step 2 will be correct.

2. Type **www.course.com/NewPerspectives/studentunion** in the Address bar; this URL is for the Student Online Companion page on the Course Technology Web site. In this tutorial, you will go to the Course Technology site and then click hyperlinks to go to individual Web pages.

TROUBLE? If a list box appears on the Address bar while you are typing a URL, just finish typing the URL. If you opened a Web site with a URL that is the same as or similar to the one you are currently entering, Internet Explorer will open the Address bar list box so that you can select the URL from a list, instead of typing the entire URL again.

3. Press the **Enter** key. After you press the Enter key, Internet Explorer adds the http:// protocol to the URL for you, and then it loads the New Perspectives Student Union Web page shown in Figure 15. When the entire page has loaded, the graphical transfer progress indicator in the status bar will stop moving, and the transfer progress report panel will display the text "Done."

| Figure 15 | NEW PERSPECTIVES STUDENT UNION WEB PAGE |

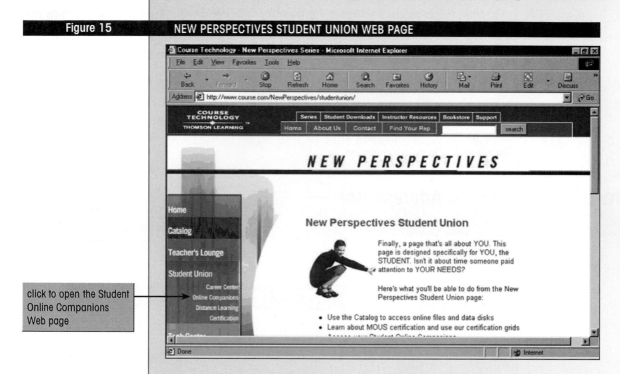

click to open the Student Online Companions Web page

TROUBLE? If a Dial-up Connection dialog box opens after you press the Enter key, click the Connect button. You must have an Internet connection to complete the steps in this tutorial.

4. Click the **Online Companions** link to open the Student Online Companions page.

5. Click the **Office XP** link to open the Microsoft Office XP Student Online Companion page.

6. Click the **Browser Basics** link to open the page that contains the links for this tutorial.

7. Click the link to the **Pennsylvania Quintet**. The Web page opens, as shown in Figure 16.

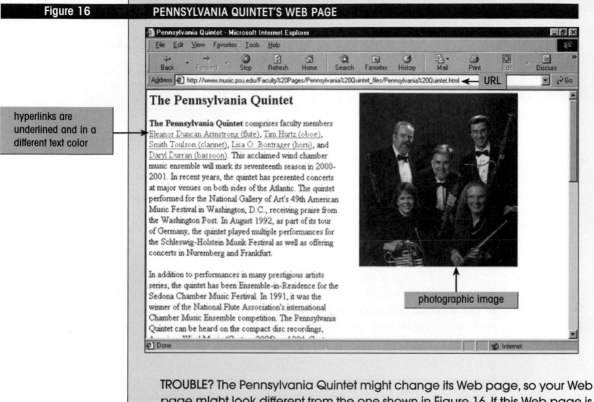

Figure 16 PENNSYLVANIA QUINTET'S WEB PAGE

hyperlinks are underlined and in a different text color

photographic image

TROUBLE? The Pennsylvania Quintet might change its Web page, so your Web page might look different from the one shown in Figure 16. If this Web page is deleted from the server, you might see an entirely different Web page. However, the steps should work in the same way.

8. Read the Web page, and then click the **Back** button ⬅ on the Standard Buttons toolbar to return to the Student Online Companion page.

You like the format of the Pennsylvania Quintet's home page, so you want to make sure that you can go back to that page later if you need to review its contents. Maggie explains that you can write down the URL so you can refer to it later, but an easier way is to use the Favorites list to store the URL for future use.

Using the Favorites Feature

Internet Explorer's **Favorites list** lets you store and organize a list of Web pages that you have visited so you can return to them easily. The **Favorites** button 🔳 on the Standard Buttons toolbar opens the Favorites Explorer bar shown in Figure 17. You can use the Favorites Explorer bar to open URLs you have stored as favorites.

Figure 17 THE FAVORITES EXPLORER BAR

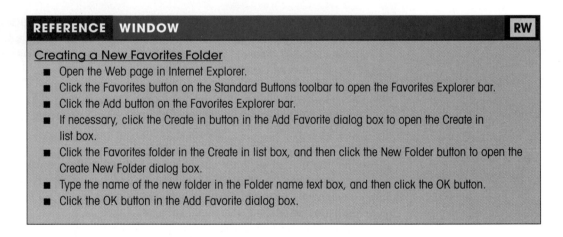

Favorites Explorer Bar

adds the currently displayed Web page to your Favorites list

closes the Explorer Bar

lets you organize your favorites into folders

Figure 17 shows the hierarchical structure of the Favorites list. For example, eight important Web links are stored in a folder named "Links." You can organize your favorites in the way that best suits your needs and working style.

You decide to save the Pennsylvania Quintet's Web page as a favorite in a new folder named Wind Quintet Information.

REFERENCE WINDOW | **RW**

Creating a New Favorites Folder
- Open the Web page in Internet Explorer.
- Click the Favorites button on the Standard Buttons toolbar to open the Favorites Explorer bar.
- Click the Add button on the Favorites Explorer bar.
- If necessary, click the Create in button in the Add Favorite dialog box to open the Create in list box.
- Click the Favorites folder in the Create in list box, and then click the New Folder button to open the Create New Folder dialog box.
- Type the name of the new folder in the Folder name text box, and then click the OK button.
- Click the OK button in the Add Favorite dialog box.

To create a new Favorites folder:

1. Click the **Forward** button ⇨ on the Standard Buttons toolbar to return to the Pennsylvania Quintet Web page.

2. Click the **Favorites** button ⊞ on the Standard Buttons toolbar to open the Favorites Explorer bar.

3. Click the **Add** button on the Favorites Explorer bar to open the Add Favorite dialog box.

4. If necessary, click the **Create in** button in the Add Favorite dialog box to open the Create in list box.

   TROUBLE? If you accidentally closed the Create in list box, click the Create in button again to open it.

5. Click the **Favorites** folder in the Create in list box to select it, and then click the **New Folder** button to open the Create New Folder dialog box.

6. Type **Wind Quintet Information** in the Folder name text box of the Create New Folder dialog box, and then click the **OK** button to close the Create New Folder dialog box. See Figure 18. Notice that the page name appears automatically in the Name text box in the Add Favorite dialog box. You can edit the page name, if necessary, by changing the suggested page name.

| Figure 18 | CREATING A NEW FAVORITES FOLDER |

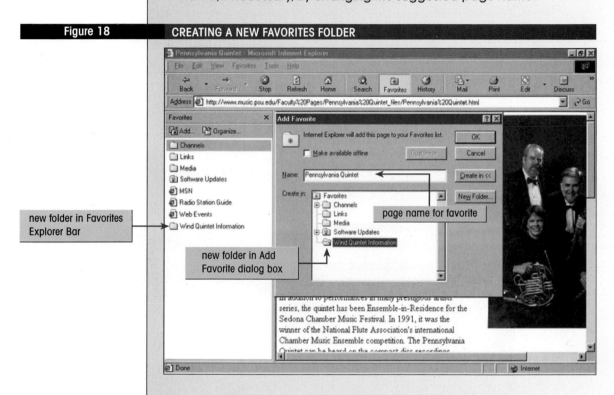

new folder in Favorites Explorer Bar

page name for favorite

new folder in Add Favorite dialog box

7. Click the **OK** button to close the Add Favorite dialog box. Now, the favorite is saved in the Wind Quintet Information folder in the Favorites Explorer Bar. You can test the favorite by opening it from the Favorites Explorer Bar.

8. Click the **Back** button ⇦ on the Standard Buttons toolbar to return to the previous page, click the **Wind Quintet Information** folder in the Favorites Explorer bar to open it, and then click **Pennsylvania Quintet**. The Pennsylvania Quintet page opens in the browser, which means that you created the favorite correctly.

TROUBLE? If the Pennsylvania Quintet page does not open, right-click the Pennsylvania Quintet favorite in the Favorites Explorer bar, and then click Properties on the shortcut menu. Click the Web Document tab and make sure that a URL appears in the URL text box. If there is no URL, click the OK button to close the dialog box, right-click the Pennsylvania Quintet favorite, click Delete on the shortcut menu, and then click the Yes button to send the favorite to the Recycle Bin. Repeat the steps to re-create the favorite, and then try again. If you still have trouble, ask your instructor or technical support person for help.

As you use the Web to find information about wind quintets and other sites of interest for the group, you might find yourself creating many favorites so you can return to sites of interest. When you start accumulating favorites, it is important to keep them organized, as you will see next.

Organizing Favorites

You explain to Maggie that you have created a new folder for Wind Quintet Information in the Favorites Explorer bar and stored the Pennsylvania Quintet's URL in that folder. Maggie suggests that you might not want to keep all of the wind quintet–related information you gather in one folder. She notes that you are just beginning your work for Marianna and the quintet and that you might be collecting all types of information for them. Maggie suggests that you might want to put information about the Pennsylvania Quintet in a separate folder named East Coast Ensembles under the Wind Quintet Information folder. As you collect information about other performers, you might add folders for Midwest and West Coast Ensembles, too.

Internet Explorer offers an easy way to organize your folders in a hierarchical structure— even after you have stored them. To rearrange URLs or even folders within folders, you use the Organize button on the Favorites Explorer bar.

REFERENCE WINDOW   **RW**

Moving an Existing Favorite into a New Folder
- Click the Favorites button on the Standard Buttons toolbar to open the Favorites Explorer bar.
- Click the Organize button on the Favorites Explorer bar to open the Organize Favorites dialog box.
- Click the folder in the list on the right of the dialog box under which you would like to create the new folder, and then click the Create Folder button.
- Type the name of the new folder, and then press the Enter key.
- Drag the favorite that you want to move into the new folder.
- Click the Close button.

To move an existing favorite into a new folder:

1. Click the **Organize** button on the Favorites Explorer bar. The Organize Favorites dialog box opens.

2. Click the **Wind Quintet Information** folder in the Organize Favorites dialog box to open it.

3. Click the **Create Folder** button in the Organize Favorites dialog box. A new folder is added to the list and its default name, "New Folder," is selected. To change the folder's name, type a new one.

4. Type **East Coast Ensembles** to replace the "New Folder" selected text, and then press the **Enter** key to rename the folder.

5. Click and drag the **Pennsylvania Quintet** favorite into the new East Coast Ensembles folder, as shown in Figure 19, and then release the mouse button. Now, the East Coast Ensembles folder contains the favorite.

Figure 19   REORGANIZING FAVORITES IN FOLDERS

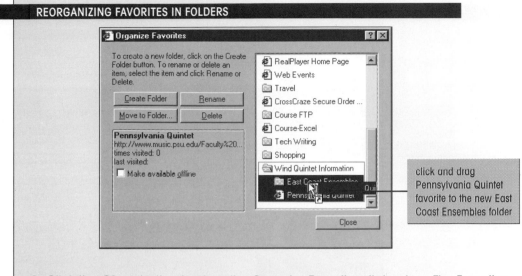

Figure 19   REORGANIZING FAVORITES IN FOLDERS

click and drag Pennsylvania Quintet favorite to the new East Coast Ensembles folder

6. Click the **Close** button to close the Organize Favorites dialog box. The Favorites Explorer bar is updated automatically to reflect your changes.

7. Click the **Favorites** button ⊞ on the Standard Buttons toolbar to close the Favorites Explorer bar.

Hyperlink **Navigation with the Mouse**

Now you know how to use the Internet to find information that will help you with the Sunset Wind Quintet. Maggie tells you that the easiest way to move from one Web page to another is to use the hyperlinks that Web page authors embed in their HTML documents, as you will see next.

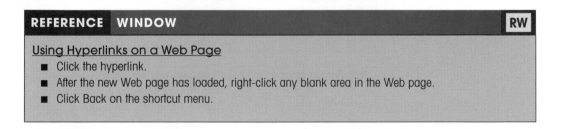

REFERENCE WINDOW   **RW**

Using Hyperlinks on a Web Page
- Click the hyperlink.
- After the new Web page has loaded, right-click any blank area in the Web page.
- Click Back on the shortcut menu.

To follow a hyperlink Web page and return:

1. Click the **Back** button ⇦ on the Standard Buttons toolbar to go back to the Student Online Companion page, click the **Cleveland Museum of Art** link to open that page, and then point to the **Collections** hyperlink shown in Figure 20, so that your pointer changes to 🖑. Notice that a ScreenTip was added to this hyperlink to display the link's name.

Figure 20   CLEVELAND MUSEUM OF ART HOME PAGE

hyperlinks

ScreenTip

2. Click the **Collections** hyperlink to load the page. Watch the first panel in the status bar—when it displays the text "Done," you know that Internet Explorer has loaded the full page.

3. Right-click any blank area in the Web page area to display the shortcut menu shown in Figure 21.

Figure 21   USING THE SHORTCUT MENU TO GO BACK TO THE PREVIOUS PAGE

shortcut menu

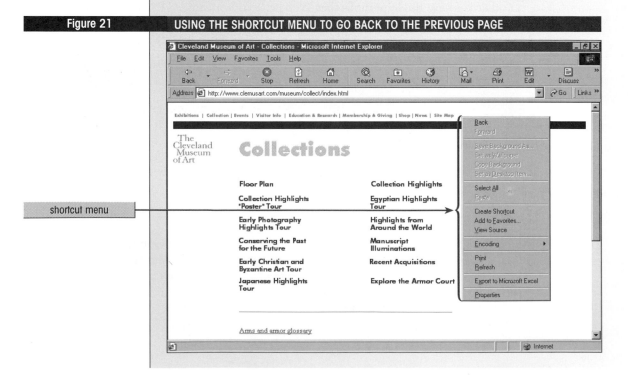

TROUBLE? If you right-click a hyperlink, your shortcut menu will display a shorter list than the one shown in Figure 21 and the Back command will not appear on the menu. If you don't see the shortcut menu shown in Figure 21, click anywhere outside the shortcut menu to close it, and then repeat Step 3.

TROUBLE? Web pages change frequently, so the Permanent Collection page you see might look different from the one shown in Figure 21, but right-clicking any blank area in the Web page will still work.

4. Click **Back** on the shortcut menu to return to the Cleveland Museum of Art home page.

You are beginning to get a good sense of how to move from one Web page to another and back again, but Maggie tells you that you have mastered only one technique of many. She explains that the Standard Buttons toolbar and the menu bar offer many tools for accessing and using Web sites.

Using the History List

In Session 1, you learned that the Back and Forward buttons let you move to and from previously visited pages. You also can use the Address bar to move to previously visited Web sites. Clicking the Address bar list arrow displays a list of Web sites that you have visited. When you click a URL in the list, Internet Explorer will load the site.

You also can open a full copy of the History list by clicking the History button 🕸 on the Standard Buttons toolbar.

To view the history list for this session:

1. Click the **History** button 🕸 on the Standard Buttons toolbar to open the History Explorer bar in the left frame of the Web page area. The History list stores each URL you have visited today, or for other specified time periods, into folders. It also maintains the hierarchy of each Web site; that is, pages you visit at a particular Web site are stored in a separate folder for that site.

2. If necessary, click the **Today** folder to open it, click the **clemusart** folder to open it, and then point to the **Cleveland Museum of Art–Collections** favorite, as shown in Figure 22.

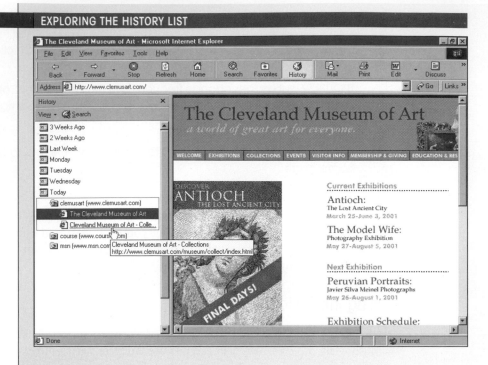

Figure 22   EXPLORING THE HISTORY LIST

To return to a particular page, click that page's entry in the list. You can see the full URL of any item in the History Explorer bar by moving the mouse pointer over the History list item, as shown in Figure 22.

TROUBLE? Your History Explorer bar might be a different size from the one that appears in Figure 22 and may contain different folders. You can resize the window by clicking and dragging its right edge either right or left to make it narrower or wider.

3. Click the **Close** button on the History Explorer bar to close it.

4. Click the **Back** button ⇐ on the Standard Buttons toolbar to return to the Student Online Companion page.

You can right-click any entry in the Internet Explorer History list and copy the URL or delete it from the list. Internet Explorer stores each history entry as a shortcut in a History folder, which is in the Windows folder.

Refreshing a Web Page

Clicking the **Refresh** button 🔃 on the Standard Buttons toolbar makes Microsoft Internet Explorer load a new copy of the current Web page that appears in the browser window. Internet Explorer stores a copy of every Web page it displays on your computer's hard drive in a Temporary Internet Files folder in the Windows folder. Storing Web pages in this folder increases the speed at which Internet Explorer can display pages as you move back and forth through the History list, because the browser can load the page from a local disk drive instead of reloading the page from the remote Web server. When you click the Refresh button, Internet Explorer contacts the Web server to see if the Web page has changed since it was stored in the cache folder. If it has changed, Internet Explorer gets the new page from the Web server; otherwise, it loads the cache folder copy.

Returning to Your Start Page

The **Home** button on the Standard Buttons toolbar displays the home (or start) page for your copy of Internet Explorer. You can change the setting for the Home toolbar button, as you will see next.

REFERENCE   WINDOW   **RW**

Changing the Home Toolbar Button Settings
- Click Tools on the menu bar, and then click Internet Options.
- Click the General tab.
- Select whether you want Internet Explorer to open with the current page, its default page, or a blank page, by clicking the corresponding button in the Home page section of the Internet Options dialog box.
- If you want to specify a home page, type the URL of that Web page in the Address text box.
- Click the OK button.

To modify your home page:

1. Click **Tools** on the menu bar, and then click **Internet Options** to open the dialog box shown in Figure 23. If necessary, click the **General** tab to display it.

Figure 23   **CHANGING THE DEFAULT HOME PAGE**

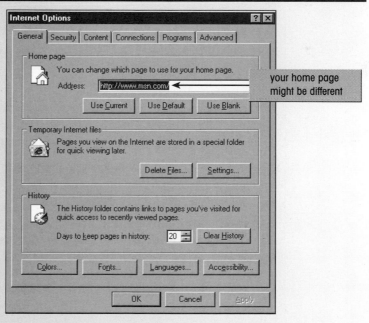

your home page might be different

To use the currently loaded Web page as your home page, click the Use Current button. To use the default home page that was installed with your copy of Internet Explorer, click the Use Default button. If you don't want a page to open when you start your browser, click the Use Blank button. If you want to specify a home page other than the current, default, or blank page, type the URL for that page in the Address text box.

> TROUBLE? You might not be able to change these settings if you are using a computer in your school lab or at your office. Some organizations set the home page defaults on all of their computers and then lock those settings.
>
> **2.** Click the **Cancel** button to close the dialog box without making any changes.

In the next section, you will learn how to print the Web page so you have a permanent record of its contents.

Printing a Web Page

The **Print** button 🖨 on the Standard Buttons toolbar lets you print the current Web frame or page. You will learn more about saving and printing Web pages later in this session, but you can use the Print command to make a printed copy of most Web pages. (Some Web pages disable the Print command.)

REFERENCE WINDOW   **RW**

<u>Printing the Current Web Page</u>
- Click the Print button on the Standard Buttons toolbar to print the current Web page with the default print settings.

or
- Click File on the menu bar, and then click Print.
- Use the Print dialog box to choose the printer you want to use, the pages you want to print, and the number of copies you want to make of each page.
- Click the OK button to print the page(s).

To print a Web page:

1. Click **File** on the menu bar, and then click **Print** to open the Print dialog box.

2. Make sure that the printer name in the Name text box is the printer you want to use; if necessary, click the **Name** list arrow to change the selection.

3. Click the **Pages** option button in the Print range section of the Print dialog box, type **1** in the from text box, press the **Tab** key, and then type **1** in the to text box to specify that you want to print only the first page.

4. Make sure that the Number of copies text box shows that you want to print one copy.

5. Click the **OK** button to print the Web page and close the Print dialog box.

Changing the Settings for Printing a Web Page

You already have seen how to print Web pages using the basic options available in the Print dialog box. Also, you have learned how to create a favorite in the Favorites list so that you can return to a Web page later. Usually, the default settings in the Print dialog box are fine for printing a Web page; however, you can use the Page Setup dialog box to change the way a Web page prints. Figure 24 shows the Page Setup dialog box, and Figure 25 describes its settings.

Figure 24 PAGE SETUP DIALOG BOX

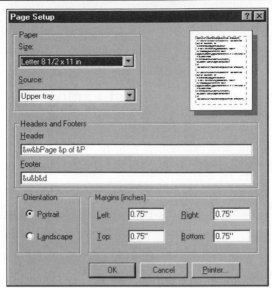

Figure 25 PAGE SETUP DIALOG BOX OPTIONS

OPTION	DESCRIPTION	USE
Paper Size	Changes the size of the printed page	Use the Letter size default unless you are printing to different paper stock, such as Legal or A4
Paper Source	Changes the printer's paper source	Use the default AutoSelect Tray unless you want to specify a different tray or manual feed for printing on heavy paper
Header	Prints the Web page's title, URL, date/time printed, and page numbers at the top of each page	To obtain details on how to specify exact header printing options, click the Header text box to select it, then press the F1 key
Footer	Prints the Web page's title, URL, date/time printed, and page numbers at the bottom of each page	To obtain details on how to specify exact footer printing options, click the Footer text box to select it, then press the F1 key
Orientation	Selects the orientation of the printed output	Portrait works best for most Web pages, but you can use landscape orientation to print the wide tables of numbers included on some Web pages
Margins	Changes the margin of the printed page	Normally you should leave the default settings, but you can change the right, left, top, or bottom margins as needed

Another print option that is extremely useful for saving paper when printing long Web pages is to reduce the font size of the Web pages before you print them. To do this, click View on the menu bar, point to Text Size, and then click either Smaller or Smallest on the Fonts menu. To make the text on a Web page larger, click either Larger or Largest.

Checking **Web Page Security Features**

You can check some of the security elements of a Web page by double-clicking the Certificates panel on the status bar. Internet Explorer will display security information for the page, if it is available, to advise you of the overall security of the page that appears in the browser window. You also can learn about how the page was encrypted. **Encryption** is a way of scrambling and encoding data transmissions that reduces the risk that a person who intercepted the Web page as it traveled across the Internet would be able to decode and read the page's contents. Web sites use encrypted transmission to send and receive information, such as credit card numbers, to ensure privacy. You are concerned about the privacy of information transmitted over the Internet, so Maggie suggests that you use Internet Explorer's Help menu to find more information about secure transactions.

Getting Help in Microsoft Internet Explorer

Maggie explains that Microsoft Internet Explorer includes a comprehensive online Help system. You can obtain help by opening the Microsoft Internet Explorer Help window. Maggie suggests that you learn about secure Web sites.

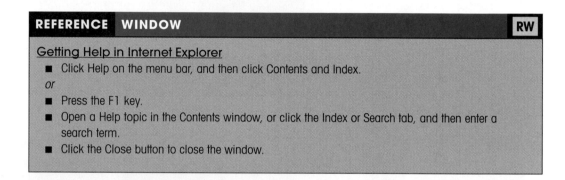

REFERENCE WINDOW   **RW**

Getting Help in Internet Explorer
- Click Help on the menu bar, and then click Contents and Index.
or
- Press the F1 key.
- Open a Help topic in the Contents window, or click the Index or Search tab, and then enter a search term.
- Click the Close button to close the window.

To open the Internet Explorer Help window:

1. Click **Help** on the menu bar, and then click **Contents and Index** to open the Microsoft Internet Explorer Help window.

2. If necessary, click the **Maximize** button ⬜ on the Microsoft Internet Explorer Help window so that it fills the desktop.

3. If necessary, click the **Contents** tab in the Contents window, click **Sending Information over the Internet Safely**, and then click **Using secure Internet sites for transactions** to open that Help topic in the Help window. Read and scroll down the page; notice that it contains a link to a related category that you can explore, as well. See Figure 26.

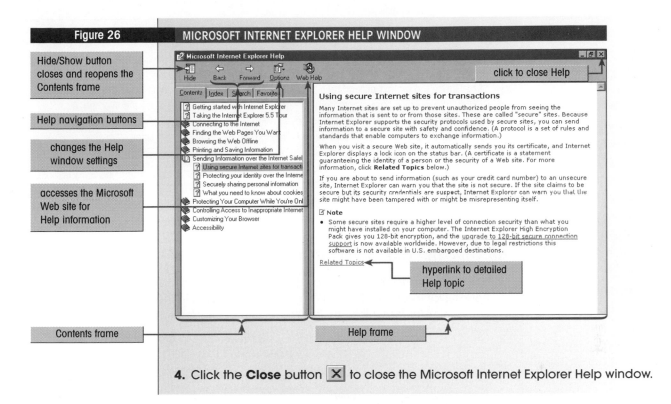

Figure 26 — MICROSOFT INTERNET EXPLORER HELP WINDOW

Hide/Show button closes and reopens the Contents frame

Help navigation buttons

changes the Help window settings

accesses the Microsoft Web site for Help information

Contents frame

Help frame

Using secure Internet sites for transactions

Many Internet sites are set up to prevent unauthorized people from seeing the information that is sent to or from those sites. These are called "secure" sites. Because Internet Explorer supports the security protocols used by secure sites, you can send information to a secure site with safety and confidence. (A protocol is a set of rules and standards that enable computers to exchange information.)

When you visit a secure Web site, it automatically sends you its certificate, and Internet Explorer displays a lock icon on the status bar. (A certificate is a statement guaranteeing the identity of a person or the security of a Web site. For more information, click **Related Topics** below.)

If you are about to send information (such as your credit card number) to an unsecure site, Internet Explorer can warn you that the site is not secure. If the site claims to be secure but its security credentials are suspect, Internet Explorer can warn you that the site might have been tampered with or might be misrepresenting itself.

☑ **Note**
- Some secure sites require a higher level of connection security than what you might have installed on your computer. The Internet Explorer High Encryption Pack gives you 128-bit encryption, and the upgrade to 128-bit secure connection support is now available worldwide. However, due to legal restrictions this software is not available in U.S. embargoed destinations.

Related Topics

click to close Help

hyperlink to detailed Help topic

4. Click the **Close** button ☒ to close the Microsoft Internet Explorer Help window.

Now you are convinced that you have all of the tools you need to find information successfully on the Web. Marianna probably will be interested in seeing the Pennsylvania Quintet Web page, but you are not sure if she will have Internet access while she's touring. Maggie says that you can save the Web page on disk, so that Marianna can open the page locally in her Web browser, using the files that you save on a disk.

Using Internet Explorer to Save a Web Page

You have learned how to use most of the Internet Explorer tools for loading Web pages and saving favorites. Now, Maggie thinks you should learn how to save a Web page. Sometimes, you will want to store entire Web pages on disk; at other times, you will only want to store selected portions of Web page text or particular graphics from a Web page. Internet Explorer lets you choose how to save the page. If you select the "Web Page, complete" option in the Save Web Page dialog box (which is the default), you will save the entire Web page, including its graphics, frames, and styles. If you select the "Web Archive for email" option, you will save a "picture" of the current Web page. Usually, you use this option when you want to send a copy of the Web page to someone in an e-mail message. The two other options—"Web Page, HTML only" and "Text File"—let you save just the HTML code or text from the Web page, respectively, without saving the graphics, frames, or styles on the Web page.

Saving a Web Page

You like the Pennsylvania Quintet's Web page and want to save all of it on disk so you can send it to Marianna. That way, she can review it without having an Internet connection. To save a Web page, you must open the page in Internet Explorer.

To save the Web page on your Data Disk:

1. Use the **Favorites** button 🔲 on the Standard Buttons toolbar to return to the Pennsylvania Quintet page. (You saved the favorite in the East Coast Ensembles folder, which is in the Wind Quintet Information folder.)

2. Click **File** on the menu bar, and then click **Save As** to open the Save Web Page dialog box.

3. Click the **Save in** list arrow, click the drive that contains your Data Disk, and then double-click the **Tutorial.01** folder to open it. You will accept the default Web page name of Pennsylvania Quintet.

4. Make sure that the Save as type list box is set to **"Web Page, complete"** and then click the **Save** button. The Save Web Page dialog box opens, and Internet Explorer saves all of the Web page's elements to your disk in a Pennsylvania Quintet_files folder. Now the Web page for the Pennsylvania Quintet's home page is saved in the Tutorial.01 folder on your Data Disk, and the page's related files are saved in the Pennsylvania Quintet_files folder. When you send the Web page and its folder to Marianna, she can open her Web browser and then use the Open command on the File menu to open the Web page's .htm file.

5. Click 🔲 on the Standard Buttons toolbar to close the Favorites Explorer bar.

If you need to save a graphic but not the text on a Web page, right-click it in the browser window, click Save Picture As on the shortcut menu, and then select the location in which to save the graphic file.

Copying Web Page Text and Saving It in a File

Maggie suggests that you might want to know how to save portions of Web page text to a file, so that you can save only the text from the Web page and use it in other programs. You will use WordPad to receive the text you will copy from a Web page, but any word processor or text editor will work.

Marianna just called to let you know that the quintet will play a concert in Cleveland on a Friday night, and she asks you to identify other opportunities for scheduling local concerts during the following weekend. Often, museums are willing to book small ensembles for weekend afternoon programs, and Marianna has given you the URL for the Cleveland Museum of Art. You will visit the site and then get the museum's address and telephone number so you can contact it about scheduling a concert.

REFERENCE WINDOW   **RW**

Copying Text from a Web Page to a WordPad Document
- Open the Web page in Internet Explorer.
- Use the mouse pointer to select the text you want to copy.
- Click Edit on the menu bar, and then click Copy.
- Start WordPad or another word processor.
- Click Edit on the menu bar, and then click Paste.
- Click the Save button on the WordPad toolbar, and then save the file to the correct folder and drive, using a filename that you specify.
- Click the Save button.

To copy text from a Web page and save it to a file:

1. Click the **Back** button ⇦ on the Standard Buttons toolbar to return to the Student Online Companion page, and then scroll down the page (if necessary) and click the **Cleveland Museum of Art** link to open that Web page in the browser window.

2. Click the **Visitor Info** hyperlink to open the Visitor Info page.

3. Click the **Hours and Address** hyperlink to open the museum information page.

4. Click and drag the **mouse pointer** over the address and telephone numbers to select them, as shown in Figure 27.

Figure 27   **SELECTING TEXT ON A WEB PAGE**

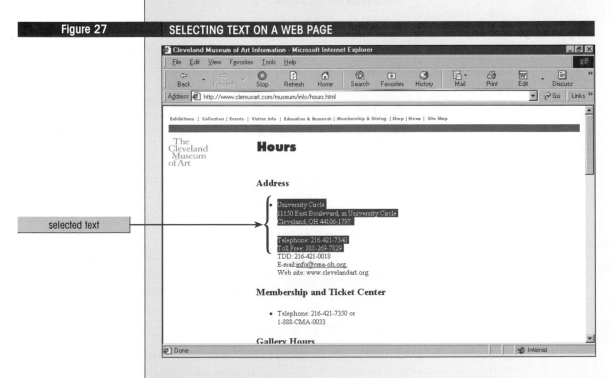

selected text

5. Click **Edit** on the menu bar, and then click **Copy** to copy the selected text to the Windows Clipboard.

Now, you can start WordPad and paste the copied text into a new document.

To start and copy the text into WordPad:

1. Click the **Start** button on the taskbar, point to **Programs**, point to **Accessories**, and then click **WordPad** to start the program and open a new document.

2. Click the **Paste** button 📋 on the WordPad toolbar to paste the text into the WordPad document, as shown in Figure 28.

Figure 28	PASTING TEXT FROM A WEB PAGE INTO A WORDPAD DOCUMENT

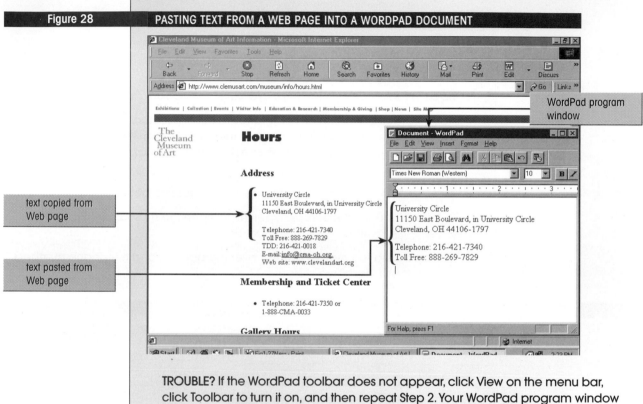

text copied from Web page

text pasted from Web page

WordPad program window

TROUBLE? If the WordPad toolbar does not appear, click View on the menu bar, click Toolbar to turn it on, and then repeat Step 2. Your WordPad program window might be a different size from the one shown in Figure 28, which does not affect the steps.

3. Click the **Save** button 💾 on the WordPad toolbar to open the Save As dialog box.

4. Click the **Save in** list arrow, change to the drive that contains your Data Disk, and then double-click the **Tutorial.01** folder.

5. Select any text that is in the File name text box, type **Address.txt**, and then click the **Save** button to save the file. Now, the address and phone number of the museum are saved in a file in the Tutorial.01 folder on your Data Disk for future reference.

6. Click the **Close** button ✕ on the WordPad title bar to close it.

7. Click the **Back** button ⬅ to return to the Visitor Info page.

Later, you will contact the museum. You notice that the Directions and Info page has a hyperlink titled "How to Get Here." This page might offer some helpful information that you could give to Marianna about where the museum is located, so you decide to save the graphic on your disk.

Saving a Web Page Graphic to Disk

Clicking the "How to Get Here" hyperlink loads a page that contains a hyperlink to a street map of the area surrounding the museum. You can save this map to your disk, as you will see next. Then, you can send the file to Marianna so that she'll have a resource for getting to the museum.

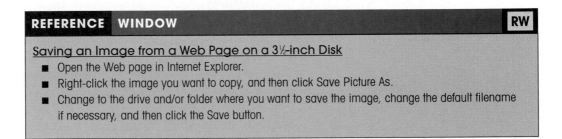

REFERENCE   WINDOW   **RW**

Saving an Image from a Web Page on a 3½-inch Disk
- Open the Web page in Internet Explorer.
- Right-click the image you want to copy, and then click Save Picture As.
- Change to the drive and/or folder where you want to save the image, change the default filename if necessary, and then click the Save button.

To save the street map image on a 3½-inch disk:

1. Click the **How to Get Here** hyperlink on the Visitor Info page, and then click the **street map** hyperlink.

2. After the map image has loaded, right-click the **map image** to open its shortcut menu, as shown in Figure 29.

Figure 29   SAVING THE MAP IMAGE TO DISK

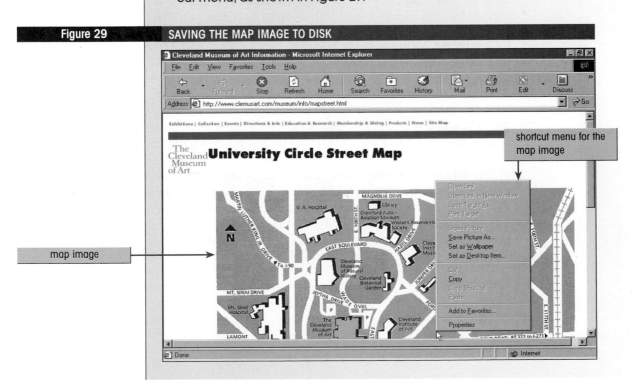

3. Click **Save Picture As** on the shortcut menu to open the Save Picture dialog box.

4. If necessary, click the **Save in** list arrow, change to the drive that contains your Data Disk, and then double-click the **Tutorial.01** folder. You will accept the default filename, mapstreet, so click the **Save** button. Now the image is saved on your Data Disk, so you can send the file to Marianna. Marianna can use her Web browser to open the image file and print it.

5. Close your Web browser.

Now, you can send a disk to Marianna so she has the Pennsylvania Quintet Web page and a map to show how to get to the museum. Maggie thinks this is a great idea, and suggests you consider using e-mail to share this information with Marianna and the other members of the Sunset Wind Quintet.

Exploring E-mail

When you use **e-mail** or electronic mail, you exchange messages with one or more users on a network, such as the Internet. Sending and receiving e-mail messages is more efficient than using ground or air mail services. Instead of composing a message on a piece of paper, inserting it in an envelope, attaching the correct postage and address to the envelope, and then depositing it in a mail box, you compose, address, and send a message directly from your computer to someone's electronic mail box. If you need to relay the same message to a number of people, such as everyone in the Sunset Wind Quintet, you can avoid making many phone calls or printing memos by sending one message to many recipients. You can also attach files, such as word-processing documents, graphics, or spreadsheets, to an e-mail message. For example, you can attach the mapstreet image to a message so you can send everyone in the quintet a copy of the map to the Cleveland Museum of Art.

Examining How E-mail Works

When you exchange e-mail, you send and receive messages with another person on your network, such as a LAN or the Internet. An **e-mail message** is a simple text document that you can compose and send using an e-mail program, such as Microsoft Outlook Express. When you send a message, it travels from your computer, through the network, and arrives at an **e-mail server**. Typically, the system administrator of your network or ISP manages the e-mail server.

The e-mail server stores the e-mail messages until the recipients request them. Then the server forwards the messages to the appropriate computers. Because e-mail uses this **store-and-forward technology**, you can send messages to anyone on the network, even if they do not have their computers turned on. When it's convenient, your recipients log on to the network and use their e-mail programs to receive and read their messages. The process of sending and receiving e-mail messages is illustrated in Figure 30.

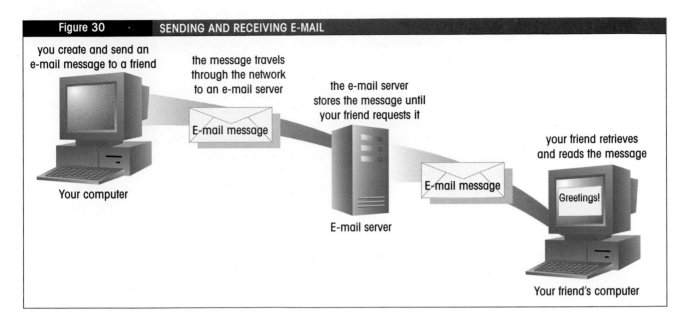

Figure 30   SENDING AND RECEIVING E-MAIL

you create and send an e-mail message to a friend

the message travels through the network to an e-mail server

the e-mail server stores the message until your friend requests it

E-mail message

Your computer

E-mail server

your friend retrieves and reads the message

E-mail message

Greetings!

Your friend's computer

As Figure 30 shows, to send and receive e-mail, you must be able to access an e-mail server on a network. If your computer is part of a network at a college or university, for example, you log on to the network to access its services. An e-mail server provides mail services to faculty, staff, and students who have access to the network. You can then send and receive e-mail any time you are logged on to the network.

If your computer is not part of a network, you can access an e-mail server on the Internet. To do so, you open an **e-mail account** with a service that provides Internet access. For example, e-mail accounts are included as part of the subscription fee for America Online (AOL) and most ISPs. E-mail accounts are also provided free of charge by advertiser-supported Web sites, such as Yahoo! and Hotmail, as illustrated in Figure 31. After you establish an e-mail account, you can connect to the Internet, most likely by using a phone line and your computer's modem, to send and receive your e-mail messages.

Figure 31   ACCESSING A FREE E-MAIL ACCOUNT

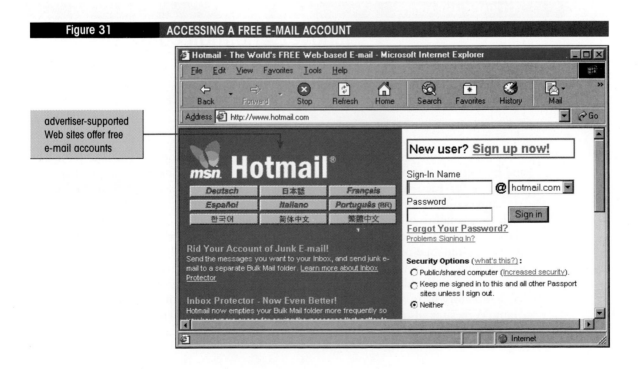

advertiser-supported Web sites offer free e-mail accounts

REFERENCE   WINDOW   RW

<u>Signing Up for a Hotmail Account</u>
- Start Internet Explorer.
- In the Address Bar, type *www.hotmail.com* to go to the Hotmail Web site.
- Click the Sign up now! hyperlink. The Registration page opens.
- Complete the Profile information. For example, type your name in the appropriate text box.
- Scroll the page until you see the Account Information heading. Read the rules to the right of the Account Information text boxes, and then enter the account information. For example, enter your new sign-in name and password.
- Click the Sign-Up button. Hotmail confirms your account information, including your new e-mail address.

You know that every quintet member can access the Internet, though they do not all belong to the same network. Therefore, you plan to open six Hotmail accounts—one for you and one for each musician. When you do, you will establish an e-mail address for each musician. An e-mail address identifies you and the location of your electronic mail box.

Finding an E-mail Address

Just as you include an address on an ordinary piece of mail, you also include an **e-mail address** on a message to make sure it arrives at its destination. Your e-mail address is included in the message as a return address, so your recipients can easily respond to your message. Anyone who has an e-mail address can send and receive electronic mail.

Sometimes, the system administrator of your e-mail server assigns you an e-mail address. Other times, such as when you sign up for a Hotmail account, you create your own e-mail address, though it must follow a particular form. An e-mail address usually starts with your user ID and an @ symbol, followed by the name of your e-mail server, as illustrated in Figure 32.

| Figure 32 | TYPICAL E-MAIL ADDRESS |

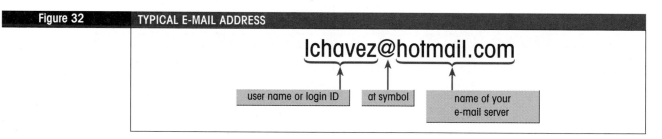

The e-mail address in Figure 32 is for Lou Chavez, the bassoonist. His user ID is lchavez and his e-mail account is on an e-mail server called hotmail.com. You plan to create e-mail addresses for each member of the quintet and follow this same pattern. For example, Marianna's e-mail address will be mrabinovich@hotmail.com.

To send mail to others outside the quintet, such as Maggie or the special events coordinator at the Cleveland Museum of Art, you must first find their e-mail addresses. The easiest way to find an e-mail address is to ask someone. For example, before you finish working with Maggie, you can ask her to write her e-mail address on her business card. You can also look up an e-mail address in a LAN or Internet directory. Most businesses and schools publish a directory listing e-mail addresses of those who have e-mail accounts on their network. Many Web sites also provide e-mail directories for people with e-mail accounts on the Internet, such as *www.worldemail.com* and *people.yahoo.com*.

When you sign up for an e-mail account, send your new e-mail address to friends, colleagues, and clients. For example, when you set up your Hotmail account, you'll send a message with your contact information to Maggie so you can keep in touch. If your e-mail address changes, such as when you use a different network or e-mail service, you can subscribe to an e-mail forwarding service so you don't miss any mail sent to your old address. For example, you can sign up for a free permanent e-mail address at *www.bigfoot.com*. Although this service does not provide you with a personal mailbox or e-mail account, as Yahoo! and Hotmail do, it does forward your mail to your current network or Internet e-mail server. That way, if someone sends a message to your old e-mail address, Bigfoot receives it and forwards it to your new e-mail address.

Contacting People on Other Networks

Maggie mentions that she has an e-mail account on AOL. She also shares with you the e-mail address of the director of the Baltimore Museum of Art, which is on a university network. You wonder if you can exchange e-mail with Maggie and the director, since they are on networks different from yours. Maggie explains that many LAN-based e-mail systems are connected to the Internet through an electronic link called a **gateway**. When you exchange e-mail with a user on another network, your messages are transferred through the gateway and relayed to their destination. Internet services such as AOL also use gateways to connect to other networks. Gateways make it easy for you to exchange e-mail with Maggie, museum directors, and anyone else on the Internet or a university, business, or government LAN. In addition, you do not need to include extra postage or pay long-distance charges to communicate with people in other cities and countries—an e-mail address is all you need to route your message to its destination anywhere in the world.

Sending and Receiving E-mail

In addition to an e-mail address, Maggie reminds you that you need an e-mail program, also called **e-mail client software**, to send and receive messages. When someone sends you a message, it is stored on your e-mail server until you log on to the network and use an e-mail program to check your mail. Then, the e-mail server transfers new messages to your electronic mailbox. You use the e-mail program to open, read, print, delete, reply to, forward, and save the mail. You also use the e-mail program to compose and send new messages and to attach a file, such as a document or graphic, to the message.

Maggie says that the computer you have been using has Microsoft Outlook Express as its e-mail program. She offers to show you how to use the program to practice sending and receiving e-mail messages. A good way to practice is to send a message to yourself and then reply to it.

Sending E-mail Messages

The Microsoft Outlook Express e-mail program installs as part of Internet Explorer. Before you practice sending e-mail messages, you should have your computer turned on, connected to the Internet, and open to the Windows desktop. You also should have an e-mail account and know your e-mail address to complete the steps in the following sections.

To start Outlook Express:

1. Click the **Start** button on the taskbar, point to **Programs**, and then click **Outlook Express**. After a moment, Outlook Express opens, as illustrated in Figure 33. Your main window might differ slightly.

Figure 33 | **OUTLOOK EXPRESS MAIN WINDOW**

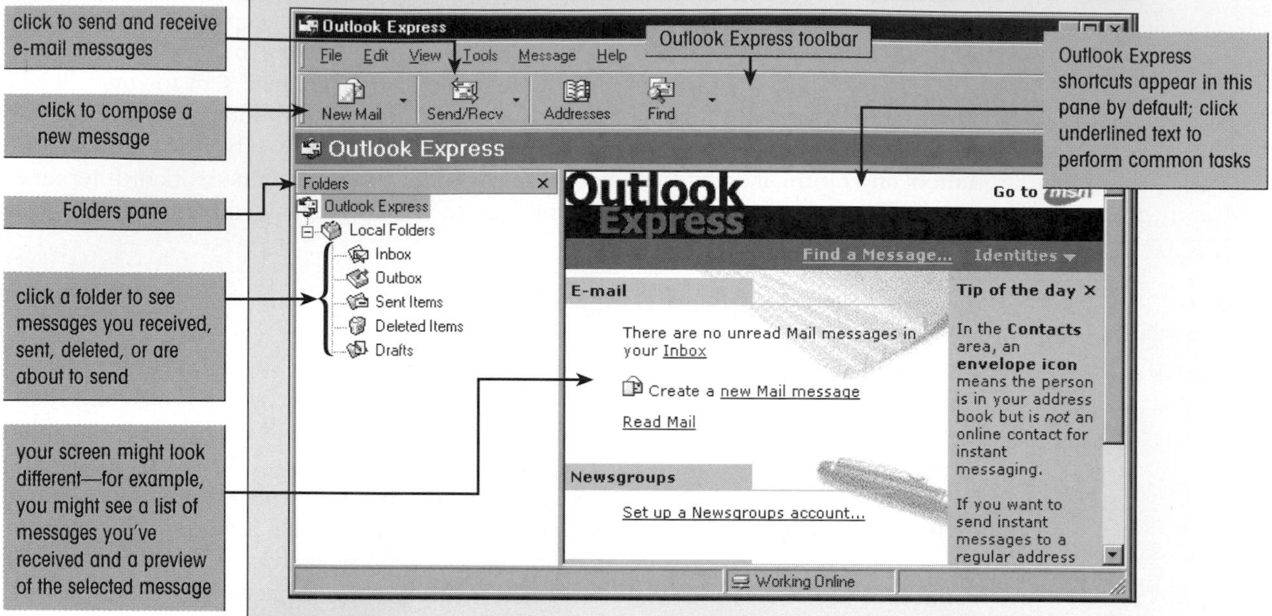

click to send and receive e-mail messages

click to compose a new message

Folders pane

click a folder to see messages you received, sent, deleted, or are about to send

your screen might look different—for example, you might see a list of messages you've received and a preview of the selected message

Outlook Express toolbar

Outlook Express shortcuts appear in this pane by default; click underlined text to perform common tasks

Outlook Express

File Edit View Tools Message Help

New Mail   Send/Recv   Addresses   Find

Outlook Express

Folders
Outlook Express
  Local Folders
    Inbox
    Outbox
    Sent Items
    Deleted Items
    Drafts

Outlook Express

Go to msn

Find a Message...   Identities ▼

E-mail

There are no unread Mail messages in your Inbox

Create a new Mail message

Read Mail

Newsgroups

Set up a Newsgroups account...

Tip of the day ×

In the **Contacts** area, an **envelope icon** means the person is in your address book but is *not* an online contact for instant messaging.

If you want to send instant messages to a regular address

Working Online

TROUBLE? If you cannot find Outlook Express on the Programs menu, check to see if an Outlook Express shortcut icon appears on the desktop or on the taskbar, and then double-click it. If you do not see the shortcut icon, ask your instructor or technical support person for help. The program might be installed in a different folder on your computer.

TROUBLE? If the title bar on the open window says "Microsoft Outlook" instead of "Microsoft Outlook Express," click the Close button to exit the program and repeat Step 1.

TROUBLE? If you see a dialog box with the message "Outlook Express is not currently your default mail client. Would you like to make it your default mail client?" click No and then continue with Step 1.

TROUBLE? If a Dial-up Connection dialog box opens, enter your user name and password into the appropriate text boxes, and then click the Connect button. If you do not know your user name or password, ask your instructor or technical support person for assistance. After you make a connection, continue with Step 1.

Maggie explains that in addition to the standard Windows components, such as the title bar, menu bar, scroll bars, Close button, and status bar, the Outlook Express window includes the following elements:

■ **Toolbar**: The Outlook Express toolbar contains buttons that let you perform common commands, such as sending or receiving mail, composing a new message, or replying to a message you received.

■ **Folders pane**: Outlook Express organizes your e-mail into several folders, including the Inbox, Outbox, and Sent Items folders. That way, you can separate the messages you send from those you receive. Click a folder in the Folders pane to open that folder.

■ **Right pane**: What appears in the right pane reflects what you selected in the Folders pane. For example, click the Outlook Express folder to see the information shown in Figure 33. Click the Inbox folder to see a list of messages you have received and a preview of the selected message.

Maggie suggests you start by sending a message to yourself. When you send a message, first you compose a basic e-mail message, and then you send it to your recipient.

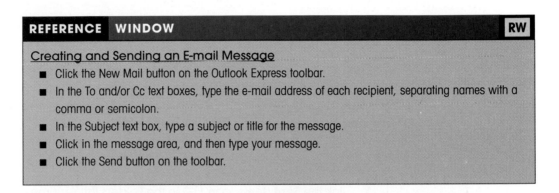

REFERENCE WINDOW **RW**

Creating and Sending an E-mail Message
■ Click the New Mail button on the Outlook Express toolbar.
■ In the To and/or Cc text boxes, type the e-mail address of each recipient, separating names with a comma or semicolon.
■ In the Subject text box, type a subject or title for the message.
■ Click in the message area, and then type your message.
■ Click the Send button on the toolbar.

To create and send an e-mail message:

1. Click the **New Mail** button 🗎 on the toolbar. You see the New Message window, shown in Figure 34.

| Figure 34 | NEW MESSAGE WINDOW IN OUTOOK EXPRESS |

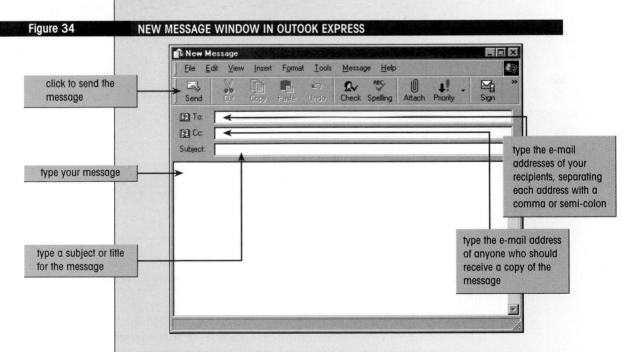

TROUBLE? If you do not see the toolbar in the Outlook Express window, click View on the menu bar, and then click Layout. In the Layout dialog box, click the Toolbar check box to insert a check, and then click OK. Return to Step 1.

2. Click in the **To** text box, and then type your e-mail address. For example, type **lchang@hotmail.com**.

3. Click in the **Subject** text box, and then type **Test**.

4. Click in the message area, and type **This is just a practice test message**. Press **Enter** five times, and then type your name.

5. Click the **Send** button [icon] on the toolbar. Outlook Express sends the message to the Outbox, and then to your e-mail address.

Maggie points out that if you wanted to send this message to many people, such as to everyone in the quintet, you could have typed more than one e-mail address in the To or Cc text box. You must separate each address with a comma or semicolon. She also mentions that if you wanted to attach a file to the message, you could click the Attach button and then select the file you want to send.

Now that you created your practice message, Maggie suggests you verify that it was sent. You can do that by opening the Sent Items folder.

To verify that Outlook Express sent your message:

1. Click the **Sent Items** icon [icon] in the Folders list. Your message appears in a separate pane at the bottom of the Sent Items list by default, as illustrated in Figure 35.

| Figure 35 | SENT ITEMS FOLDER |

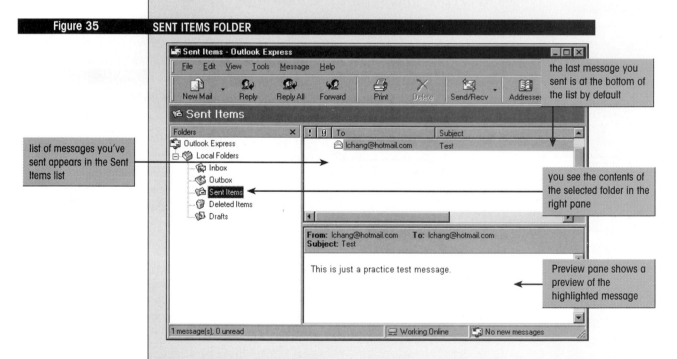

TROUBLE? If you do not see the Folders list in the Outlook Express window, click View on the menu bar, and then click Layout. In the Layout dialog box, click the Folders List check box to insert a check, and then click OK. Return to Step 1.

Maggie says you are ready to retrieve and read the message you sent. Outlook Express periodically transfers messages from your e-mail server to your Inbox, but you can also retrieve messages anytime you like.

Receiving and Reading E-mail Messages

Outlook Express transfers, or downloads, messages addressed to you from your e-mail server to your Inbox. You can then preview the message or open it to read its complete contents.

To receive and read e-mail messages:

1. Click the **Send/Recv** button on the toolbar. Outlook Express contacts your e-mail server and downloads your e-mail messages.

   TROUBLE? If you see a dialog box asking for your user name and password, enter this information and continue with Step 2. See your instructor or technical support person if you need help entering the correct user name or password.

2. Click the **Inbox** icon in the Folders list. You see a list of e-mail messages you have received appear in the upper-right pane.

3. To preview the message you sent to yourself, click the **Test message** in the Inbox. You see part of the message in the Preview pane, as shown in Figure 36.

Figure 36 **OUTLOOK EXPRESS INBOX**

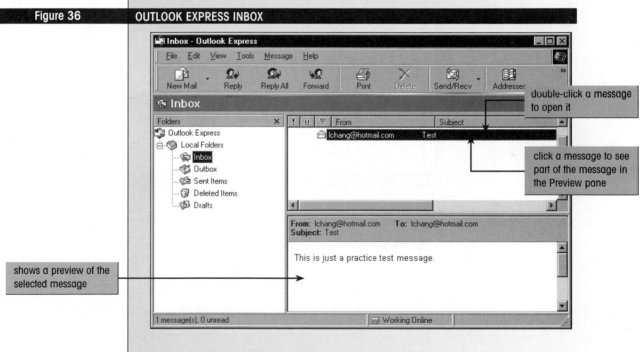

shows a preview of the selected message

double-click a message to open it

click a message to see part of the message in the Preview pane

4. Double-click the **Test message** in the Inbox to open it. The complete message appears in a new window.

Maggie wants to show you how to perform one more common e-mail task: replying to the messages you receive.

Replying to E-mail Messages

Some of the e-mail you receive asks you to provide information, answer questions, or confirm decisions. For example, you might receive a message from Marianna asking you to confirm performance dates. Instead of creating a new e-mail message, typing Marianna's e-mail address and subject, and then reminding Marianna about what she asked, you can reply directly to Marianna's message. As part of the reply, Outlook Express fills in the To and Subject lines and includes the text of the original message.

Maggie encourages you to practice replying to your own e-mail message, so you decide to give it a try.

To reply to an open e-mail message:

1. Click the **Reply** button 🔲 on the toolbar. You see the Re: Test window, as shown in Figure 37.

Figure 37	REPLYING TO A MESSAGE

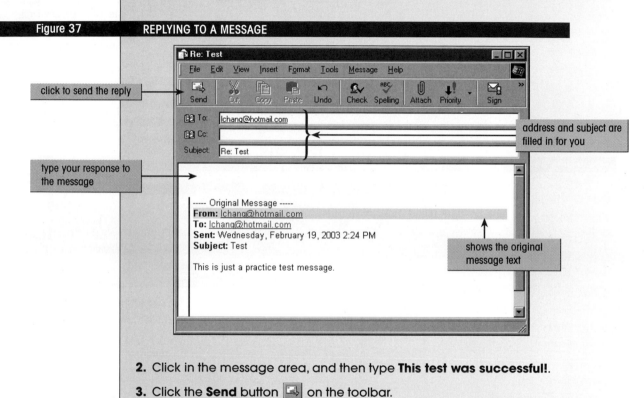

2. Click in the message area, and then type **This test was successful!**.

3. Click the **Send** button 🔲 on the toolbar.

Maggie congratulates you for completing the basic tasks of sending and receiving e-mail with Microsoft Outlook Express. Now you can exit the program and close your dial-up connection.

To exit Outlook Express and close the dial-up connection:

1. Click the **Close** button ⊠ on the title bar.

2. If you see a message asking if you want to disconnect from your Internet connection, click **Yes**. If you don't see a message, close your dial-up connection the way you usually do.

Observing E-mail Etiquette

You thank Maggie for all her help and say that you appreciate the advantages e-mail offers. With e-mail, you can send and reply to messages immediately, send the same message to many people, and receive your mail whenever you like. But Maggie cautions you that these advantages also introduce potential problems. For example, you might regret a message you send in haste or become overwhelmed by too many unread messages in your Inbox. You should also be aware that a set of customs has developed for sending and receiving e-mail, and other e-mail users expect you to observe these customs.

Maggie gives you the following guidelines for managing your e-mail:

- **Check your mail regularly**. E-mail lets you instantly respond to messages, and your correspondents expect a quick response. Check your e-mail often to take advantage of e-mail's immediacy.

- **Reply to messages only when necessary**. Although people expect you to read their e-mail messages soon after they send them, you don't have to reply to every message you receive. Doing so creates unnecessary e-mail traffic on the network and clogs up recipients' inboxes. Reply only when it's appropriate, such as when you are answering a question.

- **Let people know when you need to send a large attachment**. If you attach a large file to an e-mail message, it can take a long time for your recipient to download your message. Most e-mail servers have a limit to the size of the files you can attach; some allow files no larger than 1 MB. Check with your correspondents before sending large file attachments to find out about size restrictions and set up a convenient time to send the attachment.

- **Provide meaningful information in the Subject line**. Most e-mail programs show the Subject line, date, and sender address for incoming mail. Let your correspondents know what your message concerns by including a subject line that concisely and accurately describes the message contents. For example, a subject such as "Staff meeting rescheduled" is more informative than "Meeting." Even after people read your message, the subject line helps them quickly locate information they might need later.

- **Review your message before you send it**. Before you send a message that you may regret, such as one written in haste or anger, read it over and consider its effect. If you're still upset after reading it, set it aside for a few hours. Also, be sure to proofread your message before you send it. Most e-mail clients, including Outlook Express, include spell checkers, and some even have grammar checkers. Use standard grammar, spelling, punctuation, and capitalization to create a professional, competent impression.

- **Consider that e-mail is not private**. Your correspondents can easily forward your message to others, deliberately or inadvertently revealing information you consider confidential. Be professional and careful about what you say to and about others.

- **Follow proper netiquette**. Netiquette is jargon for "Internet etiquette"— the do's and don'ts of communicating online. For example, you should include your signature at the bottom of your message so people know who sent it. Avoid including all uppercase text because it is interpreted as shouting. Instead, use asterisks around a word, as in "Do *not* send cash," for emphasis. Be careful when using sarcasm and humor, which is easily misinterpreted in print. You can, however, use smileys such as :-) to express emotion.

Session 1.2 QUICK CHECK

1. Describe two ways to increase the Web page area in Internet Explorer.

2. You can use the _____ button in Internet Explorer to open a Web page that you opened in a Web session last week.

3. Click the _____ button on the Standard Buttons toolbar to open a search engine quickly in Internet Explorer.

4. List the names of two additional Favorites folders you might want to add to the Wind Quintet Information folder as you continue to gather information for the Sunset Wind Quintet.

5. What happens when you click the Refresh button in Internet Explorer?

6. Describe what happens when you send an e-mail message from your computer.

7. To create a message in Outlook Express, you click the _____ button.

REVIEW ASSIGNMENTS

Marianna is pleased with the information you have gathered thus far about other wind quintet Web pages and potential recital sites. In fact, she is thinking about hiring someone to create a Web page for the Sunset Wind Quintet. Marianna would like you to compile some information about the Web pages that other small musical ensembles have created so that she has some background information for her meetings with potential Web designers. Although you have searched for information about wind quintets, a large number of string quartets (two violinists, a violist, and a cellist) play similar venues.

Do the following:

1. Start your Web browser, go to the New Perspectives Student Union (*http://www.course.com/NewPerspectives/studentunion*), click the **Online Companions** link, click the **Office XP** link, click the **Browser Basics** link, and then click the **Review Assignments** link.

2. Click the hyperlinks listed under the category headings Wind Quintets, String Quartets, and Other Small Musical Ensembles to explore the Web pages for each entry.

3. Choose three interesting home pages, and print the first page of each. Create a favorite for each of these sites, and then answer the following questions for these three sites:
   a. Which sites include a photograph of the ensemble?
   b. Which photographs are in color, and which are in black and white?
   c. Which sites show the ensemble members dressed in formal concert dress?

4. Choose your favorite ensemble photograph and save it in the Tutorial.01 folder on your Data Disk.

5. Do any of the sites provide information about the ensemble's CDs? If so, which ones? Is this information on the home page, or did you click a hyperlink to find it? Start your e-mail program and create a message addressed to yourself. Write the answers to these questions as the message text, and then send the message.

6. Do any of the sites offer CDs or other products for sale? If so, which ones? Is this information on the home page, or did you click a hyperlink to find it? Create another message addressed to yourself. Write the answers to these questions as the message text, and then send the message.

7. Write a one-page report that summarizes your findings for Marianna. Include a recommendation regarding what the Sunset Wind Quintet should consider including in its Web site.

8. Close your Web browser and your Internet connection, if necessary.

CASE PROBLEMS

Case 1. Businesses on the Web Business Web sites range from very simple informational sites to comprehensive sites that offer information about the firm's products or services, history, current employment openings, and finances. An increasing number of business sites offer products or services for sale using their Web sites. You just started a position on the public relations staff of Value City Central, a large retail chain of television and appliance stores. Your first assignment is to research and report on the types of information that other large firms offer on their Web sites.

Do the following:

1. Start your Web browser, go to the New Perspectives Student Union (*http://www.course.com/NewPerspectives/studentunion*), click the **Office XP** link, click the **Online Companions** link, click the **Browser Basics** link, and then click the **Case Problems** link.

2. Use the Case Problem 1 hyperlinks to open the business sites on that page.

3. Choose three business sites that you believe would be most relevant to your assignment.

4. Print the home page for each Web site that you have chosen.

5. Select one site that you feel does the best job in each of the following five categories: overall presentation of the corporate image, description of products or services offered, presentation of the firm's history, description of employment opportunities, and presentation of financial statements or other financial information about the company.

6. Prepare a report that includes one paragraph describing why you believe each of the sites you identified in the preceding step did the best job.

7. Close your Web browser and your Internet connection, if necessary.

Case 2. Browser Wars Your employer, Bristol Mills, is a medium-sized manufacturer of specialty steel products. The firm has increased its use of computers in all of its office operations and in many of its manufacturing operations. Many of Bristol's computers currently run either Netscape Navigator or Microsoft Internet Explorer; however, the chief financial officer (CFO) has decided that the firm can support only one of these products. As the CFO's special assistant, you have been asked to recommend which Web browser the company should choose to support.

Do the following:

1. Start your Web browser, go to the New Perspectives Student Union (*http://www.course.com/NewPerspectives/studentunion*), click the **Office XP** link, click the **Browser Basics** link, and then click the **Case Problems** link.

2. Use the Case Problem 2 hyperlinks to learn more about these two widely used Web browser software packages.

3. Write a one-page memo to the CFO (your instructor) that outlines the strengths and weaknesses of each product. Recommend one program, and then support your decision using the information you collected.

4. Prepare a list of features that you would like to see in a new Web browser software package that would overcome important limitations in either Navigator or Internet Explorer. Do you think it would be feasible for a firm to develop and use such a product? Why, or why not?

5. Close your Web browser and your dial-up connection, if necessary.

Explore   *Case 3. Citizens Fidelity Bank*   You are a new staff auditor at Citizens Fidelity Bank. You have had more recent computer training than other audit staff members at Citizens, so Sally DeYoung, the audit manager, asks you to review the bank's policy on Web browser cookie settings. Some of the bank's board members have expressed concerns to Sally about the security of the bank's computers. They understand that the bank has PCs on its networks that are connected to the Internet. One of the board members learned about browser cookies and was afraid that an innocent bank employee might connect to a site that would write a dangerous cookie file on the bank's computer network. A browser **cookie** is a small file that a Web server can write to the disk drive of the computer running a Web browser. Not all Web servers write cookies, but those that do can read the cookie file the next time the Web browser on that computer connects to the Web server. Then the Web server can retrieve information about the Web browser's last connection to the server. None of the bank's board members knows very much about computers, but all of them have become concerned that a virus-laden cookie could significantly damage the bank's computer system. Sally asks you to help inform the board of directors about cookies and to establish a policy on using them.

Do the following:

1. Start your Web browser, go to the New Perspectives Student Union (*http://www.course.com/NewPerspectives/studentunion*), click the **Online Companions** link, click the **Office XP** link, click the **Browser Basics** link, and then click the **Case Problems** link.

2. Use the Internet Explorer Online Help to learn more about cookies. (*Hint*: In the Help window, open the Index tab and use the keyword "cookies.")

3. Prepare a brief outline of the content on each Web page you visit.

4. List the risks that Citizens Fidelity Bank might face by allowing cookie files to be written to its computers.

5. List the benefits that individual users obtain by allowing Web servers to write cookies to the computers that they are using at the bank to access the Web.

6. Close your Web browser and your Internet connection, if necessary.

Case 4. Columbus Suburban Area Council   The Columbus Suburban Area Council is a charitable organization devoted to maintaining and improving the general welfare of people living in Columbus suburbs. As the director of the council, you are interested in encouraging donations and other support from local citizens and would like to stay informed of grant opportunities that might benefit the council. You are especially interested in developing an informative and attractive presence on the Web.

Do the following:

1. Start your Web browser, go to the New Perspectives Student Union (*http://www.course.com/NewPerspectives/studentunion*), click the **Online Companions** link, click the **Office XP** link, click the **Browser Basics** link, and then click the **Case Problems** link.

2. Follow the Case Problem 4 hyperlinks to charitable organizations to find out more about what other organizations are doing with their Web sites.

3. Select three of the Web sites you visited and, for each, prepare a list of the site's contents. Note whether each site included financial information and whether the site disclosed how much the organization spent on administrative, or nonprogram, activities. Also note whether the site lets visitors communicate with the organization via e-mail.

4. Identify which site you believe would be a good model for the Council's new Web site. Explain why you think your chosen site would be the best example to follow.

5. Close your Web browser and your Internet connection, if necessary.

The Internet:
World Wide
Web

LAB ASSIGNMENT

One of the most popular services on the Internet is the World Wide Web. This Lab is a Web simulator that teaches you how to use Web browser software to find information. You can complete this Lab whether or not your school provides you with Internet access.

1. Click the **Steps** button to learn how to use Web browser software. As you proceed through the Steps, answer all of the Quick Check questions that appear. After you complete the Steps, you will see a Quick Check Summary Report. Follow the instructions on the screen to print this report.

2. Click the **Explore** button on the Welcome screen. Use the Web browser to locate a weather map of the Caribbean Virgin Islands. What is its URL?

3. A scuba diver named Wadson Lachouffe has been searching for the fabled treasure of Greybeard the pirate. A link from the Adventure Travel Web site *www.atour.com* leads to Wadson's Web page called "Hidden Treasure." In Explore, locate the Hidden Treasure page and answer the following questions:

   ■ What was the name of Greybeard's ship?
   ■ What was Greybeard's favorite food?
   ■ What does Wadson think happened to Greybeard's ship?

4. In the Steps, you found a graphic of Jupiter from the photo archives of the Jet Propulsion Laboratory. In the Explore section of the Lab, you can also find a graphic of Saturn. Suppose one of your friends wanted a picture of Saturn for an astronomy report. Make a list of the blue underlined links your friend must click in the correct order to find the Saturn graphic. Assume that your friend will begin at the Web Trainer home page.

5. Enter the URL **http://www.atour.com** to jump to the Adventure Travel Web site. Write a one-page description of this site. In your paper, include a description of the information at the site, the number of pages the site contains, and a diagram of the links it contains.

6. Chris Thomson is a student at UVI and has his own Web pages. In Explore, look at the information Chris has included on his pages. Suppose you could create your own Web page. What would you include? Use word-processing software to design your own Web pages. Make sure you indicate the graphics and links you would use.

QUICK CHECK ANSWERS

Session 1.1

1. False

2. format text and create hyperlinks

3. the main page of a Web site, the first page that opens when you start your Web browser, or the page that opens the first time you start a particular Web browser

4. any two: graphic image, sound clip, or video files

5. candidate's name and party affiliation, list of qualifications, biography, position statements on campaign issues, list of endorsements with hyperlinks to the Web pages of individuals and organizations that support her candidacy, audio or video clips of speeches and interviews, address and telephone number of the campaign office, and other similar information

6. A computer's IP address is a unique identifying number; its domain name is a unique name associated with the IP address on the Internet host computer responsible for that computer's domain.

7. http:// indicates use of the hypertext transfer protocol; www.savethetrees.org is the domain name and suggests a charitable or not-for-profit organization that is probably devoted to forest ecology; main.html is the name of the HTML file on the Web server.

8. A Web directory contains a hierarchical list of Web page categories; each category contains hyperlinks to individual Web pages. A Web search engine is a Web site that accepts words or expressions you enter and finds Web pages that include those words or expressions.

Session 1.2

1. Auto-hide the toolbar or press the F11 key.

2. History

3. Search

4. Midwest Ensembles, West Coast Ensembles

5. Internet Explorer contacts the Web server to see if the currently loaded Web page has changed since it was stored in the cache folder. If the Web page has changed, it obtains the new page; otherwise, it loads the cache folder copy.

6. When you send an e-mail message, it travels from your computer, through the network, and arrives at an e-mail server. The e-mail server forwards the message to the recipient when the recipient retrieves his or her messages.

7. New Mail

New Perspectives on

MICROSOFT®
OFFICE XP

TUTORIAL 1   OFF 3

Introducing Microsoft Office XP

Read This Before You Begin

To the Student

Data Disks

To complete this tutorial and the Review Assignments, you need one Data Disk. Your instructor will either provide you with the Data Disk or ask you to make your own.

If you are making your own Data Disk, you will need **one** blank, formatted high-density disk. You will need to copy a set of files and/or folders from a file server, standalone computer, or the Web onto your disk. Your instructor will tell you which computer, drive letter, and folder contain the files you need. You could also download the files by going to **www.course.com** and following the instructions on the screen.

The information below shows you which folder goes on your disk, so that you will have enough disk space to complete the tutorial and Review Assignments:

Data Disk 1

Write this on the disk label:
Data Disk 1: Introducing Office XP

Put this folder on the disk:
Tutorial.01

When you begin the tutorial, be sure you are using the correct Data Disk. Refer to the "File Finder" chart at the back of this text for more detailed information on which files are used in the tutorial. See the inside front or inside back cover of this book for more information on Data Disk files, or ask your instructor or technical support person for assistance.

Using Your Own Computer

If you are going to work through this tutorial using your own computer, you need:

■ **Computer System** Microsoft Windows 98, NT, 2000 Professional, or higher must be installed on your computer. This book assumes a typical installation of Microsoft Office XP.

■ **Data Disk** You will not be able to complete this tutorial or Review Assignments using your own computer until you have your Data Disk.

Visit Our World Wide Web Site

Additional materials designed especially for you are available on the World Wide Web.
Go to www.course.com/NewPerspectives.

To the Instructor

The Data Disk Files are available on the Instructor's Resource Kit for this title. Follow the instructions in the Help file on the CD-ROM to install the programs to your network or standalone computer. For information on creating the Data Disk, see the "To the Student" section above.

You are granted a license to copy the Data Disk Files to any computer or computer network used by students who have purchased this book.

OBJECTIVES

In this tutorial you will:

- Explore the programs that comprise Microsoft Office

- Explore the benefits of integrating data between programs

- Start programs and switch between them

- Use personalized menus and toolbars

- Save and close a file

- Open an existing file

- Print a file

- Get Help

- Close files and exit programs

INTRODUCING MICROSOFT OFFICE XP

Preparing Promotional Materials for Delmar Office Supplies

CASE

Delmar Office Supplies

Delmar Office Supplies, a company in Wisconsin founded by Nicole Delmar in 1996, sells recycled office supplies to businesses and home-based offices around the world. The demand for quality recycled papers, reconditioned toner cartridges, and renovated office furniture has been growing each year. Nicole and all her employees use Microsoft Office XP, which provides everyone in the company the power and flexibility to store a variety of information, create consistent documents, and share data. In this tutorial, you'll review some of the latest documents the company's employees have created using Microsoft Office XP.

Exploring **Microsoft Office XP**

Microsoft Office XP, or simply **Office**, is a collection of the most popular Microsoft programs: Word, Excel, PowerPoint, Access, and Outlook. Each Office program contains valuable tools to help you accomplish many tasks, such as composing reports, analyzing data, preparing presentations, and compiling information.

Microsoft Word 2002, or simply **Word**, is a **word processing program** you use to create text documents. The files you create in Word are called **documents**. Word offers many special features that help you compose and update all types of documents, ranging from letters and newsletters to reports, fliers, faxes, and even books—all in attractive and readable formats. You also can use Word to create, insert, and position figures, tables, and other graphics to enhance the look of your documents. Figure 1 shows a business letter that a sales representative composed with Word.

Figure 1	LETTER COMPOSED IN A WORD DOCUMENT

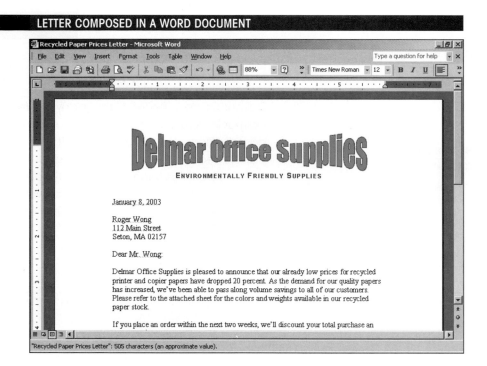

Microsoft Excel 2002, or simply **Excel**, is a **spreadsheet program** you use to display, organize, and analyze numerical information. You can do some of this in Word with tables, but Excel provides many more tools for performing calculations than Word does. Its graphics capabilities also enable you to display data visually. You might, for example, generate a pie chart or bar chart to help readers quickly see the significance of and the connections between information. The files you create in Excel are called **workbooks**. Figure 2 shows an Excel workbook with a line chart that the Operations Department uses to track the company's financial performance.

Figure 2 FINANCIAL DATA IN AN EXCEL WORKBOOK

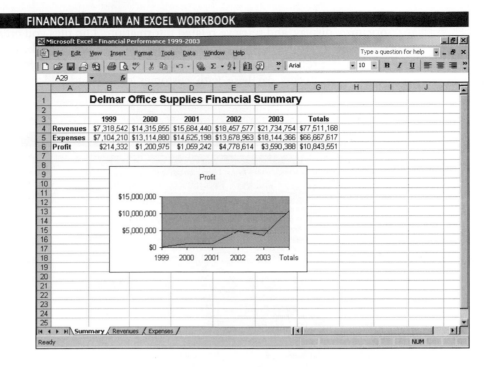

Microsoft PowerPoint 2002, or simply **PowerPoint**, is a **presentation graphics program** you use to create a collection of "slides" that can contain text, charts, pictures, and so on. The files you create in PowerPoint are called **presentations**. You can show these presentations on your computer monitor, project them onto a screen as a slide show, print them, share them over the Internet, or display them on the World Wide Web. You also can use PowerPoint to generate presentation-related documents such as audience handouts, outlines, and speakers' notes. Figure 3 shows an effective slide presentation the Sales Department created with PowerPoint to promote the latest product line.

Figure 3 SLIDE PRESENTATION CREATED IN POWERPOINT

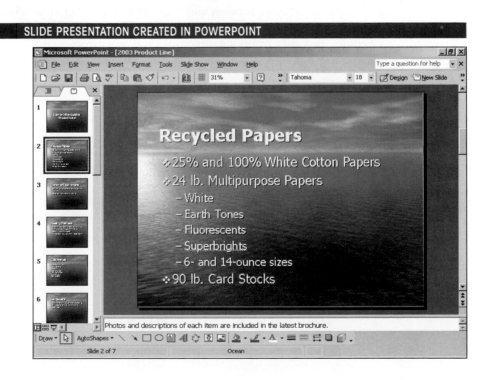

Microsoft Access 2002, or simply **Access**, is a **database program** you use to enter, organize, display, and retrieve related information. The files you create in Access are called **databases**. With Access you can create data entry forms to make data entry easier, and you can create professional reports to improve the readability of your data. Figure 4 shows a table in an Access database with customer names and addresses compiled by the Sales Department.

Figure 4 **CUSTOMER ADDRESSES COMPILED IN AN ACCESS DATABASE**

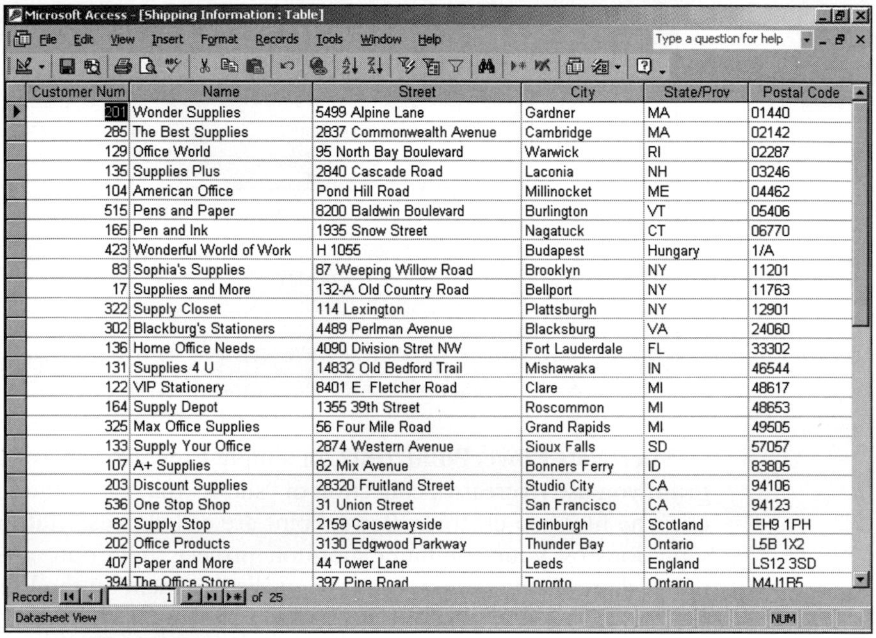

Customer Num	Name	Street	City	State/Prov	Postal Code
201	Wonder Supplies	5499 Alpine Lane	Gardner	MA	01440
285	The Best Supplies	2837 Commonwealth Avenue	Cambridge	MA	02142
129	Office World	95 North Bay Boulevard	Warwick	RI	02287
135	Supplies Plus	2840 Cascade Road	Laconia	NH	03246
104	American Office	Pond Hill Road	Millinocket	ME	04462
515	Pens and Paper	8200 Baldwin Boulevard	Burlington	VT	05406
165	Pen and Ink	1935 Snow Street	Nagatuck	CT	06770
423	Wonderful World of Work	H 1055	Budapest	Hungary	1/A
83	Sophia's Supplies	87 Weeping Willow Road	Brooklyn	NY	11201
17	Supplies and More	132-A Old Country Road	Bellport	NY	11763
322	Supply Closet	114 Lexington	Plattsburgh	NY	12901
302	Blackburg's Stationers	4489 Perlman Avenue	Blacksburg	VA	24060
136	Home Office Needs	4090 Division Stret NW	Fort Lauderdale	FL	33302
131	Supplies 4 U	14832 Old Bedford Trail	Mishawaka	IN	46544
122	VIP Stationery	8401 E. Fletcher Road	Clare	MI	48617
164	Supply Depot	1355 39th Street	Roscommon	MI	48653
325	Max Office Supplies	56 Four Mile Road	Grand Rapids	MI	49505
133	Supply Your Office	2874 Western Avenue	Sioux Falls	SD	57057
107	A+ Supplies	82 Mix Avenue	Bonners Ferry	ID	83805
203	Discount Supplies	28320 Fruitland Street	Studio City	CA	94106
536	One Stop Shop	31 Union Street	San Francisco	CA	94123
82	Supply Stop	2159 Causewayside	Edinburgh	Scotland	EH9 1PH
202	Office Products	3130 Edgwood Parkway	Thunder Bay	Ontario	L5B 1X2
407	Paper and More	44 Tower Lane	Leeds	England	LS12 3SD
394	The Office Store	397 Pine Road	Toronto	Ontario	M4J1B5

Microsoft Outlook 2002, or simply **Outlook**, is an **information management program** you use to send, receive, and organize e-mail; plan your schedule; arrange meetings; organize contacts; create a to-do list; and jot down notes. You also can use Outlook to print schedules, task lists, or phone directories and other documents. Figure 5 shows how Nicole Delmar uses Outlook to plan her schedule and create a to-do list.

Figure 5   **CALENDAR AND TASKS IN OUTLOOK**

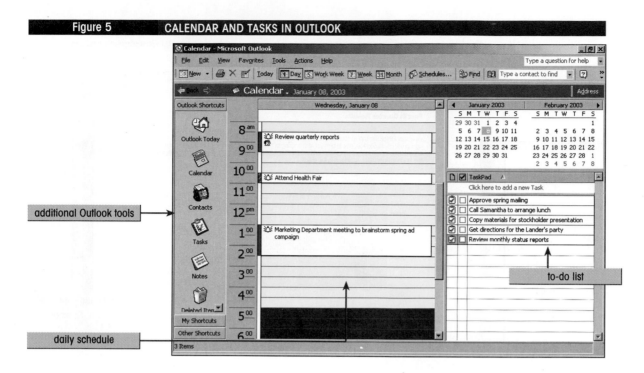

Although each Office program individually is a strong tool, their potential is even greater when used together.

Integrating Programs

One of the main advantages of Office is **integration**, the ability to share information between programs. Integration ensures consistency and accuracy, and it saves time because you don't have to re-enter the same information in several Office programs. The staff at Delmar Office Supplies uses the integration features of Office daily, including the following examples:

■ The Accounting Department created an Excel bar chart on the last two years' fourth-quarter results, which they inserted into the quarterly financial report, created in Word. They added a hyperlink to the Word report that employees can click to open the Excel workbook and view the original data. See Figure 6.

Figure 6   WORD DOCUMENT WITH AN EXCEL CHART

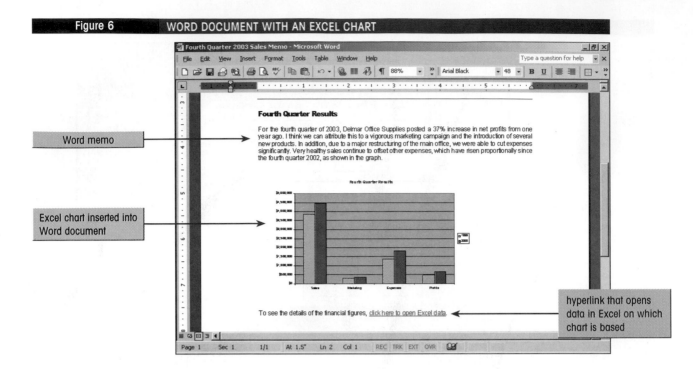

Word memo

Excel chart inserted into Word document

hyperlink that opens data in Excel on which chart is based

■ An Excel pie chart of sales percentages by divisions of Delmar Office Supplies can be duplicated on a PowerPoint slide. The slide is part of the Operations Department's presentation to stockholders. See Figure 7.

Figure 7   POWERPOINT PRESENTATION WITH AN EXCEL CHART

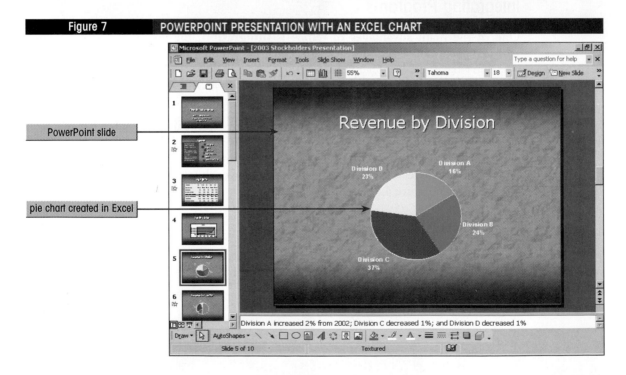

PowerPoint slide

pie chart created in Excel

■ An Access database or an Outlook contact list that stores the names and addresses of customers can be combined with a form letter that the Marketing Department created in Word, to produce a mailing promoting the company's newest products. See Figure 8.

Figure 8	WORD LETTER WITH ACCESS OR OUTLOOK DATA

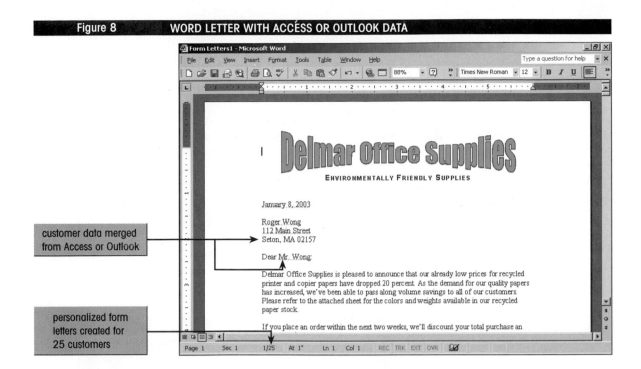

customer data merged from Access or Outlook

personalized form letters created for 25 customers

These are just a few examples of how you can take information from one Office program and integrate it into another.

Starting Office Programs

All Office programs start the same way—from the Programs menu on the Start button. You select the program you want, and then the program starts so you can immediately begin to create new files or work with existing ones.

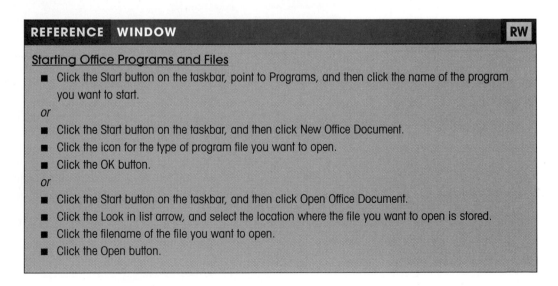

REFERENCE WINDOW   **RW**

Starting Office Programs and Files

- Click the Start button on the taskbar, point to Programs, and then click the name of the program you want to start.

or

- Click the Start button on the taskbar, and then click New Office Document.
- Click the icon for the type of program file you want to open.
- Click the OK button.

or

- Click the Start button on the taskbar, and then click Open Office Document.
- Click the Look in list arrow, and select the location where the file you want to open is stored.
- Click the filename of the file you want to open.
- Click the Open button.

You'll start Excel using the Start button.

To start Excel and open a new, blank workbook from the Start menu:

1. Make sure your computer is on and the Windows desktop appears on your screen.

   TROUBLE? Don't worry if your screen differs slightly from those shown in the figures. The figures in this book were created while running Windows 2000 in its default settings, but Office runs equally well using Windows 98 or later or Windows NT 4 with Service Pack 5. These operating systems share the same basic user interface.

2. Click the **Start** button on the taskbar, and then point to **Programs** to display the Programs menu.

3. Point to **Microsoft Excel** on the Programs menu. See Figure 9. Depending on how your computer is set up, your desktop and menu might contain different icons and commands.

Figure 9	START MENU WITH PROGRAMS MENU DISPLAYED

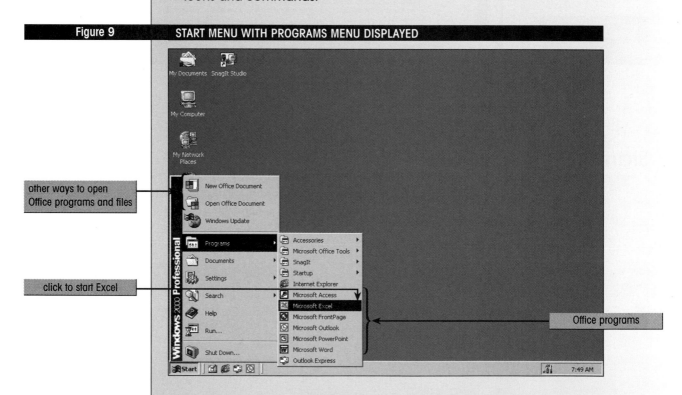

other ways to open Office programs and files

click to start Excel

Office programs

   TROUBLE? If you don't see Microsoft Excel on the Programs menu, point to Microsoft Office, and then point to Microsoft Excel. If you still don't see Microsoft Excel, ask your instructor or technical support person for help.

4. Click **Microsoft Excel** to start Excel and open a new, blank workbook. See Figure 10.

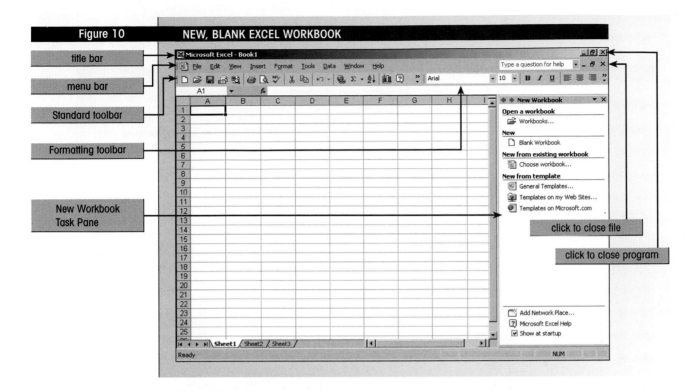

Figure 10   NEW, BLANK EXCEL WORKBOOK

title bar

menu bar

Standard toolbar

Formatting toolbar

New Workbook
Task Pane

click to close file

click to close program

An alternate method for starting programs with a blank file is to click the New Office Document command on the Start menu; the kind of file you choose determines which program opens. You'll use this method to start Word and open a new, blank document.

To start Word and open a new, blank document with the New Office Document command:

1. Leaving Excel open, click the **Start** button on the taskbar, and then click **New Office Document**. The New Office Document dialog box opens, providing another way to start Office programs. See Figure 11.

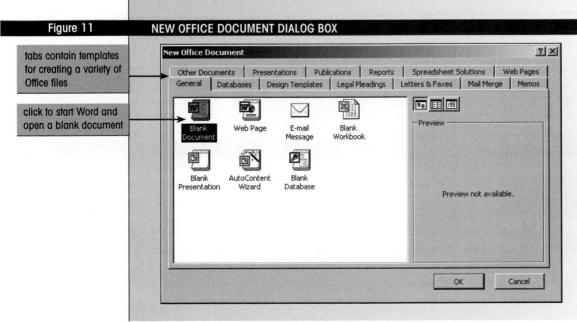

Figure 11   NEW OFFICE DOCUMENT DIALOG BOX

tabs contain templates for creating a variety of Office files

click to start Word and open a blank document

2. If necessary, click the **General** tab, click the **Blank Document** icon, and then click the **OK** button. Word opens with a new, blank document. See Figure 12.

Figure 12 NEW, BLANK DOCUMENT IN WORD

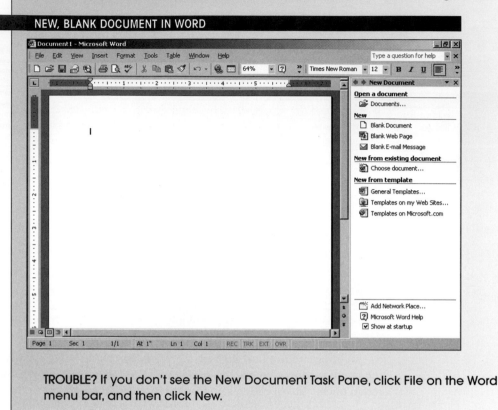

TROUBLE? If you don't see the New Document Task Pane, click File on the Word menu bar, and then click New.

You've tried two ways to start a program. There are several methods for performing most tasks in Office. This flexibility enables you to use Office in the way that fits how you like to work.

Switching Between Open Programs and Files

Two programs are running at the same time—Excel and Word. The taskbar contains buttons for both programs. When you have two or more programs running, or two files within the same program open, you can use the taskbar buttons to switch from one program or file to another. The employees at Delmar Office Supplies often work in several programs at once.

To switch between Word and Excel:

1. Click the **Microsoft Excel – Book1** button on the taskbar to switch from Word to Excel. See Figure 13.

Figure 13 EXCEL AND WORD PROGRAMS OPENED

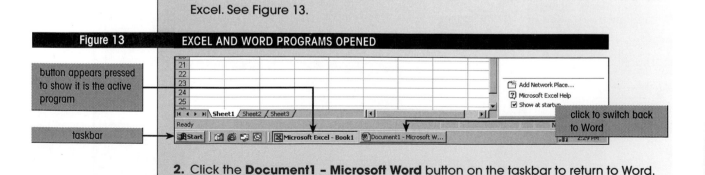

2. Click the **Document1 – Microsoft Word** button on the taskbar to return to Word.

As you can see, you can start multiple programs and switch between them in seconds.

The Office programs also share many features, so once you've learned one program, it's easy to learn the others. One of the most visible similarities among all the programs is the "personalized" menus and toolbars.

Using Personalized Menus and Toolbars

In each Office program, you perform tasks using a menu command, a toolbar button, or a keyboard shortcut. A **menu command** is a word on a menu that you click to execute a task; a **menu** is a group of related commands. For example, the File menu contains commands for managing files, such as the Open command and the Save command. A **toolbar** is a collection of **buttons** that correspond to commonly used menu commands. For example, the Standard toolbar contains an Open button and a Save button. **Keyboard shortcuts** are combinations of keys you press to perform a command. For example, Ctrl+S is the keyboard shortcut for the Save command (you hold down the Ctrl key while you press the S key). Keyboard shortcuts are displayed to the right of many menu commands.

When you first use a newly installed Office program, the menus and toolbars display only the basic and most commonly used commands and buttons, streamlining the program window. The other commands and buttons are available, but you have to click an extra button to see them (the double-arrow button on a menu and the Toolbar Options button on a toolbar). As you select commands and click buttons, the ones you use often are put on the short, personalized menu and on the visible part of the toolbars. The ones you don't use remain available on the full menus and toolbars. This means that the Office menus and toolbars might display different commands and buttons on each person's computer.

To view a personalized and full menu:

1. Click **Insert** on the Word menu bar to display the short, personalized menu. See Figure 14. The Bookmark command, for example, does not appear on the short menu.

Figure 14	SHORT, PERSONALIZED MENU

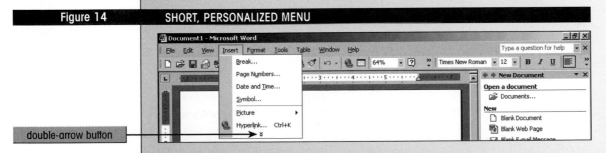

double-arrow button

TROUBLE? If the Insert menu displays different commands than shown in Figure 14, you need to reset the menus. Click Tools on the menu bar, click Customize (you might need to pause until the full menu appears to see that command), and then click the Options tab in the Customize dialog box. Click the Always show full menus check box to remove the check mark if necessary, and then click the Show full menus after a short delay check box to insert a check mark if necessary. Click the Reset my usage data button, and then click the Yes button to confirm that you want to reset the commands. Click the Close button. Repeat Step 1.

You can display the full menu in one of three ways: (1) pause until the full menu appears, which might happen as you read this; (2) click the double-arrow button at the bottom of the menu; or (3) double-click the menu name on the menu bar.

2. Pause until the full Insert menu appears, as shown in Figure 15. The Bookmark command and other commands are now visible.

| Figure 15 | EXPANDED, FULL MENU |

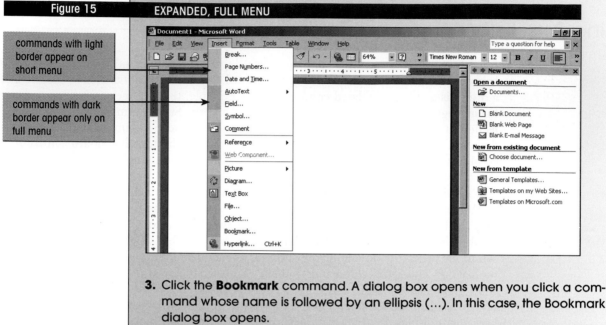

commands with light border appear on short menu

commands with dark border appear only on full menu

3. Click the **Bookmark** command. A dialog box opens when you click a command whose name is followed by an ellipsis (…). In this case, the Bookmark dialog box opens.

4. Click the **Cancel** button to close the Bookmark dialog box.

5. Click **Insert** on the menu bar again to display the short, personalized menu. The Bookmark command appears on the short, personalized menu because you used it.

6. Press the **Esc** key to close the menu.

As you can see, the menu changed based on your actions. Over time, only the commands you use frequently will appear on the personalized menu. The toolbars work similarly.

To use the personalized toolbars:

1. Observe that the Standard and Formatting toolbars appear side by side below the menu bar.

TROUBLE? If the toolbars appear on two rows, you need to reset them. Click Tools on the menu bar, click Customize, and then click the Options tab in the Customize dialog box. Click the Show Standard and Formatting toolbars on two rows check box to remove the check mark. Click the Reset my data usage button, and then click the Yes button to confirm you want to reset the commands. Click the Close button. Repeat Step 1.

The Formatting toolbar sits to the right of the Standard toolbar. You can see most of the Standard toolbar buttons, but only a few Formatting toolbar buttons.

2. Click the **Toolbar Options** button ⏩ at the right side of the Standard toolbar. See Figure 16.

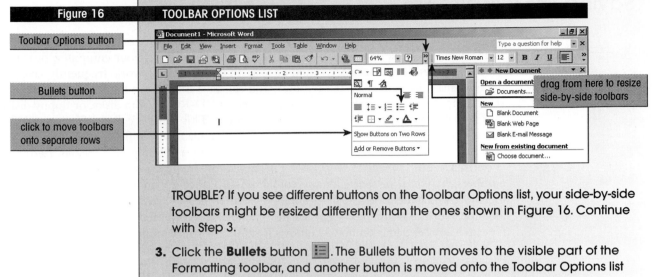

Figure 16 | **TOOLBAR OPTIONS LIST**

Toolbar Options button

Bullets button

click to move toolbars onto separate rows

drag from here to resize side-by-side toolbars

TROUBLE? If you see different buttons on the Toolbar Options list, your side-by-side toolbars might be resized differently than the ones shown in Figure 16. Continue with Step 3.

3. Click the **Bullets** button. The Bullets button moves to the visible part of the Formatting toolbar, and another button is moved onto the Toolbar Options list to make room for the new button.

   TROUBLE? If the Bullets button already appears on the Formatting toolbar, click another button on the Toolbar Options list. Then click that same button again in Step 4 to turn off that formatting.

4. Click again to turn off the Bullets formatting.

Some people like that the menus and toolbars change to meet their work habits. Others prefer to see all the menu commands or to display the toolbars on different rows so that all the buttons are always visible. You'll change the toolbar setting now.

To turn off the personalized toolbars:

1. Click the **Toolbar Options** button at the right side of the Standard toolbar.

2. Click the **Show Buttons on Two Rows command**. The toolbars move to separate rows (the Standard toolbar on top) and you can see all the buttons on each toolbar.

You can easily access any button on the toolbars with one mouse click. The drawback is that the toolbars take up more space in the program window.

Using Speech Recognition

Another way to perform tasks in Office is with your voice. Office's **speech recognition technology** enables you to say the names of the toolbar buttons, menus, menu commands, dialog box items, and so forth, rather than clicking the mouse or pressing keys to select them. The Language toolbar includes the Speech Balloon, which displays the voice command equivalents of a selected button or command. If you switch from Voice mode to Dictation mode, you can dictate the contents of your files rather than typing the text or numbers. For better accuracy, complete the Training Wizard, which helps Office learn your vocal quality, rate of talking, and speech patterns. To start using speech recognition, click Tools on the menu bar in any Office program, and then click Speech. The first time you start this feature, the Training Wizard guides you through the setup process.

Saving and Closing a File

As you create and modify Office files, your work is stored only in the computer's temporary memory, not on disk. If you were to exit the programs, turn off your computer, or experience a power failure, your work would be lost. To prevent losing work, frequently save your file to a disk—at least every ten minutes. You can save files to the hard disk located inside your computer or to portable storage disks, such as CD-ROMs, Zip disks, or floppy disks.

The first time you save a file, you need to name it. This name is called a **filename**. When you choose a filename, select a descriptive one that accurately reflects the content of the document, workbook, presentation, or database, such as "Shipping Options Letter" or "Fourth Quarter Financial Analysis." Filenames can include a maximum of 255 letters, numbers, hyphens, or spaces in any combination. Office appends a **file extension** to the filename, which identifies the program in which that file was created. The file extensions are .doc for Word, .xls for Excel, .ppt for PowerPoint, and .mdb for Access. Whether you see file extensions depends on how Windows is set up for your computer.

You also need to decide where you'll save the file—on which disk and in what folder. Choose a logical location that you'll remember whenever you want to use the file again.

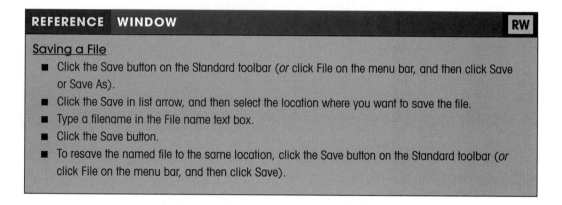

REFERENCE WINDOW   **RW**

Saving a File

- Click the Save button on the Standard toolbar (*or* click File on the menu bar, and then click Save or Save As).
- Click the Save in list arrow, and then select the location where you want to save the file.
- Type a filename in the File name text box.
- Click the Save button.
- To resave the named file to the same location, click the Save button on the Standard toolbar (*or* click File on the menu bar, and then click Save).

Nicole has asked you to start working on the agenda for the stockholder meeting. You enter text in a Word document by typing. After you type some text, you'll save the file.

To enter text in a document:

1. Type **Delmar Office Supplies**, and then press the **Enter** key. The text you typed appears on one line in the Word document.

   TROUBLE? If you make a typing error, press the Backspace key to delete the incorrect letters, and then retype the text.

2. Type **Stockholder Meeting Agenda**, and then press the **Enter** key. The text you typed appears on the second line.

The two lines of text you typed are not yet saved on disk. You'll do that now.

To save a file for the first time:

1. Insert your Data Disk in the appropriate drive.

TROUBLE? If you don't have a Data Disk, you need to get one before you can proceed. Your instructor or technical support person will either give you one or ask you to make your own by following the instructions on the "Read This Before You Begin" page at the beginning of this tutorial. See your instructor or technical support person for more information.

2. Click the **Save** button 🖫 on the Standard toolbar. The Save As dialog box opens. See Figure 17. The first few words of the first line appear in the File name text box, as a suggested filename. You'll replace this with a more descriptive filename.

Figure 17	SAVE AS DIALOG BOX

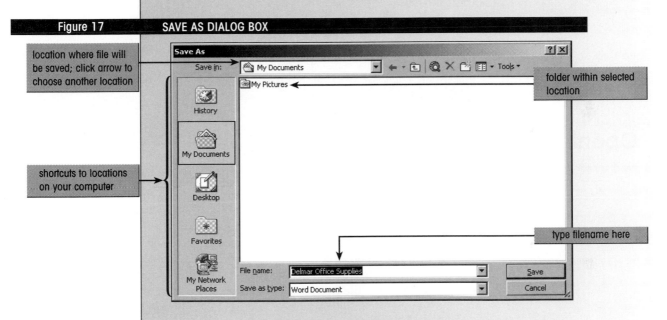

TROUBLE? If the .doc file extension appears after the filename, then your computer is configured to show file extensions. Just continue with Step 3.

3. Type **Stockholder Meeting Agenda** in the File name text box.

4. Click the **Save in** list arrow, and then click the drive that contains your Data Disk.

5. Double-click the **Tutorial.01** folder in the list box, and then double-click the **Tutorial** folder. This is the location where you want to save the document.

6. Click the **Save** button. The Save As dialog box closes, and the name of your file appears in the program window title bar.

The saved file includes everything in the document at the time you saved. Any edits or additions you then make to the document exist only in the computer's memory and are not saved in the file on the disk. As you work, remember to save frequently so that the file is updated to reflect the latest content of the document.

Because you already named the document and selected a storage location, the second and subsequent times you save, the Save As dialog box doesn't open. If you wanted to save a copy of the file with a different filename or to a different location, you would reopen the Save As dialog box by clicking File on the menu bar, and then clicking Save As. The previous version of the file remains on your disk as well.

You need to add your name to the agenda. Then you'll save your changes and close the file. You can close a file by clicking the Close command on the File menu or by clicking the Close Window button in the upper-right corner of the menu bar.

To modify, save, and close a file:

1. Type your name, and then press the **Enter** key. The text you typed appears on the next line.

2. Click the **Save** button 🖫 on the Standard toolbar.

   The updated document is saved to the file. When you're done with a file, you can close it. Although you can keep multiple files open at one time, you should close any file you are no longer working on to conserve system resources.

3. Click the **Close Window** button ⊠ on the Word menu bar to close the document. Word is still running, but no documents are open.

   TROUBLE? If a dialog box opens and asks whether you want to save the changes you made to the document, you modified the document since you last saved. Click the Yes button to save the current version and close it.

Opening a File

Once you have a program open, you can create additional new files for the open programs or you can open previously created and saved files. You can do both of these from the New Task Pane. The New Task Pane enables you to create new files and open existing ones. The name of the Task Pane varies, depending on the program you are using: Word has the New Document Task Pane, Excel has the New Workbook Task Pane, PowerPoint has the New Presentation Task Pane, and Access has the New File Task Pane.

When you want to work on a previously created file, you must open it first. Opening a file transfers a copy of the file from the storage disk (either a hard disk or a portable disk) to the computer's memory and displays it on your screen. The file is then in your computer's memory and on the disk.

REFERENCE WINDOW   RW

Opening an Existing or New File

- Click File on the menu bar, click New, and then (depending on the program) click the More documents, More workbooks, More presentations, or More files link in the New Task Pane (*or* click the Open button on the Standard toolbar *or* click File on the menu bar, and then click Open).
- Click the Look in list arrow, and then select the storage location of the file you want to open.
- Click the filename of the file you want to open.
- Click the Open button.

or

- Click File on the menu bar, click New, and then (depending on the program) click the Blank Document, Blank Workbook, Blank Presentation, or Blank Database link in the New Task Pane (*or* click the New button on the Standard toolbar).

Nicole asks you to print the agenda. To do that, you'll reopen the file. Because Word is still open, you'll use the New Document Task Pane.

To open an existing file:

1. If necessary, click **File** on the menu bar, and then click **New** to display the New Document Task Pane. See Figure 18.

| Figure 18 | NEW DOCUMENT TASK PANE |

click to open an existing document

click to open a new, blank document

click to open a copy of an existing document

click to close Task Pane

2. Click the **Documents** link in the Open a document area of the New Document Task Pane. The Open dialog box, which works similarly to the Save As dialog box, opens.

   TROUBLE? If you don't see the Documents link, look for a More Documents link below a list of recently opened files. The link name changes from Documents to More Documents after you have opened a file.

3. Click the **Look in** list arrow, and then select the **Tutorial** folder within the **Tutorial.01** folder on your Data Disk. This is the location where you saved the agenda document.

4. Click **Stockholder Meeting Agenda** in the file list. See Figure 19.

| Figure 19 | OPEN DIALOG BOX |

files in this folder are displayed below

agenda file to open and print

5. Click the **Open** button. The file you saved earlier reopens in the Word program window, and the New Document Task Pane closes.

After the file is open, you can view, edit, print, or resave it.

Printing a File

At times, you'll want a paper copy of your Office file. The first time you print during each computer session, you should use the Print menu command to open the Print dialog box so you can verify or adjust the printing settings. You can select a printer, the number of copies to print, the portion of the file to print, and so forth; the printing settings vary slightly from program to program. For subsequent print jobs you can use the Print button to print without opening the dialog box, if you want to use the same default settings.

REFERENCE WINDOW   RW
Printing a File
■ Click File on the menu bar, and then click Print.
■ Verify the print settings in the Print dialog box.
■ Click the OK button.
or
■ Click the Print button on the Standard toolbar.

You'll print the agenda document.

To print a file:

1. Make sure your printer is turned on and contains paper.

2. Click **File** on the menu bar, and then click **Print**. The Print dialog box opens. See Figure 20.

Figure 20	PRINT DIALOG BOX

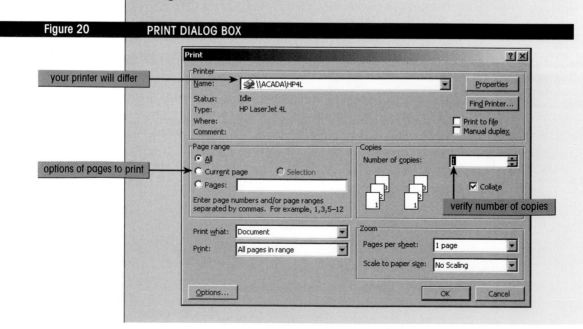

3. Verify that the correct printer appears in the Name list box. If the wrong printer appears, click the **Name** list arrow, and then click the correct printer from the list of available printers.

4. Verify that **1** appears in the Number of copies text box.

5. Click the **OK** button to print the document. See Figure 21.

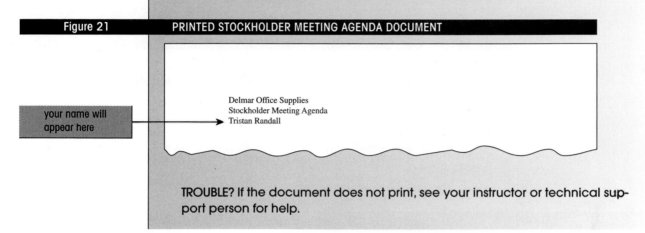

| Figure 21 | PRINTED STOCKHOLDER MEETING AGENDA DOCUMENT |

your name will appear here

Delmar Office Supplies
Stockholder Meeting Agenda
Tristan Randall

TROUBLE? If the document does not print, see your instructor or technical support person for help.

Another important aspect of Office is the ability to get help right from your computer.

Getting Help

If you don't know how to perform a task or want more information about a feature, you can turn to Office itself for information on how to use it. This information, referred to simply as **Help**, is like a huge encyclopedia stored on your computer. You can access it in a variety of ways.

There are two fast and simple methods you can use to get Help about objects you see on the screen. First, you can position the mouse pointer over a toolbar button to view its **ScreenTip**, a yellow box with the button's name. Second, you can click the **What's This?** command on the Help menu to change the pointer to ▷**?**, which you can click on any toolbar button, menu command, dialog box option, worksheet cell, or anything else you can see on your screen to view a brief description of that item.

For more in-depth help, you can use the **Ask a Question** box, located on the menu bar of every Office program, to find information in the Help system. You simply type a question using everyday language about a task you want to perform or a topic you need help with, and then press the Enter key to search the Help system. The Ask a Question box expands to show Help topics related to your query. You click a topic to open a Help window with step-by-step instructions that guide you through a specific procedure and explanations of difficult concepts in clear, easy-to-understand language. For example, you might ask how to format a cell in an Excel worksheet; a list of Help topics related to the words you typed will appear. The Help window also has Contents, Answer Wizard, and Index tabs, which you can use to look up information directly from the Help window.

If you prefer, you can ask questions of the **Office Assistant**, an interactive guide to finding information from the Help system. In addition, the Office Assistant can provide Help topics and tips on tasks as you work. For example, it might offer a tip when you select a menu command instead of clicking the corresponding toolbar button. You can turn on or off the tips, depending on your personal preference.

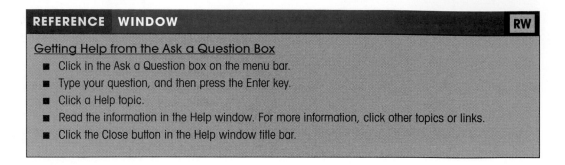

REFERENCE   WINDOW   RW

Getting Help from the Ask a Question Box
- Click in the Ask a Question box on the menu bar.
- Type your question, and then press the Enter key.
- Click a Help topic.
- Read the information in the Help window. For more information, click other topics or links.
- Click the Close button in the Help window title bar.

You'll use the Ask a Question box to obtain more information about Help.

To use the Ask a Question box:

1. Click in the **Ask a Question** box on the menu bar, and then type **How do I search help?**.

2. Press the **Enter** key to retrieve a list of topics, as shown in Figure 22.

Figure 22   ASK A QUESTION BOX WITH HELP TOPICS

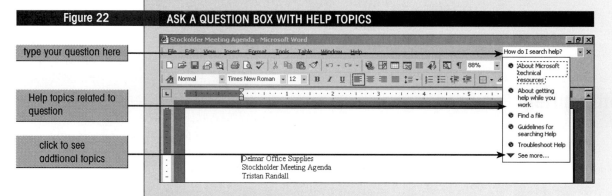

type your question here

Help topics related to question

click to see addtional topics

3. Click the **See more** link, review the additional Help topics, and then click the **See previous** link.

4. Click **About getting help while you work** to open the Help window and learn more about the various ways to obtain assistance in Office. See Figure 23.

Figure 23   HELP WINDOW

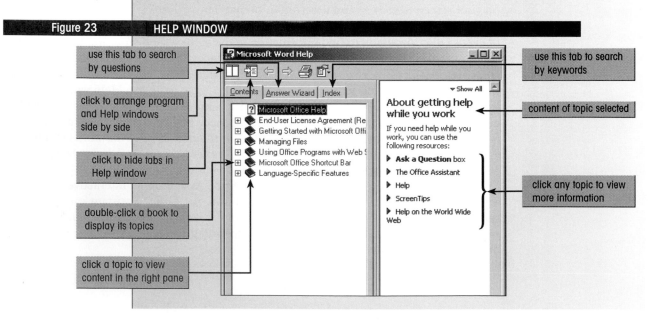

use this tab to search by questions

click to arrange program and Help windows side by side

click to hide tabs in Help window

double-click a book to display its topics

click a topic to view content in the right pane

use this tab to search by keywords

content of topic selected

click any topic to view more information

5. Click **Help** in the right pane to display information about that topic.

6. Click the other links about Help features and read the information.

7. When you're done, click the **Close** button ☒ in the Help window title bar to return to the Word window.

The Help features enable the staff at Delmar Office Supplies to get answers to questions they have about any task or procedure when they need it. The more you practice getting information from the Help system, the more effective you will be at using Office to its full potential.

Exiting Programs

Whenever you finish working with a program, you should exit it. As with many other aspects of Office, you can exit programs with a button or from a menu. You'll use both methods to close Word and Excel.

To exit a program:

1. Click the **Close** button ☒ in the upper-right corner of the screen to exit Word. Word exits, and the Excel window is visible again on your screen.

   TROUBLE? If a dialog box opens, asking whether you want to save the document, you may have inadvertently made a change to the document. Click the No button.

2. Click **File** on the menu bar, and then click **Exit**. The Excel program exits.

Exiting programs after you are done using them keeps your Windows desktop uncluttered for the next person using the computer, frees up your system's resources, and prevents data from being lost accidentally.

QUICK CHECK

1. Which Office program would you use to write a letter?
2. Which Office programs could you use to store customer names and addresses?
3. What is integration?
4. Explain the difference between Save As and Save.
5. What is the purpose of the New Task Pane?
6. When would you use the Ask a Question box?

REVIEW ASSIGNMENTS

Before the stockholders meeting at Delmar Office Supplies, you'll open and print documents for the upcoming presentation.

1. Start PowerPoint using the Start button and the Programs menu.

2. Use the Ask a Question box to learn how to change the toolbar buttons from small to large, and then do it. Use the same procedure to change the buttons back to regular size. Close the Help window when you're done.

3. Open a blank Excel workbook using the New Office Document command on the Start menu.

Explore ▶ 4. Switch to the PowerPoint window using the taskbar, and then close the presentation but leave open the PowerPoint program. (*Hint:* Click the Close Window button in the menu bar.)

Explore ▶ 5. Open a new, blank PowerPoint presentation from the New Presentation Task Pane. (*Hint:* Click Blank Presentation in the New area of the New Presentation Task Pane.)

6. Close the PowerPoint presentation and program using the Close button in the PowerPoint title bar; do not save changes if asked.

Explore ▶ 7. Open a copy of the Excel **Finances** workbook located in the **Review** folder within the **Tutorial.01** folder on your Data Disk using the New Workbook Task Pane. (*Hint:* Click File on the Excel menu bar and then click New to open the Task Pane. Click Choose Workbook in the New from existing workbook area of the New Workbook Task Pane; the dialog box functions similarly to the Open dialog box.)

8. Type your name, and then press the Enter key to insert your name at the top of the worksheet.

9. Save the worksheet as **Delmar Finances** in the **Review** folder within the **Tutorial.01** folder on your Data Disk.

10. Print one copy of the worksheet using the Print command on the File menu.

11. Exit Excel using the File menu.

Explore ▶ 12. Open the **Letter** document located in the **Review** folder within the **Tutorial.01** folder on your Data Disk using the Open Office Document command on the Start menu.

13. Use the Save As command to save the document with the filename **Delmar Letter** in the **Review** folder within the **Tutorial.01** folder on your Data Disk.

Explore ▶ 14. Press and hold the Ctrl key, press the End key, and then release both keys to move the insertion point to the end of the letter, and then type your name.

15. Use the Save button on the Standard toolbar to save the change to the Delmar Letter document.

16. Print one copy of the document, and then close the document.

17. Exit the Word program using the Close button on the title bar.

QUICK | CHECK ANSWERS

1. Word
2. Access or Outlook
3. the ability to share information between programs
4. Save As enables you to change the filename and save location of a file. Save updates a file to reflect its latest contents using its current filename and location.
5. enables you to create new files and open existing files
6. when you don't know how to perform a task or want more information about a feature

New Perspectives on

MICROSOFT®
WORD 2002

Read This Before You Begin

To the Student

Data Disks

To complete the Level I tutorials, Review Assignments, and Case Problems, you need one Data Disk. Your instructor will either provide you with the Data Disk or ask you to make your own.

If you are making your own Data Disk, you will need **one** blank, formatted high-density disk. You will need to copy a set of files and/or folders from a file server, standalone computer, or the Web onto your disk. Your instructor will tell you which computer, drive letter, and folders contain the files you need. You could also download the files by going to **www.course.com** and following the instructions on the screen.

The information below shows you which folders go on your disk, so that you will have enough disk space to complete all the tutorials, Review Assignments, and Case Problems:

Data Disk 1

Write this on the disk label:
Data Disk 1: Word 2002 Tutorials 1-4

Put these folders on the disk:
Tutorial.01, Tutorial.02, Tutorial.03, Tutorial.04, Web

When you begin each tutorial, be sure you are using the correct Data Disk. Refer to the File Finder chart at the back of this text for more detailed information on which files are used in which tutorials. See the inside front or inside back cover of this book for more information on Data Disk files, or ask your instructor or technical support person for assistance.

Course Labs

The Word Level I tutorials feature an interactive Course Lab to help you understand word processing concepts.

There are Lab Assignments at the end of Tutorial 1 that relate to this Lab.

To start a Lab, click the **Start** button on the Windows taskbar, point to **Programs**, point to **Course Labs**, point to **New Perspectives Course Labs**, and then click the name of the Lab you want to use.

Using Your Own Computer

If you are going to work through this book using your own computer, you need:

- **Computer System** Microsoft Windows 98, NT, 2000 Professional, or higher must be installed on your computer. This book assumes a typical installation of Microsoft Word.

- **Data Disk** You will not be able to complete the tutorials or exercises in this book using your own computer until you have your Data Disk.

- **Course Labs** See your instructor or technical support person to obtain the Course Lab software for use on your own computer.

Visit Our World Wide Web Site

Additional materials designed especially for you are available on the World Wide Web.
Go to www.course.com/NewPerspectives.

To the Instructor

The Data Disk Files and Course Labs are available on the Instructor's Resource Kit for this title. Follow the instructions in the Help file on the CD-ROM to install the programs to your network or standalone computer. For information on creating Data Disks or the Course Labs, see the "To the Student" section above.

You are granted a license to copy the Data Files and Course Labs to any computer or computer network used by students who have purchased this book.

Student downloads

ISBN # on title = 0 — 619-02097-0
may not need "-" 's

LAB

Word Processing

CREATING A DOCUMENT

Writing a Business Letter for Art4U Inc.

CASE

Creating a Contract Letter for Art4U Inc.

Megan Grahs is the owner and manager of Art4U Inc., a graphics design firm in Tucson, Arizona. When Megan founded Art4U in the early 1980s, the company drew most of its revenue from design projects for local magazines, newspapers, advertising circulars, and other print publications. The artists at Art4U laboriously created logos, diagrams, and other illustrations by hand, using watercolors, ink, pastels, and a variety of other media. Since the advent of the Internet, however, Art4U has become one of the Southwest's leading creators of electronic artwork. The firm's artists now work exclusively on computers, saving each piece of art as an electronic file that they can e-mail to a client in a matter of minutes.

Thanks to e-mail, Art4U is no longer limited to the local Tucson market. As a result, Art4U has nearly doubled in size over the past few years. Most of the increase in business has come from Web page designers, who continually need fresh and innovative graphics to use in their Web pages. In fact, Megan has just signed a contract with Web Time Productions agreeing to create a series of logos for a high-profile Web site. She needs to return the signed contract to Web Time's office in Chicago.

In this tutorial, you will create the cover letter that will accompany the contract. You will create the letter using Microsoft Word 2002, a popular word-processing program. Before you begin typing the letter, you will learn to start the Word program, identify and use the elements of the Word screen, and adjust some Word settings. Next you will create a new Word document, type the text of the cover letter, save the letter, and then print the letter for Megan. In the process of entering the text, you'll learn several ways to correct typing errors.

SESSION 1.1

In this session you will learn how to start Word, identify and use the parts of the Word window, and adjust some Word settings. With the skills you learn in this session, you'll be prepared to use Word to create a variety of documents, such as letters, reports, and memos.

Four Steps to a Professional Document

Word helps you produce quality work in minimal time. Not only can you type a document in Word, but you can also quickly make revisions and corrections, adjust margins and spacing, create columns and tables, and add graphics to your documents. The most efficient way to produce a document is to follow these four steps: (1) planning and creating, (2) editing, (3) formatting, and (4) printing.

In the long run, *planning* saves time and effort. First, you should determine what you want to say. State your purpose clearly and include enough information to achieve that purpose without overwhelming or boring your reader. Be sure to *organize* your ideas logically. Decide how you want your document to look as well. In this case, your letter to Web Time Productions will take the form of a standard business letter. It should be addressed to Web Time's president, Nicholas Brower. Megan has given you a handwritten note indicating what she would like you to say in the letter. This note is shown in Figure 1-1.

Figure 1-1	MEGAN'S NOTES FOR CONTRACT LETTER

Please write a cover letter for the Web Time Productions contract. In the letter please include the following questions:

- When will we receive a complete schedule for the project?
- How many preliminary designs do you require?
- Will you be available to discuss the project with our artists via a conference call next week?

Send the letter to Web Time's president, Nicholas Brower. The address is: 2210 West Sycamore Avenue, Chicago, IL 60025.

After you plan your document, you can go ahead and *create* it using Word. This generally means typing the text of your document. The next step, *editing*, consists of reading the document you've created, correcting your errors, and, finally, adding or deleting text to make the document easy to read.

Once your document is error-free, you can *format* it to make it visually appealing. Formatting features, such as adjusting margins to create white space (blank areas of a page), setting line spacing, and using boldface and italics, can help make your document easier to read. *Printing* is the final phase in creating an effective document. In this tutorial, you will preview your document before you spend time and resources to print it.

Exploring the Word Window

Before you can apply these four steps to produce a letter in Word, you need to start Word and learn about the general organization of the Word window. You'll do that now.

To start Microsoft Word:

1. Make sure Windows is running on your computer and that you can see the Windows desktop on your screen.

2. Click the **Start** button on the taskbar to display the Start menu, and then point to **Programs** to display the Programs menu.

3. Point to **Microsoft Word** on the Programs menu. Depending on how your computer is set up, you might see a small yellow box (called a ScreenTip) containing an explanation of some common uses for Microsoft Word. See Figure 1-2.

Figure 1-2	STARTING MICROSOFT WORD

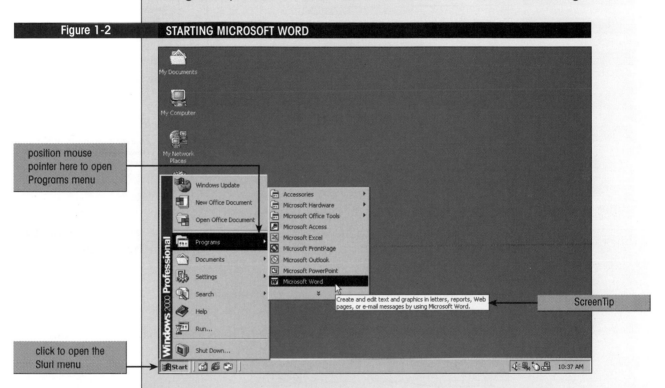

position mouse pointer here to open Programs menu

click to open the Start menu

ScreenTip

TROUBLE? Don't worry if your screen differs slightly from Figure 1-2. Although the figures in this book were created while running Windows 2000 in its default settings, Microsoft Word should run equally well using Windows 98, Windows 2000, Windows Millennium Edition, or Windows NT 4 (with Service Pack 6 installed).

TROUBLE? If you don't see the Microsoft Word option on the Programs menu, ask your instructor or technical support person for help.

TROUBLE? If the Office Shortcut Bar appears on your screen, your system is set up to display it. Because the Office Shortcut Bar is not required to complete these tutorials, it has been omitted from the figures in this text. You can close it or simply ignore it.

4. Click **Microsoft Word**. After a short pause, the Microsoft Word copyright information appears in a message box and remains on the screen until the Word program window opens. See Figure 1-3.

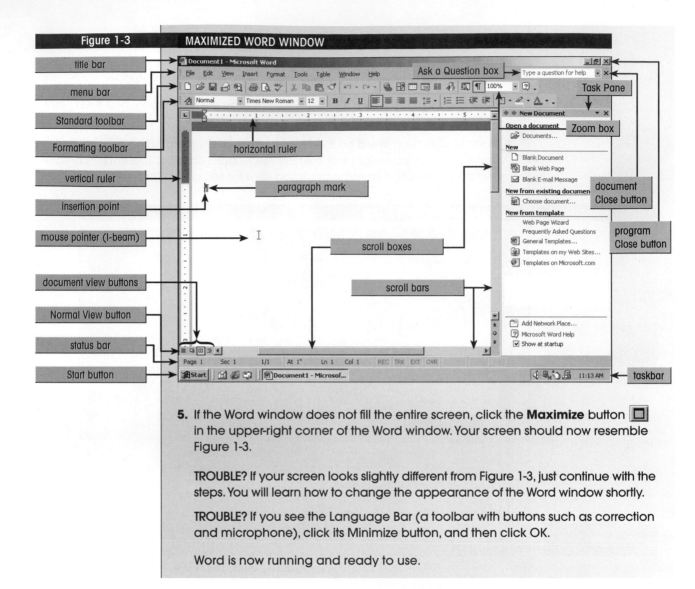

Figure 1-3 MAXIMIZED WORD WINDOW

- title bar
- menu bar
- Standard toolbar
- Formatting toolbar
- vertical ruler
- insertion point
- mouse pointer (I-beam)
- document view buttons
- Normal View button
- status bar
- Start button
- horizontal ruler
- paragraph mark
- scroll boxes
- scroll bars
- Ask a Question box
- Task Pane
- Zoom box
- document Close button
- program Close button
- taskbar

5. If the Word window does not fill the entire screen, click the **Maximize** button ☐ in the upper-right corner of the Word window. Your screen should now resemble Figure 1-3.

TROUBLE? If your screen looks slightly different from Figure 1-3, just continue with the steps. You will learn how to change the appearance of the Word window shortly.

TROUBLE? If you see the Language Bar (a toolbar with buttons such as correction and microphone), click its Minimize button, and then click OK.

Word is now running and ready to use.

The Word window is made up of a number of elements which are described in Figure 1-4. You are already familiar with some of these elements, such as the menu bar, title bar, and status bar, because they are common to all Windows programs. Don't be concerned if you don't see everything shown in Figure 1-3. You'll learn how to adjust the appearance of the Word window soon.

Figure 1-4 PARTS OF THE WORD WINDOW

SCREEN ELEMENT	DESCRIPTION
Ask a Question box	Allows you to type a question for Word Help
Document Close button	Closes the current document
Document view buttons	Switches the document between four different views: Normal view, Web Layout view, Print Layout view, and Outline view
Document window	Area where you enter text and graphics
Formatting toolbar	Contains buttons to activate common font and paragraph formatting commands

Figure 1-4	PARTS OF THE WORD WINDOW (CONTINUED)
SCREEN ELEMENT	**DESCRIPTION**
Horizontal ruler	Adjusts margins, tabs, and column widths; vertical ruler appears in Print Layout view
Insertion point	Indicates location where characters will be inserted or deleted
Menu bar	Contains lists or menus of all the Word commands. When you first display a menu, you see a short list of the most frequently used commands. To see the full list of commands in the menu, you can either click the menu and then wait a few seconds for the remaining commands to appear, or click the menu and then click or point to the downward-facing double-arrow at the bottom of the menu.
Mouse pointer	Changes shape depending on its location on the screen (i.e., I-beam pointer in text area; arrow in nontext areas)
Paragraph mark	Marks the end of a paragraph
Program Close button	Closes the current document if more than one document is open; closes Word if one or no document is open
Scroll bars	Shift text vertically and horizontally on the screen so you can see different parts of the document
Scroll box	Helps you move quickly to other pages of your document
Standard toolbar	Contains buttons to activate frequently used commands
Start button	Starts a program, opens a document, provides quick access to Windows Help
Status bar	Provides information regarding the location of the insertion point
Taskbar	Shows programs that are running and allows you to switch quickly from one program to another
Task Pane	Contains buttons and options for common tasks
Title bar	Identifies the current application (i.e., Microsoft Word); shows the filename of the current document
Zoom box	Changes the document window magnification

If at any time you would like to check the name of a Word toolbar button, position the mouse pointer over the button without clicking. A **ScreenTip**, a small yellow box with the name of the button, will appear. (If you don't see ScreenTips on your computer, click Tools on the Word menu bar, click Options, click the View tab, click the ScreenTips check box to insert a check, and then click OK.)

Keep in mind that the commands on the menu bars initially display the commands that are used most frequently on your particular computer. When you leave the menu open for a few seconds or point to the double-arrow, a complete list of commands appears. Throughout these tutorials, you should point to the double-arrow on a menu if you do not see the command you need.

Setting Up the Window Before You Begin Each Tutorial

Word provides a set of standard settings, called **default settings**, that control how the screen is set up, and how a document looks when you first start typing. These settings are appropriate for most situations. However, these settings are easily changed, and most people begin a work session by adjusting Word to make sure it is set up the way they want it.

When you become more comfortable using Word, you will learn how to customize Word to suit your needs. But to make it easier to follow the steps in these tutorials, you should take care to arrange your window to match the tutorial figures. The rest of this section explains what your window should look like and how to make it match those in the tutorials. Depending on how many people use your computer (and how much they adjust Word's appearance), you might have to set up the window to match the figures each time you start Word.

Closing the Task Pane

The **Task Pane** is part of the Word window that you can use to perform common chores, such as sending e-mail. By default, the Task Pane appears on the right side of the Word window (as in Figure 1-5) when you start Word.

Figure 1-5	TASK PANE IN THE WORD WINDOW

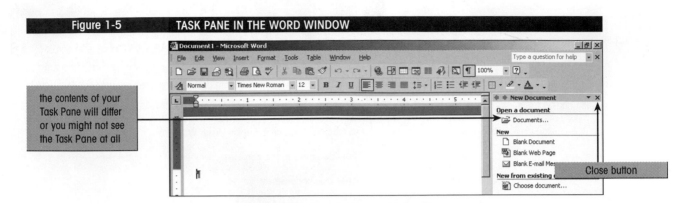

the contents of your Task Pane will differ or you might not see the Task Pane at all

Close button

Depending on how your computer is currently set up, your Task Pane might look different from the one in Figure 1-5, or you might not see the Task Pane at all. When you become a more experienced Word user, you will learn how to take advantage of the Task Pane to work more efficiently. But for now you will close it, using the Close button shown in Figure 1-5.

To close the Task Pane:

1. If the Task Pane is open on your computer, click its **Close** button ☒. The Document window expands to fill the space left by the Task Pane.

Setting the Document View to Normal

You can view your document in one of four ways—Normal, Web Layout, Print Layout, or Outline. **Web Layout view** and **Outline view** are designed for special situations that you don't need to worry about now. You will learn more about **Print Layout view**—which allows you to see a page's overall design and format—in later tutorials. In Print Layout view, Word displays both a horizontal ruler (below the toolbars) and a vertical ruler (along the left side of the Document window). For this tutorial you will use **Normal view**, which allows you to see more of the document than Print Layout view. By default, Word often displays the document in Print Layout view, just as it is in Figure 1-5. For this tutorial, you need to display the document in Normal view.

To make sure the Document window is in Normal view:

1. Click the **Normal View** button ▤ to the left of the horizontal scroll bar. See Figure 1-6. If your Document window was not in Normal view, it changes to Normal view now. The Normal View button is outlined, indicating that it is selected.

Figure 1-6   CHANGING TO NORMAL VIEW

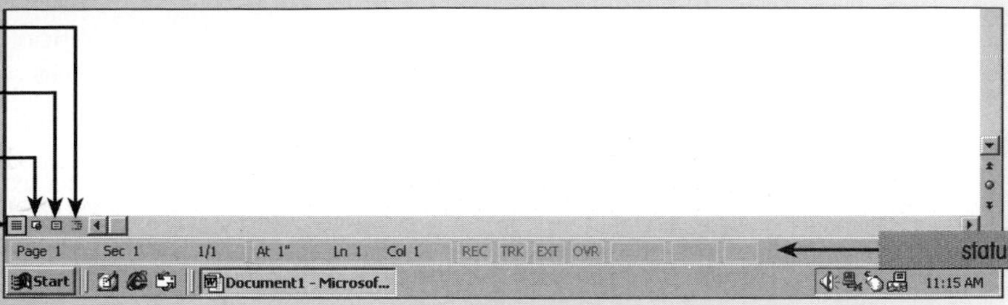

Outline View button

Print Layout button

Web Layout button

Normal View button

status bar

Page 1   Sec 1   1/1   At 1"   Ln 1   Col 1   REC TRK EXT OVR

Start   Document1 - Microsof...   11:15 AM

Displaying the Toolbars and Ruler

The Word toolbars allow you to perform common tasks quickly by clicking a button. In the Word tutorials, you will most often use the Standard toolbar and the Formatting toolbar. While working through these tutorials, you should check to make sure that only the Formatting and Standard toolbars appear on your screen. The Standard toolbar should be positioned on top of the Formatting toolbar, just as they are in Figure 1-7.

Figure 1-7   STANDARD TOOLBAR ON TOP OF FORMATTING TOOLBAR

Standard toolbar

Formatting toolbar

Depending on the settings specified by the last person to use your computer, you may not see both toolbars or your toolbars may all appear on one row. You also may see additional toolbars, such as the Drawing toolbar. In the following steps, you will make sure that your Word window shows only the Standard and Formatting toolbars. Later you will make sure that they are stacked on top of each other.

To verify that your Word window shows the correct toolbars:

1. Position the pointer over any toolbar and click the right mouse button. A shortcut menu appears. The menu lists all available toolbars with a check mark next to those currently displayed. If the Standard and Formatting toolbars are currently displayed on your computer, you should see check marks next to their names.

   TROUBLE? If you don't see any toolbars on your screen, click Tools on the menu bar, click Customize, and then click the Toolbars tab. Click the Standard and Formatting check boxes to insert a check in each, and then click Close. To gain practice using a shortcut menu, begin again with Step 1, above.

2. Verify that you see a check mark next to the word "Standard" in the shortcut menu. If you do not see a check mark, click **Standard** now. (Clicking any item on the shortcut menu closes the menu, so you will need to re-open it in the next step.)

3. Redisplay the shortcut menu, if necessary, and look for a check mark next to the word "Formatting."

4. Redisplay the shortcut menu, if necessary. If any toolbars besides the Formatting and Standard toolbars have check marks, click each one to remove the check mark and hide the toolbar. When you are finished, only the Standard and Formatting toolbars should have check marks.

If the toolbars appear on one row, perform the next steps to arrange the toolbars on two rows.

To arrange the Standard toolbar and the Formatting toolbar on two rows:

1. Click **Tools** on the menu bar, and then click **Customize**. The Customize dialog box opens.

   TROUBLE? If you don't see the Customize command on the Tools menu, point to the double arrow, as explained earlier in this tutorial, to show the full list of commands.

2. Click the **Options** tab, and then click the **Show Standard and Formatting toolbars on two rows** check box to select it (that is, to insert a check).

3. Click **Close**. The Customize dialog box closes. The toolbars on your screen should now match those shown earlier in Figure 1-7.

Displaying the Horizontal Ruler

In Normal view, you can use the **Horizontal ruler** to position text on the page. As you complete these tutorials, the ruler should be visible to help you place items precisely. If the ruler is not displayed on your screen as it is in Figure 1-8, you need to perform the following steps.

Figure 1-8	HORIZONTAL RULER DISPLAYED IN NORMAL VIEW

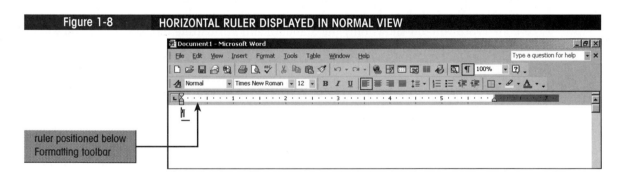

ruler positioned below Formatting toolbar

To display the ruler:

1. Click **View** on the menu bar, and then point to the **double-arrow** at the bottom of the menu to display the hidden menu commands.

2. If "Ruler" does not have a check mark next to it, click **Ruler**. The horizontal ruler should now be displayed, as shown earlier in Figure 1-8.

Selecting a Zoom Setting

You can use the **Zoom box** on the Standard toolbar to change the magnification of the Document window. (The Zoom box is shown in Figure 1-9.) This is useful when you need a close-up view of a document—especially if you have difficulty reading small print on a computer screen. You will learn how to use the Zoom box later. For now you just need to know how to make the Zoom setting match the figures in these tutorials. By default, the Zoom setting is 100% when you first start Word (as it is in Figure 1-9). But the Zoom setting you see now depends on the setting used by the last person to work with Word on your computer. If your Zoom setting is not 100%, you need to perform the following steps.

Figure 1-9   **ZOOM BOX IN STANDARD TOOLBAR**

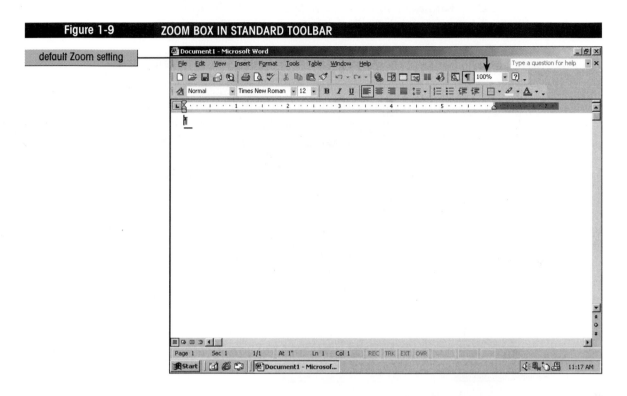

To adjust the Zoom setting:

1. Click the **list arrow** in the Zoom box. A list of settings appears.

2. Click **100%**. The list box closes, and 100% appears in the Zoom box, as shown in Figure 1-9.

Setting the Font and Font Size

A **font** is a set of characters that has a certain design, shape, and appearance. Each font has a name, such as Courier, Times New Roman, or Arial. The **font size** is the actual height of a character, measured in points, where one point equals 1/72 of an inch in height. You'll learn more about fonts and font sizes later, but for now keep in mind that most documents you create will use the Times New Roman font in a font size of 12 points. Word usually uses a default setting of Times New Roman 12 point, but someone else might have changed the setting after Word was installed on your computer. You can see your computer's current settings in the Font list box and the Font Size list box in the Formatting toolbar, as shown in Figure 1-10.

Figure 1-10   **DEFAULT FONT AND FONT SIZE SETTINGS**

If your font setting is not Times New Roman 12 point, you should change the default setting now. You'll use the menu bar to choose the commands.

To change the default font and font size:

1. Click **Format** on the menu bar, and then click **Font**. The Font dialog box opens. If necessary, click the **Font** tab. See Figure 1-11.

Figure 1-11	FONT DIALOG BOX

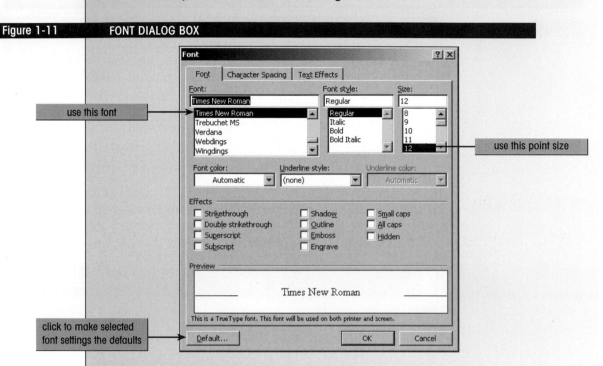

2. In the Font text box, click **Times New Roman**.

3. In the Size list box, click **12**.

4. Click the **Default** button to make Times New Roman and 12 point the default settings. Word displays a message asking you to verify that you want to make 12 point Times New Roman the default font.

5. Click **Yes**.

Displaying Nonprinting Characters

Nonprinting characters are symbols that can appear on the screen but do not show up when you print a document. You can display nonprinting characters when you are working on the appearance, or **format**, of your document. For example, one nonprinting character marks the end of a paragraph (¶), and another marks the space between words (•). It's helpful to display nonprinting characters so you can see whether you've typed an extra space, ended a paragraph, and so on.

Depending on how your computer is set up, nonprinting characters might have been displayed automatically when you started Word. In Figure 1-12, you can see the paragraph symbol (¶) in the blank Document window. Also, the Show/Hide ¶ button is outlined in the Standard toolbar. Both of these indicate that nonprinting characters are displayed. If they are not displayed on your screen, you need to perform the following steps.

Figure 1-12	NONPRINTING CHARACTERS DISPLAYED

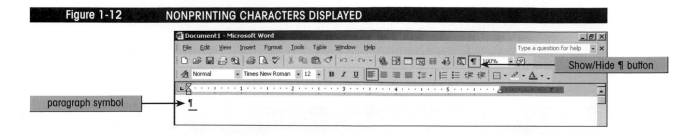

paragraph symbol →

To display nonprinting characters:

1. Click the **Show/Hide ¶** button ![¶] on the Standard toolbar. A paragraph mark (¶) appears at the top of the Document window. Your screen should now match Figure 1-12. To make sure your window always matches the figures in these tutorials, remember to complete the checklist in Figure 1-13 each time you sit down at the computer.

TROUBLE? If the Show/Hide ¶ button was already highlighted before you clicked it, you have now deactivated it. Click the Show/Hide ¶ button a second time to select it.

Figure 1-13	WORD WINDOW CHECKLIST

SCREEN ELEMENT	SETTING	CHECK
Document view	Normal view	☐
Word window	Maximized	☐
Standard toolbar	Displayed, below the menu bar	☐
Formatting toolbar	Displayed, below the Standard toolbar	☐
Other toolbars	Hidden	☐
Nonprinting characters	Displayed	☐
Font	Times New Roman	☐
Point size	12 point	☐
Ruler	Displayed	☐
Task Pane	Closed	☐
Zoom box	100%	☐

Now that you have planned your letter, opened Word, identified screen elements, and adjusted settings, you are ready to begin typing a letter. In the next session, you will create Megan's letter to Web Time Productions.

Session 1.1 QUICK CHECK

1. In your own words, list the steps in creating a document.
2. How do you start Word from the Windows desktop?
3. Define each of the following in your own words:
   a. nonprinting characters   c. font size
   b. document view buttons   d. default settings

4. Explain how to change the default font size.
5. Explain how to display or hide the Formatting toolbar.
6. Explain how to change the document view to Normal view.
7. To close the Task Pane, you need to use a command on the menu bar. True or False?

SESSION 1.2

In this session you will create a one-page document using Word. You'll correct errors and scroll through your document. You'll also name, save, preview, and print the document. Finally, you will create an envelope for the letter.

Beginning a Letter

Word Processing

You're ready to begin typing Megan's letter to Nicholas Brower at Web Time Productions. Figure 1-14 shows the completed letter printed on company letterhead. You'll begin by opening a new blank page (in case you accidentally typed something in the current page). Then you'll move the insertion point to about 2.5 inches from the top margin of the paper to allow space for the Art4U letterhead.

Figure 1-14   **COMPLETED LETTER**

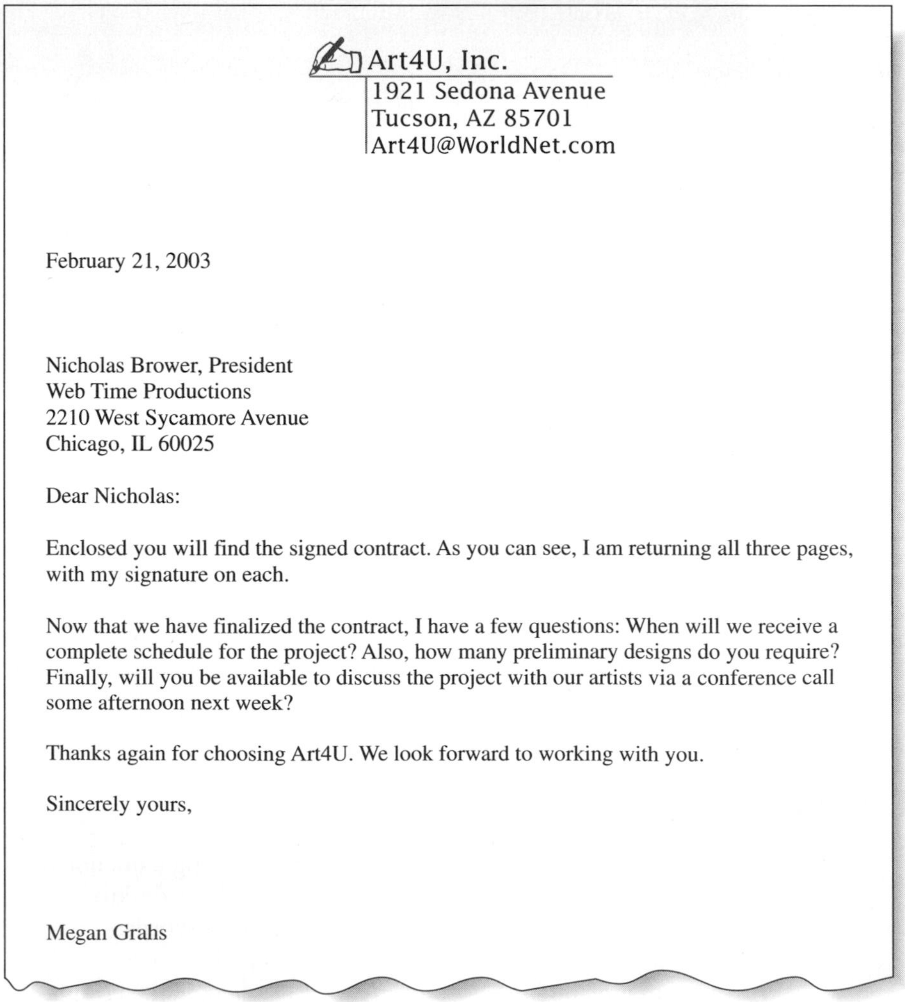

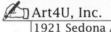 Art4U, Inc.

1921 Sedona Avenue
Tucson, AZ 85701
Art4U@WorldNet.com

February 21, 2003

Nicholas Brower, President
Web Time Productions
2210 West Sycamore Avenue
Chicago, IL 60025

Dear Nicholas:

Enclosed you will find the signed contract. As you can see, I am returning all three pages, with my signature on each.

Now that we have finalized the contract, I have a few questions: When will we receive a complete schedule for the project? Also, how many preliminary designs do you require? Finally, will you be available to discuss the project with our artists via a conference call some afternoon next week?

Thanks again for choosing Art4U. We look forward to working with you.

Sincerely yours,

Megan Grahs

To open a new document:

1. If you took a break after the previous session, make sure the Word program is running, that nonprinting characters are displayed, and that the font settings in the Formatting toolbar are set to 12 point Times New Roman. Also verify that the toolbars and the ruler are displayed. Currently, you have one document open in Word. This document is named Document1. If you have the taskbar displayed at the bottom of your screen, it should contain a button named Document1. If for some reason you need to switch between Word and another Windows program, you could click this taskbar button to redisplay the Word window. In the next steps, you'll try using this button, just for practice.

2. Click the **Minimize** button in the Word title bar. The Word window minimizes, revealing the Windows desktop. (If you couldn't see the taskbar earlier, you should see it now.)

3. Click the **Document1** button in the taskbar. The Word window maximizes again. Now you can open a new document where you can type Megan's letter.

4. Click the **New Blank Document** button on the Standard toolbar. A new document, named Document2, opens, as shown in Figure 1-15.

Figure 1-15	NEWLY OPENED DOCUMENT

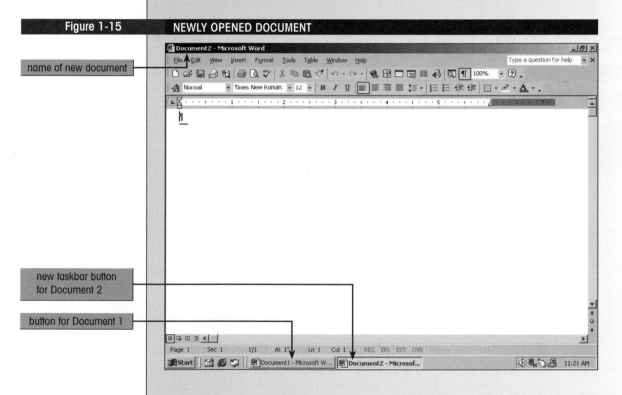

name of new document

new taskbar button for Document 2

button for Document 1

If you have the taskbar displayed at the bottom of your screen, you see an additional button for the new document. If you wanted to switch back to Document1, you could click its button on the taskbar.

Now that you have opened a new document, you need to insert some blank lines in the document so you leave enough room for the company letterhead.

To insert blank lines in the document:

1. Press the **Enter** key eight times. Each time you press the Enter key, a nonprinting paragraph mark appears. In the status bar (at the bottom of the Document window), you should see the setting "At 2.5"," indicating that the insertion point is approximately 2.5 inches from the top of the page. Another setting in the status bar should read "Ln 9," indicating the insertion point is in line 9 of the document. See Figure 1-16. (Your settings may be slightly different.)

| Figure 1-16 | DOCUMENT WINDOW AFTER INSERTING BLANK LINES |

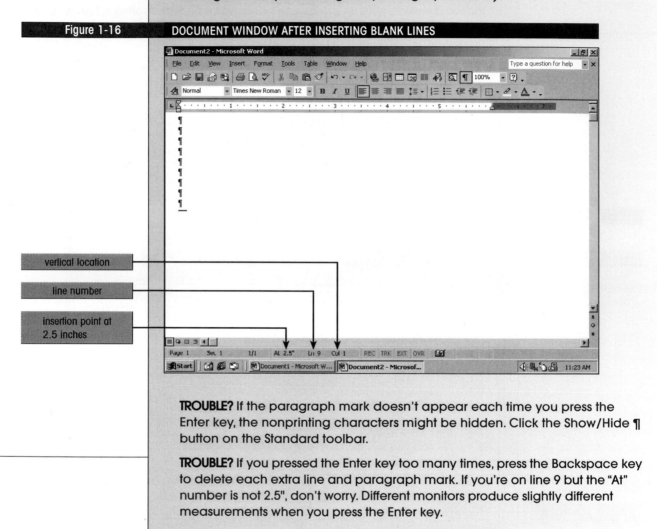

vertical location

line number

insertion point at 2.5 inches

TROUBLE? If the paragraph mark doesn't appear each time you press the Enter key, the nonprinting characters might be hidden. Click the Show/Hide ¶ button on the Standard toolbar.

TROUBLE? If you pressed the Enter key too many times, press the Backspace key to delete each extra line and paragraph mark. If you're on line 9 but the "At" number is not 2.5", don't worry. Different monitors produce slightly different measurements when you press the Enter key.

Pressing Enter is a simple, fast way to insert space in a document. When you are a more experienced Word user, you'll learn how to insert space without using the Enter key.

Entering Text

Normally, you begin typing a letter by entering the date. However, Megan tells you that she's not sure whether the contract will be ready to send today or tomorrow. So she asks you to skip the date for now and begin with the inside address. Making changes to documents is easy in Word, so you can easily add the date later.

In the following steps, you'll type the inside address (shown on Megan's note, in Figure 1-1). If you type a wrong character, press the Backspace key to delete the mistake and then retype the correct character.

To type the inside address:

1. Type **Nicholas Brower, President** and then press the **Enter** key. As you type, the nonprinting character (•) appears between words to indicate a space. Depending on how your computer is set up, you may also see a dotted underline beneath the name, Nicholas Brower, as shown in Figure 1-17. You'll learn the meaning of this underline later in this tutorial, when you type the date. For now you can just ignore it and concentrate on typing the letter.

Figure 1-17	FIRST LINE OF INSIDE ADDRESS

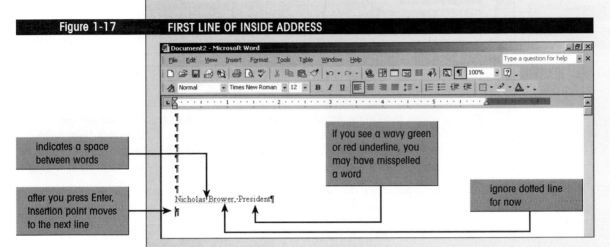

indicates a space between words

after you press Enter, insertion point moves to the next line

if you see a wavy green or red underline, you may have misspelled a word

ignore dotted line for now

Nicholas Brower, President¶

TROUBLE? If a wavy line (as opposed to a dotted line) appears beneath a word, check to make sure you typed the text correctly. If you did not, use the Backspace key to remove the error, and then retype the text correctly.

2. Type the following text, pressing the **Enter** key after each line to complete the inside address:
Web Time Productions
2210 West Sycamore Avenue
Chicago, IL 60025

Ignore the dotted underline below the street address. As mentioned earlier, you'll learn the meaning of this type of underline later in this tutorial.

3. Press the **Enter** key again to add a blank line after the inside address. (You should see a total of two paragraph marks below the inside address.) Now you can type the salutation.

4. Type **Dear Nicholas:** and press the **Enter** key twice to double space between the salutation and the body of the letter. When you press the Enter key the first time, the Office Assistant might appear, asking if you would like help writing your letter, as in Figure 1-18. (Depending on the settings on your computer, you might see a different Office Assistant.)

Figure 1-18   OFFICE ASSISTANT

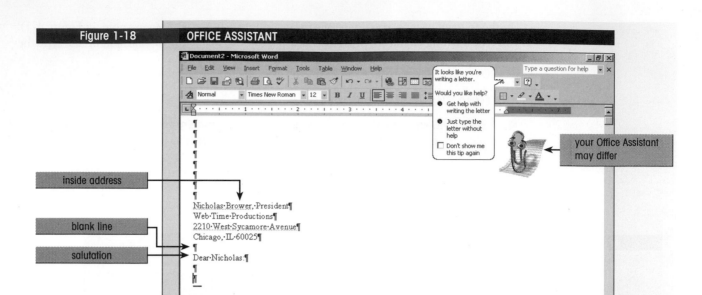

As you know, the Office Assistant is an interactive feature that sometimes appears to offer help on routine tasks. In this case, you could click "Get help with writing the letter" and have the Office Assistant lead you through a series of dialog boxes designed to set up the basic elements of a letter. For now, though, you'll close the Office Assistant and continue writing your letter.

5. Click **Just type the letter without help**. The Office Assistant closes.

   TROUBLE? If the Office Assistant remains open, right-click the Office Assistant, and then click Hide.

Before you continue with the rest of the letter, you should save what you have typed so far.

To save the document:

1. Place your Data Disk in the appropriate disk drive.

   TROUBLE? If you don't have a Data Disk, see the "Read This Before You Begin" page at the beginning of this tutorial.

2. Click the **Save** button 🔲 on the Standard toolbar. The Save As dialog box opens, similar to Figure 1-19. (Your Save As dialog box might be larger than the one shown in Figure 1-19.) Note that Word suggests using the first few words of the letter ("Nicholas Brower") as the filename. You will first replace the suggested filename with something more descriptive.

Figure 1-19   SAVE AS DIALOG BOX

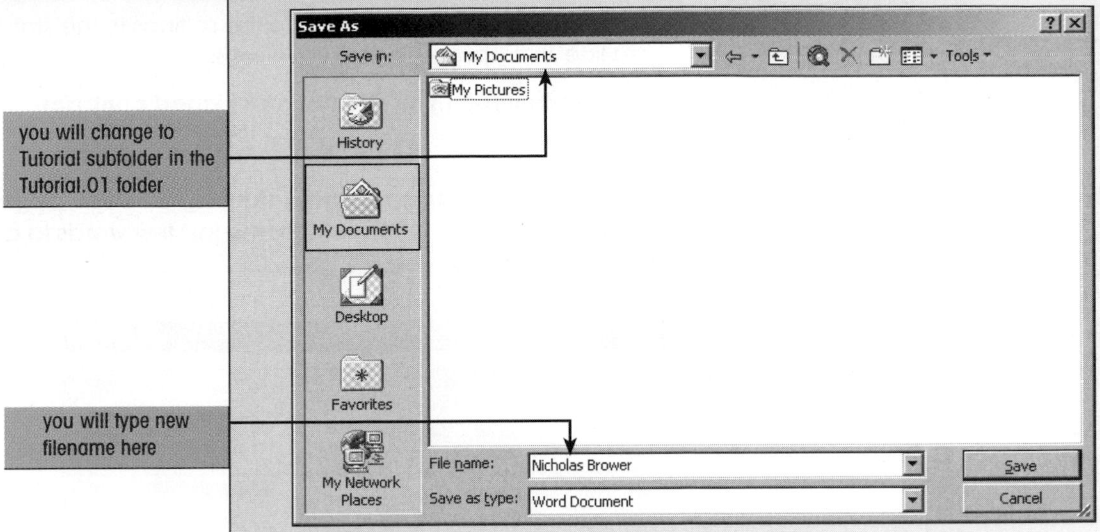

you will change to
Tutorial subfolder in the
Tutorial.01 folder

you will type new
filename here

Save As

Save in: My Documents

My Pictures

History

My Documents

Desktop

Favorites

My Network
Places

File name: Nicholas Brower

Save as type: Word Document

Save

Cancel

3. Type **Web Time Contract Letter** in the File name text box. Next, you need to tell Word where you want to save the document. In this case, you want to use the Tutorial subfolder in the Tutorial.01 folder on your Data Disk.

4. Click the **Save in** list arrow, click the drive containing your Data Disk, double-click the **Tutorial.01** folder, and then double-click the **Tutorial** folder. The word "Tutorial" is now displayed in the Save in box, indicating that the Tutorial folder is open and ready for you to save the document.

TROUBLE? If Word automatically adds the .doc extension to your filename, your computer is configured to show filename extensions. Just continue with the tutorial.

5. Click the **Save** button in the Save As dialog box. The dialog box closes, and you return to the Document window. The new document name (Web Time Contract Letter) appears in the title bar.

Note that Word automatically appends the .doc extension to the filename to identify the file as a Microsoft Word document. However, unless your computer is set up to display file extensions, you won't see the .doc extension in any of the Word dialog boxes or in the title bar. These tutorials assume that filename extensions are hidden.

Taking Advantage of Word Wrap

Now that you have saved your document, you're ready to continue working on Megan's letter. As you type the body of the letter, you do not have to press the Enter key at the end of each line. Instead, when you type a word that extends into the right margin, both the insertion point and the word moves automatically to the next line. This automatic line breaking is called **word wrap**. You'll see how word wrap works as you type the body of the letter.

To observe word wrap while typing a paragraph:

1. Make sure the insertion point is at Ln 16 (according to the settings in the status bar). If it's not, move it to line 16 by pressing the arrow keys.

2. Type the following sentence: **Enclosed you will find the signed contract.**

3. Press the **spacebar**.

4. Type the following sentence: **As you can see, I am returning all three pages, with my signature on each.** Notice how Word moves the last few words to a new line when the preceding line is full. See Figure 1-20.

Figure 1-20	WORD WRAPPING TEXT

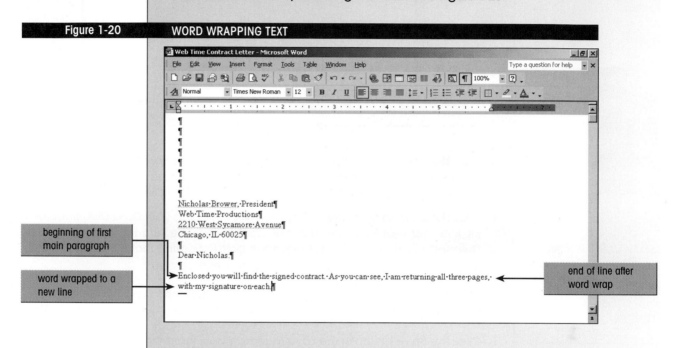

beginning of first main paragraph

word wrapped to a new line

end of line after word wrap

TROUBLE? If your screen does not match Figure 1-20 exactly, don't be concerned. The Times New Roman font can have varying letter widths and produce slightly different measurements on different monitors. As a result, the word or letter where the line wraps in your document might be different from the one shown in Figure 1-20. Continue with Step 5.

5. Press the **Enter** key to end the first paragraph, and then press the **Enter** key again to double space between the first and second paragraphs.

6. Type the following text:

   Now that we have finalized the contract, I have a few questions: When will we receive a complete schedule for the project? Also, how many preliminary designs do you require?

   When you are finished, your screen should look similar to Figure 1-21, although the line breaks on your screen might be slightly different.

Figure 1-21	BEGINNING OF SECOND MAIN PARAGRAPH

eight paragraph marks are currently visible

Nicholas·Brower,·President¶
Web·Time·Productions¶
2210·West·Sycamore·Avenue¶
Chicago,·IL·60025¶
¶
Dear·Nicholas:¶
¶
Enclosed·you·will·find·the·signed·contract.·As·you·can·see,·I·am·returning·all·three·pages,·with·my·signature·on·each.¶
¶
Now·that·we·have·finalized·the·contract,·I·have·a·few·questions.·When·will·we·receive·a· complete·schedule·for·the·project?·Also,·how·many·preliminary·designs·do·you·require?¶

line breaks might be slightly different on your screen

insertion point

last line is line 20

Page 1   Sec 1   1/1   At 4.6"   Ln 20   Col 86   REC TRK EXT OVR

Scrolling a Document

After you finish the last set of steps, the insertion point should be near the bottom of the Document window. It looks like there's not enough room to type the rest of Megan's letter. However, as you continue to add text at the end of your document, the text that you typed earlier will **scroll** (or shift up) and disappear from the top of the Document window. You'll see how scrolling works as you enter the rest of the second paragraph.

To observe scrolling while you're entering text:

1. Make sure the insertion point is positioned to the right of the question mark after the word "require" in the second main paragraph. In other words, the insertion point should be positioned at the end of line 20. (See Figure 1-21 above.)

   TROUBLE? If you are using a very large monitor, your insertion point may still be some distance from the bottom of the screen. In that case, you may not be able to perform the scrolling steps that follow. Read the steps to familiarize yourself with the process of scrolling. You'll have a chance to scroll longer documents later.

2. Press the **spacebar**, and then type the following text:

   Finally, will you be available to discuss the project with our artists via a conference call some afternoon next week?

   Notice that as you begin to type the text, Word moves the insertion point to a new line. Also, the first paragraph mark at the top of the letter scrolls off the top of the Document window to make room for the end of the question. When you are finished typing, your screen should look like Figure 1-22. (Don't worry if you make a mistake in your typing. You'll learn a number of ways to correct errors in the next section.)

Figure 1-22 **PARAGRAPH MARK SCROLLED OFF THE SCREEN**

first paragraph mark
scrolled off the screen

now only seven
paragraph marks
are visible

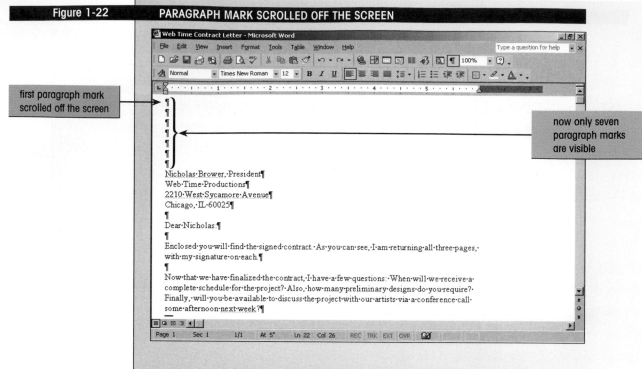

3. Press the **Enter** key twice. The document scrolls up to make room for the new lines at the bottom.

4. Type the following text:

    Thanks again for choosing Art4U. We look forward to working with you.

5. Press the **Enter** key twice.

6. Type **Sincerely yours,** (including the comma) to enter the complimentary closing.

7. Press the **Enter** key five times to allow space for a signature. Unless you have a very large monitor, part of the inside address scrolls off the top of the Document window.

8. Type **Megan Grahs**. If you see a wavy underline below Megan's name, ignore it for now. You'll learn the meaning of this underline in the next section. You've completed the letter, so you should save your work.

9. Click the **Save** button 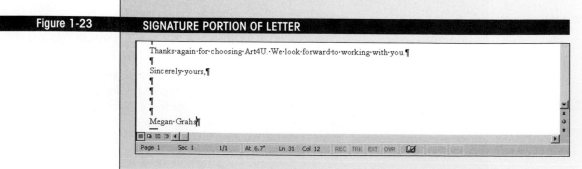 on the Standard toolbar. Word saves your letter with the same name and to the same location you specified earlier. Your letter should look like Figure 1-23. Don't be concerned about any typing errors. You'll learn how to correct them in the next section.

Figure 1-23 **SIGNATURE PORTION OF LETTER**

In the last set of steps, you watched the text at the top of your document move off your screen. You can scroll this hidden text back into view so you can read the beginning of the letter. When you do, the text at the bottom of the screen will scroll out of view. To scroll the Document window, you can click the up or down arrows in the vertical scroll bar, click anywhere in the vertical scroll bar, or drag the scroll box. Figure 1-24 summarizes these options.

Figure 1-24	SCROLLING THE DOCUMENT WINDOW

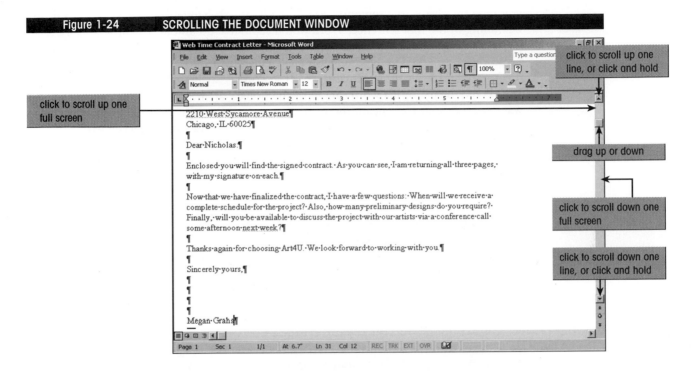

In the next set of steps, you will practice using the vertical scroll bar.

To scroll the document using the vertical scroll bar:

1. Position the mouse pointer on the up arrow at the top of the vertical scroll bar. Press and hold the mouse button to scroll the text. When the text stops scrolling, you have reached the top of the document and can see the beginning of the letter. Note that scrolling does not change the location of the insertion point in the document.

2. Click the down arrow on the vertical scroll bar. The document scrolls down one line.

3. Click anywhere in the vertical scroll bar, below the scroll box. The document scrolls down one full screen.

4. Drag the scroll box up until the first line of the inside address ("Nicholas Brower, President") is positioned at the top of the Document window.

Correcting Errors

If you discover a typing error as soon as you make it, you can press the Backspace key to erase the characters and spaces to the left of the insertion point one at a time. Backspacing erases both printing and nonprinting characters. After you erase the error, you can type the correct characters. (You can also press the Delete key to delete characters to the right of the insertion point.)

In many cases, however, Word's **AutoCorrect** feature will do the work for you. This helpful feature automatically corrects common typing errors, such as entering "adn" for "and." You might have noticed AutoCorrect at work if you forgot to capitalize the first letter in a sentence as you typed the letter. AutoCorrect automatically corrects this error as you type the rest of the sentence. For example, if you happened to type "enclosed" at the beginning of the first sentence, Word would capitalize the initial "e" automatically.

In the case of more complicated errors, you can take advantage of Word's **Spelling and Grammar** checker. This feature continually checks your document against Word's built-in dictionary and a set of grammar rules. If a word is spelled differently from how it is in Word's dictionary, or if a word isn't in the dictionary at all (for example, a person's name), a wavy *red* line appears beneath the word. A wavy red line also appears if you type duplicate words (such as "the the"). If you accidentally type an extra space between words or make a grammatical error (such as typing "He walk to the store." instead of "He walks to the store."), a wavy *green* line appears beneath the error. The easiest way to see how these features work is to make some intentional typing errors.

To correct intentional typing errors:

1. Click the **Document1** button in the taskbar.

   TROUBLE? If you closed Document1 earlier, click the New Blank Document button in the Standard toolbar to open a blank document.

2. Carefully and slowly type the following sentence exactly as it is shown, including the spelling errors and the extra space between the last two words: **microsoft Word corects teh commen typing misTakes you make.** Press the **Enter** key when you are finished typing. Notice that as you press the spacebar after the word "commen," a wavy red line appears beneath it, indicating that the word might be misspelled. Notice also that when you pressed the spacebar after the words "corects," "teh," and "misTakes," Word automatically corrected the spelling. After you pressed the Enter key, a wavy green line appeared under the last two words, alerting you to the extra space. See Figure 1-25.

Figure 1-25	DOCUMENT WITH INTENTIONAL TYPING ERRORS

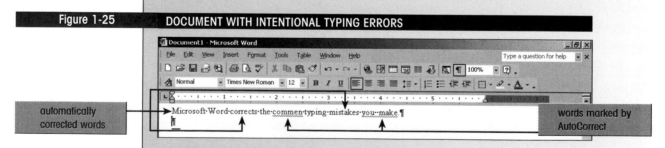

automatically corrected words

words marked by AutoCorrect

   TROUBLE? If red and green wavy lines do not appear beneath mistakes, Word is probably not set to check spelling and grammar automatically as you type. Click Tools on the menu bar, and then click Options to open the Options dialog box. Click the Spelling & Grammar tab. If necessary, insert check marks in the "Check spelling as you type" and the "Check grammar as you type" check boxes, and click OK. If Word does not automatically correct the incorrect spelling of "the," click Tools on the menu bar, click AutoCorrect Options, and make sure that all seven boxes at the top of the AutoCorrect tab have check marks. Then scroll down the AutoCorrect list to make sure that there is an entry that changes "teh" to "the," and click OK.

Working with AutoCorrect

Whenever AutoCorrect makes a change, Word inserts an **AutoCorrect Options button** in the document. You can use this button to undo a change, or to prevent AutoCorrect from making the same change in the future. To see an AutoCorrect Options button, you position the mouse pointer over a word that has been changed by AutoCorrect.

To display the AutoCorrect Options buttons:

1. Position the mouse pointer over the word "corrects." A small blue rectangle appears below the first few letters of the word, as in Figure 1-26.

   TROUBLE? If you see a blue button with a lightning bolt, you pointed to the blue rectangle after it appeared. Move the pointer so that only the rectangle is visible, and continue with the next step.

| Figure 1-26 | WORD CHANGED BY AUTOCORRECT |

small blue rectangle

2. Point to the **blue rectangle** below "corrects". The blue rectangle is replaced by the AutoCorrect Options button.

3. Click the **AutoCorrect Options** button. A menu with commands related to AutoCorrect appears. You could choose to change "corrects" back to "corects". You could also tell AutoCorrect to stop automatically correcting "corects".

4. Click anywhere in the document. The AutoCorrect menu closes.

Correcting Spelling and Grammar Errors

After you verify that AutoCorrect made changes you want, you should scan your document for wavy underlines. Again, the red underlines indicate potential spelling errors, while the green underlines indicate potential grammar or punctuation problems. In the following steps, you will learn a quick way to correct such errors.

To correct spelling and grammar errors:

1. Position the I-Beam pointer I over the word "commen" and click the right mouse button. A shortcut menu appears with suggested spellings. See Figure 1-27.

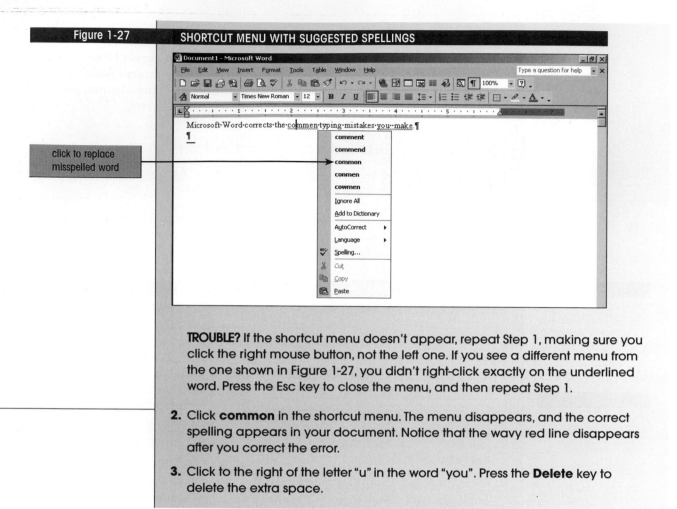

Figure 1-27 SHORTCUT MENU WITH SUGGESTED SPELLINGS

TROUBLE? If the shortcut menu doesn't appear, repeat Step 1, making sure you click the right mouse button, not the left one. If you see a different menu from the one shown in Figure 1-27, you didn't right-click exactly on the underlined word. Press the Esc key to close the menu, and then repeat Step 1.

2. Click **common** in the shortcut menu. The menu disappears, and the correct spelling appears in your document. Notice that the wavy red line disappears after you correct the error.

3. Click to the right of the letter "u" in the word "you". Press the **Delete** key to delete the extra space.

You can see how quick and easy it is to correct common typing errors with AutoCorrect and the Spelling and Grammar checker. Remember, however, to thoroughly proofread each document you create. AutoCorrect will not catch words that are spelled correctly, but used improperly (such as "your" for "you're").

Proofreading the Letter

Before you can proofread your letter, you need to close the document with the practice sentence. You don't need to save this document, because you only created it to practice correcting errors.

To close the practice document:

1. Click the **Document Close** button ⊠ (on the right end of the menu bar). You see a dialog box asking if you want to save your changes to the document.

2. Click **No**. You return to the document named Web Time Contract Letter.

Now you can proofread the letter for any typos. You can also get rid of the wavy red underline below Megan's last name.

To respond to possible spelling errors:

1. Scroll down until the signature line is visible. Because Word doesn't recognize "Grahs" as a word, it marked it as a potential error. You need to tell Word to ignore this name wherever it occurs in the letter.

2. Right-click **Grahs**. A shortcut menu opens.

3. Click **Ignore All**. The wavy red underline disappears from below "Grahs".

4. Scroll up to the beginning of the letter, and proofread it for typos. If a word has a wavy red or green underline, right-click it and choose an option in the short-cut menu. To correct other errors, click to the right or left of the error, use the Backspace or Delete key to remove it, and then type a correction.

Inserting a Date with AutoComplete

The beauty of using a word processing program such as Microsoft Word is that you can easily make changes to text you have already typed. In this case, you need to insert the current date at the beginning of the letter. Megan tells you that she wants to send the contract to Web Time Productions on February 21, so you need to insert that date into the letter now.

Before you can enter the date, you need to move the insertion point to the right location. In a standard business letter, the date belongs approximately 2.5 inches from the top. (As you recall, this is where you started the inside address earlier.) You also need to insert some blank lines to allow enough space between the date and the inside address.

To move the insertion point and add some blank lines:

1. Scroll up to display the top of the document.

2. Click to the left of the "N" in "Nicholas Brower," in the inside address. The status bar indicates that the insertion point is on line 9, 2.5 inches from the top. (Your status bar might show slightly different measurements.) You might see a square with a lowercase "i" displayed just above the name. Ignore this for now. You'll learn about this special button (called a Smart Tag Actions button) later in this tutorial.

3. Press **Enter** four times, and then press the ↑ key four times. Now the insertion point is positioned at line 9, with three blank lines between the inside address and the line where you will insert the date. See Figure 1-28.

Figure 1-28   **POSITION OF INSERTION POINT**

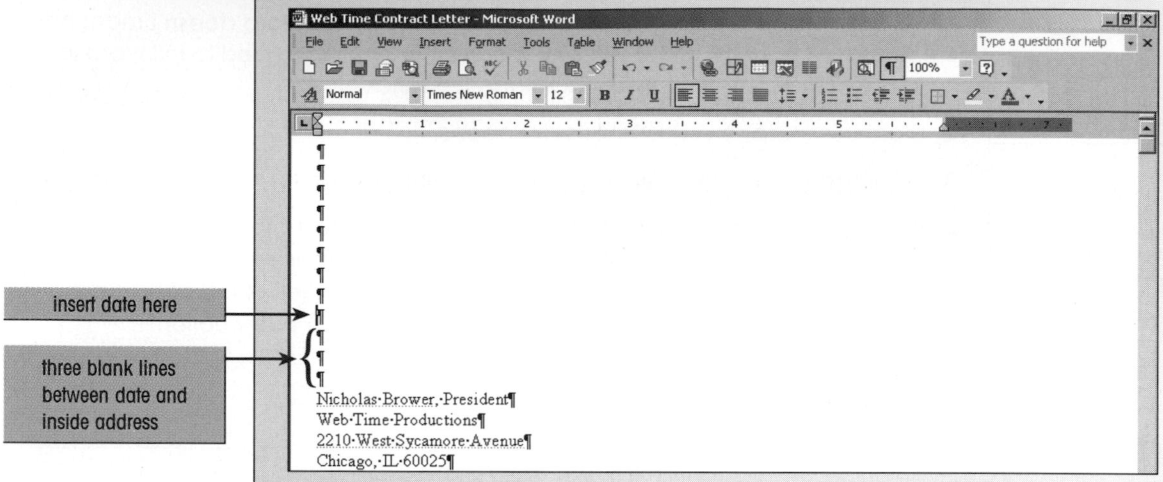

insert date here

three blank lines
between date and
inside address

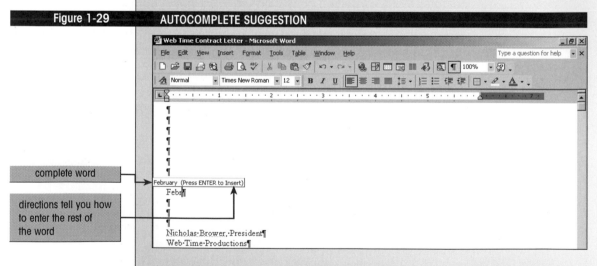

You're ready to insert the date. To do this you can take advantage of Word's **AutoComplete** feature, which automatically inserts dates and other regularly used items for you. In this case, you can type the first few characters of the month, and let Word insert the rest. (This only works for long month names like February.)

To insert the date:

1. Type **Febr** (the first four letters of February). A small yellow box, called an AutoComplete suggestion, appears above the line, as shown in Figure 1-29. If you wanted to type something other than February, you could continue typing to complete the word. In this case, though, you want to accept the AutoComplete tip, so you will press the Enter key in the next step.

Figure 1-29   **AUTOCOMPLETE SUGGESTION**

complete word

directions tell you how
to enter the rest of
the word

TROUBLE? If the AutoComplete tip doesn't appear, this feature may not be active. Click Tools on the menu bar, click AutoCorrect Options, click the AutoText tab, click the "Show AutoComplete suggestions" check box to insert a check, and then click OK.

2. Press **Enter**. The rest of the word "February" is inserted in the document.

3. Press the **spacebar** and then type **21, 2003**.

TROUBLE? If February happens to be the current month, you will see an AutoComplete suggestion displaying the current date after you press the spacebar. To accept that AutoComplete tip, press Enter. Otherwise type the rest of the date as instructed in Step 3.

4. Click one of the blank lines below the date. Depending on how your computer is set up, you may see a dotted underline below the date. (You will learn the meaning of this underline in the next section.) You have finished entering the date. See Figure 1-30.

Figure 1-30	DATE ENTERED IN THE DOCUMENT

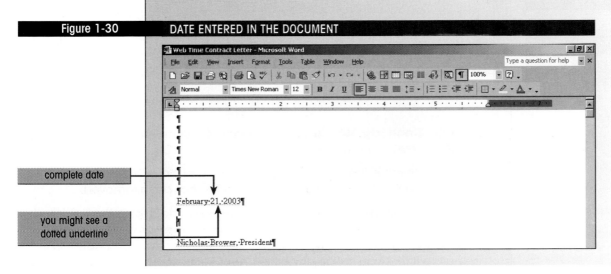

complete date

you might see a dotted underline

Removing **Smart Tags**

A dotted underline below a date, name, or address indicates that Word has inserted a Smart Tag in the document. A **Smart Tag** is a feature that that allows you to perform actions (such as sending e-mail or scheduling a meeting) that would normally require a completely different program. Word attaches Smart Tag Action buttons to certain kinds of text, including dates and names. You can click this button to open a menu (similar to a shortcut menu) where you can select commands related to that item. (For example, you might click a Smart Tag on a name to add that name to your e-mail address book.) You don't really need Smart Tags in this document, though, so you will delete them. (Your computer may not be set up to show Smart Tags at all, or it might show them on dates and addresses, but not names. If you do not see any Smart Tags in your document, simply read the following steps.)

To remove the Smart Tags from the document:

1. If you see a dotted underline below the date, position the mouse pointer over the date. A Smart Tag icon ⊚ appears over the date.

2. Move the mouse pointer over the Smart Tag icon. The Smart Tag Actions button ⊚▾ appears, as shown in Figure 1-31.

Figure 1-31   DISPLAYING THE SMART TAG ACTIONS BUTTON

Smart Tag Actions button

these items may have also been marked with Smart Tags on your computer

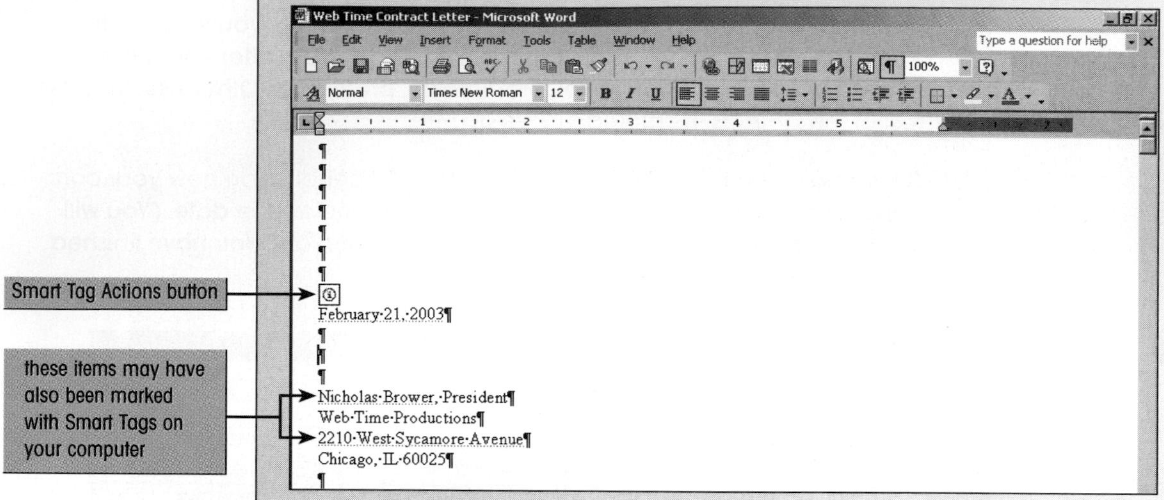

3. Click the **Smart Tag Actions** button. A menu of commands related to dates appears.

4. Click **Remove this Smart Tag**. The Smart Tag menu closes. The date is no longer underlined, indicating that the Smart Tag has been removed.

5. Remove any Smart Tags from the name and street address in the inside address. If necessary, remove the Smart Tag from the words "next week," in the second paragraph in the body of the letter, and from Megan's name in the signature line. If you notice any others, remove those also.

6. Click the **Save** button 🖫 on the Standard toolbar. Word saves your letter with the same name and to the same location you specified earlier.

Previewing and Printing a Document

Do you think the letter is ready to print? You could find out by clicking the Print button on the Standard toolbar and then reviewing the printed page. In doing so, however, you risk wasting paper and printer time. For example, if you failed to insert enough space for the company letterhead, you would have to add more space, and then print the letter all over again. To avoid wasting paper and time, you should first display the document in the Print Preview window. By default, the Print Preview window shows you the full page; there's no need to scroll through the document.

To preview the document:

1. Click the **Print Preview** button 🔍 on the Standard toolbar. The Print Preview window opens and displays a full-page version of your letter, as shown in Figure 1-32. This shows how the letter will fit on the printed page. The Print Preview toolbar includes a number of buttons that are useful for making changes that affect the way the printed page will look.

Figure 1-32	FULL PAGE DISPLAYED IN PRINT PREVIEW WINDOW

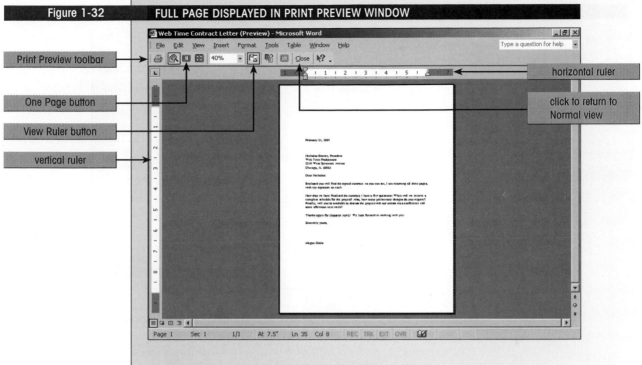

Print Preview toolbar

One Page button

View Ruler button

vertical ruler

horizontal ruler

click to return to Normal view

TROUBLE? If your letter in the Print Preview window is smaller and off to the left rather than centered in the window, click the One Page button on the Print Preview toolbar.

TROUBLE? If you don't see rulers above and to the left of the document, your rulers are not displayed. To show the rulers in the Print Preview window, click the View Rulers button on the Print Preview toolbar.

2. Click **Close** on the Print Preview toolbar to return to Normal view.

Note that it is especially important to preview documents if your computer is connected to a network so that you don't keep a shared printer tied up with unnecessary printing. In this case, the text looks well spaced and the letterhead will fit at the top of the page. You're ready to print the letter.

When printing a document, you have two choices. You can use the Print command on the File menu, which opens the Print dialog box in which you can adjust some printer settings. Or, if you prefer, you can use the Print button on the Standard toolbar, which prints the document using default settings, without opening a dialog box. In these tutorials, the first time you print from a shared computer, you should check the settings in the Print dialog box and make sure the number of copies is set to one. After that, you can use the Print button.

To print a document:

1. Make sure your printer is turned on and contains paper.

2. Click **File** on the menu bar, and then click **Print**. The Print dialog box opens. See Figure 1-33.

Figure 1-33 PRINT DIALOG BOX

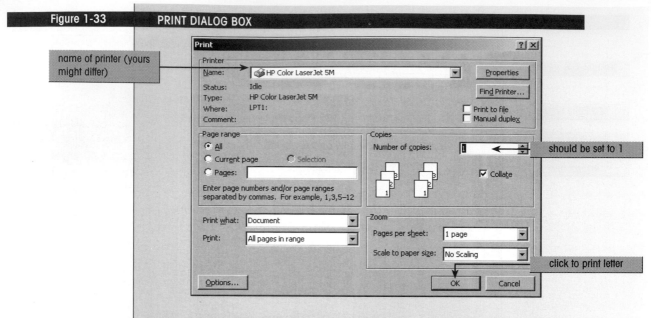

name of printer (yours might differ)

should be set to 1

click to print letter

3. Verify that your settings match those in Figure 1-33. In particular make sure the number of copies is set to 1. Also make sure the Printer section of the dialog box shows the correct printer. If you're not sure what the correct printer is, check with your instructor or technical support person.

TROUBLE? If the Print dialog box shows the wrong printer, click the Name list arrow, and then select the correct printer from the list of available printers.

4. Click **OK**. Assuming your computer is attached to a printer, the letter prints.

Your printed letter should look similar to Figure 1-14, but without the Art4U letterhead. The word wraps, or line breaks, might not appear in the same places on your letter because the size and spacing of characters vary slightly from one printer to the next.

Creating an Envelope

After you print the letter, Megan stops by your desk and asks you to print an envelope in which to mail the contracts. Creating an envelope is a simple process because Word automatically uses the inside address from the letter as the address on the envelope.

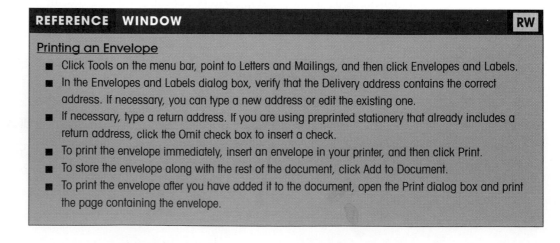

REFERENCE WINDOW **RW**

Printing an Envelope
- Click Tools on the menu bar, point to Letters and Mailings, and then click Envelopes and Labels.
- In the Envelopes and Labels dialog box, verify that the Delivery address contains the correct address. If necessary, you can type a new address or edit the existing one.
- If necessary, type a return address. If you are using preprinted stationery that already includes a return address, click the Omit check box to insert a check.
- To print the envelope immediately, insert an envelope in your printer, and then click Print.
- To store the envelope along with the rest of the document, click Add to Document.
- To print the envelope after you have added it to the document, open the Print dialog box and print the page containing the envelope.

Megan tells you that your printer is not currently stocked with envelopes. She asks you to create the envelope and add it to the document. Then she will print the envelope later, when she is ready to mail the contracts to Web Time Productions.

To create an envelope:

1. Click **Tools** on the menu bar, point to **Letters and Mailings**, and then click **Envelopes and Labels**. The Envelopes and Labels dialog box opens, as shown in Figure 1-34. By default, Word uses the inside address from the letter as the delivery address. Depending on how your computer is set up, you might see an address in the Return address box. Since you will be using Art4U's printed envelopes, you don't need to include a return address on this envelope.

Figure 1-34   **ENVELOPES AND LABELS DIALOG BOX**

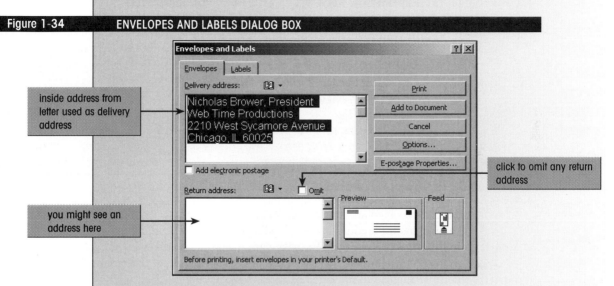

inside address from letter used as delivery address

you might see an address here

click to omit any return address

---

2. Click the **Omit** check box to insert a check, if necessary.

3. Click **Add to Document**. The dialog box closes, and you return to the Document window. The envelope is inserted at the top of the document, above a double line with the words "Section Break (Next Page)". The double line indicates that the envelope and the letter are two separate parts of the document. The envelope will print in the standard business envelope format. The letter will still print on standard 8.5 × 11-inch paper. (You'll have a chance to actually print an envelope in the exercises at the end of this tutorial.)

4. Click the **Save** button 🖫 on the Standard toolbar.

Congratulations on creating your first letter in Microsoft Word. Since you are finished with the letter and the envelope, you can close the document and exit Word.

To close the document and exit Word:

1. Click the **Close** button ☒ in the menu bar. The Web Time Contract Letter closes.

TROUBLE? If you see a dialog box with the message "Do you want to save the changes to 'Web Time Contract Letter?', you didn't save your most recent changes. Click Yes.

2. If necessary, close other open documents without saving them.

3. Click the **Close** button ☒ in the upper-right corner of the Word window. Word closes, and you return to the Windows desktop.

Session 1.2 QUICK CHECK

1. Explain how to save a document for the first time.
2. Explain how to enter the name of a month using AutoCorrect.
3. Explain how word wrap works in a Word document.
4. List the steps required to print an envelope.
5. In your own words, define each of the following:
   a. Scrolling
   b. AutoComplete
   c. AutoCorrect
   d. Print Preview
   e. Smart Tag

REVIEW ASSIGNMENTS

Megan received an e-mail from Nicholas Brower at Web Time Productions, confirming their plans for a conference call. Megan has e-mailed the graphic artists at Art4U, informing them about the call. To make sure everyone remembers, she would like you to post a memo on the bulletin board in the break room. Create the memo shown in Figure 1-35 by completing the following steps.

Figure 1-35

Art4U, Inc.
1921 Sedona Avenue
Tucson, AZ 85701
Art4U@WorldNet.com

TO: Art4U Staff Artists

FROM: Megan Grahs

DATE: February 27, 2003

SUBJECT: Conference Call

Please plan to join us for a conference call at 3 P.M. on Friday, March 1. Nicholas Brower, president of Web Time Productions, will be taking part, as will five of the company's most experienced Web page designers. This will be your chance to ask the designers some important questions.

You will be able to join the call from your desk by dialing an 800 number and a special access code. You'll receive both of these numbers via e-mail the day of the call.

1. If necessary, start Word and make sure your Data Disk is in the appropriate disk drive, and then check your screen to make sure your settings match those in the tutorials. In particular, make sure that nonprinting characters are displayed.

2. If the Office Assistant is open, hide it.

3. Click the New Blank Document button on the Standard toolbar to open a new document.

4. Press the Enter key eight times to insert enough space for the company letterhead.

5. Press the Caps Lock key, and then type "TO:" in capital letters.

Explore ▶ 6. You can use the Tab key to align text as a column. In this case, you want to align the To, From, Date, and Subject information. To begin, press the Tab key three times. Word inserts three nonprinting characters (right-pointing arrows), one for each time you pressed the Tab key.

7. Press the Caps Lock key to turn off capitalization, and then type "Art4U Staff Artists".

8. Press the Enter key twice, type "FROM:", press the Tab key twice, and then type your name in lowercase. Throughout the rest of this exercise, use the Caps Lock key as necessary to turn capitalization on and off.

9. Press the Enter key twice, type "DATE:", and then press the Tab key two times.

Explore ▶ 10. You can take advantage of AutoCorrect to type the current date. To try it now, type the name of the current month. If an AutoCorrect suggestion appears, press Enter to complete the name of the month; otherwise, continue typing. Press the spacebar. After you press the spacebar, an AutoCorrect suggestion appears with the current date. Press Enter to accept the suggestion.

11. Press the Enter key twice, type "SUBJECT:" and then press the Tab key two times. Type "Conference Call" and then press the Enter key twice.

12. Continue typing the rest of the memo as shown in Figure 1-35. (You will have a chance to correct any typing errors later.) Ignore any AutoCorrect suggestions that are not relevant to the text you are typing.

13. Save your work as **Conference Call Memo** in the Review folder for Tutorial 1.

14. Scroll to the beginning of the document and proofread your work.

15. Correct any misspelled words marked by wavy red lines. If the correct spelling of a word does not appear in the list box, press the Escape key to close the list, and then make the correction yourself. Remove any red wavy lines below words that are actually spelled correctly. Then correct any grammatical or other errors indicated by wavy green lines. Use the Backspace or Delete key to delete any extra words or spaces.

16. Remove any Smart Tags.

17. Save your most recent changes.

18. Preview and print the memo.

19. Close the document. Save any changes if necessary.

Explore ▶ 20. If you will be sending mail to someone regularly, it's helpful to add an envelope to a blank document, and then save the document, so that you can print the envelope in the future, whenever you need it. Open a new, blank document. Create an envelope for Nicholas Brower at Web Time Productions. Use the address you used as the inside address in the tutorial. For the return address, type your own address. Add the envelope to the document. If you are asked if you want to save the return address as the new default return address, click No. If your computer is connected to a printer that is stocked with envelopes, click File on the menu bar, click Print, click the Pages option button, type 1 in the Pages text box, and then click OK.

21. Save the document as **Web Time Envelope** in the Review folder for Tutorial 1.

22. Close any open documents and then exit Word.

CASE PROBLEMS

Case 1. Letter to Request Information about a Field Trip to Roaring Rapids Water Park
You are a teacher at Luis Sotelo Elementary School. Your students have been raising money all year for a trip to Roaring Rapids Water Park. Before you can plan the outing, you need to write for some information. Create the letter by doing the following:

1. If necessary, start Word, make sure your Data Disk is in the appropriate disk drive, and check your screen to make sure your settings match those in the tutorials.

2. Open a new blank document.

3. Type your name, press Enter, and then type the following address:

   Luis Sotelo Elementary School

   1521 First Avenue

   Durham, North Carolina 27701

Explore ▶

4. Press the Enter key four times, and then type the name of the current month. (If an AutoCorrect suggestion appears, press Enter to complete the name of the month.) Press the spacebar. After you press the spacebar, an AutoCorrect suggestion appears with the current date. Press Enter to accept the suggestion.

5. Press the Enter key four times after the date, and, using the proper business letter format, type the inside address: "Scott Rowland, Roaring Rapids Water Park, 2344 West Prairie Street, Durham, North Carolina 27704".

6. Double space after the inside address (that is, press the Enter Key twice), type the salutation "Dear Mr. Rowland:" and then insert another blank line. Close the Office Assistant if it opens.

7. Type the first paragraph as follows: "I'd like some information about a class field trip to Roaring Rapids Water Park. Please answer the following questions:"

8. Save your work as **Water Park Information Letter** in the Cases folder for Tutorial 1.

9. Insert one blank line, and then type these questions on separate lines with one blank line between each:
   How much is a day pass for a 10-year-old child?
   How much is a day pass for an adult?
   Can you offer a discount for a group of 25 children and 5 adults?
   Are lockers available for storing clothes and other belongings?

10. Correct any typing errors indicated by wavy lines. (*Hint*: Because "Sotelo" is spelled correctly, click Ignore All on the shortcut menu to remove the wavy red line under the word "Sotelo" and prevent Word from marking the word as a misspelling.)

11. Insert another blank line at the end of the letter, and type the complimentary closing "Sincerely," (include the comma).

12. Press the Enter key four times to leave room for the signature, and type your full name. Then press the Enter key and type "Luis Sotelo Elementary School". Notice that "Sotelo" is not marked as a spelling error this time.

13. Scroll up to the beginning of the document, and then remove any Smart Tags in the letter.

14. Save your changes to the letter, and then preview it using the Print Preview button.

15. Print the letter, close the document, and exit Word.

Case 2. Letter to Confirm Food Service During the National Purchasing Management Association Conference   As catering director for the Madison Convention and Visitors Bureau, you are responsible for managing food service at the city's convention center. The National Physical Therapy Association has scheduled a daily breakfast buffet during its annual convention (which runs July 6–10, 2003). You need to write a letter confirming plans for the daily buffet.

Create the letter using the skills you learned in the tutorial. Remember to include today's date, the inside address, the salutation, the date of the reservation, the complimentary closing, and your name and title. If the instructions show quotation marks around text you type, do not include the quotation marks in your letter. To complete the letter, do the following:

1. If necessary, start Word, make sure your Data Disk is in the appropriate disk drive, and check your screen to make sure your settings match those in the tutorials.

2. Open a new, blank document and press the Enter key until the insertion point is positioned about 2 inches from the top of the page. (Remember that you can see the exact position of the insertion point, in inches, in the status bar.)

3. Enter "June 6, 2003" as the date.

4. Press the Enter key four times after the date, and, using the proper business letter format, type the inside address: "Charles Quade, National Physical Therapy Association, 222 Sydney Street, Whitewater, WI 57332".

5. Double space after the inside address (that is, press the Enter key twice), type the salutation "Dear Mr. Quade:", and then double space again. If the Office Assistant opens, close it.

6. Write one paragraph confirming the daily breakfast buffets for July 6–10, 2003.

7. Insert a blank line and type the complimentary closing "Sincerely,".

8. Press the Enter key four times to leave room for the signature, and then type your name and title.

9. Save the letter as **Confirmation Letter** in the Cases folder for Tutorial 1.

10. Remove any Smart Tags. Reread your letter carefully, and correct any errors.

11. Save any new changes, and then preview and print the letter.

Explore   12. Create an envelope for the letter, and add it to the document. For the return address, type your own address. Add the envelope to the document. If you are asked if you want to save the return address as the new default return address, click No. If your computer is connected to a printer that is stocked with envelopes, click File on the menu bar, click Print, click the Pages option button, type 1 in the Pages text box, and then click OK.

13. Save your work and close the document, then exit Word.

Case 3. Letter Congratulating a Professor   Liza Morgan, a professor of e-commerce at Kentucky State University, was recently honored by the Southern Business Council for her series of free public seminars on developing Web sites for nonprofit agencies. She also was recently named Teacher of the Year by a national organization called Woman in Technology. As one of her former students, you need to write a letter congratulating her on these honors. To write this letter, do the following:

1. If necessary, start Word, make sure your Data Disk is in the appropriate disk drive, and check your screen to make sure your settings match those in the tutorials.

2. Write a brief letter congratulating Professor Morgan on her awards. Remember to use the four-part planning process. You should plan the content, organization, and style of the letter, and use a standard letter format. For the inside address, use the following: Professor Liza Morgan, Department of Business Administration, Kentucky State University, 1010 College Drive, Frankfort, Kentucky 40601.

3. Save the document as **Liza Morgan Letter** in the Cases folder for Tutorial 1.

4. Correct any typing errors, remove any Smart Tags, and then preview and print the memo.

Explore   5. Create an envelope for the letter, and add it to the document. For the return address, type your own address. Add the envelope to the document. If you are asked if you want to save the return address as the new default return address, click No. If your computer is connected to a printer that is stocked with envelopes, click File on the menu bar, click Print, click the Pages option button, type 1 in the Pages text box, and then click OK.

6. Save the document and close it, and then exit Word.

Case 4. Memo Created With a Template You are the office manager for Head for the Hills, a small company that sells hiking equipment over the Internet. The company has just moved to a new building which requires a special security key card after hours. Some employees have had trouble getting the key cards to work properly. You decide to hold a meeting to explain the security policies for the new building and to demonstrate the key cards. But first you need to post a memo announcing the meeting. The recently ordered letterhead (with the company's new address) has not yet arrived, so you will use a Word template to create the memo. Word provides templates—that is, models with predefined formatting—to help you create complete documents (including a professional-looking letterhead) quickly. To create the memo, do the following:

1. If necessary, start Word, make sure your Data Disk is in the appropriate disk drive, and check your screen to make sure your settings match those in the tutorials.

Explore ▶ 2. If the Task Pane is not displayed, click View on the menu bar, and then click Task Pane. The Task Pane is displayed on the right side of the Word window. You see a number of options related to creating new documents.

Explore ▶ 3. Under "New from template," click General Templates. The Templates dialog box opens.

Explore ▶ 4. Click the Memos tab, click Professional Memo, and then click the OK button. A memo template opens containing generic, placeholder text that you can replace with your own information.

5. Make sure the template is displayed in Normal View. Click at the end of the line "Company Name Here" (at the top of the document), press Backspace to delete the text, and type "Head for the Hills".

6. Click the text "Click here and type name," and in the To: line, type "All Employees". After "From," replace the current text with your name.

7. Click after "CC:" and then press Delete to delete the placeholder text. Use the Backspace key to delete the entire "CC" line. Note that Word inserts the current date automatically after the heading "Date."

8. After "Re:" type "Meeting to discuss building security".

9. Delete the placeholder text in the body of the letter, and replace it with a paragraph announcing the meeting, which is scheduled for tomorrow at 2 P.M. in the Central Conference Room.

10. Save the letter as **Meeting Memo** (in the Cases folder for Tutorial 1).

Explore ▶ 11. The memo text is in a small font, which is hard to read. To make it easier to review your work, you can change the Zoom setting in Normal view. Click the Zoom list arrow in the Standard toolbar, and then click 150%.

12. Review the memo. Correct any typos and delete any Smart Tags. Save the memo again, preview it, and then print it.

13. Close the document and exit Word.

LAB ASSIGNMENTS

The New Perspectives Labs are designed to help you master some of the key computer concepts and skills presented in each chapter of the text. If you are using your school's lab computers, your instructor or technical support person should have installed the Labs software for you. If you want to use the Labs on your home computer, ask your instructor for the appropriate software. See the Read This Before You Begin page for more information on installing and starting the Lab.

Each Lab has two parts: Steps and Explore. Use Steps first to learn and review concepts. Read the information on each page and do the numbered steps. As you work through the Lab, you will be asked to answer Quick Check questions about what you have learned. At the end of the Lab, you will see a Summary Report of your answers to the Quick Checks. If your instructor wants you to turn in this Summary Report, click the Print button on the Summary Report screen.

When you have completed the Steps, you can click the Explore button to complete the Lab Assignments. You also can use Explore to practice the skills you learned and to explore concepts on your own.

Word Processing Word-processing software is the most popular computerized productivity tool. In this Lab you will learn how word-processing software works. When you have completed this Lab, you should be able to apply the general concepts you learned to any word-processing package you use at home, at work, or in your school lab.

1. Click the Steps button to learn how word-processing software works. As you proceed through the Steps, answer all of the Quick Check questions that appear. After you complete the Steps, you will see a Quick Check Summary Report. Follow the instructions on the screen to print this report.

2. Click the Explore button to begin. Click File, and then click Open to display the Open dialog box. Click the file **Timber.tex**, and then press the Enter key to open the letter to Northern Timber Company. Make the following modifications to the letter, and then print it. You do not need to save the letter.

   a. In the first and last lines of the letter, change "Jason Kidder" to your name.
   b. Change the date to today's date.
   c. The second paragraph begins "Your proposal did not include…". Move this paragraph so it is the last paragraph in the text of the letter.
   d. Change the cost of a permanent bridge to $20,000.
   e. Spell check the letter.

3. In Explore, open the file **Stars.tex**. Make the following modifications to the document and then print it. You do not need to save the document.
   a. Center and boldface the title.
   b. Change the title font to size —16-point Arial.
   c. Boldface the DATE, SHOWER, and LOCATION.
   d. Move the January 2–3 line to the top of the list.
   e. Double-space the entire document.

4. In Explore, compose a one-page double-spaced letter to your parents or to a friend. Make sure you date the letter and check your spelling. Print the letter and sign it. You do not need to save your letter.

INTERNET ASSIGNMENTS

Student Union

The purpose of the Internet Assignments is to challenge you to find information on the Internet that you can use to create effective documents. The actual assignments are updated and maintained on the Course Technology Web site. Log on to the Internet and use your Web browser to go to the Student Union on the New Perspectives Series site at **www.course.com/NewPerspectives/studentunion**. Click the Online Companions link, and then click the link for this text.

To move text using cut and paste:

1. If necessary, scroll down until you can see the paragraph below the heading "Should I water my new tree right away?" near the bottom of page 1.

2. Double-click the word **thoroughly**. As you can see in Figure 2-14, you need to move this word to the end of the sentence.

Figure 2-14 | TEXT TO MOVE USING CUT AND PASTE

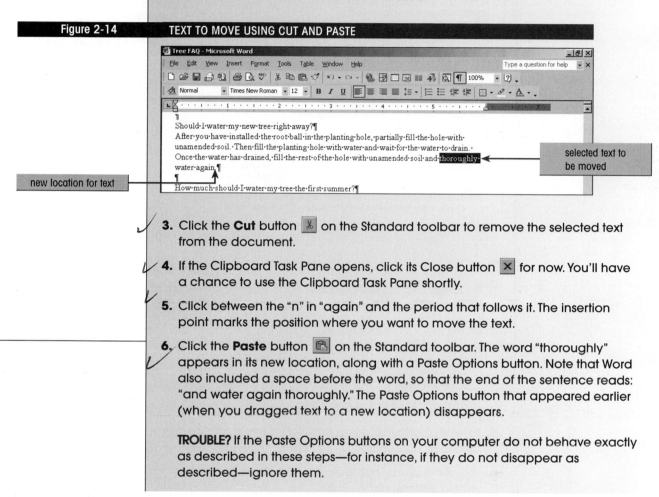

3. Click the **Cut** button on the Standard toolbar to remove the selected text from the document.

4. If the Clipboard Task Pane opens, click its Close button for now. You'll have a chance to use the Clipboard Task Pane shortly.

5. Click between the "n" in "again" and the period that follows it. The insertion point marks the position where you want to move the text.

6. Click the **Paste** button on the Standard toolbar. The word "thoroughly" appears in its new location, along with a Paste Options button. Note that Word also included a space before the word, so that the end of the sentence reads: "and water again thoroughly." The Paste Options button that appeared earlier (when you dragged text to a new location) disappears.

TROUBLE? If the Paste Options buttons on your computer do not behave exactly as described in these steps—for instance, if they do not disappear as described—ignore them.

Peter stops by your desk and mentions that he'll be using the paragraph on mulch and the paragraph on watering for the FAQ he plans to write on flowering shrubs. He asks you to copy that information and paste it in a new document that he can use as the basis for the new FAQ. You can do this using copy and paste. This technique is similar to cut and paste. In the process you'll have a chance to use the Clipboard Task Pane.

To copy and paste text:

1. Click **Edit** on the menu bar, and then click **Office Clipboard**. The Office Clipboard Task Pane opens on the right side of the Document window. It contains the message "Clipboard empty. Copy or cut to collect items." See Figure 2-15.

Figure 2-15   CLIPBOARD TASK PANE

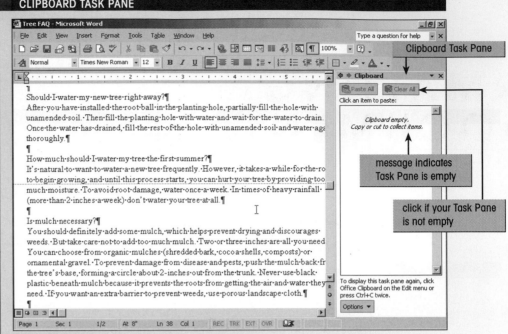

TROUBLE? If your Clipboard Task Pane does not show this message, click the Clear All button.

2. Move the mouse pointer to the selection bar and double-click next to the paragraph you edited in the last section (the paragraph that begins "After you have installed the root ball"). The entire paragraph is selected.

3. Click the **Copy** button 🖻 on the Standard toolbar. The first part of the paragraph appears in the Task Pane.

4. If necessary, scroll down until you can see the paragraph below the heading "Is mulch necessary?"

5. Select the paragraph below the heading (the paragraph that begins "You should definitely add . . . ").

6. Click 🖻. The first part of the paragraph appears in the Task Pane, as shown in Figure 2-16. An icon appears in the Windows taskbar indicating that the Clipboard Task Pane is currently active.

Figure 2-16   **ITEMS IN THE CLIPBOARD TASK PANE**

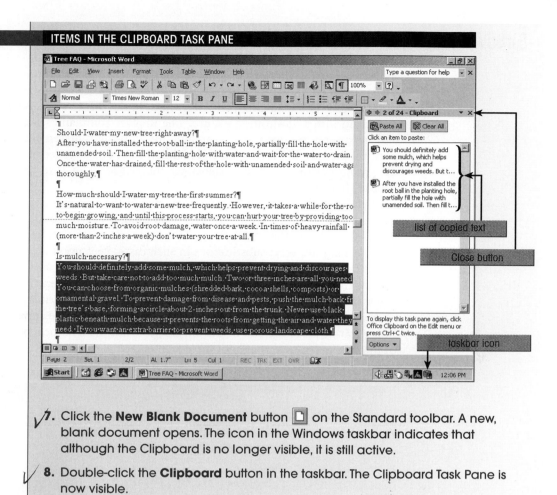

7. Click the **New Blank Document** button [ ] on the Standard toolbar. A new, blank document opens. The icon in the Windows taskbar indicates that although the Clipboard is no longer visible, it is still active.

8. Double-click the **Clipboard** button in the taskbar. The Clipboard Task Pane is now visible.

Now you can use the Clipboard Task Pane to insert the copied text into the new document.

To insert the copied text into the new document:

1. In the Clipboard Task Pane, click the item that begins "You should definitely add . . . " The text is inserted in the document.

2. Press **Enter** to insert a blank line, and then click the item that begins "After you have installed the root ball . . . " in the Task Pane. The text is inserted in the document.

3. Save the document as **Flowering Shrub FAQ** in the Tutorial folder for Tutorial 2, and then close the document. You return to the Tree FAQ document, where the Clipboard Task Pane is still open. You are finished using the Clipboard Task Pane, so you will delete its contents.

4. Click the **Clear All** button [Clear All] on the Clipboard Task Pane. The copied items are removed from the Clipboard Task Pane.

5. Click the **Close** button [X] on the Clipboard Task Pane. The Clipboard Task Pane disappears.

6. Click anywhere in the document to deselect the highlighted paragraph.

7. Save the document.

Finding and Replacing Text

When you're working with a longer document, the quickest and easiest way to locate a particular word or phrase is to use the **Find command**. If you want to replace characters or a phrase with something else, you can use the **Replace command**, which combines the Find command with a substitution feature. The Replace command searches through a document and substitutes the text you're searching for with the replacement text you specify. As you perform the search, Word stops and highlights each occurrence of the search text. You must determine whether or not to substitute the replacement text, and do so by clicking the Replace button.

If you want to substitute every occurrence of the search text with the replacement text, you can click the Replace All button. When using the Replace All button with single words, keep in mind that the search text might be found within other words. To prevent Word from making incorrect substitutions in such cases, it's a good idea to select the Find whole words only check box along with the Replace All button. For example, suppose you want to replace the word "figure" with "illustration". Unless you select the Find whole words only check box, Word would replace "configure" with "conillustration."

As you search through a document, you can search from the current location of the insertion point down to the end of the document, from the insertion point up to the beginning of the document, or throughout the document.

REFERENCE WINDOW   **RW**

Finding and Replacing Text
- Click Edit on the menu bar, and then click either Find or Replace.
- To find text, click the Find tab. To find and replace text, click the Replace tab.
- Click the More button to expand the dialog box to display additional options (including the Find whole words only option). If you see the Less button, the additional options are already displayed.
- In the Search list box, select Down if you want to search from the insertion point to the end of the document, select Up if you want to search from the insertion point to the beginning of the document, or select All to search the entire document.
- Type the characters you want to find in the Find what text box.
- If you are replacing text, type the replacement text in the Replace with text box.
- Click the Find whole words only check box to search for complete words.
- Click the Match case check box to insert the replacement text just as you specified in the Replace with text box.
- Click the Find Next button.
- Click the Replace button to substitute the found text with the replacement text and find the next occurrence.
- Click the Replace All button to substitute all occurrences of the found text with the replacement text.

Marilee wants the company initials, LMG, to be spelled out as "Long Meadow Gardens" each time they appear in the text.

To replace "LMG" with "Long Meadow Gardens":

1. Press **Ctrl+Home** to move the insertion point to the beginning of the document.

2. Click **Edit** on the menu bar, and then click **Replace**. The Find and Replace dialog box opens.

3. If you see a **More** button, click it to display the additional search options. (If you see a Less button, the additional options are already displayed.) Also, if necessary, click the **Search** list arrow, and then click **All**.

4. Click the **Find what** text box, type **LMG**, press the **Tab** key, and then type **Long Meadow Gardens** in the Replace with text box.

   TROUBLE? If you already see the text "LMG" and "Long Meadow Gardens" in your Find and Replace dialog box, someone has already performed these steps on your computer. Continue with Step 7.

5. Click the **Find whole words only** check box to insert a check.

6. Click the **Match case** check box to insert a check. This ensures that Word will insert the replacement text using initial capital letters, as you specified in the Replace with text box. Your Find and Replace dialog box should now look like Figure 2-17.

Figure 2-17	FIND AND REPLACE DIALOG BOX

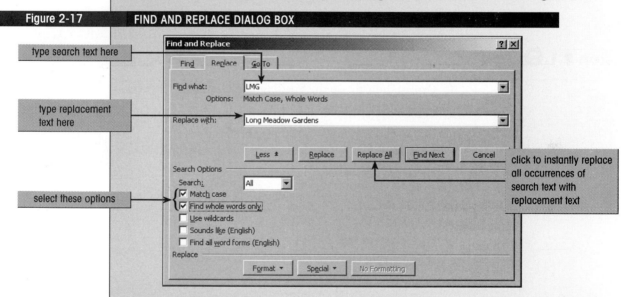

7. Click the **Replace All** button to replace all occurrences of the search text with the replacement text. When Word finishes making the replacements, you see a dialog box telling you that two replacements were made.

8. Click the **OK** button to close the dialog box, and then click the **Close** button in the Find and Replace dialog box to return to the document. The full company name has been inserted into the document, as shown in Figure 2-18. (You may have to scroll down to see this section.)

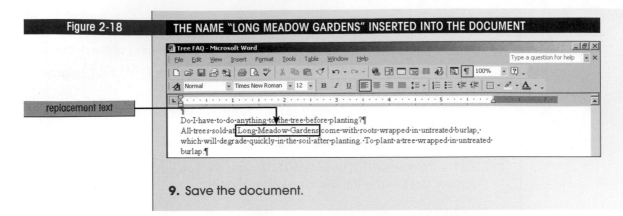

Figure 2-18   THE NAME "LONG MEADOW GARDENS" INSERTED INTO THE DOCUMENT

9. Save the document.

Note that you can also search for and replace formatting, such as bold, and special characters in the Find and Replace dialog box. Click in the Find what text box or the Replace with text box, enter any text if necessary, click the Format button, click Font to open the Font dialog box, and then select the formatting you want to find or replace. Complete the search or replace as usual.

You have completed the content changes Marilee requested. In the next session, you will make some changes that will affect the document's appearance.

Session 2.1 QUICK CHECK

1. Explain how to use the Spelling and Grammar Checker.

2. Which key(s) do you press to move the insertion point to the following places:
   a. **down one line**
   b. to the end of the document
   c. to the next screen

3. Explain how to select the following items using the mouse:
   a. one word
   b. a block of text
   c. one paragraph

4. Define the following terms in your own words:
   a. selection bar
   b. Redo button
   c. drag and drop

5. Describe a situation in which you would use the Undo button and then the Redo button.

6. True or False: You can use the Redo command to restore deleted text at a new location in your document.

7. What is the difference between cut and paste, and copy and paste?

8. List the steps involved in finding and replacing text in a document.

SESSION 2.2

In this session you will make the formatting changes Marilee suggested. You'll use a variety of formatting commands to change the margins, line spacing, text alignment, and paragraph indents. You'll also learn how to use the Format Painter, how to create bulleted and numbered lists, and how to change fonts, font sizes, and emphasis. Finally, you will add a comment to the document.

Changing the Margins

In general, it's best to begin formatting by making the changes that affect the document's overall appearance. Then you can make changes that affect only selected text. In this case, you need to adjust the document's margin settings.

Word uses default margins of 1.25 inches for the left and right margins and 1 inch for the top and bottom margins. The numbers on the ruler (displayed below the Formatting toolbar) indicate the distance in inches from the left margin, not from the left edge of the paper. Unless you specify otherwise, changes you make to the margins affect the entire document, not just the current paragraph or page.

REFERENCE WINDOW   **RW**

Changing Margins for the Entire Document
- With the insertion point anywhere in your document and no text selected, click File on the menu bar, and then click Page Setup.
- If necessary, click the Margins tab to display the margin settings.
- Use the arrows to change the settings in the Top, Bottom, Left, or Right text boxes, or type a new margin value in each text box.
- Make sure the Apply to list box displays Whole document.
- Click the OK button.

You need to change the top margin to 1.5 inches and the left margin to 1.75 inches, per Marilee's request. The left margin needs to be wider than usual to allow space for making holes so that the document can be inserted in a three-ring binder. In the next set of steps, you'll change the margins with the Page Setup command. You also can change margins in Print Layout view by dragging an icon on the horizontal ruler. You'll have a chance to practice this technique in the Review Assignments at the end of this tutorial.

To change the margins in the Tree FAQ document:

1. If you took a break after the previous session, make sure Word is running, the Tree FAQ document is open, and nonprinting characters are displayed.

2. Press **Ctrl+Home** to move the insertion point to the top of the document. This should also ensure that no text is selected in the document.

3. Click **File** on the menu bar, and then click **Page Setup** to open the Page Setup dialog box.

4. If necessary, click the **Margins** tab to display the margin settings. The Top margin setting is selected. See Figure 2-19. As you complete the following steps, keep an eye on the document preview, which will change to reflect any changes you make to the margins.

Figure 2-19	PAGE SETUP DIALOG BOX

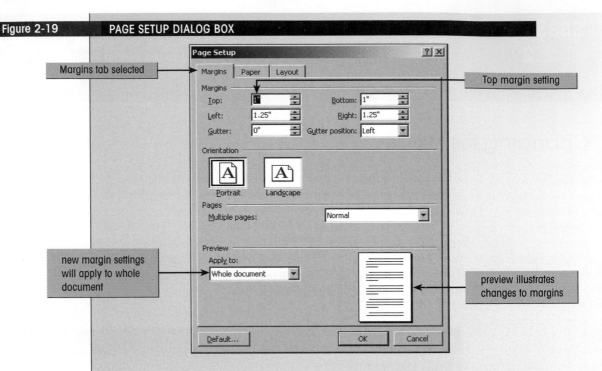

Margins tab selected
Top margin setting
new margin settings will apply to whole document
preview illustrates changes to margins

5. Type **1.5** to change the Top margin setting. (You do not have to type the inches symbol.)

6. Press the **Tab** key twice to select the Left text box and highlight the current margin setting. Notice how the text area in the Preview box moves down to reflect the larger top margin.

7. Type **1.75** and then press the **Tab** key. Watch the Preview box to see how the margin increases.

8. Make sure the **Whole document** option is selected in the Apply to list box, and then click the **OK** button to return to your document. Notice that the right margin on the ruler has changed to reflect the larger margins and the resulting reduced page area. The document text is now 5.5 inches wide. See Figure 2-20.

Figure 2-20	RULER AFTER SETTING LEFT MARGIN TO 1.75 INCHES

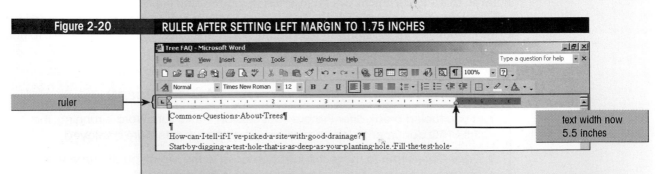

ruler
text width now 5.5 inches

TROUBLE? If a double dotted line and the words "Section Break" appear in your document, Whole document wasn't specified in the Apply to list box. If this occurs, click the Undo button on the Standard toolbar and then repeat Steps 1 through 8, making sure you select the Whole document option in the Apply to list box.

Next, you will change the amount of space between lines of text.

Changing Line Spacing

The line spacing in a document determines the amount of vertical space between lines of text. In most situations, you will want to choose from three basic types of line spacing: **single spacing** (which allows for the largest character in a particular line as well as a small amount of extra space); **1.5 line spacing** (which allows for one and one-half times the space of single spacing); and **double spacing** (which allows for twice the space of single spacing). The FAQ document is currently single-spaced because Word uses single spacing by default. Before changing the line-spacing setting, you should select the text you want to change. The easiest way to change line spacing is to use the Line Spacing button on the Formatting toolbar. You can also use the keyboard to apply single, double, and 1.5 line spacing.

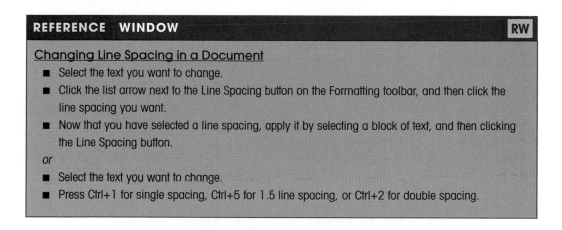

REFERENCE   WINDOW   **RW**

<u>Changing Line Spacing in a Document</u>
- Select the text you want to change.
- Click the list arrow next to the Line Spacing button on the Formatting toolbar, and then click the line spacing you want.
- Now that you have selected a line spacing, apply it by selecting a block of text, and then clicking the Line Spacing button.

or

- Select the text you want to change.
- Press Ctrl+1 for single spacing, Ctrl+5 for 1.5 line spacing, or Ctrl+2 for double spacing.

Marilee has asked you to change the line spacing for the entire FAQ document to 1.5 line spacing. You will begin by selecting the entire document.

To change the document's line spacing:

1. Triple-click in the selection bar to select the entire document.

2. Move the mouse pointer over the Line Spacing button ≣ to display its ScreenTip. You see the text "Line Spacing (1)", indicating that single spacing is currently selected.

3. Click the **Line Spacing** list arrow. A list of line spacing options appears, as shown in Figure 2-21. To double-space the document, you click 2, while to triple-space it, you click 3. In this case, you need to apply 1.5 line spacing.

| Figure 2-21 | LINE SPACING LIST BOX |

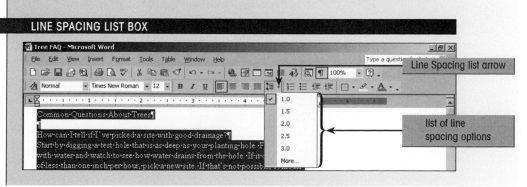

4. Click **1.5**. Notice the additional space between every line of text in the document.

5. Move the mouse pointer over [icon] to display its ScreenTip. You see the text "Line Spacing (1.5)", indicating that 1.5 spacing is currently selected.

Now you are ready to make formatting changes that affect individual paragraphs.

Aligning Text

As you begin formatting individual paragraphs in the FAQ document, keep in mind that in Word, a **paragraph** is defined as any text that ends with a paragraph mark symbol (¶). A paragraph can also be blank, in which case you see a paragraph mark alone on a single line. (The FAQ document includes one blank paragraph before each question heading.)

The term **alignment** refers to how the text of a paragraph lines up horizontally between the margins. By default, text is aligned along the left margin but is **ragged**, or uneven, along the right margin. This is called **left alignment**. With **right alignment**, the text is aligned along the right margin and is ragged along the left margin. With **center alignment**, text is centered between the left and right margins. With **justified alignment**, full lines of text are spaced between or aligned along both the left and the right margins. The paragraph you are reading now is justified. The easiest way to apply alignment settings is by clicking buttons on the Formatting toolbar.

Marilee indicates that the title of the FAQ should be centered and that the main paragraphs should be justified. First, you'll center the title.

To center-align the title:

1. Click anywhere in the title "Common Questions About Trees" at the beginning of the document.

2. Click the **Center** button [icon] on the Formatting toolbar. The text centers between the left and right margins. See Figure 2-22.

| Figure 2-22 | CENTERED TITLE |

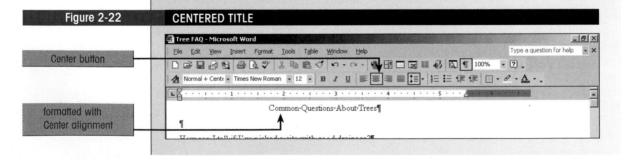

Center button

formatted with Center alignment

Next, you'll justify the text in the first two main paragraphs.

To justify the first two paragraphs using the Formatting toolbar:

1. Click anywhere in the first main paragraph, which begins "Start by digging a test hole . . . "

2. Click the **Justify** button ▤ on the Formatting toolbar. The paragraph text spreads out, so that it lines up evenly along the left and right margins.

3. Move the insertion point to anywhere in the second main paragraph, which begins "While you might be tempted . . . "

4. Click ▤ again. The text is evenly spaced between the left and right margins. See Figure 2-23.

Figure 2-23	JUSTIFIED PARAGRAPHS

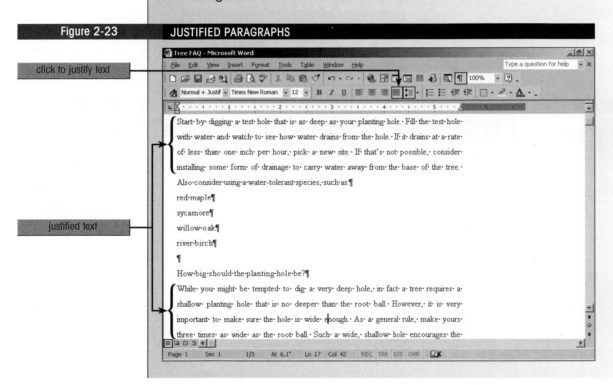

click to justify text

justified text

You'll justify the other paragraphs later. Now that you've learned how to change the paragraph alignment, you can turn your attention to indenting a paragraph.

Indenting a Paragraph

When you become a more experienced Word user, you might want to do some paragraph formatting, such as a **hanging indent** (where all lines except the first line of the paragraph are indented from the left margin) or a **right indent** (where all lines of the paragraph are indented from the right margin). You can select these types of indents on the Indents and Spacing tab of the Paragraph dialog box. (To open this dialog box, you click Format on the menu bar and then click Paragraph.)

In this document, though, you need to indent only the main paragraphs 0.5 inches from the left margin. This left indent is a simple paragraph indent, which requires only a quick click on the Formatting toolbar's Increase Indent button. According to Marilee's notes, you need to indent all of the main paragraphs.

To indent a paragraph using the Increase Indent button:

1. Click anywhere in the first main paragraph, which begins "Start by digging a test hole . . ."

2. Click the **Increase Indent** button ![icon] on the Formatting toolbar twice. (Don't click the Decrease Indent button by mistake.) The entire paragraph moves right 0.5 inches each time you click the Increase Indent button. The paragraph is indented 1 inch, 0.5 inches more than Marilee wants.

3. Click the **Decrease Indent** button ![icon] on the Formatting toolbar to move the paragraph left 0.5 inches. The paragraph is now indented 0.5 inches from the left margin. Don't be concerned about the list of tree species. You will indent it later, when you format it as a bulleted list.

4. Move the insertion point to anywhere in the second main paragraph, which begins "While you might be tempted . . ."

5. Click ![icon]. The paragraph is indented 0.5 inches. See Figure 2-24.

Figure 2-24	INDENTED PARAGRAPH

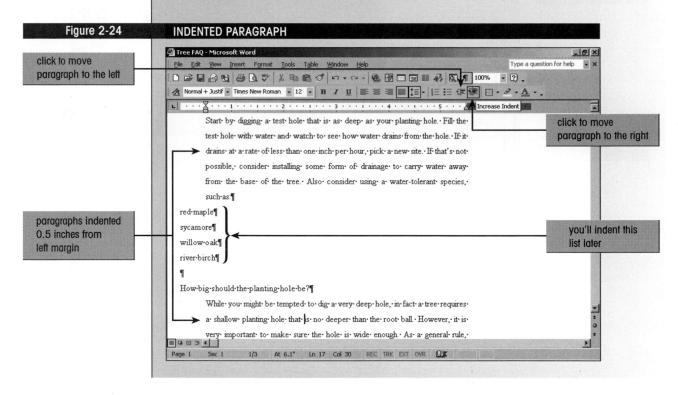

click to move paragraph to the left

click to move paragraph to the right

paragraphs indented 0.5 inches from left margin

you'll indent this list later

You can continue to indent and then justify each paragraph, or simply use the Format Painter command. The Format Painter allows you to copy both the indentation and alignment changes to all paragraphs in the document.

Using Format Painter

The **Format Painter** makes it easy to copy all the formatting features of one paragraph to other paragraphs. You can use this button to copy formatting to one or multiple items.

Use the Format Painter now to copy the formatting of the second paragraph to other main paragraphs. Begin by moving the insertion point to the paragraph whose format you want to copy.

To copy paragraph formatting with the Format Painter:

1. Verify that the insertion point is located in the second main paragraph, which begins "While you might be tempted . . . "

2. Double-click the **Format Painter** button on the Standard toolbar. The Format Painter button will stay highlighted until you click the button again. When you move the pointer over text, the pointer changes to to indicate that the format of the selected paragraph can be painted (or copied) onto another paragraph.

3. Scroll down, and then click anywhere in the third main paragraph, which begins "You may be accustomed . . . " The format of the third paragraph shifts to match the format of the first two main paragraphs. See Figure 2-25. Both paragraphs are now indented and justified. The Format Painter pointer is still visible.

Figure 2-25	FORMATS COPIED WITH FORMAT PAINTER

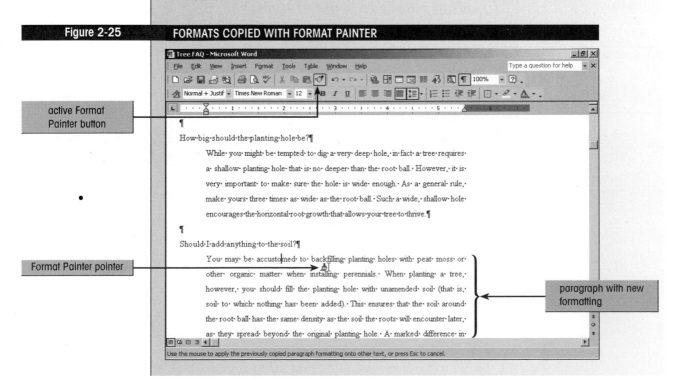

active Format Painter button

Format Painter pointer

paragraph with new formatting

4. Click the remaining paragraphs that are preceded by a question heading. Take care to click only the paragraphs below the question headings. Do not click the document title, the one-line questions, the lists, or the last paragraph in the document.

TROUBLE? If you click a paragraph and the formatting doesn't change to match the second paragraph, you single-clicked the Format Painter button rather than double-clicked it. Select a paragraph that has the desired format, double-click the Format Painter button, and then repeat Step 4.

TROUBLE? If you accidentally click a title or one line of a list, click the Undo button on the Standard toolbar to return the line to its original formatting. Then select a paragraph that has the desired format, double-click the Format Painter button, and finish copying the format to the desired paragraphs.

5. After you are finished formatting paragraphs with the Format Painter pointer, click to turn off the feature.

6. Save the document.

All the main paragraphs in the document are formatted with the correct indentation and alignment. Your next job is to make the lists easier to read by adding bullets and numbers.

Adding Bullets and Numbers

You can emphasize a list of items by adding a heavy dot, or **bullet**, before each item in the list. For consecutive items, you can use numbers instead of bullets. Marilee requests that you add bullets to the list of tree species on page 1 to make them stand out.

To apply bullets to a list of items:

1. Scroll to the top of the document until you see the list of tree species below the text "Also consider using a water-tolerant species such as:".

2. Select the four items in the list (from "red maple" to "river birch").

3. Click the **Bullets** button on the Formatting toolbar. A bullet, a dark circle, appears in front of each item. Each line indents to make room for the bullet.

4. In order to make the bullets align with the first paragraph, make sure the list is still selected, and then click the **Increase Indent** button on the Formatting toolbar. The bulleted list moves to the right.

5. Click anywhere within the document window to deselect the text. Figure 2-26 shows the indented bulleted list.

Figure 2-26 | INDENTED BULLETED LIST

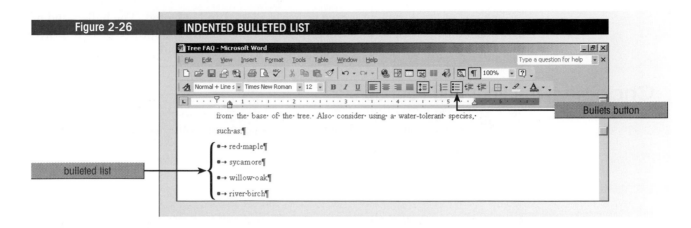

bulleted list

Next, you need to format the list of steps involved in planting a tree. Marilee asks you to format this information as a numbered list, an easy task thanks to the Numbering button, which automatically numbers selected paragraphs with consecutive numbers. If you insert a new paragraph, delete a paragraph, or reorder the paragraphs, Word automatically adjusts the numbers to make sure they remain consecutive.

To apply numbers to the list of items:

1. Scroll down until you see the list that begins "Remove any tags . . . " and ends with "of the planting hole."

2. Select the entire list.

3. Click the **Numbering** button on the Formatting toolbar. Consecutive numbers appear in front of each item in the indented list. The list is indented, similar to the bulleted list. The list would look better if it was indented to align with the paragraph.

4. Click the **Increase Indent** button on the Formatting toolbar. The list moves to the right, so that the numbers align with the preceding paragraph.

5. Click anywhere in the document to deselect the text. Figure 2-27 shows the indented and numbered list.

Figure 2-27 | INDENTED NUMBERED LIST

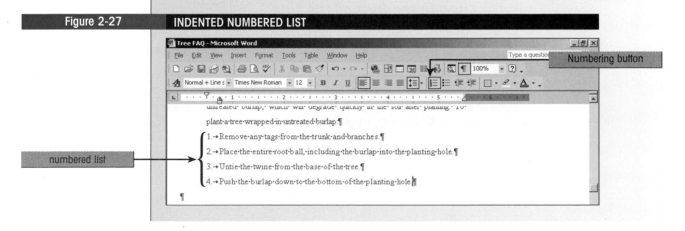

numbered list

The text of the document is now properly aligned and indented. The bullets and numbers make the lists easy to read and give readers visual clues about the type of information they contain. Next, you need to adjust the formatting of individual words.

Changing the Font and Font Size

All of Marilee's remaining changes concern changing fonts, adjusting font sizes, and emphasizing text with font styles. The first step is to change the font of the title from 12-point Times New Roman to 14-point Arial. This will make the title stand out from the rest of the text.

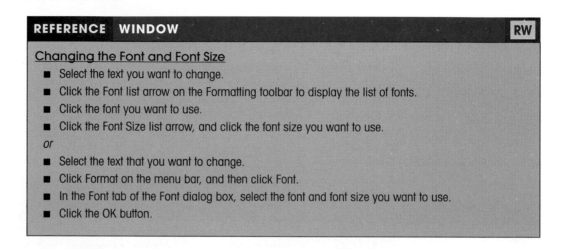

REFERENCE WINDOW **RW**

Changing the Font and Font Size
- Select the text you want to change.
- Click the Font list arrow on the Formatting toolbar to display the list of fonts.
- Click the font you want to use.
- Click the Font Size list arrow, and click the font size you want to use.

or

- Select the text that you want to change.
- Click Format on the menu bar, and then click Font.
- In the Font tab of the Font dialog box, select the font and font size you want to use.
- Click the OK button.

Marilee wants you to change the font of the title as well as its size and style. To do this, you'll use the Formatting toolbar. Marilee wants you to use a **sans serif** font, which is a font that does not have the small horizontal lines (called serifs) at the tops and bottoms of the letters. Sans serif fonts are often used in titles so they contrast with the body text. Times New Roman is a serif font, and Arial is a sans serif font. The text you are reading now is a serif font, and the text in the following steps is a sans serif font.

To change the font of the title:

1. Press **Ctrl+Home** to move the insertion point to the beginning of the document, and then select the title **Common Questions About Trees**.

2. Click the **Font** list arrow on the Formatting toolbar. A list of available fonts appears in alphabetical order, with the name of the current font in the Font text box. See Figure 2-28. (Your list of fonts might be different from those shown.) Fonts that have been used recently might appear above a double line. Note that each name in the list is formatted with the relevant font. For example, "Arial" appears in the Arial font, and "Times New Roman" appears in the Times New Roman font.

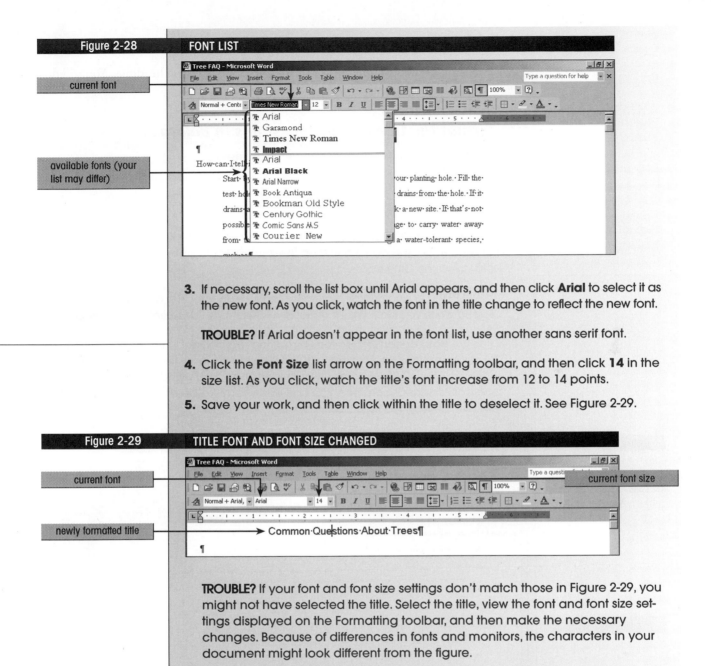

Figure 2-28 | **FONT LIST**

current font

available fonts (your list may differ)

3. If necessary, scroll the list box until Arial appears, and then click **Arial** to select it as the new font. As you click, watch the font in the title change to reflect the new font.

   TROUBLE? If Arial doesn't appear in the font list, use another sans serif font.

4. Click the **Font Size** list arrow on the Formatting toolbar, and then click **14** in the size list. As you click, watch the title's font increase from 12 to 14 points.

5. Save your work, and then click within the title to deselect it. See Figure 2-29.

Figure 2-29 | **TITLE FONT AND FONT SIZE CHANGED**

current font

current font size

newly formatted title

Common·Questions·About·Trees¶

TROUBLE? If your font and font size settings don't match those in Figure 2-29, you might not have selected the title. Select the title, view the font and font size settings displayed on the Formatting toolbar, and then make the necessary changes. Because of differences in fonts and monitors, the characters in your document might look different from the figure.

Emphasizing **Text with Boldface, Underlining, and Italics**

You can emphasize words in your document with boldface, underlining, or italics. These styles help make specific thoughts, ideas, words, or phrases stand out. (You can also add special effects such as shadows to characters.) Marilee marked a few words on the document draft (shown in Figure 2-1) that need this kind of special emphasis. You add boldface, underlining, or italics by using the relevant buttons on the Formatting toolbar. These buttons are **toggle buttons**, which means you can click them once to format the selected text, and then click again to remove the formatting from the selected text.

Bolding Text

Marilee wants to draw attention to the title and all of the question headings. You will do this by bolding them.

To format the title and the questions in boldface:

1. Select the title **Common Questions About Trees**.

2. Press and hold **Ctrl**, and then select the first question in the document ("How can I tell if I've picked a site with good drainage?"). Both the title and the first question are now selected.

3. Hold down **Ctrl** and select the remaining questions. To display more of the document, use the down arrow on the vertical scroll bar while you continue to hold down the Ctrl key.

   TROUBLE? If you accidentally select something other than a question, keep Ctrl pressed while you click the incorrect item. This should deselect the incorrect item.

4. Click the **Bold** button **B** on the Formatting toolbar, and then click anywhere in the document to deselect the text. The title and the questions appear in bold, as shown in Figure 2-30. After reviewing this change, you wonder if the title would look better without boldface. You can easily remove boldface by selecting the text and clicking the Bold button again to turn, or toggle, off boldfacing.

| Figure 2-30 | TEXT IN BOLDFACE |

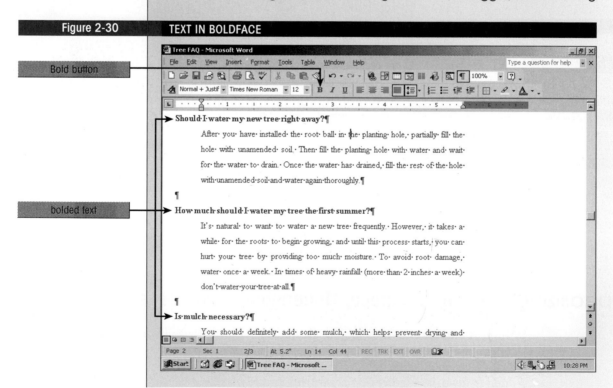

Bold button

bolded text

5. To remove the boldface, select the title, and then click **B**. The title now appears without boldface. You decide you prefer to emphasize the title with boldface after all.

6. Verify that the title is still selected, and then click **B**. The title appears in boldface again.

Underlining Text

The Underline button works in the same way as the Bold button. Marilee's edits indicate that the word "Note" should be inserted and underlined at the beginning of the final paragraph. Using the Underline button, you'll make both of these changes at the same time.

To underline text:

1. Press **Ctrl+End** to move the insertion point to the end of the document. Then move the insertion point to the left of the word "Any" in the first line of the final paragraph.

2. Click the **Underline** button **U** on the Formatting toolbar to turn on underlining. The Underline button remains highlighted. Whatever text you type now will be underlined on your screen and in your printed document.

3. Type **Note:** and then click **U** to turn off underlining. See how the Underline button is no longer pressed, and "Note:" is now underlined.

4. Press the **spacebar**. See Figure 2-31.

Figure 2-31	WORD TYPED WITH UNDERLINE

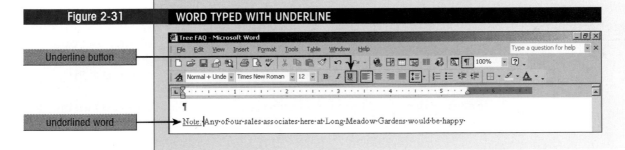

Underline button

underlined word

Italicizing Text

Next, you'll format each instance of "Long Meadow Gardens" in italics. This helps draw attention to the company name.

To italicize the company name:

1. Scroll up to the third to last question on the first page ("Do I have to do anything to the tree before planting?").

2. In the first line below the question, select **Long Meadow Gardens**.

3. Click the **Italic** button **I** on the Formatting toolbar. The company name changes from regular to italic text. In the next step, you'll learn a useful method for repeating the task you just performed.

4. Scroll down to the last paragraph of the document, select the company name, and then press the **F4** key. Keep in mind that you can use the F4 key to repeat your most recent action. It is especially helpful when formatting parts of a document.

5. Save the document.

Adding Comments

Peter stops by your desk to review your work. He's happy with the document's appearance, but wonders if he should add some information about fertilizing new trees. He asks you to insert a note to Marilee about this using Word's Comment feature. A **comment** is an electronic version of an adhesive note that you might attach to a piece of paper. To attach a comment to a Word document, select a block of text, click Comment on the Insert menu, and then type your comment in the Reviewing Pane. To display the comment, place the mouse pointer over text to which a comment has been attached. Comments are very useful when you are exchanging Word documents with co-workers electronically, either via e-mail or on floppies, because they allow you to make notes or queries without affecting the document itself.

You'll attach Peter's comment to the document title so that Marilee will be sure to see it as soon as she opens the document.

To attach a comment:

1. Scroll up to the top of the document, and then select the title **Common Questions About Trees**.

2. Click **Insert** on the menu bar, and then click **Comment**. The Reviewing Pane opens at the bottom of the document window. Depending on how your computer is set up, you might see your name, as well as the current date and time in the Reviewing Pane. The insertion point is positioned in the Reviewing Pane, ready for you to type the comment. Also, the Reviewing toolbar is displayed below the Formatting toolbar. Finally, notice that the title is enclosed in brackets. See Figure 2-32.

Figure 2-32   **INSERTING A COMMENT**

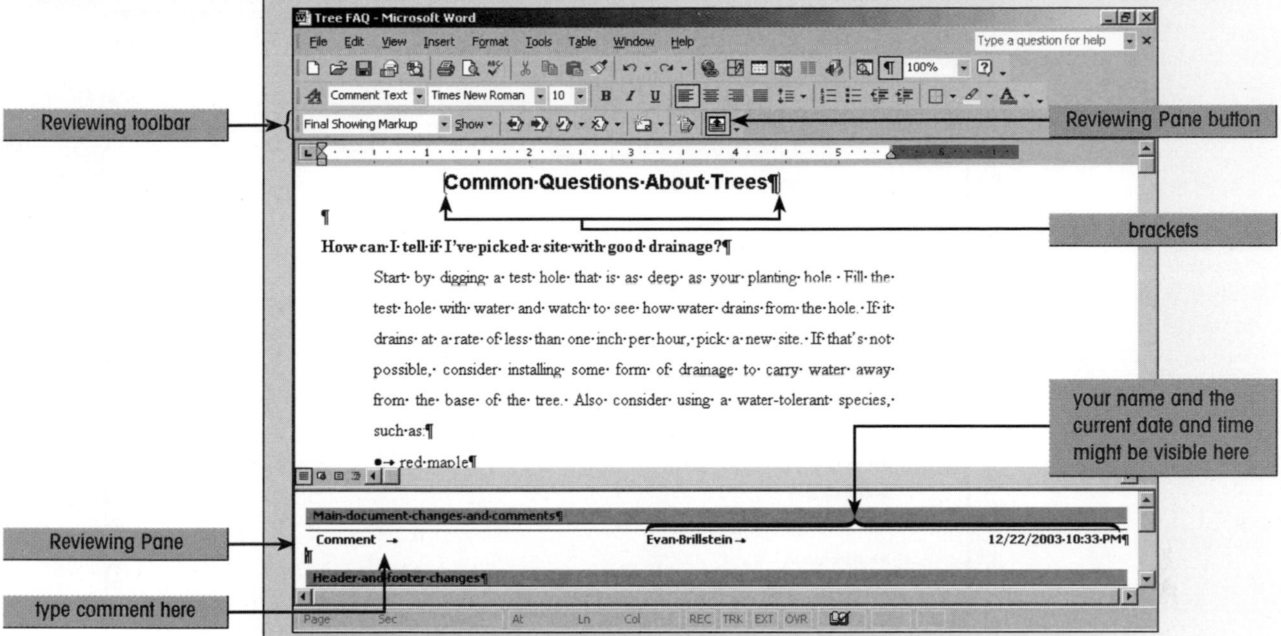

Reviewing toolbar

Reviewing Pane button

brackets

your name and the current date and time might be visible here

Reviewing Pane

type comment here

TROUBLE? The Reviewing Pane and the brackets might be a different color on your computer.

3. Type **Should we add a section on fertilizing new trees?** Now that you have typed the comment, you can close the Reviewing Pane.

4. Click the **Reviewing Pane** button 🔲 on the Reviewing toolbar. The Reviewing Pane closes.

After you insert a comment, you should display it once to make sure you included all the necessary information.

To display a comment:

1. Move the mouse pointer over the title. The comment is displayed in a box over the title. Depending on how your computer is set up, you might see your name in the comment, as well as the date and time the comment was attached. See Figure 2-33.

Figure 2-33   **VIEWING A COMMENT**

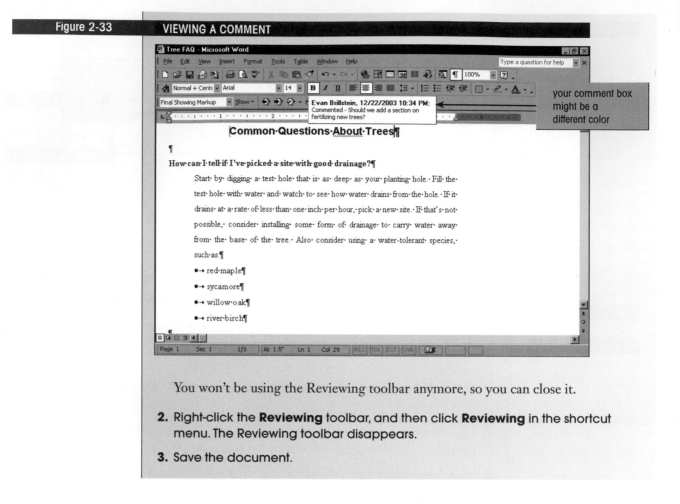

You won't be using the Reviewing toolbar anymore, so you can close it.

2. Right-click the **Reviewing** toolbar, and then click **Reviewing** in the shortcut menu. The Reviewing toolbar disappears.

3. Save the document.

Previewing Formatted Text

You have made all the editing and formatting changes that Marilee requested for the FAQ. It's helpful to preview a document after formatting it, because the Print Preview window makes it easy to spot text that is not aligned correctly.

To preview and print the document:

1. Click the **Print Preview** button on the Standard toolbar and examine the first page of the document. Notice the box in the right margin of the document, indicating that a comment has been attached to the document title. Use the vertical scroll bar to display the second page. (If you notice any formatting errors, click the Close button on the Print Preview toolbar, correct the errors in Normal view, save your changes, and then return to the Print Preview window.)

2. Click the **Print** button on the Print Preview toolbar. After a pause, the document prints. Note that the comment you inserted into the document earlier is not printed.

3. Click the **Close** button on the Print Preview toolbar.

4. Close the document and then close Word.

You now have a hard copy of the final FAQ, as shown in Figure 2-34.

Figure 2-34 **FINAL VERSION OF TREE FAQ DOCUMENT**

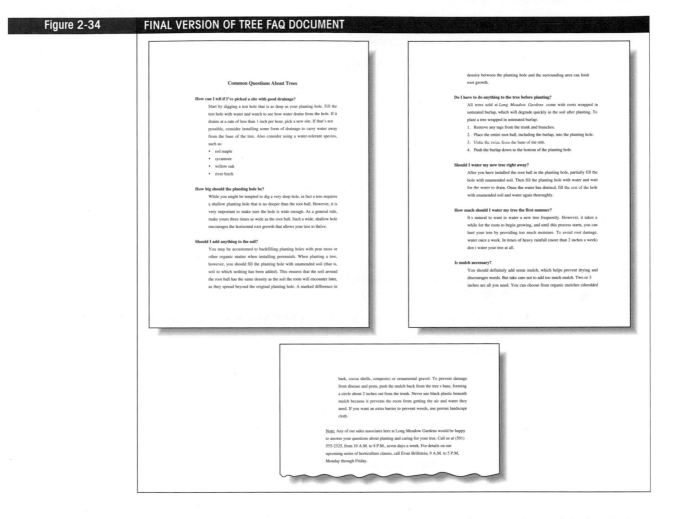

In this tutorial, you have helped Peter edit and format the FAQ that will be handed out to all customers purchasing a tree at Long Meadow Gardens. Peter will e-mail the file to Marilee later so that she can review your work and read the comment you attached.

Session 2.2 QUICK CHECK

1. What are Word's default margins for the left and right margins? For the top and bottom margins?

2. Describe the four types of text alignment.

3. Explain how to indent a paragraph 1 inch or more from the left margin.

4. Describe a situation in which you would use the Format Painter.

5. Explain how to add underlining to a word as you type it.

6. Explain how to transform a series of short paragraphs into a numbered list.

7. Explain how to format a title in 14-point Arial.

8. Describe the steps involved in changing the line spacing in a document.

REVIEW ASSIGNMENTS

Now that you have completed the FAQ, Marilee asks you to help her create a statement summarizing customer accounts for the Long Meadow Garden's wholesale nursery. She would also like you to create a document that contains contact information for Long Meadow Gardens. Remember to use the Undo and Redo buttons as you work to correct any errors.

1. If necessary, start Word, make sure your Data Disk is in the appropriate disk drive, and check your screen to make sure your settings match those in the tutorial.

2. Open the file **Statmnt** from the Review folder for Tutorial 2 on your Data Disk, and save the document as **Monthly Statement** in the same folder.

3. Use the Spelling and Grammar checker to correct any spelling or grammatical errors. If the Suggestions list box does not include the correct replacement, click outside the Spelling and Grammar dialog box, type the correction yourself, click Resume in the Spelling and Grammar dialog box, and continue checking the document.

4. Proofread the document carefully to check for any additional errors. Look for two words that are spelled correctly but used improperly.

5. Change the right margin to 2 inches using the Page Setup dialog box.

Explore

6. Change the left margin using the ruler in Print Layout view, as follows:
   a. Select the entire document.
   b. Position the pointer on the small gray square on the ruler at the left margin. A ScreenTip with the words "Left Indent" appears.
   c. Press and hold down the mouse button. A vertical dotted line appears in the document window, indicating the current left margin. Drag the margin left to the 0.5-inch mark on the ruler, and then release the mouse button.

7. Make all edits and formatting changes shown in Figure 2-35, and save your work.

Figure 2-35

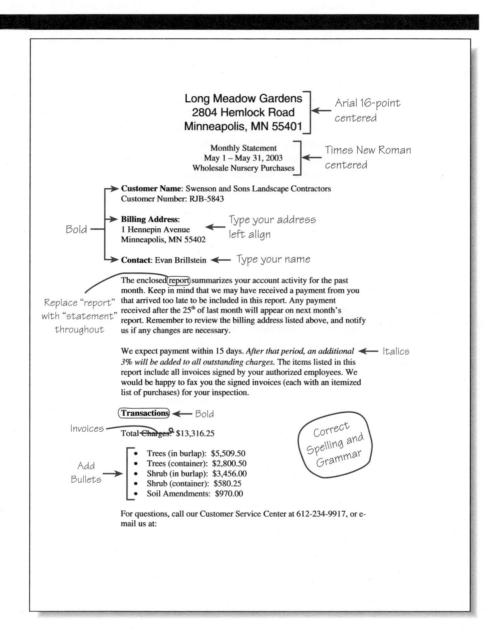

8. Remove any Smart Tags in the document.

Explore → 9. When you type Web addresses or e-mail addresses in a document, Word automatically formats them as links. When you click a Web address formatted as a link, Windows automatically opens a Web browser (such as Microsoft Internet Explorer) and, if your computer is connected to the Internet, displays that Web page. If you click an e-mail address formatted as a link, Windows opens a program where you can type an e-mail message. The address you clicked is automatically included as the recipient of the e-mail. You'll see how this works as you add a Web address and e-mail address to the statement. In the address centered at the top of the document, click at the end of the ZIP code, add a new line, and then type the address for the company's Web site: www.longmeadowgardens.com. When you are finished, press Enter. Notice that as soon as you press Enter, Word formats the address in blue with an underline, marking it as a link. Move the mouse pointer over the link and read the ScreenTip. Because this Web address is fictitious, clicking it will not actually display a Web page.

Explore → 10. Move the insertion point to the end of the document, press the spacebar, type long_meadow_gardens@worldlink.com and then press Enter. Word formats the e-mail address as a link. Press and hold the Ctrl button and then click the link. (If you see a message asking if you want to make Outlook Express your default mail client, click No.) You see a window where you could type an e-mail message to Long Meadow Gardens. (If your computer is not set up for e-mail, close any error messages that open.) Close the e-mail window without saving any changes. The link is now formatted in purple, indicating that the link has been clicked.

11 Move the last sentence of the document (which begins "For questions, call . . . ") to a new paragraph, just above the heading "Transactions".

12. Select the last Transactions portion of the document, from the heading "Transactions" down to the end of the document. Indent the selected text 1 inch by clicking the Increase Indent button twice.

13. Open the Clipboard Task Pane. Select the company name, address, and Web address at the top of the document and copy it to the Clipboard, and then copy the company e-mail address to the Clipboard.

Explore → 14. Open a new, blank document and display the Clipboard Task Pane. In the Clipboard Task Pane, click the company address to insert this information at the top of the document. Insert two blank lines, type "Send all e-mail correspondence to YOUR NAME:" (replace YOUR NAME with your first and last name). Type a space and then, in the Clipboard Task Pane, click the company e-mail address. Type a period at the end of the e-mail address.

15. Clear the contents of the Clipboard Task Pane and then close the Task Pane.

Explore ▶ 16. If necessary, switch to Print Layout view. Then attach the following comment to the company name: "Marilee, please let me know how you want this document formatted." Notice that in Print Layout view you type the comment in a small comment window directly in the margin. Switch to Normal view, and display the comment by positioning the pointer over the company name.

17. Save the document as **LMG Contact Information** in the Review folder for Tutorial 2. Print and close the document.

18. Save the Monthly Statement document, preview and print it, and then close it. Also close the Clipboard Task Pane, if necessary. Then exit Word.

CASE PROBLEMS

Case 1. Authorization Form for Gygs and Bytes Melissa Martinez is the purchasing manager for Gygs and Bytes, a wholesale distributor of computer parts based in Portland, Oregon. Most of the company's business is conducted via catalog or through the company's Web site, but local customers sometimes drop by to pick up small orders. In the past Melissa has had problems determining which of her customers' employees were authorized to sign credit invoices. To avoid confusion, she has asked all local customers to complete a form listing employees who are authorized to sign invoices. She plans to place the completed forms in a binder at the main desk, so the receptionist at Gygs and Bytes can find the information quickly.

1. Open the file **Form** from the Cases folder for Tutorial 2 on your Data Disk, and save the file as **Authorization Form** in the same folder.

Explore ▶ 2. Correct any spelling or grammar errors. Ignore any words that are spelled correctly, but that are not included in Word's dictionary. When the Spelling and Grammar Checker highlights the word "sining", click the appropriate word in the Suggestions box, and then click Change.

Explore ▶ 3. If necessary, read Steps 9 and 10 in the Review Assignments to learn about adding Web addresses and e-mail addresses to a document. Below the company's mailing address, add the company Web address in all uppercase: WWW.G&B.NET.

4. Change the top and left margins to 1.5 inches.

5. Center the first five lines of the document (containing the form title and the company address).

6. Format the first line of the document (the form title) in 16-point Arial, with italics.

7. Format lines 2 through 5 (the address, including the Web address) in 12-point Arial.

Explore   8. Replace all instances of G&B, except the first one (in the Web address), with the complete company name, Gygs and Bytes. Use the Find Next button to skip an instance of the search text.

9. Format the blank ruled lines as a numbered list. Customers will use these blank lines to write in the names of authorized employees.

Explore   10. Format the entire document using 1.5 spacing. Then triple-space the numbered list (with the blank lines) and the Signature and Title lines as follows:
   a. Select the numbered list with the blank lines.
   b. Triple-space the selected text using the line spacing button on the Formatting toolbar.
   c. Select the "Signed:" and the "Title:" lines, and then press F4.

11. Save the document.

12. Drag "Customer Number:" up to position it above "Customer Name".

Explore   13. Select "Customer Name:", "Customer Number:", and "Address:". Press Ctrl+B to format the selected text in bold. Note that it is sometimes easier to use this keyboard shortcut instead of the Bold button on the Formatting toolbar.

14. Delete the phrase "all employees" and replace it with "all authorized personnel".

Explore   15. Select the phrase "all authorized personnel will be required to show a photo I.D." Press Ctrl+I to format the selected text in italics. It is sometimes easier to use this keyboard shortcut instead of the Italic button on the Formatting toolbar.

16. Insert your name in the form, in the "Customer Name:" line. Format your name without boldface, if necessary.

17. Insert your address, left aligned, without bold, below the heading "Address:".

18. Click the Print Preview button on the Standard toolbar to check your work.

Explore   19. Click the Shrink to Fit button on the Print Preview toolbar to reduce the entire document to one page. Word reduces the font sizes slightly in order to fit the entire form on one page. Close the Print Preview window and save your work.

Explore   20. Use the Print command on the File menu to open the Print dialog box. Print two copies of the document by changing the Number of copies setting in the Print dialog box.

Explore   21. You can find out the number of words in your documents by using the Word Count command on the Tools menu. Use this command to determine the number of words in the document, and then write that number in the upper-right corner of the printout.

22. Save and close the document, and then exit Word.

Case 2. Advertising Brochure for the CCW Web Site The *Carson College Weekly* is a student-run newspaper published through the Carson College Student Services Association. The newspaper is distributed around campus each Friday. The online version of the newspaper is posted on the CCW Web site on Thursdays. Local businesses have a long-established tradition of advertising in the print version of the newspaper, and the paper's advertising manager, Noah McCormick, would like to ensure that this same tradition carries over to the online newspaper. When he sends out the monthly statements to his print advertisers, he would like to include a one-page brochure encouraging them to purchase an online ad. He has copied the text of the brochure from the CCW Web site and saved it as unformatted text in a Word document.

1. Open the file **CCW** from the Cases folder for Tutorial 2 on your Data Disk, and save the file as **CCW Brochure** in the same folder.

2. Correct any spelling or grammar errors. Take time to make sure the right correction is selected in the Suggestions list box before you click Change. Proofread for any words that are spelled correctly but used incorrectly.

Explore

3. If necessary, read Steps 9 and 10 in the Review Assignments to learn about adding Web addresses and e-mail addresses to a document. Below *Carson College Weekly*, add the newspaper's Web address in all uppercase: WWW.CARSON.CCW.EDU, and then press Enter. At the end of the document, insert a space, type "advertising@carson.ccw.edu", (without the quotation marks), type a period, and then press Enter.

4. In the second to last sentence, replace "the CCW Advertising Office" with your name.

5. Change the right margin to 1.5 inches and the left margin to 2 inches.

6. Format the entire document in 12-point Times New Roman.

7. Format the four paragraphs below "Did you know?" as a bulleted list.

8. Drag the third bullet (which begins "You can include . . . ") up to the top of the bulleted list.

9. Format the first two lines of the document using a font, font size, and alignment of your choice. Use bold or italics for emphasis.

10. Format the entire document using 1.5 line spacing.

11. Add a comment to the first line (*Carson College Weekly*) asking Noah if he would like you to leave a printed copy of the brochure in his mailbox. Close the Reviewing Pane and the Reviewing toolbar when you are finished.

12. Save your work, preview the document, and then switch back to Normal view to make any changes you think necessary.

13. Print the document.

14. Save and close the document, and then exit Word.

Case 3. *Productivity Training Summary for UpTime* Matt Patterson is UpTime's marketing director for the Northeast region. The company provides productivity training for large companies across the country. Matt wants to provide interested clients with a one-page summary of UpTime's productivity training sessions.

1. If necessary, start Word, make sure your Data Disk is in the appropriate disk drive, and check your screen to make sure your settings match those in the tutorials.

2. Open the file **UpTime** from the Tutorial 2 Cases folder on your Data Disk, and save it as **UpTime Training Summary** in the same folder.

3. Change the title at the beginning of the document to a 16-point sans serif font. Be sure to pick a font that looks professional and is easy to read. (Remember to use the Undo and Redo buttons as you work to correct any editing mistakes.)

4. Center and bold the title and Web address.

5. Delete the word "general" from the second sentence of the first paragraph after the document title.

6. Convert the list of training components following the first paragraph to an indented, numbered list.

7. Under the heading "Personal Productivity Training Seminar," delete the last sentence from the first paragraph, the one beginning with "This seminar improves".

8. Under the heading "Personal Productivity Training Seminar," delete the phrase "at the seminar" from the first sentence in the second paragraph.

9. In the first paragraph under the heading "Management Productivity Training," move the first sentence (beginning with "UpTime provides management training") to the end of the paragraph.

10. Switch the order of the first and second paragraphs under the "Field Services Technology and Training" heading.

11. Search for the text "your name", and replace it with your first and last name. Use the Bold button and the Underline button on the Formatting toolbar to format your name in boldface, with an underline.

12. Change the top margin to 1.5 inches.

13. Change the left margin to 1.75 inches.

14. Bold and italicize the heading "Personal Productivity Training Seminar" and then use the Format Painter to copy this heading's format to the headings "Management Productivity Training" and "Field Services Technology and Training". Turn off the Format Painter when you're finished.

Explore

15. Select both occurrences of the word "free" in the second paragraph under the "Field Services Technology and Training" heading. Press Ctrl+I to format the selected text in italics.

16. Save and preview the document.

17. Print the document, and then close the file, and exit Word.

Case 4. Product Description for Ridge Top   Thomas McGee is vice president of sales and marketing at Ridge Top, an outdoor and sporting-gear store in Conshohocken, Pennsylvania. Each year Thomas and his staff mail a description of new products to Ridge Top's regular customers. Thomas has asked you to edit and format the first few pages of this year's new products' description.

1. If necessary, start Word, make sure your Data Disk is in the appropriate disk drive, and check your screen to make sure your settings match those in the tutorials.

2. Open the file **Ridge** from the Tutorial 2 Cases folder on your Data Disk, and save it as **RidgeTop Guide** in the same folder.

3. Use the Spelling and Grammar checker to correct any errors in the document. Because of the nature of this document, it contains some words that the Word dictionary on your computer may not recognize. It also contains headings that the Spelling and Grammar checker may consider sentence fragments. As you use the Spelling and Grammar checker, use the Ignore All button, if necessary, to skip over brand names.

4. Delete the phrase "a great deal" from the first sentence of the paragraph below the heading "Snuggle Up to These Prices." (Remember to use the Undo and Redo buttons to correct any editing mistakes as you work.)

5. Reverse the order of the first two paragraphs under the heading, "You'll Eat Up the Prices of This Camp Cooking Gear!"

6. Cut the last sentence of the first full paragraph ("Prices are good through . . . ") from the document. Then move the insertion point to the end of the document, press the Enter key twice, and insert the cut sentence as a new paragraph. Format it in 12-point Arial, and italicize it.

7. Format the Ridge Top tip items as a numbered list.

Explore ▶ 8. Reorder the items under the "Ridge Top Tips" heading by moving the fourth product idea and the following blank paragraph to the top of the list.

9. Search for the text "your name", and replace with your first and last name.

Explore ▶ 10. Experiment with two special paragraph alignment options: first line and hanging. First, select everything from the heading "Ridge Top Guarantees Warmth at Cool Prices" through the paragraph just before the heading "Ridge Top Tips". Next, click Format on the menu bar, click Paragraph, click the Indents and Spacing tab if necessary, click the Help button in the upper-right corner of the dialog box, click the Special list arrow, and review the information on the special alignment options. Experiment with both the First line and the Hanging options. When you are finished, return the document to its original format by choosing the none option.

11. Justify all the paragraphs in the document. (*Hint*: To select all paragraphs in the document at one time, click Edit on the menu bar, and then click Select All.)

12. Replace all occurrences of "RidgeTop" with "Ridge Top". (You may have already made this correction when you checked spelling in the document.)

13. Apply a 12-point, bold, sans serif font to each of the headings. Be sure to pick a font that looks professional and is easy to read. Use the Format Painter to copy the formatting after you apply it once using the Font list box.

14. Change the title's and subtitle's font to the same font you used for the headings, except set the size to 16 point.

15. Bold the title and subtitle.

16. Underline the names and prices for all of the brand name products.

17. Save and preview the document.

18. Print the document, and then close the file, and exit Word.

INTERNET ASSIGNMENTS

Student Union

The purpose of the Internet Assignments is to challenge you to find information on the Internet that you can use to create effective documents. The actual assignments are updated and maintained on the Course Technology Web site. Log on to the Internet and use your Web browser to go to the Student Union on the New Perspectives Series site at **www.course.com/NewPerspectives/studentunion**. Click the Online Companions link, and then click the link for this text.

QUICK CHECK ANSWERS

Session 2.1

1. Click at the beginning of the document, and then click the Spelling and Grammar button on the Standard toolbar. In the Spelling and Grammar dialog box, review any errors highlighted in color. Grammatical errors appear in green; spelling errors appear in red. Review the possible corrections in the Suggestions list box. To accept a suggested correction, click it in the Suggestions list box. Then click Change to make the correction and continue searching the document for errors.

2. (a) ↓; (b) Ctrl+End; (c) Page Down

3. (a) Double-click the word; (b) click at the beginning of the block, and then drag until the entire block is selected; (c) double-click in the selection bar next to the paragraph, or triple-click in the paragraph.

4. (a) the blank space in the left margin area of the Document window that allows you to easily select entire lines or large blocks of text; (b) the button on the Standard toolbar that redoes an action you previously reversed using the Undo button; (c) the process of moving text by first selecting the text, and then pressing and holding the mouse button while moving the text to its new location in the document, and finally releasing the mouse button

5. You might use the Undo button to remove the bold formatting you had just applied to a word. You could then use the Redo button to restore the bold formatting to the word.

6. False

7. Cut and paste removes the selected material from its original location and inserts it in a new location. Copy and paste makes a copy of the selected material and inserts the copy in a new location; the original material remains in its original location.

8. Click Edit on the menu bar, click Replace, type the search text in the Find what text box, type the replacement text in the Replace with text box, click Find Next or click Replace all.

Session 2.2

1. The default top and bottom margins are 1 inch. The default left and right margins are 1.25 inches.

2. Align-left: each line flush left, ragged right; Align-right: each line flush right, ragged left; Center: each line centered, ragged right and left.; Justify: each line flush left and flush right

4. You might use the Format Painter to copy the formatting of a heading to the other headings in the document.

5. Click the Underline button on the Formatting toolbar, type the word, and then click the Underline button again to turn off underlining.

6. Select the paragraphs, and then click the Numbering button on the Formatting toolbar.

7. Select the title, click the Font list arrow, and click Arial in the list of fonts. Then click the Font Size list arrow, and click 14.

8. Select the text you want to change, click the Line Spacing list arrow on the Formatting toolbar, and then click the line spacing option you want. Or select the text, and then press Ctrl+1 for single spacing, Ctrl+5 for 1.5 line spacing, or Ctrl+2 for double spacing.

In this tutorial you will:

- Set tab stops

- Divide a document into sections

- Change the vertical alignment of a section

- Center a page between the top and bottom margins

- Create a header with page numbers

- Create a table

- Sort the rows in a table

- Modify a table's structure

- Format a table

CREATING
A MULTIPLE-PAGE
REPORT

Writing a Recommendation for Tyger Networks

CASE

Tyger Networks

Tyger Networks is a consulting company in Madison, Wisconsin that specializes in setting up computer networks for small businesses and organizations. Susan Launspach, the program director at New Hope Social Services, recently contacted Tyger Networks about linking the computer networks at New Hope's three main offices. The offices are scattered throughout southern Wisconsin in Madison, Janesville, and Milwaukee. Each office has its own self-contained computer network. To make it easier for a social worker in one office to access data stored on a computer in another office, Susan would like to establish some kind of connection between the three networks.

Caitilyn Waller, an account manager at Tyger Networks, is responsible for the New Hope account. In a phone call, she explained to Susan that connecting the three offices will create a new type of a network known as a wide area network (WAN). Because Susan is unfamiliar with networking terminology, Caitilyn offered to write a report that summarizes the options for creating this type of a network. Working with a task force of sales and technical personnel, Caitilyn compiled the necessary information in a multipage document. Now Caitilyn would like you to help her finish formatting the report. She also needs some help adding a table to the end of the report. Once the report is completed, Susan will present it to the board of directors at New Hope Social Services.

In this tutorial, you will format the report's title page so that it has a different layout from the rest of the report. The title page will contain only the title and subtitle and will not have page numbers like the rest of the report. You also will add a table to the report that summarizes the costs involved in creating a WAN.

SESSION 3.1

In this session you will review the task force's recommendation report. Then you will learn how to set tab stops, divide a document into sections, center a page between the top and bottom margins, create a header, and create a table.

Planning **the Document**

As head of the task force, Caitilyn divided the responsibility for the report among the members of the group. Each person gathered information about one topic and wrote the appropriate section of the report. Then Caitilyn compiled all the information into a coherent and unified report. In addition, she took care to follow the company's guidelines for content, organization, style, and format.

Because Caitilyn knows that some members of the New Hope board of directors will not have time to read the entire report, she began the report with an executive summary. The body of the report provides an in-depth explanation of the options for establishing a WAN. At the end of the report, she summarizes the costs of these options. The report's style follows established standards of business writing, and emphasizes clarity, simplicity, and directness.

In accordance with the company style guide, Caitilyn's report will begin with a title page, with the text centered between the top and bottom margins. Every page except the title page will include a line of text at the top, giving a descriptive name for the report, as well as the page number. The text and headings will be formatted to match all reports created at Tyger Networks, and will follow company guidelines for layout and text style.

Opening **the Report**

Caitilyn already has combined the individual sections into one document. She also has begun formatting the report by changing the font size of headings, adding elements such as bold and italics, and by indenting paragraphs. You'll open the document and perform the remaining formatting tasks on page 1, as indicated in Figure 3-1.

Figure 3-1   INITIAL DRAFT OF REPORT (PAGE 1)

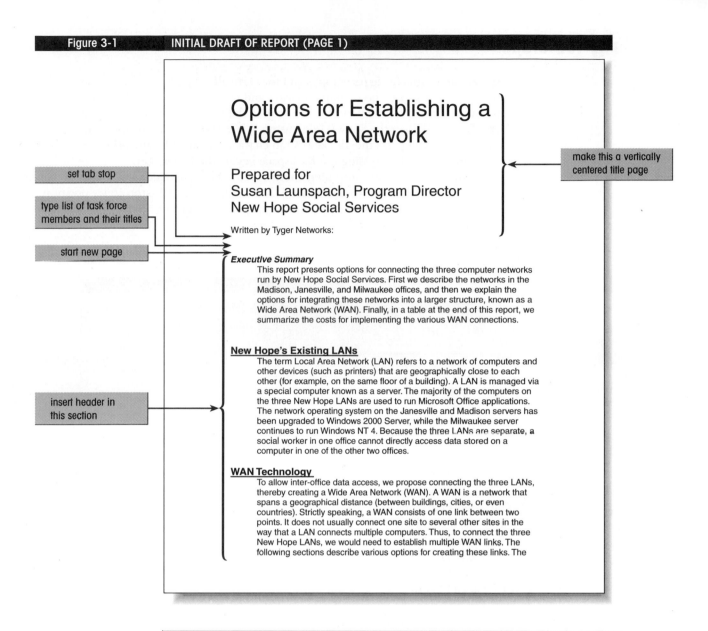

Options for Establishing a Wide Area Network

Prepared for
Susan Launspach, Program Director
New Hope Social Services

Written by Tyger Networks:

make this a vertically centered title page

set tab stop

type list of task force members and their titles

start new page

Executive Summary
This report presents options for connecting the three computer networks run by New Hope Social Services. First we describe the networks in the Madison, Janesville, and Milwaukee offices, and then we explain the options for integrating these networks into a larger structure, known as a Wide Area Network (WAN). Finally, in a table at the end of this report, we summarize the costs for implementing the various WAN connections.

New Hope's Existing LANs
The term Local Area Network (LAN) refers to a network of computers and other devices (such as printers) that are geographically close to each other (for example, on the same floor of a building). A LAN is managed via a special computer known as a server. The majority of the computers on the three New Hope LANs are used to run Microsoft Office applications. The network operating system on the Janesville and Madison servers has been upgraded to Windows 2000 Server, while the Milwaukee server continues to run Windows NT 4. Because the three LANs are separate, a social worker in one office cannot directly access data stored on a computer in one of the other two offices.

insert header in this section

WAN Technology
To allow inter-office data access, we propose connecting the three LANs, thereby creating a Wide Area Network (WAN). A WAN is a network that spans a geographical distance (between buildings, cities, or even countries). Strictly speaking, a WAN consists of one link between two points. It does not usually connect one site to several other sites in the way that a LAN connects multiple computers. Thus, to connect the three New Hope LANs, we would need to establish multiple WAN links. The following sections describe various options for creating these links. The

To open the document:

1. Start Word, and place your Data Disk in the appropriate drive.

2. Open the file **WAN** from the Tutorial folder in the Tutorial.03 folder on your Data Disk.

3. To avoid altering the original file, save the document as **New Hope WAN Report** in the Tutorial folder in the Tutorial.03 folder on your Data Disk.

4. Make sure your screen matches the figures in this tutorial. In particular, be sure to display the nonprinting characters and switch to Normal view if necessary.

Setting Tab Stops

Tabs are useful for indenting paragraphs and for vertically aligning text or numerical data in columns. A **tab** adds space between the margin and text in a column or between text in one column and text in another column. A **tab stop** is the location where text moves when you press the Tab key. When the Show/Hide button ¶ is pressed, the nonprinting tab character appears wherever you press the Tab key. A tab character is just like any other character you type; you can delete it by pressing the Backspace key or the Delete key.

Word provides several **tab-stop alignment styles**. The five major styles are left, center, right, decimal, and bar, as shown in Figure 3-2. The first three tab-stop styles position text in a similar way to the Align Left, Center, and Align Right buttons on the Formatting toolbar. The difference is that with a tab, you determine line by line precisely where the left, center, or right alignment should occur.

Figure 3-2	TAB STOP ALIGNMENT STYLES

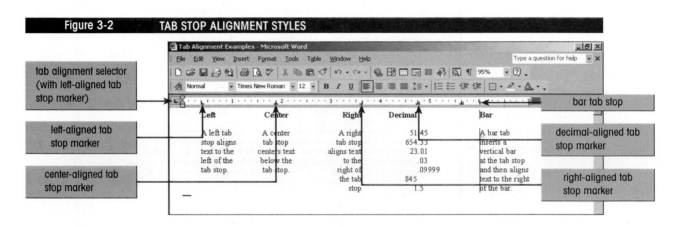

The default tab stops on the ruler are **Left tabs**, which position the left edge of text at the tab stop and extend the text to the right. **Center tabs** position text so that it's centered evenly on both sides of the tab stop. **Right tabs** position the right edge of text at the tab stop and extend the text to the left. **Decimal tabs** position numbers so that their decimal points are aligned at the tab stop. **Bar tabs** insert a vertical bar at the tab stop and then align text to the right of the bar. In addition, you also can use a **First Line Indent tab**, which indents the first line of a paragraph, and the **Hanging Indent tab**, which indents every line of a paragraph *except* the first line.

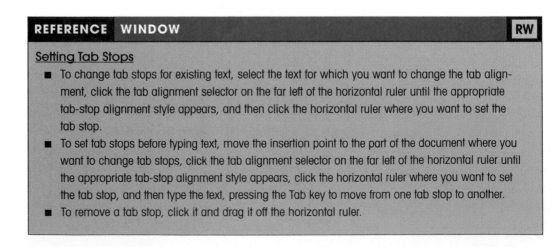

REFERENCE WINDOW **RW**

Setting Tab Stops

- To change tab stops for existing text, select the text for which you want to change the tab alignment, click the tab alignment selector on the far left of the horizontal ruler until the appropriate tab-stop alignment style appears, and then click the horizontal ruler where you want to set the tab stop.
- To set tab stops before typing text, move the insertion point to the part of the document where you want to change tab stops, click the tab alignment selector on the far left of the horizontal ruler until the appropriate tab-stop alignment style appears, click the horizontal ruler where you want to set the tab stop, and then type the text, pressing the Tab key to move from one tab stop to another.
- To remove a tab stop, click it and drag it off the horizontal ruler.

The Word default tab-stop settings are every one-half inch, as indicated by the small gray tick marks at the bottom of the ruler shown in Figure 3-3. You set a new tab stop by selecting a tab-stop alignment style (from the tab alignment selector at the left end of the horizontal ruler) and then clicking the horizontal ruler to insert the tab stop. You can remove a tab stop from the ruler by clicking it and dragging the tab stop off the ruler.

Figure 3-3	RULER WITH TAB STOPS

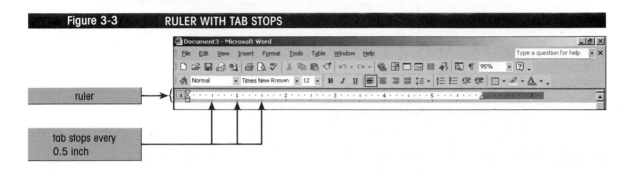

You should never try to align columns of text by adding extra spaces with the spacebar. Although the text might seem precisely aligned in the document window, it might not be aligned when you print the document. Furthermore, if you edit the text, the extra spaces might disturb the alignment. However, if you edit text aligned with tabs, the alignment remains intact. If you want to align a lot of text in many columns, it is better to use a table, as described later in this tutorial.

To align columns using tabs, you can type some text, and press the Tab key. The insertion point then moves to the next tab stop to the right, where you can type more text. You can continue in this way until you type the first row of each column. Then you can press the Enter key, and begin typing the next row of each column. However, sometimes you'll find that text in a column stretches beyond the next default tab stop, and as a result the columns fail to line up evenly.

In the Tyger Networks report, you need to type the list of task force members and their titles. As you type, you'll discover whether Word's default tab stops are appropriate for this document, or whether you need to add a new tab stop.

To enter the task force list using tabs:

1. Verify that nonprinting characters are displayed, and then move the insertion point to the line below the text "Written by Tyger Networks:."

2. Type **Caitilyn Waller** and then press the **Tab** key. A tab character appears, and the insertion point moves to the first tab stop after the *r* in "Waller." This tab stop is located at the 1.5-inch mark on the horizontal ruler. See Figure 3-4.

Figure 3-4   **TAB CHARACTER INSERTED INTO DOCUMENT**

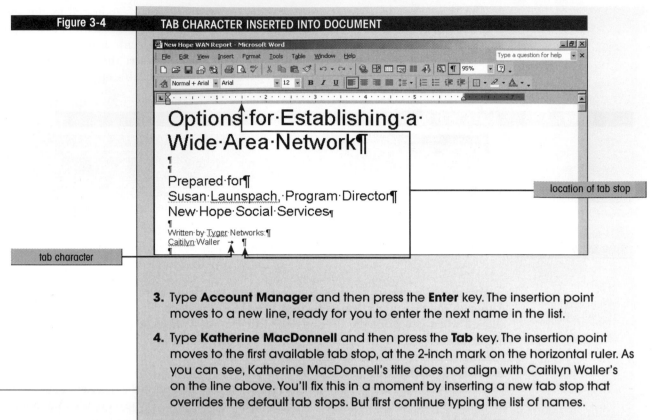

tab character

location of tab stop

3. Type **Account Manager** and then press the **Enter** key. The insertion point moves to a new line, ready for you to enter the next name in the list.

4. Type **Katherine MacDonnell** and then press the **Tab** key. The insertion point moves to the first available tab stop, at the 2-inch mark on the horizontal ruler. As you can see, Katherine MacDonnell's title does not align with Caitilyn Waller's on the line above. You'll fix this in a moment by inserting a new tab stop that overrides the default tab stops. But first continue typing the list of names.

5. Type **Product Manager** and press the **Enter** key.

6. Type **Angelo Zurlo-Cuva**, press the **Tab** key, type **Sales Engineer**, press the **Enter** key, type your first and last name, press the **Tab** key, and then type **Network Engineer**. When you are finished, your document should look like Figure 3-5.

Figure 3-5   **LIST OF TASK FORCE MEMBERS**

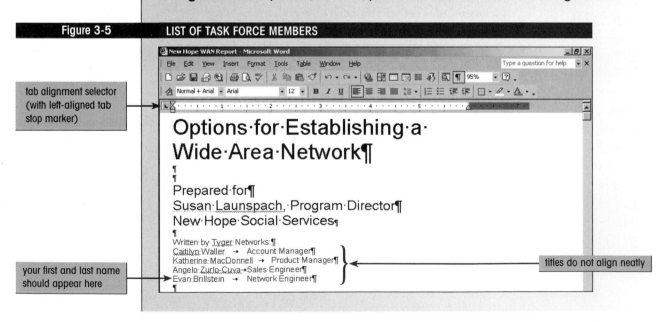

tab alignment selector (with left-aligned tab stop marker)

your first and last name should appear here

titles do not align neatly

The list of names and titles is not aligned properly. You'll fix this by inserting a new tab stop.

To add a new tab stop to the horizontal ruler:

1. Click and drag the mouse pointer to select the list of task force members and titles.

2. Make sure the current tab-stop alignment style is left tab **L**, as shown in Figure 3-5. If **L** is not selected, click the **tab alignment selector** one or more times until **L** appears.

3. Click the **tick mark** on the ruler that occurs at 2.5 inches. Word automatically inserts a left tab stop at that location and removes the tick marks to its left. The column of titles shifts to the new tab stop.

4. Deselect the highlighted text and then move the insertion point anywhere in the list of names and titles. See Figure 3-6.

| Figure 3-6 | LEFT TAB STOP ON RULER |

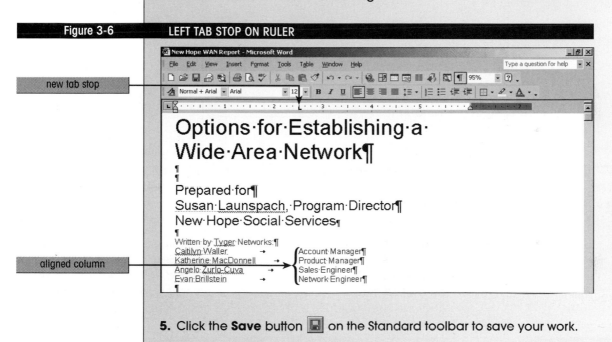

5. Click the **Save** button on the Standard toolbar to save your work.

The two columns of information are now aligned, as Caitilyn requested. Notice that Word changed the tab stops only for the selected paragraphs, not for all the paragraphs in the document. Next, you need to change the layout of the title page.

Formatting the Document in Sections

According to the company guidelines, the title page of the report should be centered between the top and bottom margins of the page. To format the title page differently from the rest of the report, you need to divide the document into sections. A **section** is a unit or part of a document that can have its own page orientation, margins, headers, footers, and vertical alignment. Each section, in other words, is like a mini-document within a document.

To divide a document into sections, you insert a **section break** (a dotted line with the words "Section Break") that marks the point at which one section ends and another begins. Sections can start on a new page or continue on the same page. You can insert a section break with the Break command on the Insert menu.

To insert a section break after the title:

1. Position the insertion point immediately to the left of the "E" in the heading "Executive Summary." You want the text above this heading to be on a separate title page and the executive summary to begin on the second page of the report.

2. Click **Insert** on the menu bar, and then click **Break** to open the Break dialog box. See Figure 3-7.

Figure 3-7	BREAK DIALOG BOX

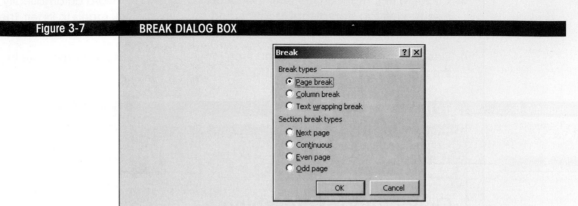

You can use this dialog box to insert several types of breaks into your document, including a **page break**, which moves the text after it onto a new page. Instead of inserting a page break, however, you will insert a section break that indicates both a new section and a new page. Later in this session, you will use another method to insert a page break into the document.

3. Under "Section break types" click the **Next page** option button, and then click the **OK** button. A double-dotted line and the words "Section Break (Next Page)" appear before the heading "Executive Summary," indicating that you have inserted a break that starts a new section on the next page. The status bar indicates that the insertion point is on page 2, section 2. See Figure 3-8.

Figure 3-8	SECTION BREAK

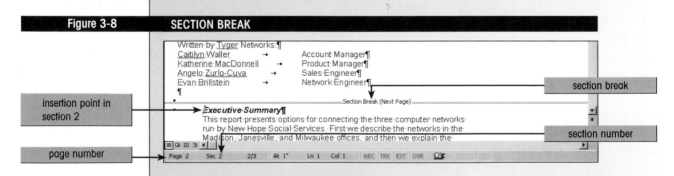

TROUBLE? If you see a single dotted line and the words "Page Break", you inserted a page break rather than a section break. Click the Undo button on the Standard toolbar, and then repeat Steps 1 through 3.

Now that the title page is a separate section and page from the rest of the report, you can make changes affecting only that section, leaving the rest of the document unchanged.

Changing **the Vertical Alignment of a Section**

You're ready to center the text of page 1 vertically on the page. But first you will switch to the Print Preview window, so you can more easily observe your changes to page 1.

To see the document in Print Preview:

1. Click the **Print Preview** button on the Standard toolbar to open the Print Preview window.

2. Click the **Multiple Pages** button on the Print Preview toolbar, and then click and drag across the top three pages in the list box to select "1 × 3 Pages." The three pages of the report are reduced in size and appear side by side. See Figure 3-9. Although you cannot read the text on the pages, you can see the general layout.

Figure 3-9	REPORT IN PRINT PREVIEW WINDOW

Print Preview toolbar

Multiple Pages button

unformatted title page

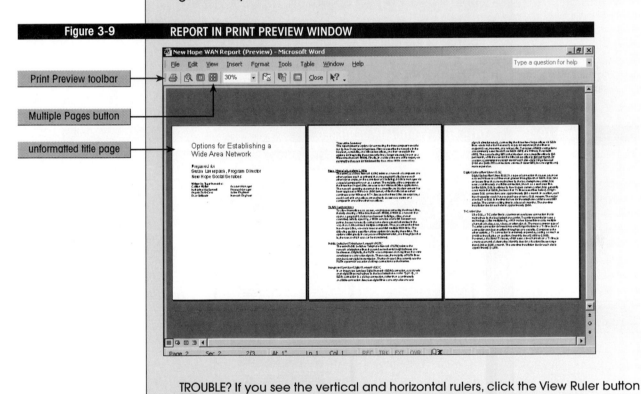

TROUBLE? If you see the vertical and horizontal rulers, click the View Ruler button on the Print Preview toolbar to hide the rulers.

Now you can change the vertical alignment to center the lines of text between the top and bottom margins. The **vertical alignment** specifies how a page of text is positioned on the page between the top and bottom margins—flush at the top, flush at the bottom, or centered between the top and bottom margins.

You'll center the title page text from within the Print Preview window.

To change the vertical alignment of the title page:

1. Click the **Magnifier** button 🔍 on the Print Preview toolbar once to deselect it.

2. Click the **leftmost page** in the Print Preview window to move the insertion point to page 1 (the title page). The status bar indicates that page 1 is the current page.

   TROUBLE? If the size of page 1 increases when you click it, you selected the Magnifier button in Step 1 instead of deselecting it. Click the Multiple Pages button on the Print Preview toolbar, drag to select "1 × 3 Pages," and then repeat Step 1.

3. Click **File** on the menu bar, and then click **Page Setup**. The Page Setup dialog box opens.

4. Click the **Layout** tab. In the Apply to list box, select **This section** (if it is not already selected) so that the layout change affects only the first section, not both sections, of your document.

5. Click the **Vertical alignment** list arrow, and then click **Center** to center the pages of the current section—in this case, just page 1—vertically between the top and bottom margins.

6. Click the **OK** button to return to the Print Preview window. The text of the title page is centered vertically, as shown in Figure 3-10.

Figure 3-10	TITLE PAGE VERTICALLY CENTERED

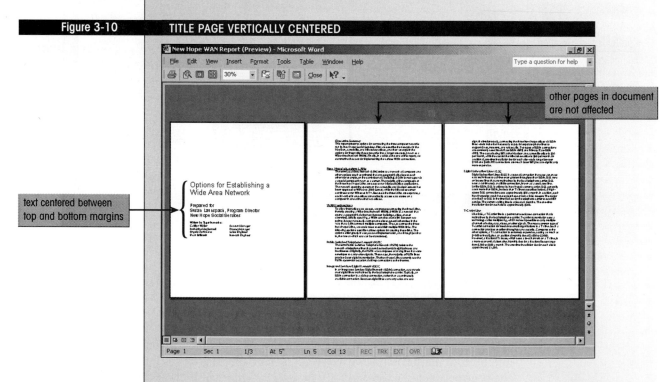

7. Click the **Close** button on the Print Preview toolbar to return to Normal view.

You have successfully centered the title page text. Next, you turn your attention to inserting a descriptive name for the report and the page number at the top of every page.

Adding **Headers**

The report guidelines at Tyger Networks require a short report title and the page number to be printed at the top of every page except the title page. Text that is printed at the top of every page is called a **header**. For example, the page number, tutorial number, and tutorial name printed at the top of the page you are reading is a header. Similarly, a **footer** is text that is printed at the bottom of every page. (You'll have a chance to work with footers in the Review Assignments at the end of this tutorial.)

When you insert a header or footer into a document, you switch to Header and Footer view. The Header and Footer toolbar is displayed, and the insertion point moves to the top of the document, where the header will appear. The main text is dimmed, indicating that it cannot be edited until you return to Normal or Print Layout view.

You'll create a header for the main body of the report (section 2) that prints "Options for Establishing a Wide Area Network" at the left margin and the page number at the right margin.

To insert a header for section 2:

1. Click anywhere after the section break, so that the insertion point is located in section 2 and not in section 1.

2. Click **View** on the menu bar, and then click **Header and Footer**. The Word window changes to Header and Footer view, and the Header and Footer toolbar appears in the document window. The header area appears in the top margin of your document surrounded by a dashed line and displays the words "Header -Section 2-". See Figure 3-11. (If the Header and Footer toolbar covers the header area, drag the toolbar below the header area, similar to its position in Figure 3-11.)

| Figure 3-11 | CREATING A HEADER |

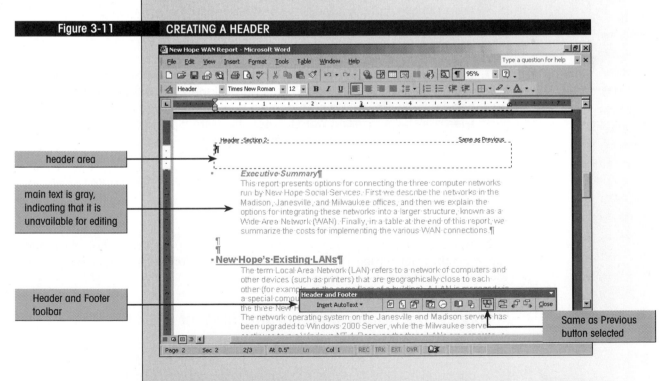

TROUBLE? If the header area displays "Header -Section 1-", click the Show Next button on the Header and Footer toolbar until the header area displays "Header -Section 2-".

TROUBLE? If the main text of the document doesn't appear on the screen, click the Show/Hide Document Text button 🔲 on the Header and Footer toolbar, and continue with Step 3.

3. Click the **Same as Previous** button 🔳 on the Header and Footer toolbar so that the button is *not* selected. When Same as Previous is selected, Word automatically inserts the same header text as for the previous section. You deselected it to ensure that the text of the current header applies only to the current section (section 2), and not to the previous section (section 1).

4. Type **Options for Establishing a Wide Area Network**. The title is automatically aligned on the left. See Figure 3-12.

Figure 3-12   **HEADER TEXT**

report title

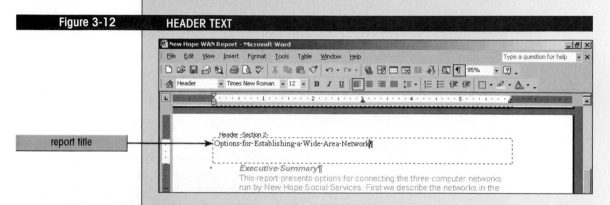

5. Press the **Tab** key to move the insertion point to the right margin of the header area. (Notice that by default the header contains center and right-align tab stops.)

6. Type the word **Page** and press the **spacebar** once.

7. Click the **Insert Page Number** button 🔳 on the Header and Footer toolbar. The page number "2" appears at the right-aligned tab. The page number in the header looks like you simply typed the number 2, but you actually inserted a special instruction telling Word to insert the correct page number on each page. Now consecutive page numbers will print on each page of the header within this section.

8. Click the **Close** button on the Header and Footer toolbar to return to Normal view, and then save your changes.

Notice that you can't see the header in Normal view. To see exactly how the header will appear on the printed page, you will switch to the Print Preview window. *Note:* you can also use Print Layout view.

To view the header and margins in Print Preview:

1. Click the **Print Preview button** 🔳 on the Standard toolbar. The three pages of the document are displayed as they were earlier in the Print Preview window, although this time you can see a line of text at the top of pages 2 and 3. To read the header text, you need to increase the magnification.

2. If necessary, click the **Magnifier** button 🔳 on the Print Preview toolbar to select it.

3. Move the pointer 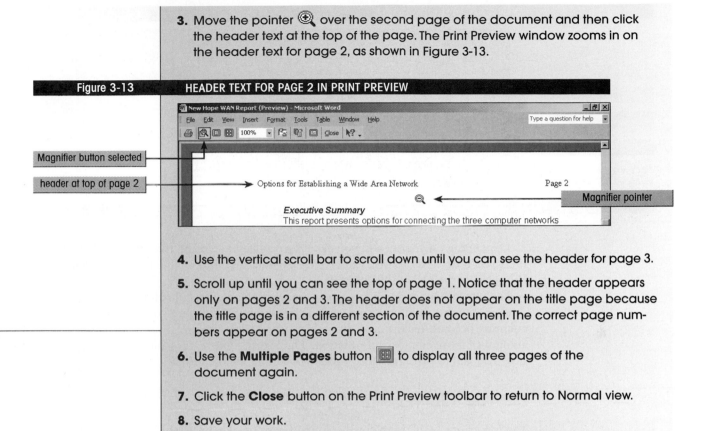 over the second page of the document and then click the header text at the top of the page. The Print Preview window zooms in on the header text for page 2, as shown in Figure 3-13.

| Figure 3-13 | HEADER TEXT FOR PAGE 2 IN PRINT PREVIEW |

Magnifier button selected

header at top of page 2

Options for Establishing a Wide Area Network   Page 2

Magnifier pointer

Executive Summary
This report presents options for connecting the three computer networks

4. Use the vertical scroll bar to scroll down until you can see the header for page 3.

5. Scroll up until you can see the top of page 1. Notice that the header appears only on pages 2 and 3. The header does not appear on the title page because the title page is in a different section of the document. The correct page numbers appear on pages 2 and 3.

6. Use the **Multiple Pages** button to display all three pages of the document again.

7. Click the **Close** button on the Print Preview toolbar to return to Normal view.

8. Save your work.

The report now has the required header. You have formatted Caitilyn's report so that the results are professional-looking, clearly presented, and easy to read. Next, you will add a table that summarizes the costs of the various WAN options.

Inserting Tables

Using Word, you can quickly organize data and arrange text in an easy-to-read table format. A **table** is information arranged in horizontal rows and vertical columns. As shown in Figure 3-14, table rows are commonly referred to by number (row 1, row 2, and so forth), while columns are commonly referred to by letter (column A on the far left, then column B and so forth). However, you do not see row and column numbers on the screen. The area where a row and column intersect is called a **cell**. Each cell is identified by a column and row label. For example, the cell in the upper-left corner of a table is cell A1 (column A, row 1), the cell to the right of that is cell B1, the cell below cell A1 is A2, and so forth. The table's structure is shown by **gridlines**, which are light gray lines that define the rows and columns. By default, gridlines do not appear on the printed page. You can emphasize specific parts of a table on the printed page by adding a **border** (a line the prints along the side of a table cell).

Figure 3-14	ELEMENTS OF A WORD TABLE

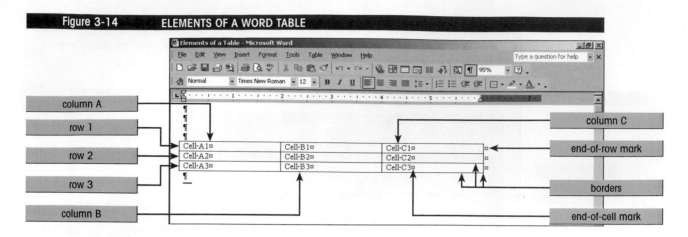

Depending on your needs, you can create a blank table and then insert information into it (as you'll do next), or you can convert existing text into a table (as you'll do in the Case Problems at the end of this tutorial).

You may be wondering why you can't use tabs to align text in columns. Tabs work well for smaller amounts of information, such as two columns with three or four rows, but tabs and columns become tedious and difficult to work with when you need to organize a larger amount of more complex information. The Word Table feature allows you to quickly organize data and to place text and graphics in a more legible format.

Creating a Table

You can create a table with equal column widths quickly by using the Insert Table button on the Standard toolbar. (You will use this technique to create the table Caitilyn requested.) You also can create a table by dragging the Draw Table pointer to draw the table structure you want. (You'll practice this method in the Case Problems.) However you create a table, you can modify it by using commands on the Table menu or the buttons on the Tables and Borders toolbar.

Caitilyn wants you to create a table that summarizes information in the Tyger Networks report. Figure 3-15 shows a sketch of what Caitilyn wants the table to look like. The table will allow the members of the New Hope board of directors to see at a glance the cost of each option. The top row of the table, called the **heading row**, identifies the type of information in each column.

Figure 3-15	TABLE SKETCH

Type of Connection	Monthly Charge
ISDN	$50 to $60
DSL	$80
T1	$1000 to $2000

Inserting a Page Break

Before you begin creating the table, you need to insert a page break so that the table will appear on a separate page.

To insert a page break:

1. Verify that the document is displayed in Normal view.

2. Press **Ctrl+End** to position the insertion point at the end of the report.

3. Press **Ctrl+Enter**. A dotted line with the words "Page Break" appears in the document window. *Note*: You also can add a page break using the Break dialog box you used earlier to insert a section break.

   TROUBLE? If you do not see the words "Page Break," check to make sure the document is displayed in Normal view.

4. Scroll down until the page break is positioned near the top of the document window.

The insertion point is now at the beginning of a new page, where you want to insert the table.

Inserting a Blank Table

You'll use the Insert Table button to insert a blank table structure into the new page. Then you can type the necessary information directly into the table.

To create a blank table using the Insert Table button:

1. Click the **Insert Table** button ⊞ on the Standard toolbar. A drop-down grid resembling a miniature table appears below the Insert Table button. The grid starts with four rows and five columns for the table. You can drag the pointer to select as many rows and columns as you need. In this case, you need four rows and two columns.

2. Position the pointer in the upper-left cell of the grid, and then click and drag the pointer down and across the grid until you highlight four rows and two columns. As you drag the pointer across the grid, Word indicates the size of the table (rows by columns) at the bottom of the grid.

3. When the table size is 4 × 2, release the mouse button. An empty table, four rows by two columns, appears in your document with the insertion point blinking in the upper-left corner (cell A1). The two columns are of equal width. Each cell contains an end-of-cell mark, and each row contains an end-of-row mark. See Figure 3-16.

| Figure 3-16 | EMPTY TABLE IN NORMAL VIEW |

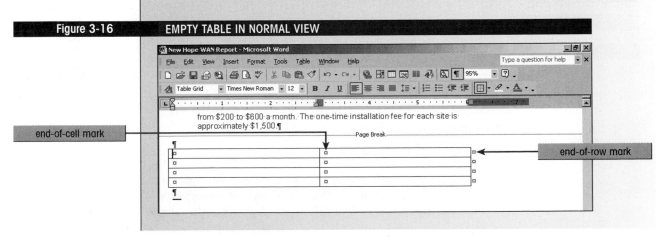

end-of-cell mark

end-of-row mark

TROUBLE? If your table is displayed in Print Layout view, switch to Normal view and then compare your table to Figure 3-16.

TROUBLE? If you don't see the end-of-cell and end-of-row marks, you need to show nonprinting characters. Click the Show/Hide button ¶ on the Standard toolbar to show nonprinting characters.

TROUBLE? If you see the Tables and Borders toolbar displayed along with the new blank table, close it. You will learn how to use the Tables and Borders toolbar later in this tutorial.

When working with tables and graphics, it's helpful to switch to Print Layout view, which allows you to get a better sense of the overall layout of the page, including the headers. Also, some special table features are only available in Print Layout view. You'll switch to Print Layout view in the following steps.

To display the table structure in Print Layout view:

1. Click the **Print Layout View** button 🔲 . If necessary, change the **Zoom** setting (in the Standard toolbar) to **100%**. The table is displayed in Print Layout view, where you can see the column widths indicated on the horizontal ruler. Also, notice that the document header is visible in Print Layout view.

2. Move the mouse pointer over the empty table. The Table Move handle appears in the table's upper-left corner, and the Table Resize handle appears in the lower-right corner. You don't need to use either of these handles now, but you should understand their function. To quickly select the entire table, you can click the Table Move handle. Then you can move the entire table by dragging the Table Move handle. To change the size of the entire table, you could drag the Table Resize handle. See Figure 3-17.

| Figure 3-17 | EMPTY TABLE IN PRINT LAYOUT VIEW |

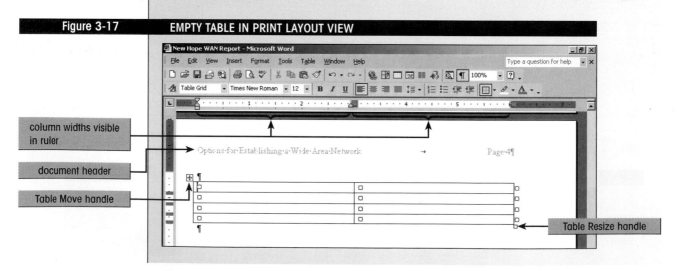

column widths visible in ruler

document header

Table Move handle

Table Resize handle

Entering Text in a Table

You can enter text in a table by moving the insertion point to a cell and typing. If the text takes up more than one line in the cell, Word automatically wraps the text to the next line and increases the height of that cell and all the cells in that row. To move the insertion point to another cell in the table, you can either click in that cell or use the Tab key. Figure 3-18 summarizes the keystrokes for moving the insertion point within a table.

Figure 3-18	KEYSTROKES FOR MOVING AROUND A TABLE

PRESS	TO MOVE THE INSERTION POINT
Tab or →	One cell to the right, or to the first cell in the next row
Shift+Tab or ←	One cell to the left, or to the last cell in the previous row
Alt+Home	To the first cell of the current row
Alt+End	To the last cell of the current row
Alt+PageUp	To the top cell of the current column
Alt+PageDown	To the bottom cell of the current column
↑	One cell up in the current column
↓	One cell down in the current column

Now you are ready to insert information into the table.

To insert data into the table:

1. Verify that the insertion point is located in cell **A1** (in the upper-left corner).

2. Type **Type of Connection**.

3. Press the **Tab** key to move to cell B1. See Figure 3-19.

Figure 3-19	ENTERING TEXT IN THE TABLE

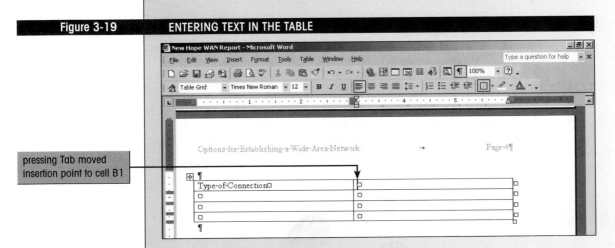

pressing Tab moved insertion point to cell B1

TROUBLE? If Word created a new paragraph in cell A1 rather than moving the insertion point to cell B1, you accidentally pressed the Enter key instead of the Tab key. Press the Backspace key to remove the paragraph mark, and then press the Tab key to move to cell B1.

4. Type **Monthly Charge** and then press the **Tab** key to move to cell A2. Notice that when you press the Tab key in the last column of the table, the insertion point moves to the first column in the next row.

You have finished entering the heading row, the row that identifies the information in each column. Now you can enter the information about the various WAN options.

To continue entering information in the table:

1. Type **ISDN** and then press the **Tab** key to move to cell B2.

2. Type **$50 to $60** and then press the **Tab** key to move the insertion point to cell A3.

3. Type the remaining information for the table, as shown in Figure 3-20, pressing the **Tab** key to move from cell to cell. Don't worry if the text in your table doesn't wrap the same way as shown here. You'll change the column widths in the next session.

Figure 3-20   **TABLE WITH COMPLETED INFORMATION**

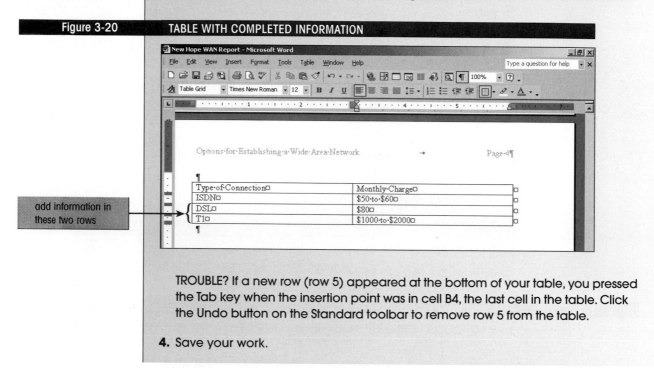

add information in these two rows

TROUBLE? If a new row (row 5) appeared at the bottom of your table, you pressed the Tab key when the insertion point was in cell B4, the last cell in the table. Click the Undo button on the Standard toolbar to remove row 5 from the table.

4. Save your work.

Keep in mind that many document-editing features, such as the Backspace key, the copy-and-paste feature, the Undo button, and the AutoCorrect feature, work the same way in a table as they do in the rest of the document. As you do in a paragraph, you must select text in a table to edit it. You will edit and format this table in the next session.

Session 3.1 QUICK CHECK

1. Define the following in your own words:
   a. tab stop
   b. cell
   c. table
   d. decimal-aligned tab stop
   e. section (of a document)

2. Explain how to center the title page vertically between the top and bottom margins.

3. What is the difference between a header and a footer?

4. Describe how to insert a blank table consisting of four columns and six rows.

5. How do you move the insertion point from one row to the next in a table?

6. How do you insert the page number in a header?

7. Explain how to insert a new tab stop.

8. Describe a situation in which you would want to divide a document into sections.

9. Describe a situation in which it would be better to use a table rather than tab stops.

10. Explain how to select an entire table.

SESSION 3.2

In this session you will learn how to change the table you just created. First, you will display the Tables and Borders toolbar and rearrange the existing rows, and then you will learn how to add and delete rows and columns. Next, you will format the table to improve its appearance.

Displaying the Tables and Borders Toolbar

The **Tables and Borders toolbar** contains a number of useful buttons that simplify the process of working with tables. You'll display the Tables and Borders toolbar in the following steps.

To open the Tables and Borders toolbar:

1. If you took a break after the previous session, make sure Word is running and that the New Hope WAN Report document is open. Check that the nonprinting characters are displayed, that the document is displayed in Print Layout view, and that the document is scrolled so that the table is visible.

2. Click the **Tables and Borders** button 🗔 on the Standard toolbar. The Tables and Borders toolbar appears.

3. Move the mouse pointer over the table. The Draw Table pointer ∅ appears. You can use this pointer to add new rows or columns in a table, and to add borders between cells. You'll have a chance to practice using this pointer in the Case Problems at the end of this tutorial. For now you'll turn it off.

4. Click the **Draw Table** button 🖉 on the Tables and Borders toolbar. The pointer changes to an I-beam pointer I.

5. If necessary, drag the Tables and Borders toolbar down and to the right, so that it doesn't block your view of the table, as shown in Figure 3-21.

Figure 3-21   **POSITIONING THE TABLES AND BORDERS TOOLBAR**

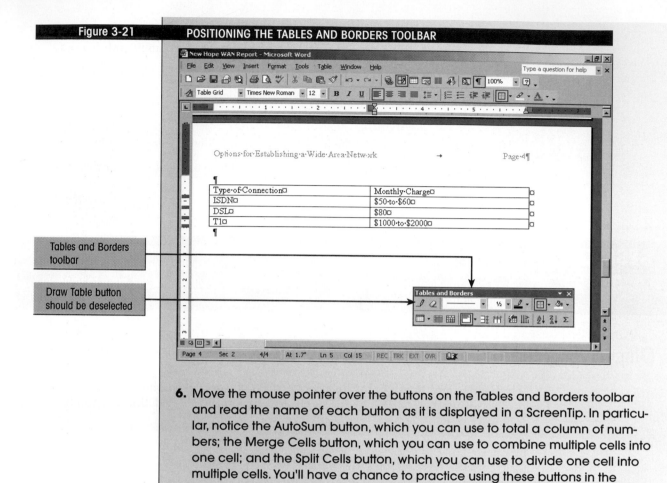

Tables and Borders toolbar

Draw Table button should be deselected

6. Move the mouse pointer over the buttons on the Tables and Borders toolbar and read the name of each button as it is displayed in a ScreenTip. In particular, notice the AutoSum button, which you can use to total a column of numbers; the Merge Cells button, which you can use to combine multiple cells into one cell; and the Split Cells button, which you can use to divide one cell into multiple cells. You'll have a chance to practice using these buttons in the Review Assignments and Case Problems at the end of this tutorial. Notice also the two Sort buttons, which you can use to rearrange the rows in a table. You will use the Sort Ascending button in the next section.

Sorting Rows in a Table

The term **sort** refers to the process of rearranging information in alphabetical, numerical, or chronological order. When you sort a table, you arrange the rows based on the contents of one of the columns. For example, you could sort the table you just created based on the contents of the Type of Connection column—either in ascending alphabetical order (from *A* to *Z*) or in descending alphabetical order (from *Z* to *A*). Alternately, you could sort the table based on the contents of the Monthly Charge column—either in descending numerical order (highest to lowest) or in ascending numerical order (lowest to highest). When you sort table data, Word usually does not sort the heading row along with the other information, but instead leaves the heading row at the top of the table.

Caitilyn would like you to sort the table in ascending alphabetical order, based on the contents of the Type of Connection column. You start by positioning the insertion point in that column.

To sort the information in the table:

1. Click cell **A2** (which contains the text "ISDN"). The insertion point is now located in the Type of Connection column.

2. Click the **Sort Ascending** button on the Tables and Borders toolbar. Rows 2 through 4 are now arranged alphabetically according to the text in the Type of Connection column. Note that Word did not sort the header row along with the other rows. The header row remains in its original position at the top of the table. See Figure 3-22.

| Figure 3-22 | TABLE AFTER BEING SORTED |

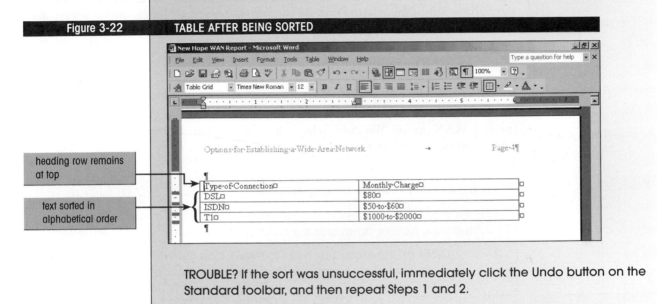

heading row remains at top

text sorted in alphabetical order

TROUBLE? If the sort was unsuccessful, immediately click the Undo button on the Standard toolbar, and then repeat Steps 1 and 2.

Caitilyn stops by and asks you to add an "Installation Fee" column. She also would like you to insert a new row with information about a Fractional T1 connection.

Modifying an Existing Table Structure

You will often need to modify a table structure by adding or deleting rows and columns. Figure 3-23 summarizes ways to insert or delete rows and columns in a table.

| Figure 3-23 | WAYS TO INSERT OR DELETE TABLE ROWS AND COLUMNS |

TO	DO THIS
Insert a row within a table	Select the row below where you want the row added, click Table on the menu bar, point to Insert, and then click Rows Above.
	Select the row below where you want the row added, and then click the Insert Rows button on the Standard toolbar.
Insert a row at the end of a table	Position the insertion point in the cell at the far right of the bottom row, then press the Tab key.
Insert a column within a table	Select the column to the right of where you want the column added, click Table on the menu bar, point to Insert, then click Columns to the Right.
	Select the column to the right of where you want the column added, then click the Insert Columns button on the Standard toolbar.
Insert a column at the end of a table	Select the end-of-row markers to the right of the table, click Table on the menu bar, point to Insert, then click Columns to the Left.
	Select the end-of-row markers to the right of the table, and then click the Insert Columns button on the Standard toolbar.
Delete a row	Select the row or rows to be deleted, click Table on the menu bar, point to Delete, and then click Rows.
Delete a column	Select the column or columns to be deleted, click Table on the menu bar, point to Delete, and then click Columns.

When you select part of a table, new buttons sometimes appear on the Standard toolbar to help you modify the table structure. For instance, when you select a column, the Insert Columns button appears to help you insert a new column in the table. In most cases, however, you'll find it easiest to use menu commands to add and delete rows and columns, because the menu commands allow you to specify exactly where you want to modify the table. For instance, by using a menu command, you can indicate whether you want to insert a column to the right or left of the selected row. By contrast, the Insert Columns button always inserts a new column to the left of the selected column.

Inserting Columns in a Table

Your first task is to insert a new column between the Type of Connection column and the Monthly Charge column. This column will contain information on the Installation Charge for each WAN option. You need to begin by selecting the column to the left of the location where you want to insert a column.

To insert a column in the table:

1. Click in cell **A1** (which contains the heading "Type of Connection") and drag the mouse pointer down until the entire Type of Connection column is selected.

2. Click **Table** on the menu bar, point to **Insert**, and then click **Columns to the Right**. A new column is inserted in the table to the right of the Type of Connection column.

   Note: If you had selected two columns in Step 1, Word would have inserted two new columns in the table. If you had selected three columns, Word would have inserted three columns, and so on.

3. Click in the new cell **B1** and enter the Installation Charge heading and data shown in Figure 3-24.

Figure 3-24 **NEW INSTALLATION CHARGE COLUMN**

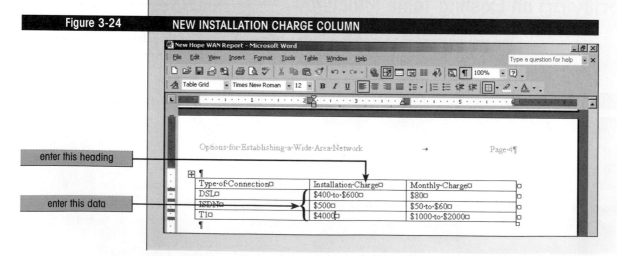

Inserting Rows in a Table

Next you need to insert a row with information on a more economical type of T1 connection, called a fractional T1 connection. You could insert this row in its alphabetical position in the table (below the DSL row). But it's quicker to add the row to the end of the table, and then resort the table.

To insert a row at the bottom of the table:

1. Click the bottom cell in the Monthly Charge column (which contains "$1000 to $2000"). The insertion point is now located in the last cell in the table.

2. Press the **Tab** key. A blank row is added to the bottom of the table.

   TROUBLE? If a blank row is not added to the bottom of the table, click the Undo button on the Standard toolbar. Check to make sure the insertion point is in the rightmost cell of the bottom row, and then press the Tab key.

3. Enter the following information in the new row:

   Type of Connection: **Fractional T1**

   Installation Charge: **$1500**

   Monthly Charge: **$200 to $600**

4. Click anywhere in the Type of Connection column, and then click the **Sort Ascending** button 🔽 on the Tables and Borders toolbar. The table rows are rearranged in alphabetical order, with the Fractional T1 row positioned below the DSL row, as shown in Figure 3-25.

Figure 3-25	SORTED TABLE WITH NEW ROW

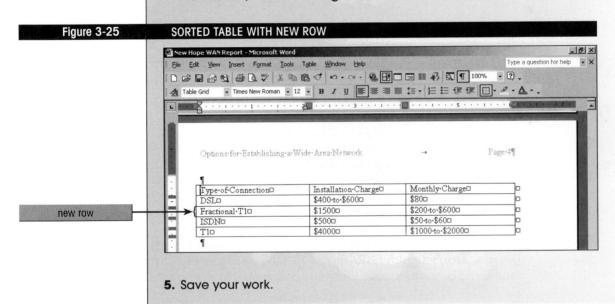

new row

5. Save your work.

After reviewing the table, Caitilyn decides not to include the information on the full T1 connection, because it is far too expensive for New Hope's current budget. She asks you to delete the T1 row.

Deleting Rows and Columns in a Table

With Word, you can delete either the contents of the cells or the structure of the cells. To delete the contents of a table, you select one or more cells, and then press the Delete key. However, to delete both the contents and structure of a selected row or column from the table entirely, you must use one of the methods described earlier in Figure 3-23. Right now you'll use a menu command to delete the T1 row.

To delete a row using the Table menu:

1. Click the selection bar next to row 5 to select the T1 row. (Select the T1 row, at the bottom of the table, *not* the Fractional T1 row.)

2. Click **Table** on the menu bar, point to **Delete**, and then click **Rows**. The selected row is deleted from the table. See Figure 3-26.

| Figure 3-26 | TABLE AFTER DELETING ROW |

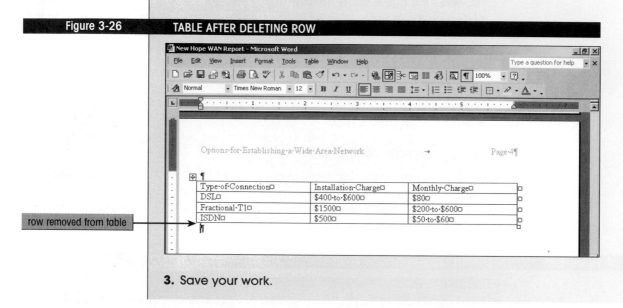

3. Save your work.

Formatting Tables

Word provides a variety of ways to enhance the appearance of the tables you create. You can alter the width of the columns and the height of the rows, or change the alignment of text within the cells or the alignment of the table between the document's left and right margins. You can also change the appearance of the table borders, and add a shaded background. If you happen to be in a hurry, you can format an entire table at one time using the **Table AutoFormat command** on the Table menu. (You'll have a chance to practice using this command in the Case Problems at the end of this tutorial.) In general, however, making formatting changes individually (using the mouse pointer along with various toolbar buttons and menu commands) gives you more options and more flexibility.

Changing Column Width and Row Height

Sometimes you'll want to adjust the column widths in a table to make the text easier to read. If you want to specify an exact width for a column, you should use the Table Properties command on the Table menu. However, it's usually easiest to drag the column's right border to a new position. Alternately, you can double-click a column border to have the column width adjust automatically to accommodate the widest entry in the column.

The Type of Connection column and the Monthly Charge column are too wide for the information they contain. You'll change these widths by dragging the column borders, using the ruler as a guide. Keep in mind that to change the width of a column, you need to drag the column's right-hand border.

To change the width of columns by dragging the borders:

1. Verify that the table is displayed in Print Layout view. Also, make sure that the insertion point is located anywhere within the table, without any part of the table selected.

2. Move the pointer over the border between columns A and B (in other words, over the right border of column A, the "Type of Connection" column). The pointer changes to ◄||►.

3. Press and hold down the **Alt** key and the mouse button. The column widths are displayed in the ruler, as shown in Figure 3-27. (The widths on your computer might differ slightly.)

| Figure 3-27 | COLUMN WIDTHS DISPLAYED IN RULER |

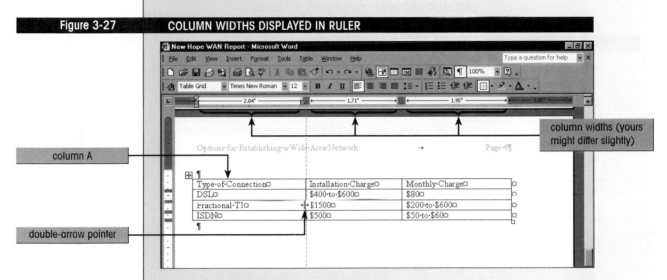

4. While holding down the **Alt** key, drag the pointer to the left until column A is about **1.4** inches wide, and then release the mouse button and the Alt key. As the width of column A decreases, the width of column B (the Installation Charge column) increases. However, the overall width of the table does not change.

   TROUBLE? If you can't get the column width to exactly 1.4 inches, make it as close to that width as possible.

Now you need to adjust the width of both columns B and C. You could do this by dragging the column border, as you did for column A. But it's much faster to double-click the right-hand border of each column.

To change the width of columns B and C:

1. Double-click the right-hand border of column B (the Installation Charge column). The column shrinks, leaving just enough room for the widest entry in the column (the column heading "Installation Charge").

2. Repeat this procedure to adjust the width of column C (the Monthly Charge column). All three columns in the table are now just wide enough to accommodate the column headings.

You also can change the height of rows by dragging a border. You'll make row 1 (the header row) taller so it is more prominent.

To change the height of row 1:

1. Position the pointer over the bottom border of the header row. The pointer changes to ÷.

2. Press and hold down the **Alt** key and the mouse button. The row heights are displayed in the vertical ruler.

3. While holding down the **Alt** key, drag the pointer down until row 1 is about **0.45** inches high, then release the mouse button and the Alt key. Notice that the height of the other rows in the table is not affected by this change. See Figure 3-28.

| Figure 3-28 | TABLE WITH NARROWER COLUMNS AND A WIDER HEADING ROW |

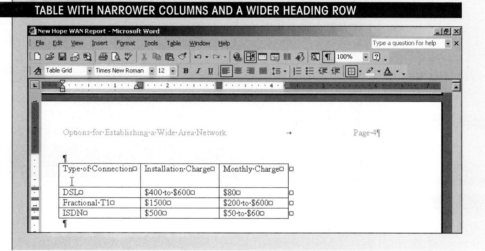

Aligning Text Within Cells

Aligning the text within the cells of a table makes the information easier to read. For example, aligning a column of numbers or percentages along the right margin helps the reader to compare the values quickly. At the same time, centering a row of headings makes a table more visually appealing. You can align text within the active cell the same way you do other text—with the alignment buttons on the Formatting toolbar. However, the Alignment buttons on the Tables and Borders toolbar provide more options.

Caitilyn would like you to align the data in the Installation Charge and Monthly Charge columns along the right side of the columns. The table also would look better with the headings centered. You'll begin by selecting and formatting all of columns B and C.

To right-align the numerical data and center the headings:

1. Move the pointer to the top of column B until the pointer changes to ↓. Press and hold the left mouse button, and then drag right to select columns B and C.

2. Click the **Align Right** button ☰ on the Formatting toolbar. The numbers line up along the right edges of the cells.

TROUBLE? If more than just the numbers and column headings are right-aligned within the table, you may have selected the wrong block of cells. Click the Undo button on the Standard toolbar, and then repeat Steps 1 through 3.

Notice that in the process of formatting columns B and C, you right-aligned two of the headings ("Installation Charge" and "Monthly Charge"). You will reformat those headings in the next step, when you center the text in row 1 both horizontally and vertically in each cell.

3. Click the selection bar next to row 1. All of row 1 is selected.

4. Click the **Align** list arrow [icon] on the Tables and Borders toolbar to display a palette of nine alignment options.

5. Click the **Align Center** button [icon] in the middle of the palette. The text is centered both horizontally and vertically in the row.

6. Click anywhere in the table to deselect the row, and then save your work. See Figure 3-29.

| Figure 3-29 | TABLE WITH NEWLY ALIGNED TEXT |

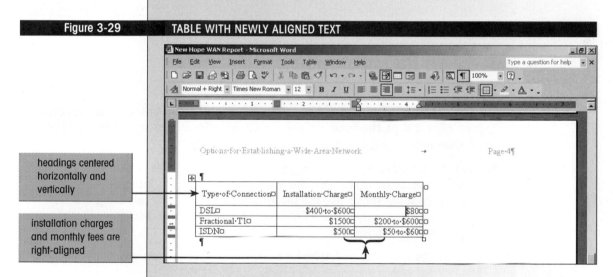

headings centered horizontally and vertically

installation charges and monthly fees are right-aligned

TROUBLE? If more than just the heading row is centered, click the Undo button on the Standard toolbar, and then repeat Steps 3 through 6.

Changing **Borders**

Gridlines and borders are different parts of a table. **Gridlines** are light gray lines that indicate the structure of the table on the screen but do not show up on the printed page. **Borders** are darker lines overlaying the gridlines, which do appear on the printed page. When you create a table using the Insert Table button, Word automatically applies a thin black border, so you can't actually see the underlying gridlines.

After you have created a table, you can add new borders or erase existing borders by using the buttons on the Tables and Borders toolbar. You can modify an existing border by changing its **line weight** (its thickness). You can also choose a different **line style**—for instance, you can change a single straight-line border to a triple dotted line.

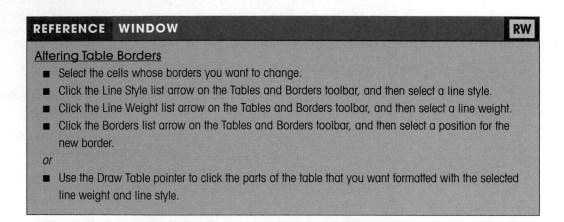

REFERENCE WINDOW   **RW**

<u>Altering Table Borders</u>
- Select the cells whose borders you want to change.
- Click the Line Style list arrow on the Tables and Borders toolbar, and then select a line style.
- Click the Line Weight list arrow on the Tables and Borders toolbar, and then select a line weight.
- Click the Borders list arrow on the Tables and Borders toolbar, and then select a position for the new border.

or

- Use the Draw Table pointer to click the parts of the table that you want formatted with the selected line weight and line style.

To modify the table's borders:

1. Select row 1 (the heading row).

2. Click the **Line Weight** list arrow ☐ on the Tables and Borders toolbar, and then click **2 ¼ pt**. Next you will examine the options available in the List Style list. Currently, a single straight-line border is selected.

3. Click the **Line Style** list arrow ☐ on the Tables and Borders toolbar, and then scroll down to view the various options. Note that you can remove borders (without removing the underlying gridlines) by selecting the No Border option. Caitilyn prefers a simple border, so you decide not to change the current selection.

4. Press the **Esc** key. The Line Style list closes. You have selected a single straight-line border, with a thickness of 2 points.

5. Click the **Borders** list arrow ☐ on the Tables and Borders toolbar. A palette of options appears. You want to insert a thick border at the bottom of Row 1, so you need to use the Bottom Border option.

6. Click the **Bottom Border** ☐ option (in the bottom row of the Borders palette, third from the left). The new border style is applied to the bottom border of row 1.

7. Click anywhere in the table to deselect the row. See Figure 3-30.

Figure 3-30	ROW 1 WITH NEW BORDER

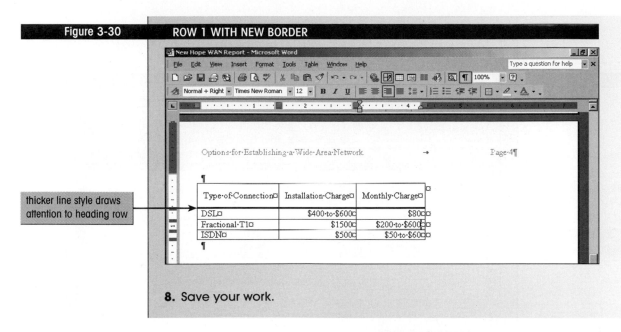

thicker line style draws
attention to heading row

8. Save your work.

Changing the borders has made the table more attractive. You'll finish formatting the table by adding shading to the cells containing the headings.

Adding Shading

Adding **shading** (a gray or colored background) is useful in tables when you want to emphasize headings, totals, or other important items. Generally, when you add shading to a table, you also need to bold the shaded text to make it easier to read.

You will now add a light gray shading to the heading row and then format the headings in bold.

To add shading to the heading row and change the headings to bold:

1. Click the selection bar to the left of row 1 to select the heading row of the table.

2. Click the **Shading Color** list arrow on the Tables and Borders toolbar. A palette of shading options opens.

3. Point to the fifth gray square from the left, in the top row. The ScreenTip "Gray-15%" appears.

4. Click the **Gray-15%** square. A light gray background appears in the heading row. Now you need to format the text in bold to make the headings stand out from the shading.

5. Click the **Bold** button **B** on the Formatting toolbar to make the headings bold. The wider letters take up more space, so Word breaks one or more of the headings into two lines within row 1.

TROUBLE? If any of the headings break incorrectly (for example, if the "n" in "Installation" moves to the next line), you might need to widen columns to accommodate the bold letters. Drag the column borders as necessary to adjust the column widths so that all the column headings are displayed correctly.

6. Click in the table to deselect row 1. Your table should look like Figure 3-31, although the line breaks in your table may differ.

Figure 3-31   BOLDED HEADINGS WITH SHADING

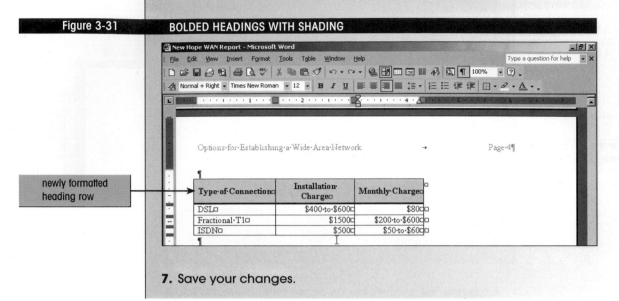

newly formatted heading row

7. Save your changes.

Centering a Table

If a table doesn't fill the entire page width, you can center it between the left and right margins. The Center button on the Formatting toolbar centers only text within each selected cell. It does not center the entire table across the page. To center a table across the page (between the left and right margins), you need to use the Table Properties command.

Caitilyn thinks the table would look better if it was centered between the left and right margins.

To center the table across the page:

1. Click anywhere in the table, click **Table** on the menu bar, and then click **Table Properties**. The Table Properties dialog box opens.

2. Click the **Table** tab if necessary.

3. In the Alignment section click the **Center** option. See Figure 3-32.

Figure 3-32   TABLE TAB OF THE TABLE PROPERTIES DIALOG BOX

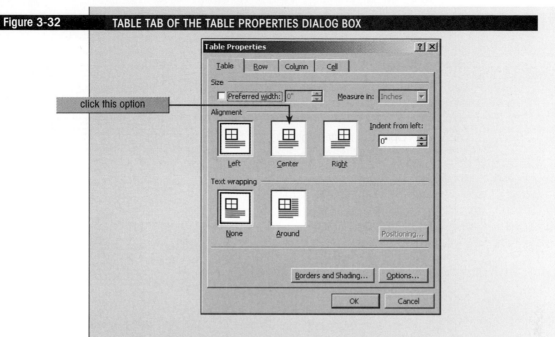

click this option

4. Click the **OK** button. The table centers between the left and right margins.

5. Save your work and then close the Tables and Borders toolbar.

Now that you're finished with the table, you want to print a copy of the full report for Caitilyn. You'll preview the report first.

To preview the report:

1. Click the **Print Preview** button 🔍 on the Standard toolbar to open the Print Preview window.

2. Use the **Multiple Pages** button ▦ on the Print Preview toolbar to display all four pages of the report. Verify that the table is properly formatted.

3. Click the **Print** button 🖨 on the Print Preview toolbar to print the report, and then close the document and exit Word.

You now have a hard copy of the New Hope report including the table, which summarizes the costs for creating a WAN. Your four-page report should look like Figure 3-33. You give the report to Caitilyn, so that she can add a brief introduction to the table.

Figure 3-33   NEW HOPE WAN REPORT

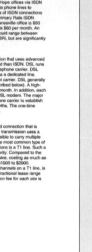
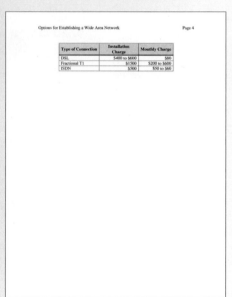

Session 3.2 QUICK CHECK

1. How do you adjust the width of the columns in a table?

2. Explain how to alter the border on the bottom of a heading row.

3. Define the following terms in your own words:
   a. line weight
   b. line style
   c. border
   d. shading

4. Explain how to add a row to the bottom of a table.

5. What's the fastest way to modify a column to accommodate the widest entry in the column?

6. In what order would the following numbers appear in a table if you sorted them in ascending numerical order: 25, 10, 75, 45?

7. How do you center a table between the left and right margins?

REVIEW ASSIGNMENTS

Susan Launspach, the program director at New Hope Social Services, has contacted Caitilyn Waller about another issue related to the agency's local area networks (LANs). Since last January, employees at the Madison office have experienced a number of problems, including malfunctioning printers and difficulty retrieving e-mail. Susan would like to hire Tyger Networks to resolve the network problems, a process known as troubleshooting. To secure the necessary funding, she needs a report outlining the basic issues, which she can then distribute to New Hope's board of directors. Working with a task force at Tyger Networks, Caitilyn has completed a draft of this report. It's your job to format the report and add a table at the end. When you're finished, she would like you to create a separate document that lists only the new equipment recommended by Tyger Networks. Complete the following:

1. If necessary, start Word, make sure your Data Disk is in the appropriate disk drive, and check your screen to make sure your settings match those in the tutorial. Display non-printing characters as necessary and switch to Print Layout view.

2. Open the file **Trouble** from the Review folder for Tutorial 3 on your Data Disk, and then save it as **Troubleshooting Report** in the same folder.

3. Select the list of task force members and their titles, and then insert a left tab stop 2.5 inches from the left margin.

4. Replace "Evan Brillstein" with your name.

5. Divide the document into two sections. Insert a section break so that the executive summary begins on a new page.

Explore 6. Vertically align the first section of the document using the Justified alignment option in the Page Setup dialog box, and view the results in Print Preview.

Explore 7. Add a footer to section 2. Click View on the menu bar, and then click Header and Footer. Use the Word online Help system to learn the functions of the buttons on the Header and Footer toolbar. Then, on the Header and Footer toolbar, click the Switch Between Header and Footer button to move to the footer area, then use the Show Next button (if necessary) to move from the section 1 footer to the section 2 footer. Click the Same as Previous button to deselect it. Using the same techniques you used to create a header in the tutorial, create a footer for section 2 that reads "Troubleshooting Network Problems Report" at the left margin. Insert the current date at the right margin. (*Hint*: Use the Insert Date button on the Header and Footer toolbar to insert the date.) Use the Formatting toolbar to format the footer and date in 9-point bold Arial.

8. Create a header for section 2 that aligns your name at the left margin and centers the page number preceded by the word "Page". Don't forget to deselect the Same as Previous button. (*Hint*: To center the page number, use the second tab stop.) Click Close on the Header and Footer toolbar, and then save your work so far.

9. Insert a page break at the end of the document, and then create the table shown in Figure 3-34.

Figure 3-34

Troubleshooting Options	Explanation	Cost
Onsite Troubleshooting	40 hours of onsite troubleshooting, at $120 an hour	$4800
Cable Checker	3 devices for each office, at $225 a piece	$675
Cable Tester	1 device to be shared among the three offices	$1300

10. Display the Tables and Borders toolbar, and then sort the Troubleshooting Options column in ascending order..

11. Insert a new row just below the Cable Tester row, and then enter the following information into the new row:

Troubleshooting option: Onsite Training

Explanation: Informational seminar for all Madison employees

Cost: $300

12. Modify the widths of columns A and C to accommodate only the widest entry in each, and then right-align the data in the Cost column.

13. Increase the height of the heading row and format it appropriately using shading and boldface. Center the headings vertically and horizontally in their cells.

Explore 14. Add a 2¼-point straight-line border around the outside of the table. (*Hint*: Select the entire table, select the line weight, and then use the Outside Border option in the Borders list box.) Add a double ½-point border at the bottom of the heading row.

15. Center the table on the page and then save your work.

16. Use the Table Move handle to select the entire table. Copy the table, open a new, blank document, and paste a copy of the table into the new document. Use the Delete command on the Table menu to delete the Onsite Training and Onsite Troubleshooting rows. Save the document as **Equipment List** in the Review folder for Tutorial 3. Close the document.

17. In the Troubleshooting Report document, insert a new row at the end of the table.

Explore 18. Select cells A6 and B6 (the two leftmost cells in the new row) and then click the Merge Cells button on the Tables and Borders toolbar. Type the text "TOTAL" into the new, merged cell, and then format the text so that it aligns on the right side of the cell. Apply boldface and shading to the new, merged cell to match the heading row.

Explore 19. Click the cell to the right of the TOTAL cell (cell C6) and then click the AutoSum button on the Tables and Borders toolbar. Word automatically sums the various costs, and displays the total ($7075.00) in cell C6.

Explore 20. Change the cost of the Onsite Training to $250, click cell C6, and then click the AutoSum button again. Word automatically updates the total.

21. Save your work, preview the report, print it, and close the document. Close the Tables and Borders toolbar, and then exit Word.

CASE PROBLEMS

Case 1. Sun Porch Bookstore Annual Report As manager of Sun Porch Bookstore in San Diego, California, you must submit an annual report to the Board of Directors. Complete the following:

1. If necessary, start Word, make sure your Data Disk is in the appropriate drive, and check your screen to make sure your settings match those in the tutorials. Switch to Print Layout view.

2. Open the file **SunRep** from the Cases folder for Tutorial 3 on your Data Disk, and save it as **Sun Porch Report** in the same folder.

3. Divide the document into two sections. Begin section 2 with the introduction on a new page.

Explore ➤ 4. Format the title ("Annual Report") and the subtitle ("Sun Porch Bookstore") using the font and font size of your choice. Center the first section vertically, and then select the title and subtitle and center them horizontally using the Center button on the Formatting toolbar. Note that you can combine horizontal and vertical alignment styles.

Explore ➤ 5. Click in section 1, and then create a header for the entire document that aligns your name on the left margin, and the current date on the right margin. Click the Show Next button on the Header and Footer toolbar to view the header text for section 2. Click the Same as Previous button to deselect it.

Explore ➤ 6. While in Header and Footer view, click the Switch between Header and Footer button to switch to the footer area for section 2. Press the Tab key to move the insertion point to the center tab stop, and then type the word "Page" followed by a space and the page number (using the Insert Page Number button on the Header and Footer toolbar). Insert a space, type the word "of", insert another space, and then click the Insert Number of Pages button on the Header and Footer toolbar to insert the total number of pages in the document. Close Header and Footer view when you are finished.

7. Select the list of members under the heading "Board of Directors." Insert a left tab stop 4.0 inches from the left margin, and then save your work.

8. Insert a page break at the end of the document, and then insert a table consisting of four rows and three columns.

9. Insert the headings "Name", "Title", and "Duties". Fill in the rows with the relevant information about the store personnel, which you will find listed in the report in the "Store Management and Personnel" section. Add new rows as needed.

10. Adjust the table column widths so the information is presented attractively.

11. Increase the height of the heading row, use the Tables and Borders toolbar to center the column headings horizontally and vertically, and then bold them.

12. Insert a row in the middle of the table, and add your name to the list of store managers. Adjust the column widths as needed.

13. Format the heading row with a light gray shading of your choice, and then change the outside border of the table to a single 2¼-point line weight.

14. Center the table on the page.

15. Save, preview, print, and close the document. Close the Tables and Borders toolbar, and then exit Word.

Case 2. Top Flight Travel's "Masterpiece Tour" Report Each year Top Flight Travel sponsors a "Masterpiece" tour, which shepherds travelers through a two-week, whirlwind tour of the artistic masterpieces of Europe. The tour director has just completed a report summarizing the most recent tour. It's your job to format the report, which includes one table. Complete the following:

1. If necessary, start Word, make sure your Data Disk is in the appropriate drive, and check your screen to make sure your settings match those in the tutorials. Switch to Print Layout view.

2. Open the file named **Tour** from the Cases folder for Tutorial 3 on your Data Disk, and then save it as **Masterpiece Tour Report** in the same folder.

3. Replace "Your Name" in the first page with your first and last name.

4. Divide the document into two sections. Begin the second section on a new page, with the summary that starts "This report summarizes and evaluates."

5. Vertically align the first section using the Center alignment option.

6. Create a header for section 2 only that contains the centered text "Top Flight Travel". (*Hint*: To center text in the header, use the second tab stop. Deselect the Same as Previous button before you begin.) Format the header text using italics and the font size of your choice.

Explore ▶ 7. On the Header and Footer toolbar, click the Switch Between Header and Footer button to move to the footer area of the document. Using the same techniques you used to create a header in the tutorial, create a footer for section 2 only that aligns "Evaluation Report" on the left margin and the date on the right margin. (*Hint*: Deselect the Same as Previous button first, and then use the Insert Date button on the Header and Footer toolbar to insert the date.) Close Header and Footer view.

Explore ▶ 8. Display the Tables and Borders toolbar. In the table, select the text in column A (the left column), bold the text, and then click the Change Text Direction button (on the Tables and Borders toolbar) twice so that text is formatted vertically, from bottom to top. Adjust the width of column A to accommodate the newly rotated text.

9. Adjust the other row and column widths as necessary.

10. Delete the blank row 2.

11. Format column A with a light colored shading of your choice.

12. Change the border around column A to 2¼-point line weight. Adjust the row heights, if necessary, to display each row heading in one line.

13. Save, preview, print, and close the document. Close the Tables and Borders toolbar, and then exit Word.

Case 3. Contact List for Flower Box Bakery Ken Yamamoto recently opened Flower Box Bakery, a wholesale bakery catering to upscale cafes and tea shops in suburban St. Louis. He has just acquired a list of potential sales contacts from the local chamber of commerce via e-mail. The information consists of names, phone numbers, and managers for a number of new cafes and restaurants in the St. Louis area. The information is formatted as simple text, with the pieces of information separated by commas. Ken asks you to convert this text into a table and then format the table to make it easy to read. Complete the following:

1. Open the file **Contacts** from the Cases folder for Tutorial 3 on your Data Disk, and then save it as **Sales Contacts** in the same folder.

Explore

2. Select the entire document, click Table on the menu bar, point to Convert, and then click Text to Table. In the Convert Text to Table dialog box, make sure the settings indicate that the table should have three columns and that the text is separated by commas. Also, select the "AutoFit to contents" option button, to ensure that columns are sized appropriately, and then click the OK button. Word converts the list into a table.

3. Replace the name "Christian Brook" with your first and last name.

4. Insert a new row at the top of the table and insert some appropriate headings.

Explore

5. When you need to format a table quickly, you can allow Word's AutoFormat command to do the work for you. Click anywhere in the table, click Table on the menu bar, and then click Table AutoFormat to open the Table AutoFormat dialog box. Scroll down the Table styles list box to see the available options. Click options that interest you, and observe the sample tables in the Preview box. Note that you can deselect the checkboxcs in the "Apply special formats to" section to remove boldface or shading from columns or rows that don't require it. Select a table style that you think is appropriate for the Contacts table, deselect check boxes as you see fit, and then click the Apply button.

6. Sort the table alphabetically by column A.

Explore

7. Place the pointer over the Table Resize handle, just outside the lower-right corner of the table. Drag the double-arrow pointer to increase the height and width of each cell to a size of your choice. Notice that all the parts of the table increase proportionally.

8. Save your work. Preview the table and then print it.

9. Close the document, and then exit Word.

Case 4. **Brochure for Camp Winnemac** Angela Freedman is the publicity director for Camp Winnemac, a sleep-away camp for girls located in Northern Michigan. She asks you to create an informational flier announcing the dates for Camp Winnemac's two summer sessions. She gives you a sketch, similar to the one shown in Figure 3-35. You decide to take advantage of the Word table features to structure the information in the sketch.

Figure 3-35

Camp Winnemac	Summer Sessions for Girls Ages 8 to 12	
	Ultimate Sports	**Equestrian Skills**
	Rock climbing, kayaking and white water rafting June 6 through July 2	Western and English style, for new and experienced riders July 6 through August 15
	Camp Winnemac is located in Michigan's Northern Peninsula, and boasts over 140 acres of forests, streams, and trails. The campgrounds include a heated pool, a modern stable, eight log cabin dormitories, and a full-sized dining hall and kitchen. For information, contact Angela Freedman at 456-818-0000.	

1. Open a new, blank document and save it as **Camp Winnemac** in the Cases folder for Tutorial 3.

2. If necessary, switch to Print Layout view and display rulers and the Tables and Borders toolbar.

3. Click the Draw Table button on the Tables and Borders toolbar, if necessary, to select the button and change the pointer to a pencil shape (the Draw Table pointer).

4. Select a single-line line style, with a line weight of 1½ points.

Explore 5. Click in the upper-left corner of the document (near the paragraph mark), and then drag down and to the right to draw a rectangle about 6 inches wide and 3.5 inches high.

Explore 6. Continue to use the Draw Table pointer to draw the columns and rows shown in Figure 3-35. For example, to draw the column border for the "Camp Winnemac" column, click at the top of the rectangle, where you want the column to begin, and drag down to the bottom of the rectangle. Use the same technique to draw rows. If you make a mistake, use the Undo button. To delete a border, click the Eraser button on the Tables and Borders toolbar, click the border you want to erase, and then click the Eraser button again to turn it off. Don't expect to draw the table perfectly the first time. You may have to practice awhile until you become comfortable with the Draw Table pointer, but once you can use it well, you will find it a helpful tool for creating complex tables. Click the Draw Table button on the toolbar again to turn it off.

Explore 7. In the left column, type the text "Camp Winnemac". With the pointer still in that cell, click the Change Text Direction button (on the Tables and Borders toolbar) twice to position the text vertically. Format the text in 26-point Times New Roman, and then center it in the cell using the Align Center option on the Tables and Borders toolbar. (*Hint*: You will probably have to adjust and readjust the row and column borders throughout this project, until all the elements of the table are positioned properly.)

8. Type the remaining text, as shown in Figure 3-35. Replace the name "Angela Freedman" with your own name. Use bold and italic as shown in Figure 3-35 to draw attention to key elements. Use the font styles, font sizes, and alignment options you think appropriate.

Explore

9. Click the Drawing button on the Standard toolbar to display the Drawing toolbar. Now you can insert the Camp Winnemac logo in the upper-right cell, using one of the tools on the Drawing toolbar. Click the upper-right cell, which at this point should be blank. Click the AutoShapes button on the Drawing toolbar, point to Basic Shapes, click the Sun shape. A box appears in the cell with the text "Create your drawing here." Click anywhere within the upper-right cell. The sun shape is inserted in the cell or somewhere nearby. The sun is selected, as indicated by the small circles, called selection handles, that surround it. If necessary, drag the sun to position it neatly within the cell. If the sun is not the right shape, click the lower-right selection handle, and drag up or down to adjust the size of the sun so that it fits within the cell borders more precisely. With the sun still selected, click the Fill Color list arrow on the Drawing toolbar, and then click a light pink square in the color palette.

10. Adjust column widths and row heights so that the table is attractive and easy to read.

Explore

11. Now that you have organized the information using the Word table tools, you can remove the borders so that the printed flier doesn't look like a table. Click the Table Move handle to select the entire table, click Table on the menu bar, click Table Properties, click the Table tab, click the Borders and Shading button, and then click the Borders tab, click the None option, click the OK button, and then click the OK button again. The borders are removed from the flier, leaving only the underlying gridlines, which will not appear on the printed page.

12. Save your work, preview the flier, make any necessary adjustments, print it, and then close the document and exit Word.

INTERNET ASSIGNMENTS

Student Union

The purpose of the Internet Assignments is to challenge you to find information on the Internet that you can use to create effective documents. The actual assignments are updated and maintained on the Course Technology Web site. Log on to the Internet and use your Web browser to go to the Student Union on the New Perspectives Series site at **www.course.com/NewPerspectives/studentunion**. Click the Online Companions link, and then click the link for this text.

QUICK CHECK ANSWERS

Session 3.1

1. **a.** the location where text moves when you press the Tab key
   b. the intersection of a row and a column in a table
   c. information arranged in horizontal rows and vertical columns
   d. a tab stop that aligns numerical data on the decimal point
   e. a unit or part of a document that can have its own page orientation, margins, headers, footers, and vertical alignment

2. Insert a section break, move the insertion point within the section you want to align, click File, click Page Setup, click the Layout tab, select Center in the Vertical alignment list box, make sure "This section" is selected in the Apply to list box, and then click OK.

3. A header appears at the top of a page, whereas a footer appears at the bottom of a page.

4. Move the insertion point to the location where you want the table to appear. Click the Insert Table button on the Standard toolbar. In the grid, click and drag to select four columns and six rows, and then release the mouse button.

5. If the insertion point is in the cell at the far right in a row, press the Tab key. Otherwise, press the ↓ key.

6. Click View on the menu bar, click Header and Footer, verify that the insertion point is located in the Header area, press Tab to move the insertion point to where you want the page number to appear, and then click the Insert Page Number button on the Header and Footer toolbar.

7. Select the text whose tab alignment you want to change, click the tab alignment selector on the far left of the horizontal ruler until the appropriate tab stop alignment style appears, and then click in the horizontal ruler where you want to set the new tab stop.

8. You may want to divide a document into sections if you wanted to center only part of the document between the top and bottom margins.

9. It's better to use a table rather than tab stops when you need to organize more than a few columns of information.

10. Click the Table Move handle.

Session 3.2

1. Drag the right border of each column to a new position.

2. Select the row. Click the Line Style list arrow on the Tables and Borders toolbar and select a line style. Click the Line Weight list arrow on the Tables and Borders toolbar and select a line weight. Click the Borders list arrow on the Tables and Borders toolbar and then click the Bottom Border option.

3. **a.** the thickness of the line used to create a border

   b. the style of the line used to create a border

   c. the outline of a row, cell, column, or table

   d. a gray or colored background used to highlight parts of a table

4. Click the cell at the far right in the bottom row of the table, and then press the Tab key.

5. Double-click the column's right-hand border.

6. 10, 25, 45, 75

7. Click anywhere in the table, click Table on the menu bar, click Table Properties, click the Table tab, click Center, and then click OK.

In this tutorial you will:

- Identify desktop-publishing features

- Create a title with WordArt

- Work with hyperlinks

- Create newspaper-style columns

- Insert and edit graphics

- Wrap text around a graphic

- Incorporate drop caps

- Use symbols and special typographic characters

- Add a page border

DESKTOP PUBLISHING A NEWSLETTER

Creating a Newsletter for Wide World Travel

CASE

Wide World Travel, Inc.

Wide World Travel, Inc. hosts international tours for travelers of all ages. Recently, the company has expanded its business by selling clothes and shoes specifically designed for the frequent traveler. Max Stephenson, one of the Wide World tour guides, has taken on the job of managing this new retail venture. In order to generate business, he wants to include an informational newsletter with each set of airline tickets mailed from the main office. He has asked you to help him create the newsletter.

Max has already written the text of the newsletter, which describes some of the most popular items sold by Wide World Travel. Now Max wants you to transform this text into an eye-catching publication that is neat, organized, and professional looking. He would like the newsletter to contain headings (so the customers can scan it quickly for interesting items) as well as a headline that will give the newsletter a memorable look. He wants you to include a picture that will reinforce the newsletter content.

In this tutorial, you'll plan the layout of the newsletter and then add some information about the Wide World Travel Web site. Then you'll get acquainted with the desktop-publishing features and elements you'll need to use to create the newsletter. Also, you'll learn how desktop publishing differs from other word-processing tasks and from Web page design. You'll format the title using an eye-catching design and divide the document into newspaper-style columns to make it easier to read. To add interest and focus to the text, you'll include a piece of art. You'll then fine-tune the newsletter layout, give it a more professional appearance with typographic characters, and put a border around the page to give the newsletter a finished look.

SESSION 4.1

In this session you will see how Max planned his newsletter and learn about desktop-publishing features and elements. Then you will add and remove a hyperlink, create the newsletter title using WordArt, modify the title's appearance, and format the text of the newsletter into newspaper-style columns.

Planning the Document

The newsletter will provide a brief overview of some popular items sold by Wide World Travel. Like most newsletters, it will be written in an informal style that conveys information quickly. The newsletter title will be eye-catching and will help readers quickly identify the document. Newsletter text will be split into two columns to make it easier to read, and headings will help readers scan the information quickly. A picture will add interest and illustrate the newsletter's content. Drop caps and other desktop-publishing elements will help draw readers' attention to certain information and make the newsletter design attractive and professional.

Elements of Desktop Publishing

Desktop publishing is the production of commercial-quality printed material using a desktop computer system from which you can enter and edit text, create graphics, compose or lay out pages, and print documents. In addition to newsletters, you can desktop publish brochures, posters, and other documents that include text and graphics. In the Case Problems, you'll have to create a brochure. The following elements are commonly associated with desktop publishing:

- High-quality printing. A laser printer or high-resolution inkjet printer produces final output.
- Multiple fonts. Two or three font types and sizes provide visual interest, guide the reader through the text, and convey the tone of the document.
- Graphics. Graphics, such as horizontal or vertical lines (called rules), boxes, electronic art, and digitized photographs help illustrate a concept or product, draw a reader's attention to the document, and make the text visually appealing.
- Typographic characters. Typographic characters such as typographic long dashes, called em dashes (—), in place of double hyphens (--), separate dependent clauses; typographic medium-width dashes, called en dashes (–), are used in place of hyphens (-) as minus signs and in ranges of numbers; and typographic bullets (•) signal items in a list.
- Columns and other formatting features. Columns of text, pull quotes (small portions of text pulled out of the main text and enlarged), page borders, and other special formatting features that you don't frequently see in letters and other documents distinguish desktop-published documents.

You'll incorporate many of these desktop-publishing elements into the Wide World Travel newsletter for Max.

Word's Desktop-Publishing Features

Successful desktop publishing requires that you first know what elements professionals use to desktop publish a document. Figure 4-1 defines some of the desktop-publishing features included in Word. Max wants you to use these features to produce the final newsletter shown in Figure 4-2. The newsletter includes some of the typical desktop-publishing elements that you can add to a document using Word.

Figure 4-1   **WORD DESKTOP PUBLISHING FEATURES**

ELEMENT	DESCRIPTION
Columns	Two or more vertical blocks of text that fit on one page
WordArt	Text modified with special effects, such as rotated, curved, bent, shadowed, or shaded letters
Clip art	Prepared graphic images that are ready to be inserted into a document
Drop cap	Oversized first letter of word beginning a paragraph that extends vertically into two or more lines of the paragraph
Typographic symbols	Special characters that are not part of the standard keyboard, such as em dashes (—), copyright symbols (©), or curly quotation marks (")

Figure 4-2   **WIDE WORLD TRAVEL NEWSLETTER**

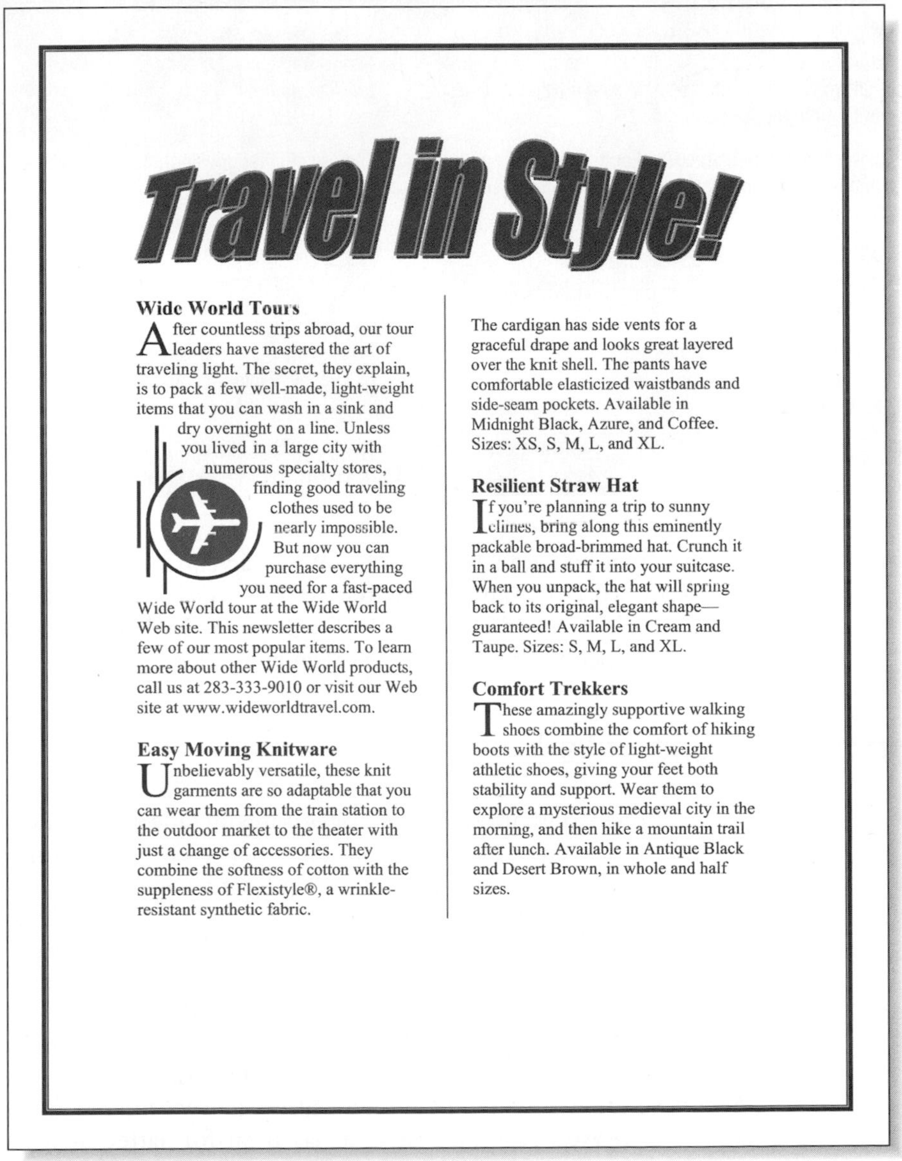

Travel in Style!

Wide World Tours

After countless trips abroad, our tour leaders have mastered the art of traveling light. The secret, they explain, is to pack a few well-made, light-weight items that you can wash in a sink and dry overnight on a line. Unless you lived in a large city with numerous specialty stores, finding good traveling clothes used to be nearly impossible. But now you can purchase everything you need for a fast-paced Wide World tour at the Wide World Web site. This newsletter describes a few of our most popular items. To learn more about other Wide World products, call us at 283-333-9010 or visit our Web site at www.wideworldtravel.com.

Easy Moving Knitware

Unbelievably versatile, these knit garments are so adaptable that you can wear them from the train station to the outdoor market to the theater with just a change of accessories. They combine the softness of cotton with the suppleness of Flexistyle®, a wrinkle-resistant synthetic fabric.

The cardigan has side vents for a graceful drape and looks great layered over the knit shell. The pants have comfortable elasticized waistbands and side-seam pockets. Available in Midnight Black, Azure, and Coffee. Sizes: XS, S, M, L, and XL.

Resilient Straw Hat

If you're planning a trip to sunny climes, bring along this eminently packable broad-brimmed hat. Crunch it in a ball and stuff it into your suitcase. When you unpack, the hat will spring back to its original, elegant shape—guaranteed! Available in Cream and Taupe. Sizes: S, M, L, and XL.

Comfort Trekkers

These amazingly supportive walking shoes combine the comfort of hiking boots with the style of light-weight athletic shoes, giving your feet both stability and support. Wear them to explore a mysterious medieval city in the morning, and then hike a mountain trail after lunch. Available in Antique Black and Desert Brown, in whole and half sizes.

Desktop Publishing Versus Web Page Design

In many ways, desktop-published documents are similar to another kind of document known as a Web page. As you probably know, a **Web page** is a document that can contain specially formatted text, graphics, video, and audio. A Web page is stored on a computer as a collection of electronic files and is designed to be viewed in a special program called a **browser**. You probably have experience using a browser such as Microsoft Internet Explorer to explore Web pages on the Internet.

Like desktop-published documents, Web pages often include drop caps, multiple fonts, and graphics. However, you must use these elements differently when designing a Web page than when desktop publishing a document. Figure 4-3 summarizes some basic distinctions between desktop publishing and Web page design.

Figure 4-3	DESKTOP-PUBLISHED DOCUMENTS COMPARED TO WEB PAGES
DESKTOP PUBLISHING	**WEB PAGE DESIGN**
Reader sees the entire page at one time. Large areas of white space or uneven columns are therefore very noticeable in a desktop-published document.	Reader sees only the portion of the Web page that is displayed in the browser window.
Use of color increases printing costs. For this reason, many desktop-published documents are designed to be printed on a black and white printer.	The use of color does not affect the cost of producing the Web page.
The quality of the printer greatly affects the appearance of graphics in the printed page. Thus, desktop publishers usually prefer simple graphics that print well on laser printers.	The quality of graphics is most affected by the type of electronic file in which the graphic is stored.
The page is static. The only devices that can be used to catch the reader's attention are desktop-publishing elements, such as headlines, columns, and graphics.	Parts of the page can be animated, or include video. Also, Web pages often convey information or attract the reader's attention by using sound.
The reader cannot interact with a desktop-published document.	The reader can interact with a Web page by clicking links that display other Web pages or by entering information into a form on the Web page.

Now that you are familiar with some basic concepts related to desktop publishing, you can begin work on Max's newsletter. Your first task is to insert some information about the Wide World Travel Web site in the first section. To do this, you need to understand how to work with specially formatted text called hyperlinks.

Working with Hyperlinks

As mentioned in Figure 4-3, Web pages often include special text called **hyperlinks** (or simply **links**) that you can click to display other Web pages. You can also use hyperlinks in Word documents that will be read **online** (that is, on a computer).

For example, if you type an e-mail address and then press Enter, Word will automatically format the e-mail address as a hyperlink. (Hyperlink text is usually formatted in blue with an underline.) When you press Ctrl and click an e-mail hyperlink, an e-mail program opens automatically, ready for you to type a message. (If you completed the Review Assignments for Tutorial 2, you already have experience using e-mail hyperlinks.)

In the same way, Word will automatically format a Web page address, or **URL**, as a hyperlink. (One example of a Web address is www.microsoft.com.) When you press Ctrl and click a Web page address that has been formatted as a hyperlink, your computer's browser opens automatically and attempts to display that Web page. (The browser may not actually be able to display the Web page if your computer is not currently connected to the Internet, or if the Web page is unavailable for some other reason.)

Including hyperlinks in a Word document is very useful when you plan to distribute it via e-mail and have others read it online. For instance, if you include your e-mail address in a memo to a potential customer, the customer can click the e-mail address to begin typing an e-mail message to you in reply. However, when you know that your document will only be distributed on paper, it's a good idea to remove any hyperlinks so that the e-mail address or Web address is formatted the same as the rest of the document. This helps ensure that a desktop-published document has a uniform look. To remove a hyperlink, right-click the hyperlink and then click Remove Hyperlink in the shortcut menu. Once you remove the hyperlink, the Web address or e-mail address remains in the document, but is no longer formatted in blue with an underline.

Max would like you to complete the newsletter text by adding a reference to the Wide World Travel Web site. He does not want the company's Web address formatted as a hyperlink, so you will have to remove the hyperlink after typing the Web address. He has saved the newsletter text in a document named Clothes. You'll begin by opening the document that contains the unformatted text of the newsletter, often called **copy**.

To open the newsletter document and add the Web address:

1. Start Word, and place your Data Disk in the appropriate drive. Make sure your screen matches the figures in this tutorial. In particular, be sure to display non-printing characters and switch to Normal view.

2. Open the file **Clothes** from the Tutorial folder in the Tutorial.04 folder on your Data Disk.

3. To avoid altering the original file, save the document as **Travel Clothes** in the Tutorial folder in the Tutorial.04 folder on your Data Disk.

4. If necessary, change the Zoom setting (in the Standard toolbar) to 100% and switch to Normal view.

5. Click at the end of the second paragraph (after the phone number) press the **spacebar**, and then type the following: **or visit our Web site at www.wideworldtravel.com**

6. Type a period at the end of the Web address, and then press the **Enter** key. The Web address is formatted as a hyperlink, in a blue font with an underline.

7. Move the mouse pointer over the hyperlink. A ScreenTip appears, with the complete URL (including some extra characters that a browser needs to display the Web page). The ScreenTip also displays instructions for displaying the Wide World Travel Web site. See Figure 4-4.

Figure 4-4	HYPERLINK WITH SCREENTIP

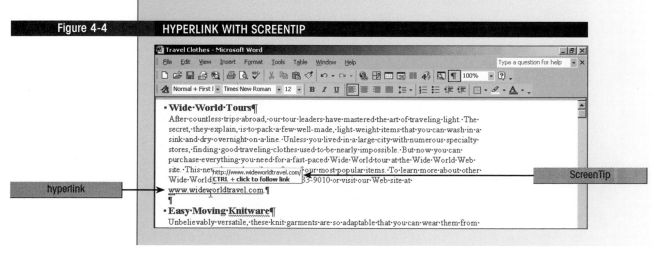

Max tells you that the Wide World Travel Web site is being updated, so it is not yet available online. So instead of clicking the link to test it, you will remove the hyperlink. This will ensure that the Web address is formatted to match the rest of the paragraph.

To remove the hyperlink:

1. Right-click the text **www.wideworldtravel.com**. A shortcut menu opens, as shown in Figure 4-5.

Figure 4-5	HYPERLINK MENU

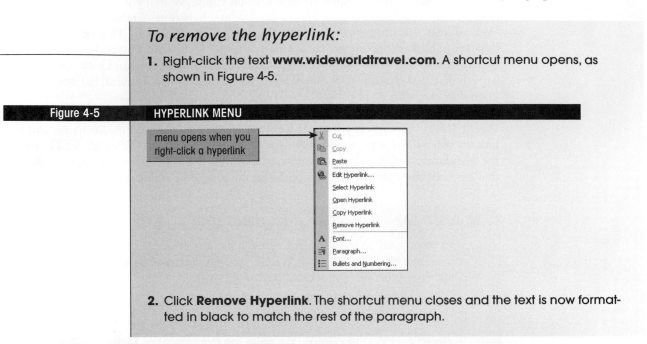

2. Click **Remove Hyperlink**. The shortcut menu closes and the text is now formatted in black to match the rest of the paragraph.

You have finished adding the information about the company's Web site to the newsletter. Now that the newsletter contains all the necessary details, you can turn your attention to adding a headline.

Using WordArt to Create a Headline

Max wants the title of the newsletter, "Travel in Style," to be eye-catching and dramatic, as shown earlier in Figure 4-2. WordArt, available in Word and other Microsoft Office programs, provides great flexibility in designing text with special effects that expresses the image or mood you want to convey in your printed documents. With WordArt, you can apply color and shading, as well as alter the shape and size of the text. You can easily "wrap" the document text around WordArt shapes.

Note that you begin creating WordArt by clicking a button on the Drawing toolbar. When you first display the Drawing toolbar, Word switches to Print Layout view. As a rule, Print Layout view is the most appropriate view to use when you are desktop publishing with Word because it shows you exactly how the text and graphics fit on the page. The vertical ruler that appears in Print Layout view helps you position graphical elements more precisely.

REFERENCE WINDOW   **RW**

<u>Creating Special Text Effects Using WordArt</u>

- Click the Drawing button on the Standard toolbar to display the Drawing toolbar.
- Click the Insert WordArt button on the Drawing toolbar.
- Click the style of text you want to insert, and then click the OK button.
- Type the text you want in the Edit WordArt Text dialog box.
- Click the Font and Size list arrows to select the font and font size you want.
- If you want, click the Bold or Italic button, or both.
- Click the OK button.
- With the WordArt selected, drag any handle to reshape and resize it. To keep the text in the same proportions as the original, press and hold down the Shift key while you drag a handle.

You're ready to use WordArt to create the newsletter title. First you will display the Drawing toolbar. Then you will choose a WordArt style and type the headline text.

To create the title of the newsletter using WordArt:

1. Press **Ctrl+Home** to move the insertion point to the beginning of the document.

2. If the Drawing toolbar is not displayed on your screen, click the **Drawing** button on the Standard toolbar. The Drawing toolbar appears at the bottom of the screen. Word switches to Print Layout view.

   TROUBLE? If the Drawing toolbar is not positioned at the bottom of the Document window, drag it there by its title bar. If you do not see the Drawing toolbar anywhere, right-click the Standard toolbar, and then click Drawing on the shortcut menu.

3. If necessary, click **View** on the menu bar and then click **Ruler** to display the vertical and horizontal rulers, and then verify that the Zoom setting is 100%.

4. Click the **Insert WordArt** button on the Drawing toolbar. The WordArt Gallery dialog box opens, displaying 30 different WordArt styles.

5. Click the WordArt style in the second row from the top, second column from the right, as shown in Figure 4-6.

Figure 4-6   **WORDART STYLES**

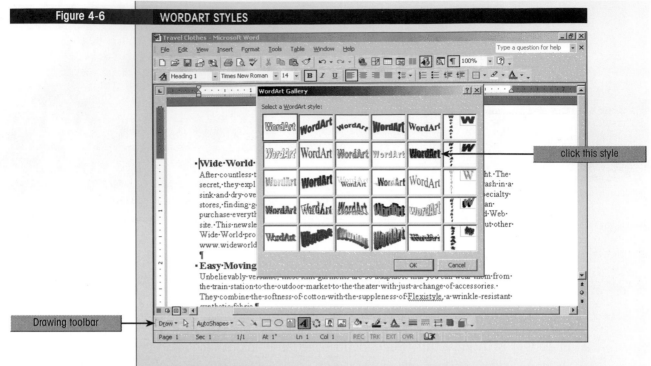

6. Click the **OK** button. The Edit WordArt Text dialog box opens, displaying the default text "Your Text Here," which you will replace with the newsletter title.

7. Type **Travel in Style** to replace the default text with the newsletter title. Notice the toolbar at the top of the Edit WordArt Text dialog box, which you could use to apply boldface and italics, or to change the font or font style. You don't need to use these options now, but you might choose to when creating headlines for other documents.

8. Click the **OK** button. The Edit WordArt Text dialog box closes and the WordArt image is inserted at the beginning of the newsletter. The "Wide World Tours" heading moves to the right to accommodate the new headline. See Figure 4-7.

   TROUBLE? If you see a border around the headline, the WordArt is currently selected. Click anywhere outside of the border to deselect the WordArt.

Figure 4-7   **WORDART HEADLINE INSERTED INTO DOCUMENT**

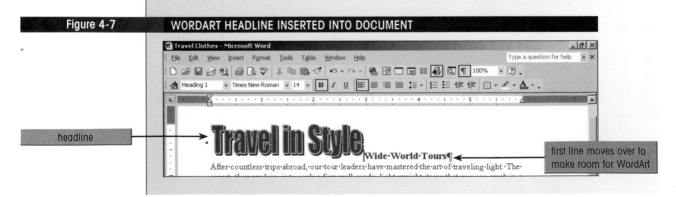

Eventually, you will position the headline so that it appears at the very top of the document, stretching from margin to margin. But for now, you can leave it in its current position.

Selecting a WordArt Object

The WordArt image you have created is not regular text. You cannot edit it as you would other text, by moving the insertion point to it and typing new letters, or by selecting part of it and using the buttons on the Formatting toolbar. Unlike regular text, a WordArt headline is considered an **object**—that is, something that lies on top of the document. To edit a WordArt object in Word, you must first click it to select it. Then you can make changes using special toolbar buttons and dialog boxes, or by dragging it with the mouse.

Max would like you to make several changes to the newsletter headline. Before you can do this, you need to select it.

To select the WordArt headline:

1. Click the WordArt headline. The headline is surrounded by a black border with eight small black squares (called resize handles). The WordArt toolbar also appears. See Figure 4-8.

Figure 4-8   **SELECTED HEADLINE**

Editing a WordArt Object

Now that the WordArt object is selected, you can modify its appearance (color, shape, size, and so forth) using the buttons on the Drawing toolbar or the WordArt toolbar. First of all, Max would like you to edit the WordArt by adding an exclamation mark at the end of the headline. While you're making that change, he would like you to format the headline in italics.

To change the font and formatting of the WordArt object:

1. Verify that the WordArt object is selected, as indicated by the resize handles.

2. Click the **Edit Text** button on the WordArt toolbar. The Edit WordArt Text dialog box opens. As you recall, you used this dialog box earlier when you first created the WordArt headline.

3. Click at the end of the headline (after the "e" in Style") and type **!** (an exclamation mark).

4. Click the **Italic** button in the Edit WordArt Text dialog box. The headline in the Text box is now formatted in italics, with an exclamation mark at the end.

5. Click the **OK** button. The Edit WordArt Text dialog box closes, allowing you to see the edited headline in the document.

Changing the Shape of a WordArt Object

You can quickly change the shape of a WordArt object using the **WordArt Shape** button on the WordArt toolbar. Right now, the WordArt headline has a straight shape, without any curve to it. Max wants to use an arched shape.

To change the shape of the WordArt object:

1. Verify that the WordArt headline is selected, and then click the **WordArt Shape** button ![Abc] on the WordArt toolbar.

2. Move the mouse pointer over the options in the palette to display a ScreenTip with the name of each shape. As you can see, the Plain Text shape (a straight line) is currently selected.

3. Click the **Inflate Top** shape (fourth row down, fifth column from the left), as shown in Figure 4-9.

Figure 4-9	WORDART SHAPES

Plain Text shape

Inflate Top shape

The newsletter title changes to the new WordArt shape.

The headline has the shape you want. Now you can take care of positioning the WordArt object above the newsletter text.

Wrapping Text Below the WordArt Object

At this point, the WordArt object is on the same line as the heading "Wide World Tours." Max would like you to set the WordArt on its own line at the top of the document. To do this, you need to change the way the text flows, or **wraps**, around the WordArt object.

You can wrap text around objects many different ways in Word. For example, you can have the text wrap above and below the object, through it, or wrap the text to follow the shape of the object, even if it has an irregular shape. Text wrapping is often used in newsletters to prevent text and graphics from overlapping, to add interest, and to prevent excessive open areas, called white space, from appearing on the page. The Text Wrapping button on the WordArt or Picture toolbar provides some basic choices, whereas the Layout tab of the Format Picture dialog box provides more advanced options. Because you want to use a relatively simple option—wrapping text so that it flows below the WordArt headline—you'll use the Text Wrapping button on the WordArt toolbar. You'll have a chance to use the Format Picture dialog box in the Case Problems at the end of this tutorial.

To wrap the newsletter text below the WordArt headline:

1. With the WordArt object selected, click the **Text Wrapping** button ![icon] on the WordArt toolbar. A menu of text wrapping options opens.

2. Click **Top and Bottom**. The text drops below the newsletter title. The WordArt is still selected, but instead of handles in the shape of square boxes, you see small circles. A number of other items appear around the WordArt object, as shown in Figure 4-10. You can use the handles shown in Figure 4-10 to change the size and position of the WordArt object. You'll learn the meaning of the anchor symbol shortly. Don't be concerned if yours is not in the same position as the one in Figure 4-10.

Figure 4-10	WORDART AFTER WRAPPING TEXT

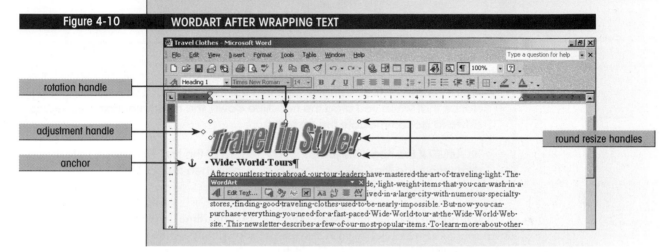

Positioning and Sizing the WordArt Object

After you choose a text wrap style for a WordArt object, you can adjust its size and position in the document. To position a WordArt object, click it and drag it with the mouse pointer. To widen any WordArt object, drag one of its resize handles. To keep the object the same proportion as the original, hold down the Shift key as you drag the resize handle. This prevents "stretching" the object more in one direction than the other.

Max asks you to widen the headline so it fits neatly within the newsletter margins. As you enlarge the headline, you can practice dragging the WordArt object to a new position.

To position and enlarge the WordArt object:

1. Move the mouse pointer over the headline.

2. Use the ↔‍↕ pointer to drag the WordArt object to the right, until it is centered over the top of the newsletter.

3. Click the **Undo** button on the Standard toolbar to undo the move. The headline returns to its original position, aligned along the left-hand margin. Note that you can use this same technique to drag a WordArt object to any location in a document. (You'll learn more about dragging objects later in this tutorial, when you insert a picture into the newsletter.)

4. With the WordArt object still selected, position the pointer over its lower-right resize handle. The pointer changes to ↖.

5. Press and hold the **Shift** key while you drag the resize handle to the right margin, using the horizontal ruler as a guide. See Figure 4-11. As you drag the handle, the pointer changes to ┼. If necessary, repeat the procedure to make the exclamation mark line up with the right margin.

Figure 4-11   **RESIZING THE WORDART OBJECT**

top margin marker →

right margin marker

resizing pointer

6. If necessary, use the ⊹ pointer to drag the headline down slightly, so that the top of the headline does not extend into the top margin, as shown in Figure 4-11. Notice that when you drag the headline down, the newsletter text also moves down to accommodate the headline.

TROUBLE? If the headline jumps to the middle of the first paragraph of text, you dragged it too far. Click the Undo button, and then repeat Step 6.

In addition to moving and resizing the WordArt headline, you can drag the rotation handle to rotate the headline. You can also use the adjustment handle to increase or decrease the arch at the top of the headline. You'll have a chance to practice these techniques in the Review Assignments at the end of this tutorial. Right now you need to turn your attention to the anchor symbol on the left side of the WordArt object.

Anchoring **the WordArt Object**

At some point after you wrap text around a document, you need to make sure the WordArt object is properly positioned within the document as a whole—a process known as **anchoring**. The process draws its name from the anchor symbol in the left margin, which indicates the position of the WordArt relative to the text. (The anchor symbol is only visible after you wrap text around the document.) To ensure that changes to the text (such as section breaks) do not affect the WordArt, you need to anchor the WordArt to a blank paragraph before the text. At this point, the WordArt anchor symbol is probably located to the left of the first paragraph (the heading "Wide World Tours"). However, yours may be in a different position (for instance, it might be positioned above and to the left of the WordArt). In the next set of steps, you will move the anchor to a new, blank paragraph at the beginning of the document.

To anchor the WordArt object to a blank paragraph:

1. Press **Ctrl+Home**. The insertion point moves to the beginning of the newsletter text (that is, to the left of the first "W" in the heading "Wide World Tours"). The WordArt object is no longer selected; you cannot see the anchor at this point.

2. Press the **Enter** key. A new paragraph symbol is inserted at the beginning of the document.

3. Click the WordArt object. The selection handles and the anchor symbol appear.

4. Click the anchor and drag it to the left of the new, blank paragraph, as shown in Figure 4-12.

Figure 4-12	PROPERLY ANCHORED WORDART

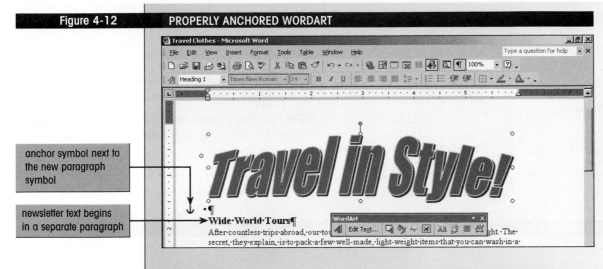

anchor symbol next to the new paragraph symbol

newsletter text begins in a separate paragraph

TROUBLE? If your WordArt headline is positioned below the new paragraph symbol, drag it up slightly to position it above the new paragraph symbol. If you notice any other differences between your headline and the one shown in Figure 4-12, edit the headline to make it match the figure. For example, you may need to drag the WordArt left or right slightly, or you may need to adjust its size by dragging one of its resize handles.

5. Click anywhere in the newsletter to deselect the WordArt, and then save your work.

Your WordArt is now finished. Max congratulates you on your excellent work. The headline will definitely draw attention to the newsletter, encouraging potential customers to read the entire document.

Formatting Text in Newspaper-Style Columns

Because newsletters are meant for quick reading, they are usually laid out in newspaper-style columns. In newspaper-style columns, a page is divided into two or more vertical blocks, or columns. Text flows down one column, continues at the top of the next column, flows down that column, and so forth. The narrow columns and small type size allow the eye to take in a lot of text, thus allowing a reader to scan a newspaper quickly for interesting information.

When formatting a document in columns, you can click where you want the columns to begin and then click the Columns button on the Formatting toolbar. However, the Columns command on the Formatting menu offers more options. Using the Columns command, you can insert a vertical line between columns. The Columns command also gives you more control over exactly what part of the document will be formatted in columns.

Max wants you to divide the text below the title into two columns and add a vertical line between them.

To apply newspaper-style columns to the body of the newsletter:

1. Position the insertion point at the beginning of the second paragraph (to the left of the first "W" in "Wide World Tours").

2. Click **Format** on the menu bar, and then click **Columns**. The Columns dialog box opens.

3. In the Presets section, click the **Two** icon.

4. Click the **Line between** check box to select it. The text in the Preview box changes to a two-column format with a vertical rule between the columns.

   You want these changes to affect only the paragraphs after the WordArt headline, so you'll need to insert a section break and apply the column formatting to the text after the insertion point.

5. Click the **Apply to** list arrow, and then click **This point forward** to have Word automatically insert a section break at the insertion point. See Figure 4-13.

Figure 4-13   COMPLETED COLUMNS DIALOG BOX

creates two columns of the same width

places a line between columns

shows how columns will look with current settings

adds section break at insertion point

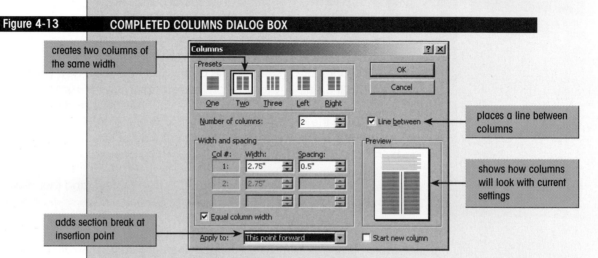

6. Click the **OK** button to return to the Document window. A continuous section break appears below the WordArt title. The word "continuous" indicates that the new section continues on the same page as the preceding page—in other words, the newsletter text and the WordArt title will print on the same page, even though they lie in different sections. The text in Section 2 is formatted in two columns.

To get a good look at the columns, you need to change the zoom setting so you can see the entire page at one time.

To zoom out to display the whole page:

1. Click the **Zoom** list arrow on the Standard toolbar, and then click **Whole Page**. Word displays the entire page of the newsletter so that you can see how the two-column format looks on the page. See Figure 4-14. Note that the Whole Page Zoom setting is only available in Print Layout view. You should use it whenever you want to have the entire page displayed as you edit it.

Figure 4-14	WHOLE PAGE VIEW SHOWING TWO COLUMNS

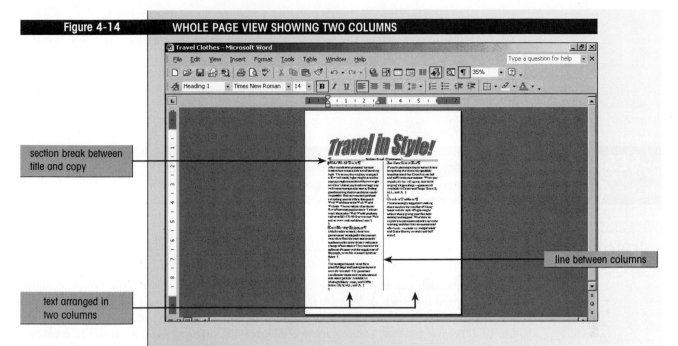

section break between title and copy

line between columns

text arranged in two columns

TROUBLE? Your columns may break at a slightly different line from those shown in the figure. This is not a problem; just continue with the tutorial.

The newsletter headline is centered on the page, and the copy is in a two-column format. The text fills the left column but not the right column. You'll fix this later, after you add a graphic and format some of the text.

2. Click the **Zoom** list arrow again, and then click **Page Width**. The Page Width option reduces the zoom setting enough to make the page span the width of the document window. Now you can read the text again.

3. Save your work.

Keep in mind that you can modify the structure of columns in a document by reformatting the document with three or more columns, or return the document to its original format by formatting it as one column. You can also insert column breaks to force text to move from one column to the next. You'll have a chance to practice modifying the columns in the Case Problems at the end of this tutorial.

Session 4.1 QUICK | CHECK

1. Describe four elements commonly associated with desktop publishing.

2. Describe at least two differences between a desktop-published document and a Web page.

3. In your own words, define the following terms:

    a. desktop publishing

    b. Web page

    c. copy

    d. anchor

4. True or False: When using Word's desktop-publishing features, you should display your document in Normal view.

5. True or False: You can edit WordArt just as you would edit any other text in Word.
6. How do you change the text of a WordArt object after you have inserted it into a Word document?
7. What is the purpose of the WordArt Shape button on the WordArt toolbar?
8. True or False: When you first format a document into newspaper-style columns, the columns will not necessarily be of equal length.

SESSION 4.2

In this session you will insert, resize, and crop clip art, and change the way the text wraps around the clip art. Then you'll create drop caps, insert typographic symbols, balance columns, place a border around the newsletter, and print the newsletter.

Inserting Graphics

Graphics, which can include drawings, paintings, photographs, charts, tables, designs, or even designed text such as WordArt, add variety to documents and are especially appropriate for newsletters. Word allows you to draw pictures in your document, using the buttons on the Drawing toolbar. To produce professional-looking graphics, it's easier to create a picture in a special graphics program and then save the picture as an electronic file. (You may already be familiar with one graphics program, **Paint**, which is included as part of the Windows operating system.)

Instead of creating your own art in a graphics program, you can take a piece of art on a piece of paper (such as a photograph) and scan it—that is, run it through a special machine called a scanner. A **scanner** is similar to a copy machine except that it saves a copy of the image as an electronic file, instead of reproducing it on a piece of paper. (As you may know, many modern copy machines also function as scanners.) You can also use a digital camera to take a photograph that is then stored as an electronic file.

Electronic files come in several types, many of which were developed for use in Web pages. In desktop publishing, you will most commonly work with **bitmaps**—a type of file that stores an image as a collection of tiny dots, which, when displayed on a computer monitor or printed on a page, make up a picture. There are several types of bitmap files, the most common of which are:

- ■ BMP: Used by Microsoft Paint to store graphics you create. These files, which have the .bmp file extension, tend to be very large.
- ■ GIF: Suitable for most types of simple art. A GIF file is compressed, so it doesn't take up much room on your computer. A GIF file has the file extension .gif.
- ■ JPEG: Suitable for photographs and drawings. Even more compressed than GIF files. A JPEG file has the file extension .jpg.
- ■ TIFF: Commonly used for photographs or scanned images. TIFF files have the file extension .tif and are usually much larger than GIF or JPEG files.

Once you have stored a piece of art as an electronic file, you can insert it into a document using the Picture commands on the Insert menu. You'll have a chance to explore some of these commands in the Review Assignments and Case Problems at the end of this tutorial.

If you don't have time to prepare your own art work, you can take advantage of **clip art**—a collection of pre-made, copyright-free images included along with Word. A number of clip art selections are stored on your computer when you install Microsoft Word. You can also download additional clip art from the Web. (You'll have a chance to look for clip art on the Web in the Case Problems at the end of this tutorial.) You begin inserting clip art by opening the Clip Art Task Pane. From there you can open the Clip Organizer, which gives you access to a series of folders containing various categories of clip art. Then you copy an image to the Office Clipboard, close the Clip Organizer, and paste the image into the document.

To add visual appeal to the Wide World Travel newsletter, you will insert a piece of clip art now. Max wants you to use a graphic that reflects the newsletter content.

To insert the clip art image of an airplane into the newsletter:

1. If you took a break after the previous session, make sure Word is still running, the Travel Clothes newsletter is open, the document is in Print Layout view, and the nonprinting characters are displayed. Also verify that the Drawing toolbar is displayed.

2. Click the **Insert Clip Art** button 🖼 on the Drawing toolbar. The Insert Clip Art Task Pane opens, as shown in Figure 4-15. You can use the top part of this Task Pane to search for graphics related to a specific topic. You can also click the Clip Organizer option (near the bottom) to open a dialog box where you can browse among the various images stored on your computer. You'll use the Clip Organizer in the next step.

Figure 4-15	INSERT CLIP ART TASK PANE

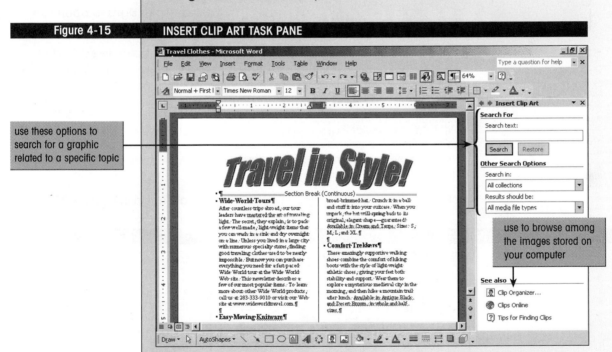

use these options to search for a graphic related to a specific topic

use to browse among the images stored on your computer

TROUBLE? If you see the Add Clips to Organizer dialog box, click Now. This will organize the clip art installed on your computer into folders, so that you can then use the Clip Organizer dialog box to select a piece of clip art. This dialog box will appear the first time you attempt to use clip art on your computer.

3. Click **Clip Organizer** near the bottom of the Task Pane. The Microsoft Clip Organizer opens, with the Favorites folder selected in the Collection List. This dialog box works similar to Windows Explorer. You click the plus signs next to folders to display subfolders. The images stored in subfolders are displayed in the right-hand pane. Clip art in Word is stored in subfolders within the Office Collections folder. See Figure 4-16. (You might see different folders from those shown in Figure 4-16, but you should see the Office Collections folder.)

Figure 4-16 MICROSOFT CLIP ORGANIZER

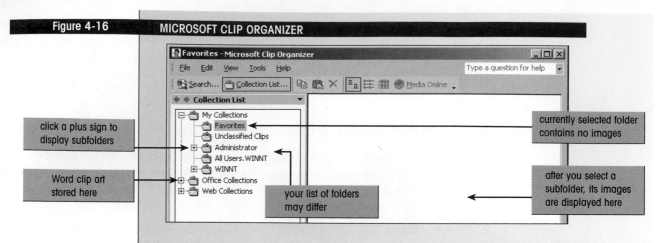

click a plus sign to display subfolders

Word clip art stored here

your list of folders may differ

currently selected folder contains no images

after you select a subfolder, its images are displayed here

4. Click the plus sign next to the **Office Collections** folder. A list of subfolders within the Office Collections folder appears. This list of folders, which is created when you install Word, organizes clip art images into related categories. The folders with plus signs next to them contain subfolders or clip art images.

5. Scroll down and examine the list of folders. Click any plus signs to open subfolders, and then click folders to display clip art images in the right-hand pane.

6. Click the plus sign next to the **Transportation** folder to display its subfolders, and then click the **Transportation** folder to select it. Three images stored in the Transportation folder are displayed in the right-hand pane.

   TROUBLE? If you don't see any images in the Transportation folder, click the Travel folder to select it and display an image of an airplane in a blue circle.

7. Move the pointer over the image of the airplane in the blue circle. An arrow button appears.

8. Click the arrow button. A menu of options opens, as shown in Figure 4-17.

Figure 4-17 IMAGE IN THE TRANSPORTATION FOLDER SELECTED

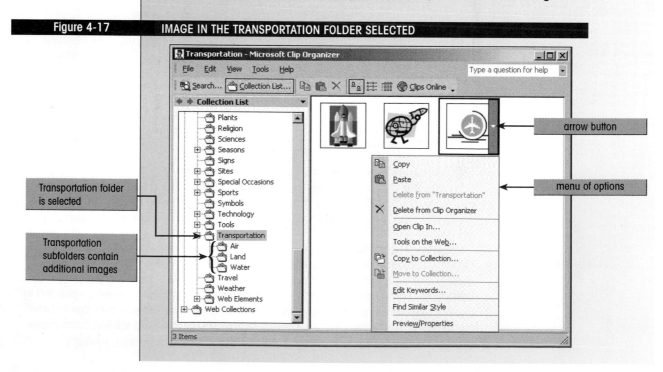

arrow button

menu of options

Transportation folder is selected

Transportation subfolders contain additional images

9. Click **Copy** in the menu. The image is copied to the Office Clipboard.

10. Click the **Close** button [X] to close the Microsoft Clip Organizer, and then click **Yes** when you see a dialog box asking if you want to save the item on the Clipboard. You return to the Document window.

Now that you have copied the image to the Clipboard, you can paste it into the document at the insertion point. Max asks you to insert the graphic in the paragraph below the heading "Tours." Before you insert the image, you will close the Task Pane.

To paste the clip art into the document:

1. Close the Insert Clip Art Task Pane.

2. Position the insertion point to the left of the word "After" in the beginning of the first paragraph below the heading "Wide World Tours."

3. Click the **Paste** button [icon] on the Standard toolbar. The image is inserted into the document at the insertion point. The image nearly fills the left column.

4. Save the document.

5. Click the airplane image to select it. Like the WordArt object you worked with earlier, the clip art image is an object with resize handles that you can use to change its size. The Picture toolbar appears whenever the clip art object is selected. See Figure 4-18.

Figure 4-18	NEWSLETTER WITH THE CLIP ART OBJECT INSERTED

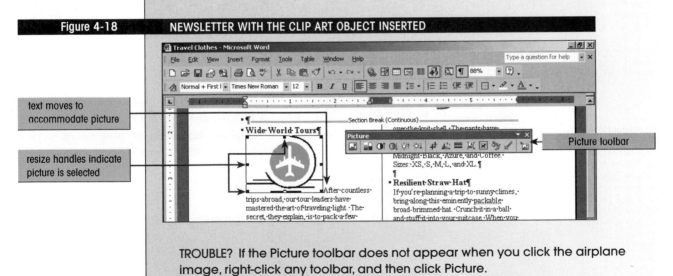

text moves to accommodate picture

resize handles indicate picture is selected

Picture toolbar

TROUBLE? If the Picture toolbar does not appear when you click the airplane image, right-click any toolbar, and then click Picture.

Max would like the image to be smaller so it doesn't distract attention from the text. You'll make that change in the next section.

Resizing a Graphic

You often need to change the size of a graphic so that it fits better into your document. This is called **scaling** the image. You can resize a graphic by either dragging its resize handles or, for more precise control, by using the Format Picture button on the Picture toolbar.

For Max's newsletter, the dragging technique will work fine.

To resize the clip art graphic:

1. Make sure the clip art graphic is selected.

2. Drag the lower-right resize handle up and to the left until the dotted outline forms a rectangle about 1.5 inches wide. Remember to use the horizontal ruler as a guide. See Figure 4-19. *Note:* You don't have to hold down the Shift key, as you do with WordArt, to resize the picture proportionally.

Figure 4-19	RESIZING THE GRAPHIC

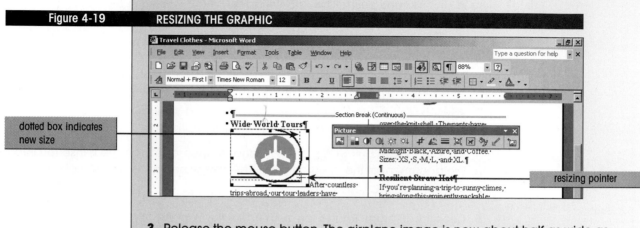

dotted box indicates new size

resizing pointer

3. Release the mouse button. The airplane image is now about half as wide as the left-hand column.

Max wonders if the graphic would look better if you deleted part of the horizontal line on the left side of the image. You'll make that change in the next section.

Cropping a Graphic

You can **crop** the graphic—that is, cut off one or more of its edges—using either the Crop button on the Picture toolbar or the Format Picture dialog box. Once you crop a graphic, the part you cropped is hidden from view. It remains a part of the graphic image, so you can change your mind and restore a cropped graphic to its original form.

To crop the airplane graphic:

1. If necessary, click the clip art to select it. The resize handles appear.

2. Click the **Crop** button on the Picture toolbar. The pointer changes to. To crop the graphic, you must position this pointer over a middle handle on any side of the graphic.

3. Position the pointer directly over the middle resize handle on the left side of the picture.

4. Press and hold down the mouse button. The pointer changes to ⊣.

5. Drag the handle to the right. As you drag, a dotted outline appears to indicate the new shape of the graphic. Position the left border of the dotted outline along the left border of the blue circle. See Figure 4-20.

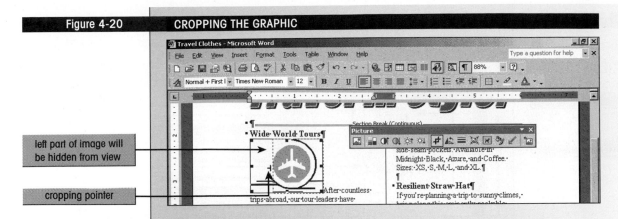

Figure 4-20   CROPPING THE GRAPHIC

left part of image will be hidden from view

cropping pointer

6. Release the mouse button.

Max decides he prefers to display the whole airplane, so he asks you to return to the original image.

7. Click the **Undo** button on the Standard toolbar. The cropping action is reversed, and the full image reappears.

Rotating a Graphic

Max still isn't happy with the appearance of the graphic, because of the amount of white space on the left side. He suggests rotating the image, so that the airplane is positioned horizontally on the page. Use the Rotate Left button on the Picture toolbar to rotate the image.

To rotate the airplane graphic:

1. If necessary, click the clip art to select it. The resize handles appear.

2. Click the **Rotate Left** button on the Picture toolbar. The graphic rotates 90 degrees to the left. The resize handles change to circles, just as they did when you adjusted the position of the WordArt headline earlier. You can drag the green rotation handle to rotate the graphic, but it's easier to continue using the Rotate Left button.

3. Click again. The graphic rotates another 90 degrees, leaving the airplane upside down.

4. Click again. The graphic rotates another 90 degrees. Now the airplane appears to be flying across the page from left to right. See Figure 4-21.

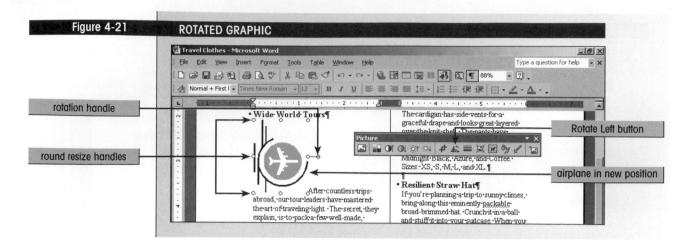

Figure 4-21   ROTATED GRAPHIC

rotation handle

round resize handles

Rotate Left button

airplane in new position

Now Max wants you to make the text wrap to the right of the graphic, making the airplane look as if it's flying into the text.

Wrapping Text Around a Graphic

For the airplane to look as though it flies into the newsletter text, you need to make the text wrap around the image. Earlier, you used the Top and Bottom text wrapping to position the WordArt title above the columns of text. Now you'll try the Tight text wrapping option to make the text follow the shape of the plane.

To wrap text around the airplane graphic:

1. Verify that the airplane graphic is selected.

2. Click the **Text Wrapping** button ▦ on the Picture toolbar. A menu of text wrapping options appears.

3. Click **Tight**. The text wraps to the right of the airplane, following its shape.

4. Click anywhere in the text to deselect the graphic, and then save the newsletter. Your screen should look similar to Figure 4-22.

Figure 4-22   TEXT WRAPPED AROUND GRAPHIC

text flows around irregular shape

The Text Wrapping button should provide all the options you need for most situations. In some cases, however, you might want to use the more advanced options available in the Format Picture or Format WordArt dialog box. You'll have a chance to explore these options in one of the Case Problems.

Moving a Graphic

Finally, Max asks you to move the graphic down to the middle of the paragraph, so that it is not so close to the heading. You can do this by dragging the graphic to a new position. Like WordArt, a clip art graphic is anchored to a specific paragraph in a document. When you drag a graphic (including WordArt) to a new paragraph, the anchor symbol moves to the top of that paragraph. When you drag a graphic to a new position within the same paragraph, the anchor symbol remains in its original position and only the graphic moves. You'll see how this works when you move the airplane graphic.

To move the graphic:

1. Verify that the graphic is selected. You should see an anchor symbol to the left of the graphic, indicating that the graphic is anchored to the first paragraph below the heading "Wide World Tours." (It may look like the graphic is actually anchored to the heading.)

2. Move the mouse pointer over the graphic.

3. Click and drag the pointer down. As you move the pointer, a dotted outline appears indicating the new position of the graphic.

4. Position the dotted outline in the middle of the paragraph, aligned along the left margin, and then release the mouse button. The graphic moves to its new position, but the anchor remains at the top of the paragraph. See Figure 4-23.

| Figure 4-23 | GRAPHIC IN NEW POSITION |

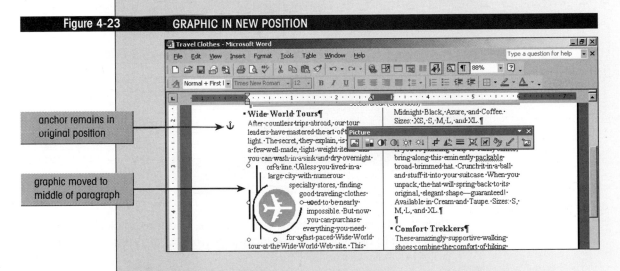

anchor remains in original position

graphic moved to middle of paragraph

5. Click anywhere outside the graphic to deselect it.

TROUBLE? If paragraph text wraps to the left of the graphic, you need to drag the graphic further to the left, so that it aligns along the left-hand margin.

The image of the airplane draws the reader's attention to the beginning of the newsletter, but the rest of the text looks plain. Max suggests adding a drop cap at the beginning of each section.

Inserting Drop Caps

A **drop cap** is a large, capital letter that highlights the beginning of the text of a newsletter, chapter, or some other document section. The drop cap usually extends from the top of the first line of the paragraph down two or three succeeding lines of the paragraph. The text of the paragraph wraps around the drop cap. Word allows you to create a drop cap for the first letter of the first word of a paragraph.

You will create a drop cap for the first paragraph following each heading in the newsletter. The drop cap will extend two lines into the paragraph.

To insert drop caps in the newsletter:

1. Click in the paragraph below the heading "Wide World Tours" (the paragraph where you inserted the graphic).

2. Click **Format** on the menu bar, and then click **Drop Cap**. The Drop Cap dialog box opens.

3. In the Position section, click the **Dropped** icon.

4. Click the **Lines to drop** down arrow once to change the setting from 3 to 2. You don't need to change the default distance from the text. See Figure 4-24.

Figure 4-24   DROP CAP DIALOG BOX

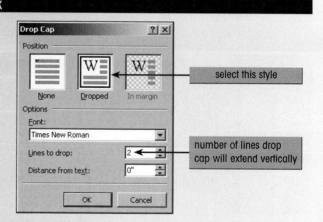

A large *W* in the Dropped position, with arrows labeled "select this style" pointing to the Dropped style, and "number of lines drop cap will extend vertically" pointing to the Lines to drop value of 2.

5. Click the **OK** button to close the dialog box, and then click anywhere in the newsletter to deselect the new drop cap. Word formats the first character of the paragraph as a drop cap.

6. Click anywhere in the newsletter text to deselect the drop cap.

   Note: Word re-wraps the text around the graphic to accommodate the drop cap above. If the paragraph text wraps to the left of the graphic, drag it closer to the left margin. See Figure 4-25.

   TROUBLE? Don't be concerned if Word now marks the "fter" of "After" as a grammatical error. Word considers drop caps to be objects, not regular text. By formatting the *A* in "After" as a drop cap, you essentially deleted the regular character *A*. Because the remaining regular characters "fter" do not appear in the dictionary, Word marks it as a potential error.

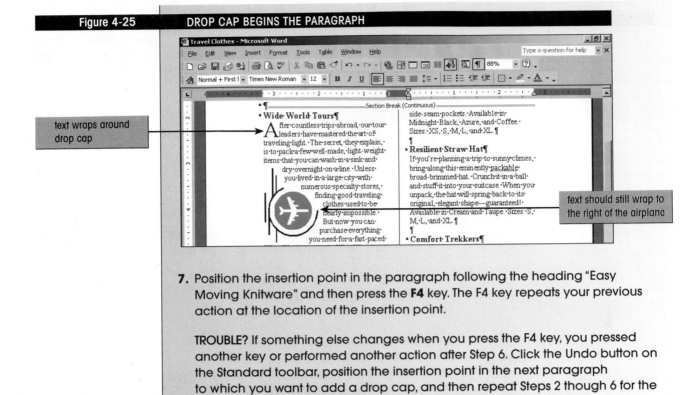

Figure 4-25   **DROP CAP BEGINS THE PARAGRAPH**

text wraps around drop cap

text should still wrap to the right of the airplane

7. Position the insertion point in the paragraph following the heading "Easy Moving Knitware" and then press the **F4** key. The F4 key repeats your previous action at the location of the insertion point.

   TROUBLE? If something else changes when you press the F4 key, you pressed another key or performed another action after Step 6. Click the Undo button on the Standard toolbar, position the insertion point in the next paragraph to which you want to add a drop cap, and then repeat Steps 2 though 6 for the paragraph specified in Step 7.

8. Continue using the **F4** key to add drop caps to the paragraphs following the remaining two headings.

The newsletter looks more lively with the drop caps. Next, you turn your attention to inserting a registered trademark symbol beside a trademark name.

Inserting Symbols and Special Characters

In printed publications, it is customary to change some of the characters available on the standard keyboard into more polished looking characters called **typographic symbols**. For instance, while you might type two hyphens to indicate a dash, in a professionally produced version of that document the two hyphens would be changed to one long dash (called an em dash because it is approximately as wide as the letter "m"). In the past, desktop publishers had to rely on special software to insert and print a document containing typographic symbols, but now you can let Microsoft Word do the work for you.

Word's AutoCorrect feature automatically converts some standard characters into more polished looking typographic symbols as you type. For instance, as Max typed the information on the Resilient Straw Hat, he typed two hyphens after the words "elegant shape." As he began to type the next word "guaranteed," Word automatically converted the two hyphens into an em dash. Figure 4-26 lists some of the other characters that AutoCorrect automatically converts to typographic symbols. In most cases you need to press the spacebar and type more characters before Word will insert the appropriate symbol. You'll have a chance to practice using AutoCorrect to insert typographic symbols in the Review Assignments at the end of this tutorial.

Figure 4-26   COMMON TYPOGRAPHIC SYMBOLS

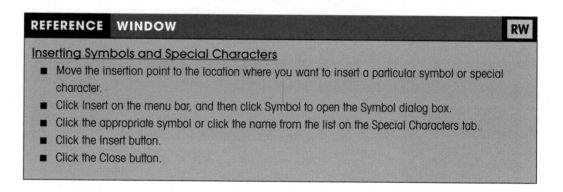

TO INSERT THIS SYMBOL OR CHARACTER	TYPE	WORD CONVERTS IT TO
em dash	word--word	word—word
smiley	:)	☺
copyright symbol	(c)	©
registered trademark symbol	(r)	®
trademark symbol	(tm)	™
ordinal numbers	1st, 2nd, 3rd, etc.	1st, 2nd, 3rd, etc.
fractions	1/2, 1/4	½, ¼
arrows	--> or <--	→ or ←

To insert typographic characters into a document after you've finished typing it, you can use the Symbol command on the Insert menu.

REFERENCE   WINDOW   RW

Inserting Symbols and Special Characters
- Move the insertion point to the location where you want to insert a particular symbol or special character.
- Click Insert on the menu bar, and then click Symbol to open the Symbol dialog box.
- Click the appropriate symbol or click the name from the list on the Special Characters tab.
- Click the Insert button.
- Click the Close button.

Max noticed that he forgot to insert a registered trademark symbol (®) after the trademarked name "Flexistyle." He asks you to insert this symbol now, using the Symbol command on the Insert menu.

To insert the registered trademark symbol:

1. Scroll down to display the paragraph below the heading "Easy Moving Knitware," and then click to the right of the word "Flexistyle." (Take care to click between the final "e" and the comma.)

2. Click **Insert** on the menu bar, and then click **Symbol** to open the Symbol dialog box.

3. If necessary, click the **Special Characters** tab. See Figure 4-27.

Figure 4-27	INSERTING A TYPOGRAPHIC SYMBOL

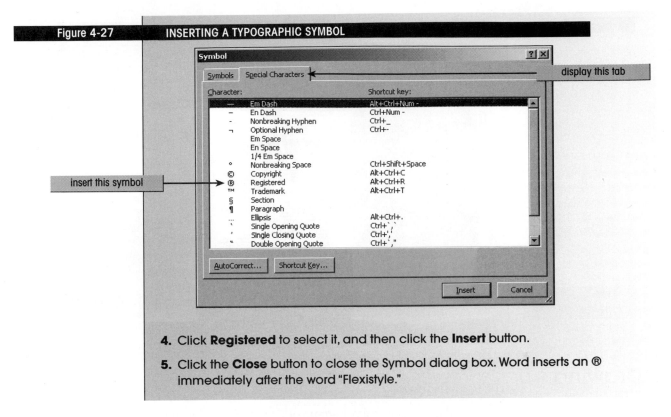

4. Click **Registered** to select it, and then click the **Insert** button.

5. Click the **Close** button to close the Symbol dialog box. Word inserts an ® immediately after the word "Flexistyle."

Next, you decide to adjust the columns of text so they are approximately the same length.

Balancing the Columns

You can shift text from one column to another by adding blank paragraphs to move the text into the next column or by deleting blank paragraphs to shorten the text so it will fit into one column. The problem with this approach is that any edits you make could throw off the balance. Instead, Word can automatically **balance** the columns, or make them of equal length.

To balance the columns:

1. Position the insertion point at the end of the text in the right column, just after the period following the word "sizes."

Next, you need to change the zoom to Whole Page so you can see the full affect of the change.

2. Click the **Zoom** list arrow on the Standard toolbar, and then click **Whole Page**.

3. Click **Insert** on the menu bar, and then click **Break**. The Break dialog box opens.

4. Below "section break types," click the **Continuous** option button.

5. Click the **OK** button. Word inserts a continuous section break at the end of the text. As shown in Figure 4-28, Word balances the text between the two section breaks.

Figure 4-28   NEWSLETTER WITH BALANCED COLUMNS

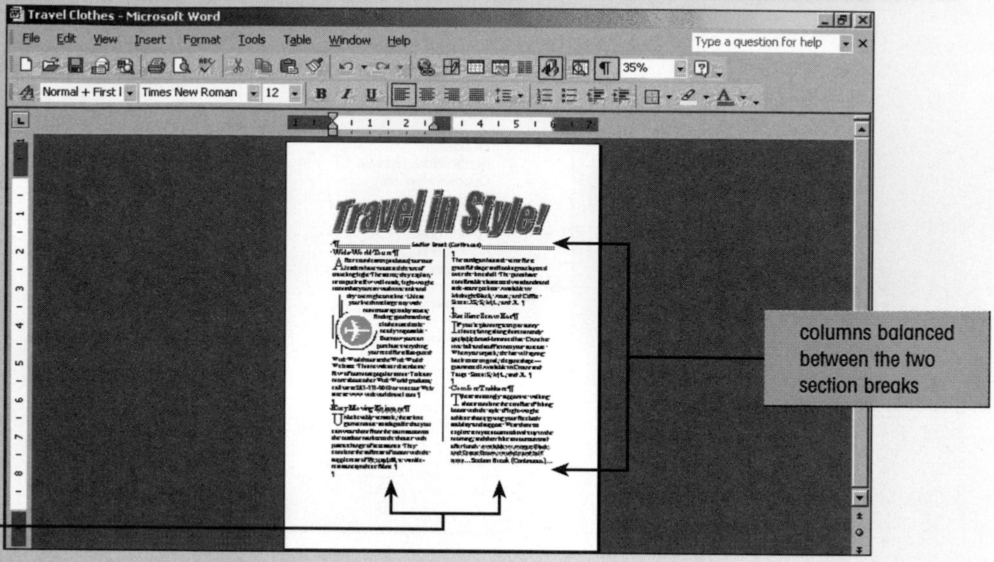

columns balanced between the two section breaks

approximately equal length

Drawing a Border Around the Page

You can add definition to a paragraph or an entire page by adding a border. Right now, Max wants to add a border around the newsletter. (In the Case Problems at the end of this tutorial, you'll learn how to add a border around individual paragraphs.)

To draw a border around the newsletter:

1. Make sure the document is in Print Layout view and that the zoom setting is set to Whole Page so that you can see the entire newsletter.

2. Click **Format** on the menu bar, and then click **Borders and Shading**. The Borders and Shading dialog box opens.

3. Click the **Page Border** tab. You can use the Setting options on the left side to specify the type of border you want. In this case, you want a simple box.

4. In the Setting section, click the **Box** option. Now that you have selected the type of border you want, you can choose the style of line that will be used to create the border.

5. In the Style list box, scroll down and select the ninth style down from the top (the thick line with the thin line underneath), and then verify that the Apply to list option is set to **Whole document**. See Figure 4-29. (While the Borders and Shading dialog box is open, notice the Shading tab, which you can use to add a colored background to a page. You'll have a chance to use this tab in the Case Problems at the end of this tutorial.)

Figure 4-29	ADDING A BORDER TO THE NEWSLETTER

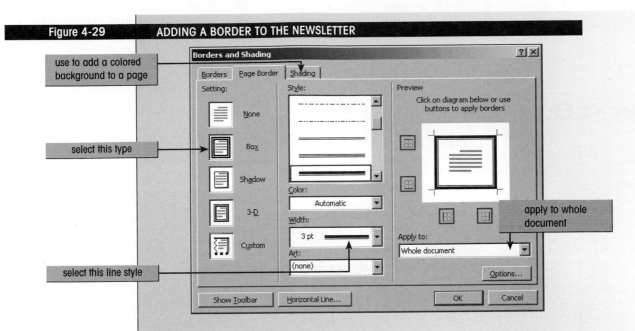

- use to add a colored background to a page
- select this type
- select this line style
- apply to whole document

6. Click the **OK** button, and then save your work. The newsletter is now surrounded by an attractive border, as shown in Figure 4-30.

Figure 4-30	NEWSLETTER WITH BORDER

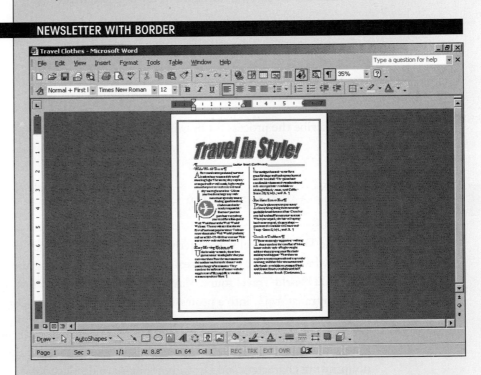

7. Create a footer that centers **Prepared by your name** and the current date at the bottom of the document. Be sure to replace **your name** with your first and last name. Format the footer in a small font to make it as unobtrusive as possible.

8. Preview the newsletter and then print it. Unless you have a color printer, the WordArt headline and the airplane will print in black and white.

9. If necessary, click the **Close** button on the Print Preview toolbar to return to Print Layout view, then close the newsletter and exit Word.

You give the printed newsletter to Max, along with a copy on disk. He thinks it looks great and thanks you for your help. He'll print it later on a high-quality color printer (to get the best resolution for printing multiple copies).

Session 4.2 QUICK CHECK

1. Define the following in your own words:

   a. drop cap

   b. scaling

   c. clip art

   d. balance

2. Explain how to insert a clip art graphic in Word.

3. Describe a situation in which you would want to scale a graphic. Describe a situation in which you would want to crop a graphic.

4. True or False: When inserting a drop cap, you can specify the number of lines you want the drop cap to extend into the document vertically.

5. Describe two different methods for inserting the registered trademark symbol in a document.

6. Besides the Symbol command on the Insert menu, what is another way of entering typographic symbols?

7. Describe the process for drawing a border around the page.

REVIEW ASSIGNMENTS

Max's Wide World Travel newsletter was a success; the sales for the advertised items were brisk. Now he has been asked to create a newsletter describing the highlights of some recent Wide World Travel tours. Max has already written the text of the newsletter and asks you to transform it into a professional-looking newsletter. Complete the following:

1. If necessary, start Word and make sure your Data Disk is in the appropriate disk drive. Check your screen to make sure your settings match those in the tutorial and that the nonprinting characters and Drawing toolbar are displayed.

2. Open the file **Travel** from the Review folder for Tutorial 4 on your Data Disk, and then save it as **Travel Highlights** in the same folder.

3. In the first paragraph after the heading "Wide World Tours," replace "YOUR NAME" with your first and last name.

4. In the first paragraph after the heading "Wide World Tours" (after the phone number), insert the following: "or visit our Web site at www.wideworldtravel.com." Then press Enter to insert a blank line. Remove the hyperlink from the Web address.

5. At the top of the document, create the headline "Wide World Highlights" using WordArt. In the WordArt Gallery, choose the third style from the right in the third row down from the top (the rainbow style with the shadow).

6. Change the shape of the WordArt object to Triangle Up, and then edit the WordArt text to add italics.

7. Apply the Top and Bottom wrapping style to the WordArt object.

8. Insert a blank paragraph at the beginning of the document, anchor the WordArt headline to the new paragraph, and then save your work. If the WordArt moves below the new paragraph symbol, drag it up above the new paragraph. When you are finished, the anchor symbol should be positioned to the left of the new paragraph symbol, with the WordArt object positioned above the new paragraph symbol.

9. If necessary, enlarge the WordArt object to span the entire width of the page. Be sure to hold down the Shift key while you drag. When you are finished, the WordArt object should be approximately .5 inches high on the left end, and about 1 inch tall at the center.

Explore ▷ 10. Practice dragging the adjustment handle (the yellow diamond on the left) up and down to change the slope of the WordArt image. Click the Undo button to undo each change. When you are finished, the adjustment handle should be located to the left of the middle resize handle on the left edge of the WordArt object.

Explore ▷ 11. Practice dragging the rotation handle to rotate the WordArt object. When you are finished, return the headline to its original, horizontal position.

12. Position the insertion point to the left of the first word in the first heading, and then format the newsletter text in two columns using the Columns dialog box. Insert a section break so that the columns formatting is applied to the part of the newsletter after the insertion point. Do not insert a line between columns. View the new columns in Print Layout view, using the Whole Page zoom setting.

13. Return to Page Width zoom, and then click to the left of the paragraph that begins "We prefaced our adventure . . . "

14. Insert the clip art graphic of the Eiffel Tower from the Buildings folder.

15. Select and resize the graphic so it is approximately 1.5 inches square.

16. Crop the image vertically on the left and right. When you are finished, the image

should be approximately 1 inch wide.

17. Use the Undo button to undo the cropping.

18. Wrap text around the graphic using the Tight wrapping option.

19. Add a drop cap for the first paragraph following each heading, using the default settings for the Dropped position.

Explore 20. Scroll to display the paragraph below the heading "Wide World Tours." Click after the last "s" in "Wide World Adventures," press the spacebar, and then type "(tm)" (without the quotation marks). Word's AutoCorrect feature converts the letters in parentheses to the trademark symbol. Save your work and then open a new, blank document, and practice using AutoCorrect to insert the typographic symbols shown earlier in Figure 4-26. When you are finished, close the document without saving your changes.

Explore 21. You can change the alignment of text in newspaper-style columns using the alignment buttons on the Formatting toolbar. Select both columns of text by clicking before the first word of the heading "Wide World Tours," pressing and holding down the Shift key, and then clicking after the last word of text in the second column ("square"). Use the Justify button on the Formatting toolbar to justify the text.

22. Balance the columns. If the words in the last line of the newsletter text are spaced too far apart after you insert the section break, click at the end of the line and then press Enter to move the section break to the next line.

23. Add a border around the page using a border style of your choice.

24. Preview, save, and print the newsletter. When you are finished, close the document and exit word.

CASE PROBLEMS

Case 1. City of Santa Fe, New Mexico Caroline Hestwood is the manager of information systems for the city of Santa Fe. She and her staff, along with the city manager, have just decided to convert all city computers from the Windows 98 operating system to Windows 2000 and to standardize applications software on the latest version of Microsoft Office. Caroline writes a monthly newsletter on computer operations and training, so this month she decides to devote the newsletter to the conversion. Complete the following:

1. If necessary, start Word, make sure your Data Disk is in the appropriate drive, and check your screen to make sure your settings match those in the tutorial.

2. Open the file **Convert** from the Cases folder for Tutorial 4 on your Data Disk, and then save the file as **Software Conversion** in the same folder.

Explore

3. If the text you want to format as WordArt has already been typed, you can begin creating your WordArt by selecting the text in the document. Select the text of the newsletter title, "Software Update." (Do not select the paragraph symbol at the end of the title.) Click the Insert WordArt button on the Drawing toolbar, and then choose the WordArt style in the third row down, first column on the left. Verify that "Software Update" appears in the Edit WordArt Text dialog box, and then click OK.

4. Set the wrapping style to Top and Bottom, insert a new paragraph, and then anchor the WordArt to the new paragraph.

5. Edit the WordArt object to set the font to 32-point Arial bold, and then apply the Arch Up (Curve) shape to the object. Resize the WordArt object so that it spans the width of the page from left margin to right margin and so that its maximum height is about 1 inch. (*Hint*: Use the resize handles while watching the horizontal and vertical rulers in Print Layout view to adjust the object to the appropriate size.)

6. Center and italicize the subtitle of the newsletter, "Newsletter from the Santa Fe Information Management Office."

7. Replace "INSERT YOUR NAME HERE" with your name, then center and italicize the line containing your name.

8. Insert a continuous section break before the subtitle.

Explore

9. You can emphasize paragraphs within a document by putting a border around one or more paragraphs and by adding shading. To learn how, select the subtitle and the line after it (containing your name). Click Format on the menu bar, and then click Borders and Shading. In the Borders and Shading dialog box, select the Box style on the Borders tab, click the Shading tab, select a light, see-through color from the Fill grid, such as Gray-15%, and then click OK.

10. Select everything in the newsletter from the heading "The Big Switch" through the last word in the document. Then use the Columns button in the Standard toolbar to format the body of the newsletter into two newspaper-style columns. Examine the newsletter to find the new section break.

Explore

11. Position the insertion point at the beginning of the first paragraph under the heading "Training on MS Office," and then open the Insert Clip Art Task Pane. In the Search text box, type Computer and then click Search. A group of clip art images appears in the Insert Clip Art Task Pane. Click an image that illustrates the newsletter content. The image is inserted into the newsletter. Close the Insert Clip Art Task Pane.

Explore

12. Resize the picture so that it is 35% of its original size. Instead of dragging the resize handles as you did in the tutorial, select the picture, and then click the Format Picture button on the Picture toolbar to open the Format Picture dialog box. Click the Size tab. Adjust the Height and Width settings to 35% in the Scale section, and make sure the Lock aspect ratio check box is selected. Click OK.

13. Use the appropriate Picture toolbar button to select the Tight wrapping option.

Explore ▶ 14. You can use the Replace command to replace standard word processing characters with typographic characters. To replace every occurrence of two dashes (– –) with an em dash (—), position the insertion point at the beginning of the first paragraph of text. Click Edit on the menu bar, and then click Replace. In the Find what text box, type two hyphens (--), and then press the Tab key to move the insertion point to the Replace with text box. Click the More button to display additional options, and then click the Special button at the bottom of the dialog box. Click Em Dash in the list. Word displays the special code for em dashes in the Replace with text box. Click the Replace All button. When the operation is complete, click the OK button, and then click the Close button.

Explore ▶ 15. Preview the newsletter. If it does not fit on one page, click the Shrink to Fit button on the Print Preview toolbar.

16. Insert a border around the newsletter. Use a border style of your choice.

17. If necessary, balance the columns.

18. Save and print the newsletter, and then close it and exit Word.

Case 2. *Morning Star Movers* Martin Lott is the executive secretary to Whitney Kremer, director of personnel for Morning Star Movers (MSM), a national moving company with headquarters in Minneapolis, Minnesota. Whitney assigned you the task of preparing the monthly newsletter News and Views, which provides news about MSM employees. You decide to update the layout and to use the desktop-publishing capabilities of Word to design the newsletter. You will use text assembled by other MSM employees for the body of the newsletter. Complete the following:

1. If necessary, start Word, make sure your Data Disk is in the appropriate drive, and check your screen to make sure your settings match those in the tutorial.

2. Open the file **Movers** from the Cases folder for Tutorial 4 on your Data Disk, and then save it as **Movers Newsletter** in the same folder.

3. Use the Find and Replace command to replace all instances of the name "Katrina" with your first name. Then replace all instances of "Pollei" with your last name.

4. Click at the end of the first section (to the right of the space after "contact her at") and then type "thurlow@msm.net" (without the quotes) followed by a period. Press Enter to insert a blank line, and then remove the hyperlink.

5. Create a "News and Views" WordArt title for the newsletter. Use the WordArt style in the third row down, fourth column from the left, and set the font to 24-point Arial bold. Set the wrapping style to Top and Bottom, and then anchor the WordArt to a new, blank paragraph.

6. Resize the WordArt object proportionally so that the title spans the width of the page from left margin to right margin and so that the height of the title is about 1 inch. (*Hint*: Use the resize handles while watching the horizontal and vertical rulers in Print Layout view to adjust the object to the appropriate size.)

7. Make sure the WordArt object is positioned above the new paragraph, and then format the body of the newsletter into two newspaper-style columns. Place a vertical rule between the columns.

Explore ▷ 8. You can change the structure of a newsletter by reformatting it with additional columns. Change the number of columns from two to three using the same technique you used in the previous step (that is, the Columns command on the Format menu). Make sure that the Equal column width check box is selected.

Explore ▷ 9. You can insert your own graphics, stored as an electronic file, just as quickly as you can insert clip art. Position the insertion point at the beginning of the paragraph below the heading "MSM Chess Team Takes Third." Click Insert on the menu bar, point to Picture, and then click From File. Look in the Cases folder for Tutorial 4 on your Data Disk, select the file named Knight, and then click the Insert button.

Explore ▷ 10. You can delete a graphic by selecting it, and then pressing the Delete key. To practice this technique, click the Knight graphic to select it, and then press the Delete key. To reinsert the graphic, click the Undo button.

11. Scale the height and the width of the picture to 60% of its original size. (*Hint*: To scale the size, click the Format Picture button on the Picture toolbar, and then set the Scale values on the Size tab, making sure the Lock aspect ratio check box is selected.) Close the Format Picture dialog box when you are finished.

Explore ▷ 12. In addition to cropping a picture with the Crop button, you can use the Format Picture dialog box. Using this dialog box allows you to be more precise because you can specify exact cropping measurements. To try it now, click the Format Picture button on the Picture toolbar, click the Picture tab, and change the values in the Crop from text boxes. Crop 0.3, 0.4, 0.2, and 0.4 inches from the left, right, top, and bottom of the picture, respectively.

Explore ▷ 13. You already know how to wrap text around a graphic or WordArt object using the Text Wrapping button. In some situations, however, you might need additional options to gain even more control over how text wraps in a document. To view these options now, click the Format Picture button on the Picture toolbar, click the Layout tab, and then click Advanced. Click the Tight icon, and notice the additional settings at the bottom of the Advanced Layout dialog box. Among other things, you can specify to what side the text should wrap and the distance to preserve between the text and the graphic. Click the Right only option button, click OK, and then click OK again. Keep in mind that you can also access the Advanced Layout dialog box from the Format WordArt dialog box.

Explore   14. Format drop caps in the first paragraph after each heading except the "MSM Chess Team Takes Third" heading. Use the default settings for number of lines, but change the font of the drop cap to Arial.

15. View the entire page. If necessary, decrease the height of the WordArt title or change the page margins until the entire newsletter fits onto one page and until each column starts with a heading.

16. Add a border around the entire page of the newsletter using the Page Border command.

17. Save the newsletter, and then preview and print it. Close the document and exit Word.

Case 3. *Wild Grains Grocery Cooperative* Mary Ann Hansen is the publicity director for Wild Grains Grocery Cooperative in Athens, Georgia. Local residents pay a membership fee to join the co-op, and then receive a 10% discount on all purchases. Many members don't realize that they can take advantage of other benefits—such as free cooking classes and monthly mailings with recipe cards and coupons. To spread the word, Mary Ann would like to create a brochure describing the benefits of joining the co-op. She has already written the text of the brochure. She would like the brochure to consist of one piece of paper folded in three parts, like a standard business letter, with text on both sides of the paper. Complete the following:

1. If necessary, start Word, make sure your Data Disk is in the appropriate drive, and check your screen to make sure your settings match those in the tutorial.

2. Open the file **Grains** from the Cases folder for Tutorial 4 on your Data Disk, and then save it as **Wild Grains Brochure**.

3. Below the cornucopia graphic, click after the Web address, insert a blank line and then type your first and last name. Remove the hyperlink from the Web address.

4. Format the entire document in three columns of equal width. Do not include a vertical line between columns. Don't be concerned that part of the text overflows onto a second page.

5. Click at the end of the list of member benefits (after the word "country") and press Ctrl+Enter to insert a page break. Click the Bullets button to remove the bullet from the new paragraph.

Explore   6. You are already familiar with adding section breaks and page breaks to a document. You can also add a column break, which forces the text after the insertion point to move to the next column. Click at the beginning of the heading "Join Now!" (just to the left of the "J"), click Insert on the menu bar and then click Break. Under Break Types, click Column break, and then click OK. Insert another column break before the heading "Member Benefits." On the second page, click at the top of the left-hand column, press Enter a few times to insert some blank paragraphs, and then insert another column break. (Don't be concerned if the new paragraph marks don't align.) Press Ctrl+End to move the insertion point to the end of the document and insert another column break.

7. Change the zoom setting to Whole Page and review your work. The document should consist of two pages, with three columns each. The graphic and the co-op address should appear in the middle column on the second page.

Explore

8. Click the cornucopia graphic in the second page, click the Copy button on the Standard toolbar, click to the left of the heading "Join Now!" and then add two blank paragraphs. Click in the first new paragraph (at the top of the column) and then click the Paste button on the Standard toolbar. The middle column of the first page now contains the graphic, with the heading "Join Now!" below, followed by two paragraphs of text.

9. Click in the left-hand column of page 2, and then delete all but one of the paragraph marks. With the insertion point located at the only remaining paragraph mark in the left-hand column, insert the WordArt text "WHY JOIN?" In the WordArt Gallery select the style in the fourth column from the left, third row down (the rainbow style with a shadow). Be sure to type "WHY JOIN?" in all uppercase letters in the Edit WordArt Text dialog box, and format the text in boldface. Save your work.

Explore

10. Select the WordArt object, and then click the WordArt Vertical Text button on the WordArt toolbar. The heading is positioned vertically in the left-hand column of page 2.

11. Increase the size of the WordArt object (by dragging a resize handle) so that the WordArt spans the height of the column—do *not* press Shift as you drag the handle—and the letters spread out to fill the height of the column. When you are finished, the WordArt object should be approximately 6 inches high. If you increase the size too much, the WordArt will jump to the next column. If that happens, click the Undo button and try again.

Explore

12. Click the Format WordArt button on the WordArt toolbar. In the Format WordArt dialog box, click the Colors and Lines tab, click the Color list arrow, click the black square in the upper-left hand corner of the palette, and then click OK. The WordArt changes from a rainbow style to all black. Save your work.

Explore

13. Use the Copy button on the Formatting toolbar to copy the "WHY JOIN?" WordArt object to the Office Clipboard. Paste a copy of the WordArt object in the right-hand column of page 2, and then change the text to "WILD GRAINS". When you are finished, page 2 should consist of the "WHY JOIN?" WordArt in the left-hand column, the graphic and address information in the middle column, and the "WILD GRAINS" WordArt in the right-hand column. Zoom to Whole Page view and examine your work.

14. If necessary, add paragraph breaks to the center column to center the graphic and the text vertically in relation to the WordArt titles. Adjust the size of the WordArt as necessary.

15. Use the Page Setup command on the File menu to center both pages vertically. (*Hint*: Use the Vertical alignment setting in the Layout tab.)

Explore 16. To print the brochure, you need to print the first page and print the second page on the reverse side. Click File on the menu bar, click Print, click the Pages option button, type 1, and then click OK. Retrieve the printed page, and then insert it into your printer's paper tray so that "WHY JOIN?" prints on the reverse side of the list of member benefits; likewise, "WILD GRAINS" should print on the reverse side of the "Welcome to Wild Grains" text. Whether you should place the printed page upside down or right-side up depends on your printer. You may have to print a few test pages until you get it right. When you finish, you should be able to turn page 1 (the page with the heading "Welcome to Wild Grains") face up, and then fold it inward like a business letter, along the two column borders. Fold the brochure so that the "WILD GRAINS" column lies on top.

17. Save and close the document, and then exit Word.

Case 4. New Job Newsletter You've just moved to a new part of the country and decide to send out a newsletter to friends and family describing your new job. In the one-page newsletter, you'll include articles about you and your colleagues, your new job, your new responsibilities, and future plans. You'll desktop publish the copy into a professional-looking newsletter. Complete the following:

1. If necessary, start Word, make sure your Data Disk is in the appropriate drive, and check your screen to make sure your settings match those in the tutorial.

2. Write two articles to include in the newsletter; save each article in a separate file.

3. Plan the general layout of your newsletter.

4. Create a title for your newsletter with WordArt.

5. Save the document as **New Job** in the Cases folder for Tutorial 4.

Explore 6. Insert the current date and your name as author below the title.

7. Insert the articles you wrote into your newsletter. Position the insertion point where you want the first article to appear, click Insert on the menu bar, click File, select the article you want to insert, and then click the Insert button. Repeat to insert the second article.

Explore 8. Format your newsletter with multiple columns.

9. Insert at least one clip art picture into your newsletter. If your computer is connected to the Internet, use the Clips Online option in the Insert Clip Art Task Pane to access Microsoft's online collection of clip art. Follow the directions on the screen to search for an image that illustrates the content of your newsletter. Download the image to your computer, and then insert it into the newsletter.

Explore 10. Wrap text around the graphic, and then add at least two drop caps in the newsletter.

11. Create a border around the page and then add shading to the entire document using the Shading tab in the Borders and Shading dialog box. (*Hint*: Press Ctrl+A to select the entire document, open the Borders and Shading dialog box, select a page border, click the Shading tab, select a light, transparent color from the Fill grid, such as Gray-15%, and then click OK.)

12. Save and print the newsletter, and then close the document and exit Word.

INTERNET ASSIGNMENTS

Student Union

The purpose of the Internet Assignments is to challenge you to find information on the Internet that you can use to create effective documents. The actual assignments are updated and maintained on the Course Technology Web site. Log on to the Internet and use your Web browser to go to the Student Union on the New Perspectives Series site at **www.course.com/NewPerspectives/studentunion**. Click the Online Companions link, and then click the link for this text.

QUICK CHECK ANSWERS

Session 4.1

1. List any four of the following: The printing is of high-quality; the document uses multiple fonts; the document incorporates graphics; the document uses typographic characters; the document uses columns and other special formatting features.

2. List any two of the following: In desktop publishing the reader sees the entire page at one time while in a Web page the reader sees only part of the page at a time; in desktop publishing the use of color increases printing costs, while in Web design, color itself does not affect the cost of producing a Web page; in desktop publishing the quality of the printer greatly affects the appearance of graphics in the printed page, while in Web design the quality of graphics is most affected by the type of electronic file in which the graphic is stored; in desktop publishing the page is static, while in Web design parts of the page can be animated, or include video and audio; the reader cannot interact with a desktop-published document, while it is possible to interact with a Web page by clicking hyperlinks.

3. (a) Using a desktop computer system to produce commercial-quality printed material. With desktop publishing, you can enter and edit text, create graphics, lay out pages, and print documents. (b) A document that can contain specially for-matted text, graphics, video, and audio. A Web page is stored on a computer as a collection of electronic files and is designed to be viewed in a special program called a browser. (c) Unformatted text (d) A symbol that appears in the left mar-gin, which shows a WordArt object's position in relation to the text.

4. False

5. False

6. To resize a WordArt object, select the object and drag its resize handles. To resize the WordArt object proportionally, press and hold the Shift key as you drag a resize handle.

   To change the text of a WordArt object, click the object to select it, click the Edit Text button on the WordArt toolbar, edit the text in the Edit WordArt Text dialog box, and then click OK.

7. The WordArt Shape button allows you to change the basic shape of a WordArt object.

8. True

Session 4.2

1. (a) a large, uppercase letter that highlights the beginning of the text of a newsletter, chapter, or some other document section; (b) resizing an image to better fit a document; (c) existing, copyright-free artwork that you can insert into your document; (d) to make columns of equal length

2. Position the insertion point at the location where you want to insert the image, click the Insert Clip Art button on the Drawing toolbar, click Clip Organizer in the Task Pane, open the folder containing the image you want, click the arrow button on the image, click Copy, and then close the Clip Organizer. Finally, paste the graphic into the document.

3. You might scale a graphic to better fit the width of a column of text. You might crop a graphic to emphasize or draw attention to a particular part of the image or to eliminate unnecessary borders.

4. True

5. Click where you want to insert the symbol in the document, click Insert on the menu bar, click Symbol, click the Special Characters tab in the Symbol dialog box, click Registered Trademark in the list, click the Insert button, and then click the Close button. Type "(tm)".

6. using the AutoCorrect feature, which lets you type certain characters and then changes those characters into the corresponding symbol

7. Click Format on the menu bar, click Borders and Shading, click the Page Border tab in the Borders and Shading dialog box, select the border type you want in the Setting section, choose a line style from the Style list box, make sure Whole document appears in the Apply to list box, and then click OK.

In this tutorial you will:

- Create a new Web page

- Convert a Word document to a Web page

- Display your Web pages in a browser

CREATING WEB PAGES WITH WORD

Creating a Web Page for Bayside Health Inc.

Bayside Health Inc.

Bayside Health Inc. provides a variety of health-related services for corporations and other social service organizations. Susan Dague, publications director, is often asked to develop newsletters on a variety of topics related to health and fitness. To broaden the audience for these newsletters, she would like to transform them into Web pages and allow clients to read them over the World Wide Web.

Web pages are special documents designed to be viewed in a program called a **browser**. The two most popular browsers are **Microsoft Internet Explorer** and **Netscape Navigator**. Whatever type you use, a browser retrieves files from a special kind of computer called a **Web server** and displays those files on your computer in the form of a Web page.

Browsers work by sending messages to and receiving messages from a Web server. The messages travel back and forth between the browser and the Web server via a computer network. Because Susan's computer is connected to the Bayside Health computer network, she can use her browser to retrieve company Web pages from a Web server just down the hall from her office. At the same time, Susan's computer is also connected to the largest, most widely used computer network in the world, the **Internet**. The part of the Internet that transfers and displays Web pages is called the **World Wide Web**, or simply, the **Web**. Each Web page has its own specific **address** (or **URL**), such as *www.microsoft.com* or *www.cnn.com*. A group of related Web pages is called a **Web site**. The main Web page within a Web site (the one that is usually displayed first) is called a **home page**. When Susan uses a browser to access well-known, national Web sites (such as *www.microsoft.com* or *www.cnn.com*), she is accessing the World Wide Web.

Creating a Web Page

Professional Web page designers use programs specifically designed for creating Web pages, such as Microsoft FrontPage. However, for simple Web pages, Microsoft Word is a good option. As you'll see, many of the word-processing skills you have already mastered transfer easily to Web page design.

Susan asks you to open a blank Web page in Word now, so that you can begin creating a Health News home page.

To open a blank Web page:

1. Start Word. If paragraph marks are not visible, click the **Show/Hide ¶** button ¶ on the Standard toolbar to display them.

2. If you see the New Document Task Pane, click **Blank Web Page** in the Task Pane. Otherwise click **File** on the menu bar, click **New**, and then click **Blank Web Page** in the Task Pane. A blank document opens, similar to a regular Word document. The only difference you can see is that the Web Layout View button (rather than the Normal View or Print Layout View button) is selected in the lower-left corner of the Document window.

3. Click **File** on the menu bar, and then click **Save as Web Page**.

4. In the Save As dialog box, click the **Save as type** list arrow.

   The Save as type list shows that you can save this document as a Web archive, a file format that saves all the elements of a Web site, including text and graphics, in a single file. This format is useful if you need to e-mail an entire Web site to someone else to review, for example. You do not need to be concerned with this file format now.

5. Click **Web Page**, if necessary.

6. Save the Web page in the Web folder on your Data Disk as **Health News Home Page**.

Susan asks you to start typing the text of the home page. As you will see, Word's basic editing and formatting features work the same in a Web page as they do in a regular Word document.

To type the text of the home page:

1. Type **Bayside Health Inc.**, and then press the **Enter** key twice.

2. Type **Welcome to Our Health News Home Page**, and then press the **Enter** key twice, type **Our Health News Reports give you quick updates on these important topics:**, press the **Enter** key twice, click the **Bullets** button ≣ on the Formatting toolbar, and then type the following list:

   - **Exercise**
   - **Pain management**
   - **Low-fat cooking**

3. Select the heading "Bayside Health Inc." and the subheading "Welcome to our Health News Home Page" and then format them in 26-point Arial. Click the **Font Color** list arrow ▲▾ on the Formatting toolbar, and then click the red square in the third row from the top, first column on the left. Finally, center the heading and subheading. Click outside of the headings to deselect them.

Now that you have formatted the text, you can transform the look of the Web page itself by selecting a collection of formatting options known as a theme.

4. Click **Format** on the menu bar, and then click **Theme** to open the Theme dialog box.

5. In the Choose a Theme list box, click **Blends**.

6. If you see a message indicating that the Blends theme is not installed on your computer, select another theme. Otherwise click the **OK** button. The Web page is now formatted as shown in Figure 1.

| Figure 1 | FORMATTED WEB PAGE |

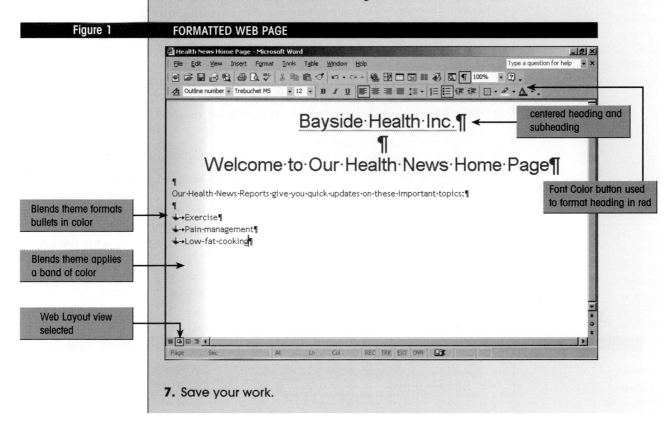

7. Save your work.

Converting a Word Document to a Web Page

Now that you have created the Web page, you are ready to add a hyperlink that will open an additional Web page. First you have to prepare the Web page that you want the hyperlink to open. The information on exercise is currently stored as a desktop-published newsletter. Susan would like you to convert that Word document to a Web page.

To open the Exercise newsletter:

1. Open the document named **Exercise** in the Web folder on your Data Disk, and then display the document in Print Layout view, zoomed to Whole Page.

As you can see, this document contains a WordArt headline, a border, formatted headings, and a graphic (taken from Word's clip art collection). To find out exactly what the document will look like as a Web page, you can use Web Layout view.

To preview a Web page in Web Layout view:

1. Click the **Web Layout View** button 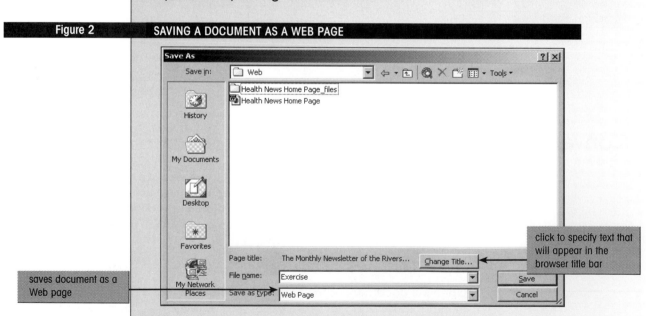. The two-column portion of the document changes to a single column, and the border is hidden. The graphic (which was originally near the end of the document, in the bottom of the right column) moves to the top of the second section, under the heading "Excessive Hype Over Exercise Type."

As you examine the document in Web Layout view, you can see that not all the features of the desktop-published document will survive the conversion to a Web page. After you convert a Word document to a Web page, you often need to update the formatting and adjust the position of graphics. You'll do that after you convert the document to a Web page.

To convert the document to a Web page:

1. Click **File** on the menu bar, and then click **Save as Web Page**. The Save As dialog box opens.

2. If necessary, navigate to the Web folder on your Data Disk.

3. Click the **Save as type** list arrow, and then click **Web Page**. The Health News Home Page appears in the file list box, along with a folder named "Health News Home Page_files." Word created this folder when you first saved the home page, in order to store special files associated with a Web page. You can just ignore it. Also notice that the Change Title button appears above the File name text box, as shown in Figure 2. You can use this button to specify the text that appears in the browser title bar each time the Web page is displayed. Unless you make a selection, the first few lines of text are used by default. In this case, you will only change the actual filename.

Figure 2	SAVING A DOCUMENT AS A WEB PAGE

saves document as a Web page

Page title: The Monthly Newsletter of the Rivers...   Change Title...

click to specify text that will appear in the browser title bar

File name: Exercise

Save as type: Web Page

4. Change the filename to **Exercise Web Page** and then click the **Save** button. A message informs you that some features of the original document (the desktop-published newsletter) will not survive the conversion to a Web page because they cannot be displayed in Internet Explorer and Netscape Navigator.

5. Click **Continue**. The document is saved as a Web page. It looks the same as it did in Web Layout view, except that it has a new filename. See Figure 3. Now you need to move the graphic, which shifted after Word removed the newspaper-style columns.

| Figure 3 | DOCUMENT SAVED AS WEB PAGE |

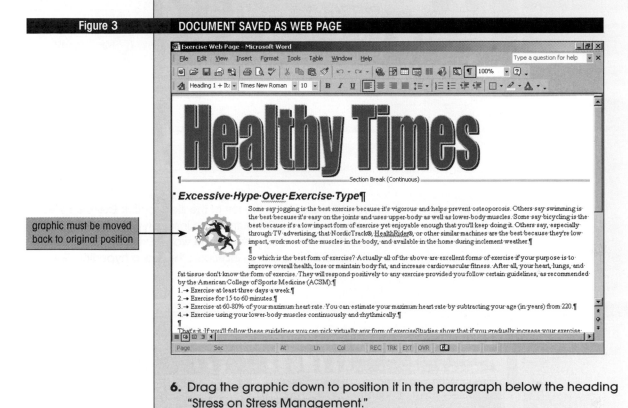

graphic must be moved back to original position

6. Drag the graphic down to position it in the paragraph below the heading "Stress on Stress Management."

Susan explains that to give a Web site a coherent look and feel, you should format the Web pages in the site similarly. Eventually, she plans to format the Exercise Web page using the Blends theme you used earlier for the home page, and make other changes, such as changing the WordArt headline to plain text formatted in red.

Adding a Hyperlink

Susan wants you to format the "Exercise" bullet in the home page as a hyperlink that will open the Exercise Web page.

To add a hyperlink to the home page:

1. Save and close the Exercise Web Page, and, if necessary, open the Health News Home Page.

2. Select the text "Exercise" in the first bullet, click **Insert** on the menu bar, and then click **Hyperlink**. The Insert Hyperlink dialog box opens. You use this dialog box (shown in Figure 4) to specify what you want to happen when you click the word "Exercise."

| Figure 4 | INSERT HYPERLINK DIALOG BOX |

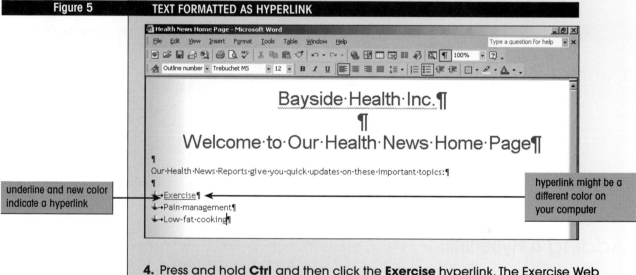

click to display the files in the same folder as the current document

click to have the link open a file or Web page that you have already created

use to have the link perform other functions

automatically created when you saved Exercise Web page

automatically created when you saved home page

file list with content of current folder

3. Verify that "Current Folder" is selected to the left of the file list, click **Exercise Web Page** in the file list, and then click the **OK** button. The Insert Hyperlink dialog box closes, and you return to the home page, where the word "Exercise" is formatted in a different color, with an underline, which indicates that it is a hyperlink. See Figure 5.

| Figure 5 | TEXT FORMATTED AS HYPERLINK |

underline and new color indicate a hyperlink

hyperlink might be a different color on your computer

4. Press and hold **Ctrl** and then click the **Exercise** hyperlink. The Exercise Web page opens in Internet Explorer.

5. Close Internet Explorer. You return to the home page, where the Exercise link has changed to a different color, indicating that the link has been used.

6. Save the home page, and then close Word.

Susan explains that she will eventually add more links to the home page, as well as to the Exercise Web page.

Viewing **Web Pages in a Web Browser**

Now that you are finished with your work on the Web pages, Susan would like you to see how they look in the browser window. Susan explains that the computers at Bayside Health run Microsoft Internet Explorer, the browser that comes with the Windows operating system. Because you will be using Internet Explorer to retrieve files stored on your computer, you don't have to worry about connecting to the Internet. (If your computer is already connected to the Internet, that's fine too.)

To start Internet Explorer:

1. Verify that your computer is turned on, and that the Windows desktop is visible. Notice the Launch Internet Explorer Browser icon in the taskbar, as shown in Figure 6.

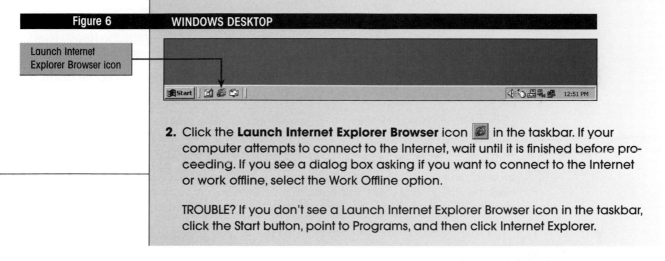

Figure 6	WINDOWS DESKTOP

Launch Internet
Explorer Browser icon

🏁Start 　🗐 🌍 🗒 ◁🔊🔅🖳🖥️ 12:51 PM

2. Click the **Launch Internet Explorer Browser** icon 🌍 in the taskbar. If your computer attempts to connect to the Internet, wait until it is finished before proceeding. If you see a dialog box asking if you want to connect to the Internet or work offline, select the Work Offline option.

   TROUBLE? If you don't see a Launch Internet Explorer Browser icon in the taskbar, click the Start button, point to Programs, and then click Internet Explorer.

Now that you have opened Internet Explorer, you can use it to display the Web page you just created. To open Web pages stored on another computer on a network, you generally use the Address text box near the top of the browser window. However, to open a file on your computer, it's easier to use the Open command on the File menu.

To open your Web pages in Internet Explorer:

1. Click **File** on the menu bar, click **Open**, click **Browse** in the Open dialog box, navigate to the Web folder on your Data Disk, click **Health News Home Page**, click the **Open** button, and then click the **OK** button. The home page opens in the browser window, as shown in Figure 7.

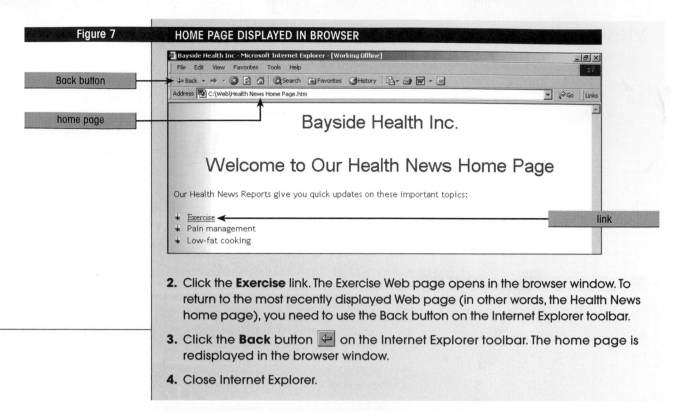

Figure 7   HOME PAGE DISPLAYED IN BROWSER

Back button

home page

link

2. Click the **Exercise** link. The Exercise Web page opens in the browser window. To return to the most recently displayed Web page (in other words, the Health News home page), you need to use the Back button on the Internet Explorer toolbar.

3. Click the **Back** button on the Internet Explorer toolbar. The home page is redisplayed in the browser window.

4. Close Internet Explorer.

You have finished creating two Web pages in Microsoft Word. You tested them in the browser, and tested the link to make sure it works correctly. Now Susan can build on your work by adding more text and links. She will ultimately store your Web pages on a Web server so that Bayside's clients can access them through the Internet.

REVIEW ASSIGNMENTS

Susan is pleased with your preliminary work on the Health News Web site and asks you to help her on a similar project. Bayside Health has recently contracted to host a series of lectures on vegetarian cooking for college students. She asks you to begin creating a Web site that provides information on the classes. You'll need to use a desktop-published flier as the basis for one of the Web pages. Complete the following:

1. Open a new Web page. Add headings explaining the purpose of the Web page, and then type a paragraph of text introducing a series of vegetarian cooking classes. Add a bulleted list of class topics. Include "The Fast Art of Stir-Frying" as one of the topics. Format the Web page using a theme of your choice. Adjust fonts and font sizes as necessary. Save your work as a Web page in the Web folder on your Data Disk with the filename **Cooking Classes Home Page**.

Explore 2. Open the Word document **Stir-Fry** from the Web folder on your Data Disk and review it in Print Preview, zoomed to Whole Page. Preview the document in Web Layout view and then save it as a Web page named **Stir-Fry Class** in the Web folder on your Data Disk.

3. Format the new Web page to match the home page, save your changes, and then close it.

4. Add a hyperlink to the home page that opens the Stir-Fry Class Web page, save your work, test the link, and then close Word.

5. Open the new home page in Internet Explorer, and then test the hyperlink. Close Internet Explorer.

New Perspectives on

MICROSOFT®
EXCEL 2002

Read This Before You Begin

To the Student

Data Disks

To complete the Level 1 tutorials, Review Assignments, and Case Problems, you need three Data Disks. Your instructor will either provide you with these Data Disks or ask you to make your own.

If you are making your own Data Disks, you will need **three** blank, formatted high-density disks. You will need to copy a set of files and/or folders from a file server, standalone computer, or the Web onto your disks. Your instructor will tell you which computer, drive letter, and folders contain the files you need. You could also download the files by going to www.course.com and following the instructions on the screen.

The information below shows you which folders go on each of your disks, so that you will have enough disk space to complete all the tutorials, Review Assignments, and Case Problems:

Data Disk 1

Write this on the disk label:
Data Disk 1: Excel 2002 Tutorials 1 and 2

Put these folders on the disk:
Tutorial.01
Tutorial.02

Data Disk 2

Write this on the disk label:
Data Disk 2: Excel 2002 Tutorials 3 and 4

Put these folders on the disk:
Tutorial.03
Tutorial.04

Data Disk 3

Write this on the disk label:
Data Disk 3: Excel 2002 — Creating Web Pages

Put this folder on the disk:
Web

When you begin each tutorial, be sure you are using the correct Data Disk. Refer to the "File Finder" chart at the back of this text for more detailed information on which files are used in which tutorials. See the inside front or inside back cover of this book for more information on Data Disk files, or ask your instructor or technical support person for assistance.

Course Labs

The Excel Level I tutorials feature an interactive Course Lab to help you understand spreadsheet concepts. There are Lab Assignments at the end of Tutorial 1 that relate to this Lab.

To start a Lab, click the **Start** button on the Windows taskbar, point to **Programs**, point to **Course Labs**, point to **New Perspectives Course Labs**, and then click the name of the Lab you want to use.

Using Your Own Computer

If you are going to work through this book using your own computer, you need:

- **Computer System** Microsoft Windows 98, NT, 2000 Professional, or higher must be installed on your computer. This book assumes a typical installation of Microsoft Excel.

- **Data Disks** You will not be able to complete the tutorials or exercises in this book using your own computer until you have your Data Disks.

- **Course Labs** See your instructor or technical support person to obtain the Course Lab software for use on your own computer.

Visit Our World Wide Web Site

Additional materials designed especially for you are available on the World Wide Web.
Go to www.course.com/NewPerspectives.

To the Instructor

The Data Disk Files and Course Labs are available on the Instructor's Resource Kit for this title. Follow the instructions in the Help file on the CD-ROM to install the programs to your network or standalone computer. For information on creating Data Disks or the Course Labs, see the "To the Student" section above.

You are granted a license to copy the Data Files and Course Labs to any computer or computer network used by students who have purchased this book.

OBJECTIVES

In this tutorial you will:

- Identify major components of the Excel window

- Navigate within and between worksheets

- Select and move worksheet cells

- Insert text, values, and formulas into a worksheet

- Insert and delete worksheet rows and columns

- Resize worksheet rows and columns

- Insert, move, and rename worksheets

- Print a workbook

LAB

Spreadsheets

USING EXCEL TO MANAGE FINANCIAL DATA

Creating an Income Statement

CASE

Lawn Wizards

Lawn Wizards is a small company that specializes in lawn, bush, and tree care. The company started out as a two-person operation, but in recent years the service has gained in popularity. In the last few months, Lawn Wizards has added three employees—two of them full-time workers. The sudden growth in his small business has caught the owner of the company, Mike Bennett, by surprise. Up to now, he has been entering his financial records using a paper financial ledger. However, he realizes that with the growth of his business he needs to store his documents in electronic form.

Mike has just purchased Microsoft Excel 2002 for the business. He has come to you for help. He has many projects for you to work on, but first he needs help with electronic spreadsheets so he can pre-pare his income figures. Mike needs to know what electronic spread-sheets can do, and he needs to become familiar with the basics of Excel.

In this tutorial you will use Excel to help Mike understand electronic spreadsheets. You will explain the different parts of the Excel document window and show him how to move around an Excel work-sheet. You will show him how Excel works by modifying an Excel workbook that contains some of the monthly income figures for Mike's lawn service business.

SESSION 1.1

In this session, you will learn about electronic spreadsheets and how they can be used in business. You will explore the components of the Excel window and learn how to move around within an Excel worksheet. Finally, you will select cells and cell ranges and move the selections to a new location within the worksheet.

Introducing Excel

Mike has just purchased Excel and has loaded it on one of his computers. Before working with his financial records, you and Mike sit down to learn about the fundamental parts of Excel. Understanding why electronic spreadsheets such as Excel have become an essential tool for businesses will help Mike to use Excel more fully and help him run his business efficiently.

Understanding Spreadsheets

Excel is a computerized spreadsheet. A **spreadsheet** is an important business tool that helps you report and analyze information. Spreadsheets are often used for cash flow analysis, budgeting, inventory management, market forecasts, and decision making. For example, an accountant might use a spreadsheet like the one shown in Figure 1-1 to record budget information.

Figure 1-1	BUDGET SPREADSHEET

Cash Budget Forecast

	January Estimated	January Actual
Cash in Bank (Start of Month)	$1,400.00	$1,400.00
Cash in Register (Start of Month)	100.00	100.00
Total Cash	$1,500.00	$1,500.00
Expected Cash Sales	$1,200.00	$1,420.00
Expected Collections	400.00	380.00
Other Money Expected	100.00	52.00
Total Income	$1,700.00	$1,852.00
Total Cash and Income	$3,200.00	$3,352.00
All Expenses (for Month)	$1,200.00	$1,192.00
Cash Balance at End of Month	$2,000.00	$2,160.00

In this spreadsheet, the accountant has recorded predicted and observed income and expenses for the month of January. Each line, or row, in this spreadsheet displays a different income or expense. Each column contains the predicted or observed values or text that describes those values. The accountant has also entered the income and expense totals, perhaps having used a calculator to do the calculations.

Figure 1-2 shows the same spreadsheet in Excel. The spreadsheet is now laid out in a grid in which the rows and columns are easily apparent. As you will see later, calculations are also part of this electronic spreadsheet, so that the expense and income totals are calculated automatically rather than entered manually. If an entry in the spreadsheet is changed, the spreadsheet will automatically update any calculated values based on that entry. Thus an electronic spreadsheet provides more flexibility in entering and analyzing your data than the paper version.

Figure 1-2	BUDGET SPREADSHEET IN EXCEL

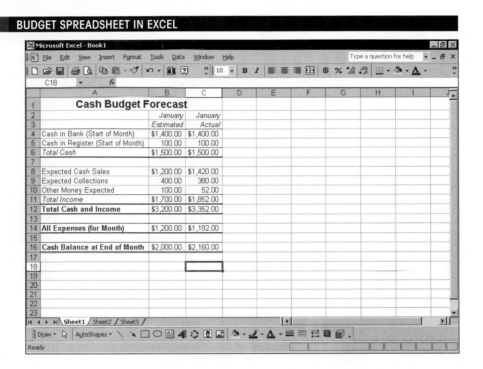

Excel stores electronic spreadsheets in documents called **workbooks**. Each workbook is made up of individual **worksheets**, or **sheets**, just as Mike's spiral-bound ledger is made up of sheets of paper. You will learn more about multiple worksheets later in this tutorial. For now, just keep in mind that the terms *worksheet* and *sheet* are used interchangeably.

Parts of the Excel Window

Excel displays workbooks within a window that contains many tools for entering, editing, and viewing the data. You will view some of these tools after starting Excel. By default, Excel will open with a blank workbook.

To start Excel:

1. Make sure Windows is running on your computer and the Windows desktop appears on your screen.

2. Click the **Start** button on the taskbar to display the Start menu, and then point to **Programs** to display the Programs menu.

3. Point to **Microsoft Excel** on the Programs menu. See Figure 1-3.

Figure 1-3	STARTING EXCEL

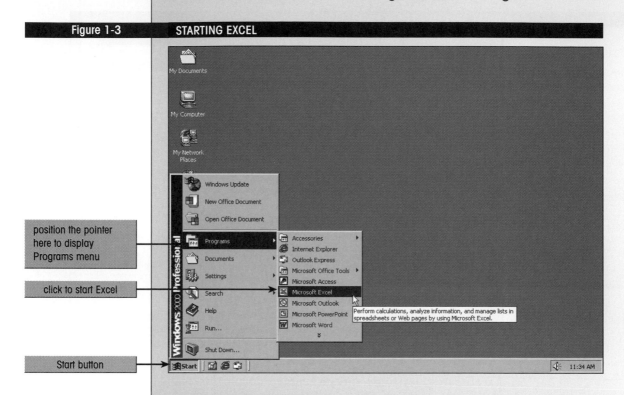

position the pointer here to display Programs menu

click to start Excel

Start button

TROUBLE? Do not worry if your screen differs slightly. Although the figures in this book were created while running Windows 2000 in its default settings, the Windows 98 and Windows NT operating systems share the same basic user interface as Windows 2000, and Excel runs equally well using any of these.

TROUBLE? Depending on how your system was set up, the menu entry for Excel may appear in a different location on the Programs menu. If you cannot locate Excel, ask your instructor for assistance.

4. Click **Microsoft Excel**. After a short pause, the Excel program window and a blank workbook appear. See Figure 1-4.

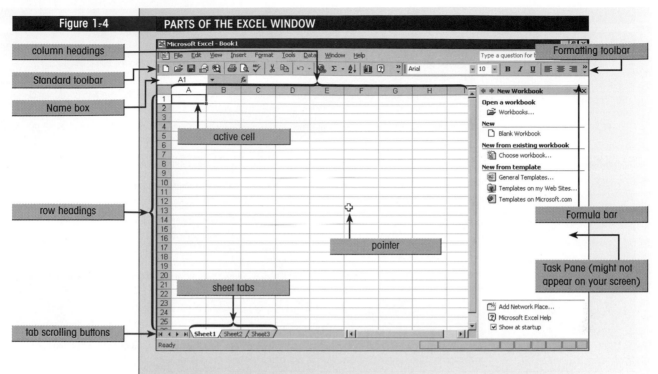

Figure 1-4   **PARTS OF THE EXCEL WINDOW**

column headings

Standard toolbar

Name box

active cell

row headings

pointer

sheet tabs

tab scrolling buttons

Formatting toolbar

Formula bar

Task Pane (might not appear on your screen)

TROUBLE? Depending on your Excel configuration, the Task Pane might not appear in the Excel window. To display the Task Pane, click View on the menu bar, and then click Task Pane.

The Excel window has features similar to other Windows programs. It contains a title bar, menu bar, scroll bars, and a status bar. The Excel window also contains features that are unique to the program itself. Within the Excel program window is the document window, which is also referred to as the **workbook window** or **worksheet window**. The worksheet window provides a grid of columns and rows in which the intersection of a column and row is called a **cell**. Figure 1-4 identifies many of the other components of the Excel window. Take a look at each of these components so you are familiar with their location and purpose. Figure 1-5 summarizes the properties of each of these components.

Figure 1-5	EXCEL WINDOW COMPONENTS
FEATURE	**DESCRIPTION**
Active cell	The **active cell** is the cell in which you are currently working. A dark border outlining the cell identifies the active cell.
Column headings	**Column headings** list the columns in the worksheet. Columns are listed alphabetically from A to IV (a total of 256 possible columns).
Formula bar	The **Formula bar**, which is located immediately below the toolbars, displays the contents of the active cell. As you type or edit data, the changes appear in the Formula bar.
Name box	The **Name box** displays the location of the currently active cell in the workbook window.
Pointer	The **pointer** indicates the current location of your mouse pointer. The pointer changes shape to reflect the type of task you can perform at a particular location in the Excel window.
Row headings	**Row headings** list the rows in the worksheet. Rows are numbered consecutively from 1 up to 65,536.
Sheet tabs	Each worksheet in the workbook has a **sheet tab** that identifies the sheet's name. To move between worksheets, click the appropriate sheet tab.
Task Pane	The **Task Pane** appears when you initially start Excel, and it displays a list of commonly used tasks. The Task Pane will disappear once you open a workbook.
Tab scrolling buttons	The **tab scrolling buttons** are used to move between worksheets in the workbook.
Toolbars	**Toolbars** provide quick access to the most commonly used Excel menu commands. The **Standard toolbar** contains buttons for Excel commands such as Save and Open. The **Formatting toolbar** contains buttons used to format the appearance of the workbook. Additional toolbars are available.

Now that you are familiar with the basic layout of an Excel workbook, you can try moving around within the workbook.

Navigating in a Workbook

You can navigate in a workbook by moving from worksheet to worksheet or in a worksheet by moving from cell to cell. Each cell is identified by a **cell reference**, which indicates its row and column location. For example, the cell reference B6 indicates that the cell is located where column B and row 6 intersect. The column letter is always first in the cell reference. B6 is a correct cell reference; 6B is not. One cell in the worksheet, called the **active cell**, is always selected and ready for receiving data. Excel identifies the active cell with a dark border outlining it. In Figure 1-4, cell A1 is the active cell. Notice that the cell reference for the active cell appears in the Name box next to the Formula bar. You can change the active cell by selecting another cell in the worksheet.

Navigating Within a Worksheet

Excel provides several ways of moving around in the worksheet. The most direct way is to use your mouse. To change the active cell, move the mouse pointer over a different cell and click anywhere within the cell with your left mouse button. If you need to move to a cell that is not currently displayed in the workbook window, use the vertical and horizontal scroll bars to display the area of the worksheet containing the cell.

The second way of moving around the worksheet is through your keyboard. Excel provides you with many keyboard shortcuts for moving to different cells within the worksheet. Figure 1-6 describes some of these keyboard shortcuts.

Figure 1-6	KEYS FOR NAVIGATING WITHIN A WORKSHEET
KEYSTROKE	**ACTION**
↑ , ↓ , ← , →	Moves the active cell up, down, left, or right one cell
Enter	Moves the active cell down one cell
Tab	Moves the active cell to the right one cell
Page Up	Moves the active cell up one full screen
Page Down	Moves the active cell down one full screen
Home	Moves the active cell to column A of the current row
Ctrl + Home	Moves the active cell to cell A1
F5 (function key)	Opens the Go To dialog box in which you can enter the cell address of the cell that you want to make active

Finally, you can enter a cell reference in the Name box to move directly to that cell in the worksheet.

Explore these techniques by moving around the worksheet using your keyboard and mouse.

To move around the worksheet:

1. Position the mouse pointer over cell E8, and then click the left mouse button to make cell E8 the active cell.

   Notice that cell E8 is surrounded by a black border, indicating it is the active cell, and that the Name box displays the cell reference "E8." Note also that the row and column headings for row 8 and column E are highlighted, giving another visual indication about the location of the active cell.

2. Click cell **B4** to make it the active cell.

3. Press the → key on your keyboard to make cell C4 the active cell.

4. Press the ↓ key to make cell C5 the active cell. See Figure 1-7.

Figure 1-7	MAKING CELL C5 THE ACTIVE CELL

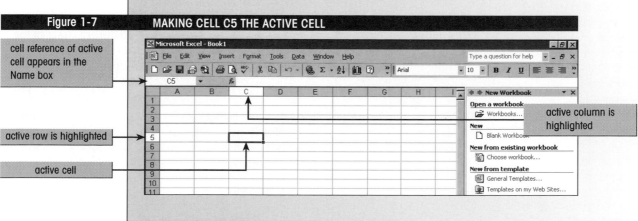

cell reference of active cell appears in the Name box

active row is highlighted

active cell

active column is highlighted

5. Press the **Home** key to move to cell A5, the first cell in the current row.

6. Press **Ctrl + Home** to make cell A1 the active cell.

So far you have moved around the portion of the worksheet displayed in the workbook window. The content of many worksheets will not fit into the workbook window, so you may have to move to cells that are not currently displayed by Excel. You can do this using your keyboard or the scroll bars.

To bring other parts of the worksheet into view:

1. Press the **Page Down** key on your keyboard to move the display down one screen. The active cell is now A26 (the active cell on your screen may be different). Notice that the row numbers on the left side of the worksheet indicate you have moved to a different area of the worksheet. See Figure 1-8.

Figure 1-8	MOVING TO A DIFFERENT AREA OF THE WORKSHEET

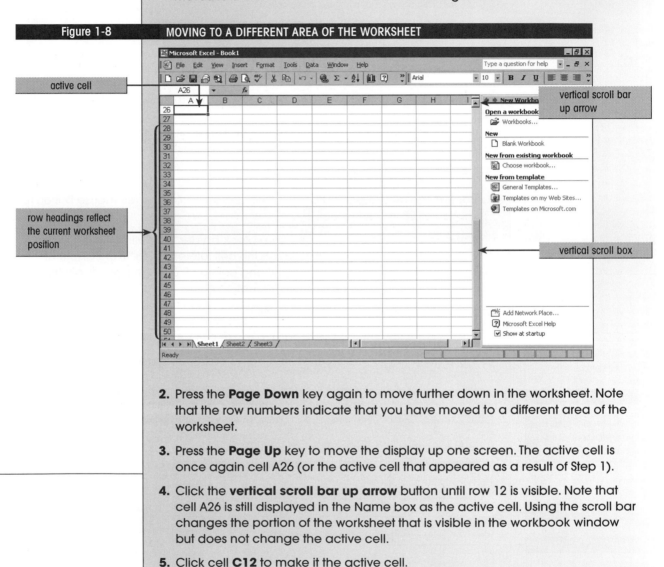

active cell

row headings reflect the current worksheet position

vertical scroll bar up arrow

vertical scroll box

2. Press the **Page Down** key again to move further down in the worksheet. Note that the row numbers indicate that you have moved to a different area of the worksheet.

3. Press the **Page Up** key to move the display up one screen. The active cell is once again cell A26 (or the active cell that appeared as a result of Step 1).

4. Click the **vertical scroll bar up arrow** button until row 12 is visible. Note that cell A26 is still displayed in the Name box as the active cell. Using the scroll bar changes the portion of the worksheet that is visible in the workbook window but does not change the active cell.

5. Click cell **C12** to make it the active cell.

6. Click the blank area above the vertical scroll box to move up one full screen, and then click the blank area below the vertical scroll box to move down a full screen.

7. Click the **vertical scroll box** and drag it to the top of the scroll bar to again change the area of the worksheet being displayed in the window.

You can also use the Go To dialog box and the Name box to jump directly to a specific cell in the worksheet, whether the cell is currently visible in the workbook window or not. Try this now.

To use the Go To dialog box and Name box:

1. Press the **F5** key to open the Go To dialog box.

2. Type **K55** in the Reference text box, and then click the **OK** button. Cell K55 is now the active cell.

3. Click the **Name** box, type **E6**, and then press the **Enter** key. Cell E6 becomes the active cell.

4. Press **Ctrl + Home** to make cell A1 the active cell.

Navigating Between Worksheets

A workbook is usually composed of several worksheets. The workbook shown in Figure 1-8 contains three worksheets (this is the default for new blank workbooks) labeled Sheet1, Sheet2, and Sheet3. To move between the worksheets, you click the sheet tab of the worksheet you want to display.

To move between worksheets:

1. Click the **Sheet2** tab. Sheet2, which is blank, appears in the workbook window. Notice that the Sheet2 tab is now white with the name "Sheet2" in a bold font. This is a visual indicator that Sheet2 is the active worksheet.

2. Click the **Sheet1** tab to return to the first sheet in the workbook.

Some workbooks will contain so many worksheets that some sheet tabs will be hidden from view. If that is the case, you can use the tab scrolling buttons located in the lower-left corner of the workbook window to scroll through the list of sheet tabs. Figure 1-9 describes the actions of the four tab scrolling buttons. Note that clicking the tab scrolling buttons does not change the active sheet; clicking the tab scrolling buttons allows you to view the other sheet tabs in the workbook. To change the active sheet, you must click the sheet tab itself.

Figure 1-9	TAB SCROLLING BUTTONS

first sheet → previous sheet

last sheet / next sheet

Now that you have some basic skills navigating through a worksheet and a workbook, you can begin working with Mike's financial records. Some of the figures from the Lawn Wizards' April income statement have already been entered in an Excel workbook.

Opening and Saving a Workbook

There are several ways of accessing a saved workbook. To open a workbook, you can click the Open command on Excel's File menu or you can click the Open button found on the Standard toolbar. You can also click the Workbooks link found in the Task Pane (if the Task Pane is visible to you). Any of these methods will display the Open dialog box. Once the Open dialog box is displayed, you have to navigate through the hierarchy of folders and drives on your computer or network to locate the workbook file.

Mike has saved the income statement with the filename "Lawn1." Locate and open this file now.

To open the Lawn1 workbook:

1. Place your Excel Data Disk in the appropriate drive.

   TROUBLE? If you don't have a Data Disk, you need to contact your instructor or technical support person who will either give you one or give you instructions for creating your own. You can also review the instructions on the Read This Before You Begin page located at the front of this book.

2. Click the **Open** button 📂 on the Standard toolbar. The Open dialog box is displayed. See Figure 1-10.

Figure 1-10	OPEN DIALOG BOX

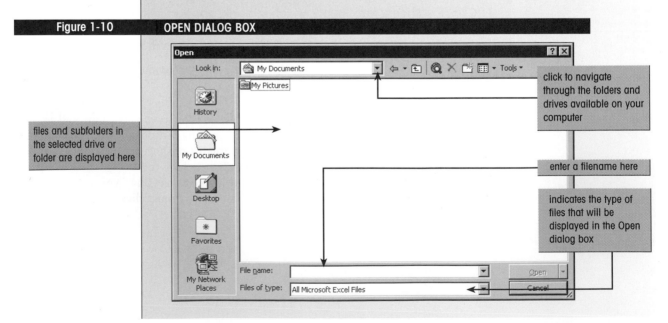

files and subfolders in the selected drive or folder are displayed here

click to navigate through the folders and drives available on your computer

enter a filename here

indicates the type of files that will be displayed in the Open dialog box

3. Click the **Look in** list arrow to display the list of available drives. Locate the drive that contains your Data Disk. This text assumes your Data Disk is a 3½-inch disk in drive A.

4. Click the drive that contains your Data Disk. A list of documents and folders on your Data Disk appears in the list box.

5. In the list of file and folder names, double-click **Tutorial.01**, double-click **Tutorial** to display the contents of the folder, and then click **Lawn1**.

6. Click the **Open** button (you could also have double-clicked Lawn1 to open the file). The workbook opens, displaying the income figures in the Sheet1 worksheet. Note that if the Task Pane was previously visible, it has now disappeared. See Figure 1-11.

Figure 1-11	LAWN1 WORKBOOK

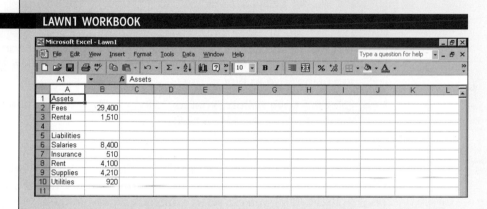

Sometimes you will want to open a new blank workbook. Excel allows you to have several workbooks open at the same time. To create a new blank workbook, you can click the New button on the Standard toolbar.

Before going further in the Lawn1 workbook, you should make a copy of the file with a new name. This will allow you to go back to the original version of the file if necessary.

Mike suggests that you save the file with the name "Lawn2."

To save the workbook with a different name:

1. Click **File** on the menu bar, and then click **Save As**. The Save As dialog box opens with the current workbook name in the File name text box. Note that the Tutorial folder on your Data Disk is automatically opened, so you do not have to navigate through your computer's hierarchy of folders and drives.

2. Click immediately to the right of "Lawn1" in the File name text box, press the **Backspace** key, and then type **2**.

3. Make sure that "Microsoft Excel Workbook" is displayed in the Save as type list box. See Figure 1-12.

Figure 1-12   SAVE AS DIALOG BOX

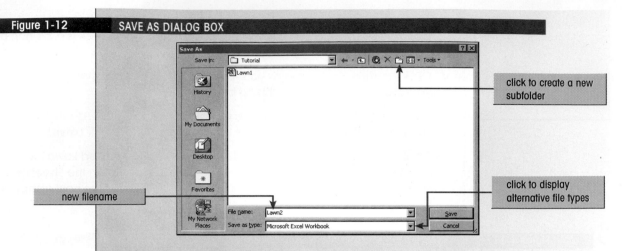

Note that if you want to save the file to a new folder, you can create a new folder "on the fly" by clicking the Create New Folder button 📝 located at the top of the Save As dialog box.

4. Click the **Save** button. Excel saves the workbook under the new name and closes the Save As dialog box.

By default, Excel saves the workbooks in Microsoft Excel Workbook format. If you are creating a report that will be read by applications other than Excel (or versions of Excel prior to Excel 2002), you can select a different type from the Save as type list box in the Save (or Save As) dialog box.

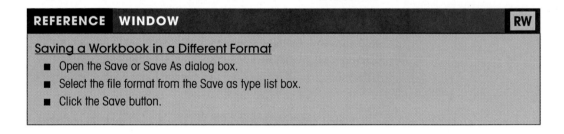

REFERENCE WINDOW   **RW**

Saving a Workbook in a Different Format
- Open the Save or Save As dialog box.
- Select the file format from the Save as type list box.
- Click the Save button.

Figure 1-13 displays a partial list of the other formats you can save your workbook as. You can add other formats by running the Excel 2002 or Office XP installation program. Note that some of the formats described in Figure 1-13 save only the active worksheet, not the entire workbook.

Figure 1-13   SOME OF THE FILE FORMATS SUPPORTED BY EXCEL

FORMAT	DESCRIPTION
CSV (Comma delimited)	Saves the active worksheet as a text file with columns separated by commas
DBF2, DBF3, DBF4	Saves the active worksheet as a dBASE table in the different versions of dBASE
Formatted Text (Space delimited)	Saves the active worksheet as a text file with columns separated by spaces
Microsoft Excel 2.1, 3.0, 4.0 Worksheet	Saves the workbook in the earliest versions of Excel
Microsoft Excel 5.0, 95, 97, 2000 Workbook	Saves the workbook in an earlier version of Excel
Text (Tab delimited)	Saves the active worksheet as a text file with columns separated by tabs
Web Archive	Saves the workbook as a Web site, enclosed within a single file
Web Page	Saves the workbook in HTML format, suitable for use as a Web page
WK1, WK2, WK3	Saves the active worksheet as a Lotus 1-2-3 spreadsheet
WK4 (1-2-3)	Saves the workbook as a Lotus 1-2-3 document
WQ1	Saves the active worksheet as a Quattro Pro spreadsheet
XML Spreadsheet	Saves the workbook in XML format, suitable for use in Web queries

In this text you will use only the Microsoft Excel Workbook format.

Working with Ranges

The data in the Lawn2 workbook contains the assets and liabilities for Lawn Wizards during the month of April, 2003. Mike would like to include this information in a title at the top of the worksheet. To make room for the title, you have to move the current content down a few rows. To move a group of cells in a worksheet, you have to first understand how Excel handles cells.

A group of worksheet cells is called a **cell range**, or **range**. Ranges can be either adjacent or nonadjacent. An **adjacent range** is a single rectangular block such as all of the data entered in cells A1 through B10 of the Lawn2 workbook. A **nonadjacent range** is comprised of two or more separate adjacent ranges. You could view the Lawn2 workbook as containing two nonadjacent ranges: the first range, cell A1 through cell B3, contains the company's assets, and the second range, cell A5 through cell B10, displays the company's liabilities.

Just as a cell reference indicates the location of the cell on the worksheet, a range reference indicates the location and size of the range. For adjacent ranges, the range reference identifies the cells in the upper-left and lower-right corners of the rectangle, with the individual cell references separated by a colon. For example, the range reference for Mike's income statement is A1:B10. If the range is nonadjacent, a semicolon separates the rectangular blocks, such as A1:B3;A5:B10, which refers to data in Mike's income statement, but does not include the blank row (row 4), which separates the assets from the liabilities.

Selecting Ranges

Working with ranges of cells makes working with the data in a worksheet easier. Once you know how to select ranges of cells, you can move and copy the data anywhere in the worksheet or workbook.

REFERENCE WINDOW   RW

Selecting Adjacent or Nonadjacent Ranges of Cells

To select an adjacent range of cells:

■ Click a cell in the corner of the rectangle that comprises the adjacent range.

■ Press and hold down the left mouse button, and drag the pointer through the cells you want selected.

■ Release the mouse button.

To select a nonadjacent range of cells:

■ Select an adjacent range of cells.

■ Press and hold down the Ctrl key, and then select another adjacent cell range.

■ With the Ctrl key still pressed, continue to select other cell ranges until all of the ranges are selected.

■ Release the mouse button and the Ctrl key.

Next you'll select the adjacent range A1 through B10.

To select the range A1:B10:

1. Click cell **A1** (if necessary) to make it the active cell, and then press and hold down the left mouse button.

2. With the mouse button still pressed, drag the pointer to cell **B10**.

3. Release the mouse button. All of the cells in the range A1:B10 are now high-lighted, indicating that they are selected. See Figure 1-14.

| Figure 1-14 | SELECTING RANGE A1:B10 |

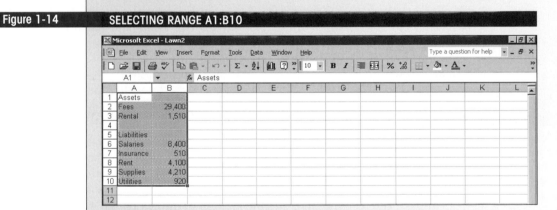

To deselect the range, you can click any cell in the worksheet.

4. Click cell **C1** to deselect the range.

To select a nonadjacent range, you begin by selecting an adjacent range, and then you press and hold down the Ctrl key and select other adjacent ranges. Release the Ctrl key and the mouse button when you are finished. Next you'll select the assets and then select the lia-bilities in the income statement.

To select the nonadjacent range A1:B3;A5:B10:

1. Select the range **A1:B3**.

2. Press and hold down the **Ctrl** key.

3. Select the range **A5:B10**. See Figure 1-15.

Figure 1-15	SELECTING THE NONADJACENT RANGE A1:B3;A5:B10

4. Click any cell in the worksheet to deselect the range.

Other Selection Techniques

To select a large range of data, Excel will automatically scroll horizontally or vertically to display additional cells in the worksheet. Selecting a large range of cells using the mouse drag technique can be slow and frustrating. For this reason, Excel provides keyboard shortcuts to quickly select large blocks of data without having to drag through the worksheet to select the necessary cells. Figure 1-16 describes some of these selection techniques.

Figure 1-16	OTHER RANGE SELECTION TECHNIQUES

TO SELECT...	ACTION
A large range of cells	Click the first cell in the range, press and hold down the Shift key, and then click the last cell in the range. All of the cells between the first and last cell are selected.
All cells on the worksheet	Click the Select All button, the gray rectangle in the upper-left corner of the worksheet where the row and column headings meet.
All cells in an entire row or column	Click the row or column heading.
A range of cells containing data	Click the first cell in the range, press and hold down the Shift key, and then double-click the side of the active cell in which you want to extend the selection. Excel extends the selection up to the first empty cell.

Try some of the techniques described in Figure 1-16 using the income statement.

To select large ranges of cells:

1. Click cell **A1** to make it the active cell.

2. Press and hold down the **Shift** key, and then click cell **B10**. Note that all of the cells between A1 and B10 are selected.

TROUBLE? If the range A1:B10 is not selected, try again, but make sure you hold down the Shift key while you click cell B10.

3. Release the Shift key.

4. Click cell **A1** to remove the selection.

5. Press and hold down the **Shift** key, and move the pointer to the bottom edge of cell A1 until the mouse pointer changes to ⭲.

6. Double-click the bottom edge of cell **A1**. The selection extends to cell A3, the last cell before the blank cell A4.

7. With the Shift key still pressed, move the pointer to the right edge of the selection until, once again, the pointer changes to ⭲.

8. Double-click the right edge of the selection. The selection extends to the last non-blank column in the worksheet.

9. Click the **A** column heading. All of the cells in column A are selected.

10. Click the **1** row heading. All of the cells in the first row are selected.

Moving a Selection of Cells

Now that you know various ways to select a range of cells, you can move the income statement data to another location in the worksheet. To move a cell range, you first select it and then position the pointer over the selection border and drag the selection to a new location. Copying a range of cells is similar to moving a range. The only difference is that you must press the Ctrl key while you drag the selection to its new location. A copy of the original data appears at the location of the pointer when you release the mouse button.

You can also move a selection to a new worksheet in the current workbook. To do this, you press and hold down the Alt key and then drag the selection over the sheet tab of the new worksheet. Excel will automatically make that worksheet the active sheet, so you can drag the selection into its new location on the worksheet.

Next you'll move the cells in the range A1:B10 to a new location, beginning at cell A5.

To move the range A1:B10 down four rows:

1. Select the range **A1:B10**.

2. Move the pointer over the bottom border of the selection until the pointer changes to ⭲.

3. Press and hold down the left mouse button, and then drag the selection down four rows. A ScreenTip appears indicating the new range reference of the selection. See Figure 1-17.

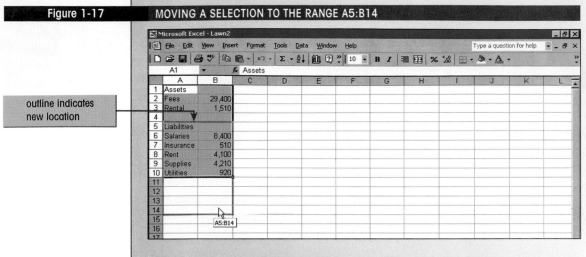

Figure 1-17   MOVING A SELECTION TO THE RANGE A5:B14

outline indicates
new location

4. When the ScreenTip displays "A5:B14", release the left mouse button. The income statement is now moved to range A5:B14.

5. Click cell **A1** to remove the selection.

At this point, you have made space for a title and other information to be placed above the income statement. In the next session you will learn how to enter the new text into the worksheet, as well as how to edit the contents already there.

To exit Excel:

1. Click **File** on the menu bar, and then click **Exit**.

2. When Excel prompts you to save your changes, click the **Yes** button. Excel saves the changes to the workbook and closes.

Session 1.1 QUICK CHECK

1. A(n) _____ is the place on the worksheet where a column and row intersect.

2. Cell _____ refers to the intersection of the fourth column and second row.

3. What combination of keys can you press to make A1 the active cell in the worksheet?

4. To make Sheet2 the active worksheet, you _____.

5. Describe the two types of cell ranges in Excel.

6. What is the cell reference for the rectangular group of cells that extends from cell A5 down to cell F8?

7. Describe how you move a cell range from the Sheet1 worksheet to the Sheet2 worksheet.

In this session, you will enter text and values into a worksheet. You will also enter formulas using basic arithmetic operators. You will use Excel's edit mode to change the value in a cell. You will insert rows and columns into a worksheet and modify the width of a column. You will insert, delete, and move worksheets, and you will rename sheet tabs. Finally, you will create a hard copy of your workbook by sending its contents to a printer.

Entering Information into a Worksheet

In the previous session, you learned about the different parts of Excel's workbook window, and you learned how to work with cells and cell ranges. Now you will enter some new information in Mike's April income statement. The information that you enter in the cells of a worksheet can consist of text, values, or formulas. Mike wants you to enter text that describes the income statement located on Sheet1.

Entering Text

Text entries include any combination of letters, symbols, numbers, and spaces. Although text is sometimes used as data, text is more often used to describe the data contained in the workbook. For example, the range A5:A14 of the income statement indicates the various asset and liability categories.

To enter text in a worksheet, you click the cell in which you want the text placed and then type the text you want entered. Excel automatically aligns text with the left edge of the cell. Mike wants you to enter the text labels "Lawn Wizards" in cell A1 and "Income Statement" in cell A2.

To enter labels in cell A1 and A2:

1. If you took a break after the previous session, make sure Excel is running and the Lawn2 workbook is open.

2. Verify that Sheet1 is the active worksheet in the Lawn2 workbook.

3. Click cell **A1** if necessary to make it the active cell.

4. Type **Lawn Wizards** and then press the **Enter** key.

5. In cell A2, type **Income Statement** and then press the **Enter** key. See Figure 1-18.

   TROUBLE? If you make a mistake as you type, you can correct the error with the Backspace key. If you realize you made an error after pressing the Enter key, reenter the text by repeating Steps 3 through 5.

Figure 1-18 | **ADDING NEW TEXT TO THE INCOME STATEMENT**

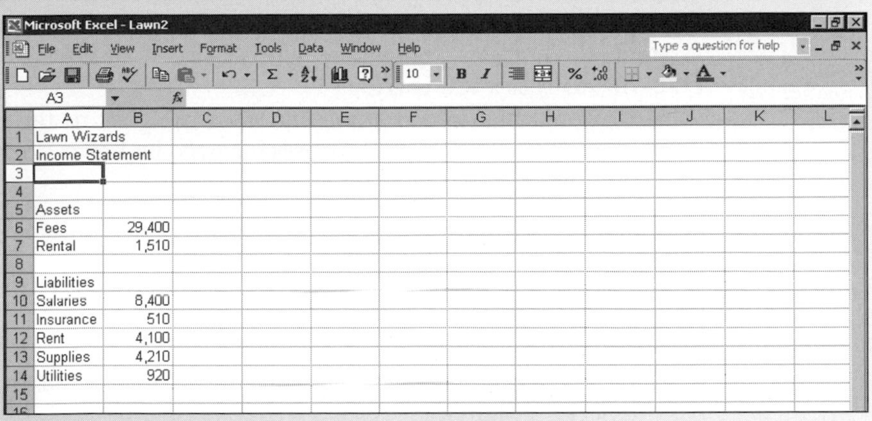

Note that even though you entered text in cells A1 and A2, the text appears to flow into cells B1 and B2. When you enter a text string longer than the width of the active cell, Excel will display the additional text if the cells to the right of the active cell are blank. If those cells are not blank, then Excel will truncate the display (though the entire text is still present in the cell). As you will see later, you can increase the width of the column if the text is cut off.

Entering Dates

Dates are treated as separate from text in Excel. As you will learn later, Excel includes several special functions and commands to work with dates. For example, you can insert a function that will calculate the number of days between two dates (you will learn more about this in the next tutorial). To enter a date, separate the parts of the date with a slash or hyphen. For example, the date April 1, 2003 can be entered as either "4/1/2003" or "1-Apr-2003".

You can also enter the date as the text string "April 1, 2003", in which case Excel might automatically convert the text to "1-Apr-2003". You can change the format used by Excel to display dates by changing the cell's format. You will learn about date formats in Tutorial 3.

Mike wants the date "4/1/2003" to appear in cell A3.

To insert the date in cell A3:

1. Verify that cell A3 is the active cell.

2. Type **4/1/2003** and then press the **Enter** key.

TROUBLE? Your system may be set up to display dates using the mm/dd/yy format; therefore, you may see the date displayed as 4/1/03 rather than 4/1/2003.

Entering Values

Values are numbers that represent a quantity of some type: the number of units in an inventory, stock prices, an exam score, and so on. Values can be numbers such as 378 and 25.275, or negative numbers such as –55.208. Values can also be expressed as currency ($4,571.25) or percentages (7.5%). Dates and times are also values, though that fact is hidden from you by the way Excel displays date information.

As you type information into a cell, Excel determines whether the information you have entered can be treated as a value. If so, Excel will automatically recognize the value type and right-align the value within the cell. Not all numbers are treated as values. For example, Excel treats a telephone number (1-800-555-8010) or a Social Security number (372-70-9654) as a text entry.

Mike would like to add a miscellaneous category to the list of monthly liabilities. In April, the total miscellaneous expenses incurred by Lawn Wizards totaled $351.

To add the miscellaneous expenses:

1. Click cell **A15** and then type **Misc** as the category.

2. Press the **Tab** key to move to the next column.

3. Type **351** and then press the **Enter** key. Figure 1-19 shows the new entry in the income statement.

| Figure 1-19 | ADDING A NEW CATEGORY AND VALUE TO THE INCOME STATEMENT |

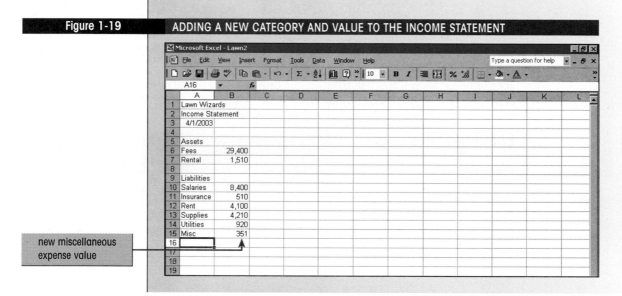

new miscellaneous expense value

Entering Formulas

A **formula** is an expression that is used to calculate a value. You can enter a formula by typing the expression into the active cell, or in special cases Excel will automatically insert the formula for you. Excel formulas always begin with an equal sign (=) followed by an expression that calculates a value. If you do not start with an equal sign, Excel will treat the expression you enter as text. The expression can contain one or more **arithmetic operators**, such as +, −, *, or /, that are applied to either values or cells in the workbook. Figure 1-20 gives some examples of Excel formulas.

Figure 1-20 — **ARITHMETIC OPERATORS USED IN FORMULAS**

ARITHMETIC OPERATION	ARITHMETIC OPERATOR	EXAMPLE	DESCRIPTION
Addition	+	=10+A5 =B1+B2+B3	Adds 10 to the value in cell A5 Adds the values of cells B1, B2, and B3
Subtraction	–	=C9–B2 =1–D2	Subtracts the value in B2 from the value in cell C9 Subtracts the value in cell D2 from 1
Multiplication	*	=C9*B9 =E5*0.06	Multiplies the value in cell C9 by the value in cell B9 Multiplies the value in cell E5 by 0.06
Division	/	=C9/B9 =D15/12	Divides the value in cell C9 by the value in cell B9 Divides the value in cell D15 by 12
Exponentiation	^	=B5^3 =3^B5	Raises the value in cell B5 to the third power Raises 3 to the power specified in cell B5

REFERENCE WINDOW   RW

Entering a Formula

- Click the cell where you want the formula value to appear.
- Type = and then type the expression that calculates the value you want.
- For formulas that include cell references, such as B2 or D78, you can type the cell reference or you can use the mouse or arrow keys to select each cell.
- When the formula is complete, press the Enter key.

If an expression contains more than one arithmetic operator, Excel performs the calculation in the order of precedence. The **order of precedence** is a set of predefined rules that Excel follows to unambiguously calculate a formula by determining which operator is applied first, which operator is applied second, and so forth. First, Excel performs exponentiation (^). Second, Excel performs multiplication (*) or division (/). Third, Excel performs addition (+) or subtraction (-).

For example, because multiplication has precedence over addition, the formula =3+4*5 has the value 23. If the expression contains two or more operators with the same level of precedence, Excel applies them going from left to right in the expression. In the formula =4*10/8, Excel first multiplies 4 by 10 and then divides the product by 8 to return the value 5.

You can add parentheses to a formula to make it easier to interpret or to change the order of operations. Excel will calculate any expression contained within the parentheses before any other part of the formula. The formula =(3+4)*5 first calculates the value of 3+4 and then multiplies the total by 5 to return the value 35 (note that without the parentheses, Excel would return a value of 23 as noted in the previous paragraph). Figure 1-21 shows other examples of Excel formulas in which the precedence order is applied to return a value.

Figure 1-21	EXAMPLES ILLUSTRATING ORDER OF PRECEDENCE RULES	
FORMULA VALUE A1=10, B1=20, C1=3	**ORDER OF PRECEDENCE RULE**	**RESULT**
=A1+B1*C1	Multiplication before addition	70
=(A1+B1)*C1	Expression inside parentheses executed before expression outside	90
=A1/B1+C1	Division before addition	3.5
=A1/(B1+C1)	Expression inside parentheses executed before expression outside	.435
=A1/B1*C1	Two operators at same precedence level, leftmost operator evaluated first	1.5
=A1/(B1*C1)	Expression inside parentheses executed before expression outside	.166667

The Lawn2 workbook contains the asset and liability values for various categories, but it doesn't include the total assets and liabilities, nor does it display Lawn Wizards' net income (assets minus liabilities) for the month of April. Mike suggests that you add formulas to calculate these values now.

To calculate the total assets for the month of April:

1. Click cell **A8** to make it the active cell.

2. Type **Total** and then press the **Tab** key twice.

3. In cell C8, type **=B6+B7** (the income from fees and rental for the month).

Note that as you type in the cell reference, Excel surrounds each cell with a different colored border that matches the color of the cell reference in the formula. As shown in Figure 1-22, Excel surrounds cell B6 with a blue border matching the blue used for the cell reference. Green is used for the B7 cell border and cell reference.

Figure 1-22	TYPING A FORMULA INTO A CELL

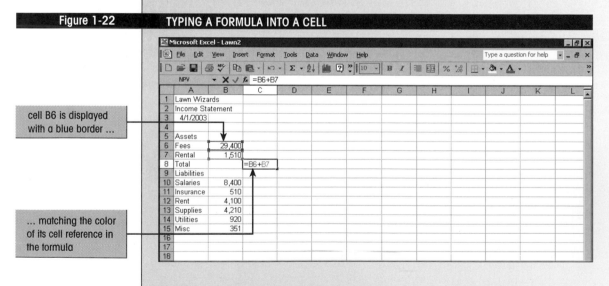

cell B6 is displayed with a blue border ...

... matching the color of its cell reference in the formula

4. Press the **Enter** key.

The total assets value displayed in cell C8 is 30,910.

You can also enter formulas interactively by clicking each cell in the formula rather than typing in the cell reference. Using this approach reduces the possibility of error caused by typing in an incorrect cell reference.

To enter a formula by pointing and clicking:

1. Click cell **A16** to make it the active cell.
2. Type **Total** and then press the **Tab** key twice.

   TROUBLE? Note that when you started to type the word "Total" in cell A16, Excel automatically completed it for you. Since some worksheets will repeat the same word or phrase several times within a row or column, this AutoComplete feature can save you time.

3. In cell C16, type = and then click cell **B10**. Excel automatically inserts the reference to cell B10 into your formula.
4. Type + and then click cell **B11**.
5. Type + and then click cell **B12**.
6. Continue to select the rest of the liabilities in the range B13:B15, so that the formula in cell C16 reads **=B10+B11+B12+B13+B14+B15**. Do not type an equal sign after you click cell B15.
7. Press the **Enter** key. The total liabilities value "18,491" appears in cell C16.

   Now you can calculate the net income for the month of April.

8. In cell A18, enter **Net Income** and then press the **Tab** key twice.
9. In cell C18, enter the formula **=C8-C16** by clicking to select the cell references, and then press the **Enter** key. Figure 1-23 shows the completed formulas in the income statement.

Figure 1-23 TOTAL ASSETS, LIABILITIES, AND NET INCOME

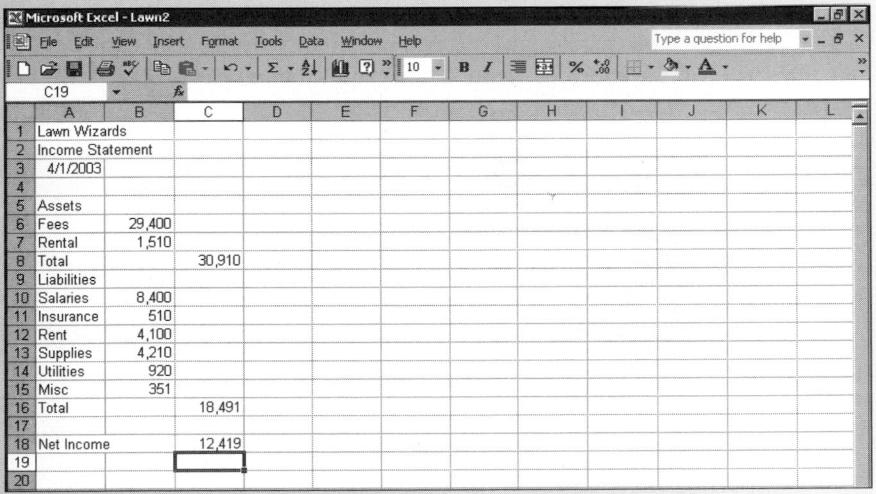

	A	B	C
1	Lawn Wizards		
2	Income Statement		
3	4/1/2003		
4			
5	Assets		
6	Fees	29,400	
7	Rental	1,510	
8	Total		30,910
9	Liabilities		
10	Salaries	8,400	
11	Insurance	510	
12	Rent	4,100	
13	Supplies	4,210	
14	Utilities	920	
15	Misc	351	
16	Total		18,491
17			
18	Net Income		12,419
19			
20			

Working with Rows and Columns

Mike examines the worksheet and points out that it is difficult to separate the assets from the liabilities. He would like you to insert a blank row between row 8 and row 9. You could do this by moving the cell range A9:C18 down one row, but there is another way. Excel allows you to insert rows or columns into your worksheet.

Inserting a Row or Column

To insert a new row, you select a cell in the row where you want the new row placed. You then select Rows from the Insert menu. Excel will shift that row down, inserting a new blank row in its place. Inserting a new column follows the same process. Select a cell in the column where you want the new column inserted, and click Columns on the Insert menu. Excel will shift that column to the right, inserting a new blank column in its place.

To insert multiple rows or columns, select multiple cells before applying the Insert command. For example, to insert two new blank rows, select two adjacent cells in the same column, and click Rows on the Insert menu. To insert three new blank columns, select three adjacent cells in the same row, and click Columns on the Insert menu.

You can also insert individual cells within a row or column (rather than an entire row or column). To do this, select the range where you want the new cells placed, and click Cells on the Insert menu. Excel provides four options:

■ **Shift cells right**	Inserts new blank cells into the selected region, and moves the selected cells to the right. The new cells will have the same number of rows and columns as the selected cells.
■ **Shift cells down**	Inserts new blank cells into the selected region, and moves the selected cells down. The new cells will have the same number of rows and columns as the selected cells.
■ **Entire row**	Inserts an entire blank row.
■ **Entire column**	Inserts an entire blank column.

You can also insert rows and columns by right-clicking the selected cells and choosing Insert on the shortcut menu. This is equivalent to clicking the Cells command on the Insert menu.

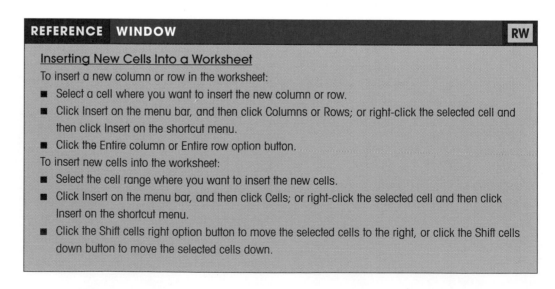

REFERENCE WINDOW   **RW**

Inserting New Cells Into a Worksheet

To insert a new column or row in the worksheet:
- Select a cell where you want to insert the new column or row.
- Click Insert on the menu bar, and then click Columns or Rows; or right-click the selected cell and then click Insert on the shortcut menu.
- Click the Entire column or Entire row option button.

To insert new cells into the worksheet:
- Select the cell range where you want to insert the new cells.
- Click Insert on the menu bar, and then click Cells; or right-click the selected cell and then click Insert on the shortcut menu.
- Click the Shift cells right option button to move the selected cells to the right, or click the Shift cells down button to move the selected cells down.

Now that you have seen how to insert new cells into your worksheet, you'll insert three new blank cells into the range A9:C9.

To insert three new cells into the worksheet:

1. Select the range **A9:C9**.

2. Click **Insert** on the menu bar, and then click **Cells**.

3. Click the **Shift cells down** option button, if necessary. See Figure 1-24.

Figure 1-24	INSERT DIALOG BOX

4. Click the **OK** button.

Excel inserts new blank cells in the range A9:C9 and shifts the rest of the income statement down one row.

TROUBLE? Excel displays an Insert Options button on the lower-right corner of cell C9. You can use this button to define how the new cells should be formatted. You will learn about formatting in Tutorial 3.

When you insert a new row, the formulas in the worksheet are automatically updated to reflect the changing position. For example, the formula for Net Income has changed from =C8–C16 to =C8–C17 to reflect the new location of the total liabilities cell. You will learn more about how formulas are adjusted in Tutorial 2.

Clearing or Deleting a Row or Column

Mike wants to make one further change to the income statement. He wants to consolidate the supplies and miscellaneous categories into one entry. Your first task will be to remove the current contents of the range A14:B14 (the supplies category). Excel provides two ways of removing data. One way, called **clearing**, simply deletes the contents of the cells. To clear the contents of a cell, you use either the Delete key or the Clear command on the Edit menu. Clearing the contents of a cell does not change the structure of the workbook; that is, the row is not removed from the worksheet. Do not press the spacebar to enter a blank character in an attempt to clear a cell's content. Excel treats a blank character as text, so even though the cell appears to be empty, it is not.

To remove the supplies category data:

1. Select the range **A14:B14**.

2. Press the **Delete** key. The text and values in the range A14:B14 are cleared.

   Now you can enter the text for the supplies and miscellaneous category.

3. In cell A14, type **Supplies & Misc.** and then press the **Tab** key.

   Now enter the total for the new category.

4. In cell B14, type **4,561** and then press the **Enter** key.

   TROUBLE? Do not worry that the Supplies & Misc category label in cell A14 appears to be cut off. The adjacent cell is no longer empty, and cell A14 is not wide enough to display the entire text entry. You will correct this problem shortly.

Now you need to delete the miscellaneous category from the income statement. Excel provides similar options for deleting rows, columns, and cells as it does for inserting them. To delete a row, column, or cell from the worksheet, you first select the cell or range and then click Delete on the Edit menu (you can also right-click the selected range and choose Delete on the shortcut menu). Excel provides you with the following delete options:

- **Shift cells left**   Deletes the selected cells and shifts cells from the right into the selected region
- **Shift cells up**   Deletes the selected cells and shifts cells from the bottom up into the selected region
- **Entire row**   Deletes the entire row
- **Entire column**   Deletes the entire column

Because you no longer need the miscellaneous category, you will delete the cell range A16:C16.

To delete the cell range A16:C16:

1. Select the range **A16:C16**.

2. Click **Edit** on the menu bar, and then click **Delete**.

3. Select the **Shift cells up** option button if necessary, and then click the **OK** button. Excel deletes the contents of the cell range and moves the cells below up one row. See Figure 1-25.

Figure 1-25	DELETING THE MISCELLANEOUS CATEGORY FROM THE INCOME STATEMENT

width of column A
needs to be increased

#REF! indicates that
there is an invalid cell
reference in the formula

Mike immediately sees two problems. One problem is that the text entry in cell A14 is cut off. The second is that the liabilities total in cell C16 and the net income in cell C18 have been replaced with *#REF!* The *#REF!* entry is Excel's way of indicating that there is an invalid cell reference in a formula. Because Excel cannot calculate the formula's value, Excel displays this text as a warning. The invalid cell reference occurred when the miscellaneous total was deleted. Since that cell no longer exists, any formula that is based on that cell, such as the formula that calculates the liability, will return an error message, and since the total liability now returns an error message, the formula for the net income on which the total liability value is based also returns an error.

So you need to do two things: 1) increase the width of column A so that no text is truncated, and 2) revise the formula in cell C16 to remove the error message. First you will change the width of column A.

Increasing the Width of a Column or the Height of a Row

Excel provides several methods for changing the width of a column or the height of a row. You can click the dividing line of the column or row, or you can drag the dividing line to change the width of the column or the height of the row. You can also double-click the border of a column heading, and the column will increase in width to match the length of the longest entry in the column. Widths are expressed either in terms of the number of characters or the number of screen pixels.

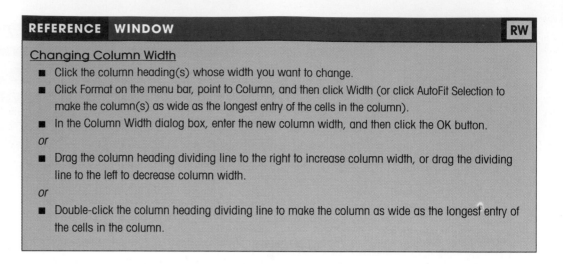

Changing Column Width

- Click the column heading(s) whose width you want to change.
- Click Format on the menu bar, point to Column, and then click Width (or click AutoFit Selection to make the column(s) as wide as the longest entry of the cells in the column).
- In the Column Width dialog box, enter the new column width, and then click the OK button.

or

- Drag the column heading dividing line to the right to increase column width, or drag the dividing line to the left to decrease column width.

or

- Double-click the column heading dividing line to make the column as wide as the longest entry of the cells in the column.

You'll drag the dividing line between columns A and B to increase the width of column A enough to display the complete text in cell A14.

To increase the width of column A:

1. Move the mouse pointer to the dividing line between the column A and column B headings until the pointer changes to ↔.

2. Click and drag the pointer to the right to a length of about **15** characters (or 110 pixels).

3. Release the mouse button. The entire text in cell A14 should now be visible. See Figure 1-26.

Figure 1-26   **INCREASING THE WIDTH OF COLUMN A**

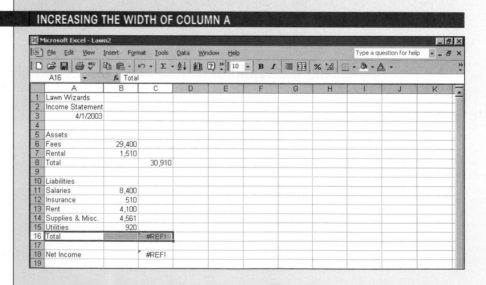

TROUBLE? If the text in cell A14 is still truncated, drag the dividing line further to the right.

Editing **Your Worksheet**

When you work in Excel you might make mistakes that you want to correct or undo. You have an error in the Lawn2 workbook of an invalid cell reference in cell C16. You could simply delete the formula in cell C16 and reenter the formula from scratch. However, there may be times when you will not want to change the entire contents of a cell, but merely edit a portion of the entry. For example, if a cell contains a large block of text or a complicated formula, you might not want to retype the text or formula completely. Instead, you can edit a cell by either selecting the cell and then clicking in the Formula bar to make the changes or by double-clicking the cell to open the cell in **edit mode**.

Working in Edit Mode

When you are working in edit mode or editing the cell using the Formula bar, some of the keys on your keyboard act differently than they do when you are not editing the content of a cell. For example, the Home, Delete, Backspace, and End keys do not move the insertion point to different cells in the worksheet; rather they move the insertion point to different locations within the cell. The Home key, for example, moves the insertion point to the beginning of whatever text has been entered into the cell. The End key moves the insertion point to the end of the cell's text. The left and right arrow keys move the insertion point backward and forward through the text in the cell. The Backspace key deletes the character immediately to the left of the insertion point, and the Delete key deletes the character at the location of the insertion point. Once you are finished editing the cell, press the Enter key to leave editing mode or to remove the insertion point from the Formula bar.

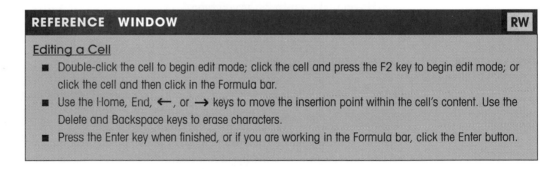

REFERENCE WINDOW   `RW`

Editing a Cell
- Double-click the cell to begin edit mode; click the cell and press the F2 key to begin edit mode; or click the cell and then click in the Formula bar.
- Use the Home, End, ←, or → keys to move the insertion point within the cell's content. Use the Delete and Backspace keys to erase characters.
- Press the Enter key when finished, or if you are working in the Formula bar, click the Enter button.

Now you'll use edit mode to change the formula in cell C16.

To edit the formula in cell C16:

1. Double-click cell **C16**.

An insertion point appears in the cell, indicating where new text will be inserted into the current cell expression. Note that the formula appears fine except for the *+#REF!* at the end of the expression. See Figure 1-27. This notation indicates that the cell reference used in the formula no longer points to a valid cell reference. In this case, the cell referenced was deleted. You can fix the error by deleting the *+#REF!* from the formula.

Figure 1-27 | **EDITING THE FORMULA IN CELL C16**

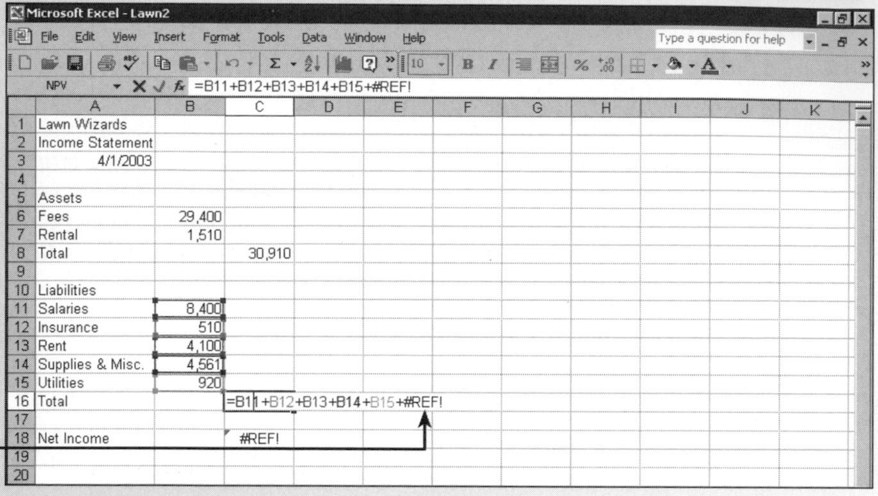

#REF! indicates a cell reference that no longer exists

2. Press the **End** key to move the blinking insertion point to the end of the cell.

3. Press the **Backspace** key six times to delete *+#REF!* from the formula.

4. Press the **Enter** key. The value 18,491 appears in cell C16, and the net income for the company is 12,419.

If you make a mistake as you type, you can press the Esc key or click the Cancel button on the Formula bar to cancel all changes you made while in edit mode.

Undoing an Action

Another way of fixing a mistake is to undo the action. Undoing an action cancels it, returning the workbook to its previous state. To undo an action, click the Undo button located on the Standard toolbar. As you work, Excel maintains a list of your actions, so you can undo most of the actions you perform on your workbook during your current session. To reverse more than one action, click the list arrow next to the Undo button and click the action you want to undo from the list. To see how this works, use the Undo button to remove the edit you just made to cell C16.

To undo your last action:

1. Click the **Undo** button [↶] on the Standard toolbar. The value *#REF!* appears again in cells C16 and C18 indicating that your last action, editing the formula in cell C16, has been undone.

If you find that you have gone too far in undoing your previous actions, you can go forward in the action list and redo those actions. To redo an action, you click the Redo button on the Standard toolbar. Use the Redo button now to return the formula in cell C16 to its edited state.

To redo your last action:

1. Click the **Redo** button ⟳ on the Standard toolbar. The edited formula has been reinserted into cell C16 and the value 18,491 again appears in the cell.

TROUBLE? If you don't see the Redo button, click the Toolbar Options button ⟩⟩ located on the right edge of the Standard toolbar, and then click ⟳ to repeat the delete (the Redo button will now appear on the toolbar). You can also click the Repeat Delete command on the Edit menu (you might have to wait a few seconds for Excel to display the full Edit menu). After you undo an action, the Repeat command changes to reflect the action that has been undone so you can choose to repeat the action if undoing the action does not give you the result you want.

Through the use of edit mode and the Undo and Redo buttons, you should be able to correct almost any mistake you make in your Excel session.

Working with Worksheets

By default, Excel workbooks contain three worksheets labeled Sheet1, Sheet2, and Sheet3. You can add new worksheets or remove old ones. You can also give your worksheets more descriptive names. In the Lawn2 workbook, there is no data entered in the Sheet2 or Sheet3 worksheets. Mike suggests that you remove these sheets from the workbook.

Adding and Removing Worksheets

To delete a worksheet, you first select its sheet tab to make the worksheet the active sheet; then right-click the sheet tab and choose Delete from the shortcut menu. Try this now by deleting the Sheet2 and Sheet3 worksheets.

To delete the Sheet2 and Sheet3 worksheets:

1. Click the **Sheet2** tab to make Sheet2 the active sheet.

2. Right-click the sheet tab, and then click **Delete** on the shortcut menu. Sheet2 is deleted and Sheet3 becomes the active sheet.

3. Right-click the **Sheet3** tab, and then click **Delete**.

There is now only one worksheet in the workbook.

After you have deleted the two unused sheets, Mike informs you that he wants to include a description of the workbook content and purpose. In other words, Mike wants to include a **documentation sheet**, a worksheet that provides information about the content and purpose of the workbook. A documentation sheet can be any information that you feel is important, for example, the name of the person who created the workbook or instructions on how to use the workbook. A documentation sheet is a valuable element if you intend to share the workbook with others. The documentation sheet is often the first worksheet in the workbook, though in this case Mike wants to place it at the end of the workbook.

To insert a new worksheet, you can either use the Insert Worksheet command or the right-click method. Using either method will insert a new worksheet before the active sheet.

To insert a new worksheet in the workbook:

1. Click **Insert** on the menu bar.

2. Click **Worksheet**. A new worksheet with the name "Sheet2" is placed at the beginning of your workbook.

Mike wants the documentation sheet to include the following information:

- The company name
- The date the workbook was originally created
- The person who created it
- The purpose of the workbook

You'll add this information to the new sheet in the Lawn2 workbook.

To insert the documentation information in the new worksheet:

1. Click cell **A1** if necessary, and then type **Lawn Wizards**.

2. Click cell **A3**, type **Date:** and then press the **Tab** key.

3. Enter the current date using the date format, mm/dd/yyyy. For example, if the date is April 5, 2003, enter the text string "4/5/2003." Press the **Enter** key.

4. In cell A4, type **Created By:** and then press the **Tab** key.

5. Enter your name in cell B4, and then press the **Enter** key.

6. Type **Purpose:** in cell A5, and then press the **Tab** key.

7. In cell B5, type **To record monthly income statements for the Lawn Wizards,** and then press the **Enter** key.

8. Increase the width of column A to **15** characters. Figure 1-28 shows the completed documentation sheet (your sheet will display a different name and date).

| Figure 1-28 | CREATING A DOCUMENTATION SHEET |

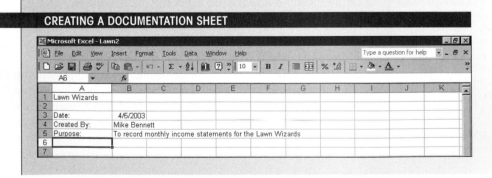

Renaming a Worksheet

The current sheet names "Sheet2" and "Sheet1" are not very descriptive. Mike suggests that you rename Sheet2 "Documentation" and Sheet1 "April Income". To rename a worksheet, you double-click the sheet tab to select the sheet name, and then you type a new name for the sheet.

Rename the sheet tabs using more meaningful names.

To rename the worksheets:

1. Double-click the **Sheet2** tab. Note that the name of the sheet is selected.

2. Type **Documentation** and then press the **Enter** key. The width of the sheet tab adjusts to the length of the name you type.

3. Double-click the **Sheet1** tab.

4. Type **April Income** and then press the **Enter** key.

Moving a Worksheet

Finally, Mike wants the Documentation sheet to appear last in the workbook. He feels that the actual data should be displayed first. To move the position of a worksheet in the workbook, you click the worksheet's sheet tab, and drag and drop it to a new location relative to the other worksheets.

You can create a copy of the entire worksheet by holding down the Ctrl key as you drag and drop the sheet tab. When you release the mouse button, a copy of the original worksheet will be placed at the new location, while the original sheet will stay at its initial position in the workbook.

REFERENCE WINDOW   **RW**

Moving or Copying a Worksheet
- Click the sheet tab of the worksheet you want to move (or copy).
- Drag the sheet tab along the row of sheet tabs until the small arrow appears in the desired location. To create a copy of the worksheet, press and hold down the Ctrl key as you drag the sheet tab to the desired location.
- Release the mouse button. Release the Ctrl key if necessary.

You'll move the Documentation sheet now.

To move the Documentation worksheet:

1. Click the **Documentation** tab to make it the active worksheet.

2. Click the **Documentation** tab again, and then press and hold down the left mouse button so the pointer changes to ▯. A small arrow appears in the upper-left corner of the sheet tab.

3. Drag the pointer to the right of the April Income tab, and then release the mouse button. The Documentation sheet is now the second sheet in the workbook.

Printing a Worksheet

Now that you are finished editing the Lawn2 workbook, you can create a hard copy of its contents for your records. You can print the contents of your workbook using either the Print command on the File menu or by clicking the Print button on the Standard toolbar. If you use the Print command, Excel displays a dialog box in which you can specify which worksheets you want to print, the number of copies, and the print quality (or resolution). If you click the Print button, you will not have a chance to set these options, but if you do not need to do so, clicking the Print button is a faster way of generating your output. Finally, you can also choose the Print Preview command on the File menu or click the Print Preview button on the Standard toolbar to see what your page will look like before it is sent to the printer. You can print directly from Print Preview.

If you are printing to a shared printer on a network, many other people might be sending print jobs at the same time you do. To avoid confusion, you will print the contents of both the Documentation sheet and the April Income sheet. You will use the Print command on the File menu since you need to print the entire workbook and not just the active worksheet (which is the default print setting). You will learn more about the Print Preview command in the next tutorial.

To print the contents of the Lawn2 workbook:

1. Click **File** on the menu bar, and then click **Print** to open the Print dialog box. See Figure 1-29.

Figure 1-29	PRINT DIALOG BOX

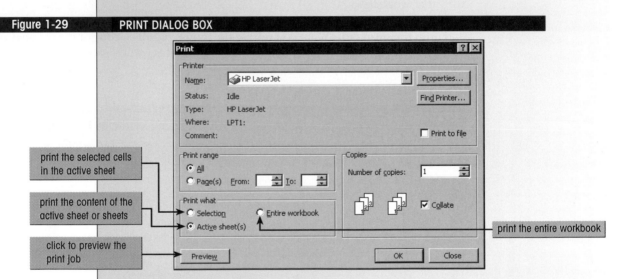

print the selected cells in the active sheet

print the content of the active sheet or sheets

click to preview the print job

print the entire workbook

2. Click the **Name** list box, and then select the printer to which you want to print.

   Now you need to select what to print. To print the complete workbook, select the Entire workbook option button. To print the active worksheet, select the Active sheet(s) option button. To print the selected cells on the active sheet, click the Selection option button.

3. Click the **Entire workbook** option button.

4. Make sure "1" appears in the Number of copies list box, since you only need to print one copy of the workbook.

5. Click the **OK** button to send the workbook to the printer.

TROUBLE? If the workbook does not print, see your instructor or technical resource person for help.

You have completed your work on the Lawn2 workbook, so you can save your changes and exit Excel.

6. Click the **Save** button 🖫 on the Standard toolbar, and then click the **Close** button ☒ on the title bar.

You give Mike the hard copy of the Lawn2 workbook. He will file the report for later reference. If he needs to add new information to the workbook or if he needs you to make further changes to the structure of the workbook, he will contact you.

Session 1.2 QUICK CHECK

1. Indicate whether Excel treats the following cell entries as a value, text, or a formula:
   a. 11/09/2003
   b. Net Income
   c. 321
   d. =C11*225
   e. 201-19-1121
   f. =D1-D9
   g. 44 Evans Avenue

2. What formula would you enter to divide the value in cell E5 by the value in cell E6?

3. What formula would you enter to raise the value in cell E5 to the power of the value in cell E6?

4. When you insert a new row into a worksheet, the selected cells are moved _____.

5. When you insert a new column into a worksheet, the selected cells are moved _____.

6. To change the name of a worksheet, double-click the _____.

7. Which key do you press to clear the contents of the active cell?

8. How does clearing a cell differ from deleting a cell?

REVIEW ASSIGNMENTS

Mike has another workbook in which he wants you to make some changes. This workbook contains the income and expense figures for May. Mike has already done some work on the file, but wants you to make some modifications and additions. To complete this task:

1. Start Excel and open the workbook **Income1** located in the Tutorial.01/Review folder on your Data Disk.

2. Save the workbook as **Income2** in the same folder.

3. Change the date in cell A3 to 5/1/2003.

4. Insert new cells in the range A12:C12, shifting the other cells down. In cell A12, enter the text "Rent". In cell B12, enter the value "4,100".

Explore   5. Edit the formula in cell C16 so that the formula includes the cost of rent in the liabilities total.

Explore   6. There is a mistake in the formula for the net income. Fix the formula so that it displays the difference between the assets and the liabilities in the month of May.

7. Move the income statement values in the range A5:C18 to the range C1:E14.

8. Resize the width of column C to 15 characters.

9. Insert a sheet named "Documentation" at the beginning of the workbook.

10. In the Documentation sheet, enter the following text:
    - Cell A1: Lawn Wizards
    - Cell A3: Date:
    - Cell B3: *Enter the current date*
    - Cell A4: Created By:
    - Cell B4: *Enter your name*
    - Cell A5: Purpose:
    - Cell B5: To record income and expenses for the month of May

11. Increase the width of column A in the Documentation worksheet to 20 characters.

12. Rename Sheet1 as **May Income**.

13. Delete Sheet2 and Sheet3.

14. Print the entire contents of the Income2 workbook.

15. Save and close the workbook, and then exit Excel.

CASE PROBLEMS

Case 1. Cash Flow Analysis at Madison Federal Lisa Wu is a financial consultant at Madison Federal. She is working on a financial plan for Tom and Carolyn Watkins. Lisa has a cash flow analysis for the couple, and she wants you to record this information for her. Here are the relevant financial figures:

Receipts
- Employment Income: 95,000
- Other Income: 5,000

Disbursements
- Insurance: 940
- Savings/Retirement: 8,400
- Living Expenses: 63,000
- Taxes: 16,300

Lisa wants you to calculate the total receipts and total disbursements and then to calculate the income surplus (receipts minus disbursements) in an Excel workbook that she has already started. To complete this task:

1. Open the **CFlow1** workbook located in the Tutorial.01/Cases folder on your Data Disk, and then save the workbook as **CFlow2** in the same folder.

2. Move the contents of the range A1:C12 to the range A3:C14.

3. Insert the text "Cash Flow Analysis" in cell A1.

4. Increase the width of column A to 130 pixels, the width of column B to 160 pixels, and the width of column C to 130 pixels.

5. Insert the financial numbers listed earlier into the appropriate cells in column C.

6. In cell C6, insert a formula to calculate the total receipts.

7. In cell C12, insert a formula to calculate the total disbursements.

8. Insert a formula to calculate the surplus in cell C14.

9. Rename Sheet1 as **Cash Flow**.

10. Insert a worksheet at the beginning of the workbook named "Documentation".

11. In the Documentation sheet, enter the following text:

    ■ Cell A1: Cash Flow Report
    ■ Cell A3: Date:
    ■ Cell B3: *Enter the current date*
    ■ Cell A4: Created By:
    ■ Cell B4: *Enter your name*
    ■ Cell A5: Purpose:
    ■ Cell B5: Cash flow analysis for Tom and Carolyn Watkins

12. Increase the width of column A in the Documentation worksheet to 20 characters.

13. Delete Sheet2 and Sheet3.

14. Print the contents of the entire workbook.

Explore ▶ 15. What would the surplus be if the couple's taxes increased to 18,500? Enter this value into the Cash Flow worksheet, and then print just the Cash Flow worksheet.

16. Save and close the workbook, and then exit Excel.

Case 2. Financial Report for EMS Industries Lee Evans is an agent at New Haven Financial Services. His job is to maintain financial information on stocks for client companies. He has the annual balance sheet for a company named EMS Industries in an Excel workbook and needs your help in finishing the workbook layout and contents. To complete this task:

1. Open the **Balance1** workbook located in the Tutorial.01/Cases folder on your Data Disk, and then save the workbook as **Balance2** in the same folder.

2. Select the cells A1:C2 and insert two new rows into the worksheet.

3. Insert the text "Annual Balance Sheet for EMS Industries" in cell A1.

4. Move the contents of the range A19:C33 to the range E3:G17.

5. Move the contents of the range B36:C38 to the range B19:C21.

6. Change the width of column B to 150 pixels, the width of column D to 20 pixels, and the width of column F to 150 pixels.

7. Insert a formula in cell C10 to calculate the total current assets, in cell C17 to calculate the total noncurrent assets, in cell G10 to calculate the total current liabilities, and in cell G17 to calculate the total noncurrent liabilities.

8. In cell C19, insert a formula to calculate the total of the current and noncurrent assets.

9. In cell C20, insert a formula to calculate the total of the current and noncurrent liabilities.

10. In cell C21, insert a formula to calculate the annual balance (the total assets minus the total liabilities).

11. Rename Sheet1 as **Annual Balance Sheet**.

12. Delete Sheet2 and Sheet3.

13. Insert a worksheet named "Documentation" at the front of the workbook.

14. Enter the following text into the Documentation sheet:

- Cell A1: Annual Balance Report
- Cell A3: Company:
- Cell B3: EMS Industries
- Cell A4: Date:
- Cell B4: *Enter the current date*
- Cell A5: Recorded By:
- Cell B5: *Enter your name*
- Cell A6: Summary:
- Cell B6: Annual Balance Sheet

15. Increase the width of column A in the Documentation worksheet to 20 characters.

16. Print the entire contents of the workbook.

17. Save and close the workbook, and then exit Excel.

Case 3. Analyzing Sites for a New Factory for Kips Shoes   Kips Shoes is planning to build a new factory. The company has narrowed the site down to four possible cities. Each city has been graded on a 1-to-10 scale for four categories: the size of the local market, the quality of the labor pool, the local tax base, and the local operating expenses. Each of these four factors is given a weight with the most important factor given the highest weight. After the sites are analyzed, the scores for each factor will be multiplied by their weights, and then a total weighted score will be calculated.

Gwen Sanchez has entered the weights and the scores for each city into an Excel workbook. She needs you to finish the workbook by inserting the formulas to calculate the weighted scores and the total overall score for each city. To complete this task:

1. Open the **Site1** workbook located in the Tutorial.01/Cases folder on your Data Disk, and then save the workbook as **Site2** in the same folder.

2. Switch to the Site Analysis sheet.

3. In cell B12, calculate the weighted Market Size score for Waukegan by inserting a formula that multiplies the value in cell B5 by the value in cell C5.

4. Insert formulas to calculate the weighted scores for the rest of the cells in the range B12:E15.

5. Insert formulas in the range B17:E17 that calculate the totals of the weighted scores for each of the four cities. Which city has the highest weighted score?

6. Switch to the Documentation sheet, and enter your name and the date in the appropriate location on the sheet.

7. Print the entire workbook.

Explore

8. Gwen reports that Brockton's score for market size should be 6 and not 5. Modify this entry in the table, and then print just the Site Analysis worksheet with the new total scores. Does this change your conclusions about which city is most preferable for the new factory?

9. Save and close the workbook, and then exit Excel.

Case 4. Cash Counting Calculator   Rob Stuben works at a local town beach in Narragansett where a fee is collected for parking. At the end of each day, the parking attendants turn in the cash they have collected with a statement of the daily total. Rob is responsible for receiving the daily cash from each attendant, checking the accuracy of the daily total, and taking the cash deposit to the bank.

Rob wants to set up a simple cash counter using Excel, so that he can insert the number of bills of each denomination into a worksheet so the total cash is automatically computed. By a simple cash counter method, he only has to count and enter the number of one-dollar bills, the number of fives, and so on. To complete this task:

1. Save a new workbook with the name **CashCounter** in the Tutorial.01/Cases folder on your Data Disk.

Explore

2. In the workbook, create a worksheet named **Counter** with the following properties:

   ■ All currency denominations (1, 5, 10, 20, 50, 100) should be listed in the first column of the worksheet.

   ■ In the second column, you will enter the number of bills of each denomination, but this column should be left blank initially.

   ■ In the third column, insert the formulas to calculate totals for each denomination, (that is, the number of bills multiplied by the denomination of each bill).

   ■ In a blank cell at the bottom of the third column, which contains the formulas for calculating the totals of each denomination, a formula that calculates the grand total of the cash received should be entered.

3. Create a Documentation sheet. The sheet should include the title of the workbook, the date the workbook was created, your name, and the purpose of the workbook. Make this worksheet the first worksheet in the workbook.

4. Adjust the widths of the columns, if necessary. Delete any blank worksheets from the workbook.

Explore

5. On Rob's first day using the worksheet, the cash reported by an attendant was $1,565. Rob counted the bills and separated them by denomination. Enter the following values into the worksheet:

   ■ 5 fifties

   ■ 23 twenties

   ■ 41 tens

   ■ 65 fives

   ■ 120 ones

6. Print the entire contents of your workbook.

Explore 7. On Rob's second day, the cash reported by an attendant was $1,395. Again, Rob counted the money and separated the bills by denomination. Clear the previous values, and then enter the new values for the distribution of the bills into the worksheet:

  - 2 hundreds
  - 4 fifties
  - 17 twenties
  - 34 tens
  - 45 fives
  - 90 ones

8. Print just the Counter worksheet.

9. Save and close the workbook, and then exit Excel.

LAB ASSIGNMENTS

The New Perspectives Labs are designed to help you master some of the key computer concepts and skills presented in each chapter of the text. If you are using your school's lab computers, your instructor or technical support person should have installed the Labs software for you. If you want to use the Labs on your home computer, ask your instructor for the appropriate software. See the Read This Before You Begin page for more information on installing and starting the Lab.

Each Lab has two parts: Steps and Explore. Use Steps first to learn and review concepts. Read the information on each page and do the numbered steps. As you work through the Lab, you will be asked to answer Quick Check questions about what you have learned. At the end of the Lab, you will see a Summary Report of your answers to the Quick Checks. If your instructor wants you to turn in this Summary Report, click the Print button on the Summary Report screen.

When you have completed Steps, you can click the Explore button to complete the Lab Assignments. You can also use Explore to practice the skills you learned and to explore concepts on your own.

SPREADSHEETS Spreadsheet software is used extensively in business, education, science, and humanities to simplify tasks that involve calculations. In this Lab you will learn how spreadsheet software works. You will use spreadsheet software to examine and modify worksheets, as well as to create your own worksheets.

1. Click the Steps button to learn how spreadsheet software works. As you proceed through the Steps, answer all of the Quick Check questions that appear. After you complete the Steps, you will see a Quick Check Summary Report. Follow the instructions on the screen to print this report.

2. Click the Explore button to begin this assignment. Click OK to display a new worksheet. Click File on the menu bar, and then click Open to display the Open dialog box. Click the file **Income.xls** and then press the Enter key to open the **Income and Expense Summary** workbook. Notice that the worksheet contains labels and values for income from consulting and training. It also contains labels and values for expenses

such as rent and salaries. The worksheet does not, however, contain formulas to calculate Total Income, Total Expenses, or Profit. Do the following:

a. Calculate the Total Income by entering the formula =SUM(C4:C5) in cell C6.
b. Calculate the Total Expenses by entering the formula =SUM(C9:C12) in C13.
c. Calculate Profit by entering the formula =C6-C13 in cell C15.
d. Manually check the results to make sure you entered the formulas correctly.
e. Print your completed worksheet showing your results.

3. You can use a spreadsheet to keep track of your grades in a class and to calculate your grade average. In Explore, click File on the menu bar, and then click Open to display the Open dialog box. Click the file **Grades.xls** to open the workbook. The worksheet contains the labels and formulas necessary to calculate your grade average based on four test scores. You receive a score of 88 out of 100 on the first test. On the second test, you score 42 out of 48. On the third test, you score 92 out of 100. You have not taken the fourth test yet. Enter the appropriate data in the **Grades.xls** worksheet to determine your grade average after taking three tests. Print out your worksheet.

4. Worksheets are handy for answering "what if" questions. Suppose you decide to open a lemonade stand. You're interested in how much profit you can make each day. What if you sell 20 cups of lemonade? What if you sell 100? What if the cost of lemons increases?

In Explore, open the file **Lemons.xls** and use the worksheet to answer questions a through d. Then print the worksheet for question e:

a. What is your profit if you sell 20 cups a day?
b. What is your profit if you sell 100 cups a day?
c. What is your profit if the price of lemons increases to $.07 and you sell 100 cups?
d. What is your profit if you raise the price of a cup of lemonade to $.30? (Lemons still cost $.07 and assume you sell 100 cups.)
e. Suppose your competitor boasts that she sold 50 cups of lemonade in one day and made exactly $12.00. On your worksheet adjust the cost of cups, water, lemons, and sugar, and the price per cup to show a profit of exactly $12.00 for 50 cups sold. Print this worksheet.

5. It is important to make sure the formulas in your worksheet are accurate. An easy way to test this is to enter 1's for all the values on your worksheet, then check the calculations manually. In Explore, open the file **Receipt.xls**, which contains a formula that calculates sales receipts. Enter "1" as the value for Item 1, Item 2, Item 3, and Sales Tax %. Now manually calculate what you would pay for three items that each cost $1.00 in a state where sales tax is 1% (.01). Do your manual calculations match those of the worksheet? If not, correct the formulas in the worksheet, and then print out a *formula report* of your revised worksheet.

6. In Explore, create your own worksheet showing your household budget for one month. Make up the numbers for the budget. Put a title at the top of the worksheet. Use formulas to calculate your total income and expenses for the month. Add another formula to calculate how much money you were able to save. Print a formula report of your worksheet. Also, print your worksheet showing realistic values for one month.

INTERNET ASSIGNMENTS

Student Union

The purpose of the Internet Assignments is to challenge you to find information on the Internet that you can use to create effective spreadsheets. The actual assignments are updated and maintained on the Course Technology Web site. Log on to the Internet and use your Web browser to go to the Student Union on the New Perspectives Series site at **www.course.com/NewPerspectives/studentunion**. Click the Online Companions link, and then click the link for this text.

QUICK CHECK ANSWERS

Session 1.1

1. cell
2. D2
3. Ctrl + Home
4. Click the Sheet2 tab.
5. Adjacent and nonadjacent. An adjacent range is a rectangular block of cells. A nonadjacent range consists of two or more separate adjacent ranges.
6. A5:F8
7. Select the cells you want to move, and then press and hold down the Alt key and drag the selection over the Sheet2 tab. When Sheet2 becomes the active sheet, continue to drag the selection to position it in its new location in the worksheet, and then release the left mouse button and the Alt key.

Session 1.2

1. **a.** value
   b. text
   c. value
   d. formula
   e. text
   f. formula
   g. text
2. =E5/E6
3. =E5^E6
4. down
5. to the right
6. sheet tab and then type the new name to replace the highlighted sheet tab name
7. Delete key
8. Clearing a cell deletes the cell's contents but does not affect the position of other cells in the workbook. Deleting a cell removes the cell from the worksheet, and other cells are shifted into the deleted cell's position.

WORKING WITH FORMULAS AND FUNCTIONS

Analyzing a Mortgage

CASE

Prime Realty

You work as an assistant at Prime Realty (PR) selling real estate. One of the agents at PR, Carol Malloy, has asked you to help her develop an Excel workbook that calculates mortgages. The workbook needs to include three values: the size of the loan, the number of payments, and the annual interest rate. Using this information in the workbook, you will be able to determine the monthly payment needed to pay off the loan and the total cost of the mortgage over the loan's history. Carol wants the workbook to display a table showing the monthly payments with information describing how much of the payment is for interest and how much is applied toward the principal. Carol also wants the workbook to be flexible enough so that if a client intends on making additional payments, beyond the required monthly payment, the workbook will show how the cost of the loan and subsequent payments are affected.

In this tutorial, you will use Excel's financial functions to create the workbook for the mortgage calculations.

SESSION 2.1

In this session, you will learn about Excel's functions. You will insert functions and function arguments. You will copy and paste formulas and functions into your workbook. Finally, you will learn about absolute and relative references and how to insert them into your formulas.

Working **with** Excel Functions

Carol has already started the loan workbook. She has not entered any values yet, but she has entered some text and a documentation sheet. Open her workbook now.

To open Carol's workbook:

1. Start Excel and then open the **Loan1** workbook located in the Tutorial.02/Tutorial folder on your Data Disk.

2. On the Documentation sheet, enter your name in cell B3.

3. Click the **Mortgage** tab to make the sheet the active worksheet. See Figure 2-1.

Figure 2-1   **THE LOAN WORKBOOK**

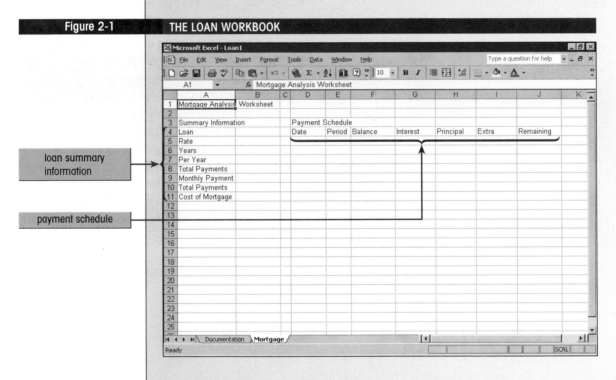

4. Save the workbook as **Loan2** in the Tutorial.02/Tutorial folder on your Data Disk.

The Mortgage worksheet is divided into two sections. The Summary Information section is the area in which you will enter the basic information about the loan, including the amount of the loan, the current interest rate, and the length of the mortgage. Figure 2-2 provides a description of the information that you will enter in the cells in that section.

Figure 2-2   CELLS IN THE SUMMARY INFORMATION SECTION

CELL	DESCRIPTION
B4	Enter the amount of the loan
B5	Enter the interest rate
B6	Enter the length of the mortgage in years
B7	Enter the number of periods (months) that the interest will be compounded each year
B8	Calculate the total number of periods in the loan
B9	Calculate the monthly payment
B10	Calculate the total payments on the loan
B11	Calculate the cost of the loan (total payments minus the amount of the loan)

The other section of the worksheet contains the payment schedule; it indicates how much is paid toward the principal and how much is paid in interest each month. The schedule also indicates the balance remaining on the loan each month. Figure 2-3 describes the values to be placed in each column.

Figure 2-3   COLUMNS IN THE PAYMENT SCHEDULE

COLUMN	DESCRIPTION
Date	Date that loan payment is due
Period	Loan payment period
Balance	Balance of loan remaining to be paid
Interest	Interest due
Principal	Portion of the monthly payment used to reduce the principal
Extra	Extra payments beyond the scheduled monthly payment
Remaining	Balance of loan remaining after the monthly payment

To make this worksheet operational, you need to use financial functions that are provided in Excel.

Function Syntax

In the previous tutorial you used formulas to calculate values. For example, the formula =*A1+A2+A3+A4* totals the values in the range A1:A4 and places the sum in the active cell. Although calculating sums this way for small ranges works fine, a formula that calculates the sum of 100 cells would be so large that it would become unmanageable. In Excel you can easily calculate the sum of a large number of cells by using a function. A **function** is a pre-defined, or built-in, formula for a commonly used calculation.

Each Excel function has a name and syntax. The **syntax** specifies the order in which you must enter the different parts of the function and the location in which you must insert commas, parentheses, and other punctuation. The general syntax for an Excel function is =FUNCTION(*argument1, argument2, ...*), where FUNCTION is the name of the Excel function, and *argument1*, *argument2*, and so on are **arguments**—the numbers, text, or cell references used by the function to calculate a value. Some arguments are **optional arguments** because they are not necessary for the function to return a value. If you omit an optional argument, Excel assumes a default value for it. By convention, optional arguments will appear in this text within square brackets along with the default value. For example, in the function =FUNCTION(*argument1*,[*argument2=value*]), the second argument is optional, and *value* is the default value assigned to *argument2* if a value is omitted from the argument list. A convention that you will follow in this text is to display function names in uppercase letters; however, when you enter formulas into your own Excel worksheets, you can use either uppercase or lowercase letters.

Excel supplies over 350 different functions organized into 10 categories:

- Database functions
- Date and Time functions
- Engineering functions
- Financial functions
- Information functions
- Logical functions
- Lookup functions
- Math functions
- Statistical functions
- Text and Data functions

You can learn about each function using Excel's online Help. Figure 2-4 describes some of the more important math and statistical functions that you may often use in your workbooks.

Figure 2-4	MATH AND STATISTICAL FUNCTIONS
FUNCTION	**DESCRIPTION**
AVERAGE(*values*)	Calculates the average value in a set of numbers, where *values* is either a cell reference or a collection of cell references separated by commas
COUNT(*values*)	Counts the number of cells containing numbers, where *values* is either a cell reference or a range of cell references separated by commas
MAX(*values*)	Calculates the largest value in a set of numbers, where *values* is either a cell reference or a range of cell references separated by commas
MIN(*values*)	Calculates the smallest value in a set of numbers, where *values* is either a cell reference or a range of cell references separated by commas
ROUND(*number, num_digits*)	Rounds a *number* to a specified number of digits, indicated by the *num_digits* arguments
SUM(*numbers*)	Calculates the sum of a collection of numbers, where *numbers* is either a cell or a range reference or a series of numbers separated by commas

For example, the SUM function calculates the total for the values in a range of cells. The SUM function has only one argument, the cell reference containing the values to be totaled. To calculate the total of the cells in the range A1:A100, you would insert the expression =SUM(A1:A100) into the active cell.

Functions can also be combined with formulas. For example, the expression =MAX(A1:A100)/100 returns the maximum value in the range A1:A100 and then divides the value by 100. One function can also be nested inside the other. The expression =ROUND(AVERAGE(A1:A100),1) uses the AVERAGE function to calculate the average of the values in the range A1:A100 and then uses the ROUND function to round the average value off to the first decimal place.

By combining functions and formulas, you can create very sophisticated expressions to handle almost any situation.

Financial Functions

In Carol's workbook, you will use one of Excel's financial functions to calculate information about the loan. Figure 2-5 describes a few of Excel's financial functions in more detail.

Figure 2-5	FINANCIAL FUNCTIONS
FUNCTION	**DESCRIPTION**
FV(*rate,nper,pmt,*[*pv=*0],[*type=*0])	Calculates the future value of an investment based on periodic, constant payments, and a constant interest rate, where *rate* is the interest rate per period, *nper* is the number of periods, *pmt* is the payment per period, *pv* is the present value of the investment, and *type* indicates when payments are due (*type=*0 for payments at the end of each period, *type=*1 for payments at the beginning of each period)
IPMT(*rate,per,nper pv,*[*fv=*0],[*type=*0])	Calculates the interest payment for a given period for an investment based on period cash payments and a constant interest rate, where *fv* is the future value of the investment
PMT(*rate,nper,pv,*[*fv=*0],[*type=*0]	Calculates the payment for a loan based on constant payments and a constant interest rate
PPMT(*rate,per,nper,pv,*[*fv=*0],[*type=*0])	Calculates the payment on the principal for a given period for an investment based on period cash payments and a constant interest rate
PV(*rate,nper,pmt,*[*fv=*0],[*type=*0])	Calculates the present value of an investment

You need a function to calculate the monthly payment that will pay off a loan at a fixed interest rate. You can use Excel's PMT function to do just that. The syntax of the PMT function is PMT(*rate,nper,pv,*[*fv=*0],[*type=*0]) where *rate* is the interest rate per period of the loan, *nper* is the total number of periods, *pv* is the present value of the loan, *fv* is the future value, and *type* specifies whether the payment is made at the beginning of each period (*type=*1) or at the end of each period (*type=*0). Note that both the *fv* and *type* arguments are optional arguments. If you omit the *fv* argument, Excel assumes that the future value will be 0, in other words that the loan will be completely paid off. If you omit the *type* argument, Excel assumes a type value of 0 so that the loan is paid off at the end of each period.

For example, if Carol wanted to know the monthly payment for a $50,000 loan at 9% annual interest compounded monthly over 10 years, the arguments for the PMT function would be *PMT(0.09/12,10*12,50000)*. Note that the yearly interest rate is divided by the number of periods (months) for the interest rate per period. Similarly, the number of periods (months) is multiplied by the number of years in order to arrive at the total number of periods.

The value returned by the PMT function is –633.38, indicating that a client would have to spend $633.38 per month to pay off the loan in 10 years. Excel uses a negative value to indicate that the value is an expense rather than income.

You can also use the PMT function for annuities other than loans. For example, if you want to determine how much money to save at a 6% annual interest rate compounded monthly so that you will have $5000 at the end of five years, you use the following PMT function: *=PMT(0.06/12,5*12,0,5000)*. Note that the present value is 0 (since you are starting out with no money in the account) and the future value is 5000 (since that is the amount you want to have after 5 years). In this case, Excel will return a value of –71.66, indicating that you would have to invest $71.66 per month to achieve $5000 in your savings account after 5 years.

Inserting a Function

Carol wants to calculate the monthly payment for a 20-year loan of $150,000 at 7.5% annual interest compounded monthly. First you need to enter this information into the workbook. You also need to enter a formula that will calculate the total number of monthly payments.

To add the loan information:

1. Click cell **B4**, type **$150,000** and then press the **Enter** key. Even though you have added a dollar symbol in writing the loan amount, Excel still interprets cell B4 as a numeric value and not a text string.

2. In cell B5, type **7.5%** and then press the **Enter** key. Note that when you type a percentage into a worksheet cell, Excel interprets the percentage as a value. The actual value in cell B5 is 0.075; the value is just *formatted* to appear with the percent sign. You will learn more about how Excel formats numbers in the next tutorial.

3. In cell B6, type **20** and then press the **Enter** key.

4. In cell B7, type **12** since there are 12 payment periods in each year, and then press the **Enter** key.

   Note that in this text you can *enter* a cell reference in a formula or function by clicking the cell or by typing the cell reference.

5. In cell B8, enter the formula **=B6*B7** for the total number of payments in the mortgage, and then press the **Enter** key. The value 240 appears in cell B8, and cell B9 is now the active cell.

Now you will use the PMT function to calculate the required monthly payment to pay off the loan under the terms of the mortgage. You could simply type the function and its arguments into the cell, but you will often find that you have forgotten which arguments are required by the function and the correct order in which the arguments need to be entered. To assist you, Excel provides the Insert Function button on the Formula bar. Clicking this button displays a dialog box from which you can choose the function you want to enter. Once you choose a function, another dialog box opens in which you specify values for all of the function's arguments.

REFERENCE WINDOW   **RW**

Inserting a Function

- Click the cell in which you will insert the function.
- Click the Insert Function button on the Formula bar.
- Select the type of function you want from the select a category list box, and then select the function category; or type information about the function in the Search for a function text box, and then click the Go button.
- Select the function in the Select a function list box.
- Click the OK button to view the arguments for the selected function.
- Enter values for each required argument in the Function Arguments dialog box.
- Click the OK button.

You will insert the PMT function in the Summary Information section of the Mortgage worksheet to determine the monthly payment required to pay off a mortgage. You will use the Insert Function button on the Formula bar to insert the PMT function.

To insert the PMT function:

1. With cell B9 as the active cell, click the **Insert Function** button 𝑓ₓ on the Formula bar. The Insert Function dialog box opens. See Figure 2-6.

Figure 2-6   **INSERT FUNCTION DIALOG BOX**

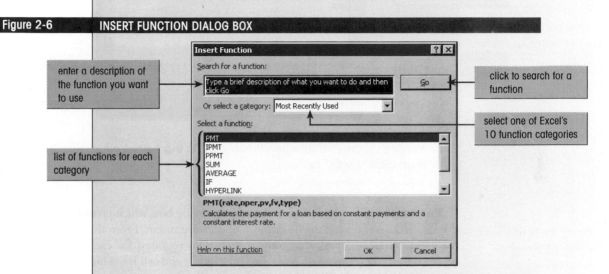

There are two ways to select a function using this dialog box. If you know something about the function but are not sure in which category the function belongs, enter a text description in the Search for a function text box and click the Go button. Excel will search for the functions that match your description. If you know the general category, select the category from the select a category list box; then Excel will list all of the functions in that category. Browse through the function list to find the function you need.

2. Type **calculate mortgage payments** in the Search for a function text box, and then click the **Go** button. Excel returns the PMT, IPMT, and NPER functions in the Select a function list box. Note that a description of the selected function and its arguments appears at the bottom of the dialog box. See Figure 2-7.

Figure 2-7   SEARCHING FOR A FUNCTION

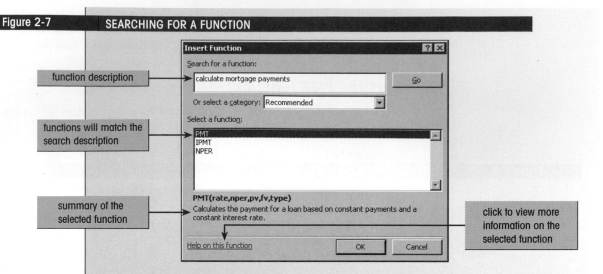

function description

functions will match the
search description

summary of the
selected function

click to view more
information on the
selected function

3. Verify that the PMT function is selected in the Select a function list box, and then click the **OK** button.

Excel next displays the Function Arguments dialog box, which provides all of the arguments in the selected function and the description of each argument. From this dialog box, you can select the cells in the workbook that contain the values required for each argument. Note that the expression =*PMT()* appears in both the Formula bar and cell B9. This display indicates that Excel is starting to insert the PMT function for you. You have to use the Function Arguments dialog box to complete the process.

You will start by entering the value for the Rate argument. Remember that rate refers to the interest rate per period. In this case, that value is 7.5% divided by 12, or if you use the cells in the worksheet, the value in cell B5 is divided by the value in cell B7. You can enter the cell references either by typing them into the appropriate argument boxes or by pointing to a cell with the mouse pointer, in which case Excel will automatically insert the cell reference into the appropriate box.

To insert values into the PMT function:

1. With the blinking insertion point in the Rate argument box, click cell **B5**, type **/**, and then click cell **B7**. The expression *B5/B7* appears in the box and the value 0.00625 appears to the right of the box.

   TROUBLE? If necessary, move the dialog box to view column B before clicking cell B5.

2. Press the **Tab** key to move to the Nper argument box.

3. Click cell **B8** for the 240 total payments needed for this loan, and then press the **Tab** key.

   The present value of the loan is $150,000, which is found in cell B4.

4. Click cell **B4** to enter the value of the loan in the Pv argument box. Figure 2-8 shows the completed Function Arguments dialog box.

Figure 2-8   **ENTERING ARGUMENT VALUES**

interest rate per period

total payment periods

the present value (the loan amount)

value that will be returned by the PMT function

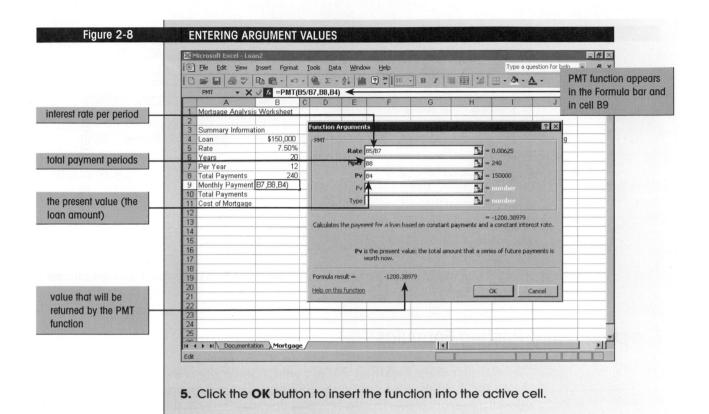

PMT function appears in the Formula bar and in cell B9

5. Click the **OK** button to insert the function into the active cell.

Excel displays the value ($1,208.39) with a red colored font in cell B9. This is a general format that Excel uses to display negative currency values. Carol would rather have the monthly payment appear as a positive value, so you will have to insert a negative sign in front of the PMT function to switch the monthly payment to a positive value. You will also complete the rest of the Summary Information section.

To complete the Summary Information section:

1. Double-click cell **B9** to enter edit mode.

2. Click directly to the right of the = (equal sign), type – so that the expression changes to =–PMT(B5/B7,B8,B4), and then press the **Enter** key.

3. In cell B10, enter **=B9*B8** and then press the **Enter** key.

4. In cell B11, enter **=B10-B4** and then press the **Enter** key. Figure 2-9 shows the complete summary information for this loan.

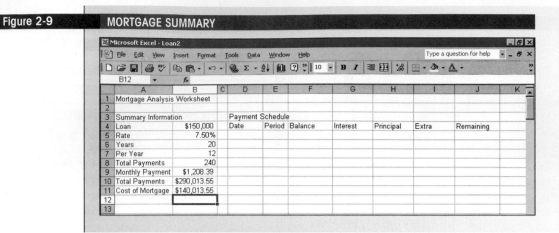

Figure 2-9   MORTGAGE SUMMARY

The required monthly payment for this loan will be $1,208.39. The total interest payments will be $140,013.55.

Copying and Pasting Formulas

The next part of the worksheet that you need to work with is the payment schedule, which details the monthly payments on the mortgage. Before entering values into the payment schedule, you should consider the functions that you will use in the schedule. Each row of the payment schedule represents the condition of the loan for a single month of the mortgage.

The Date column (column D in the worksheet) will contain the date on which a payment is due. At this point you will not enter any date information (you will do that later in the tutorial). The Period column specifies the number of periods in the mortgage. The first month is period 1, the second month is period 2, and so forth. Since there are 240 payment periods, this payment schedule will extend from row 5 down to row 244 in the worksheet. The Balance column displays the balance left on the loan at the beginning of each period. The initial balance value is the amount of the loan, which is found in cell B4. After the initial period, the balance will be equal to the remaining balance from the previous period.

The Interest column is the amount of interest due on the balance, which is equal to: Balance * Interest rate per period. In this example, the interest rate per period is the annual interest rate (in cell B5) divided by the number of periods in a year (in cell B7).

Subtracting the interest due from the monthly payment (cell B9) tells you how much is paid toward reducing the principal. This value is placed in column H of the worksheet. Carol knows that sometimes clients will want to make extra payments each month in order to pay off the loan quicker (and thereby reduce the overall cost of the mortgage). The Extra column (column I in the worksheet) is used for recording these values. Finally, the remaining balance will be equal to the balance at the beginning of the month minus the payment toward the principal and any extra payments.

Now that you have reviewed what values and functions will go into each column of the payment schedule, you are ready to insert the first row of the schedule.

To insert the first row of values in the payment schedule:

1. Click cell **E5**, type **1** and then press the **Tab** key.

   Now you will enter the initial balance, which is equal to the amount of the loan found in cell B4. Rather than typing in the value itself, you will enter a reference to the cell. If you change the amount of the loan, this change will be automatically reflected in the payment schedule.

2. In cell F5, enter **=B4** and then press the **Tab** key.

   Next you will enter the interest due in this period, which is equal to the balance multiplied by the interest rate per period (cell B5 divided by cell B7).

3. In cell G5, enter **=F5*B5/B7** and then press the **Tab** key.

   TROUBLE? Note that if the values in cells F5 and G5 are displayed with a different number of decimal places, do not worry. You will learn more about formatting cells in Tutorial 3.

   The payment toward the principal is equal to the monthly payment (cell B9) minus the interest payment (cell G5).

4. In cell H5, enter **=B9-G5** and then press the **Tab** key.

   At this point there are no extra payments toward the mortgage so you will enter $0 in the Extra column. The balance remaining is equal to the present balance minus the payment towards the principal and any extra payments.

5. In cell I5, type **$0** and then press the **Tab** key.

6. In cell J5, enter **=F5-(H5+I5)** and then press the **Enter** key. Figure 2-10 shows the first period values in the payment schedule.

Figure 2-10	FIRST PERIOD VALUES IN THE PAYMENT SCHEDULE

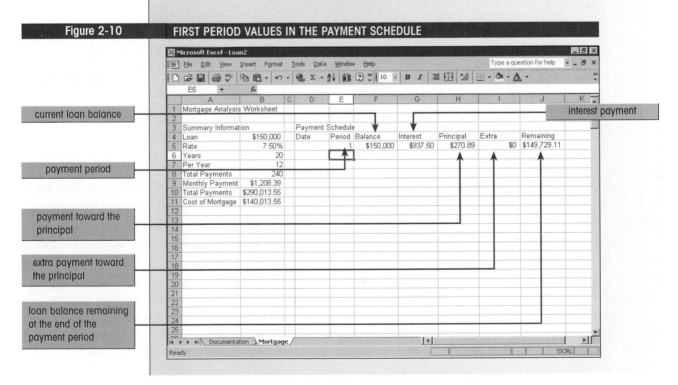

current loan balance

interest payment

payment period

payment toward the principal

extra payment toward the principal

loan balance remaining at the end of the payment period

You could have also calculated the monthly interest payment using Excel's IPMT function and the monthly payment toward the principal using the PPMT function. However, both of these functions assume that there will be no extra payments toward the principal. This assumption is something that Carol does not want to omit in her payment schedule.

The second row of the payment schedule is similar to the first. The only difference is that the balance (to be displayed in cell F6) will be carried over from the remaining balance (displayed in cell J5) in the previous row. At this point, you could retype the formulas that you used in the first row of the payment schedule. However, it is much easier and more efficient to copy and paste the formulas. When you **copy** the contents of a range, Excel places the formulas and values in those cells in a memory location called the **Clipboard**. The contents remain on the Clipboard until you **paste** them. You can paste the contents of the selected cells into another location on your worksheet, into a different worksheet or workbook, or even into another Windows application.

REFERENCE WINDOW   **RW**

Copying and Pasting a Cell or Range
- Select the cell or range to be copied.
- Click the Copy button on the Standard toolbar.
- Select the cell or range into which you want to copy the selection.
- Click the Paste button on the Standard toolbar.
- If necessary, click the Paste Options button to apply a paste-related option to the pasted selection.
- Press the Esc key to deselect the selection.

Next you will copy and paste a range of values in the worksheet.

To insert the second row of values in the payment schedule:

1. Click cell **E6**, type **2** and then press the **Tab** key.

2. In cell F6, enter **=J5** (since the remaining balance needs to be carried over into the second payment period), and then press the **Enter** key.

   Now you will copy the formulas from the range G5:J5 to the range G6:J6.

3. Select the range **G5:J5** and then click the **Copy** button on the Standard toolbar.

   TROUBLE? If you do not see the Copy button on the Standard toolbar, click the Toolbar Options button on the Standard toolbar, and then click.

   Note that the range that you copied has a moving border surrounding it. This moving border is a visual reminder of what range values are currently in the paste buffer.

4. Click cell **G6** to make it the active cell, and then click the **Paste** button on the Standard toolbar. Note that you did not have to select a range of cells equal to the range you were copying because the cells adjacent to cell G6 were empty and could accommodate the pasted range.

The formulas from the G5:J5 range are pasted into the G6:J6 range. See Figure 2-11.

Figure 2-11   COPYING AND PASTING FORMULAS

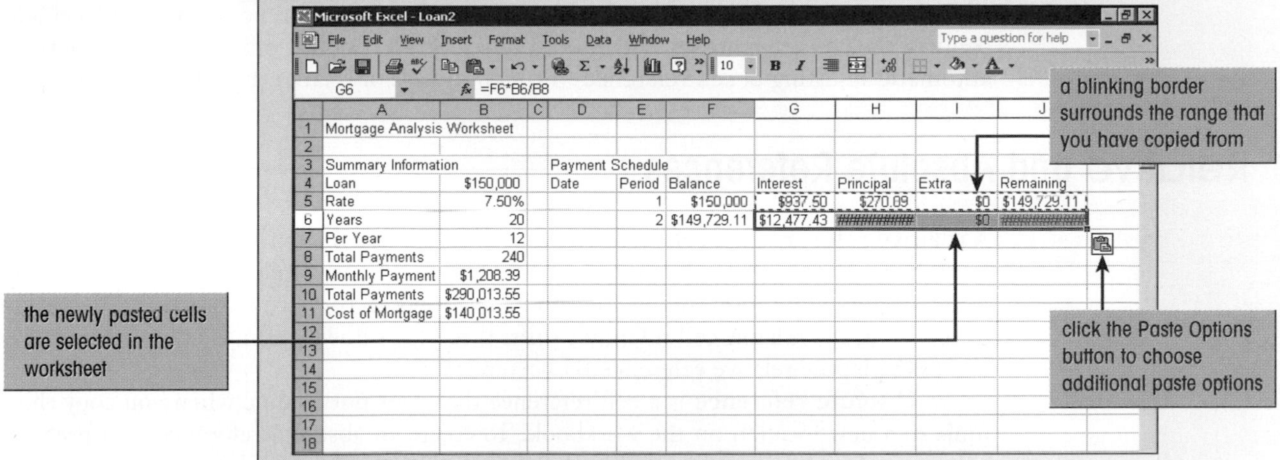

the newly pasted cells are selected in the worksheet

a blinking border surrounds the range that you have copied from

click the Paste Options button to choose additional paste options

Note that next to the pasted range is the Paste Options button. You can click this button to apply one of the available options for pasting cell values into the new range. By default, Excel pastes the values and formulas along with the format used to display those values and formulas. You will learn more about the Paste Options button in the next session.

5. Press the **Esc** key to remove the moving border.

Apparently something is wrong. Note that the interest payment in cell G6 has jumped to $12,477.43, and the principal payment in cell H6 and the remaining balance are represented with ########. Excel uses this string of symbols to represent a value that is so large that it cannot be displayed within the width of the cell. To view the value in the cell, you must either increase the width of the column or hover your mouse pointer over the cell.

To view the value in cell H6:

1. Hover your mouse pointer over cell H6. After a brief interval, the value $277,536.12 appears in a ScreenTip.

2. Click cell **G6** to make it the active cell. The Formula bar displays the formula =F6*B6/B8.

The interest payment value jumped to $12,477.43 and the payment on the principal became $277,536.12. The absurdity of these values results from the way in which Excel copies formulas. When Excel copies formulas to a new location, Excel automatically adjusts the cell references in those formulas. For example, to calculate the remaining balance for the first payment period in cell J5, the formula is =F5-(H5+I5). For the second payment period, the remaining balance in cell J6 uses the formula =F6-(H6+I6). The cell references are shifted down one row.

This automatic update of the cell references works fine for this formula, but the updating does not work for the calculation of the interest payment. The interest payment should be the balance multiplied by the interest rate per period; therefore, for the first three rows of the payment schedule, the formulas should be =F5*B5/B7, =F6*B5/B7, and =F7*B5/B7.

However, when you copied the first formula to the second row, *all* of the cell references shifted down one row and the formula automatically became *=F6*B6/B8*. You have a different formula; therefore, the result is a nonsensical value. Note that this is an issue only when copying a cell, not moving a cell. When you move a cell, Excel does *not* modify the cell references.

You need to be able to control how Excel adjusts cell references, so that Excel adjusts some of the cell references in the interest due formula, but not others. You can control this automatic adjusting of cell references through the use of relative and absolute references.

Relative and Absolute References

A **relative reference** is a cell reference that shifts when you copy it to a new location on the worksheet. As you saw in the preceding set of steps, a relative reference changes in relation to the change of location. If you copy a formula to a cell three rows down and five columns to the right, the relative cell reference shifts three rows down and five columns to the right. For example, the relative reference B5 becomes G8.

An **absolute reference** is a cell reference that does not change when you copy the formula to a new location on the workbook. To create an absolute reference, you preface the column and row designations with a dollar sign ($). For example, the absolute reference for B5 would be $B$5. No matter where you copy the formula, this cell reference would stay the same. (Relative references do not include dollars signs.)

A **mixed reference** combines both relative and absolute cell references. A mixed reference for B5 would be either $B5 or B$5. In the case of $B5, the row reference would shift, but the column reference would not. In the case of B$5, only the column reference shifts.

You can switch between absolute, relative, and mixed references by selecting the cell reference in the formula (either using edit mode or the Formula bar) and then pressing the F4 key on your keyboard repeatedly.

The problem you have encountered with the payment schedule formulas is that you need a relative reference for the remaining balance but an absolute reference for the interest rate divided by the payment periods per year (since those values are always located in the same place in the worksheet). So instead of the formula *=F5*B5/B7*, you need to use the formula *=F5*$B$5/$B$7*.

Next you will revise the formulas in the payment schedule to use relative and absolute references, and then copy the revised formulas.

To use relative and absolute references in the payment schedule:

1. Double-click cell **G5** to enter edit mode, use an arrow key to position the insertion point to the left of the column heading B if necessary, and then type **$**. Continue to use the arrow keys to position the insertion point in the formula before typing three more **$** to change the formula to *=F5*$B$5/$B$7*. Press the **Enter** key.

   You also have to change the formula in cell H5, so that the formula subtracts the interest payment from the required monthly payment to calculate the payment toward the principal. Instead of typing the dollar signs to change a relative reference to an absolute reference, you will use the F4 key.

2. Double-click cell **H5**, make sure the insertion point is positioned in the B9 cell reference, and then press the **F4** key to change the formula to *=$B$9–G5*. Press the **Enter** key.

   Now copy these new formulas into the second row of the payment schedule. Note that you do not have to delete the contents of the range into which you are copying the updated formulas.

3. Select the range **G5:H5**, and then click the **Copy** button 🔳 on the Standard toolbar.

4. Click cell **G6** and then click the **Paste** button 📋 on the Standard toolbar.

The new values are much more reasonable. The interest payment has decreased to $935.81, and the payment toward the principal has increased to $272.58. You will now add one more row to the payment schedule and copy the formulas.

To add a third row to the payment schedule:

1. Click cell **E7**, type **3** and then press the **Tab** key.

2. Select the range **F6:J6**, and then click the **Copy** button 🔳 on the Standard toolbar.

3. Click cell **F7** and then click the **Paste** button 📋 on the Standard toolbar.

Figure 2-12 shows the first three rows of the payment schedule.

| Figure 2-12 | PASTING THE THIRD ROW OF THE PAYMENT SCHEDULE |

4. Examine the formulas in cells G5, G6, and G7. Note that the relative reference to the balance remaining on the loan changes from F5 to F6 to F7 as you proceed down the schedule, but the interest rate per period keeps the same absolute reference, $B$5/$B$7.

As you would expect, the interest payment schedule decreases as the remaining balance decreases, and the monthly payment that goes to the principal steadily increases. Carol would like you to complete the rest of the payment schedule for all 240 payment periods. You will explore how to complete the rest of the payment schedule in a quick and efficient way in the next session.

To close the Loan2 workbook:

1. Click **File** on the menu bar, and then click **Exit**.

2. When prompted to save your changes to Loan2.xls, click the **Yes** button.

Session 2.1 QUICK CHECK

1. Which function would you enter to calculate the minimum value in the range B1:B50?

2. What function would you enter to calculate the ratio between the maximum value in the range B1:B50 and the minimum value?

3. A 5-year loan for $10,000 has been taken out at 7% interest compounded quarterly. What function would you enter to calculate the quarterly payment on the loan?

4. Which function would you use to determine the amount of interest due in the second quarter of the first year of the loan discussed in question 3?

5. In the formula *A8+$C$1*, *$C$1* is an example of a(n) _____ reference.

6. Cell A10 contains the formula *=A1+B1*. If the contents of this cell were copied to cell B11, what formula would be inserted into that cell?

7. Cell A10 contains the formula *=$A1+B$1*. If this cell were copied to cell B11, what formula would be inserted into that cell? What would the formula be if you moved cell A10 to B11?

SESSION 2.2

In this session you will use Excel's Auto Fill feature to automatically fill in formulas, series, and dates. You will use Excel's logical functions to create functions that return different values based on different conditions. Finally, you will learn how Excel stores dates, and then you will work with dates using Excel's library of date and time functions.

Filling in Formulas and Values

So far you have entered only three periods of the 240 total payment periods into the payment schedule. You used the copy and paste technique to enter the values for the second and third rows. You could continue to copy and paste the remaining rows of the payment schedule, but you can use a more efficient technique—the fill handle. The **fill handle** is a small black square located in the lower-right corner of a selected cell or range. When you drag the fill handle, Excel automatically fills in the formulas or formats used in the selected cells. This technique is also referred to as **Auto Fill**.

REFERENCE WINDOW   **RW**

Copying Formulas Using Auto Fill
- Select the range that contains the formulas you want to copy.
- Click and drag the fill handle in the direction you want to copy the formulas.
- Release the mouse button.
- If necessary, click the Auto Fill Options button, and then select the Auto Fill option you want to apply to the selected range.

Copying Formulas

Carol wants you to copy the formulas from the range F6:J7 into the larger range F7:J244. Copying the formulas into the larger range will, in effect, calculate the monthly payments for all 240 periods of the loan—all 20 years of the mortgage.

To copy the formulas using the fill handle:

1. If you took a break after the previous session, make sure Excel is running and the Loan2 workbook is open.

2. Verify that the Mortgage sheet is the active worksheet.

3. Select the range **F6:J7**.

4. Position the pointer over the fill handle (the square box in the lower-right corner of cell J7) until the pointer changes to ↓.

5. Click and drag the fill handle down the worksheet to cell **J244**. As you drag the fill handle, an outline appears displaying the selected cells, and the worksheet automatically scrolls down.

6. Release the mouse button. By default, Excel copies the values and formulas found in the original range F6:J7 into the new range F7:J244. See Figure 2-13.

Figure 2-13	FILLING IN THE REST OF THE PAYMENT SCHEDULE VALUES

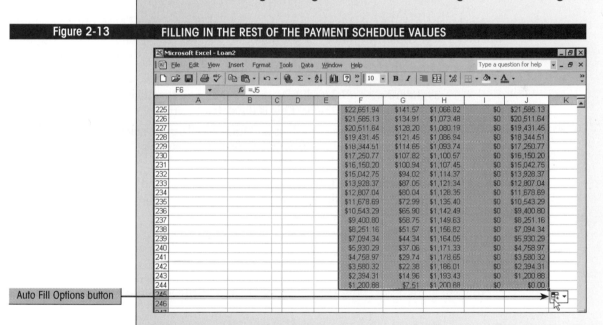

Auto Fill Options button

TROUBLE? It is very easy to "overshoot the mark" when dragging the fill handle down. If this happens, you can either click the Undo button ↺ on the Standard toolbar and try again, or simply select the extras formulas you created and delete them.

Excel has copied the formulas from the first few rows of the payment schedule into the rest of the rows and has also automatically adjusted any relative references in the formulas. For example, the formula in cell G244 is *=F244*$B$5/$B$7*, which is the interest due on the last loan payment, an amount of $7.51. The last row in the payment schedule shows a remaining balance of $0.00 in cell J244. The loan is paid off.

Note that to the right of the filled values is the Auto Fill Options button. Clicking this button displays the available options that you can choose from to specify how Excel should perform the Auto Fill. Click this button now to view the options.

To view the Auto Fill options:

1. Click the **Auto Fill Options** button 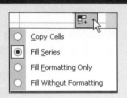 to the right of cell J244. Excel displays the Auto Fill Options menu, as shown in Figure 2-14.

Figure 2-14	AUTO FILL OPTIONS

Copy Cells
Fill Series
Fill Formatting Only
Fill Without Formatting

2. Click anywhere outside of the menu to hide it.

As shown in Figure 2-14, there are four Auto Fill options. These options determine whether Excel copies the values or formulas, or whether Excel simply copies the formats used to display those values and formulas. The four options and their descriptions are:

- **Copy Cells**: Copies the values and formulas into the selected range, as well as the formats used to display those values and formulas. Relative references are adjusted accordingly. This is the default option.
- **Fill Series**: Copies the values and formulas into the selected range, and completes any arithmetic or geometric series. Relative references are adjusted accordingly.
- **Fill Formatting Only**: Copies only the formats used to display the values or formulas in the cells. Values and formulas are not copied into the selected range.
- **Fill Without Formatting**: Copies the values and formulas into the selected range. The formats used to display those values and formulas are not copied. Relative references are adjusted accordingly.

You will learn more about formatting values and formulas in the next tutorial.

Filling a Series

Missing from the payment schedule are the numbers in column E. There should be a sequence of numbers starting with the value 1 in cell E5 and ending with the value 240 in cell E244. Since these numbers are all different, you cannot simply copy and paste the values. You can, however, use the fill handle to complete a series of numbers, as long as you include the first few numbers of the series. If the numbers increase by a constant value in an arithmetic series, dragging the fill handle will continue that same increase over the length of the newly selected cells.

Use the fill handle to enter the numbers for the Period column in the payment schedule.

To fill in the payment period values:

1. Press **Ctrl + Home** to return to the top of the worksheet.

2. Select the range **E5:E7**.

3. Click and drag the fill handle down to cell **E244**. Note that as you drag the fill handle a label appears indicating the current value in the series. When you reach cell E244, the label displays the value *240*.

4. Release the mouse button. Figure 2-15 shows the values in the payment schedule through the 240th payment.

Figure 2-15   FILLING IN THE PAYMENT PERIOD NUMBERS

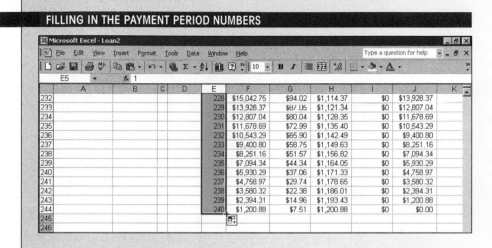

Filling In Dates

You can also use the fill handle to fill in dates—the one part of the payment schedule you have not entered yet. As with filling in a series, if you specify the initial date or dates, Excel will automatically insert the rest of the dates. The series of dates that Excel fills in depends on the dates you start with. If you start with dates that are separated by a single day, Excel will fill in a series of days. If you start with dates separated by a single month, Excel will fill in a series of months and so forth. You can also specify how to fill in the date values using the Auto Fill Options button.

Next you will insert an initial date for the loan as August 1, 2003, and then specify that each payment period is due at the beginning of the next month.

To insert the payment dates:

1. Type **8/1/2003** in cell D5, and then click the **Enter** button ☑ on the Formula bar. Note that clicking the Enter button on the Formula bar inserts the value in the cell and keeps it the active cell.

2. Drag the fill handle down to cell **D244**, and then release the mouse button. Note that as you drag the fill handle down, the date appears in the pop-up label; the date *3/27/2004* appears when you reach cell D244.

   TROUBLE? Don't worry if your computer is set up to display dates in a different format. The format doesn't affect the date value.

   By default, Excel created a series of consecutive days. You need to change the consecutive days to consecutive months.

3. Click the **Auto Fill Options** button 🔳 located to the lower-right corner of cell D244.

4. Click the **Fill Months** option button. Excel fills in consecutive months in the payment schedule. The last payment date is 7/1/2023. See Figure 2-16.

Figure 2-16   ADDING DATES TO THE PAYMENT SCHEDULE

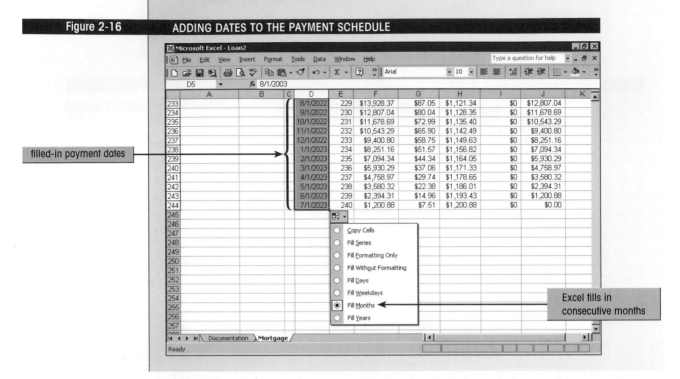

Excel provides other techniques for automatically inserting series of numbers into your worksheets. You can even create your own customized fill series. You can use the online Help to learn how to use the other Auto Fill options. For now though, you have completed the payment schedule.

Carol wants to verify that the numbers you have inserted into the payment schedule are correct. She suggests that, as a check, you add up the interest payments in column G. The total should match the cost of the mortgage that you calculated in cell B11.

To calculate the total interest payments:

1. Click cell **A13**, and type **Observed Payments**, and then press the **Enter** key.

2. In cell A14, type **Cost of Mortgage**, and then press the **Tab** key. The observed cost of the mortgage is the sum of interest payments in the range G5:G244.

3. In cell B14, type **=SUM(G5:G244)**, and then press the **Enter** key. As shown in Figure 2-17, the total cost of the interest payments in the payment schedule, $140,013.55, matches what was calculated in cell B11.

Figure 2-17 **TOTAL INTEREST PAYMENTS FROM THE PAYMENT SCHEDULE**

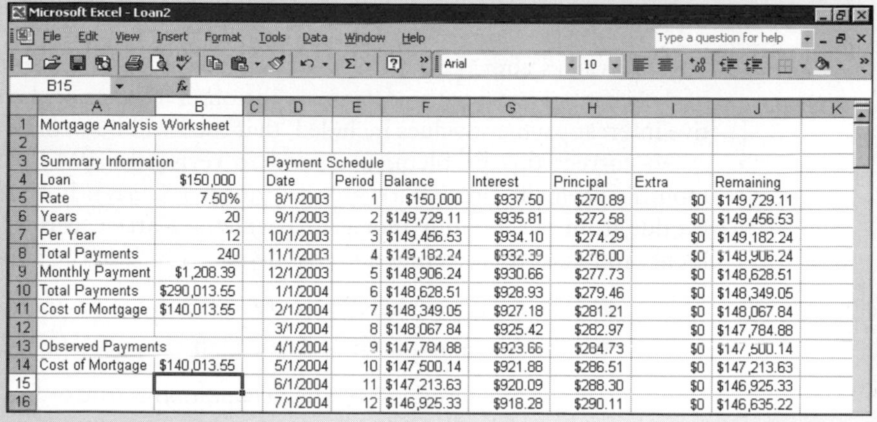

	A	B	C	D	E	F	G	H	I	J	K
1	Mortgage Analysis Worksheet										
2											
3	Summary Information			Payment Schedule							
4	Loan	$150,000		Date	Period	Balance	Interest	Principal	Extra	Remaining	
5	Rate	7.50%		8/1/2003	1	$150,000	$937.50	$270.89	$0	$149,729.11	
6	Years	20		9/1/2003	2	$149,729.11	$935.81	$272.58	$0	$149,456.53	
7	Per Year	12		10/1/2003	3	$149,456.53	$934.10	$274.29	$0	$149,182.24	
8	Total Payments	240		11/1/2003	4	$149,182.24	$932.39	$276.00	$0	$148,906.24	
9	Monthly Payment	$1,208.39		12/1/2003	5	$148,906.24	$930.66	$277.73	$0	$148,628.51	
10	Total Payments	$290,013.55		1/1/2004	6	$148,628.51	$928.93	$279.46	$0	$148,349.05	
11	Cost of Mortgage	$140,013.55		2/1/2004	7	$148,349.05	$927.18	$281.21	$0	$148,067.84	
12				3/1/2004	8	$148,067.84	$925.42	$282.97	$0	$147,784.88	
13	Observed Payments			4/1/2004	9	$147,784.88	$923.66	$284.73	$0	$147,500.14	
14	Cost of Mortgage	$140,013.55		5/1/2004	10	$147,500.14	$921.88	$286.51	$0	$147,213.63	
15				6/1/2004	11	$147,213.63	$920.09	$288.30	$0	$146,925.33	
16				7/1/2004	12	$146,925.33	$918.28	$290.11	$0	$146,635.22	

Using Excel's Logical Functions

So far you have assumed that there are no extra payments toward the principal. In fact, the PMT function assumes constant periodic deposits with no additional payments. If extra payments were made, they would reduce the cost of the mortgage and speed up the payment of the loan. Carol would like to see what the effect would be on the payment schedule and the cost of the mortgage if an extra payment were made.

To add an extra payment to the schedule:

1. Click cell **I22**, which corresponds to the payment period for 1/1/2005.

   Now assume that a client makes an extra payment of $20,000 toward the principal on this date.

2. Type **$20,000** in cell I22, and then press the **Enter** key. The observed cost of the mortgage shown in cell B14 drops to $80,262.15.

3. Scroll down the worksheet until row **190** comes into view (corresponding to the date of 1/1/2019). See Figure 2-18.

Figure 2-18 **NEGATIVE INTEREST PAYMENTS**

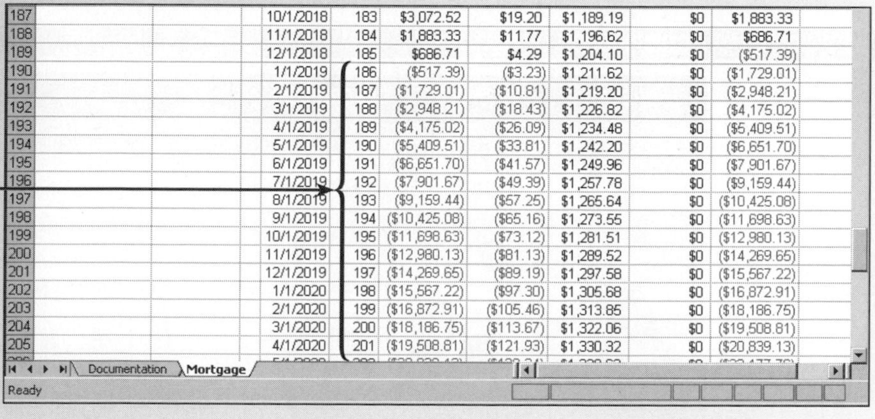

after 12/1/2018, the remaining balance on the loan appears as a negative value

	D	E	F	G	H	I	J
187	10/1/2018	183	$3,072.52	$19.20	$1,189.19	$0	$1,883.33
188	11/1/2018	184	$1,883.33	$11.77	$1,196.62	$0	$686.71
189	12/1/2018	185	$686.71	$4.29	$1,204.10	$0	($517.39)
190	1/1/2019	186	($517.39)	($3.23)	$1,211.62	$0	($1,729.01)
191	2/1/2019	187	($1,729.01)	($10.81)	$1,219.20	$0	($2,948.21)
192	3/1/2019	188	($2,948.21)	($18.43)	$1,226.82	$0	($4,175.02)
193	4/1/2019	189	($4,175.02)	($26.09)	$1,234.48	$0	($5,409.51)
194	5/1/2019	190	($5,409.51)	($33.81)	$1,242.20	$0	($6,651.70)
195	6/1/2019	191	($6,651.70)	($41.57)	$1,249.96	$0	($7,901.67)
196	7/1/2019	192	($7,901.67)	($49.39)	$1,257.78	$0	($9,159.44)
197	8/1/2019	193	($9,159.44)	($57.25)	$1,265.64	$0	($10,425.08)
198	9/1/2019	194	($10,425.08)	($65.16)	$1,273.55	$0	($11,698.63)
199	10/1/2019	195	($11,698.63)	($73.12)	$1,281.51	$0	($12,980.13)
200	11/1/2019	196	($12,980.13)	($81.13)	$1,289.52	$0	($14,269.65)
201	12/1/2019	197	($14,269.65)	($89.19)	$1,297.58	$0	($15,567.22)
202	1/1/2020	198	($15,567.22)	($97.30)	$1,305.68	$0	($16,872.91)
203	2/1/2020	199	($16,872.91)	($105.46)	$1,313.85	$0	($18,186.75)
204	3/1/2020	200	($18,186.75)	($113.67)	$1,322.06	$0	($19,508.81)
205	4/1/2020	201	($19,508.81)	($121.93)	$1,330.32	$0	($20,839.13)

Documentation Mortgage

Ready

Something is wrong. With the extra payment, the loan is paid off early, at the end of the 185th payment period; but starting with 12/1/2018, the payment schedule no longer makes sense. It appears that the client is still making payments on a loan that is already paid off.

The effect of this error is that the remaining balance and the interest payments appear as negative values after the loan is paid off. But remember, in cell B14, you calculated the sum of the interest payments to determine the observed cost of the mortgage. With those negative interest payment values included, that total will be wrong.

To correct this problem, you need to revise the PMT function that determines the monthly payment directed toward the principal. Currently, this function subtracts the interest due from the monthly mortgage payment to arrive at the amount of the principal payment. You need to use a function that decides which of the two following situations is true:

- The remaining balance is greater than the payment toward the principal.
- The remaining balance is less than the payment toward the principal.

A function that determines whether a condition is true or false is called a **logical function**. Excel supports several logical functions, which are described in Figure 2-19.

Figure 2-19	EXCEL'S LOGICAL FUNCTIONS
FUNCTION	**DESCRIPTION**
AND(*logical1*,[*logical2*], ...)	Returns the value TRUE if all arguments are true; returns FALSE if one or more arguments is false
FALSE()	Returns the value FALSE
IF(*logical_test*,*value_if_true*,*value_if_false*)	Returns *value_if_true* if the *logical_test* argument is true; returns the *value_if_false* if the *logical_test* argument is false
NOT(*logical*)	Returns the value TRUE if *logical* is false; returns the value FALSE if *logical* is true
OR(*logical1*,[*logical2*], ...)	Returns the value TRUE if at least one argument is true; returns FALSE if all arguments are false
TRUE()	Returns the value TRUE

In this loan workbook, you will be using an IF function. The syntax of the IF function is =IF(*logical_test*,*value_if_true*,*value_if_false*) where *logical_test* is an expression that is either true or false, *value_if_true* is an expression that Excel will run if the *logical_test* is true, and *value_if_false* is an expression that runs when the *logical_test* is false. The logical test is constructed using a comparison operator. A **comparison operator** checks whether two expressions are equal, whether one is greater than the other, and so forth. Figure 2-20 describes the six comparison operators supported by Excel.

Figure 2-20	COMPARISON OPERATORS	
OPERATOR	**EXAMPLE**	**DESCRIPTION**
=	A1=B1	Checks if the value in cell A1 equals the value in cell B1
>	A1>B1	Checks if the value in cell A1 is greater than B1
<	A1<B1	Checks if the value in cell A1 is less than B1
>=	A1>=B1	Checks if the value in cell A1 is greater than or equal to B1
<=	A1<=B1	Checks if the value in cell A1 is less than or equal to B1
<>	A1<>B1	Checks if the value in cell A1 is not equal to the value in cell B1

For example, the function *=IF(A1=10,20,30)* tests whether the value in cell A1 is equal to 10. If so, the function returns the value 20, otherwise the function returns the value 30. You can also use cell references in place of values.

The function *=IF(A1=10,B1,B2)* returns the value from cell B1 if A1 equals 10, otherwise the function returns the value stored in cell B2.

You can also make comparisons with text strings. When you do, the text strings must be enclosed in quotation marks. For example, the function *=IF(A1="RETAIL",B1,B2)* tests whether the text RETAIL has been entered into cell A1. If so, the function returns the value from cell B1, otherwise it returns the value from cell B2.

Because some functions are very complex, you might find it easier to enter a logical function, such as the IF function, using Excel's Insert Function option. You will use the Insert Function option to enter an IF function in the first row of the payment schedule.

To enter the IF function in the first row of the payment schedule:

1. Click cell **H5** in the payment schedule, and then press the **Delete** key to clear the cell contents.

2. Click the **Insert Function** button *fx* on the Formula bar.

3. Click the **Or select a category** list arrow, and then click **Logical** in the list of categories displayed.

4. Click **IF** in the Select a Function list box, and then click the **OK** button to open the Function Arguments dialog box.

   First, you need to enter the logical test. The test is whether the remaining balance in cell F5 is greater than the usual amount of payment toward the principal, which is equal to the monthly loan payment ($B$9) minus the interest payment (G5). The logical test is therefore *F5>($B$9–G5)*.

5. In the Logical_test argument box, enter **F5>($B$9–G5)**, and then press the **Tab** key.

   If the logical test is true (in other words, if the remaining balance is greater than the principal payment), Excel should return the usual principal payment. In this case, that value is the expression *$B$9–G5*.

6. In the Value_if_true argument box, enter **$B$9–G5**, and then press the **Tab** key.

   If the logical test is false (which means that the balance remaining is *less* than the usual principal payment), the payment should be set equal to the remaining balance—which has the effect of paying off the loan. In this case, Excel should return the value in cell F5.

7. In the Value_if_false argument box, enter **F5**. Figure 2-21 shows the completed dialog box.

Figure 2-21   INSERTING THE IF FUNCTION

tests whether the remaining balance is greater than the payment toward the principal

if true, the principal payment is equal to the monthly loan payment minus the interest due

if false, the payment is equal to the remaining balance

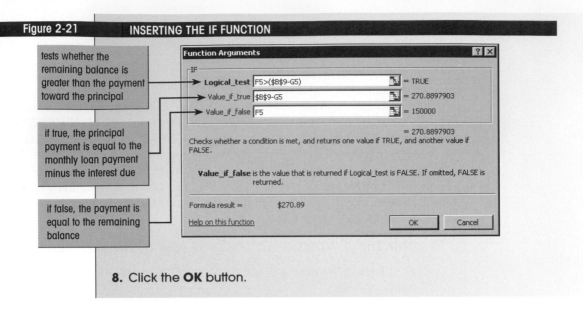

8. Click the **OK** button.

Now copy this new formula into the rest of the payment schedule.

To fill in the rest of the payment schedule:

1. With cell H5 the active cell, click the fill handle and drag it down to cell **H244**.

2. Scroll up to row **190**. As shown in Figure 2-22, the payment schedule now accurately shows that once the remaining balance reaches $0, the interest payments and the payments toward the principal also become $0.

Figure 2-22   NEW PAYMENT VALUES

after the loan is paid off, the remaining balance and monthly payments are equal to $0

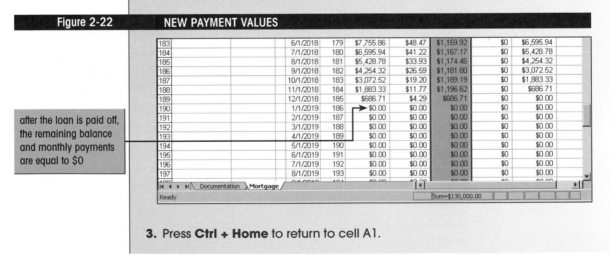

3. Press **Ctrl + Home** to return to cell A1.

Note that with the extra payment, the observed cost of the mortgage is $93,034.73. Thus, if a client were to make an extra payment of $20,000 on 1/1/2005, Carol could tell the client that there would be a savings of almost $47,000 over the history of the loan.

Making an extra payment or payments will greatly affect the number of payment periods. From the payment schedule, you can tell that the number of payment periods would be 185. The question is how can you include this information in the summary section at the top of the worksheet. To include the information, you will have to make the following change to the payment period values in column E of the payment schedule:

■ If the balance is greater than 0, the period number should be one higher than the previous period number.

■ If the balance is 0, set the period number to 0.

You'll make this change to the payment schedule now.

To add an IF function that adjusts the period numbers in case of extra payments:

1. Click cell **E6** to make it the active cell, and then press the **Delete** key.

2. Click the **Insert Function** button *fx* on the Formula toolbar.

3. Click **IF** in the Select a function list box, and then click the **OK** button.

   The logical test is whether the balance (in cell F6) is greater than $0 or not.

4. In the Logical_test argument box, enter **F6>0**, and then press the **Tab** key.

   If the logical test is true, the period number should be equal to the previous period number (E5) plus 1.

5. In the Value_if_true argument box, enter **E5+1**, and then press the **Tab** key.

   If the logical test is false, the balance is 0. Set the period number to 0.

6. In the Value_if_false argument box, type **0**, and then click the **OK** button.

7. Verify that E6 is still the active cell, and then click and drag the fill handle down to cell **E244**.

8. Scroll up the worksheet to row **190**. Note that once the loan is paid off, the period number is equal to 0. See Figure 2-23.

| Figure 2-23 | NEW PAYMENT PERIOD NUMBERS |

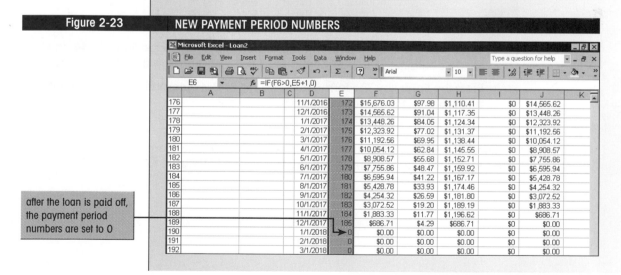

after the loan is paid off, the payment period numbers are set to 0

Using the AutoSum Button

Since the period numbers are all equal to zero after the loan is paid off, the last period number in the payment schedule will also be the largest. You can, therefore, use the MAX function to calculate the maximum, or last, payment period in the schedule. You can enter the MAX function either by typing the function directly into the active cell or by using the

Insert Function button on the Formula bar. However, Excel also provides the AutoSum button on the Standard toolbar to give you quick access to the SUM, AVERAGE, COUNT, MIN, and MAX functions. The AutoSum button can be a real timesaver, so you will use it in this situation.

To use the AutoSum button to calculate the maximum payment period:

1. Scroll to the top of the worksheet.

2. Click cell **A15**, type **Total Payments** and then press the **Tab** key.

3. Click the **list arrow** for the AutoSum button Σ ▾ on the Standard toolbar to display a list of summary functions. See Figure 2-24.

Figure 2-24	USING THE AUTOSUM BUTTON

AutoSum button

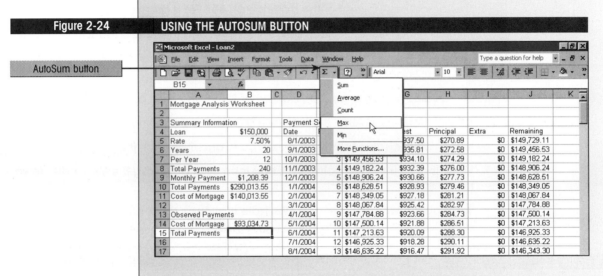

4. Click **Max** in the list, and then drag the pointer over the range **E5:E244** (the range containing the payment period numbers from the payment schedule).

5. Press the **Enter** key. The formula *=MAX(E5:E244)* is automatically entered into cell B15, and the value 185 appears in the cell.

Carol suggests you test the new payment schedule one more time. She asks what the effect would be if the extra payment on 1/1/2005 was increased from $20,000 to $25,000.

To test the new payment figures:

1. Click cell **I22**.

2. Type **$25,000** and then press the **Enter** key.

The cost of the mortgage decreases to $84,368.07 and the number of payments decreases to 174.

Using Excel's Date Functions

Excel stores dates as integers, where the integer values represent the number of days since January 1, 1900. For example, the integer value for the date January 1, 2008 is 39448 because that date is 39,448 days after January 1, 1900. Most of the time you do not see these values because Excel automatically formats the integers to appear as dates, such as 1/1/2008. This method of storing the dates allows you to work with dates in the same way you work with numbers. For example, if you subtract one date from another, the answer will be the number of days separating the two dates.

In addition to creating simple formulas with date values, you can use Excel's date functions to create dates or to extract information about date values. To insert the current date into your workbook, you could use the TODAY function, for example. To determine which day of the week a particular date falls on, you could use the WEEKDAY function. Note that the date functions use your computer's system clock to return a value. Figure 2-25 describes some of Excel's more commonly used date functions.

Figure 2-25	EXCEL'S DATE FUNCTIONS
FUNCTION	**DESCRIPTION**
DATE(*year, month, day*)	Returns the integer for the date represented by the *year*, *month*, and *day* arguments
DAY(*date*)	Extracts the day of the month from the *date* value
MONTH(*date*)	Extracts the month number from the *date* value, where January=1, February=2, and so forth
NOW(), TODAY()	Returns the integer for the current date and time
WEEKDAY(*date*)	Calculates the day of the week using the *date* value, where Sunday=1, Monday=2, and so forth
YEAR(*date*)	Extracts the year number from the *date* value

On the Documentation sheet, there is a cell for entering the current date. Rather than typing the date in manually, you will enter it using the TODAY function.

To use the TODAY function:

1. Click the **Documentation** tab to make it the active worksheet, and then click cell **B4**.

2. Click the **Insert Function** button f_x on the Formula bar.

3. Select **Date & Time** from the function category list.

4. Scroll down the list, click **TODAY**, and then click the **OK** button twice. Note that the second dialog box indicated that there are no arguments for the TODAY function. The current date is entered into cell B4 (your date will most likely be different). See Figure 2-26.

| Figure 2-26 | INSERTING THE CURRENT DATE |

the TODAY function inserts the current date into the cell

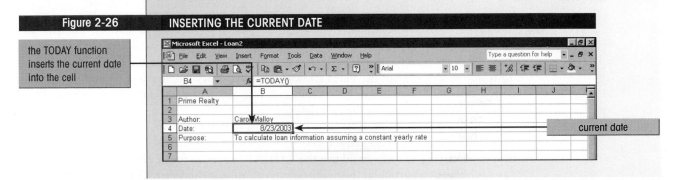

current date

The TODAY and NOW functions will always display the current date and time. Thus, if you reopen this workbook on a different date, the date in cell B4 will be updated to reflect that change. If you want a permanent date (that might reflect when the workbook was initially developed), you enter the date directly into the cell without using a function.

You have completed your work on the Loan workbook. Carol will examine the workbook and get back to you with more assignments. For now, you can close Excel and save your work.

To save your work:

1. Click **File** on the menu bar, and then click **Exit**.

2. Click the **Yes** button when prompted to save your changes.

Session 2.2 QUICK CHECK

1. Describe how you would create a series of odd numbers from 1 to 99 in column A of your worksheet.

2. Describe how you would create a series of yearly dates, ranging from 1/1/2003 to 1/1/2030, in column A of your worksheet.

3. What function would you enter to return the text string "Yes" if cell A1 is greater than cell B1 and "No" if cell A1 is not greater than cell B1?

4. Describe three ways of entering the SUM function into a worksheet cell.

5. Which function would you enter to extract the year value from the date entered into cell A1?

6. Which function would you enter to display the current date in the worksheet?

7. Which function would you enter to determine which day of the week a date entered into cell A1 falls on?

REVIEW ASSIGNMENTS

Carol has another workbook for you to examine. Although the loan workbook was helpful, Carol realizes that most of the time she will be working with clients who can make only a specified monthly payment. She wants to have a workbook in which she enters a specific monthly payment and from that amount determine how large a mortgage her client can afford.

To determine this information, you will use the PV function: PV(*rate*,*nper*,*pmt*,[*fv*=0],[*type*=0]) where *rate* is the interest per period, *nper* is the number of payment periods, *pmt* is the monthly payment, *fv* is the future value of the loan (assumed to be 0), and *type* specifies when the loan will be paid (assumed to be 0 at the beginning of each payment period). For a loan, the *pmt* argument must be a negative number since it represents an expense and not income. The PV function then returns the present value of the loan or annuity. In Carol's workbook, the return would be the largest mortgage her clients can afford for a given monthly payment.

As with the previous workbook, Carol wants this new workbook to contain a payment schedule. The current annual interest rate is 7.5% compounded monthly. Carol wants the payment schedule to assume a 20-year mortgage with a monthly payment of $950. What is the largest mortgage her clients could get under those conditions, and how much would the interest payments total?

To complete this task:

1. Start Excel and open the **Mort1** workbook located in the Tutorial.02/Review folder on your Data Disk.

2. Save the workbook as **Mort2** in the same folder.

3. Enter your name and the current date in the Documentation sheet (use a function to automatically insert the date). Switch to the Mortgage worksheet.

4. Enter "$950" for the monthly payment in cell B4, "7.5%" as the interest rate in cell B5, "20" as the number of years, and "12" as the number of periods per year.

5. Enter a formula in cell B8 to calculate the total number of payments over the history of the loan.

Explore ▷ 6. In cell B10, use the PV function to calculate the largest mortgage a client could receive under those conditions. Remember that you need to make the monthly payment, which appears in cell B4, a negative, so the return is a positive number.

7. Complete the first row of the payment schedule, with the following formulas:

   ■ The initial value of the payment period should be equal to 1.
   ■ The initial balance should be equal to the amount of the mortgage.
   ■ The interest due should be equal to the balance multiplied by the interest rate per period.
   ■ Use the IF function to test whether the balance is greater than the monthly payment minus the interest due. If so, the principal payment should be equal to the monthly payment minus the interest due. If not, the principal payment should be equal to the balance.
   ■ Set the extra payment value to $0.
   ■ The remaining balance should be equal to the initial balance minus the principal payment and any extra payment.

8. Complete the second row of the payment schedule with the following formulas:

   ■ Carry the remaining balance from cell J3 into the current balance in cell F4.
   ■ If the current balance is equal to 0, set the period number to 0, otherwise set the period number equal to cell E3 plus 1.
   ■ Copy the formulas in the range G3:J3 to the range G4:J4.

9. Select the range E4:J4 and then drag the fill handle down to fill range E242:J242. What happens to the values in the Extra column when you release the mouse button?

Explore ▷ 10. Click the Auto Fill Options button next to the filled in values. Which option button is selected? Does this help you understand what happened in the previous step? Click the Copy Cells option button to fix the problem.

11. In cell D3, enter the initial date of the loan as "4/1/2003".

12. Payments are due at the beginning of each month. Fill in the rest of the payment dates in the range D3:D242 using the appropriate Auto Fill option.

13. In cell B11, enter the cost of the mortgage, which is equal to the sum of the interest payments in the payment schedule.

14. In cell B12, enter the number of observed payments, which is equal to the maximum payment period number in the payment schedule.

Explore 15. If a client pays an extra $100 for each period of the first five years of the loan, what is the cost of the mortgage and how many months will it take to pay off the loan? On what date will the loan be paid?

16. Print the entire Mort2 workbook.

17. Save and close the workbook, and then exit Excel.

CASE PROBLEMS

Case 1. Setting Up a College Fund   Lynn and Peter Chao have recently celebrated the birth of their first daughter. The couple is acutely aware of how expensive a college education is. Although the couple does not have much money, they realize that if they start saving now, they can hopefully save a nice sum for their daughter's education. They have asked you for help in setting up a college fund for their daughter.

The couple has set a goal of saving $75,000 that they will use in 18 years for college. Current annual interest rates for such funds are 6.5% compounded monthly. Lynn and Peter want you to determine how much money they would have to set aside each month to reach their goal. They would also like you to create a schedule so they can see how fast their savings will grow over the next few years.

You can calculate how fast monthly contributions to a savings account will grow using the same financial functions used to determine how fast monthly payments can pay back a loan. In this case, the present value is equal to 0 (since the couple is starting out with no savings in the college fund) and the future value is $75,000 (the amount that the couple wants to have saved after 18 years.)

To complete this task:

1. Open the **School1** workbook located in the Tutorial.02/Cases folder on your Data Disk, and then save the workbook as **School2** in the same folder.

2. Enter your name and the current date in the Documentation sheet. Switch to the College Fund worksheet.

3. Enter the Chaos' saving goal in cell B3 and the assumed annual interest rate in cell B4. Enter the number of years they plan to save in cell B5 and the number of payments per year in cell B6.

4. Enter a formula to calculate the total number of payments in cell B7.

Explore 5. In cell B9, use the PMT function to calculate the monthly payment required for the Chaos to meet their savings goal. Express your answer as a positive value rather than a negative value.

6. Begin filling out the savings schedule. In the first row, enter the following information:

   - The initial date is 1/1/2003.
   - The payment period is 1.
   - The starting balance is equal to the first monthly payment.

   Explore ▶

   - Calculate the accrued interest using the IPMT function, assuming that payments are made at the beginning of each month. (*Hint:* Scroll the IPMT arguments list to display all the necessary arguments.)
   - Calculate the ending balance, which is equal to the starting balance plus the interest accrued in the current month.

7. Enter the second row of the table, using the following guidelines:

   - The date is one month later than the previous date.
   - The payment period is 2.
   - The starting balance is equal to the previous month's ending balance plus the monthly payment.
   - Use the IPMT function to calculate the interest for the second payment period.
   - The ending balance is once again equal to the starting balance plus the accrued interest.

8. Use the fill handle to fill in the remaining 214 months of the savings schedule. Choose the appropriate fill options to ensure that the values in the dates and the period and interest values fill in correctly.

9. Save your changes.

10. Print a copy of the College Fund worksheet, and then indicate on the printout how much the couple will have to save each month to reach their savings goal.

11. Save and close the workbook, and then exit Excel.

Case 2. Payroll Information at Sonic Sounds Jeff Gwydion manages the payroll at Sonic Sounds. He has asked you for help in setting up a worksheet to store payroll values. The payroll contains three elements: the employee's salary, the 401(k) contribution, and the employee's health insurance cost. The company's 401(k) contribution is 3% of the employee's salary for employees who have worked for the company at least one year; otherwise the company's contribution is zero. Sonic Sounds also supports two health insurance plans: Premier and Standard. The cost of the Premier plan is $6,500, and the cost of the Standard plan is $5,500.

The workbook has already been set up for you. Your job is to enter the functions and formulas to calculate the 401(k) contributions and health insurance costs for each employee.

To complete this task:

1. Open the **Sonic1** workbook located in the Tutorial.02/Cases folder on your Data Disk, and save the workbook as **Sonic2** in the same folder.

2. Enter your name and the current date (calculated using a function) in the Documentation sheet. Switch to the Payroll worksheet.

3. In cell C13, determine the number of years the employee Abbot has been employed by subtracting the date Abbot was hired from the current date and then dividing the difference by 365.

4. Use the fill handle to compute the years employed for the rest of the employees.

Explore

5. Use an IF function to compute the 401(k) contribution for each employee (*Note*: Remember that an employee must have worked at Sonic for at least one year to be eligible for the 401(k) contribution.)

Explore

6. Use an IF function to calculate the health insurance cost for each employee at the company. (*Hint*: Test whether the employee's health plan listed in column E is equal to the value in cell B4. If so, the employee is using the Premier plan, and the health cost is equal to the value in cell C4. If not, the employee is using the Standard plan, and the health cost is equal to the value in cell C5.)

7. Calculate the total salaries, total 401(k) contributions, and total health insurance expenses for all of the employees at Sonic Sounds. Place the functions in the range B7:B9.

8. Print the contents of the **Sonic2** workbook.

9. Redo the analysis, assuming that the cost of the Premier plan has risen to $7,000 and the cost of the Standard plan has risen to $6,100. What is the total health insurance cost to the company's employees?

10. Print just the Payroll sheet.

11. Save and close the workbook, and then exit Excel.

Case 3. Depreciation at Leland Hospital Leland Hospital in Leland, Ohio, has purchased a new x-ray machine for its operating room. Debra Sanchez in purchasing wants your assistance in calculating the yearly depreciation of the machine. **Depreciation** is the declining value of an asset over its lifetime. To calculate the depreciation, you need the initial cost of the asset, the number of years or periods that the asset will be used, and the final or salvage value of the asset. The new x-ray machine costs $450,000. The hospital expects that the x-ray machine will be used for 10 years and that at the end of the 10-year period the salvage value will be $50,000. Debra wants you to calculate the depreciation of the machine for each year in that 10-year period.

Accountants use several different methods to calculate depreciation. The difference between each method lies in how fast the asset declines in value. Figure 2-27 describes four Excel functions that you can use to calculate depreciation.

Figure 2-27	EXCEL'S DEPRECIATION FUNCTIONS	
METHOD	**FUNCTION**	**DESCRIPTION**
Straight-line	SLN(*cost, salvage, life*)	The straight-line method distributes the depreciation evenly over the life of the asset, so that the depreciation is the same in each period. The argument *cost* is the cost of the asset, *salvage* is the salvage value at the end of the life of the asset, and *life* is the number of periods that the asset is being depreciated.
Sum-of-years	SYD(*cost, salvage, life, per*)	The sum-of-years method concentrates the most depreciation in the earliest periods of the lifetime of the asset. The argument *per* is the period that you want to calculate the depreciation for.
Fixed-declining balance	DB(*cost, salvage, life, period, [month=12]*)	The fixed-declining balance method is an accelerated depreciation method in which the highest depreciation occurs in the earliest periods. The argument *month* is an optional argument that specifies the number of months in the first year (assumed to be 12).
Double-declining balance	DDB(*cost, salvage, life, period, [factor=2]*)	The double-declining balance method is an accelerated method in which the highest depreciation occurs in the earliest periods. The optional *factor* argument controls that rate at which the balance declines.

Debra wants you to calculate the depreciation using all four methods so that she can see the impact on each method on the asset's value. She has already created the workbook containing the basic figures; she needs you to add the formulas.

To complete this task:

1. Open the **Leland1** workbook located in the Tutorial.02/Cases folder on your Data Disk and save the workbook as **Leland2** in the same folder.

2. Enter your name and the current date (calculated using a function) in the Documentation sheet. Switch to the Depreciation worksheet.

3. Enter the cost of the x-ray machine in cell B3, the lifetime of the machine in cell B4, and the salvage value in B5.

Explore   4. In the range B9:B18, enter the depreciation of the x-ray machine using the straight-line method.

5. In the range C9:C18, enter the yearly value of the machine after the depreciation is applied (*Hint*: After the first year, you must subtract the yearly depreciation from the previous year's value).

Explore   6. In the range F9:F18, enter the depreciation using the sum-of-years method.

7. In the range G9:G18, calculate the yearly value of the machine after the sum-of-years depreciation.

Explore   8. In the range B22:B31, calculate the fixed-declining depreciation for each year.

9. In the range C22:C31, calculate the value of the x-ray machine after applying the fixed-declining depreciation.

Explore 10. In the range F22:F31, calculate the double-declining depreciation for each year.

11. In the range G22:G31, calculate the yearly value of the x-ray machine after applying the double-declining depreciation.

12. Print the entire workbook.

13. Save and close the workbook, and then exit Excel.

Case 4. Analyzing Faculty Salaries at Glenmore Junior College A complaint has been raised at Glenmore Junior College, a liberal arts college in upstate New York, that female faculty members are being paid less than their male counterparts. Professor Lawton, a member of the faculty senate, has asked you to compile basic statistics on faculty salaries, broken down by gender. The current salary figures are shown in Figure 2-28.

Figure 2-28	**FACULTY SALARIES**

MALE FACULTY	**MALE FACULTY**	**MALE FACULTY**	**FEMALE FACULTY**	**FEMALE FACULTY**
$40,000	$55,000	$75,000	$25,000	$60,000
$45,000	$55,000	$75,000	$30,000	$60,000
$45,000	$60,000	$75,000	$35,000	$60,000
$45,000	$60,000	$75,000	$40,000	$60,000
$45,000	$60,000	$80,000	$42,000	$62,000
$45,000	$62,000	$85,000	$45,000	$62,000
$45,000	$62,000	$95,000	$47,000	$65,000
$50,000	$65,000	$115,000	$50,000	$65,000
$50,000	$65,000		$55,000	$67,000
$52,000	$65,000		$55,000	$70,000
$55,000	$70,000		$57,000	$75,000

To complete this task:

1. Create a new workbook named **JrCol** and store it in the Tutorial.02/Cases folder on your Data Disk.

2. Insert a Documentation sheet into the workbook containing your name, the current date (calculated using a function), and the purpose of the workbook.

3. Rename Sheet1 as "Statistical Analysis" and delete any unused worksheets.

4. In the Statistical Analysis worksheet, enter the male and female faculty salaries in two separate columns labeled "Male Faculty" and "Female Faculty."

Explore

5. Use Excel's statistical functions to create a table of the following statistics for all faculty members, male faculty members, and female faculty members:

- the count
- the sum of the salaries
- the average salary
- the median salary
- the minimum salary
- the maximum salary
- the range of salary values (maximum minus minimum)
- the standard deviation of the salary values
- the standard error of the salary values (the standard deviation divided by the square root of the number of salaries)

6. Compare the average male salary to the average female salary. Is there evidence that the female faculty members are paid significantly less?

7. Average values can sometimes be skewed by high values. Compare the median male salary to the median female salary. Is the evidence supporting the complaint stronger or weaker using the median salary figures?

Explore

8. Select the cell range containing the statistics you calculated, and then print only that selected range.

9. Save and close the workbook, and then exit Excel.

INTERNET ASSIGNMENTS

Student Union

The purpose of the Internet Assignments is to challenge you to find information on the Internet that you can use to create effective spreadsheets. The actual assignments are updated and maintained on the Course Technology Web site. Log on to the Internet and use your Web browser to go to the Student Union on the New Perspectives Series site at **www.course.com/NewPerspectives/studentunion**. Click the Online Companions link, and then click the link for this text.

QUICK CHECK ANSWERS

Session 2.1

1. =MIN(B1:B50)
2. =MAX(B1:50)/MIN(B1:B50)
3. =PMT(0.07/4,20,10000)
4. =IPMT(0.07/4,2,20,10000)
5. absolute reference
6. =B2+C2
7. =$A2+C$1; if moved, the formula would stay the same, =$A1+B$1

Session 2.2

1. Enter the values *1* and *3* in the first two rows of column A. Select the two cells and then drag the fill handle down to complete the rest of the series.

2. Enter *1/1/2003* in the first cell. Select the first cell and then drag the fill handle down 27 rows. Click the Auto Fill Options button, and then click the Fill Years option button.

3. =IF(A1>B1,"Yes","No")

4. Type the SUM function directly into the cell while in edit mode, using the Insert Function button on the Formula bar or using the AutoSum button on the Standard toolbar.

5. =YEAR(A1)

6. =TODAY()

7. =WEEKDAY(A1)

OBJECTIVES

In this tutorial you will:

- Format data using different fonts, sizes, and font styles

- Align cell contents

- Add cell borders and backgrounds

- Merge cells and hide rows and columns

- Format the worksheet background and sheet tabs

- Find and replace formats within a worksheet

- Create and apply styles

- Apply an AutoFormat to a table

- Format a printout using Print Preview

- Create a header and footer for a printed worksheet

- Define a print area and add a page break to a printed worksheet

DEVELOPING A PROFESSIONAL-LOOKING WORKSHEET

Formatting a Sales Report

CASE

NewGeneration Monitors

NewGeneration Monitors is a computer equipment company that specializes in computer monitors. Joan Sanchez has been entering sales data on three of the company's monitors into an Excel workbook. She plans on including the sales data in a report to be presented later in the week. Joan has made no attempt to make this data presentable to her coworkers. She has simply entered the numbers. She needs you to transform her raw figures into a presentable report.

To create a professional-looking document, you will learn how to work with Excel's formatting tools to modify the appearance of the data in each cell, the cell itself, and the entire worksheet. You will also learn how to format printouts that Joan wants to generate based on her workbook. You will learn how to create headers and footers, and control which parts of the worksheet are printed on which pages.

SESSION 3.1

In this session, you will format the contents of individual cells in your worksheet by modifying the font used in the cell or by changing the font size or style. You will also use color in your worksheet, modifying the background color of worksheet cells as well as the color of the text in a cell. You will also have an opportunity to examine various Excel commands that you can use to control text alignment and to wrap a line of text within a single cell. Finally, you will create borders around individual cells and cell ranges.

Formatting Worksheet Data

The data for Joan's sales report has already been stored in an Excel workbook. Before going further, open the workbook and save it with a new filename.

To open the Sales report workbook:

1. Start Excel, and open the **Sales1** workbook located in the Tutorial.03/Tutorial folder on your Data Disk.

2. On the Documentation worksheet, enter your name in cell B3, and enter the current date in cell B4.

3. Save the workbook as **Sales2** in the Tutorial.03/Tutorial folder on your Data Disk.

4. Click the **Sales** tab. Figure 3-1 shows the current appearance of the sales report, which is unformatted.

| Figure 3-1 | THE UNFORMATTED SALES WORKSHEET |

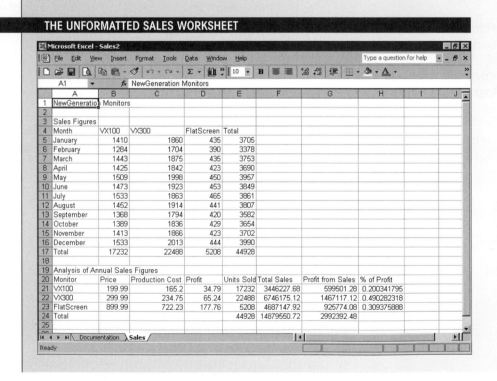

The Sales worksheet contains two tables. The first table displays the monthly sales for three of NewGeneration's monitors: the VX100, VX300, and the FlatScreen. The second table presents an analysis of these sales figures, showing the profit from the monitor sales and the percentage that each monitor contributes to the overall profit. In its current state, the worksheet is difficult to read and interpret. This is a problem that Joan wants you to solve by using Excel's formatting tools.

Formatting is the process of changing the appearance of your workbook. A properly formatted workbook can be easier to read, appear more professional, and help draw attention to important points you want to make. Formatting changes only the appearance of the data; formatting does not affect the data itself. For example, if a cell contains the value 0.124168, and you format the cell to display only up to the thousandths place (for example, 0.124), the cell still contains the precise value, even though you cannot see it displayed in the worksheet.

Up to now, Excel has been automatically formatting your cell entries using a formatting style called the General format. The **General format** aligns numbers with the right edge of the cell without dollar signs or commas, uses the minus sign for negative values, and truncates any trailing zeros to the right of the decimal point. For more control over your data's appearance, you can choose from a wide variety of other number formats. Formats can be applied using either the Formatting toolbar or the Format menu from Excel's menu bar. Formats can also be copied from one cell to another, giving you the ability to apply a common format to different cells in your worksheet.

Using the Formatting Toolbar

The Formatting toolbar is the fastest way to format your worksheet. By clicking a single button on the Formatting toolbar you can increase or decrease the number of decimal places displayed in a selected range of cells, display a value as a currency or percentage, or change the color or size of the font used in a cell.

When Joan typed in the monthly sales figures for the three monitors, she neglected to include a comma to separate the thousands from the hundreds and so forth. Rather than retype these values, you can use the Comma Style button on the Formatting toolbar to format the values with a comma. You can use the Increase Decimal or Decrease Decimal button on the Formatting toolbar to change the number of decimal places displayed in a number.

To apply the Comma format and adjust the number of decimal places displayed:

1. Select the range **B5:E17** in the Sales worksheet.

2. Click the **Comma Style** button [⊞] on the Formatting toolbar. Excel adds the comma separator to each of the values in the table and displays the values with two digits to the right of the decimal point.

   TROUBLE? If you do not see the Comma Style button on the Formatting toolbar, click the Toolbar Options button [»] on the Formatting toolbar, and then click [⊞].

   TROUBLE? If the Standard and Formatting toolbars appear on separate rows on your computer, then the Toolbar Options button might look slightly different from the Toolbar Options button [»] used throughout this text. If you are unsure about the function of a toolbar button, hover the pointer over the button to display its name.

   Because all of the sales figures are whole numbers, you will remove the zeros.

3. Click the **Decrease Decimal** button [.00→.0] on the Formatting toolbar twice to remove the zeros. See Figure 3-2.

Figure 3-2 — APPLYING THE COMMA STYLE TO THE SALES FIGURES

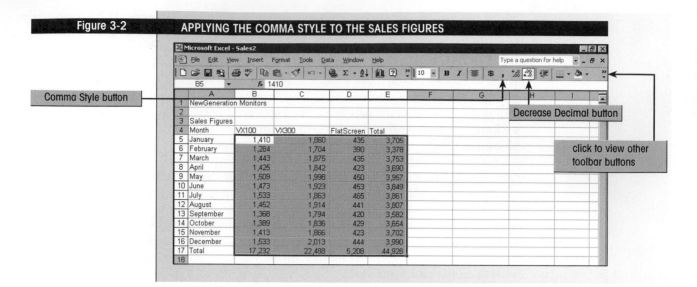

Joan's worksheet also displays the price and production cost of each monitor as well as last year's total sales and profit. She wants this information displayed using dollar signs, commas, and two decimal places. To format the values with these attributes, you can apply the Currency style.

To apply the Currency format:

1. Select the nonadjacent range **B21:D23;F21:G24**.

   TROUBLE? To select a nonadjacent range, select the first range, press and hold the Ctrl key, and then select the next range.

2. Click the **Currency Style** button $ on the Formatting toolbar. Excel adds the dollar signs and commas to the currency values and displays each value (price) to two decimal places. See Figure 3-3.

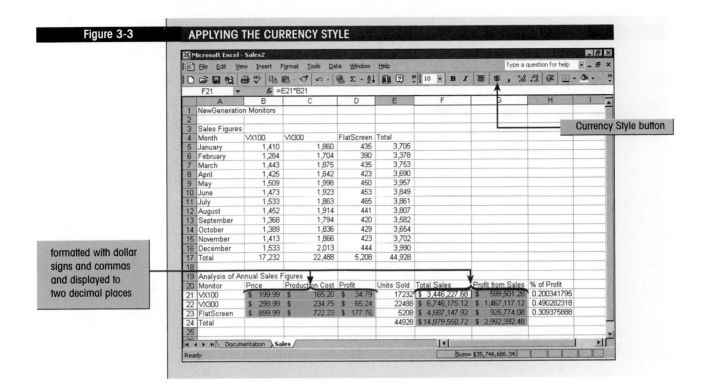

Figure 3-3   **APPLYING THE CURRENCY STYLE**

Currency Style button

formatted with dollar signs and commas and displayed to two decimal places

Finally, the range H21:H23 displays the percentage that each monitor contributes to the overall profit from sales. Joan wants these values displayed with a percent sign and to two decimal places. You will apply the Percent format; however, Excel, by default, does not display any decimal places with the Percent format. You need to increase the number of decimal places displayed.

To apply the Percent format and increase the number of decimal places:

1. Select the range **H21:H23**.

2. Click the **Percent Style** button on the Formatting toolbar.

3. Click the **Increase Decimal** button on the Formatting toolbar twice to display the percentages to two decimal places. See Figure 3-4.

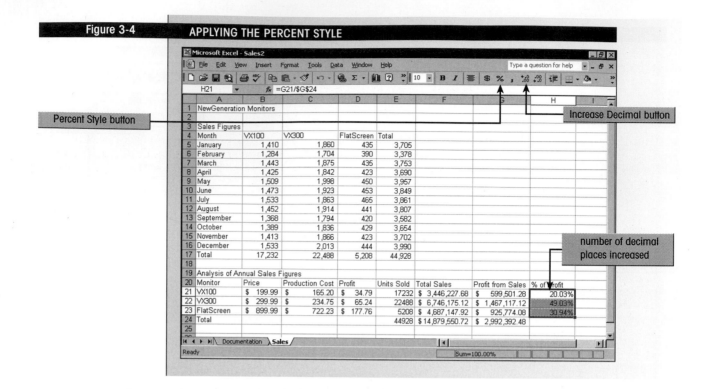

Figure 3-4   APPLYING THE PERCENT STYLE

By displaying the percent values using the Percent format, you can quickly see that one monitor, the VX300, accounts for almost half of the profit from monitor sales.

Copying Formats

As you look over the sales figures, you see that one area of the worksheet still needs to be formatted. The Units Sold column in the range E21:E24 still does not display the comma separator you used in the sales figures table. To fix a formatting problem like this one, you can use one of the methods that Excel provides for copying a format from one location to another.

One of these methods is the Format Painter button located on the Standard toolbar. When you use the Format Painter option, you "paint" a format from one cell to another cell or to a range of cells. You can also use the fill handle and its Auto Fill options to copy a format from one cell to another. Another method for copying a format is using the Copy and Paste commands, which are available on both the Standard toolbar and the Edit menu. The Copy and Paste method requires you to click the Formatting Only option button that appears when you paste the selected cell, so that only the formatting of the pasted cell, not its content, is applied. Using the Format Painter button does all of this in fewer steps.

You will use the Format Painter button to copy the format used in the sales figures table and to paste that format into the range E21:E24.

To copy the format using the Format Painter button:

1. Select cell **B5**, which contains the formatting that you want to copy. You do not have to copy the entire range, because the range is formatted in the same way.

2. Click the **Format Painter** button 🖌 on the Standard toolbar.

As you move the pointer over the worksheet area, the pointer changes to ➕🖌.

> **TROUBLE?** If you do not see the Format Painter button, click the Toolbar Options button on the Standard toolbar, and then click.
>
> **3.** Select the range **E21:E23**. The format that you used in the sales figures table is applied to the cells in the range E21:E23.

You have not applied the format to cell E24 yet. Rather than using the Format Painter button again, you can drag the fill handle down over the cell. Recall that you can use the fill handle to copy formulas and values from one range into another. You can also use the fill handle to copy formats.

To copy the format using the fill handle:

1. Click and drag the fill handle down to the range **E21:E24**.

When you release the mouse button, the word "Price" appears. This occurs because the default action of the fill handle in this case is to fill the values in the range E21:E23 into cell E24. You'll override this default behavior by choosing a different option from the list of Auto Fill options.

2. Click the **Auto Fill Options** button located at the lower-right corner of the selected range.

3. Click the **Fill Formatting Only** option button. Excel extends the format from the range E21:E23 into cell E24.

The Formatting toolbar is a fast and easy way to copy and apply cell formats, but there are other ways of formatting your data.

Using the Format Cells Dialog Box

Joan stops by to view your progress. She agrees that formatting the values has made the worksheet easier to read, but she has a few suggestions. She does not like the way the currency values are displayed with the dollar signs ($) placed at the left edge of the cell, leaving a large blank space between the dollar sign and the numbers. She would like to have the dollar sign placed directly to the left of the dollar amounts, leaving no blank spaces.

The convenience of the Formatting toolbar's one-click access to many of the formatting tasks you will want to perform does have its limits. As you can see in the worksheet, when you use the Formatting toolbar, you cannot specify how the format is applied. To make the change that Joan suggests, you need to open the Format Cells dialog box, which gives you more control over the formatting.

To open the Format Cells dialog box:

1. Select the nonadjacent range **B21:D23;F21:G24**.

2. Click **Format** on the menu bar, and then click **Cells**. The Format Cells dialog box opens. See Figure 3-5.

Figure 3-5   FORMAT CELLS DIALOG BOX

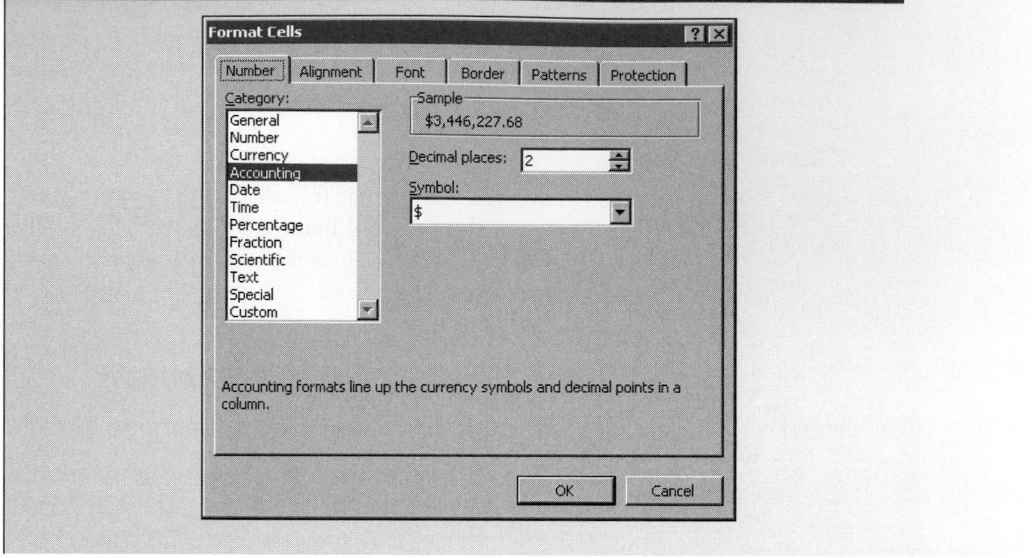

The Format Cells dialog box contains the following six tabs, each dedicated to a different set of format properties:

- **Number**—used to format the appearance of text and values within selected cells
- **Alignment**—used to control how text and values are aligned within a cell
- **Font**—used to choose the font type, size, and style
- **Border**—used to create borders around selected cells
- **Patterns**—used to create and apply background colors and patterns for selected cells
- **Protection**—used to lock or hide selected cells, preventing other users from modifying the cells' contents

So far, you have worked with number formats only. Excel supports several categories of number formats, ranging from Accounting and Currency formats to Scientific formats that might be used for recording engineering data. Figure 3-6 describes some of the number format categories.

Figure 3-6   NUMBER FORMAT CATEGORIES

CATEGORY	DESCRIPTION
General	Default format; numbers are displayed without dollar signs, commas, or trailing decimal places
Number	Used for a general display of numbers
Currency, Accounting	Used for displaying monetary values; use Accounting formats to align decimal points within a column
Date, Time	Used for displaying date and time values
Percentage	Used for displaying decimal values as percentages
Fraction, Scientific	Used for displaying values as fractions or in scientific notation
Text	Used for displaying values as text strings
Special	Used for displaying zip codes, phone numbers, and social security numbers

As shown in Figure 3-5, Excel applied an Accounting format, displaying the dollar sign and two decimal places, to the sales figures. The Accounting format differs from the Currency format; the Accounting format lines up the decimal points and the dollar signs for values within a column so that all the dollar signs appear at the left edge of the cell border. To align the dollar signs closer to the numbers, you can change the format to the Currency format.

To apply the Currency format:

1. On the Number tab, click **Currency** in the Category list box.

As shown in the Negative numbers list box, Excel displays negative currency values either with a minus sign (-) or with a combination of a red font and parentheses. Joan wants any negative currency values to be displayed with a minus sign.

2. Click the first entry in the Negative numbers list box.

3. Click the **OK** button. Excel changes the format of the currency values, removing the blank spaces between the dollar signs and the currency values, rather than having the dollar signs lined up within each column.

By using the Format Cells dialog box, you can control the formatting to ensure that text and values are displayed the way you want them to be.

Working **with Fonts and Colors**

A **font** is the design applied to characters, letters, and punctuation marks. Each font is identified by a **font name** (or **typeface**). Some of the more commonly used fonts are Arial, Times Roman, and Courier. Each font can be displayed using one of the following styles: regular, italic, bold, or bold italic. Fonts can also be displayed with special effects, such as strikeout, underline, and color.

Fonts can also be rendered in different sizes. Sizes are measured using "points." By default, Excel displays characters using a 10-point Arial font in a regular style. To change the font used in a selected cell, you either click the appropriate buttons on the Formatting toolbar or select options in the Format Cells dialog box.

In the logo that the company uses on all its correspondence and advertising materials, the name "NewGeneration Monitors" appears in a large Times New Roman font. Joan wants you to modify the title in cell A1 to reflect this company-wide format.

To change the font and font size of the title:

1. Click cell **A1** to make it the active cell.

2. Click the **list arrow** for the Font button `Arial ▾` on the Formatting toolbar, scroll down the list of available fonts, and then click **Times New Roman**.

TROUBLE? If you do not have the Times New Roman font installed on your computer, choose a different Times Roman font or choose MS Serif in the list.

3. Click the **list arrow** for the Font Size button `10 ▾` on the Formatting toolbar, and then click **18**. Figure 3-7 shows the revised format for the title in cell A1.

Figure 3-7 CHANGING THE FONT AND FONT SIZE

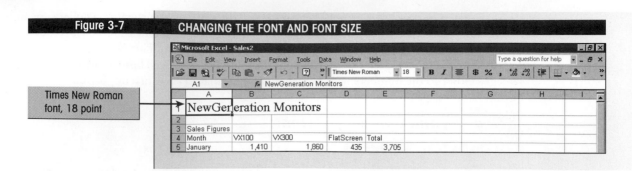

Times New Roman font, 18 point

Joan wants the column titles of both tables displayed in bold font and the word "Total" in both tables displayed in italics. To make these modifications, you will again use the Formatting toolbar.

To apply the bold and italic styles:

1. Select the nonadjacent range **A4:E4;A20:H20**.

2. Click the **Bold** button **B** on the Formatting toolbar. The titles in the two tables now appear in a boldface font.

3. Select cell **A17**, press and hold the **Ctrl** key, and then click cell **A24**.

4. Click the **Italic** button **I** on the Formatting toolbar. The word "Total" in cells A17 and A24 is now italicized.

Joan points out that NewGeneration's logo usually appears in a red font. Color is another one of Excel's formatting tools. Excel allows you to choose a text color from a palette of 40 different colors. If the color you want is not listed, you can modify Excel's color configuration to create a different color palette. Excel's default color settings will work for most situations, so in this case you will not modify Excel's color settings.

To change the font color of the title to red:

1. Click cell **A1** to make it the active cell.

2. Click the **list arrow** for the Font Color button **A·** on the Formatting toolbar. A color palette appears. See Figure 3-8.

Figure 3-8 CHOOSING A RED FONT COLOR

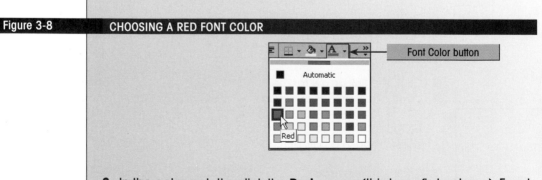

Font Color button

3. In the color palette, click the **Red** square (third row, first column). Excel changes the color of the font in cell A1 to red. See Figure 3-9.

Figure 3-9   **CHANGING FONT COLOR**

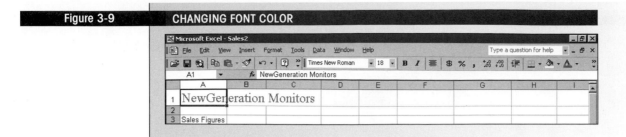

Aligning **Cell Contents**

When you enter numbers and formulas into a cell, Excel automatically aligns them with the cell's right edge and bottom border. Text entries are aligned with the left edge and bottom border. The default Excel alignment does not always create the most readable worksheets. As a general rule, you should center column titles, format columns of numbers so that the decimal places are lined up within a column, and align text with the left edge of the cell. You can change alignment using the alignment tools on the Formatting toolbar or the options on the Alignment tab in the Format Cells dialog box.

Joan wants the column titles centered above the values in each column.

To center the column titles using the Formatting toolbar:

1. Select the nonadjacent range **B4:E4;B20:H20**.

2. Click the **Center** button ▤ on the Formatting toolbar. Excel centers the text in the selected cells in each column.

The Formatting toolbar also provides the Align Left button and the Align Right button so that you can left- and right-align cell contents. If you want to align the cell's contents vertically, you have to open the Format Cells dialog box and choose the vertical alignment options on the Alignment tab.

Another alignment option available in the Format Cells dialog box is the Merge and Center option, which centers the text in one cell across a range of cells. Joan wants the company logo to be centered at the top of the worksheet. In other words, she wants the contents of cell A1 to be centered across the range A1:H1.

To center the text across the range A1:H1:

1. Select the range **A1:H1**.

2. Click **Format** on the menu bar, and then click **Cells**.

3. Click the **Alignment** tab.

4. Click the **Horizontal** list arrow in the Text alignment pane, and then click **Center Across Selection**. See Figure 3-10.

Figure 3-10   ALIGNMENT TAB

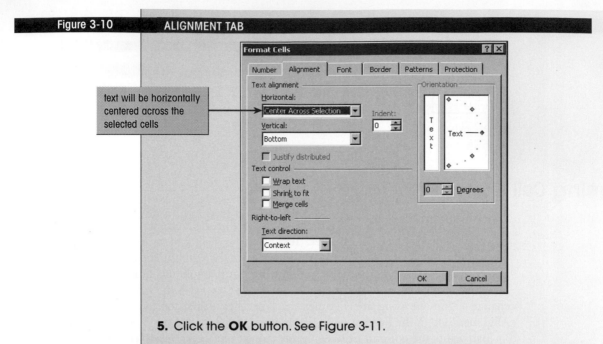

text will be horizontally centered across the selected cells

5. Click the OK button. See Figure 3-11.

Figure 3-11   CENTERING TEXT WITHIN CELLS AND ACROSS COLUMNS

text is centered across the range A1:H1

text is centered within each cell

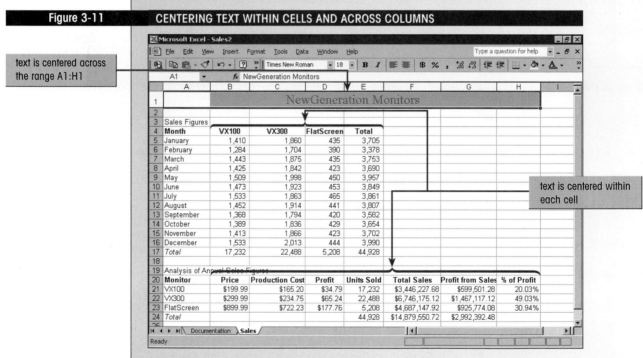

Indenting and Wrapping Text

Sometimes you will want a cell's contents offset, or indented, a few spaces from the cell's edge. This is particularly true for text entries that are aligned with the left edge of the cell. Indenting is often used for cell entries that are considered "subsections" of your worksheet. In the sales figures table, Joan wants you to indent the names of the months in the range A5:A16 and the monitor titles in the range A21:A23.

To indent the months and monitor titles:

1. Select the nonadjacent range **A5:A16;A21:A23**.

2. Click the **Increase Indent** button on the Formatting toolbar. Excel shifts the contents of the selected cells to the right.

   TROUBLE? You may have to click the Toolbar Options button, and then choose the Add or Remove Buttons option before you can click the Increase Indent button. As you use more buttons on the Formatting toolbar, they are added to the toolbar. If your Standard and Formatting toolbars now appear on separate rows, that is okay. The rest of the figures in this book might not look exactly like your screen, but this will not affect your work.

Clicking the Increase Indent button increases the amount of indentation by roughly one character. To decrease or remove an indentation, click the Decrease Indent button or modify the indent value using the Format Cells dialog box.

If you enter text that is too wide for a cell, Excel either extends the text into the adjoining cells (if the cells are empty) or truncates the display of the text. You can also have Excel wrap the text within the cell so that the excess text is displayed on additional lines within the cell. To wrap text, you use the Format Cells dialog box.

Joan notes that some of the column titles in the second table are long. For example, the "Production Cost" label in cell C20 is much longer than the values below it. This formatting has caused some of the columns to be wider than they need to be. Joan suggests that you wrap the text within the column titles and then reduce the width of the columns.

To wrap the title text within a cell and reduce the column widths:

1. Select the cell range **A20:H20**.

2. Click **Format** on the menu bar, and then click **Cells**.

3. Click the **Wrap text** check box in the Text control pane.

4. Click the **OK** button. The text in cells C20 and G20 now appears on two rows within the cells.

5. Reduce the width of column **C** to about **10** characters.

6. Reduce the width of column **G** to about **12** characters.

7. Reduce the width of column **H** to about **8** characters. See Figure 3-12.

Figure 3-12	WRAPPING TEXT WITHIN A CELL

long column titles wrap to a new line and the widths of the columns are reduced

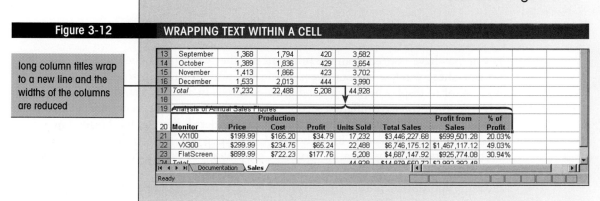

> **TROUBLE?** Different monitors have different screen resolutions and column widths. If your screen does not match Figure 3-12, resize the columns accordingly.

Other Formatting Options

Excel supports even more formatting options than have been discussed so far. For example, instead of wrapping the text, you can have Excel shrink it to fit the size of the cell. If you reduce the cell later on, Excel will automatically resize the text to match. You can also rotate the contents of the cell, displaying the cell entry at almost any angle (see Figure 3-13). Joan does not need to use either of these options in her workbook, but they might be useful later on another project.

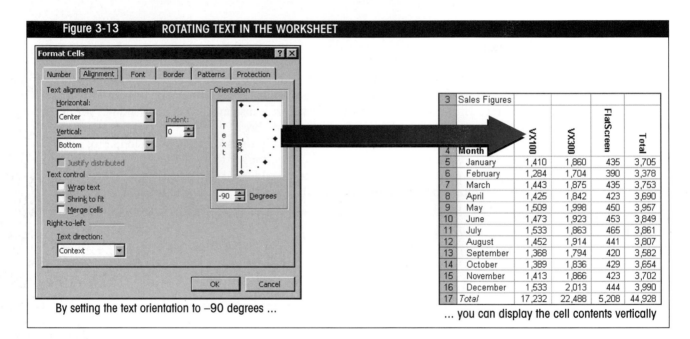

Figure 3-13   ROTATING TEXT IN THE WORKSHEET

By setting the text orientation to –90 degrees ...

... you can display the cell contents vertically

Working with Cell Borders and Backgrounds

Up to now, all the formatting you have done has been applied to the contents of a cell. Excel also provides a range of tools to format the cells themselves. Specifically, you can add borders to the cells and color the cell backgrounds.

Adding a Cell Border

As you may have noticed from the printouts of other worksheets, the gridlines that appear in the worksheet window are not displayed on the printed page. In some cases, however, you might want to display borders around individual cells in a worksheet. This would be particularly true when you have different sections or tables in a worksheet, as in Joan's Sales worksheet.

You can add a border to a cell using either the Borders button on the Formatting toolbar or the options on the Border tab in the Format Cells dialog box. The Borders button allows you to create borders quickly, whereas the Format Cells dialog box lets you further refine your choices.

Joan wants you to place a border around each cell in the two tables in the worksheet. You'll select the appropriate border style from the list of available options on the Borders palette.

To create a grid of cell borders in the two tables:

1. Select the nonadjacent range **A4:E17;A20:H24**.

2. Click the **list arrow** for the Borders button ▭ ▾ on the Formatting toolbar. See Figure 3-14.

Figure 3-14	BORDER OPTIONS

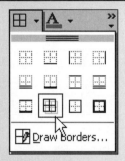

3. Click the **All Borders** option (third row, second column) in the gallery of border options. A thin border appears around each cell in the selected range.

4. Click cell **A1** to deselect the range.

You can also place a border around the entire range itself (and not the individual cells) by selecting a different border style. Try this by creating a thick border around the cell range.

To create a thick border around the selected range:

1. Select the range **A4:E17;A20:H24** again.

2. Click the **list arrow** for the Borders button ▭ ▾ on the Formatting toolbar, and then click the **Thick Box Border** option (third row, fourth column) in the border gallery.

3. Click cell **A2**. Figure 3-15 shows the two tables with their borders.

Figure 3-15   BORDERS WITHIN AND AROUND THE TWO SALES TABLES

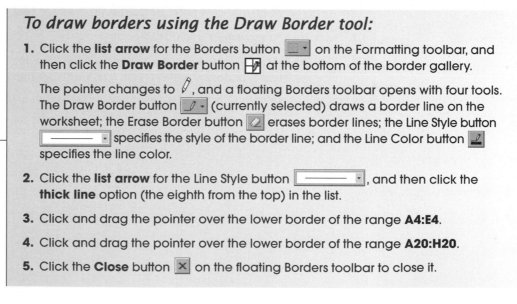

If you want a more interactive way of drawing borders on your worksheet, you can use the Draw Border button, which is also one of the options on the Borders palette. To see how this option works, you will add a thick black line under the column titles in both of the tables.

To draw borders using the Draw Border tool:

1. Click the **list arrow** for the Borders button on the Formatting toolbar, and then click the **Draw Border** button at the bottom of the border gallery.

   The pointer changes to , and a floating Borders toolbar opens with four tools. The Draw Border button (currently selected) draws a border line on the worksheet; the Erase Border button erases border lines; the Line Style button specifies the style of the border line; and the Line Color button specifies the line color.

2. Click the **list arrow** for the Line Style button , and then click the **thick line** option (the eighth from the top) in the list.

3. Click and drag the pointer over the lower border of the range **A4:E4**.

4. Click and drag the pointer over the lower border of the range **A20:H20**.

5. Click the **Close** button on the floating Borders toolbar to close it.

Finally, you will add a double line above the Total row in each table. You will add the line using the options in the Format Cells dialog box.

To create the double border lines:

1. Select the nonadjacent range **A16:E16;A23:H23**.

2. Click **Format** on the menu bar, and then click **Cells**.

3. Click the **Border** tab. The Border tab displays a diagram showing what borders, if any, are currently surrounding the selected cells.

   The bottom border is currently a single thin line. You want to change this to a double line.

4. Click the **double line** style in the Line Style list box located on the right side of the tab.

5. Click the **bottom border** in the border diagram. The bottom border changes to a double line. See Figure 3-16.

Figure 3-16 | **BORDER TAB**

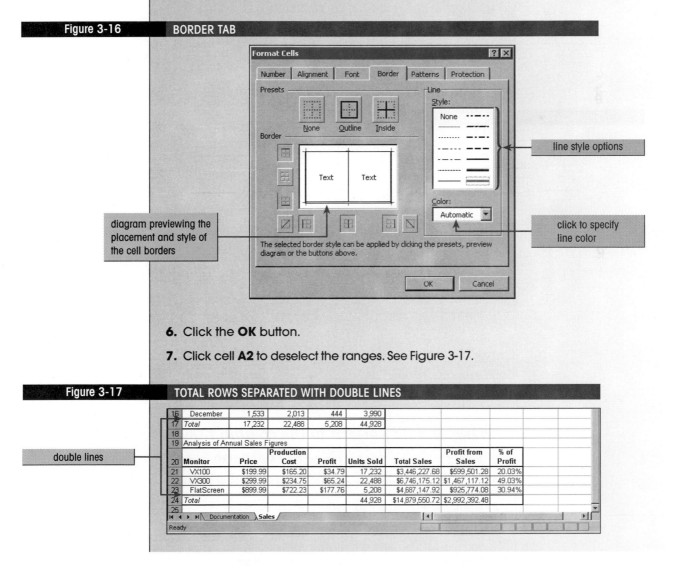

diagram previewing the placement and style of the cell borders

line style options

click to specify line color

6. Click the **OK** button.

7. Click cell **A2** to deselect the ranges. See Figure 3-17.

Figure 3-17 | **TOTAL ROWS SEPARATED WITH DOUBLE LINES**

double lines

			Production				Profit from	% of	
16	December	1,533	2,013	444	3,990				
17	Total	17,232	22,488	5,208	44,928				
18									
19	Analysis of Annual Sales Figures								
20	Monitor	Price	Production Cost	Profit	Units Sold	Total Sales	Profit from Sales	% of Profit	
21	VX100	$199.99	$165.20	$34.79	17,232	$3,446,227.68	$599,501.28	20.03%	
22	VX300	$299.99	$234.75	$65.24	22,488	$6,746,175.12	$1,467,117.12	49.03%	
23	FlatScreen	$899.99	$722.23	$177.76	5,208	$4,687,147.92	$925,774.08	30.94%	
24	Total				44,928	$14,879,550.72	$2,992,392.48		
25									

Documentation \ Sales /

Ready

You can also specify a color for the cell borders by using the Color list box located on the Border tab (see Figure 3-16). Joan does not need to change the border colors, but she would like you to change the background color for the column title cells.

Setting the Background Color and Pattern

Patterns and color can be used to enliven a dull worksheet or provide visual emphasis to the sections of the worksheet that you want to stress. If you have a color printer or a color projection device, you might want to take advantage of Excel's color tools. By default, worksheet cells are not filled with any color (the white you see in your worksheet is not a fill color for the cells). To change the background color in a worksheet, you can use the Fill Color button on the Formatting toolbar, or you can use the Format Cells dialog box, which also provides patterns that you can apply to the background.

Joan wants to change the background color of the worksheet. When she makes her report later in the week, she will be using the company's color laser printer. So she would like you to explore using background color in the column titles for the two sales tables. She suggests that you try formatting the column titles with a light yellow background.

To apply a fill color to the column titles:

1. Select the nonadjacent range **A4:E4;A20:H20**.

2. Click the **list arrow** for the Fill Color button 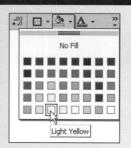 on the Formatting toolbar.

3. Click the **Light Yellow** square (fifth row, third column). See Figure 3-18.

Figure 3-18 | SELECTING A FILL COLOR

4. Click cell **A2** to deselect the column titles. The column titles now have light yellow backgrounds.

Joan would also like to investigate whether you can apply a pattern to the fill background. Excel supports 18 different fill patterns. To create and apply a fill pattern, you have to open the Format Cells dialog box.

To apply a fill pattern to the column titles:

1. Select the nonadjacent range **A4:E4;A20:H20**.

2. Click **Format** on the menu bar, and then click **Cells**.

3. Click the **Patterns** tab.

4. Click the **Pattern** list arrow. Clicking the Pattern list arrow displays a gallery of patterns and a palette of colors applied to the selected pattern. The default pattern color is black. You will choose just a pattern now.

5. Click the **50% Gray** pattern (first row, third column) in the pattern gallery. See Figure 3-19.

Figure 3-19	SELECTING A FILL PATTERN

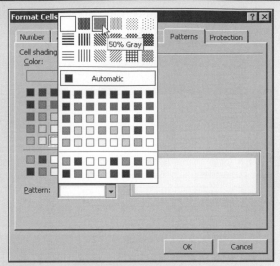

6. Click the **OK** button.

7. Click cell **A2** to deselect the ranges and to see the pattern.

The background pattern you have chosen overwhelms the text in these column titles. You can improve the appearance by changing the color of the pattern itself from black to a light orange.

To change the pattern color:

1. Select the range **A4:E4;A20:H20** again.

2. Click **Format** on the menu bar, and then click **Cells**.

3. Click the **Pattern** list arrow. The default (or automatic) color of a selected pattern is black. You can choose a different color for the pattern using the color palette below the patterns.

4. Click the **Light Orange** square (third row, second column) in the color palette.

5. Click the **OK** button.

6. Click cell **A2** to deselect the ranges. Figure 3-20 shows the patterned background applied to the column titles. Note that the light orange pattern does not overwhelm the column titles.

Figure 3-20 **COLUMN TITLES WITH FORMATTED BACKGROUND**

background pattern
with a new color

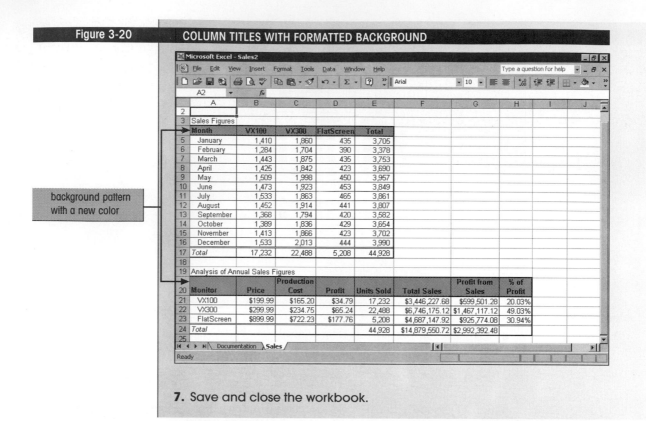

7. Save and close the workbook.

Joan is pleased with the progress you have made. In the next session, you will explore other formatting features.

Session 3.1 QUICK CHECK

1. Describe two ways of applying a Currency format to cells in your worksheet.

2. If the number 0.05765 has been entered into a cell, what will Excel display if you:
   a. format the number using the Percent format with one decimal place?
   b. format the number using the Currency format with two decimal places and a dollar sign?

3. Which two buttons can you use to copy a format from one cell range to another?

4. A long text string in one of your worksheet cells has been truncated. List three ways to correct this problem.

5. How do you center the contents of a single cell across a range of cells?

6. Describe three ways of creating a cell border.

7. How would you apply a background pattern to a selected cell range?

SESSION 3.2

In this session, you will format a worksheet by merging cells, hiding rows and columns, inserting a background image, and finding and replacing formats. You will also be introduced to styles. You will see how to create and apply styles, and you will learn how styles can be used to make formatting more efficient. You will also learn about Excel's gallery of AutoFormats. Finally, you will work with the Print Preview window to control the formatting applied to your printed worksheets.

Formatting the Worksheet

In the previous session you formatted individual cells within the worksheet. Excel also provides tools for formatting the entire worksheet or the entire workbook. You will explore some of these tools as you continue to work on Joan's Sales report.

Merging Cells into One Cell

Joan has reviewed the Sales worksheet and has a few suggestions. She would like you to format the titles for the two tables in her report so that they are centered in a bold font above the tables. You could do this by centering the cell title across a cell range, as you did for the title in the last session. Another way is to merge several cells into one cell and then center the contents of that single cell. Merging a range of cells into a single cell removes all of the cells from the worksheet, except the cell in the upper-left corner of the range. Any content in the other cells of the range is deleted. To merge a range of cells into a single cell, you can use the Merge option on the Alignment tab in the Format Cells dialog box or click the Merge and Center button on the Formatting toolbar.

> ### To merge and center the cell ranges containing the table titles:
>
> 1. If you took a break after the previous session, start Excel and open the Sales2 workbook.
>
> 2. In the Sales worksheet, select the range **A3:E3**.
>
> 3. Click the **Merge and Center** button ⊞ on the Formatting toolbar. The cells in the range A3:E3 are merged into one cell at the cell location, A3. The text in the merged cell is centered as well.
>
> 4. Click the **Bold** button **B** on the Formatting toolbar.
>
> 5. Select the range **A19:H19**, click ⊞, and then click **B**.
>
> 6. Click cell **A2** to deselect the range. Figure 3-21 shows the merged and centered table titles.

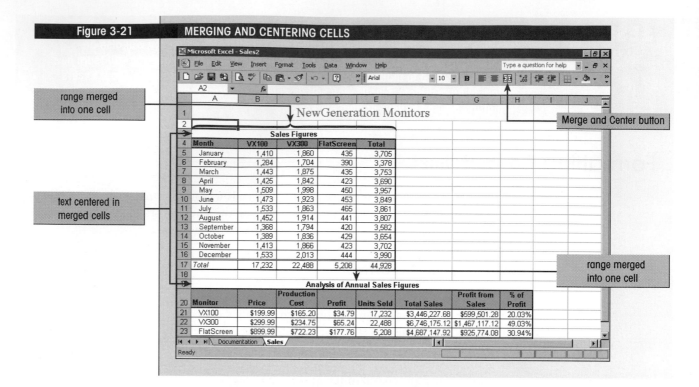

Figure 3-21 — MERGING AND CENTERING CELLS

To split a merged cell back into individual cells, regardless of the method you used to merge the cells, you select the merged cell and then click the Merge and Center button again. You can also merge and unmerge cells using the Alignment tab in the Format Cells dialog box.

Hiding Rows and Columns

Sometimes Joan does not need to view the monthly sales for the three monitors. She does not want to remove this information from the worksheet, but she would like the option of temporarily hiding that information. Excel provides this capability. Hiding a row or column does not affect the data stored there, nor does it affect any other cell that might have a formula referencing a cell in the hidden row or column. Hiding part of your worksheet is a good way of removing extraneous information, allowing you to concentrate on the more important data contained in your worksheet. To hide a row or column, first you must select the row(s) or column(s) you want to hide. You can then use the Row or Column option on the Format menu or right-click the selection to open its shortcut menu.

You will hide the monthly sales figures in the first table in the worksheet.

To hide the monthly sales figures:

1. Select the headings for rows **5** through **16**.

2. Right-click the selection, and then click **Hide** on the shortcut menu. Excel hides rows 5 through 16. Note that the total sales figures in the range B17:E17 are not affected by hiding the monthly sales figures. See Figure 3-22.

Figure 3-22   **HIDING WORKSHEET ROWS**

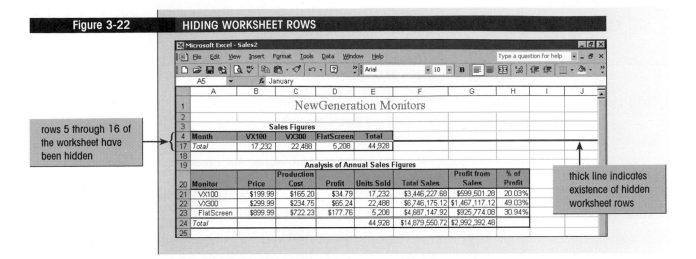

rows 5 through 16 of the worksheet have been hidden

thick line indicates existence of hidden worksheet rows

To unhide a hidden row or column, you must select the headings of the rows or columns that border the hidden area; then you can use the right-click method or the Row or Column command on the Format menu. You will let Joan know that it is easy to hide any row or column that she does not want to view. But for now you will redisplay the hidden sales figures.

To unhide the monthly sales figures:

1. Select the row headings for rows **4** and **17**.

2. Right-click the selection, and then click **Unhide** on the shortcut menu. Excel redisplays rows 5 through 16.

3. Click cell **A2** to deselect the rows.

Hiding and unhiding a column follows the same process, except that you select the worksheet column headings rather than the row headings.

Formatting the Sheet Background

In the previous session you learned how to create a background color for individual cells within the worksheet. Excel also allows you to use an image file as a background. The image from the file is tiled repeatedly until the images fill up the entire worksheet. Images can be used to give the background a textured appearance, like that of granite, wood, or fibered paper. The background image does not affect the format or content of any cell in the worksheet, and if you have already defined a background color for a cell, Excel displays the color on top, hiding that portion of the image.

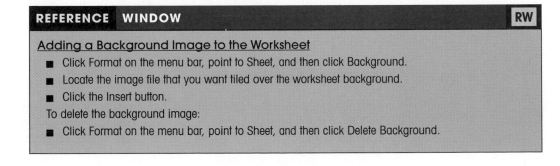

REFERENCE WINDOW   **RW**

Adding a Background Image to the Worksheet
- Click Format on the menu bar, point to Sheet, and then click Background.
- Locate the image file that you want tiled over the worksheet background.
- Click the Insert button.

To delete the background image:
- Click Format on the menu bar, point to Sheet, and then click Delete Background.

Joan wants you to experiment with using a background image for the Sales worksheet. She has an image file that she wants you to try.

To add a background image to the worksheet:

1. Click **Format** on the menu bar, point to **Sheet**, and then click **Background**.

2. Locate and select the **Back** image file in the Tutorial.03/Tutorial folder on your Data Disk, and then click the **Insert** button.

   The Back image file is tiled over the worksheet, creating a textured background for the Sales sheet. Notice that the tiling is hidden in the cells that already contained a background color. In order to make the sales figures easier to read, you'll change the background color of those cells to white.

3. Select the nonadjacent range **A5:E17;A21:H24**.

4. Click the **list arrow** for the Fill Color button 🎨▾ on the Formatting toolbar, and then click the **White** square (last row, last column) in the color palette.

5. Click cell **A2**. Figure 3-23 shows the Sales worksheet with the formatted background.

Figure 3-23   ADDING A BACKGROUND IMAGE

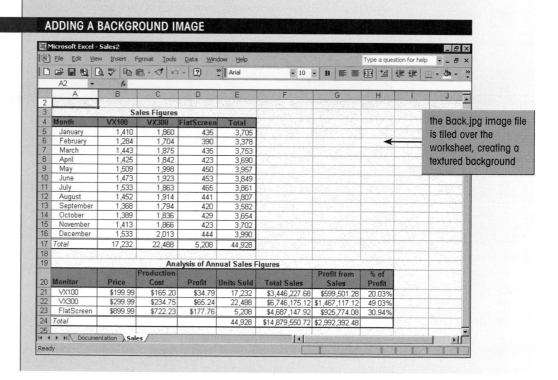

the Back.jpg image file is tiled over the worksheet, creating a textured background

Note that you cannot apply a background image to all of the sheets in a workbook at the same time. If you want to apply the same background to several sheets, you must format each sheet separately.

Formatting Sheet Tabs

In addition to the sheet background, you can also format the background color of worksheet tabs. This color is only visible when the worksheet is not the active sheet in the workbook; the background color for the active sheet is always white. You can use tab colors to better organize the various sheets in your workbook. For example, worksheets that contain sales information could be formatted with blue tabs, and sheets that describe the company's cash flow or budget could be formatted with green tabs.

If Joan's workbook contained many sheets, it would be easier to locate information if the sheet tabs were different colors. To explore how to color sheet tabs, you will change the tab color of the Sales worksheet to light orange.

To change the tab color:

1. Right-click the **Sales** tab, and then click **Tab Color** on the shortcut menu.

2. Click the **Light Orange** square (third row, second column) in the color palette.

3. Click the **OK** button. A light orange horizontal stripe appears at the bottom of the tab, but because Sales is the active worksheet, the background color is still white.

4. Click the **Documentation** tab. Now that Documentation is the active sheet, you can see the light orange color of the Sales sheet tab.

5. Click the **Sales** tab to make it the active sheet again.

Clearing and Replacing Formats

Sometimes you might want to change or remove some of the formatting from your workbooks. As you experiment with different formats, you will find a lot of use for the Undo button on the Standard toolbar as you remove formatting choices that did not work out as well as you expected. Another choice is to clear the formatting from the selected cells, returning the cells to their initial, unformatted appearance. To see how this option works, you will remove the formatting from the company name in cell A1 on the Sales worksheet.

To clear the format from cell A1:

1. Click cell **A1** to select it.

2. Click **Edit** on the menu bar, point to **Clear**, and then click **Formats**. Excel removes the formatting that was applied to the cell text and removes the formatting that centered the text across the range A1:H1.

3. Click the **Undo** button 🔄 on the Standard toolbar to undo your action, restoring the formats you cleared.

Sometimes you will want to make a formatting change that applies to several different cells. If those cells are scattered throughout the workbook, you may find it time-consuming to search and replace the formats for each individual cell. If the cells share a common format that you want to change, you can use the Find and Replace command to locate the formats and modify them.

Finding and Replacing a Format

- Click Edit on the menu bar, and then click Replace.
- Click the Options >> button, if necessary, to display the format choices.
- Click the top Format list arrow, and then click Format.
- Specify the format you want to find in the Find Format dialog box, and then click the OK button.
- Click the bottom Format list arrow, and then click Format.
- Enter a new format with which you want to replace the old format, and then click the OK button.
- Click the Replace All button to replace all occurrences of the old format; or click the Replace button to replace the currently selected cell containing the old format; or click the Find Next button to find the next occurrence of the old format before replacing it.
- Click the Close button.

For example, in the Sales worksheet, the table titles and column titles are displayed in a bold font. After seeing how the use of color has made the worksheet come alive, Joan wants you to change the titles to a boldface blue. Rather than selecting the cells that contain the table and column titles and formatting them, you can replace all occurrences of the boldface text with blue boldface text.

To find and replace formats:

1. Click **Edit** on the menu bar, and then click **Replace**. The Find and Replace dialog box opens. You can use this dialog box to find and replace the contents of the cells. In this case, you will use it only for finding and replacing formats, leaving the contents of the cells unchanged.

2. Click the **Options >>** button to display additional find and replace options. See Figure 3-24.

TROUBLE? If the button on your workbook appears as Options <<, the additional options are already displayed, and you do not need to click any buttons.

Figure 3-24	FIND AND REPLACE DIALOG BOX

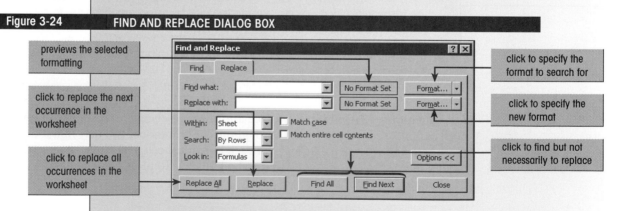

The dialog box expands to display options that allow you to find and replace cell formats. It also includes options to determine whether to search within the active sheet or the entire workbook. Currently no format options have been set.

3. Click the top **Format** list arrow, and then click **Format**.

The Find Format dialog box opens. Here is where you specify the format you want to search for. In this case, you are searching for cells that contain boldface text.

4. Click the **Font** tab, and then click **Bold** in the Font style list box. See Figure 3-25.

| Figure 3-25 | FIND FORMAT DIALOG BOX |

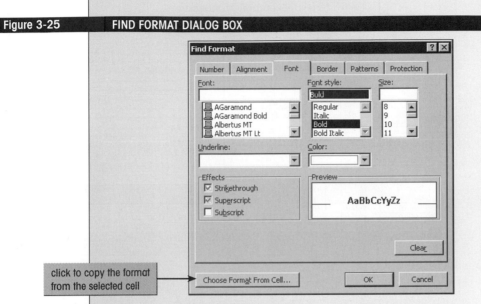

click to copy the format from the selected cell

5. Click the **OK** button.

Next, you have to specify the new format that you want to use to replace the boldface text. In this case, you need to specify a blue boldface text.

6. Click the bottom **Format** list arrow, and then click **Format**.

7. Click **Bold** in the Font style list box.

8. Click the **Color** list box, and then click the **Blue** square (second row, sixth column) in the color palette.

9. Click the **OK** button.

10. Click the **Replace All** button to replace all boldface text in the worksheet with boldface blue text. Excel indicates that it has completed its search and made 15 replacements.

11. Click the **OK** button, and then click the **Close** button. See Figure 3-26.

Figure 3-26 SALES WORKSHEET WITH BOLDFACE BLUE TEXT

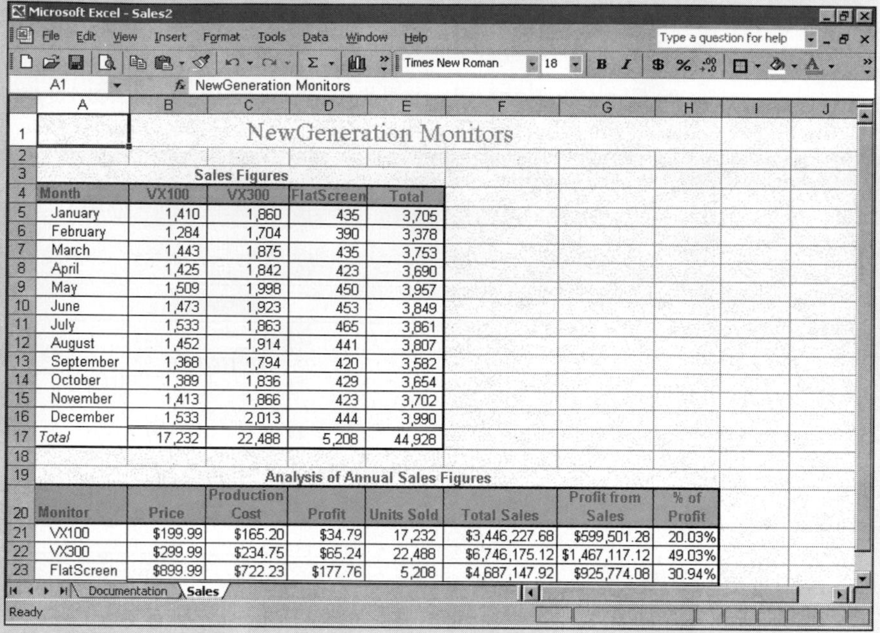

NewGeneration Monitors

Sales Figures

Month	VX100	VX300	FlatScreen	Total
January	1,410	1,860	435	3,705
February	1,284	1,704	390	3,378
March	1,443	1,875	435	3,753
April	1,425	1,842	423	3,690
May	1,509	1,998	450	3,957
June	1,473	1,923	453	3,849
July	1,533	1,863	465	3,861
August	1,452	1,914	441	3,807
September	1,368	1,794	420	3,582
October	1,389	1,836	429	3,654
November	1,413	1,866	423	3,702
December	1,533	2,013	444	3,990
Total	17,232	22,488	5,208	44,928

Analysis of Annual Sales Figures

Monitor	Price	Production Cost	Profit	Units Sold	Total Sales	Profit from Sales	% of Profit
VX100	$199.99	$165.20	$34.79	17,232	$3,446,227.68	$599,501.28	20.03%
VX300	$299.99	$234.75	$65.24	22,488	$6,746,175.12	$1,467,117.12	49.03%
FlatScreen	$899.99	$722.23	$177.76	5,208	$4,687,147.92	$925,774.08	30.94%

Using **Styles**

If you have several cells that employ the same format, you can create a style for those cells. A **style** is a saved collection of formatting options—number formats; text alignment; font sizes and colors; borders; and background fills—that can be applied to cells in the worksheet. When you apply a style, Excel remembers which styles are associated with which cells in the workbook. If you want to change the appearance of a particular type of cell, you need only modify the specifications for the style, and the appearance of any cell associated with that style would be automatically changed to reflect the new style.

You can create a style in one of two ways: by selecting a cell from the worksheet and basing the style definition on the formatting choices already defined for that cell or by manually entering the style definitions into a dialog box. Once you create and name a style, you can apply it to cells in the workbook.

Excel has eight built-in styles named Comma, Comma [0], Currency, Currency [0], Followed Hyperlink, Hyperlink, Normal, and Percent. You have been using styles all of this time without knowing it. Most cells are formatted with the Normal style, but when you enter a percentage, Excel formats it using the Percent style. Similarly, currency values are automatically formatted using the Currency style, and so forth.

Creating a Style

Joan wants you to further modify the appearance of the worksheet by changing the background color of the months in the first table and the monitor names in the second table to yellow. Rather than applying new formatting to the cells, you decide to create a new style called "Category" that you will apply to the category columns of the tables in your workbook. You will create the style using the format already applied to cell A5 of the worksheet as a basis.

To create a style using a formatted cell:

1. Click cell **A5** to select it. The format applied to this cell becomes the basis of the new style that you want to create.

2. Click **Format** on the menu bar, and then click **Style**. The Style dialog box opens. All of the formatting options associated with the style of the active cell are listed. For example, the font is 10-point Arial.

   To create a new style for this cell, you simply type a different name into the list box.

3. Verify that Normal is highlighted in the Style name list box, and then type **Category**. See Figure 3-27.

Figure 3-27	STYLE DIALOG BOX

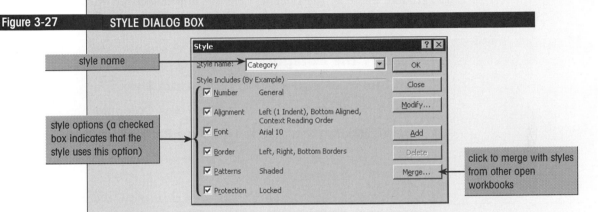

If you do not want all of these formatting options to be part of the Category style, you can deselect the options you no longer want included. You can also modify a current format option or add a new format option. You'll change the background color in the Category style to yellow.

4. Click the **Modify** button. The Format Cells dialog box opens.

5. Click the **Patterns** tab, and then click the **Yellow** square (fourth row, second column) in the color palette.

6. Click the **OK** button to close the Format Cells dialog box.

   If you click the OK button in the Style dialog box, the style definition changes and the updated style is applied to the active cell. If you click the Add button in the dialog box, the change is added, or saved, to the style definition but the updated style is not applied to the active cell.

7. Click the **OK** button. The background color of cell A5 changes to yellow.

Now you need to apply this style to other cells in the workbook.

Applying a Style

To apply a style to cells in a worksheet, you first select the cells you want associated with the style and then open the Styles dialog box.

To apply the Category style:

1. Select the nonadjacent range **A6:A16;A21:A23**.

2. Click **Format** on the menu bar, and then click **Style**.

3. Click the **Style name** list arrow, and then click **Category**.

4. Click the **OK** button, and then click cell **A2** to deselect the cells. A yellow background color is applied to all of the category cells in the two tables.

The yellow background appears a bit too strong. You decide to change it to a light yellow background. Since all the category cells are now associated with the Category style, you need only modify the definition of the Category style to make this change.

To modify the Category style:

1. Click **Format** on the menu bar, and then click **Style**.

2. Click the **Style name** list arrow, and then click **Category**.

3. Click the **Modify** button, and then click the **Patterns** tab, if necessary.

4. Click the **Light Yellow** square (fifth row, second column) in the color palette, and then click the **OK** button.

5. Click the **Add** button. Excel changes the background color of all the cells associated with the Category style.

   TROUBLE? Do not click the OK button. Clicking the OK button will apply the Category style only to the active cell.

6. Click the **Close** button. See Figure 3-28.

Figure 3-28   **CATEGORY STYLE IN THE SALES WORKSHEET**

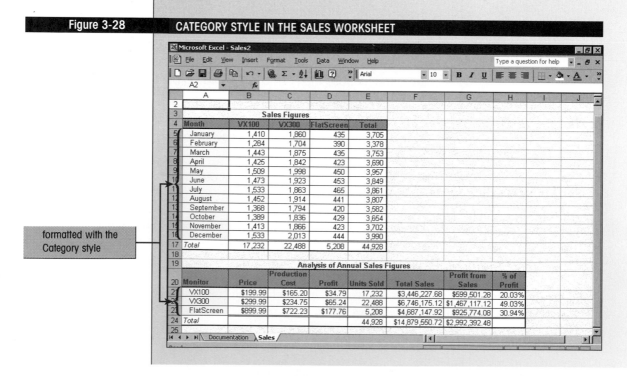

formatted with the Category style

You can also copy styles from one workbook to another. Copying styles allows you to create a collection of workbooks that share a common look and feel.

Using AutoFormat

Excel's **AutoFormat** feature lets you choose an appearance for your worksheet cells from a gallery of 17 predefined formats. Rather than spending time testing different combinations of fonts, colors, and borders, you can apply a professionally designed format to your worksheet by choosing one from the AutoFormat Gallery. You have done a lot of work already formatting the data in the Sales workbook to give it a more professional and polished look, but you decide to see how the formatting you have done compares to one of Excel's AutoFormat designs.

Apply an AutoFormat to the Sales Figures table so that you can compare the professionally designed format to the format you have worked on.

To apply an AutoFormat to the table:

1. Select the range **A3:E17**.

2. Click **Format** on the menu bar, and then click **AutoFormat**. The AutoFormat dialog box opens. See Figure 3-29.

Figure 3-29	AUTOFORMAT GALLERY

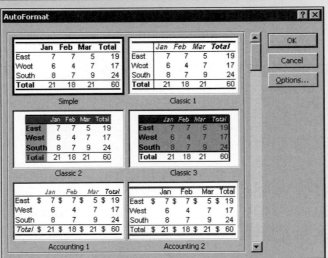

The dialog box displays a preview of how each format will appear when applied to cells in a worksheet.

3. Click **Classic 3** in the list of available designs, and then click the **OK** button.

4. Click cell **A2** to remove the highlighting from the first table. Figure 3-30 shows the appearance of the Classic 3 design in your workbook.

Figure 3-30   **APPLYING AN AUTOFORMAT**

table formatted with the Classic 3 design

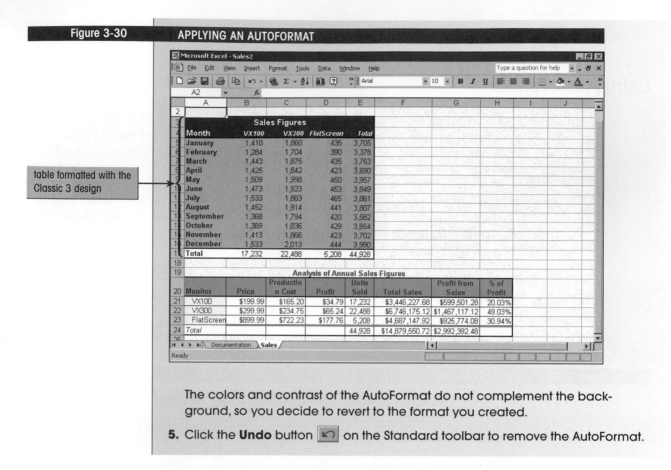

The colors and contrast of the AutoFormat do not complement the background, so you decide to revert to the format you created.

5. Click the **Undo** button on the Standard toolbar to remove the AutoFormat.

Although you will not use an AutoFormat in this case, you can see how an AutoFormat can be used as a starting point. You could start with Excel's professional design and then make modifications to the worksheet to fit your own needs.

Formatting the Printed Worksheet

You have settled on an appearance for the Sales worksheet—at least the appearance that is displayed on your screen. But that is only half of your job. Joan also wants you to format the appearance of this worksheet when it is printed out. You have to decide how to arrange the report on the page, the size of the page margins, the orientation of the page, and whether the page will have any headers or footers. You can make many of these choices through Excel's Print Preview.

Opening the Print Preview Window

As the name implies, the **Print Preview window** shows you how each page of your worksheet will look when it is printed. From the Print Preview window, you can make changes to the page layout before you print your worksheet.

To preview the Sales worksheet printout:

1. Click the **Print Preview** button on the Standard toolbar. The Print Preview window opens, displaying the worksheet as it will appear on the printed page. See Figure 3-31.

Figure 3-31	PRINT PREVIEW

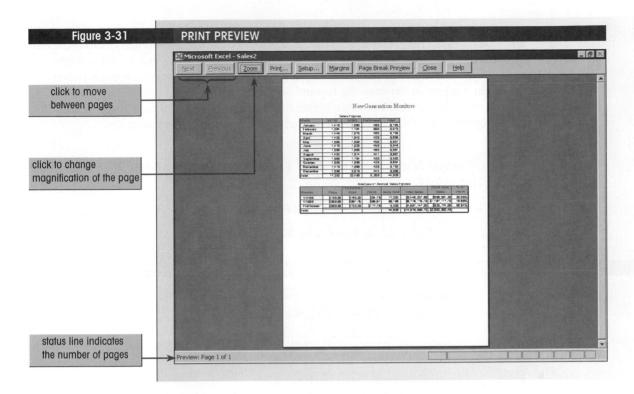

click to move
between pages

click to change
magnification of the page

status line indicates
the number of pages

Excel displays the full page in the Print Preview window. You might have difficulty reading the text because it is so small. Do not worry if the preview is not completely readable. One purpose of Print Preview is to see the overall layout of the worksheet. If you want a better view of the text, you can increase the magnification by either using the Zoom button on the Print Preview toolbar or by clicking the page with the 🔍 pointer. Clicking the Zoom button again, or clicking the page a second time with the pointer, reduces the magnification, bringing the whole page back into view.

To enlarge the preview:

1. Click the **Zoom** button on the Print Preview toolbar.

2. Use the horizontal and vertical scroll bars to move around the worksheet.

3. Click anywhere within the page with the pointer to reduce the magnification.

You can also make changes to the layout of a worksheet page using the Setup and Margins buttons on the Print Preview toolbar.

Defining the Page Setup

You can use the Page Setup dialog box to control how a worksheet is placed on a page. You can adjust the size of the **margins**, which are the spaces between the page content and the edges of the page. You can center the worksheet text between the top and bottom margins (horizontally) or between the right and left margins (vertically). You can change the **page orientation**, which determines if the page is wider than it is tall or taller than it is wide. You can also use the Page Setup dialog box to display text that will appear at the top (a header) or bottom (a footer) of each page of a worksheet. You can open the Page Setup dialog box using the File menu or using the Print Preview toolbar.

By default, Excel places a 1-inch margin above and below the report and a ¾-inch margin to the left and right. Excel also aligns column A in a worksheet at the left margin and row 1 at the top margin. Depending on how many columns and rows there are in the worksheet, you might want to increase or decrease the page margins or center the worksheet between the left and right margins or between the top and bottom margins.

You want to increase the margin size for the Sales worksheet to 1 inch all around. You also want the worksheet to be centered between the right and left margins.

To change the margins and center the worksheet horizontally on the page:

1. Click the **Setup** button on the Print Preview toolbar.

2. Click the **Margins** tab. See Figure 3-32.

| Figure 3-32 | MARGINS TAB |

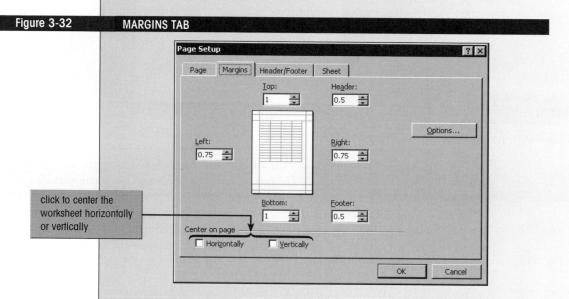

click to center the worksheet horizontally or vertically

The Margins tab provides a diagram showing the placement of the worksheet on the page. In addition to adjusting the sizes of the margins, you can also adjust the space allotted to the header and footer.

3. Click the **Left** up arrow to set the size of the left margin to **1** inch.

4. Click the **Right** up arrow to increase the size of the right margin to **1** inch.

5. Click the **Horizontally** check box, and then click the **OK** button.

The left and right margins change, but there is now less room for the worksheet. As indicated in the status line located in the lower-left corner of the Print Preview window, the worksheet now covers two pages instead of one; the last column in the Sales Analysis table has been moved to the second page. You can restore the margins to their default sizes, and the worksheet will once again fit on a single page. Another option is to change the orientation of the page from portrait to landscape. **Portrait orientation** (which is the default) displays the page taller than it is wide. **Landscape orientation** displays the page wider than it is tall.

You want to change the page orientation to landscape so the last column of the Sales Analysis table will fit on the same page as the rest of the columns in the table.

To change the page orientation:

1. Click the **Setup** button, and then click the **Page** tab.

2. Click the **Landscape** option button. See Figure 3-33.

Figure 3-33	PAGE SETUP DIALOG BOX

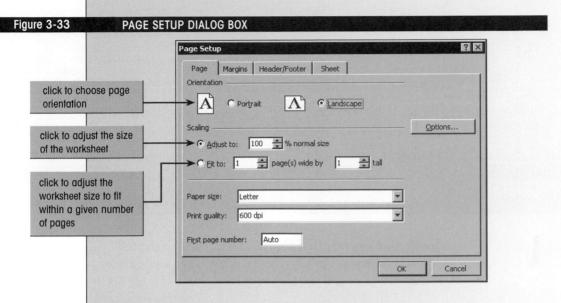

click to choose page orientation

click to adjust the size of the worksheet

click to adjust the worksheet size to fit within a given number of pages

3. Click the **OK** button. Excel changes the orientation to landscape. Note that the entire report now fits on a single page.

The Page tab in the Page Setup dialog box contains other useful formatting features. You can reduce or increase the size of the worksheet on the printed page. The default size is 100%. You can also have Excel automatically reduce the size of the report to fit within a specified number of pages.

Working with Headers and Footers

Joan wants you to add a header and footer to the report. A **header** is text printed in the top margin of every worksheet page. A **footer** is text printed at the bottom of every page. Headers and footers can add important information to your printouts. For example, you can create a header that displays your name and the date the report was created. If the report covers multiple pages, you can use a footer to display the page number and the total number of pages. You use the Page Setup dialog box to add headers and footers to a worksheet.

Excel tries to anticipate headers and footers that you might want to include in your worksheet. Clicking the Header or Footer list arrow displays a list of possible headers or footers (the list is the same for both). For example, the "Page 1" entry inserts the page number of the worksheet prefaced by the word "Page" in the header; the "Page 1 of ?" displays the page number and the total number of pages. Other entries in the list include the name or the worksheet or workbook.

If you want to use a header or footer not available in the lists, you click the Custom Header or Custom Footer button and create your own header and footer. The Header dialog box and the Footer dialog box are similar. Each dialog box is divided into three sections, left, center, and right. If you want to enter information such as the filename or the day's date into the header or footer, you can either type the text or click one of the format buttons located above the three section boxes. Figure 3-34 describes the format buttons and the corresponding format codes.

Figure 3-34   HEADER/FOOTER FORMATTING BUTTONS

BUTTON	NAME	FORMATTING CODE	ACTION
A	Font	None	Sets font, text style, and font size
#	Page number	&[Page]	Inserts page number
	Total pages	&[Pages]	Inserts total number of pages
	Date	&[Date]	Inserts current date
	Time	&[Time]	Insert current time
	Path	&[Path]&[File]	Inserts path and filename
	Filename	&[File]	Insert filename
	Sheet name	&[Tab]	Inserts name of active worksheet
	Picture	&[Picture]	Inserts an image file
	Format picture	None	Formats the picture inserted into the header/footer

Joan wants a header that displays the filename at the left margin and today's date at the right margin. She wants a footer that displays the name of the workbook author, with the text aligned at the right margin of the footer. You'll create the header and footer now.

To add a custom header to the workbook:

1. Click the **Setup** button on the Print Preview toolbar, and then click the **Header/Footer** tab.

2. Click the **Custom Header** button. The Header dialog box opens. See Figure 3-35.

Figure 3-35   HEADER DIALOG BOX

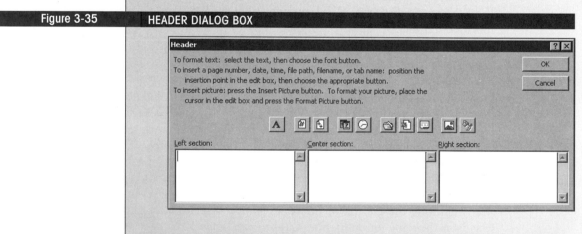

3. In the Left section box, type **Filename:** and then press the **spacebar**.

4. Click the **Filename** button ⬚ to insert the format code. The formatting code for the name of the file, &(File), appears after the text string that you entered in the Left section box.

5. Click the **Right section** box, and then click the **Date** button ⬚. Excel inserts the &(DATE) format code into the section box.

6. Click the **OK** button to close the Header dialog box.

7. Click the **Custom Footer** button. The Footer dialog box opens.

8. Click the **Right section** box, type **Prepared by:** and then type your name.

9. Click the **OK** button. The Page Setup dialog box displays the custom header and footer that you created.

10. Click the **OK** button. The Print Preview window displays the worksheet with the new header and footer.

11. Click the **Close** button on the Print Preview toolbar.

Working with the Print Area and Page Breaks

When you displayed the worksheet in the Print Preview window, how did Excel know which parts of the active worksheet you were going to print? The default action is to print all parts of the active worksheet that contain text, formulas, or values, which will not always be what you want. If you want to print only a part of the worksheet , you can define a **print area** that contains the content you want to print. To define a print area, you must first select the cells you want to print, and then select the Print Area option on the File menu.

A print area can include an adjacent range or nonadjacent ranges. You can also hide rows or columns in the worksheet in order to print nonadjacent ranges. For her report, Joan might decide against printing the sales analysis information. To remove those cells from the printout, you need to define a print area that excludes the cells for the second table.

To define the print area:

1. Select the range **A1:H17**.

2. Click **File** on the menu bar, point to **Print Area**, and then click **Set Print Area**.

3. Click cell **A2**. Excel places a dotted black line around the selected cells of the print area. This is a visual indicator of what parts of the worksheet will be printed.

4. Click the **Print Preview** button 🔍 on the Standard toolbar. The Print Preview window displays only the first table. The second table has been removed from the printout because it is not in the defined print area.

5. Click the **Close** button on the Print Preview toolbar.

Another approach that Joan might take is to place the two tables on separate pages. You can do this for her by creating a **page break**, which forces Excel to place a portion of a worksheet on a new page.

Before inserting a page break, you must first redefine the print area to include the second table.

To redefine the print area, and then insert a page break:

1. Select the range **A1:H24**.

2. Click **File** on the menu bar, point to **Print Area**, and then click **Set Print Area**.

Before you insert the page break, you need to indicate where in the worksheet you want the break to occur. Because you want to print the second table on a separate page, you will set the page break at cell A18, which will force rows 18 through 24 to a new page.

3. Click cell **A18**, click **Insert** on the menu bar, and then click **Page Break**. Another blank dotted line appears—this time above cell A18, indicating there is a page break at this point in the print area. See Figure 3-36.

Figure 3-36   ADDING A PAGE BREAK TO THE PRINT AREA

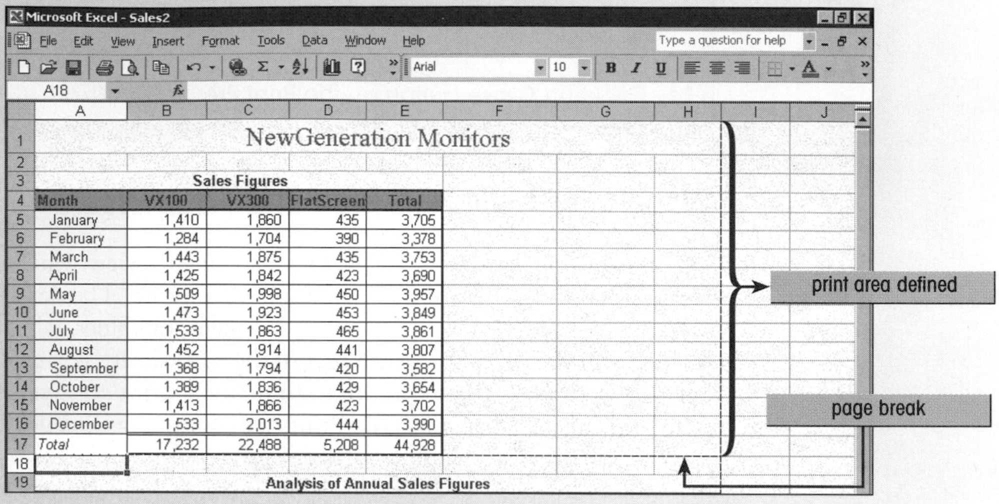

print area defined

page break

4. Click the **Print Preview** button [icon] on the Standard toolbar. Excel displays the first table on page 1 in the Print Preview window.

5. Click the **Next** button to display page 2.

6. Click the **Close** button on the Print Preview toolbar.

You show the print preview to Joan and she notices that the name of the company, "NewGeneration Monitors," appears on the first page, but not on the second. That is not surprising because the range that includes the company name is limited to the first page of the printout. However, Joan would like to have this information repeated on the second page.

You can repeat information, such as the company name, by specifying which cells in the print area should be repeated on each page. This is particularly useful in long tables which extend over many pages. In such cases, you can have the column titles repeated for each page in the printout.

To set rows or columns to repeat on each page, you have to open the Page Setup dialog box from the worksheet window.

To repeat the first row on each page:

1. Click **File** on the menu bar, and then click **Page Setup**.

2. Click the **Sheet** tab. See Figure 3-37.

> You have created the two charts that Alicia wanted, so you can save your
> work, and then close the workbook and Excel.
>
> 5. Click the **Save** button 🖫 on the Standard toolbar, and then click the **Close**
>   button ☒ on the title bar to exit the program.

Rotating the pie and exploding a pie slice are both examples of formatting the appearance
of an Excel chart after it has been created with the Chart Wizard. In the next session you
will learn about the other formatting tools available to you.

Session 4.1 QUICK CHECK

1. What is the difference between a chart type and a chart sub-type?

2. Which chart would you most likely use to track the daily values of a stock?

3. What is a data series?

4. What is the difference between the plot area and the chart area?

5. What are gridlines?

6. Describe the two types of chart locations.

7. A chart that shows the contribution of each data value to the whole is called a(n)
   _____ chart.

8. A pie chart in which all slices are separated from one another is called a(n)
   _____ chart.

SESSION 4.2

In this session, you will modify the properties of the charts you created in the first
session. You will change the chart's data source, location, options, and type. You
will format individual chart elements and apply color fills. You will also work with
3-D charts and create drawing objects that you can place on your chart sheets or
worksheets. Finally, you print a chart sheet.

Modifying a Chart

In the last session you used the Chart Wizard to create two charts. Although the Chart
Wizard presents you with a variety of choices concerning your chart's appearance, the wizard does not provide every possibility. To make further modifications to your charts, you can
use the formatting tools and commands available on the Chart toolbar and the Chart menu.

Editing the Data Source

After you create a chart, you can change the data that is used in the chart. You might need
to change the data if the wrong information has been used or if you decide to display a different data series.

REFERENCE WINDOW

<u>Editing a Chart's Data Source</u>
- Click Chart on the menu bar, and then click Source Data.
- Click the Series tab.
- To remove a data series, select the data series in the Series list box, and click the Remove button.
- To add a data series, click the Add button, and then select the cell references for the new data series.
- To revise a data series, select the data series in the Series list box, click the reference box for the data series, and then select a new cell reference.
- Click the OK button.

Alicia can see from the charts that 16-inch telescopes comprise a small portion of Vega's sales due to their size and expense. For this reason, she wants you to remove the NightVision 16 from the two charts you created. You will begin by removing the NightVision 16 data series from the column chart.

To remove the NightVision 16 data series:

1. If you took a break after the previous session, make sure Excel is running and the Vega2 workbook is open. Click the **Sales** tab.

2. Click the embedded column chart to select it.

3. Click **Chart** on the menu bar, and then click **Source Data**. The Source Data dialog box opens.

4. Click the **Series** tab.

5. Click **NightVision 16** in the Series list box.

6. Click the **Remove** button.

7. Click the **OK** button. The NightVision 16 sales data is no longer represented in the column chart. See Figure 4-20.

Figure 4-20   REMOVING THE NIGHTVISION 16 FROM THE COLUMN CHART

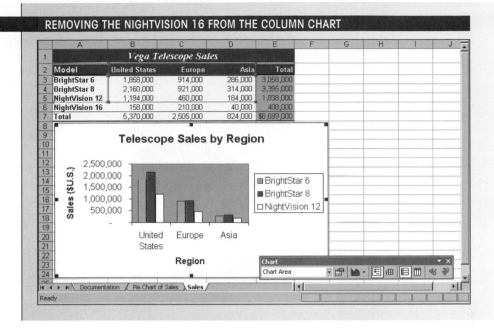

Removing the NightVision 16 pie slice from the pie chart presents a slightly different problem. Unlike the column chart (which has multiple data series), the pie chart has only one data series—there is not a separate data series for each model. To remove the NightVision 16 from the pie chart, you have to change the cell reference of the data series to exclude the NightVision 16 row.

To remove the NightVision 16 from the pie chart:

1. Click the **Pie Chart of Sales** tab.

2. Click **Chart** on the menu bar, and then click **Source Data**.

   There is only one data series, named "Total," in this chart. The cell reference for the values for this data series is found in the range E3:E6 on the Sales worksheet. The corresponding labels for the data series are found in the range A3:A6 on the same worksheet. To exclude the NightVision 16 from the chart, you have to change the references to range E3:E5 and range A3:A5, respectively.

3. Click the **Collapse Dialog Box** button ▦ for the Values box. Clicking the Collapse Dialog Box button collapses the dialog box so you can drag the pointer over a range of cells in the Sales worksheet that you need to select.

4. Select the range **E3:E5** and then click the **Expand Dialog Box** button ▦.

5. Click ▦ for the Category Labels box.

6. Select the range **A3:A5** and then click ▦.

7. Click the **OK** button. Figure 4-21 shows the revised pie chart.

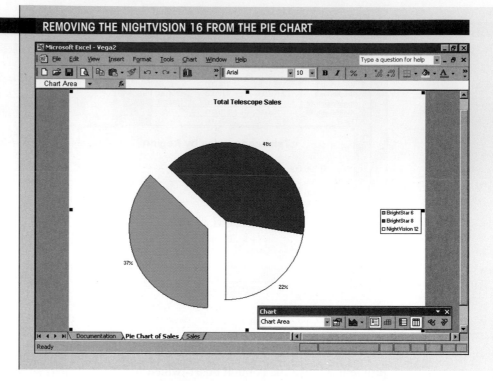

Figure 4-21   **REMOVING THE NIGHTVISION 16 FROM THE PIE CHART**

Note that, when you removed the NightVision 16 from the data series, the percentages in the pie chart changed as well to reflect a total sales figure based on only three models rather than on four.

Changing the Chart Location

Alicia has decided that she prefers the chart sheet to the embedded chart. She wants you to move the embedded column chart on the Sales worksheet to a chart sheet. Rather than re-creating the chart using the Chart Wizard, you will use the Location command on the Chart menu.

You will move the embedded chart to a chart sheet, which you will name "Column Chart of Sales."

To change the location of the column chart:

1. Click the **Sales** tab.

2. Verify that the embedded column chart is selected in the worksheet.

3. Click **Chart** on the menu bar, and then click **Location**.

4. Click the **As new sheet** option button, and then type **Column Chart of Sales** as the name of the chart sheet.

5. Click the **OK** button. The column chart moves into its own chart sheet.

Changing Chart Options

You may have noticed that the dialog boxes to change the chart's data source and location looked identical to the dialog boxes from steps 2 and 4 of the Chart Wizard. Dialog boxes from the remaining two Chart Wizard steps are also available through commands on the Chart menu. Recall that the third step of the Chart Wizard allowed you to format the chart's appearance by adding or removing chart titles, gridlines, legends, and labels.

Alicia wants to revisit some of the chart options selected earlier. After seeing that the percent labels in the pie chart provided useful information, she wants you to add labels to the column chart displaying the actual sales values on top of each column.

To revise the chart options for the column chart:

1. Click **Chart** on the menu bar, and then click **Chart Options**. The Chart Options dialog box opens. Note that the dialog box is identical to Step 3 of the Chart Wizard.

2. Click the **Data Labels** tab, if necessary.

3. Click the **Value** check box, and then click the **OK** button. The sales figures for each model now appear above the corresponding column. See Figure 4-22.

Figure 4-22   ADDING LABELS TO THE COLUMNS

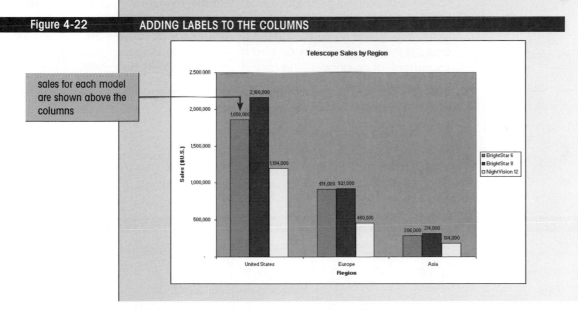

sales for each model are shown above the columns

Alicia has a few changes that she wants you to make to the chart labels. You cannot make these changes by modifying the chart options. Instead you have to format the individual elements within the chart.

Formatting **Chart Elements**

So far, all of the formatting that you have done has applied to the chart as a whole. You can also select and format individual chart elements, such as the chart title, legend, and axes. To format an individual chart element, you can click the element to select it and then format its appearance using the same tools on the Formatting toolbar you used to format worksheet cells; you can double-click the chart element to open a dialog box containing formatting shortcut menu to open the dialog box. Using the Formatting toolbar is usually quicker, but opening a format dialog box will provide you with more options and more control over the element's appearance.

Formatting Chart Text

Alicia wants you to change the alignment of the chart labels. She feels that the labels would look better if you changed their alignment from horizontal to vertical. Alicia also points out that the chart's background is gray. She is concerned that the black label text will be difficult to read for some people. She suggests that yellow text might show up better against the gray background.

To format the chart labels:

1. Double-click the chart label **1,858,000**, located above the first column in the chart. The Format Data Labels dialog box opens.

   The 1,858,000 chart label is part of the set of labels for the BrightStar 6 model. Any changes you make in this dialog box will apply to all of the labels for the BrightStar 6 telescope sales data (and not to the other labels on the chart). The Format Data Labels dialog box has four tabs. You use the Font and Number tabs to change font-related options to text and values and to apply number formats to values as you did in the previous tutorial. You use the Patterns tab to change the fill color, patterns, and borders around labels. You use the Alignment tab to change the alignment of the text in the label.

2. Click the **Color** list box, and then click the **Yellow** square located in the fourth row and third column of the color palette.

3. Click the **Alignment** tab.

4. Click the **red diamond** ✦ in the Orientation box, and then drag the diamond counterclockwise until the value in the Degrees box displays **90**. The text changes to a vertical orientation with an angle of 90 degrees. See Figure 4-23.

Figure 4-23   CHANGING THE ORIENTATION OF THE COLUMN LABELS

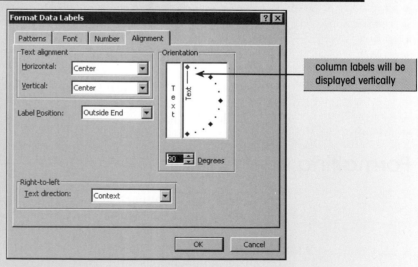

5. Click the **OK** button. The labels for the BrightStar 6 sales data have been rotated 90 degrees and now appear in a yellow font.

6. Double-click the **2,160,000** label above the second column in the chart, and then change the label to a yellow font, rotated 90 degrees.

7. Double-click the **1,194,000** label above the third column, and then format the label as you did the previous two labels. Figure 4-24 shows the revised labels.

Figure 4-24	FORMATTED COLUMN LABELS

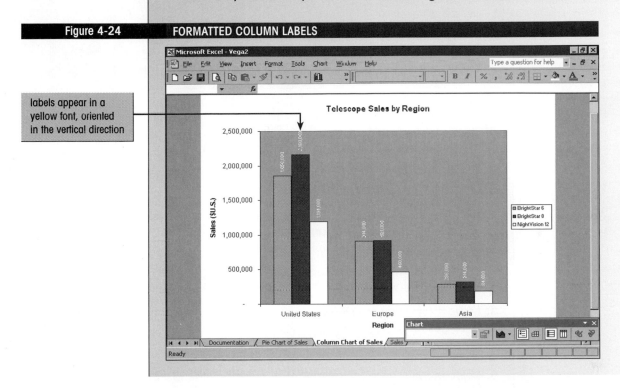

labels appear in a yellow font, oriented in the vertical direction

Inserting New Chart Text

Excel classifies chart text in three categories: label text, attached text, and unattached text. **Label text** includes the category names, the tick mark labels, and the legend text. Label text often is linked to cells in the worksheet. **Attached text** includes the chart title and the axes titles. Although the text appears in a predefined position, you can edit and move it. Unlike label text, attached text is not linked to any cells in the worksheet. Finally, **unattached text** is any additional text that you want to include in the chart. Unattached text can be positioned anywhere within the chart area and formatted with the same tools you use to format label and attached text.

To enter unattached text, you type the text in the Formula bar. Excel automatically creates a text box for the text entry and places the text box on the chart. You can then resize the text box and move it to another location in the chart area. You can format the text using the Format Text Box dialog box.

REFERENCE   WINDOW   **RW**

<u>Inserting Unattached Text into a Chart</u>
- Select the chart.
- In the Formula bar, type the text that you want to include in the chart.
- To resize the new unattached text box, click and drag one of the text box's selection handles.
- To move the unattached text box, click the border of the text box, and drag the text box to a new location in the chart area.
- To format the unattached text, select the text box and click the appropriate formatting buttons on the Formatting toolbar; or double-click the border of the text box to open the Format Text Box dialog box, and use the options provided on the dialog box tabs, and then click the OK button.

Alicia wants you to add the text "Vega Sales from the Last Fiscal Year" to the upper-right corner of the plot area. She wants the text in a yellow Arial font.

To create an unattached text entry:

1. With the chart still selected, type **Vega Sales from the Last Fiscal Year** in the Formula bar above the chart, and then press the **Enter** key. Excel places a text box containing the new unattached text in the middle of the plot area.

2. Click the **list arrow** for the **Font Color** button on the Formatting toolbar, and then click the **Yellow** square (fourth row, third column) in the color palette.

3. Move the pointer over the edge of the unattached text box until the pointer changes to ⭭.

4. Drag the text box to the upper-right corner of the chart area.

5. Release the mouse button and click outside of the text box to deselect it. See Figure 4-25.

Figure 4-25   **FORMATTED COLUMN LABELS**

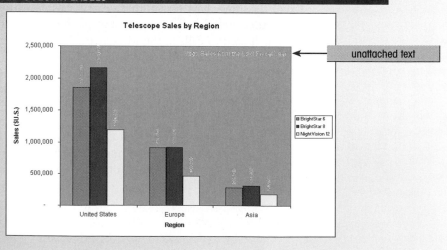

You can double-click an unattached text box at any time to open the Format Text Box dialog box in which you can change the font format, alignment, and color. You can also create a border around the text. Try this now by creating a yellow border.

To create a border for the text box:

1. Double-click the border of the selected text box.

   TROUBLE? If you double-clicked the text in the text box, the Format Text Box dialog box did not open. Double-click the border of the text box.

2. Click the **Colors and Lines** tab.

3. Click the **Color** list box in the Line section, and then click the **Yellow** square (fourth row, third column) in the color palette.

4. Click the **OK** button and then click outside the chart to deselect it. Figure 4-26 shows the revised text box with the yellow border.

Figure 4-26   **FORMATTED COLUMN LABELS**

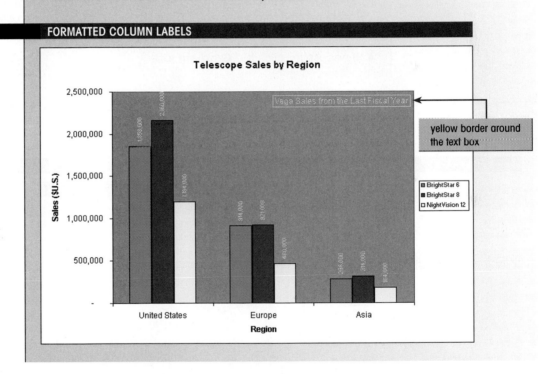

Now that you have formatted the chart labels and have added unattached text, you can turn to some of the other features of Excel charts that need modifying.

Working with Colors and Fills

You solved the problems with the chart labels, but Alicia feels that the column chart lacks visual appeal. Alicia has seen objects filled with a variety of colors that gradually blend from one color to another. She wonders if you can do the same thing for the columns in the column chart.

When you want to fill a column (or area) in a chart with a pattern or color, you are actually modifying the appearance of the data marker in the chart. You will concentrate only on the fill color used in the data marker. Other data markers have other patterns that you can modify. For example, in a scatter chart, the data markers are points that appear in the plot. You can specify the color of those data points, their size, whether a line will connect the data points, and if so the color, thickness, and style of that line.

To format the fill color of the chart columns:

1. Double-click the first column in the chart. The Format Data Series dialog box opens with the tabs that you can use to control one or more aspects of the selected data marker.

2. Click the **Patterns** tab. You can use the options provided on this tab to control the border style that appears around the column as well as the appearance of the column's interior. Currently, the column is formatted with a black border and filled with a pale blue color.

3. Click the **Fill Effects** button. The Fill Effects dialog box opens. The tabs in this dialog box provide a full range of options that you can use to create sophisticated and lush colors and patterns.

4. If necessary, click the **Gradient** tab.

You use the options on the Gradient tab to create fill effects that blend together different and varying amounts of color. Figure 4-27 displays the Gradient tab.

Figure 4-27	FILL EFFECTS

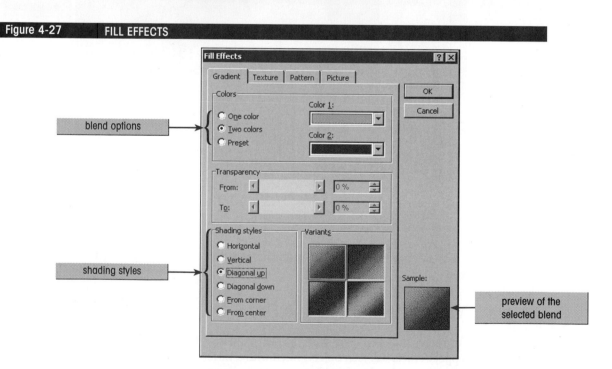

Note that you have three color options from which to choose:

- **One color**—Creates a blend that uses different shades of one color. You select the range of shades using a scroll bar.
- **Two colors**—Creates a blend from one color into another.
- **Preset**—Provides a list of predefined blend styles, including Early Sunset, Nightfall, Ocean, Rainbow, and Chrome.

You can also specify the direction of the blending effect, choosing from horizontal, vertical, diagonal up, diagonal down, from corner, and from center. For the selected column in the current chart, you will create a blend fill effect using a single color starting from a dark shade of the pale blue color. You will use a horizontal shading style to give the color dimension.

To create the fill effect:

1. Click the **One color** option button.

2. Drag the scroll box to the Dark end of the shading scale. Note that as you change the shading scale, the images in the Variants pane reflect the degree of shading.

3. Verify that the **Horizontal** option button in the Shading styles section is selected.

4. Click the **OK** button twice. Excel displays the first column series with a dark blue color at the bottom of the column, blending into the light blue color at the top.

   Create similar blends for the other columns.

5. Double-click the second column in the chart.

6. Click the **Fill Effects** button.

7. Click the **One color** option button, drag the shading scroll bar to the Dark end of the scale, and then click the **OK** button twice.

8. Double-click the third column, and then create the same blend fill effect you created for the first two data series, going from the dark end of the yellow scale to the light end.

9. Click outside the chart area. Figure 4-28 shows the revised column chart with blends for each of the three data series.

Figure 4-28   COLUMNS WITH BLENDED COLORS

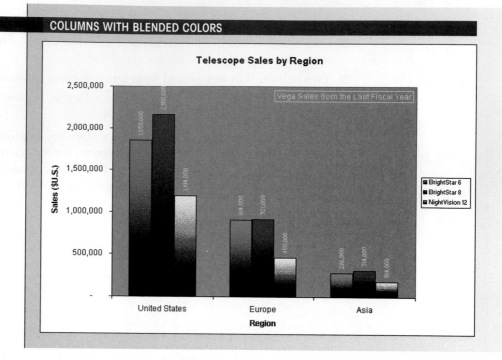

Using a Graphic Image as a Background

Alicia likes the change you made to the columns and now wants to change the background. Rather than just a solid gray background, she wants to use a graphic image in the background. She has a graphic file that shows an image from the Hubble telescope that she thinks would work well with the theme of telescope sales.

To insert this image into the chart, you need to change the fill options for the plot area of the chart.

To change the plot area fill:

1. Double-click any blank space inside the plot area (do not click one of the chart columns).

2. Click the **Fill Effects** button on the Patterns tab.

3. Click the **Picture** tab, and then click the **Select Picture** button.

4. Locate the Tutorial.04/Tutorial folder on your Data Disk, and then select the **Space** file.

5. Click the **Insert** button.

6. Click the **OK** button twice, and then click outside the chart area. Figure 4-29 shows the revised column chart with the new background image.

Figure 4-29	CHART WITH SPACE BACKGROUND IMAGE

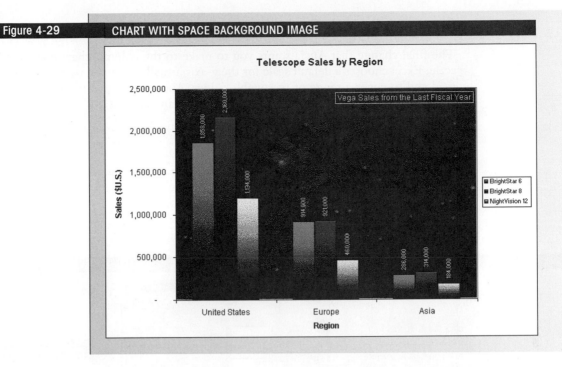

Graphic images can be applied to other elements in the chart. For example, you can replace the columns in the column chart with graphic images. To do so, you select the column and use the same Fill Effects dialog box that you used to create the background image for the chart. However, before you close the Fill Effects dialog box, you can also choose one of the stacking or stretching options available for the image in place of the column. Figure 4-30 shows the effect of the two Format options provided in the Fill Effects dialog box.

Figure 4-30	REPLACING COLUMNS WITH GRAPHICS

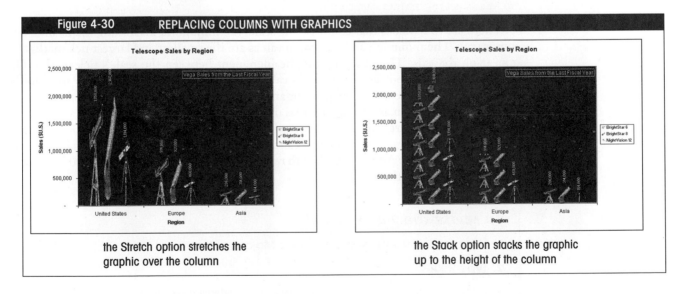

the Stretch option stretches the graphic over the column

the Stack option stacks the graphic up to the height of the column

Alicia is pleased with the appearance of the columns and does not require any additional changes to them.

Changing the Axis Scale

The final change that Alicia wants you to make to the column chart concerns the chart's scale. Excel chooses a default scale for the y-axis, usually designed to make the scale easy to read and to cover a range of reasonable values. Alicia wants you to examine the scale that Excel chose for this chart to see if a change is warranted.

To view the y-axis scale:

1. Double-click any of the values on the y-axis. The Format Axis dialog box opens. You can use this dialog box to format the scale's appearance and to change the range and increments used in the scale.

2. Click the **Scale** tab. See Figure 4-31.

Figure 4-31   SCALE TAB

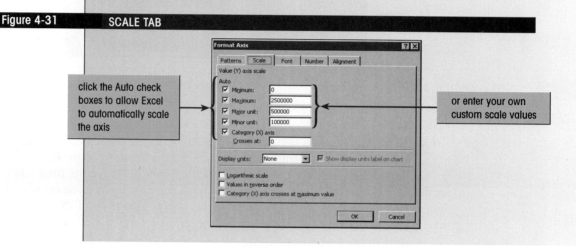

click the Auto check boxes to allow Excel to automatically scale the axis

or enter your own custom scale values

There are four values that comprise the scale: the minimum, maximum, major unit, and minor unit. The minimum and maximum values are the smallest and largest tick marks that appear on the axis. The major unit is the increment between the scale's tick marks. The chart also has a second set of tick marks called **minor tick marks** that may or may not be displayed. The difference between major and minor tick marks is that major tick marks are displayed alongside an axis value, whereas minor tick marks are not.

In the current chart, the scale that Excel displayed ranges from 0 to 2,500,000 in increments of 500,000. The minor tick mark increment is 100,000, but these tick marks are not displayed on the axes. Alicia would like to reduce the increment value to 250,000 in order to show more detail on the chart.

To revise the y-axis scale:

1. Double-click the current entry in the Major unit box.

2. Type **250000**.

3. Click the **OK** button. Figure 4-32 shows the revised y-axis scale.

| Figure 4-32 | REVISED SCALE FOR THE Y-AXIS |

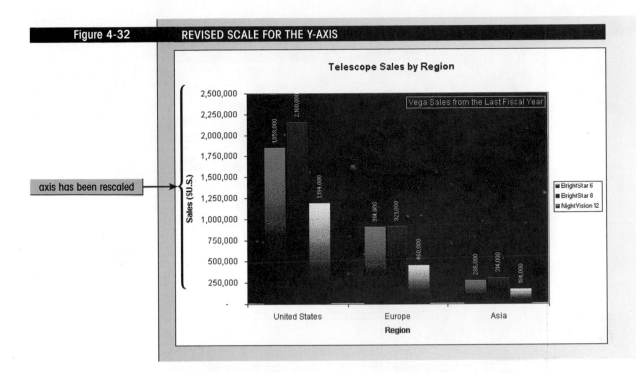

axis has been rescaled

Alicia is happy with the latest version of the column chart. She now wants you to go back to the pie chart and make some modifications there.

Working **with Three-Dimensional Charts**

Many of the Excel charts can be displayed either as two-dimensional "flat" charts or as charts that appear three-dimensional. Alicia wants you to change the pie chart to a three-dimensional pie chart. To do this, you have to change the chart type.

> ### To change the pie chart to 3-D:
>
> **1.** Click the **Pie Chart of Sales** tab.
>
> **2.** Click **Chart** on the menu bar, and then click **Chart Type**.
>
> **3.** Click the second chart sub-type in the top row. See Figure 4-33.

Figure 4-33   CHANGING TO A 3-D PIE CHART

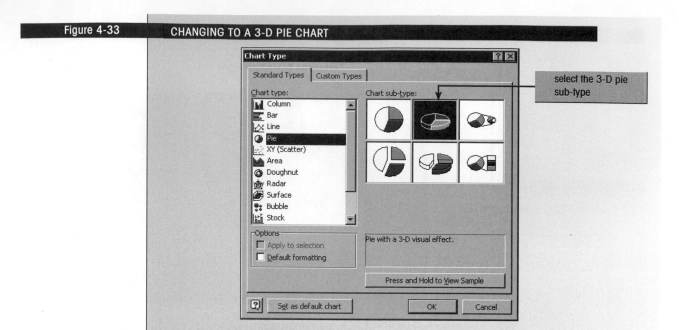

select the 3-D pie
sub-type

4. Click the **OK** button. Excel displays the pie chart in three dimensions. Note that
   Excel has retained the rotation you applied to the chart in the last session, and
   the BrightStar 6 slice is still exploded. See Figure 4-34.

Figure 4-34   3-D PIE CHART

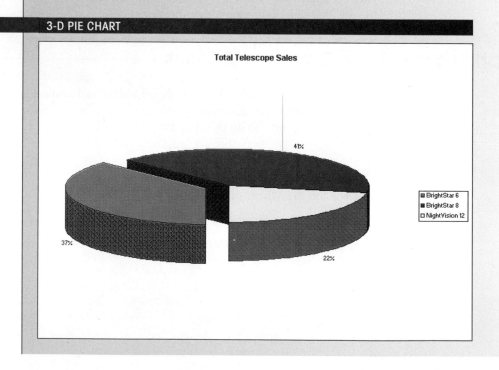

In a 3-D chart, you have several options to modify the 3-D effect. One of these is **elevation**,
the illusion that you're looking at the 3-D chart from a particular height either above or below
the chart. Another of these is **perspective**, which is the illusion that parts of the 3-D chart that
are "farther" away from you decrease in size. Finally, you can rotate a 3-D chart to bring different parts of the chart to the forefront. In a pie chart, you can change the elevation and rotation,
but not the perspective.

Alicia likes the 3-D view of the pie chart but feels that the angle of the pie is too low, causing the pie to appear flat despite its three dimensions. She wants the angle of the pie to be a little higher.

To increase the elevation above the pie chart:

1. Click **Chart** on the menu bar, and then click **3-D View**.

2. Click the **Elevation Up** button twice to increase the elevation to 25 degrees. See Figure 4-35.

Figure 4-35	3-D VIEW DIALOG BOX

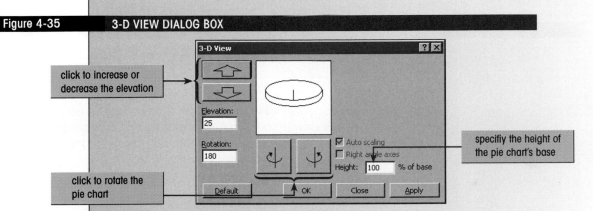

Note that there are also buttons that you can use to rotate the pie chart. Clicking one of the rotation buttons is similar to the rotation setting that you applied to the pie chart at the end of the first session.

3. Click the **OK** button. Excel redraws the pie chart, giving the illusion that the observer is at a higher elevation above the chart.

Alicia is happy with the appearance of the column chart and does not want you to apply any 3-D effects to that chart.

Using the Drawing Toolbar

One of the big stories from the past fiscal year was the successful introduction of the NightVision scopes, and Alicia wants to highlight the fact that the company had in excess of $1,800,000 in sales of the NightVision 12. She has seen charts that contain shapes, like star bursts and block arrows, that give added emphasis to details and facts that the chart author wants to include. Alicia wants to do something similar with the pie chart.

To create a graphical shape, Excel provides the Drawing toolbar. The Drawing toolbar is a common feature of all Office XP products. You can use the Drawing toolbar to add text boxes, lines, block arrows and other objects to charts and worksheets. A whole tutorial could be spent examining all of the features of the Drawing toolbar, but this tutorial just examines how to create and format a drawing object.

Displaying the Drawing Toolbar

Depending on your Excel configuration, the Drawing toolbar may or may not be displayed in the Excel window when you start Excel. (The default is to not show the toolbar.) As with all toolbars, you can choose to display or hide the Drawing toolbar.

To display the Drawing toolbar:

1. Click **View** on the menu bar, point to **Toolbars**, and then click **Drawing**. The Drawing toolbar appears, as shown in Figure 4-36.

Figure 4-36	DRAWING TOOLBAR

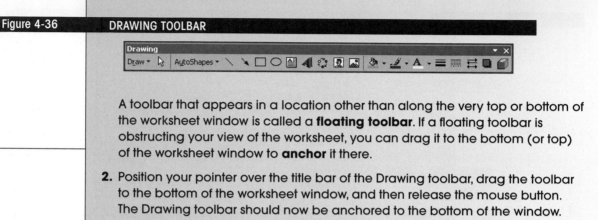

A toolbar that appears in a location other than along the very top or bottom of the worksheet window is called a **floating toolbar**. If a floating toolbar is obstructing your view of the worksheet, you can drag it to the bottom (or top) of the worksheet window to **anchor** it there.

2. Position your pointer over the title bar of the Drawing toolbar, drag the toolbar to the bottom of the worksheet window, and then release the mouse button. The Drawing toolbar should now be anchored to the bottom of the window.

Now you will use the Drawing toolbar to add a drawing object to the pie chart.

Working with AutoShapes

The Drawing toolbar contains a list of predefined shapes called **AutoShapes**. These AutoShapes can be simple squares or circles or more complicated objects such as flow chart objects and block arrows. Once you insert an AutoShape into a chart or worksheet, you can resize and move it, like any other object. You can modify the fill color of an AutoShape, change the border style, and even insert text.

REFERENCE WINDOW   **RW**

Inserting an AutoShape
- Click the AutoShapes list arrow on the Drawing toolbar.
- Point to the AutoShape category that you want to use, and then click the AutoShape that you want to create.
- Position the crosshair pointer over the location for the AutoShape in the chart or worksheet, and then drag the pointer over the area where you want the shape to appear. To draw an AutoShape in the same proportion as the shape on the palette, press and hold the Shift key as you drag the pointer to draw the shape.
- Release the mouse button.
- To resize an AutoShape, click the shape to select it, and then drag one of the nine selection handles.
- To rotate an AutoShape, click the green rotation handle that is connected to the shape, and drag the handle to rotate the shape.
- To change the shape of the AutoShape, click the yellow diamond tool, and drag the tool to change the shape.

Alicia wants to add a multi-pointed star to the pie chart to highlight the success of the NightVision 12 telescope.

To add a multi-pointed star to the pie chart:

1. Click the **AutoShapes** list arrow on the Drawing toolbar.

2. Point to **Stars and Banners**, and then click the **16-Point Star** AutoShape located in the second row and second column of the AutoShapes palette.

   As you move the pointer over the worksheet, the pointer shape will change to $+$.

3. Move the pointer to the upper-right corner of the chart area, about one inch to the right of the chart title.

   To draw an AutoShape in the same proportion as the shape on the palette, you must press and hold the Shift key as you drag the pointer to draw the shape.

4. Press the **Shift** key as you drag the pointer down and to the right about one and one-half inches.

   Note that pressing the Shift key allows you to create a perfect 16-point star. If you do not press the Shift key as you drag the pointer, your star might be slightly lopsided.

5. Release the mouse button. A 16-point star appears in the upper-right corner of the chart area. See Figure 4-37.

   TROUBLE? If the AutoShape on your screen does not match the size and shape of the AutoShape shown in the figure, you can resize the object again by pressing and holding the Shift key as you drag a selection handle. Or click the Undo button on the Standard toolbar to delete the object, and then repeat Steps 1 through 5 to redraw the AutoShape. Make sure that you press and hold down the Shift key to draw the object proportionally.

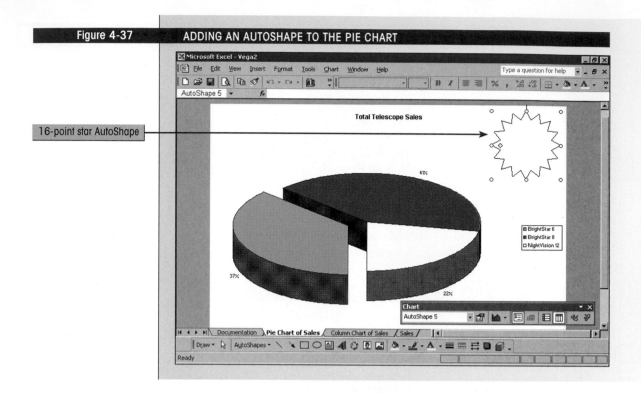

Figure 4-37   ADDING AN AUTOSHAPE TO THE PIE CHART

16-point star AutoShape

You probably noticed that the selection handles of the AutoShape appear as open circles and that there is also a diamond tool ⬦. You can use the ⬦ to change the shape of the AutoShape. For example, you can change the size of the jagged points of the star by dragging the diamond tool either in towards the center of the star (to increase the size of the points) or away from the star's center (to decrease the size of the points). You may have also noticed a green selection handle that is attached to the AutoShape through a vertical line. This is a rotation handle. By clicking and dragging this handle, you can rotate the AutoShape.

Formatting an AutoShape

In addition to modifying the shape, size, or rotation of an AutoShape, you can add text to it. To add text to an AutoShape, you first select it and then start typing the desired text. The text will be automatically placed within the boundaries of the shape.

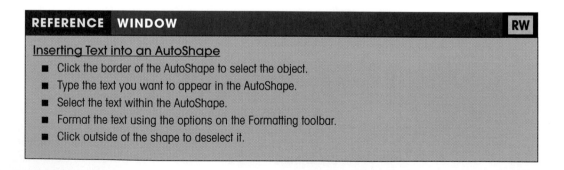

REFERENCE WINDOW   **RW**

Inserting Text into an AutoShape
- Click the border of the AutoShape to select the object.
- Type the text you want to appear in the AutoShape.
- Select the text within the AutoShape.
- Format the text using the options on the Formatting toolbar.
- Click outside of the shape to deselect it.

Alicia wants to add text to the AutoShape star that highlights the success of the NightVision 12.

To add text to the 16-point star:

1. Verify that the 16-point star AutoShape is still selected.

2. Type **NightVision 12 Sales Exceed $1,800,000!** (do *not* press the Enter key).

3. Click the **Center** button ▤ on the Formatting toolbar.

4. Click outside of the AutoShape to deselect it.

> **TROUBLE?** If the text does not wrap logically within the boundaries of the AutoShape, resize the star to better accommodate the text.

The star with the text adds value to the overall appearance of the chart. However, the star could use some background color to make it more visually interesting. You decide to format the AutoShape by adding a yellow background.

To change the background color of the AutoShape:

1. Click the border of the 16-point star AutoShape to select it.

2. Click the **list arrow** for the **Fill Color** button ▨▾ on the Drawing toolbar, and then click the **Yellow** square (fourth row, third column) in the color palette.

> **TROUBLE?** If the background color does not change to yellow, you may have selected the text in the star rather than the star itself. Click the Undo button ↺, and then repeat Steps 1 and 2.

The AutoShape definitely looks better with the yellow background. You decide to try one more thing: you want to see if adding a shadow effect to the start will be too much or will add depth to the object. To add a shadow effect to an object, you can choose one of the available shadow effects provided on the Drawing toolbar.

To add a drop shadow:

1. Verify that the 16-point star is still selected.

2. Click the **Shadow Style** button ▣ on the Drawing toolbar to display the gallery of shadow options. See Figure 4-38.

Figure 4-38   SHADOW STYLE OPTIONS

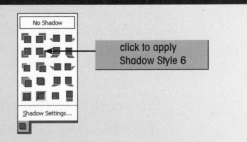

3. Click **Shadow Style 6** (second row, second column) in the shadow gallery.

4. Click outside the star to deselect it. Figure 4-39 shows the revised pie chart with the formatted AutoShape.

Figure 4-39   THE PIE CHART WITH THE STAR AUTOSHAPE

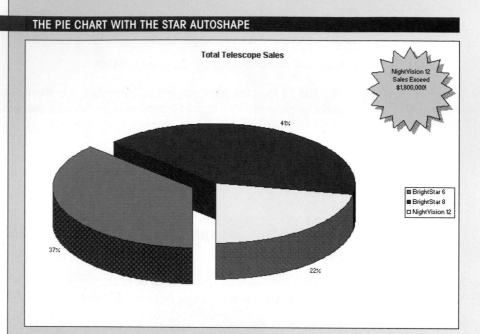

There are no other changes to be made, so you will hide the Drawing toolbar, which will increase the workspace on your screen. There are other shapes and objects on the Drawing toolbar that you can use to augment your charts and worksheets. For now though, Alicia is satisfied with the present appearance of the chart.

5. Click the **Drawing** button ![icon] on the Formatting toolbar. The Drawing toolbar closes.

Printing Your Charts

Now that you have completed your work on the two charts for Alicia, you will make hard copies of them. Printing a chart sheet is similar to printing a worksheet. As when printing a worksheet, you should preview the printout before sending the worksheet to the printer. From the Print Preview window, you can add headers and footers and control the page layout, just as you do for printing the contents of your worksheets. You also have the added option of resizing the chart to fit within the confines of a single printed page.

To print more than one chart sheet at a time, you select both chart sheets, and then open the Print Preview window. Each chart will print on its own page.

To set up the two charts for printing:

1. Make sure the Pie Chart of Sales worksheet is the current sheet.

2. Press and hold the **Shift** key, and then click the **Column Chart of Sales** tab. Both chart sheets are selected.

3. Click the **Print Preview** button on the Standard toolbar. The Print Preview window opens, showing the pie chart on the first of two pages.

4. Click the **Setup** button on the Print Preview toolbar to open the Page Setup dialog box. The Page Setup options are similar to the options for printing a worksheet, except that a new dialog box tab, Chart, has been added.

5. Click the **Chart** tab. Figure 4-40 shows the Chart tab.

Figure 4-40   CHART TAB

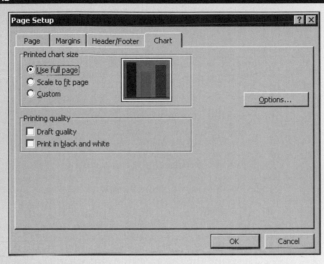

Excel provides three choices for defining the size of a chart printout. These are:

- **Use full page** in which the chart is resized to fit the full page, extending out to the borders of all four margins. The proportions of the chart may change since it is extended in all directions to fit the page. This is the default option.
- **Scale to fit page** in which the chart is resized until one of the edges reaches a margin border. The proportions of the chart remained unchanged, but it might not fit the entire page.
- **Custom** in which the dimensions of the printed chart are specified on the chart sheet outside of the Print Preview window.

You will use the Scale to fit page option because you do not want to have the charts resized disproportionately.

To set the size of the charts:

1. Click the **Scale to fit page** option button, and then click the **OK** button.

2. Click the **Next** button to preview the column chart printout.

3. Click the **Setup** button.

4. On the Chart tab, click the **Scale to fit page** option button, and then click the **OK** button.

5. Click the **Print** button to open the Print dialog box, and then send both chart sheets to the printer.

Now that you have finished your work, you can close the Vega2 workbook and exit Excel.

6. Click the **Save** button 🖫 on the Standard toolbar, and then click the **Close** button ⊠ on the title bar.

You show your final product to Alicia. She is pleased with the results. Alicia will get back to you with any other tasks she might need you to do before the sales meeting next week.

Session 4.2 QUICK CHECK

1. Describe how you would remove a data series from a column chart.

2. How would you change the location (either embedded or as a chart sheet) for a chart?

3. What is the difference between label text, attached text, and unattached text?

4. What is the difference between major tick marks and minor tick marks?

5. How would you change a column chart into a 3-D column chart?

6. What is an AutoShape?

7. Describe the three options for sizing a chart on the printed page.

REVIEW ASSIGNMENTS

Alicia has another workbook that shows the monthly United States sales for the three major telescope models. She wants you to create a chart for this worksheet, but this time a line chart. She wants the line chart to show the change in sales over the course of the last fiscal year. She prefers having a separate sheet for the chart with the legend placed at the bottom of the page.

To complete this task:

1. Start Excel and open the **VegaUSA1** workbook located in the Tutorial.04/Review folder on your Data Disk.

2. Save the workbook as **VegaUSA2** to the same folder.

3. Enter your name and the current date in the Documentation sheet, and then switch to the Monthly Sales worksheet.

4. Select the range A2:D14, and then start the Chart Wizard.

5. Use the Chart Wizard to create a line chart, using the first chart sub-type. Specify "United States Telescope Sales" as the chart title, "Month" as the x-axis title, and "Sales ($U.S.)" as the y-axis title. Position the legend at the bottom of the chart area. Place the chart on a chart sheet named "Monthly Sales Chart".

6. Format the x-axis labels, changing the alignment to 90 degrees.

Explore 7. Double-click the line for the BrightStar 6 model, and within the Patterns dialog box, change the color of the line to white.

8. Change the fill effect for the plot area to the preset fill style Nightfall.

Explore   9. Double-click the legend box, and change the fill color to dark blue and the color of the legend text to white.

Explore   10. Use the Drawing toolbar to create an 8-point star located in the upper-left corner of the chart area.

11. Insert the text "NightVision 12 sales remained high in Autumn!" into the 8-point star you just created.

12. Change the fill color of the 8-point star to tan, and apply Shadow Style 1 to the shape.

13. In the Print Preview window, scale the chart to fit the page.

14. Add a footer to the chart displaying your name and the date in the lower-right corner of the page. Save your changes, and then print the chart.

15. Close the workbook and exit Excel.

CASE PROBLEMS

Case 1. Cast Iron Concepts   Andrea Puest, the regional sales manager of Cast Iron Concepts (CIC), a distributor of cast iron stoves, is required to present a report of the company's sales in her sales region, which includes the states of New Hampshire, Vermont, and Maine. She sells four major models: Star Windsor, Box Windsor, West Windsor, and Circle Windsor. The Circle Windsor is CIC's latest entry in the cast iron stove market.

Andrea will make a presentation of her sales figures next month and has asked for your help in creating a chart showing the sales results. She wants to create a 3-D column chart with each column representing the sales for a particular model and region.

To complete this task:

1. Open the **CIC1** workbook located in the Tutorial.04/Cases folder of your Data Disk, and then save the file as **CIC2** to the same folder.

2. Enter your name and the current date in the Documentation sheet. Switch to the Sales worksheet.

3. Select the range A2:D6, and then start the Chart Wizard.

4. Use the Chart Wizard to create an embedded 3-D Column chart that compares values across categories and across series. The data series in the chart should be organized by columns, not rows. Specify "Windsor Stove Sales" as the chart title. Do not specify titles for the axes. Do not include a legend.

5. Move the embedded chart so that the upper-left corner of the chart is located in cell A8, and then resize the chart so that it covers the range A8:E29.

6. Change the font of the chart title to a 14-point, bold, dark blue Arial.

7. Change the color of the chart area to tan.

Explore   8. Change the 3-D view of the chart so that its elevation equals 10 degrees, its rotation equals 120 degrees, and its perspective equals 15.

9. Change the font of the y-axis labels (the names of the state) to an 8-point regular Arial font.

10. Change the font of the x-axis labels (the model names) to an 8-point regular Arial font, displayed at a -90 degree angle.

Explore   11. Select the walls of the 3-D plot, and change the wall color to white.

12. Center the contents of the worksheet horizontally on the page, and then add a header that displays your name and the date in the upper-right corner of the worksheet.

13. Save your changes, and then print the worksheet.

14. Close the workbook, and then close Excel.

Case 2. Dantalia Baby Powder Kemp Wilson is a quality control engineer for Dantalia Baby Powder. Part of the company's manufacturing process involves a machine called a "filler," which pours a specified amount of powder into bottles. Sometimes the filling heads on the filler become partially clogged, causing the bottles to be under filled. If that happens, the bottles must be rejected. On each assembly line, there are a certain number of bottles rejected during each shift.

Kemp's job is to monitor the number of defective bottles and locate the fillers that may have clogged filler heads. One of the tools he uses to do this is a Pareto chart. A **Pareto chart** is a column chart in which each column represents the total number of defects assigned to different parts of the production process. In this case, the columns would represent the 24 different fillers in the assembly line. The columns are sorted so that the part that caused the most defects is displayed first; the second-most is displayed second, and so forth. Superimposed on the columns is a line that displays the cumulative percentage of defects for all of the parts. Thus by viewing the cumulative percentages, you can determine, for example, what percentages of the total defects are due to the three worst parts. In this way, Kemp can isolate the problem filler heads and report how much they contribute to the total defects.

Kemp has a worksheet listing the number of defects per filler head from a recent shift. The data is already sorted going from the filler head with the most defects to the one with the fewest. The cumulative percent values have also been already calculated. Kemp wants you to create a Pareto chart based on this data.

To complete this task:

1. Open the **Powder1** workbook located in the Tutorial.04/Cases folder of your Data Disk, and then save the file as **Powder2** to the same folder.

2. Enter your name and the current date in the Documentation sheet. Switch to the Quality Control worksheet.

3. Select the range A1:C25, and then start the Chart Wizard.

Explore ▷ 4. Use the Chart Wizard to create a custom chart, selecting the Line – Column on 2 Axes in the Custom Types list box. Specify "Filler Head Under Fills" as the chart title. Specify "Filler Head" as the x-axis title, "Count of Under Fills" as the y-axis title, and "Cumulative Percentage" as the second y-axis title. Do not include a legend. Place the chart on a chart sheet named "Pareto Chart".

5. Change the alignment of the x-axis labels to an angle of 90 degrees.

6. Change the alignment of the second y-axis title to –90 degrees.

Explore ▷ 7. Change the scale of the second y-axis so that the values range from 0 to 1.0.

Explore ▷ 8. Select the data series that displays the number of defects for each filler head, and add data labels that display the number of defects above each column. Do *not* display labels above the lines that represent the cumulative percentages. (*Hint*: Use the Data Labels tab in the Format Data Series dialog box.)

Explore ▷ 9. From the Format Data Series dialog box for the chart's columns, use the Options tab to reduce the gap separating the columns to 0 pixels.

10. Change the fill color of the chart columns and the plot area to white.

11. Examine the Pareto chart, and determine approximately what percentage of the total number of defects can be attributed to the three worst filler heads.

12. Add a header that displays your name and the date in the upper-right corner of the worksheet.

13. Save your changes to the file, and then print the Pareto chart.

14. Close the workbook, and then close Excel.

Case 3. Charting Stock Activity You work with Lee Whyte, a stock analyst who plans to publish a Web site on stocks. One component of the Web site will be a five-week record of the activity of various key stocks. Lee has asked for your help in setting up an Excel workbook to keep a running record of the trading volume, open, high, low, and close values of some of the stocks he's tracking.

Lee wants you to create a stock market chart of the activity of the Pixal Inc. stock as a sample. The last six weeks of the stock's performance have been saved in a workbook. He wants you to create a chart sheet for the data that has been entered.

To complete this task:

1. Open the **Pixal1** workbook located in the Tutorial.04/Cases folder of your Data Disk, and then save the file as **Pixal2** to the same folder.

2. Enter your name and the current date in the Documentation sheet. Switch to the Pixal Data worksheet.

3. Select the range A9:G39, and then start the Chart Wizard.

4. Use the Chart Wizard to create a stock chart using the Volume-Open-High-Low-Close sub-type. Specify "Pixal Inc." as the chart title. Specify "Date" as the x-axis title, "Volume (mil)" as the y-axis title, and "Price" as the second y-axis title. Remove the gridlines and do not include the legend. Place the chart in a chart sheet named "Pixal Chart".

5. Change the scale of the first y-axis so that the scale ranges from 0 to 5 with a major unit of 0.5.

6. Change the scale of the second y-axis so that the scale ranges from 15 to 21 with a major unit of 1.

7. Change the alignment of the second y-axis title to −90 degrees.

Explore 8. Change the scale of the x-axis so that the major unit occurs every seven days.

9. Double-click the column data series that displays the volume of shares traded, and using the Options tab, reduce the gap between adjacent columns to 0 pixels.

10. Change the fill color of the plot area to light yellow.

11. Change the font size of the chart title to 16 points.

Explore 12. In the upper-right corner of the plot area, insert the Rounded Rectangular Callout AutoShape from the Drawing toolbar. Enter "Pixal Inc. is experiencing a tough first quarter" in the area of the AutoShape, and then on a new line, enter "-Stock Reviews". Format the text in a bold red 14-point font. Resize the AutoShape if necessary.

13. Add the Shadow Style 6 drop shadow to the AutoShape.

14. Add your name and the date to the right section of the header. Scale the chart to fit the page in landscape orientation.

15. Save the changes, and then print the chart sheet.

Explore 16. Lee has a new week's worth of data for the Pixal worksheet. Enter the data shown in Figure 4-41 to the table of stock activity, and then modify that chart's data source to include the new data values for each data series.

Figure 4-41

DATE	VOLUME (MIL)	OPEN	HIGH	LOW	CLOSE
2/17/2003	0.35	16.30	16.95	16.75	16.85
2/18/2003	0.45	16.85	17.20	17.05	17.15
2/19/2003	0.52	17.15	17.45	17.25	17.25
2/20/2003	0.40	17.25	17.35	16.95	17.25
2/21/2003	0.38	17.25	17.55	16.75	16.95

17. Save your changes, and then reprint the chart sheet with the new data values.

18. Close the workbook and Excel.

Case 4. *Relating Cancer Rates to Temperature* A 1965 study analyzed the relationship between the mean annual temperature in 16 regions in Great Britain and the annual mortality rates in those regions for a certain type of breast cancer. Lynn Watson, a researcher at a British university, has asked you to chart the data from the sample. Figure 4-42 shows the sample values.

Figure 4-42

REGION	TEMPERATURE	MORTALITY
1	31.8	67.3
2	34.0	52.5
3	40.2	68.1
4	42.1	84.6
5	42.3	65.1
6	43.5	72.2
7	44.2	81.7
8	45.1	89.2
9	46.3	78.9
10	47.3	88.6
11	47.8	95.0
12	48.4	87.0
13	49.2	95.9
14	49.9	104.5
15	50.0	100.4
16	51.3	102.5

To complete this task:

1. Create a new workbook named **BCancer** that contains a Documentation sheet displaying your name, the date, and the purpose of the workbook, and a worksheet named "Breast Cancer Data" that contains the data from Figure 4-42 entered in the range A1:C17.

2. Select the temperature and mortality data, and then start the Chart Wizard.

3. Use the Chart Wizard to create an embedded XY (Scatter) chart with no data points connected. Specify "Mortality vs. Temperature" as the chart title. Specify "Temperature" as the title of the x-axis and "Mortality Index" as the title of the y-axis. Remove the gridlines. Do not include the legend. The scatter chart should be embedded on the Breast Cancer Data worksheet, with the chart covering the cell range D1:K23.

4. Change the scale of the x-axis to cover the temperature range 30 to 55 degrees.

5. Change the scale of the y-axis to cover the mortality index range 50 to 110.

Explore

6. Double-click one of the data points in the chart to open the Format Data Series dialog box, and make the following changes to the appearance of the data points:

   ■ Change the marker style to a circle that is 7 points in size.
   ■ Change the background color of the circle to white.
   ■ Change the foreground color of the circle to red.

Explore

7. Click Chart on the menu bar, and then click Add Trendline. On the Type tab, click the Linear trend line, and then click the OK button. The purpose of the linear trend line is to display whether a linear relationship exists between the 16 regions' mean annual temperature and their annual mortality index. Does it appear that such a relationship exists? What does a high mean annual temperature imply about the annual mortality index?

8. Change the fill color of the plot area to light yellow.

9. Set up the worksheet to print in landscape orientation. Center the worksheet horizontally and vertically on the page. Enter your name and the date in the right section of the page's header. Print the chart.

10. Save and close the workbook, and then close Excel.

INTERNET ASSIGNMENTS

Student Union

The purpose of the Internet Assignments is to challenge you to find information on the Internet that you can use to create effective spreadsheets. The actual assignments are updated and maintained on the Course Technology Web site. Log on to the Internet and use your Web browser to go to the Student Union on the New Perspectives Series site at **www.course.com/NewPerspectives/studentunion**. Click the Online Companions link, and then click the link for this text.

QUICK | CHECK ANSWERS

Session 4.1

1. A chart type is one of the 14 styles of charts supported by Excel. Each chart type has various alternate formats, called chart sub-types.

2. stock chart

3. A data series is a range of data values that is plotted on the chart.

4. The plot area contains the actual data values that are plotted in the chart, as well as any background colors or images for that plot. The chart area contains the plot area and any other element (such as titles and legend boxes) that may be included in the chart.

5. Gridlines are lines that extend out from the tick marks on either axis into the plot area.

6. embedded charts, which are placed within a worksheet, and chart sheets, which contain only the chart itself

7. pie

8. exploded pie

Session 4.2

1. Click Chart on the menu bar, click Source Data, and then click the Series tab. Select the data series in the Series list box, and click the Remove button.

2. Click Chart on the menu bar, and then click Location. Select a new location from the dialog box.

3. Label text is text that consists of category names, tick mark labels, and legend text. Attached text is text that is attached to other elements of the chart, such as the chart title or axes titles. Unattached text is additional text that is unassociated with any particular element of the chart.

4. Major tick marks are tick marks that appear on the axis alongside the axis values. Minor tick marks do not appear alongside any axis value, but instead are used to provide a finer gradation between major tick marks.

5. Click Chart on the menu bar, and then click Chart Type. Select one of the 3-D chart sub-types for the column chart.

6. An AutoShape is a predefined shape available on the Drawing toolbar. You can add an AutoShape to any worksheet or chart. You can change the size or shape of an AutoShape, and you can change its fill color.

7. a) Use full page, which resizes the chart to fit the full size of the printed page; the proportions of the chart may change in the resizing, b) Scale to fit page, in which the chart is resized to fit the page, but it retains its proportions, c) Custom, in which the dimensions of the printed chart are specified in the chart sheet

In this tutorial you will:

- Learn about the Internet and the World Wide Web

- Create a non-interactive Web page based on an Excel workbook

- Create an interactive Web page based on an Excel workbook

CREATING WEB PAGES WITH EXCEL

Publishing Workbooks to the Web

CASE

Premier Finance

David Kowlske is a financial officer at Premier Finance, a lending company that is increasing its presence on the World Wide Web. David wants to add a page to the company's Web site in which customers can view the current cost of a 20-year mortgage with a fixed interest rate. He also wants to create a second Web page in which customers can enter different values for the interest rate, the size of the mortgage, and the length of the loan to see how those values affect the cost of the mortgage. He has already created two Excel workbooks containing the values and formulas he wants to see transferred to the Web.

The most far-reaching and popular extended network today is the **Internet**. To share network information, the Internet uses hypertext documents. A **hypertext document** is an electronic file that contains elements called links that provide easy access to other hypertext documents. The collection of these hypertext documents is called the **World Wide Web**, or **Web** for short. Each hypertext document is referred to as a **Web page**; a collection of Web pages is called a **Web site**; Web sites are stored on computers called **Web servers**; and to view a Web page, a user must have a software program called a **Web browser** that retrieves the hypertext document from the Web server and then displays the document on the user's computer. The two major browsers are Netscape Navigator and Microsoft Internet Explorer.

David has asked for your help in creating the two Web pages.

Publishing a Non-Interactive Web Site

Microsoft provides tools to convert Excel workbooks into Web pages that can be placed on the Web to be viewed by others. You can create two types of Web pages: non-interactive and interactive. The **non-interactive Web page** allows users to scroll through the contents of an Excel workbook, but they cannot make any changes to the values displayed in the Web page. The **interactive Web page** provides tools to modify and format the values displayed in the Web page, though any changes a user makes in the Web page do not affect the original workbook, nor do those changes last from one browser session to another.

Your first task is to convert David's mortgage data into a non-interactive Web page that will display the current values for a $100,000 mortgage for twenty years at a fixed 7.50% annual interest rate. David has already placed this data into a workbook named "Mortgage1". Use this workbook as a basis for the non-interactive Web page.

To open the Mortgage1 workbook:

1. Start Excel, if necessary, and open the **Mortgage1** workbook located in the Web/Tutorial folder on your Data Disk.

2. On the Documentation sheet, enter the current date and your name.

3. Save the workbook as **Mortgage2** in the Web/Tutorial folder on your Data Disk.

4. Click the other sheet tabs to view the contents of the rest of the workbook, and then return to the Documentation sheet.

The Loan Values worksheet displays the current mortgage cost of a $100,000 loan along with two embedded charts that show the declining remaining balance on the principal over 240 payments and the breakdown between total interest payments and total principal payments. The Schedule worksheet displays a sample payment schedule for a 20-year mortgage.

Setting the Publishing Options

The process of creating a Web page based on a workbook involves opening the Save As dialog box. The first task you'll perform in that dialog box is to choose a non-interactive format for the Web page.

To start creating a non-interactive Web page:

1. Click **File** on the menu bar, and then click **Save as Web Page**. The Save As dialog box opens. See Figure 1.

Figure 1	SAVE AS DIALOG BOX

Save As

Save in: Tutorial

History

My Documents

Desktop

Favorites

My Network Places

click to publish either the selected sheet or the whole workbook

click to create an interactive Web page

click to specify publishing options for the Web page

click to change the Web page's title

Save: ⦿ Entire Workbook   ○ Selection: Sheet   Publish...

☐ Add interactivity

Page title: Change Title...

File name: Mortgage2.htm   Save

Save as type: Web Page (*.htm; *.html)   Cancel

2. Verify that the Add interactivity check box is *not* selected.

Web pages will usually have a page title that appears in the title bar of the Web browser. You can set the page title for David's page in the Save As dialog box.

To specify the page title:

1. Click the **Change Title** button.

2. In the Set Page Title dialog box, type **Sample Mortgage Values**, and then click the **OK** button. The page title is displayed in the Save As dialog box above the File name list box.

To avoid confusion with the Mortgage2 Excel workbook, you decide to change the filename of the Web page to Mortgage3.

3. Click the File name list box, and change the name of the Web page file to **Mortgage3.htm**.

The next step in setting up the page for publishing on the Web is to choose which components of the workbook to publish. From the current dialog box, you can choose from two option buttons to publish either the entire workbook or the current selection in the active worksheet. You can also click the Publish button, which opens the Publish as Web Page dialog box. From that dialog box you can further refine your publishing choices. You can publish the entire workbook; a selected worksheet in the workbook; an item on a selected worksheet, such as an embedded chart or pivot table; an adjacent range of cells in a worksheet; or a previously published selection from the workbook.

David wants only the Loan Values worksheet published to the company's Web site, and he wants to include both of the embedded charts on the sheet.

To select the Loan Values worksheet:

1. Click the **Publish** button. The Publish as Web Page dialog box opens. You use this dialog box to specify which components of the workbook to publish.

2. Click the **Choose** list arrow at the top of the dialog box. Excel displays a list of possible publishing options.

3. Click **Items on Loan Values** in the list. Excel displays three more options—each of which are based on the Loan Values worksheet. You can publish all of the contents of the Loan Values worksheet or either of the two embedded charts.

4. Click **Sheet All contents of Loan Values** in the list. See Figure 2.

| Figure 2 | SELECTING THE ITEMS TO PUBLISH |

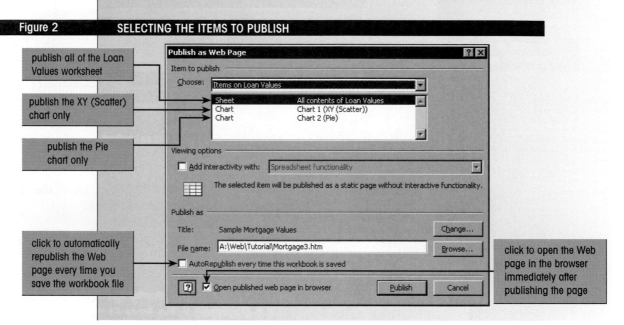

Now that you've defined what you want to publish, you are ready to publish the Loan Values worksheet as a Web page.

Publishing the Web Page

David knows that he might need to update this particular workbook in the future. He wants the Web page to be updated automatically so that it always matches any changes made to the source workbook. You can ensure that the Web page will be automatically updated by turning on the **AutoRepublish** option. Enabling this option republishes the Web page with any changes that have been made to a workbook whenever the workbook is saved.

To turn on the AutoRepublish feature:

1. Click the **AutoRepublish every time this workbook is saved** check box.

   Rather than hunting around for the Web page after you publish it, you can have Excel launch your browser automatically.

2. Click the **Open published web page in browser** check box.

   You're now ready to publish the Web page.

3. Click the **Publish** button. Excel opens a Web page based on the contents of the Loan Values worksheet.

4. Click the **Maximize** button ⬜ to maximize the browser window. Figure 3 shows the contents of the Web page.

Figure 3 | **THE LOAN VALUES WEB PAGE**

Web page title

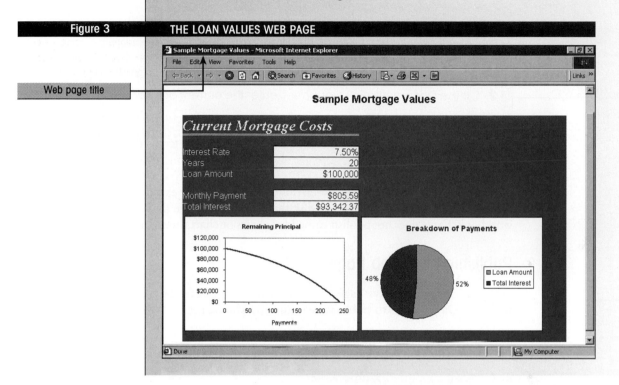

Note that, unlike the previewed version you opened earlier, this Web page does not display boxes or symbols. These navigation tools are not needed because this Web page displays a single worksheet, not an entire workbook. Also note that the page title you specified, "Sample Mortgage Values," appears in the browser's title bar and above the worksheet.

You show the completed page to David, so you can close your Web browser and workbook.

To close your work:

1. Click the **Close** button ☒ to close the Web browser and return to the Mortgage2 workbook.

2. Click the **Save** button 🖫 on the Standard toolbar.

Excel prompts you whether to disable or enable the AutoRepublish feature. Because you aren't about to make any additional changes to this workbook, you can safely disable the feature.

3. Verify that the Disable the AutoRepublish feature while this workbook is open option button is selected, and then click the **OK** button.

4. Click **File** on the menu bar, and then click **Close**.

Now that you've created a non-interactive Web page, you can create an interactive page.

Publishing an Interactive Web Site

David wants an interactive Web page in which customers can enter different mortgage values to see how the values affect the overall cost of the mortgage. He has created a workbook that you can use to create the interactive Web page.

To open the Calc1 workbook:

1. Open the file **Calc1**, located in the Web/Tutorial folder on your Data Disk.

2. On the Documentation worksheet, enter the current date and your name.

3. Save the workbook as **Calc2** in the Web/Tutorial folder on your Data Disk.

4. Review the contents of the workbook, and then return to the Documentation sheet.

There are a few differences between this workbook and the earlier Mortgage workbook. You can test different mortgage values using this workbook. Note that there are no charts in this workbook. Excel does not publish embedded charts or chart sheets in its interactive Web pages.

Publishing the Web Page

You publish an interactive page in the same way you published the non-interactive page. In this case, David wants to publish the entire workbook, not just one worksheet.

To begin publishing the Calc2 workbook:

1. Make sure the Documentation sheet is the active sheet.

2. Click **File** on the menu bar, and then click **Save as Web Page**.

3. Verify that the Entire Workbook option button is selected.

4. Click the **Add interactivity** check box.

5. Click the **Change Title** button, type **Mortgage Calculator** in the Set Title dialog box, and then click the **OK** button.

6. Click the File name list box, and change the name of the Web page file to **Calc3.htm**.

   As with the other workbook, David wants to republish the Web page each time the Calc2 workbook is saved.

7. Click the **Publish** button, and then click the **AutoRepublish every time this workbook is saved** check box.

8. Verify that the Open published Web page in the browser check box is selected.

9. Click the **Publish** button. The Web page opens in your Web browser.

   TROUBLE? If Netscape is your default browser, you will not be able to view the interactive Web page.

   TROUBLE? It may take a minute or so to create the interactive Web page based on this workbook.

Working with the Published Page

In an interactive Web page, the contents of the workbook are placed on the page as a Web component called the **spreadsheet component**. The initial size of the spreadsheet component is chosen to fit the initial dimensions of the Web browser window. If you change the size of the Web browser window, you might need to refresh the window to resize the workbook object to fit the new dimensions.

To view the interactive Web page:

1. Click the **Maximize** button ▢ on the Web browser. The Web browser enlarges to fit the entire monitor screen, but the spreadsheet component does not change size.

2. Click **View** on the menu bar, and then click **Refresh**. The spreadsheet component enlarges to match the new dimensions of the browser window. See Figure 4.

Figure 4	INTERACTIVE WEB PAGE

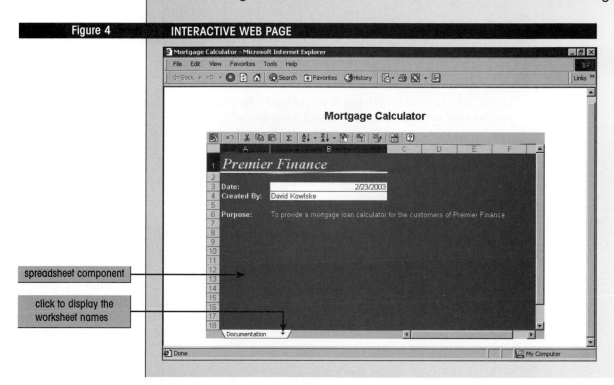

spreadsheet component

click to display the worksheet names

The spreadsheet component is a fully functioning object. You can enter new values or formulas, resize the rows or columns, and format the appearance of worksheet cells. The spreadsheet component does not have different tabs for the various worksheets. Instead you move between worksheets by selecting the worksheet from the single tab. You decide to test the interactive workbook by placing new values on the Calculator page.

To test the interactive workbook:

1. Click the **list arrow** for the Documentation tab, and then click **Calculator** in the list of worksheet names.

2. Select the current value in the Years box, type **15**, and then press the **Enter** key. The value of the monthly payment increases to $927.01, and the overall cost of the mortgage decreases to $66,862.22.

3. Click the **Close** button ☒ to close your Web browser and return to the Calc2 workbook in Excel.

You've completed your work for David. Save and close the Calc2 workbook before exiting Excel.

4. Click the **Save** button 🖫 on the Standard toolbar.

5. Close the workbook and then exit Excel.

The interactivity of this Web page also extends to the appearance of the workbook. You can sort the worksheet cells, filter the data, or export the data from the Web page back to an Excel workbook. You can also change the fill colors, fonts, or borders of individual cells in the workbook. However, none of the changes that you make to the workbook from the Web browser are permanent. The workbook will go back to its original appearance the next time you open the Web page.

REVIEW ASSIGNMENTS

David has placed the Web pages you helped him create on the company's Web server, and they've met with great success. David has a few additional workbooks that he wants you to convert to Web pages. These workbooks display sample values for a proposed college fund. David wants customers to have the ability to view the return from monthly investments in a college savings plan. As before, you'll create both a non-interactive and an interactive version of David's workbooks.

To complete this task:

1. Open the **Fund1** workbook located in the Web/Review folder on your Data Disk. Enter your name and the date in the workbook's Documentation sheet, and then save the workbook as **Fund2** in the same folder.

2. Create a non-interactive Web page based on the workbook using the following guidelines: a) enter "Sample College Fund" as the page title, b) enter **Fund3.htm** as the new filename, c) publish only the contents of the Fund Values worksheet, d) republish the Web page every time the Fund2 workbook is saved, and e) open the published Web page in the browser automatically.

3. Maximize the browser window so you can review the Web page, and then close your browser.

4. Close the workbook, saving your changes.

5. Open the **FCalc1** workbook located in the Web/Review folder on your Data Disk. Enter your name and the date in the Documentation sheet, and then save the workbook as **FCalc2** in the same folder.

6. Create an interactive Web page of the entire workbook with the page title "Fund Calculator" and the filename **FCalc3.htm**. Make sure the Web page is republished each time the FCalc2 workbook is saved, and make sure the Web page opens in the browser window automatically.

7. Maximize the browser window, refresh the screen, and then display the Calculator sheet.

8. Close your browser.

9. Save and close the **FCalc2** workbook, and then exit Excel.

New Perspectives on

INTEGRATING MICROSOFT® OFFICE XP

Read This Before You Begin

To the Student

Data Disks

To complete this tutorial, Review Assignments, and Case Problems, you need one Data Disk. Your instructor will either provide you with the Data Disk or ask you to make your own.

If you are making your own Data Disk, you will need **one** blank, formatted high-density disk. You will need to copy a set of files and/or folders from a file server, standalone computer, or the Web onto your disk. Your instructor will tell you which computer, drive letter, and folders contain the files you need. You could also download the files by going to www.course.com and following the instructions on the screen.

The information below shows you which folders go on your disk, so that you will have enough disk space to complete the tutorial, Review Assignments, and Case Problems:

Data Disk 1

Write this on the disk label:
Integrating Office XP: Tutorial 1 Data Disk

Put this folder on the disk:
Tutorial.01

When you begin each tutorial, be sure you are using the correct Data Disk. Refer to the "File Finder" chart at the back of this text for more detailed information on which files are used in which tutorials. See the inside front or inside back cover of this book for more information on Data Disk files, or ask your instructor or technical support person for assistance.

Using Your Own Computer

If you are going to work through this book using your own computer, you need:

- **Computer System** Microsoft Windows 98, NT, 2000 Professional, or higher must be installed on your computer. This book assumes a typical installation of Microsoft Office XP.

- **Data Disk** You will not be able to complete the tutorials or exercises in this book using your own computer until you have your Data Disk.

Visit Our World Wide Web Site

Additional materials designed especially for you are available on the World Wide Web. Go to www.course.com/NewPerspectives.

To the Instructor

The Data Disk Files are available on the Instructor's Resource Kit for this title. Follow the instructions in the Help file on the CD-ROM to install the programs to your network or standalone computer. For information on creating Data Disks, see the "To the Student" section above.

You are granted a license to copy the Data Files to any computer or computer network used by students who have purchased this book.

In this tutorial you will:

- Learn about object linking and embedding (OLE)

- Embed an Excel chart in a Word document

- Edit an embedded Excel chart in Word

- Link an Excel worksheet to a Word document

- Update a linked Excel worksheet

- Test and break a link

INTEGRATING WORD AND EXCEL

Creating a Customer Letter that Includes a Chart and Table for Country Gardens

CASE

Country Gardens

Nearly 17 years ago, Sue Dickinson began selling plants and herbs cultivated on her farm in Bristol, New Hampshire. At her customers' urging, she eventually opened a small shop that she named Country Gardens. The business has since grown to include three shops, which are located in Derry, New Hampshire; Dunstable, Massachusetts; and the newest one in Burlington, Vermont. This year, Country Gardens received the much-prized recognition as the largest grower and greens supplier in New England, a title established by NEGHA (the New England Growers and Horticultural Association).

Sue has now decided to offer her existing products and introduce new products through a mail-order catalog so she can better monitor market trends and customer needs by tracking order amounts and timing.

Sue plans to send a letter to her customers to announce the new mail-order catalog. She has drafted the body of the letter, which highlights the company's recent recognition by NEGHA and introduces the mail-order catalog. She also wants the letter to include a chart NEGHA has supplied, depicting the company's status as the top grower in the area, and a table outlining the 10 new products to be offered in the catalog.

You'll complete the letter for Sue using Microsoft Office XP. She created the letter in Word, but the chart and table were created in Excel. Fortunately, in Office XP you can share information between individual programs, including Word, Excel, PowerPoint, Access, and Outlook.

Object Linking and Embedding

Sue's letter requires the NEGHA chart and the new products table. The letter is a Word document, and both the chart and table are Excel files, as shown in Figure 1-1.

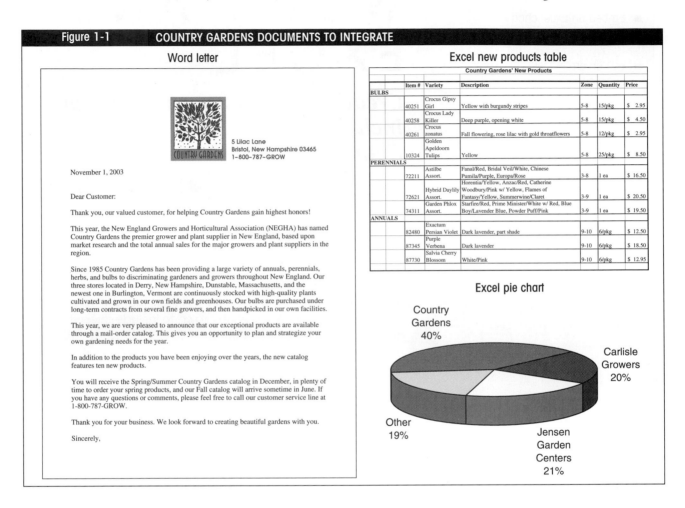

Figure 1-1   COUNTRY GARDENS DOCUMENTS TO INTEGRATE

Putting all these pieces together into one Word document is possible because Office XP supports **object linking and embedding** (OLE, pronounced "oh-lay"), a type of transferring and sharing of information between programs. OLE is often referred to as **integration**, which is a general term for sharing information (the terms are often used interchangeably.) An **object** is the specific information that you want to share between programs and can be anything from a chart or a table (as in Sue's case) to a picture, video, or sound clip, or almost anything else you can create on a computer. The program you used to create the object is called the **source program**, and the program that created the file where you want to insert the object is called the **destination program**. Likewise, the file that initially contains the object is called the **source file**, and the file where you want to insert the object is called the **destination file**.

Both linking and embedding involve inserting an object into a destination file; the difference lies in where their respective objects are stored. With **embedding**, a copy of the object becomes part of the destination file. If you want to make changes to the object, you can—in either the destination file or the source file—but the changes you make in one file do not appear in the other file. This is helpful if you want to leave the original object unchanged. Embedding enables you to edit an object using its source program's commands, unlike regular copying and pasting.

With **linking**, the object does not exist as a separate object in the destination file. Instead, OLE creates a direct connection, or **link**, between the source and destination programs, so that the object exists in only one place—the source file—but the link displays the object in the destination file as well. You can edit the object from either file, and the link ensures that any changes made to the object appear in both files. Figure 1-2 summarizes embedding and linking and compares their advantages and disadvantages.

Figure 1-2	COMPARING INTEGRATION METHODS	
	EMBEDDING	**LINKING**
Description	Displays and stores an object in the destination file	Displays an object in the destination file along with the source file's location; stores the object in the source file
Use if you want to	Include the object in the destination file, and edit the object using the source program without affecting the source file.	Include the same object in more than one document, and edit the object in either the source file or the destination file and have the changes appear in the other file.
Advantages	Source file and destination file can be stored separately. Use source program commands to make changes to object in destination file.	Destination file size remains fairly small. Source and destination files remain identical.
Disadvantages	Destination file size increases to reflect addition of source file.	Source and destination files must be stored together.

Figure 1-3 illustrates the differences between embedding and linking.

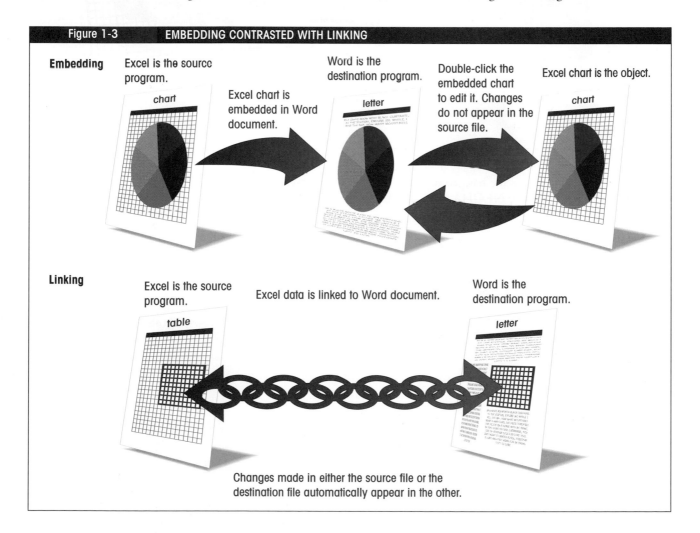

Figure 1-3   EMBEDDING CONTRASTED WITH LINKING

Embedding

Excel is the source program.

chart

Excel chart is embedded in Word document.

Word is the destination program.

letter

Double-click the embedded chart to edit it. Changes do not appear in the source file.

Excel chart is the object.

chart

Linking

Excel is the source program.

table

Excel data is linked to Word document.

Word is the destination program.

letter

Changes made in either the source file or the destination file automatically appear in the other.

In the case of the Country Gardens customer letter, the NEGHA pie chart needs to be integrated into the customer letter. Sue knows that the data in the chart will not change, but she might want to modify the chart's size and appearance once it is integrated into the letter. Sue asks you to embed the pie chart in the letter, as shown in Figure 1-4, so she can use the Excel commands to modify the chart. Because the prices of some products might change, Sue asks you to link the new products table between the Word document and the Excel workbook, as shown in Figure 1-4. This way, Sue can update the prices from either the letter or the table, and both files will show the latest prices.

Figure 1-4   INTEGRATING EXCEL OBJECTS INTO WORD

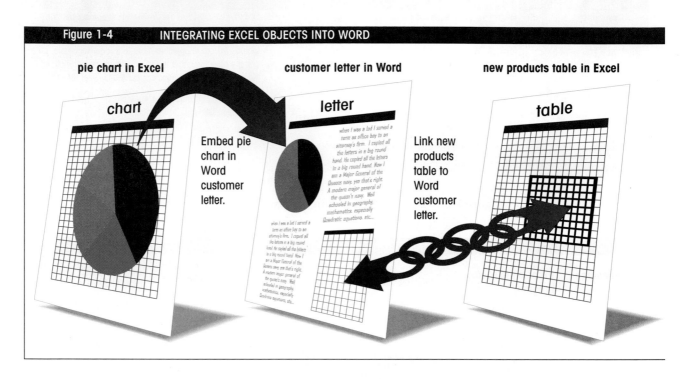

Sue has given you the Word file containing her letter. The first thing you'll do is embed the NEGHA pie chart. You need to first start Word and then open the letter.

To start Word and open the letter:

1. Start Word as usual.

2. Make sure your Data Disk is in the appropriate drive, and then open the **Letter** document, which is located in the Tutorial folder in the Tutorial.01 folder on your Data Disk. The letter appears in Print Layout view. See Figure 1-5.

| Figure 1-5 | COUNTRY GARDENS CUSTOMER LETTER |

make sure nonprinting characters are visible

Standard and Formatting toolbars display on separate rows

make sure view is Print Layout

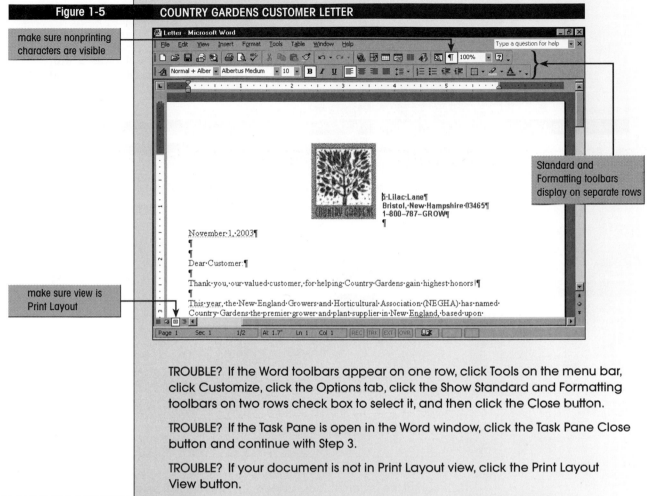

TROUBLE? If the Word toolbars appear on one row, click Tools on the menu bar, click Customize, click the Options tab, click the Show Standard and Formatting toolbars on two rows check box to select it, and then click the Close button.

TROUBLE? If the Task Pane is open in the Word window, click the Task Pane Close button and continue with Step 3.

TROUBLE? If your document is not in Print Layout view, click the Print Layout View button.

TROUBLE? If your document does not show the nonprinting characters, click the Show/Hide ¶ button on the Standard toolbar.

Next, you'll save the file with a new name. That way, the original letter remains intact on your Data Disk, in case you want to restart the tutorial.

3. Click **File** on the menu bar, and then click **Save As** to display the Save As dialog box.

4. Save the file as **Customer Letter** in the Tutorial folder in the Tutorial.01 folder on your Data Disk.

You're ready to embed the Excel chart provided by NEGHA that identifies Country Gardens as the top grower in New England. To do this, you need to have access to both Word and Excel. The customer letter is already open, so now you need to start Excel and open the file containing the pie chart.

To open the chart in Excel:

1. Start Excel as usual.

2. Open the **NEGHA** workbook, which is located in the Tutorial folder of the Tutorial.01 folder on your Data Disk. The workbook opens with a pie chart visible. See Figure 1-6.

| Figure 1-6 | NEGHA PIE CHART |

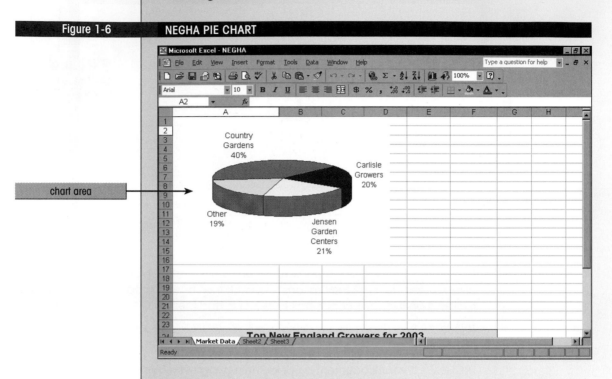

chart area

TROUBLE? If the Excel toolbars appear on one row, click Tools on the menu bar, click Customize, click the Options tab, click the Show Standard and Formatting toolbars on two rows check box to select it, and then click the Close button.

TROUBLE? If the Task Pane is open in the Excel window, click the Task Pane Close button and continue with Step 3.

Again, you'll save the file with a new name to keep the original workbook intact on your Data Disk.

3. Click **File** on the menu bar, and then click **Save As** to display the Save As dialog box.

4. Save the file as **Pie Chart** in the Tutorial folder in the Tutorial.01 folder on your Data Disk.

With both programs and files open, you can embed the pie chart into the letter.

Embedding an Excel Chart in a Word Document

Sue wants her letter to include the pie chart from NEGHA showing Country Gardens as the top grower in the area for 2003. The data for the chart will not change, so you'll embed the pie chart from the source file into her Word letter. That way, if Sue wants to resize the pie chart in the customer letter, she can make these changes using Excel commands without affecting the source file. (Recall that when you embed an object, you automatically have access to the object's source program commands and features to manipulate the embedded object in the destination program.)

REFERENCE WINDOW   **RW**

Embedding an Object

- Start the source program, open the file containing the object to be embedded, select the object or information you want to embed in the destination program, and then click the Copy button on the Standard toolbar.
- Start the destination program, open the file that will contain the embedded object, position the insertion point where you want to place the object, click Edit on the menu bar, and then click Paste Special.
- Click the Paste option button, select the option you want in the As list box, and then click the OK button.

Now you can embed the pie chart in the customer letter using the Paste Special dialog box.

To embed the Excel chart in the Word document:

1. The pie chart should appear on your screen. Click the chart area (the white area around the pie) to select the chart. When the chart is selected, handles appear around the chart area.

2. Click the **Copy** button 🖳 on the Excel Standard toolbar to copy the chart to the Clipboard. The chart now appears with a rotating dashed line around its frame, indicating that it has been copied.

   TROUBLE? If the Copy button is not available, you probably clicked the chart instead of the chart area. Click any cell in the worksheet to deselect the chart item, click the white area around the chart, and then repeat Step 2.

3. Click the **Customer Letter - Microsoft Word** button on the taskbar to return to the Customer Letter document.

4. Click to the left of the paragraph mark immediately above the paragraph that begins "Since 1985" to position the insertion point where you need to embed the pie chart. See Figure 1-7.

Figure 1-7	PLACEMENT FOR THE PIE CHART IN THE CUSTOMER LETTER

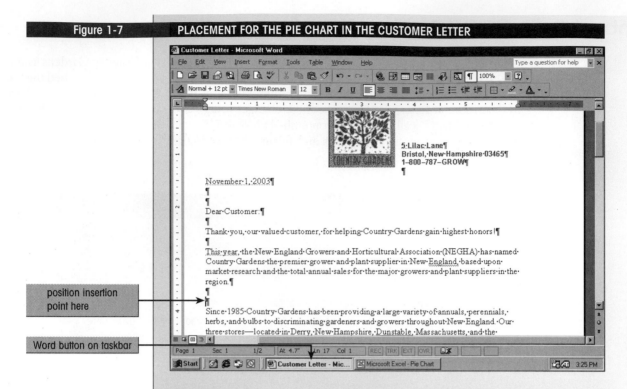

position insertion point here

Word button on taskbar

5. Click **Edit** on the menu bar, and then click **Paste Special**. The Paste Special dialog box opens. See Figure 1-8.

Figure 1-8	PASTE SPECIAL DIALOG BOX

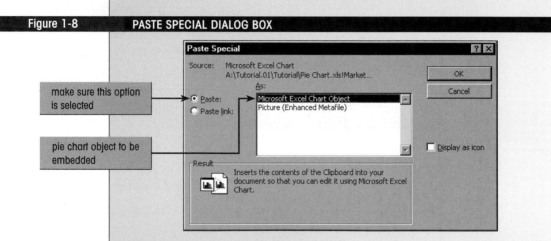

make sure this option is selected

pie chart object to be embedded

TROUBLE? If the Clipboard Task Pane is open in the Word window, click the Task Pane Close button, and continue with Step 6.

6. In the As list box, click **Microsoft Excel Chart Object**, if necessary, to select the chart as the object to embed.

TROUBLE? If the Microsoft Excel Chart Object option does not appear in the As list box, you might not have selected and copied the chart correctly. Click the Cancel button, and then repeat Steps 1 through 6, making sure that when you select the chart, handles appear around the chart area, and that when you copy the chart, a rotating dashed line appears around the chart area.

7. Make sure the **Paste** option button is selected. This option will embed the chart. If you wanted to link the chart, you would click the Paste link option button.

8. Click the **OK** button. The Paste Special dialog box closes, and after a few moments, the Excel pie chart appears in the letter. See Figure 1-9.

| Figure 1-9 | PIE CHART EMBEDDED IN THE CUSTOMER LETTER |

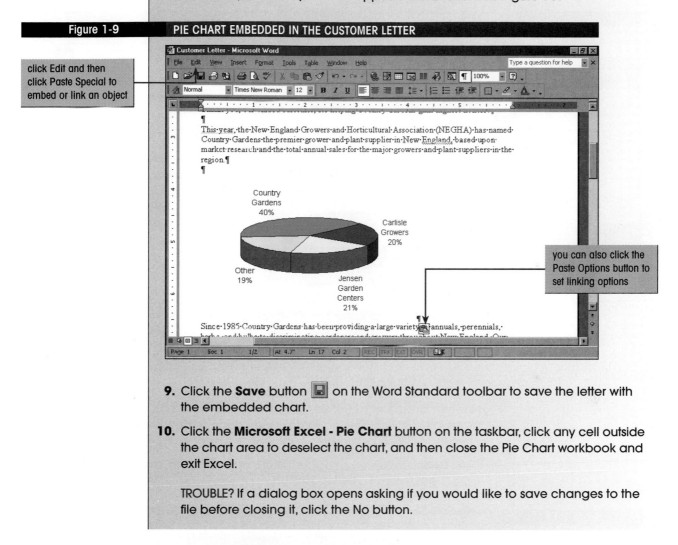

click Edit and then click Paste Special to embed or link an object

you can also click the Paste Options button to set linking options

9. Click the **Save** button 🖫 on the Word Standard toolbar to save the letter with the embedded chart.

10. Click the **Microsoft Excel - Pie Chart** button on the taskbar, click any cell outside the chart area to deselect the chart, and then close the Pie Chart workbook and exit Excel.

TROUBLE? If a dialog box opens asking if you would like to save changes to the file before closing it, click the No button.

After reviewing the letter with the embedded pie chart, Sue decides that the pie chart would be more impressive if it were rotated so that the pie slice showing Country Gardens' market percentage appeared in front. Because you embedded the chart, you can use Excel chart commands from within the Word document to modify the chart.

Modifying **an Embedded Object**

When you edit an embedded object within the destination program, the changes affect only the embedded object; the original object in the source program remains unchanged. When you select an embedded object, the destination program's menu bar and commands change to the menu bar and commands of the embedded object's source program, which you use to modify the embedded object.

Now that you have embedded the pie chart in Word, you can rotate the chart so that the Country Gardens pie wedge appears in front.

To edit the pie chart from within Word:

1. Double-click the chart. After a moment, a dashed border appears around the chart, and the Excel menus and toolbars replace those of Word. See Figure 1-10.

| Figure 1-10 | SELECTED EXCEL CHART IN THE CUSTOMER LETTER |

Word menu displays Excel Chart commands

selected chart appears in an Excel window

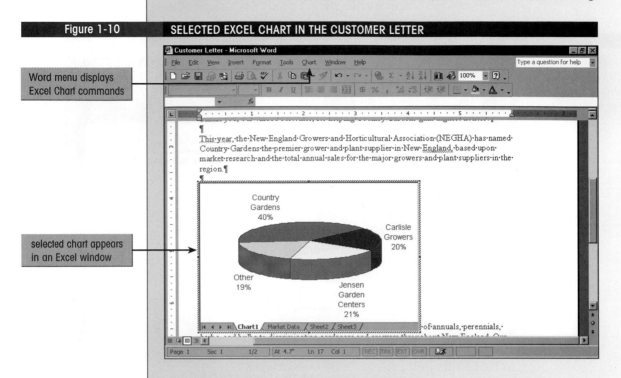

TROUBLE? If the floating Chart toolbar appears, click its Close button to close it.

Now you can modify the chart. The chart is a 3-D pie chart, and you want to rotate it so that the Country Gardens pie wedge appears in front. You do this using the 3-D View dialog box.

2. Click **Chart** on the menu bar, and then click **3-D View**. The 3-D View dialog box opens. See Figure 1-11.

| Figure 1-11 | 3-D VIEW DIALOG BOX |

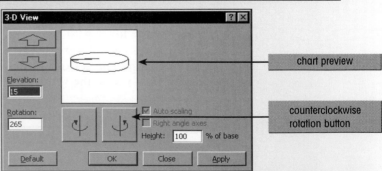

chart preview

counterclockwise rotation button

The Rotation text box shows the current value of 265, and the chart preview shows the median line pointing left. You want to move the Country Gardens wedge from the back of the pie to the front of the pie, so you need to move the median line counterclockwise, from the left to the right.

3. Click the **counterclockwise rotation** button until the Rotation text box shows the value 95. As you click the counterclockwise rotation button, watch the pie chart move in the preview box.

4. Click the **Apply** button, and then click the **OK** button. The Country Gardens pie wedge appears at the front of the pie chart. See Figure 1-12.

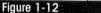

Figure 1-12   **REVISED EMBEDDED PIE CHART**

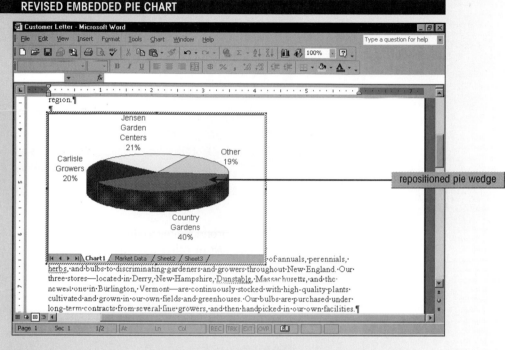

5. Click in the letter to deselect the chart and return to Word's menus and toolbars.

6. Click the **Save** button 🖫 on the Standard toolbar to save the document.

If you were to open the Pie Chart workbook, you would see that the pie chart there remained unchanged. Your final task is to include the table of new products in the letter. To do this, you will link the table from Excel to Word.

Linking an Object from Excel to Word

Sue tracks her product and pricing information in an Excel workbook named Products. Unlike the information in the pie chart, the product and pricing information is subject to change. Sue has yet to receive the current bulb prices from her supplier. Because she wants you to finish setting up the letter now, you'll link the table from the Products workbook to the Customer Letter document instead of embedding it as you did the chart. This way, you can make any price changes from either the Excel workbook or the Word document, and the changes will automatically appear in the other file. This will keep the information up to date in both files.

REFERENCE WINDOW   **RW**

Linking an Object

- Start the source program, open the file containing the object to be linked, select the object or information you want to link to the destination program, and then click the Copy button on the Standard toolbar.
- Start the destination program, open the file that will contain the link to the copied object, position the insertion point where you want the linked object to appear, click Edit on the menu bar, and then click Paste Special.
- Click the Paste link option button, select the option you want in the As list box, and then click the OK button.

or

- In the source file, select the object or information you want to link, and then click the Copy button on the Standard toolbar.
- Start the destination program, open the file that will contain the linked object, position the insertion point where you want to place the object, and then click the Paste button on the Standard toolbar.
- Click the Paste Options button, and then select a command from the Paste Options menu.

Now you will link the product table to the letter using the Paste Options button. This button appears when you paste text or other information from one Office document to another. You first need to open the Products workbook, and then select the table object for linking.

To link the product table to the customer letter:

1. Start Excel, and then open the **Products** workbook in the Tutorial folder in the Tutorial.01 folder on your Data Disk.

   TROUBLE? If the New Workbook Task Pane is open in the Excel window, click the Task Pane Close button and continue with Step 2.

2. Save the workbook as **New Products** in the same folder.

3. Select cells **A1** through **H17**, and then click the **Copy** button 🖺 on the Excel Standard toolbar to copy the data to the Clipboard.

4. Click the **Customer Letter - Microsoft Word** button on the taskbar to return to the customer letter.

5. Scroll the document and position the insertion point to the left of the paragraph mark above the paragraph that begins "You will receive." This is where you want the product and pricing data to appear. See Figure 1-13.

Figure 1-13   PLACEMENT FOR LINKING THE EXCEL WORKSHEET TO THE CUSTOMER LETTER

position insertion point here

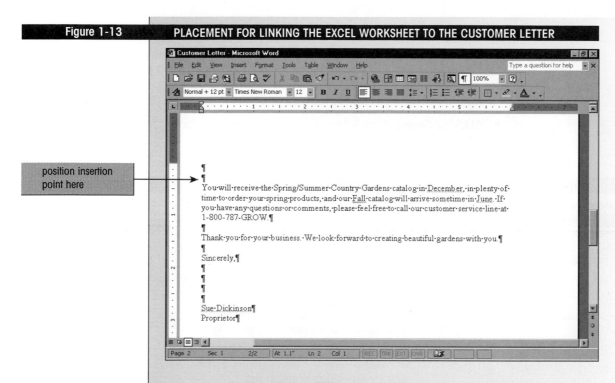

6. Click the **Paste** button 🖹 on the Word Standard toolbar. The Country Gardens New Products table from Excel is inserted in the customer letter. Notice the Paste Options button appears just below the new products table. You will use this button to link the original new products table contained in the Excel worksheet and the new products table embedded in the letter.

7. Click the **Paste Options** button 🖹 to open the Paste Options menu. See Figure 1-14.

Figure 1-14   LINKED NEW PRODUCTS TABLE

click one of these options to paste without linking

linked table would look the same if embedded

click one of these options to link the table

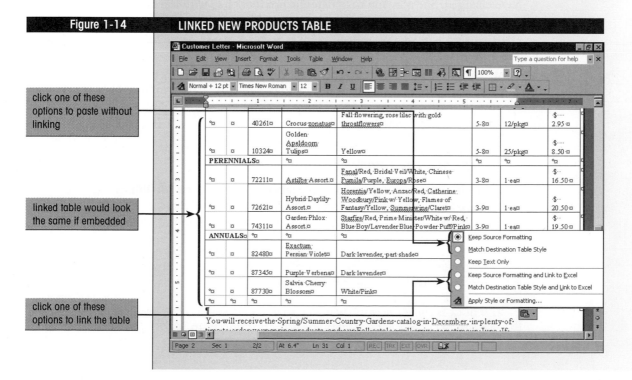

Figure 1-15 describes the commands on the Paste Options menu.

8. Click the **Match Destination Table Style and Link to Excel** option button. This means that the table will be linked, rather than embedded, and that its format will match the default table style in Word. The products table in Word is now formatted in Times New Roman 12-pt. text and linked to the Excel worksheet.

9. Click the **Save** button 🖫 on the Word Standard toolbar to save the customer letter.

Figure 1-15	PASTE OPTIONS COMMANDS
CHOOSE THIS PASTE OPTIONS COMMAND:	**TO DO THE FOLLOWING:**
Keep Source Formatting	Paste the object without linking and match the formatting in the source file
Match Destination Table Style	Paste the object without linking and format the object in the Word default table style
Keep Text Only	Paste the object as text only, not as a table or other formatted object; Word separates table columns with tab characters and table rows with paragraph symbols
Keep Source Formatting and link to Excel	Link the paste object to Excel and match the formatting in the Excel source file; any formatting changes you make to the pasted object remain when you change the data in the source file
Match Destination Table Style and Link to Excel	Link the pasted objects to Excel and format the linked data in the Word default table style; any formatting changes you make to the paste object remain when you change the data in the source file
Apply Style or Formatting	Open the Style and Formatting Task Pane to select styles to apply to the pasted text

Note that the table is too wide for the page. You will have a chance to fine-tune the format of the table later.

Sue just received the latest bulb prices from her supplier. As she expected, some prices have changed. She asks you to update the product table with the new prices.

Updating Linked Objects

Now that you have linked the product table from the workbook to the customer letter, you can edit the information from either the source file (the Excel workbook) or the destination file (the Word document), and the changes will automatically appear in the other file. When making changes, you can have one or both files open.

To update the product table in Excel:

1. Right-click a blank area of the taskbar and then click **Tile Windows Horizontally** on the shortcut menu. The source and destination files each appear in a reduced window, stacked one on top of the other.

   TROUBLE? If the range A1 to H17 is still selected in the Excel worksheet, click anywhere in the Excel window to make this the active window, and then press the Esc key to deselect the range.

2. If necessary, scroll each window so you can see the first item in the table. The price of Crocus Gipsy Girl bulbs has changed from $2.95 to $3.95.

3. In the Excel window, click cell **H5**, type **3.95**, and then press the **Enter** key. As you press the Enter key, watch the customer letter. Because you linked the table from Excel to Word, the change you just made to the price of product 40251, Crocus Gipsy Girl bulbs, also appears here in the destination document. See Figure 1-16.

| Figure 1-16 | LINKED DOCUMENTS TILED HORIZONTALLY |

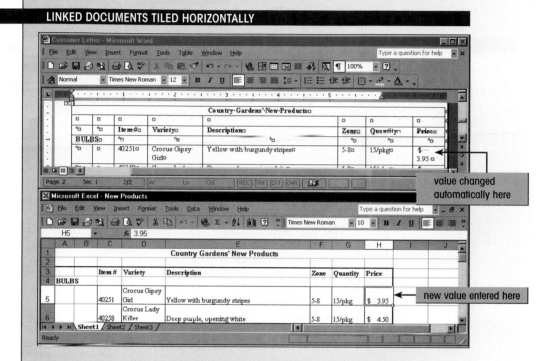

4. Right-click a blank area of the taskbar, and then click **Undo Tile** to view just one program window at a time.

5. Click the **Customer Letter - Microsoft Word** button on the taskbar to switch to the customer letter.

6. Click the **Save** button on the Standard toolbar to save the customer letter.

What would happen if you were working on the new product table in Excel without the Word document open? Would the information still be updated in the customer letter? To find out, make the remaining changes to the prices for bulbs with the customer letter closed. You can then reopen the customer letter to verify that the changes appear there as well.

To edit the linked object with the Word document closed:

1. Close the customer letter and exit Word.

2. If necessary, click the **Microsoft Excel - New Products** button on the taskbar to make the New Products workbook active.

3. Enter **4.95** in cell H6, and then enter **3.25** in cell H7.

4. Click the **Save** button on the Standard toolbar.

5. Start Word, click **File** on the menu bar, and then click **1 Customer Letter** to open the letter.

TROUBLE? If the customer letter is not listed as 1 Customer Letter, it might be listed with the drive and folder name preceding it. If you still cannot find it, use the Open command on the File menu to open the Customer Letter document.

6. Scroll the document to view the linked table. Notice that the new bulb prices appear in the linked table in Word. See Figure 1-17.

Figure 1-17	VALUES UPDATED IN LINKED DOCUMENT

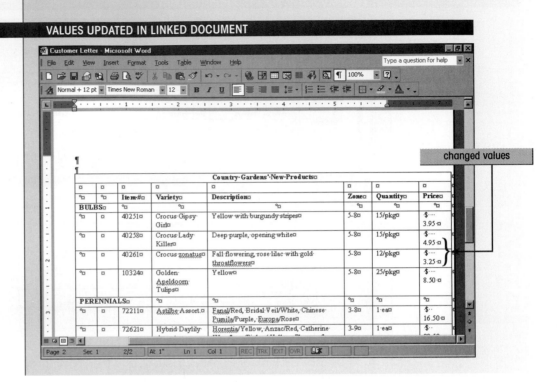

Linked documents are effective in many cases, but sometimes you'll want to break the link.

Breaking Links

Once you are finished working with linked documents, you can break the link between the two documents. You do this by using the Links command on the Edit menu in the destination file. Once you break a link, the only changes you can make to the object in the destination file are resizing, moving, and deleting. Also, any such changes you make to the object in the source file no longer appear in the destination file once the link is broken. In other words, when you break the link, the object acts as a pasted picture in the destination file.

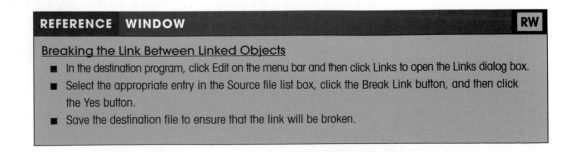

REFERENCE WINDOW   **RW**

Breaking the Link Between Linked Objects
- In the destination program, click Edit on the menu bar and then click Links to open the Links dialog box.
- Select the appropriate entry in the Source file list box, click the Break Link button, and then click the Yes button.
- Save the destination file to ensure that the link will be broken.

You are finished updating the new product prices and are ready to give Sue the finished letter to send to her customers. Because the bulb prices are final, Sue asks you to break the link between the Customer Letter document and the New Products workbook, so she can store the letter and workbook separately.

To break the link:

1. In the Word window, click **Edit** on the menu bar, and then click **Links** to open the Links dialog box. There should be just one entry in the Source file list box, and it should be selected. If not, click the entry to select it. See Figure 1-18.

Figure 1-18   LINKS DIALOG BOX

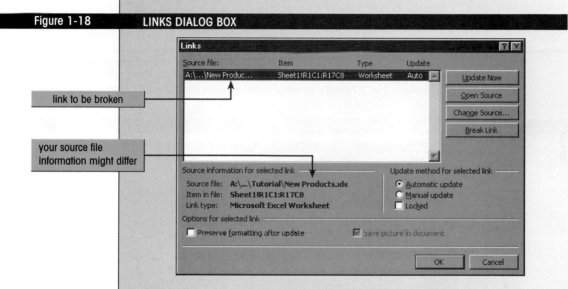

link to be broken

your source file information might differ

TROUBLE? Depending on the disk drive used for your Data Disk, your entry in the Links dialog box might be different from the one shown in Figure 1-18.

2. Click the **Break Link** button. A dialog box opens, asking you to confirm that you want to break the link.

3. Click the **Yes** button. The link is broken, and the dialog box closes. You'll confirm that the link is indeed broken by editing the new products table in Excel, and then verifying that the change is not made in Word.

4. Switch to the Excel workbook.

5. Enter **9.5** in cell H8.

6. Switch to the customer letter. Note that the price of Golden Apeldoorn Tulips in the table did not change from $8.50 to $9.50. This confirms that the link between the two files is broken.

7. Switch to the Excel window, click **File** on the menu bar, click **Close**, and then click the **No** button when prompted to save the changes to the file. You do not want to save the change you made to the price, because this change was made simply to test the broken link.

8. Exit Excel.

9. Save the Customer Letter document.

If you had closed the Customer Letter document without saving it, the link to the Excel object would still be intact. Because you saved the letter, the link remains broken.

Sue asks you to print a copy of the letter so that she can review it before mailing out any letters.

To preview and print the letter:

1. At the bottom of the letter, replace Sue Dickinson's name with your own and use the **Move Table Column** icons in the horizontal ruler to resize the new products table so that it fits attractively on the page.

2. Click the **Table Select** icon above the upper-left corner of the table, and then change the size of the table text to 10 points.

3. Click the **Print Preview** button 🔍 on the Standard toolbar to preview the letter.

4. If necessary, click the **Multiple Pages** button 🔡 on the Print Preview toolbar and select **1 x 2 Pages** to view both pages of the letter. See Figure 1-19.

Figure 1-19	PREVIEW OF COMPLETED CUSTOMER LETTER

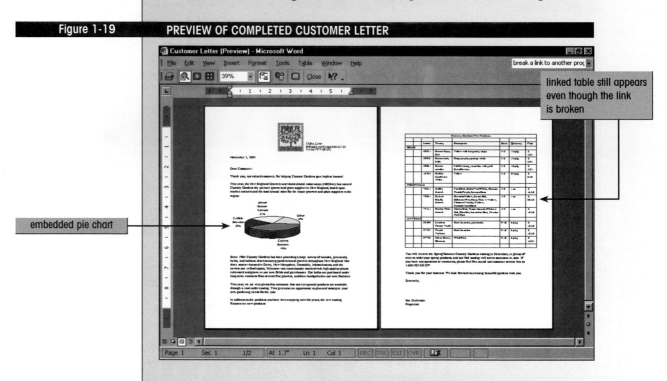

embedded pie chart

linked table still appears even though the link is broken

TROUBLE? If your letter has three pages, click File on the menu bar, click Page Setup, click the Margins tab, set the left, right, and bottom margins to .75, and then click the OK button.

5. Print the letter.

TROUBLE? If your printed letter contains a table of data instead of the pie chart, click the pie chart, click Edit on the menu bar, point to Chart Object, and then click Convert to open the Convert dialog box. Click the Activate as option button, click Microsoft Excel Chart, and then click the OK button. Save the document, and then reprint.

6. Close the letter and exit Word. You return to the Windows desktop.

You have integrated the NEGHA pie chart and the new products table from Excel into the customer letter Sue created in Word. She is pleased with the finished customer letter and is ready to send it to her customers.

QUICK CHECK

1. What is an object?

2. What is the difference between embedding an object and linking an object?

3. When an object is embedded between two programs, how many copies of the object exist?

4. If an Excel chart is linked to a Word document, which program is the source program?

5. True or False: Any changes you make to a linked object appear in both the destination and source files.

6. If you no longer want an object linked between two documents, what should you do?

7. If you break the link between the source Excel file and the destination Word file, change the price of Astilbe Assortment from $16.50 to $17.50 in the Excel file, and then close the Word file without saving changes, what will the price be when you reopen the Word file? Why?

REVIEW ASSIGNMENTS

Sue wants to send a memo to all Country Gardens employees introducing the plans for the catalog, the new products, and Country Gardens' status as the top grower in New England.

To create the memo:

1. Start Word, and then open the **Memo** document in the Review folder of the Tutorial.01 folder on your Data Disk.

2. Save the document as **Employee Memo** in the Review folder.

3. Start Excel, and then open the **PieChart** workbook in the Review folder of the Tutorial.01 folder on your Data Disk.

4. Save the workbook as **PieChart2** in the Review folder.

5. Embed the chart from the **PieChart2** workbook into the **Employee Memo** document on the blank line above the New Catalog! heading of the memo.

Explore   6. Double-click a blank area of the chart. Describe what happens. Why does this occur?

Explore   7. Explode the Country Gardens wedge of the pie, and then deselect the chart. (*Hint*: Single-click the Country Gardens wedge twice to select only that wedge, and then click and drag the wedge to explode it.)

8. Switch to Excel, and then close the **PieChart2** file without saving changes.

9. Open the **Products** workbook in the Review folder of the Tutorial.01 folder on your Data Disk, and then save it as **New Products2** in the Review folder.

10. Use the Paste Options button to link the new products table to the employee memo, and place it in the blank paragraph mark above the paragraph that begins "Once again." Keep the formatting of the source file when you link the table.

11. Switch to Excel, deselect the table, and change the price of Crocus Gipsy Girl to $4.75, and the price of Golden Apeldoorn Tulips to $9.20.

12. Switch back to the **Employee Memo** document. Notice that the changes are reflected in both the workbook and the memo.

13. Replace Sue Dickinson's name at the top and bottom of the memo with your own. Fine-tune the format of the table.

14. Save the memo, and then preview and print it. (*Hint*: If the table splits the text of the New Products paragraph, drag the table down slightly to move it below the complete paragraph.)

15. Break the link between the employee memo and the table.

16. Test that the link is broken by changing the price of the Astilbe Assortment from $16.50 to $17.50 in the table in the Excel window.

17. Exit Word and Excel. When prompted to save files, click the Yes button.

CASE PROBLEMS

Case 1. Cable-Ease Company Jose Rivera is the sales supervisor for the Cable-Ease Company in Washington, D.C. Cable-Ease leases mainframe computer cables and wiring. The company recently began to provide leasing quotes to customers over the phone. To ensure that both parties clearly understand the quotes, Jose wants all salespeople to follow up each telephone quote with a confirmation letter that provides a written quotation. The company uses an Excel workbook to calculate all quotations. If the customer later changes the quote specifications, Jose wants to be able to update the confirmation letter easily. However, he also wants to control when the letter is updated, so that changes aren't reflected until the customer confirms the order. To accomplish this, you'll link the quote from the Excel workbook into the confirmation letter, and then use the Office Help to find out about manually updating links.

1. Start Word, and then open the **Price** document in the Cases folder of the Tutorial.01 folder on your Data Disk.

2. Save the document as **Quote** in the Cases folder.

3. Change the name in the inside address and salutation from Mr. Clyde Davis to your own.

4. Start Excel, and then open the **Costs** workbook in the Cases folder of the Tutorial.01 folder on your Data Disk.

5. Save the workbook as **Charges** in the Cases folder.

6. Copy cells A1 through G6 to the Clipboard.

7. Switch to Word.

8. Link the Excel worksheet object into the Word document in the blank paragraph between paragraphs one and three of the body of the letter, matching the style of the Quote letter, and then save the document.

9. Switch to Excel.

10. Change the quantity ordered for all three items to 4.

11. Save the changes to **Charges**, switch to Word, and save the changes to **Quote**.

Explore ► 12. In the online Help, find information about manually updating links.

    a. Click the Ask a Question text box, and then type "How do I manually update links" in the Search text box.

    b. Press Enter, and then select the topic "Control how linked objects are updated."

    c. Click the "Change a linked object's setting to automatic or manual updating" hyperlink, and then read the information.

    d. Click the "Manually update a linked object when you choose" hyperlink, read the information, and then exit the Help window.

Explore ► 13. In the Word document, change the type of link for the Excel worksheet object to manual.

14. Save the Word document as **Confirm** in the Cases folder of the Tutorial.01 folder on your Data Disk.

15. Switch to Excel, and then change the quantity ordered for Item 1 to 3.

16. Save the workbook, and then exit Excel. Note that the change you just made in the previous step is not reflected in the Word document.

Explore ► 17. Based on what you learned from Office Help in Step 12, manually update the link to the Excel worksheet object. Note that the change you made to Item 1 is now reflected in the Word document.

Explore ► 18. Save and print the **Confirm** document, and then exit Word.

Case 2. Admissions at San Francisco University Darren Parnell, a senior at San Francisco University, works in the Admissions office. His supervisor, Fabia Hazan, asked him to help create an information packet to be sent to freshmen and their parents. Along with information on housing, meal plans, course selection, campus facilities, and so on, he needs to provide summary information on typical student expenditures (separate from tuition expenses). He decides to use Word and Excel to create a letter that includes a chart showing the average student expenditures at San Francisco University for the last few years, and a table of the typical expenditures students can expect this year. The information he collected is shown in Figure 1-20.

Figure 1-20

EXPENDITURES	2000	2001	2002	2003 (ESTIMATED)
Books	$750	$775	$850	$850
Dorm fees	$185	$185	$195	$255
Lab fees	$40	$40	$45	$55
Supplies	$105	$125	$135	$150
Library fees	$60	$75	$75	$75
TOTAL	$1140	$1200	$1300	$1385

You'll use Word and Excel to create the letter for Darren.

1. Start Word, and create a new document. Write a letter to parents of incoming freshmen of San Francisco University. Briefly outline the purpose of the letter, which is to provide the new students with an idea of typical student expenditures separate from tuition fees. Mention that the university realizes these expenditures can be difficult to meet, given the cost of tuition, and that over the last three years, the school and faculty have worked to keep increases to these expenses at a minimum. Type your name and address in the inside address. Remember to include a proper salutation and closing.

2. Save the file as **SFU Expenses Letter** in the Cases folder of the Tutorial.01 folder on your Data Disk.

3. Start Excel, and create a new worksheet. Rename Sheet1 as "Line Chart", and then enter the data for just 2000-2002, as shown in Figure 1-20.

4. Create a line chart based on the data, showing how minor the expense increases were over the last three years.

5. Save the workbook as **Estimated Expenses** in the Cases folder of the Tutorial.01 folder on your Data Disk.

Explore   6. Link the line chart to the **SFU Expenses Letter** document in an appropriate place.

7. In the Excel worksheet, change the Books amount for 2001 from $775 to $795.

Explore   8. On Sheet2 of the **Estimated Expenses** workbook, create a worksheet that shows the estimated expenses (but not the total) for 2003 in Figure 1-20. Rename the worksheet as "Expenses".

9. Embed the Expenses worksheet in the **SFU Expenses Letter** document in an appropriate place.

Explore   10. Insert a row into the embedded expenses worksheet that totals the expense amounts.

11. Save, preview, and then print the letter.

12. Close Word and Excel, saving files as needed.

Quick | Check answers

1. the specific information that you want to share between programs, such as a chart, table, picture, video or sound clip, or almost anything else you can create on a computer

2. Embedding stores a copy of the object in the destination file, and any changes do not appear in the source file; linking stores the object in the source file but displays it in the destination file, and any changes to the object made from either file appear in both files.

3. two

4. Excel

5. True

6. break the link

7. $17.50; closing the Word document without saving keeps the link intact

New Perspectives on

MICROSOFT®
ACCESS 2002

Read This Before You Begin

To the Student

Data Disks

To complete the Level I tutorials, Review Assignments, and Case Problems, you need six Data Disks. Your instructor will either provide you with these Data Disks or ask you to make your own.

If you are making your own Data Disks, you will need **six** blank, formatted high-density disks. You will need to copy a set of files and/or folders from a file server, standalone computer, or the Web onto your disks. Your instructor will tell you which computer, drive letter, and folders contain the files you need. You could also download the files by going to www.course.com and following the instructions on the screen.

The information below shows you which folders go on each of your disks, so that you will have enough disk space to complete all the tutorials, Review Assignments, and Case Problems:

Data Disk 1
Write this on the disk label:
Data Disk 1: Access Tutorial Files
Put this folder on the disk:
Tutorial

Data Disk 2
Write this on the disk label:
Data Disk 2: Access Review Assignments
Put this folder on the disk:
Review

Data Disk 3
Write this on the disk label:
Data Disk 3: Access Case Problem 1
Put this folder on the disk:
Cases

Data Disk 4
Write this on the disk label:
Data Disk 4: Access Case Problem 2
Put this folder on the disk:
Cases

Data Disk 5
Write this on the disk label:
Data Disk 5: Access Case Problem 3
Put this folder on the disk:
Cases

Data Disk 6
Write this on the disk label:
Data Disk 6: Access Case Problem 4
Put this folder on the disk:
Cases

When you begin each tutorial, be sure you are using the correct Data Disk. Refer to the "File Finder" chart at the back of this text for more detailed information on which files are used in which tutorials, and make sure you carefully read the note above the chart. See the inside front or inside back cover of this book for more information on Data Disk files, or ask your instructor or technical support person for assistance.

Course Labs

The Access Level I tutorials feature an interactive Course Lab to help you understand database concepts. There are Lab Assignments at the end of Tutorial 1 that relate to this Lab.

To start a Lab, click the **Start** button on the Windows taskbar, point to **Programs**, point to **Course Labs**, point to **New Perspectives Course Labs**, and then click the name of the Lab you want to use.

Using Your Own Computer

If you are going to work through this book using your own computer, you need:

- **Computer System** Microsoft Windows 98, NT, 2000 Professional, or higher must be installed on your computer. This book assumes a typical installation of Microsoft Access.

- **Data Disks** You will not be able to complete the tutorials or exercises in this book using your own computer until you have your Data Disks.

- **Course Labs** See your instructor or technical support person to obtain the Course Lab software for use on your own computer.

Visit Our World Wide Web Site

Additional materials designed especially for you are available on the World Wide Web.
Go to www.course.com/NewPerspectives.

To the Instructor

The Data Disk Files and Course Labs are available on the Instructor's Resource Kit for this title. Follow the instructions in the Help file on the CD-ROM to install the programs to your network or standalone computer. For information on creating Data Disks or the Course Labs, see the "To the Student" section above.

You are granted a license to copy the Data Files and Course Labs to any computer or computer network used by students who have purchased this book.

In this tutorial you will:

- Define the terms field, record, table, relational database, primary key, and foreign key

- Open an existing database

- Identify the components of the Access and Database windows

- Open and navigate a table

- Learn how Access saves a database

- Open an existing query, and create, sort, and navigate a new query

- Create and navigate a form

- Create, preview, and navigate a report

- Learn how to manage a database by backing up, restoring, compacting, and converting a database

LAB

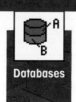

Databases

INTRODUCTION TO MICROSOFT ACCESS 2002

Viewing and Working with a Table Containing Employer Data

CASE

Northeast Seasonal Jobs International (NSJI)

During her high school and college years, Elsa Jensen spent her summers working as a lifeguard for some of the most popular beaches on Cape Cod, Massachusetts. Throughout those years, Elsa met many foreign students who had come to the United States to work for the summer, both at the beaches and at other seasonal businesses, such as restaurants and hotels. Elsa formed friendships with several students and kept in contact with them beyond college. Through discussions with her friends, Elsa realized that foreign students often have a difficult time finding appropriate seasonal work, relying mainly on "word-of-mouth" references to locate jobs. Elsa became convinced that there must be an easier way.

Several years ago, Elsa founded Northeast Seasonal Jobs, a small firm located in Boston that served as a job broker between foreign students seeking part-time, seasonal work and resort businesses located in New England. Recently Elsa expanded her business to include resorts in the eastern provinces of Canada, and consequently she changed her company's name to Northeast Seasonal Jobs International (NSJI). At first the company focused mainly on summer employment, but as the business continued to grow, Elsa increased the scope of operations to include all types of seasonal opportunities, including foliage tour companies in the fall and ski resorts in the winter.

Elsa depends on computers to help her manage all areas of NSJI's operations, including financial management, sales, and information management. Several months ago the company upgraded to Microsoft Windows and **Microsoft Access 2002** (or simply **Access**), a computer program used to enter, maintain, and retrieve related data in a format known as a database. Elsa and her staff use Access to maintain data such as information about employers, positions they have available for seasonal work, and foreign students seeking employment. Elsa recently created a database named Seasonal to track the company's employer customers and data about their available positions. She asks for your help in completing and maintaining this database.

<table>
<tr><td>**SESSION
1.1**</td><td>In this session, you will learn key database terms and concepts, open an existing data-
base, identify components of the Access and Database windows, open and navigate a
table, and learn how Access saves a database.</td></tr>
</table>

Introduction to Database Concepts

Databases

Before you begin working on Elsa's database and using Access, you need to understand a few key terms and concepts associated with databases.

Organizing Data

Data is a valuable resource to any business. At NSJI, for example, important data includes employers' names and addresses, and available positions and wages. Organizing, storing, maintaining, retrieving, and sorting this type of data are critical activities that enable a business to find and use information effectively. Before storing data on a computer, however, you first must organize the data.

Your first step in organizing data is to identify the individual fields. A **field** is a single characteristic or attribute of a person, place, object, event, or idea. For example, some of the many fields that NSJI tracks are employer ID, employer name, employer address, employer phone number, position, wage, and start date.

Next, you group related fields together into tables. A **table** is a collection of fields that describe a person, place, object, event, or idea. Figure 1-1 shows an example of an Employer table consisting of four fields: EmployerID, EmployerName, EmployerAddress, and PhoneNumber.

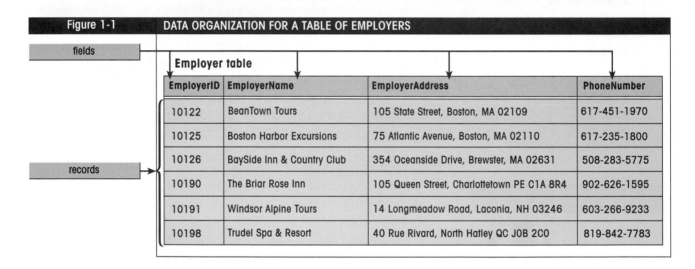

Figure 1-1   DATA ORGANIZATION FOR A TABLE OF EMPLOYERS

fields

Employer table

EmployerID	EmployerName	EmployerAddress	PhoneNumber
10122	BeanTown Tours	105 State Street, Boston, MA 02109	617-451-1970
10125	Boston Harbor Excursions	75 Atlantic Avenue, Boston, MA 02110	617-235-1800
10126	BaySide Inn & Country Club	354 Oceanside Drive, Brewster, MA 02631	508-283-5775
10190	The Briar Rose Inn	105 Queen Street, Charlottetown PE C1A 8R4	902-626-1595
10191	Windsor Alpine Tours	14 Longmeadow Road, Laconia, NH 03246	603-266-9233
10198	Trudel Spa & Resort	40 Rue Rivard, North Hatley QC J0B 2C0	819-842-7783

records

The specific value, or content, of a field is called the **field value**. In Figure 1-1, the first set of field values for EmployerID, EmployerName, EmployerAddress, and PhoneNumber are, respectively: 10122; BeanTown Tours; 105 State Street, Boston, MA 02109; and 617-451-1970. This set of field values is called a **record**. In the Employer table, the data for each employer is stored as a separate record. Figure 1-1 shows six records; each row of field values is a record.

Databases and Relationships

A collection of related tables is called a **database**, or a **relational database**. NSJI's Seasonal database contains two related tables: the Employer and NAICS tables, which Elsa created. (The NAICS table contains North American Industry Classification System codes, which are used to classify businesses by the type of activity in which they are engaged.) In Tutorial 2, you will create a Position table to store information about the available positions at NSJI's employer clients.

Sometimes you might want information about employers and their available positions. To obtain this information, you must have a way to connect records in the Employer table to records in the Position table. You connect the records in the separate tables through a **common field** that appears in both tables.

In the sample database shown in Figure 1-2, each record in the Employer table has a field named EmployerID, which is also a field in the Position table. For example, BaySide Inn & Country Club is the third employer in the Employer table and has an EmployerID of 10126. This same EmployerID field value, 10126, appears in three records in the Position table. Therefore, BaySide Inn & Country Club is the employer with these three positions available.

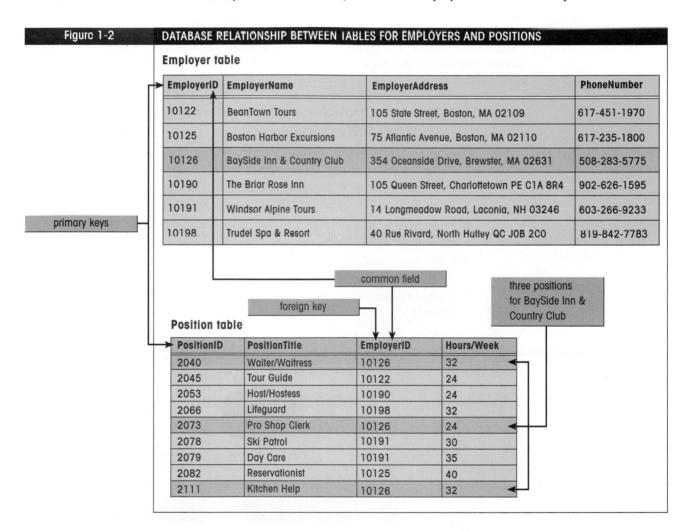

Figure 1-2	DATABASE RELATIONSHIP BETWEEN TABLES FOR EMPLOYERS AND POSITIONS

Employer table

EmployerID	EmployerName	EmployerAddress	PhoneNumber
10122	BeanTown Tours	105 State Street, Boston, MA 02109	617-451-1970
10125	Boston Harbor Excursions	75 Atlantic Avenue, Boston, MA 02110	617-235-1800
10126	BaySide Inn & Country Club	354 Oceanside Drive, Brewster, MA 02631	508-283-5775
10190	The Briar Rose Inn	105 Queen Street, Charlottetown PE C1A 8R4	902-626-1595
10191	Windsor Alpine Tours	14 Longmeadow Road, Laconia, NH 03246	603-266-9233
10198	Trudel Spa & Resort	40 Rue Rivard, North Hatley QC J0B 2C0	819-842-7783

primary keys

common field

three positions for BaySide Inn & Country Club

foreign key

Position table

PositionID	PositionTitle	EmployerID	Hours/Week
2040	Waiter/Waitress	10126	32
2045	Tour Guide	10122	24
2053	Host/Hostess	10190	24
2066	Lifeguard	10198	32
2073	Pro Shop Clerk	10126	24
2078	Ski Patrol	10191	30
2079	Day Care	10191	35
2082	Reservationist	10125	40
2111	Kitchen Help	10126	32

Each EmployerID in the Employer table must be unique, so that you can distinguish one employer from another and identify the employer's specific positions available in the Position table. The EmployerID field is referred to as the primary key of the Employer table. A **primary key** is a field, or a collection of fields, whose values uniquely identify each record in a table. In the Position table, PositionID is the primary key.

When you include the primary key from one table as a field in a second table to form a relationship between the two tables, it is called a **foreign key** in the second table, as shown in Figure 1-2. For example, EmployerID is the primary key in the Employer table and a foreign key in the Position table. Although the primary key EmployerID has unique values in the Employer table, the same field as a foreign key in the Position table does not have unique values. The EmployerID value 10126, for example, appears three times in the Position table because the BaySide Inn & Country Club has three available positions. Each foreign key value, however, must match one of the field values for the primary key in the other table. In the example shown in Figure 1-2, each EmployerID value in the Position table must match an EmployerID value in the Employer table. The two tables are related, enabling users to connect the facts about employers with the facts about their employment positions.

Relational Database Management Systems

To manage its databases, a company purchases a database management system. A **database management system (DBMS)** is a software program that lets you create databases and then manipulate data in them. Most of today's database management systems, including Access, are called relational database management systems. In a **relational database management system**, data is organized as a collection of tables. As stated earlier, a relationship between two tables in a relational DBMS is formed through a common field.

A relational DBMS controls the storage of databases on disk by carrying out data creation and manipulation requests. Specifically, a relational DBMS provides the following functions, which are illustrated in Figure 1-3:

- It allows you to create database structures containing fields, tables, and table relationships.
- It lets you easily add new records, change field values in existing records, and delete records.
- It contains a built-in query language, which lets you obtain immediate answers to the questions you ask about your data.
- It contains a built-in report generator, which lets you produce professional-looking, formatted reports from your data.
- It provides protection of databases through security, control, and recovery facilities.

| Figure 1-3 | RELATIONAL DATABASE MANAGEMENT SYSTEM |

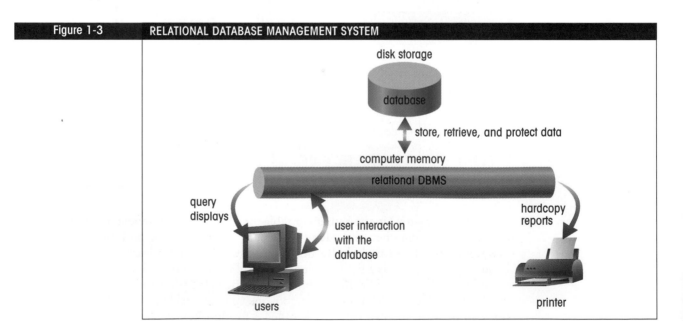

A company such as NSJI benefits from a relational DBMS because it allows users working in different departments to share the same data. More than one user can enter data into a database, and more than one user can retrieve and analyze data that was entered by others. For example, NSJI will store only one copy of the Employer table, and all employees will be able to use it to meet their specific requests for employer information.

Finally, unlike other software programs, such as spreadsheets, a DBMS can handle massive amounts of data and can easily form relationships among multiple tables. Each Access database, for example, can be up to two gigabytes in size and can contain up to 32,768 objects (tables, queries, and so on).

Opening an Existing Database

Now that you've learned some database terms and concepts, you're ready to start Access and open the Seasonal database.

To start Access and open the Seasonal database:

1. Click the **Start** button on the taskbar, point to **Programs**, and then point to **Microsoft Access**. See Figure 1-4.

Figure 1-4   **STARTING MICROSOFT ACCESS**

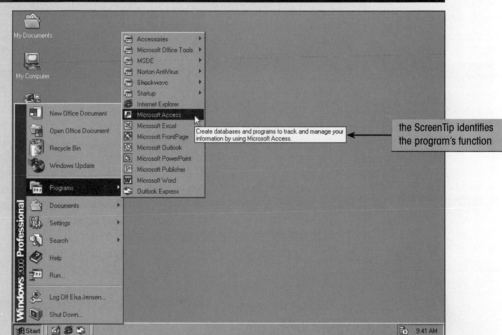

the ScreenTip identifies the program's function

TROUBLE? If your screen differs slightly from the figure, don't worry. Although the figures in this tutorial were created on a computer running Windows 2000 in its default settings, the different Windows operating systems share the same basic user interface, and Microsoft Access runs equally well using Windows 98, Windows NT, Windows 2000, or Windows XP.

TROUBLE? If you don't see the Microsoft Access option on the Programs menu, you might need to click the double arrow on the Programs menu to display more options. If you still cannot find the Microsoft Access option, ask your instructor or technical support person for help.

2. Click **Microsoft Access** to start Access. After a short pause, the Access copyright information appears in a message box and remains on the screen until the Access window opens. See Figure 1-5.

| Figure 1-5 | MICROSOFT ACCESS WINDOW |

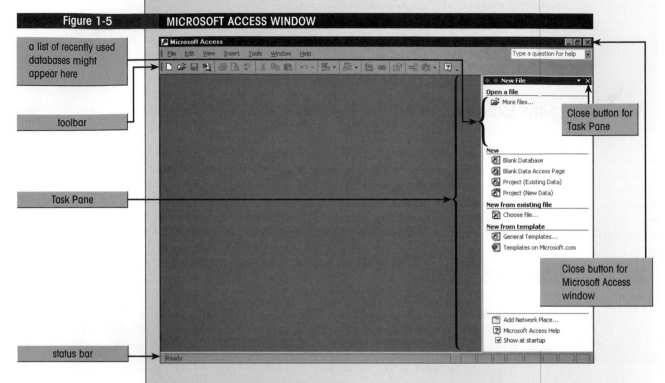

a list of recently used databases might appear here

toolbar

Close button for Task Pane

Task Pane

Close button for Microsoft Access window

status bar

When you start Access, the Access window contains a Task Pane that allows you to create a new database or to open an existing database. You can click the "Blank Database" option in the "New" section of the Task Pane to create a new database on your own, or you can click the "General Templates" option in the "New from template" section of the Task Pane to let Access guide you through the steps for creating one of the standard databases provided by Microsoft. In this case, you need to open an existing database.

To open an existing database, you can select the name of a database in the list of recently opened databases (if the list appears), or you can click the "More files" option to open a database not listed. You need to open an existing database—the Seasonal database on your Data Disk.

3. Make sure you have created your copy of the Access Data Disk, and then place your Data Disk in the appropriate disk drive.

TROUBLE? If you don't have a Data Disk, you need to get one before you can proceed. Your instructor will either give you one or ask you to make your own. (See your instructor for more information.) In either case, be sure that you have made a backup copy of your Data Disk before you begin working, so that the original Data Files will be available on the copied disk in case you need to start over because of an error or problem.

4. In the "Open a file" section of the Task Pane, click the **More files** option. The Open dialog box is displayed. See Figure 1-6.

Figure 1-6	OPEN DIALOG BOX

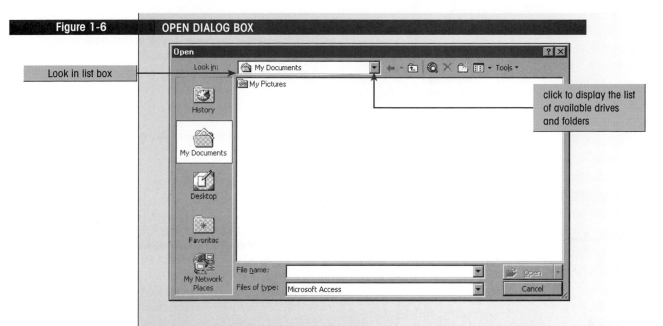

Look in list box

click to display the list of available drives and folders

TROUBLE? The list of folders and files on your screen might be different from the list in Figure 1-6.

5. Click the **Look in** list arrow, and then click the drive that contains your Data Disk.

6. Click **Tutorial** in the list box (if necessary), and then click the **Open** button to display a list of the files in the Tutorial folder.

7. Click **Seasonal** in the list box, and then click the **Open** button. The Seasonal database opens in the Access window. See Figure 1-7.

Figure 1-7	ACCESS AND DATABASE WINDOWS

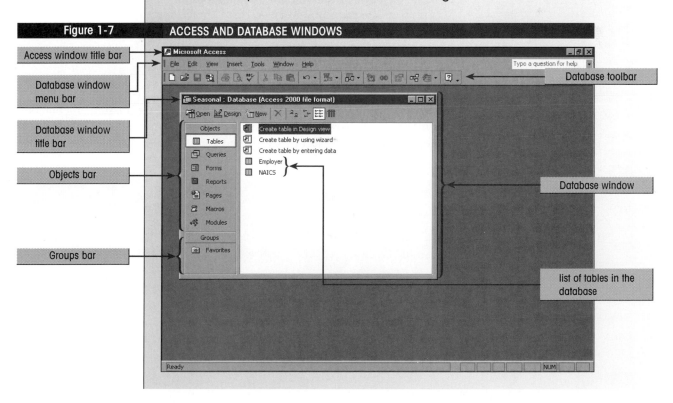

Access window title bar

Database window menu bar

Database window title bar

Objects bar

Groups bar

Database toolbar

Database window

list of tables in the database

TROUBLE? The filename on your screen might be Seasonal.mdb instead of Seasonal, depending on your computer's default settings. The extension ".mdb" identifies the file as a Microsoft Access database.

TROUBLE? If Tables is not selected in the Objects bar of the Database window, click it to display the list of tables in the database.

Before you can begin working with the database, you need to become familiar with the components of the Access and Database windows.

The Access and Database Windows

The **Access window** is the program window that appears when you start the program. The **Database window** appears when you open a database; this window is the main control center for working with an open Access database. Except for the Access window title bar, all screen components now on your screen are associated with the Database window (see Figure 1-7). Most of these screen components—including the title bars, window sizing buttons, menu bar, toolbar, and status bar—are the same as the components in other Windows programs.

Notice that the Database window title bar includes the notation "(Access 2000 file format)." By default, databases that you create in Access 2002 use the Access 2000 database file format. This feature ensures that you can use and share databases originally created in Access 2002 without converting them to Access 2000, and vice versa. (You'll learn more about database file formats and converting databases later in this tutorial.)

The Database window provides a variety of options for viewing and manipulating database objects. Each item in the **Objects bar** controls one of the major object groups—such as tables, queries, forms, and reports—in an Access database. The **Groups bar** allows you to organize different types of database objects into groups, with shortcuts to those objects, so that you can work with them more easily. The Database window also provides buttons for quickly creating, opening, and managing objects, as well as shortcut options for some of these tasks.

Elsa has already created the Employer and NAICS tables in the Seasonal database. She asks you to open the Employer table and view its contents.

Opening an Access Table

As noted earlier, tables contain all the data in a database. Tables are the fundamental objects for your work in Access. To view, add, change, or delete data in a table, you first open the table. You can open any Access object by using the Open button in the Database window.

REFERENCE WINDOW	RW
Opening an Access Object	
■ In the Objects bar of the Database window, click the type of object you want to open.	
■ If necessary, scroll the object list box until the object name appears, and then click the object name.	
■ Click the Open button in the Database window.	

You need to open the Employer table, which is one of two tables in the Seasonal database.

To open the Employer table:

1. In the Database window, click **Employer** to select it.

2. Click the **Open** button in the Database window. The Employer table opens in Datasheet view on top of the Database and Access windows. See Figure 1-8.

Figure 1-8	EMPLOYER TABLE DISPLAYED IN DATASHEET VIEW

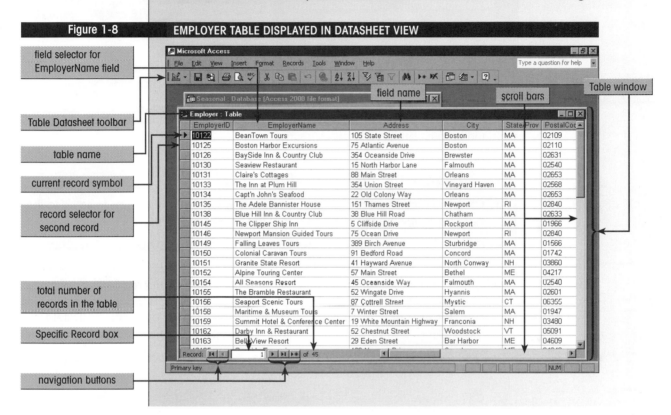

field selector for EmployerName field

field name

scroll bars

Table window

Table Datasheet toolbar

table name

current record symbol

record selector for second record

total number of records in the table

Specific Record box

navigation buttons

Datasheet view shows a table's contents as a **datasheet** in rows and columns, similar to a table or spreadsheet. Each row is a separate record in the table, and each column contains the field values for one field in the table. Each column is headed by a field name inside a field selector, and each row has a record selector to its left. Clicking a **field selector** or a **record selector** selects that entire column or row (respectively), which you then can manipulate. A field selector is also called a **column selector**, and a record selector is also called a **row selector**.

Navigating an Access Datasheet

When you first open a datasheet, Access selects the first field value in the first record. Notice that this field value is highlighted and that a darkened triangle symbol, called the current record symbol, appears in the record selector to the left of the first record. The **current record symbol** identifies the currently selected record. Clicking a record selector or field value in another row moves the current record symbol to that row. You can also move the pointer over the data on the screen and click one of the field values to position the insertion point.

The Employer table currently has 13 fields and 45 records. To view fields or records not currently visible in the datasheet, you can use the horizontal and vertical scroll bars shown in Figure 1-8 to navigate through the data. The **navigation buttons**, also shown in Figure 1-8, provide another way to move vertically through the records. Figure 1-9 shows which record becomes the current record when you click each navigation button. The **Specific Record box**, which appears between the two sets of navigation buttons, displays the current record number. The total number of records in the table appears to the right of the navigation buttons.

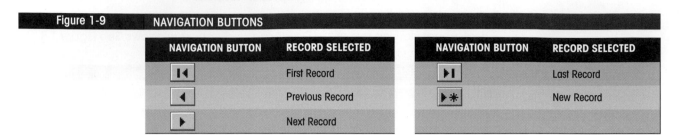

Figure 1-9		NAVIGATION BUTTONS	

NAVIGATION BUTTON	RECORD SELECTED	NAVIGATION BUTTON	RECORD SELECTED
◀	First Record	▶▌	Last Record
◀	Previous Record	▶✳	New Record
▶	Next Record		

Elsa suggests that you use the various navigation techniques to move through the Employer table and become familiar with its contents.

To navigate the Employer datasheet:

1. Click the right scroll arrow in the horizontal scroll bar a few times to scroll to the right and view the remaining fields in the Employer table.

2. Drag the scroll box in the horizontal scroll bar all the way to the left to return to the previous display of the datasheet.

3. Click the **Next Record** navigation button [▶]. The second record is now the current record, as indicated by the current record symbol in the second record selector. Also, notice that the second record's value for the EmployerID field is highlighted, and "2" (for record number 2) appears in the Specific Record box.

4. Click the **Last Record** navigation button [▶▌]. The last record in the table, record 45, is now the current record.

5. Click the **Previous Record** navigation button [◀]. Record 44 is now the current record.

6. Click the **First Record** navigation button [◀]. The first record is now the current record.

Saving a Database

Notice the Save button 🖫 on the Table Datasheet toolbar. Unlike the Save buttons in other Windows programs, this Save button does not save the active document (database) to your disk. Instead, you use the Save button to save the design of an Access object, such as a table, or to save datasheet format changes. Access does not have a button or option you can use to save the active database.

Access saves changes to the active database to your disk automatically, when a record is changed or added and when you close the database. If your database is stored on a disk in drive A, you should never remove the disk while the database file is open. If you remove the disk, Access will encounter problems when it tries to save the database, which might damage the database.

Now that you've viewed the Employer table, you can exit Access.

To exit Access:

1. Click the **Close** button ☒ on the Access window title bar. The Employer table and the Seasonal database close, Access closes, and you return to the Windows desktop.

Now that you've become familiar with Access and the Seasonal database, in the next session, you'll be ready to work with the data stored in the database.

Session 1.1 QUICK CHECK

1. A(n) _____ is a single characteristic of a person, place, object, event, or idea.

2. You connect the records in two separate tables through a(n) _____ that appears in both tables.

3. The _____, whose values uniquely identify each record in a table, is called a(n) _____ when it is placed in a second table to form a relationship between the two tables.

4. In a table, the rows are also called _____, and the columns are also called _____.

5. The _____ identifies the selected record in an Access table.

6. Describe two methods for navigating through a table.

SESSION 1.2

In this session, you will open an existing query and create and navigate a new query; create and navigate a form; and create, preview, and navigate a report. You will also learn how to manage databases by backing up and restoring, compacting and repairing, and converting databases.

Working with Queries

A **query** is a question you ask about the data stored in a database. In response to a query, Access displays the specific records and fields that answer your question. When you create a query, you tell Access which fields you need and what criteria Access should use to select the records. Then Access displays only the information you want, so you don't have to navigate through the entire database for the information.

Before creating a new query, you will open a query that Elsa created recently so that she could view information in the Employer table in a different way.

Opening an Existing Query

Queries that you create and save appear in the Queries list of the Database window. To see the results of a query, you simply open, or run, the query. Elsa created and saved a query named "Contacts" in the Seasonal database. This query shows all the fields from the Employer table, but in a different order. Elsa suggests that you open this query to see its results.

To open the Contacts query:

1. Insert your Data Disk into the appropriate disk drive.

2. Start Access, and then click the **More files** option in the Task Pane to display the Open dialog box.

3. Click the **Look in** list arrow, click the drive that contains your Data Disk, click **Tutorial** in the list box, and then click the **Open** button to display the list of files in the Tutorial folder.

4. Click **Seasonal** in the list box, and then click the **Open** button.

5. Click **Queries** in the Objects bar of the Database window to display the Queries list. The Queries list box contains one object—the Contacts query. See Figure 1-10.

Figure 1-10	LIST OF QUERIES IN THE SEASONAL DATABASE

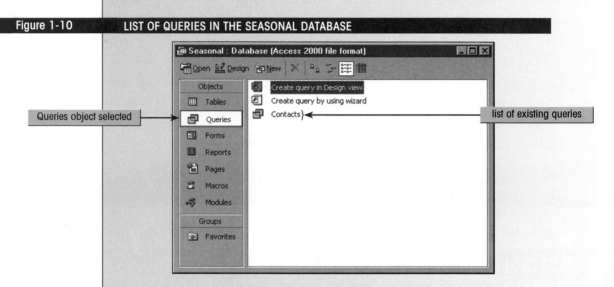

Now you will run the Contacts query by opening it.

6. Click **Contacts** to select it, and then click the **Open** button in the Database window. Access displays the results of the query in Datasheet view. See Figure 1-11.

Figure 1-11	RESULT OF RUNNING THE CONTACTS QUERY

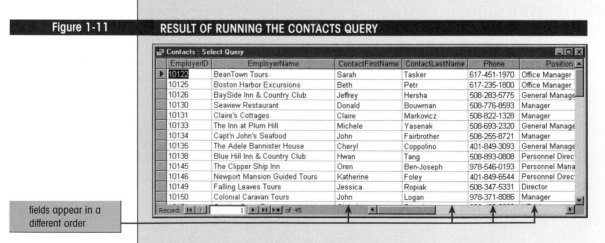

> Notice that the query displays the fields from the Employer table, but in a different order. For example, the first and last names of each contact, as well as the contact's phone number, appear next to the employer name. This arrangement lets Elsa view pertinent contact information without having to scroll through the table. Rearranging the display of table data is one task you can perform with queries, so that table information appears in a different order to suit how you want to work with the information.
>
> **7.** Click the **Close** button ☒ on the Query window title bar to close the Contacts query.

Even though a query can display table information in a different way, the information still exists in the table as it was originally entered. If you opened the Employer table, it would still show the fields in their original order.

Zack Ward, the director of marketing at NSJI, wants a list of all employers so that his staff can call them to check on their satisfaction with NSJI's services and recruits. He doesn't want the list to include all the fields in the Employer table (such as PostalCode and NAICSCode). To produce this list for Zack, you need to create a query using the Employer table.

Creating, Sorting, and Navigating a Query

You can design your own queries or use an Access **Query Wizard**, which guides you through the steps to create a query. The Simple Query Wizard allows you to select records and fields quickly, and it is an appropriate choice for producing the employer list Zack wants. You can choose this Wizard either by clicking the New button, which opens a dialog box from which you can choose among several different Wizards to create your query, or by double-clicking the "Create query by using wizard" option, which automatically starts the Simple Query Wizard.

To start the Simple Query Wizard:

1. Double-click **Create query by using wizard**. The first Simple Query Wizard dialog box opens. See Figure 1-12.

| Figure 1-12 | FIRST SIMPLE QUERY WIZARD DIALOG BOX |

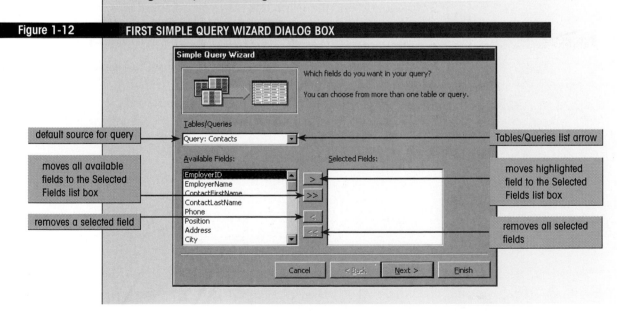

default source for query

moves all available fields to the Selected Fields list box

removes a selected field

Tables/Queries list arrow

moves highlighted field to the Selected Fields list box

removes all selected fields

Because Contacts is the only query object currently in the Seasonal database, it is listed in the Tables/Queries box by default. You need to base the query you're creating on the Employer table.

2. Click the **Tables/Queries** list arrow, and then click **Table: Employer** to select the Employer table as the source for the new query. The Available Fields list box now lists the fields in the Employer table.

You need to select fields from the Available Fields list to include them in the query. To select fields one at a time, click a field and then click the $\boxed{>}$ button. The selected field moves from the Available Fields list box on the left to the Selected Fields list box on the right. To select all the fields, click the $\boxed{>>}$ button. If you change your mind or make a mistake, you can remove a field by clicking it in the Selected Fields list box and then clicking the $\boxed{<}$ button. To remove all selected fields, click the $\boxed{<<}$ button.

Each Wizard dialog box contains buttons on the bottom that allow you to move to the previous dialog box (Back button), move to the next dialog box (Next button), or cancel the creation process (Cancel button) and return to the Database window. You can also finish creating the object (Finish button) and accept the Wizard's defaults for the remaining options.

Zack wants his list to include data from only the following fields: EmployerName, City, State/Prov, ContactFirstName, ContactLastName, and Phone. You need to select these fields to include them in the query.

To create the query using the Simple Query Wizard:

1. Click **EmployerName** in the Available Fields list box, and then click the $\boxed{>}$ button. The EmployerName field moves to the Selected Fields list box.

2. Repeat Step 1 for the fields **City**, **State/Prov**, **ContactFirstName**, **ContactLastName**, and **Phone**, and then click the **Next** button. The second, and final, Simple Query Wizard dialog box opens and asks you to choose a name for your query. This name will appear in the Queries list in the Database window. You'll change the suggested name (Employer Query) to "Employer List."

3. Click at the end of the highlighted name, use the Backspace key to delete the word "Query," and then type **List**. Now you can view the query results.

4. Click the **Finish** button to complete the query. Access displays the query results in Datasheet view.

5. Click the **Maximize** button 🗖 on the Query window title bar to maximize the window. See Figure 1-13.

| Figure 1-13 | QUERY RESULTS |

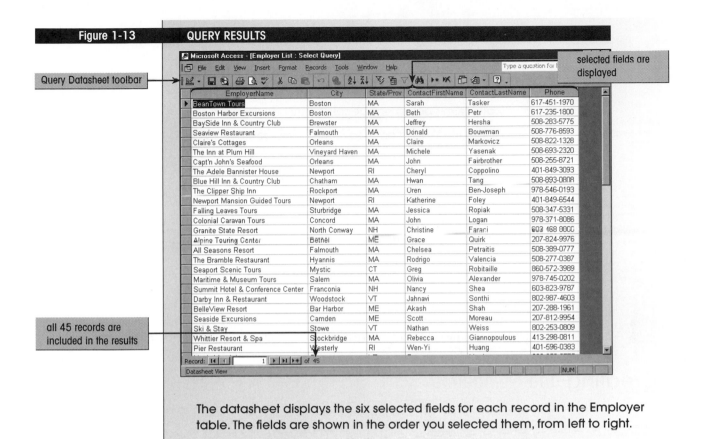

Query Datasheet toolbar →

selected fields are displayed

all 45 records are included in the results

EmployerName	City	State/Prov	ContactFirstName	ContactLastName	Phone
BeanTown Tours	Boston	MA	Sarah	Tasker	617-451-1970
Boston Harbor Excursions	Boston	MA	Beth	Petr	617-235-1800
BaySide Inn & Country Club	Brewster	MA	Jeffrey	Hersha	508-283-5775
Seaview Restaurant	Falmouth	MA	Donald	Bouwman	508-776-8593
Claire's Cottages	Orleans	MA	Claire	Markovicz	508-822-1328
The Inn at Plum Hill	Vineyard Haven	MA	Michele	Yasenak	508-693-2320
Capt'n John's Seafood	Orleans	MA	John	Fairbrother	508-255-8721
The Adele Bannister House	Newport	RI	Cheryl	Coppolino	401-849-3093
Blue Hill Inn & Country Club	Chatham	MA	Hwan	Tang	508-893-0808
The Clipper Ship Inn	Rockport	MA	Oren	Ben-Joseph	978-546-0193
Newport Mansion Guided Tours	Newport	RI	Katherine	Foley	401-849-6544
Falling Leaves Tours	Sturbridge	MA	Jessica	Ropiak	508-347-5331
Colonial Caravan Tours	Concord	MA	John	Logan	978-371-8086
Granite State Resort	North Conway	NH	Christine	Farari	603 468 8000
Alpine Touring Center	Bethel	ME	Grace	Quirk	207-824-9976
All Seasons Resort	Falmouth	MA	Chelsea	Petraitis	508-389-0777
The Bramble Restaurant	Hyannis	MA	Rodrigo	Valencia	508-277-0387
Seaport Scenic Tours	Mystic	CT	Greg	Robitaille	860-572-3989
Maritime & Museum Tours	Salem	MA	Olivia	Alexander	978-745-0202
Summit Hotel & Conference Center	Franconia	NH	Nancy	Shea	603-823-9787
Darby Inn & Restaurant	Woodstock	VT	Jahnavi	Sonthi	802-987-4603
BelleView Resort	Bar Harbor	ME	Akash	Shah	207-288-1961
Seaside Excursions	Camden	ME	Scott	Moreau	207-812-9954
Ski & Stay	Stowe	VT	Nathan	Weiss	802-253-0809
Whittier Resort & Spa	Stockbridge	MA	Rebecca	Giannopoulous	413-298-0811
Pier Restaurant	Westerly	RI	Wen-Yi	Huang	401-596-0383

Record: 1 of 45

Datasheet View — NUM

The datasheet displays the six selected fields for each record in the Employer table. The fields are shown in the order you selected them, from left to right.

The records are currently listed in order by the primary key field (EmployerID from the Employer table). This is true even though the EmployerID field is not included in the display of the query results. Zack prefers the records listed in order by state or province, so that his staff members can focus on all records for the employers in a particular state or province. To display the records in the order Zack wants, you need to sort the query results by the State/Prov field.

To sort the query results:

1. Click to position the insertion point anywhere in the State/Prov column. This establishes the State/Prov column as the current field.

2. Click the **Sort Ascending** button on the Query Datasheet toolbar. Now the records are sorted in ascending alphabetical order by the values in the State/Prov field. All the records for Connecticut (CT) are listed first, followed by the records for Massachusetts (MA), Maine (ME), and so on.

   Notice that the navigation buttons are located at the bottom of the window. You navigate through a query datasheet in the same way that you navigate through a table datasheet.

3. Click the **Last Record** navigation button. The last record in the query datasheet, for the Darby Inn & Restaurant, is now the current record.

4. Click the **Previous Record** navigation button. Record 44 in the query datasheet is now the current record.

5. Click the **First Record** navigation button ⏮. The first record is now the current record.

6. Click the **Close Window** button ✕ on the menu bar to close the query.

A dialog box opens and asks if you want to save changes to the design of the query. This box opens because you changed the sort order of the query results.

7. Click the **Yes** button to save the query design changes and return to the Database window. Notice that the Employer List query now appears in the Queries list box. In addition, because you maximized the Query window, now the Database window is also maximized. You need to restore the window.

8. Click the **Restore Window** button 🗗 on the menu bar to restore the Database window.

The query results are not stored in the database; however, the query design is stored as part of the database with the name you specified. You can re-create the query results at any time by running the query again. You'll learn more about creating and running queries in Tutorial 3.

After Zack views the query results, Elsa then asks you to create a form for the Employer table so that her staff members can use the form to enter and work with data in the table easily.

Creating and Navigating a Form

A **form** is an object you use to maintain, view, and print records in a database. Although you can perform these same functions with tables and queries, forms can present data in many customized and useful ways.

In Access, you can design your own forms or use a Form Wizard to create your forms automatically. A **Form Wizard** is an Access tool that asks you a series of questions, and then creates a form based on your answers. The quickest way to create a form is to use an **AutoForm Wizard**, which places all the fields from a selected table (or query) on a form automatically, without asking you any questions, and then displays the form on the screen.

Elsa wants a form for the Employer table that will show all the fields for one record at a time, with fields listed one below another in a column. This type of form will make it easier for her staff to focus on all the data for a particular employer. You'll use the AutoForm: Columnar Wizard to create the form.

To create the form using an AutoForm Wizard:

1. Click **Forms** in the Objects bar of the Database window to display the Forms list. The Forms list box does not contain any forms yet.

2. Click the **New** button in the Database window to open the New Form dialog box. See Figure 1-14.

Figure 1-14	NEW FORM DIALOG BOX

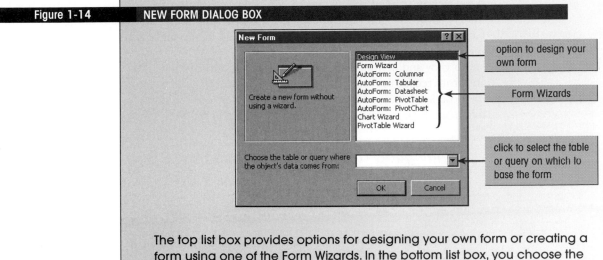

The top list box provides options for designing your own form or creating a form using one of the Form Wizards. In the bottom list box, you choose the table or query that will supply the data for the form.

3. Click **AutoForm: Columnar** to select this AutoForm Wizard.

4. Click the list arrow for choosing the table or query on which to base the form, and then click **Employer**.

5. Click the **OK** button. The AutoForm Wizard creates the form and displays it in Form view. See Figure 1-15.

Figure 1-15	FORM CREATED BY THE AUTOFORM: COLUMNAR WIZARD

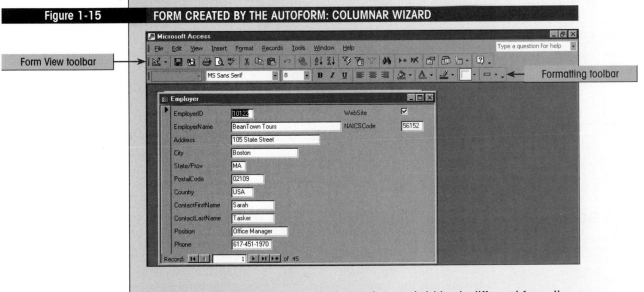

TROUBLE? The background of your form might look different from the one shown in Figure 1-15, depending on your computer's settings. If so, don't worry. You will learn how to change the form's style later in this text. For now, continue with the tutorial.

The form displays one record at a time in the Employer table. Access displays the field values for the first record in the table and selects the first field value (EmployerID). Each field name appears on a separate line (spread over two columns) and on the same line as its field value, which appears in a box. The widths of the boxes are different to accommodate the different sizes of the displayed field values; for example, compare the small box for the State/Prov field value with the larger box for the EmployerName field value. The AutoForm: Columnar Wizard automatically placed the field names and values on the form and supplied the background style.

To view and maintain data using a form, you must know how to move from field to field and from record to record. Notice that the Form window contains navigation buttons, similar to those available in Datasheet view, which you can use to display different records in the form. You'll use these now to navigate through the form; then you'll save and close the form.

To navigate, save, and close the form:

1. Click the **Next Record** navigation button ▶. The form now displays the values for the second record in the Employer table.

2. Click the **Last Record** navigation button ▶| to move to the last record in the table. The form displays the information for record 45, Lighthouse Tours.

3. Click the **Previous Record** navigation button ◀ to move to record 44.

4. Click the **First Record** navigation button |◀ to return to the first record in the Employer table.

    Next, you'll save the form with the name "Employer Data" in the Seasonal database. Then the form will be available for later use. You'll learn more about creating and customizing forms in Tutorial 4.

5. Click the **Save** button 🖫 on the Form View toolbar. The Save As dialog box opens.

6. In the Form Name text box, click at the end of the highlighted word "Employer," press the **spacebar**, type **Data**, and then press the **Enter** key. Access saves the form as Employer Data in the Seasonal database and closes the dialog box.

7. Click the **Close** button ✕ on the Form window title bar to close the form and return to the Database window. Note that the Employer Data form is now listed in the Forms list box.

After attending a staff meeting, Zack returns with another request. He wants the same employer list you produced earlier when you created the Employer List query, but he'd like the information presented in a more readable format. You'll help Zack by creating a report.

Creating, Previewing, and Navigating a Report

A **report** is a formatted printout (or screen display) of the contents of one or more tables in a database. Although you can print data appearing in tables, queries, and forms, reports provide you with the greatest flexibility for formatting printed output. As with forms, you can design your own reports or use a Report Wizard to create reports automatically.

Zack wants a report showing the same information contained in the Employer List query that you created earlier. However, he wants the data for each employer to be grouped together, with one employer record below another, as shown in the report sketch in Figure 1-16.

Figure 1-16   **SKETCH OF ZACK'S REPORT**

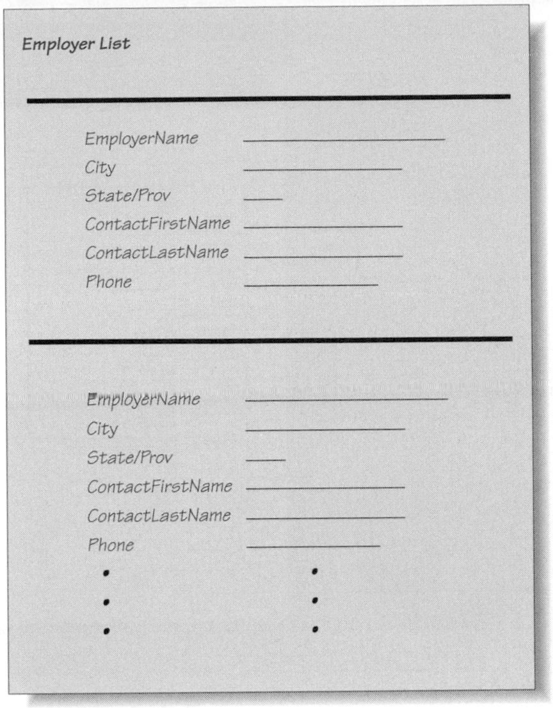

Employer List

EmployerName _____
City _____
State/Prov _____
ContactFirstName _____
ContactLastName _____
Phone _____

EmployerName _____
City _____
State/Prov _____
ContactFirstName _____
ContactLastName _____
Phone _____

To produce the report for Zack, you'll use the AutoReport: Columnar Wizard, which is similar to the AutoForm: Columnar Wizard you used earlier when creating the Employer Data form.

To create the report using the AutoReport: Columnar Wizard:

1. Click **Reports** in the Objects bar of the Database window, and then click the **New** button in the Database window to open the New Report dialog box, which is similar to the New Form dialog box you saw earlier.

2. Click **AutoReport: Columnar** to select this Wizard for creating the report.

   Because Zack wants the same data as in the Employer List query, you need to choose that query as the basis for the report.

3. Click the list arrow for choosing the table or query on which to base the report, and then click **Employer List**.

4. Click the **OK** button. The AutoReport Wizard creates the report and displays it in Print Preview, which shows exactly how the report will look when printed.

   To view the report better, you'll maximize the window and change the Zoom setting so that you can see the entire page.

5. Click the **Maximize** button ▢ on the Report window title bar, click the **Zoom** list arrow (to the right of the value 100%) on the Print Preview toolbar, and then click **Fit**. The entire first page of the report is displayed in the window. See Figure 1-17.

Figure 1-17 | **FIRST PAGE OF THE REPORT IN PRINT PREVIEW**

report title taken from query name

fields grouped for each record

lines separate records

page navigation buttons

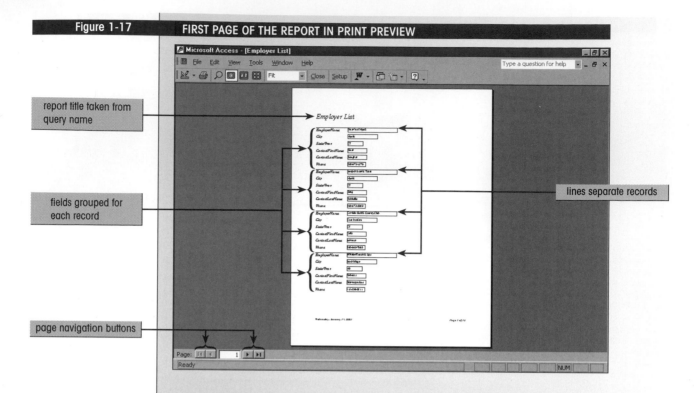

TROUBLE? The fonts used in your report might look different from the ones shown in Figure 1-17, depending on your computer's settings. If so, don't worry. You will learn how to change the report's style later in this text.

Each field from the Employer List query appears on its own line, with the corresponding field value to the right and in a box. Horizontal lines separate one record from the next, visually grouping all the fields for each record. The name of the query—Employer List—appears as the report's title.

Notice that the Print Preview window provides page navigation buttons at the bottom of the window, similar to the navigation buttons you've used to move through records in a table, query, and form. You use these buttons to move through the pages of a report.

6. Click the **Next Page** navigation button ▶. The second page of the report is displayed in Print Preview.

7. Click the **Last Page** navigation button ▶│ to move to the last page of the report. Note that this page contains the fields for only one record. Also note that the box in the middle of the navigation buttons displays the number "12"; there are 12 pages in this report.

TROUBLE? Depending on the printer you are using, your report might have more or fewer pages. If so, don't worry. Different printers format reports in different ways, sometimes affecting the total number of pages.

8. Click the **First Page** navigation button │◀ to return to the first page of the report.

At this point, you could close the report without saving it because you can easily re-create it at any time. In general, it's best to save an object—report, form, or query—only if you anticipate using the object frequently or if it is time-consuming to create, because these objects use considerable storage space on your disk. However, Zack wants to show the report to his staff members, so he asks you to save it.

To close and save the report:

1. Click the **Close Window** button ⊠ on the menu bar. *Do not* click the Close button on the Print Preview toolbar.

   TROUBLE? If you clicked the Close button on the Print Preview toolbar, you switched to Design view. Simply click the Close Window button ⊠ on the menu bar, and then continue with the steps.

   A dialog box opens and asks if you want to save the changes to the report design.

2. Click the **Yes** button. The Save As dialog box opens.

3. Click to the right of the highlighted text in the Report Name text box, press the **spacebar** once, type **Report**, and then click the **OK** button. Access saves the report as "Employer List Report" and returns to the Database window.

You'll learn more about creating and customizing reports in Tutorial 4.

Managing a Database

One of the main tasks involved in working with database software is managing your databases and the data they contain. By managing your databases, you can ensure that they operate in the most efficient way, that the data they contain is secure, and that you can work with the data effectively. Some of the activities involved in database management include backing up and restoring a database, compacting and repairing a database, and converting a database for use in other versions of Access.

Backing Up and Restoring a Database

You make a backup copy of a database file to protect your database against loss or damage. You can make the backup copy using one of several methods: Windows Explorer, My Computer, Microsoft Backup, or other backup software. If you back up your database file to a floppy disk, and the file size exceeds the size of the disk, you cannot use Windows Explorer or My Computer; you must use Microsoft Backup or some other backup software so that you can copy the file over more than one disk.

To restore a backup database file, choose the same method you used to make the backup copy. For example, if you used the Microsoft Backup tool (which is one of the System Tools available from the Programs menu and Accessories submenu in Windows 2000), you must choose the Restore option for this tool to copy the database file to your database folder. If the existing database file and the backup copy have the same name, restoring the backup copy might replace the existing file. If you want to save the existing file, rename it before you restore it.

Compacting and Repairing a Database

Whenever you open an Access database and work in it, the size of the database increases. Likewise, when you delete records and when you delete or replace database objects—such as queries, forms, and reports—the space that had been occupied on the disk by the deleted or replaced records or objects does not become available for other records or objects. To make the space available, you must compact the database. **Compacting** a database rearranges the data and objects in a database to decrease its file size. Unlike making a copy of a database file, which you do to protect your database against loss or damage, you compact a database to make it smaller, thereby making more space available on your disk and speeding up the process of opening and closing the database. Figure 1-18 illustrates the compacting process; the orange colored elements in the figure represent database records and objects.

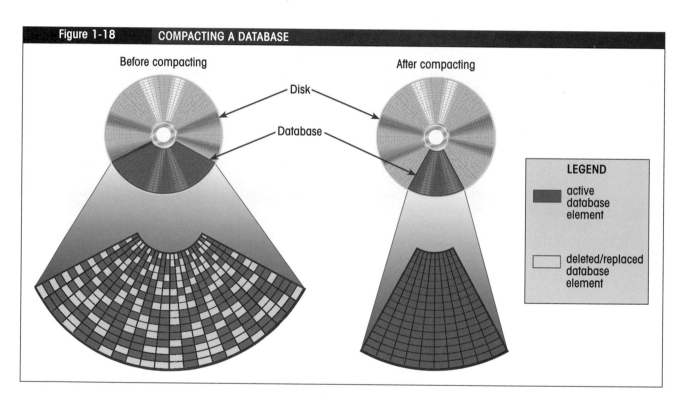

Figure 1-18   COMPACTING A DATABASE

When you compact a database, Access repairs the database at the same time. In many cases, Access detects that a database is damaged when you try to open it and gives you the option to compact and repair it at that time. If you think your database might be damaged because it is behaving unpredictably, you can use the "Compact and Repair Database" option to fix it. With your database file open, point to the Database Utilities option on the Tools menu, and then choose the Compact and Repair Database option.

Compacting a Database Automatically

Access also allows you to set an option for your database file so that every time you close the database, it will be compacted automatically.

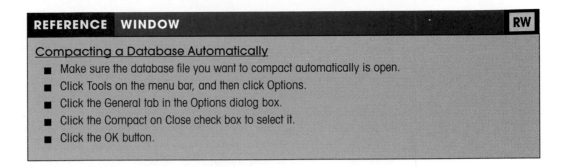

You'll set the compact option now for the Seasonal database. Then, every time you subsequently close the Seasonal database, Access will compact the database file for you. After setting this option, you'll exit Access.

To set the option for compacting the Seasonal database:

1. Make sure the Seasonal Database window is open on your screen.

2. Click **Tools** on the menu bar, and then click **Options**. The Options dialog box opens.

3. Click the **General** tab in the dialog box, and then click the **Compact on Close** check box to select it. See Figure 1-19.

Figure 1-19	GENERAL TAB OF THE OPTIONS DIALOG BOX

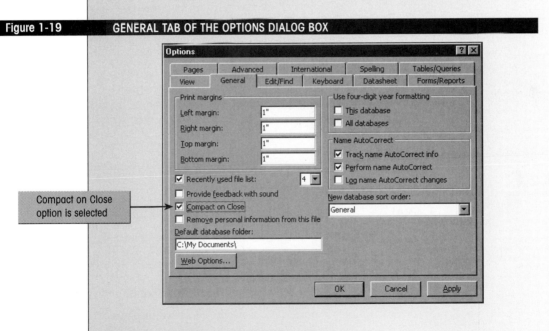

Compact on Close option is selected

4. Click the **OK** button to set the option.

5. Click the **Close** button 🗙 on the Access window title bar to exit Access. When you exit, Access closes the Seasonal database file and compacts it automatically.

Converting an Access 2000 Database

Another important database management task is converting a database so that you can work with it in a different version of Access. As noted earlier in this tutorial, the default file format for databases you create in Access 2002 is Access 2000. This enables you to work with the database in either the Access 2000 or 2002 versions of the software, without having to convert it. This compatibility makes it easy for multiple users working with different versions of the software to share the same database and work more efficiently.

Sometimes, however, you might need to convert an Access 2000 database to another version. For example, if you needed to share an Access 2000 database with a colleague who worked on a laptop computer with Access 97 installed on it, you could convert the Access 2000 database to the Access 97 format. Likewise, you might want to convert an Access 2000 database to the Access 2002 file format if the database becomes very large in size. Access 2002 is enhanced so that large databases run faster in the Access 2002 file format, making it more efficient for you to work with the information contained in them.

To convert a database, follow these steps:

1. Make sure the database you want to convert is closed and the Access window is open.

2. Click Tools on the menu bar, point to Database Utilities, point to Convert Database, and then choose the format you want to convert to—To Access 97 File Format, To Access 2000 File Format, or To Access 2002 File Format.

3. In the Database to Convert From dialog box, select the name of the database you want to convert, and then click the Convert button.

4. In the Convert Database Into dialog box, enter a new name for the converted database in the File name text box, and then click the Save button.

After converting a database, you can use it in the version of Access to which you converted the file. Note, however, that when you convert to a previous file format, such as converting from the Access 2000 file format to the Access 97 file format, you might lose some of the advanced features of the newer version and you might need to make some adjustments to the converted database.

With the Employer and NAICS tables in place, Elsa can continue to build the Seasonal database and use it to store, manipulate, and retrieve important data for NSJI. In the following tutorials, you'll help Elsa complete and maintain the database, and you'll use it to meet the specific information needs of other NSJI employees.

Session 1.2 QUICK | CHECK

1. A(n) _____ is a question you ask about the data stored in a database.

2. Unless you specify otherwise, the records resulting from a query are listed in order by the _____.

3. The quickest way to create a form is to use a(n) _____.

4. Describe the form created by the AutoForm: Columnar Wizard.

5. After creating a report, the AutoReport Wizard displays the report in _____.

6. _____ a database rearranges the data and objects in a database to decrease its file size.

REVIEW ASSIGNMENTS

In the Review Assignments, you'll work with the **Seasons** database, which is similar to the database you worked with in the tutorial. Complete the following:

1. Make sure your Data Disk is in the disk drive.

2. Start Access and open the **Seasons** database, which is located in the Review folder on your Data Disk.

Explore   3. Open the Microsoft Access Help window, and then display the Contents tab. Double-click the topic "Microsoft Access Help" (if necessary), and then double-click the topic "Queries," and then click "About types of queries." Read the displayed information, and then click "Select queries." Read the displayed information. In the Contents tab, double-click the topic "Forms," and then click the topic "About forms." Read the displayed information. In the Contents tab, scroll down and double-click the topic "Reports and Report Snapshots," and then click the topic "About reports." Read the displayed information. When finished reading all the topics, close the Microsoft Access Help window. Use Notepad, Word, or some other text editor to write a brief summary of what you learned.

Explore   4. Use the "Ask a Question" box to ask the following question: "How do I rename an object?" Click the topic "Rename a database object" and read the displayed information. Close the Microsoft Access Help window. Then, in the **Seasons** database, rename the **Table1** table as **Employers**.

5. Open the **Employers** table.

Explore   6. Open the Microsoft Access Help window, and then display the Index tab. Type the keyword "print" in the Type keywords text box, and then click the Search button. Click the topic "Set page setup options for printing" and then click "For a table, query, form, or report." Read the displayed information. Close the Microsoft Access Help window. Set the option for printing in landscape orientation, and then print the first page only of the **Employers** table datasheet. Close the **Employers** table.

Explore   7. Use the Simple Query Wizard to create a query that includes the City, EmployerName, ContactFirstName, ContactLastName, and Phone fields (in that order) from the **Employers** table. Name the query **Employer Phone List**. Sort the query results in ascending order by City. Set the option for printing in landscape orientation, and then print the second page only of the query results. Close and save the query.

8. Use the AutoForm: Columnar Wizard to create a form for the **Employers** table.

Explore   9. Use context-sensitive Help to find out how to move to a particular record and display it in the form. Click the What's This? command from the Help menu, and then use the Help pointer to click the number 1 in the Specific Record box at the bottom of the form. Read the displayed information. Click to close the Help box, and then use the Specific Record box to move to record 42 (for Whitney's Resort & Spa) in the **Employers** table.

Explore   10. Print the form for the current record (42). (*Hint:* Click the Selected Record(s) option in the Print dialog box to print the current record.)

11. Save the form as **Employer Info**, and then close the form.

Explore   12. Use the AutoReport: Tabular Wizard to create a report based on the **Employers** table. Print the first page of the report, and then close and save the report as **Employers**.

13. Set the option for compacting the **Seasons** database on close.

Explore   14. Convert the **Seasons** database to Access 2002 file format, saving the converted file as **Seasons2002** in the Review folder. Then convert the **Seasons** database to Access 97 file format, saving the converted file as **Seasons97** in the Review folder. Using Windows Explorer or My Computer, view the contents of your Review folder, and note the file sizes of the three versions of the **Seasons** database. Describe the results.

15. Exit Access.

CASE PROBLEMS

Case 1. Lim's Video Photography Several years ago, Youngho Lim left his position at a commercial photographer's studio and started his own business, Lim's Video Photography, located in San Francisco, California. Youngho quickly established a reputation as one of the area's best videographers, specializing in digital video photography. Youngho offers customers the option of storing edited videos on CD or DVD. His video shoots include weddings and other special events, as well as recording personal and commercial inventories for insurance purposes.

As his business continues to grow, Youngho relies on Access to keep track of information about clients, contracts, and so on. Youngho recently created an Access database named **Videos** to store data about his clients. You'll help Youngho complete and maintain the **Videos** database. Complete the following:

1. Make sure your Data Disk is in the disk drive.

2. Start Access and open the **Videos** database, which is located in the Cases folder on your Data Disk.

3. Open the **Client** table, print the table datasheet, and then close the table.

4. Use the Simple Query Wizard to create a query that includes the ClientName, Phone, and City fields (in that order) from the **Client** table. Name the query **Client List**. Print the query results, and then close the query.

Explore   5. Use the AutoForm: Tabular Wizard to create a form for the **Contract** table. Print the form, save it as **Contract Info**, and then close it.

Explore   6. Use the AutoReport: Columnar Wizard to create a report based on the **Contract** table. Maximize the Report window and change the Zoom setting to Fit. Use the Two Pages button on the Print Preview toolbar to view the first two pages of the report in Print Preview. Print the first page of the report, and then close and save it as **Contracts**.

7. Set the option for compacting the **Videos** database on close.

Explore   8. Convert the **Videos** database to Access 2002 file format, saving the converted file as **Videos2002** in the Cases folder. Then convert the **Videos** database to Access 97 file format, saving the converted file as **Videos97** in the Cases folder. Using Windows Explorer or My Computer, view the contents of your Cases folder, and note the file sizes of the three versions of the **Videos** database. Describe the results.

9. Exit Access.

Case 2. DineAtHome.course.com After working as both a concierge in a local hotel and a manager of several restaurants, Claire Picard founded DineAtHome.course.com in Naples, Florida. Her idea for this e-commerce company was a simple one: to provide people with an easy-to-use, online service that would allow them to order meals from one or more area restaurants and have the meals delivered to their homes. DineAtHome acts as a sort of broker between restaurants and customers. The participating restaurants offer everything from simple fare to gourmet feasts. Claire's staff performs a variety of services, from simply picking up and delivering the meals to providing linens and table service for more formal occasions.

Claire created the **Meals** database in Access to maintain information about participating restaurants and their menu offerings. She needs your help in working with this database. Complete the following:

1. Make sure your Data Disk is in the disk drive.

2. Start Access and open the **Meals** database, which is located in the Cases folder on your Data Disk.

Explore 3. Open the **Restaurant** table, print the table datasheet in landscape orientation, and then close the table.

4. Use the Simple Query Wizard to create a query that includes the RestaurantName, OwnerFirstName, OwnerLastName, and City fields (in that order) from the **Restaurant** table. Name the query **Owner List**.

Explore 5. Sort the query results in descending order by the City field. (*Hint*: Use a toolbar button.)

Explore 6. Use the "Ask a Question" box to ask the following question: "How do I select multiple records?" Click the topic "Select fields and records," and then click the topic "Select fields and records in a datasheet." Read the displayed information, and then close the Help window. Select the four records with "Marco Island" as the value in the City field, and then print just the selected records. (*Hint*: Use the Selected Record(s) option in the Print dialog box to print them.) Close the query, and save your changes to the design.

Explore 7. Use the AutoForm: Columnar Wizard to create a form for the **Restaurant** table. Use context-sensitive Help to find out how to move to a particular record and display it in the form. Click the What's This? command from the Help menu, and then use the Help pointer to click the number 1 in the Specific Record box at the bottom of the form. Read the displayed information. Click to close the Help box, use the Specific Record box to move to record 11 (for The Gazebo), and then print the form for the current record only. (*Hint*: Use the Selected Record(s) option in the Print dialog box to print the current record.) Save the form as **Restaurant Info**, and then close the form.

8. Use the AutoReport: Columnar Wizard to create a report based on the **Restaurant** table. Maximize the Report window and change the Zoom setting to Fit.

Explore 9. Use the View menu to view all eight pages of the report at the same time in Print Preview.

10. Print just the first page of the report, and then close and save the report as **Restaurants**.

11. Set the option for compacting the **Meals** database on close.

Explore 12. Convert the **Meals** database to Access 2002 file format, saving the converted file as **Meals2002** in the Cases folder. Then convert the **Meals** database to Access 97 file format, saving the converted file as **Meals97** in the Cases folder. Using Windows Explorer or My Computer, view the contents of your Cases folder, and note the file sizes of the three versions of the **Meals** database. Describe the results.

13. Exit Access.

Case 3. Redwood Zoo   The Redwood Zoo is a small zoo located in the picturesque city of Gig Harbor, Washington, on the shores of Puget Sound. The zoo is ideally situated, with the natural beauty of the site providing the perfect backdrop for the zoo's varied exhibits. Although there are larger zoos in the greater Seattle area, the Redwood Zoo is considered to have some of the best exhibits of marine animals. The newly constructed polar bear habitat is a particular favorite among patrons.

Michael Rosenfeld is the director of fundraising activities for the Redwood Zoo. The zoo relies heavily on donations to fund both ongoing exhibits and temporary displays, especially those involving exotic animals. Michael created an Access database named **Redwood** to keep track of information about donors, their pledges, and the status of funds. You'll help Michael maintain the **Redwood** database. Complete the following:

1. Make sure your Data Disk is in the disk drive.

2. Start Access and open the **Redwood** database, which is located in the Cases folder on your Data Disk.

3. Open the **Donor** table, print the table datasheet, and then close the table.

Explore ▶ 4. Use the Simple Query Wizard to create a query that includes all the fields in the **Donor** table *except* the MI field. (*Hint*: Use the >> and < buttons to select the necessary fields.) Name the query **Donors**.

Explore ▶ 5. Sort the query results in descending order by the Class field. (*Hint*: Use a toolbar button.) Print the query results, and then close and save the query.

Explore ▶ 6. Use the AutoForm: Columnar Wizard to create a form for the **Fund** table. Use context-sensitive Help to find out how to move to a particular record and display it in the form. Click the What's This? command from the Help menu, and then use the Help pointer to click the number 1 in the Specific Record box at the bottom of the form. Read the displayed information. Click to close the Help box, use the Specific Record box to move to record 7 (Polar Bear Park), and then print the form for the current record only. (*Hint*: Use the Selected Record(s) option in the Print dialog box to print the current record.) Save the form as **Fund Info**, and then close it.

7. Use the AutoReport: Columnar Wizard to create a report based on the **Donor** table. Maximize the Report window and change the Zoom setting to Fit.

Explore ▶ 8. Use the View menu to view all seven pages of the report at the same time in Print Preview.

9. Print just the first page of the report, and then close and save the report as **Donors**.

10. Set the option for compacting the **Redwood** database on close.

Explore ▶ 11. Convert the **Redwood** database to Access 2002 file format, saving the converted file as **Redwood2002** in the Cases folder. Then convert the **Redwood** database to Access 97 file format, saving the converted file as **Redwood97** in the Cases folder. Using Windows Explorer or My Computer, view the contents of your Cases folder, and note the file sizes of the three versions of the **Redwood** database. Describe the results.

12. Exit Access.

Case 4. Mountain River Adventures   Several years ago, Connor and Siobhan Dempsey moved to Boulder, Colorado, drawn by their love of the mountains and their interest in outdoor activities of all kinds. This interest led them to form the Mountain River Adventures center. The center began as a whitewater rafting tour provider, but quickly grew to encompass other activities, such as canoeing, hiking, camping, fishing, and rock climbing.

From the beginning, Connor and Siobhan have used computers to help them manage all aspects of their business. They recently installed Access and created a database named **Trips** to store information about clients, equipment, and the types of guided tours they provide. You'll work with the **Trips** database to manage this information. Complete the following:

1. Make sure your Data Disk is in the disk drive.

2. Start Access and open the **Trips** database, which is located in the Cases folder on your Data Disk.

3. Open the **Client** table.

Explore 4. Print the **Client** table datasheet in landscape orientation, and then close the table.

5. Use the Simple Query Wizard to create a query that includes the ClientName, City, State/Prov, and Phone fields (in that order) from the **Client** table. Name the query **Client Info**.

Explore 6. Sort the query results in descending order by State/Prov. (*Hint*: Use a toolbar button.)

7. Print the query results, and then close and save the query.

Explore 8. Use the AutoForm: Columnar Wizard to create a form for the **Client** table. Use context-sensitive Help to find out how to move to a particular record and display it in the form. Click the What's This? command from the Help menu, and then use the Help pointer to click the number 1 in the Specific Record box at the bottom of the form. Read the displayed information. Click to close the Help box, use the Specific Record box to move to record 18, and then print the form for the current record only. (*Hint:* Use the Selected Record(s) option in the Print dialog box to print the current record.) Save the form as **Client Info**, and then close it.

Explore 9. Use the AutoReport: Tabular Wizard to create a report based on the **Client** table. Maximize the Report window and change the Zoom setting to Fit. Use the Two Pages button on the Print Preview toolbar to view both pages of the report in Print Preview. Print the first page of the report in landscape orientation, and then close and save the report as **Clients**.

10. Set the option for compacting the **Trips** database on close.

Explore 11. Convert the **Trips** database to Access 2002 file format, saving the converted file as **Trips2002** in the Cases folder. Then convert the **Trips** database to Access 97 file format, saving the converted file as **Trips97** in the Cases folder. Using Windows Explorer or My Computer, view the contents of your Cases folder, and note the file sizes of the three versions of the **Trips** database. Describe the results.

12. Exit Access.

LAB ASSIGNMENTS

Databases

These Lab Assignments are designed to accompany the interactive Course Lab called Databases. To start the Databases Lab, click the Start button on the Windows taskbar, point to Programs, point to Course Labs, point to New Perspectives Course Labs, and then click Databases. If you do not see Course Labs on your Programs menu, see your instructor or technical support person.

Databases   This Databases Lab demonstrates the essential concepts of file and database management systems. You will use the Lab to search, sort, and report the data contained in a file of classic books.

1. Click the Steps button to review basic database terminology and to learn how to manipulate the classic books database. As you proceed through the Steps, answer all of the Quick Check questions that appear. After you complete the Steps, you will see a Quick Check summary report. Follow the instructions on the screen to print this report.

2. Click the Explore button. Make sure you can apply basic database terminology to describe the classic books database by answering the following questions:
   a. How many records does the file contain?
   b. How many fields does each record contain?

   c. What are the contents of the Catalog # field for the book written by Margaret Mitchell?

   d. What are the contents of the Title field for the record with Thoreau in the Author field?

   e. Which field has been used to sort the records?

3. In Explore, manipulate the database as necessary to answer the following questions:

   a. When the books are sorted by title, what is the first record in the file?

   b. Use the Search button to search for all the books in the West location. How many do you find?

   c. Use the Search button to search for all the books in the Main location that are checked in. What do you find?

4. Use the Report button to print out a report that groups the books by Status and sorts them by Title. On your report, circle the four field names. Draw a box around the summary statistics showing which books are currently checked in and which books are currently checked out.

INTERNET ASSIGNMENTS

Student Union

The purpose of the Internet Assignments is to challenge you to find information on the Internet that you can use to create effective documents. The actual assignments are updated and maintained on the Course Technology Web site. Log on to the Internet and use your Web browser to go to the Student Union on the New Perspectives Series site at **www.course.com/NewPerspectives/studentunion**. Click the Online Companions link, and then click the link for this text.

QUICK CHECK ANSWERS

Session 1.1

1. field

2. common field

3. primary key; foreign key

4. records; fields

5. current record symbol

6. Use the horizontal and vertical scroll bars to view fields or records not currently visible in the datasheet; use the navigation buttons to move vertically through the records.

Session 1.2

1. query

2. primary key

3. AutoForm Wizard

4. The form displays each field name to the left of its field value, which appears in a box; the widths of the boxes represent the size of the fields.

5. Print Preview

6. Compacting

OBJECTIVES

In this tutorial you will:

- Learn the guidelines for designing databases and setting field properties

- Create a new database

- Create and save a table

- Define fields and specify a table's primary key

- Add records to a table

- Modify the structure of a table

- Delete, move, and add fields

- Change field properties

- Copy records and import tables from another Access database

- Delete and change records

CREATING
AND MAINTAINING
A DATABASE

Creating the Northeast Database, and Creating, Modifying, and Updating the Position Table

CASE

Northeast Seasonal Jobs International (NSJI)

The Seasonal database contains two tables—the Employer table and the NAICS table. These tables store data about NSJI's employer customers and the NAICS codes for pertinent job positions, respectively. Elsa Jensen also wants to track information about each position that is available at each employer's place of business. This information includes the position title and wage. Elsa asks you to create a third table, named Position, in which to store the position data.

Because this is your first time creating a new table, Elsa suggests that you first create a new database, named "Northeast," and then create the new Position table in this database. This will keep the Seasonal database intact. Once the Position table is completed, you then can import the Employer and NAICS tables from the Seasonal database into your new Northeast database.

Some of the position data Elsa needs is already stored in another NSJI database. After creating the Position table and adding some records to it, you'll copy the records from the other database into the Position table. Then you'll maintain the Position table by modifying it and updating it to meet Elsa's specific data requirements.

SESSION 2.1

In this session, you will learn the guidelines for designing databases and setting field properties. You'll also learn how to create a new database, create a table, define the fields for a table, select the primary key for a table, and save the table structure.

Guidelines for Designing Databases

A database management system can be a useful tool, but only if you first carefully design the database so that it meets the needs of its users. In database design, you determine the fields, tables, and relationships needed to satisfy the data and processing requirements. When you design a database, you should follow these guidelines:

- **Identify all the fields needed to produce the required information.** For example, Elsa needs information about employers, NAICS codes, and positions. Figure 2-1 shows the fields that satisfy these information requirements.

Figure 2-1	ELSA'S DATA REQUIREMENTS

EmployerID	ContactFirstName
PositionID	ContactLastName
PositionTitle	Position
EmployerName	Wage
Address	Hours/Week
City	NAICSCode
State/Prov	NAICSDesc
PostalCode	StartDate
Country	EndDate
Phone	ReferredBy
Openings	WebSite

- **Group related fields into tables.** For example, Elsa grouped the fields relating to employers into the Employer table and the fields related to NAICS codes into the NAICS table. The other fields are grouped logically into the Position table, which you will create, as shown in Figure 2-2.

Figure 2-2	ELSA'S FIELDS GROUPED INTO TABLES

Employer table	NAICS table	Position table
EmployerID	NAICSCode	PositionID
EmployerName	NAICSDesc	PositionTitle
Address		Wage
City		Hours/Week
State/Prov		Openings
PostalCode		ReferredBy
Country		StartDate
ContactFirstName		EndDate
ContactLastName		
Position		
Phone		
WebSite		

■ **Determine each table's primary key.** Recall that a primary key uniquely identifies each record in a table. Although a primary key is not mandatory in Access, it's usually a good idea to include one in each table. Without a primary key, selecting the exact record that you want can be a problem. For some tables, one of the fields, such as a Social Security or credit card number, naturally serves the function of a primary key. For other tables, two or more fields might be needed to function as the primary key. In these cases, the primary key is referred to as a **composite key.** For example, a school grade table would use a combination of student number and course code to serve as the primary key. For a third category of tables, no single field or combination of fields can uniquely identify a record in a table. In these cases, you need to add a field whose sole purpose is to serve as the table's primary key.

For Elsa's tables, EmployerID is the primary key for the Employer table, NAICSCode is the primary key for the NAICS table, and PositionID will be the primary key for the Position table.

■ **Include a common field in related tables.** You use the common field to connect one table logically with another table. For example, Elsa's Employer and Position tables will include the EmployerID field as a common field. Recall that when you include the primary key from one table as a field in a second table to form a relationship, the field is called a foreign key in the second table; therefore, the EmployerID field will be a foreign key in the Position table. With this common field, Elsa can find all positions available at a particular employer; she can use the EmployerID value for an employer and search the Position table for all records with that EmployerID value. Likewise, she can determine which employer has a particular position available by searching the Employer table to find the one record with the same EmployerID value as the corresponding value in the Position table.

■ **Avoid data redundancy.** Data redundancy occurs when you store the same data in more than one place. With the exception of common fields to connect tables, you should avoid redundancy because it wastes storage space and can cause inconsistencies, if, for instance, you type a field value one way in one table and a different way in the same table or in a second table. Figure 2-3, which contains portions of potential data to be stored in the Employer and Position tables, shows an example of incorrect database design that has data redundancy in the Position table; the EmployerName field is redundant, and one value was entered incorrectly, in three different ways.

Figure 2-3 INCORRECT DATABASE DESIGN WITH DATA REDUNDANCY

Employer table

EmployerID	EmployerName	Address	Phone
10122	BeanTown Tours	105 State Street, Boston, MA 02109	617-451-1970
10125	Boston Harbor Excursions	75 Atlantic Avenue, Boston, MA 02110	617-235-1800
10126	BaySide Inn & Country Club	354 Oceanside Drive, Brewster, MA 02631	508-283-5775
10190	The Briar Rose Inn	105 Queen Street, Charlottetown PE C1A 8R4	902-626-1595
10191	Windsor Alpine Tours	14 Longmeadow Road, Laconia, NH 03246	603-266-9233
10198	Trudel Spa & Resort	40 Rue Rivard, North Hatley QC J0B 2C0	819-842-7783

data redundancy

Position table

PositionID	EmployerID	EmployerName	PositionTitle	Hours/Week
2040	10126	DaySide Inn & Country Club	Waiter/Waitress	32
2045	10122	BeanTown Tours	Tour Guide	24
2053	10190	The Briar Rose Inn	Host/Hostess	24
2066	10198	Trudel Spa & Resort	Lifeguard	32
2073	10126	Baside Inn & Country Club	Pro Shop Clerk	24
2078	10191	Windsor Alpine Tours	Ski Patrol	30
2079	10191	Windsor Alpine Tours	Day Care	35
2082	10125	Boston Harbor Excursions	Reservationist	40
2111	10126	BaySide Inn Club	Kitchen Help	32

inconsistent data

■ **Determine the properties of each field.** You need to identify the **properties**, or characteristics, of each field so that the DBMS knows how to store, display, and process the field values. These properties include the field's name, maximum number of characters or digits, description, valid values, and other field characteristics. You will learn more about field properties later in this tutorial.

The Position table you need to create will contain the fields shown in Figure 2-2, plus the EmployerID field as a foreign key. Before you create the new Northeast database and the Position table, you first need to learn some guidelines for setting field properties.

Guidelines for Setting Field Properties

As just noted, the last step of database design is to determine which values to assign to the properties, such as the name and data type, of each field. When you select or enter a value for a property, you **set** the property. Access has rules for naming fields, choosing data types, and setting other properties for fields.

Naming Fields and Objects

You must name each field, table, and other object in an Access database. Access then stores these items in the database, using the names you supply. It's best to choose a field or object name that describes the purpose or contents of the field or object, so that later you can easily remember what the name represents. For example, the three tables in the Northeast database will be named Employer, NAICS, and Position, because these names suggest their contents.

The following rules apply to naming fields and objects:

- A name can be up to 64 characters long.
- A name can contain letters, numbers, spaces, and special characters, except for a period (.), exclamation mark (!), accent grave (`), and square brackets ([ ]).
- A name cannot start with a space.
- A table or query name must be unique within a database. A field name must be unique within a table, but it can be used again in another table.

In addition, experienced users of databases follow these conventions for naming fields and objects:

- Capitalize the first letter of each word in the name.
- Avoid extremely long names because they are difficult to remember and reference.
- Use standard abbreviations, such as Num for Number, Amt for Amount, and Qty for Quantity.
- Do not use spaces in field names because these names will appear in column headings on datasheets and on labels in forms and reports. By not using spaces, you'll be able to show more fields in these objects at one time.

Assigning Field Data Types

You must assign a data type for each field. The **data type** determines what field values you can enter for the field and what other properties the field will have. For example, the Position table will include a StartDate field, which will store date values, so you will assign the date/time data type to this field. Then Access will allow you to enter and manipulate only dates or times as values in the StartDate field.

Figure 2-4 lists the 10 data types available in Access, describes the field values allowed for each data type, explains when you should use each data type, and indicates the field size of each data type.

Figure 2-4	DATA TYPES FOR FIELDS	
DATA TYPE	**DESCRIPTION**	**FIELD SIZE**
Text	Allows field values containing letters, digits, spaces, and special characters. Use for names, addresses, descriptions, and fields containing digits that are not used in calculations.	0 to 255 characters; 50 characters default
Memo	Allows field values containing letters, digits, spaces, and special characters. Use for long comments and explanations.	1 to 65,535 characters; exact size is determined by entry
Number	Allows positive and negative numbers as field values. Numbers can contain digits, a decimal point, commas, a plus sign, and a minus sign. Use for fields that you will use in calculations, except calculations involving money.	1 to 15 digits
Date/Time	Allows field values containing valid dates and times from January 1, 100 to December 31, 9999. Dates can be entered in mm/dd/yy (month, day, year) format, several other date formats, or a variety of time formats, such as 10:35 PM. You can perform calculations on dates and times, and you can sort them. For example, you can determine the number of days between two dates.	8 bytes
Currency	Allows field values similar to those for the number data type. Unlike calculations with number data type decimal values, calculations performed using the currency data type are not subject to round-off error.	Accurate to 15 digits on the left side of the decimal separator and to 4 digits on the right side

Figure 2-4	DATA TYPES FOR FIELDS, CONTINUED	
DATA TYPE	**DESCRIPTION**	**FIELD SIZE**
AutoNumber	Consists of integers with values controlled by Access. Access automatically inserts a value in the field as each new record is created. You can specify sequential numbering or random numbering, which guarantees a unique field value, so that such a field can serve as a table's primary key.	9 digits
Yes/No	Limits field values to yes and no, on and off, or true and false. Use for fields that indicate the presence or absence of a condition, such as whether an order has been filled or whether an employee is eligible for the company dental plan.	1 character
OLE Object	Allows field values that are created in other programs as objects, such as photographs, video images, graphics, drawings, sound recordings, voice-mail messages, spreadsheets, and word-processing documents. These objects can be linked or embedded.	1 gigabyte maximum; exact size depends on object size
Hyperlink	Consists of text used as a hyperlink address. A hyperlink address can have up to three parts: the text that appears in a field or control; the path to a file or page; and a location within the file or page. Hyperlinks help you to connect your application easily to the Internet or an intranet.	Up to 64,000 characters total for the three parts of a hyperlink data type
Lookup Wizard	Creates a field that lets you look up a value in another table or in a predefined list of values.	Same size as the primary key field used to perform the lookup

Setting Field Sizes

The **Field Size** property defines a field value's maximum storage size for text, number, and AutoNumber fields only. The other data types have no Field Size property because their storage size is either a fixed, predetermined amount or is determined automatically by the field value itself, as shown in Figure 2-4. A text field has a default field size of 50 characters; you can also set its field size by entering a number from 0 to 255. For example, the PositionTitle and ReferredBy fields in the Position table will be text fields with a size of 30 each.

When you use the number data type to define a field, you should set the field's Field Size property based on the largest value that you expect to store in that field. Access processes smaller data sizes faster using less memory, so you can optimize your database's performance and its storage space by selecting the correct field size for each field. For example, it would be wasteful to use the Long Integer setting when defining a field that will store only whole numbers ranging from 0 to 255, because the Long Integer setting will use four bytes of storage space. A better choice would be the Byte setting, which uses one byte of storage space to store the same values. Field Size property settings for number fields are as follows:

- **Byte:** Stores whole numbers (numbers with no fractions) from 0 to 255 in one byte
- **Integer:** Stores whole numbers from −32,768 to 32,767 in two bytes
- **Long Integer** (default): Stores whole numbers from −2,147,483,648 to 2,147,483,647 in four bytes
- **Single:** Stores positive and negative numbers to precisely seven decimal places and uses four bytes
- **Double:** Stores positive and negative numbers to precisely 15 decimal places and uses eight bytes
- **Replication ID:** Establishes a unique identifier for replication of tables, records, and other objects and uses 16 bytes
- **Decimal:** Stores positive and negative numbers to precisely 28 decimal places and uses 12 bytes

Elsa documented the design for the new Position table by listing each field's name, data type, size (if applicable), and description, as shown in Figure 2-5. Note that Elsa assigned the text data type to the PositionID, PositionTitle, EmployerID, and ReferredBy fields; the currency data type to the Wage field; the number data type to the Hours/Week and Openings fields; and the date/time data type to the StartDate and EndDate fields.

Figure 2-5	DESIGN FOR THE POSITION TABLE			
	Field Name	Data Type	Field Size	Description
	PositionID	Text	4	Primary key
	PositionTitle	Text	30	
	EmployerID	Text	5	Foreign key
	Wage	Currency		Rate per hour
	Hours/Week	Number	Integer	Work hours per week
	Openings	Number	Integer	Number of openings
	ReferredBy	Text	30	
	StartDate	Date/Time		Month and day
	EndDate	Date/Time		Month and day

With Elsa's design in place, you're ready to create the new Northeast database and the Position table.

Creating a New Database

Access provides two ways for you to create a new database: using a Database Wizard or creating a blank database. When you use a Wizard, the Wizard guides you through the database creation process and provides the necessary tables, forms, and reports for the type of database you choose—all in one operation. Using a Database Wizard is an easy way to start creating a database, but only if your data requirements closely match one of the supplied templates. When you choose to create a blank database, you need to add all the tables, forms, reports, and other objects after you create the database file. Creating a blank database provides the most flexibility, allowing you to define objects in the way that you want, but it does require that you define each object separately. Whichever method you choose, you can always modify or add to your database after you create it.

The following steps outline the process for creating a new database using a Database Wizard:

1. If necessary, click the New button on the Database toolbar to display the Task Pane.

2. In the "New from template" section of the Task Pane, click General Templates. The Templates dialog box opens.

3. Click the Databases tab, and then choose the Database Wizard that most closely matches the type of database you want to create. Click the OK button.

4. In the File New Database dialog box, choose the location in which to save the new database, specify its name, and then click the Create button.

5. Complete each of the Wizard dialog boxes, clicking the Next button to move through them after making your selections.

6. Click the Finish button when you have completed all the Wizard dialog boxes.

None of the Database Wizards matches the requirements of the new Northeast database, so you'll use the Blank Database option to create it.

To create the Northeast database:

1. Place your Data Disk in the appropriate disk drive, and then start Access.

2. In the New section of the Task Pane, click **Blank Database**. The File New Database dialog box opens. This dialog box is similar to the Open dialog box.

3. Click the **Save in** list arrow, and then click the drive that contains your Data Disk.

4. Click **Tutorial** in the list box, and then click the **Open** button.

5. In the File name text box, double-click the text **db1** to select it, and then type **Northeast**.

   TROUBLE? Your File name text box might contain an entry other than "db1." Just select whatever text is in this text box, and continue with the steps.

6. Click the **Create** button. Access creates the Northeast database in the Tutorial folder on your Data Disk, and then displays the Database window for the new database with the Tables object selected.

Now you can create the Position table in the Northeast database.

Creating a Table

Creating a table consists of naming the fields and defining the properties for the fields, specifying a primary key (and a foreign key, if applicable) for the table, and then saving the table structure. You will use Elsa's design (Figure 2-5) as a guide for creating the Position table in the Northeast database.

To begin creating the Position table:

1. Click the **New** button in the Database window. The New Table dialog box opens. See Figure 2-6.

Figure 2-6	NEW TABLE DIALOG BOX

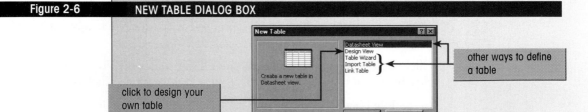

TROUBLE? If the Task Pane opens and displays "New File" at the top, you clicked the New button on the Database toolbar instead of the New button in the Database window. Click the Close button to close the Task Pane, and then repeat Step 1.

In Access, you can create a table from entered data (Datasheet View), define your own table (Design View), use a Wizard to automate the table creation process (Table Wizard), or use a Wizard to import or link data from another database or other data source (Import Table or Link Table). For the Position table, you will define your own table.

2. Click **Design View** in the list box, and then click the **OK** button. The Table window opens in Design view. (Note that you can also double-click the "Create table in Design view" option in the Database window to open the Table window in Design view.) See Figure 2-7.

Figure 2-7	TABLE WINDOW IN DESIGN VIEW

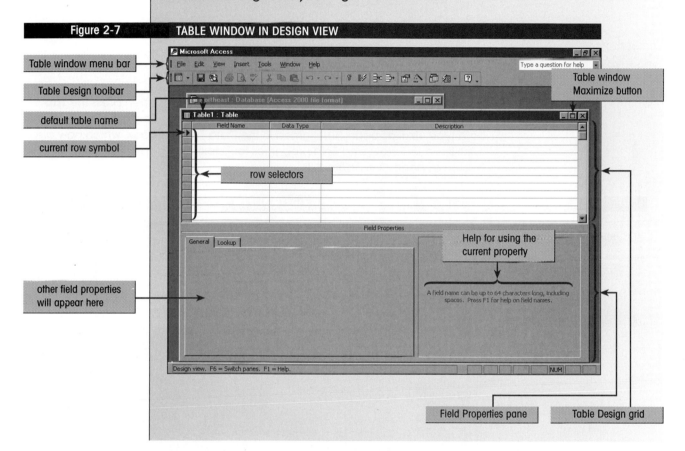

You use Design view to define or modify a table structure or the properties of the fields in a table. If you create a table without using a Wizard, you enter the fields and their properties for your table directly in the Table window in Design view.

Defining Fields

Initially, the default table name, Table1, appears on the Table window title bar, the current row symbol is positioned in the first row selector of the Table Design grid, and the insertion point is located in the first row's Field Name box. The purpose or characteristics of the current property (Field Name, in this case) appear in the right side of the Field Properties pane. You can display more complete information about the current property by pressing the F1 key.

You enter values for the Field Name, Data Type, and Description field properties in the Table Design grid. You select values for all other field properties, most of which are optional, in the Field Properties pane. These other properties will appear when you move to the first row's Data Type text box.

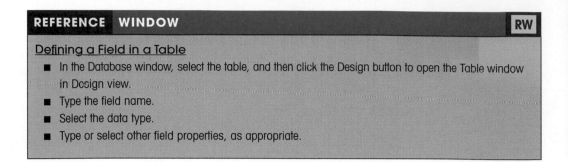

REFERENCE WINDOW **RW**

Defining a Field in a Table
■ In the Database window, select the table, and then click the Design button to open the Table window in Design view.
■ Type the field name.
■ Select the data type.
■ Type or select other field properties, as appropriate.

The first field you need to define is PositionID.

To define the PositionID field:

1. Type **PositionID** in the first row's Field Name text box, and then press the **Tab** key (or press the **Enter** key) to advance to the Data Type text box. The default data type, Text, appears highlighted in the Data Type text box, which now also contains a list arrow, and field properties for a text field appear in the Field Properties pane. See Figure 2-8.

Figure 2-8   **TABLE WINDOW AFTER ENTERING THE FIRST FIELD NAME**

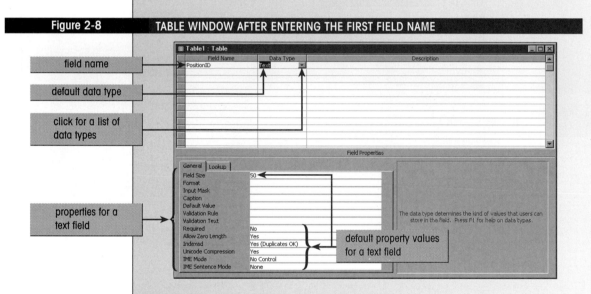

Notice that the right side of the Field Properties pane now provides an explanation for the current property, Data Type.

TROUBLE? If you make a typing error, you can correct it by clicking the mouse to position the insertion point, and then using either the Backspace key to delete characters to the left of the insertion point or the Delete key to delete characters to the right of the insertion point. Then type the correct text.

Because the PositionID numbers will not be used in calculations, you will assign the text data type (as opposed to the number data type) to the PositionID field.

2. Press the **Tab** key to accept Text as the data type and to advance to the Description text box.

Next you'll enter the Description property value as "Primary key." You can use the Description property to enter an optional description for a field to explain its purpose or usage. A field's Description property can be up to 255 characters long, and its value appears on the status bar when you view the table datasheet.

3. Type **Primary key** in the Description text box.

Notice the Field Size property for the text field. The default setting of "50" is displayed. You need to change this number to "4" because all PositionID values at NSJI contain only 4 digits. (Refer to the Access Help system for a complete description of all the properties available for the different data types.)

4. Double-click the number **50** in the Field Size property box to select it, and then type **4**. The definition of the first field is completed. See Figure 2-9.

Figure 2-9	PositionID FIELD DEFINED

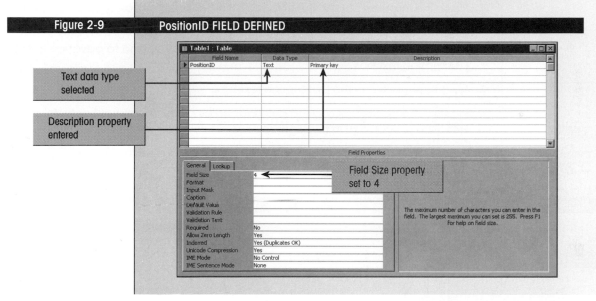

Text data type selected

Description property entered

Elsa's Position table design shows PositionTitle as the second field. You will define PositionTitle as a text field with a Field Size of 30, which is a sufficient length for any title values that will be entered.

To define the PositionTitle field:

1. Place the insertion point in the second row's Field Name text box, type **PositionTitle** in the text box, and then press the **Tab** key to advance to the Data Type text box.

2. Press the **Tab** key to accept Text as the field's data type.

According to Elsa's design (Figure 2-5), you do not need to enter a description for this field. If you've assigned a descriptive field name and the field does not fulfill a special function (such as primary key), you usually do not enter a value for the optional Description property. PositionTitle is a field that does not require a value for its Description property.

Next, you'll change the Field Size property to 30. Note that when defining the fields in a table, you can move between the Table Design grid and the Field Properties pane of the Table window by pressing the F6 key.

3. Press the **F6** key to move to the Field Properties pane. The current entry for the Field Size property, 50, is highlighted.

4. Type **30** to set the Field Size property. You have completed the definition of the second field.

The third field in the Position table is the EmployerID field. Recall that this field will serve as the foreign key in the Position table, allowing you to relate data from the Position table to data in the Employer table. The field must be defined in the same way in both tables—that is, a text field with a field size of 5.

To define the EmployerID field:

1. Place the insertion point in the third row's Field Name text box, type **EmployerID** in the text box, and then press the **Tab** key to advance to the Data Type text box.

2. Press the **Tab** key to accept Text as the field's data type and to advance to the Description text box.

3. Type **Foreign key** in the Description text box.

4. Press the **F6** key to move to the Field Properties pane. The current entry for the Field Size property, 50, is highlighted.

5. Type **5** to set the Field Size property. You have completed the definition of the third field. See Figure 2-10.

| Figure 2-10 | TABLE WINDOW AFTER DEFINING THE FIRST THREE FIELDS |

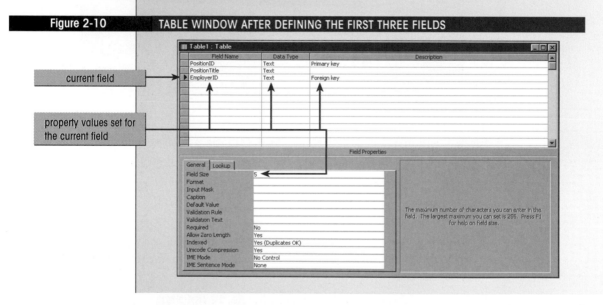

The fourth field is the Wage field, which will display values in the currency format.

To define the Wage field:

1. Place the insertion point in the fourth row's Field Name text box, type **Wage** in the text box, and then press the **Tab** key to advance to the Data Type text box.

2. Click the **Data Type** list arrow, click **Currency** in the list box, and then press the **Tab** key to advance to the Description text box.

3. Type **Rate per hour** in the Description text box.

Elsa wants the Wage field values to be displayed with two decimal places, and she does not want any value to be displayed by default for new records. So, you need to set the Decimal Places and Default Value properties accordingly.

4. Click the **Decimal Places** text box to position the insertion point there. A list arrow appears on the right side of the Decimal Places text box.

When you position the insertion point or select text in many Access text boxes, Access displays a list arrow, which you can click to display a list box with options. You can display the list arrow and the list box simultaneously if you click the text box near its right side.

5. Click the **Decimal Places** list arrow, and then click **2** in the list box to specify two decimal places for the Wage field values.

Next, notice the Default Value property, which specifies the value that will be automatically entered into the field when you add a new record. Currently this property has a setting of 0. Elsa wants the Wage field to be empty (that is, to contain *no* default value) when a new record is added. Therefore, you need to change the Default Value property to the setting "Null." Setting the Default Value property to "Null" tells Access to display no value in the Wage field, by default.

6. Select **0** in the Default Value text box either by dragging the pointer or double-clicking the mouse, and then type **Null**.

The next two fields in the Position table—Hours/Week and Openings—are number fields with a field size of Integer. Also, for each of these fields, Elsa wants the values displayed with no decimal places, and she does not want a default value displayed for the fields when new records are added. You'll define these two fields next.

To define the Hours/Week and Openings fields:

1. Position the insertion point in the fifth row's Field Name text box, type **Hours/Week** in the text box, and then press the **Tab** key to advance to the Data Type text box.

2. Click the **Data Type** list arrow, click **Number** in the list box, and then press the **Tab** key to advance to the Description text box.

3. Type **Work hours per week** in the Description text box.

4. Click the right side of the **Field Size** text box, and then click **Integer** to choose this setting. Recall that the Integer field size stores whole numbers in two bytes.

5. Click the right side of the **Decimal Places** text box, and then click **0** to specify no decimal places.

6. Select the value **0** in the Default Value text box, and then type **Null**.

7. Repeat Steps 1 through 6 to define the **Openings** field as the sixth field in the Position table. For the Description, enter the text **Number of openings**.

According to Elsa's design (Figure 2-5), the final three fields to be defined in the Position table are ReferredBy, a text field, and StartDate and EndDate, both date/time fields. You'll define these three fields next.

To define the ReferredBy, StartDate, and EndDate fields:

1. Position the insertion point in the seventh row's Field Name text box, type **ReferredBy** in the text box, press the **Tab** key to advance to the Data Type text box, and then press the **Tab** key again to accept the default Text data type.

2. Change the default Field Size of 50 to **30** for the ReferredBy field.

3. Position the insertion point in the eighth row's Field Name text box, type **StartDate**, and then press the **Tab** key to advance to the Data Type text box.

4. Click the **Data Type** list arrow, click **Date/Time** to select this type, press the **Tab** key, and then type **Month and day** in the Description text box.

   Elsa wants the values in the StartDate field to be displayed in a format showing only the month and day, as in the following example: 03/11. You use the Format property to control the display of a field value.

5. In the Field Properties pane, click the right side of the **Format** text box to display the list of predefined formats. As noted in the right side of the Field Properties pane, you can either choose a predefined format or enter a custom format.

   TROUBLE? If you see a list arrow instead of a list of predefined formats, click the list arrow to display the list.

   None of the predefined formats matches the layout Elsa wants for the StartDate values. Therefore, you need to create a custom date format. Figure 2-11 shows some of the symbols available for custom date and time formats. (A complete description of all the custom formats is available in Help.)

Figure 2-11   **SYMBOLS FOR SOME CUSTOM DATE FORMATS**

SYMBOL	DESCRIPTION
/	date separator
d	day of the month in one or two numeric digits, as needed (1 to 31)
dd	day of the month in two numeric digits (01 to 31)
ddd	first three letters of the weekday (Sun to Sat)
dddd	full name of the weekday (Sunday to Saturday)
w	day of the week (1 to 7)
ww	week of the year (1 to 53)
m	month of the year in one or two numeric digits, as needed (1 to 12)
mm	month of the year in two numeric digits (01 to 12)
mmm	first three letters of the month (Jan to Dec)
mmmm	full name of the month (January to December)
yy	last two digits of the year (01 to 99)
yyyy	full year (0100 to 9999)

Elsa wants the dates to be displayed with a two-digit month (mm) and a two-digit day (dd). You'll enter this custom format now.

6. Click the **Format** list arrow to close the list of predefined formats, and then type **mm/dd** in the Format text box. See Figure 2-12.

Figure 2-12   **SPECIFYING THE CUSTOM DATE FORMAT**

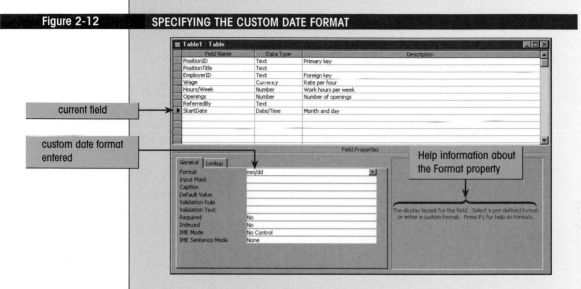

current field

custom date format
entered

Next, you'll define the ninth and final field, EndDate. This field will have the same definition and properties as the StartDate field.

7. Place the insertion point in the ninth row's Field Name text box, type **EndDate**, and then press the **Tab** key to advance to the Data Type text box.

You can select a value from the Data Type list box as you did for the StartDate field. Alternately, you can type the property value in the text box or type just the first character of the property value.

8. Type **d**. The value in the ninth row's Data Type text box changes to "date/Time," with the letters "ate/Time" highlighted. See Figure 2-13.

Figure 2-13   **SELECTING A VALUE FOR THE DATA TYPE PROPERTY**

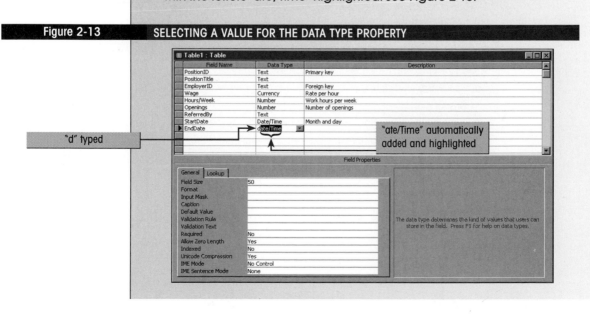

"d" typed

9. Press the **Tab** key to advance to the Description text box, and then type **Month and day**. Note that Access changes the value for the Data Type property to Date/Time.

10. In the Format text box, type **mm/dd** to specify the custom date format for the EndDate field.

You've finished defining the fields for the Position table. Next, you need to specify the primary key for the table.

Specifying the Primary Key

Although Access does not require a table to have a primary key, including a primary key offers several advantages:

- A primary key uniquely identifies each record in a table.
- Access does not allow duplicate values in the primary key field. If a record already exists with a PositionID value of 1320, for example, Access prevents you from adding another record with this same value in the PositionID field. Preventing duplicate values ensures the uniqueness of the primary key field.
- When a primary key has been specified, Access forces you to enter a value for the primary key field in every record in the table. This is known as **entity integrity**. If you do not enter a value for a field, you have actually given the field what is known as a **null value**. You cannot give a null value to the primary key field because entity integrity prevents Access from accepting and processing that record.
- Access stores records on disk in the same order as you enter them but displays them in order by the field values of the primary key. If you enter records in no specific order, you are ensured that you will later be able to work with them in a more meaningful, primary key sequence.
- Access responds faster to your requests for specific records based on the primary key.

REFERENCE WINDOW | **RW**

Specifying a Primary Key for a Table
- In the Table window in Design view, click the row selector for the field you've chosen to be the primary key.
- If the primary key will consist of two or more fields, press and hold down the Ctrl key, and then click the row selector for each additional primary key field.
- Click the Primary Key button on the Table Design toolbar.

According to Elsa's design, you need to specify PositionID as the primary key for the Position table.

To specify PositionID as the primary key:

1. Position the pointer on the row selector for the PositionID field until the pointer changes to a ➡ shape. See Figure 2-14.

Figure 2-14	SPECIFYING PositionID AS THE PRIMARY KEY

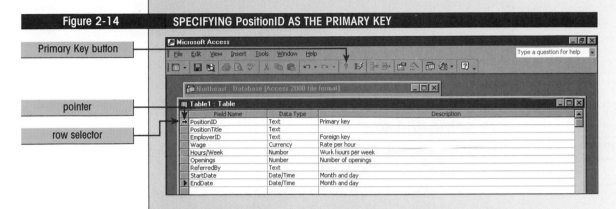

2. Click the mouse button. The entire first row of the Table Design grid is highlighted.

3. Click the **Primary Key** button 🔑 on the Table Design toolbar, and then click a row other than the first to deselect the first row. A key symbol appears in the row selector for the first row, indicating that the PositionID field is the table's primary key. See Figure 2-15.

Figure 2-15	PositionID SELECTED AS THE PRIMARY KEY

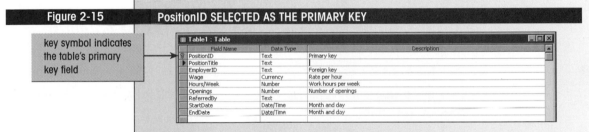

TROUBLE? Your insertion point might be in a different location from the one shown in the figure, depending on where you clicked to deselect the first row.

If you specify the wrong field as the primary key, or if you later change your mind and do not want the designated primary key field to be the table's primary key, you can select the field and then click the Primary Key button on the Table Design toolbar again, which will remove the key symbol and the primary key designation from the field. Then you can choose another field to be the primary key, if necessary.

You've defined the fields for the Position table and specified its primary key, so you can now save the table structure.

Saving the Table Structure

The last step in creating a table is to name the table and save the table's structure on disk. Once the table is saved, you can use it to enter data in the table.

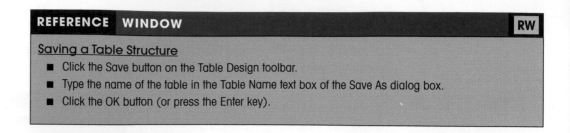

According to Elsa's plan, you need to save the table you've defined as "Position."

To name and save the Position table:

1. Click the **Save** button 💾 on the Table Design toolbar. The Save As dialog box opens.

2. Type **Position** in the Table Name text box, and then press the **Enter** key. Access saves the table with the name Position in the Northeast database on your Data Disk. Notice that Position now appears instead of Table1 in the Table window title bar.

Recall that in Tutorial 1 you set the Compact on Close option for the Seasonal database so that it would be compacted automatically each time you closed it. Now you'll set this option for your new Northeast database, so that it will be compacted automatically.

To set the option for compacting the Northeast database automatically:

1. Click **Tools** on the menu bar, and then click **Options**. The Options dialog box opens.

2. Click the **General** tab in the dialog box, and then click the **Compact on Close** check box to select it.

3. Click the **OK** button to set the option.

The Position table is now complete. In Session 2.2, you'll continue to work with the Position table by entering records in it, modifying its structure, and maintaining data in the table. You will also import two tables, Employer and NAICS, from the Seasonal database into the Northeast database.

Session 2.1 QUICK CHECK

1. What guidelines should you follow when designing a database?
2. What is the purpose of the Data Type property for a field?
3. For which three types of fields can you assign a field size?

4. In Design view, which key do you press to move between the Table Design grid and the Field Properties pane?

5. You use the _____ property to control the display of a field value.

6. A(n) _____ value, which results when you do not enter a value for a field, is not permitted for a primary key.

SESSION 2.2

In this session, you will add records to a table; modify the structure of an existing table by deleting, moving, and adding fields and changing field properties; copy records from another Access database; import tables from another Access database; and update an existing database by deleting and changing records.

Adding Records to a Table

You can add records to an Access table in several ways. A table datasheet provides a simple way for you to add records. As you learned in Tutorial 1, a datasheet shows a table's contents in rows and columns. Each row is a separate record in the table, and each column contains the field values for one field in the table. If you are currently working in Design view, you first must change from Design view to Datasheet view in order to view the table's datasheet.

Elsa asks you to add the two records shown in Figure 2-16 to the Position table. These two records contain data for positions that have recently become available at two employers.

Figure 2-16	RECORDS TO BE ADDED TO THE POSITION TABLE								
PositionID	PositionTitle	EmployerID	Wage	Hours/Week	Openings	ReferredBy	StartDate	EndDate
2021	Waiter/Waitress	10155	9.50	30	1	Sue Brown	6/30	9/15
2017	Tour Guide	10149	15.00	20	1	Ed Curran	9/21	11/1

To add the records in the Position table datasheet:

1. If you took a break after the previous session, make sure that Access is running and that the Position table of the Northeast database is open in Design view. To open the table in Design view from the Database window, right-click the **Position** table, and then click **Design View** on the shortcut menu.

   Access displays the fields you defined for the Position table in Design view. Now you need to switch to Datasheet view so that you can enter the two records for Elsa.

2. Click the **View** button for Datasheet view 🔲 on the Table Design toolbar. The Table window opens in Datasheet view. See Figure 2-17.

| Figure 2-17 | TABLE WINDOW IN DATASHEET VIEW |

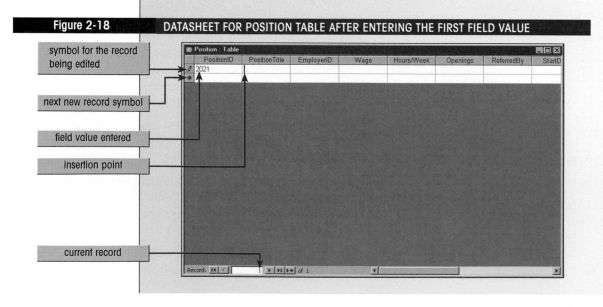

current record symbol

field names

Table window

Description property for
the current field

The table's nine field names appear at the top of the datasheet. Some of the
field names might not be visible. The current record symbol in the first row's
record selector identifies the currently selected record, which contains no data
until you enter the first record. The insertion point is located in the first row's
PositionID field, whose Description property appears on the status bar.

3. Type **2021**, which is the first record's PositionID field value, and then press the
Tab key. Each time you press the Tab key, the insertion point moves to the right
to the next field in the record. See Figure 2-18.

| Figure 2-18 | DATASHEET FOR POSITION TABLE AFTER ENTERING THE FIRST FIELD VALUE |

symbol for the record
being edited

next new record symbol

field value entered

insertion point

current record

TROUBLE? If you make a mistake when typing a value, use the Backspace key to delete characters to the left of the insertion point or the Delete key to delete characters to the right of the insertion point. Then type the correct value. If you want to correct a value by replacing it entirely, double-click the value to select it, and then type the correct value.

The pencil symbol in the first row's record selector indicates that the record is being edited. The star symbol in the second row's record selector identifies the second row as the next one available for a new record. Notice that all the fields are initially empty; this occurs because you set the Default Value property for the fields (as appropriate) to Null.

4. Type **Waiter/Waitress** in the PositionTitle field, and then press the **Tab** key. The insertion point moves to the EmployerID field.

5. Type **10155** and then press the **Tab** key. The insertion point moves to the right side of the Wage field.

   Recall that the PositionID, PositionTitle, and EmployerID fields are all text fields and that the Wage field is a currency field. Field values for text fields are left-aligned in their boxes, and field values for number, date/time, and currency fields are right-aligned in their boxes.

6. Type **9.5** and then press the **Tab** key. Access displays the field value with a dollar sign and two decimal places ($9.50), as specified by the currency format. You do not need to type the dollar sign, commas, or decimal point (for whole dollar amounts) because Access adds these symbols automatically for you.

7. In the Hours/Week field, type **30**, press the **Tab** key, type **1** in the Openings field, and then press the **Tab** key.

8. Type **Sue Brown** in the ReferredBy field, and then press the **Tab** key. Depending on your monitor's resolution and size, the display of the datasheet might shift so that the next field, StartDate, is completely visible.

9. Type **6/30** in the StartDate field, and then press the **Tab** key. Access displays the value as 06/30, as specified by the custom date format (mm/dd) you set for this field. The insertion point moves to the final field in the table, EndDate.

10. Type **9/15** in the EndDate field, and then press the **Tab** key. Access displays the value as 09/15, shifts the display of the datasheet back to the left, stores the first completed record in the Position table, removes the pencil symbol from the first row's record selector, advances the insertion point to the second row's PositionID text box, and places the current record symbol in the second row's record selector.

    Now you can enter the values for the second record.

11. Refer to Figure 2-16, and repeat Steps 3 through 10 to add the second record to the table. Access saves the record in the Position table, and moves the insertion point to the beginning of the third row. See Figure 2-19.

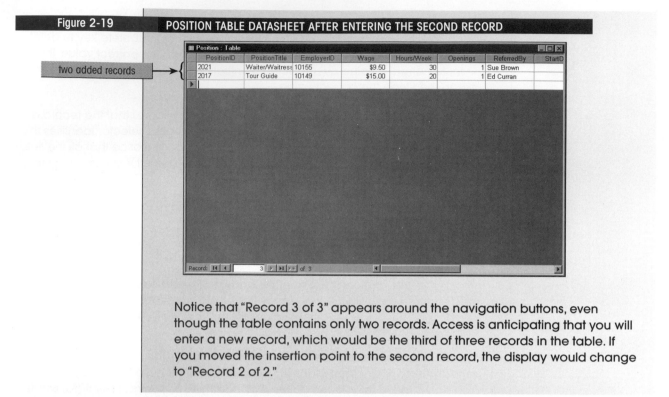

Figure 2-19   POSITION TABLE DATASHEET AFTER ENTERING THE SECOND RECORD

two added records

Notice that "Record 3 of 3" appears around the navigation buttons, even though the table contains only two records. Access is anticipating that you will enter a new record, which would be the third of three records in the table. If you moved the insertion point to the second record, the display would change to "Record 2 of 2."

Notice that the two records are currently listed in the order in which you entered them. However, once you close the table or change to another view, and then redisplay the table datasheet, the records will be listed in primary key order by the values in the PositionID field.

Modifying the Structure of an Access Table

Even a well-designed table might need to be modified. For example, the government at all levels and competitors place demands on a company to track more data and to modify the data it already tracks. Access allows you to modify a table's structure in Design view: you can add and delete fields, change the order of fields, and change the properties of the fields.

After holding a meeting with her staff members and reviewing the structure of the Position table and the format of the field values in the datasheet, Elsa has several changes she wants you to make to the table. First, she has decided that it's not necessary to keep track of the name of the person who originally requested a particular position, so she wants you to delete the ReferredBy field. Also, she thinks that the Wage field should remain a currency field, but she wants the dollar signs removed from the displayed field values in the datasheet. She also wants the Openings field moved to the end of the table. Finally, she wants you to add a new yes/no field, named Experience, to the table to indicate whether the available position requires that potential recruits have prior experience in that type of work. The Experience field will be inserted between the Hours/Week and StartDate fields. Figure 2-20 shows Elsa's modified design for the Position table.

Figure 2-20	MODIFIED DESIGN FOR THE POSITION TABLE			

Field Name	Data Type	Field Size	Description
PositionID	Text	4	Primary key
PositionTitle	Text	30	
EmployerID	Text	5	Foreign key
Wage	Currency		Rate per hour
Hours/Week	Number	Integer	Work hours per week
Experience	Yes/No		Experience required
StartDate	Date/Time		Month and day
EndDate	Date/Time		Month and day
Openings	Number	Integer	Number of openings

You'll begin modifying the table by deleting the ReferredBy field.

Deleting a Field

After you've defined a table structure and added records to the table, you can delete a field from the table structure. When you delete a field, you also delete all the values for the field from the table. Therefore, you should make sure that you need to delete a field and that you delete the correct field.

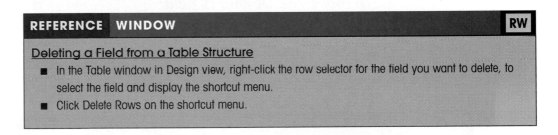

REFERENCE WINDOW **RW**

Deleting a Field from a Table Structure
- In the Table window in Design view, right-click the row selector for the field you want to delete, to select the field and display the shortcut menu.
- Click Delete Rows on the shortcut menu.

You need to delete the ReferredBy field from the Position table structure.

To delete the ReferredBy field:

1. Click the **View** button for Design view [icon] on the Table Datasheet toolbar. The Table window for the Position table opens in Design view.

2. Position the pointer on the row selector for the ReferredBy field until the pointer changes to a ➡ shape.

3. Right-click to select the entire row for the ReferredBy field and display the short-cut menu, and then click **Delete Rows**.

   A dialog box opens asking you to confirm the deletion.

4. Click the **Yes** button to close the dialog box and to delete the field and its values from the table. See Figure 2-21.

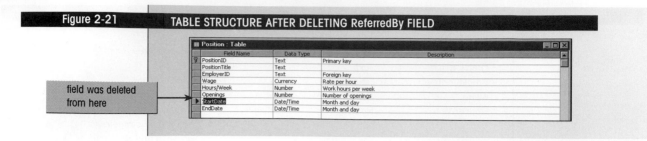

Figure 2-21   TABLE STRUCTURE AFTER DELETING ReferredBy FIELD

field was deleted
from here

You have deleted the ReferredBy field in the Table window, but the change doesn't take place in the table on disk until you save the table structure. Because you have other modifications to make to the table, you'll wait until you finish them all before saving the modified table structure to disk.

Moving a Field

To move a field, you use the mouse to drag it to a new location in the Table window in Design view. Your next modification to the Position table structure is to move the Openings field to the end of the table, as Elsa requested.

To move the Openings field:

1. Click the **row selector** for the Openings field to select the entire row.

2. Place the pointer in the row selector for the Openings field, click the ⬚ pointer, and then drag the ⬚ pointer to the row selector below the EndDate row selector. See Figure 2-22.

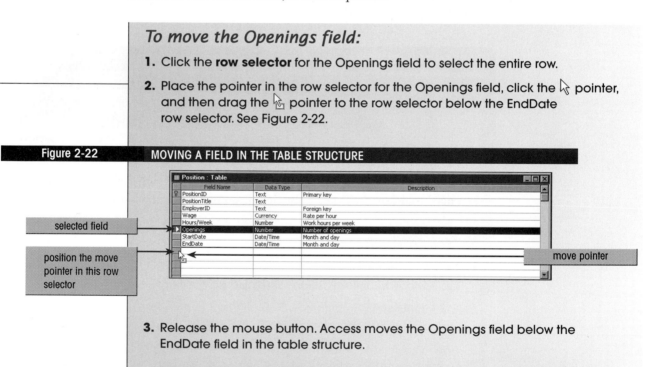

Figure 2-22   MOVING A FIELD IN THE TABLE STRUCTURE

selected field

position the move
pointer in this row
selector

move pointer

3. Release the mouse button. Access moves the Openings field below the EndDate field in the table structure.

   TROUBLE? If the Openings field did not move, repeat Steps 1 through 3, making sure you firmly hold down the mouse button during the drag operation.

Adding a Field

Next, you need to add the Experience field to the table structure between the Hours/Week and StartDate fields. To add a new field between existing fields, you must insert a row. You begin by selecting the field that will be below the new field you want to insert.

To add the Experience field to the Position table:

1. Right-click the **row selector** for the StartDate field to select this field and display the shortcut menu, and then click **Insert Rows**. Access adds a new, blank row between the Hours/Week and StartDate fields. See Figure 2-23.

| Figure 2-23 | AFTER INSERTING A ROW IN THE TABLE STRUCTURE |

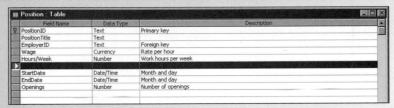

You'll define the Experience field in the new row of the Position table. Access will add this new field to the Position table structure between the Hours/Week and StartDate fields.

2. Click the **Field Name** text box for the new row, type **Experience**, and then press the **Tab** key.

   The Experience field will be a yes/no field that will specify whether prior work experience is required for the position.

3. Type **y**. Access completes the data type as "yes/No."

4. Press the **Tab** key to select the yes/no data type and to move to the Description text box.

   Notice that Access changes the value in the Data Type text box from "yes/No" to "Yes/No."

5. Type **Experience required** in the Description text box.

   Elsa wants the Experience field to have a Default Value property value of "No," so you need to set this property.

6. In the Field Properties pane, click the **Default Value** text box, type **no**, and then click somewhere outside of the Default Value text box to deselect the value. Notice that Access changes the Default Value property value from "no" to "No." See Figure 2-24.

Figure 2-24   **EXPERIENCE FIELD ADDED TO THE POSITION TABLE**

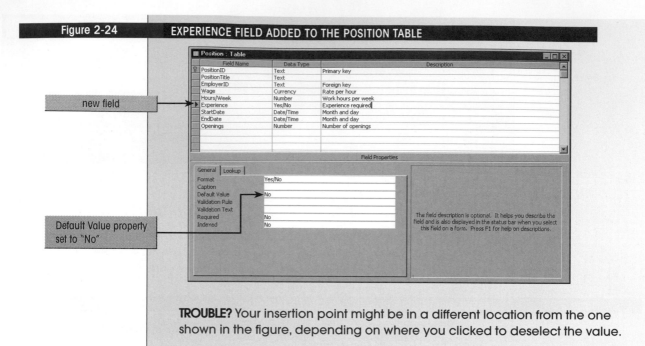

new field

Default Value property
set to "No"

TROUBLE? Your insertion point might be in a different location from the one shown in the figure, depending on where you clicked to deselect the value.

You've completed adding the Experience field to the Position table in Design view. As with the other changes you've made in Design view, however, the Experience field is not added to the Position table in the Northeast database until you save the changes to the table structure.

Changing Field Properties

Elsa's last modification to the table structure is to remove the dollar signs from the Wage field values displayed in the datasheet—repeated dollar signs are unnecessary and they clutter the datasheet. As you learned earlier when defining the StartDate and EndDate fields, you use the Format property to control the display of a field value.

To change the Format property of the Wage field:

1. Click the **Description** text box for the Wage field. The Wage field is now the current field.

2. Click the right side of the **Format** text box to display the Format list box. See Figure 2-25.

Figure 2-25	FORMAT LIST BOX FOR THE WAGE FIELD

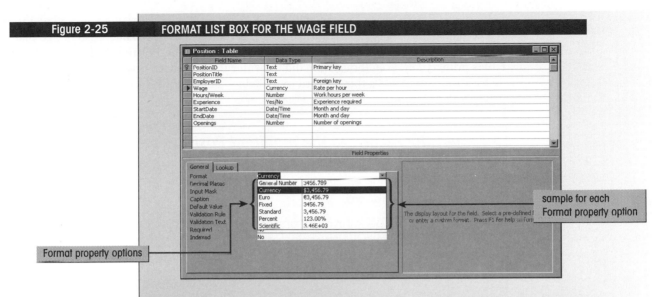

To the right of each Format property option is a field value whose appearance represents a sample of the option. The Standard option specifies the format Elsa wants for the Wage field.

3. Click **Standard** in the Format list box to accept this option for the Format property.

Elsa wants you to add a third record to the Position table datasheet. Before you can add the record, you must save the modified table structure, and then switch to the Position table datasheet.

To save the modified table structure, and then switch to the datasheet:

1. Click the **Save** button 🖫 on the Table Design toolbar. The modified table structure for the Position table is stored in the Northeast database. Note that if you forget to save the modified structure and try to close the table or switch to another view, Access will prompt you to save the table before you can continue.

2. Click the **View** button for Datasheet view 🖩 on the Table Design toolbar. The Position table datasheet opens. See Figure 2-26.

Figure 2-26	DATASHEET FOR THE MODIFIED POSITION TABLE

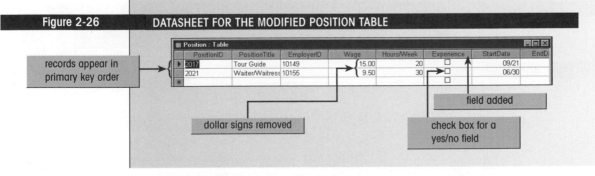

Notice that the ReferredBy field no longer appears in the datasheet, the Openings field is now the rightmost column (you might need to scroll the datasheet to see it), the Wage field values do not contain dollar signs, and the Experience field appears between the Hours/Week and StartDate fields. The Experience column contains check boxes to represent the yes/no field values. Empty check boxes signify "No," which is the default value you assigned to the Experience field. A check mark in the check box indicates a "Yes" value. Also notice that the records appear in ascending order based on the value in the PositionID field, the Position table's primary key, even though you did not enter the records in this order.

Elsa asks you to add a third record to the table. This record is for a position that requires prior work experience.

To add the record to the modified Position table:

1. Click the **New Record** button ▶✳ on the Table Datasheet toolbar. The insertion point moves to the PositionID field for the third row, which is the next row available for a new record.

2. Type **2020**. The pencil symbol appears in the row selector for the third row, and the star appears in the row selector for the fourth row. Recall that these symbols represent a record being edited and the next available record, respectively.

3. Press the **Tab** key. The insertion point moves to the PositionTitle field.

4. Type **Host/Hostess**, press the **Tab** key to move to the EmployerID field, type **10163**, and then press the **Tab** key. The Wage field is now the current field.

5. Type **18.5** and then press the **Tab** key. Access displays the value as "18.50" (with no dollar sign).

6. Type **32** in the Hours/Week field, and then press the **Tab** key. The Experience field is now the current field.

   Recall that the default value for this field is "No," which means the check box is initially empty. For yes/no fields with check boxes, you press the Tab key to leave the check box unchecked; you press the spacebar or click the check box to add or remove a check mark in the check box. Because this position requires experience, you need to insert a check mark in the check box.

7. Press the **spacebar**. A check mark appears in the check box.

8. Press the **Tab** key, type **6/15** in the StartDate field, press the **Tab** key, and then type **10/1** in the EndDate field.

9. Press the **Tab** key, type **1** in the Openings field, and then press the **Tab** key. Access saves the record in the Position table and moves the insertion point to the beginning of the fourth row. See Figure 2-27.

| Figure 2-27 | POSITION TABLE DATASHEET WITH THIRD RECORD ADDED |

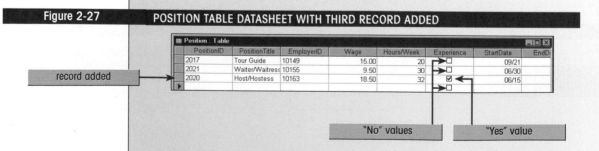

As you add records, Access places them at the end of the datasheet. If you switch to Design view and then return to the datasheet, or if you close the table and then open the datasheet, Access will display the records in primary key sequence.

For many of the fields, the columns are wider than necessary for the field values. You can resize the datasheet columns so that they are only as wide as needed to display the longest value in the column, including the field name. Resizing datasheet columns to their best fit improves the display of the datasheet and allows you to view more fields at the same time.

To resize the Position datasheet columns to their best fit:

1. Place the pointer on the line between the PositionID and PositionTitle field names until the pointer changes to a ✛ shape.

2. Double-click the pointer. The PositionID column is resized so that it is only as wide as the longest value in the column (the field name, in this case).

3. Double-click the ✛ pointer on the line to the right of each remaining field name to resize all the columns in the datasheet to their best fit. See Figure 2-28.

| Figure 2-28 | DATASHEET AFTER RESIZING ALL COLUMNS TO THEIR BEST FIT |

Notice that all nine fields in the Position table are now visible in the datasheet.

You have modified the Position table structure and added one record. Next you need to obtain the rest of the records for this table from another database, and then import the two tables from the Seasonal database (Employer and NAICS) into your Northeast database.

Obtaining Data from Another Access Database

Sometimes the data you need for your database might already exist in another Access database. You can save time in obtaining this data by copying and pasting records from one database table into another or by importing an entire table from one database into another.

Copying Records from Another Access Database

You can copy and paste records from a table in the same database or in a different database only if the tables have the same structure—that is, the tables contain the same fields in the same order. Elsa's NEJobs database in the Tutorial folder on your Data Disk has a table named Available Positions that has the same table structure as the Position table. The records in the Available Positions table are the records Elsa wants you to copy into the Position table.

Other programs, such as Microsoft Word and Microsoft Excel, allow you to have two or more documents open at a time. However, you can have only one Access database open at a time. Therefore, you need to close the Northeast database, open the Available Positions table in the NEJobs database, select and copy the table records, close the NEJobs database, reopen the Position table in the Northeast database, and then paste the copied records. (*Note*: If you have a database open and then open a second database, Access will automatically close the first database for you.)

To copy the records from the Available Positions table:

1. Click the **Close** button ☒ on the Table window title bar to close the Position table. A message box opens asking if you want to save the changes to the layout of the Position table. This box appears because you resized the datasheet columns to their best fit.

2. Click the **Yes** button in the message box.

3. Click ☒ on the Database window title bar to close the Northeast database.

4. Click the **Open** button 🗁 on the Database toolbar to display the Open dialog box.

5. If necessary, display the list of files on your Data Disk, and then open the **Tutorial** folder.

6. Open the database file named **NEJobs**. The Database window opens. Notice that the NEJobs database contains only one table, the Available Positions table. This table contains the records you need to copy.

7. Click **Available Positions** in the Tables list box (if necessary), and then click the **Open** button in the Database window. The datasheet for the Available Positions table opens. See Figure 2-29. Note that this table contains a total of 62 records.

Figure 2-29	DATASHEET FOR THE NEJobs DATABASE'S AVAILABLE POSITIONS TABLE

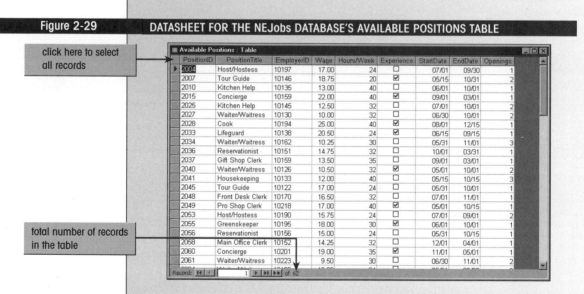

click here to select all records

total number of records in the table

Elsa wants you to copy all the records in the Available Positions table. You can select all records by clicking the row selector for the field name row.

8. Click the **row selector** for the field name row (see Figure 2-29). All the records in the table are now highlighted, which means that Access has selected all of them.

9. Click the **Copy** button 📋 on the Table Datasheet toolbar. All the records are copied to the Windows Clipboard.

    TROUBLE? If a Clipboard panel opens in the Task Pane, click its Close button to close it, and then continue with Step 10.

10. Click ☒ on the Table window title bar. A dialog box opens asking if you want to save the data you copied to the Windows Clipboard.

11. Click the **Yes** button in the dialog box. The dialog box closes, and then the table closes.

12. Click [X] on the Database window title bar to close the NEJobs database.

To finish copying and pasting the records, you must open the Position table and paste the copied records into the table.

To paste the copied records into the Position table:

1. Click **File** on the menu bar, and then click **Northeast** in the list of recently opened databases. The Database window opens, showing the tables for the Northeast database.

2. In the Tables list box, click **Position** (if necessary), and then click the **Open** button in the Database window. The datasheet for the Position table opens.

You must paste the records at the end of the table.

3. Click the **row selector** for row four, which is the next row available for a new record.

4. Click the **Paste** button [📋] on the Table Datasheet toolbar. A dialog box opens asking if you are sure you want to paste the records (62 in all).

5. Click the **Yes** button. All the records are pasted from the Windows Clipboard, and the pasted records remain highlighted. See Figure 2-30. Notice that the table now contains a total of 65 records—the three original records plus the 62 copied records.

Figure 2-30	TABLE AFTER COPYING AND PASTING RECORDS

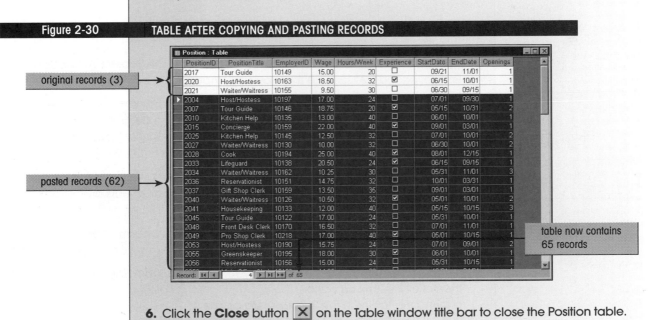

6. Click the **Close** button [X] on the Table window title bar to close the Position table.

Importing a Table from Another Access Database

When you import a table from one Access database to another, you place a copy of the table—including its structure, field definitions, and field values—in the database into which you import it. There are two ways to import a table from another Access database into your current database: using the Get External Data option on the File menu, or using the Import Table Wizard, which is available in the New Table dialog box. You'll use both methods to import the two tables from the Seasonal database into your Northeast database.

To import the Employer and NAICS tables:

1. Make sure the Northeast Database window is open on your screen.

2. Click **File** on the menu bar, position the pointer on the double-arrow at the bottom of the File menu to display the full menu (if necessary), point to **Get External Data**, and then click **Import**. The Import dialog box opens. This dialog box is similar to the Open dialog box.

3. Display the list of files in your Tutorial folder, click **Seasonal**, and then click the **Import** button. The Import Objects dialog box opens. See Figure 2-31.

Figure 2-31	IMPORT OBJECTS DIALOG BOX

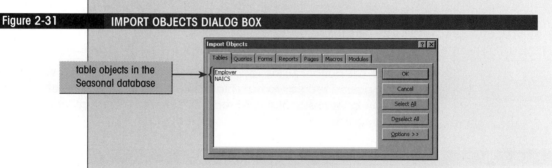

table objects in the Seasonal database

The Tables tab of the dialog box lists both tables in the Seasonal database—Employer and NAICS. Note that you can import other objects as well (queries, forms, reports, and so on).

4. Click **Employer** in the list of tables, and then click the **OK** button. The Import Objects dialog box closes, and the Employer table is now listed in the Northeast Database window.

Now you'll use the Import Table Wizard to import the NAICS table. (Note that you could also use the Select All button in the Import Objects dialog box to import all the objects listed on the current tab at the same time.)

5. Click the **New** button in the Database window, click **Import Table** in the New Table dialog box, and then click the **OK** button. The Import dialog box opens.

6. If necessary, display the list of files in your Tutorial folder, click **Seasonal**, and then click the **Import** button. The Import Objects dialog box opens, again displaying the tables in the Seasonal database.

7. Click **NAICS** in the list of tables, and then click the **OK** button to import the NAICS table into the Northeast database.

Now that you have all the records in the Position table and all three tables in the Northeast database, Elsa examines the records to make sure they are correct. She finds one record in the Position table that she wants you to delete and another record that needs changes to its field values.

Updating a Database

Updating, or **maintaining**, a database is the process of adding, changing, and deleting records in database tables to keep them current and accurate. You've already added records to the Position table. Now Elsa wants you to delete and change records.

Deleting Records

To delete a record, you need to select the record in Datasheet view, and then delete it using the Delete Record button on the Table Datasheet toolbar or the Delete Record option on the shortcut menu.

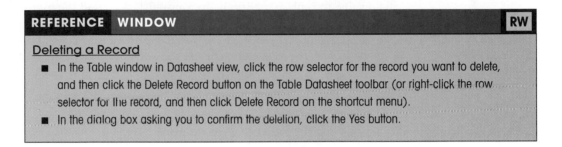

REFERENCE WINDOW   **RW**

Deleting a Record

- In the Table window in Datasheet view, click the row selector for the record you want to delete, and then click the Delete Record button on the Table Datasheet toolbar (or right-click the row selector for the record, and then click Delete Record on the shortcut menu).
- In the dialog box asking you to confirm the deletion, click the Yes button.

Elsa asks you to delete the record whose PositionID is 2015 because this record was entered in error; the position for this record does not exist. The fourth record in the table has a PositionID value of 2015. This record is the one you need to delete.

To delete the record:

1. Open the Position table in Datasheet view.

2. Right-click the **row selector** for row four. Access selects the fourth record and displays the shortcut menu. See Figure 2-32.

| Figure 2-32 | DELETING A RECORD |

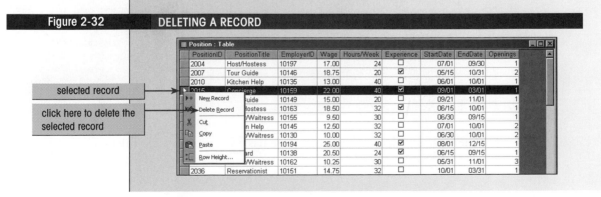

3. Click **Delete Record** on the shortcut menu. Access deletes the record and opens a dialog box asking you to confirm the deletion. Because the deletion of a record is permanent and cannot be undone, Access prompts you to make sure that you want to delete the record.

TROUBLE? If you selected the wrong record for deletion, click the No button. Access ends the deletion process and continues to display the selected record. Repeat Steps 2 and 3 to delete the correct record.

4. Click the **Yes** button to confirm the deletion and close the dialog box.

Elsa's final update to the Position table involves changes to field values in one of the records.

Changing Records

To change the field values in a record, you first must make the record the current record. Then you position the insertion point in the field value to make minor changes or select the field value to replace it entirely. In Tutorial 1, you used the mouse with the scroll bars and the navigation buttons to navigate through the records in a datasheet. You can also use keystroke combinations and the F2 key to navigate a datasheet and to select field values.

The **F2 key** is a toggle that you use to switch between navigation mode and editing mode:

- In **navigation mode**, Access selects an entire field value. If you type while you are in navigation mode, your typed entry replaces the highlighted field value.
- In **editing mode**, you can insert or delete characters in a field value based on the location of the insertion point.

Figure 2-33 shows some of the navigation mode and editing mode keystroke techniques.

Figure 2-33	NAVIGATION MODE AND EDITING MODE KEYSTROKE TECHNIQUES	
PRESS	**TO MOVE THE SELECTION IN NAVIGATION MODE**	**TO MOVE THE INSERTION POINT IN EDITING MODE**
←	Left one field value at a time	Left one character at a time
→	Right one field value at a time	Right one character at a time
Home	Left to the first field value in the record	To the left of the first character in the field value
End	Right to the last field value in the record	To the right of the last character in the field value
↑ or ↓	Up or down one record at a time	Up or down one record at a time and switch to navigation mode
Tab or Enter	Right one field value at a time	Right one field value at a time and switch to navigation mode
Ctrl + Home	To the first field value in the first record	To the left of the first character in the field value
Ctrl + End	To the last field value in the last record	To the right of the last character in the field value

The record Elsa wants you to change has a PositionID field value of 2125. Some of the values were entered incorrectly for this record, and you need to enter the correct values.

To modify the record:

1. Make sure the PositionID field value for the fourth record is still highlighted, indicating that the table is in navigation mode.

2. Press **Ctrl + End**. Access displays records from the end of the table and selects the last field value in the last record. This field value is for the Openings field.

3. Press the **Home** key. The first field value in the last record is now selected. This field value is for the PositionID field.

4. Press the ↑ key. The PositionID field value for the previous record (PositionID 2125) is selected. This record is the one you need to change.

   Elsa wants you to change these field values in the record: PositionID to 2124, EmployerID to 10163, Wage to 14.50, Experience to "Yes" (checked), and EndDate to 10/15.

5. Type **2124**, press the **Tab** key twice, type **10163**, press the **Tab** key, type **14.5**, press the **Tab** key twice, press the **spacebar** to insert a check mark in the Experience check box, press the **Tab** key twice, and then type **10/15**. The changes to the record are complete. See Figure 2-34.

Figure 2-34	TABLE AFTER CHANGING FIELD VALUES IN A RECORD

field values changed

You've completed all of Elsa's updates to the Position table. Now you can exit Access.

6. Click the **Close** button ⊠ on the Access window title bar to close the Position table and the Northeast database, and to exit Access.

Elsa and her staff members approve of the revised table structure for the Position table. They are confident that the table will allow them to easily track position data for NSJI's employer customers.

Session 2.2 Quick Check

1. What does a pencil symbol in a datasheet's row selector represent? A star symbol?

2. What is the effect of deleting a field from a table structure?

3. How do you insert a field between existing fields in a table structure?

4. A field with the _____ data type can appear in the table datasheet as a check box.

5. Describe the two ways in which you can display the Import dialog box, so that you can import a table from one Access database to another.

6. In Datasheet view, what is the difference between navigation mode and editing mode?

REVIEW ASSIGNMENTS

Elsa needs a database to track data about the students recruited by NSJI and about the recruiters who find jobs for the students. She asks you to create the database by completing the following:

1. Make sure your Data Disk is in the appropriate disk drive, and then start Access.

2. Create a new, blank database named **Recruits** and save it in the Review folder on your Data Disk.

Explore

3. Use the Table Wizard to create a new table named **Recruiter** in the **Recruits** database, as follows:
   a. Base the new table on the Employees sample table, which is one of the sample tables in the Business category.
   b. Add the following fields to your table (in the order shown): SocialSecurityNumber, Salary, FirstName, MiddleName, and LastName.
   c. Click SocialSecurityNumber in the "Fields in my new table" list, and then use the Rename Field button to change the name of this field to SSN. Click the Next button.
   d. Name the new table **Recruiter**, and choose the option for setting the primary key yourself. Click the Next button.
   e. Specify SSN as the primary key field and accept the default data type. Click the Next button.
   f. In the final Table Wizard dialog box, click the Finish button to display the table in Datasheet view. (*Note:* The field names appear with spaces between words; this is how the Table Wizard is set up to format these field names when they appear in Datasheet view.)

4. Add the recruiter records shown in Figure 2-35 to the **Recruiter** table. (*Note:* You do not have to type the dashes in the SSN field values or commas in the Salary field values; the Table Wizard formatted these fields so that these symbols are entered automatically for you.)

Figure 2-35

SSN	Salary	First Name	Middle Name	Last Name
892-77-1201	40,000	Kate	Teresa	Foster
901-63-1554	38,500	Paul	Michael	Kirnicki
893-91-0178	40,000	Ryan	James	DuBrava

5. Make the following changes to the structure of the **Recruiter** table:
   a. Move the Salary field so that it appears after the LastName field.
   b. Add a new field between the LastName and Salary fields, using the following properties:
Field Name:	BonusQuota
Data Type:	Number
Description:	Number of recruited students needed to receive bonus
Field Size:	Byte
Decimal Places:	0
   c. Change the format of the Salary field so that commas are displayed, dollar signs are not displayed, and no decimal places are displayed in the field values.
   d. Save the revised table structure.

6. Use the **Recruiter** datasheet to update the database as follows:
   a. Enter these BonusQuota values for the three records: 60 for Kate Foster; 60 for Ryan DuBrava; and 50 for Paul Kirnicki.
   b. Add a record to the **Recruiter** datasheet with the following field values:
SSN:	899-40-2937
First Name:	Sonia
Middle Name:	Lee
Last Name:	Xu
BonusQuota:	50
Salary:	39,250

7. Close the **Recruiter** table, and then set the option for compacting the **Recruits** database on close.

8. Elsa created a database with her name as the database name. The **Recruiter Employees** table in that database has the same format as the **Recruiter** table you created. Copy all the records from the **Recruiter Employees** table in the **Elsa** database (located in the Review folder on your Data Disk) to the end of the **Recruiter** table in the **Recruits** database.

Explore

9. Because you added a number of records to the database, its size has increased. Compact the database manually using the Compact and Repair Database option.

10. Delete the MiddleName field from the **Recruiter** table structure, and then save the table structure.

11. Resize all columns in the datasheet for the **Recruiter** table to their best fit.

12. Print the **Recruiter** table datasheet, and then save and close the table.

13. Create a table named **Student** using the Import Table Wizard. The table you need to import is named **Student**, which is one of the tables in the **Elsa** database located in the Review folder on your Data Disk.

14. Make the following modifications to the structure of the **Student** table in the **Recruits** database:

   a. Enter the following Description property values:
      StudentID: Primary key
      SSN: Foreign key value of the recruiter for this student
   b. Change the Field Size property for both the FirstName field and the LastName field to 15.
   c. Move the BirthDate field so that it appears between the Nation and Gender fields.
   d. Change the format of the BirthDate field so that it displays only two digits for the year instead of four.
   e. Save the table structure changes. (Answer "Yes" to any warning messages about property changes and lost data.)

15. Switch to Datasheet view, and then resize all columns in the datasheet to fit the data.

16. Delete the record with the StudentID DRI9901 from the **Student** table.

17. Save, print, and then close the **Student** datasheet.

18. Close the **Recruits** database, and then exit Access.

CASE PROBLEMS

Case 1. Lim's Video Photography Youngho Lim uses the **Videos** database to maintain information about the clients, contracts, and events for his video photography business. Youngho asks you to help him maintain the database by completing the following:

1. Make sure your Data Disk is in the appropriate disk drive.

2. Start Access and open the **Videos** database located in the Cases folder on your Data Disk.

Explore

3. Use Design view to create a table using the table design shown in Figure 2-36.

Figure 2-36

Field Name	Data Type	Description	Field Size	Other Properties
Shoot#	Number	Primary key	Long Integer	Decimal Places: 0 Default Value: Null
ShootType	Text		2	
ShootTime	Date/Time			Format: Medium Time
Duration	Number	# of hours	Single	Default Value: Null
Contact	Text	Person who booked shoot	30	
Location	Text		30	
ShootDate	Date/Time			Format: mm/dd/yyyy
Contract#	Number	Foreign key	Integer	Decimal Places: 0 Default Value: Null

4. Specify Shoot# as the primary key, and then save the table as **Shoot**.

5. Add the records shown in Figure 2-37 to the **Shoot** table.

Figure 2-37

Shoot#	ShootType	ShootTime	Duration	Contact	Location	ShootDate	Contract#
927032	AP	4:00 PM	3.5	Ellen Quirk	Elm Lodge	9/27/2003	2412
103031	HP	9:00 AM	3.5	Tom Bradbury	Client's home	10/30/2003	2611

6. Youngho created a database named **Events** that contains a table with shoot data named **Shoot Events**. The **Shoot** table you created has the same format as the **Shoot Events** table. Copy all the records from the **Shoot Events** table in the **Events** database (located in the Cases folder on your Data Disk) to the end of the **Shoot** table in the **Videos** database.

7. Modify the structure of the **Shoot** table by completing the following:

   a. Delete the Contact field.

   b. Move the ShootDate field so that it appears between the ShootType and ShootTime fields.

8. Switch to Datasheet view and resize all columns in the datasheet for the **Shoot** table to their best fit.

9. Use the **Shoot** datasheet to update the database as follows:

   a. For Shoot# 421032, change the ShootTime value to 7:00 PM, and change the Location value to Le Bistro.

   b. Add a record to the **Shoot** datasheet with the following field values:
   Shoot#:   913032
   ShootType: SE
   ShootDate: 9/13/2003
   ShootTime: 1:00 PM
   Duration: 2.5
   Location: High School football field
   Contract#:   2501

10. Switch to Design view, and then switch back to Datasheet view so that the records appear in primary key sequence by Shoot#. Resize any datasheet columns to their best fit, as necessary.

11. Print the **Shoot** table datasheet, and then save and close the table.

Explore   12. Create a table named **ShootDesc**, based on the data shown in Figure 2-38 and according to the following steps:

Figure 2-38

ShootType	ShootDesc
AP	Anniversary Party
BM	Bar/Bat Mitzvah
BP	Birthday Party
CP	Insurance Commercial Property
DR	Dance Recital
GR	Graduation
HP	Insurance Home Property
LS	Legal Services
RC	Religious Ceremony
SE	Sports Event
WE	Wedding

   a. Select the Datasheet View option in the New Table dialog box.

   b. Enter the 11 records shown in Figure 2-38. (Do *not* enter the field names at this point.)

   c. Switch to Design view, supply the table name, and then answer "No" if asked if you want to create a primary key.

    d. Type the following field names and set the following properties for the two text fields:

       ShootType

Description:	Primary key
Field Size:	2

       ShootDesc

Description:	Description of shoot
Field Size:	30

    e. Specify the primary key, save the table structure changes, and then switch back to Datasheet view. If you receive any warning messages, answer "Yes" to continue.

    f. Resize both datasheet columns to their best fit; then save, print, and close the datasheet.

  13. Close the **Videos** database, and then exit Access.

Case 2. DineAtHome.course.com Claire Picard uses the **Meals** database to track information about local restaurants and orders placed at the restaurants by the customers of her e-commerce business. You'll help her maintain this database by completing the following:

  1. Make sure your Data Disk is in the appropriate disk drive.

  2. Start Access and open the **Meals** database located in the Cases folder on your Data Disk.

  3. Use Design view to create a table using the table design shown in Figure 2-39.

Figure 2-39

Field Name	Data Type	Description	Field Size	Other Properties
Order#	Number	Primary key	Long Integer	Decimal Places: 0 Default Value: Null
Restaurant#	Number	Foreign key	Long Integer	Decimal Places: 0
OrderAmt	Currency	Total amount of order		Format: Fixed

  4. Specify Order# as the primary key, and then save the table as **Order**.

  5. Add the records shown in Figure 2-40 to the **Order** table.

Figure 2-40

Order#	Restaurant#	OrderAmt
3117	131	155.35
3123	115	45.42
3020	120	85.50

Explore

  6. Modify the structure of the **Order** table by adding a new field between the Restaurant# and OrderAmt fields, with the following properties:

Field Name:	OrderDate
Data Type:	Date/Time
Format:	Long Date

  7. Use the revised **Order** datasheet to update the database as follows:

    a. Enter the following OrderDate values for the three records: 1/15/03 for Order# 3020, 4/2/03 for Order# 3117, and 5/1/03 for Order# 3123.

    b. Add a new record to the **Order** datasheet with the following field values:

Order#:	3045
Restaurant#:	108
OrderDate:	3/16/03
OrderAmt:	50.25

  8. Claire created a database named **Customer** that contains a table with order data named **Order Records**. The **Order** table you created has the same format as the **Order Records** table. Copy all the records from the **Order Records** table in the **Customer** database (located in the Cases folder on your Data Disk) to the end of the **Order** table in the **Meals** database.

9. Resize all columns in the datasheet for the **Order** table to their best fit.

10. For Order# 3039, change the OrderAmt value to 87.30.

11. Delete the record for Order# 3068.

12. Print the **Order** table datasheet, and then save and close the table.

13. Close the **Meals** database, and then exit Access.

Case 3. Redwood Zoo Michael Rosenfeld continues to track information about donors, their pledges, and the status of funds to benefit the Redwood Zoo. Help him maintain the **Redwood** database by completing the following:

1. Make sure your Data Disk is in the appropriate disk drive.

2. Start Access and open the **Redwood** database located in the Cases folder on your Data Disk.

3. Create a table named **Pledge** using the Import Table Wizard. The table you need to import is named **Pledge Records**, which is located in the **Pledge** database in the Cases folder on your Data Disk.

Explore 4. After importing the **Pledge Records** table, use the shortcut menu to rename the table to **Pledge** in the Database window.

Explore 5. Modify the structure of the **Pledge** table by completing the following:

a. Enter the following Description property values:

Pledge#:	Primary key
DonorID:	Foreign key
FundCode:	Foreign key

b. Change the format of the PledgeDate field to mm/dd/yyyy.

c. Change the Data Type of the TotalPledged field to Currency with the Standard format.

d. Specify a Default Value of B for the PaymentMethod field.

e. Specify a Default Value of F for the PaymentSchedule field.

f. Save the modified table structure.

6. Switch to Datasheet view, and then resize all columns in the datasheet to their best fit.

7. Use the **Pledge** datasheet to update the database as follows:

a. Add a new record to the **Pledge** table with the following field values:

Pledge#:	2695
DonorID:	59045
FundCode:	P15
PledgeDate:	7/11/2003
TotalPledged:	1000
PaymentMethod:	B
PaymentSchedule:	M

b. Change the TotalPledged value for Pledge# 2499 to 150.

c. Change the FundCode value for Pledge# 2332 to B03.

8. Print the **Pledge** table datasheet, and then save and close the table.

9. Close the **Redwood** database, and then exit Access.

Case 4. Mountain River Adventures Connor and Siobhan Dempsey use the **Trips** database to track the data about the guided tours they provide. You'll help them maintain this database by completing the following:

1. Make sure your Data Disk is in the appropriate disk drive.

2. Start Access and open the **Trips** database located in the Cases folder on your Data Disk.

Explore 3. Use the Import Spreadsheet Wizard to create a new table named **Rafting Trip**. The data you need to import is contained in the **Rafting** workbook, which is a Microsoft Excel file located in the Cases folder on your Data Disk.

a. Select the Import Table option in the New Table dialog box.

b. Change the entry in the Files of type list box to display the list of Excel workbook files in the Cases folder.

    c. Select the **Rafting** file and then click the Import button.

    d. In the Import Spreadsheet Wizard dialog boxes, choose the Sheet1 worksheet; choose the option for using column headings as field names; select the option for choosing your own primary key; specify Trip# as the primary key; and enter the table name (**Rafting Trip**). Otherwise, accept the Wizard's choices for all other options for the imported data.

4. Open the **Rafting Trip** table and resize all datasheet columns to their best fit.

5. Modify the structure of the **Rafting Trip** table by completing the following:

    a. For the Trip# field, enter a Description property of "Primary key", change the Field Size to Long Integer, and set the Decimal Places property to 0.

    b. For the River field, change the Field Size to 45.

    c. For the TripDistance field, enter a Description property of "Distance in miles", change the Field Size to Integer, and set the Decimal Places property to 0.

    d. For the TripDays field, enter a Description property of "Number of days for the trip", and change the Field Size to Single.

    e. For the Fee/Person field, change the Data Type to Currency and set the Format property to Fixed.

    f. Save the table structure. If you receive any warning messages about lost data or integrity rules, click the Yes button.

6. Use the **Rafting Trip** datasheet to update the database as follows:

    a. For Trip# 3142, change the TripDistance value to 20.

    b. Add a new record to the **Rafting Trip** table with the following field values:

Trip#:	3675
River:	Colorado River (Grand Canyon)
TripDistance:	110
TripDays:	2.5
Fee/Person:	215

    c. Delete the record for Trip# 3423.

7. Print the **Rafting Trip** table datasheet, and then close the table.

8. Use Design view to create a new table named **Booking** using the table design shown in Figure 2-41.

Figure 2-41

Field Name	Data Type	Description	Field Size	Other Properties
Booking#	Number	Primary key	Long Integer	Decimal Places: 0 Default Value: Null
Client#	Number	Foreign key	Integer	Decimal Places: 0
TripDate	Date/Time			Format: Short Date
Trip#	Number	Foreign key	Long Integer	Decimal Places: 0
People	Number	Number of people in the group	Byte	Decimal Places: 0

9. Specify Booking# as the primary key, and then save the table as **Booking**.

10. Add the records shown in Figure 2-42 to the **Booking** table.

Figure 2-42

Booking#	Client#	TripDate	Trip#	People
410	330	6/5/03	3529	4
403	315	7/1/03	3107	7
411	311	7/5/03	3222	5

11. Connor created a database named **Groups** that contains a table with booking data named **Group Info**. The **Booking** table you created has the same format as the **Group Info** table. Copy all the records from the **Group Info** table in the **Groups** database (located in the Cases folder on your Data Disk) to the end of the **Booking** table in the **Trips** database.

12. Resize all columns in the **Booking** datasheet to their best fit.

13. Print the **Booking** datasheet, and then save and close the table.

14. Close the **Trips** database, and then exit Access.

INTERNET ASSIGNMENTS

Student Union

The purpose of the Internet Assignments is to challenge you to find information on the Internet that you can use to create effective documents. The actual assignments are updated and maintained on the Course Technology Web site. Log on to the Internet and use your Web browser to go to the Student Union on the New Perspectives Series site at **www.course.com/NewPerspectives/studentunion**. Click the Online Companions link, and then click the link for this text.

QUICK CHECK ANSWERS

Session 2.1

1. Identify all the fields needed to produce the required information, group related fields into tables, determine each table's primary key, include a common field in related tables, avoid data redundancy, and determine the properties of each field.

2. The Data Type property determines what field values you can enter for the field and what other properties the field will have.

3. text, number, and AutoNumber fields

4. F6

5. Format

6. null

Session 2.2

1. the record being edited; the next row available for a new record

2. The field and all its values are removed from the table.

3. In Design view, right-click the row selector for the row above which you want to insert the field, click Insert Rows on the shortcut menu, and then define the new field.

4. yes/no

5. Make sure the database into which you want to import a table is open, click the File menu, point to Get External Data, and then click Import; or, click the New button in the Database window, click Import Table in the New Table dialog box, and then click the OK button.

6. In navigation mode, the entire field value is selected, and anything you type replaces the field value; in editing mode, you can insert or delete characters in a field value based on the location of the insertion point.

OBJECTIVES

In this tutorial you will:

- Learn how to use the Query window in Design view

- Create, run, and save queries

- Update data using a query

- Define a relationship between two tables

- Sort data in a query

- Filter data in a query

- Specify an exact match condition in a query

- Change a datasheet's appearance

- Use a comparison operator to match a range of values

- Use the And and Or logical operators

- Use multiple undo and redo

- Perform calculations in a query using calculated fields, aggregate functions, and record group calculations

QUERYING A DATABASE

Retrieving Information About Employers and Their Positions

CASE

Northeast Seasonal Jobs International (NSJI)

At a recent company meeting, Elsa Jensen and other NSJI employees discussed the importance of regularly monitoring the business activity of the company's employer clients. For example, Zack Ward and his marketing staff track employer activity to develop new strategies for promoting NSJI's services. Matt Griffin, the manager of recruitment, needs to track information about available positions, so that he can find student recruits to fill those positions. In addition, Elsa is interested in analyzing other aspects of the business, such as the wage amounts paid for different positions at different employers. All of these informational needs can be satisfied by queries that retrieve information from the Northeast database.

SESSION 3.1

In this session, you will use the Query window in Design view to create, run, and save queries; update data using a query; define a one-to-many relationship between two tables; sort data with a toolbar button and in Design view; and filter data in a query datasheet.

Introduction to Queries

As you learned in Tutorial 1, a query is a question you ask about data stored in a database. For example, Zack might create a query to find records in the Employer table for only those employers located in a specific state or province. When you create a query, you tell Access which fields you need and what criteria Access should use to select the records.

Access provides powerful query capabilities that allow you to:

- display selected fields and records from a table
- sort records
- perform calculations
- generate data for forms, reports, and other queries
- update data in the tables in a database
- find and display data from two or more tables

Most questions about data are generalized queries in which you specify the fields and records you want Access to select. These common requests for information, such as "Which employers are located in Quebec?" or "How many waiter/waitress positions are available?" are called **select queries**. The answer to a select query is returned in the form of a datasheet. The result of a query is also referred to as a **recordset**, because the query produces a set of records that answers your question.

More specialized, technical queries, such as finding duplicate records in a table, are best formulated using a Query Wizard. A Query Wizard prompts you for information by asking a series of questions and then creates the appropriate query based on your answers. In Tutorial 1, you used the Simple Query Wizard to display only some of the fields in the Employer table; Access provides other Query Wizards for more complex queries. For common, informational queries, it is easier for you to design your own query than to use a Query Wizard.

Zack wants you to create a query to display the employer ID, employer name, city, contact first name, contact last name, and Web site information for each record in the Employer table. He needs this information for a market analysis his staff is completing on NSJI's employer clients. You'll open the Query window to create the query for Zack.

Query Window

You use the Query window in Design view to create a query. In Design view, you specify the data you want to view by constructing a query by example. When you use **query by example (QBE)**, you give Access an example of the information you are requesting. Access then retrieves the information that precisely matches your example.

For Zack's query, you need to display data from the Employer table. You'll begin by starting Access, opening the Northeast database, and displaying the Query window in Design view.

To start Access, open the Northeast database, and open the Query window in Design view:

1. Place your Data Disk in the appropriate disk drive.

2. Start Access and open the **Northeast** database located in the Tutorial folder on your Data Disk. The Northeast database is displayed in the Database window.

3. Click **Queries** in the Objects bar of the Database window, and then click the **New** button. The New Query dialog box opens. See Figure 3-1.

Figure 3-1	NEW QUERY DIALOG BOX

You'll design your own query instead of using a Query Wizard.

4. If necessary, click **Design View** in the list box.

5. Click the **OK** button. Access opens the Show Table dialog box on top of the Query window. (Note that you could also have double-clicked the "Create query in Design view" option in the Database window.) Notice that the title bar of the Query window shows that you are creating a select query.

The query you are creating will retrieve data from the Employer table, so you need to add this table to the Select Query window.

6. Click **Employer** in the Tables list box (if necessary), click the **Add** button, and then click the **Close** button. Access places the Employer table's field list in the Select Query window and closes the Show Table dialog box.

To display more of the fields you'll be using for creating queries, you'll maximize the Select Query window.

7. Click the **Maximize** button ☐ on the Select Query window title bar. See Figure 3-2.

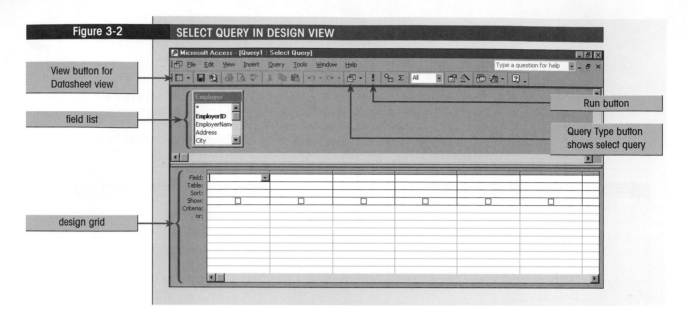

Figure 3-2 — SELECT QUERY IN DESIGN VIEW

In Design view, the Select Query window contains the standard title bar, the menu bar, the status bar, and the Query Design toolbar. On the toolbar, the Query Type button shows a select query; the icon on this button changes according to the type of query you are creating. The title bar on the Select Query window displays the query type (Select Query) and the default query name (Query1). You'll change the default query name to a more meaningful one later when you save the query.

The Select Query window in Design view contains a field list and the design grid. The **field list** contains the fields for the table you are querying. The table name appears at the top of the list box, and the fields are listed in the order in which they appear in the table. You can scroll the field list to see more fields; or, you can expand the field list to display all the fields and the complete field names by resizing the field list box.

In the **design grid**, you include the fields and record selection criteria for the information you want to see. Each column in the design grid contains specifications about a field you will use in the query. You can choose a single field for your query by dragging its name from the field list to the design grid in the lower portion of the window. Alternatively, you can double-click a field name to place it in the next available design grid column.

When you are constructing a query, you can see the query results at any time by clicking the View button or the Run button on the Query Design toolbar. In response, Access displays the datasheet, which contains the set of fields and records that results from answering, or **running**, the query. The order of the fields in the datasheet is the same as the order of the fields in the design grid. Although the datasheet looks just like a table datasheet and appears in Datasheet view, a query datasheet is temporary, and its contents are based on the criteria you establish in the design grid. In contrast, a table datasheet shows the permanent data in a table. However, you can update data while viewing a query datasheet, just as you can when working in a table datasheet or form.

If the query you are creating includes every field from the specified table, you can use one of the following three methods to transfer all the fields from the field list to the design grid:

■ Click and drag each field individually from the field list to the design grid. Use this method if you want the fields in your query to appear in an order that is different from the order in the field list.

- Double-click the asterisk in the field list. Access places the table name followed by a period and an asterisk (as in "Employer.*") in the design grid, which signifies that the order of the fields will be the same in the query as it is in the field list. Use this method if you don't need to sort the query or specify conditions for the records you want to select. The advantage of using this method is that you do not need to change the query if you add or delete fields from the underlying table structure. Such changes are reflected automatically in the query.

- Double-click the field list title bar to highlight all the fields, and then click and drag one of the highlighted fields to the design grid. Access places each field in a separate column and arranges the fields in the order in which they appear in the field list. Use this method when you need to sort your query or include record selection criteria.

Now you'll create and run Zack's query to display selected fields from the Employer table.

Creating and Running a Query

The default table datasheet displays all the fields in the table, in the same order as they appear in the table. In contrast, a query datasheet can display selected fields from a table, and the order of the fields can be different from that of the table.

Zack wants the Employer table's EmployerID, EmployerName, City, ContactFirstName, ContactLastName, and WebSite fields to appear in the query results. You'll add each of these fields to the design grid.

To select the fields for the query, and then run the query:

1. Drag **EmployerID** from the Employer field list to the design grid's first column Field text box, and then release the mouse button. See Figure 3-3.

Figure 3-3	FIELD ADDED TO THE DESIGN GRID

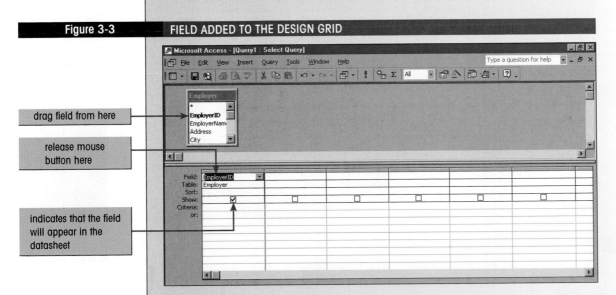

In the design grid's first column, the field name EmployerID appears in the Field text box, the table name Employer appears in the Table text box, and the check mark in the Show check box indicates that the field will be displayed in the datasheet when you run the query. Sometimes you might not want to display a field and its values in the query results. For example, if you are creating a query to show all employers located in Massachusetts, and you assign the name "Employers in Massachusetts" to the query, you do not need to include the State/Prov field value for each record in the query results—every State/Prov field value would be "MA" for Massachusetts. Even if you choose not to include a field in the display of the query results, you can still use the field as part of the query to select specific records or to specify a particular sequence for the records in the datasheet.

2. Double-click **EmployerName** in the Employer field list. Access adds this field to the second column of the design grid.

3. Scrolling the Employer field list as necessary, repeat Step 2 for the **City**, **ContactFirstName**, **ContactLastName**, and **WebSite** fields to add these fields to the design grid in that order.

TROUBLE? If you double-click the wrong field and accidentally add it to the design grid, you can remove the field from the grid. Select the field's column by clicking the pointer ↓ on the bar above the Field text box for the field you want to delete, and then press the Delete key (or click Edit on the menu bar, and then click Delete Columns).

Having selected the fields for Zack's query, you now can run the query.

4. Click the **Run** button ❗ on the Query Design toolbar. Access runs the query and displays the results in Datasheet view. See Figure 3-4.

Figure 3-4	DATASHEET DISPLAYED AFTER RUNNING THE QUERY

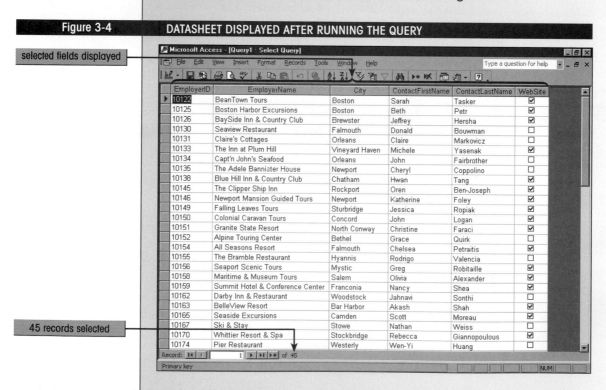

The six fields you added to the design grid appear in the datasheet, and the records are displayed in primary key sequence by EmployerID. Access selected a total of 45 records for display in the datasheet.

Zack asks you to save the query as "Employer Analysis" so that he can easily retrieve the same data again.

5. Click the **Save** button 🖫 on the Query Datasheet toolbar. The Save As dialog box opens.

6. Type **Employer Analysis** in the Query Name text box, and then press the **Enter** key. Access saves the query with the specified name in the Northeast database on your Data Disk and displays the name in the title bar.

When viewing the results of the query, Zack noticed a couple of changes that need to be made to the data in the Employer table. The Adele Bannister House recently developed a Web site, so the WebSite field for this record needs to be updated. In addition, the contact information has changed for the Alpine Touring Center.

Updating Data Using a Query

Although a query datasheet is temporary and its contents are based on the criteria in the query design grid, you can update the data in a table using a query datasheet. In this case, Zack has changes he wants you to make to records in the Employer table. Instead of making the changes in the table datasheet, you can make them in the Employer Analysis query datasheet. The underlying Employer table will be updated with the changes you make.

To update data using the Employer Analysis query datasheet:

1. For the record with EmployerID 10135 (The Adele Bannister House), click the check box in the WebSite field to place a check mark in it.

2. For the record with EmployerID 10152 (Alpine Touring Center), change the ContactFirstName field value to **Mary** and change the ContactLastName field value to **Grant**.

3. Click the **Close Window** button ☒ on the menu bar to close the query. Note that the Employer Analysis query appears in the list of queries.

4. Click the **Restore Window** button 🗗 on the menu bar to return the Database window to its original size.

Now you will check the Employer table to verify that the changes you made in the query datasheet were also made to the Employer table records.

5. Click **Tables** in the Objects bar of the Database window, click **Employer** in the list of tables, and then click the **Open** button. The Employer table datasheet opens.

6. For the record with EmployerID 10135, scroll the datasheet to the right to verify that the WebSite field contains a check mark. For the record with EmployerID 10152, scroll to the right to see the new contact information (Mary Grant).

7. Click the **Close** button ☒ on the Employer table window to close it.

Matt also wants to view specific information in the Northeast database. However, he needs to see data from both the Employer table and the Position table at the same time. To view data from two tables at the same time, you need to define a relationship between the tables.

Defining Table Relationships

One of the most powerful features of a relational database management system is its ability to define relationships between tables. You use a common field to relate one table to another. The process of relating tables is often called performing a **join**. When you join tables that have a common field, you can extract data from them as if they were one larger table. For example, you can join the Employer and Position tables by using the EmployerID field in both tables as the common field. Then you can use a query, a form, or a report to extract selected data from each table, even though the data is contained in two separate tables, as shown in Figure 3-5. In the Positions query shown in Figure 3-5, the PositionID, PositionTitle, and Wage columns are fields from the Position table, and the EmployerName and State/Prov columns are fields from the Employer table. The joining of records is based on the common field of EmployerID. The Employer and Position tables have a type of relationship called a one-to-many relationship.

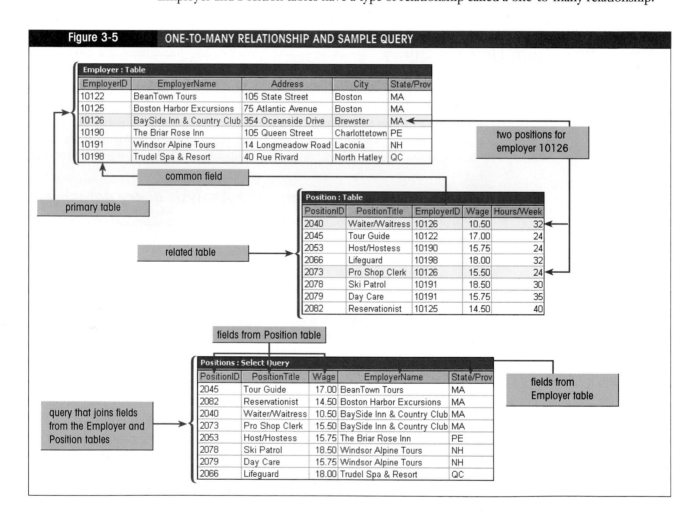

Figure 3-5   ONE-TO-MANY RELATIONSHIP AND SAMPLE QUERY

One-to-Many Relationships

A **one-to-many relationship** exists between two tables when one record in the first table matches zero, one, or many records in the second table, and when one record in the second table matches exactly one record in the first table. For example, as shown in Figure 3-5, employers 10126 and 10191 each have two available positions, and employers 10122, 10125, 10190, and 10198 each have one available position. Every position has a single matching employer.

Access refers to the two tables that form a relationship as the primary table and the related table. The **primary table** is the "one" table in a one-to-many relationship; in Figure 3-5, the Employer table is the primary table because there is only one employer for each available position. The **related table** is the "many" table; in Figure 3-5, the Position table is the related table because there can be many positions offered by each employer.

Because related data is stored in two tables, inconsistencies between the tables can occur. Consider the following scenarios:

- Matt adds a position record to the Position table for a new employer, Glen Cove Inn, using EmployerID 10132. Matt did not first add the new employer's information to the Employer table, so this position does not have a matching record in the Employer table. The data is inconsistent, and the position record is considered to be an **orphaned** record.

- Matt changes the EmployerID in the Employer table for BaySide Inn & Country Club from 10126 to 10128. Two orphaned records for employer 10126 now exist in the Position table, and the database is inconsistent.

- Matt deletes the record for Boston Harbor Excursions, employer 10125, in the Employer table because this employer is no longer an NSJI client. The database is again inconsistent; one record for employer 10125 in the Position table has no matching record in the Employer table.

You can avoid these problems by specifying referential integrity between tables when you define their relationships.

Referential Integrity

Referential integrity is a set of rules that Access enforces to maintain consistency between related tables when you update data in a database. Specifically, the referential integrity rules are as follows:

- When you add a record to a related table, a matching record must already exist in the primary table, thereby preventing the possibility of orphaned records.

- If you attempt to change the value of the primary key in the primary table, Access prevents this change if matching records exist in a related table. However, if you choose the **cascade updates** option, Access permits the change in value to the primary key and changes the appropriate foreign key values in the related table, thereby eliminating the possibility of inconsistent data.

- When you delete a record in the primary table, Access prevents the deletion if matching records exist in a related table. However, if you choose the **cascade deletes** option, Access deletes the record in the primary table and also deletes all records in related tables that have matching foreign key values.

Now you'll define a one-to-many relationship between the Employer and Position tables so that you can use fields from both tables to create a query that will retrieve the information Matt needs. You will also define a one-to-many relationship between the NAICS (primary) table and the Employer (related) table.

Defining a Relationship Between Two Tables

When two tables have a common field, you can define a relationship between them in the Relationships window. The **Relationships window** illustrates the relationships among a database's tables. In this window, you can view or change existing relationships, define new relationships between tables, and rearrange the layout of the tables in the window.

You need to open the Relationships window and define the relationship between the Employer and Position tables. You'll define a one-to-many relationship between the two tables, with Employer as the primary table and Position as the related table, and with EmployerID as the common field (the primary key in the Employer table and a foreign key in the Position table). You'll also define a one-to-many relationship between the NAICS and Employer tables, with NAICS as the primary table and Employer as the related table, and with NAICSCode as the common field (the primary key in the NAICS table and a foreign key in the Employer table).

To define the one-to-many relationship between the Employer and Position tables:

1. Click the **Relationships** button [icon] on the Database toolbar. The Show Table dialog box opens on top of the Relationships window. See Figure 3-6.

| Figure 3-6 | SHOW TABLE DIALOG BOX |

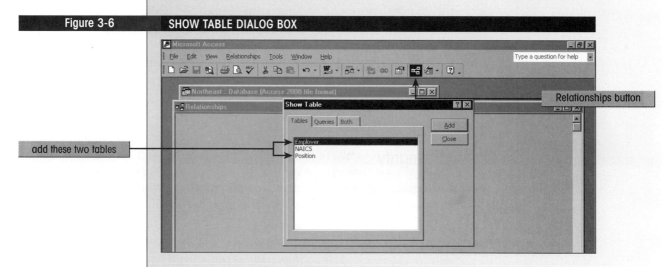

You must add each table participating in a relationship to the Relationships window.

2. Click **Employer** (if necessary), and then click the **Add** button. The Employer field list is added to the Relationships window.

3. Click **Position**, and then click the **Add** button. The Position field list is added to the Relationships window.

4. Click the **Close** button in the Show Table dialog box to close it and reveal the entire Relationships window.

To form the relationship between the two tables, you drag the common field of EmployerID from the primary table to the related table. Then Access opens the Edit Relationships dialog box, in which you select the relationship options for the two tables.

5. Click **EmployerID** in the Employer field list, and drag it to **EmployerID** in the Position field list. When you release the mouse button, the Edit Relationships dialog box opens. See Figure 3-7.

Figure 3-7	EDIT RELATIONSHIPS DIALOG BOX

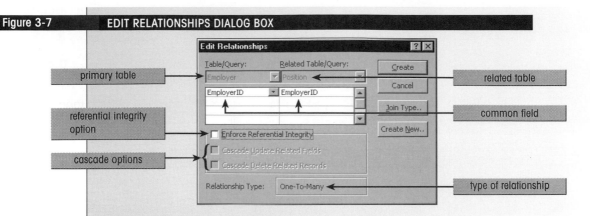

primary table

related table

referential integrity option

common field

cascade options

type of relationship

The primary table, related table, and common field appear at the top of the dialog box. The type of relationship, One-To-Many, appears at the bottom of the dialog box. When you click the Enforce Referential Integrity check box, the two cascade options become available. If you select the Cascade Update Related Fields option, Access will change the appropriate foreign key values in the related table when you change a primary key value in the primary table. If you select the Cascade Delete Related Records option, when you delete a record in the primary table, Access will delete all records in the related table that have a matching foreign key value.

6. Click the **Enforce Referential Integrity** check box, click the **Cascade Update Related Fields** check box, and then click the **Cascade Delete Related Records** check box. **Note:** You should select this option with caution because you might inadvertently delete records you do not want deleted.

7. Click the **Create** button to define the one-to-many relationship between the two tables and to close the dialog box. The completed relationship appears in the Relationships window. See Figure 3-8.

Figure 3-8	DEFINED RELATIONSHIP IN THE RELATIONSHIPS WINDOW

"one" side of the relationship

"many" side of the relationship

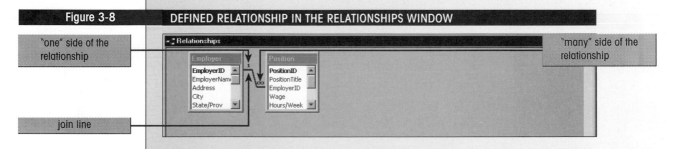

join line

The **join line** connects the EmployerID fields, which are common to the two tables. The common field joins the two tables, which have a one-to-many relationship. The "one" side of the relationship has the digit 1 at its end, and the "many" side of the relationship has the infinity symbol ∞ at its end. The two tables are still separate tables, but you can use the data in them as if they were one table.

Now you need to define the one-to-many relationship between the NAICS and Employer tables. In this relationship, NAICS is the primary ("one") table because there is only one code for each employer. Employer is the related ("many") table because there are multiple employers with the same NAICS code.

To define the one-to-many relationship between the NAICS and Employer tables:

1. Click the **Show Table** button  on the Relationship toolbar. The Show Table dialog box opens on top of the Relationships window.

2. Click **NAICS** in the list of tables, click the **Add** button, and then click the **Close** button to close the Show Table dialog box. The NAICS field list appears in the Relationships window to the right of the Position field list. To make it easier to define the relationship, you'll move the NAICS field list below the Employer and Position field lists.

3. Click the NAICS field list title bar and drag the list until it is below the Position table (see Figure 3-9), and then release the mouse button.

4. Scroll the Employer field list until the NAICSCode field is visible. Because the NAICS table is the primary table in this relationship, you need to drag the NAICSCode field from the NAICS field list to the Employer field list. Notice that the NAICSCode field in the NAICS table appears in a bold font; this indicates that the field is the table's primary key. On the other hand, the NAICSCode field in the Employer table is not bold, which is a reminder that this field is the foreign key in this table.

5. Click and drag the **NAICSCode** field in the NAICS field list to the **NAICSCode** field in the Employer field list. When you release the mouse button, the Edit Relationships dialog box opens.

6. Click the **Enforce Referential Integrity** check box, click the **Cascade Update Related Fields** check box, and then click the **Cascade Delete Related Records** check box. You now have selected all the necessary relationship options.

7. Click the **Create** button to define the one-to-many relationship between the two tables and close the dialog box. The completed relationship appears in the Relationships window. See Figure 3-9.

Figure 3-9	BOTH RELATIONSHIPS DEFINED

With both relationships defined, you have connected the data among the three tables in the Northeast database.

8. Click the **Save** button on the Relationship toolbar to save the layout in the Relationships window.

9. Click the **Close** button on the Relationships window title bar. The Relationships window closes, and you return to the Database window.

Creating a Multi-table Query

Now that you have joined the Employer and Position tables, you can create a query to produce the information Matt wants. To help him determine his recruiting needs, Matt wants a query that displays the EmployerName, City, and State/Prov fields from the Employer table and the Openings, PositionTitle, StartDate, and EndDate fields from the Position table.

To create, run, and save the query using the Employer and Position tables:

1. Click **Queries** in the Objects bar of the Database window, and then double-click **Create query in Design view**. The Show Table dialog box opens on top of the Query window in Design view.

   You need to add the Employer and Position tables to the Query window.

2. Click **Employer** in the Tables list box (if necessary), click the **Add** button, click **Position**, click the **Add** button, and then click the **Close** button. The Employer and Position field lists appear in the Query window, and the Show Table dialog box closes. Note that the one-to-many relationship that exists between the two tables is shown in the Query window. Also, notice that the join line is thick at both ends; this signifies that you selected the option to enforce referential integrity. If you had not selected this option, the join line would be thin at both ends and neither the "1" nor the infinity symbol would appear, even though there is a one-to-many relationship between the two tables.

   You need to place the EmployerName, City, and State/Prov fields from the Employer field list into the design grid, and then place the Openings, PositionTitle, StartDate, and EndDate fields from the Position field list into the design grid.

3. Double-click **EmployerName** in the Employer field list to place EmployerName in the design grid's first column Field text box.

4. Repeat Step 3 to add the **City** and **State/Prov** fields from the Employer table, so that these fields are placed in the second and third columns of the design grid.

5. Repeat Step 3 to add the **Openings**, **PositionTitle**, **StartDate**, and **EndDate** fields (in that order) from the Position table, so that these fields are placed in the fourth through seventh columns of the design grid.

   The query specifications are completed, so you now can run the query.

6. Click the **Run** button [!] on the Query Design toolbar. Access runs the query and displays the results in the datasheet.

7. Click the **Maximize** button [□] on the Query window title bar. See Figure 3-10.

Figure 3-10   DATASHEET FOR THE QUERY BASED ON THE EMPLOYER AND POSITION TABLES

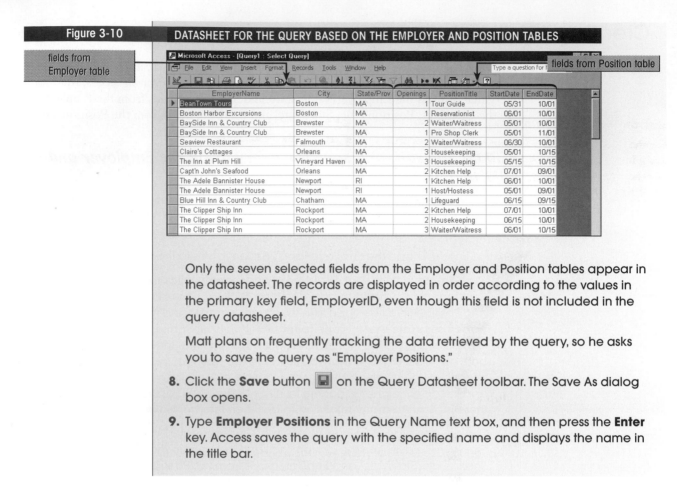

fields from Employer table

fields from Position table

Only the seven selected fields from the Employer and Position tables appear in the datasheet. The records are displayed in order according to the values in the primary key field, EmployerID, even though this field is not included in the query datasheet.

Matt plans on frequently tracking the data retrieved by the query, so he asks you to save the query as "Employer Positions."

8. Click the **Save** button 🖫 on the Query Datasheet toolbar. The Save As dialog box opens.

9. Type **Employer Positions** in the Query Name text box, and then press the **Enter** key. Access saves the query with the specified name and displays the name in the title bar.

Matt decides he wants the records displayed in alphabetical order by employer name. Because the query displays data in order by the field value of EmployerID, which is the primary key for the Employer table, you need to sort the records by EmployerName to display the data in the order Matt wants.

Sorting Data in a Query

Sorting is the process of rearranging records in a specified order or sequence. Sometimes you might need to sort data before displaying or printing it to meet a specific request. For example, Matt might want to review position information arranged by the StartDate field because he needs to know which positions are available earliest in the year. On the other hand, Elsa might want to view position information arranged by the Openings field for each employer, because she monitors employer activity for NSJI.

When you sort data in a query, you do not change the sequence of the records in the underlying tables. Only the records in the query datasheet are rearranged according to your specifications.

To sort records, you must select the **sort key**, which is the field used to determine the order of records in the datasheet. In this case, Matt wants the data sorted by the employer name, so you need to specify the EmployerName field as the sort key. Sort keys can be text, number, date/time, currency, AutoNumber, yes/no, or Lookup Wizard fields, but not memo, OLE object, or hyperlink fields. You sort records in either ascending (increasing) or descending (decreasing) order. Figure 3-11 shows the results of each type of sort for different data types.

Figure 3-11	SORTING RESULTS FOR DIFFERENT DATA TYPES	
DATA TYPE	**ASCENDING SORT RESULTS**	**DESCENDING SORT RESULTS**
Text	A to Z	Z to A
Number	lowest to highest numeric value	highest to lowest numeric value
Date/Time	oldest to most recent date	most recent to oldest date
Currency	lowest to highest numeric value	highest to lowest numeric value
AutoNumber	lowest to highest numeric value	highest to lowest numeric value
Yes/No	yes (check mark in check box) then no values	no then yes values

Access provides several methods for sorting data in a table or query datasheet and in a form. One method, clicking a toolbar sort button, lets you sort the displayed records quickly.

Using a Toolbar Button to Sort Data

The **Sort Ascending** and **Sort Descending** buttons on the toolbar allow you to sort records immediately, based on the values in the selected field. First you select the column on which you want to base the sort, and then you click the appropriate sort button on the toolbar to rearrange the records in either ascending or descending order. Unless you save the datasheet or form after you've sorted the records, the rearrangement of records is temporary.

Recall that in Tutorial 1 you used the Sort Ascending button to sort query results by the State/Prov field. You'll use this same button to sort the Employer Positions query results by the EmployerName field.

To sort the records using a toolbar sort button:

1. Click any visible EmployerName field value to establish the field as the current field (if necessary).

2. Click the **Sort Ascending** button 📊 on the Query Datasheet toolbar. The records are rearranged in ascending order by employer name. See Figure 3-12.

Figure 3-12	SORTING RECORDS ON A SINGLE FIELD IN A DATASHEET

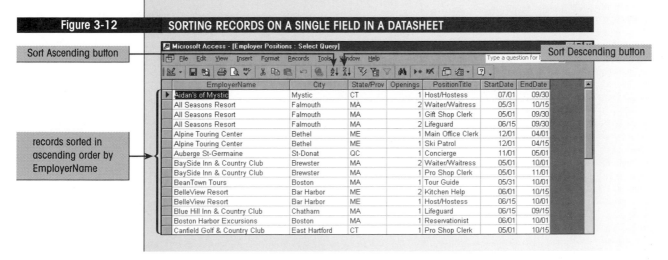

Sort Ascending button

Sort Descending button

records sorted in ascending order by EmployerName

After viewing the query results, Matt decides that he'd prefer to see the records arranged by the value in the PositionTitle field, so that he can identify the types of positions he needs to fill. He also wants to display the records in descending order according to the value of the Openings field, so that he can easily see how many openings there are for each position. To do this you need to sort using two fields.

Sorting Multiple Fields in Design View

Sort keys can be unique or nonunique. A sort key is **unique** if the value of the sort key field for each record is different. The EmployerID field in the Employer table is an example of a unique sort key because each employer record has a different value in this field. A sort key is **nonunique** if more than one record can have the same value for the sort key field. For example, the PositionTitle field in the Position table is a nonunique sort key because more than one record can have the same PositionTitle value.

When the sort key is nonunique, records with the same sort key value are grouped together, but they are not in a specific order within the group. To arrange these grouped records in a specific order, you can specify a **secondary sort key**, which is a second sort key field. The first sort key field is called the **primary sort key**. Note that the primary sort key is *not* the same as a table's primary key field. A table has at most one primary key, which must be unique, whereas any field in a table can serve as a primary sort key.

Access lets you select up to 10 different sort keys. When you use the toolbar sort buttons, the sort key fields must be in adjacent columns in the datasheet. You highlight the adjacent columns, and Access sorts first by the first column and then by each other highlighted column in order from left to right.

Matt wants the records sorted first by the PositionTitle field and then by the Openings field. The two fields are adjacent, but not in the correct left-to-right order, so you cannot use the toolbar buttons to sort them. You could move the Openings field to the right of the PositionTitle field in the query datasheet. However, you can specify only one type of sort—either ascending or descending—for selected columns in the query datasheet. This is not what Matt wants; he wants the PositionTitle field values to be sorted in ascending alphabetical order and the Openings field values to be sorted in descending order.

In this case, you need to specify the sort keys for the query in Design view. Any time you want to sort on multiple fields that are nonadjacent or in the wrong order, but do not want to rearrange the columns in the query datasheet to accomplish the sort, you must specify the sort keys in Design view.

In the Query window in Design view, Access first uses the sort key that is leftmost in the design grid. Therefore, you must arrange the fields you want to sort from left to right in the design grid, with the primary sort key being the leftmost sort key field. In Design view, multiple sort fields do not have to be adjacent to each other, as they do in Datasheet view; however, they must be in the correct left-to-right order.

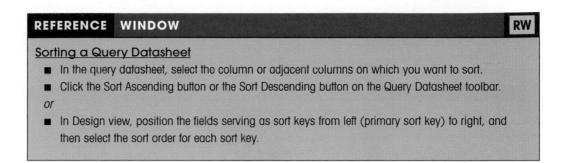

To achieve the results Matt wants, you need to switch to Design view, move the Openings field to the right of the EndDate field, and then specify the sort order for the two fields.

To select the two sort keys in Design view:

1. Click the **View** button for Design view ⬚ on the Query Datasheet toolbar to open the query in Design view.

   First, you'll move the Openings field to the right of the EndDate field. Remember, in Design view, the sort fields do not have to be adjacent, and non-sort key fields can appear between sort key fields. So, you will move the Openings field to the end of the query design, following the EndDate field.

2. If necessary, click the right arrow in the design grid's horizontal scroll bar a few times to scroll to the right so that both the Openings and EndDate fields are completely visible.

3. Position the pointer in the Openings field selector until the pointer changes to a ⬇ shape, and then click to select the field. See Figure 3-13.

Figure 3-13   **SELECTED OPENINGS FIELD**

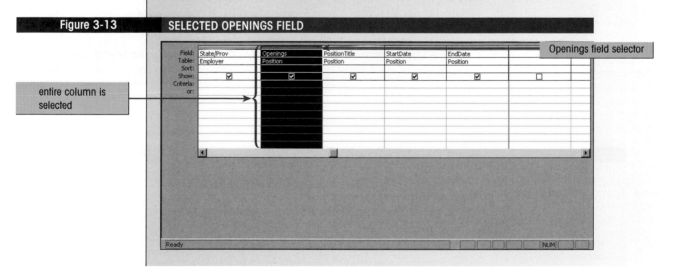

Openings field selector

entire column is selected

4. Position the pointer in the Openings field selector, and then click and drag the pointer ⬚ to the right until the vertical line on the right of the EndDate field is highlighted. See Figure 3-14.

Figure 3-14   **DRAGGING THE FIELD IN THE DESIGN GRID**

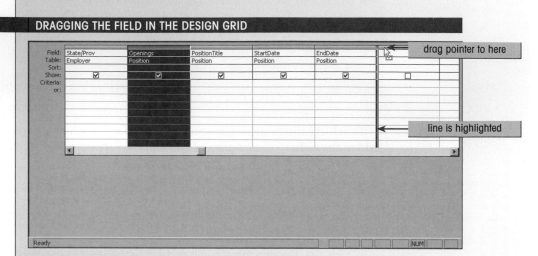

drag pointer to here

line is highlighted

5. Release the mouse button. The Openings field moves to the right of the EndDate field.

The fields are now in the correct order for the sort. Next, you need to specify an ascending sort order for the PositionTitle field and a descending sort order for the Openings field.

6. Click the right side of the **PositionTitle Sort** text box to display the list arrow and the sort options, and then click **Ascending**. You've selected an ascending sort order for the PositionTitle field, which will be the primary sort key. The PositionTitle field is a text field, and an ascending sort order will display the field values in alphabetical order.

7. Click the right side of the **Openings Sort** text box, click **Descending**, and then click in one of the empty text boxes to the right of the Openings field to deselect the setting. You've selected a descending sort order for the Openings field, which will be the secondary sort key, because it appears to the right of the primary sort key (PositionTitle) in the design grid. See Figure 3-15.

Figure 3-15   **SELECTING TWO SORT KEYS IN DESIGN VIEW**

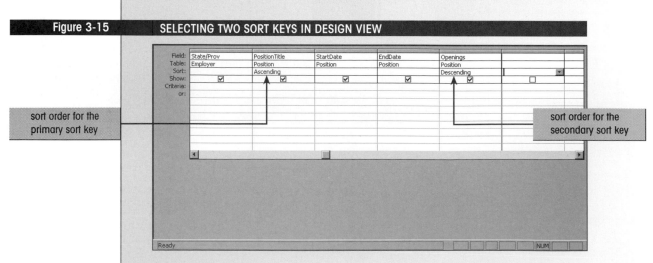

sort order for the
primary sort key

sort order for the
secondary sort key

You have finished your query changes, so now you can run the query and then save the modified query with the same query name.

8. Click the **Run** button ! on the Query Design toolbar. Access runs the query and displays the query datasheet. The records appear in ascending order, based on the values of the PositionTitle field. Within groups of records with the same PositionTitle field value, the records appear in descending order by the values of the Openings field. See Figure 3-16.

Figure 3-16	DATASHEET SORTED ON TWO FIELDS

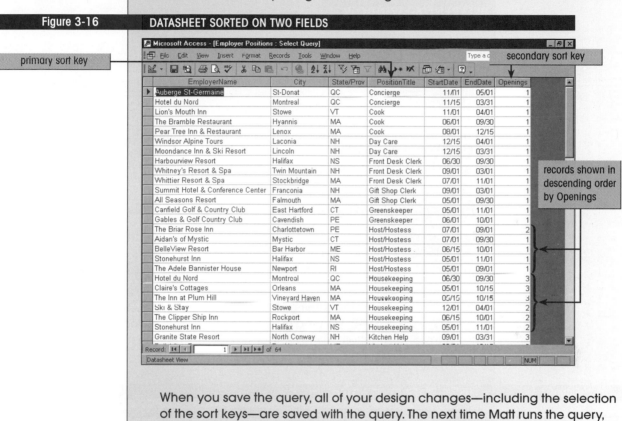

primary sort key

secondary sort key

records shown in descending order by Openings

When you save the query, all of your design changes—including the selection of the sort keys—are saved with the query. The next time Matt runs the query, the records will appear sorted by the primary and secondary sort keys.

9. Click the **Save** button 🖫 on the Query Datasheet toolbar to save the revised Employer Positions query.

Matt wants to concentrate on the positions in the datasheet with a start date sometime in May, to see how many recruits he will need to fill these positions. Selecting only the records with a StartDate field value in May is a temporary change that Matt wants in the datasheet, so you do not need to switch to Design view and change the query. Instead, you can apply a filter.

Filtering Data

A **filter** is a set of restrictions you place on the records in an open datasheet or form to *temporarily* isolate a subset of the records. A filter lets you view different subsets of displayed records so that you can focus on only the data you need. Unless you save a query or form with a filter applied, an applied filter is not available the next time you run the query or open the form.

The simplest technique for filtering records is Filter By Selection. **Filter By Selection** lets you select all or part of a field value in a datasheet or form, and then display only those records that contain the selected value in the field. Another technique for filtering records is to use **Filter By Form**, which changes your datasheet to display empty fields. Then you can select a value from the list arrow that appears when you click any blank field to apply a filter that selects only those records containing that value.

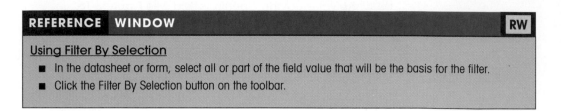

REFERENCE WINDOW   RW

Using Filter By Selection
- In the datasheet or form, select all or part of the field value that will be the basis for the filter.
- Click the Filter By Selection button on the toolbar.

For Matt's request, you need to select just the beginning digits "05" in the StartDate field, to view all the records with a May start date, and then use Filter By Selection to display only those query records with this same partial value.

To display the records using Filter By Selection:

1. In the query datasheet, locate the first occurrence of a May date in the StartDate field, and then select **05** in that field value.

2. Click the **Filter By Selection** button 🦅 on the Query Datasheet toolbar. Access displays the filtered results. Only the 17 query records that have a StartDate field value with the beginning digits "05" appear in the datasheet. The status bar's display (FLTR), the area next to the navigation buttons, and the selected Remove Filter button on the toolbar all indicate that the records have been filtered. See Figure 3-17.

Figure 3-17   USING FILTER BY SELECTION

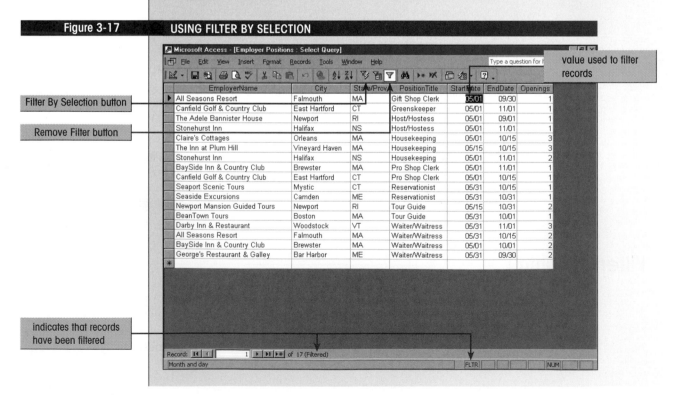

TROUBLE? If you are unable to select only the digits "05" in the StartDate field because the entire field value (including a four-digit year) is displayed when you click in the field, your Windows date settings might be affecting the display of the field values. In this case, you can either read through the remaining steps on this page without completing them, or ask your instructor for assistance.

Next, Matt wants to view only those records with a StartDate value of 05/01, because he needs to fill those positions before the other May positions. So, you need to filter by the complete field value of 05/01.

3. Click in any StartDate field value of **05/01**, and then click ▼⁄. The filtered display now shows only the 9 records with a value of 05/01 in the StartDate field.

Now you can redisplay all the query records by clicking the Remove Filter button; this button works as a toggle to switch between the filtered and nonfiltered displays.

4. Click the **Remove Filter** button ▼ on the Query Datasheet toolbar. Access redisplays all the records in the query datasheet.

5. Click the **Save** button 🖫 on the Query Datasheet toolbar, and then click the **Close Window** button ✕ on the menu bar to save and close the query and return to the Database window.

6. Click the **Restore Window** button 🗗 on the menu bar to return the Database window to its original size.

The queries you've created will help NSJI employees retrieve just the information they want to view. In the next session, you'll continue to create queries to meet their information needs.

Session 3.1 QUICK CHECK

1. What is a select query?

2. Describe the field list and the design grid in the Query window in Design view.

3. How are a table datasheet and a query datasheet similar? How are they different?

4. The _____ is the "one" table in a one-to-many relationship, and the _____ is the "many" table in the relationship.

5. _____ is a set of rules that Access enforces to maintain consistency between related tables when you update data in a database.

6. For a date/time field, how do the records appear when sorted in ascending order?

7. When must you define multiple sort keys in Design view instead of in the query datasheet?

8. A(n) _____ is a set of restrictions you place on the records in an open datasheet or form to isolate a subset of records temporarily.

SESSION 3.2

In this session, you will specify an exact match condition in a query, change a datasheet's appearance, use a comparison operator to match a range of values, use the And and Or logical operators to define multiple selection criteria for queries, use multiple undo and redo, and perform calculations in queries.

Defining Record Selection Criteria for Queries

Matt wants to display employer and position information for all positions with a start date of 07/01, so that he can plan his recruitment efforts accordingly. For this request, you could create a query to select the correct fields and all records in the Employer and Position tables, select a StartDate field value of 07/01 in the query datasheet, and then click the Filter By Selection button to filter the query results to display only those positions starting on July 1. However, a faster way of displaying the data Matt needs is to create a query that displays the selected fields and only those records in the Employer and Position tables that satisfy a condition.

Just as you can display selected fields from a database in a query datasheet, you can display selected records. To tell Access which records you want to select, you must specify a condition as part of the query. A **condition** is a criterion, or rule, that determines which records are selected. To define a condition for a field, you place the condition in the field's Criteria text box in the design grid.

A condition usually consists of an operator, often a comparison operator, and a value. A **comparison operator** asks Access to compare the value in a database field to the condition value and to select all the records for which the relationship is true. For example, the condition >15.00 for the Wage field selects all records in the Position table having Wage field values greater than 15.00. Figure 3-18 shows the Access comparison operators.

Figure 3-18	ACCESS COMPARISON OPERATORS	
OPERATOR	**MEANING**	**EXAMPLE**
=	equal to (optional; default operator)	="Hall"
<	less than	<#1/1/99#
<=	less than or equal to	<=100
>	greater than	>"C400"
>=	greater than or equal to	>=18.75
<>	not equal to	<>"Hall"
Between ... And...	between two values (inclusive)	Between 50 And 325
In ()	in a list of values	In ("Hall", "Seeger")
Like	matches a pattern that includes wildcards	Like "706*"

Specifying an Exact Match

For Matt's request, you need to create a query that will display only those records in the Position table with the value 07/01 in the StartDate field. This type of condition is called an **exact match** because the value in the specified field must match the condition exactly in order for the record to be included in the query results. You'll use the Simple Query Wizard to create the query, and then you'll specify the exact match condition.

To create the query using the Simple Query Wizard:

1. If you took a break after the previous session, make sure that Access is running, the Northeast database is open, and the Queries object Is selected in the Database window.

2. Double-click **Create query by using wizard**. Access opens the first Simple Query Wizard dialog box, in which you select the tables (or queries) and fields for the query.

3. Click the **Tables/Queries** list arrow, and then click **Table: Position**. The fields in the Position table appear in the Available Fields list box. Except for the PositionID and EmployerID fields, you will include all fields from the Position table in the query.

4. Click the >> button. All the fields from the Available Fields list box move to the Selected Fields list box.

5. Scroll up and click **PositionID** in the Selected Fields list box, click the < button to move the PositionID field back to the Available Fields list box, click **EmployerID** in the Selected Fields list box, and then click the < button to move the EmployerID field back to the Available Fields list box.

   Matt also wants certain information from the Employer table included in the query results. Because he wants the fields from the Employer table to appear in the query datasheet to the right of the fields from the Position table fields, you need to click the last field in the Selected Fields list box so that the new Employer fields will be inserted below it In the list.

6. Click **Openings** in the Selected Fields list box.

7. Click the **Tables/Queries** list arrow, and then click **Table: Employer**. The fields in the Employer table now appear in the Available Fields list box. Notice that the fields you selected from the Position table remain in the Selected Fields list box.

8. Click **EmployerName** in the Available Fields list box, and then click the > button to move EmployerName to the Selected Fields list box, below the Openings field.

9. Repeat Step 8 to move the **State/Prov**, **ContactFirstName**, **ContactLastName**, and **Phone** fields into the Selected Fields list box. (Note that you can also double-click a field to move it from the Available Fields list box to the Selected Fields list box.)

10. Click the **Next** button to open the second Simple Query Wizard dialog box, in which you choose whether the query will display records from the selected tables or a summary of those records. Summary options show calculations such as average, minimum, maximum, and so on. Matt wants to view the details for the records, not a summary.

11. Make sure the **Detail (shows every field of every record)** option button is selected, and then click the **Next** button to open the last Simple Query Wizard dialog box, in which you choose a name for the query and complete the Wizard. You need to enter a condition for the query, so you'll want to modify the query's design.

12. Type **July 1 Positions**, click the **Modify the query design** option button, and then click the **Finish** button. Access saves the query as July 1 Positions and opens the query in Design view. See Figure 3-19.

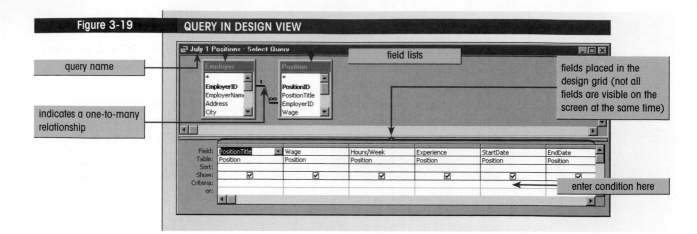

Figure 3-19 — QUERY IN DESIGN VIEW

The field lists for the Employer and Position tables appear in the top portion of the window, and the join line indicating a one-to-many relationship connects the two tables. The selected fields appear in the design grid. Not all of the fields are visible in the grid; to see the other selected fields, you need to scroll to the right using the horizontal scroll bar.

To display the information Matt wants, you need to enter the condition for the StartDate field in its Criteria text box. Matt wants to display only those records with a start date of 07/01.

To enter the exact match condition, and then run the query:

1. Click the **StartDate Criteria** text box, type **7/01**, and then press the **Enter** key. The condition changes to #7/01/2003#.

   TROUBLE? If your date is displayed with a two-digit year, or if it shows a different year, don't worry. You can customize Windows to display different date formats.

   Access automatically placed number signs (#) before and after the condition. You must place date and time values inside number signs when using these values as selection criteria. If you omit the number signs, however, Access will include them automatically.

2. Click the **Run** button ![run] on the Query Design toolbar. Access runs the query and displays the selected field values for only those records with a StartDate field value of 07/01. A total of 9 records are selected and displayed in the datasheet. See Figure 3-20.

   TROUBLE? If your query does not produce the results shown in Figure 3-20, you probably need to specify the year "01" as part of the StartDate criteria. To do so, return to the query in Design view, enter the criteria "7/01/01" for the StartDate, and then repeat Step 2.

| Figure 3-20 | DATASHEET DISPLAYING SELECTED FIELDS AND RECORDS |

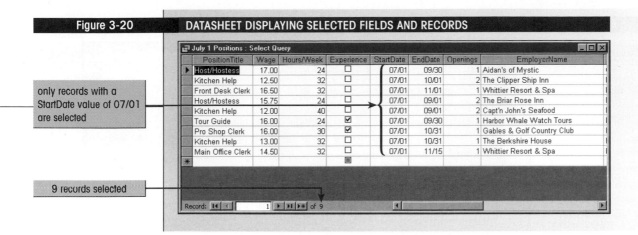

only records with a StartDate value of 07/01 are selected

9 records selected

Matt would like to see more fields and records on the screen at one time. He asks you to maximize the datasheet, change the datasheet's font size, and resize all the columns to their best fit.

Changing a Datasheet's Appearance

You can change the characteristics of a datasheet, including the font type and size of text in the datasheet, to improve its appearance or readability. As you learned in Tutorial 2, you can also resize the datasheet columns to view more columns on the screen at the same time.

You'll maximize the datasheet, change the font size from the default 10 points to 8, and then resize the datasheet columns.

To change the font size and resize columns in the datasheet:

1. Click the **Maximize** button 🔲 on the Query window title bar.

2. Click **Format** on the menu bar, and then click **Font** to open the Font dialog box.

3. Scroll the Size list box, click **8**, and then click the **OK** button. The font size for the entire datasheet changes to 8.

   Next you need to resize the columns to their best fit, so that each column is just wide enough to fit the longest value in the column. Instead of resizing each column individually, as you did in Tutorial 2, you'll select all the columns and resize them at the same time.

4. Position the pointer in the PositionTitle field selector. When the pointer changes to a ⬇ shape, click to select the entire column.

5. Click the right arrow on the horizontal scroll bar until the Phone field is fully visible, and then position the pointer in the Phone field selector until the pointer changes to a ⬇ shape.

6. Press and hold the **Shift** key, and then click the mouse button. All the columns are selected. Now you can resize all of them at once.

7. Position the pointer at the right edge of the Phone field selector until the pointer changes to a ↔ shape. See Figure 3-21.

Figure 3-21   PREPARING TO RESIZE ALL COLUMNS TO THEIR BEST FIT

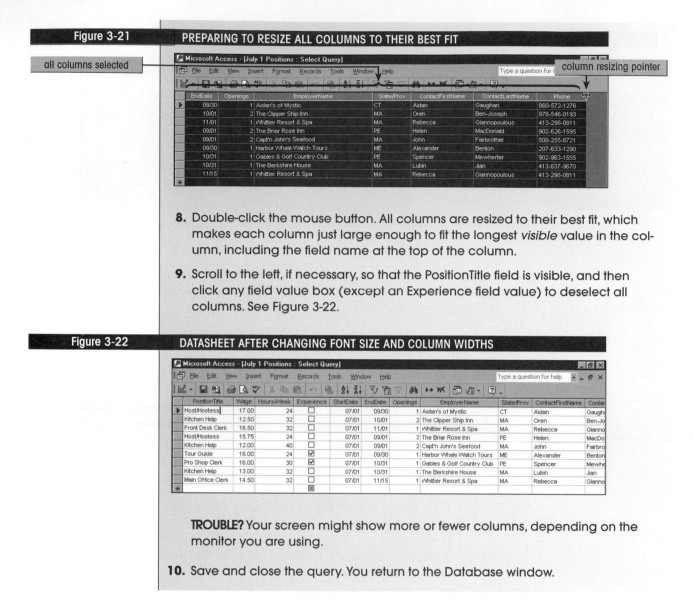

8. Double-click the mouse button. All columns are resized to their best fit, which makes each column just large enough to fit the longest *visible* value in the column, including the field name at the top of the column.

9. Scroll to the left, if necessary, so that the PositionTitle field is visible, and then click any field value box (except an Experience field value) to deselect all columns. See Figure 3-22.

Figure 3-22   DATASHEET AFTER CHANGING FONT SIZE AND COLUMN WIDTHS

TROUBLE? Your screen might show more or fewer columns, depending on the monitor you are using.

10. Save and close the query. You return to the Database window.

After viewing the query results, Matt decides that he would like to see the same fields, but only for those records whose Wage field value is equal to or greater than 17.00. He needs this information when he recruits students who will require a higher wage per hour for the available positions. To create the query needed to produce these results, you need to use a comparison operator to match a range of values—in this case, any Wage value greater than or equal to 17.00.

Using a Comparison Operator to Match a Range of Values

Once you create and save a query, you can click the Open button to run it again, or you can click the Design button to change its design. Because the design of the query you need to create next is similar to the July 1 Positions query, you will change its design, run the query to test it, and then save the query with a new name, which keeps the July 1 Positions query intact.

To change the July 1 Positions query design to create a new query:

1. Click the **July 1 Positions** query in the Database window (if necessary), and then click the **Design** button to open the July 1 Positions query in Design view.

2. Click the **Wage Criteria** text box, type **>=17**, and then press the **Tab** key three times. See Figure 3-23.

Figure 3-23	CHANGING A QUERY'S DESIGN TO CREATE A NEW QUERY

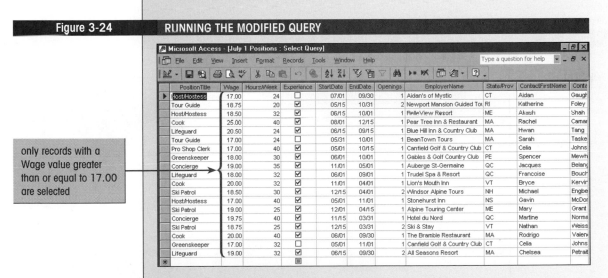

new condition

condition to delete

Matt's new condition specifies that a record will be selected only if its Wage field value is 17.00 or higher. Before you run the query, you need to delete the condition for the StartDate field.

3. With the StartDate field condition highlighted, press the **Delete** key. Now there is no condition for the StartDate field.

4. Click the **Run** button ![run] on the Query Design toolbar. Access runs the query and displays the selected fields for only those records with a Wage field value greater than or equal to 17.00. A total of 19 records are selected. See Figure 3-24.

Figure 3-24	RUNNING THE MODIFIED QUERY

only records with a Wage value greater than or equal to 17.00 are selected

PositionTitle	Wage	Hours/Week	Experience	StartDate	EndDate	Openings	EmployerName	State/Prov	ContactFirstName	Conta
Host/Hostess	17.00	24	☐	07/01	09/30	1	Aidan's of Mystic	CT	Aidan	Gaugh
Tour Guide	18.75	20	☑	05/15	10/31	2	Newport Mansion Guided Tou	RI	Katherine	Foley
Host/Hostess	18.50	32	☑	06/15	10/01	1	BelleView Resort	ME	Akash	Shah
Cook	25.00	40	☑	08/01	12/15	1	Pear Tree Inn & Restaurant	MA	Rachel	Camar
Lifeguard	20.50	24	☑	06/15	09/15	1	Blue Hill Inn & Country Club	MA	Hwan	Tang
Tour Guide	17.00	24	☐	05/31	10/01	1	BeanTown Tours	MA	Sarah	Taske
Pro Shop Clerk	17.00	40	☑	05/01	10/15	1	Canfield Golf & Country Club	CT	Celia	Johns
Greenskeeper	18.00	30	☑	06/01	10/01	1	Gables & Golf Country Club	PE	Spencer	Mewh
Concierge	19.00	35	☑	11/01	05/01	1	Auberge St-Germaine	QC	Jacques	Belang
Lifeguard	18.00	32	☑	06/01	09/01	1	Trudel Spa & Resort	QC	Francoise	Bouch
Cook	20.00	32	☑	11/01	04/01	1	Lion's Mouth Inn	VT	Bryce	Kervir
Ski Patrol	18.50	30	☑	12/15	04/01	2	Windsor Alpine Tours	NH	Michael	Engbe
Host/Hostess	17.00	40	☑	05/01	11/01	1	Stonehurst Inn	NS	Gavin	McDor
Ski Patrol	19.00	25	☑	12/01	04/15	1	Alpine Touring Center	ME	Mary	Grant
Concierge	19.75	40	☑	11/15	03/31	1	Hotel du Nord	QC	Martine	Norma
Ski Patrol	18.75	25	☑	12/15	03/31	2	Ski & Stay	VT	Nathan	Weiss
Cook	20.00	40	☑	06/01	09/30	1	The Bramble Restaurant	MA	Rodrigo	Valen
Greenskeeper	17.00	32	☐	05/01	11/01	1	Canfield Golf & Country Club	CT	Celia	Johns
Lifeguard	19.00	32	☑	06/15	09/30	2	All Seasons Resort	MA	Chelsea	Petrait

So that Matt can display this information again, as necessary, you'll save the query as High Wage Amounts.

5. Click **File** on the menu bar, click the double-arrow at the bottom of the menu to display the full menu (if necessary), and then click **Save As** to open the Save As dialog box.

6. In the text box for the new query name, type **High Wage Amounts**. Notice that the As text box specifies that you are saving the data as a query.

7. Click the **OK** button to save the query using the new name. The new query name appears in the title bar.

8. Close the Query window and return to the Database window.

Elsa asks Matt for a list of the positions with a start date of 07/01 for only the employers in Prince Edward Island. She wants to increase NSJI's business activity throughout eastern Canada (Prince Edward Island in particular), especially in the latter half of the year. To produce this data, you need to create a query containing two conditions—one for the position's start date and another to specify only the employers in Prince Edward Island (PE).

Defining **Multiple Selection Criteria for Queries**

Multiple conditions require you to use **logical operators** to combine two or more conditions. When you want a record selected only if two or more conditions are met, you need to use the **And logical operator**. In this case, Elsa wants to see only those records with a StartDate field value of 07/01 *and* a State/Prov field value of PE. If you place conditions in separate fields in the *same* Criteria row of the design grid, all conditions in that row must be met in order for a record to be included in the query results. However, if you place conditions in *different* Criteria rows, a record will be selected if at least one of the conditions is met. If none of the conditions is met, Access does not select the record. When you place conditions in different Criteria rows, you are using the **Or logical operator**. Figure 3-25 illustrates the difference between the And and Or logical operators.

Figure 3-25	LOGICAL OPERATORS And AND Or FOR MULTIPLE SELECTION CRITERIA

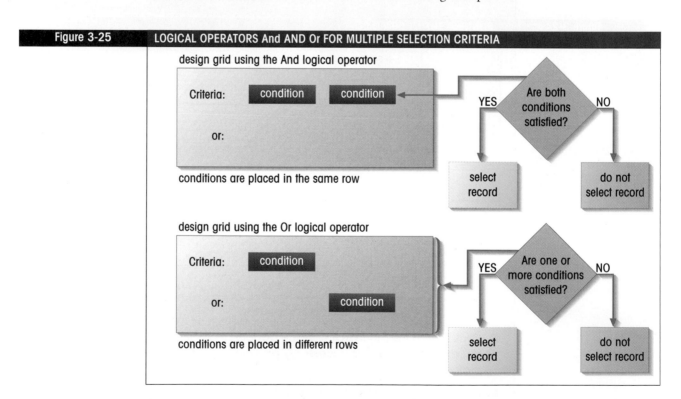

The And Logical Operator

To create Elsa's query, you need to modify the existing July 1 Positions query to show only the records for employers located in Prince Edward Island and offering positions starting on 07/01. For the modified query, you must add a second condition in the same Criteria row. The existing condition for the StartDate field finds records for positions that start on July 1; the new condition "PE" in the State/Prov field will find records for employers in Prince Edward Island. Because the conditions appear in the same Criteria row, the query will select records only if both conditions are met.

After modifying the query, you'll save it and then rename it as "PE July 1 Positions," overwriting the July 1 Positions query, which Matt no longer needs.

To modify the July 1 Positions query and use the And logical operator:

1. With the Queries object selected in the Database window, click **July 1 Positions** (if necessary), and then click the **Design** button to open the query in Design view.

2. Scroll the design grid to the right, click the **State/Prov Criteria** text box, type **PE**, and then press the ↓ key. See Figure 3-26.

Figure 3-26	QUERY TO FIND POSITIONS IN PE THAT START ON 07/01

And logical operator; conditions entered in the same row

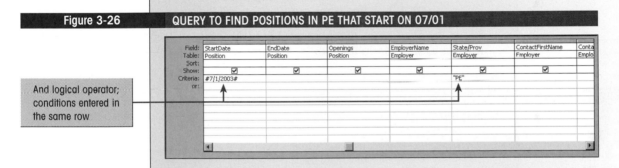

Notice that Access added quotation marks around the entry "PE"; you can type the quotation marks when you enter the condition, but if you forget to do so, Access will add them for you automatically.

The condition for the StartDate field is already entered, so you can run the query.

3. Run the query. Access displays in the datasheet only those records that meet both conditions: a StartDate field value of 07/01 and a State/Prov field value of PE. Two records are selected. See Figure 3-27.

Figure 3-27	RESULTS OF QUERY USING THE AND LOGICAL OPERATOR

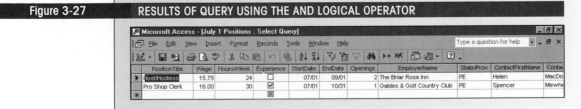

Now you can save the changes to the query and rename it.

4. Save and close the query. You return to the Database window.

5. Right-click **July 1 Positions** in the Queries list box, and then click **Rename** on the shortcut menu.

6. Click to position the insertion point to the left of the word "July," type **PE**, press the **spacebar**, and then press the **Enter** key. The query name is now PE July 1 Positions.

Using Multiple Undo and Redo

In previous versions of Access, you could not undo certain actions. Now Access allows you to undo and redo multiple actions when you are working in Design view for tables, queries, forms, reports, and so on. For example, when working in the Query window in Design view, if you specify multiple selection criteria for a query, you can use the multiple undo feature to remove the criteria—even after you run and save the query.

To see how this feature works, you will reopen the PE July 1 Positions query in Design view, delete the two criteria, and then reinsert them using multiple undo.

To modify the PE July 1 Positions query and use the multiple undo feature:

1. Open the **PE July 1 Positions** query in Design view.

2. Select the StartDate Criteria value, **#7/1/2003#**, and then press the **Delete** key. The StartDate Criteria text box is now empty.

3. Press the **Tab** key four times to move to and select **"PE"**, the State/Prov Criteria value, and then press the **Delete** key.

4. Run the query. Notice that the results display all records for the fields specified in the query design grid.

5. Switch back to Design view.

Now you will use multiple undo to reverse the edits you made and reinsert the two conditions.

6. Click the **list arrow** for the Undo button 🖮 on the Query Design toolbar. A menu appears listing the actions you can undo. See Figure 3-28.

Figure 3-28	USING MULTIPLE UNDO

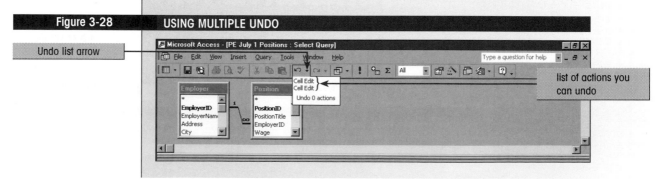

Undo list arrow

list of actions you can undo

Two items, both named "Cell Edit," are listed in the Undo list box. These items represent the two changes you made to the query design—first deleting the StartDate condition and then deleting the State/Prov condition. If you select an action that is below other items in the list, you will undo all the actions above the one you select, in addition to the one you select. Currently no actions are selected, so the list box indicates "Undo 0 actions."

7. Position the pointer over the second occurrence of **Cell Edit** in the list. Notice that both undo actions are highlighted, and the list box indicates that you can undo two actions.

8. Click the second occurrence of **Cell Edit**. Both actions are "undone," and the two conditions are redisplayed in the query design grid. The multiple undo feature makes it easy for you to test different criteria for a query and, when necessary, to undo your actions based on the query results.

   Notice that the Redo button and list arrow are now available. You can redo the actions you've just undone.

9. Click the **list arrow** for the Redo button on the Query Design toolbar. The Redo list box indicates that you can redo the two cell edits.

10. Click the **list arrow** for the Redo button again to close the Redo list box without selecting any option.

11. Close the query. Click the **No** button in the message box that opens, asking if you want to save your changes. You return to the Database window.

Matt has another request for information. He knows that it can be difficult to find student recruits for positions that offer fewer than 30 hours of work per week or that require prior work experience. So that his staff can focus on such positions, Matt wants to see a list of those positions that provide less than 30 hours of work or that require experience. To create this query, you need to use the Or logical operator.

The Or Logical Operator

For Matt's request, you need a query that selects a record when either one of two conditions is satisfied or when both conditions are satisfied. That is, a record is selected if the Hours/Week field value is less than 30 *or* if the Experience field value is "Yes" (checked). You will enter the condition for the Hours/Week field in one Criteria row and the condition for the Experience field in another Criteria row, thereby using the Or logical operator.

To display the information Matt wants to view, you'll create a new query containing the EmployerName and City fields from the Employer table and the PositionTitle, Hours/Week, and Experience fields from the Position table. Then you'll specify the conditions using the Or logical operator.

To create the query and use the Or logical operator:

1. In the Database window, double-click **Create query in Design view**. The Show Table dialog box opens on top of the Query window in Design view.

2. Click **Employer** in the Tables list box (if necessary), click the **Add** button, click **Position**, click the **Add** button, and then click the **Close** button. The Employer and Position field lists appear in the Query window and the Show Table dialog box closes.

3. Double-click **EmployerName** in the Employer field list to add the EmployerName field to the design grid's first column Field text box.

4. Repeat Step 3 to add the **City** field from the Employer table, and then add the **PositionTitle**, **Hours/Week**, and **Experience** fields from the Position table.

   Now you need to specify the first condition, <30, in the Hours/Week field.

5. Click the **Hours/Week Criteria** text box, type **<30** and then press the **Tab** key.

   Because you want records selected if either of the conditions for the Hours/Week or Experience fields is satisfied, you must enter the condition for the Experience field in the "or" row of the design grid.

6. Press the ↓ key, and then type **Yes** in the "or" text box for Experience. See Figure 3-29.

Figure 3-29	QUERY WINDOW WITH THE OR LOGICAL OPERATOR

Or logical operator; conditions entered in different rows

Field:	EmployerName	City	PositionTitle	Hours/Week	Experience		
Table:	Employer	Employer	Position	Position	Position		
Sort:							
Show:	☑	☑	☑	☑	☑	☐	
Criteria:				<30			
or:					Yes		

7. Run the query. Access displays only those records that meet either condition: an Hours/Week field value less than 30 or an Experience field value of "Yes" (checked). A total of 35 records are selected.

   Matt wants the list displayed in alphabetical order by EmployerName. The first record's EmployerName field is highlighted, indicating the current field.

8. Click the **Sort Ascending** button [⬇] on the Query Datasheet toolbar.

9. Resize all datasheet columns to their best fit. Scroll through the entire datasheet to make sure that all values are completely displayed. Deselect all columns when you are finished resizing them, and then return to the top of the datasheet. See Figure 3-30.

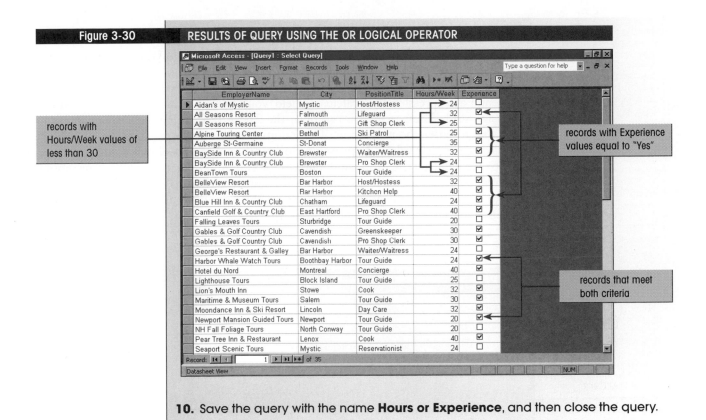

Figure 3-30 RESULTS OF QUERY USING THE OR LOGICAL OPERATOR

records with Hours/Week values of less than 30

records with Experience values equal to "Yes"

records that meet both criteria

10. Save the query with the name **Hours or Experience**, and then close the query.

Next, Elsa wants to use the Northeast database to perform calculations. She is considering offering a 2% bonus per week to the student recruits in higher paid positions, based on employer recommendation, and she wants to know exactly what these bonuses would be.

Performing **Calculations**

In addition to using queries to retrieve, sort, and filter data in a database, you can use a query to perform calculations. To perform a calculation, you define an **expression** containing a combination of database fields, constants, and operators. For numeric expressions, the data types of the database fields must be number, currency, or date/time; the constants are numbers such as .02 (for the 2% bonus); and the operators can be arithmetic operators (+ − * /) or other specialized operators. In complex expressions, you can enclose calculations in parentheses to indicate which one should be performed first. In expressions without parentheses, Access calculates in the following order of precedence: multiplication and division before addition and subtraction. When operators have equal precedence, Access calculates them in order from left to right.

To perform a calculation in a query, you add a calculated field to the query. A **calculated field** is a field that displays the results of an expression. A calculated field appears in a query datasheet or in a form or report; however, it does not exist in a database. When you run a query that contains a calculated field, Access evaluates the expression defined by the calculated field and displays the resulting value in the datasheet, form, or report.

Creating a Calculated Field

To produce the information Elsa wants, you need to open the High Wage Amounts query and create a calculated field that will multiply each Wage field value by each Hours/Week value, and then multiply that amount by .02 to determine the 2% weekly bonus Elsa is considering.

To enter an expression for a calculated field, you can type it directly in a Field text box in the design grid. Alternately, you can open the Zoom box or Expression Builder and use either one to enter the expression. The **Zoom box** is a large text box for entering text, expressions, or other values. **Expression Builder** is an Access tool that contains an expression box for entering the expression, buttons for common operators, and one or more lists of expression elements, such as table and field names. Unlike a Field text box, which is too small to show an entire expression at one time, the Zoom box and Expression Builder are large enough to display lengthy expressions. In most cases, Expression Builder provides the easiest way to enter expressions.

REFERENCE WINDOW RW

Using Expression Builder

- Open the query in Design view.
- In the design grid, position the insertion point in the Field text box of the field for which you want to create an expression.
- Click the Build button on the Query Design toolbar.
- Use the expression elements and common operators to build the expression, or type the expression directly.
- Click the OK button.

You'll begin by copying, pasting, and renaming the High Wage Amounts query, keeping the original query intact. You'll name the new query "High Wages with Bonus." Then you'll modify this query in Design view to show only the information Elsa wants to view.

To copy the High Wage Amounts query and paste the copy with a new name:

1. Right-click the **High Wage Amounts** query in the list of queries, and then click **Copy** on the shortcut menu.

2. Right-click an empty area of the Database window, and then click **Paste** on the shortcut menu. The Paste As dialog box opens.

3. Type **High Wages with Bonus** in the Query Name text box, and then press the **Enter** key. The new query appears in the query list, along with the original High Wage Amounts query.

Now you're ready to modify the High Wages with Bonus query to create the calculated field for Elsa.

To modify the High Wages with Bonus query:

1. Open the **High Wages with Bonus** query in Design view.

   Elsa wants to see only the EmployerName, PositionTitle, and Wage fields in the query results. First, you'll delete the unnecessary fields, and then you'll move the EmployerName field so that it appears first in the query results.

2. Scroll the design grid to the right until the Hours/Week and EmployerName fields are visible at the same time.

3. Position the pointer on the Hours/Week field until the pointer changes to a ↓ shape, click and hold down the mouse button, drag the mouse to the right to highlight the Hours/Week, Experience, StartDate, EndDate, and Openings fields, and then release the mouse button.

4. Press the **Delete** key to delete the five selected fields.

5. Repeat Steps 3 and 4 to delete the State/Prov, ContactFirstName, ContactLastName, and Phone fields from the query design grid.

   Next you'll move the EmployerName field to the left of the PositionTitle field so that the Wage values will appear next to the calculated field values in the query results.

6. Scroll the design grid back to the left (if necessary), select the **EmployerName** field, and then use the pointer ⥂ to drag the field to the left of the PositionTitle field. See Figure 3-31.

| Figure 3-31 | MODIFIED QUERY BEFORE ADDING THE CALCULATED FIELD |

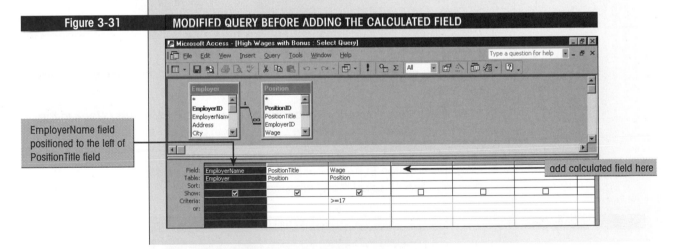

EmployerName field positioned to the left of PositionTitle field

add calculated field here

Now you're ready to use Expression Builder to enter the calculated field in the High Wages with Bonus query.

To add the calculated field to the High Wages with Bonus query:

1. Position the insertion point in the Field text box to the right of the Wage field, and then click the **Build** button ⚒ on the Query Design toolbar. The Expression Builder dialog box opens. See Figure 3-32.

Figure 3-32   INITIAL EXPRESSION BUILDER DIALOG BOX

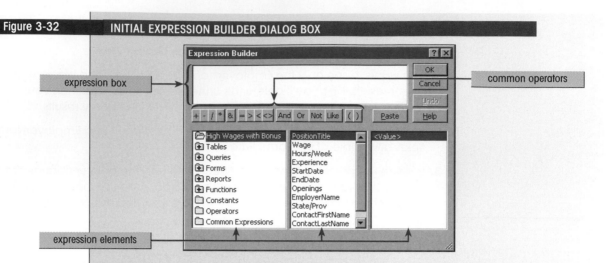

You use the common operators and expression elements to help you build an expression. Note that the High Wages with Bonus query is already selected in the list box on the lower left; the fields included in the original version of the query are listed in the center box.

The expression for the calculated field will multiply the Wage field values by the Hours/Week field values, and then multiply that amount by the numeric constant .02 (which represents a 2% bonus). To include a field in the expression, you select the field and then click the Paste button. To include a numeric constant, you simply type the constant in the expression.

2. Click **Wage** in the field list, and then click the **Paste** button. [Wage] appears in the expression box.

To include the multiplication operator in the expression, you click the asterisk (*) button.

3. Click the * button in the row of common operators, click **Hours/Week** in the field list, and then click the **Paste** button. The expression multiplies the Wage values by the Hours/Week values.

4. Click the * button in the row of common operators, and then type **.02**. You have finished entering the expression. See Figure 3-33.

Figure 3-33   COMPLETED EXPRESSION FOR THE CALCULATED FIELD

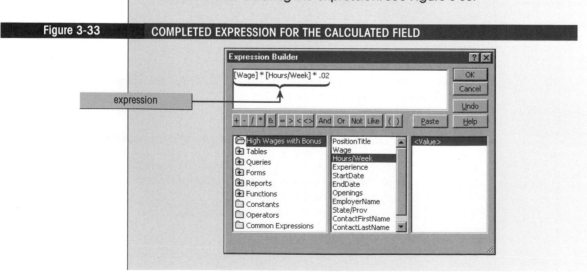

Note that you also could have typed the expression directly into the expression box, instead of clicking the field names and the operator.

5. Click the **OK** button. Access closes the Expression Builder dialog box and adds the expression to the design grid in the Field text box for the calculated field.

    Next, you need to specify a name for the calculated field as it will appear in the query results.

6. Press the **Home** key to position the insertion point to the left of the expression.

    You'll enter the name WeeklyBonus, which is descriptive of the field's contents; then you'll run the query.

7. Type **WeeklyBonus:**. *Make sure you include the colon following the field name.* The colon is needed to separate the field name from its expression.

8. Run the query. Access displays the query datasheet, which contains the three specified fields and the calculated field with the name "WeeklyBonus." Resize all datasheet columns to their best fit. See Figure 3-34.

Figure 3-34	DATASHEET DISPLAYING THE CALCULATED FIELD

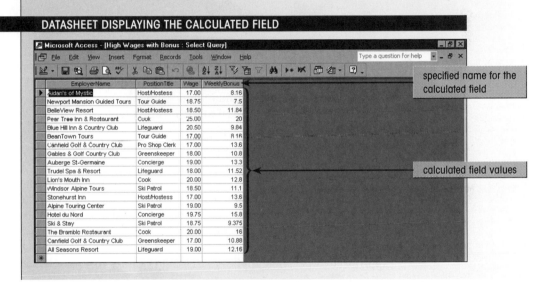

Notice the WeeklyBonus value for Ski & Stay; the value appears with three decimal places (9.375). Currency values should have only two decimal places, so you need to format the WeeklyBonus calculated field so that all values appear in the Fixed format with two decimal places.

To format the calculated field:

1. Switch to Design view.

2. Right-click the **WeeklyBonus** calculated field in the design grid to open the shortcut menu, and then click **Properties**. The property sheet for the selected field opens. The property sheet for a field provides options for changing the display of field values in the datasheet.

3. Click the right side of the **Format** text box to display the list of formats, and then click **Fixed**.

4. Click the right side of the **Decimal Places** text box, and then click **2**.

5. Click in the **Description** text box to deselect the Decimal Places setting. See Figure 3-35.

Figure 3-35	PROPERTY SHEET SETTINGS TO FORMAT THE CALCULATED FIELD

Now that you have formatted the calculated field, you can run the query.

6. Close the Field Properties window, and then save and run the query. The value for Ski & Stay now correctly appears as 9.38.

7. Close the query.

Elsa prepares a report on a regular basis that includes a summary of information about the wages paid to student recruits. She lists the minimum hourly wage paid, the average wage amount, and the maximum hourly wage paid. She asks you to create a query to determine these statistics from data in the Position table.

Using Aggregate Functions

You can calculate statistical information, such as totals and averages, on the records selected by a query. To do this, you use the Access aggregate functions. **Aggregate functions** perform arithmetic operations on selected records in a database. Figure 3-36 lists the most frequently used aggregate functions. Aggregate functions operate on the records that meet a query's selection criteria. You specify an aggregate function for a specific field, and the appropriate operation applies to that field's values for the selected records.

Figure 3-36	FREQUENTLY USED AGGREGATE FUNCTIONS	
AGGREGATE FUNCTION	**DETERMINES**	**DATA TYPES SUPPORTED**
Avg	Average of the field values for the selected records	AutoNumber, Currency, Date/Time, Number
Count	Number of records selected	AutoNumber, Currency, Date/Time, Memo, Number, OLE Object, Text, Yes/No
Max	Highest field value for the selected records	AutoNumber, Currency, Date/Time, Number, Text
Min	Lowest field value for the selected records	AutoNumber, Currency, Date/Time, Number, Text
Sum	Total of the field values for the selected records	AutoNumber, Currency, Date/Time, Number

To display the minimum, average, and maximum of all the wage amounts in the Position table, you will use the Min, Avg, and Max aggregate functions for the Wage field.

To calculate the minimum, average, and maximum of all wage amounts:

1. Double-click **Create query in Design view**, click **Position**, click the **Add** button, and then click the **Close** button. The Position field list is added to the Query window and the Show Table dialog box closes.

   To perform the three calculations on the Wage field, you need to add the field to the design grid three times.

2. Double-click **Wage** in the Position field list three times to add three copies of the field to the design grid.

   You need to select an aggregate function for each Wage field. When you click the Totals button on the Query Design toolbar, a row labeled "Total" is added to the design grid. The Total row provides a list of the aggregate functions that you can select.

3. Click the **Totals** button Σ on the Query Design toolbar. A new row labeled "Total" appears between the Table and Sort rows in the design grid. See Figure 3-37.

Figure 3-37	TOTAL ROW INSERTED IN THE DESIGN GRID

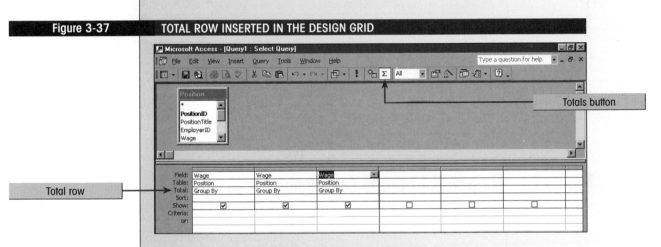

In the Total row, you specify the aggregate function you want to use for a field.

4. Click the right side of the first column's **Total** text box, and then click **Min**. This field will calculate the minimum amount of all the Wage field values.

   When you run the query, Access automatically will assign a datasheet column name of "MinOfWage" for this field. You can change the datasheet column name to a more descriptive or readable name by entering the name you want in the Field text box. However, you must also keep the field name Wage in the Field text box, because it identifies the field whose values will be calculated. The Field text box will contain the datasheet column name you specify followed by the field name (Wage) with a colon separating the two names.

5. Position the insertion point to the left of Wage in the first column's Field text box, and then type **MinimumWage:**. Be sure that you type the colon.

6. Click the right side of the second column's **Total** text box, and then click **Avg**. This field will calculate the average of all the Wage field values.

7. Position the insertion point to the left of Wage in the second column's Field text box, and then type **AverageWage:**.

8. Click the right side of the third column's **Total** text box, and then click **Max**. This field will calculate the maximum amount of all the Wage field values.

9. Position the insertion point to the left of Wage in the third column's Field text box, and then type **MaximumWage:**.

The query design is completed, so you can run the query.

10. Run the query. Access displays one record containing the three aggregate function values. The single row of summary statistics represents calculations based on the 64 records selected by the query.

You need to resize the three columns to their best fit to see the column names.

11. Resize all columns to their best fit, and then position the insertion point in the field value in the first column. See Figure 3-38.

| Figure 3-38 | RESULTS OF THE QUERY USING AGGREGATE FUNCTIONS |

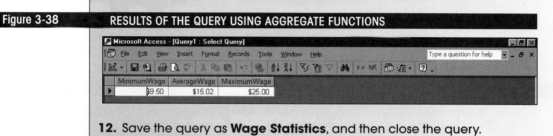

12. Save the query as **Wage Statistics**, and then close the query.

Elsa also wants her report to include the same wage statistics (minimum, average, and maximum) for each type of position. She asks you to display the wage statistics for each different PositionTitle value in the Position table.

Using Record Group Calculations

In addition to calculating statistical information on all or selected records in selected tables, you can calculate statistics for groups of records. For example, you can determine the number of employers in each state or province, or the average wage amount by position.

To create a query for Elsa's latest request, you can modify the current query by adding the PositionTitle field and assigning the Group By operator to it. The **Group By operator** divides the selected records into groups based on the values in the specified field. Those records with the same value for the field are grouped together, and the datasheet displays one record for each group. Aggregate functions, which appear in the other columns of the design grid, provide statistical information for each group.

You need to modify the current query to add the Group By operator for the PositionTitle field. This will display the statistical information grouped by position for the 64 selected records in the query. As you did earlier, you will copy the Wage Statistics query and paste it with a new name, keeping the original query intact, to create the new query.

To copy and paste the query, and then add the PositionTitle field with the Group By operator:

1. Right-click the **Wage Statistics** query in the list of queries, and then click **Copy** on the shortcut menu.

2. Right-click an empty area of the Database window, and then click **Paste** on the shortcut menu.

3. Type **Wage Statistics by Position** in the Query Name text box, and then press the **Enter** key.

   Now you're ready to modify the query design.

4. Open the **Wage Statistics by Position** query in Design view.

5. Double-click **PositionTitle** in the Position field list to add the field to the design grid. Group By, which is the default option in the Total row, appears for the PositionTitle field.

   You've completed the query changes, so you can run the query.

6. Run the query. Access displays 16 records—one for each PositionTitle group. Each record contains the three aggregate function values and the PositionTitle field value for the group. Again, the summary statistics represent calculations based on the 64 records selected by the query. See Figure 3-39.

Figure 3-39	AGGREGATE FUNCTIONS GROUPED BY PositionTitle

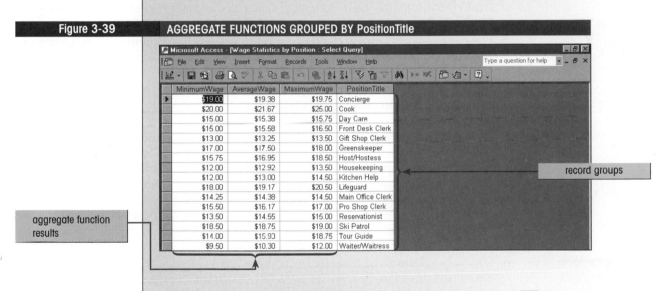

7. Save and close the query, and then click the **Close** button ☒ on the Access window title bar to close the Northeast database and to exit Access.

   TROUBLE? If a dialog box opens and asks if you want to empty the Clipboard, click the Yes button.

The queries you've created and saved will help Elsa, Zack, Matt, and other employees to monitor and analyze the business activity of NSJI's employer customers. Now any NSJI staff member can run the queries at any time, modify them as needed, or use them as the basis for designing new queries to meet additional information requirements.

Session 3.2 QUICK CHECK

1. A(n) _____ is a criterion, or rule, that determines which records are selected for a query datasheet.
2. In the design grid, where do you place the conditions for two different fields when you use the And logical operator? The Or logical operator?

3. To perform a calculation in a query, you define a(n) _____ containing a combination of database fields, constants, and operators.

4. How does a calculated field differ from a table field?

5. What is an aggregate function?

6. The _____ operator divides selected records into groups based on the values in a field.

REVIEW ASSIGNMENTS

Elsa needs information from the **Recruits** database, and she asks you to query the database by completing the following:

1. Make sure your Data Disk is in the appropriate disk drive, start Access, and then open the **Recruits** database located in the Review folder on your Data Disk.

2. Create a select query based on the **Student** table. Display the StudentID, FirstName, and LastName fields in the query results; sort in ascending order based on the LastName field values; and select only those records whose Nation value equals Ireland. (*Hint*: Do not display the Nation field values in the query results.) Save the query as **Students from Ireland**, run the query, and then print the query datasheet.

3. Use the **Students from Ireland** datasheet to update the **Student** table by changing the FirstName field value for StudentID OMA9956 to Richard. Print the query datasheet, and then close the query.

4. Define a one-to-many relationship between the primary **Recruiter** table and the related **Student** table. Select the referential integrity option and both cascade options for the relationship.

5. Use Design view to create a select query based on the **Recruiter** and **Student** tables. Select the fields FirstName (from the **Student** table), LastName (from the **Student** table), City, Nation, BonusQuota, Salary, and SSN (from the **Student** table), in that order. Sort in ascending order based on the Nation field values. Select only those records whose SSN equals "977071798." (*Hint*: Do not type the dashes for the SSN criterion, and do not display the SSN field values in the query results.) Save the query as **Wolfe Recruits**, and then run the query. Resize all columns in the datasheet to fit the data. Print the datasheet, and then save the query.

Explore 6. Use Help to learn about Filter By Form. In the Ask a Question box, type, "How do I create a filter?" and then click the topic "Create a filter." Read the portions of the topic pertaining to Filter By Selection and Filter By Form, and then close the Microsoft Access Help window.

Explore 7. Use the Filter By Form button on the Query Datasheet toolbar to filter the records in the **Wolfe Recruits** datasheet that have a Nation field value of "Spain," and then apply the filter. Print the query datasheet.

Explore 8. Remove the filter to display all records, and then save and close the query.

Explore 9. Use Design view to create a query based on the **Recruiter** table that shows all recruiters with a BonusQuota field value between 40 and 50, and whose Salary field value is greater than 35000. (*Hint*: Refer to Figure 3-18 to determine the correct comparison operator to use.) Display all fields except SSN from the **Recruiter** table. Save the query as **Bonus Info**, and then run the query.

Explore 10. Switch to Design view for the **Bonus Info** query. Create a calculated field named RaiseAmt that displays the net amount of a 3% raise to the Salary values. Display the results in descending order by RaiseAmt. Save the query as **Salaries with Raises**, run the query, resize all columns in the datasheet to fit the data, print the query datasheet, and then save and close the query.

11. In the Database window, copy the **Students from Ireland** query, and then paste it with the new name **Students from Holland Plus Younger Students**. Open the new query in Design view. Modify the query to display only those records with a Nation field value of Holland or with a BirthDate field value greater than 1/1/84. Also, modify the query to include the Nation field values in the query results. Save and run the query. Resize all columns in the datasheet to fit the data, print the query datasheet, and then save and close the query.

12. Create a new query based on the **Recruiter** table. Use the Min, Max, and Avg aggregate functions to find the lowest, highest, and average values in the Salary field. Name the three aggregate fields LowestSalary, HighestSalary, and AverageSalary, respectively. Save the query as **Salary Statistics**, and then run the query. Resize all columns in the datasheet to fit the data, print the query datasheet, and then save and close the query.

13. Open the **Salary Statistics** query in Design view. Modify the query so that the records are grouped by the BonusQuota field. Save the query as **Salary Statistics by BonusQuota**, run the query, print the query datasheet, and then close the query.

14. Close the **Recruits** database, and then exit Access.

CASE PROBLEMS

Case 1. Lim's Video Photography   Youngho Lim wants to view specific information about his clients and video shoot events. He asks you to query the **Videos** database by completing the following:

1. Make sure your Data Disk is in the appropriate disk drive, start Access, and then open the **Videos** database located in the Cases folder on your Data Disk.

Explore

2. Define the necessary one-to-many relationships between the database tables, as follows: between the primary **Client** table and the related **Contract** table, between the primary **Contract** table and the related **Shoot** table, and between the primary **ShootDesc** table and the related **Shoot** table. (*Hint*: Add all four tables to the Relationships window, and then define the three relationships.) Select the referential integrity option and both cascade options for each relationship.

3. Create a select query based on the **Client** and **Contract** tables. Display the ClientName, City, ContractDate, and ContractAmt fields, in that order. Sort in ascending order based on the ClientName field values. Run the query, save the query as **Client Contracts**, and then print the datasheet.

4. Use Filter By Selection to display only those records with a City field value of Oakland in the **Client Contracts** datasheet. Print the datasheet and then remove the filter. Save and close the query.

5. Open the **Client Contracts** query in Design view. Modify the query to display only those records with a ContractAmt value greater than or equal to 600. Run the query, save the query as **Contract Amounts**, and then print the datasheet.

6. Switch to Design view for the **Contract Amounts** query. Modify the query to display only those records with a ContractAmt value greater than or equal to 600 and with a City value of San Francisco. Also modify the query so that the City field values are not displayed in the query results. Run the query, save it as **SF Contract Amounts**, print the datasheet, and then close the query.

7. Close the **Videos** database, and then exit Access.

Case 2. DineAtHome.course.com   Claire Picard is completing an analysis of the orders placed at restaurants that use her company's services. To help her find the information she needs, you'll query the **Meals** database by completing the following:

1. Make sure your Data Disk is in the appropriate disk drive, start Access, and then open the **Meals** database located in the Cases folder on your Data Disk.

2. Define a one-to-many relationship between the primary **Restaurant** table and the related **Order** table. Select the referential integrity option and both cascade options for the relationship.

3. Use Design view to create a select query based on the **Restaurant** and **Order** tables. Display the fields RestaurantName, City, OrderAmt, and OrderDate, in that order. Sort in descending order based on the OrderAmt field values. Select only those records whose OrderAmt is greater than 150. Save the query as **Large Orders**, and then run the query.

4. Use the **Large Orders** datasheet to update the **Order** table by changing the OrderAmt value for the first record in the datasheet to 240.25. Print the datasheet, and then close the query.

5. Use Design view to create a select query based on the **Restaurant** and **Order** tables. For all orders placed on 03/21/2003, display the Order#, OrderAmt, OrderDate, and RestaurantName fields. Save the query as **March 21 Orders**, and then run the query. Switch to Design view, modify the query so that the OrderDate values do not appear in the query results, and then save the modified query. Run the query, print the query results, and then close the query.

6. Use Design view to create a select query based on the **Restaurant** table. For all restaurants that have a Website and are located in Naples, display the RestaurantName, OwnerFirstName, OwnerLastName, and Phone fields. Save the query as **Naples Restaurants with Websites**, run the query, print the query results, and then close the query.

7. Use Design view to create a select query based on the **Restaurant** and **Order** tables. For all orders placed on 03/14/2003 or 03/15/2003, display the fields OrderDate, OrderAmt, RestaurantName, and Restaurant# (from the **Restaurant** table). Display the results in ascending order by OrderDate and then in descending order by OrderAmt. Save the query as **Selected Dates**, run the query, print the query datasheet, and then close the query.

Explore ▶ 8. Use the **Order** table to display the highest, lowest, total, average, and count of the OrderAmt field for all orders. Then do the following:

   a. Specify column names of HighestOrder, LowestOrder, TotalOrders, AverageOrder, and #Orders. Use the property sheet for each column (except #Orders) to format the results as Fixed with two decimal places. Save the query as **Order Statistics**, and then run the query. Resize all datasheet columns to their best fit, save the query, and then print the query results.

   b. Change the query to display the same statistics grouped by RestaurantName. (*Hint*: Use the Show Table button on the Query Design toolbar to add the **Restaurant** table to the query.) Save the query as **Order Statistics by Restaurant**. Run the query, print the query results, and then close the query.

9. Close the **Meals** database, and then exit Access.

Case 3. Redwood Zoo   Michael Rosenfeld wants to find specific information about the donors and their pledge amounts for the Redwood Zoo. You'll help them find the information in the **Redwood** database by completing the following:

1. Make sure your Data Disk is in the appropriate disk drive, start Access, and then open the **Redwood** database located in the Cases folder on your Data Disk.

Explore ▶ 2. Define the necessary one-to-many relationships between the database tables, as follows: between the primary **Donor** table and the related **Pledge** table, and between the primary **Fund** table and the related **Pledge** table. (*Hint*: Add all three tables to the Relationships window, and then define the two relationships.) Select the referential integrity option and both cascade options for each relationship.

3. Use Design view to create a select query that, for all pledges with a TotalPledged field value of greater than 200, displays the DonorID (from the **Donor** table), FirstName, LastName, Pledge#, TotalPledged, and FundName fields. Sort the query in ascending order by TotalPledged. Save the query as **Large Pledges**, and then run the query.

4. Use the **Large Pledges** datasheet to update the **Pledge** table by changing the TotalPledged field value for Pledge# 2976 to 750. Print the query datasheet, and then close the query.

5. Use Design view to create a select query that, for all donors who pledged less than $150 or who donated to the Whale Watchers fund, displays the Pledge#, PledgeDate, TotalPledged, FirstName, and LastName fields. Save the revised query as **Pledged or Whale Watchers**, run the query, and then print the query datasheet. Change the query to select all donors who pledged less than $150 and who donated to the Whale Watchers fund. Save the revised query as **Pledged and Whale Watchers**, and then run the query. Close the query.

Explore ▶ 6. Use Design view to create a select query that displays the DonorID (from the **Donor** table), TotalPledged, PaymentMethod, PledgeDate, and FundName fields. Save the query as **Pledges after Costs**. Create a calculated field named Overhead that displays the results of multiplying the TotalPledged field values by 15% (to account for overhead costs). Save the query, and then create a second calculated field named NetPledge that displays the results of subtracting the Overhead field values from the TotalPledged field values.

Format the calculated fields as Fixed. Display the results in ascending order by TotalPledged. Save the modified query, and then run the query. Resize all datasheet columns to their best fit, print the query results, and then save and close the query.

Explore 7. Use the **Pledge** table to display the sum, average, and count of the TotalPledged field for all pledges. Then do the following:

   a. Specify column names of TotalPledge, AveragePledge, and #Pledges.
   b. Change properties so that the values in the TotalPledge and AveragePledge columns display two decimal places and the Fixed format.
   c. Save the query as **Pledge Statistics**, run the query, resize all datasheet columns to their best fit, and then print the query datasheet. Save the query.
   d. Change the query to display the sum, average, and count of the TotalPledged field for all pledges by FundName. (*Hint*: Use the Show Table button on the Query Design toolbar to add the **Fund** table to the query.) Save the query as **Pledge Statistics by Fund**, run the query, print the query datasheet, and then close the query.

8. Close the **Redwood** database, and then exit Access.

Case 4. Mountain River Adventures   Connor and Siobhan Dempsey want to analyze data about their clients and the rafting trips they take. Help them query the **Trips** database by completing the following:

1. Make sure your Data Disk is in the appropriate disk drive, start Access, and then open the **Trips** database located in the Cases folder on your Data Disk.

Explore 2. Define the necessary one-to-many relationships between the database tables, as follows: between the primary **Client** table and the related **Booking** table, and between the primary **Rafting Trip** table and the related **Booking** table. (*Hint*: Add all three tables to the Relationships window, and then define the two relationships.) Select the referential integrity option and both cascade options for each relationship.

3. For all clients, display the ClientName, City, State/Prov, Booking#, and TripDate fields. Save the query as **Client Trip Dates**, and then run the query. Resize all datasheet columns to their best fit. In Datasheet view, sort the query results in ascending order by the TripDate field. Print the query datasheet, and then save and close the query.

4. For all clients from Colorado (CO), display the ClientName, City, State/Prov, Trip#, People, and TripDate fields. Sort the query in ascending order by City. Save the query as **Colorado Clients**, and then run the query. Modify the query to remove the display of the State/Prov field values from the query results. Save the modified query, run the query, print the query datasheet, and then close the query.

Explore 5. For all clients who are not from Colorado or who are taking a rafting trip in the month of July 2003, display the ClientName, City, State/Prov, Booking#, TripDate, and Trip# fields. (*Hint*: Refer to Figure 3-18 to determine the correct comparison operators to use.) Sort the query in descending order by TripDate. Save the query as **Out of State or July**, run the query, and then print the query datasheet. Change the query to select all clients who are not from Colorado and who are taking a rafting trip in the month of July 2003. Sort the query in ascending order by State/Prov. Save the query as **Out of State and July**, run the query, print the query datasheet, and then close the query.

6. For all bookings, display the Booking#, TripDate, Trip# (from the **Booking** table), River, People, and Fee/Person fields. Save the query as **Trip Cost**. Then create a calculated field named TripCost that displays the results of multiplying the People field values by the Fee/Person field values. Display the results in descending order by TripCost. Run the query, resize all datasheet columns to their best fit, print the query datasheet, and then save and close the query.

Explore 7. Use the **Rafting Trip** table to determine the minimum, average, and maximum Fee/Person for all trips. Use the Ask a Question box to ask the question, "What is a caption?" and then locate and click the topic "Change a field name in a query." Read the displayed information, and then click and read the subtopic "Change a field's caption."

Close the Help window. Set the Caption property of the three fields to Lowest Fee, Average Fee, and Highest Fee, respectively. Also set the properties so that the results of the three fields are displayed as Fixed with two decimal places. Save the query as **Fee Statistics**, run the query, resize all datasheet columns to their best fit, print the query datasheet, and then save the query again. Revise the query to show the fee statistics grouped by People. (*Hint*: Use the Show Table button on the Query Design toolbar to display the Show Table dialog box.) Save the revised query as **Fee Statistics by People**, run the query, print the query datasheet, and then close the query.

Explore

8. Use the Ask a Question box to ask the following question: "How do I create a Top Values query?" Click the topic "Show only the high or low values in a query." Read the displayed information, and then close the Help window. Open the **Trip Cost** query in Design view, and then modify the query to display only the top five values for the TripCost field. Save the query as **Top Trip Cost**, run the query, print the query datasheet, and then close the query.

9. Close the **Trips** database, and then exit Access.

INTERNET ASSIGNMENTS

Student Union

The purpose of the Internet Assignments is to challenge you to find information on the Internet that you can use to create effective documents. The actual assignments are updated and maintained on the Course Technology Web site. Log on to the Internet and use your Web browser to go to the Student Union on the New Perspectives Series site at **www.course.com/NewPerspectives/studentunion**. Click the Online Companions link, and then click the link for this text.

QUICK CHECK ANSWERS

Session 3.1

1. a general query in which you specify the fields and records you want Access to select
2. The field list contains the table name at the top of the list box and the table's fields listed in the order in which they appear in the table; the design grid displays columns that contain specifications about a field you will use in the query.
3. A table datasheet and a query datasheet look the same, appearing in Datasheet view, and can be used to update data in a database. A table datasheet shows the permanent data in a table, whereas a query datasheet is temporary and its contents are based on the criteria you establish in the design grid.
4. primary table; related table
5. Referential integrity
6. oldest to most recent date
7. when you want to perform different types of sorts (both ascending and descending, for example) on multiple fields, and when you want to sort on multiple fields that are nonadjacent or in the wrong order, but you do not want to rearrange the columns in the query datasheet to accomplish the sort
8. filter

Session 3.2

1. condition
2. in the same Criteria row; in different Criteria rows
3. expression
4. A calculated field appears in a query datasheet, form, or report but does not exist in a database, as does a table field.
5. a function that performs an arithmetic operation on selected records in a database
6. Group By

OBJECTIVES

In this tutorial you will:

- Create a form using the Form Wizard

- Change a form's AutoFormat

- Find data using a form

- Preview and print selected form records

- Maintain table data using a form

- Check the spelling of table data using a form

- Create a form with a main form and a subform

- Create a report using the Report Wizard

- Insert a picture in a report

- Preview and print a report

CREATING FORMS AND REPORTS

Creating a Position Data Form, an Employer Positions Form, and an Employers and Positions Report

Northeast Seasonal Jobs International (NSJI)

Elsa Jensen wants to continue enhancing the Northeast database to make it easier for NSJI employees to find and maintain data. In particular, she wants the database to include a form based on the Position table to make it easier for employees to enter and change data about available positions. She also wants the database to include a form that shows data from both the Employer and Position tables at the same time. This form will show the position information for each employer along with the corresponding employer data, providing a complete picture of NSJI's employer clients and their available positions.

In addition, Zack Ward would like the database to include a formatted report of employer and position data so that his marketing staff members will have printed output when completing market analyses and planning strategies for selling NSJI's services to employer clients. He wants the information to be formatted attractively, perhaps by including a picture or graphic image on the report for visual interest.

SESSION 4.1

In this session, you will create a form using the Form Wizard, change a form's AutoFormat, find data using a form, preview and print selected form records, maintain table data using a form, and check the spelling of table data using a form.

Creating a Form Using the Form Wizard

As you learned in Tutorial 1, a form is an object you use to maintain, view, and print records in a database. In Access, you can design your own forms or use a Form Wizard to create them for you automatically.

Elsa asks you to create a new form that her staff can use to view and maintain data in the Position table. In Tutorial 1, you used the AutoForm Wizard to create the Employer Data form in the Seasonal database. The AutoForm Wizard creates a form automatically, using all the fields in the selected table or query. To create the form for the Position table, you'll use the Form Wizard. The **Form Wizard** allows you to choose some or all of the fields in the selected table or query, choose fields from other tables and queries, and display the selected fields in any order on the form. You can also apply an existing style to the form to format its appearance quickly.

To open the Northeast database and activate the Form Wizard:

1. Place your Data Disk in the appropriate disk drive.

2. Start Access and open the **Northeast** database located in the Tutorial folder on your Data Disk.

3. Click **Forms** in the Objects bar of the Database window.

4. Click the **New** button in the Database window. The New Form dialog box opens.

5. Click **Form Wizard**, click the list arrow for choosing a table or query, click **Position** to select this table as the source for the form, and then click the **OK** button. The first Form Wizard dialog box opens. See Figure 4-1.

Figure 4-1	FIRST FORM WIZARD DIALOG BOX

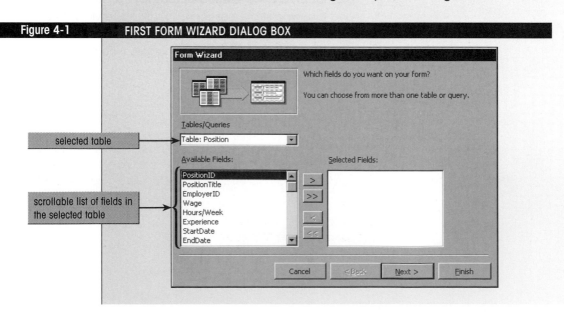

selected table

scrollable list of fields in the selected table

Elsa wants the form to display all the fields in the Position table, but in a different order. She would like the Experience field to appear at the bottom of the form so that it stands out more, making it easier to determine if a position requires prior work experience.

To finish creating the form using the Form Wizard:

1. Click **PositionID** in the Available Fields list box (if necessary), and then click the [>] button to move the field to the Selected Fields list box.

2. Repeat Step 1 to select the **PositionTitle, EmployerID, Wage, Hours/Week, StartDate, EndDate, Openings,** and **Experience** fields, in that order. Remember, you can also double-click a field to move it from the Available Fields list box to the Selected Fields list box.

3. Click the **Next** button to display the second Form Wizard dialog box, in which you select a layout for the form. See Figure 4-2.

Figure 4-2	CHOOSING A LAYOUT FOR THE FORM

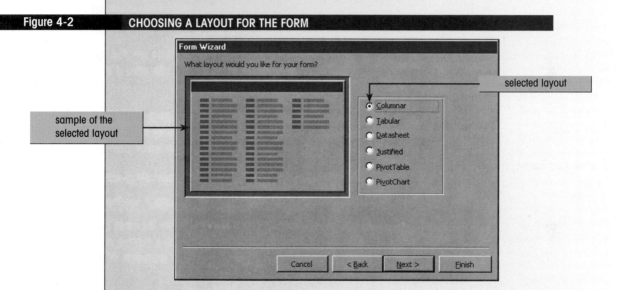

The layout choices are Columnar, Tabular, Datasheet, Justified, PivotTable, and PivotChart. A sample of the selected layout appears on the left side of the dialog box.

4. Click each of the option buttons and review the corresponding sample layout.

The Tabular and Datasheet layouts display the fields from multiple records at one time, whereas the Columnar and Justified layouts display the fields from one record at a time. The PivotTable and PivotChart layouts display summary and analytical information. Elsa thinks the Columnar layout is the appropriate arrangement for displaying and updating data in the table, so you'll choose this layout.

5. Click the **Columnar** option button (if necessary), and then click the **Next** button. Access displays the third Form Wizard dialog box, in which you choose a style for the form. See Figure 4-3.

Figure 4-3   CHOOSING A STYLE FOR THE FORM

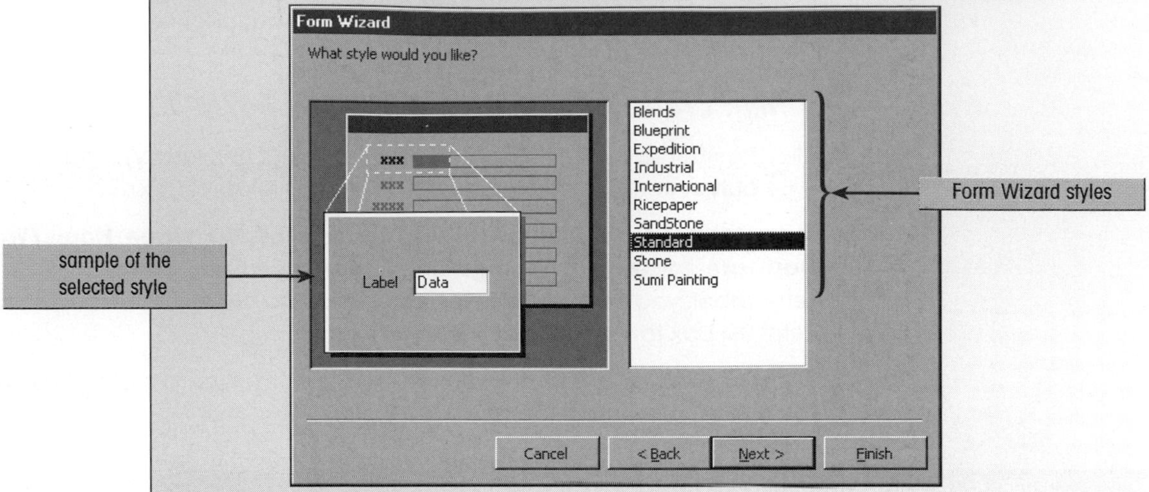

sample of the selected style

Form Wizard styles

A sample of the selected style appears in the box on the left. If you choose a style, which is called an **AutoFormat**, and decide you'd prefer a different one after the form is created, you can change it.

TROUBLE? Don't worry if a different form style is selected in your dialog box instead of the one shown in Figure 4-3. The dialog box displays the most recently used style, which might be different on your computer.

6. Click each of the styles and review the corresponding sample.

Elsa likes the Expedition style and asks you to use it for the form.

7. Click **Expedition** and then click the **Next** button. Access displays the final Form Wizard dialog box and shows the Position table's name as the default form name. "Position" is also the default title that will appear in the form's title bar. See Figure 4-4.

Figure 4-4   FINAL FORM WIZARD DIALOG BOX

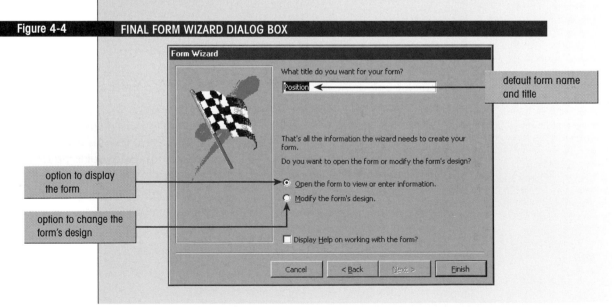

default form name and title

option to display the form

option to change the form's design

You'll use "Position Data" as the form name and, because you don't need to change the form's design at this point, you'll display the form.

8. Click the insertion point to the right of Position in the text box, press the **spacebar**, type **Data**, and then click the **Finish** button. The completed form opens in Form view. See Figure 4-5.

Figure 4-5	COMPLETED FORM FOR THE POSITION TABLE

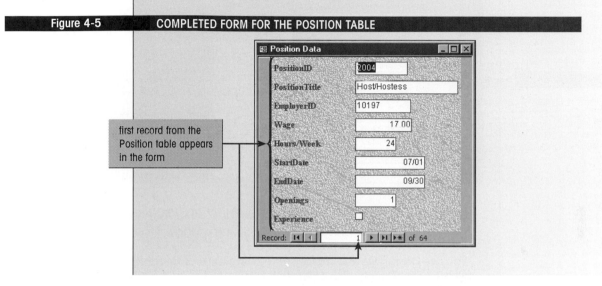

first record from the Position table appears in the form

After viewing the form, Elsa decides that she doesn't like the form's style; the background makes the field names a bit difficult to read. She asks you to change the form's style.

Changing a Form's AutoFormat

You can change a form's appearance by choosing a different AutoFormat for the form. As you learned when you created the Position Data form, an AutoFormat is a predefined style for a form (or report). The AutoFormats available for a form are the ones you saw when you selected the form's style using the Form Wizard. To change an AutoFormat, you must switch to Design view.

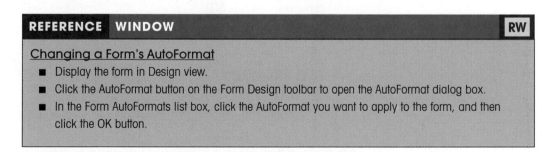

REFERENCE WINDOW   **RW**

Changing a Form's AutoFormat
- Display the form in Design view.
- Click the AutoFormat button on the Form Design toolbar to open the AutoFormat dialog box.
- In the Form AutoFormats list box, click the AutoFormat you want to apply to the form, and then click the OK button.

To change the AutoFormat for the Position Data form:

1. Click the **View** button for Design view on the Form View toolbar. The form is displayed in Design view. See Figure 4-6.

Figure 4-6	FORM DISPLAYED IN DESIGN VIEW

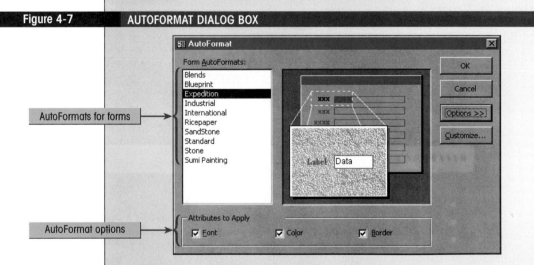

Form window

AutoFormat button

TROUBLE? If your screen displays any window other than those shown in Figure 4-6, click the Close button ⊠ on the window's title bar to close it.

You use Design view to modify an existing form or to create a form from scratch. In this case, you need to change the AutoFormat for the Position Data form.

2. Click the **AutoFormat** button 🔲 on the Form Design toolbar. The AutoFormat dialog box opens.

3. Click the **Options** button to display the AutoFormat options. See Figure 4-7.

Figure 4-7	AUTOFORMAT DIALOG BOX

AutoFormats for forms

AutoFormat options

A sample of the selected AutoFormat appears to the right of the Form AutoFormats list box. The options at the bottom of the dialog box let you apply the selected AutoFormat or just its font, color, or border.

Elsa decides that she prefers the Standard AutoFormat, because its field names and field values are easy to read.

4. Click **Standard** in the Form AutoFormats list box, and then click the **OK** button. The AutoFormat dialog box closes, the Standard AutoFormat is applied to the form, and the Form window in Design view becomes the active window.

5. Click the **View** button for Form view 🖾 on the Form Design toolbar. The form is displayed in Form view with the new AutoFormat. See Figure 4-8.

| Figure 4-8 | FORM DISPLAYED WITH THE NEW AUTOFORMAT |

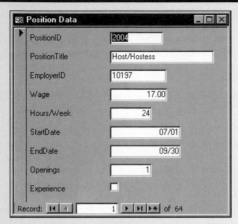

You have finished modifying the format of the form and can now save it.

6. Click the **Save** button 🖫 on the Form View toolbar to save the modified form.

Elsa wants to use the Position Data form to view some data in the Position table. To view data, you need to navigate through the form. As you learned in Tutorial 1, you navigate through a form in the same way that you navigate through a table datasheet. Also, the navigation mode and editing mode keystroke techniques you used with datasheets in Tutorial 2 are the same when navigating a form.

To navigate through the Position Data form:

1. Press the **Tab** key to move to the PositionTitle field value, and then press the **End** key to move to the Experience field. Because the Experience field is a yes/no field, its value is not highlighted; instead, a dotted outline appears around the field name to indicate that it is the current field.

2. Press the **Home** key to move back to the PositionID field value. The first record in the Position table still appears in the form.

3. Press **Ctrl + End** to move to the Experience field for record 64, which is the last record in the table. The record number for the current record appears in the Specific Record box between the navigation buttons at the bottom of the form.

4. Click the **Previous Record** navigation button ◄ to move to the Experience field in record 63.

5. Press the ↑ key twice to move to the EndDate field in record 63.

6. Click the insertion point between the numbers "1" and "5" in the EndDate field value to switch to editing mode, press the **Home** key to move the insertion point to the beginning of the field value, and then press the **End** key to move the insertion point to the end of the field value.

7. Click the **First Record** navigation button ![◄] to move to the EndDate field value in the first record. The entire field value is highlighted because you have switched from editing mode to navigation mode.

8. Click the **Next Record** navigation button ![►] to move to the EndDate field value in record 2, the next record.

Elsa asks you to display the records for The Clipper Ship Inn, whose EmployerID is 10145, because she wants to review the available positions for this employer.

Finding Data Using a Form

The **Find** command lets you search for data in a form or datasheet so you can display only those records you want to view. You choose a field to serve as the basis for the search by making that field the current field; then you enter the value you want Access to match in the Find and Replace dialog box. You can use the Find command by clicking the toolbar Find button or by using the Edit menu.

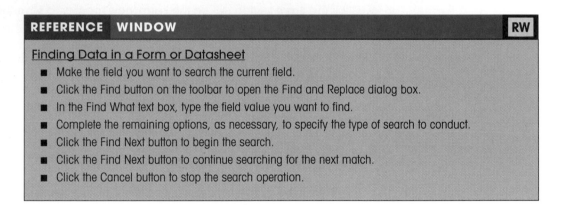

REFERENCE WINDOW   **RW**

Finding Data in a Form or Datasheet
- Make the field you want to search the current field.
- Click the Find button on the toolbar to open the Find and Replace dialog box.
- In the Find What text box, type the field value you want to find.
- Complete the remaining options, as necessary, to specify the type of search to conduct.
- Click the Find Next button to begin the search.
- Click the Find Next button to continue searching for the next match.
- Click the Cancel button to stop the search operation.

You need to find all records in the Position table for The Clipper Ship Inn, whose EmployerID is 10145.

To find the records using the Position Data form:

1. Click in the **EmployerID** field value box. This is the field that you will search for matching values.

2. Click the **Find** button ![binoculars] on the Form View toolbar. The Find and Replace dialog box opens. Note that the Look In list box shows the name of the field that Access will search (in this case, the current EmployerID field), and the Match list box indicates that Access will find values that match the entire entry in the field. You could choose to match only part of a field value or only the beginning of each field value.

3. If the Find and Replace dialog box covers the form, move the dialog box by dragging its title bar. If necessary, move the Position Data form window so that you can see both the dialog box and the form at the same time. See Figure 4-9.

Figure 4-9	FIND AND REPLACE DIALOG BOX

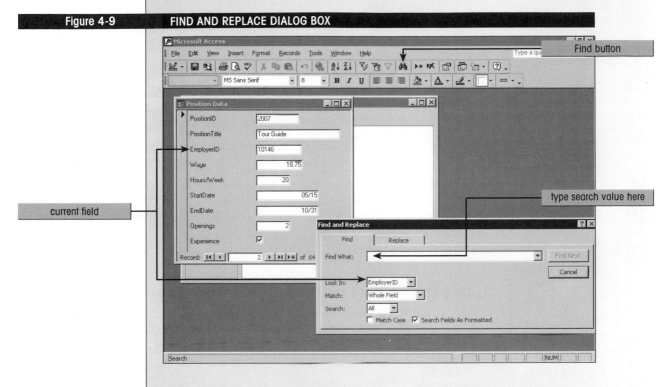

4. In the Find What text box, type **10145** and then click the **Find Next** button. Access displays record 7, which is the first record for EmployerID 10145.

5. Click the **Find Next** button. Access displays record 47, which is the second record for EmployerID 10145.

6. Click the **Find Next** button. Access displays record 48, which is the third record for EmployerID 10145.

7. Click the **Find Next** button. Access displays a dialog box informing you that the search is finished.

8. Click the **OK** button to close the dialog box.

The search value you enter can be an exact value, such as the EmployerID 10145 you just entered, or it can include wildcard characters. A **wildcard character** is a placeholder you use when you know only part of a value or when you want to start or end with a specific character or match a certain pattern. Figure 4-10 shows the wildcard characters you can use when finding data.

Figure 4-10	WILDCARD CHARACTERS	
WILDCARD CHARACTER	**PURPOSE**	**EXAMPLE**
*	Match any number of characters. It can be used as the first and/or last character in the character string.	th* finds *the, that, this, therefore,* and so on
?	Match any single alphabetic character.	a?t finds *act, aft, ant, apt,* and *art*
[]	Match any single character within the brackets.	a[fr]t finds *aft* and *art* but not *act, ant,* and *apt*
!	Match any character not within brackets.	a[!fr]t finds *act, ant,* and *apt* but not *aft* and *art*
-	Match any one of a range of characters. The range must be in ascending order (a to z, not z to a).	a[d-p]t finds *aft, ant,* and *apt* but not *act* and *art*
#	Match any single numeric character.	#72 finds *072, 172, 272, 372,* and so on

Elsa wants to view the position records for two employers: George's Restaurant & Galley (EmployerID 10180) and Moondance Inn & Ski Resort (EmployerID 10185). Matt Griffin, the manager of recruitment, knows of some student recruits with prior work experience who are interested in working for these employers. Elsa wants to see which positions, if any, require experience. You'll use the * wildcard character to search for these employers' positions.

To find the records using the * wildcard character:

1. Click **10145** in the Find What text box to select the entire value, and then type **1018***.

   Access will match any field value in the EmployerID field that starts with the digits 1018.

2. Click the **Find Next** button. Access displays record 64, which is the first record found for EmployerID 10185. Note that the Experience field value is unchecked, indicating that this position does not require experience.

3. Click the **Find Next** button. Access displays record 25, which is the first record found for EmployerID 10180. Again, the Experience field value is unchecked.

4. Click the **Find Next** button. Access displays record 42, which is the second record found for EmployerID 10185. In this case, the Experience field value is checked, indicating that this position requires prior work experience.

5. Click the **Find Next** button. Access displays a dialog box informing you that the search is finished.

6. Click the **OK** button to close the dialog box.

7. Click the **Cancel** button to close the Find and Replace dialog box.

Of the three positions, only one requires experience—PositionID 2089. Elsa asks you to use the form to print the data for record 42, which is for PositionID 2089, so that she can give the printout to Matt.

Previewing and Printing Selected Form Records

Access prints as many form records as can fit on a printed page. If only part of a form record fits on the bottom of a page, the remainder of the record prints on the next page. Access allows you to print all pages or a range of pages. In addition, you can print the currently selected form record.

Before printing record 42, you'll preview the form record to see how it will look when printed. Notice that the current record number (in this case, 42) appears in the Specific Record box at the bottom of the form.

To preview the form and print the data for record 42:

1. Click the **Print Preview** button 🔍 on the Form View toolbar. The Print Preview window opens, showing the form records for the Position table in miniature. If you clicked the Print button now, all the records for the table would be printed, beginning with the first record.

2. Click the **Maximize** button ▢ on the form's title bar.

3. Click the **Zoom** button 🔍 on the Print Preview toolbar, and then use the vertical scroll bar to view the entire page. Each record from the Position table appears in a separate form. See Figure 4-11.

| Figure 4-11 | PRINT PREVIEW WINDOW DISPLAYING FORM RECORDS |

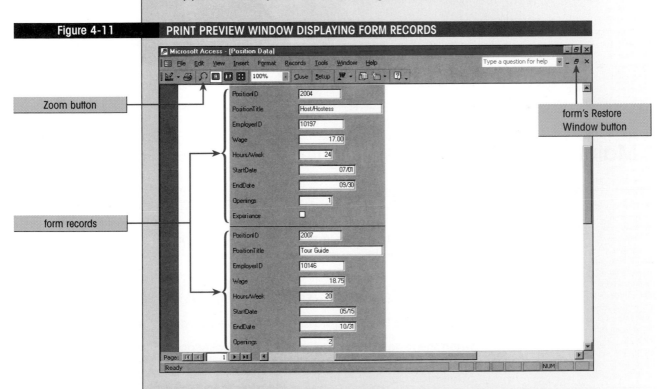

4. Click the **Restore Window** button 🗗 on the Print Preview menu bar, and then click the **Close** button on the Print Preview toolbar to return to the table in Form view.

The record that you need to print, PositionID 2089, appears in the form. To print selected records you need to use the Print dialog box.

5. Click **File** on the menu bar, and then click **Print**. The Print dialog box opens.

6. Click the **Selected Record(s)** option button to print the current form record (record 42).

7. Click the **OK** button to close the dialog box and to print the selected record.

Elsa has identified several updates, as shown in Figure 4-12, that she wants you to make to the Position table. You'll use the Position Data form to update the data in the Position table.

| Figure 4-12 | UPDATES TO THE POSITION TABLE |

PositionID	Update Action
2033	Change Hours/Week to 35 Change StartDate to 6/30
2072	Delete record
2130	Add new record for PositionID 2130: PositionTitle = Housekeeping EmployerID = 10151 Wage = 12.50 Hours/Week = 30 StartDate = 6/1 EndDate = 10/15 Openings = 2 Experience = No

Maintaining **Table Data Using a Form**

Maintaining data using a form is often easier than using a datasheet, because you can concentrate on all the changes required to a single record at one time. You already know how to navigate a form and find specific records. Now you'll make the changes Elsa requested to the Position table, using the Position Data form.

First, you'll update the record for PositionID 2033.

To change the record using the Position Data form:

1. Make sure the Position Data form is displayed in Form view.

   When she reviewed the position data to identify possible corrections, Elsa noted that 10 is the record number for PositionID 2033. If you know the number of the record you want to display, you can type the number in the Specific Record box and press the Enter key to go directly to that record.

2. Select **42** in the Specific Record box, type **10**, and then press the **Enter** key. Record 10 (PositionID 2033) is now the current record.

   You need to change the Hours/Week field value to 35 and the StartDate field value to 6/30 for this record.

3. Click the insertion point to the left of the number 2 in the Hours/Week field value, press the **Delete** key twice, and then type **35**. Note that the pencil symbol appears in the upper-left corner of the form, indicating that the form is in editing mode.

4. Press the **Tab** key to move to and select the StartDate field value, type **6/30**, and then press the **Enter** key. See Figure 4-13.

Figure 4-13	POSITION RECORD AFTER CHANGING FIELD VALUES

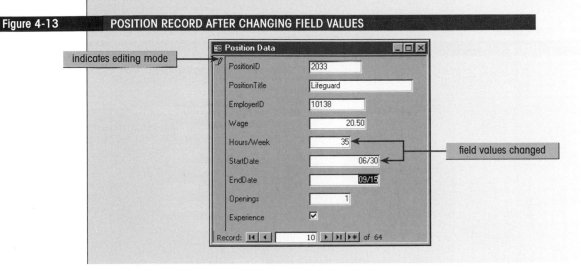

You have completed the changes for PositionID 2033. Elsa's next update is to delete the record for PositionID 2072. The employer client recently informed Elsa that a full-time, permanent employee has been hired for this position, so it is no longer available for student recruits.

To delete the record using the Position Data form:

1. Click anywhere in the PositionID field value to make it the current field.

2. Click the **Find** button 🔍 on the Form View toolbar. The Find and Replace dialog box opens.

3. Type **2072** in the Find What text box, click the **Find Next** button, and then click the **Cancel** button. The record for PositionID 2072 is now the current record.

4. Click the **Delete Record** button ✖ on the Form View toolbar. A dialog box opens, asking you to confirm the record deletion.

5. Click the **Yes** button. The dialog box closes, and the record for PositionID 2072 is deleted from the table.

Elsa's final maintenance change is to add a record for a new position available at the Granite State Resort.

To add the new record using the Position Data form:

1. Click the **New Record** button ▸✱ on the Form View toolbar. Record 64, the next record available for a new record, becomes the current record. All field value boxes are empty, and the insertion point is positioned at the beginning of the field value box for PositionID.

2. Refer to Figure 4-14 and enter the value shown for each field. Press the **Tab** key to move from field to field.

Figure 4-14   COMPLETED FORM FOR THE NEW RECORD

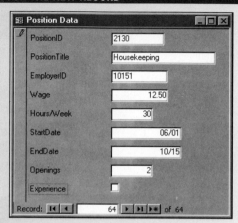

TROUBLE? Compare your screen with Figure 4-14. If any field value is wrong, correct it now, using the methods described earlier for editing field values.

3. After entering the value for Openings, press the **Tab** key twice (if necessary). Record 65, the next record available for a new record, becomes the current record, and the record for PositionID 2130 is saved in the Position table.

You've completed Elsa's changes to the Position table, so you can close the Position Data form.

4. Click the **Close** button ✖ on the form's title bar. The form closes and you return to the Database window. Notice that the Position Data form is listed in the Forms list box.

Checking the Spelling of Table Data Using a Form

You can check the spelling of table data using a table or query datasheet or a form that displays the table data. The Spelling feature searches through the data and identifies any words that are not included in its dictionary. Sometimes the word is misspelled, and you can correct it; other words are spelled correctly, but they are not listed in the spelling dictionary.

Elsa wants to make sure that the position data contains no spelling errors. You'll use the Position Data form to check the spelling of data in the Position table.

To check the spelling of data using the Position Data form:

1. Double-click **Position Data** to open the form in Form view. The form displays data for the first record.

2. Click the **Spelling** button on the Form View toolbar. The Spelling dialog box opens, identifying the word "Reservationist" as not in its dictionary. See Figure 4-15.

| Figure 4-15 | SPELLING DIALOG BOX |

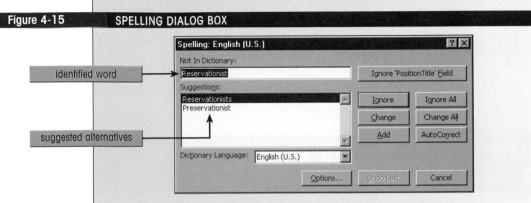

identified word

suggested alternatives

TROUBLE? If the word "Reservationist" is not identified by the Spelling feature, it was probably added to your dictionary. Just continue with the steps.

Note that the dialog box provides buttons for ignoring the word or changing it to one of the suggested alternatives, plus an option for ignoring all entries in the selected field (PositionTitle, in this case). The word is spelled correctly, so you will ignore all occurrences of this word in the Position table.

3. Click the **Ignore All** button. Next, the Spelling dialog box identifies the word "Greenskeeper" as not in its dictionary, and suggests the spelling should be two words, "Greens keeper." You'll change to the suggested spelling.

4. Click the **Change All** button. All occurrences of the word "Greenskeeper" are changed to the words "Greens keeper" in the Position table.

A dialog box opens, informing you that the spell check is complete.

5. Click the **OK** button to close the dialog box.

6. Close the form.

You can customize how the Spelling feature works in Access by changing the settings on the Spelling tab of the Options dialog box, which you open by choosing Options from the Tools menu. For example, you can choose another language for the main dictionary, and you can create custom dictionaries to contain words or phrases specific to the type of data in your database. Adding frequently used words to a custom dictionary will prevent the Spelling feature from identifying those words as not in its dictionary, thereby speeding up the spell check process.

The Position Data form will enable Elsa and her staff to enter and maintain data easily in the Position table. In the next session, you'll create another form for working with data in both the Position and Employer tables at the same time. You'll also create a report showing data from both tables.

Session 4.1 QUICK CHECK

1. Describe the difference between creating a form using the AutoForm Wizard and creating a form using the Form Wizard.

2. What is an AutoFormat, and how do you change one for an existing form?

3. Which table record is displayed in a form when you press Ctrl + End while you are in navigation mode?

4. You can use the Find command to search for data in a form or _____.

5. Which wildcard character matches any single alphabetic character?

6. How many form records does Access print by default on a page?

SESSION 4.2

In this session, you will create a form with a main form and a subform, modify a form in Design view, create a report using the Report Wizard, insert a picture in a report, and preview and print a report.

Elsa would like you to create a form so that she can view the data for each employer and its available positions at the same time. The type of form you need to create will include a main form and a subform.

Creating a Form with a Main Form and a Subform

To create a form based on two tables, you must first define a relationship between the two tables. In Tutorial 3, you defined a one-to-many relationship between the Employer (primary) and Position (related) tables, so you are ready to create the form based on both tables.

When you create a form containing data from two tables that have a one-to-many relationship, you actually create a main form for data from the primary table and a subform for data from the related table. Access uses the defined relationship between the tables to join the tables automatically through the common field that exists in both tables.

Elsa and her staff will use the form when contacting employers about their available positions. The main form will contain the employer ID and name, contact first and last names, and phone number for each employer. The subform will contain the position ID and title, wage, hours/week, experience, start and end dates, and number of openings for each position.

You'll use the Form Wizard to create the form.

To create the form using the Form Wizard:

1. If you took a break after the previous session, make sure that Access is running and the Northeast database is open.

2. Make sure the Forms object is selected in the Database window, and then click the **New** button. The New Form dialog box opens.

   When creating a form based on two tables, you first choose the primary table and select the fields you want to include in the main form; then you choose the related table and select fields from it for the subform.

3. Click **Form Wizard**, click the list arrow for choosing a table or query, click **Employer** to select this table as the source for the main form, and then click the **OK** button. The first Form Wizard dialog box opens, in which you select fields in the order you want them to appear on the main form.

Elsa wants the form to include only the EmployerID, EmployerName, ContactFirstName, ContactLastName, and Phone fields from the Employer table.

4. Click **EmployerID** in the Available Fields list box (if necessary), and then click the > button to move the field to the Selected Fields list box.

5. Repeat Step 4 for the **EmployerName**, **ContactFirstName**, **ContactLastName**, and **Phone** fields.

The EmployerID field will appear in the main form, so you do not have to include it in the subform. Otherwise, Elsa wants the subform to include all the fields from the Position table.

6. Click the **Tables/Queries** list arrow, and then click **Table: Position**. The fields from the Position table appear in the Available Fields list box. The quickest way to add the fields you want to include is to move all the fields to the Selected Fields list box, and then to remove the only field you don't want to include (EmployerID).

7. Click the >> button to move all the fields from the Position table to the Selected Fields list box.

8. Click **Position.EmployerID** in the Selected Fields list box, and then click the < button to move the field back to the Available Fields list box. Note that the table name (Position) is included in the field name to distinguish it from the same field (EmployerID) in the Employer table.

9. Click the **Next** button. The next Form Wizard dialog box opens. See Figure 4-16.

Figure 4-16	CHOOSING A MAIN/SUBFORM FORMAT

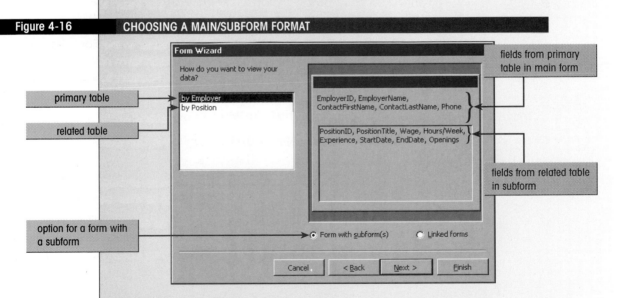

In this dialog box, the list box on the left shows the order in which you will view the selected data: first by data from the primary Employer table, and then by data from the related Position table. The form will be displayed as shown in the right side of the dialog box, with the fields from the Employer table at the top in the main form, and the fields from the Position table at the bottom in the sub-form. The selected option button specifies a main form with a subform. The Linked forms option creates a form structure where only the main form fields are displayed. A button with the subform's name on it appears on the main form; you can click this button to display the associated subform records.

The default options shown in Figure 4-16 are correct for creating a form with Employer data in the main form and Position data in the subform.

To finish creating the form:

1. Click the **Next** button. The next Form Wizard dialog box opens, in which you choose the subform layout.

   The Tabular layout displays subform fields as a table, whereas the Datasheet layout displays subform fields as a table datasheet. The PivotTable and PivotChart layouts display summary and analytical information. The layout choice is a matter of personal preference. You'll use the Datasheet layout.

2. Click the **Datasheet** option button (if necessary), and then click the **Next** button. The next Form Wizard dialog box opens, in which you choose the form's style.

   Elsa wants all forms in the Northeast database to have the same style, so you will choose Standard, which is the same style you applied to the Position Data form.

3. Click **Standard** (if necessary), and then click the **Next** button. The next Form Wizard dialog box opens, in which you choose names for the main form and the subform.

   You will use the name "Employer Positions" for the main form and the name "Position Subform" for the subform.

4. Click the insertion point to the right of the last letter in the Form text box, press the **spacebar**, and then type **Positions**. The main form name is now Employer Positions. Note that the default subform name, Position Subform, is the name you want, so you don't need to change it.

   You have answered all the Form Wizard's questions.

5. Click the **Finish** button. After a few moments, the completed form opens in Form view.

   Some of the columns in the subform are not wide enough to display the field names entirely. You need to resize the columns to their best fit.

6. Double-click the pointer ++ at the right edge of each column in the subform, scrolling the subform to the right, as necessary, to display additional columns. Scroll the subform all the way back to the left. The columns are resized to their best fit. See Figure 4-17.

Figure 4-17	MAIN FORM WITH SUBFORM IN FORM VIEW

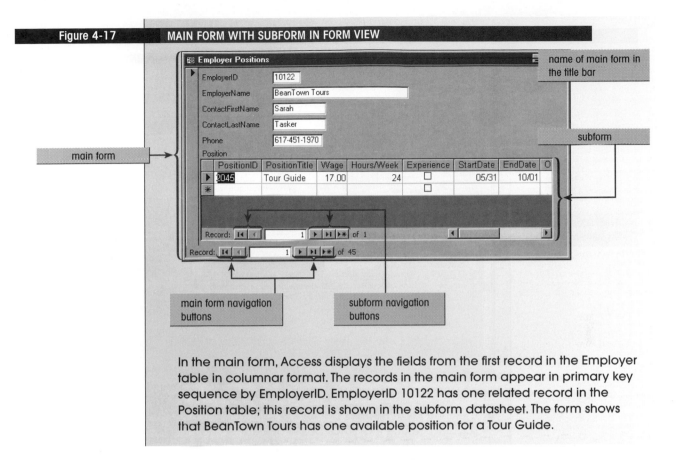

In the main form, Access displays the fields from the first record in the Employer table in columnar format. The records in the main form appear in primary key sequence by EmployerID. EmployerID 10122 has one related record in the Position table; this record is shown in the subform datasheet. The form shows that BeanTown Tours has one available position for a Tour Guide.

Notice that the subform is not wide enough to display all the fields from the Position table. Although the subform includes a horizontal scroll bar, which allows you to view the other fields, Elsa wants all the fields from the Position table to be visible in the subform at the same time. Even if you maximized the Form window, the subform would still not display all of the fields. You need to widen the main form and the subform in Design view.

Modifying a Form in Design View

Just as you use Design view to modify the format and content of tables and queries, you use Design view to modify a form. You can change the fields that are displayed on a form, and modify their size, location, format, and so on. You need to open the Employer Positions form in Design view and resize the Position subform to display all the fields at the same time.

To widen the Position subform:

1. Click the **View** button for Design view ▨ on the Form View toolbar to display the form in Design view.

2. Click the **Maximize** button ▢ to enlarge the window. See Figure 4-18.

Figure 4-18   FORM DISPLAYED IN DESIGN VIEW

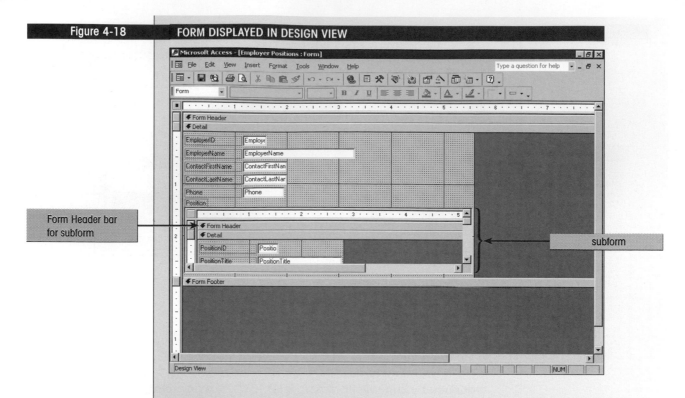

Form Header bar
for subform

subform

3. Click the **Form Header** bar for the subform (refer to Figure 4-18) to select the subform. Notice that small boxes appear around the subform's border. These boxes, which are called **handles**, indicate that the subform is selected and can be manipulated. See Figure 4-19.

Figure 4-19   SUBFORM SELECTED IN DESIGN VIEW

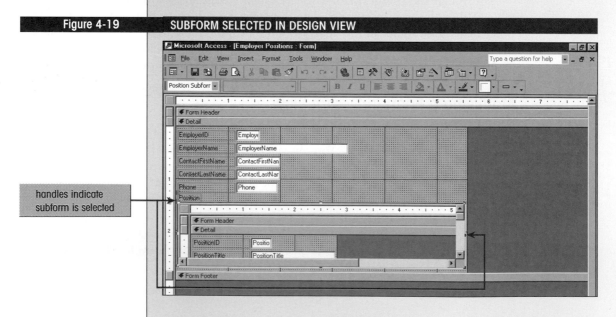

handles indicate
subform is selected

4. Position the pointer on the right-center sizing handle so it changes to a ↔ shape, and then click and drag the handle to the right to the **6.5**-inch mark on the horizontal ruler. See Figure 4-20.

Figure 4-20	RESIZING THE POSITION SUBFORM

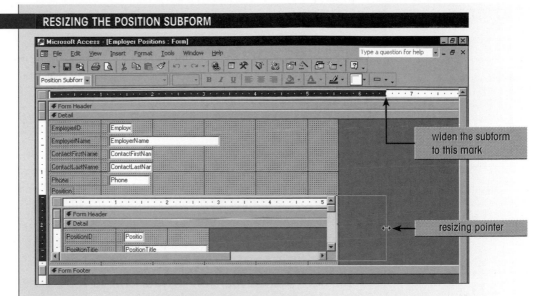

5. **Release the mouse button.** The subform section is resized. Notice that the main form section is also resized.

6. **Switch back to Form view.** Notice that all the field names in the Position Subform are now visible.

7. Click the **Restore Window** button on the menu bar to restore the form to its original size. Now you need to resize the Form window in Form view so that all the fields will be displayed when the Form window is not maximized.

8. Position the pointer on the right edge of the form so it changes to a ↔ shape, and then click and drag the right edge of the form to resize it so that it matches the form shown in Figure 4-21.

Figure 4-21	FORM WITH ALL SUBFORM FIELDS VISIBLE

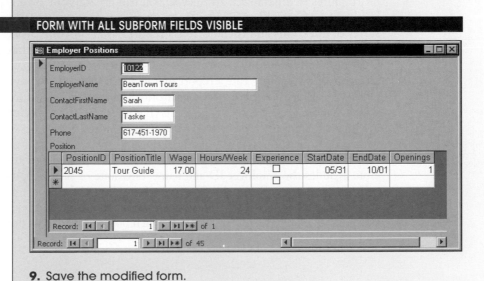

9. **Save the modified form.**

Two sets of navigation buttons appear at the bottom of the Form view window. You use the top set of navigation buttons to select records from the related table in the subform, and the bottom set to select records from the primary table in the main form.

You'll use the navigation buttons to view different records.

> ### To navigate to different main form and subform records:
>
> 1. Click the **Last Record** navigation button ▶| in the main form. Record 45 in the Employer table for Lighthouse Tours becomes the current record in the main form. The subform shows that this employer has one available Tour Guide position.
>
> 2. Click the **Previous Record** navigation button ◀ in the main form. Record 44 in the Employer table for Harbor Whale Watch Tours becomes the current record in the main form.
>
> 3. Select **44** in the Specific Record box for the main form, type **32**, and then press the **Enter** key. Record 32 in the Employer table for Windsor Alpine Tours becomes the current record in the main form. This employer has two available positions.
>
> 4. Click the **Last Record** navigation button ▶| in the subform. Record 2 in the Position table becomes the current record in the subform.
>
>   You have finished your work with the form, so you can close it.
>
> 5. Close the form. Notice that both the main form, Employer Positions, and the subform, Position Subform, appear in the Forms list box.

Zack would like a report showing data from both the Employer and Position tables so that all the pertinent information about employer clients and their positions is available in one place. To satisfy Zack's request, you'll create the report using the Report Wizard.

Creating a Report Using the Report Wizard

As you learned in Tutorial 1, a report is a formatted printout of the contents of one or more tables in a database. In Access, you can create your own reports or use the Report Wizard to create them for you. Like the Form Wizard, the **Report Wizard** asks you a series of questions and then creates a report based on your answers. Whether you use the Report Wizard or design your own report, you can change the report's design after you create it.

Zack wants you to create a report that includes selected employer data from the Employer table and all the available positions from the Position table for each employer. Zack has sketched a design of the report he wants (Figure 4-22). Like the Employer Positions form you just created, which includes a main form and a subform, the report will be based on both tables, which are joined in a one-to-many relationship through the common EmployerID field. As shown in the sketch in Figure 4-22, the selected employer data from the primary Employer table includes the employer ID and name, city, state or province, contact first and last names, and phone number. Below the data for each employer, the report will include the position ID and title, wage, hours/week, experience, start and end dates, and openings data from the related Position table. The set of field values for each position is called a **detail record**.

| Figure 4-22 | REPORT SKETCH FOR THE EMPLOYERS AND POSITIONS REPORT |

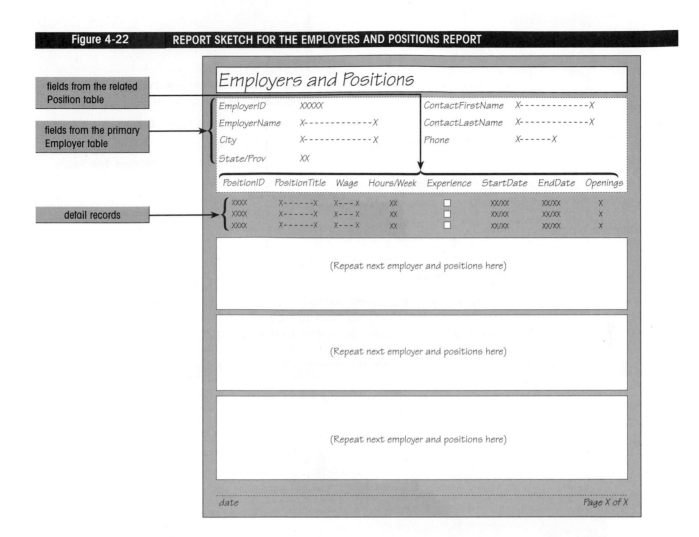

fields from the related Position table

fields from the primary Employer table

detail records

You'll use the Report Wizard to create the report according to the design in Zack's sketch.

To start the Report Wizard and select the fields to include in the report:

1. Click **Reports** in the Objects bar of the Database window to display the Reports list box. You have not yet created any reports.

2. Click the **New** button in the Database window. The New Report dialog box opens.

   As was the case when you created the form with a subform, initially you can choose only one table or query to be the data source for the report. Then you can include data from other tables. You will select the primary Employer table in the New Report dialog box.

3. Click **Report Wizard**, click the list arrow for choosing a table or query, and then click **Employer**.

4. Click the **OK** button. The first Report Wizard dialog box opens.

   In the first Report Wizard dialog box, you select fields in the order you want them to appear on the report. Zack wants the EmployerID, EmployerName, City,

State/Prov, ContactFirstName, ContactLastName, and Phone fields from the Employer table to appear on the report.

5. Click **EmployerID** in the Available Fields list box (if necessary), and then click the ⟩ button. The field moves to the Selected Fields list box.

6. Repeat Step 5 to add the **EmployerName**, **City**, **State/Prov**, **ContactFirstName**, **ContactLastName**, and **Phone** fields to the report.

7. Click the **Tables/Queries** list arrow, and then click **Table: Position**. The fields from the Position table appear in the Available Fields list box.

The EmployerID field will appear on the report with the employer data, so you do not have to include it in the detail records for each position. Otherwise, Zack wants all the fields from the Position table to be included in the report.

8. Click the ⟩⟩ button to move all the fields from the Available Fields list box to the Selected Fields list box.

9. Click **Position.EmployerID** in the Selected Fields list box, click the ⟨ button to move the selected field back to the Available Fields list box, and then click the **Next** button. The second Report Wizard dialog box opens. See Figure 4-23.

Figure 4-23	CHOOSING A GROUPED OR UNGROUPED REPORT

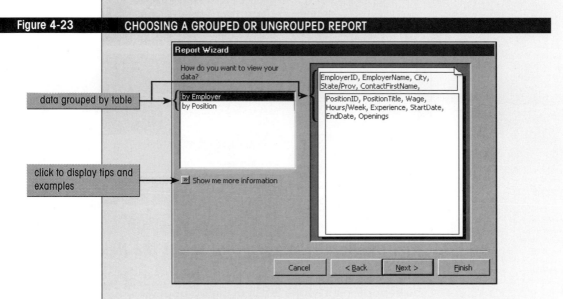

data grouped by table

click to display tips and examples

You can choose to arrange the selected data grouped by table, which is the default, or ungrouped. For a grouped report, the data from a record in the primary table appears as a group, followed on subsequent lines of the report by the joined records from the related table. For the report you are creating, data from a record in the Employer table appears in a group, followed by the related records for each employer from the Position table. An example of an ungrouped report would be a report of records from the Employer and Position tables in order by PositionID. Each position and its associated employer data would appear together on one or more lines of the report; the data would not be grouped by table.

You can display tips and examples for the choices in the Report Wizard dialog box by clicking the "Show me more information" button ⟩⟩ .

To display tips about the options in the Report Wizard dialog box:

1. Click the ⏩ button. The Report Wizard Tips dialog box opens. Read the information shown in the dialog box.

You can display examples of different grouping methods by clicking the ⏩ button ("Show me examples").

2. Click ⏩. The Report Wizard Examples dialog box opens. See Figure 4-24.

Figure 4-24 **REPORT WIZARD EXAMPLES DIALOG BOX**

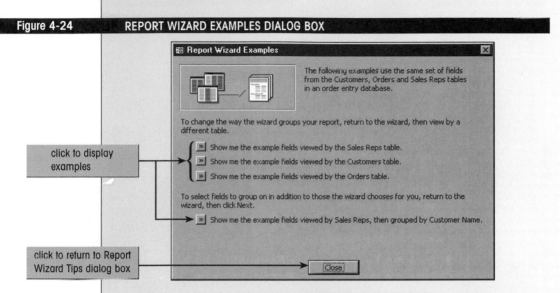

click to display examples

click to return to Report Wizard Tips dialog box

You can display examples of different grouping methods by clicking the ⏩ buttons.

3. Click each ⏩ button in turn, review the displayed example, and then click the **Close** button to return to the Report Wizard Examples dialog box.

4. Click the **Close** button to return to the Report Wizard Tips dialog box, and then click the **Close** button to return to the second Report Wizard dialog box.

The default options shown on your screen are correct for the report Zack wants, so you can continue responding to the Report Wizard questions.

To finish creating the report using the Report Wizard:

1. Click the **Next** button. The next Report Wizard dialog box opens, in which you choose additional grouping levels.

Two grouping levels are shown: one for an employer's data, and the other for an employer's positions. Grouping levels are useful for reports with multiple levels, such as those containing monthly, quarterly, and annual totals, or for those containing city and country groups. Zack's report contains no further grouping levels, so you can accept the default options.

2. Click the **Next** button. The next Report Wizard dialog box opens, in which you choose the sort order for the detail records. See Figure 4-25.

Figure 4-25   **CHOOSING THE SORT ORDER FOR DETAIL RECORDS**

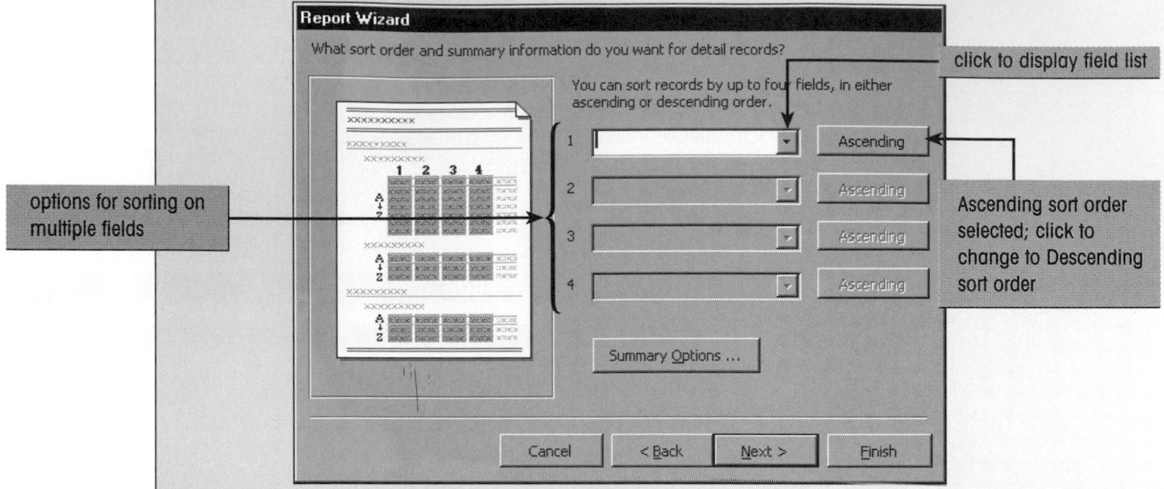

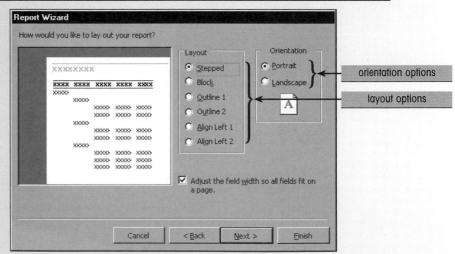

options for sorting on multiple fields

click to display field list

Ascending sort order selected; click to change to Descending sort order

The records from the Position table for an employer represent the detail records for Zack's report. He wants these records to appear in increasing, or ascending, order by the value in the PositionID field. The Ascending option is already selected by default. To change to descending order, you simply click this button, which acts as a toggle between the two sort orders. Also, notice that you can sort on multiple fields, as you can with queries.

3. Click the **1** list arrow, click **PositionID**, and then click the **Next** button. The next Report Wizard dialog box opens, in which you choose a layout and page orientation for the report. See Figure 4-26.

Figure 4-26   **CHOOSING THE REPORT LAYOUT AND PAGE ORIENTATION**

orientation options

layout options

A sample of each layout appears in the box on the left.

4. Click each layout option and examine each sample that appears.

You'll use the Outline 2 layout option because it resembles the layout shown in Zack's sketch of the report. Also, because of the number of fields in the Position table, the information would fit better in a wide format; therefore, you'll choose the landscape orientation.

5. Click the **Outline 2** option button, click the **Landscape** option button, and then click the **Next** button. The next Report Wizard dialog box opens, in which you choose a style for the report.

   A sample of the selected style, or AutoFormat, appears in the box on the left. You can always choose a different AutoFormat after you create the report, just as you can when creating a form. Zack likes the appearance of the Corporate AutoFormat, so you'll choose this one for your report.

6. Click **Corporate** (if necessary), and then click the **Next** button. The last Report Wizard dialog box opens, in which you choose a report name, which also serves as the printed title on the report.

   According to Zack's sketch, the report title you need to specify is "Employers and Positions."

7. Type **Employers and Positions** and then click the **Finish** button. The Report Wizard creates the report based on your answers and saves it as an object in the Northeast database. Then Access opens the Employers and Positions report in Print Preview.

   To view the report better, you need to maximize the Report window.

8. Click the **Maximize** button 🔲 on the Employers and Positions title bar.

   To view the entire page, you need to change the Zoom setting.

9. Click the **Zoom** list arrow on the Print Preview toolbar, and then click **Fit**. The first page of the report is displayed in Print Preview. See Figure 4-27.

Figure 4-27	REPORT DISPLAYED IN PRINT PREVIEW

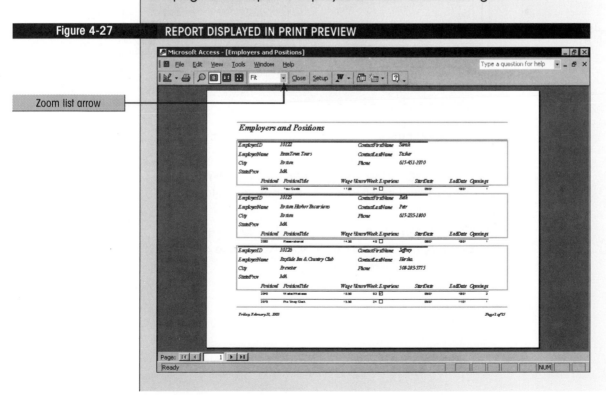

Zoom list arrow

When a report is displayed in Print Preview, you can use the pointer to toggle between a full-page display and a close-up display of the report. Zack asks you to check the report to see if any adjustments need to be made. For example, some of the field titles or values might not be displayed completely, or you might need to move fields to enhance the report's appearance. To do so, you need to view a close-up display of the report.

To view a close-up display of the report and make any necessary corrections:

1. Click the pointer 🔍 at the top center of the report. The display changes to show a close-up view of the report. See Figure 4-28.

Figure 4-28   CLOSE-UP VIEW OF THE REPORT

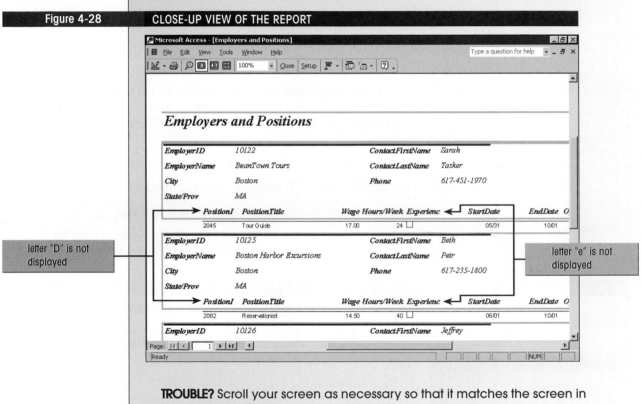

letter "D" is not displayed

letter "e" is not displayed

TROUBLE? Scroll your screen as necessary so that it matches the screen in Figure 4-28.

The letter "D" at the end of the PositionID field name and the letter "e" at the end of the Experience field name are not visible. To fix this, you need to switch to Design view.

2. Click the **View** button for Design view 📐 on the Print Preview toolbar. Access displays the report in Design view. See Figure 4-29.

| Figure 4-29 | REPORT DISPLAYED IN DESIGN VIEW |

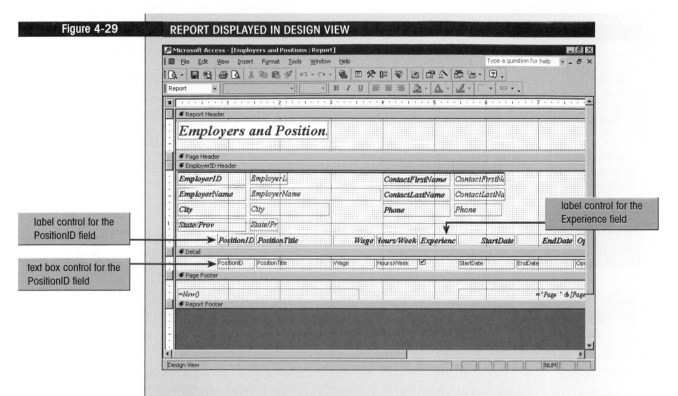

label control for the
PositionID field

text box control for the
PositionID field

label control for the
Experience field

TROUBLE? If your screen displays any window other than those shown in Figure 4-29, click the Close button ☒ on the window's title bar to close it.

You use the Report window in Design view to modify existing reports and to create custom reports.

Each item on a report in Design view is called a **control**. For example, the PositionID field consists of two controls: the label "PositionID," which appears on the report to identify the field value, and the PositionID text box, in which the actual field value appears. You need to widen the label control for the PositionID field so that the entire field name is visible in the report.

3. Click the label control for the PositionID field to select it. Handles appear on the border around the control, indicating that the control is selected and can be manipulated.

4. Position the pointer on the center-left handle of the PositionID label control until the pointer changes to a ↔ shape. See Figure 4-30.

Figure 4-30   RESIZING THE PositionID LABEL CONTROL

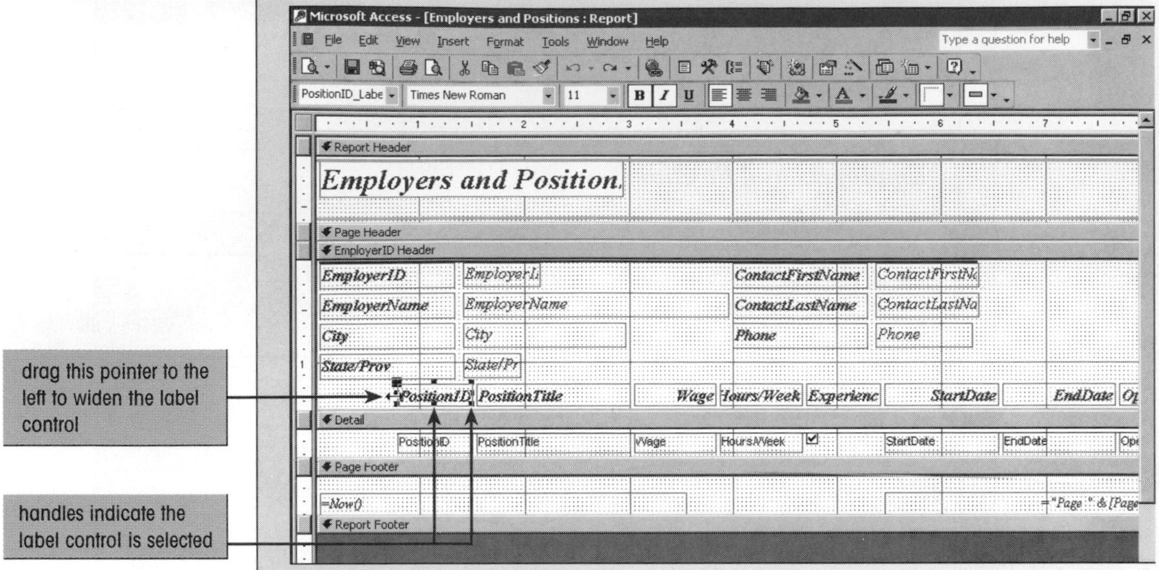

drag this pointer to the left to widen the label control

handles indicate the label control is selected

5. Click and drag the pointer to the left until the left edge of the control is aligned with the **0.75**-inch mark on the horizontal ruler, and then release the mouse button.

   To correct the problem with the Experience field name, you'll use the center-right handle.

6. Position the pointer on the center-right handle of the Experience label control until the pointer changes to a ↔ shape, click and drag the pointer to the right until the right edge is aligned with the 5.5-inch mark on the horizontal ruler, and then release the mouse button.

   Now you need to switch back to Print Preview and make sure that the complete names for the PositionID and Experience fields are visible.

7. Click the **View** button for Print Preview 🔍 on the Report Design toolbar. The report appears in Print Preview. Notice that the PositionID and Experience field names in the label controls are now completely displayed.

8. Click **File** on the menu bar, and then click **Save** to save the modified report.

Zack decides that he wants the report to include a graphic image to the right of the report title, for visual interest. You can add the graphic to the report by inserting a picture.

Inserting a Picture in a Report

In Access, you can insert a picture or other graphic image in a report or form to enhance the appearance of the report or form. Sources of graphic images include files created in Microsoft Paint and other drawing programs, and scanned files. The file containing the picture you need to insert is named Globe, and it is located in the Tutorial folder on your Data Disk.

To insert the picture in the report:

1. Click the **Close** button on the Print Preview toolbar to display the report in Design view. See Figure 4-31.

Figure 4-31	INSERTING A PICTURE IN DESIGN VIEW

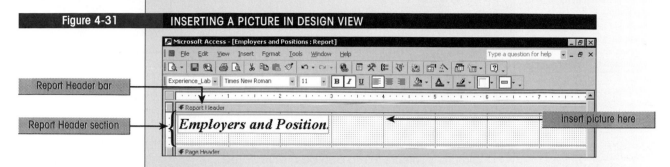

Zack wants the picture to appear on the first page of the report only; therefore, you need to insert the picture in the Report Header section (see Figure 4-31). Any text or picture placed in this section appears once at the beginning of the report.

2. Click the **Report Header** bar to select this section of the report. The bar is highlighted to indicate that the section is selected.

3. Click **Insert** on the menu bar, and then click **Picture**. The Insert Picture dialog box opens. If necessary, open the **Tutorial** folder on your Data Disk. See Figure 4-32.

Figure 4-32	INSERT PICTURE DIALOG BOX

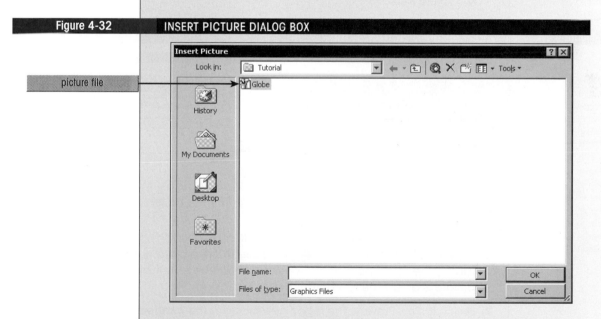

4. Click **Globe** to select the picture for the report, and then click the **OK** button. The picture is inserted in the left side of the Report Header section, covering some of the report title text. See Figure 4-33.

Figure 4-33   PICTURE INSERTED IN THE REPORT

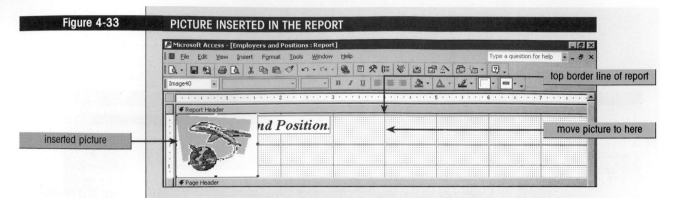

Notice that handles appear around the picture's border, indicating that the picture is selected and can be manipulated.

Zack wants the picture to appear to the right of the report title, so you need to move the picture using the mouse.

5. Position the pointer on the picture until the pointer changes to a ✋ shape, and then click and drag the mouse to move the picture to the right so that its left edge aligns with the 4-inch mark on the horizontal ruler and its top edge is just below the top border line above the report title (see Figure 4-33).

6. Release the mouse button. The picture appears in the new position. Notice that the height of the Report Header section increased slightly to accommodate the picture. See Figure 4-34.

Figure 4-34   REPOSITIONED PICTURE IN THE REPORT

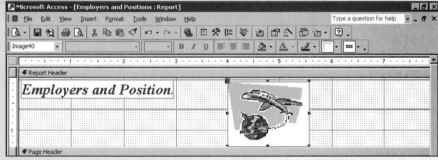

TROUBLE? If your picture appears in a different location from the one shown in Figure 4-34, use the pointer ✋ to reposition the picture until it is in approximately the same position shown in the figure. Be sure that the top edge of the picture is below the top border line of the report.

7. Switch to Print Preview. The report now includes the inserted picture. If necessary, click the **Zoom** button 🔍 on the Print Preview toolbar to display the entire report page. See Figure 4-35.

| Figure 4-35 | PRINT PREVIEW OF REPORT WITH PICTURE |

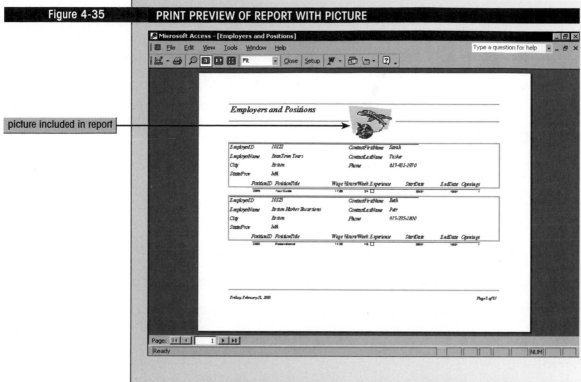

picture included in report

TROUBLE? If the picture covers the gray line at the top of the report, switch to Design view and use the pointer to position the picture in the correct location. Then repeat Step 7.

8. Save the modified report.

The report is now completed. You'll print just the first page of the report so that Zack can review the report layout and the inserted picture.

To print page 1 of the report:

1. Click **File** on the menu bar, and then click **Print**. The Print dialog box opens.

2. In the Print Range section, click the **Pages** option button. The insertion point now appears in the From text box so that you can specify the range of pages to print.

3. Type **1** in the From text box, press the **Tab** key to move to the To text box, and then type **1**. These settings specify that only page 1 of the report will be printed.

4. Click the **OK** button. The Print dialog box closes, and the first page of the report is printed.

Zack approves of the report layout and contents, so you can close the report.

5. Click the **Close Window** button ☒ on the menu bar.

TROUBLE? If you click the Close button on the Print Preview toolbar by mistake, you switch to Design view. Click the Close Window button ☒ on the menu bar.

6. Exit Access.

Elsa is satisfied that the forms you created—the Position Data form and the Employer Positions form—will make it easier to enter, view, and update data in the Northeast database. The Employers and Positions report presents important information about NSJI's employer clients in an attractive and professional format, which will help Zack and his staff in their marketing efforts.

Session 4.2 QUICK CHECK

1. In a form that contains a main form and a subform, what data is displayed in the main form and what data is displayed in the subform?

2. Describe how you use the navigation buttons to move through a form containing a main form and a subform.

3. When you use the Report Wizard, the report name is also used as the _____.

4. Each item on a report in Design view is called a(n) _____.

5. To insert a picture in a report, the report must be displayed in _____.

6. Any text or pictures placed in the _____ section of a report will appear only on the first page of the report.

REVIEW ASSIGNMENTS

Elsa wants to enhance the **Recruits** database with forms and reports, and she asks you to complete the following:

1. Make sure your Data Disk is in the appropriate disk drive, start Access, and then open the **Recruits** database located in the Review folder on your Data Disk.

2. If your **Recruits** database is stored on drive A, you will need to delete the files **Seasons97.mdb** and **Seasons2002.mdb** from your disk so you will have enough room to complete the steps. If your database is stored on a hard or network drive, no action is necessary.

3. Use the Form Wizard to create a form based on the **Student** table. Select all fields for the form, the Columnar layout, the SandStone style, and the title **Student Data** for the form.

4. Use the form you created in the previous step to print the fifth form record. Change the AutoFormat to Sumi Painting, save the changed form, and then print the fifth form record again.

5. Use the **Student Data** form to update the **Student** table as follows:

   a. Use the Find command to move to the record with StudentID STO1323. Change the field values for FirstName to Nathaniel, City to Perth, and BirthDate to 4/2/85 for this record.

   b. Use the Find command to move to the record with StudentID KIE2760, and then delete the record.

   c. Add a new record with the following field values:
   StudentID: SAN2540
   FirstName: Pedro
   LastName: Sandes

City:	Barcelona
Nation:	Spain
BirthDate:	5/1/85
Gender:	M
SSN:	977-07-1798

    d. Print only this form record, and then close the form.

Explore

6. Use the AutoForm: Columnar Wizard to create a form based on the **Salaries with Raises** query. Save the form as **Salaries with Raises**, and then close the form.

Explore

7. Use the Form Wizard to create a form containing a main form and a subform. Select the FirstName, LastName, and SSN fields from the **Recruiter** table for the main form, and select all fields except SSN from the **Student** table for the subform. Use the Datasheet layout and the Sumi Painting style. Specify the title **Recruiter Students** for the main form and the title **Student Subform** for the subform. Resize all columns in the subform to their best fit. Use Design view to resize the main form and the subform so that all fields are visible in the subform at the same time. Resize the Form window in Form view, as necessary, so that all fields are visible at the same time. Print the fourth main form record and its subform records. Save and close the form.

Explore

8. Use the Report Wizard to create a report based on the primary **Recruiter** table and the related **Student** table. Select all fields from the **Recruiter** table, and select all fields from the **Student** table except SSN, in the following order: FirstName, LastName, City, Nation, BirthDate, Gender, StudentID. In the third Report Wizard dialog box, specify the Nation field as an additional grouping level. Sort the detail records in ascending order by City. Choose the Align Left 2 layout and the Formal style for the report. Specify the title **Recruiters and Students** for the report.

Explore

9. Display the **Recruiters and Students** report in Design view and maximize the Report window. In the Nation Header section, change the Student_FirstName label control to "FirstName" and change the Student_LastName label control to "LastName." Widen both the Gender and StudentID label controls so that the labels are fully visible in the report. (*Hint*: You can resize the Gender control to both the left and the right, and the borders of adjacent controls can touch each other.)

10. Insert the **Travel** picture, which is located in the Review folder on your Data Disk, in the Report Header section of the **Recruiters and Students** report. Position the picture so that its left edge aligns with the 4-inch mark on the horizontal ruler and its top edge is just below the top border line of the report.

11. Print only the first page of the report, and then close and save the modified report.

12. If your database is stored on drive A, you will need to turn off the Compact on Close feature before closing the **Recruits** database because there isn't enough room on the disk to compact the database. If your database is stored on a hard or network drive, no action is necessary.

13. Close the **Recruits** database, and then exit Access.

CASE PROBLEMS

Case 1. Lim's Video Photography Youngho Lim wants the **Videos** database to include forms and reports that will help him track and view information about his clients and their video shoot events. You'll create the necessary forms and reports by completing the following:

1. Make sure your Data Disk is in the appropriate disk drive, start Access, and then open the **Videos** database located in the Cases folder on your Data Disk.

2. Use the Form Wizard to create a form based on the **Client** table. Select all fields for the form, the Columnar layout, and the Blends style. Specify the title **Client Data** for the form.

3. Change the AutoFormat for the **Client Data** form to Standard.

4. Use the Find command to move to the record with Client# 338, and then change the Address field value for this record to 2150 Brucewood Avenue.

5. Use the **Client Data** form to add a new record with the following field values:

   Client#:   351
   ClientName: Peters, Amanda
   Address: 175 Washington Street
   City: Berkeley
   State: CA
   Zip: 94704
   Phone: 510-256-1007

   Print only this form record, and then save and close the form.

6. Use the Form Wizard to create a form containing a main form and a subform. Select all the fields from the **Client** table for the main form, and select all fields except Client# from the **Contract** table for the subform. Use the Tabular layout and the Standard style. Specify the title **Contracts by Client** for the main form and the title **Contract Subform** for the subform.

7. Print the seventh main form record and its subform records, and then close the **Contracts by Client** form.

8. Use the Report Wizard to create a report based on the primary **Client** table and the related **Contract** table. Select all the fields from the **Client** table, and select all the fields from the **Contract** table except Client#. Sort the detail records in ascending order by Contract#. Choose the Align Left 2 layout and the Casual style. Specify the title **Client Contracts** for the report.

9. Insert the **Camcord** picture, which is located in the Cases folder on your Data Disk, in the Report Header section of the **Client Contracts** report. Position the picture so that its left edge aligns with the 4-inch mark on the horizontal ruler and its top edge is just below the top border line of the report.

10. Print only the first page of the report, and then close and save the modified report.

11. Close the **Videos** database, and then exit Access.

Case 2. DineAtHome.course.com Claire Picard continues her work with the **Meals** database to track and analyze the business activity of the restaurants she works with and their customers. To help her, you'll enhance the **Meals** database by completing the following:

1. Make sure your Data Disk is in the appropriate disk drive, start Access, and then open the **Meals** database located in the Cases folder on your Data Disk.

2. Use the Form Wizard to create a form containing a main form and a subform. Select the Restaurant#, RestaurantName, City, Phone, and Website fields from the **Restaurant** table for the main form, and select all fields except Restaurant# from the **Order** table for the subform. Use the Datasheet layout and the Industrial style. Specify the title **Restaurant Orders** for the main form and the title **Order Subform** for the subform. Resize all columns in the subform to their best fit. Print the first main form record and its displayed subform records.

3. For the form you just created, change the AutoFormat to SandStone, save the changed form, and then print the first main form record and its subform records.

4. Navigate to the third record in the subform for the first main record, and then change the OrderAmt field value to 107.80.

5. Use the Find command to move to the record with the Restaurant# 118, and then delete the record. Answer Yes to any warning messages about deleting the record.

Explore 6. Use the appropriate wildcard character to find all records with the word "House" anywhere in the restaurant name. (*Hint*: You must enter the wildcard character before and after the text you are searching for.) How many records did you find? Close the **Restaurant Orders** form.

Explore 7. Use the Report Wizard to create a report based on the primary **Restaurant** table and the related **Order** table. Select the Restaurant#, RestaurantName, Street, City, OwnerFirstName, and OwnerLastName fields from the **Restaurant** table, and select all fields from the **Order** table except Restaurant#. In the third Report Wizard dialog box, specify the OrderDate field as an additional grouping level. Sort the detail records by OrderAmt in *descending* order. Choose the Align Left 1 layout and the Bold style for the report. Specify the title **Orders by Restaurants** for the report.

8. Insert the **Server** picture, which is located in the Cases folder on your Data Disk, in the Report Header section of the **Orders by Restaurants** report. Leave the picture in its original position at the left edge of the Report Header section.

Explore 9. Use the Ask a Question box to ask the following question: "How do I move a control in front of or behind other controls?" Click the topic "Move one or more controls to a new position," and then click the subtopic "Move a control in front of or behind other controls." Read the information and then close the Help window. Make sure the **Server** picture is still selected, and then move it behind the Orders by Restaurants title.

Explore 10. Use the Ask a Question box to ask the following question: "How do I change the background color of a control?" Click the topic "Change the background color of a control or section." Read the information and then close the Help window. Select the Orders by Restaurant title object, and then change its background color to Transparent.

11. Display the report in Print Preview. Print just the first page of the report, and then close and save the report.

12. Close the **Meals** database, and then exit Access.

Case 3. Redwood Zoo Michael Rosenfeld wants to create forms and reports for the **Redwood** database. You'll help him create these database objects by completing the following:

1. Make sure your Data Disk is in the appropriate disk drive, start Access, and then open the **Redwood** database located in the Cases folder on your Data Disk.

2. If your **Redwood** database is stored on drive A, you will need to delete the files **Redwood97.mdb** and **Redwood2002.mdb** from your disk so you will have enough room to complete the steps. If your database is stored on a hard or network drive, no action is necessary.

3. Use the Form Wizard to create a form based on the **Pledge** table. Select all fields for the form, the Columnar layout, and the Blueprint style. Specify the title **Pledge Info** for the form.

4. Use the **Pledge Info** form to update the **Pledge** table as follows:

   a. Use the Find command to move to the record with Pledge# 2490, and then change the FundCode to B11 and the TotalPledged amount to 75.

   b. Add a new record with the following values:

Pledge#:	2977
DonorID:	59021
FundCode:	M23
PledgeDate:	12/15/2003
TotalPledged:	150
PaymentMethod:	C
PaymentSchedule:	S

   c. Print just this form record.

   d. Delete the record with Pledge# 2900.

5. Change the AutoFormat of the **Pledge Info** form to Expedition, save the changed form, and then use the form to print the last record in the **Pledge** table. Close the form.

6. Use the Form Wizard to create a form containing a main form and a subform. Select all the fields from the **Donor** table for the main form, and select the Pledge#, FundCode, PledgeDate, and TotalPledged fields from the **Pledge** table for the subform. Use the Tabular layout and the Expedition style. Specify the title **Donors and Pledges** for the main form and the title **Pledge Subform** for the subform.

7. Display record 11 in the main form. Print the current main form record and its subform records, and then close the **Donors and Pledges** form.

Explore 8. Use the Report Wizard to create a report based on the primary **Donor** table and the related **Pledge** table. Select the DonorID, FirstName, LastName, and Class fields from the **Donor** table, and select all fields from the **Pledge** table except DonorID. In the third Report Wizard dialog box, specify the FundCode field as an additional grouping level. Sort the detail records in *descending* order by TotalPledged. Choose the Align Left 2 layout, Landscape orientation, and the Soft Gray style. Specify the title **Donors and Pledges** for the report.

9. Insert the **Animals** picture, which is located in the Cases folder on your Data Disk, in the Report Header section of the **Donors and Pledges** report. Position the picture so that its left edge aligns with the 4-inch mark on the horizontal ruler and its top edge is just below the top border line of the report.

Explore 10. Use the Ask a Question box to ask the following question: "How do I add a special effect to an object?" Click the topic "Make a control appear raised, sunken, shadowed, chiseled, or etched." Read the information, and then close the Help window. Add the Shadowed special effect to the **Animals** picture, and then save the report.

Explore 11. Print only pages 1 and 7 of the report, and then close it.

12. If your database is stored on drive A, you will need to turn off the Compact on Close feature before closing the **Redwood** database because there isn't enough room on the disk to compact the database. If your database is stored on a hard or network drive, no action is necessary.

13. Close the **Redwood** database, and then exit Access.

Case 4. Mountain River Adventures Connor and Siobhan Dempsey want to create forms and reports that will help them track and analyze data about their customers and the rafting trips they take. Help them enhance the **Trips** database by completing the following:

1. Make sure your Data Disk is in the appropriate disk drive, start Access, and then open the **Trips** database located in the Cases folder on your Data Disk.

2. Use the Form Wizard to create a form containing a main form and a subform. Select the Client#, ClientName, City, State/Prov, and Phone fields from the **Client** table for the main form, and select all fields except Client# from the **Booking** table for the subform. Use the Datasheet layout and the Standard style. Specify the title **Clients and Bookings** for the main form and the title **Booking Subform** for the subform. Resize all columns in the subform to their best fit. Print the ninth main form record and its subform records.

3. For the form you just created, change the AutoFormat to Stone, save the changed form, and then print the ninth main form record and its subform records.

4. Navigate to the second record in the subform for the ninth main record, and then change the People field value to 7.

5. Use the Find command to move to the record with Client# 330, and then delete the record. Answer Yes to any warning messages about deleting the record.

6. Use the appropriate wildcard character to find all records with a City value that begins with the letter "D." How many records did you find? Close the form.

7. Use the Report Wizard to create a report based on the primary **Client** table and the related **Booking** table. Select all fields from the **Client** table, and select all fields except Client# from the **Booking** table. Sort the detail records by the TripDate field in ascending order. Choose the Outline 1 layout and the Compact style. Specify the title **Client Bookings** for the report.

Explore   8. Display the **Client Bookings** report in Design view, and then widen the Phone text box control so that the Phone field values are completely displayed in the report.

9. Insert the **Raft** picture, which is located in the Cases folder on your Data Disk, in the Report Header section of the **Client Bookings** report. Position the picture so that its left edge aligns with the 2-inch mark on the horizontal ruler and its top edge is just below the top border line of the report. (If the picture blocks part of the bottom border line of the header, that is fine.)

Explore   10. Insert the same **Raft** picture in the Report Footer section of the **Client Bookings** report. (Items placed in the Report Footer section appear only once, at the end of the report.) Position the picture so that its right edge aligns with the right edge of the report, at approximately the 6.5-inch mark on the horizontal ruler. Save the report.

Explore   11. View the first two pages of the report in Print Preview at the same time. (*Hint*: Use a toolbar button.) Use the Page navigation buttons to move through the report, displaying two pages at a time. Print only the first and last pages of the report, and then close the report.

12. Close the **Trips** database, and then exit Access.

INTERNET ASSIGNMENTS

Student Union

The purpose of the Internet Assignments is to challenge you to find information on the Internet that you can use to create effective documents. The actual assignments are updated and maintained on the Course Technology Web site. Log on to the Internet and use your Web browser to go to the Student Union on the New Perspectives Series site at **www.course.com/NewPerspectives/studentunion**. Click the Online Companions link, and then click the link for this tutorial.

QUICK CHECK ANSWERS

Session 4.1

1. The AutoForm Wizard creates a form automatically using all the fields in the selected table or query; the Form Wizard allows you to choose some or all of the fields in the selected table or query, choose fields from other tables and queries, and display fields in any order on the form.

2. An AutoFormat is a predefined style for a form (or report). To change a form's AutoFormat, display the form in Design view, click the AutoFormat button on the Form Design toolbar, click the new AutoFormat in the Form AutoFormats list box, and then click the OK button.

3. the last record in the table

4. datasheet

5. the question mark (?)

6. as many form records as can fit on a printed page

Session 4.2

1. The main form displays the data from the primary table, and the subform displays the data from the related table.

2. You use the top set of navigation buttons to select and move through records from the related table in the subform, and the bottom set to select and move through records from the primary table in the main form.

3. report title

4. control

5. Design view

6. Report Header

CREATING WEB PAGES WITH ACCESS

Creating Web Pages to Display Employer and Position Data

CASE

Northeast Seasonal Jobs International (NSJI)

Elsa Jensen recognizes the value of the data stored in the Northeast database, both for promoting NSJI's business activities and for maintaining important information about NSJI's employer clients and student recruits. To increase efficiency and facilitate the sharing of information, Elsa wants to display certain information in the form of Web pages. **Web pages** are special documents you can view using a program called a **browser**. The two most popular browsers are **Microsoft Internet Explorer** and **Netscape Navigator**. The browser retrieves files from a type of computer called a **Web server** and displays those files on a computer in the form of a Web page.

Web pages are connected to each other through **hyperlinks**, which are words, phrases, or graphic images that you click to move to another location in the same Web page or a different page. Text hyperlinks are usually underlined and appear in a different color than the rest of the text in the page. The collection of linked Web pages that reside on computers throughout the world is called the **World Wide Web**, or simply, the **Web**. These computers form the largest and most widely used computer network in the world—the **Internet**. Most companies maintain a **Web site**, which is a group of related Web pages that provides information about the company and allows interaction with it. Each Web site has its own Internet address, which is called a **Uniform Resource Locator (URL)**. For example, the URL www.microsoft.com is the address for Microsoft Corporation. Most companies, including NSJI, also maintain internal private networks, called **intranets**, for sharing information only with other members of the organization.

Most Web pages are created using a programming language called **HTML (Hypertext Markup Language)**. You can create a Web page by typing all of the necessary HTML code into a text document and saving the document with the .htm or .html file extension. Because a Web page contains HTML code, it is also called an **HTML document**. Some programs, including Access, have built-in tools that convert objects to HTML documents for viewing on the Web. In this tutorial, you will use these built-in tools to convert objects in the Northeast database to HTML documents.

Working with the Web

When you create Web pages based on Access database objects, the pages can be either static or dynamic. A **static Web page** shows the state of the database object at the time the page was created; any subsequent changes made to the object, such as updates to field values in a record, are not reflected in the Web page. A **dynamic Web page** is updated automatically each time the page is viewed and reflects the current state of the database object at that time. The type of Web page you create depends on how you want the information to be shared and manipulated by other users.

Creating and Viewing a Static Web Page

Elsa wants you to create a Web page based on the Employer Positions query, which shows selected fields from both the Employer and Position tables. She wants this information to be available to NSJI employees when they work out of the office and make a dial-up connection to NSJI's intranet from their laptop computers. Because Elsa does not want the employees to be able to make changes to this information, you'll create a static Web page.

In Access, you create a static Web page by exporting a database object to an HTML document.

> ### To export the Employer Positions query as an HTML document:
>
> **1.** Place your Data Disk in the appropriate disk drive, start Access, and then open the **Northeast** database located in the Tutorial folder on your Data Disk.
>
> **2.** Click **Queries** in the Objects bar of the Database window, right-click **Employer Positions** to display the shortcut menu, and then click **Export**. The Export dialog box opens, displaying the type and name of the object you are exporting in its title bar (in this case, the Employer Positions query). In this dialog box you specify the filename, file type, and location for the exported object. You need to save the Employer Positions query as an HTML document in the Tutorial folder.
>
> **3.** Make sure that the Save in list box displays the Tutorial folder on your Data Disk.
>
> **4.** Click the **Save as type** list arrow, and then scroll down the list and click **HTML Documents**. The query name is added to the File name text box automatically. See Figure 1.

Figure 1   **EXPORT DIALOG BOX**

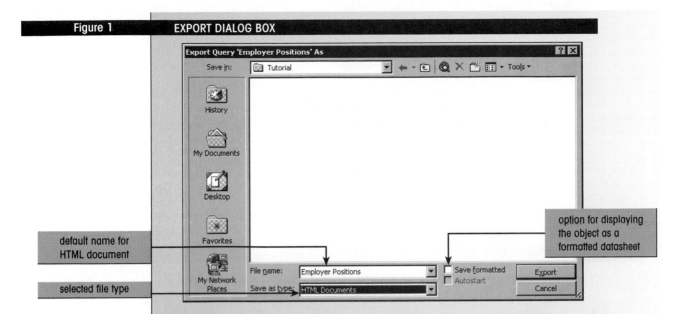

default name for
HTML document

selected file type

option for displaying
the object as a
formatted datasheet

Notice the Save formatted option. This option allows you to display the object
in a format similar to its appearance in Datasheet view, with all the column
headings, shading, and so on. If you do not choose this option, the object will
appear without the field names as column headings and the appropriate
spacing between columns. Elsa wants the Employer Positions query to appear
in datasheet format.

5. Click the **Save formatted** check box, and then click the **Export** button. The
   HTML Output Options dialog box opens. See Figure 2.

Figure 2   **HTML OUTPUT OPTIONS DIALOG BOX**

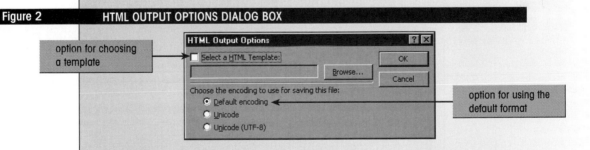

option for choosing
a template

option for using the
default format

This dialog box provides options for choosing an HTML template in which to
display the Web page, or for using the default format. A **template** is a file that
contains special instructions for creating and displaying a Web page with both
text and graphics. Elsa does not want to use a template for the Employer
Positions query, so you can accept the default settings.

6. Make sure that the **Default encoding** option button is selected, and then click
   the **OK** button. Access exports the Employer Positions query to an HTML document named Employer Positions in the Tutorial folder. The HTML document does
   not exist in the Northeast database as a database object; it is a separate file
   stored on your Data Disk.

NSJI uses Microsoft Internet Explorer as its Web browser. You will now use Internet
Explorer to view the Web page you just created.

To view the Employer Positions query Web page:

1. Click **View** on the menu bar, point to **Toolbars**, and then click **Web**. Access displays the Web toolbar.

2. Click the **Go** button on the Web toolbar, and then click **Open Hyperlink**. Access displays the Open Internet Address dialog box, in which you can specify the URL of the Web site or the name of the HTML document you want to view.

3. Click the **Browse** button. The Browse dialog box opens.

4. Make sure that the Look in list box displays the Tutorial folder on your Data Disk, click **Employer Positions** in the list, and then click the **Open** button. The Address list box in the Open Internet Address dialog box now displays the address for the Employer Positions HTML document. See Figure 3.

Figure 3	OPEN INTERNET ADDRESS DIALOG BOX

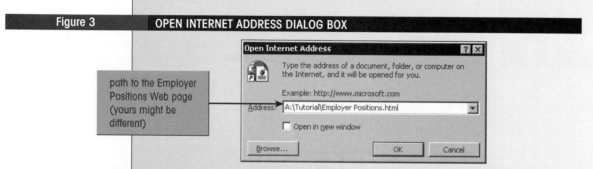

path to the Employer Positions Web page (yours might be different)

5. Click the **OK** button. Internet Explorer starts and opens the Employer Positions Web page. See Figure 4.

Figure 4	EMPLOYER POSITIONS QUERY DATASHEET IN THE INTERNET EXPLORER WINDOW

HTML document filename appears as the Web page title

address for the Employer Positions Web page (yours might be different)

records from the Employer Positions query datasheet

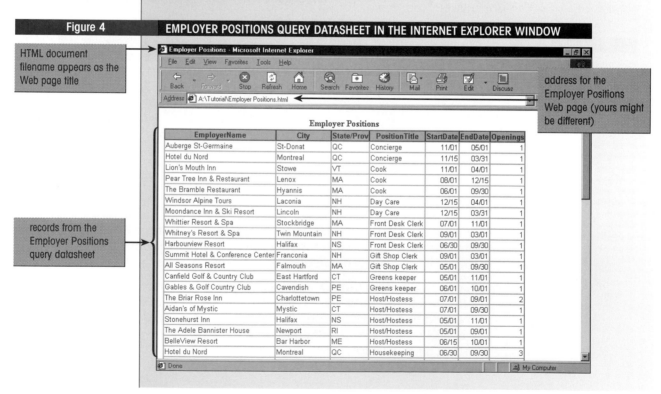

Employer Positions

EmployerName	City	State/Prov	PositionTitle	StartDate	EndDate	Openings
Auberge St-Germaine	St-Donat	QC	Concierge	11/01	05/01	1
Hotel du Nord	Montreal	QC	Concierge	11/15	03/31	1
Lion's Mouth Inn	Stowe	VT	Cook	11/01	04/01	1
Pear Tree Inn & Restaurant	Lenox	MA	Cook	08/01	12/15	1
The Bramble Restaurant	Hyannis	MA	Cook	06/01	09/30	1
Windsor Alpine Tours	Laconia	NH	Day Care	12/15	04/01	1
Moondance Inn & Ski Resort	Lincoln	NH	Day Care	12/15	03/31	1
Whittier Resort & Spa	Stockbridge	MA	Front Desk Clerk	07/01	11/01	1
Whitney's Resort & Spa	Twin Mountain	NH	Front Desk Clerk	09/01	03/01	1
Harbourview Resort	Halifax	NS	Front Desk Clerk	06/30	09/30	1
Summit Hotel & Conference Center	Franconia	NH	Gift Shop Clerk	09/01	03/01	1
All Seasons Resort	Falmouth	MA	Gift Shop Clerk	05/01	09/30	1
Canfield Golf & Country Club	East Hartford	CT	Greens keeper	05/01	11/01	1
Gables & Golf Country Club	Cavendish	PE	Greens keeper	06/01	10/01	1
The Briar Rose Inn	Charlottetown	PE	Host/Hostess	07/01	09/01	2
Aidan's of Mystic	Mystic	CT	Host/Hostess	07/01	09/30	1
Stonehurst Inn	Halifax	NS	Host/Hostess	05/01	11/01	1
The Adele Bannister House	Newport	RI	Host/Hostess	05/01	09/01	1
BelleView Resort	Bar Harbor	ME	Host/Hostess	06/15	10/01	1
Hotel du Nord	Montreal	QC	Housekeeping	06/30	09/30	3

> TROUBLE? If your computer has Netscape Navigator installed as its default browser, Netscape Navigator will start automatically and open the Employer Positions Web page. If this is the case, your screens will look slightly different from those shown in the figures.
>
> TROUBLE? If your computer does not have a browser installed on it, ask your instructor or technical support person for assistance.
>
> **6.** Scroll through the Employer Positions Web page to view its contents. Notice the Print button on the Standard Buttons toolbar, which you could use to print the Web page, if necessary.
>
> **7.** Click the **Close** button ☒ on the title bar to close Internet Explorer. You return to the Northeast database in the Microsoft Access window.

Because you exported the query object to an HTML document, you created a static Web page. Therefore, any future changes made to the underlying data in the Employer and Positions tables will not appear in the Employer Positions Web page. Elsa will need to export this information periodically, perhaps once a week, so that the NSJI employees who view this page will have updated information.

Next, Elsa wants you to create a Web page showing the information in the Employer table. She wants this page to be dynamic, so that any changes made to the data in the Employer table will be reflected in the Web page. Furthermore, Elsa wants NSJI employees to be able to use the Web page to make changes to the Employer table. To meet Elsa's needs, you'll create a data access page.

Creating and Viewing a Data Access Page

A **data access page** is a dynamic HTML document that you can open with a browser to view or update current data in the Access database object on which the data access page is based. Unlike an exported HTML document, such as the one you just created, a data access page exists as a database object with a link to the HTML document on which it is based. This HTML document, however, is stored outside the database.

You can create a data access page either in Design view or by using a Wizard. To create the data access page for the Employer table, you'll use the AutoPage: Columnar Wizard.

> ### To create the data access page for the Employer table:
>
> **1.** Click **Pages** in the Objects bar of the Database window to display the Pages list. The list box does not contain any pages.
>
> **2.** Click the **New** button in the Database window. The New Data Access Page dialog box opens. This dialog box is similar to ones you have used to create new forms and reports.
>
> **3.** Click **AutoPage: Columnar** to select this Wizard, click the list arrow for choosing the table or query as the basis for the page, click **Employer**, and then click the **OK** button. After a few moments, the AutoPage: Columnar Wizard creates the data access page and displays it in Page view. See Figure 5.

Figure 5 DATA ACCESS PAGE CREATED BY THE AUTOPAGE: COLUMNAR WIZARD

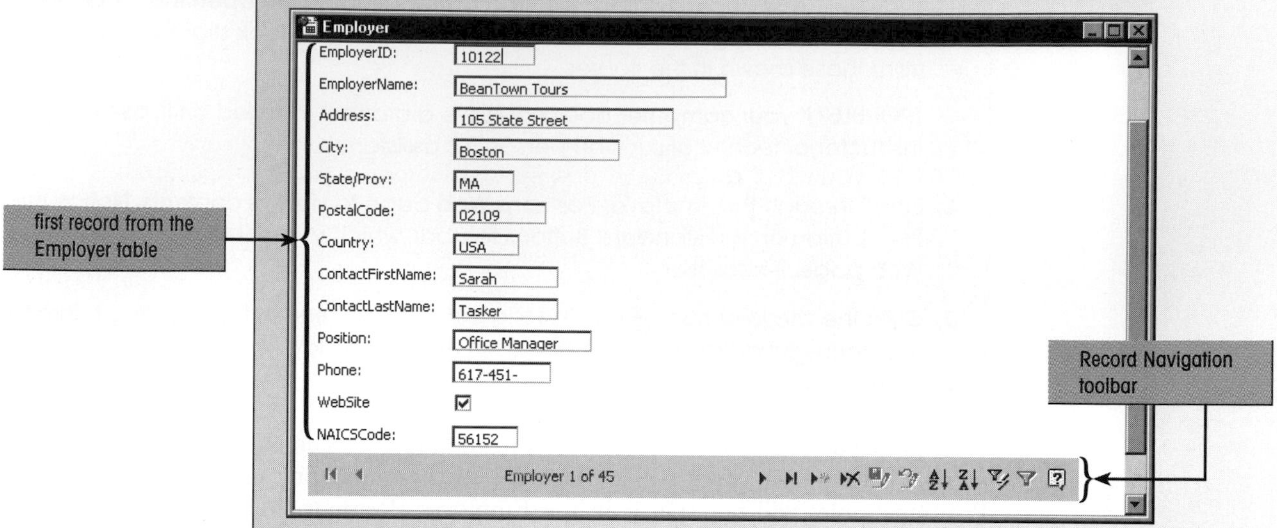

first record from the Employer table

Record Navigation toolbar

TROUBLE? Your data access page might appear with an AutoFormat applied to it. This will not affect your work with the page; simply continue with the steps.

Notice that the Phone field value is not completely visible. You can fix this quickly in Design view.

4. Click the **View** button for Design view 🖳 on the Page View toolbar. The data access page opens in Design view.

5. Click the **Phone** field's text box to select it (handles will appear around it), place the pointer on the center-right handle until the pointer changes to a ↔ shape, and then click and drag the pointer to the right until the Phone text box is approximately the same size as the Position text box above it. Then release the mouse button.

6. Click the **View** button for Page View 🖾 on the Page Design toolbar to switch back to Page view. The Phone field value is now completely visible.

The data access page displays the fields for the first record in the Employer table in a format that is similar to a form. Notice the Record Navigation toolbar, which appears below the record. This toolbar provides buttons for moving between table records, similar to the buttons you use to move between records in a form, and buttons for adding and deleting records, sorting and filtering data, and so on.

Elsa has a change to make to one of the records in the Employer table. The Bayside Inn & Country Club has a new General Manager, so the contact first and last names for this employer need to be changed. You can make the necessary changes directly in the data access page, which at the same time will update the Employer table in the Northeast database. Before making the changes, you will save the data access page.

To save the data access page and update the contact information in Page view:

1. Click the **Save** button 🖫 on the Page View toolbar. The Save As Data Access Page dialog box opens.

2. Make sure that the Save in list box displays the Tutorial folder on your Data Disk, and then click the **Save** button to save the data access page with the default name "Employer."

TROUBLE? If a message box opens with a warning about the connection string, click the OK button and continue with the steps.

Now you will change the necessary field values in the Employer table.

3. Use the Record Navigation toolbar to move to record 3 (for the Bayside Inn & Country Club), double-click the entry **Jeffrey** in the ContactFirstName field, type **Mary**, double-click the entry **Hersha** in the ContactLastName field, and then type **Russell**.

You can save changes you make to a record in a data access page either by moving to another record or by clicking the Save button on the Record Navigation toolbar. You'll save your changes.

4. Click the **Save** button ![Save icon] on the Record Navigation toolbar.

5. Click the **Close** button ![X] on the Employer window title bar. The data access page closes, and you return to the Database window. Notice that the Employer data access page is listed in the Pages list box.

You have created the data access page and viewed it in Page view. Now, you'll see how the page looks in Internet Explorer.

To view the Employer data access page in Internet Explorer:

1. Right-click **Employer** in the Pages list box, and then click **Web Page Preview**. Internet Explorer starts and opens the Employer data access page. See Figure 6.

| Figure 6 | DATA ACCESS PAGE IN THE INTERNET EXPLORER WINDOW |

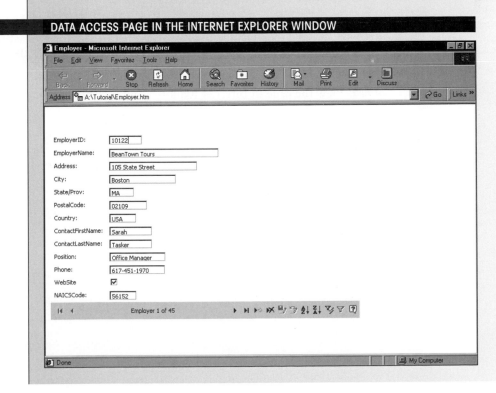

Now NSJI employees can use the company's intranet to view and update Employer data in Internet Explorer. Any changes that employees make using the Employer data access page will also be made to the Employer table.

2. Close Internet Explorer. You return to the Database window.

To confirm that the changes you made earlier to the contact information are reflected in the Employer table, you'll open the table now and view the record.

3. Click **Tables** in the Objects bar of the Database window, and then open the **Employer** table in Datasheet view. Scroll to the right and notice that the contact information for the Bayside Inn & Country Club is now Mary Russell.

4. Exit Access.

REVIEW ASSIGNMENTS

Elsa is pleased with the Web pages you created for the **Northeast** database. Now she would like to you create Web pages based on objects in the **Recruits** database. Complete the following:

1. Make sure your Data Disk is in the appropriate disk drive, start Access, and then open the **Recruits** database located in the Review folder on your Data Disk.

2. Create a static Web page named **Recruiter** based on the **Recruiter** table. Specify the option for displaying the data in a datasheet format and do not use a template. View the resulting Web page in Internet Explorer, use the Print button on the Standard Buttons toolbar to print the page, and then close Internet Explorer.

3. Use the AutoPage: Columnar Wizard to create a data access page based on the **Student** table.

4. Use the Record Navigation toolbar to move to the last record in the **Student** table (record 34), and then change the BirthDate field value for the last record to 11/16/84. Save your change using the appropriate Record Navigation toolbar button.

5. Save the data access page with the name **Student** in the Review folder on your Data Disk. View the page in Internet Explorer, and use the Print button on the Standard Buttons toolbar to print the page.

6. Close Internet Explorer, and then exit Access.

New Perspectives on

INTEGRATING
MICROSOFT®
OFFICE XP

TUTORIAL 2   INT 2.03

Integrating Word, Excel, and Access

Read This Before You Begin

To the Student

Data Disks

To complete this tutorial, Review Assignments, and Case Problems, you need one Data Disk. Your instructor will either provide you with the Data Disk or ask you to make your own.

If you are making your own Data Disk, you will need **one** blank, formatted high-density disk. You will need to copy a set of files and/or folders from a file server, standalone computer, or the Web onto your disk. Your instructor will tell you which computer, drive letter, and folders contain the files you need. You could also download the files by going to **www.course.com** and following the instructions on the screen.

The information below shows you which folders go on your disk, so that you will have enough disk space to complete the tutorial, Review Assignments, and Case Problems:

Data Disk 1

Write this on the disk label:
Integrating Office XP: Tutorial 2 Data Disk

Put this folder on the disk:
Tutorial.02

When you begin each tutorial, be sure you are using the correct Data Disk. Refer to the "File Finder" chart at the back of this text for more detailed information on which files are used in which tutorials. See the inside front or inside back cover of this book for more information on Data Disk files, or ask your instructor or technical support person for assistance.

Using Your Own Computer

If you are going to work through this book using your own computer, you need:

- **Computer System** Microsoft Windows 98, NT, 2000 Professional, or higher must be installed on your computer. This book assumes a typical installation of Microsoft Office XP.

- **Data Disk** You will not be able to complete the tutorials or exercises in this book using your own computer until you have your Data Disk.

Visit Our World Wide Web Site

Additional materials designed especially for you are available on the World Wide Web.
Go to **www.course.com/NewPerspectives**.

To the Instructor

The Data Disk Files are available on the Instructor's Resource Kit for this title. Follow the instructions in the Help file on the CD-ROM to install the programs to your network or standalone computer. For information on creating Data Disks, see the "To the Student" section above.

You are granted a license to copy the Data Files to any computer or computer network used by students who have purchased this book.

INTEGRATING WORD, EXCEL, AND ACCESS

Creating a Brochure for Country Gardens

Country Gardens

Last season, Sue Dickinson, the proprietor of the Country Gardens shops in New Hampshire, Vermont, and Massachusetts, created a mail-order catalog to make it easier for her customers to order gardening supplies and plants. The catalog was a big success and played a significant role in enhancing Country Gardens' status as the top grower and greens supplier in New England. Now Sue wants to turn her attention to the one segment of her business that hasn't increased—bulbs, including tulips, daffodils, and crocuses. Last spring, Sue created special collections of tulip bulbs that she selected according to growing season and color. She then offered these bulb collections at a special price for any customer who placed an advance order for their fall plantings. The tulip collections sold moderately.

This year, Sue wants to promote the tulip collections by creating a brochure that she will mail to anyone who ordered more than 50 bulbs last spring—her best customers. Sue has drafted the text for the brochure, including information on Country Gardens and the descriptions of the tulip collections. Sue still needs to insert the company logo into the brochure. Sue also wants to include a table summarizing the most popular collections from last year. Finally, she wants to include a price list for the complete collection. The company logo and the complete bulb price list are contained in other Office documents, such as a Word letter and an Excel workbook. To create the table showing the most popular bulb collections, Sue can use sales data she has stored in an Excel workbook. To do this, she needs to import the information into an Access database where she can use Access tools to analyze the data, and then she can export the information into the brochure.

You'll complete sections of the brochure for Sue using the special tools and features of Microsoft Office XP that let you integrate information created in Word, Excel, and Access.

Planning the Brochure

Sue has already created a draft of the tulip brochure in a Word document but needs to pull in graphics and data from other sources. To insert this information, you can copy and paste it from one Office document to the tulip brochure. Figure 2-1 shows Sue's plan for the tulip brochure.

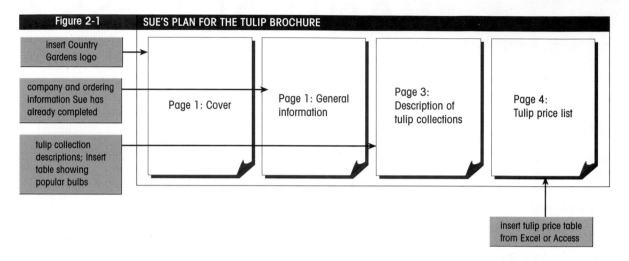

Figure 2-1 SUE'S PLAN FOR THE TULIP BROCHURE

insert Country Gardens logo

company and ordering information Sue has already completed

tulip collection descriptions; Insert table showing popular bulbs

Page 1: Cover

Page 1: General information

Page 3: Description of tulip collections

Page 4: Tulip price list

insert tulip price table from Excel or Access

First Sue needs to insert the company logo on the cover of the brochure. She can do this by copying and pasting the logo from the customer letter you worked with in the first Integration tutorial. Secondly, Sue needs to insert a table listing the prices for the complete bulb collection. She cannot recall if she created this table using Excel or Access. Once she finds the table, she can copy and paste it onto page four of the brochure.

On page three of the brochure, Sue wants to include a table showing the most popular bulb collections. To create this table, Sue will need to analyze sales data from last year, which she has stored in an Excel workbook. Sue realizes the analysis of this sales data would be easier if the data was in the form of a table in her Sales Access database, thereby allowing her to use the more sophisticated analytical tools available in Access. To use Access to analyze the tulip bulb sales data, Sue needs to import the data into her Sales database. Importing data is different than the OLE methods you learned about in the first integration tutorial. Recall that OLE is used to *share* data between Office programs. When you **import** data from one Office program to another, you are actually converting the data from its original source program format to a format that is supported by the destination program, which allows you to then use the destination program's tools and features to view and manipulate the data in a new way. Once Sue has imported the sales data from the Excel workbook into Access, she can create a query to determine the top selling bulb collections and then export that information as a table into the tulip brochure. **Exporting**, like importing, converts data from one program's format to another. However, when you import, you start in the destination program and import from the source program. Exporting reverses this process—you start in the source program and export to the destination program.

Now, however, your first task is to collect the logo and the bulb price list to insert into the brochure. You'll use the Office Task Panes to streamline the process of finding and collecting information from different Office documents.

Using the Task Panes

Sue knows that she can find some of the information she needs in other Office documents. The company logo has been used in some promotional letters she has written to customers. She also knows that she has created a table of tulip prices in either an Excel worksheet or Access database.

Sue asks you to find these two pieces of information—the company logo and the tulip bulb price table—and insert them in the brochure where they belong. To integrate this material, you can use the Office **Task Panes**. Every Office program contains a number of Task Panes, including the New File, Clipboard, and Search Task Panes. The Task Panes integrate related options that you need to perform common tasks, such as simple and advanced options for finding a file.

You can start by using the Clipboard Task Pane to copy and paste the company logo into the brochure. Then you can use the Search Task Pane to find the tulip price table and insert that in the brochure.

Collecting Information on the Clipboard Task Pane

You use the **Clipboard Task Pane** to collect text and other items from Office documents and then paste those items into any Office document. The Clipboard Task Pane—also called the Clipboard—works with the standard Copy and Paste commands. You copy an item to the Clipboard to add it to your collection and then paste it into any Office document. The collected items stay on the Clipboard until you clear the Clipboard or exit Office.

For Sue's tulip brochure, you'll copy the Country Gardens logo from one document and use the Clipboard to paste it into the brochure. First, you'll start Word and open the brochure document.

To start Word and open the brochure document:

1. Start Word as usual.

   TROUBLE? If the New Document Task Pane opens, leave it open and continue to Step 2.

2. Make sure your Data Disk is in the appropriate drive, and then open the **Brochure** document, which is located in the Tutorial folder in the Tutorial.02 folder on your Data Disk. The brochure opens in Print Layout view. If necessary, display the nonprinting characters.

   Next, you'll save the file with a new name. That way, the original brochure remains intact on your Data Disk in case you want to restart the tutorial.

3. Click **File** on the menu bar, and then click **Save As** to open the Save As dialog box.

4. Save the file as **Tulip Brochure** in the Tutorial folder in the Tutorial.02 folder on your Data Disk.

Sue's draft of the tulip brochure includes four pages. The first page includes a placeholder for the company logo. The second page provides general information about ordering tulips from Country Gardens. The third page lists the tulip collections Sue is offering. She will add the table showing the most popular bulb collections to this page later, after she creates this table using Access. The fourth page is where Sue wants to include the tulip price table. You'll start by copying the Country Gardens logo from a letter.

To copy the logo from a Word document:

1. Open the **Customer Letter** document which is located in the Tutorial folder in the Tutorial.02 folder on your Data Disk. This is the document that contains the Country Gardens logo.

2. Click **Edit** on the menu bar, and then click **Office Clipboard**. The Clipboard Task Pane opens.

3. Click the **logo** to select it, as shown in Figure 2-2.

   TROUBLE? If the Picture toolbar displays, click its Close button to close it.

Figure 2-2	COUNTRY GARDENS LOGO SELECTED

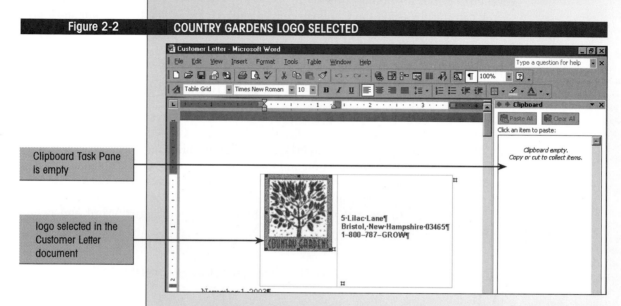

Clipboard Task Pane is empty

logo selected in the Customer Letter document

4. Click the **Copy** button on the Standard toolbar. Word copies the logo to the Clipboard Task Pane, as shown in Figure 2-3.

Figure 2-3	COPIED LOGO IN THE CLIPBOARD TASK PANE

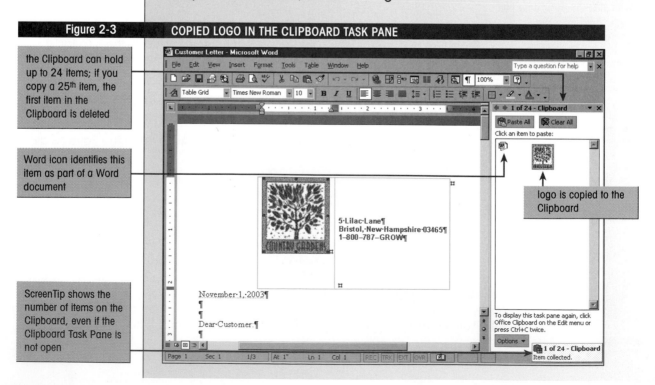

the Clipboard can hold up to 24 items; if you copy a 25th item, the first item in the Clipboard is deleted

Word icon identifies this item as part of a Word document

logo is copied to the Clipboard

ScreenTip shows the number of items on the Clipboard, even if the Clipboard Task Pane is not open

5. Close the Customer Letter document without saving any changes.

The Clipboard Task Pane now contains one item—the company logo. Before you paste the logo into the Tulip Brochure document, you need to collect one more item—the tulip price table.

Finding Files with the Search Task Pane

Sue created the tulip price table last season and remembers only that she stored it in either an Excel worksheet or Access database. Before you can collect this table, you must find the document that contains it. You can use the **Search Task Pane** to find the right file.

You use the Search Task Pane to find files that contain text you specify. This type of search is called a **basic search**. You can also use the Search Task Pane to find files based on their properties, such as who created the file or when. This type of search is called an **advanced search**. In either type of search, you enter your **search criteria**—the text or properties of the files you want to find. Sue wants to find the document that contains the text "tulip price table," so you will perform a basic search using the Search Task Pane.

To find the tulip price table document:

1. In the Tulip Brochure document, click the **Search** button 🔍 on the Standard toolbar. The Search Task Pane opens, as shown in Figure 2-4.

Figure 2-4	SEARCH TASK PANE

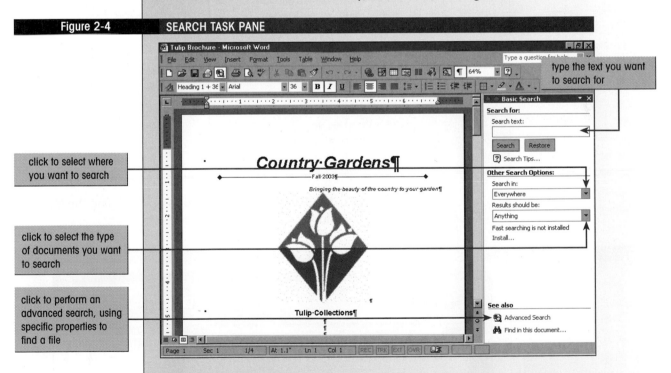

click to select where you want to search

click to select the type of documents you want to search

click to perform an advanced search, using specific properties to find a file

type the text you want to search for

2. Click in the **Search text** text box and type **tulip price table**. Sue knows that the document contains this text, so you can use it to find the file.

3. Click the **Search in** list arrow, click to clear the **Everywhere** check box and click the **My Computer** check box to select it. Then click outside of the Search in list to close the list box.

If necessary, you could select only certain locations to narrow your search and speed up the search process. You can also narrow the search by selecting what type of document you want to find. Sue knows that the tulip price table is in either an Excel workbook or an Access database, so you can select only those types of documents to search.

4. Click the **Results should be** list arrow, and then click the **plus sign (+)** next to Anything to expand the list, if necessary.

5. Click to select only Excel and Access files and to deselect all other options. If necessary, scroll the list to deselect the Outlook items and Web pages. Then click outside the list box to close it. Your Search Task Pane should look similar to the one shown in Figure 2-5.

Figure 2-5	SEARCH TASK PANE WITH SEARCH CRITERIA

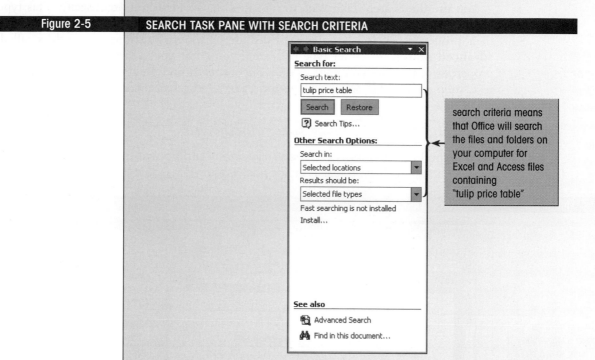

search criteria means that Office will search the files and folders on your computer for Excel and Access files containing "tulip price table"

6. Click the **Search** button. The Search Results Task Pane opens, listing the files it found based on the criteria you entered. See Figure 2-6.

Figure 2-6	SEARCH RESULTS TASK PANE

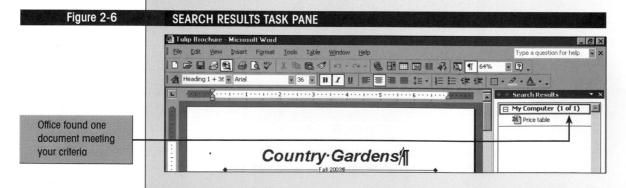

Office found one document meeting your criteria

TROUBLE? If more than one file is listed in the Search Results Task Pane, make sure one is the Excel Price table workbook.

Your search found an Excel workbook containing the text "tulip price table." Now you can open the workbook and copy the table to the Clipboard.

To open the workbook and copy the tulip price table:

1. In the Search Results Task Pane, click the **Price table workbook**. Excel starts and the Price table workbook opens in the workbook window.

2. If necessary, select cells **A1** to **G12**, as shown in Figure 2-7. These are the cells containing the tulip price table.

| Figure 2-7 | CELLS TO COPY FROM EXCEL |

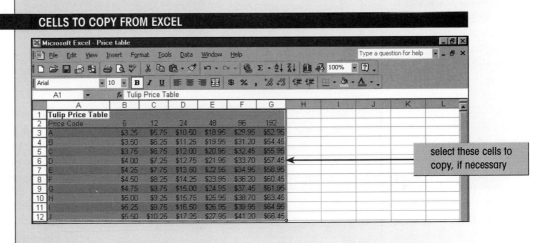

3. Click the **Copy** button 🖹 on the Excel Standard toolbar to copy the price table to the Clipboard, and then press **Enter**.

4. Close the Price table and exit Excel. If a dialog box opens asking you to save changes, click the **No** button. The information you copied remains on the Clipboard even after you exit Excel.

You have collected two items for the brochure—the company logo and the tulip price table. Now you can paste these items into the Tulip Brochure document for Sue.

Pasting Items from the Clipboard Task Pane

To paste an item from the Clipboard Task Pane to a document, you open the document, click where you want to insert the item, and then click the item in the Clipboard Task Pane. The text or object appears in the document. When you paste text, the **Paste Options button** appears in the program window. You use the Paste Options button to determine how the information you pasted should be formatted in the Word document. When you paste the tulip price table into the Tulip Brochure document, you want to be sure the inserted text matches the other text in the brochure. If it doesn't, you'll use the Paste Options button to change the formatting.

You are ready to paste the selections you collected on the Clipboard.

To paste items from the Clipboard:

1. With the Tulip Brochure document open in Word, click the **Other Task Panes** list arrow, and then click **Clipboard** to open the Clipboard, which should contain two items, as shown in Figure 2-8.

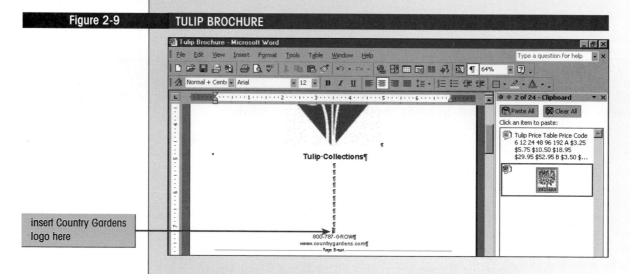

Figure 2-8   **CLIPBOARD WITH TWO ITEMS FOR TULIP BROCHURE**

tulip price table copied from Excel

company logo copied from Word letter

To complete the first page of the brochure, insert the logo you copied from the customer letter.

2. Scroll the document until you see the phone number for Country Gardens. Place the insertion point to the left of the paragraph marker (¶) that appears above the phone number. See Figure 2-9.

Figure 2-9   **TULIP BROCHURE**

insert Country Gardens logo here

3. In the Clipboard Task Pane, click the **Country Gardens logo**. Word pastes the logo at your insertion point. See Figure 2-10.

Figure 2-10   LOGO COPIED INTO BROCHURE

click the logo item in the Clipboard Task Pane to insert the logo in the document

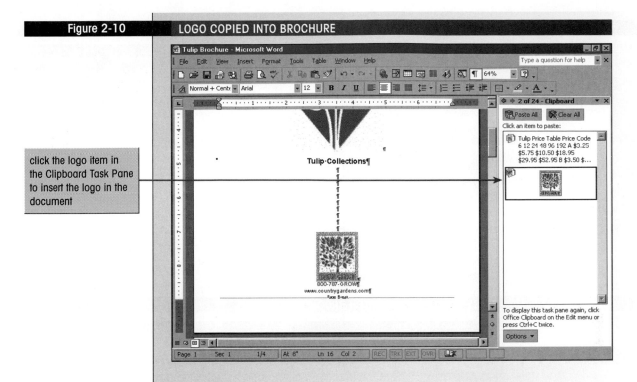

Now you can paste the tulip price table into page four of the Tulip Brochure.

4. Press **Ctrl+End** to go to the last page in the brochure, which is page four. The insertion point appears to the left of the second paragraph marker.

5. In the Clipboard Task Pane, click the Excel item that begins **"Tulip Price Table."** Word pastes the price table into the Tulip Brochure document, retaining the formatting of the original Excel worksheet, as shown in Figure 2-11.

Figure 2-11   TULIP PRICE TABLE IN BROCHURE

table retains formatting from the original Excel worksheet

click to see a list of Paste Options commands

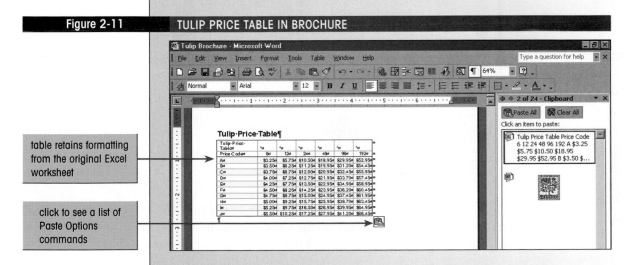

Notice that the format of the table does not match the format of the other text in the brochure—the table text is smaller, for example. You can choose a command from the Paste Options menu to have the table text match the format of the other brochure text.

6. Click the **Paste Options** button 📋. You see the options described in Figure 2-12.

Figure 2-12   **PASTE OPTIONS COMMANDS WHEN PASTING TEXT INTO WORD**

CHOOSE THIS COMMAND	TO DO THIS
Keep Source Formatting	Retain the formatting of the pasted text
Match Destination Table Style	Change the formatting of the pasted text to match other similar text in the destination document
Keep Text Only	Paste the text witout any formatting; choose this command when you want to paste table text without the table structure
Apply Style or Formatting	Choose the style or formatting you want to apply

7. Click the **Match Destination Table Style** option button. The format of the tulip price table text now matches the format of the other paragraphs in the brochure—all are Arial 12 point and use the same line spacing. The tulip price table appears as in Figure 2-13.

Figure 2-13   **TABLE FORMATTED TO MATCH BROCHURE TEXT**

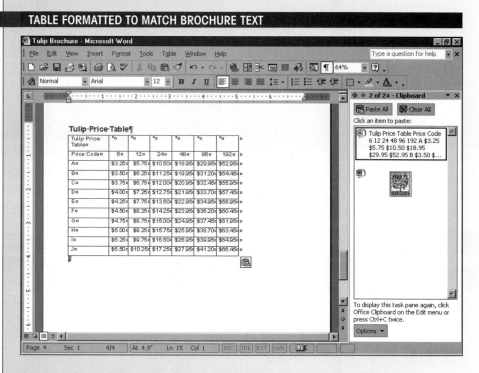

8. Save the Tulip Brochure document.

You have added all the information Sue needs in the first part of the brochure. Now Sue needs you to create the table listing the most popular bulb collections, which you will then insert into the third page of the brochure.

presentation you want, the AutoContent Wizard creates a general outline for you to follow and formats the slides using a built-in design template. A **design template** is a file that contains the colors and format of the background and the type style of the titles, accents, and other text. Once you start creating a presentation with a given design template, you can change to any other PowerPoint design template or create a custom design template. In this tutorial, you'll use the AutoContent Wizard to sell your idea, the donation of time or money for humanitarian projects. Because "Selling Your Ideas" is predefined, you'll use the AutoContent Wizard, which will automatically create a title slide and standard outline that you then can edit to fit Miriam's needs.

To create the presentation with the AutoContent Wizard:

1. Start PowerPoint, and then click **From AutoContent Wizard** on the New Presentation Task Pane on the right side of the PowerPoint window. The first of several AutoContent Wizard dialog boxes opens. See Figure 1-8.

Figure 1-8	OPENING DIALOG BOX OF AUTOCONTENT WIZARD

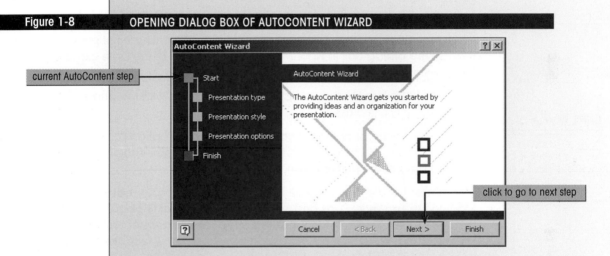

TROUBLE? If the New Presentation Task Pane doesn't appear on your screen, click View on the menu bar, and then click Task Pane. If the Task Pane isn't New Presentation, click the Other Task Panes list arrow at the top of the Task Pane, click New from Existing Presentation, and then click From AutoContent Wizard.

2. Read the information in the AutoContent Wizard dialog box, and then click the **Next** button to display the next dialog box of the AutoContent Wizard. This dialog box allows you to select the type of presentation.

3. Click the **Carnegie Coach** button (which provides AutoContent presentations based upon Dale Carnegie Training principles), and then, if necessary, click **Selling Your Ideas**. See Figure 1-9.

Figure 1-9   SELECTING TYPE OF PRESENTATION IN AUTOCONTENT WIZARD

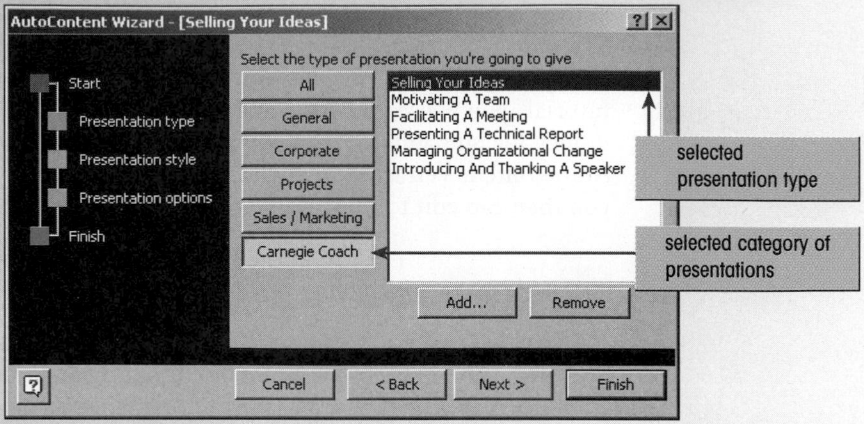

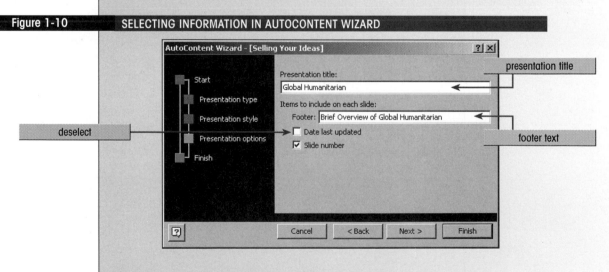

The **Carnegie Coach** is a special feature of PowerPoint in which the AutoContent Wizard can help you create different types of presentations (listed in the dialog box in Figure 1-9) using principles of the Dale Carnegie Training system.

4. Click the **Next** button to display the dialog box with the question, "What type of output will you use?"

5. If necessary, click the **On-screen presentation** option button to select it, and then click the **Next** button. In this dialog box, you'll specify the title and footer (if any) of the presentation.

6. Click Ⅰ in the **Presentation title** text box and type **Global Humanitarian**, click Ⅰ in the **Footer** text box and type **Brief Overview of Global Humanitarian**, and then click the **Date last updated** check box to deselect it. Leave the Slide Number box checked. The dialog box should now look like Figure 1-10.

Figure 1-10   SELECTING INFORMATION IN AUTOCONTENT WIZARD

7. Click the **Next** button. The final AutoContent Wizard dialog box opens, letting you know that you completed the AutoContent Wizard.

8. Click the **Finish** button. PowerPoint now displays the AutoContent outline in the Outline tab and the title slide (Slide 1) in the Slide Pane. See Figure 1-11. The

AutoContent Wizard automatically displays the presenter's name (actually the name of the computer's owner) below the title in Slide 1. The name that appears on your screen will be different from the one in Figure 1-11.

Figure 1-11	OUTLINE AND SLIDE AFTER COMPLETING AUTOCONTENT WIZARD

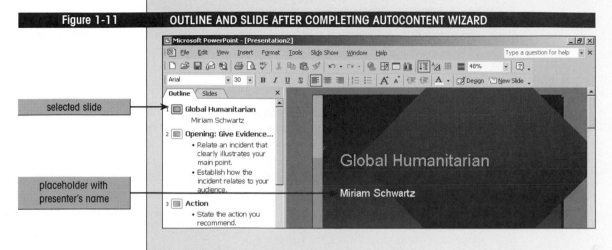

TROUBLE? If you can't see the Outline tab and the Slide Pane as shown in Figure 1-11, click the Normal View button on the View toolbar.

Now that you've used the AutoContent Wizard, you're ready to edit its default outline to fit Miriam's specific presentation needs.

Editing AutoContent Slides

The AutoContent Wizard automatically creates the title slide, as well as other slides, with suggested text located in placeholders. A **placeholder** is a region of a slide, or a location in an outline, reserved for inserting text or graphics. To edit the AutoContent outline to fit Miriam's needs, you must select the placeholders one at a time, and then replace them with other text.

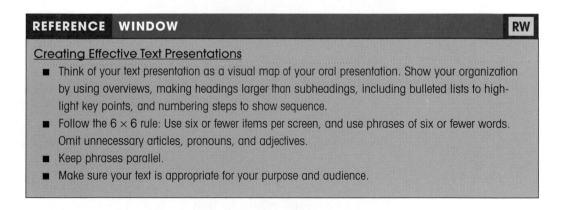

REFERENCE WINDOW		RW

Creating Effective Text Presentations
- Think of your text presentation as a visual map of your oral presentation. Show your organization by using overviews, making headings larger than subheadings, including bulleted lists to highlight key points, and numbering steps to show sequence.
- Follow the 6 × 6 rule: Use six or fewer items per screen, and use phrases of six or fewer words. Omit unnecessary articles, pronouns, and adjectives.
- Keep phrases parallel.
- Make sure your text is appropriate for your purpose and audience.

You'll now begin to edit and replace the text to fit Miriam's presentation. The first text you'll change is the presenter's name placeholder.

To edit and replace text in a slide:

1. In the Slide Pane, drag Ⓘ across the text of the presenter's name (currently the computer owner's name) to select it. When the text is selected, it appears as black text on a violet background.

2. Type your first and last name (so your instructor can identify you as the author of this presentation), and then click anywhere else on the slide. As soon as you start to type, the placeholder disappears, and the typed text appears in its place. The figures in this book will leave the name as Miriam Schwartz.

TROUBLE? If PowerPoint marks your name with a red wavy underline, this indicates that the word is not found in the PowerPoint dictionary. In most cases, this means the word might be misspelled. If that were the case here, you would right-click the red wavy underlined word to display a list of suggested spellings, and then click the correct word, or simply edit the misspelled word. In this case, however, you want to tell PowerPoint to ignore what it thinks is a misspelling.

3. If your name was marked as a misspelling, right-click the word to display the shortcut menu, and then click **Ignore All**.

You have made substantial progress in creating Miriam's presentation. Now you'll create a folder for your presentation files, and save this presentation. Then, you'll exit PowerPoint.

Creating a Folder for Saving Presentations

As a general rule, you should save your PowerPoint work often, about every 15 minutes (or as often as your instructor recommends), so you won't lose your work in case of a power outage, a power surge, or some other computer or software glitch.

To create a folder and save a presentation for the first time:

1. If necessary, place your Data Disk into the appropriate drive.

2. Click the **Save** button 🖫 on the Standard toolbar. The Save As dialog box opens.

3. Click the **Save in** list arrow, and then click the drive that contains your Data Disk.

4. Double-click the **Tutorial.01** folder, and then double-click **Tutorial** to open that folder.

5. Click the **Create New Folder** button 🗖 on the Save As dialog box toolbar. The New Folder dialog box opens.

6. Type **My Files** (see Figure 1-12), and click the **OK** button, edit the default filename (probably Global Humanitarian) in the File name text box so that it becomes **Global Humanitarian Overview**, and then click the **Save** button. PowerPoint saves the presentation to the disk using the filename Global Humanitarian Overview. That name now appears in the title bar of the PowerPoint window. Now that you have saved your work, you're ready to exit PowerPoint.

Figure 1-12 | CREATING A NEW FOLDER

> **New Folder** ? X
>
> OK
>
> Name: My Files   Cancel

7. Click the **Close** button on the PowerPoint window to exit PowerPoint.

In addition to the Save command, PowerPoint also has a Save As command, which allows you to save the current presentation to a new file. For example, if you make modifications to an existing presentation but you want to keep the old version and save the new version to the disk, you would use the Save As command to save the modified presentation with a new filename.

In the next session, you'll continue to edit the text of Miriam's presentation, as well as create notes.

Session 1.1 QUICK CHECK

1. In one to three sentences, describe the purpose of PowerPoint and the components of a presentation that you can create with this program.

2. Name and describe the PowerPoint tabs and panes visible within Normal View.

3. Define or describe the following:
   a. gradient fill
   b. footer
   c. slide transition
   d. custom animation
   e. placeholder
   f. bulleted list

4. Why should you plan a presentation before you create it? What are some of the presentation elements that should be considered?

5. Describe the purpose of the AutoContent Wizard.

6. What is the 6×6 rule?

7. What does a red wavy underline indicate?

8. Why is it important to save your work frequently?

SESSION 1.2

In this session, you'll learn how to move from one slide to the next, modify bulleted lists, add new slides with a specified layout, delete slides, change the order of slides, promote and demote outline text, create notes, use the Style Checker, and preview and print a presentation.

Modifying a Presentation

Miriam reviewed your presentation and she has several suggestions for improvement. First, she wants you to replace text in the placeholders with information about Global Humanitarian. Most of the slides in the presentation contain two placeholder text boxes.

The slide **title text** is a text box at the top of the slide that gives the title of the information on that slide; the slide **main text** (also called **body text**) is a large text box in which you type a bulleted or numbered list. In this presentation, you'll modify or create title text and main text in all but the title slide (Slide 1).

Editing Slides

You'll now edit Slides 2 through 5 by replacing the placeholder text and by adding new text.

To edit the text in the slides:

1. If you took a break after the previous session, start PowerPoint, and then open the presentation **Global Humanitarian Overview** located in the My Files folder of the Tutorial.01\Tutorial folder. Notice that this filename appears in the New Presentation Task Pane, so you can click the filename to open the presentation.

2. With Slide 1 in the Slide Pane, click the **Next Slide** button ⬇.

3. Select the title text ("Opening: Give Evidence...") so that the title text box becomes active (as indicated by the hatched lines around the box and the resize handles at each corner and on each side of the text box) and the text becomes highlighted. See Figure 1-13. Now you're ready to type the desired title.

Figure 1-13	SELECTING TITLE TEXT

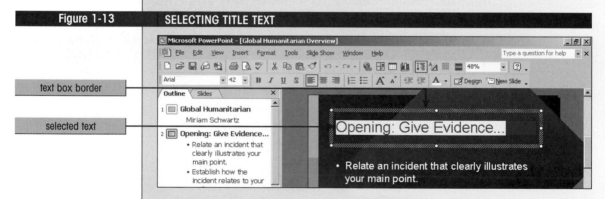

text box border

selected text

4. Type **Are You Rich?** and click in a blank space just outside the edge of the slide to deselect the text box. The hatched lines and resize handles disappear. This title is meant to give evidence of the ability and need to help villagers in less-developed countries. Now you're ready to replace the placeholder text in the bulleted list on this slide.

   TROUBLE? If you click somewhere on the slide that selects another item, such as the main text, click another place, preferably just outside the edge of the slide, to deselect all items.

5. Within the main text box, select the text of the first bulleted item, **Relate an incident that clearly illustrates your main point**, and then type **If you live in a non dirt floor home, top 50%**. Don't include a period at the end of the phrase. Notice how this bulleted item is an incomplete sentence, short for "If you live in a home with a non dirt floor, you're in the top 50% of wealthiest people on earth." Keep in mind that the bulleted lists are not meant to be the complete presentation; instead they remind the speaker of key points and to emphasize the key points to the audience. In all your presentations, you should follow the 6 × 6 rule as much as possible: keep each bulleted item as close to six words as possible, and if possible, have six or fewer bulleted items.

6. Select the text of the second bulleted item, then and type **Home has window and more than one room, top 20%** (without a period). With the insertion point at the end of the second bulleted item, you're ready to create additional bulleted items.

7. Press the **Enter** key. PowerPoint creates a new bullet and leaves the insertion point to the right of the indent after the bullet, waiting for you to type the text.

8. Type **If you can read and have more than one pair of shoes, top 5%**, press the **Enter** key, and then type the last two bulleted items, as shown in Figure 1-14. Notice that as you add more text to a bulleted list, PowerPoint automatically adjusts the font size to fit in the main text placeholder.

TROUBLE? If the font size doesn't automatically adjust so that the text fits within the main text placeholder, click the AutoFit icon and then click AutoFit Text to Placeholder.

Figure 1-14	SLIDE 2 AFTER ADDING TEXT

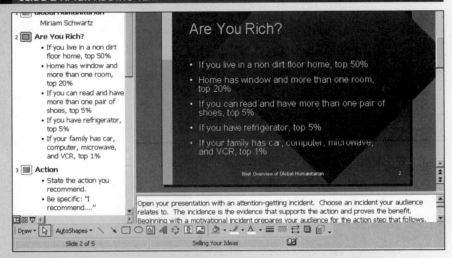

9. Click in a blank area of the slide to deselect the bulleted list text box. The completed Slide 2 should look like Figure 1-14.

You're now ready to go to other slides and edit text.

To edit the other slides:

1. Click the **Next Slide** button ⬇ to go to Slide 3.

2. Select the title placeholder ("Action") and type **How You Can Help** (with no punctuation).

3. Select all the text in the main text placeholder, and type **Become a member of Global Humanitarian**, press the **Enter** key, and then type **Contribute to humanitarian projects**. Now you'll add some sub-bullets (second-level bulleted items) beneath the current (first-level) bulleted item.

4. Press the **Enter** key to insert a new bullet, and then press the **Tab** key to indent. The bullet changes to a second-level bullet (a dash in this case).

5. Type **Health**, press the **Enter** key (the bullet stays second level), type **Education**, press the **Enter** key, type **Water and Environment**, press the **Enter** key, type **Income Generation and Agriculture**, press the **Enter** key, and type **Leaderships and Cultural Enhancement**. Now you want the next bullet to return to the first level.

6. Press the **Enter** key to create a new second-level bullet, and then click the **Decrease Indent** button 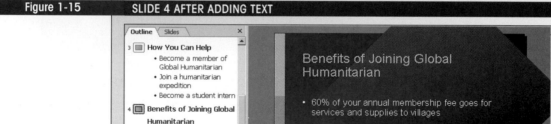 on the Formatting toolbar to convert the item to a first-level bullet. You can also press the Shift + Tab key combination. Type the remaining two bulleted items: **Join a humanitarian expedition** and **Become a student intern**. The slide exceeds the 6 × 6 rule in the number of bulleted items, but you'll fix that later.

You have completed editing and adding text to Slide 3. Now you'll edit the other slides and save your work.

To edit the slides and save the presentation:

1. Go to Slide 4 and edit the title text to read **Benefits of Joining Global Humanitarian**.

2. Select all the text, not just the text of the first bulleted item, in the main text placeholder, and then add the bulleted items, as shown in Figure 1-15.

Figure 1-15   **SLIDE 4 AFTER ADDING TEXT**

---

3. Go to Slide 5 (currently the last slide in the presentation), and then modify the title and text boxes so that the slide looks like Figure 1-16.

Figure 1-16	COMPLETED SLIDE 5

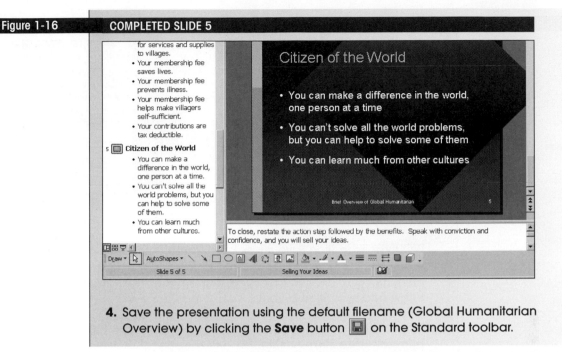

4. Save the presentation using the default filename (Global Humanitarian Overview) by clicking the **Save** button on the Standard toolbar.

You have completed the first draft of the Global Humanitarian presentation. Now you'll add a slide to provide additional information about Global Humanitarian.

Adding a New Slide and Choosing a Layout

Miriam wants you to add a new slide at the end of the presentation explaining how individuals and families can join Global Humanitarian. When you add a new slide, PowerPoint formats the slide using a **slide layout**, which is an arrangement of placeholders. PowerPoint supports four **text layouts**: Title Slide (placeholders for a title and a subtitle, usually used as the first slide in a presentation); Title Only (a title placeholder but not main text placeholder); Text (the default slide layout, with a title and a main text placeholder); and 2 Column Text (same as Text, but with two columns). PowerPoint also supports several **content layouts**—slide layouts that contain from zero to four charts, diagrams, images, tables, or movie clips. In addition, PowerPoint supports combination layouts, called **text and content layouts**, and several other types of layouts. When you add a new Slide 6, you'll use the Text layout.

To insert a new slide:

1. Because you want to add a slide after Slide 5, make sure Slide 5 is still in the Slide Pane. In general, when you add a new slide, it will appear immediately after the current one.

2. Click the **New Slide** button on the Formatting toolbar. The new slide appears in the Slide Pane. See Figure 1-17. The Slide Layout Task Pane appears, with the Text layout as the default for the new slide. You'll accept the default layout for this slide. If you wanted a different layout, you would click the desired layout in the Slide Layout Task Pane.

Figure 1-17   NEW SLIDE

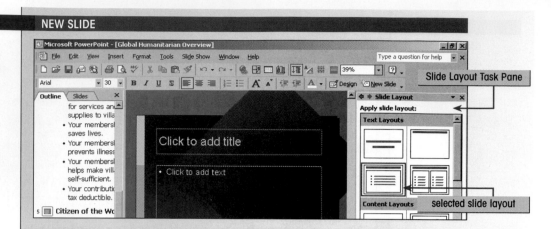

TROUBLE? If the Slide Layout Task Pane doesn't automatically appear in the PowerPoint window, make sure the Task Pane is in view by clicking View on the menu bar and clicking Task Pane. Then If necessary, click the Task Pane list arrow, and click Slide Layout.

3. Click anywhere in the title placeholder, and then type the title **Global Humanitarian Membership**.

4. Click in the main text placeholder. The insertion point appears just to the right of the first bullet.

5. Type **$75 per year individual membership**, press the **Enter** key to start a new bulleted item, type **$150 per year family membership**, press the **Enter** key, type **Visit our Web site at www.globalhumanitiarian.org** (which PowerPoint will automatically mark as a link by changing its color and underlining it), press the Enter key, and then type **Call 523–555–SERV**.

You have inserted a new slide at the end of the presentation and added text to the slide. Next you'll create a new slide by promoting text in the Outline tab.

Promoting, Demoting, and Moving Outline Text

To **promote** an item means to increase the outline level of that item—for example, to change a bulleted item into a slide title or to change a sub-bullet (a second-level bullet) into a first-level bullet. To **demote** an item means to decrease the outline level—for example, to change a slide title into a bulleted item within another slide or to change a bulleted item into a sub-bulleted item. You'll begin by promoting a bulleted item to a slide title, thus creating a new slide.

To create a new slide by promoting outline text:

1. Go to Slide 3 by dragging the Slide Pane scroll bar up until the ScreenTip displays "Slide: 3 of 6" and the title "How You Can Help." Notice that the text of that slide appears in the Outline tab. You can modify text of a slide not only in the Slide Pane, but also in the Outline tab. Currently, the Outline tab is so narrow that you can't see much of the text. One way to increase its size is to close the Task Pane.

2. Click the **Close** button ☒ at the top of the Task Pane.

TROUBLE? If you accidentally click the Close button of the PowerPoint window or Presentation window, PowerPoint will ask you if you want to save the changes to your presentation. Click the Cancel button so that the presentation doesn't close, and then click the correct Close button so that the Task Pane closes.

3. In the Outline tab, move the pointer to the bullet to the left of "Contribute to humanitarian projects" so that the pointer becomes ↔↕↔, and then click the bullet. The text for that bullet and all its sub-bullets becomes selected. You have to do this in the Outline tab rather than the Slide Pane so that you can decrease indent (promote) the text to a new slide. Now you'll promote that text so that it becomes title text and first-level bullets.

4. Click the **Decrease Indent** button ⊯ on the Formatting toolbar. PowerPoint promotes the text to a slide title, and automatically creates a new Slide 4. See Figure 1-18. As you can see, the new slide appears with the title text "Contribute to humanitarian projects." Now you'll edit this text, and then move some of the bulleted items to another slide.

Figure 1-18	PROMOTING A BULLETED ITEM TO BECOME A NEW SLIDE

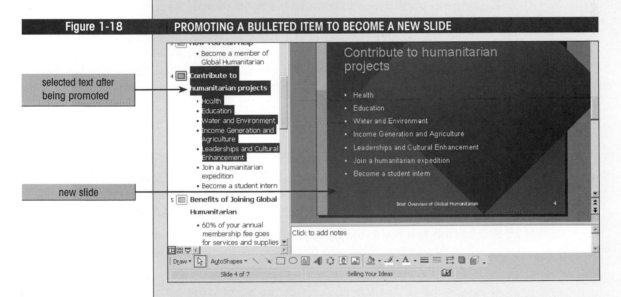

selected text after being promoted

new slide

5. Edit the title of the new Slide 4 to **Types of Humanitarian Projects in Third-World Villages**. You can make these changes either in the Slide Pane or Outline tab.

6. In the Outline tab, click ↔↕↔ on the bullet to the left of "Join a humanitarian expedition." While holding down the left mouse button, drag the bullet and its text up until the horizontal line position marker is just under the bulleted item "Become a member of Global Humanitarian" in Slide 3, as shown in Figure 1-19, and then release the mouse button.

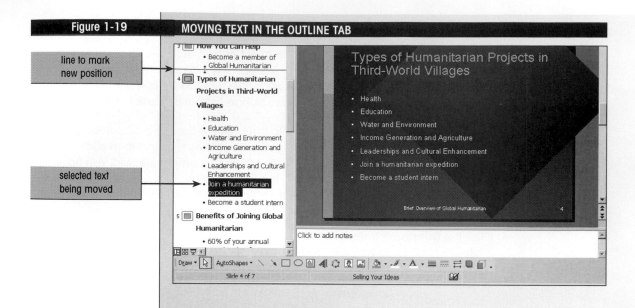

Figure 1-19   MOVING TEXT IN THE OUTLINE TAB

line to mark
new position

selected text
being moved

7. Using the same procedure, move the bulleted item "Become a student intern" from the end of Slide 4 to the end of Slide 3 in the Outline tab.

As you review your slides, you notice that in Slide 5, the phrase "Your membership fee" is unnecessarily repeated three times. You decide to fix the problem by demoting some of the text.

To demote text:

1. Go to Slide 5 in the Outline tab, "Benefits of Joining Global Humanitarian."

2. Click immediately to the right of "Your membership fee" in the second bulleted item, and then press the **Enter** key. Notice that "saves lives" becomes a new bulleted item, but you want that item to appear indented at a lower outline level.

3. Press the **Tab** key to indent "saves lives," and then delete any spaces to the left of "saves lives." You can also click the Increase Indent button on the Formatting toolbar.

4. Now, in the Outline tab, click on the bullet to the left of "Your membership fee prevents illness," press and hold down the **Shift** key, and then click the bullet to the left of "Your membership fee helps make villagers self-sufficient." This selects both bulleted items at the same time.

5. Click the **Increase Indent** button on the Formatting toolbar to demote the two bulleted items.

6. Delete the phrase "Your membership fee" and the space after it from the two items that you just demoted. Your slide now looks like Figure 1-20.

Figure 1-20	SLIDE 5 AFTER DEMOTING TEXT TO SUB-BULLETS

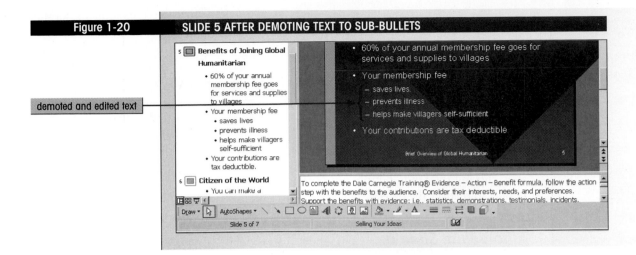

Miriam looks at your presentation and suggests that you move the current Slide 4 ahead of Slide 3. You could make this change by clicking ↕ on the slide icon ▣ and dragging it up above the slide icon for Slide 3. Instead, you'll move the slide in Slide Sorter View.

Moving Slides in Slide Sorter View

In Slide Sorter View, PowerPoint displays all the slides as thumbnails, so that 12 or more slides can appear on the screen at once. This view not only provides you with a good overview of your presentation, but also allows you to easily change the order of the slides and modify the slides in other ways.

To move the slide:

1. Click the **Slide Sorter View** button 🔠 on the View toolbar. You now see your presentation in Slide Sorter view. Move the pointer ⍀ over Slide 4. As you can see, a frame appears around the slide.

2. Click **Slide 4**. Notice that the frame around the slide becomes thicker, indicating that the slide is selected.

3. Press and hold down the left mouse button, drag the slide to the left so that the vertical line position marker appears on the other side of Slide 3, as shown in Figure 1-21, and then release the mouse button. The old Slides 3 and 4 switch places.

Figure 1-21	MOVING A SLIDE IN SLIDE SORTER VIEW

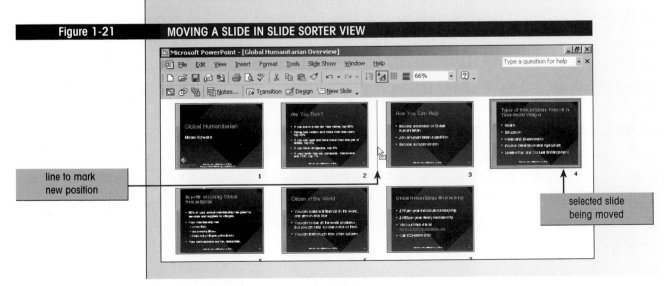

Miriam is pleased with your presentation, but suggests that you delete one of the slides.

Deleting Slides

When creating a presentation, you'll often delete slides. The AutoContent Wizard may create slides that you don't think are necessary, or you may create slides that you no longer want. For this presentation, Miriam asks you to delete Slide 6, titled "Citizen of the World." You can delete slides in the Outline tab by clicking the slide icon and pressing the Delete key, in Slide Sorter View by selecting the slide and pressing the Delete key, or in Normal View by using the menus. Keep in mind that once you delete a slide, you can recover it by immediately clicking the Undo button, but once you've done several other operations, you may not be able to recover the deleted slide. Now you'll use the menu method to delete a slide.

To delete Slide 6:

1. In Slide Sorter View, click **Slide 6**, and then click the **Normal View** button ⊞. This step causes Slide 6 to appear in the Slide Pane in Normal View. Now you're ready to delete the slide.

2. Click **Edit** on the menu bar, and then, if necessary, point to the double-arrow (at the bottom of the menu) to display the hidden menu items. PowerPoint, like other Office programs, initially displays the commands that are used most frequently on that computer. When you leave the menu open for a few seconds, or click the double-arrow, PowerPoint anticipates that you are looking for an item not currently displayed, and it expands the list of possible options. For the rest of these tutorials, click the double-arrow if you don't see the option you're looking for.

3. Click **Delete Slide**. The entire slide is deleted from the presentation. The slide that was Slide 7 becomes Slide 6 and appears in the Slide Pane.

This completes the presentation slides. Your next task is to use the Style Checker to check consistency and style within your presentation.

Using the Style Checker

The **Style Checker** automatically checks your presentation for consistency and style, and marks problems on a slide with a light bulb 💡. For the Style Checker to be active in your PowerPoint program, you might have to turn on the Style Checker.

To turn on the Style Checker:

1. Click **Tools** on the menu bar, click **Options** to open the Options dialog box, and click the **Spelling and Style** tab.

   TROUBLE? If you get the message about the Style Checker using the Office Assistant, click the Enable Assistant button.

2. Make sure the **Check style** check box is selected. If it's not checked, click the check box. Now you'll check to make sure the desired Style Checker options are selected.

3. Click the **Style Options** button on the Options dialog box, make sure each item is checked or unchecked, as shown in Figure 1-22, and then click the **OK** button.

| Figure 1-22 | STYLE OPTIONS DIALOG BOX |

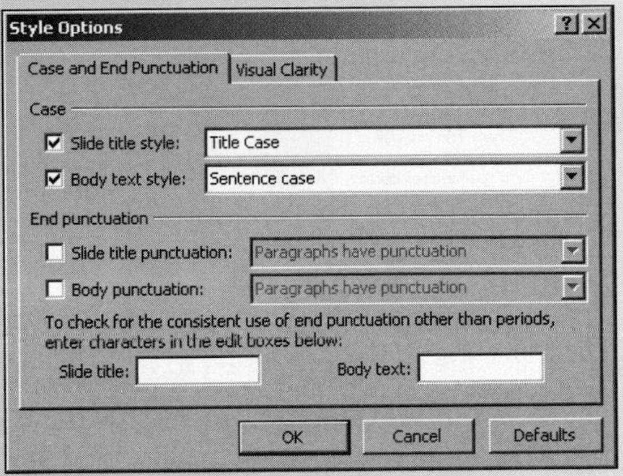

Style Options

Case and End Punctuation | Visual Clarity

Case
☑ Slide title style: Title Case
☑ Body text style: Sentence case

End punctuation
☐ Slide title punctuation: Paragraphs have punctuation
☐ Body punctuation: Paragraphs have punctuation

To check for the consistent use of end punctuation other than periods, enter characters in the edit boxes below:
Slide title: [   ]   Body text: [   ]

OK | Cancel | Defaults

4. Click the **OK** button on the Options dialog box.

You don't have to show the Office Assistant for the style checking to work, but the Office Assistant will automatically appear on the screen when you click 💡 to view the style error. From now on, PowerPoint will check the style in your presentation as you display each slide in the Slide Pane. Now you'll go through your presentation and check for style problems. As you display a slide, PowerPoint will mark any potential style errors with 💡.

To fix the problems marked by the Style Checker:

1. Go to Slide 1. As you can see, no style error occurs on this slide.

2. Go to Slide 2, where you will find no style error marked, and then to Slide 3, where 💡 appears next to the title. Often you won't know the style problem, but you can determine it by clicking the light bulb.

TROUBLE? If, in this or subsequent steps, the light bulb doesn't appear by the main text, go to the next or the previous slide, and then return to the current slide as a way of telling the Office Assistant to recheck the slide.

3. Click 💡. The Office Assistant appears and displays the problem. See Figure 1-23. The Style Checker can automatically fix the problem if you clicks the blue bullet of the first option in the Office Assistant dialog box.

Figure 1-23 **USING THE STYLE CHECKER**

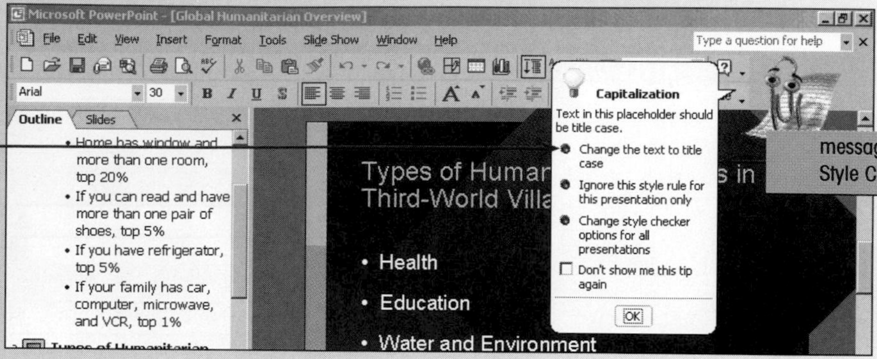

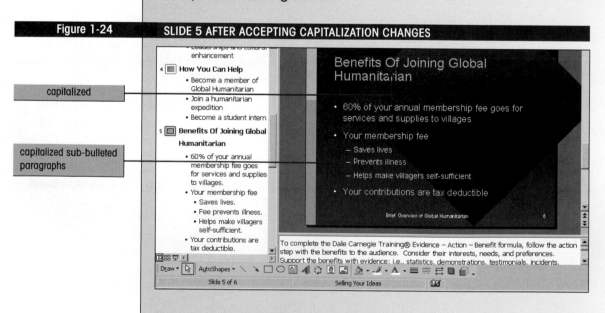

click to accept
suggested changes

message from
Style Checker

4. Click the **Change the text to title case** option button. The words "Of" and "In" are capitalized. Now the light bulb appears by the main text (the bulleted list).

5. Click 💡 to see the error in the bulleted list, and then click **Change the text to sentence case**. All the words (except the first word in each bulleted item) in the last three bulleted items are converted to lowercase; that is, all the bulleted items are converted to sentence case.

6. Go to Slide 4. Here the Style Checker detects that the first bulleted item is in mixed case (Global Humanitarian is capitalized), but you don't want to make any changes here. Click 💡 to read the error, but don't click any of the bulleted options. Instead, just click the **OK** button. When you click OK without selecting any of the other options, PowerPoint ignores the style for that slide.

7. Go to Slide 5 and use the same method to correct the capitalization problems in the title. Notice that in the main body of this slide, the sub-bullets need to be capitalized. See Figure 1-24.

Figure 1-24 **SLIDE 5 AFTER ACCEPTING CAPITALIZATION CHANGES**

capitalized

capitalized sub-bulleted paragraphs

8. Continue to the last slide, but click the **OK** button in this case to tell the Style Checker to ignore the suggested style error because you don't want to change the capitalization on this slide.

As you create your own presentations, watch for the problems marked by the Style Checker. Of course, in some cases, you might want a certain capitalization that the Style Checker detects as an error. In these cases, just ignore the light bulb, or click it, and then click the OK button. The light bulb never appears on the screen during a slide show or when you print a presentation.

Creating **Speaker Notes**

When you show the presentation to Miriam, she is satisfied. Now you're ready to prepare the other parts of Miriam's presentation: the notes (also called speaker notes) and audience handouts (a printout of the slides). **Notes** are printed pages that contain a picture of and notes about each slide. They help the speaker remember what to say while a particular slide appears during the presentation.

You'll create notes, or modify existing notes, for only two of the slides in the presentation.

To create notes:

1. Go to Slide 1. As you can see, notes already appear in the Notes Pane, just below the Slide Pane. First you'll delete them.

2. Click anywhere in the Notes Pane, press **Ctrl + A** to select all the text in the Notes Pane, and then press the **Delete** key. The current notes, which gave hints on how to sell your ideas to your audience, disappear from the pane. Now you're ready to type your own notes. Miriam wants to remember to acknowledge special guests or Global Humanitarian executives at any meeting where she might use this presentation.

3. Type **Acknowledge special guests and Global Humanitarian executives.** See Figure 1-25.

Figure 1-25   NOTES ON SLIDE 1

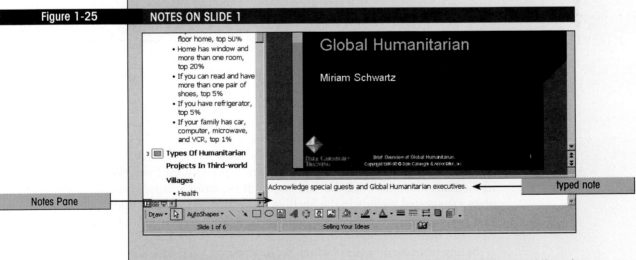

4. Go to Slide 2, delete all the current text from the Notes Pane, and then type **Everyone in this room is in the top 99th percentile of wealthy people who have ever lived on earth**.

5. Go to Slide 3, click in the Notes Pane, and then type **Give an example of each of these project types**. These are all the notes that Miriam wants.

6. Go through the rest of the slides in the presentation and delete any comments currently found in the Notes Pane.

7. Make sure your Data Disk is still in the disk drive, go back to Slide 1, and then save the presentation using the default filename. An updated copy of your presentation is now on your Data Disk.

Before Miriam gives her presentation, she'll print the Notes Panes of the presentation so she'll have the notes available during her presentations. Miriam also might want the Notes Panes to include headers and footers. Similar to a footer, a **header** is a word or phrase that appears at the top of each page. You'll practice inserting a footer (through the AutoContent Wizard) in an exercise at the end of the tutorial.

You can now view the completed presentation to make sure that it is accurate, informative, and visually pleasing.

To view the slide show:

1. Click the **Slide Show View** button ⬚.

2. Proceed through the slide show as you did earlier, clicking the left mouse button or pressing the spacebar to advance from one slide to the next.

3. When you reach the end of your slide show, press the **spacebar** to move to the blank screen, and then press the **spacebar** again to return to Normal View.

If you see a problem on one of your slides, press the Esc key to abort the slide show. The slide on the screen at the time you press the Esc key will appear in the Slide Pane. After you fix any problems, save the completed presentation again.

Now you're ready to preview and print your presentation.

Previewing and Printing the Presentation

Before you print or present a slide show, you should always do a final spell check of all the slides and speaker notes by clicking the Spelling button to start the PowerPoint Spell Checker feature. If PowerPoint finds a word that's not in its dictionary, the word is marked in the Slide Pane, and the Spelling dialog box appears. If the word is actually spelled correctly, but not found in the PowerPoint dictionary, you can click the Ignore button to tell the Spell Checker to ignore that occurrence of the word, or click Ignore All to tell the Spell Checker to ignore all occurrences of the word. If you want PowerPoint to add the word to its dictionary, you can click the Add button. If the word is misspelled, PowerPoint often displays a suggested spelling in the Spelling dialog box; in that case, you would click the correct suggestion, and then click Change or Change All to correct that occurrence or all occurrences of the misspelled word.

Before printing on your black-and-white printer, you should preview the presentation to make sure the text is legible in grayscale (shades of black and white).

To preview the presentation in grayscale:

1. Make sure Slide 1 appears in the Slide Pane, click the **Color/Grayscale** button ▦ on the Standard toolbar, and then click **Grayscale**. See Figure 1-26.

Figure 1-26 | **SLIDE 1 IN GRAYSCALE**

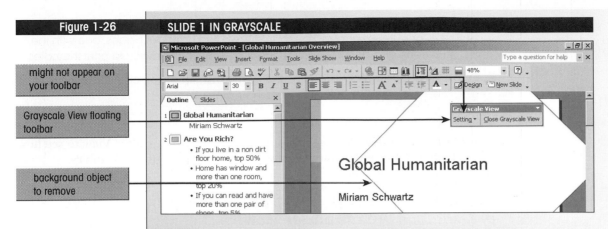

might not appear on your toolbar

Grayscale View floating toolbar

background object to remove

2. Look at the text on each slide to make sure it is legible. Depending on your Windows printer driver, the background graphics (a square tipped on a corner, in this case) might make some of the text hard to read, so you might want to omit the graphics from the slides.

3. Click **Format** on the menu bar, click **Background** to display the Background dialog box, click the **Omit background graphics from master** check box, and then click the **Apply to All** button. The slide appears as before, but without the background graphics.

4. Click **File** on the menu bar, and then click **Print** to open the Print dialog box. PowerPoint provides several printing options. For example, you can print the slides in color using a color printer; print in grayscale using a black-and-white printer; print handouts with 2, 3, 4, 6, or 9 slides per page; or print the Notes Pages (printed notes below a picture of the corresponding slide). You can also format and then print the presentation onto overhead transparency film (available in most office supply stores).

5. Click the **Print what** list arrow, click **Handouts**, then in the Handouts section, click the **Slides per page** list arrow, and then click **4**. Make sure the Frame slides check box is selected, and the Color/grayscale text box is set to Grayscale. See Figure 1-27.

Figure 1-27 | **PRINT DIALOG BOX**

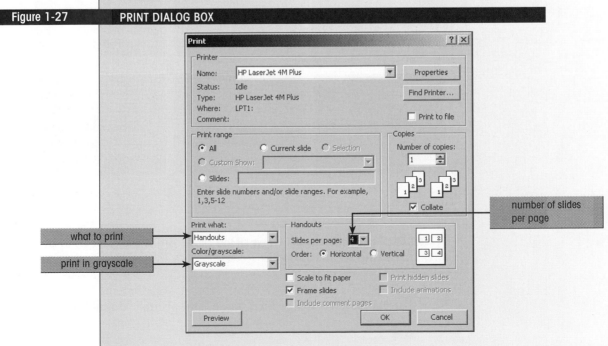

what to print

print in grayscale

number of slides per page

6. Make sure all the other options are set as in Figure 1-27, and then click the **OK** button to print the handouts. You should have two handout pages, one with the first four slides, and another with the last two. Now you're ready to print the notes.

7. Display the Print dialog box, click the **Print what** list arrow, click **Notes Pages**, and then click the **OK** button to print the notes.

Your last task is to view the completed presentation in Slide Sorter View to see how all the slides look together. First, however, you'll restore the background graphics.

To restore the background graphics and view the completed presentation in Slide Sorter View:

1. Click the **Color/Grayscale** button ▦ on the Standard toolbar, and then click **Color** to return to color view.

2. Click **Format** on the menu bar, click **Background**, click the **Omit background graphics from master** check box to deselect it, and then click the **Apply to All** button. The background graphics are restored to the slides.

3. Click the **Slide Sorter View** button ▦ on the View toolbar.

4. To see the slides better, click the **Zoom** list arrow on the Standard toolbar, and change the Zoom to **100%**. Compare your handouts with the six slides shown in Figure 1-28.

| Figure 1-28 | COMPLETED PRESENTATION IN SLIDE SORTER VIEW |

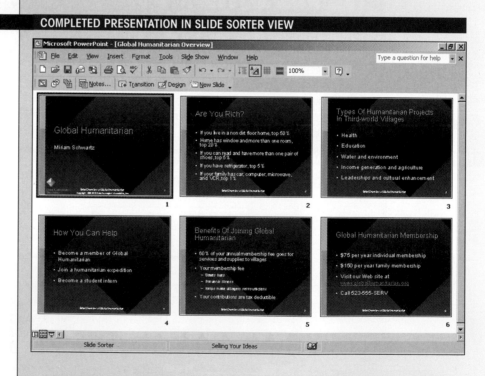

TROUBLE? If the thumbnail views of the slides are too big for all to be seen at once, set the Zoom to a lower value.

Now that you have created, edited, saved, and printed Miriam's presentation, you can exit PowerPoint.

To exit PowerPoint:

1. Click ☒ in the upper-right corner of the PowerPoint window. Because you have made changes since the last time you saved the presentation, PowerPoint displays a dialog box with the message "Do you want to save the changes you made to Global Humanitarian Overview.ppt?"

2. Click the **No** button to exit PowerPoint without saving the current version of the presentation, because you already saved the final version.

You have created a presentation using the AutoContent Wizard, edited it according to Miriam's wishes, and created and printed notes and handouts. Miriam thanks you for your help; she believes that your work will enable her to make an effective presentation.

Session 1.2 QUICK CHECK

1. Explain how to do the following in the Outline tab:
   a. move text up
   b. delete a slide
   c. promote text
   d. edit text

2. What does it mean to promote a bulleted item in the Outline tab? To demote a bulleted item?

3. Explain a benefit of using the Outline tab rather than the Slide Pane, and a benefit of using the Slide Pane rather than the Outline tab.

4. Explain how to add a slide to a presentation.

5. What is the Style Checker? What is an example of a consistency or style problem that it might mark?

6. What are speaker notes? How do you create them?

7. Why is it beneficial to preview a presentation before printing it?

REVIEW ASSIGNMENTS

Miriam Schwartz, the managing director of the Austin, Texas, headquarters of Global Humanitarian, asks you to prepare a PowerPoint presentation explaining the Village Outreach Program to potential donors and volunteers. She gives you a disk with a rough draft of a PowerPoint presentation that provides most of the information about the Village Outreach Program. Your job is to edit the presentation. Complete the following:

1. Start PowerPoint and make sure your Data Disk is in the disk drive.

Explore
2. Open the presentation **VillagOP** in the Review folder of the Tutorial.01 folder, and then save the file using the new filename **Village Outreach Program** in the same Review folder. (*Hint*: To save a file with a different filename, click File on the menu bar, and then click Save As.)

3. In Slide 1, change the subtitle placeholder ("Global Humanitarian") to your name.

4. In Slide 2, use the Outline tab to demote the bulleted items "Health," "Education," "Clean water and environment," and "Leadership" and make them sub-bulleted items. (*Hint*: Select all four items at once by clicking the bullet of the first item, pressing and holding down the Shift key, and clicking the bullet of the last item.)

5. Below the sub-bulleted item "Clean water and environment," insert another sub-bulleted item "Agriculture and Income Generation."

6. In Slide 3, delete all occurrences of the word "the" to approach the 6 × 6 rule by reducing the number of words in each bulleted item.

7. Use the Outline tab to move the last bulleted item ("Assist villagers in organizing health committees") so it becomes the second bulleted item in the main text.

8. In Slide 4, right-click the misspelled word (marked with the wavy red underline), and then click the correctly spelled word.

9. In the Outline tab of Slide 5, promote the bulleted item "Agriculture and Income Generation" so it becomes the title of a new slide (Slide 6).

10. Return to Slide 5 and promote the last three sub-bulleted items so they become bullets on the same level as "Help villagers construct."

Explore 11. Still in Slide 5, tell PowerPoint Spell Checker to ignore all occurrences of the word "catchment," which is not found in PowerPoint's dictionary. (*Hint*: Right-click the word.)

12. In the new Slide 6, edit the typographical error "load," which should be "loan." (This exercise is to remind you of the importance of proofreading your presentation. Don't leave it to the PowerPoint Spell Checker to find all your errors.)

13. Edit the final bulleted item so that each phrase after "Encourage weekly meetings to discuss" is a sub-bulleted item with no punctuation. You should end up with five sub-bulleted items.

14. Go to Slide 7, and then add a new Slide 8.

15. In Slide 8, type the title "Household Interventions."

16. Type the following as bulleted items in Slide 8: "Wells," "Pumps," "Greenhouses," "Lorena Stoves," "First aid supplies," and "Bookkeeping supplies."

17. In Slide 2, add the following speaker note: "Relate personal experiences for each of these items."

18. In Slide 3, add the following speaker note: "Remind audience that we need volunteer physicians, dentists, optometrists, nurses, and social workers."

Explore 19. Make sure the Style Checker is turned on, and then set the Style Options for Visual Clarity so that the maximum number of bullets should not exceed six, the number of lines per title should not exceed two, and number of lines per bulleted item should not exceed two. (*Hint*: Use the Legibility section of the Visual Clarity tab on the Style Options dialog box.)

20. Go through each slide of the presentation to see if the Style Checker marks any potential problems. When you see the light bulb, click it, and assess whether you want to accept or reject the suggested change. For example, in Slide 2, make sure you keep "Village Outreach Programs" capitalized.

Explore 21. If any of the bulleted text (for example, the text in Slide 7) doesn't fit on the slide, but drops below the main text box, set the text box to AutoFit. (*Hint*: Select the text box, click the AutoFit icon ⊡, which appears near the lower-left corner of the text box, and select the desired option.)

Explore 22. Add to the presentation the design template called "Cliff," which has a green gradient-filled background. (*Hint*: Open the Task Pane, if necessary, and change the Task Pane to Slide Design—Design Templates using the drop-down menu. Then move the pointer over a design template thumbnail so the design template name appears. Click the thumbnail of the desired template.) If you can't find the "Cliff" design template, choose a different design template.

23. Spell check the presentation by clicking the Spelling button.

24. View the presentation in Slide Show View.

25. Save the presentation using its default filename.

Explore 26. View the presentation again in Slide Show View, except this time start with Slide 4 and go only to Slide 6. (*Hint*: The slide show starts with the slide in the Slide Pane. To terminate a slide show, press the Esc key.)

27. Preview the presentation in grayscale.

28. Print the presentation in grayscale as handouts with four slides per page.

29. Close the file, and then exit PowerPoint.

CASE PROBLEMS

Case 1. e-Commerce Consultants   Two years ago, Whitney Harris of Rockford, Illinois, founded a consulting business that helps local businesses with their e-commerce needs, including Web page design, order fulfillment, and security. Whitney asks you to prepare a presentation to businesses to sell the services of e-Commerce Consultants. Do the following:

1. Create a new onscreen PowerPoint presentation and start the AutoContent Wizard.

2. In the Sales/Marketing category, select Selling a Product or Service.

3. Type the presentation title as "e-Commerce: Your Strategy for the Future," and type the footer as "e-Commerce Consultants."

4. Omit the Date last updated from the presentation, but include the slide number.

5. In Slide 1, change the subtitle placeholder, if necessary, to your name.

6. In Slide 2 ("Objective"), include the following bulleted items (here and in the other slides, delete the current items in the main text placeholder): "How to manage change," "How to overcome barriers to e-commerce," "How to change managerial styles," "How to set up your Web site," "How to manage orders," and "What we offer to your business."

7. In Slide 3 ("Customer Requirements"), keep the radial diagram that automatically appears here, and then include the following bulleted items: "Company management issues," "Web site design and set-up," "Order taking and fulfillment," "Security," and "Other?"

Explore 8. Go to Slide 4, open the Slide Layout Task Pane, and change the slide layout to Text. (*Hint*: Click the slide layout thumbnail that contains only a title and a bulleted list.)

9. Delete the three pyramid diagrams by clicking each one and pressing the Delete key.

10. In Slide 4, change the title to "Meeting Your Needs," and then include the following bulleted items: "We supply labor or help you find employees," "We provide know-how, graphic design, software, programming, security systems," "We can help promote your product, secure startup funding, arrange for credit card accounts," and "We can answer all your questions."

11. Delete Slides 5 and 6.

12. In the new Slide 5 ("Key Benefits"), include the following bulleted items: "You focus on your products, your services, your bottom line," and "We help you sell your product on the Internet."

13. In Slide 6, ("Next Steps"), include the following bulleted items: "Make a list of the things that you want us to do," "Draw up an agreement," "Set a timeline for implementation," "Establish your order-fulfillment operation," and "Launch your Web site and e-commerce system."

14. Save the presentation to the Cases folder in the Tutorial.01 folder using the filename **e-Commerce Consultants**.

15. In Slide 1, delete the space between "e-Commerce:" and "Your," and then press Enter to move the phrase "Your Strategy for the Future" to the second line of the title.

Explore 16. Center the text in the title text box. (*Hint*: Use the Answer Wizard of the Help system and ask the question, "How do I center a paragraph?")

17. In Slide 2, move "manage change" down to a new bulleted item, indent (demote) that item so it is a sub-bullet under "How to," delete "How to" from the next four bulleted items, and then make them sub-bullets under "How to."

18. In Slide 4, edit the second bulleted item to be "We provide," and then make sub-bulleted items of "know how," "graphic design," "software," "programming," and "security systems."

19. Similarly in Slide 4, do the same type of editing for the next bulleted item, making "We can help" the main bullet and the other phrases the sub-bullets.

Explore   20. Still in Slide 4, move the third bullet "We can help" (along with all its sub-bullets) up to become the second bullet. (*Hint*: In the Outline tab or Slide Pane, when you select a bulleted item, PowerPoint automatically selects all its sub-bullets.)

21. Move the last bulleted item "We can answer all your questions" up to become the first bulleted item.

22. Promote the bulleted item "We provide" (and all its sub-bullets) to become a new separate slide, and then add the word "What" at the beginning of the slide title.

23. In Slide 6 ("Key Benefits"), edit the first bulleted item to be "You focus on your," and then make sub-bulleted items of "products," "services," and "bottom line."

24. In Slide 7 ("Next Steps"), delete excess words like "a," "an," "the," and "that" to achieve the 6 × 6 rule as closely as possible.

Explore   25. Make sure the Style Checker is turned on, and then set the Style Options for Visual Clarity so that the maximum number of bullets should not exceed six, the number of lines per title should not exceed two, and the number of lines per bulleted item should not exceed two. (*Hint*: Use the Legibility section of the Visual Clarity tab on the Style Options dialog box.)

26. Go through each slide of the presentation to see if the Style Checker marks any potential problems. When you see the light bulb, click it, and assess whether you want to accept or reject the suggested change. You'll want to accept most of the suggested changes, but make sure you leave words like "Web" and "Internet" capitalized.

27. Spell check the presentation by clicking the Spelling button.

28. View the presentation in Slide Show View.

30. Save the current version of the presentation using its default filename, preview the presentation in grayscale, and then print the presentation in grayscale as handouts with four slides per page.

31. Close the file, and then exit PowerPoint.

Case 2. Northeast Seafoods   Paul Neibaur is president of Northeast Seafoods, a seafood distribution company with headquarters in Halifax, Nova Scotia. He buys fish and other seafood from suppliers and sells to restaurant and grocery store chains. Although his company has been in business and profitable for 27 years, Paul wants to sell the company and retire. He wants you to help him create a PowerPoint presentation to prospective buyers. Do the following:

1. Open the file **Seafoods** in the Cases folder in the Tutorial.01 folder of your Data Disk, and save it back to the same folder using the filename **Northeast Seafoods**.

2. In Slide 1, replace the subtitle placeholder ("Paul Neibaur") with your name.

3. In Slide 2, add the speaker's note "Mention that the regular customers are all large grocery store and restaurant chains."

Explore   4. Run the Spell Checker. Tell it to ignore all occurrences of the word "preapproved" which are not found in the PowerPoint dictionary. (*Hint*: Click the Ignore All button on the Spelling dialog box.) Do the same for other correctly spelled words, if any, not found in the PowerPoint dictionary. Correct all the misspelled words.

Explore   5. Move the third bulleted item ("19% to 28% profit . . .") from Slide 2 to become the last bulleted item in Slide 4. (*Hint*: You can use the Outline tab to drag the bullet, or you can use the cut-and-paste method.)

6. In Slide 3, edit the third bulleted item so that "freezers," "saws," "packagers," and "other equipment" are sub-bulleted items below the main bullet.

7. Do the same for the items after the colon in the fifth main bulleted item, and then delete the colon.

8. Move the last bulleted item ("Contracts with . . .") to become the second bulleted item.

9. Promote the bulleted item "Experienced employees" and its sub-bullets so that they become a new separate slide.

Explore   10. Use the Slides tab to move Slide 4 ("Experienced Employees") to become Slide 3. (*Hint*: Drag and drop the slide.)

11. In Slide 5, find the typographical error (if you haven't already) and correct it. This demonstrates the importance of proofreading your presentation carefully, because PowerPoint doesn't pick up this type of error.

12. Make sure the Style Checker is turned on, and then go through all the slides correcting problems of case (capitalization). Be sure not to let the Style Checker change the case for "Small Business Administration;" otherwise, accept the Style Checker's suggested case changes.

Explore   13. Add to the presentation the design template called "Ocean," which has a blue gradient-filled background with lighter colors near the upper-left corner. (*Hint*: Open the Task Pane, if necessary, and change the Task Pane to Slide Design—Design Templates. Then move the pointer over a design template thumbnail so the design template name appears. Click the thumbnail of the desired template.) If you can't find the "Ocean" design template, choose a different design template.

14. View the presentation in Slide Show View.

15. Save the presentation using its default filename.

16. Preview the presentation in grayscale.

17. Print the presentation in grayscale as handouts with four slides per page.

18. Close the file and then exit PowerPoint.

Case 3. Magnolia Gardens Eye Center   Dr. Carol Wang, the head ophthalmologist at the Magnolia Gardens Eye Center in Charleston, South Carolina, performs over 20 surgeries per week using laser in situ keratomileusis, also called laser-assisted in situ keratomileusis (LASIK), to correct vision problems of myopia (nearsightedness), hyperopia (farsightedness), and astigmatism. She asks you to help prepare a PowerPoint presentation to those interested in learning more about LASIK. Do the following:

1. Open the file **LASIK** in the Cases folder in the Tutorial.01 folder of your Data Disk, and save it back to the same folder using the filename **Magnolia LASIK**.

2. In Slide 1, replace the subtitle placeholder ("Magnolia Gardens Eye Center") with your name.

3. In Slide 2, move the third bulleted item up to become the first bulleted item.

4. Add a fourth bulleted item with the text "Improves how patients see without corrective lenses."

5. Edit the third bulleted item so that "myopia," "hyperopia," and "astigmatism" are sub-bulleted items below the main bullet.

Explore   6. In Slide 3, change the bulleted list to a numbered list.

Explore   7. Have PowerPoint automatically split Slide 3 into two slides. (*Hint*: With the main text box selected, click the AutoFit Options icon ⬓ and select the appropriate option.)

Explore   8. On the new Slide 4, change the numbering so it starts at 5 rather than 1, to continue from the previous slide. (*Hint*: Select the numbered text box, click Format on the menu bar, click Bullets and Numbering, click the Numbered tab, and change the Start at value.)

9. At the end of the title in Slide 4, add a space and "(cont.)," the abbreviation for continued.

10. In Slide 5, demote the two bullets under "With low to moderate myopia," so they become sub-bullets.

11. In Slide 6, demote the final two bullets to become sub-bullets.

12. In Slide 7, move the sixth bulleted item ("Greater the correction, longer the time to heal") to become the second item.

13. In Slide 8, edit the bulleted item ("Analysis of . . .") so that "eye pressure," "shape of cornea," and "thickness of cornea" are sub-bullets below "Analysis of."

14. Add a Slide 9. Select the Title Only layout in the Text Layout section of the Slide Layout Task Pane.

Explore ▶ 15. In Slide 9, add the title "Magnolia Gardens Eye Center," and then create a new text box near the center of the slide, with the address and phone number ("8184 Magnolia Drive" on the first line, "Charleston, SC 29406" on the second line, and "(843) 555-EYES" on the third line). (*Hint*: Click the Text Box button on the Drawing toolbar, and then click on the slide at the desired location.)

Explore ▶ 16. Change the font size of the new text box on Slide 9 so that it's 32 points. If you're not sure how to do it, use the Help system to get help on changing the font size. If necessary, drag the edge of the text box so the box is positioned near the center of the slide.

Explore ▶ 17. Make sure the Style Checker is turned on, and then set the Style Options for Visual Clarity so that the maximum number of bullets should not exceed six, the number of lines per title should not exceed two, and the number of lines per bulleted item should not exceed two. Also turn on body punctuation, so that the Style Checker checks for punctuation at the end of paragraphs in the main text, but make sure title punctuation is turned off. (*Hint*: Use the Legibility section of the Visual Clarity tab and the Body punctuation section of the Case and End Punctuation tab on the Style Options dialog box.)

18. Go through all the slides, correcting problems of case (capitalization) and punctuation. Be sure not to let the Style Checker change the case for proper nouns; otherwise, accept the Style Checker's suggested case changes. Let the Style Checker correct end punctuation for complete sentences, but you shouldn't allow (or you should remove) punctuation for words or phrases that don't form complete sentences.

Explore ▶ 19. Add to the presentation the design template called "Watermark," which has a white background with violet circles. (*Hint*: Open the Task Pane, if necessary, and change the Task Pane to Slide Design – Design Templates. Then move the pointer over a design template thumbnail so the design template name appears. Click the thumbnail of the desired template. The Watermark template is the last one in the Task Pane.) If you can't find the "Watermark" design template, choose a different design template.

20. View the presentation in Slide Show View.

21. Save the presentation using its default filename.

22. Preview the presentation in grayscale.

23. Print the presentation in grayscale as handouts with four slides per page.

24. Close the files and then exit PowerPoint.

Case 4. Textbook Review   Your English teacher asks you to prepare a book review for presentation to the class. The teacher asks you to review any textbook for any class, current or past. To help you give your class presentation, you want to use PowerPoint slides. Your task is to prepare a presentation of at least six PowerPoint slides. Do the following:

1. Use the AutoContent Wizard to begin developing slides based on "Generic" from the General category of presentation types.

2. Make the presentation "Review of" followed by your textbook title, and make the footer "Review of" followed by the textbook subject. For example, the title might be "Review of *Earth's Dynamic Systems*" and the footer "Review of Geology Textbook."

3. In the footer, include both the date and the slide number.

4. Edit Slide 1 so that the textbook title is italicized. If you don't know how to italicize existing text, use PowerPoint's Help.

5. Also in Slide 1, if necessary, change the subtitle to your name.

6. In Slide 2 ("Introduction"), include the following type of information in the bulleted list: title, authors, publisher, publication year, number of pages, and college course using the book.

7. In Slide 3 ("Topics of Discussion"), include the categories used in reviewing the book; for example, "Level of writing," "Clarity of explanations," "Completeness of explanations," "Figures and tables," "End-of-chapter materials," and "End-of-book supplementary material."

8. Delete Slides 4 through 9. (*Hint*: The easiest way to delete many slides at once is to select the slides in Slide Sorter View.)

9. Create at least one slide for each of the topics you listed on Slide 3, and then include bulleted lists explaining that topic.

10. Create a slide titled "Summary and Recommendation" as the last slide in your presentation, giving your overall impression of the book and your recommendation for whether or not it should be continued.

Explore ▶ 11. Make sure the Style Checker is turned on, and then set the Style Options for Visual Clarity so that the maximum number of bullets should not exceed six, the number of lines per title should not exceed two, and the number of lines per bulleted item should not exceed two. Also turn on body punctuation, so that the Style Checker checks for punctuation at the end of paragraphs in the main text, but make sure title punctuation is turned off. (*Hint*: Use the Legibility section of the Visual Clarity tab and the End punctuation section of the Case and End Punctuation tab on the Style Options dialog box.)

12. Go through all the slides, correcting problems of case (capitalization), punctuation, number of bulleted items per slide, and the number of lines per bulleted item. Be sure not to let the Style Checker change the case for proper nouns. Let the Style Checker correct end punctuation for complete sentences, but you shouldn't allow (or you should remove) punctuation for words or phrases that don't form complete sentences.

Explore ▶ 13. Add to the presentation an appropriate design template. For example, if you're reviewing a geology textbook, you might apply the "Globe" design style. (*Hint*: Open the Task Pane, if necessary, and change the Task Pane to Slide Design – Design Templates.)

14. Check the spelling of your presentation.

15. View the presentation in Slide Show View. If you see any typographical errors or other problems, stop the slide show, correct the problems, and then continue the slide show.

16. If necessary, change the order of the bulleted items on slides, or change the order of slides.

17. If you find slides with more than six bulleted items, split the slide in two.

18. If you find slides that aren't necessary, delete them.

19. Save the presentation in the Cases folder of the Tutorial.01 folder, using the filename **Textbook Review**.

20. Preview the presentation in grayscale.

21. Print the presentation in grayscale as handouts with four slides per page.

22. Close the file, and then exit PowerPoint.

INTERNET ASSIGNMENTS

Student Union

The purpose of the Internet Assignments is to challenge you to find information on the Internet that you can use to create effective documents. The actual assignments are updated and maintained on the Course Technology Web site. Log on to the Internet and use your Web browser to go to the Student Union on the New Perspectives Series site at **www.course.com/NewPerspectives/studentunion**. Click the Online Companions link, and then click the link for this text.

QUICK CHECK ANSWERS

Session 1.1

1. PowerPoint provides everything you need to produce a presentation that consists of black-and-white or color overheads, 35-mm slides, or on-screen slides. The presentation's components can consist of individual slides, speaker notes, an outline, and audience handouts.

2. The Outline tab shows an outline of your presentation, including titles and text of each slide. The Slides tab displays thumbnails of each slide in your presentation. The Slide Pane shows the slide as it will look during your slide show. The Notes Pane contains any notes that you might prepare on each slide. The Task Pane displays lists or sets of tasks that you can apply to your slide.

3. a. gradient fill: a type of shading in which one color blends into another
   b. footer: a word or phrase that appears at the bottom of each slide in the presentation
   c. slide transition: the special effect of how a slide appears on the monitor screen
   d. custom animation: user-defined motion or appearance of items on the slide
   e. placeholder: a region of a slide, or a location in an outline, reserved for inserting text or graphics
   f. bulleted list: a list of paragraphs with a special character (dot, circle, box, star, or other character) to the left of each paragraph

4. Planning improves the quality of your presentation, makes your presentation more effective and enjoyable, and saves you time and effort. You should answer several questions: What is my purpose or objective? What type of presentation is needed? What is the physical location of my presentation? What is the best format for presenting the information?

5. The AutoContent Wizard lets you choose a presentation category and then creates a general outline of the presentation.

6. Use six or fewer items per screen, and use phrases of six or fewer words

7. a word that is not located in the PowerPoint dictionary, usually a misspelled word.

8. so that you won't lose all your work if, for example, a power failure suddenly shuts down your computer

Session 1.2

1. a. Click a slide or bullet icon, and drag the selected item up.
   b. Select the slide to be deleted, click Edit on the menu bar, and then click Delete Slide. Or, select the slide to be deleted and press the Delete key.
   c. Unindent or move it from a lower to a higher outline level.
   d. Drag the I-beam pointer to select the text, and then delete or retype it.

2. Promote means to decrease the level (for example, from level 2 to level 1) of an outline item; demote means to increase the level (for example, from level 1 to level 2) of an outline item.

3. In the Outline tab you can see the text of several slides at once, which makes it easier to work with text. In the Slide Pane, you can see the design and layout of the slide.

4. Click the New Slide button on the Standard toolbar, then select the desired layout from the New Slide dialog box. You can also promote (unindent) a bulleted item using the Outline tab.

5. The Style Checker automatically checks your presentation for consistency and style. For example, it will check for consistency in punctuation.

6. Speaker notes are printed pages that contain a picture of and notes about each slide. Create them by typing text into the Notes Pane.

7. By previewing your presentation, you make sure that the slides are satisfactory, and that the presentation is legible in grayscale if you use a monochrome printer.

OBJECTIVES

In this tutorial you will:

- Create, resize, and move text boxes and graphics boxes

- Add a design template and modify the design using the Slide Masters

- Insert tab stops to align text

- Change the layouts of existing slides

- Insert and resize pictures and clip-art images

- Create a table and a diagram

- Draw and manipulate a simple graphic using AutoShapes

- Create a summary slide

APPLYING
AND MODIFYING TEXT AND GRAPHIC OBJECTS

Presentation on Preparing for an Expedition to Peru

CASE

Global Humanitarian, Lima Office

The objectives of Global Humanitarian's expeditions are to help villagers build homes, schools, greenhouses, wells, culinary water systems, and Lorena adobe stoves; to provide medical and dental services; and to teach basic hygiene, literacy, and gardening skills. The village council of Paqarimuy, a small village in the *puna* (also called the *altiplano* or high-altitude plains of the Andes Mountains), requested help in accomplishing some of these objectives. Therefore, Pablo Fuentes, the managing director of Global Humanitarian in Lima, Peru, is organizing a service expedition to that village. He asks you to help prepare a PowerPoint presentation to prospective expedition participants. Pablo already wrote most of the text in a blank presentation, and wants you to enhance the text with special formatting and graphics.

In this tutorial, you'll open the text presentation, and then enhance the presentation by adding graphics to the slides. A **graphic** is a picture, clip art, photograph, shape, design, graph, chart, or diagram that you can add to a slide. A graphic is an example of an **object**, which is an element of a slide. A slide element can be a graphic, text box, border, or background.

SESSION 2.1

In this session, you'll apply a design template to a presentation, use the Slide Master and Title Master to modify the presentation design, insert footers and slide numbering, change the slide layout, edit and format text, add and modify tab stops, and modify and insert graphics into the presentation slides.

Planning a Presentation

Before creating his text presentation, Pablo and his staff planned the presentation as follows:

- **Purpose of the presentation**: To convince potential volunteers to apply for a position in the Peru Expedition
- **Type of presentation**: An onScreen (electronic) information presentation
- **Audience**: Students, health professionals, and other people interested in serving villages in an LDC
- **Location of presentation**: A conference room at the offices of Global Humanitarian, as well as classrooms and business offices
- **Audience needs**: To recognize the services they can provide and the adventure they can enjoy as expedition volunteers
- **Format**: One speaker presenting an onScreen slide show consisting of 7 to 10 slides

After planning the presentation, Pablo quickly types the text into PowerPoint without worrying about the appearance of the presentation. He now asks you to make the presentation more interesting and effective by changing the format and adding graphics.

Applying a Design Template

Plain white slides with normal text (such as black Times New Roman or Arial) often fail to hold the audience's attention. In today's information age, your audiences expect more interesting color schemes, fonts, and other effects. You'll begin enhancing Pablo's presentation by changing the design template.

A **design template** is a file that contains the color scheme, attributes, and format for the titles, main text, other text, and background in the presentation. Pablo's current presentation was created using the Default Design template, as shown on the status bar in Figure 2-1. Pablo wants a color scheme with a dark blue background and a color gradient. You'll change the design template now.

REFERENCE WINDOW   RW

Applying a Design Template
- If necessary, open the Task Pane by clicking View on the menu bar, and then clicking Task Pane.
- Display the Slide Design tasks in the Task Pane by clicking the Slide Design button on the Formatting toolbar.
- Scroll through the design template thumbnails until you see one you'd like to apply, and then click it. The design is immediately applied to all the slides in the presentation.

Figure 2-1 **SLIDE 1 OF THE PRESENTATION**

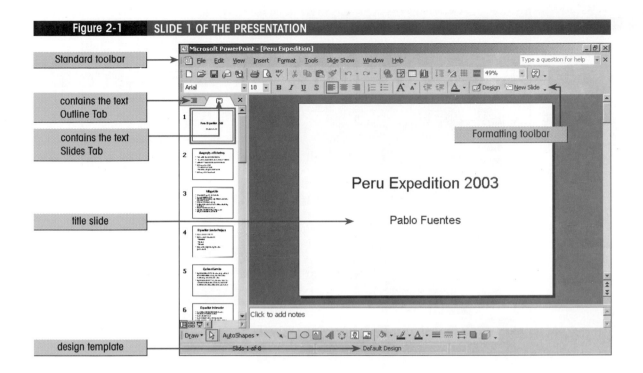

To change the design template:

1. Start PowerPoint and open the presentation file **PeruExp** from the Tutorial folder of the Tutorial.02 folder on your Data Disk.

2. Save the file back to the same folder using the filename **Peru Expedition**. As you can see in Figure 2-1, the design template is called Default Design, in which the slides have black Arial text on a plain white background. To apply a different design template, you have to open the Task Pane.

3. Click the **Slide Design** button 🖾 on the Formatting toolbar. This opens the Task Pane with the Slide Design templates.

4. Scroll down through the thumbnail views of the design templates, and move over the thumbnails to view the ScreenTips with the names of the templates until you find Mountain Top. The design templates appear in the Task Pane in alphabetical order, so Mountain Top is about halfway down.

5. Click the design template **Mountain Top**. The design template of Peru Expedition changes from Default Design to Mountain Top. See Figure 2-2.

Figure 2-2   SLIDE AFTER APPLYING DESIGN TEMPLATE

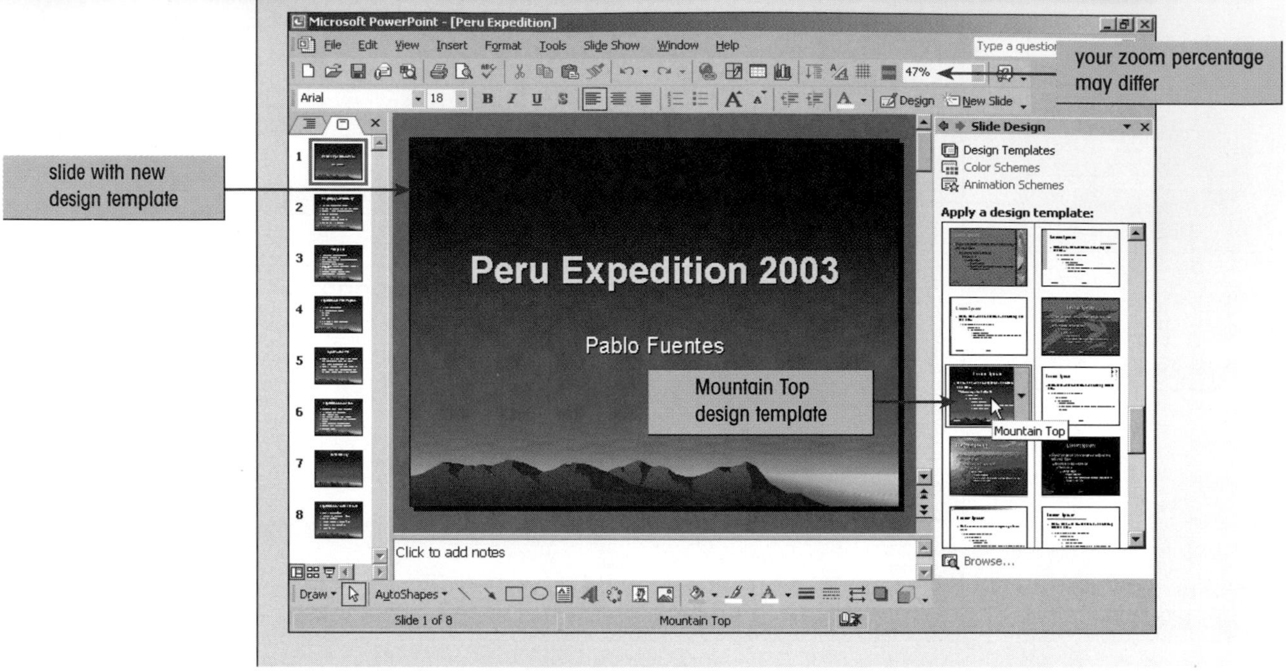

As you can see, the title slide (Slide 1 of the presentation) has a dark blue background with a color gradient, and a background graphic of a mountain top along the bottom of the slide.

Modifying **the Slide Masters**

Instead of using the current background graphic of the Mountain Top design template, Pablo prefers an actual photograph of the Andes Mountains, in the form of a bitmap image. He also wants you to modify some other elements of the design template. You'll begin by removing the background graphics from the Slide Masters. A **master** is a slide that contains the text and other objects that appear on all the slides of the same type. Masters, however, never appear when you show or print a presentation. PowerPoint presentations usually have two types of masters: the **Title Master**, which contains the objects that appear on the title slide (most presentations have only one title slide, but some have more than one), and the **Slide Master**, which contains the objects that appear on all the slides except the title slide. Now you'll modify the two types of masters.

Inserting a Bitmap Image on the Slide Masters

Graphics add information, clarification, emphasis, variety, and even pizzazz to a PowerPoint presentation. PowerPoint enables you to include many types of graphics in your presentation: graphics created using another Windows program, scanned photographs, drawings, cartoons, and other picture files located on a CD or other disk. You can also create graphics using the Drawing tools in PowerPoint. Finally, you can add graphical bullets.

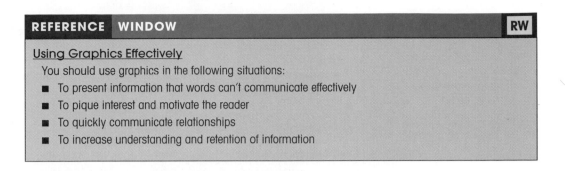

To use a picture in a PowerPoint presentation, the picture must be a computer file located on an electronic medium, such as a CD or hard disk. Picture files are generated by taking photographs with a digital camera, scanning photographs taken with conventional cameras, or drawing pictures using graphics software (such as Microsoft Paint). To get a computer file of Global Humanitarian's logo, Pablo hired a graphic artist to create the file using graphics software. To get a picture of the Andes Mountains, Pablo scanned a picture he took with a 35mm film camera.

Now you'll delete the current background graphic in the Title Master and insert a new one.

To modify the Title Master:

1. Click **View** on the menu bar, point to **Master**, and then click **Slide Master**. See Figure 2-3. Even though you clicked Slide Master, the Title Master appears because the title slide was in the Slide Pane when you switched your view.

   As you can see from the thumbnail slides on the left, the Slide Master View includes two slides, the Slide Master and the Title Master. The Title Master contains the background graphics and text placeholders for the title slide. Now you'll delete the background graphics.

Figure 2-3	TITLE MASTER VIEW

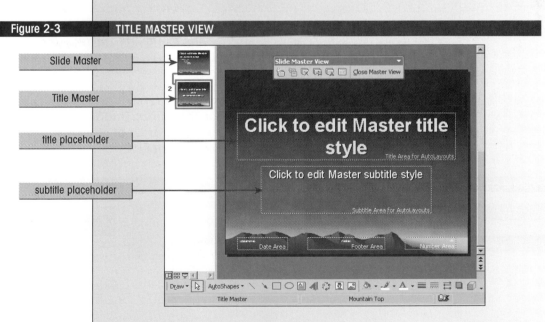

2. Click the graphic containing the mountain tops at the bottom of the slide to select it, and then press the **Delete** key to delete the graphic. With the old background graphics deleted, you're ready to insert the new bitmap image.

TROUBLE? If the entire mountain top graphic doesn't disappear, make sure you select the section still visible, and then press the Delete key again.

3. Click the **Insert Picture** button 🖾 on the Drawing toolbar. You also click this button to insert a picture into any slide in Normal View.

4. If necessary, change the **Look in** folder to Tutorial in the Tutorial.02 folder on your Data Disk.

5. Click **MntTop** (or **MntTop.jpg**, whichever appears in the dialog box), the bitmap image file of a mountain top, and click the **Insert** button. The picture is inserted into your Title Master in the middle of the slide. Now you have to move and resize the image to fit along the bottom of the Title Master.

6. Drag the mountain top image to the lower-left corner of the slide. See Figure 2-4.

TROUBLE? If the floating Picture toolbar covers the lower-left corner, drag the toolbar to another location on the screen.

As you can see, the selected bitmap image has resize handles in each corner and on each side of the picture. A **resize handle** is a small circle in the corner or on the edge of an object (picture, text box, and so forth) that, when dragged with the pointer, changes the size of the box. You'll drag a resize handle to resize the image to the width of the slide.

Figure 2-4	MODIFIED TITLE MASTER

resize handle

bitmap image

7. Drag the upper-right resize handle up and to the right until the width of the bitmap image is the same as the width of the slide, and approximately double its original height, as shown in Figure 2-5.

You have two tasks left to perform on the bitmap image. First, you'll set a **transparent color**, which is a color on the bitmap image that becomes transparent (invisible). Second, you'll change the order of objects so that the bitmap image is behind the footer placeholder.

Figure 2-5	RESIZING THE BITMAP IMAGE

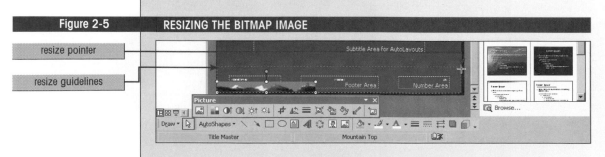

resize pointer

resize guidelines

8. Click **Set Transparent Color** on the Picture toolbar, and then click ✐ any-where in the blue sky above the mountain tops in the bitmap image. The sky disappears so that the gradient slide background color appears in its place. Now you want to make sure the mountain top picture is behind the three text box placeholders at the bottom of the slide.

9. Click the **Draw** button on the Drawing toolbar near the bottom of the PowerPoint window, point to **Order**, and then click **Send to Back** on the submenu. This sends the bitmap image to the back of all the objects on the Title Master.

As you can see, changing the drawing of mountain tops to a digital photograph of Andes Mountain tops makes the background graphic more realistic. Now you'll make the same changes on the Slide Master that you just made on the Title Master.

To change the background graphic on the Slide Master:

1. Click the resized bitmap image that you just added to the Title Master to select it, if necessary, and click the **Copy** button 🖺 on the Standard toolbar. This puts the image on the Clipboard so you can copy it to the Slide Master.

2. Drag the **Scroll bar** button up to make the Slide Master appear in the Slide Pane. As you can see, the original drawing of the mountain top appears at the bottom of the slide.

3. Delete the original mountain top drawing, and then click the **Paste** button 🖺 to paste the bitmap image on the slide.

4. Send the image to the back so that it's behind all the other objects on the Slide Master. Now both the Title Master and Slide Master have the Andes Mountain tops' bitmap image as a background picture in the design template.

Modifying Text on the Slide Master

Next, Pablo wants you to replace the current subtitle and body text font (Arial) with a different font (Times New Roman), and change the color of the title text from a very light violet to light blue. When you make these changes on the Title or Slide Master, the changes take effect on all the slides in the presentation. You can use the same procedure, however, to change the font on just one slide by making the change in the Slide Pane in Normal View.

To modify the fonts on the masters:

1. Click the dotted-line edge of the body placeholder labeled "Click to edit Master text style" on the Slide Master. The box surrounding the placeholder becomes a thick, gray line with resize handles.

2. Click the **Font** list arrow on the Formatting toolbar, and then click **Times New Roman** to change the title font from Arial to Times New Roman.

3. Click the dotted-line edge of the placeholder labeled "Click to edit Master title style," click the **Font Color** list arrow 🅰▾ on the Drawing or Formatting toolbar, click **More Colors** to open the Colors dialog box, and then click the **Standard** tab. You can now see a honeycomb of color tiles from which to select a new font color. See Figure 2-6.

TROUBLE? If you can't see the Font Color button on the Formatting toolbar, the Formatting and Standard toolbars might be on the same row. Move the Formatting toolbar onto its own row by dragging the double vertical bars that are to the left of the Font text box down and to the left.

Figure 2-6   COLORS DIALOG BOX

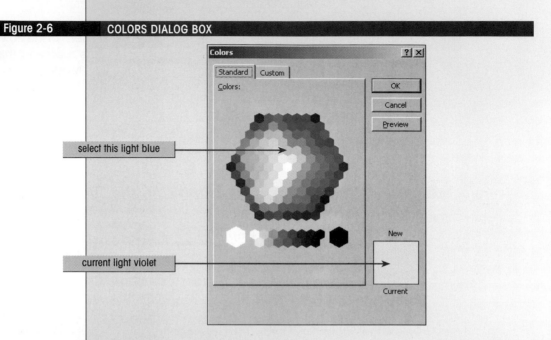

select this light blue

current light violet

4. Click the light blue tile, as marked in Figure 2-6, and then click the **OK** button. The font color of the title changes from very light violet to light blue.

You decide to modify the title text box so you can insert the Global Humanitarian logo near the title.

Resizing a Text Box on the Slide Master

You'll resize the title text box on the Slide Master by dragging the left-center resize handle.

To resize the text box:

1. Make sure the title text box of the Slide Master is still selected. The resize handles appear.

2. Drag the left-center resize handle to the right approximately 1 inch, as shown in Figure 2-7, and then release the mouse button. This leaves room for the logo, which will go in the upper-left corner of the slide, to the left of the title text box. Now you'll change the text alignment so that the title text on the Slide Master is left-aligned rather than centered.

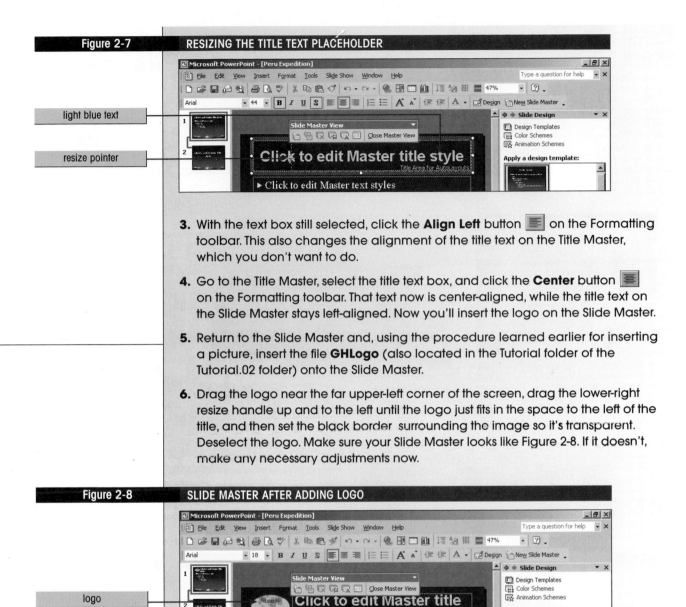

| Figure 2-7 | RESIZING THE TITLE TEXT PLACEHOLDER |

light blue text

resize pointer

3. With the text box still selected, click the **Align Left** button ▤ on the Formatting toolbar. This also changes the alignment of the title text on the Title Master, which you don't want to do.

4. Go to the Title Master, select the title text box, and click the **Center** button ▤ on the Formatting toolbar. That text now is center-aligned, while the title text on the Slide Master stays left-aligned. Now you'll insert the logo on the Slide Master.

5. Return to the Slide Master and, using the procedure learned earlier for inserting a picture, insert the file **GHLogo** (also located in the Tutorial folder of the Tutorial.02 folder) onto the Slide Master.

6. Drag the logo near the far upper-left corner of the screen, drag the lower-right resize handle up and to the left until the logo just fits in the space to the left of the title, and then set the black border surrounding the image so it's transparent. Deselect the logo. Make sure your Slide Master looks like Figure 2-8. If it doesn't, make any necessary adjustments now.

| Figure 2-8 | SLIDE MASTER AFTER ADDING LOGO |

logo

left aligned text box

This completes your work on the Slide Masters. Now you'll return to Normal View.

7. Click the **Normal View** button ▣ on the View toolbar.

8. Save the presentation using the default name and location.

Applying a Second Design Template

Normally all your slides in one presentation will have the same design template. On occasion, however, you might want to apply a second design template to only one, or a few, of the slides in your presentation. For example, Pablo wants you to change the design template for Slide 8, "Expedition Costs (Per Person)" from the modified Mountain Top design to Globe design.

To change the design template for one slide:

1. Go to Slide 8 by clicking the thumbnail of that slide in the Slides tab. When you want to apply a design template to only one slide, you'll usually want that slide to appear in the Slide Pane.

2. Go through the same procedure as you did for applying a design template (click the Slide Design button on the Formatting toolbar), except don't click the design thumbnail; instead, click the **Design Template** list arrow of the Globe design. See Figure 2-9. (If you just click the Globe design, it will appear on all the slides rather than just the selected slide.)

Figure 2-9	APPLYING A DESIGN TEMPLATE TO ONE SLIDE

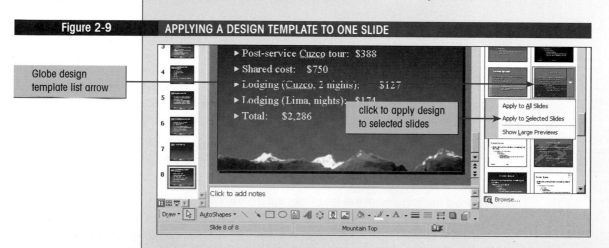

Globe design template list arrow

click to apply design to selected slides

3. Click **Apply to Selected Slides**. Because Slide 8 is the only selected slide in the Slides tab, it's the only one to which the design template is applied. See Figure 2-10. If you want more slides with that design, you can Shift-click to select a range of slides in the Slides tab, or Ctrl-click to select additional slides in the Slides tab.

Figure 2-10	SLIDE AFTER APPLYING GLOBE DESIGN TEMPLATE

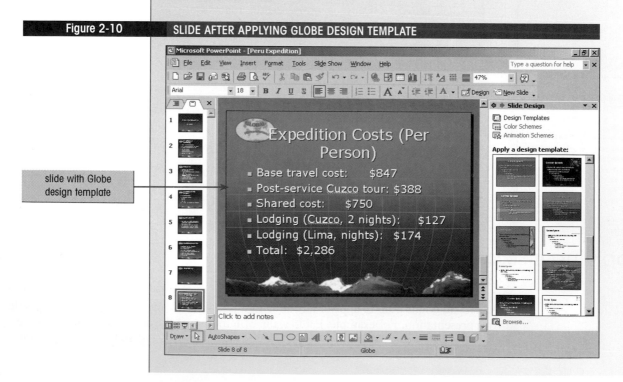

slide with Globe design template

TROUBLE? If you click the design thumbnail instead of the Design Template list arrow, or if you click the list arrow and then click Apply to All Slides, you should click the Undo button on the Standard toolbar, and then repeat Steps 1, 2, and 3.

You applied the Globe design template to only one slide in the presentation. The modified Mountain Top design remains on the other slides.

Adding and Modifying Tab Stops

A **tab** adds space between the left margin and the beginning of the text on a particular line, or between the text in one column and the text in another column. (When you create several long columns of data, however, you probably want to use a table instead of tabs.) For example, in Slide 8 ("Expedition Costs"), Pablo typed the cost description and a colon, pressed the Tab key to add space, and then typed the dollar amounts for each expense. However, Pablo kept the default tab stops. A **tab stop** is the location where the insertion point moves (including any text to the right of it) when you press the Tab key. PowerPoint supports **tab-stop alignment styles**. The four styles are left ⌊, center ⌊, right ⌋, and decimal ⌊, as shown in Figure 2-11. The default tab stops on the ruler are left tabs, which position the left edge of text at the tab stop and extend the text to the right. However, you want to align the right sides of the dollar amounts in Slide 8, so you want to use a right tab stop ⌋, which positions the right edge of text at the tab stop and extends the text to the left.

Figure 2-11	TAB STOP ALIGNMENT STYLES

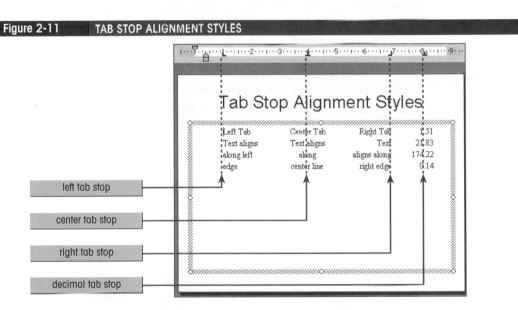

Your task now is to add a right tab stop in Slide 8 so that the dollar amounts are aligned on the right side of the slide.

To change the tab stops:

1. Close the Task Pane, if necessary, by clicking the **Close** button ⊠ in the Task Pane.

2. If the ruler doesn't appear above the Slide Pane, click **View** on the menu bar, and then click **Ruler**. The ruler appears on the screen. Click anywhere in the body text placeholder so that the ruler displays the default tab stops. See Figure 2-12.

Figure 2-12 **RULER IN POWERPOINT WINDOW**

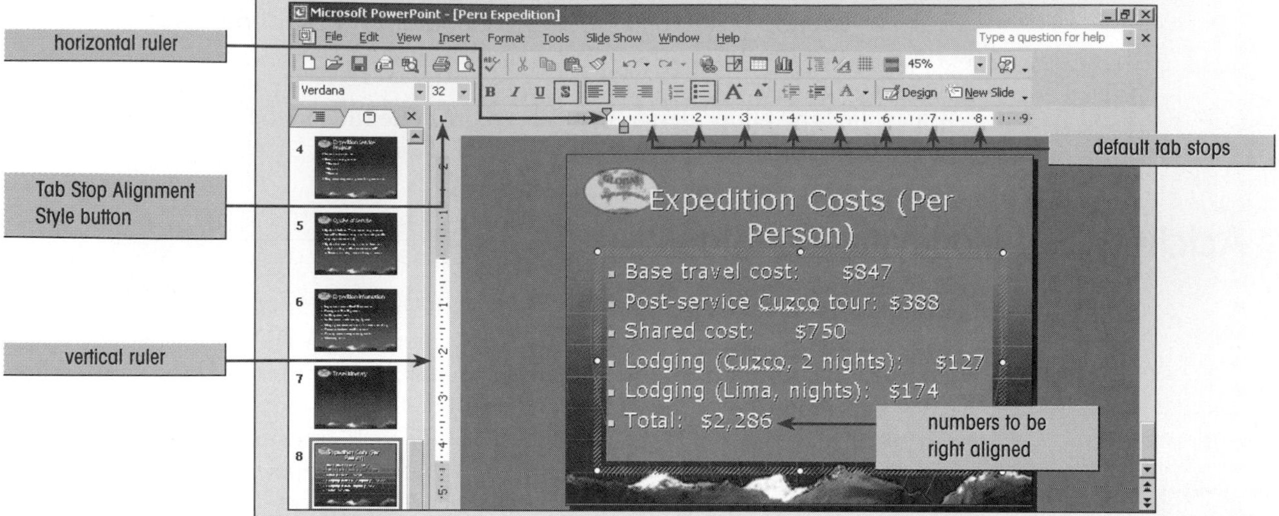

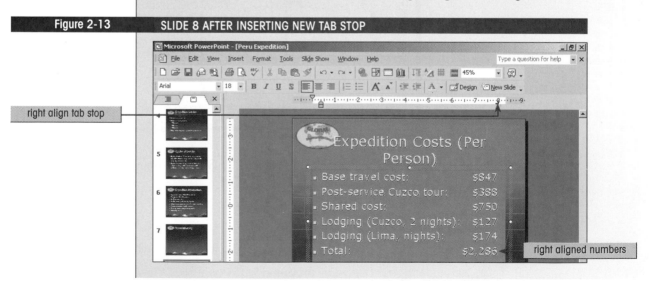

Notice that the default tab stops are marked with light gray rectangles, or hash marks, under the ruler bar. (Depending upon your screen colors, these may be difficult to see.) When you add a tab stop, PowerPoint automatically deletes all the default tab stops to the left of the one you added, and marks the user-placed tab stop with the corresponding tab-stop character.

3. Click the **Tab Stop Alignment Style** button, located in the upper-left corner of the ruler, as shown in Figure 2-12, until the right tab stop appears there. Normally you have to click the button twice, but you might have to click it more or fewer times depending on the current tab-stop style appearing there. (As you click, you will cycle through the four alignment styles.)

4. Click just below the 8-inch marker in the white area of the horizontal ruler at the top of the Slide Pane. The new right tab stop appears at the location you clicked, the default tab stops left of the new tab stop disappear, and the dollar amounts in the body text box become right-aligned. See Figure 2-13.

Figure 2-13 **SLIDE 8 AFTER INSERTING NEW TAB STOP**

TROUBLE? If you used the wrong tab-stop alignment style, drag the new tab stop off the ruler to delete it, and repeat Steps 3 and 4. If you used the correct tab-stop style but clicked in the wrong place, drag the tab-stop character to the right or left until it's positioned where you want it.

5. Click **View** on the menu bar, and then click **Ruler** to deselect it. The ruler disappears from the PowerPoint window.

If you need to adjust the location of a tab stop on the ruler, drag the tab-stop character to the right or left until it's positioned where you want it. To do this now, you'd have to redisplay the ruler, select the body text box, and then drag ▣ to the right or left along the ruler.

Inserting **Footers and Slide Numbers**

As part of the overall slide design, Pablo wants you to include footers on each slide, except the title slide. As you recall, a **footer** is a word or phrase that appears at the bottom of each page, and similarly, a **header** is a word or phrase that appears at the top of each page. You can create headers and footers by adding text boxes to the Slide Masters, but PowerPoint already provides header and footer placeholders. Now you'll use the footer placeholder to add a footer, including slide numbers, to each of the slides (except the title slide).

To insert a footer into your presentation:

1. Go to **Slide 2**, click **View** on the menu bar, click **Header and Footer** to open the Header and Footer dialog box, and then click the **Slides** tab, if necessary, to display the slide header and footer information.

2. Make sure the **Date and time** check box is deselected because you don't want that information to appear in the slide.

3. Click the **Slide number** check box because you do want the slide number to appear on each slide.

4. Click the **Footer** check box, and then click Ⅰ in the Footer text box.

5. Type **Peru Expedition 2003**, which becomes the footer text, and click the **Don't show on title slide** check box so that the title slide doesn't include the footer. See Figure 2-14.

Figure 2-14   HEADER AND FOOTER DIALOG BOX

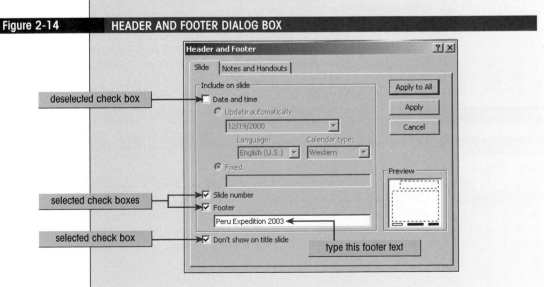

6. Click the **Apply to All** button on the Header and Footer dialog box. All the slides (except Slide 1) now contain a footer. See Figure 2-15.

Figure 2-15   SLIDE 2 AFTER INSERTING FOOTER AND SLIDE NUMBERING

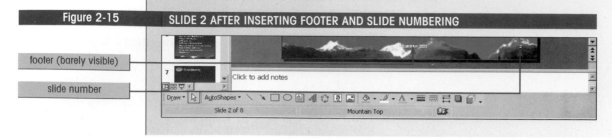

footer (barely visible)

slide number

The problem with the footer is that its text isn't legible. Specifically, the font is too small and its white color makes it unreadable against the white peak of an Andean mountaintop. You can solve this problem by changing the position and size of the footer on the Slide Master.

To modify the position and font of a footer:

1. Display the Slide Master in the PowerPoint window using the procedure you learned earlier in this presentation. First you'll move the footer placeholder to the left corner of the slide where the date and time placeholder is currently located.

2. Click the edge of the date and time placeholder (labeled Date Area) in the lower-left corner of the slide, and press the **Delete** key to remove the placeholder from the slide.

3. Select the footer placeholder (labeled Footer Area), currently located in the bottom middle of the slide, and then press the ← key until the placeholder is aligned on the left with the body text placeholder. By using the ← key, rather than dragging and dropping, you ensure that you move the placeholder horizontally but not vertically.

4. Click the **Align Left** button [icon] so the text in the footer placeholder is aligned on the left edge rather than centered in the placeholder.

5. Shift-click the slide number placeholder (labeled Number Area) in the lower-right corner of the slide, so that both the footer and the slide number placeholders are selected.

6. Press the ↓ key two or three times until the bottoms of the two placeholders are on the bottom of the slide, as shown in Figure 2-16. Use the ↓ key to nudge the placeholders in small increments so you can position the objects exactly where you want them.

Figure 2-16   SLIDE MASTER AFTER ADJUSTING PLACEHOLDERS

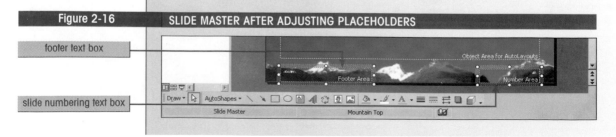

footer text box

slide numbering text box

7. With the footer and slide number placeholders still selected, click the **Font Size** list arrow, click **24** to change the font size to 24 point. The problem now is that the footer placeholder is too small to contain all the footer text on one line (a fact that you would observe if you switched back to Normal View), so you'll expand the footer placeholder.

8. Deselect the two placeholders, select just the footer placeholder, and then drag the right-center resize handle of the footer placeholder to the right until the right of the text box is near the center of the slide, and then click the **Normal View** button to return to Slide 2. You can now easily read the footer and slide number. See Figure 2-17.

Figure 2-17	SLIDE 2 WITH MODIFIED FOOTER AND SLIDE NUMBER

footer now legible

slide number

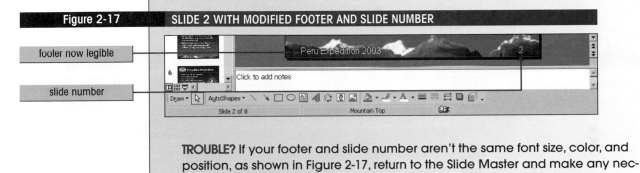

TROUBLE? If your footer and slide number aren't the same font size, color, and position, as shown in Figure 2-17, return to the Slide Master and make any necessary adjustments.

9. Save the presentation using the default filename.

Now as you look through all the slides you see footers on all of them.

Inserting and Modifying Clip Art

Slide 6, "Expedition Information," has eight bulleted items of text. Pablo wants to include some clip art to add interest to this slide. (In PowerPoint, **clip art** refers specifically to images in the Media Gallery that accompanies Office XP.) He decides that an image of a globe would help emphasize the global aspects of the expedition.

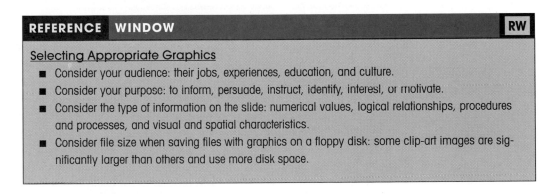

REFERENCE WINDOW **RW**

Selecting Appropriate Graphics
- Consider your audience: their jobs, experiences, education, and culture.
- Consider your purpose: to inform, persuade, instruct, identify, interest, or motivate.
- Consider the type of information on the slide: numerical values, logical relationships, procedures and processes, and visual and spatial characteristics.
- Consider file size when saving files with graphics on a floppy disk: some clip-art images are significantly larger than others and use more disk space.

Inserting Clip Art

To add clip art to a slide, you can use a PowerPoint predefined slide layout (Text & Clip Art or Clip Art & Text), or you can insert it as you would a picture. For Slide 6, you'll first change the existing slide layout before adding clip art.

To change the layout of the slide and add clip art:

1. Go to Slide 6, "Expedition Information."

2. Display the Task Pane and then the Slide Layout by clicking the **Other Task Panes** list arrow and then **Slide Layout**, scroll down the Task Pane until you see Other Layouts, click the layout with the description Title, Text, and Clip Art (first row, left column, below Other Layouts). See Figure 2-18. Notice that PowerPoint automatically reduces the size of text in the bulleted list (from 28-point to 20-point text) so that it would fit properly within the reduced text box.

   TROUBLE? If the font size doesn't automatically change, click the AutoFit Options list arrow (near the lower-left corner of the bulleted text) and click AutoFit Text of Placeholder.

Figure 2-18   SLIDE 6 AFTER CHANGING LAYOUT

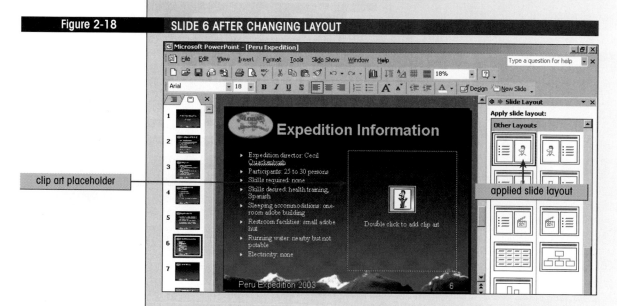

clip art placeholder

3. Double-click the clip-art placeholder. PowerPoint displays the Select Picture dialog box. If necessary, drag the box up so you can see all of it. See Figure 2-19. Now you'll search for a clip-art image that relates to a globe.

Figure 2-19   SELECT PICTURE DIALOG BOX

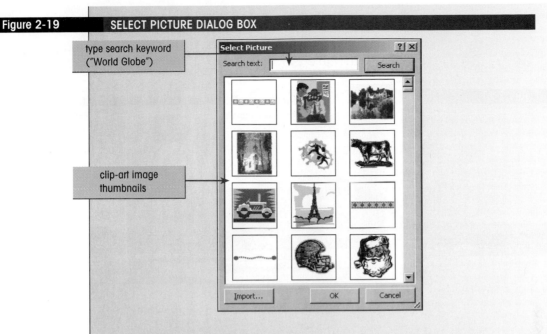

type search keyword
("World Globe")

clip-art image
thumbnails

4. Click I, if necessary, in the **Search** text box near the top of the dialog box, type **world globe**, and then click the **Search** button. PowerPoint displays several clip-art images with a representation of a world globe.

5. Double-click the image with a globe in the center and a red circular background. The clip art appears in the slide. See Figure 2-20.

Figure 2-20   SLIDE 6 WITH CLIP-ART IMAGE

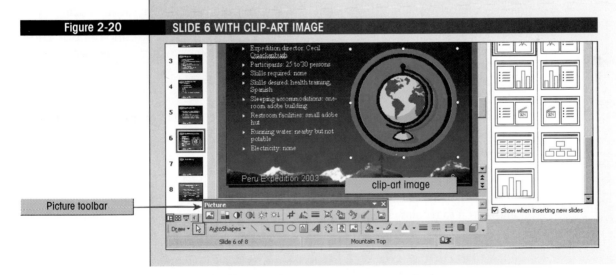

Picture toolbar

clip-art image

Now you'll modify this clip-art image by changing its size and some of its colors.

Resizing Clip Art

Pablo thinks the clip art is too big—making the font size in the bulleted list too small. You can reduce the clip art size by dragging a resize handle.

To resize the clip-art image:

1. Drag a resize handle of the globe clip-art image until the image is the relative size shown in Figure 2-21. Don't worry about getting the exact size.

Figure 2-21 | SLIDE 6 WITH RESIZED CLIP-ART IMAGE

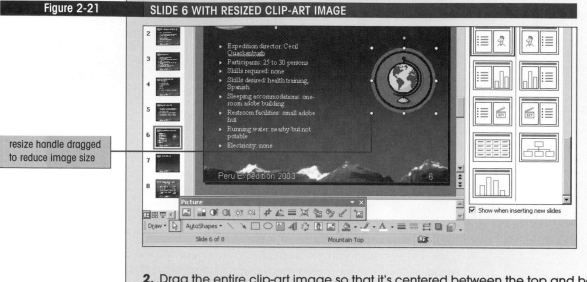

resize handle dragged to reduce image size

2. Drag the entire clip-art image so that it's centered between the top and bottom of the slide, but still near the right edge of the slide.

3. Select the bulleted list text box by clicking anywhere in the box, and then drag the right-center resize handle to the right until it just touches the left edge of the clip art. The font in the bulleted list should automatically increase in size.

   TROUBLE? If the font size doesn't expand to fit the resized placeholder box, click the AutoFit button [⬍] (located near the lower-left corner of the placeholder), and click AutoFit Text to Placeholder.

With the clip-art image inserted and resized, you're ready to change some of the colors.

Recoloring Clip Art

Pablo thinks the red colors on the clip art don't match the blue hues of the design template and the Global Humanitarian logo, so he asks you to change the red to dark blue. PowerPoint allows you to recolor clip-art images, but not bitmap images or other types of pictures.

To recolor a clip-art image:

1. Make sure the clip art in Slide 6 is still selected by clicking it. The resize handles appear around the image, and the floating Picture toolbar is on the screen.

   TROUBLE? If the Picture toolbar doesn't appear automatically, click View on the menu bar, point to Toolbars, and click Picture.

2. Click the **Recolor Picture** button [🖼] on the Picture toolbar to display the Recolor Picture dialog box. See Figure 2-22.

Figure 2-22	RECOLOR PICTURE DIALOG BOX

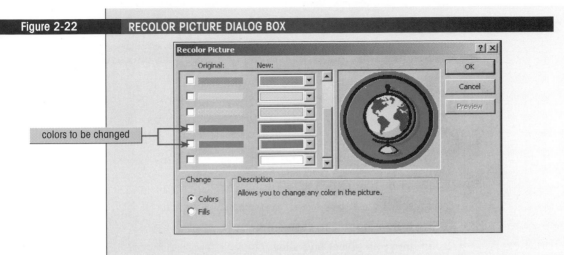

colors to be changed

3. Drag the scroll button down to the bottom of the scroll bar in the dialog box so you see the red and off-red tiles, as shown in Figure 2-22.

4. Click the off-red color tile list arrow, and then click the light violet tile on the palette of default colors. The default colors are those colors associated with the overall color scheme of the design template.

5. In a similar manner, change the red tile on the Recolor Picture dialog box to the blue tile (but not the dark blue tile) on the palette of automatic colors.

6. Click the **OK** button, and then click outside the selected object to deselect it. The clip-art image has been recolored. See Figure 2-23.

Figure 2-23	SLIDE 6 AFTER RECOLORING CLIP-ART IMAGE

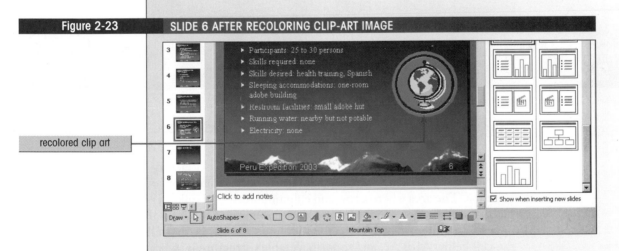

recolored clip art

7. Save the presentation using the default filename Peru Expedition.

Pablo is pleased with how well the colors of the globe clip-art image match the colors on Slide 6.

You completed most of Pablo's presentation. In Session 2.2 you'll finalize the slides by creating a table, diagram, and simple drawing.

Session 2.1 QUICK CHECK

1. List four situations in which you can use graphics effectively.

2. Explain the meaning of the following terms:
   a. text box
   b. graphic
   c. object
   d. resize handle

3. Describe how to do the following:
   a. select a text box so that resize handles appear
   b. scale a graphic to change its size
   c. move an object on a slide
   d. apply a second design template to only one slide
   e. insert a clip-art image
   f. recolor a clip-art image

4. What is the Title Master? The Slide Master?

5. What are tabs? What are tab stops? Describe how to insert a right tab stop on the ruler.

6. What is the Media Gallery?

7. List three criteria for selecting an appropriate type of graphic.

SESSION 2.2

In this session, you'll learn how to create a table, a cycle diagram, text boxes, graphic shapes, and a summary slide.

Creating a Table in a Slide

Pablo wants you to create a table in Slide 7 of the travel itinerary for the Peru Expedition of Global Humanitarian. A **table** is information arranged in horizontal rows and vertical columns. The area where a row and column intersect is called a **cell**. Each cell contains one piece of information and is identified by a column and row label. For example, the cell in the upper-left corner of a table is cell A1 (column A, row 1), the cell to the right of that is B1, the cell below A1 is A2, and so forth. A table's structure is indicated by **borders**, which are lines that outline the rows and columns.

The table you'll create will have four columns, one for the date of travel, one for the departure or arrival city, one for the time of departure or arrival, and one for the flight number. The table will have nine rows: one row for labels, and eight rows for information about the travel departures and arrivals. Now you'll create the travel itinerary table.

To create a table:

1. If you took a break after the previous session, make sure PowerPoint is running and the file **Peru Expedition** is open in Normal View.

2. Go to Slide 7 ("Travel Itinerary"), make sure the Slide Layout Task Pane is open, scroll down the slide layouts down so you can see the Other Layouts section at the bottom, and click the **Title and Table** layout (next-to-the-last row, first column) to see the Insert Table placeholder.

3. Double-click the table placeholder in Slide 7. The Insert Table dialog box opens.

4. Set the number of columns to **4** and the number of rows to **9**, click the **OK** button to insert the table, and then click anywhere in the table to select it. PowerPoint automatically displays the Tables and Borders toolbar when you select the table. See Figure 2-24.

Figure 2-24	SLIDE 7 WITH EMPTY TABLE

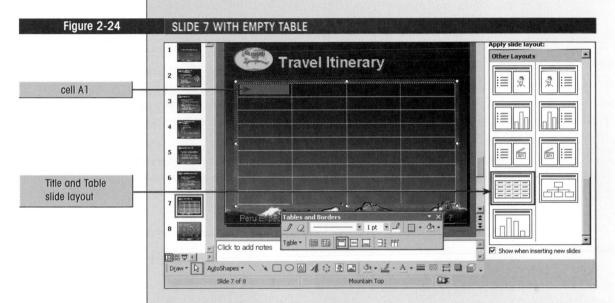

cell A1

Title and Table slide layout

TROUBLE? If the table doesn't have four columns and nine rows, click the Undo button on the Standard toolbar to undo your creation of the table, and then repeat Steps 3 and 4.

TROUBLE? If the Tables and Borders toolbar doesn't appear on the screen, click View on the main menu, point to Toolbars, and then click Tables and Borders.

With the blank table in the slide, you're ready to change the border below the top rows so that it separates the label on the top row from the information in the other rows.

To draw a border:

1. Make sure the **Draw Table** pointer is selected. If necessary, click the **Draw Table** button on the Tables and Borders toolbar.

2. On the Tables and Borders toolbar, click the **Border Width** list arrow, and then click **3 pt** to change the border line width to three points.

3. Click the **Border Color** button on the Tables and Borders toolbar, and then click the light blue tile (the custom color below the main row of tiles). Now when you draw a border, it will be a 3-point, light blue line.

4. Drag ✏ from the border below cell A1 to cell D1, along the border between the first and second rows. When you release the mouse button, the light blue line appears.

5. Close the Task Pane so the Slide Pane is larger and you can see your table better.

In addition to changing the vertical and horizontal border lines, you can also add and change diagonal lines within cells of a table. First click the Table button on the Tables and Borders toolbar, click Borders and Fill, click the Borders tab, and then click one or both of the Diagonal Line buttons (if you click both buttons, PowerPoint displays a large "X" through the cell).

Now you're ready to fill the blank cells with information.

To add information to the table:

1. Click the **Draw Table** button 📝 on the Tables and Borders toolbar to deselect it. The pointer should be ⬚ while it's in a blank area of the slide in the Slide Pane, or ⊺ when it's in a cell.

2. Click ⊺ in cell A1 (upper-left corner of the table) and type **Date**, press the **Tab** key to move to cell B1, type **City**, press the **Tab** key to move to cell C1, then type **Time**, press the **Tab** key to move to cell D1 (upper-right corner of the table), and type **Flight**. This completes the table labels.

3. Press the **Tab** key to move to cell A2, type **December 25**, tab to cell B2, type **Lv Dallas** (short for "Leave Dallas"), tab to cell C2, type **4:22 PM**, tab to cell D2, and type **AA 982** (short for American Airlines flight 982). This completes the first row of data.

4. Complete the information in the other cells, as shown in Figure 2-25, and then click in a blank area of the slide to deselect the table.

Figure 2-25	SLIDE 7 WITH FILLED-IN TABLE

blue border

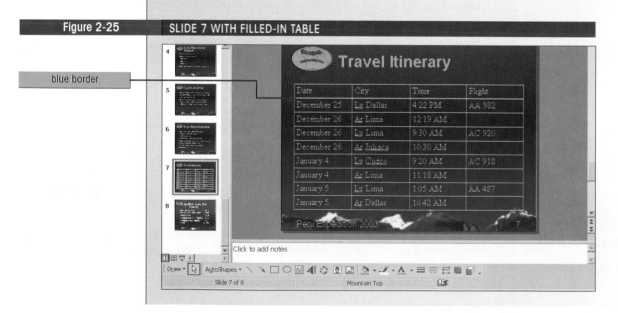

The table looks fine to Pablo, except that he wants text in the top row to be a light blue bold Arial font.

To modify the table font:

1. Drag I across all the text in the top row to select it.

2. Change the font to Arial, as you would any other type of text, change the attribute to bold, and then change the font color by clicking the **Font Color** list arrow ▲ ⋅ on the Formatting toolbar, and then click the light blue tile located below the main row of tiles (the same color tile as the border below the top row).

3. Click anywhere in a blank area of the Slide Pane to deselect the table. See Figure 2-26.

| Figure 2-26 | SLIDE 7 AFTER MODIFYING TABLE |

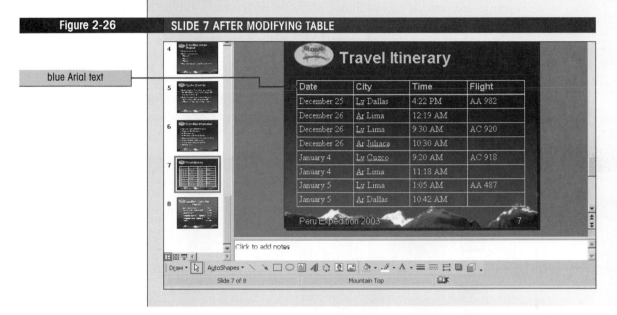

blue Arial text

You completed the table that shows the flight itinerary for the Peru expedition. If you want to add a new row at the bottom of the table, you can move the insertion point to the lower-right corner (the last cell) in the table, and press the Tab key. The Tables and Borders toolbar also lets you remove rows, add and remove columns, combine cells, split cells, and perform other modifications to the table. If you want to do any of these tasks, use PowerPoint's Help.

Your next task is to create a cycle diagram on Slide 5.

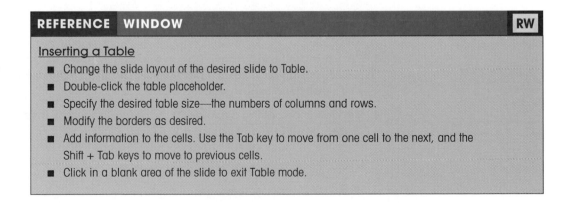

REFERENCE   WINDOW   **RW**

Inserting a Table

- Change the slide layout of the desired slide to Table.
- Double-click the table placeholder.
- Specify the desired table size—the numbers of columns and rows.
- Modify the borders as desired.
- Add information to the cells. Use the Tab key to move from one cell to the next, and the Shift + Tab keys to move to previous cells.
- Click in a blank area of the slide to exit Table mode.

Creating a Cycle Diagram

A **cycle diagram** is a diagram used to show a process that has a continuous cycle. The latest version of PowerPoint allows you to create not only cycle diagrams, but also other types of diagrams using the new Diagram Gallery. The Diagram Gallery allows you to create organizational charts, radial diagrams (used to show relationships of a core element), pyramid diagrams (used to show foundation-based relationships), Venn diagrams (overlapping circles used to show areas of overlap between elements), target diagrams (used to show steps toward a goal), as well as cycle diagrams. In the Peru Expedition presentation, Pablo wants you to convert the text in Slide 5 ("Cycles of Service") into actual cycle diagrams to show the vicious cycle of failure when service is performed badly, and the positive cycle of success when service is performed properly. Now you'll create the cycle diagrams.

To create a cycle diagram:

1. Go to Slide 5, open the Slide Layout tasks in the Task Pane, and click the layout **Title and 2 Content over Text** in the Text and Content Layouts section. See Figure 2-27.

| Figure 2-27 | SLIDE 5 WITH NEW SLIDE LAYOUT |

two pieces of content above text

selected slide layout

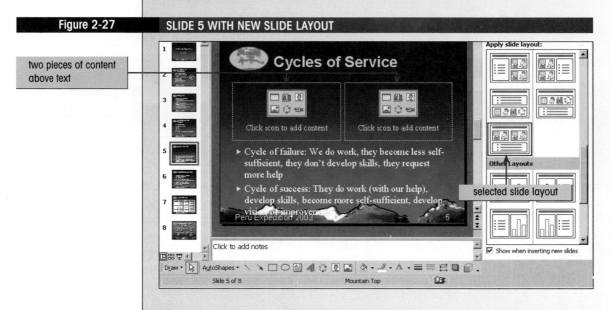

2. Click the **Insert Diagram or Organization Chart** button on the left content placeholder. The Diagram Gallery dialog box opens.

3. Click the **Cycle Diagram** icon (on the top row, center), and then click the **OK** button. PowerPoint draws a blank cycle diagram in the left placeholder. Now you'll edit the diagram with the desired text.

4. Right-click any of the cycle diagram arrows and click **Insert Shape** so that the diagram has four arrows instead of three, click in the upper-right text box (located in clock directions at about 2 o'clock), and type **We do work** (which is the first item in the "Cycle of failure," as shown in the bulleted list).

TROUBLE? If your cycle diagram displays bent rectangles instead of arrows, don't worry. Just leave the shapes as they are. The early release of PowerPoint 2002 might create curved rectangles instead of curved arrows.

5. Click in the lower-right text box (at 4 o'clock), type **They become less**, press the **Enter** key, type **self-sufficient**, and then insert the remainder of the text into the diagram, as shown in Figure 2-28.

6. Using the same procedure, create the cycle diagram on the right in the slide, as shown in Figure 2-28.

7. Click the edge of the bulleted-list text box, press the **Delete** key, and then change the slide layout to **Title and 2 Content** (located in the Content Layouts section of the Slide Layout Task Pane). Your slide should now look like Figure 2-28.

| Figure 2-28 | COMPLETED SLIDE 5 WITH TWO CYCLE DIAGRAMS |

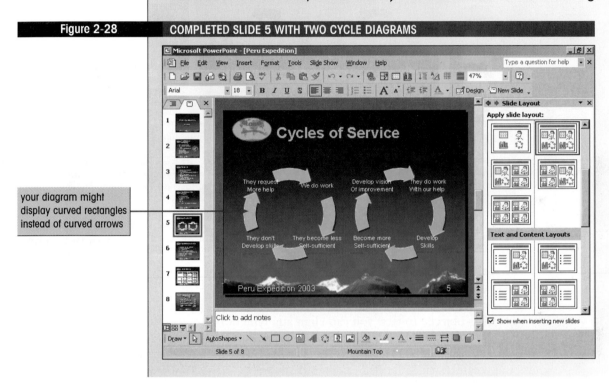

your diagram might display curved rectangles instead of curved arrows

Now you'll label each cycle diagram by adding new text boxes in the slide.

Adding Text Boxes

Adding a text box in a PowerPoint slide is easy: you simply use the Text Box button on the Drawing toolbar. For Pablo's presentation, you want to add text above both diagrams.

To add text boxes in the slide:

1. Click the **Text Box** button [icon] on the Drawing toolbar, click the text box pointer ↓ centered above the left cycle diagram, click the **Center** button [icon] on the Formatting toolbar, and then type **Cycle of Failure**.

2. Repeat Step 1, except center the text box above the right cycle diagram and type **Cycle of Success**.

3. Move the two text boxes so they are as close to the positions shown in Figure 2-29 as possible.

Figure 2-29   **SLIDE 5 WITH TWO ADDED TEXT BOXES**

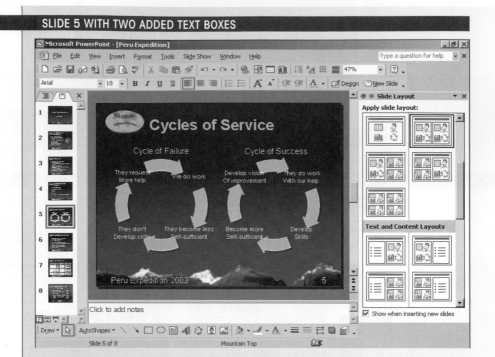

4. To make sure the two text boxes are aligned vertically on the slide, select both text boxes (select one, and then Shift-click the other), click the **Draw** button on the Drawing toolbar, point to **Align or Distribute**, and then click **Align Bottom**.

These steps demonstrate two important PowerPoint features: adding text boxes and aligning objects. In fact, you can align any type of object (text boxes, graphics boxes, diagrams, and so forth) using this same alignment method.

Pablo likes the two cycle diagrams in Slide 5, and now asks you to insert a new Slide 6, and create a shape in the slide.

Creating and Manipulating a Shape

For the last graphic to be included in his presentation, Pablo asks you to add an inverted isosceles triangle with text to a new Slide 6. His hand-drawn sketch of how he wants the graphic to appear is shown in Figure 2-30. The text lists the three components of the Global Humanitarian strategy—Village Outreach Projects, Expeditions, and Internships—that you'll place along each side of the triangle. Pablo chose an isosceles triangle to point out that each of the three strawtegies is equally important. This graphic will be a strong visual reminder to potential Global Humanitarian contributors and volunteers of this threefold strategy.

Figure 2-30	PABLO'S SKETCH

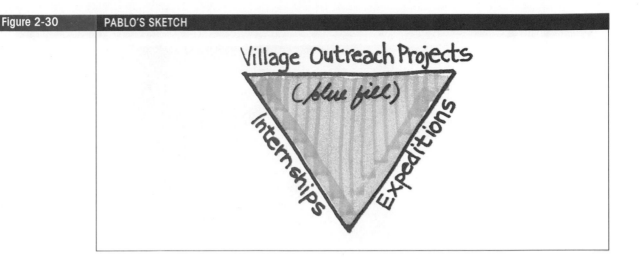

Inserting and Recoloring a Shape

To create the triangle, you'll use PowerPoint AutoShapes which includes several categories of shapes: lines, connectors, basic shapes (for example, rectangles and triangles), block arrows, flowcharts, stars and banners, callouts, and action buttons.

To insert a shape in a slide, using AutoShapes:

1. Insert a new Slide 6, change the slide layout to **Title Only**, and type the slide title **Global Humanitarian Strategy** in the title placeholder.

2. Click the **AutoShapes** list arrow on the Drawing toolbar, and then point to **Basic Shapes**. PowerPoint displays the Basic Shapes palette. See Figure 2-31.

Figure 2-31	SELECTING AN AUTOSHAPE

3. Click the **Isosceles Triangle** button △ on the Basic Shapes palette. The pointer will now change to ┼ when you move it into the Slide Pane.

4. Position ┼ approximately 1 inch below the "a" in "Strategy" (in the title of the slide), press and hold down the **Shift** key, and then click the mouse button and drag the pointer down and to the right. The outline of a triangle appears as you drag. (The Shift key makes the triangle equilateral—three sides of equal length.)

5. Release the mouse button and then the Shift key when your triangle is approximately the same size and shape as the one shown in Figure 2-32. The yellow diamond above the triangle is like a resize handle except that, if you drag it, the position of the tip of the triangle changes without changing the overall size of the object box. The green circle above the triangle is the rotation handle, which allows you to rotate the shape.

Figure 2-32   SLIDE 6 WITH ISOSCELES TRIANGLE

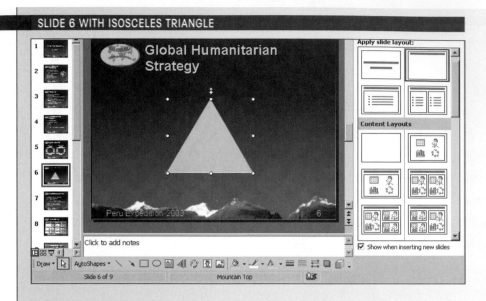

TROUBLE? If your triangle doesn't look like the one in Figure 2-32, you can move it by dragging it to a new location, resize or change its shape by dragging one or more of the resize handles, change the location of the triangle tip by dragging the yellow diamond, or you can press the Delete key to delete your triangle, and then repeat Steps 2 through 5 to redraw it.

The default color of the drawn object is cyan, but Pablo prefers blue, to match the blues in the background.

To change the fill color of the AutoShape:

1. With the triangle still selected, click the **Fill Color** list arrow [icon] on the Drawing toolbar. A box with color tiles appears on the screen.

2. Click the blue tile (not the dark blue tile, but the second tile from the right), which displays the ScreenTip message "Follow Accent and Hyperlink Scheme Color" to let you know this color matches the current color scheme. The fill color of the triangle automatically changes to blue.

The triangle is the desired size and color, but, looking at Pablo's sketch, you realize you need to flip (invert) the triangle so that it points down instead of up.

To flip an object:

1. With the triangle still selected, click the **Draw** button on the Drawing toolbar, point to **Rotate or Flip**, and then click the **Flip Vertical** button. (Alternately, you can use the rotate handle at the top of the triangle to rotate it to the desired position.)

2. Click in a blank region in the slide to deselect the triangle. Your triangle should be positioned, colored, sized, and oriented like the one shown in Figure 2-33.

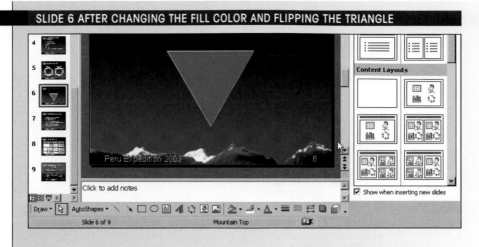

Figure 2-33   SLIDE 6 AFTER CHANGING THE FILL COLOR AND FLIPPING THE TRIANGLE

3. Save the presentation.

The shape is now in its final form.

Adding Text to the Diagram

You're ready to add the text naming the three strategies of Global Humanitarian on each side of the triangle. In this case, you'll add text outside the triangle, but in other cases you might want to add text to the inside of an AutoShape graphic. To do the latter, select the Text Box tool, click on the inside of the shape, type the text, and then turn on the word wrap text in AutoShape feature. PowerPoint then automatically formats the text so it stays within the selected AutoShape.

You'll now add three text boxes around the AutoShape triangle you just created.

To add a text box to the slide:

1. Click the **Text Box** button 🖺 on the Drawing toolbar, move ↓ so it is just above and centered on the upper edge of the triangle, and then click there. (The position doesn't have to be exact.)

2. Click the **Center** button 🖺 on the Formatting toolbar, and then type **Village Outreach Projects**.

3. Click 🖺, click ↓ to the right of the triangle, and then type **Expeditions**.

4. Create a third text box to the left of the triangle with the text **Internships**.

5. Select all three text boxes by Ctrl-clicking them, and then change the font size to 24 points.

6. Click in a blank area of the slide to deselect the text boxes. Your slide should now look like Figure 2-34.

Figure 2-34   TEXT BOXES ADDED NEAR TRIANGLE

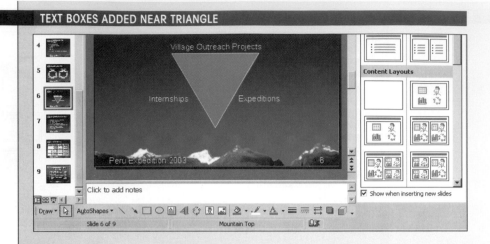

TROUBLE? If the text boxes you added to the sides of the triangle are not in the same position as the text in the figure, don't worry. You'll move the text boxes in the next set of steps.

Next you'll rotate the text boxes to make them parallel to the sides of the triangle.

Rotating and Moving Text Boxes

The method for rotating text is similar to the one for rotating graphics (or rotating any other object): you drag the rotate handle on the object.

To rotate and move the text boxes:

1. Select the text box that contains "Expeditions" by clicking anywhere within the text box. The resize handles and rotate handle appear around the box.

2. Position the pointer over the rotate handle. The pointer becomes ↻.

3. Press and hold the **Shift** key, and then press and hold the mouse button. Holding down the Shift key makes the rotation occur in 15-degree increments.

4. Drag the rotate handle counterclockwise until the top edge of the box is parallel to the lower-right edge of the triangle. See Figure 2-35. Release the mouse button, and then the Shift key.

Figure 2-35   ROTATING A TEXT BOX

rotate pointer

outline of rotated text box

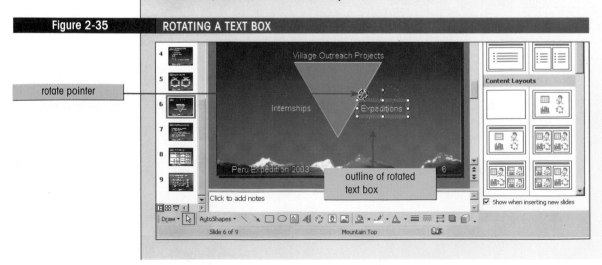

5. Drag the "Expeditions" text box until it's against and centered on the lower-right edge of the triangle.

TROUBLE? If the edge of the text box isn't parallel to the edge of the triangle, you can repeat Steps 2–5 to fix the rotation. If necessary, try not pressing the Shift key.

TROUBLE? If the text box jumps from one location to another as you drag it, and you can't position it exactly where you want it, hold down the Alt key as you drag the box. (The Alt key temporarily disables the Snap to Grid feature, which allows objects to move only to invisible gridlines, not to positions between gridlines.)

6. Click the text box that contains "Internships," repeat Steps 2–5, but this time rotate the box clockwise until it's parallel to the lower-left edge of the triangle, and then position the text box so it's close to and centered on the left edge of the triangle. Deselect the text box. Your slide should look like Figure 2-36.

Figure 2-36	SLIDE 6 WITH COMPLETED DIAGRAM

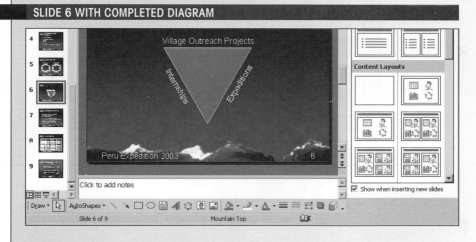

7. Save the presentation.

You have completed Slide 6. Pablo asks you to perform one final task before the presentation is finished. He wants you to add a summary at the end of the presentation.

Adding a Summary Slide

A **summary slide** is a slide containing the slide titles of selected slides in the presentation. PowerPoint helps you automatically create a summary slide.

To create a summary slide:

1. Click the **Slide Sorter View** button ⊞ on the View toolbar to view your presentation in Slide Sorter View.

2. Close the Task Pane so you can see more of the slides in the Slide Sorter Pane.

3. Select all the slides except the first one by clicking Slide 2, pressing and holding the **Shift** key, and clicking Slide 9. PowerPoint marks the selected slides by drawing dark boxes around each of them.

4. Click the **Summary Slide** button on the Slide Sorter toolbar. PowerPoint creates a new Slide 2 with the title "Summary Slide," and bulleted items of the titles of the selected slides.

5. Move Slide 2 to the end of your presentation by dragging it to the right of Slide 10, and then return to Normal View to view and edit the Summary Slide (the new Slide 10).

6. In Slide 10, delete "Slide" so the title becomes "Summary." See Figure 2-37.

   You completed the entire presentation, so you should save the final version to the disk.

| Figure 2-37 | SUMMARY SLIDE AT END OF PRESENTATION |

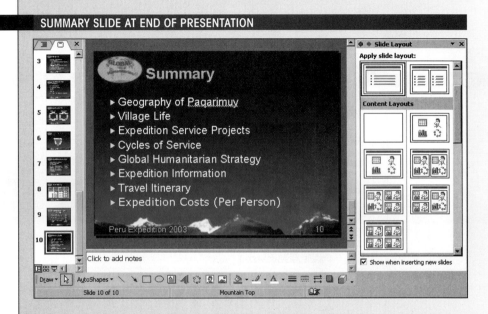

7. With your Data Disk still in the disk drive, click the **Save** button 🔲. PowerPoint saves the file using its current filename.

As usual, you should finish up your presentation by checking its spelling and style, viewing it in Slide Show View, and printing it.

To check, view, and print the presentation:

1. Check the spelling of your presentation by clicking the **Spelling** button 🔤 on the Standard toolbar, and handling each word not found in the PowerPoint dictionary. In most cases, you should click the **Ignore All** button because the words are proper nouns (like "Paqarimuy" and "Cuzco").

2. Make sure the Style Checker is turned on, and then go through each of the slides in Normal View. In most cases, you can just ignore the style checks.

3. View the presentation in Slide Show View. If you see any problems, press the **Esc** key to get out of Slide Show View and return to Normal View. Make the corrections and return to Slide Show View. If you do make any changes to your presentation, make sure you save it again to the Data Disk.

4. Print the presentation in grayscale as handouts, with six slides per page. Don't worry that the footers and one of the graphics are illegible in grayscale.

5. Close the presentation and PowerPoint.

Pablo is pleased with the additions and modifications you made to the presentation. He and others are anxious to use it to recruit volunteers for the next Peru Expedition.

Session 2.2 QUICK | CHECK

1. How do you add a table to a slide?

2. Where is cell A1 in a table?

3. What is a cycle diagram? Give an example.

4. How do you add a text box to a slide?

5. How do you use AutoShapes to draw a shape, such as a rectangle or circle?

6. How do you invert a triangle so that it points down instead of up?

7. How do you rotate an object?

8. What is the Summary Slide feature in PowerPoint?

REVIEW ASSIGNMENTS

One of the questions that potential volunteers often ask when Pablo presents information about the Peru Expedition is, "What items will I need for the trip?" In other words, they want to see a packing list to give them an idea of what they'll have to purchase and pack if they decide to go on the trip. So, Pablo wants to give a presentation to all volunteers regarding what they must take on the service expedition. Therefore, he asks you to create a PowerPoint presentation on the Peru Expedition packing list. Do the following:

1. If necessary, start PowerPoint and make sure your Data Disk is in the appropriate disk drive.

2. Open **PackList** from the Tutorial.02 Review folder on your Data Disk, and then save the file back to the same folder using the filename **Peru Packing List**.

3. Apply the design template titled "Shimmer," and then replace the subtitle in Slide 1 with your name.

4. In the Title Master, insert the logo file **GHLogo**, located in the Tutorial folder in the Tutorial.02 folder on the Data Disk, and position the graphic near the lower-right corner of the slide, just above the Number Area (slide number placeholder).

5. Add the footer "Packing List" and slide numbering to all the slides except Slide 1.

6. Change the title font color from white to yellow on both the Title Master and Slide Master.

Explore

7. In Slide 2, change the slide layout so you can place a clip-art image to the right of the bulleted list, and then insert appropriate clip art that deals with money. (*Hint*: Use the clip-art search feature and use the search word "money.")

8. Recolor the clip art so that it matches one or more of the current slide colors of blue or yellow.

Explore ▶ 9. In Slide 3, insert the bit map image file **slpbag** ("sleeping bag") located in the Review folder. (*Hint*: Rather than changing the slide layout and then inserting the image, just click the Insert Picture button on the Drawing toolbar, and then select the picture to be inserted. This will automatically change the slide layout.)

10. Use the resize handles of the bitmap image to increase its size so it fills more of the space on the right side of the slide.

Explore ▶ 11. In Slides 4 through 8, repeat Steps 9 and 10, except insert an appropriate bitmap image from the Review folder. (*Hint*: Use the preview window of the Insert Picture dialog box to match a bitmap image with the text on the slide.)

12. In Slide 9, insert a clip-art image to the left of the bulleted list. Pick clip art that deals with food or water.

13. Recolor the clip art to match the color scheme of your slide presentation.

14. Add a new Slide 10 and apply the Title Only slide layout.

15. Select the title box and type the slide title "Four Areas of Personal Preparation."

Explore ▶ 16. Draw a square in the middle of the blank area of the slide below the title, and change the fill color to light blue. (*Hint*: To draw a square, hold down the Shift key while using the Rectangle tool.)

17. Add text just outside the box on each of its four sides, using the words "Physical," "Mental," "Social," and "Spiritual." It doesn't matter which word you place on which side.

18. Rotate the text on the right side of the box so it reads top to bottom, and rotate the text on the left side so it reads bottom to top.

19. Adjust the text around the box so that each word is centered along the box edge, and almost resting on the box.

20. Add a new Slide 11 and apply the Table slide layout.

21. Insert the slide title "Discount Items." Now you'll create a table that shows some of the discount prices available to Global Humanitarian volunteers at a local retail store.

22. Insert a table with three columns and five rows. Add the text as follows:

Item	Regular Price	Discount Price
Boots	$220	$106
Sleeping bag	$180	$95
Water filter	$46	$28
Flashlight	$22	$12

Explore ▶ 23. Right-align the text and numbers in columns 2 and 3. If you're not sure how, use PowerPoint Help.

24. Draw a yellow, 4.5-point border below the top row, and change the top row text to yellow, 28-point text.

Explore ▶ 25. Drag the bottom-center resize handle of the table up so that the table stays the same width but decreases in height so the text fits better in the cells of the table.

26. Create a summary slide that includes titles from all the slides except Slide 1, and change the title to "Summary." Notice that PowerPoint creates two summary slides.

27. Change the slide layout of the first summary slide to Title and 2 Column Text, move items from the second summary slide to the second column of the first summary slide, delete the second summary slide, and then move some of the times in the left column of the summary slide to the right column so that each column has about the same number of lines of text. Keep the items in the same order as the slides.

28. To Slide 10 only, apply the design template titled "Textured."

29. Preview, spell check, and save the presentation using the default filename.

30. Print the presentation as grayscale handouts with four slides per page.

31. Close the file and exit PowerPoint.

CASE PROBLEMS

Case 1. MyBodyTrainer.com Several years ago, Gary Raddatz received an M.S. degree in Exercise Physiology and became a board-certified strength and conditioning specialist (CSCS). Recently he started a new e-commerce company called MyBodyTrainer.com, which provides services and products for health, fitness, weight loss, and sports conditioning. The services include personalized programs, and the products include fitness equipment and dietary supplements. Gary's business is expanding rapidly, but he needs capital to hire three more CSCS employees and several other employees to process orders, and to purchase additional inventory, and rent additional warehouse and office space. He asks you to help him prepare a PowerPoint presentation giving an overview of his business. He will give the presentation to bankers and investors to help him raise money for his company. Do the following:

1. Open **MyBody** from the Tutorial.02 Cases folder on your Data Disk, and then save the file back to the same folder using the filename **MyBodyTrainer**.

2. Apply the design template titled "Competition," and then replace the subtitle in Slide 1 with your name.

3. In the Slide Master, change the title text box so it is left-aligned rather than center-aligned. You'll then have to change the title in the Title Master back to center-aligned.

4. Also in the Slide Master, draw a straight horizontal line across the slide (from one edge to the next) between the title placeholder and the body text placeholder. (*Hint*: Use the Line tool on the Drawing toolbar.)

Explore 5. With the horizontal line selected, change its thickness to 3 points and its color to gold (the "Follow Accent and Hyperlink Scheme Color"). (*Hint*: Use the Line Color and Line Style buttons on the Drawing toolbar.)

Explore 6. In Slides 7 and 8, include the text and two bitmap images. In Slide 7, use **weights** and **strmach** (strength machines), and in Slide 8 use **excyle** (exercise cycle) and **treadmil** (treadmill). These bitmap images are located in the Tutorial.02 Cases folder. (*Hint*: Adjust the slide layout for Title, Text and 2 Content.)

7. In Slide 8, adjust the two images so they are side-by-side and fill the area to the right of the text. Similarly, in Slide 7, adjust the size and position of the images so they are visible and attractive.

8. In Slide 9, include the bitmap image **vitamins**.

9. In Slide 3, insert either an appropriate clip-art or bitmap image.

10. If necessary, recolor the clip-art image so it matches the design template color scheme.

Explore   11. In Slide 4 ("Five Sides to Fitness"), draw a large equilateral regular pentagon in the middle of the blank area of the slide below the title. (*Hint*: Hold down the Shift key while using the Regular Pentagon tool.)

12. Invert the pentagon so it's pointed down.

13. Add white, 18-point Arial text just outside the box on each of its fives sides, using the phrases (starting at the top of the pentagon and going clockwise): "Motivation," "Strength Training," "Cardio Exercise," "Nutrition," and "Flexibility."

14. Rotate the text boxes so they are parallel to their respective sides of the pentagon. Adjust the size of the pentagon and the position of the text so that each phrase is centered along the box edge, and almost resting on the shape.

15. In Slide 11, insert a table with two columns and five rows. Add the text as follows:

Expense Item	Amount Needed
CSCS Employees	$140,000
Other Employees	$215,000
Inventory	$145,000
Rent	$20,000

Explore   16. Add a new row with "Total" in the left column and "$520,000" in the right column. (*Hint*: To add a row to an existing table, move to the lower-right cell, in this case B5, and press the Tab key.)

Explore   17. Drag the bottom-center resize handle of the table up so that the table stays the same width but decreases in height. This makes the text fit better in the cells of the table, and the table fit better on the slide.

18. Right-align the text and numbers in column 2. If you're not sure how to do this, use PowerPoint Help.

19. Change the fill color of the top row of the table to dark amber—the Automatic fill color of the Fill button on the Tables and Borders toolbar.

20. Create a summary slide that includes titles from Slides 5 through 10, and change the title to "Products and Services." Leave the slide as the new Slide 5 in the presentation.

21. Preview, spell check, and save the presentation using the default filename.

22. Print the presentation as grayscale handouts with six slides per page.

23. Close the file and exit PowerPoint.

Case 2. Payroll Partners Payroll Partners, founded by Thora Ostvig, is a Wichita, Kansas–based accountancy office that helps small businesses process payroll and perform other financial tasks. Recently Thora was approached by lawyers of a national chain of payroll-processing offices who expressed interest in buying her business. Thora is interested in exploring the idea, and asks you to prepare a presentation that she can use to present to the board of directors of the national chain in hopes of getting the best deal possible. Do the following:

1. Open **Payroll** from the Tutorial.02 Cases folder on your Data Disk, and then save the file back to the same folder using the filename **Payroll Partners**.

2. Apply the design template titled "Proposal," and then replace the subtitle in Slide 1 with your name.

3. In the Title Master, change the title text so it's the same color as the title text in the Slide Master.

Explore

4. In the Slide Master, add a black 3-point border around the title text box. (*Hint*: Use the Line Color and Line Style tools on the Drawling toolbar.)

5. Add the footer "Payroll Partners" and slide numbering to all the slides except Slide 1.

Explore

6. Change the slide layout of Slide 3 to Content, and then insert a Venn diagram, which is a diagram showing areas of overlap between elements. It consists of two or more over-lapping circles. In this case, you want to include three circles.

7. Add text next to each of the circles (in the designated placeholders): "Software Development," "Accounting," and "Small Business Payroll."

8. Near the bottom of the slide and centered below the Venn diagram, insert a text box with the phrase "Niche Region." Change the text to 32-point purple text.

Explore

9. Draw a black 3-point arrow from this text box to the center of the Venn diagram where the three circles overlap. (*Hint*: Use the Arrow tool and Line Style tool on the Drawing toolbar.)

10. In Slide 5, insert a clip-art image that deals with money. If necessary, recolor the image to match the slide color scheme. If necessary, use the AutoFit option to fit the text in the placeholder.

11. In Slide 6, change the font color of the asking price to purple.

12. In Slide 7, insert a table with three columns and five rows.

13. Insert the following text into the table:

Year	Gross Revenues	Earnings
1999	$180,000	$70,000
2000	$270,000	$122,000
2001	$350,000	$188,000
2002	$510,000	$238,000

Explore

14. Drag the bottom-center resize handle of the table up so that the table stays the same width but decreases in height. This makes the text fit better in the cells of the table.

Explore

15. Select the top row of text, and change the vertical alignment so the text appears at the bottom of each cell in the row. Use the Align Bottom button on the Tables and Borders toolbar.

16. Right-align the text and numbers in columns 2 and 3. If you're not sure how to do this, use PowerPoint Help.

17. Change the fill color of the top row of the table to purple—the Automatic fill color of the Fill button on the Tables and Borders toolbar—and then change the font color to white.

18. Create a summary slide that includes titles from Slides 3 through 8, move the slide to the end of the presentation (so it becomes Slide 9), and change the title to "Summary."

19. Preview, fix any problems you see, spell check, and save the presentation using the default filename.

20. Print the presentation as grayscale handouts with six slides per page.

21. Close the file and exit PowerPoint.

Case 3. Sally's Scrapbooking   Four years ago, Brian and Sally DiQuattro started a home business called Sally's Scrapbooking Supplies, which distributes scrapbooking supplies to retail stores in the Atlanta, Georgia, area. More recently, Brian and Sally opened their own specialty store (called Sally's Scrapbooking) and stocked it with scrapbooking supplies, which includes binders, paper and plastic sheets and protectors, colored pens and markers, stickers and die cuts, stencils, scissors and cutting boards, glues and adhesives, and miscellaneous items. As part of their marketing, Brian and Sally give presentations to scrapbooking clubs, women's clubs, crafts clubs, church groups, genealogical societies, and others interested in preserving their family histories through picture scrapbooks. The DiQuattros ask you to prepare a presentation for members of these organizations. Do the following:

1. Start PowerPoint, open the presentation file **Scrapbk** from the Tutorial.02 Cases folder, and save the file back to the same folder using the filename **Sally's Scrapbooking**.

2. In Slide 1, change the names under "Sally's Scrapbooking" in the subtitle to your name.

3. Apply an appropriate design template of your choice.

4. Add a footer and slide numbers to the slide presentation.

5. Modify the Slide Master and the Title Master to enhance the design template in any way you see fit.

6. In most slides, add a bitmap graphic. The Tutorial.02 Cases folder has several graphics that start with "sb" (for "scrapbook"); use any or all of these pictures. You'll want to include two or more pictures on some of the slides, and possibly none on other slides. Match the picture to the slide text.

7. Include at least one clip-art image in your presentation. Recolor the image, if necessary, to match your presentation's color scheme.

8. In Slide 9, insert a table that includes sale items, retail prices, and discount prices (three columns), and include at least five items (six rows, a header row, and five item rows). Choose any of the items that appear in the presentation. Make up fictitious but reasonable prices.

9. Add arrows and text boxes to one slide to label items in a photo. For example, in Slide 7, you might include the pictures of pens (sbpens) and scissors (sbsciss), and then label each photo with an arrow and text boxes at the end of the arrows. Rotate one or more of the text boxes.

10. Create a summary slide for Slides 3 through 9, and move the summary slide to the end of the presentation. Change its title to "Scrapbooking Summary."

11. Preview, spell check, and save the presentation using the default filename.

12. Print the presentation as grayscale handouts with six slides per page.

13. Close the file and exit PowerPoint.

Case 4. College Honor Society   Honor societies recognize students who distinguish themselves

Explore

in academics and leadership. Your assignment is to prepare a PowerPoint presentation on an honor society at your college or university. Do the following:

1. Gather information on an honor society from honor society advisors, college advisement centers, or the office of the Dean of Students. For the names, locations, and phone numbers, call information at your college, or consult your student directory or catalog. You can also gather information from the World Wide Web. For general information about members of the Association of College Honor Societies, including a list of most honor societies in the United States and Canada, consult www.achsnatl.org. For information on a specific national, non-discipline-specific honor society, Phi Kappa Phi, consult www.phikappaphi.org. For a national freshman honor society, Phi Eta Sigma, consult www.phietasigma.org.

2. Begin to create your PowerPoint presentation by typing the name of the society on the title slide, and your name as the subtitle.

3. Create at least eight slides with information about the society. Information on your slides might include local and national names and addresses of advisors and officers, purposes, eligibility, activities, scholarships, recognition programs, famous members, history, meetings, local and national conventions, merchandise, and publications.

4. Apply an appropriate design template to the presentation.

5. Modify the Slide Master by adding a text box or graphics object, changing the font attributes, or making some other desired change that will appear on all the slides.

6. Include an appropriate footer and slide number on each slide (except the first title slide). In the Slide Master, change the font style, size, color, or position of the footer and slide number text.

7. Include in your presentation at least four graphics, at least one of which should be a clip-art image. (If you choose to describe Phi Kappa Phi or Phi Eta Sigma, bitmap images of their logos are in the Tutorial.02 Cases folder.) You can acquire images from the Web, or from your local chapter of the honor society.

8. Recolor the clip art to match the color scheme or the other graphics in your presentation.

9. Include a table, cycle diagram, or Venn diagram in your presentation. (For information on Venn diagrams, use PowerPoint Help.) For example, you might include: a table with the name, description, location, and dates of chapter activities; a table listing the chapter merchandise and prices; a table with names, addresses, phone numbers, and e-mail addresses of chapter officers. You might include a cycle diagram showing the cycle of academic achievement, academic honors, encouragement to excel academically, association with other academically outstanding students, which in turn encourages more academic achievement. You might include a Venn diagram showing the overlap between local officer activities, national officer leadership, and member participation.

10. Include a drawing that you create from lines, arrows, AutoShapes, or text boxes. For example, you might create a diagram showing the procedure for becoming a member of the honor society, using text boxes and arrows.

11. Apply a second design template to one of the slides.

12. Create a summary slide, and change its title to "Summary of Phi Kappa Phi" (but use the name of your selected honor society).

13. Preview, spell check, and save the presentation using the filename Honor Society.

14. Print the presentation as grayscale handouts with six slides per page.

15. Close the file and exit PowerPoint.

INTERNET ASSIGNMENTS

Student Union

The purpose of the Internet Assignments is to challenge you to find information on the Internet that you can use to create effective documents. The actual assignments are updated and maintained on the Course Technology Web site. Log on to the Internet and use your Web browser to go to the Student Union on the New Perspectives Series site at **www.course.com/NewPerspectives/studentunion**. Click the Online Companions link, and then click the link for this text.

QUICK | CHECK ANSWERS

Session 2.1

1. (a) to present information that words can't communicate effectively; (b) to interest and motivate the reader; (c) to quickly communicate relationships; and (c) to increase understanding and retention

2. (a) region of the slide that contains text (b) a picture, clip art, graph, chart, diagram, bitmap image, etc. (c) any item (text box, clip art, graphic, and so forth) on a slide that you can select, move, resize, rotate, or otherwise manipulate (d) small circles on the box around an object; when you drag a resize handle with the pointer, the size of the object changes

3. (a) Click anywhere in the text box. (b) Drag a resize handle. (c) Drag the object (or in the case of a text box, the edge of the box). (d) Display the slide in the Slide Pane, click the list arrow of the desired design template in the Design Template Task Pane, and click Apply to selected slides. (e) Click the Insert Clip Art button on the Drawing toolbar, click (or double-click) the desired clip-art image. (f) Select the clip-art image, click the Recolor Picture button on the Picture toolbar, and modify the original colors to new colors.

4. The Title Master is a slide that contains the objects that appear on the title slide of the presentation. The Slide Master is a slide that contains the objects that appear on all the slides except the title slide.

5. Tabs add space between the left margin and the beginning of the text on a particular line, or between the text in one column and the text in another column. Tab stops are the locations where text moves when you press the Tab key. Click the Tab Stop Alignment Styles button until the right tab marker appears, and then click the desired location on the ruler.

6. a collection of clip-art images (as well as sound clips and movie clips)

7. Consider (a) your audience (jobs, experiences, education, culture); (b) your purpose (to inform, instruct, identify, motivate); and (c) the type of information on the slide (numerical values, logical relationships, procedures and processes, and visual and spatial characteristics).

Session 2.2

1. Change the slide layout to Table, double-click the table placeholder, set the desired number of columns and rows, insert information into the cells, and modify the table format as desired.

2. upper-left corner

3. a diagram used to show a process that has a continuous cycle; for example, a diagram to show the vicious cycle of failure when service is performed badly, or the positive cycle of success when service is performed properly

4. Click the Text Box button on the Drawing toolbar, and click at the desired location in the slide.

5. Click the AutoShapes list arrow on the Drawing toolbar, point to the appropriate tool (such as Basic Shapes), click the desired shape, move the pointer into the Slide Pane, and drag the pointer to draw the figure.

6. Select the triangle, click the Draw button on the Drawing toolbar, point to Rotate or Flip, and click Flip Vertical. Or, you can use the rotate handle.

7. Drag the rotate handle (little green circle) of the object in the Slide Pane.

8. a method for automatically creating a slide with the titles of the slides selected in the Slide Sorter Pane

OBJECTIVES

In this tutorial you will:

- Learn about the World Wide Web

- Create hyperlinks

- Publish a presentation on the Web

- View a presentation using a Web browser

CREATING
WEB PAGES WITH
POWERPOINT

Creating a Web Page for Global Humanitarian

CASE

Global Humanitarian Web Site

Miriam Schwartz, the managing director of Global Humanitarian in Austin, Texas, recently saw the presentation Peru Expedition Report that you helped Pablo Fuentes prepare. She would like to share a modified version of this PowerPoint presentation with potential volunteers and contributors, so she decides to make the presentation available on the Internet.

The **Internet** is the largest and most widely used computer network in the world. It's really a network of thousands of smaller networks, all joined together electronically. Part of the Internet is a global information-sharing system called the **World Wide Web** (also called the "Web" or WWW). The Web allows you to find and view electronic documents, called **Web pages**. Organizations and individuals make their Web pages available by placing them on a **Web server**, a dedicated network computer with high-capacity hard disks. The World Wide Web, then, is a connected network of these Web servers. The location of a particular set of Web pages on a server is called a **Web site**. You can access a particular Web site by specifying its address, also called its **Uniform Resource Locator** (**URL**). To specify URLs and to view Web pages, you use a **Web browser**, which is a software program that sends requests for Web pages, retrieves them, and then interprets them for display on the computer screen. Two of the most popular browsers are Microsoft Internet Explorer and Netscape Navigator.

Most Web sites contain a **home page**, a Web page that contains general information about the site. Home pages are like "home base"—they are a starting point for online viewers. They usually contain hyperlinks. A **hyperlink** (short for "hypertext link," also called a "hot link" or just a "link") is a word, phrase, or graphic image that you click to display another location, called the **target**. Text hyperlinks are usually underlined and appear in a different color than the rest of the document. The target of a hyperlink can be a location within the document (presentation), a different document, or a page on the World Wide Web.

Publishing a Presentation on the Web

Normally, you and the organization for which you work would create Web pages using software specifically designed for that purpose, such as Microsoft FrontPage, which is a **Web page editor**. But sometimes you want to publish a PowerPoint presentation, for example, as a link to the organization's home page. Global Humanitarian, similar to most large organizations, has its own Web page, but Miriam thinks the pictures and information in the Peru Expedition Report would make an excellent resource for prospective volunteers and contributors.

To prepare Miriam's PowerPoint presentation (or any presentation) for viewing on the World Wide Web, you first have to convert it to a file format called HTML, with the filename extension .htm or .html. **HTML** (Hypertext Markup Language) is a special language for describing the format of a Web page so that Web browsers can interpret and display the pages. The HTML markings in a file tell the browser how to format the text, graphics, tables, and other objects. Fortunately, you don't have to learn the Hypertext Markup Language to create HTML documents; PowerPoint does the work for you. You can easily save any PowerPoint presentation as an HTML document using the PowerPoint "Save as Web Page" command. This command automatically creates a set of HTML documents (or pages), one page for each slide, plus an index page. The **index page** includes hyperlinks to all the slides in the presentation. Furthermore, if your presentation includes any type of graphics, PowerPoint usually converts them to separate files, in GIF or JPEG format. Finally, PowerPoint creates additional files that help users view and navigate through the Web pages. All these files are stored in a separate folder, which is given a name based on the original PowerPoint presentation file.

If you want to edit the resulting HTML documents, you'll have to use either a word processor that supports HTML editing (for example, Microsoft Word 2002) or a dedicated HTML editor (for example, Microsoft FrontPage). PowerPoint doesn't support direct editing of HTML documents.

You'll now open a modified version of the Peru Expedition Report (called PeruExp) and save it as a Web page, that is, as a set of HTML documents.

To save the presentation as a Web page:

1. Open the presentation file **PeruExp** located in the Web folder on your Data Disk, and then use the Save As command on the File menu to save it back to the same folder using the filename **PeruExpedition**. You must give the presentation a filename with no spaces in anticipation of publishing it as a Web page, because some browsers can't handle filenames with spaces.

2. Take a minute to go through the presentation so you're familiar with its content. Note that it's similar, but certainly not identical, to the Peru Expedition Report you helped create in an earlier tutorial.

3. Click **File** on the menu bar, and then click **Save as Web Page**. The Save As dialog box opens. See Figure 1.

Figure 1	SAVE AS DIALOG BOX TO SAVE PRESENTATION AS A WEB PAGE

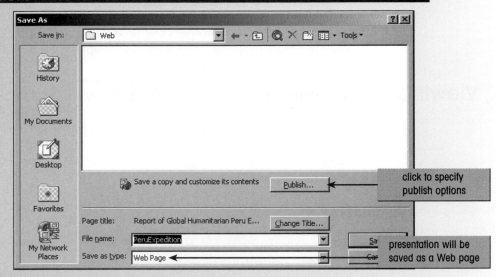

4. Click the **Publish** button on the dialog box. This opens the Publish as Web Page dialog box where you can specify options for your Web page. See Figure 2. You'll publish your Web page for Microsoft Internet Explorer and for Netscape Navigator.

Figure 2	PUBLISH AS WEB PAGE DIALOG BOX

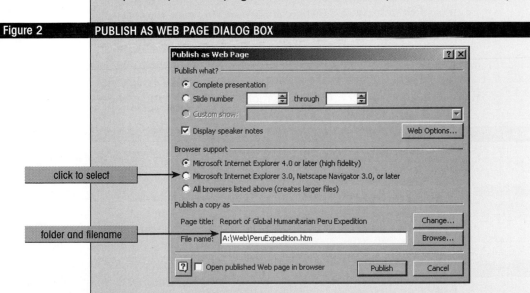

5. Click **Microsoft Internet Explorer 3.0, Netscape Navigator 3.0, or later** in the Browser support section of the dialog box. Leave all the other options, as shown in Figure 2. Make sure the Save in folder is Web (on your Data Disk), with the File name set to **PeruExpedition.htm**.

6. Click the **Publish** button. PowerPoint creates and opens an HTML page named PeruExpedition, with the filename extension *.htm. This is the index page for the presentation. PowerPoint also creates a new directory named PeruExpedition_files, which contains many kinds of files, including an HTML file for each slide, a .GIF or .JPG file for each graphic, and other types of files required by the Web pages.

This completes all the steps necessary to create a Web page using PowerPoint. Having saved Peru Expedition as an HTML file, you should now view it in your Web browser to verify that it has been converted correctly. You might want to test this and other Web pages you create using other browsers and browser versions to make sure the pages appear how you want them to appear to everyone who might try to view them.

Viewing a Presentation in a Web Browser

Eventually, Miriam will give a copy of the Web page and its accompanying folders to Global Humanitarian's computer support technician, who will post the files on the company Web server. For now, however, you can still view the presentation in a browser.

To view the presentation in Internet Explorer:

1. Click **File** on the menu bar, and then click **Web Page Preview**. PowerPoint opens your Web browser (in this example, Microsoft Internet Explorer) with the Web page in the browser window.

   TROUBLE? If your computer uses Netscape Navigator or some other browser, your screen will look different than those shown here, where Internet Explorer was used.

   TROUBLE? If no browser opens, consult your instructor or your technical support person.

2. If necessary, maximize the browser window so it fills the screen. See Figure 3.

   TROUBLE? If PowerPoint opened another program, such as Microsoft Word, or if you received an error message, a Web browser might not be installed on your computer. Consult your instructor or technical support person for assistance.

| Figure 3 | SLIDE 1 OF THE PRESENTATION WEB PAGES |

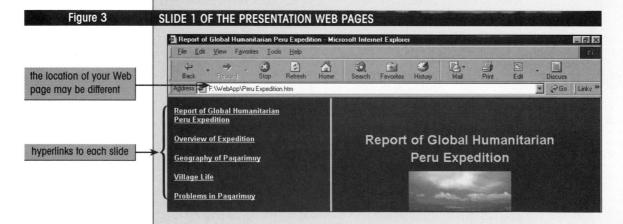

the location of your Web page may be different

hyperlinks to each slide

As you can see, the first slide of your presentation appears in the main frame of the browser, an outline of the slides appears along the left edge in the contents frame. Each outline item is a hyperlink to its corresponding slide. Also, a toolbar appears at the bottom of the window. These hyperlinks and the toolbar help you navigate through the presentation.

TROUBLE? If you don't see the outline, click the Outline button at the bottom of the screen. You should also be aware that your Web page might look different if your default browser isn't Microsoft Internet Explorer.

3. Click the **Next Slide** button ⏩ on the toolbar at the bottom of the Web page. The browser now displays Slide 2 of the presentation.

4. Click the hyperlink **Taught Hygiene Classes**. See Figure 4. As you can see, the browser now displays the Taught Hygiene Classes slide. This shows that when you saved your original presentation as a Web page, PowerPoint automatically translated the slide hyperlinks to Web page hyperlinks.

Figure 4	SLIDE 9 OF THE PRESENTATION WEB PAGES

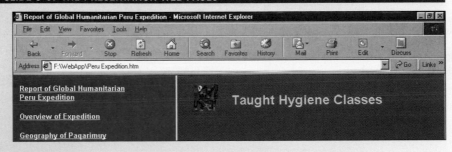

5. Click the **Previous Slide** button ◀ on the Web page toolbar. You should now be looking at Slide 8 "Helped Build Greenhouse." As you can see, the navigation buttons help you easily move one slide forward or backwards, whereas the outline hyperlinks allow you to jump from one slide to any other in any order.

6. Look through the Web page as you desire, then close your Web browser.

Miriam is pleased with the resulting Web page, but after going through it, she asks you to add a hyperlink from the phrase "expedition volunteers" in Slide 2 to the picture of some of the expedition volunteers in Slide 10. She also would like you to create a hyperlink from the last slide to the first slide.

Creating Hyperlinks

In the Peru Expedition file, the text phrase "expedition volunteers" in Slide 2 will become a hyperlink, and will appear as underlined text in a color different from normal text. Besides text, however, you could use digital images, shapes, clip art, and other objects as hyperlinks.

The target of your hyperlink will be another slide in the same presentation, but you could make the target another PowerPoint file, an e-mail address, or a Web page. You'll now create the hyperlink.

To create a hyperlink:

1. Go to Slide 2, "Overview of Expedition."

2. Select the phrase **expedition volunteers** by dragging I from the beginning of "expedition" to the end of "volunteer." The text is now highlighted in blue.

3. Click the **Insert Hyperlink** button 🔗 on the Standard toolbar. The Insert Hyperlink dialog box opens. Now you have to select the type of hyperlink you want. In this case, you'll make a hyperlink to a place in the current document, that is, in this presentation file.

4. Click the **Place in This Document** button in the Insert Hyperlink dialog box. See Figure 5.

Figure 5   INSERT HYPERLINK DIALOG BOX

select this

drag down to display Slide 10

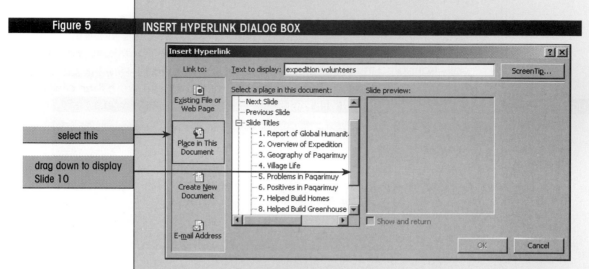

5. Drag the **Select a place in this document** vertical scroll button down to the bottom of the vertical scroll bar, and then click **10. Expedition Volunteers** located under Slide Titles.

6. Click the **OK** button, and then deselect the text box in Slide 2. See Figure 6.

Figure 6   SLIDE 2 WITH HYPERLINK TO SLIDE 10

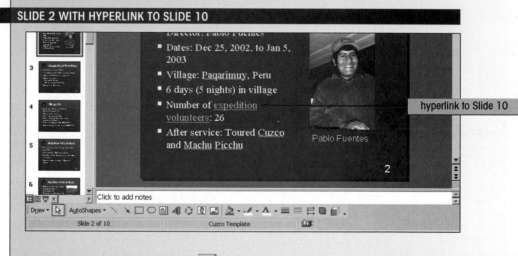

hyperlink to Slide 10

7. To test the hyperlink, click 🖵 to start the slide show with Slide 2 on the screen.

8. Move the mouse so a pointer appears, and then move the pointer 🖑 over the hyperlink, and click the mouse button. The presentation jumps to Slide 10, "Expedition Volunteers."

TROUBLE? If the hyperlink didn't work, carefully repeat all the above steps, making sure you select the correct target.

9. Press the **Esc** key to end the slide show and return to Normal View.

You've created the first hyperlink, and now you're ready to create the second one, which will point from Slide 10 to Slide 1. You'll insert a text box as the hyperlink.

To create another hyperlink:

1. With Slide 10 in the Slide Pane, click the **Text Box** button 🖼 on the Drawing toolbar, click ↓ in the bottom center of the slide, directly below the space between the caption words "Expedition" and "volunteers," and then click the **Center** button 🖳 so that the text will be centered as you type it.

2. Type **Return to First Slide**. You're now ready to make this text a hyperlink back to Slide 1.

3. Select the text **Return to First Slide**, click the **Insert Hyperlink** button 🖳 to display the Insert Hyperlink dialog box, make sure the **Place in This Document** button is depressed, and click **1. Report of Global Humanitarian** under Slide Titles in the "Select a place in this document" section of the dialog box.

4. Click the **OK** button, and then deselect the text box in Slide 10. See Figure 7. Make sure your hyperlink text appears, as shown in Figure 7.

| Figure 7 | SLIDE 10 WITH HYPERLINK TO SLIDE 1 |

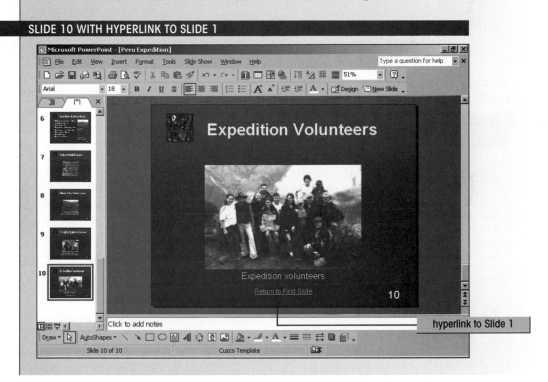

Having created the new hyperlink, you're ready to test the hyperlink, save the new version of the file as a Web page, and then test the hyperlink in your Web browser.

To test the hyperlink:

1. Click 🖵 to get into Slide Show View, and then with 🖑, click the hyperlink **Return to First Slide**. The Slide Show immediately jumps to Slide 1.

2. Press the **Esc** key to return to Normal View.

3. Save the presentation as a normal PowerPoint file.

4. Save the presentation as a Web Page, with the **Microsoft Internet Explorer 3.0, Netscape Navigator 3.0, or later** feature selected in the Publish as a Web Page dialog box, to the Web folder. When you're asked if you want to replace the Web page that already exists, click the **Yes** button. The new version of the Web page is now in the Web folder. You can now view it with a Web browser.

5. Close Peru Expedition, but leave PowerPoint open if you're completing the Review Assignments at this time.

6. Open **Peru Expedition** into your Web browser; click [≫] to go to Slide 2.

7. Click the hyperlink **expedition volunteers**. The Web page jumps to Slide 10.

8. Click the hyperlink **Return to First Slide**. The Web page jumps to Slide 1.

   TROUBLE? If the hyperlinks don't work, go back through this section of the tutorial, repeating the steps carefully to make sure you create the hyperlinks properly. If you still have trouble, consult your instructor or technical support person.

9. Look through as much of the presentation in your browser as you'd like, and then close your Web browser.

The Web page is now complete. Miriam will follow through on having it placed on the Global Humanitarian's Web site.

REVIEW ASSIGNMENTS

Miriam Schwartz, the managing director of Global Humanitarian in Austin, Texas, likes the result of sharing the Peru Expedition text and pictures on the World Wide Web. But she is aware that potential volunteers often choose a Global Humanitarian expedition to Peru because of the tour of Cuzco and Machu Picchu following the service in a needy village. So she asks you to help her create a Web page giving a brief tour of Cuzco and Machu Picchu, similar to the presentation you might have helped prepare previously. Do the following:

1. Start PowerPoint, if necessary, and open the presentation file **MPTour** located in the Web folder on your Data Disk, and then save it as **MachuPicchuTour**.

2. Go through the presentation in Slide Show View so you are familiar with its content.

3. In Slide 1, create a text box near the lower-right corner with the text **Go to Machu Picchu**.

4. Create a hyperlink of the text in this new text box, with Slide 4 as the target.

5. Check the hyperlink in Slide Show View.

6. Save the presentation as a Web page, making sure the filename is **Machu Picchu Tour.htm** in the Publish as Web Page dialog box, and not MPTour.htm.

7. Open the presentation in your Web browser.

8. Go through the presentation using the browser. Check to make sure your hyperlink works.

9. Close your Web browser and PowerPoint.

New Perspectives on

INTEGRATING MICROSOFT® OFFICE XP

TUTORIAL 3   INT 3.03

Integrating Word, Excel, Access and PowerPoint

Read This Before You Begin

To the Student

Data Disks

To complete this tutorial, Review Assignments, and Case Problems, you need one Data Disk. Your instructor will either provide you with the Data Disk or ask you to make your own.

If you are making your own Data Disk, you will need **one** blank, formatted high-density disk. You will need to copy a set of files and/or folders from a file server, standalone computer, or the Web onto your disk. Your instructor will tell you which computer, drive letter, and folders contain the files you need. You could also download the files by going to **www.course.com** and following the instructions on the screen.

The information below shows you which folders go on your disk, so that you will have enough disk space to complete the tutorial, Review Assignments, and Case Problems:

Data Disk 1

Write this on the disk label:
Integrating Office XP: Tutorial 3 Data Disk

Put this folder on the disk:
Tutorial.03

When you begin each tutorial, be sure you are using the correct Data Disk. Refer to the "File Finder" chart at the back of this text for more detailed information on which files are used in which tutorials. See the inside front or inside back cover of this book for more information on Data Disk files, or ask your instructor or technical support person for assistance.

Using Your Own Computer

If you are going to work through this book using your own computer, you need:

- **Computer System** Microsoft Windows 98, NT, 2000 Professional, or higher must be installed on your computer. This book assumes a typical installation of Microsoft Office XP.

- **Data Disk** You will not be able to complete the tutorials or exercises in this book using your own computer until you have your Data Disk.

Visit Our World Wide Web Site

Additional materials designed especially for you are available on the World Wide Web.
Go to **www.course.com/NewPerspectives**.

To the Instructor

The Data Disk Files are available on the Instructor's Resource Kit for this title. Follow the instructions in the Help file on the CD-ROM to install the programs to your network or standalone computer. For information on creating Data Disks, see the "To the Student" section above.

You are granted a license to copy the Data Files to any computer or computer network used by students who have purchased this book.

In this tutorial you will:

- Merge an Access query with a Word document

- View merged documents

- Preview and print a merged document

- Create a Word outline

- Create PowerPoint slides from a Word outline

- Copy and paste an Access query into a PowerPoint presentation

- Link an Excel chart to a PowerPoint presentation

INTEGRATING
WORD, EXCEL, ACCESS, AND POWERPOINT

Creating a Form Letter and Integrated Presentation for Country Gardens

CASE

Country Gardens

Sue Dickinson is ready to expand the marketing and promotional activities of her plant supply company, Country Gardens. She wants to send out a promotional letter she's written that announces the new mail-order catalog, highlights her company's recognition by NEGHA (the New England Growers and Horticultural Association), and introduces its new products. Sue plans to create three separate mailings to coincide with promotional events at each of her company's three stores. The Derry, New Hampshire store has an open house next month, so Sue first wants to send the letter only to New Hampshire customers. Later, she will create a second mailing for Vermont customers to coincide with the Burlington store's grand opening, and then a third mailing to Massachusetts customers to coincide with the Dunstable store's participation in a town fair.

Sue also needs to prepare a presentation for next month's Eastern Regional Growers Conference, which is sponsored by NEGHA. The conference provides a good opportunity for Country Gardens and other area greens suppliers to share information and promote their companies and products.

In this tutorial, you'll complete two separate tasks. First, you'll merge the promotional letter with the names and addresses of Country Gardens' New Hampshire customers, which are stored in an Access database. After completing the form letter, you'll create a presentation for Sue to use at the conference. You'll use the outline feature in Word to create an outline of the topics she wants to cover, and then you'll create a PowerPoint presentation from the outline. The presentation will also include the Excel pie chart showing Country Gardens as the largest area grower and an Access query listing the company's ten new products. You'll use different integration methods to include these items in the presentation.

Planning the Form Letter

A **form letter** is a Word document that contains standard paragraphs of text and a minimum of variable text, such as the names and addresses of the letter recipients. The **main document** of a form letter contains the text and other information (including punctuation, spaces, and graphics) that you want to keep the same in each letter. It also includes **merge fields**, which are special instructions that tell Word where to print the variable information. The variable information is contained in a **data source**, which can be a Word table, an Access database, or some other source. When you merge the main document with the data source, Word replaces the merge fields with the appropriate information from the data source. The process of combining the main document with the data source is called a **merge**. The term **mail merge** is used when you are merging a main document with a list of addresses from any data source.

In this case, Sue's promotional letter is the main document, and the Access database containing the names and addresses of Country Gardens' customers is the data source. Figure 3-1 shows Sue's plan for the form letter.

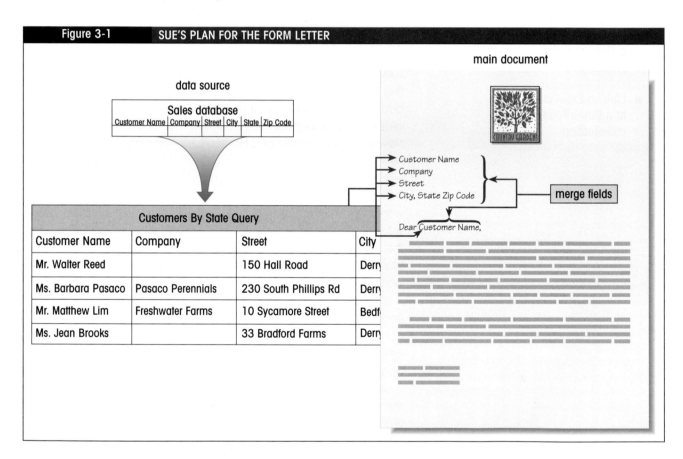

Figure 3-1   SUE'S PLAN FOR THE FORM LETTER

Note that the data source is actually a query in the Sales database. This query, which Sue created and saved as "Customers by State," retrieves name, company, and address of her customers. You'll follow Sue's plan to merge the Access data with the Word document to create the form letter.

Merging **Access Data with a Word Document**

The first step in completing the mail merge is to specify the type of document you want to create, such as a form letter. Next you select the main document, which Word also calls the starting document. Then you select recipients from the data source, which is often in the form of a list. When you use an Access database as the data source for a mail merge, you can select any table or query defined in the database as the actual data source. Next, you insert items containing merge fields in the main document. These items, such as the Address block, are placeholders for the information that changes from one letter to another. If necessary, you can match the fields in the Address block with those from your data source so that they correspond. Finally, you preview the letters, make any necessary changes, and merge the main document and the data source to produce customized form letters.

Selecting a Starting Document and Recipients

A mail-merge starting document can be a new or existing Word document. In this case, the starting document is Sue's existing promotional letter. The document, which is named Letter2 and is stored on your Data Disk, is a slightly modified version of the document you worked with in the first integration tutorial. You'll begin by starting Word and opening the letter document.

To start Word and open the letter document:

1. Start Word as usual.

2. Make sure your Data Disk is in the appropriate drive, and then open the **Letter2** document, which is located in the Tutorial folder in the Tutorial.03 folder on your Data Disk. The letter opens in Print Layout view. If necessary, display the nonprinting characters.

   Next you'll save the file with a new name. That way, the original letter remains intact on your Data Disk in case you want to restart the tutorial.

3. Click **File** on the menu bar, and then click **Save As** to open the Save As dialog box.

4. Save the file as **Main Letter** in the Tutorial folder in the Tutorial.03 folder on your Data Disk.

5. Replace Sue Dickinson's name at the end of the letter with your own.

6. Press **Ctrl+Home** to return to the beginning of the letter, and then save the document.

You need to start by selecting the type of document you want to create.

To select the document type:

1. Click **Tools** on the menu bar, point to **Letters and Mailings**, and then click **Mail Merge Wizard**. The Mail Merge Task Pane opens. See Figure 3-2.

Figure 3-2   MAIL MERGE TASK PANE

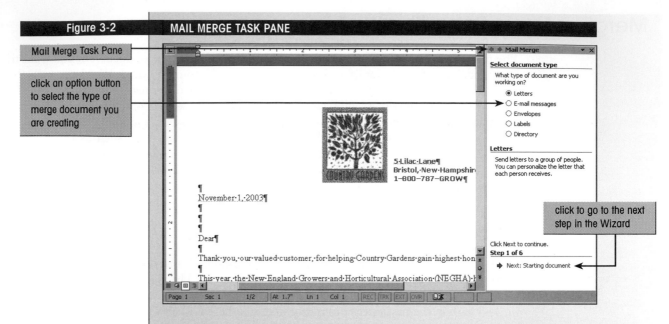

Mail Merge Task Pane

click an option button to select the type of merge document you are creating

click to go to the next step in the Wizard

TROUBLE? If the Mail Merge Task Pane does not open, click View on the menu bar, and then click Task Pane. If you see a Task Pane other than the Mail Merge Task Pane, click the Other Task Panes list arrow, and then click Mail Merge.

The Mail Merge Task Pane guides you through the six steps of creating a merge document. In Step 1, you select the type of document you want to create. The Letters option button is selected by default, but you can also use the Mail Merge Wizard to create e-mail messages, envelopes, labels, or a directory.

2. Click the **Letters** option button, if necessary, and then click **Next: Starting document** to continue. The Mail Merge Task Pane shows the options for Step 2: Select starting document. You want to use the current document, Sue's customer letter, as the starting document.

3. Click the **Use the current document** option button, if necessary, and then click **Next: Select recipients**. The Mail Merge Task Pane shows the options for Step 3: Select recipients, as in Figure 3-3.

Figure 3-3   STEP 3 OF 6 IN THE MAIL MERGE WIZARD

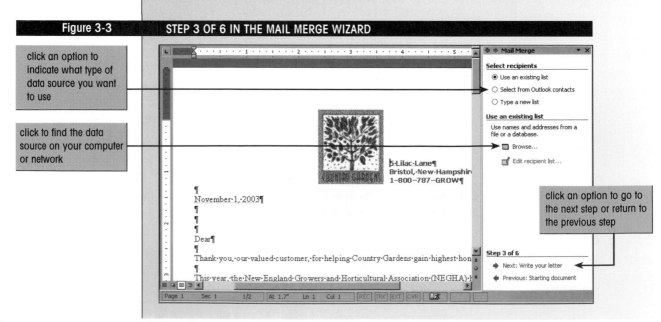

click an option to indicate what type of data source you want to use

click to find the data source on your computer or network

click an option to go to the next step or return to the previous step

You want to select recipients from an existing list in an Access database.

4. Click the **Use an existing list** option button, if necessary, and then click **Browse** to find the customer list, the Customers by State query in the Sales database. The Select Data Source dialog box opens.

5. Open the **Sales** database, which is in the Tutorial folder in the Tutorial.03 folder on your Data Disk. The Select Table dialog box opens, which lets you choose a table or query in the selected database as the data source.

6. Click **Customers by State** to select it, if necessary, and then click the **OK** button. The Mail Merge Recipients dialog box opens, as shown in Figure 3-4.

Figure 3-4   **MAIL MERGE RECIPIENTS DIALOG BOX**

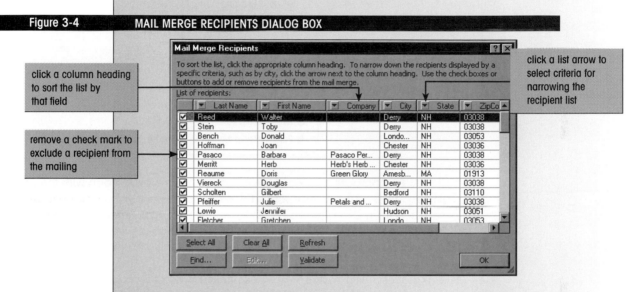

You use the Mail Merge Recipients dialog box to select the people who will receive Sue's customer letter. You can sort this list by any field. For example, if you were doing a large mass mailing, you could sort the list by zip code. You can also narrow the list to select only a subset. For example, she wants to send letters only to those customers who live in New Hampshire.

7. Click the **State** list arrow, and then click **NH**. The list of recipients changes to include only those customers in New Hampshire. Sue will change this setting to "VT" and then to "MA" when she completes the other two mailings to customers in Vermont and then Massachusetts.

   TROUBLE? If you clicked the State column heading instead of the State list arrow, you sorted the list according to state. Click OK to close the dialog box, click Select a different list in the Mail Merge Task Pane, and then repeat steps 5–7.

8. Click the **OK** button to close the Mail Merge Recipients dialog box. The Use an existing list section of the Mail Merge Task Pane now indicates that Word will select your recipients from the Customers by State query in Sales.mdb. Your screen should look similar to Figure 3-5.

Figure 3-5   RECIPIENTS SELECTED

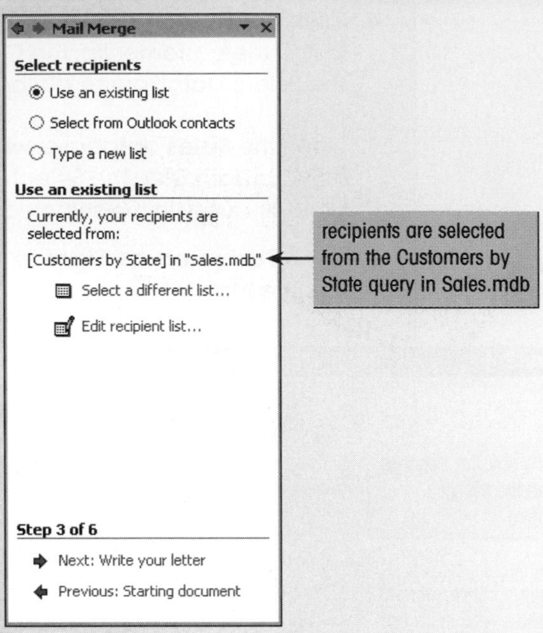

recipients are selected from the Customers by State query in Sales.mdb

TROUBLE? Compare the Mail Merge Task Pane on your screen with the one shown in Figure 3-5. If your screen does not show that your recipients are selected from Customers by State in Sales.mdb, click Select a different list in the Mail Merge Task Pane, and then repeat steps 5–7.

Merging Access data with a Word document creates a type of link different from those you've already created between Office programs. A standard link, such as from Excel to Word, establishes a two-way connection between the source and destination programs so that you can update information from either program and have it reflected in the other. However, to ensure database integrity and enforce database security, all updates to an Access database must occur from within Access. Therefore, you cannot create a two-way link between Access and another program. The mail merge between Word and Access creates a one-way link, which means that any changes you make to the Access data are reflected in the mail merge results in Word, but any changes you make to the merged data in Word are not reflected in the Access data.

Inserting the Merge Fields

As noted earlier, a merge field is a special instruction that tells Word where to insert the variable information from the data source into a form letter. For example, right now the letter doesn't have an inside address (the address for the recipient) at the top, as business letters usually do. Because this information will be different for each letter, you'll use merge fields to tell Word what information to pull from the Access query.

The Mail Merge Wizard includes items, such as an Address block and Greeting line, that contain merge fields commonly used for form letters. To complete Sue's form letter, you need to insert two items—the Address block and Greeting line—and then check the merge fields to make sure they correspond with the fields in the Customers by State query.

To insert the merge fields in the letter document:

1. With the Mail Merge Task Pane showing Step 3 of 6, click **Next: Write your letter**. The Mail Merge Task Pane displays Step 4 of the Mail Merge Wizard in which you write or edit your letter. Sue has already written the letter, but you need to add the recipient's name and address and a greeting line to personalize each copy of the letter. To do so, you will insert items into the letter that contain merge fields.

2. Position the insertion point just before the second paragraph marker below the date. This is where the customer's name and address will appear.

3. In the Mail Merge Task Pane, click **Address block**. The Insert Address Block dialog box opens, as shown in Figure 3-6.

Figure 3-6	INSERT ADDRESS BLOCK DIALOG BOX

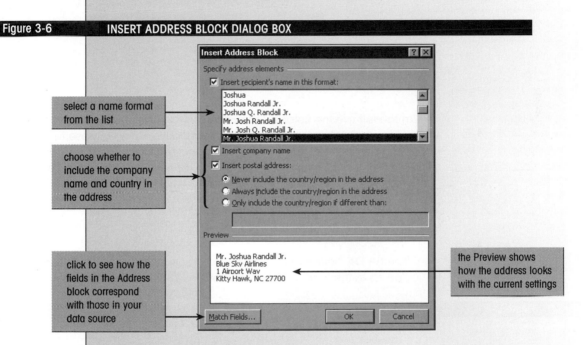

select a name format from the list

choose whether to include the company name and country in the address

click to see how the fields in the Address block correspond with those in your data source

the Preview shows how the address looks with the current settings

You use this dialog box to choose the format of the recipient's name and to specify whether to include the company name and country in the address. The content, tone, and style of the writing in Sue's customer letter is friendly and professional, so Sue suggests using a simple first and last name format.

4. Click **Joshua Randall Jr.** in the recipient's name list.

TROUBLE? If the recipient's name list is dimmed, first click the Insert recipient's name in this format check box to insert a check, and then repeat step 4.

After selecting address elements, check to see how the fields in the Address block correspond to the fields in the Customers by State query.

5. Click the **Match Fields** button. The Match Fields dialog box opens, as shown in Figure 3-7.

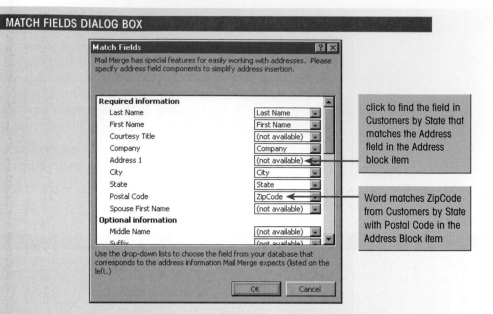

Figure 3-7   MATCH FIELDS DIALOG BOX

On the left are the fields Word expects in the Address block. On the right are the fields in the data source. Word automatically matches those fields that have the same or similar name. For example, it matches Postal Code with ZipCode. Note that Word has not found a match for the Address 1 field. You want Word to match the Address 1 field with the Street field in the Access query.

6. Click the **Address 1** list arrow and then click **Street**. The Street field from the Access query contains the same information—the street address—that Word uses in the Address 1 field. Click the **OK** button to close the Match Fields dialog box.

7. Click the **OK** button to close the Address Block dialog box. The Address block appears in the letter between double chevrons (« »), as in Figure 3-8.

Figure 3-8   ADDDRESS BLOCK INSERTED

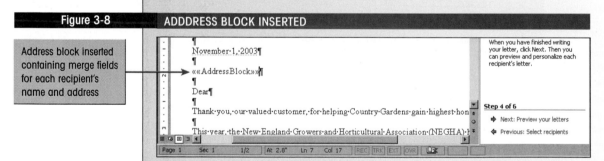

Address block inserted containing merge fields for each recipient's name and address

TROUBLE? If the Address block appears between curly braces and includes additional text, such as {ADDRESSBLOCK /f}, Word is displaying field codes. Click Tools on the menu bar, click Options, click the View tab in the Options dialog box, and then click the Field codes check box to remove the check mark.

Now you can insert the greeting line to personalize the salutation.

8. Position the insertion point between the "r" in the word "Dear" and the paragraph symbol, and then press the **spacebar**. You need a space between "Dear" and the name that follows.

9. In the Mail Merge Task Pane, click **Greeting line**. The Greeting Line dialog box opens, as shown in Figure 3-9.

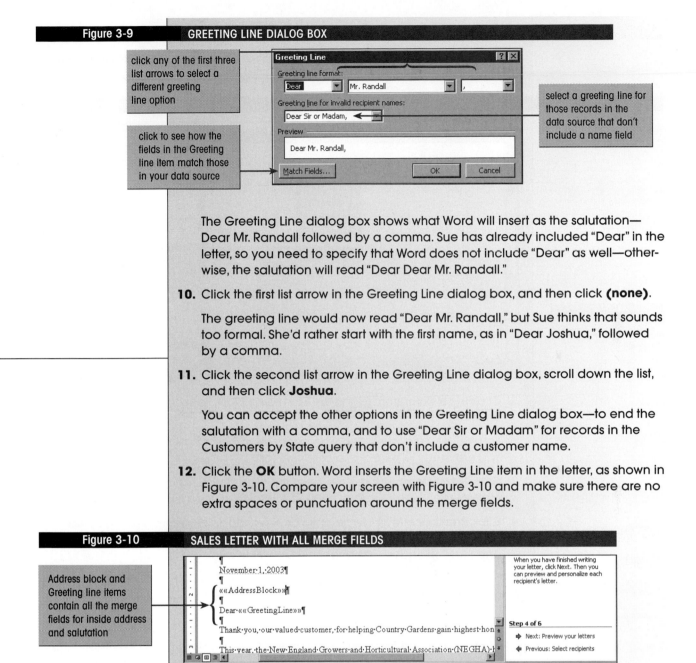

Figure 3-9   GREETING LINE DIALOG BOX

click any of the first three list arrows to select a different greeting line option

click to see how the fields in the Greeting line item match those in your data source

select a greeting line for those records in the data source that don't include a name field

The Greeting Line dialog box shows what Word will insert as the salutation—Dear Mr. Randall followed by a comma. Sue has already included "Dear" in the letter, so you need to specify that Word does not include "Dear" as well—otherwise, the salutation will read "Dear Dear Mr. Randall."

10. Click the first list arrow in the Greeting Line dialog box, and then click **(none)**.

The greeting line would now read "Dear Mr. Randall," but Sue thinks that sounds too formal. She'd rather start with the first name, as in "Dear Joshua," followed by a comma.

11. Click the second list arrow in the Greeting Line dialog box, scroll down the list, and then click **Joshua**.

You can accept the other options in the Greeting Line dialog box—to end the salutation with a comma, and to use "Dear Sir or Madam" for records in the Customers by State query that don't include a customer name.

12. Click the **OK** button. Word inserts the Greeting Line item in the letter, as shown in Figure 3-10. Compare your screen with Figure 3-10 and make sure there are no extra spaces or punctuation around the merge fields.

Figure 3-10   SALES LETTER WITH ALL MERGE FIELDS

Address block and Greeting line items contain all the merge fields for inside address and salutation

Performing the Mail Merge

With the starting document and merge fields in place, you're ready to perform the mail merge. You can choose to merge the data to a new Word document or directly to the printer. In this case, Sue wants the merge results placed in a new document so that she can check the merged form letters before printing them. The final result will be a Word document with many pages, made of one letter for each of the 21 customers in New Hampshire. Each letter will be identical, except for the merge fields, which will have the individual names and addresses.

Before you merge to a new document, preview the letters and make sure they are complete and contain all the information you want.

To complete the mail merge:

1. With the Mail Merge Task Pane showing Step 4 of 6, click **Next: Preview your letters**. See Figure 3-11.

Figure 3-11	PREVIEW OF THE PERSONALIZED FORM LETTER

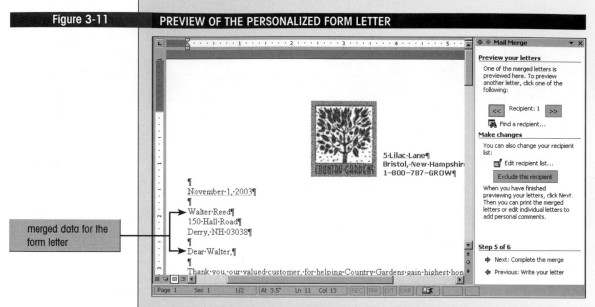

merged data for the form letter

2. Click the **Next** button >> in the Mail Merge Task Pane to preview the next recipient.

   You show the preview to Sue, who approves of the format of the form letter. You are ready to print a copy of the letter.

3. Click **Next: Complete the merge** in the Mail Merge Task Pane. Step 6 of the Mail Merge Wizard displays in the Task Pane.

4. Click **Print** in the Mail Merge Task Pane. A dialog box opens where you can specify the records you want to print. Make sure you are connected to a printer and that it is loaded with paper and ready to print.

5. Click the **Current record** option button, and then click the **OK** button. Word prints one copy of the form letter.

6. Save the Main Letter document.

   Now you can create a new document containing all of the form letters.

7. In the Mail Merge Task Pane, click **Edit individual letters**. The Merge to New Document dialog box opens.

8. Click the **All** option button, if necessary, and then click the **OK** button. Word opens a single new document that contains all the individual letters. This merged document contains the form letter for each of the 21 recipients; each letter is separated from the next by a section break. These 21 recipients are the New Hampshire customers, as determined by your selection in the Mail Merge Recipients dialog box.

9. Click the **Next Page** and **Previous Page** buttons in the vertical scroll bar to page through the merged document and see the merged addresses and salutations. Word replaced each merge field with the appropriate Access data, as shown in Figure 3-12.

Figure 3-12	COMPLETED MERGE LETTER

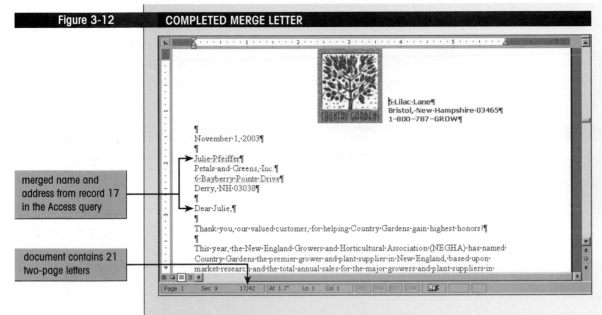

merged name and address from record 17 in the Access query

document contains 21 two-page letters

Notice that the merged document contains 42 pages. Each letter is two pages long, and there are 21 letters in all.

10. Click **File** on the menu bar, and then click **Save As**. Save the document as **Merged Letters** in the Tutorial folder in the Tutorial.03 folder on your Data Disk, and then close the document. You return to the starting document.

11. Save and close the Main Letter document.

Sue plans to review the printed letter with her assistants to make sure everyone approves it before she prints and mails the form letters. While she does that, Sue asks you to prepare her presentation for the Eastern Regional Growers Conference to be held next month. In her presentation, Sue wants to promote her company's new products and new mail-order catalog, as well as highlight the NEGHA recognition as the area's top grower and greens supplier.

Sue has already created the PowerPoint presentation file, selected a suitable template for the presentation, and created the first slide, which shows the Country Gardens logo and slogan. One of her assistants, Judy Pon, created a Word document in which she entered the text for the remaining slides based on notes she took during a meeting with Sue. To complete the presentation, you first need to create a Word outline from Judy's document.

Creating a Word Outline

You can create an outline in Word by typing text directly in Outline view in a new document. When you do, Word assigns heading styles to the text to format it as an outline. You can also format the text in an existing document by displaying it in Outline view and assigning each paragraph an appropriate heading style. The document created by Sue's assistant is named Outline and is stored on your Data Disk. You'll format this document as an outline and then create slides 2 through 7 in Sue's PowerPoint presentation from the outline.

To open the document and display it in Outline view:

1. Open the **Outline** document located in the Tutorial folder in the Tutorial.03 folder on your Data Disk.

2. Save the document as **Outline for Slides** in the same folder.

To format the document's text as an outline, you first need to switch to Outline view.

3. Click the **Outline View** button located to the left of the horizontal scroll bar. The document switches to Outline view, and the Outlining toolbar is displayed. See Figure 3-13.

Figure 3-13	DOCUMENT DISPLAYED IN OUTLINE VIEW

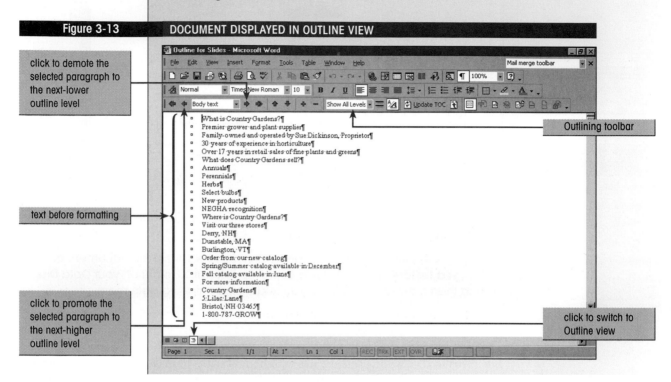

click to demote the selected paragraph to the next-lower outline level

Outlining toolbar

text before formatting

click to promote the selected paragraph to the next-higher outline level

click to switch to Outline view

To format text as an outline, you use the Promote and Demote buttons on the Outlining toolbar. The **Promote** button moves the selected paragraph to the next-higher outline level. The **Demote** button moves the selected paragraph to the next-lower outline level. (Word refers to any text marked by a nonprinting, end-of-paragraph mark as a paragraph, even if the text consists of only one or two words.)

The easiest way to format the text for Sue's outline is to select all of it and promote it to the first outline level. Then you can demote text as necessary. When you create PowerPoint slides from an outline, paragraphs at the first outline level become slide titles; paragraphs at the second outline level become first-level slide text; paragraphs at the third outline level become second-level slide text, and so on. This is why using an outline is the most efficient way to integrate a Word document into a PowerPoint presentation.

To format the text as a Word outline:

1. Click **Edit** on the menu bar, and then click **Select All**.

2. Click the **Promote** button on the Outlining toolbar. Word changes each paragraph to a first-level heading.

3. Click anywhere in the document to deselect the text. See Figure 3-14.

Figure 3-14 · PARAGRAPHS AFTER BEING PROMOTED

indicates heading style of selected paragraph

indicates outline level

all paragraphs are outline Level 1

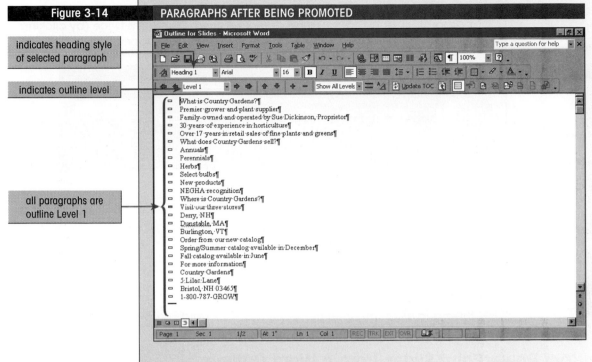

Now you need to demote the necessary paragraphs to the next level.

4. Position the insertion point anywhere in the second paragraph (beginning with the word "Premier").

5. Click the **Demote** button ⬜ on the Outlining toolbar. The paragraph moves to the next-lower outline level.

Notice that the first paragraph now includes a plus sign to its left. This indicates that the first paragraph has subitems (paragraphs at a lower level) associated with it.

6. Repeat Step 5 to format the next three paragraphs as subitems of the first paragraph.

7. Refer to Figure 3-15 to format the next seven paragraphs as indicated.

Figure 3-15 · FIRST PART OF FORMATTED OUTLINE

Level 2 paragraphs

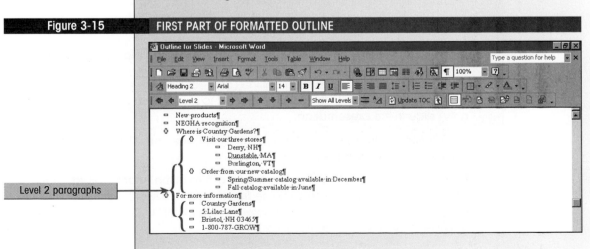

8. Scroll the document, and then refer to Figure 3-16 to format the remaining paragraphs. Note that you must demote some paragraphs twice (by clicking the Demote button two times) to move them to the appropriate level.

| Figure 3-16 | REMAINDER OF FORMATTED OUTLINE |

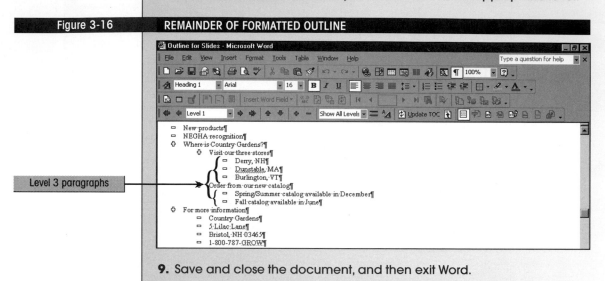

Level 3 paragraphs

9. Save and close the document, and then exit Word.

Creating PowerPoint Slides from a Word Outline

When you create slides from a Word outline, PowerPoint uses the heading styles in the Word document to determine how to format the text. For example, each paragraph formatted with the Heading 1 style becomes the title of a new slide, each Heading 2 becomes the first level of text on a slide, and so on. You can use an outline to create new slides in an existing presentation or to create an entirely new PowerPoint presentation. Now you can open Sue's PowerPoint presentation and create new slides from the outline you created.

To create new PowerPoint slides from the Word outline:

1. Start PowerPoint, and then open the **Growers** presentation located in the Tutorial folder in the Tutorial.03 folder on your Data Disk. The presentation opens and displays its first and only slide, which contains the Country Gardens logo and slogan.

2. Save the presentation as **Growers Conference** in the same folder.

TROUBLE? If the Task Pane opens, click its Close button to close the Task Pane.

When you create slides from an outline (or other file), PowerPoint inserts them after the current slide. In this case, you want to insert them after the first (and only) slide in the presentation.

3. Click **Insert** on the menu bar, and then click **Slides from Outline**. The Insert Outline dialog box opens.

4. Make sure the dialog box displays the list of files in the Tutorial folder, click **Outline for Slides**, and then click the **Insert** button. PowerPoint inserts and formats the text of the Word outline to create slides 2 through 7 and displays the first new slide (slide 2). See Figure 3-17.

Figure 3-17 | **FIRST SLIDE INSERTED FROM OUTLINE**

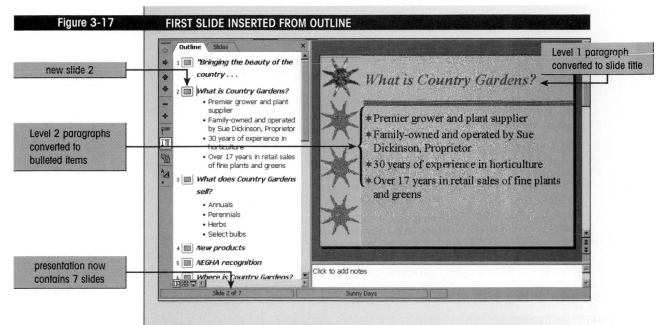

TROUBLE? If you see a message box that you must first install a converter before inserting an outline, insert your Office XP CD and then click Yes, or ask your instructor or technical support person for help.

5. Click the **Previous Slide** and **Next Slide** buttons in the slide pane scroll bar to view each slide.

   Notice that each Level 1 paragraph in the Word outline became a slide title, each Level 2 paragraph became a bulleted item, and each Level 3 paragraph became a subitem in a bulleted list. Also, note that PowerPoint automatically assigned the Bulleted List layout to each slide.

6. Save the presentation.

With the text for all the slides in place, you can now complete the presentation by adding the new products table (created in Access) and the NEGHA pie chart (created in Excel).

Copying and Pasting an Access Query in a PowerPoint Presentation

Sue wants the "New products" slide (slide 4) to include the list of Country Gardens' 10 new products being offered this year. This information is stored as an Access query in the Sales database. To include this information, you can copy and paste the Access query into the PowerPoint presentation.

Sue knows that the list of Country Gardens' 10 new products will not change before the conference, so she asks you to copy and paste the query on slide 4.

To prepare to copy and paste the query:

1. Move to slide **4** in the presentation.

   This slide will include only the title "New products" and the pasted Access query data. Therefore, the current layout of the slide, Bulleted List, is inappropriate. You need to change the layout of the slide before you copy and paste the query.

2. Click **Format** on the menu bar, and then click **Slide Layout**. The Slide Layout Task Pane opens.

3. Click the **Title Only** layout (column 2, row 1 in the Text Layouts section). PowerPoint applies the layout to the slide.

4. Close the Slide Layout Task Pane.

Now you can copy and paste the Access query on the slide.

To copy and paste the New Products query on slide 4:

1. Start Access and open the **Sales** database located in the Tutorial folder in the Tutorial.03 folder on your Data Disk.

2. Click **Queries** in the Database window, if necessary, to display the list of queries in the database, and then double-click **New Products**. Access displays the results of the query in Datasheet view. See Figure 3-18.

Figure 3-18	NEW PRODUCTS QUERY RESULTS

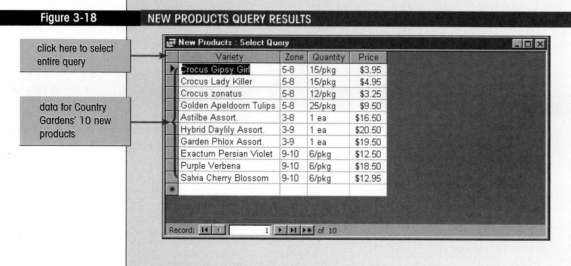

click here to select entire query

data for Country Gardens' 10 new products

Sue wants all the data from the query to appear on the slide.

3. Click the selector to the left of the column headings (refer to Figure 3-18). Access selects the entire query.

4. Click the **Copy** button 📋 on the Query Datasheet toolbar to copy the query results to the Clipboard.

5. Close the query and the database, and then exit Access. You return to the presentation.

Now you can paste the query on slide 4.

6. Click the **Paste** button 📋 on the PowerPoint Standard toolbar. PowerPoint inserts the query results as a table on the slide. You need to reposition it on the slide.

7. Click the table to select it. Make sure the table has a dotted outline, as in Figure 3-19. The dotted outline indicates you can make changes to the entire table. A dashed outline indicates you can select parts of the table to change.

Figure 3-19   **ACCESS TABLE SELECTED ON POWERPOINT SLIDE**

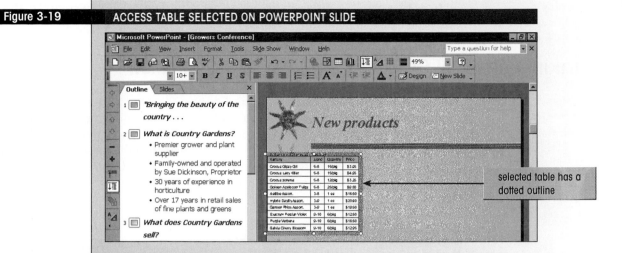

selected table has a dotted outline

TROUBLE? If your table does not have a dotted outline as in Figure 3-19, press and hold the Shift key and then click the table to select it.

8. Use the mouse pointer ✛ to drag the table so that it is left aligned and below the decorative line.

   TROUBLE? If the Tables and Borders toolbar appears, drag it out of the way or close it. If you see the query title "New Products" on the slide, click New Products until it is surrounded with a dotted outline, and then press the Delete key.

   So that the table is easier to read, you need to enlarge the table and then the text in the table.

9. Click the table to select it, if necessary. Drag the lower-right sizing handle to enlarge the table to fill the remaining space in the slide.

10. Right-click the selected table, click **Font** on the shortcut menu, click **18** in the Size list box, and then click the **OK** button. Click an empty area on the slide to deselect the table. See Figure 3-20.

Figure 3-20   **FINAL QUERY TABLE IN SLIDE**

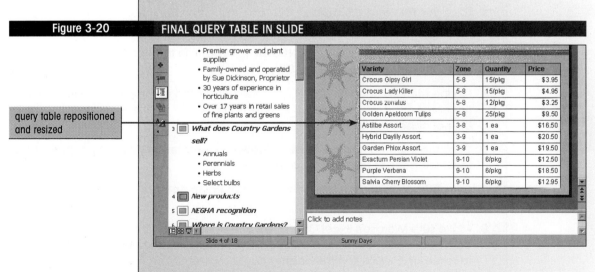

query table repositioned and resized

11. Save the presentation.

Now that you have inserted the Access query in slide 4, you can complete the slide presentation by adding other information to slide 5.

Linking an Excel Chart to a PowerPoint Presentation

Sue wants the Excel pie chart showing Country Gardens as the area's top grower to be included on the "NEGHA recognition" slide (slide 5). Recall that the chart shows sales data for the top growers. Sue has been reviewing the fourth quarter sales, and she thinks that the sales figures for the year might come in even higher than the figures the NEGHA used to create the pie chart. Because Sue might need to revise the Country Gardens data series in the pie chart to reflect the new sales figures, she asks you to link the chart to the presentation. This way the new figures will be automatically reflected in her presentation.

REFERENCE WINDOW   **RW**

Linking Excel Data to a PowerPoint Presentation
- In Excel, select the information you want to insert into a PowerPoint presentation, and then click the Copy button on the Standard toolbar.
- In PowerPoint, click where you want to insert the Excel data, click Edit on the menu bar, and then click Paste Special.
- In the Paste Special dialog box, click Microsoft Excel Chart Object, if necessary, click the Paste link option button, and then click the OK button.

To link the Excel pie chart to the presentation:

1. Move to slide **5** in the presentation. First you need to change the slide layout to one appropriate for displaying the slide title and the linked pie chart.

2. Click **View** on the menu bar, and then click **Task Pane**. The Slide Layout Task Pane opens.

3. Click the **Title and Content** layout (column 1, row 2 in the Content Layouts section), and then close the Slide Layout Task Pane.

4. Start Excel and then open the **NEGHA** workbook in the Tutorial folder in the Tutorial.03 folder on your Data Disk.

5. On the Market Data worksheet, click the chart area of the pie chart to select the entire chart, and then click the **Copy** button on the Standard toolbar. Do not close the NEGHA workbook.

6. Click the **Microsoft PowerPoint—(Growers Conference)** button on the taskbar to switch back to the presentation.

7. Click **Edit** on the menu bar, and then click **Paste Special**. The Paste Special dialog box opens.

8. Make sure Microsoft Excel Chart Object is selected, click the **Paste link** option button, and then click the **OK** button. The chart is linked to the slide. You need to resize and reposition the chart.

9. Use the corner sizing handles and the pointer to resize and reposition the chart so that it looks like the one shown in Figure 3-21. When you're finished, click an empty area on the slide to deselect the chart.

Figure 3-21   **LINKED CHART AFTER REPOSITIONING AND RESIZING**

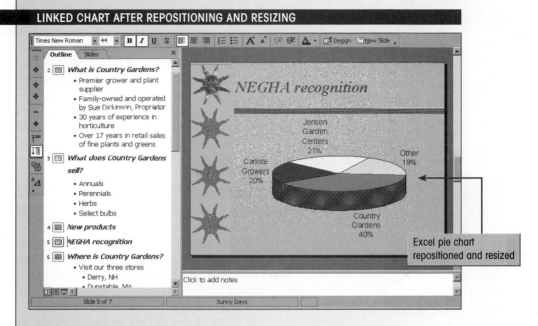

10. Save and close the presentation, and close all open programs.

Sue is pleased with the finished letter and presentation, and she is confident that both will contribute to the successful promotion of Country Gardens. The integration features of Office make it easy for Sue to work with information created in different programs to produce exactly the results she wants.

QUICK CHECK

1. Describe how a mail merge works.
2. What is a merge field?
3. Why is a query a good data source for a mail merge?
4. Explain why you store the form letter with the merge fields in one document and the personalized form letter with individual names and addresses in another document.
5. How do you change heading levels in Outline view in Word?
6. What does the plus sign to the left of a paragraph in Outline view in Word indicate?
7. Describe the slide or slides that PowerPoint would create from a Word outline that has one Level 1 paragraph and three Level 2 paragraphs.

REVIEW ASSIGNMENTS

Now that the promotional letter is completed, Sue is ready to send it to her customers. To do so, she wants to print the customers' names and addresses on mailing labels that can be placed on the envelopes. Also, Sue wants to prepare a brief presentation to give to her employees at the next staff meeting. The presentation will be about the upcoming Eastern Regional Growers Conference.

1. Start Word as usual, and make sure your Data Disk is in the appropriate disk drive.

Explore ▶ 2. Start the Mail Merge Wizard, and select labels as your starting document.

Explore ▶ 3. On Step 2 of the Mail Merge Wizard, open the Label Options dialog box to set the label options. Select Avery standard labels. Scroll down and choose product number 5160 - Address. Accept all other defaults in this dialog box.

4. In Step 3 of the Wizard, select recipients from an existing list in the Customers by State query in the **Sales** database, which is stored in the Review folder in the Tutorial.03 folder on your Data Disk.

5. In the Mail Merge Recipients dialog box, select only those customers in New Hampshire.

6. In Step 4 of the Wizard, lay out the first label by inserting the Address block item. Accept the defaults in the Insert Address Block dialog box. Match the Last Name, First Name, Company, City, and State fields to those with the same names. Match Address 1 to Street and Postal Code to Zip Code.

Explore ▶ 7. After you insert the Address block in the first label, click the Update all labels button to copy the layout of the first label to the other labels on the page.

8. Preview the labels. Replace the name and address in the first label with your own.

9. Complete the merge by printing one copy of the label. Then click Edit individual labels, and merge all of them to a new document. Save the document containing the merged labels as **Merged labels** in the Review folder on your Data Disk, and then close the document.

10. Save the main document (the one with the merge fields) as **Main Labels** in the Review folder on your Data Disk, and then close the document.

11. Open the **Topics** document in the Review folder on your Data Disk, and save it as **Topics Outline**.

12. Format the Topics Outline document as an outline. Format the following paragraphs as Level 1 headings: About the Conference, Company Booth, New Products, Estimated Breakdown of Participants, Assignments.

13. Format all other paragraphs as Level 2 headings, except the following four paragraphs, which should be formatted as Level 3 headings: Make presentation, Attend the owners' meeting, Manage the booth, Lead breakout group discussion.

Explore ▶ 14. Point to the buttons on the Outlining toolbar, and use the ScreenTips to find the Move Up and Move Down buttons. Use the What's This? command on the Help menu to learn about the Move Up and Move Down buttons on the Outlining toolbar. Then reposition the paragraph "Estimated Breakdown of Participants" as the third Level 1 paragraph in the outline.

15. Save and close the Topics Outline document.

16. Start PowerPoint and create a new presentation using the Maple design template. Choose the Title Slide layout for the first slide.

17. On the first slide, type the title "Staff Meeting" and the subtitle "Preparing for the Eastern Regional Growers Conference."

18. Create new slides from the Topics Outline document. The new slides should be inserted after the first slide.

Explore ▶ 19. Add a footer to the presentation that displays your name, the date, and the slide numbers. (*Hint*: Click View on the menu bar, click Header and Footer, and then make the appropriate changes in the Header and Footer dialog box.)

20. On slide 2, use the Tab key to align the words "Durham, NH" below the words "The New England Center," and then delete the comma after the word "Center."

21. Save the presentation as **Staff Meeting** in the Review folder on your Data Disk.

22. Move to slide 4 and complete the following:

    a. Change the layout of the slide to Content.

    b. Open the **Groups** workbook in the Review folder on your Data Disk, and then link the pie chart in the workbook to slide 4.

    c. Resize and reposition the chart so that it is centered on the slide.

23. Move to slide 5 and complete the following:
    a. Change the layout of the slide to Title Only.
    b. Open the Sales database in the Review folder on your Data Disk, and then copy and paste the data in the New Products query to slide 5.
    c. Change the text of the data to 18 point.
    d. Resize and reposition the data so that it is centered on the slide.
24. Save the presentation, and then print it using the Handouts (6 slides per page) option.
25. Exit all open programs.

CASE PROBLEMS

Case 1. Cable-Ease Company Jose Rivera, the sales supervisor for the Cable-Ease Company, has printed several follow-up letters to customers, providing written quotations. Now he needs to send the letters to the customers. You'll use the mail-merge feature to create the envelopes for the mailing.

1. Start Word as usual, and make sure your Data Disk is in the appropriate drive.

Explore 2. Start the Mail Merge Wizard, and select Envelopes as the type of document you want to create.

Explore 3. Change the document layout by selecting envelope options and then accepting the default settings in the Envelope Options dialog box.

4. Select recipients for the envelopes by using the Customers table in the **Leases** database, which is stored in the Tutorial.03 Cases folder on your Data Disk.

Explore 5. In the Mail Merge Recipients dialog box, make sure the recipients are sorted by customer number.

6. Arrange your envelopes by typing your name and address as the return address and inserting the Address block in the middle of the envelope. Set the following options in the Address Block dialog box:
    a. Accept all the default settings in the Insert Address Block dialog box.
    b. Match the following fields:

Last Name	CustomerName
First Name	(not available)
Courtesy Title	(not available)
Company	Company
Address 1	Street
City	City
State	State
Postal Code	ZipCode

7. Preview the envelopes. (You might see a space before the customer name, which you can ignore.)

8. Complete the merge by merging the records to a new document. Save the document as **Merged Envelopes** in the Tutorial.03 Cases folder on your Data Disk.

9. Save the main document as **Main Envelopes** in the Cases folder in the Tutorial.03 folder on your Data Disk.

10. Return to the preview of the envelopes, Step 5 of 6 in the Mail Merge Wizard, and view the data for recipient 19, Ms. Nicole Vitale.

Explore 11. Position the insertion point to the left of the word "Boulevard" in the address on the envelope, delete the word "Boulevard," and then type "Street." Switch to Access and open the Customers table in the Leases database. View the data for record 19. Was the change you made in Word reflected in the Access table? Why, or why not? Switch back to Word, and then save and close the **Main Envelopes** document.

Explore   12. In Access, change the entry in the Street field for record 20 to "25 Wilson Road." Close the Customers table. Switch to Word and then open the **Main Envelopes** document. Open the Mail Merge toolbar, and then view the data for record 20 from the main document. Was the change you made in Access reflected in the Word document? Why, or why not?

Explore   13. Print the envelope for recipient 19 (Nicole Vitale) on regular paper. Exit Word. Do not save changes to the Main Envelopes document.

Case 2. Admissions at San Francisco University Darren Parnell has been asked by his supervisor, Fabia Hazan, the head of the Admissions office, to prepare a presentation to give to incoming freshmen and their parents during orientation. You'll prepare the presentation for Darren by completing the following:

1. Create an outline document in Word containing the topics to present during orientation. Review Case Problem 2 in the first integration tutorial for ideas on presentation topics. Include enough topics for five or six presentation slides. Be sure to include several first-level headings and second-level headings in the outline. Save the document as **Orientation Outline** in the Cases folder in the Tutorial.03 folder on your Data Disk. Close the document and exit Word.

2. Create a PowerPoint presentation using a template of your choice. Create a title slide for the presentation using text of your choice. Save the presentation as **Slides for Orientation** in the Cases folder in the Tutorial.03 folder on your Data Disk.

Explore   3. Create a footer on the presentation that includes your name, the date, and the slide numbers. (*Hint*: Click View on the menu bar, click Header and Footer, and then make the appropriate changes in the Header and Footer dialog box.)

4. Create new slides from the Orientation Outline document you created in Step 1.

5. In Case Problem 2 in the first integration tutorial, you created a line chart in Excel (in a workbook named **Estimated Expenses**). Link this chart to an appropriate slide in your presentation. Or, create a new line chart in Excel, and link this chart to an appropriate slide. Move and resize the chart so that it is easy to read.

Explore   6. Insert an appropriate picture from the Insert Clip Art Task Pane on one or more individual slides or on the slide master so that the picture appears on each slide in the presentation. If necessary, use the Ask a Question box or Office Assistant to find out how to insert a picture from the Clip Art Task Pane on a slide.

7. Save the presentation, and then run the slide show.

Explore   8. Print the presentation slides using the Handouts (6 slides per page) option.

9. Close any open programs.

Quick | Check answers

1. A mail merge combines a main or starting document that contains standard text and merge fields that indicate where to print variable information with a data source that contains the variable information.

2. special instructions that tell Word where to print the variable information

3. so that the merge will use your latest query instructions to retrieve the data

4. You use the form letter with the merge fields document to print other letters with a different data source or when the list of names and addresses in the data source changes. You use the personalized form letter to print and send to each recipient.

5. Click the Promote or Demote button on the Outlining toolbar.

6. that the paragraph has subitems (paragraphs at a lower level) associated with it

7. It becomes a slide with a title and three bullets of text.

moving within document
  dragging and dropping,
    WD 2.12–2.14
  in general, WD 2.12
nonprinting characters,
  WD 1.12–1.13
outline text, promoting, demoting,
  moving, PPT 1.22–1.25
previewing, WD 2.36–2.37
scrolling, WD 1.21–1.23
slide
  body text, PPT 1.18
  main text, PPT 1.18
  title text, PPT 1.18
text and content layout, PPT 1.21
text layout, PPT 1.21
typeface toggle buttons, WD 2.31
underlining, WD 2.33
word wrap, WD 1.19–1.21,
  WD 4.10–4.11
  around graphic, WD 4.22
Zoom box, AC 3.34
text, WIN 2000 2.04–07
blocks, WIN 2000 2.06
error correction, WIN 2000 2.04
inserting characters,
  WIN 2000 2.07
insertion point versus pointer,
  WIN 2000 2.05–06
selecting, WIN 2000 2.06
typing, WIN 2000 2.04–05
word wrap, WIN 2000 2.04
text box
adding, PPT 2.24–2.25
border, EX 4.27
resizing, PPT 2.08–2.09
rotating and moving, PPT 2.29–2.30
text boxes, WIN 2000 1.24
**Thumbnails view, WIN 2000 2.18,
  WIN 2000 2.19**
tick marks, chart, EX 4.09, EX 4.32
title
centering, EX 3.11
for chart, EX 4.09
color and pattern for, 3.18–3.20
Slide Master slide, PPT 2.04
Title Master slide, PPT 2.04
  modifying, PPT 2.05–2.07
title text, PPT 1.18
wrapping within cell, EX 3.13
**title bar, WIN 2000 1.16,
  WIN 2000 1.17**
TODAY function, EX 2.28
toggle button
text, WD 2.31
toolbar, BEB 21
toolbar. *See also* Drawing toolbar;
  Formatting toolbar
hiding and showing, BEB 20–21
Office, OFF 13–16
  personalized, OFF 14–15
toggling, BEB 21
understanding, PPT 1.07
Word, WD 1.09–1.10

**toolbars, WIN 2000 1.14,
  WIN 2000 1.16, WIN 2000 1.17,
  WIN 2000 1.22–23.** *See also*
  specific toolbars
controlling display,
  WIN 2000 2.17–18
displaying, WIN 2000 2.17–18
displaying button functions,
  WIN 2000 1.22
selecting buttons, WIN 2000 1.23
**top–level directories,
  WIN 2000 2.21**
touch pads, WIN 2000 1.06
trackballs, WIN 2000 1.06
transfer protocol, BEB 11
**triangular arrow, menus,
  WIN 2000 1.21**
typeface, EX 3.09
typing text, WIN 2000 2.04–05
typographic characters, WD 4.02
**typographic symbols, inserting in
  text, WD 4.25–4.27**

U

underlining text. *See also* **text**
  procedure, WD 2.33
Undo button. *See also* **error
  correction**
  using, WD 2.11–2.12
**Undo command, multiple,
  AC 3.30–3.31**
**Uniform Resource Locator (URL),
  POWERPOINT WEB 1,
  WD 4.04.** *See also* **address**
  discussed, BEB 10–11
  entering in Address bar, BEB 21–23
**Up button, Standard toolbar,
  WIN 2000 2.23**
URL. *See* **Uniform Resource
  Locator**

V

values
category values, EX 4.06
definition, EX 1.21
entering into worksheet,
  EX 1.21–1.22
filling in, in general, EX 2.16
X values, EX 4.06
vertical alignment. *See also*
  document
  changing, WD 3.09–3.10
viewing. *See* **displaying**

W

Web. *See* **World Wide Web**
Web browser, EXCEL WEB 1
client/server structure of Web,
  BEB 4
favorites, BEB 15
in general, BEB 4, BEB 12,
  WD 4.04, EXCEL WEB 1

Home button, BEB 14
Internet Service Provider, BEB 12
menu bar, BEB 14
scroll bar, BEB 13
status bar, BEB 13–14
title bar, BEB 13
History list, BEB 15–16
hypertext, links, hypermedia,
  BEB 5–7
viewing presentation in,
  POWERPOINT WEB 4–5
viewing Web page in, ACCESS
  WEB 7–8
Web client, BEB 4
Web design. *See also* **desktop
  publishing**
vs. desktop publishing, WD 4.04
Web directory, BEB 15
**Web page, BEB 6, WORD WEB 1,
  WD 4.04.** *See also* **document**
adding hyperlink to, POWER-
  POINT WEB 5–6
address (URL), WD 4.04, WORD
  WEB 1
converting Word document to,
  WORD WEB 3–5
copying, BEB 36–39
copyright law and, BEB 16–17
creating, WEB 2–3
opening, in Internet Explorer,
  ACCESS WEB 7–8
printing, BEB 16, BEB 32–33
publishing presentation as, POW-
  ERPOINT WEB 2–4
refreshing, BEB 15, BEB 30
reloading, BEB 15
returning to, BEB 16, BEB 31–32
saving, BEB 16
  in Internet Explorer, BEB 35–40
  to disk, BEB 39–40
spreadsheet component, EXCEL
  WEB 7
start page, BEB 8, BEB 31–32
stopping page transfer, BEB 15
viewing in Web browser, WORD
  WEB 7–8
Web site and, BEB 7–8
**Web page editor, POWERPOINT
  WEB 2**
Web server, BEB 4, WORD WEB 1
Web site, WEB 1. *See also*
  non–interactive Web site
interactive, publishing, EXCEL
  WEB 6–8
Web page and, BEB 7–8
Web style, WIN 2000 2.21
What's This? command, OFF 21
Windows
shutting down, WIN 2000 1.15–16
starting, WIN 2000 1.04
windows. *See also* **specific windows**
controls, WIN 2000 1.16–17
maximizing, WIN 2000 1.18,
  WIN 2000 1.19

X

Z

TASK	PAGE #	RECOMMENDED METHOD
Absolute reference, change to relative	EX 2.14	Edit the formula, deleting the $ before the column and row references; or press F4 to switch between absolute, relative, and mixed references
Access query, copy and paste into PowerPoint	INT 3.18	Display the query results, click the selector to the left of the column headings to select paste the entire query, click ▣ , switch to the PowerPoint PowerPoint slide, click ▣
Access, exit	AC 1.13	Click ✕ on the program window
Access, start	AC 1.07	Click Start, point to Programs, click Microsoft Access
Action, redo	WD 2.11	Click ↶ or list arrow
Action, undo	WD 2.11	Click ↶ or list arrow
Actions, redo several	EX 1.33	Click the list arrow for ↶ ▾ , select the action(s) to redo
Actions, undo several	EX 1.32	Click the list arrow for ↶ ▾ , select the action(s) to undo
Aggregate functions, use in a query	AC 3.38	Display the query in Design view, click Σ
Auto Fill, copy formulas	EX 2.16	See Reference Window: Copying Formulas Using Auto Fill
Auto Fill, create series	EX 2.18	Select the range, drag the fill handle down, release mouse button, click ▣ , click the option button to complete series
AutoContent Wizard, run	PPT 1.13	Click File, click New, click From AutoContent Wizard on New Presentation Task Pane, follow instructions
AutoCorrect, use	WD 1.25	Click ▧ ▾ , click correct spelling
AutoFormat, apply	EX 3.31	Select the range, click Format, click AutoFormat, select an AutoFormat design, click OK
AutoFormat, change	AC 4.05	See Reference Window: Changing a Form's AutoFormat
AutoShape, add text to	EX 4.38	See Reference Window: Inserting Text into an AutoShape
AutoShape, insert, reshape, resize and rotate	EX 4.37	See Reference Window: Inserting an AutoShape
AutoSum, apply	EX 2.25	Click the cell in which you want the final value to appear, click the list arrow for Σ ▾ , select the AutoSum function to apply
Background color, apply	EX 3.18	Select the range, click the list arrow for ▧ ▾ , select a color square in the color palette
Background pattern, apply	EX 3.18	Open the Format Cells dialog box, click the Patterns tab, click the Pattern list arrow, click a pattern in the pattern gallery, click OK
Boldface, add to text	WD 2.32	Select text, click B
Border, change in table	WD 3.28	See Reference Window: Altering Table Borders
Border, create	EX 3.15	Click the list arrow for ▦ ▾ , select a border in the border gallery
Border, draw	EX 3.16	Click the list arrow for ▦ ▾ , click ▨ , draw the border using the Pencil tool
Border, draw around page	WD 4.28	Click Format, click Borders and Shading, click Page Border tab, click Box, click apply to Whole Document
Border of table, draw	PPT 2.21	Click ✎ set desired border style and border width on Tables and Borders toolbar, drag ✎ along border
Bullets, add to paragraphs	WD 2.28	Select paragraphs, click ▤
Calculated field, add to a query	AC 3.34	See Reference Window: Using Expression Builder
Cell, clear contents of	EX 1.27	Click Edit, click Clear; or press Delete
Cell, edit	EX 1.31	See Reference Window: Editing a Cell
Cells, delete from worksheet	EX 1.27	Select the cell or range, click Edit, click Delete, select a delete option, click OK; or select the cell or range, click-right the selection, click Delete, select a delete option, click OK
Cells, insert into worksheet	EX 1.26	See Reference Window: Inserting New Cells into a Worksheet

TASK	PAGE #	RECOMMENDED METHOD
Cells, merge	EX 3.21	Select the adjacent cells, open the Format Cells dialog box, click the Alignment tab, select the Merge check box, click OK
Cells, merge and center	EX 3.21	Select the adjacent cells, click ▦▾
Character, insert	WIN 2000 2.07	Click where you want to insert the text, type the character
Chart, add data label	EX 4.23	Select a data marker(s) or data series, click Chart, click Chart Options, click the Data Labels tab, select the data label type, click OK
Chart, add gridline	EX 4.23	Select the chart, click Chart, click Chart Options, click the Gridlines tab, click the check box for gridline option you want to select, click OK
Chart, add, remove, revise data series	EX 4.20	See Reference Window: Editing a Chart's Data Source
Chart axis title, add or edit	EX 4.23	Select the chart, click Chart, click Chart Options, click the Titles tab, click the Category (X) axis text box and type the text for the title, click the Values (Y) axis text box and type the text for the title, click OK
Chart, change 3-D elevation	EX 4.35	Select a 3-D chart, click Chart, click 3-D View, enter the elevation value or click the Elevation Up or Elevation Down button, click OK
Chart, change location	EX 4.22	Select the chart, click Chart, click Location, specify the new location, click OK
Chart, change scale	EX 4.32	Double-click a value on the y-axis, click the Scale tab, enter the minimum and maximum values for the scale, click OK
Chart, change to 3-D	EX 4.33	Select the chart, click Chart, click Chart Type, select a 3-D sub-type, click OK
Chart, create with Chart Wizard	EX 4.04	See Reference Window: Creating a Chart with the Chart Wizard
Chart data markers, change fill color	EX 4.28	Double-click the data marker, click the Patterns tab, click Fill Effects, click the Gradient tab, select the color and related color options, click OK
Chart, format data marker	EX 4.28	Double-click the data marker, select the formatting options using the tabs in the Format Data Series dialog box
Chart, move	EX 4.13	Select the chart, move the pointer over the chart area, drag the chart to its new location, release the mouse button
Chart, resize	EX 4.13	Select the chart, move the pointer over a selection handle, drag the handle to resize the chart, release the mouse button
Chart, select	EX 4.12	Move pointer over a blank area of the chart, and then click
Chart text, format	EX 4.24	Select the chart label, click a button on the Formatting toolbar; or double-click the chart label, select the formatting options using the tabs in the Format Data Labels dialog box
Chart text, insert new unattached	EX 4.25	See Reference Window: Inserting Unattached Text into a Chart
Chart title, add or edit	EX 4.26	Select the chart, click Chart, click Chart Options, click the Titles tab, click in the Chart title text box, type the text for title, click OK
Chart, update	EX 4.14	Enter new values for the chart's data source and the chart is automatically updated
Chart, use background image in	EX 4.30	Double-click the plot area, click the Patterns tab, click the Fill Effects, click the Picture tab, click Select Picture, locate and select the background image file, click Insert, click OK twice
Chart Wizard, start	EX 4.04	Click ▦
Clip art, crop	WD 4.20	Click clip art, click ⌖, drag picture border to crop
Clip art, find	WD 4.17	Click ▦ on Drawing toolbar, type search criteria, click Search
Clip art, insert	PPT 2.16	Change slide layout to a Content layout, click ▦ in content placeholder, click clipart image, click OK
Clip art, insert in document	WD 4.17	Click ▦ on Drawing toolbar, click Clip Organizer, click picture, click Copy, click in document, click ▦

TASK	PAGE #	RECOMMENDED METHOD
Clip art, recolor	PPT 2.18	Click clipart image, click [icon], click color list arrow of color to change, click desired color, click OK
Clip art, resize	WD 4.20	Click clip art, drag resize handle
Clip art, rotate	WD 4.21	Click clip art, click [icon] on the Picture toolbar
Clip art, wrap text around	WD 4.22	Click clip art, click [icon] button on the Picture toolbar, click text wrapping option
Clipboard Task Pane, open	WD 2.15	Click Edit, click Office Clipboard
Clipboard Task Pane, open	INT 2.06	Click Edit, click Office Clipboard
Clipboard Task Pane, use to cut, copy, and paste	WD 2.16	See Reference Window: Cutting or Copying and Pasting Text
Column, change width	EX 1.30	See Reference Window: Changing Column Width
Column, delete from worksheet	EX 1.27	Select the column, click Edit, click Delete; or select the column, click-right the selection, click Delete
Column, hide	EX 3.22	Select the headings for the columns you want to hide, right-click the selection, click Hide
Column, insert in table	WD 3.22	Click Table, point to Insert, click Columns to Right or Columns to Left
Column, insert into worksheet	EX 1.30	See Reference Window: Inserting Cells into a Worksheet
Column, resize width in a datasheet	AC 2.29	Double-click ↔ on the right border of the column heading
Column, select	EX 1.19	Click the column heading of the column you want to select; to select more than one column, hold down the Ctrl key and click each individual column heading; to select a range of columns, click the first column heading in the range, hold down the Shift key and click the last column in the range
Column, unhide	EX 3.23	Select the column headings left and right of the hidden columns, right-click the selection, click Unhide
Column width, change in table	WD 3.25	Double-click or drag border between columns; to see measurements, press and hold Alt while dragging
Columns, balance	WD 4.27	Click the end of the right-most column, click Insert, click Break, click Continuous, click OK
Columns, format text in	WD 4.13	Click where you want to insert columns, or select text to divide into columns, click Format, click Columns, select options, click OK
Columns, repeat in printout	EX 3.38	Open the Page Setup dialog box, click the Sheet tab, click the Column to repeat at left box, click the column that contain the information you want repeated, click OK
Comment, add or edit	WD 2.35	Click comment, click [icon]
Comment, display	WD 2.35	Point to comment
Comment, insert	WD 2.35	Click Insert, click Comment
Data, check spelling of	AC 4.15	Click [icon]
Data Disk, create	WIN 2000 2.15	Click [Start], point to Programs, point to NP on Microsoft Windows 2000 – Level I, click Disk 1, click OK
Data, find	AC 4.08	See Reference Window: Finding Data in a Form or Datasheet
Database, compact and repair	AC 1.24	Click Tools, point to Database Utilities, click Compact and Repair Database
Database, compact on close	AC 1.25	See Reference Window: Compacting a Database Automatically
Database, convert to another Access version	AC 1.26	Close the database to convert, click Tools, point to Database Utilities, point to Convert Database, click the format to convert to
Database, create a blank	AC 2.07	Click [icon] on the Database toolbar, click Blank Database in the Task Pane, type the database name, select the drive and folder, click Create
Database, create using a Wizard	AC 2.07	Click [icon] on the Database toolbar, click General Templates in the Task Pane, click the Databases tab, select a template, click OK, type the database name, select the drive and folder, click Create, follow the instructions in the Wizard

TASK	PAGE #	RECOMMENDED METHOD
Database, open	AC 1.07	Click [icon]
Datasheet view, switch to	AC 2.19	Click [icon]
Date, insert current	EX 2.28	Insert the TODAY() or NOW() function
Date, insert with AutoComplete	WD 1.28	Start typing date, press Enter
Dates, fill in with Auto Fill	EX 2.19	Select the cell containing the initial date, drag and drop the fill handle to fill in the rest of the dates; click the Auto Fill options button [icon] and choose whether to fill in days, weekdays, months, or years
Design Template, apply	PPT 2.03	Click [icon], click design thumbnail in Task Pane
Design Template, apply to one slide or selected slides	PPT 2.10	Click [icon], selected slide(s) click design thumbnail list arrow, click Apply to Selected Slides
Design view, switch to	AC 2.23	Click [icon]
Desktop, access	WIN 2000 1.14	Click [icon] on the Quick Launch toolbar
Diagram, create	PPT 2.23	Change slide layout to a Content layout, click [icon] in content placeholder, click desired diagram type, click OK, modify diagram as desired
Disk, format	WIN 2000 2.03	Right-click the 3 1/2 Floppy icon in My Computer, click Format on the shortcut menu, specify the capacity and file system of the disk, click Start
Document, close	WD 1.33	Click [icon]
Document, open	WD 2.03	Click [icon], select drive and folder, click filename, click open
Document, open new	WD 1.15	Click [icon]
Document, preview	WD 1.36	Click [icon]
Document, print	WD 1.30	Click [icon]
Document, save with new name	WD 2.04	Click File, click Save As, select drive and folder, enter new filename, click Save
Document, save with same name	WD 1.18	Click [icon]
Drawing toolbar, display	EX 4.36	Click View, point to Toolbars, click Drawing; or click [icon]
Drawing toolbar, open	WD 4.07	Click [icon]
Drop cap, insert	WD 4.24	Click in paragraph, click Format, click Drop Cap, select options, click OK
E-mail message, create	BEB 46	Click [icon]
E-mail message, send	BEB 47	Click [icon]
E-mail messages, receive and send	BEB 48	Click [icon]
E-mail messages, reply to	BEB 49	Click [icon]
Embedded object, create	INT 1.09	See Reference Window: Embedding an Object
Embedded object, edit	INT 1.12	Double-click the object, and then edit it using the source program's commands
Envelope, create	WD 1.33	Click Tools, point to Letters and Mailings, click Envelopes and Labels, click Envelopes tab, type delivery and return addresses, click Print
Excel chart, link to a PowerPoint slide	INT 3.20	Display the Excel chart, click the chart area to select the entire chart, click [icon], switch to the PowerPoint slide, click Edit, click Paste Special, click Microsoft Excel Chart Object, click the Paste Link option button, click OK
Excel data, import into Access	INT 2.14	Open Access database, click File, point to Get External Data, click Import, click Files of type list arrow, click Microsoft Excel, click Import, and then follow the instructions in the Access Import Spreadsheet Wizard
Excel, exit	EX 1.19	Click File and then click Exit
Excel, start	EX 1.05	Click Start, point to Programs, click Microsoft Excel

TASK	PAGE #	RECOMMENDED METHOD
Favorite, move to a new folder	BEB 26	See Reference Window: Moving an Existing Favorite into a New Folder
Favorites Explorer Bar, open	BEB 24	Click [icon]
Favorites folder, create	BEB 24	See Reference Window: Creating a New Favorites Folder
Field, add to a database table	AC 2.25	See Reference Window: Adding a Field Between Two Existing Fields
Field, define in a database table	AC 2.10	See Reference Window: Defining a Field in a Table
Field, delete from a database table	AC 2.23	See Reference Window: Deleting a Field from a Table Structure
Field, move to a new location in a database table	AC 2.24	Display the table in Design view, click the field's row selector, drag the field with the pointer
File, close	OFF 1.19	Click [X]
File, copy	WIN 2000 2.24	See Reference Window: Moving and Copying a File
File, delete	WIN 2000 2.26	See Reference Window: Deleting a File
File, move	WIN 2000 2.24	See Reference Window: Moving and Copying a File
File, open	OFF 1.20	See Reference Window: Opening an Existing or New File
File, open from My Computer	WIN 2000 2.11	Open My Computer, open the window containing the file, click the file, press Enter
File, open from within a program	WIN 2000 2.12	Start the program, click File, click Open, select the file in the Open dialog box, click Open
File, print	OFF 1.21	See Reference Window: Printing a File
File, print	WIN 2000 2.13	Click [icon]
File, rename	WIN 2000 2.25	See Reference Window: Renaming a File
File, save	OFF 1.17	See Reference Window: Saving a File
File, save	WIN 2000 2.07	Click [icon]
Files, find	INT 2.07	Click [icon], type search text in the Search Task Pane, set other search options, and then click Search
Files, view as large icons	WIN 2000 2.18	Click View, click Large Icons
Files, view as small icons	WIN 2000 2.18	Click View, click Small Icons
Files, view details	WIN 2000 2.18	Click View, click Details
Files, view in list	WIN 2000 2.18	Click View, click List
Files, view thumbnails	WIN 2000 2.18	Click View, click Thumbnails
Fill color, change	PPT 2.28	Click object to select it, click [icon], select desired color
Filter By Selection, activate	AC 3.20	See Reference Window: Using Filter By Selection
Find and replace text	WD 2.18	See Reference Window: Finding and Replacing Text
Floppy disk, copy	WIN 2000 2.28	See Reference Window: Copying a Disk
Folder hierarchy, move back in the	WIN 2000 2.23	Click the Back button [icon]
Folder hierarchy, move forward in the	WIN 2000 2.23	Click the Forward button [icon]
Folder hierarchy, move up the	WIN 2000 2.23	Click the Up button [icon]
Folder options, restore default settings	WIN 2000 2.21	Click Tools, click Folder Options, click the General tab, click the Restore Defaults button; click the View tab, click the Restore Defaults button, click OK
Folder, create	WIN 2000 2.22	See Reference Window: Creating a Folder
Folder, create	PPT 1.16	Click File, click Save As, click [icon], type folder name, click OK

TASK	PAGE #	RECOMMENDED METHOD
Font, change color	EX 3.10	Click the list arrow for A ▾ , select a color from the color palette
Font, change size	EX 3.09	Click the list arrow for 10 ▾ , click a size
Font, change style	EX 3.10	Select the text, click B , click I , or click U
Font, change typeface	EX 3.09	Click the list arrow for Arial ▾ button, click a font
Font, modify	PPT 2.07	Click edge of text box, click Font list arrow, click font
Font, select	WD 1.10	Click Format, click Font, click font name
Font and font size, change	WD 2.30	See Reference Window: Changing the Font and Font Size
Font color, modify	PPT 2.07	Click edge of text box, click Font Color list arrow, click color (or click More Colors and click color, click OK)
Font size, select	WD 1.11	Click Format, click Font, click font size
Footer, add	WD 3.11	Click View, click Header and Footer, click 🔲 , type footer text, click Close
Footers, create	PPT 2.13	Click View, click Header and Footer, make sure there is a check mark in the Footer Check box, click ⌶ in Footer text box, type text, click Apply to All
Form Wizard, activate	AC 4.02	Click Forms in the Objects bar, click New, click Form Wizard, choose the table or query for the form, click OK
Format, apply currency style, percent style, or comma style	EX 3.03	Click $, click % , or click , or open the Format Cells dialog box, click the Number tab, select a style, specify style-related options, click OK
Format, clear	EX 3.25	Click Edit, point to Clear, click Formats
Format, copy	WD 2.27	Select text with desired format, double-click 🖌 , select paragraphs to format, click 🖌
Format, copy using fill handle	EX 3.07	Select the cell or range that contains the formatting you want to copy, drag the fill handle down, click 🔳 , click the Fill Formatting Only option button
Format, copy using Format Painter	EX 3.06	Select the cell or range that contains the formatting you want to copy, click 🖌 , drag the pointer over the cell or range to apply the formatting
Format, decrease decimal places	EX 3.03	Click
Format, find and replace	EX 3.26	See Reference Window: Finding and Replacing a Format
Format, increase decimal places	EX 3.05	Click
Format Cells dialog box, open	EX 3.07	Click Format, click Cells
Formula, copy	EX 2.12	See Reference Window: Copying and Pasting a Cell or Range
Formula, copy with Auto Fill	EX 2.16	See Reference Window: Copying Formulas Using Auto Fill
Formula, enter using keyboard	EX 1.23	See Reference Window: Entering a Formula
Formula, enter using mouse	EX 1.23	See Reference Window: Entering a Formula
Function, insert	EX 2.06	See Reference Window: Inserting a Function
Graphic, crop	WD 4.20	Click graphic, click 📐 , drag to crop
Graphic, find	WD 4.17	Click 🔍 on Drawing toolbar, type search criteria, click Search
Graphic, resize	WD 4.20	Click graphic, drag resize handle
Graphic, rotate	WD 4.21	Click graphic, click 🔄 on the Picture toolbar
Graphic, wrap text around	WD 4.22	Click graphic, click 🔲 button on the Picture toolbar, click text wrapping option
Grayscale, preview presentation in	PPT 1.30	Click 🔲
Handouts, print	PPT 1.31	Click File, click Print, click Print what list arrow, click Handouts, click Slides per page list arrow, click number, click OK
Header, add	WD 3.11	Click View, click Header and Footer, type header text, click Close
Header/footer, create	EX 3.35	Open the Page Setup dialog box, click the Header/Footer tab, click list arrow for the Header button or the Footer button, select an available header or footer, click OK

TASK	PAGE #	RECOMMENDED METHOD
Header/footer, create custom	EX 3.36	Open Page Setup dialog box, click the Header/Footer tab, click the Custom Header or Customer Footer button, complete the header/footer related boxes, click OK
Help, display topic from Contents tab	WIN 2000 1.26	In Help, click the Contents tab, click 📖 until you see the topic you want, click ❓ to display topic
Help, display topic from Index tab	WIN 2000 1.27	In Help, click the Index tab, scroll to locate topic, click topic, click Display
Help, get from Ask a Question box	OFF 1.23	See Reference Window: Getting Help from the Ask a Question Box
Help, get in Internet Explorer	BEB 34	See Reference Window: Getting Help in Internet Explorer
Help, return to previous Help topic	WIN 2000 1.28	Click ⬅
Help, start	WIN 2000 1.25	See Reference Window: Starting Windows 2000 Help
History Explorer Bar, open	BEB 29	Click 🕑
Home page, change default	BEB 31	See Reference Window: Changing the Home Toolbar Button Settings
Home page, return to	BEB 31	Click 🏠
Hyperlink, add in document	WD 4.05	Type e-mail address or URL, press spacebar
Hyperlink, remove	WD 4.06	Right-click hyperlink, click Remove Hyperlink
Hyperlink, use	WD 4.05	Press Ctrl and click the hyperlink
Insertion point, move	WIN 2000 2.05	Click the location in the document to which you want to move
Internet Explorer, close	BEB 13	Click ✕
Internet Explorer, start	BEB 18	Click the Start button, point to Programs, click Internet Explorer
Internet Explorer window, maximize	BEB 18	Click ☐
Italics, add to text	WD 2.33	Select text, click *I*
Line spacing, change	WD 2.23	Select text to change, press Ctrl+1 for single spacing, Ctrl+5 for 1.5 line spacing, or Ctrl+2 for double spacing
Linked object, break	INT 1.18	See Reference Window: Breaking the Link Between Linked Objects
Linked object, create	INT 1.14	See Reference Window: Linking an Object
Linked object, reestablish	INT 1.20	Close the destination program without saving the link changes by clicking File, Close, and then No
Linked object, update	INT 1.16	Make changes in the source program, or double-click the linked object to make changes from the destination file
List box, scroll	WIN 2000 1.23	Click ▼ to scroll down the list box
Mail Merge Wizard, start	INT 3.05	Click Tools, point to Letters and Mailings, click Mail Merge Wizard
Margins, change	WD 2.21	Click File, click Page Setup, click Margins tab, enter margin values, click OK
Master, slide or title, modify	PPT 2.05	Shift-click ▣, make modifications, click ▣
Menu option, select	WIN 2000 1.08, WIN 2000 1.21	Click the menu option, or, if it is a submenu, point to it
My Computer, open	WIN 2000 2.16	Click My Computer on the desktop, press Enter
Nonprinting characters, show	WD 1.12	Click Show/Hide ¶
Normal view, change to	WD 1.08	Click ≡
Notes, create	PPT 1.29	Click in Notes Pane, type text
Notes, print	PPT 1.32	Click File, click Print, click Print what list arrow, click Notes Pages, click OK

TASK	PAGE #	RECOMMENDED METHOD
Numbering, add to paragraphs	WD 2.29	Select paragraphs, click [icon]
Numbering, slide	PPT 2.13	Click View, click Header and Footer, click Slide Number check box
Object, change order	PPT 2.07	Click object, click Draw, list arrow, point to Order, click desired layering order
Object, open	AC 1.10	Click the object's type in the Objects bar, click the object's name, click Open
Object, resize	PPT 2.17	Click object, drag resize handle
Object, rotate	PPT 2.28	Click object to select it, drag rotate handle
Object, save	AC 1.20	Click [icon], type the object name, click OK
Office files, open	OFF 1.09	See Reference Window: Starting Office Programs and Files
Office programs, start	OFF 1.09	See Reference Window: Starting Office Programs and Files
Outline text, demote	PPT 1.24	Click Outline tab (if necessary), click paragraph, click [icon]
Outline text, promote	PPT 1.23	Click Outline tab (if necessary), click paragraph, click [icon]
Outlook Express, close	BEB 49	Click [icon]
Outlook Express, start	BEB 44	Click the Start button, point to Programs, and then click Outlook Express
Page, change orientation	EX 3.35	Open the Page Setup dialog box, click the Page tab, click either the Landscape or the Portrait option button
Page, preview more than one	WD 3.09	Click [icon], click [icon]
Page, set margins	EX 3.34	Open the Page Setup dialog box, click the Margins tab, specify the width of the margins, click OK
Page, vertically align	WD 3.10	Click File, click Page Setup, click Layout tab, click Vertical alignment list arrow, click Center
Page, view whole	WD 4.14	Click Zoom list arrow, click Whole Page
Page break, insert	EX 3.37	Click the cell below where you want the page break to appear, click Insert, click Page Break
Page break, insert	WD 3.15	Click where you want to break the page, press Ctrl+Enter
Page number, insert	WD 3.12	Open header or footer, click [icon] on Header/Footer toolbar
Page print settings, change	BEB 33	Click File, click Page Setup
Page Setup dialog box, open	EX 3.33	Click File, click Page Setup; or click the Setup button on the Print Preview toolbar
Paragraph, decrease indent	WD 2.26	Click [icon]
Paragraph, indent	WD 2.26	Click [icon]
Paragraph, move to the next-higher outline level	INT 3.14	Click [icon] on the Outlining toolbar
Paragraph, move to the next-lower outline level	INT 3.15	Click [icon] on the Outlining toolbar
Paste options, select	WD 2.14	Click [icon]
Paste options, set	INT 2.12	Paste object into Word, click [icon], click option button
Personalized menus and toolbars, turn on or off	OFF 1.15	Click Tools, click Customize, click the Options tab, check or uncheck options, click Close
Picture, insert clip art	WD 4.17	Click [icon] on Drawing toolbar, click Clip Organizer, click picture, click Copy, click in document, click Paste
Pie chart, create	EX 4.15	Select the row or column of data values to be charted, click [icon], select Pie in the list of chart types, select a sub-type, complete the remaining Chart Wizard dialog boxes
Pie chart, explode piece(s)	EX 4.18	See Reference Window: Creating an Exploded Pie Chart

TASK	PAGE #	RECOMMENDED METHOD
Pie chart, rotate	EX 4.17	Double-click the pie in the pie chart, click the Options tab, enter a new value in the Angle of first slice box, click OK
PowerPoint, exit	PPT 1.12	Click [X] of PowerPoint window
PowerPoint, start	PPT 1.04	Click Start button, point to Programs, click Microsoft PowerPoint
Presentation, close	PPT 1.12	Click [X] on presentation window
Presentation, open	PPT 1.05	Click [🗁], select disk and folder, click filename, click Open
Primary key, specify	AC 2.16	See Reference Window: Specifying a Primary Key for a Table
Print area, define	EX 3.37	Select the range, click File, point to Print Area, click Set Print Area
Print layout view, change to	WD 3.16	Click [▤]
Print Preview, open	EX 3.32	Click [🔍]
Program, close	WIN 2000 1.11	Click [X]
Program, close inactive	WIN 2000 1.14	Right-click program button, click Close
Program, exit	OFF 1.25	Click [X]
Program, start	WIN 2000 1.10	See Reference Window: Starting a Program
Program, switch to another	WIN 2000 1.13	See Reference Window: Switching Between Programs
Programs, switch between	OFF 1.12	Click the program button on the taskbar
Property sheet, open	AC 3.37	Right-click the object or control, click Properties
Query, create	INT 2.17	Open Access database, click Queries in the Objects list, double-click Create query by using wizard, and then following the instructions in the Simple Query Wizard
Query, define	AC 3.03	Click Queries in the Objects bar, click New, click Design View, click OK
Query, export from Access to Word	INT 2.20	Create and save query in Access, click File, click Export, click Files of type list arrow, click Rich Text Format, click Export All, open Word document, click Insert, click File, click Save as type list arrow, click RichText Format, click file, click Insert
Query, run	AC 3.06	Click [!]
Query results, sort	AC 3.17	See Reference Window: Sorting a Query Datasheet
Range, copy	EX 1.18	Select the cell or range, hold down the Ctrl key and drag the selection to the new location, release the mouse button and Ctrl
Range, move	EX 1.18	Select the cell or range, drag the selection to the new location, release the mouse button
Range, select adjacent	EX 1.16	See Reference Window: Selecting Adjacent or Nonadjacent Ranges of Cells
Range, select non-adjacent	EX 1.16	See Reference Window: Selecting Adjacent or Nonadjacent Ranges of Cells
Record, add a new one	AC 2.28	Click [▶*]
Record, delete	AC 2.33	See Reference Window: Deleting a Record
Record, move to a specific one	AC 1.11	Type the record number in the Specific Record box, press Enter
Record, move to first	AC 1.12	Click [◀◀]
Record, move to last	AC 1.12	Click [▶▶]
Record, move to next	AC 1.12	Click [▶]
Record, move to previous	AC 1.12	Click [◀]
Records, redisplay all after filter	AC 3.21	Click [▽]
Redo command, use to redo multiple operations in a database object	AC 3.31	Click the list arrow for [↷], click the action(s) to redo
Relationship, define between database tables	AC 3.10	Click [⧉]

TASK	PAGE #	RECOMMENDED METHOD
Relative reference, change to absolute	EX 2.14	Type $ before the column and row references; or press F4 to insert $
Reviewing pane, open or close	WD 2.35	Click [icon] on Reviewing toolbar
Row, change height	EX 1.30	Move the pointer over the row heading border until the pointer changes to ┼, click and drag the border to increase or decrease the height of the row
Row, delete from table	WD 3.24	Select the rows you want to delete, click Table, point to Rows, click Delete
Row, delete from worksheet	EX 1.27	Select the row, click Edit, click Delete; or select the row, click-right the selection, click Delete
Row, hide	EX 3.22	Select the headings for the rows you want to hide, right-click the selection, click Hide
Row, insert in table	WD 3.23	Press Tab at the end of a table
Row, insert into worksheet	EX 1.30	See Reference Window: Inserting Cells into a Worksheet
Row, select	EX 1.19	Click the heading of the row you want to select; to select more than one row, hold down the Ctrl key and click each individual row heading; to select a range of rows, click the first row heading in the range, hold down the Shift key and click the last row in the range
Row, unhide	EX 3.23	Select the rows headings above and below the hidden rows, right-click the selection, click Unhide
Rows, repeat in printout	EX 3.38	Open the Page Setup dialog box, click the Sheet tab, click the Row to repeat at top box, click the row that contains the information
Row height, change in table	WD 3.26	Drag divider between rows; to see measurements, press and hold Alt while dragging
Ruler, display	WD 1.10	Click View, click Ruler
Ruler, view (or hide)	PPT 2.11	Click View, click Ruler
ScreenTips, view	WIN 2000 1.07	Position the pointer over the item
Search Task Pane, open	INT 2.07	Click [icon]
Section, insert in document	WD 3.08	Click where you want to insert a section break, click Insert, click Break, click Section break types option button, click OK
Section, vertically align	WD 3.09	Click File, click Page Setup, click Layout, click This Section, click Vertical alignment list arrow, click Center, click OK
Shading, apply to table	WD 3.29	Select table area to shade, click Shading Color list arrow on Tables and Borders toolbar, click a color
Shape, create	PPT 2.26	Click AutoShapes list arrow, point to shape type, click desired shape, drag ┼ in slide
Sheet tabs, format	EX 3.25	Right-click the sheet tab, click Tab Color, select a color from the color palette
Slide, add new	PPT 1.21	Click [icon]
Slide, delete	PPT 1.26	In Slide Pane, click Edit, click Delete Slide. In Outline Tab, click [icon], press Delete; in Slide Tab, click slide, click Delete
Slide, go to next	PPT 1.18	Click [icon]
Slide Show, view	PPT 1.08	Click [icon]
Slide Sorter View, switch to	PPT 1.25	Click [icon]
Smart Tag, remove	WD 1.29	Click [icon], click Remove this Smart Tag
Sort, specify ascending in datasheet	AC 3.15	Click [icon]
Sort, specify descending in datasheet	AC 3.15	Click [icon]
Speaker Notes, create	PPT 1.29	Click in Notes Pane, type text
Special character, insert	WD 4.26	Click Insert, click Symbol, click Special Characters tab, click special character, click Insert, click Close

TASK	PAGE #	RECOMMENDED METHOD
Spelling, correct individual word	WD 1.25	Right-click misspelled word (as indicated by a wavy red line), click correctly spelled word
Spelling and grammar, check	WD 2.05	See Reference Window: Checking a Document for Spelling and Grammatical Errors
Spelling and grammar, check document	WD 2.05	Click ![ABC], click correction, click change; click Ignore once to skip an item
Start menu, open	WIN 2000 1.07	Click ![Start]
Style, apply	EX 3.29	Select the range, click Format, click Style, select a style, click OK
Style, create	EX 3.29	Select the cell that contains the formatting you want to use as the basis of the new style, click Format, click Style, type a name for the style, click Modify, specify format options using the Format Cells dialog box, click OK, click OK
Style, modify	EX 3.30	Select the range, click Format, click Style, click Modify, change style attributes, click OK
Style Checker, fix style problem	PPT 1.27	Click ![icon], click option to fix style problem
Style Checker, set options	PPT 1.27	Click Tools, click Options, click Spelling and Style tab, click Style Options, set options, click OK, then click OK in the Options dialog box
Style Checker, turn on	PPT 1.26	Click Tools, click Options, click Spelling and Style tab, click Check style check box, click OK
Symbol, insert	WD 4.26	Click Insert, click Symbol, click desired symbol, click Insert, click Close
Tab stop, add	PPT 2.12	Select text box, click View, click Ruler, click tab stop alignment selector button to select desired tab stop style, click location on ruler
Tab stop, set	WD 3.05	Click tab alignment selector, click ruler
Table, center on page	WD 3.30	Click in table, click Table, click Table Properties, click Table tab, click Center alignment option, click OK
Table, create	PPT 2.20	Change slide layout to a Content layout or to Title and Table layout, click ![icon], set number of columns and rows, fill in and format cells as desired
Table, create	WD 3.15	Click ![icon], drag to select columns and rows; or click ![icon] on Tables and Borders toolbar, draw columns and rows
Table, create in a database	AC 2.08	Click Tables in the Objects bar, click New, click Design View, click OK
Table, import from another Access database	AC 2.32	Click File, point to Get External Data, click Import, select the folder, click Import, select the table, click OK
Table, open in a database	AC 1.10	Click Tables in the Objects bar, click the table name, click Open
Table, sort	WD 3.20	Click in the column you want to sort, click ![icon] or ![icon] on Tables and Borders toolbar
Table structure, save in a database	AC 2.18	See Reference Window: Saving a Table Structure
Tables and Borders toolbar, display	WD 3.19	Click ![icon]
Task Pane, close	WD 1.08	Click ![X]
Text, align	WD 2.24	Select text, click ![icon], ![icon], ![icon], or ![icon]
Text, align in table	WD 3.26	Click Align list arrow on Tables and Borders toolbar, click alignment option
Text, align within a cell	EX 3.11	Click ![icon], click ![icon], click ![icon], click ![icon], or click ![icon]; or open Format Cells dialog box, click the Alignment tab, select a text alignment, click OK
Text, bold	WD 2.32	Select text, click **B**
Text, change indent	EX 3.11	Click ![icon], or ![icon]
Text, copy and paste	WD 2.16	Select text, click ![icon], move to target location, click ![icon]
Text, delete	WD 2.10	Press Backspace to delete character to left of insertion point; press Delete to delete character to the right; press Ctrl+Backspace to delete to beginning of word; press Ctrl+Delete to delete to end of word
Text, enter into cell	EX 1.20	Click the cell, type text entry, press Enter

TASK	PAGE #	RECOMMENDED METHOD
Text, italicize	WD 2.33	Select text, click *I*
Text, move by cut and paste	WD 2.15	Select text, click ✂, move to target location, click 📋
Text, move by drag and drop	WD 2.13	Select text, drag pointer to target location, release mouse button
Text, replace	WD 2.18	See Reference Window: Finding and Replacing Text
Text, select	WIN 2000 2.06	Drag the pointer over the text
Text, select a block of	WD 2.09	Click at beginning of block, press and hold Shift and click at end of block
Text, select entire document	WD 2.09	Press Ctrl and click in selection bar
Text, select multiple adjacent lines	WD 2.09	Click and drag in selection bar
Text, select multiple nonadjacent lines	WD 2.09	Select text, press and hold Ctrl, and select next text
Text, select multiple paragraphs	WD 2.09	Double-click and drag in selection bar
Text, select paragraph	WD 2.09	Double-click in selection bar next to paragraph
Text, select sentence	WD 2.09	Press Ctrl and click in sentence
Text, underline	WD 2.33	Select text, click U
Text, wrap around WordArt	WD 4.22	Click WordArt, click 📷 on the WordArt toolbar, click text wrap option
Text, wrap in cell	EX 3.13	Open the Format Cells dialog box, click the Alignment tab, select the Text wrap check box, click OK
Text box, add	PPT 2.25	Click 📄, click ↓ in slide, type text
Text box, resize	PPT 2.08	Click text box, drag resize handle
Toolbar, display	WD 1.09	Right-click any visible toolbar, click toolbar name
Toolbar, hide or show	BEB 20	See Reference Window: Hiding and Restoring the Toolbars
Toolbars, control display	WIN 2000 2.17	Click View, point to Toolbars, select the toolbar options you want
Toolbar button, select	WIN 2000 1.22	Click the toolbar button
Transparent color, picture, set	PPT 2.07	Click picture, click 🖉, click color in picture
Underline, add to text	WD 2.33	Select text, click U
Undo command, use to undo multiple operations in a database object	AC 3.30	Click the list arrow for ↩, click the action(s) to undo
URL, enter and go to	BEB 21	See Reference Window: Entering a URL in the Address Bar
Web page, add page title	EXCEL WEB 3	Click File, click Save as Web Page, click the Change Title button, enter the page title, click OK
Web page, print all pages	BEB 32	Click 🖨
Web page, print one or a few pages	BEB 32	See Reference Window: Printing the Current Web Page
Web page, publish a workbook	EXCEL WEB 6	Click File, click Save as Web Page, select the Entire Workbook option button, specify a title, click Publish, click the AutoRepublish every time this workbook is saved check box (optional), click the Open published Web page in the browser check box (optional), click Publish
Web page, publish a worksheet	EXCEL WEB 3	Click File, click Save as Web Page, select the Selection: Sheet option button, specify a title, click Publish, specify the items to publish, specify the Web page as interactive or non-interactive, click the AutoRepublish every time this work-book is saved check box (optional), click the Open published web page in the browser check box (optional), click Publish

TASK	PAGE #	RECOMMENDED METHOD
Web page, publish interactive	EXCEL WEB 2	Click File, click Save as Web Page, select the Add Interactivity check box, click Publish
Web page, publish non-interactive	EXCEL WEB 2	Click File, click Save as Web Page, clear the Add Interactivity check box
Web page, refresh	BEB 30	Click [icon]
Web page, republish automatically with updates	EXCEL WEB 4	Click File, click Save as Web Page, click Publish, select the AutoRepublish every time this workbook is saved check box
Web page, save to floppy disk	BEB 36	See Reference Window: Saving a Web Page to a Disk
Web page, stop loading	BEB 15	Click [icon]
Web page graphic, save	BEB 39	See Reference Window: Saving an Image from a Web Page on a 3 1/2-inch Disk
Web page in history list, move forward to next	BEB 15	Click [icon]
Web page in history list, return to previous	BEB 15	Click [icon]
Web page text, save	BEB 37	See Reference Window: Copying Text from a Web Page to a WordPad Document
Window, close	WIN 2000 1.18	Click [icon]
Window, maximize	WIN 2000 1.18	Click [icon]
Window, minimize	WIN 2000 1.18	Click [icon]
Window, move	WIN 2000 1.20	Drag the title bar
Window, resize	WIN 2000 1.20	Drag [icon]
Window, restore	WIN 2000 1.18	Click [icon]
Windows 2000, shut down	WIN 2000 1.15	Click [Start], click Shut Down click the list arrow, click Shut Down, click OK
Windows 2000, start	WIN 2000 1.04	Turn on the computer
Word, exit	WD 1.33	Click [icon]
Word, start	WD 1.05	Click [Start], point to Programs, click Microsoft Word
WordArt, change shape	WD 4.10	Click WordArt, click [icon] on the WordArt toolbar, click shape
WordArt, edit text	WD 4.09	Click WordArt, click Edit Text button on WordArt toolbar, edit text, click OK
WordArt, insert	WD 4.07	Click [icon], click WordArt style, click OK, type WordArt text, select font, size, and style, click OK
WordArt, wrap text	WD 4.22	Click WordArt, click [icon] on the WordArt toolbar, click text wrap option
Workbook, open	EX 1.12	Click [icon]; (or click File and click Open or click the Workbook link in the Task Pane), locate the drive and folder that contains the workbook, click the file- name, click Open (or double-click the workbook file name in the Task Pane)
Workbook, print	EX 1.36	Click [icon]; or click File, click Print, select printer and print-related options, click OK
Workbook, save for first time	EX 1.14	Click [icon] (or click File, click Save or Save As), locate the folder and drive in which to store the file, type a filename, click Save
Workbook, save in a different format	EX 1.14	See Reference Window: Saving a Workbook in a Different Format
Workbook, save to update	EX 1.14	Click [icon]; or click File, click Save
Workbook, save with new name	EX 1.14	Click File, click Save As, locate the folder and drive in which to store the file, type a filename, click Save
Worksheet, add background image	EX 3.23	See Reference Window: Adding a Background Image to the Worksheet
Worksheet, copy	EX 1.35	See Reference Window: Moving or Copying a Worksheet
Worksheet, delete	EX 1.33	Click the sheet tab, click Edit, click Delete Sheet; or right-click the sheet tab, click Delete

TASK	PAGE #	RECOMMENDED METHOD
Worksheet, insert	EX 1.34	Click Insert, click Worksheet; or right-click a sheet tab, click Insert, click Worksheet icon, click Insert
Worksheet, move	EX 1.35	See Reference Window: Moving or Copying a Worksheet
Worksheet, rename	EX 1.35	Double-click the sheet tab that you want to rename, type a new name, press Enter
Worksheets, move between	EX 1.11	Click the sheet tab for the worksheet you want to view; or click one of the tab scrolling buttons, click the sheet tab
Zoom setting, change	WD 1.11	Click Zoom list arrow, click zoom percentage

Windows 2000 File Finder

Location in Tutorial	Name and Location of Data File	Student Saves File As...	Student Creates New File
Tutorial 2 Session 2.1			Practice Text.doc
Session 2.2 *Note:* Students copy the contents of Disk 1 onto Disk 2 in this session.	Agenda.doc Budget2001.xls Budget2001.xls Budget2002.xls Exterior.bmp Interior.bmp Logo.bmp Members.wdb Minutes.wps Newlogo.bmp Opus27.mid Parkcost.wks Proposal.doc Resume.doc Sales.wks Sample Text.doc Tools.wks Travel.wps Practice Text.doc *(Saved from Session 2.1)*		
Review Assigments & Projects	*Note:* Students continue to use the Data Disks they used in the Tutorial. For certain Assignments, they will need a 3rd blank disk.	Woods Resume .doc *(Saved from Resume.doc)*	Letter.doc Song.doc Poem.doc

Browser and E-mail Basics File Finder

Location in Tutorial	Name and Location of Data File	Student Saves File As...	Student Creates New File
BROWSER AND E-MAIL BASICS DISK 1 Session 2			Tutorial.01\Pennsylvania Tutorial.01\Address.txt Tutorial.01\mapstreet.gif
Review Assignments			*Student disks will vary*
Case Problem 1			*Student disks will vary*
Case Problem 2			*Student disks will vary*

Introducing Microsoft Office XP File Finder

Location in Tutorial	Name and Location of Data File	Student Saves File As...	Student Creates File from Scratch
Page OFF 17			Tutorial.01\Tutorial\ Stockholder Meeting Agenda.doc
Review Assignments	Tutorial.01\Review\Finances.xls	Tutorial.01\Review\Delmar Finances.xls	
Review Assignments	Tutorial.01\Review\Letter.doc	Tutorial.01\Review\Delmar Letter.doc	

Word 2002 Level I File Finder

Location in Tutorial	Name and Location of Data File	Student Saves File As...	Student Creates New File
Tutorial 1	(No file)		
Session 1.1			
Session 1.2			Tutorial.01\Tutorial\Web Time Contract Letter
Review Assignments			Tutorial.01\Review\Conference Call Memo
			Tutorial.01\Review\Web Time Envelope
Case Problem 1			Tutorial.01\Cases\Water Park Information Letter
Case Problem 2			Tutorial.01\Cases\Confirmation Letter
Case Problem 3			Tutorial.01\Cases\Liza Morgan Letter
Case Problem 4			Tutorial.01\Cases\Meeting Memo
Tutorial 2			
Session 2.1	Tutorial.02\Tutorial\FAQ	Tutorial.02\Tutorial\Tree FAQ	
Session 2.2	(Continued from Session 2.1)		
Review Assignments	Tutorial.02\Review\Statmnt	Tutorial.02\Review\Monthly Statement	Tutorial.02\Review\LMG Contact Information
Case Problem 1	Tutorial.02\Cases\Form	Tutorial.02\Cases\Authorization Form	
Case Problem 2	Tutorial.02\Cases\CCW	Tutorial.02\Cases\CCW Brochure	
Case Problem 3	Tutorial.02\Cases\UpTime	Tutorial.02\Cases\UpTime Training Summary	
Case Problem 4	Tutorial.02\Cases\Ridge	Tutorial.02\Cases\Ridge Top Guide	
Tutorial 3			
Session 3.1	Tutorial.03\Tutorial\WAN	Tutorial.03\Tutorial\New Hope WAN Report	
Session 3.2	(Continued from Session 3.1)		
Review Assignments	Tutorial.03\Review\Trouble	Tutorial.03\Review\Troubleshooting Report	Tutorial.03\Review\Equipment List
Case Problem 1	Tutorial.03\Cases\SunRep	Tutorial.03\Cases\Sun Porch Report	
Case Problem 2	Tutorial.03\Cases\Tour	Tutorial.03\Cases\Masterpiece Tour Report	
Case Problem 3	Tutorial.03\Cases\Contacts	Tutorial.03\Cases\Sales Contacts	
Case Problem 4			Tutorial.03\Cases\Camp Winnemac
Tutorial 4			
Session 4.1	Tutorial.04\Tutorial\Clothes	Tutorial.04\Tutorial\Travel Clothes	
Session 4.2	(Continued from Session 4.1)		
Review Assignments	Tutorial.04\Review\Travel	Tutorial.04\Review\Travel Highlights	
Case Problem 1	Tutorial.04\Cases\Convert	Tutorial.04\Cases\Software Conversion	
Case Problem 2	Tutorial.04\Cases\Movers	Tutorial.04\Cases\Movers Newsletter	
Case Problem 3	Tutorial.04\Cases\Grains	Tutorial.04\Cases\Wild Grains Brochure	
Case Problem 4			Tutorial.04\Cases\New Job
Web			
Tutorial	Web\Exercise	Web\Exercise Web Page.htm	Web\Health News Home Page.htm
Review Assignments	Web\Stir-Fry	Web\Stir-Fry Class.htm	Web\Cooking Classes Home Page.htm

Excel 2002 Level I File Finder

Location in Tutorial	Name and Location of Data File	Student Saves File As...	Student Creates New File
Tutorial 1			
Session 1.1	Tutorial.01\Tutorial\Lawn1.xls	Lawn2.xls	
Session 1.2	(Continued from Session 1.1)		
Review Assignments	Tutorial.01\Review\Income1.xls	Income2.xls	
Case Problem 1	Tutorial.01\Cases\CFlow1.xls	CFlow2.xls	
Case Problem 2	Tutorial.01\Cases\Balance1.xls	Balance2.xls	
Case Problem 3	Tutorial.01\Cases\Site1.xls	Site2.xls	
Case Problem 4			CashCounter.xls
Tutorial 2			
Session 2.1	Tutorial.02\Tutorial\Loan1.xls	Loan2.xls	
Session 2.2	(Continued from Session 2.1)		
Review Assignments	Tutorial.02\Review\Mort1.xls	Mort2.xls	
Case Problem 1	Tutorial.02\Cases\School1.xls	School2.xls	
Case Problem 2	Tutorial.02\Cases\Sonic1.xls	Sonic2.xls	
Case Problem 3	Tutorial.02\Cases\Leland1.xls	Leland2.xls	
Case Problem 4			JrCol.xls
Tutorial 3			
Session 3.1	Tutorial.03\Tutorial\Sales1.xls	Sales2.xls	
Session 3.2	(Continued from Session 3.1)		
Review Assignments	Tutorial.03\Review\Region1.xls	Region2.xls	
Case Problem 1	Tutorial.03\Cases\Running1.xls	Running2.xls	
Case Problem 2	Tutorial.03\Cases\WBus1.xls	WBus2.xls	
Case Problem 3	Tutorial.03\Cases\Blades1.xls	Blades2.xls	
Case Problem 4			Payroll.xls
Tutorial 4			
Session 4.1	Tutorial.04\Tutorial\Vega1.xls	Vega2.xls	
Session 4.2	(Continued from Session 4.1)		
Review Assignments	Tutorial.04\Review\VegaUSA1.xls	VegaUSA2.xls	
Case Problem 1	Tutorial.04\Cases\CIC1.xls	CIC2.xls	
Case Problem 2	Tutorial.04\Cases\Powder1.xls	Powder2.xls	
Case Problem 3	Tutorial.04\Cases\Pixal1.xls	Pixal2.xls	
Case Problem 4			BCancer.xls
Web			
Tutorial	Web\Tutorial\Mortgage1.xls Web\Tutorial\Calc1.xls	Mortgage2.xls Calc2.xls	Mortgage3.htm Mortgage3_files\filelist.xml Mortgage3_files\Mortgage2_*30888_image001*.gif Mortgage3_files\Mortgage2_*30888_image002*.gif Calc3.htm
Review Assignments	Web\Review\Fund1.xls Web\Review\FCalc1.xls	Fund2.xls FCalc2.xls	Fund3.htm Fund3_files\filelist.xml Fund3_files\Fund2_*7971_image001*.gif FCalc3.htm

Note: GIF files will have different filenames for different users.

Integration Tutorial 1 File Finder

Location in Tutorial	Name and Location of Data File	Student Saves File As...	Student Creates New File
Tutorial 1			
Tutorial	Tutorial.01\Tutorial\Letter.doc	Tutorial.01\Tutorial\Customer Letter.doc	
	Tutorial.01\Tutorial\NEGHA.xls	Tutorial.01\Tutorial\PieChart.xls	
	Tutorial.01\Tutorial\Products.xls	Tutorial.01\Tutorial\New Products.xls	
Review Assignments	Tutorial.01\Review\Memo.doc	Tutorial.01\Review\Employee Memo.doc	
	Tutorial.01\Review\PieChart.xls	Tutorial.01\Review\PieChart2.xls	
	Tutorial.01\Review\Products.xls	Tutorial.01\Review\NewProducts2.xls	
Case Problem 1	Tutorial.01\Cases\Price.doc	Tutorial.01\Cases\Quote.doc and Tutorial.01\Cases\Confirm.doc	
	Tutorial.01\Cases\Costs.xls	Tutorial.01\Cases\Charges.xls	
Case Problem 2			Tutorial.01\Cases\SFU Expenses Letter.doc
			Tutorial.01\Cases\Estimated Expenses.xls

Access 2002 Level I File Finder

Note: *The Data Files supplied with this book and listed in the chart below are starting files for Tutorial 1. You will begin your work on each subsequent tutorial with the files that you created in the previous tutorial. For example, after completing Tutorial 1, you begin Tutorial 2 with your ending files from Tutorial 1. The Review Assignments and Case Problems also build on the starting Data Files in this way. You must complete each tutorial, Review Assignment, and Case Problem in order and finish them completely before continuing to the next tutorial, or your Data Files will not be correct for the next tutorial.*

Location in Tutorial	Name and Location of Data File	Student Creates New File
Tutorial 1		
Session 1.1	Disk1\Tutorial\Seasonal.mdb	
Session 1.2	Disk1\Tutorial\Seasonal.mdb (*continued from Session 1.1*)	
Review Assignments	Disk2\Review\Seasons.mdb	Disk2\Review\Seasons2002.mdb
		Disk2\Review\Seasons97.mdb
Case Problem 1	Disk3\Cases\Videos.mdb	Disk3\Cases\Videos2002.mdb
		Disk3\Cases\Videos97.mdb
Case Problem 2	Disk4\Cases\Meals.mdb	Disk4\Cases\Meals2002.mdb
		Disk4\Cases\Meals97.mdb
Case Problem 3	Disk5\Cases\Redwood.mdb	Disk5\Cases\Redwood.mdb
		Disk5\Cases\Redwood.mdb
Case Problem 4	Disk6\Cases\Trips.mdb	Disk6\Cases\Trips2002.mdb
		Disk6\Cases\Trips97.mdb
Tutorial 2		
Session 2.1		Disk1\Tutorial\Northeast.mdb
Session 2.2	Disk1\Tutorial\Northeast.mdb (*continued from Session 2.1*)	
	Disk1\Tutorial\NEJobs.mdb	
	Disk1\Tutorial\Seasonal.mdb (*continued from Tutorial 1*)	
Review Assignments	Disk2\Review\Elsa.mdb	Disk2\Review\Recruits.mdb
Case Problem 1	Disk3\Cases\Videos.mdb (*continued from Tutorial 1*)	
	Disk3\Cases\Events.mdb	
Case Problem 2	Disk4\Cases\Meals.mdb (*continued from Tutorial 1*)	
	Disk4\Cases\Customer.mdb	
Case Problem 3	Disk5\Cases\Redwood.mdb (*continued from Tutorial 1*)	
	Disk5\Cases\Pledge.mdb	
Case Problem 4	Disk6\Cases\Trips.mdb (*continued from Tutorial 1*)	
	Disk6\Cases\Rafting.xls	
	Disk6\Cases\Groups.mdb	
Tutorial 3		
Session 3.1	Disk1\Tutorial\Northeast.mdb (*continued from Session 2.2*)	
Session 3.2	Disk1\Tutorial\Northeast.mdb (*continued from Session 3.1*)	

Access 2002 Level I File Finder (continued)

Location in Tutorial	Name and Location of Data File	Student Creates New File
Review Assignments	Disk 2\Review\Recruits.mdb *(continued from Tutorial 2)*	
Case Problem 1	Disk3\Cases\Videos.mdb *(continued from Tutorial 2)*	
Case Problem 2	Disk4\Cases\Meals.mdb *(continued from Tutorial 2)*	
Case Problem 3	Disk5\Cases\Redwood.mdb *(continued from Tutorial 2)*	
Case Problem 4	Disk6\Cases\Trips.mdb *(continued from Tutorial 2)*	
Tutorial 4		
Session 4.1	Disk1\Tutorial\Northeast.mdb *(continued from Session 3.2)*	
Session 4.2	Disk1\Tutorial\Northeast.mdb *(continued from Session 4.1)* Disk1\Tutorial\Globe.bmp	
Review Assignments	Disk2\Review\Recruits.mdb *(continued from Tutorial 3)* Disk2\Review\Travel.bmp	
Case Problem 1	Disk3\Cases\Videos.mdb *(continued from Tutorial 3)* Disk3\Cases\Camcord.bmp	
Case Problem 2	Disk4\Cases\Meals.mdb *(continued from Tutorial 3)* Disk4\Cases\Server.bmp	
Case Problem 3	Disk5\Cases\Redwood.mdb *(continued from Tutorial 3)* Disk5\Cases\Animals.bmp	
Case Problem 4	Disk6\Cases\Trips.mdb *(continued from Tutorial 3)* Disk6\Cases\Raft.gif	
Web		Disk 1\Tutorial\Employer Positions.htm
Tutorial		Disk 1\Tutorial\Employer.htm
Review Assignments		Disk 2\Review\Recruiter.htm Disk 2\Review\Student.htm

Integration Tutorial 2 File Finder

Location in Tutorial	Name and Location of Data File	Student Saves File As...	Student Creates New File
Tutorial 2			
Tutorial	Tutorial.02\Tutorial\Brochure.doc	Tutorial.02\Tutorial\Tulip Brochure.doc	
	Tutorial.02\Tutorial\Customer Letter.doc		
	Tutorial.02\Tutorial\Price Table.xls		
	Tutorial.02\Tutorial\Order List.xls	Tutorial.02\Tutorial\Tulip Order List.xls	
	Tutorial.02\Tutorial\Sales.mdb	Tutorial.02\Tutorial\Sales.mdb	
Review Assignments	Tutorial.02\Review\Instructions.doc		
	Tutorial.02\Review\Tulip Instructions.doc		
	Tutorial.02\Review\Bulb Tips.doc		
	Tutorial.02\Review\Zones.xls		
	Tutorial.02\Review\Regions.xls	Tutorial.02\Review\Delivery Regions.xls	
Case Problem 1	Tutorial.02\Cases\Memo.doc	Tutorial.02\Cases\Marketing Memo.doc	
	Tutorial.02\Cases\Stationery.doc		
Case Problem 2	Tutorial.02\Cases\Admissions.xls	Tutorial.02\Cases\Admissions by Region.xls	
			Tutorial.02\Cases\SFU Admissions.mdb
	Tutorial.02\Cases\Admissions Memo.doc	Tutorial.02\Cases\Top Admissions.doc	

PowerPoint 2002 Level I File Finder

Location in Tutorial	Name and Location of Data File	Student Saves File As...	Student Creates New File
Tutorial 1			
Session 1.1	Tutorial.01\Tutorial\Lorena.ppt		Tutorial.01\My Files\ Global Humanitarian Overview.ppt
Session 1.2	Tutorial.01\My Files\Global Humanitarian Overview.ppt	Tutorial.01\My Files\Global Humanitarian Overview.ppt	
Review Assignments	Tutorial.01\Review\Village OP.ppt	Tutorial.01\Review\Village Outreach Program.ppt	
Case Problem 1			Tutorial.01\Cases\e-Commerce Consultants.ppt
Case Problem 2	Tutorial.01\Cases\Seafoods.ppt	Tutorial.01\Cases\Northeast Seafoods.ppt	
Case Problem 3	Tutorial.01\Cases\LASIK.ppt	Tutorial.01\Cases\Magnolia LASIK.ppt	
Case Problem 4			Tutorial.01\Cases\Textbook Review.ppt
Tutorial 2			
Session 2.1	Tutorial.02\Tutorial\PeruExp.ppt	Tutorial.02\Tutorial\Peru Expedition.ppt	
Session 2.2		Tutorial.02\Tutorial\Peru Expedition.ppt	
Review Assignments	Tutorial.02\Review\PackList.ppt	Tutorial.02\Review\Peru Packing List.ppt	
Case Problem 1	Tutorial.02\Cases\MyBody.ppt	Tutorial.02\Cases\MyBodyTrainer.ppt	
Case Problem 2	Tutorial.02\Cases\Payroll.ppt	Tutorial.02\Cases\Payroll Partners.ppt	
Case Problem 3	Tutorial.02\Cases\Scrapbk.ppt	Tutorial.02\Cases\Sally's Scrapbooking.ppt	
Case Problem 4			Tutorial.02\Cases\Honor Society.ppt
Web			
Tutorial	Web\PeruExp.ppt	Web\PeruExpedition.ppt	Web\PeruExpedition.htm
Review Assignments	Web\MPTour.ppt	Web\MachuPicchuTour.ppt	Web\Machu Picchu Tour.htm

Integration Tutorial 3 File Finder

Location in Tutorial	Name and Location of Data File	Student Saves File As...	Student Creates New File
Tutorial 3			
Tutorial	Tutorial.03\Tutorial\Letter2.doc	Tutorial.03\Tutorial\Main Letter.doc and Tutorial.03\Tutorial\Merged Letters.doc	
	Tutorial.03\Tutorial\Sales.mdb		
	Tutorial.03\Tutorial\Outline.doc	Tutorial.03\Tutorial\Outline for Slides.doc	
	Tutorial.03\Tutorial\Growers.ppt	Tutorial.03\Tutorial\Growers Conference.ppt	
	Tutorial.03\Tutorial\NEGHA.xls		
Review Assignments	Tutorial.03\Review\Sales.mdb		Tutorial.03\Review\Merged Labels.doc and Main Labels.doc
	Tutorial.03\Review\Topics.doc	Tutorial.03\Review\Topics Outline.doc	
	Tutorial.03\Review\Groups.xls		Tutorial.03\Review\Staff Meeting.ppt
Case Problem 1	Tutorial.03\Cases\Leases.mdb		Tutorial.03\Cases/Merged Envelopes.doc and Tutorial.03\Cases/Main Envelopes.doc
Case Problem 2			Tutorial.03\Cases\Orientation Outline.doc
			Tutorial.03\Cases\Slides for Orientation.ppt

Microsoft Word 2002 MOUS Certification Grid

Note: This grid contains a complete list of the Word 2002 Core and Expert skills. These skills are covered in one or more of the following texts: *New Perspectives on Microsoft Office XP First Course*, *New Perspectives on Microsoft Office XP Second Course*, and *New Perspectives on Microsoft Office XP Third Course*.

Core — Standardized Coding Number	Certification Skill Activity — Activity	Courseware Reqs	End-of-Tutorial Pages	End-of-Tutorial Practice — Tutorial Pages	Exercise	Step Number
W2002-1	**Inserting and Modifying Text**					
W2002-1-1	Insert, modify and move text and symbols	Insert, cut, copy, paste and paste special	1.16–1.18 (insert)	1.35	RA	1–9, 11
				1.36	CP1	3–7
				1.36–1.37	CP2	3–8
				1.37	CP3	2
				1.38	CP4	5–8
			2.14–2.17 (cut, copy, paste)	2.40	RA	14
				2.44	CP4	6
			7.55 (Paste Special)		CP2	3
		Finding and	2.17–2.19	2.38	RA	7
				2.41	CP1	8
				2.42	CP2	4
				2.43	CP3	11
				2.44	CP4	12
		Using AutoCorrect to insert frequently used text	1.23–1.25	1.35	RA	10
				1.36	CP1	4
W2002-1-2	Apply and modify text formats	Applying and modifying character formats	2.31–2.34	2.38	RA	7
				2.41	CP1	6, 13 15, 16
				2.42	CP2	9
				2.43	CP3	4, 11 14, 15
				2.44–2.45	CP4	13, 15 16
W2002-1-3	Correct spelling and grammar usage	Using Spelling and Grammar checks	1.24–1.26	1.35	RA	15
				1.36	CP1	10
			2.05–2.06	2.38	RA	3
				2.41	CP1	2
				2.42	CP2	2
				2.44	CP4	3
		Using the Thesaurus	5.05–5.06	5.45	RA	5
				5.48	CP1	8
				5.50	CP3	6
W2002-1-4	Apply font and text effects	Applying character effects (superscript, subscript, etc.) and text effects (animation)	5.36	5.45	RA	8, 10
				5.48	CP1	
			7.34–7.35 (animation)	7.49	RA	15

Standardized Coding Number	Certification Skill Activity Activity	Courseware Reqs	End–of–Tutorial Pages	End–of–Tutorial Practice		
				Tutorial Pages	Step Exercise	Number
		Applying highlights	2.08–2.09 (select)	2.40	RA	13, 14
				2.41	CP1	13, 15
				2.43	CP3	15
				2.44	CP4	11
			5.35–5.36 (color)	5.46	RA	16
				5.47	CP1	6
				5.50	CP3	10
W2002-1-5	Enter and format Date and Time	Inserting date/time fields and modifying field formats	1.27–1.29 (Auto Complete)	1.35	RA	10
				1.36	CP1	4
			5.34–5.35	5.46	RA	17
				5.49	CP2	13
				5.51	CP4	8
W2002-1-6	Apply character styles	Applying character styles	5.15	5.45	RA	9
W2002-2	**Creating and Modifying Paragraphs**					
W2002-2-1	Modify paragraph formats	Applying paragraph formats	2.23–2.25 2.27–2.28	2.38	RA	7
				2.41	CP1	5, 10
				2.42	CP2	10
				2.43	CP3	14
				2.44	CP4	11
		Applying borders and shading to paragraphs	5.19 4.28–29	2.32	CP1	9
		Indenting paragraphs	2.25–2.26	2.38–2.40	RA	6, 13
				2.42	CP3	6
				2.44	CP4	10
W2002-2-2	Set and modify tabs	Setting and modifying tabs	3.04–3.07	3.33	RA	3
				3.35	CP1	7
W2002-2-3	Apply bullet, outline, and numbering format to paragraphs	Applying bullets and numbering	2.28–2.29	2.38	RA	7
				2.41	CP1	9
				2.42	CP2	7
				2.43	CP3	6
				2.44	CP4	7
		Creating outlines	5.24–5.27	5.46	RA	11–13
				5.47	CP1	2
				5.49	CP2	7
				5.50	CP3	3–4
				5.51	CP4	3–6
W2002-2-4	Apply paragraph styles	Applying paragraph styles (e.g.; Heading 1)	5.16	5.45	RA	7
				5.49	CP2	4, 6

Standardized Coding Number	Certification Skill Activity / Activity	Courseware Reqs	End-of-Tutorial Pages	End-of-Tutorial Practice		
				Tutorial Pages	Exercise	Step Number
W2002-3	**Formatting Documents**					
W2002-3-1	Create and modify a header and footer	Creating and modifying document headers and footers	3.11–3.13	3.33 3.35 3.36	RA CP1 CP2	7, 8 5, 6 6, 7
W2002-3-2	Apply and modify column settings	Applying columns and modifying text alignment	4.13–4.14 4.27–4.28	4.31 4.32 4.34 4.35	RA CP1 CP2 CP3	12, 21 10 8 6
		Creating newsletter columns	4.13–4.14	4.31 4.32	RA CP1	12 10
		Revising column layout	4.27–4.28	4.31 4.34 4.35	RA CP2 CP3	21 8 6
W2002-3-3	Modify document layout and Page Setup options	Inserting page breaks	3.14–3.15	3.34 3.35	RA CP1	8 8
		Inserting page numbers	3.12	3.33 3.35	RA CP1	8 6
		Modifying page margins, page orientation	2.20–2.22 (margins)	2.38 2.41 2.42 2.43	RA CP1 CP2 CP3	5, 6 4 5 12, 13
W2002-3-4	Create and modify tables	Creating and modifying tables	3.13–3.18 3.21–3.27	3.34 3.35 3.36 3.37 3.38	RA CP1 CP2 CP3 CP4	8, 10–12 10–12 8, 9 4, 7 6, 7
		Applying AutoFormats to tables	3.24	3.37	CP3	5
		Modifying table borders and shading	3.27–3.30	3.34 3.35 3.36 3.38	RA CP1 CP2 CP4	12, 13 13 11 6
		Revise tables (insert and delete rows and columns, modify cell formats)	3.21–3.27 3.35 3.36 3.37	3.34	RA CP1 CP2 CP3	10–12 17,18 12 10 4
W2002-3-5	Preview and Print documents, envelopes, and labels	Using Print Preview	1.30–1.31	1.35 1.36 1.37 1.37 1.38	RA CP1 CP2 CP3 CP4	18 14 11 4 12
		Printing documents, envelopes, and labels	1.31–1.32 (documents)	1.35 1.36 1.37 1.37 1.38	RA CP1 CP2 CP3 CP4	18 14 11 4 12

Standardized Coding Number	Certification Skill Activity — Activity	Courseware Reqs	End-of-Tutorial Pages	End-of-Tutorial Practice — Tutorial Pages	Exercise	Step Number
			1.32 (envelopes)	1.35	RA	20
				1.37	CP2	12
				1.37	CP3	5
W2002-4	**Managing Documents**					
W2002-4-1	Manage files and folders for documents	Creating folders for document storage	5.04–5.05	5.45	RA	3
				5.50	CP3	2
W2002-4-2	Create documents using templates	Creating a document from a template	5.22 5.47	5.47	RA	24
W2002-4-3	Save documents using different names and file formats	Using Save, Save As	1.18–1.19 (Save)	1.35	RA	13, 17 21
				1.36	CP1	8, 14
				1.37	CP2	9, 13
				1.37	CP3	3, 6
				1.38	CP4	10, 12
			2.04 (Save As)	2.38	RA	2, 18
				2.41	CP1	1
				2.42	CP2	1
				2.43	CP3	2
				2.44	CP4	2
W2002-5	**Working with Graphics**					
W2002-5-1	Insert images and graphics	Adding images to document	4.16–4.19	4.31	RA	14
				4.33	CP1	11
				4.34	CP2	9
				4.36	CP4	9
W2002-5-2	Create and modify diagrams and charts	Creating and modifying charts and diagrams	7.17–7.23	7.48 (charts)	RA	8
					CP1	3–5
				7.55 (diagrams)	CP4	18
W2002-6	**Workgroup Collaboration**					
W2002-6-1	Compare and Merge documents	Compare and Merge documents	7.2–7.6	7.48	RA	3–5
W2002-6-2	Insert, view and edit comments	Insert, view and edit comments	2.34–2.35	2.40	RA	17
				2.42	CP2	11
	Convert documents into Web pages	Previewing as documents as web pages	7.46–7.47	7.49, 7.50	RA	11, 21
				7.51	CP1	7
				7.52	CP2	9
		Saving documents as web pages	7.38–7.39	7.49	RA	17
				7.52	CP2	10
				7.53	CP3	7
				7.55	CP4	10

Expert Standardized Coding Number	Certification Skill Activity Activity	Courseware Reqs	End-of-Tutorial Pages	End-of-Tutorial Practice		
				Tutorial Pages	Exercise	Step Number
W2002e-1	**Customizing Paragraphs**					
W2002e-1-1	Control Pagination	Managing orphans and widows	10.14–10.17	10.68 10.71	RA CP1	8–9 7–8
		Setting line and page breaks	10.15–10.18 3.08 3.14	10.72 3.33 3.35 3.36	CP1 RA CP1 CP2	6 5 8 4
W2002e-1-2	Sort paragraphs In lists and tables	Using the Sort feature	3.20–3.21, 3.23	3.34 3.37 10.114	RA CP3 CP1	10 6 32
W2002e-2	**Formatting documents**					
W2002e-2-1	Create and format document sections	Using Page Setup options to format sections	3.09–3.10	3.33 3.35 3.36	RA CP1 CP2	5–6 3–4 4–5
		Verifying paragraph formats	5.10, 5.15 8.10–8.12	5.47 5.49–5.50 8.64	RA CP2 CP3	23 5, 15 5
		Clearing Formats	5.33, 5.39	5.46 5.49	RA CP2	16, 18 11
W2002e-2-2	Create and apply character and paragraph styles	Creating and applying character and paragraph styles	8.10–8.13 5.09–5.11 5.15–5.16 5.19–5–21	8.58 8.60 8.64 5.45 5.49 5.50	RA CP1 CP3 RA CP2 CP3	3–4 8 5 7–9 4–6 9
W2002e-2-3	Create and update document indexes and tables of contents, figures, and authorities	Inserting an index	10.55–10.62 10.74–10.77 10.78	10.70–10.71 CP2 CP3	RA 6, 31, 33 	23–30 3, 9–10
		Inserting a table of contents, table of figures, or tables of authorities	5.39–5.41 10.62–10.65	5.47 5.48 5.50 10.70 10.74 10.77 10.78–10.79 10.80	RA CP1 CP3 RA CP1 CP2 CP3 CP4	18 12 11 26–27 31 29 8, 14–16 14
W2002e-2-4	Create cross-references	Inserting cross-references	10.29–10.31	10.69–10.70 10.73 10.77 10.80	RA CP1 CP2 CP4	12, 24 28 32 6
W2002e-2-5	Add and revise endnotes and footnotes	Create, format, and edit footnotes and endnotes	5.29–5.31	5.48 5.48 5.50	RA CP1 CP3	14 9 7

Standardized Coding Number	Certification Skill Activity / Activity	Courseware Reqs	End-of-Tutorial Pages	End-of-Tutorial Practice Tutorial Pages	Exercise	Step Number
W2002e-2-6	Create and manage master documents and subdocuments	Creating master documents with three or more subdocuments	10.02–10.14, 10.19–10.20	10.68–10.70 10.71 10.75 10.77–10.78	RA CP1 CP2 CP3	4–7, 29 3–6 7–8 1–5
W2002e-2-7	Move within documents	Using automation features for document navigation (bookmarks and Document Map)	7.27–7.30 8.45–8.46 9.37–9.42	7.49 8.61 8.63 8.65 9.54	RA CP1 CP2 CP3 RA	12, 14–15 15 11 15 11–20
W2002e-2-8	Create and modify forms using various form controls	Creating custom forms using two or more form controls	9.1–9.53	9.53–9.55 9.56 9.59–9.60 9.60–9.61	RA CP1 CP3 CP4	1–27 1–25 1–22 1–23
W2002e-2-9	Create forms and prepare forms for distribution	Protecting forms	9.26–9.27 9.42–9.44	9.54 9.56 9.58 9.60 9.61	RA CP1 CP2 CP3 CP4	23 21 21 22 19
		Distributing forms	9.48–9.50	9.58	CP2	22
W2002e-3	**Customizing Tables**					
W2002e-3-1	Use Excel data in tables	Using object linking to display Excel worksheet data as a Word table or worksheet object	7.17–7.18	7.52 7.57	RA CP2	8 3
W2002e-3-1	Perform calculations in Word tables	Use formulas in tables	 9.35–9.37	3.34 9.54 9.58 9.59 9.61	RA RA CP2 CP3 CP4	18, 19 17 17 8–9 11
		Modifying table formats by merging and/or splitting table cells	9.11–9.14	9.53 9.56 9.59–9.60 9.60 3.34	RA CP1 CP3 CP4 RA	7, 10 9 5, 13 6 17
W2002e-4	**Creating and Modifying Graphics**					
W2002e-4-1	Create, modify, and position graphics	Creating and inserting graphics in documents	4.06–4.13 4.16–4.23 9.10–9.11	4.31 4.33 4.34 4.36 4.38 9.53	RA CP1 CP2 CP3 CP4 RA	5, 6, 14–16 3–5, 11–13 5, 6, 9–13 8–10 4, 9–10 3

Standardized Coding Number	Certification Skill Activity — Activity	Courseware Reqs	End-of-Tutorial Pages	End-of-Tutorial Practice		
				Tutorial Pages	Exercise	Step Number
		Modifying graphics	4.16–4.23	4.31	RA	5, 6, 14–16
				4.33	CP1	3–5, 11–13
				4.34	CP2	5, 6, 9–13
				4.36	CP3	8–10
					CP4	9–10
W2002e-4-2	Create and modify charts using data from other applications	Creating and revising charts using Excel or Access data	7.17–7.23	7.48	RA	7–8
				7.51	CP1	3–5
W2002e-4-3	Align text and graphics	Using advanced text wrapping and layout options with graphics	4.22	4.31	RA	18
				4.33	CP1	13
				4.34	CP2	13
				4.36	CP4	10
W2002e-5	**Customizing Word**					
W2002e-5-1	Create, edit, and run macros	Creating macros	8.32–8.46	8.59	RA	15, 16
				8.61	CP1	15
				8.63	CP2	11
			9.37–9.42	9.54	RA	19
				9.60	CP3	17
		Editing a macro using the Visual Basic Editor	8.42–8.44	8.59	RA	17
				8.63	CP2	12
		Running macros	8.50–8.52	8.59	RA	16, 17
				8.61	CP1	15
				8.63	CP2	11
			9.44–9.47	9.54	RA	19
				9.60	CP3	17
W2002e-5-2	Customize menus and toolbars	Creating a custom menu	8.4–8.5	8.60–8.62	CP1	4, 21
		Adding and removing buttons from a toolbar	8.22–8.24	8.58–59	RA	10–11 16, 22
W2002e-6	**Workgroup Collaboration**					
W2002e-6-1	Track, accept, and reject changes to documents	Tracking changes	7.07–7.08	7.50	RA	4–5
			10.31–10.36	10.69	RA	13–18
				10.72–10.73	CP1	13–21
				10.75–10.76	CP2	11–23
		Reviewing changes by type and reviewer	10.37	10.80	CP4	12
		Responding to proposed changes	7.07–7.08	7.50	RA	4–5
			10.36–10.39	10.69	RA	18
				10.73	CP1	21
				10.76	CP2	23

MOUS CERTIFICATION GRID

Standardized Coding Number	Certification Skill Activity — Activity	Courseware Reqs	End-of-Tutorial Pages	End-of-Tutorial Practice — Tutorial Pages	Exercise	Step Number
W2002e-6-2	Merge input from several reviewers	Distributing documents for revision via e-mail	7.25–7.26	7.50	RA	24
				7.51	CP1	13
			9.48–9.50			
			10. 41	10.80	CP4	16
		Merging three or more revisions of the same document	7.02–7.05	7.48	RA	3
			10.39	10.80	CP4	5
W2002e-6-3	Insert and modify hyperlinks to other documents and Web pages	Inserting and modifying hyperlinks	4.04–4.07	4.30	RA	4
				4.33	CP2	4
				4.35	CP3	3
			7.27–7.32	7.49	RA	12, 13, 14
				7.51	CP1	9, 10
				7.52	CP2	12
				7.53	CP3	9
				7.54	CP4	3, 5, 7, 11
W2002e-6-4	Create and edit Web documents in Word	Opening Web pages in Word	7.38–7.39 7.45–7.47	7.49–7.50	RA	17, 21
				7.53	CP2	10, 11, 13
				7.53–7.54	CP3	1, 7, 11
		Saving Word documents to the Web	7.37–7.40	7.49	RA	17
				7.53	CP2	10, 11
				7.53–7.54	CP3	7
W2002e-6-5	Create document versions	Creating versions of documents	10.39–10.40	10.73	CP1	19
				10.80	CP4	3
W2002e-6-6	Protect documents	Set document protection	10.32–10.33	10.75–10.76	CP2	10, 22
				10.78	CP3	11
				10.79	CP4	3
W2002e-6-7	Define and modify default file locations for workgroup templates	Modify and re-post HTML documents	5.22	5.46–5.47	RA	21, 24
				10.70	RA	23
W2002e-6-8	Attach digital signatures to documents	Using digital signatures to authenticate documents	10.44–10.47	10.70	RA	29
				10.73	CP1	22
				10.81	CP4	7, 9
W2002e-7	**Using Mail Merge**					
W2002e-7-1	Merge letters with a Word, Excel, or Access data source	Completing an entire mail merge process for form letters	6.2–6.29	6.38	RA	1–10
				6.40–41	CP1	2–10
				6.41–42	CP2	2–10
				6.43–44	CP3	6–12, 16
W2002e-7-2	Merge labels with a Word, Excel, or Access data source	Completing an entire mail merge process for mailing labels	6.29–6.34	6.42	CP2	11–14
W2002e-7-3	Use Outlook data as mail merge data source	Completing a mail merge using Outlook information as the data source	6.08	6.45	CP4	15

Microsoft Excel 2002 MOUS Certification Grid

Note: This grid contains a complete list of the Excel 2002 Core and Expert skills. These skills are covered in one or more of the following texts: *New Perspectives on Microsoft Office XP First Course, New Perspectives on Microsoft Office XP Second Course,* and *New Perspectives on Microsoft Office XP Third Course.*

Core Standardized Coding Number	Certification Skill Activity — Activity	Tutorial Pages	End-of-Tutorial Practice — End-of-Tutorial Pages	Exercise	Step Number
Ex2002-1-1	Insert, delete, and move cells	1.18	1.38	Review Assignment	7
			1.39	Case Problem 1	2
			1.39	Case Problem 2	4–5
		1.26–1.28	1.38	Review Assignment	4
Ex2002-1-2	Enter and edit cell data including text, numbers, and formulas	1.20–1.25, 1.31	1.38	Review Assignment	3–6,10
			1.39	Case Problem 1	3,5–8, 11,15
			1.39,1.40	Case Problem 2	3,7–10, 14
			1.40–1.41	Case Problem 3	3–6
			1.41,1.42	Case Problem 4	2,3,5,7
Ex2002-1-3	Check spelling	7.02–7.04	7.49	Review Assignment	2
			7.52	Case Problem 3	5
			7.53	Case Problem 4	4
Ex2002-1-4	Find and replace cell data and formats	3.25–3.27			
		5.09–5.10	5.50	Case Problem 2	5
Ex2002-1-5	Work with a subset of data by filtering lists	5.18–5.20	5.48	Review Assignment	8,10
			5.50	Case Problem 2	10
Ex2002-2	**Managing Workbooks**				
Ex2002-2-1	Manage workbook files and folders	1.12–1.14	1.38	Review Assignment	1
			1.39	Case Problem 1	1
			1.39	Case Problem 2	1
			1.40	Case Problem 3	1
Ex2002-2-2	Create workbooks using templates	6.14–6.16			
Ex2002-2-3	Save workbooks using different names and file formats	1.12–1.15	1.38	Review Assignment	2
			1.39	Case Problem 1	1
			1.39	Case Problem 2	1
			1.40	Case Problem 3	1
			1.41	Case Problem 4	1
Ex2002-3	**Formatting and Printing Worksheets**				
Ex2002-3-1	Apply and modify cell formats	3.03–3.14	3.41	Review Assignment	4,6,7, 9–17
			3.42	Case Problem 1	4
			3.43	Case Problem 2	3–8
			3.44	Case Problem 3	3–8
			3.45	Case Problem 4	6
Ex2002-3-2	Modify row and column settings	1.26–1.28	1.40	Case Problem 2	2
		3.22–3.23			
		5.06–5.07	5.49	Case Problem 1	3
			5.50	Case Problem 2	4
			5.51	Case Problem 3	4
			5.52	Case Problem 4	3

Standardized Coding Number	Certification Skill Activity / Activity	Tutorial Pages	End-of-Tutorial Pages	Exercise	Step Number
			End-of-Tutorial Practice		
Ex2002-3-3	Modify row and column formats	1.29–1.30	1.38	Review Assignment	8,11
			1.39	Case Problem 1	4,12
			1.40	Case Problem 2	6,15
			1.41	Case Problem 4	4
		3.11–3.14	3.44	Review Assignment	4
				Case Problem 3	4
Ex2002-3-4	Apply styles	3.28–3.31	3.42	Case Problem 1	5
Ex2002-3-5	Use automated tools to format worksheets	3.31–3.32	3.41	Review Assignment	5
			6.38	Review Assignment	7
			6.40	Case Problem 1	6
			6.40	Case Problem 2	5
Ex2002-3-6	Modify Page Setup options for worksheets	3.33–3.39	3.41	Review Assignment	19
			3.42	Case Problem 1	6
			3.43	Case Problem 2	9,12
			3.44	Case Problem 3	10
Ex2002-3-7	Preview and print worksheets and workbooks	1.36	1.38	Review Assignment	14
			1.39	Case Problem 1	14
			1.40	Case Problem 2	16
			1.41	Case Problem 3	7
			1.42	Case Problem 4	6,8
		3.32–3.33	3.34	Case Problem 2	13
		3.37	3.41, 3.42	Review Assignment	18,22
			3.43	Case Problem 2	10,13
			3.44	Case Problem 3	9,12
			3.46	Case Problem 4	9
		4.38–4.40	4.43	Review Assignment	13,14
			4.45	Case Problem 2	13
			4.45	Case Problem 3	15
Ex2002-4	**Modifying Workbooks**				
Ex2002-4-1	Insert and delete worksheets	1.33–1.34	1.38	Review Assignment	9,13
			1.39	Case Problem 1	10,13
			1.40	Case Problem 2	12,13
			1.42	Case Problem 4	3,4
Ex2002-4-2	Modify worksheet names and positions	1.35	1.38	Review Assignment	9,12
			1.39	Case Problem 1	9,10
			1.40	Case Problem 2	11,13
			1.41	Case Problem 4	3
		3.24–3.25			
Ex2002-4-3	Use 3-D references	6.06–6.08, 6.22–6.25	6.38	Review Assignment	4,6
			6.39, 6.40	Case Problem 1	2,5
			6.40	Case Problem 2	4
			6.41	Case Problem 3	2,4
			6.41, 6.42	Case Problem 4	3,7

Standardized Coding Number	Certification Skill Activity		Tutorial Pages	End-of-Tutorial Practice		
		Activity		End-of-Tutorial Pages	Exercise	Step Number
Ex2002-5	**Creating and Revising Formulas**					
Ex2002-5-1	Create and revise formulas		2.03–2.20	2.30–2.31	Review Assignment	5–10, 13,14
				2.31–2.32	Case Problem 1	5,6,7,8
				2.34	Case Problem 2	4,6
				2.35	Case Problem 3	11
Ex2002-5-2	Use statistical, date and time, in formulas		2.03–2.29	2.30,2.31	Review Assignment	3,6–8, 14–15
				2.31–2.32	Case Problem 1	4–7
				2.33	Case Problem 1	5–7
				2.34–2.35	Case Problem 3	4,6, 8–10
				2.36	Case Problem 4	5
				5.48	Review Assignment	8
				5.50	Case Problem 2	10
				5.51	Case Problem 3	3
Ex2002-6	**Creating and Modifying Graphics**					
Ex2002-6-1	Create, modify, position and print charts		4.03–4.35	4.42–4.43	Review Assignment	4–9
				4.43–4.44	Case Problem 1	3–12
				4.44	Case Problem 2	3–10
				4.45	Case Problem 3	4–11
				4.47	Case Problem 4	2–8
Ex2002-6-2	Create, modify and position graphics		4.35–4.40	4.43	Review Assignment	10–12
				4.45	Case Problem 3	12–13
Ex2002-7	**Workgroup Collaboration**					
Ex2002-7-1	Convert worksheets into web pages		7.36–7.44	7.50	Review Assignment	14–15
				7.51	Case Problem 1	8
				7.51–7.52	Case Problem 2	7–9
				7.53	Case Problem 3	8
				7.54	Case Problem 4	6
Ex2002-7-2	Create hyperlinks		7.44–7.47	7.50	Review Assignment	13
				7.50–7.51	Case Problem 1	6–7
				7.51	Case Problem 2	6
				7.53	Case Problem 3	9
Ex2002-7-3	View and edit comments		7.16–7.19	7.49,7.50	Review Assignment	5,9,10
				7.52	Case Problem 3	7
				7.53	Case Problem 4	5

Expert **Standardized Coding Number**	**Certification Skill Activity** Activity	**Tutorial Pages**	**End-of-Tutorial Practice**		
			End-of-Tutorial Pages	**Exercise**	**Step Number**
Ex2002e-1	**Importing and Exporting Data**				
Ex2002e-1-1	Import data to Excel	11.05–11.09	11.50–11.51	Review Assignment	4–14
			11.51	Case Problem 1	2–7
			11.52	Case Problem 2	2–10
			11.53	Case Problem 3	3–10
			11.54	Case Problem 4	3–7
			A2.13	Case Problem 2	2–6
Ex2002e-1-2	Export data from Excel	A2.04–A2.08	A2.11	Review Assignment	2–6
			A2.12	Case Problem 1	2–5
Ex2002e-1-3	Publish worksheets and workbooks to the Web	7.38–7.44	7.50	Review Assignment	14–15
			7.50	Case Problem 1	8
			7.51	Case Problem 2	7–9
			7.53	Case Problem 3	8
			7.53	Case Problem 4	6
		A4.09–A4.11	A4.18	Review Assignment	2
			A4.19	Case Problem 1	2
			A4.19	Case Problem 2	2
Ex2002e-2	**Managing Workbooks**				
Ex2002e-2-1	Create, edit, and apply templates	6.13–6.22	6.40	Review Assignment	11
			6.41	Case Problem 1	10
			6.42	Case Problem 2	9
Ex2002e-2-2	Create workspaces	6.37–6.39	6.44	Case Problem 4	10
Ex2002e-2-3	Use Data Consolidation	6.08–6.11	6.40	Review Assignment	4
			6.41	Case Problem 1	2
			6.42	Case Problem 2	4
			6.43	Case Problem 3	2
Ex2002e-3	**Formatting Numbers**				
Ex2002e-3-1	Create and apply custom number formats	9-16–9.17	9.39	Review Assignment	6
		A3.03–A3.09	A3.12–A3.13	Review Assignment	2–7
			A3.13	Case Problem 1	2–6
			A3.13–A3.14	Case Problem 2	2–4
Ex2002e-3-2	Use conditional formats	5.22–5.25	5.48	Review Assignment	9
			5.49	Case Problem 1	6
			5.50	Case Problem 2	8
			5.51	Case Problem 3	7
			5.52	Case Problem 4	7
Ex2002e-4	**Working with Ranges**				
Ex2002e-4-1	Use named ranges in formulas	8.15–8.24	8.48	Review Assignment	6–8
			8.53	Case Problem 2	3–4
			8.55	Case Problem 3	2–5
		12.27–12.31			
Ex2002e-4-2	Use Lookup and Reference functions	6.32–6.37	6.40	Review Assignment	6
			6.41	Case Problem 1	5
			6.43	Case Problem 3	4,5
			6.44	Case Problem 4	3,7

Standardized Coding Number	Certification Skill Activity — Activity	Tutorial Pages	End-of-Tutorial Practice — End-of-Tutorial Pages	Exercise	Step Number
			8.56	Case Problem 4	5
			12.62	Case Problem 2	3
Ex2002e-5	**Customizing Excel**				
Ex2002e-5-1	Customize toolbars and menus	12.44–12.54	12.60	Review Assignment	9–11
Ex2002e-5-2	Create, edit, and run macros	8.27–8.46	8.48	Review Assignment	11–22
			8.51	Case Problem 1	8–12
			8.53	Case Problem 2	7–12
			8.56	Case Problem 4	7–10
		12.03–12.04;	12.59	Review Assignment	4–7
		12.12–12.19;	12.62	Case Problem 1	2–5
		12.28–12.31;	12.63–12.64	Case Problem 2	4–7
		12.39–12.43	12.65	Case Problem 3	3–9
			12.66	Case Problem 4	2–7
Ex2002e-6	**Auditing Worksheets**				
Ex2002e-6-1	Audit formulas	7.04–7.08	7.49	Review Assignment	3
			7.50	Case Problem 1	5
Ex2002e-6-2	Locate and resolve errors	7.08–7.16	7.49	Review Assignment	4
			7.50	Case Problem 1	5
			7.52	Case Problem 3	6
Ex2002e-6-3	Identify dependencies in formulas	7.08–7.16	7.49	Review Assignment	3
			7.50	Case Problem 1	5
Ex2002e-7	**Summarizing Data**				
Ex2002e-7-1	Use subtotals with lists and ranges	5.25–5.28	5.48	Review Assignment	7
			5.49	Case Problem 1	5
			5.50	Case Problem 2	9
			5.51	Case Problem	8–9
Ex2002e-7-2	Define and apply filters	5.20–5.21	5.50	Case Problem 2	6
			5.51	Case Problem 3	6
Ex2002e-7-3	Add group and outline criteria to ranges	5.28–5.29	5.48	Review Assignment	12
			5.51	Case Problem 3	10
Ex2002e-7-4	Use data validation	8.04–8.10	8.48	Review Assignment	4
			8.50	Case Problem 1	3–4
			8.56	Case Problem 4	3
Ex2002e-7-5	Retrieve external data and create queries	11.12–11.32	11.50–11.51	Review Assignment	4–16
			11.51	Case Problem 1	2–7
			11.52	Case Problem 2	2–10
			11.53	Case Problem 3	3–10
			11.54	Case Problem 4	3–7
Ex2002e-7-6	Create Extensible Markup Language (XML) Web queries	11.13-11.22	11.50	Review Assignment	4–6
			11.52	Case Problem 2	2–5
			11.54	Case Problem 4	2–6

Standardized Coding Number	Certification Skill Activity Activity	Tutorial Pages	End-of-Tutorial Practice End-of-Tutorial Pages	Exercise	Step Number
Ex2002e-8	**Analyzing Data**				
Ex2002e-8-1	Create PivotTables, PivotCharts, and PivotTable/PivotChart Reports	5.31–5.47	5.48	Review Assignment	11–14
			5.49	Case Problem 1	10–11
			5.50	Case Problem 2	11
			5.51	Case Problem 3	10–11
			5.52	Case Problem 4	8–9, 11–13
		9.35–9.38	9.40	Review Assignment	11
			9.43	Case Problem 2	8
		A4.05–4.10	A4.18	Review Assignment	2
Ex2002e-8-2	Forecast values with what-if analysis	9.23–9.24	9.41	Case Problem 1	3
Ex2002e-8-3	Create and display scenarios	9.22–9.32	9.39	Review Assignment	8–12
			9.40–9.42	Case Problem 1	7–9
			9.42–9.43	Case Problem 2	3–7
			9.43–9.44	Case Problem 3	5–6
			9.44–9.46	Case Problem 4	6–7
Ex2002e-9	**Workgroup Collaboration**				
Ex2002e-9-1	Modify passwords, protections, and properties	8.10–8.15	8.48	Review Assignment	9,10
			8.51	Case Problem 1	7,15
			8.53	Case Problem 2	10–11
			8.55	Case Problem 3	6
			8.57	Case Problem 4	4,6
Ex2002e-9-2	Create a shared workbook	7.19–7.23	7.49	Review Assignment	6,11
			7.51	Case Problem 2	5
			7.52	Case Problem 3	4
			7.53	Case Problem 4	1,4
Ex2002e-9-3	Track, accept and reject changes to workbooks	7.24–7.32	7.50	Review Assignment	8
			7.50	Case Problem 1	3
			7.51	Case Problem 2	4,5
			7.52	Case Problem 3	2,3
Ex2002e-9-4	Merge workbooks	7.34–7.36	7.50	Case Problem 1	2
			7.51	Case Problem 2	2
			7.53	Case Problem 4	2

Microsoft Access 2002 MOUS Certification Grid

Note: This grid contains a complete list of the Access 2002 Core and Expert skills. These skills are covered in one or more of the following texts: *New Perspectives on Microsoft Office XP First Course, New Perspectives on Microsoft Office XP Second Course,* and *New Perspectives on Microsoft Office XP Third Course.*

Core	Certification Skill Activity		Tutorial Number (page numbers)	End-of-Tutorial Practice	
Standardized Coding Number		Activity		Exercise	Step Number
AC2002-1		**Creating and Using Databases**			
Ac2002-1-1		Create Access databases	2 (2.07)	Review Assignment	2
Ac2002-1-2		Open database objects in multiple views	1 (1.10–1.11, 1.13–1.14, 1.18–1.19, 1.20–1.21) 2	1: Review Assignment	5
				Case Problem 1	3–6
				Case Problem 2	3, 4, 6–9
				Case Problem 3	3–9
				Case Problem 4	3–9
				2: Review Assignment	3–6, 9
				Case Problem 1	3, 6–10
				Case Problem 2	3–11
				Case Problem 3	5–7
				Case Problem 4	4–6, 8–12
Ac2002-1-3		Move among records	1 (1.11–1.12, 1.17–1.18, 1.20–1.22) 2 4 (4.07–4.08) 5 (5.33)	1: Review Assignment	9
				Case Problem 2	6, 7
				Case Problem 3	8
				Case Problem 4	16
				2: Review Assignment	9
				Case Problem 1	7, 11
				Case Problem 2	7
				Case Problem 3	6
				Case Problem 4	
Ac2002-1-4		Format datasheets	2 (2.29) 3 (3.25–3.26)	2: Review Assignment	11, 15
				Case Problem 1	8, 10, 12
				Case Problem 3	6
				Case Problem 4	12
				3: Review Assignment	10–12
				Case Problem 2	8
				Case Problem 3	6, 7
				Case Problem 4	3, 6
Ac2002-2		**Creating and Modifying Tables**			
Ac2002-2-1		Create and modify tables	2 (2.09)	Review Assignment	3, 13
				Case Problem 3	3
				Case Problem 4	3
Ac2002-2-2		Add a pre-defined input mask to a field	5 (5.10–5.13)	Review Assignment	5
				Case Problem 1	3
				Case Problem 2	2
				Case Problem 4	3
				Case Problem 5	13
Ac2002-2-3		Create Lookup fields	5 (5.01–5.09)	Review Assignment	2
				Case Problem 1	2
				Case Problem 3	2
				Case Problem 4	2
				Case Problem 5	15

Standardized Coding Number	Certification Skill Activity — Activity	Tutorial Number (page numbers)	End-of-Tutorial Practice — Exercise	Step Number
Ac2002-2-4	Modify field properties	2 (2.22–2.27) 5 (5.10–5.13)	2: Review Assignment Case Problem 1 Case Problem 2 Case Problem 3 Case Problem 4 5: Review Assignment Case Problem 1 Case Problem 2 Case Problem 4	5, 10, 14 7 6 5 5 5 3 2 3
Ac2002-3 Ac2002-3-1	**Creating and Modifying Queries** Create and modify Select queries	1 (1.13–1.17) 3 (3.02–3.07, 3–23–3.24) 5 (5.15–5.16)	1: Review Assignment Case Problem 1 Case Problem 2 Case Problem 3 Case Problem 4 3: Review Assignment Case Problem 1 Case Problem 2 Case Problem 3 Case Problem 4 5: Review Assignment Case Problem 1 Case Problem 2 Case Problem 3 Case Problem 4	7 4 4 4 5 2, 5, 9, 12 3 3, 5–8 3, 5–7 3–7 6, 8–10 5, 6, 8 5, 8 5, 7, 8 5, 7, 8
Ac2002-3-2	Add calculated fields to Select queries	3 (3.34–3.38, 3.38–3.39)	Review Assignment Case Problem 2 Case Problem 3 Case Problem 4	10 8 6, 7 4
Ac2002-4 Ac2002-4-1	**Creating and Modifying Forms** Create and display forms	1 (1.18–1.20) 4 (4.02–4.07, 4.16–4.19) 5 (5.23–5.58)	1: Review Assignment Case Problem 1 Case Problem 2 Case Problem 3 Case Problem 4 4: Review Assignment Case Problem 1 Case Problem 2 Case Problem 3 Case Problem 4 5: Review Assignment Case Problem 1 Case Problem 2 Case Problem 3 Case Problem 4 Case Problem 5	8 5 7 6 8 3, 6, 7 2, 6 2 3, 6 2 11 9 9, 12, 13 9 9, 12, 13 8

Standardized Coding Number	**Certification Skill Activity** Activity	Tutorial Number (page numbers)	**End-of-Tutorial Practice** Exercise	Step Number
Ac2002-4-2	Modify form properties	5 (5.31–5.32, 5.33–5.35, 5.37–5.39, 5.40–5.42, 5.46–5.47, 5.51)	Review Assignment Case Problem 1 Case Problem 2 Case Problem 3 Case Problem 4 Case Problem 5	11 9 9, 12, 13 9 9, 12, 13 8
Ac2002-5	**Viewing and Organizing Information**			
Ac2002-5-1	Enter, edit, and delete records	2 (2.19–2.22, 2.23–2.24, 2.28) 3 (3.07) 4 (4.12–4.13)	2: Review Assignment Case Problem 1 Case Problem 2 Case Problem 3 Case Problem 4 3: Review Assignment Case Problem 2 Case Problem 3 4: Review Assignment Case Problem 1 Case Problem 2 Case Problem 3 Case Problem 4	4, 6, 16 5, 9, 12 5, 7, 11 7 6, 10 3 4 4 5 5 4, 5 4 4, 5
Ac2002-5-2	Create queries	1 (1.15–1.18) 3 (3.02–3.07, 3.13–3.14, 3.23–3.24, 3.32–3.33, 3.39–3.41) 5 (5.15–5.16)	1: Review Assignment Case Problem 1 Case Problem 2 Case Problem 3 Case Problem 4 3: Review Assignment Case Problem 1 Case Problem 2 Case Problem 3 Case Problem 4 5: Review Assignment Case Problem 1 Case Problem 2 Case Problem 3 Case Problem 4	7 4 4 4 5 2, 5, 9, 12 3 3, 5–8 3, 5–7 3–8 6, 8–10 5, 6, 8 5, 8 5, 7, 8 5, 7, 8
Ac2002-5-3	Sort records	3 (3.14–3.20, 3.33)	Review Assignment Case Problem 1 Case Problem 2 Case Problem 3 Case Problem 4	5, 10 3 3, 7 3 3–5
Ac2002-5-4	Filter records	3 (3.20–3.21) 5 (5.53–5.58)	3: Review Assignment Case Problem 1 5: Review Assignment Case Problem 2 Case Problem 4	6–8 4 12, 13 10, 11 10, 11
Ac2002-6	**Defining Relationships**			
Ac2002-6-1	Create one-to-many relationships	3 (3.08–3.13)	Review Assignment Case Problem 1 Case Problem 2 Case Problem 3 Case Problem 4	4 2 2 2 2

Standardized Coding Number	Activity	Tutorial Number (page numbers)	Exercise	Step Number
Ac2002-6-2	Enforce referential integrity	3 (3.09, 3.11–3.12)	Review Assignment	4
			Case Problem 1	2
			Case Problem 2	2
			Case Problem 3	2
			Case Problem 4	2
Ac2002-7	**Producing Reports**			
Ac2002-7-1	Create and format reports	1 (1.20–1.23)	1: Review Assignment	12
		4 (4.22–4.30)	Case Problem 1	6
		6 (6.02–6.57)	Case Problem 2	8
			Case Problem 3	7
			Case Problem 4	9
			4: Review Assignment	8
			Case Problem 1	8
			Case Problem 2	7
			Case Problem 3	8
			Case Problem 4	7
			6: Review Assignment	2-7
			Case Problem 1	3-9
			Case Problem 2	3-5
			Case Problem 3	3-8
			Case Problem 4	3-9
			Case Problem 5	3-4
Ac2002-7-2	Add calculated controls to reports	6 (6.08–6.10, 6.29–6.32, 6.36–6.40)	Case Problem 1	7e, 7g
			Case Problem 2	3h, 3i
			Case Problem 3	7f, 7g
			Case Problem 4	6f, 7e, 7f
			Case Problem 5	3
Ac2002-7-3	Preview and print reports	4 (4.27–4.30, 4.32–4.33)	4: Review Assignment	11
		6 (6.20–6.21, 6.49–6.50, 6.54)	Case Problem 1	10
			Case Problem 2	11
			Case Problem 3	11
			Case Problem 4	11
			6: Review Assignment	7
			Case Problem 1	8, 9e
			Case Problem 2	4, 5g
			Case Problem 3	8
			Case Problem 4	8, 9e
			Case Problem 5	4
Ac2002-8	**Integrating with Other Applications**			
Ac2002-8-1	Import data to Access	2 (2.29–2.33)	2: Review Assignment	8
		7 (7.46–7.48)	Case Problem 1	6
			Case Problem 2	8
			Case Problem 3	3
			Case Problem 4	3, 11
			7: Case Problem 2	7
Ac2002-8-2	Export data from Access	7 (7.02–7.05, 7.49–7.54)	Review Assignment	2, 7, 8
			Case Problem 1	2, 7, 8
			Case Problem 2	2, 8, 9
			Case Problem 3	2, 7, 8
			Case Problem 4	2, 7, 8
			Case Problem 5	2, 6
Ac2002-8-3	Create a simple data access page	7 (7.08–7.11)	Case Problem 4	4

Expert	Certification Skill Activity		End-of-Tutorial Practice	
Standardized Coding Number	**Activity**	**Tutorial Number (page numbers)**	**Exercise**	**Step Number**
Ac2002e-1	**Creating And Modifying Tables**			
Ac2002e-1-1	Use data validation	5 (5.13–5.14)	Review Assignment	3
			Case Problem 2	3
			Case Problem 3	3
			Case Problem 5	14
Ac2002e-1-2	Link tables	11 (11.08–11.12)	Case Problem 1	4–5
			Case Problem 2	4
			Case Problem 3	4
Ac2002e-1-3	Create lookup fields and modify Lookup field properties	5 (5.04–5.09)	Review Assignment	2
			Case Problem 1	2
			Case Problem 3	2
			Case Problem 4	2
			Case Problem 5	15
Ac2002e-1-4	Create and modify input masks	5 (5.10–5.13)	Review Assignment	5
			Case Problem 1	3
			Case Problem 2	2
			Case Problem 4	3
			Case Problem 5	13
Ac2002e-2	**Creating And Modifying Forms**			
Ac2002e-2-1	Create a form in Design View	5 (5.23–5.52)	Review Assignment	11
			Case Problem 1	9
			Case Problem 2	9, 12, 13
			Case Problem 3	9
			Case Problem 4	9, 12, 13
			Case Problem 5	7, 8
Ac2002e-2-2	Create a Switchboard and set startup options	9 (9.02–9.04, 9.39–9.54) 11 (11.23–11.25)	9: Review Assignment	3–5
			Case Problem 1	2–5
			Case Problem 2	2–4
			Case Problem 3	2–5
			Case Problem 4	2–6
			Case Problem 5	2–4
			11: Review Assignment	6
			Case Problem 1	6
			Case Problem 2	5
			Case Problem 3	6
			Case Problem 5	5
Ac2002e-2-3	Add Subform controls to Access forms	5 (5.48–5.52)	Review Assignment	11
			Case Problem 1	9
			Case Problem 2	12
			Case Problem 4	12, 13
			Case Problem 5	8
Ac2002e-3	**Refining Queries**			
Ac2002e-3-1	Specify multiple query criteria	3 (3.28–3.33) 5 (5.19–5.20)	3: Review Assignment	9, 11
			Case Problem 1	6
			Case Problem 2	7
			Case Problem 3	5
			Case Problem 4	5
			5: Review Assignment	6, 7
			Case Problem 2	7
			Case Problem 3	7

Standardized Coding Number	**Certification Skill Activity** Activity	Tutorial Number (page numbers)	End-of-Tutorial Practice Exercise	Step Number
Ac2002e-3-2	Create and apply advanced filters	8 (8.29–8.31)	Review Assignment	11
			Case Problem 1	9
			Case Problem 2	9
			Case Problem 3	11
Ac2002e-3-3	Create and run parameter queries	5 (5.20–5.22)	Review Assignment	10
			Case Problem 1	8
			Case Problem 2	8
			Case Problem 3	8
			Case Problem 4	8
Ac2002e-3-4	Create and run action queries	8 (8.16–8.28)	Review Assignment	7–10
			Case Problem 1	8
			Case Problem 2	8
			Case Problem 3	8–10
			Case Problem 4	7–9
			Case Problem 5	11–12
Ac2002e-3-5	Use aggregate functions in queries	3 (3.38–3.41)	Review Assignment	12
			Case Problem 2	8
			Case Problem 3	7
			Case Problem 4	7
Ac2002e-4	**Producing Reports**			
Ac2002e-4-1	Create and modify reports	6 (6.10–6.40)	Review Assignment	2–7
			Case Problem 1	3–8, 9
			Case Problem 2	3–4, 5
			Case Problem 3	3–8
			Case Problem 4	3–8, 9
			Case Problem 5	3–4
Ac2002e-4-2	Add Subreport controls to Access reports	6 (6.22–6.32)	Review Assignment	5
			Case Problem 1	6
			Case Problem 3	6
			Case Problem 4	6
Ac2002e-4-3	Sort and group data in reports	6 (6.12–6.13)	Review Assignment	4h, 5i
			Case Problem 1	5d, 6h, 9d
			Case Problem 2	3a, 5d
			Case Problem 3	5a
			Case Problem 4	5b, 6e, 9d
			Case Problem 5	3b
Ac2002e-5	**Defining Relationships**			
Ac2002e-5-1	Establish one-to-many relationships	3 (3.08–3.12) 8 (8.32–8.39)	3: Review Assignment	4
			Case Problem 1	2
			Case Problem 2	2
			Case Problem 3	2
			Case Problem 4	2
			8: Review Assignment	3
			Case Problem 1	3, 4
			Case Problem 2	3, 4
			Case Problem 3	3
			Case Problem 4	3
			Case Problem 5	3
Ac2002e-5-2	Establish many-to-many relationships	3 (3.08–3.12) 8 (8.32–8.39)	3: Review Assignment	4
			Case Problem 1	2
			Case Problem 2	2
			Case Problem 3	2
			Case Problem 4	2

Standardized Coding Number	Certification Skill Activity — Activity	Tutorial Number (page numbers)	End-of-Tutorial Practice — Exercise	Step Number
			8: Review Assignment	3
			Case Problem 1	3, 4
			Case Problem 2	3, 4
			Case Problem 3	3
			Case Problem 4	3
			Case Problem 5	3
Ac2002e-6	**Operating Access on the Web**			
Ac2002e-6-1	Create and Modify a Data Access Page	7 (7.14–7.24)	Review Assignment	5
			Case Problem 1	5
			Case Problem 2	5
			Case Problem 3	5
			Case Problem 4	5
			Case Problem 5	5
Ac2002e-6-2	Save PivotTables and PivotCharts views to Data Access Pages	7 (7.25–7.45)	Review Assignment	6
			Case Problem 1	6
			Case Problem 2	6
			Case Problem 3	6
			Case Problem 4	6
			Case Problem 5	6
Ac2002e-7	**Using Access tools**			
Ac2002e-7-1	Import XML documents into Access	7 (7.46–7.48)	Case Problem 2	7
Ac2002e-7-2	Export Access data to XML documents	7 (7.49–7.51)	Review Assignment	7
			Case Problem 1	7
			Case Problem 2	8
			Case Problem 3	7
			Case Problem 4	7
			Case Problem 5	6
Ac2002e-7-3	Encrypt and decrypt databases	11 (11.25–11.27)	Review Assignment	7
			Case Problem 1	7
			Case Problem 2	6
			Case Problem 3	7
Ac2002e-7-4	Compact and repair databases	1 (1.24–1.25) 5	1: Review Assignment 5: Case Problem 5	7, 9 12
Ac2002e-7-5	Assign database security	11 (27–11.38)	Case Problem 2	6
			Case Problem 4	5
Ac2002e-7-6	Replicate a database	11 (11.13–11.18)	Review Assignment	4
			Case Problem 3	5
			Case Problem 4	4
			Case Problem 5	4
Ac2002e-8	**Creating Database Applications**			
Ac2002e-8-1	Create Access Modules	10 (10.02–10.04, 10.10–10.14, 10.16–10.32, 10.36–10.41)	Review Assignment	2, 3
			Case Problem 1	2
			Case Problem 2	2
			Case Problem 3	2, 3
			Case Problem 4	2–4
			Case Problem 5	2, 3
Ac2002e-8-2	Use the Database Splitter	11 (11.19–11.22)	Review Assignment	5
			Case Problem 1	5
Ac2002e-8-3	Create an MDE file	11 (11.38–11.39)	Review Assignment	8
			Case Problem 1	7
			Case Problem 2	8
			Case Problem 3	8
			Case Problem 5	6

Microsoft PowerPoint 2002 MOUS Certification Grid

Note: This grid contains a complete list of the PowerPoint 2002 MOUS skills. These skills are covered in one or more of the following texts: *New Perspectives on Microsoft Office XP First Course, New Perspectives on Microsoft Office XP Second Course,* and *New Perspectives on Microsoft Office XP Third Course.*

Standardized Coding Number	Skill Sets and Skills Being Measured	Activity	End-of-Tutorial Practice		
			Tutorial Pages	Exercise	Step Number
PP2002-1	**Creating Presentations**				
PP2002-1-1	Create presentations (manually and using automated tools)	Creating presentations from a blank presentation	2.02	CP4 (2.38) CP4 (3.49)	2 3
		Creating presentations using the AutoContent Wizard	1.12	CP1 (1.35) CP4 (1.38)	1, 2 1
		Creating presentations using Design templates	2.02	RA (2.33) CP1 (2.35) CP2 (2.36)	3 2 2
PP2002-1-2	Add slides to and delete slides from presentations	Adding slides to presentations	1.21	CP3 (1.38) RA (2.34)	14 14, 20
		Delete slides from a presentation	1.26	CP1 (1.35) CP4 (1.39)	11 8
PP2002-1-3	Modify headers and footers in the Slide Master	Adding information to the Footer area, Date/Time area, or Number Area of the Slide Master	2.06, 2.13	RA (2.33) CP2 (2.37) CP4 (2.39)	5 5 6
PP2002-2	**Inserting and Modifying Text**				
PP2002-2-1	Import text from Word	Open a Word outline as a presentation	4.06	RA (4.33) CP1 (4.35) CP2 (4.36) CP4 (4.39)	1 1 4 1
PP2002-2-2	Insert, format, and modify text	Adding text to slides	1.22	RA (1.34)	5, 15, 16
		Edit and format text on slides	1.18 3.10	RA (1.34) RA (3.43)	6, 12 4
PP2002-3	**Inserting and Modifying Visual Elements**				
PP2002-3-1	Add tables, charts, clip art, and bitmap images to slides	Creating tables on slides	2.20	RA (2.34) CP1 (2.36) CP2 (2.37)	22 15 13
		Adding ClipArt images to slides	2.15	RA (2.33) CP1 (2.35) CP2 (2.37)	7, 12 9 10
		Adding charts and bitmap images to slides	2.06, 3.17, 3.22, 3.27	RA (2.33) CP1 (2.35) CP4 (2.39) RA (3.43) CP1 (3.45) CP1 (4.35)	4, 9 6, 8 9 15, 17 7, 9,14 8, 10, 11, 13
PP2002-3-2	Customize slide backgrounds	Adding bitmap graphics to slides or backgrounds	3.13, 6.10	RA (3.43) CP1 (6.37)	7 1
PP2002-3-3	Add OfficeArt elements to slides	Creating OfficeArt elements and adding them to slides	2.27	RA (2.34) CP1 (2.36)	16

Standardized Coding Number	Skill Sets and Skills Being Measured	Activity	Tutorial Pages	Exercise	Step Number
PP2002-3-4	Apply custom formats to tables	Applying user-defined formats to tables	2.22	RA (2.34) CP1 (2.36) CP2 (2.37)	24, 25 18, 19 15–17
PP2002-4	**Modifying Presentation Formats**				
PP2002-4-1	Apply formats to presentations	Formatting slides differently in a single presentation	2.16, 2.24	RA (2.33) CP2 (2.37)	7, 14 6
		Modifying presentation templates	2.05	RA (2.33) CP1 (2.35)	3,4,6 2, 3–5
		Modifying the format of slides independent of other slides	3.20	CP2 (3.47) CP3 (3.48)	23 14
		Applying more than one design template to presentations	2.10	CP4 (3.29)	11
PP2002-4-2	Apply animation schemes	Applying an animation scheme to a single slide, group of slides, or an entire presentation	3.33, 3.34 5.10	RA (3.44) CP1 (3.45) CP2 (3.47) RA (5.38) CP1 (5.40)	20, 21 17 22 5 7
PP2002-4-3	Apply slide transitions	Applying transition effects to a single slide, group of slides, or an entire presentation	3.31, 5.29	RA (3.43) CP1 (3.45) CP2 (3.47) RA (5.40)	19 16 21 11
PP2002-4-4	Customize slide formats	Customizing slides	5.06 (changing placeholder sizes), 5.26 (customizing background)	RA (5.39) CP1 (5.40)	11, 13 9
PP2002-4-5	Customize slide templates	Customizing templates	3.07, 6.02	RA (3.43) RA (6.36)	3–8, 27 4, 5, 7, 13
PP2002-4-6	Manage a Slide Master	Creating and managing multiple Slide Masters	6.10	CP3 (6.40)	5
PP2002-4-7	Rehearse timing	Rehearsing presentations	4.22, 5.30	CP2 (4.37) RA (5.39)	16 18
PP2002-4-8	Rearrange slides	Changing the order of slides in presentations	1.25	CP2 (1.37)	10
PP2002-4-9	Modify slide layout	Changing the layout of individual slides	2.16	RA (2.33) CP2 (2.37)	7, 14 6
PP2002-4-10	Add links to a presentation	Adding hyperlinks to slides	4.16, 5.09	RA (4.34) RA (5.39)	15 13
PP2002-5	**Printing Presentations**				
PP2002-5-1	Preview and print slides, outlines, handouts, and speaker notes	Printing slides	1.30	CP4 (6.40)	10
		Printing handouts	1.31	RA (1.35) CP1 (1.36)	28 30
		Printing Speaker Notes	1.32	CP3 (6.39)	10
		Printing comments pages	6.29	CP3 (6.39)	10

Standardized Coding Number	Skill Sets and Skills Being Measured	Activity	End-of-Tutorial Practice		
			Tutorial Pages	Exercise	Step Number
PP2002-6	**Working with Data from Other Sources**				
PP2002-6-1	Import Excel charts to slides	Inserting Excel charts on slides (either as embedded or linked objects)	4.13	CP1 (4.35)	8
PP2002-6-2	Add sound and video to slides	Adding sound effects to slides	3.19, 5.20	RA (3.43) CP1 (3.45)	12, 13 15
PP2002-6-3	Insert Word tables on slides	Inserting Word tables on slides (either as embedded or linked objects)	4.10	RA (4.33) CP1 (4.35)	8 6
PP2002-6-4	Export a presentation as an outline	Saving slide presentations as RTF outlines	6.16	CP3 (6.39)	11
PP2002-7	**Managing and Delivering Presentations**				
PP2002-7-1	Set up slide shows	Setting-up presentations for delivery	5.29 (deliver as self-running)	RA (5.39)	19
PP2002-7-2	Deliver presentations	Preparing slide shows	3.31ff. for delivery (transitions, animations, etc.)	RA (3.43)	19, 20, 22
		Running slide shows	1.08	RA (1.36) CP1 (1.37)	28 14
PP2002-7-3	Manage files and folders for presentations	Creating folders for storing presentations	1.16, 3.04	RA (3.42)	1
PP2002-7-4	Work with embedded fonts	Embedding fonts in presentations	3.41	CP2 (3.47)	24
PP2002-7-5	Publish presentations to the Web	Publishing presentations to the Web (Save as HTML),	4.26	RA (4.34) CP2 (4.37)	21 20
PP2002-7-6	Use Pack and Go	Preparing presentation for remote delivery using Pack and Go	3.41	RA (3.44) CP2 (3.47)	25 26
PP2002-8	**Workgroup Collaboration**				
PP2002-8-1	Set up a review cycle	Setting up a review cycle and sending presentations for review	6.27	6.28–6.29	1–3
PP2002-8-2	Review presentation comments	Reviewing and accepting and rejecting changes from multiple reviewers	6.30, 6.31	6.28–6.29	1–8
PP2002-8-3	Schedule and deliver presentation broadcasts	Setting-up and scheduling online broadcasts	4.31	4.32	1–8 (in Reference Window)
PP2002-8-4	Publish presentations to the Web	Saving presentations as a web pages (using the Publish option)	4.26	RA (4.34) CP2 (4.37)	21 20